# The New York Times
# Current History

# THE
# EUROPEAN
# WAR

## VOLUME XVII.
### OCTOBER—NOVEMBER—DECEMBER, 1918

With Alphabetical and Analytical Index
Illustrations, Maps and Diagrams

NEW YORK
THE NEW YORK TIMES COMPANY

# INDEX AND TABLE OF CONTENTS

## Volume XVII.

[Titles of articles appear in *italics*]

# Portraits

# Illustrations

# Maps

# Cartoons

# THE EUROPEAN WAR

## Period October, 1918—December, 1918

# INTRODUCTION

THE period under review was one of the most momentous in human history, because it marked the virtual ending of the world war. The strategy of Marshal Foch and the ceaseless hammering of the allied armies against the crumbling enemy lines brought about a situation where the only alternatives for Germany were capitulation or an overwhelming disaster in the field. She chose the former, and negotiations were begun that resulted in the signing of an armistice on Nov. 11, 1918, the terms of which made resumption of the war by the Central Powers impossible.

### THE ALLIED ADVANCE

The battles of the late Summer and early Fall of 1918 had established an incontestable military superiority on the part of the Entente. On the far-flung western front Germany was everywhere in retreat. The armies of the Crown Prince, balked in their thrust at Paris, had been thrown back across the Vesle and nearly to the Aisne. More slowly Rupprecht of Bavaria was yielding before the impact of the great offensive launched by Haig in Picardy and Flanders.

Not for a day did the pressure relax. Not once in the period of sanguinary fighting that followed was the enemy permitted a breathing spell. From the perimeters of the three salients—the Picardy, Lys, and Marne—Foch made a series of crushing attacks, sometimes in succession, again simultaneously, but always in accordance with one coherent, strategic plan, whose brilliancy evoked the admiration even of his foes.

The Picardy offensive, on a line from Arras to Soissons, aimed at forcing the withdrawal of the Germans to and beyond the Hindenburg line. Engaged in this operation were three British armies under Horne, Byng, and Rawlinson, and French armies led by Debeney, Humbert, and Mangin, the latter having brigaded with him the 32d American Division. The immediate objectives of the British were Albert, Bapaume, and Péronne; of the French, Roye and Noyon. The struggles that resulted in the successful attainment of these have been described in the preceding volume.

On Sept. 5, in one of the most dashing operations of the war, the British crossed the Canal du Nord on a fifteen-mile front. The next day the whole line swept forward to an average depth of eight miles. Chauny and Ham fell into the Allies' hands. By Sept. 18 a steady advance had carried the British to their old intrenchments near St. Quentin, while the French also had reached at La Fère the points from which they had been driven in the German offensive of March 21.

In the meantime, the pressure of the American forces against the Crown Prince's army beyond the Vesle bore fruit, Sept. 4, in a German retreat on a twenty-mile front between Condé and Jonchery, and on the 5th the enemy right wing was driven across the Aisne. Contemporary with this was a smashing advance of Mangin's Fourth Army between Soissons and the Oise that penetrated nearly three miles into the enemy lines, captured 8,000 prisoners, and opened the way for the subsequent envelopment of Laon. In this movement the French were greatly assisted by the brilliant exploit of the Americans in taking Juvigny, where one American division met and conquered four crack German divisions and gained possession of the Juvigny Plateau and the St. Quentin-Soissons highway. By Sept. 8 the combined American and French forces were in sight of Laon, and in conjunction with Humbert's army began the clearing of the St. Gobain Forest, ten miles from the city. A large part of the task had been accomplished by the 16th, and on the same date a formidable threat was developed against the Chemin des Dames.

Still more significant of Germany's waning fortunes at this juncture was the sweeping American victory at St. Mihiel in the Lorraine sector. Here the famous salient held by the Germans since 1914 had formed an insuperable obstacle to an invasion of Lorraine and attack upon Metz. For weeks a great American army had been gathering there, and when the attack was begun on Sept. 12 it resulted in one of the most signal and complete victories of the war. In two days the salient had been pinched out and the enemy were in swift retreat; in a week an area of 200 square miles had been reclaimed, with captures of 20,000 prisoners and 100 guns. The plan of Pershing was carried out with the precision of clockwork, and the American losses were negligible. It was a convincing proof of what American aid in the struggle meant to the cause of the Entente, and the news of the victory sent a thrill through the allied world.

While Pershing was consolidating his positions and developing his lines in the direction of Metz and the Briey Basin, the British and French closed in upon Cambrai and Laon, two strongholds of the Hindenburg line. On Sept. 27 Byng's army, including American forces, together with Horne's army, advanced on a fourteen-mile front in the direction of Cambrai, and the next day captured Marcoing, Noyelles, and Cantaing, with 10,000 prisoners and 200 guns. Rawlinson had an equally spectacular success on the 29th, when his troops forced the crossing of the Scheldt Canal, while the Americans under his command took Bellecourt and Nauroy. The way to Cambrai was now cleared, and on Oct. 9, after fierce fighting, it was occupied by the allied troops.

Meanwhile, Mangin's unrelenting pressure had resulted in the taking of Fort de Malmaison on Sept. 28, an achievement which placed him on the left and rear of the Chemin des Dames. In the next two days he advanced two miles against stubborn resistance, and on Oct. 2 captured the massif of St. Thierry. Berthelot, co-operating with him on the right, captured Berry-au-Bac, the great German supply depot, on Oct. 7. By the 12th the Germans were retreating from the Craonne Plateau, and on the 13th they evacuated Laon. This completed the obliteration of the salient and linked up Mangin's army with Debeney and Rawlinson on his left and Gouraud and Pershing on his right. From the date of that junction the German cause was doomed beyond recall.

The capture of St. Quentin by Debeney and Rawlinson completed the destruction of the Hindenburg line, and the occupation of part of the Hunding line in the rear of the former. Events in this sector moved with great rapidity. By Sept. 22 Debeney had captured the woods near Lys Fontaine, while his advance guards had reached the Oise. Two days later he stormed the famous Epine de Dallon. On the 25th the British took Selency, and after heavy fighting at Thorigny and Le Tronquoy, St. Quentin was taken on Oct. 1. It was a deserted city, for the entire civil population of 56,000 had been carried away by the Germans in their retreat.

Closely allied with the preceding operations, both chronologically and strategically, was the joint Franco-American drive begun on Sept. 26, involving the co-operation of the French under General Gouraud, from the Suippe east to the Argonne Forest, with the First American Army from the forest east to the Meuse, north of Verdun.

The terrain was difficult and the opposition bitter, but the attack was launched with an élan and determination that carried it far in the initial stages. The Americans advanced from five to six miles on the first day, capturing Gercourt, Montfauçon, and Verennes. The French made a penetration of four miles, taking Servon, together with Butte de Mesnil and Mazarin Farm. Ten thousand prisoners fell into the hands of the Allies before the end of the second day. Pressing their advantage, the French on Sept 28 captured Somme-Py, while the Americans, sweeping down the Aire, came in contact with the Kriemhilde line. Six days later they cut the line, defeating Prussian Guard divisions that sought to hold it. In the meantime, Gouraud, by a rapid advance, had occupied Challerange and come within two miles of Vouziers. Here the German line broke, and on Oct. 6 was driven back eight miles in the direction of the Suippe.

The next day the Americans stormed the heights commanding the Aire Valley, and on the 11th began to develop a new advance east of the Meuse. By the 15th they were fighting fiercely at and beyond St. Juvin, and expanding their positions on the right bank of the Meuse. The following day Grand Pré, at the vortex of the Argonne Forest, was occupied, and on the 17th, by taking the defenses of Romagne, they gained complete control over the Côte de Chatillon. Meanwhile, the army of Gouraud had captured Vouziers, and was developing an advance toward Rethel. At that time the operations of the two armies had netted over 30,000 prisoners and 800 guns, besides gaining ground of great strategical importance and inflicting a telling blow on the rapidly diminishing German morale.

While Northern France was thus being rapidly cleared of the enemy, a great offensive was launched on the Belgian front between Dixmude and the Passchendaele Ridge, north of Ypres. On Sept. 28 the British fleet bombarded the defenses on the Belgian coast from Nieuport to Zeebrugge, and at the same time the Belgian Army under King Albert, in conjunction with Plumer's Second British Army, penetrated the German lines to a depth of five miles, capturing 4,000 prisoners. By Sept. 30 Roulers had fallen into the Belgians' hands, and the British had advanced to within two miles of the important railway junction of Menin. On Oct. 2 the Allies were joined by French forces under General Degoutte, and the united armies began a great encircling movement against Lille. Between the 2d and the 14th Armentières was occupied, and the allied positions consolidated. Then began a general rolling up of the enemy lines and a German retreat that gave all the signs of developing into a débâcle.

On the 16th important advances were made by all the Allies. French cavalry came within seven miles of the Ghent-Bruges Canal. The British captured Quesnoy, and crossed the Lys near Comines. The Belgians gained control of the roads from Thoumont to Ostend and Bruges.

Oct. 17 was one of the epochal days of the war. Lille, the most important city in occupied France, was taken by the British Fifth Army under General Birdwood. Ostend and Zeebrugge, the rendezvous for German submarines, were evacuated. The important cities of Bruges, Lophem, Thielt, Meulebeke, Courtrai, Tourcoing, and Roubaix fell into the hands of the Allies, and the redemption of the Belgian seacoast became an accomplished fact.

The immediate objective was the line of the Scheldt, which it was desired to reach before the fortifications which the Germans were constructing there could be completed. The attainment of this end proved easy beyond expectation. With rare exceptions there was no pretense of real opposition to the swinging advance of the Allies. All that was attempted was a series of rearguard actions to retard the pursuers, while the main German armies continued swiftly to retreat. Every day brought its record of Entente successes in the capture of miles of territory, thousands of prisoners, and scores of guns. Between Oct. 20 and 25 the Belgians and French crossed the Lys Canal toward Ghent, the First British Army gained control of the Forest of Raismes, while to the south the Third British Army took eight miles of the Valenciennes-Avesnes railway. On the last day of the month the American 30th Division, with Byng's Third Army, made a slashing and successful attack on a fifteen-mile front between the Lys and the Scheldt, capturing numerous towns and prisoners. On the same day the Second British Army, co-operating with French and Belgians, drove in the enemy's lines toward Audenarde. On Nov. 3 the Belgian Army, in a ten-mile advance, reached the Terneuzen Canal, while the British attained the right bank of the Scheldt, thus bringing the allied armies within five miles of Ghent.

On the other side of the border the armies that had taken Cambrai and St. Quentin were advancing swiftly in the direction of Valenciennes, Maubeuge, and Hirson. By Oct. 22 the British forces had reached the suburbs of Valenciennes. Spirited fighting here held up the advance for a few days, but on Nov. 2 Valenciennes was entered by Canadian troops, after having been under German rule since August of 1914. In an irresistible attack on Nov. 4 the British, with two American divisions, took Landrecies and Catillon, with 10,000 prisoners and 200 guns, while simultaneously Debeney forced a passage of the Oise-Sambre Canal, with great captures of men and materials.

These important successes were duplicated by Mangin, who, after the capture of Laon, had pressed rapidly forward between the Oise and the Aisne in the direction of Guise. On Oct. 25 he pierced the Hunding line in conjunction with Guillaumat. By the end of the month he had crossed the Peron River, and by Nov. 7 had reached the railway between La Capelle and Hirson. On the 9th Hirson was stormed, and lines of investment were drawn closely about Mézières.

If these victories seem remarkable and the swiftness of the allied advance difficult to understand, the explanation is to be found not wholly in the diminishing morale of the German armies. It lies rather in the tremendous task assigned the American forces in the Argonne and beyond, and the characteristic way in which they performed it. For there it was that the German High Command made its most formidable stand, and concentrated its greatest re-

sources, thus making the work of the Allies easier on other parts of the front. It was Germany's last desperate effort to stave off impending defeat. If she lost there she lost everywhere.

The reason was obvious. The possession of the Argonne by the Americans constituted a direct threat against the Longuyon-Sedan-Mézières railway. This was the principal artery of communication of the German armies. If it were taken, all the enemy forces would be bottled up, leaving as their only means of egress the gateway through Liége. For that reason the choicest divisions at the disposal of the German leaders were gathered to oppose the American advance. But the Americans were not to be denied, and the epic fighting that followed shed new lustre on their arms.

On Oct. 19-20 the Americans advanced in the region of Bourrot. On the 21st they took Brieulles and the Bois de Forêt. Two days later they crushed the Freya defenses, and on the 26th began the bombardment of the railway with the huge naval guns that were one of the surprises of the war. They stormed the Ancreville Ridge on the 30th. By this time the co-operating army of Gouraud had crossed the Aisne between Vouziers and Rethel, and engaged the enemy on the Alleux Plateau. The following day the Freya line was taken almost for its entire length, and by the 4th the railway line was cut at Montmedy and Conflans. On the 6th the Americans, after fierce fighting, took the historic city of Sedan, and shortly after occupied the heights of the Woevre, from which they were in a position to make a powerful attack upon Metz.

## THE COLLAPSE OF BULGARIA

After a long period of quiescence the Macedonian front sprang into life on Sept. 16. The date of the allied attack was timed with sound judgment, for it coincided with the period when Germany was battling for her life on the western front and could send no help to this smallest of her allies. The offensive developed with startling suddenness, and within two weeks resulted in the withdrawal of Bulgaria from the war.

Three armies co-operated in this culminating drive. British and Greek troops attacked in the vicinity of Lake Doiran, Serbians and French drove at the enemy's centre, and Italians assailed the Albanian front. Despite the strength of the enemy positions and the enormous natural difficulties offered by the mountainous country, the allied preparations had been so complete and the impetus of their attack was so great that the Bulgarians broke and fled on all portions of their lines. By Sept. 23 a wedge had been driven between the First and Second Bulgarian Armies. Doiran and Prilep had been captured, and the First Bulgarian Army was in rout. The following day the Serbians crossed the Vardar River, and the Second Bulgarian Army was fleeing before them in disorder.

On the 25th the British and Greek forces crossed the Bulgarian border, and the next day captured the important fortress of Strumnitza, which was the key to Sofia, the Bulgarian capital. Uskub was entered by the Serbians and French on the 30th, thus assuring the capture of the First Bulgarian Army, which had no way of escape from the allied forces closing in upon both sides. The enemy troops were by this time nothing more than disorganized mobs. Nothing stood in the way of the complete overrunning of Bulgaria by the triumphant allied forces led by Franchet d'Esperey. Militarily, the end had come for Bulgaria.

In Sofia there was mad terror and confusion. Anarchy threatened. The King and his advisers were bitterly denounced by crowds who besieged the palace and demanded that the country surrender. Frantic appeals were made to Berlin and Vienna for assistance. These were fruitless. On Sept. 25 the Bulgarian Government dispatched an emissary to General d'Esperey with the request that hostilities be suspended for forty-eight hours pending the arrival of accredited representatives of the Government, who would be authorized to negotiate a treaty of peace. Fearing a ruse, and not willing to forego or weaken his military advantage, d'Esperey refused to halt his operations, but expressed his willingness to receive and listen to the delegates.

These presented themselves at Saloniki on Sept. 28. Discussions ensued and on Sept. 29 a provisional armistice was signed by d'Esperey and the Commissioners. The terms were presented to and approved by the allied Governments at once, and on Sept. 30 at noon the armistice went into effect.

The terms involved nothing less than unconditional surrender. They were purely military in character. Consideration of political and territorial matters was postponed until the signing of a final treaty of peace. Bulgaria agreed to evacuate all occupied territory in Greece and Serbia; to demobilize her army at once; to surrender all means of transport on land and on the Danube to the Allies; to permit their unhindered passage through Bulgaria for the development of military operations; to surrender all arms and ammunition; to permit the occupation by the Allies of all strategic points, and to withdraw as a belligerent from the war. No stipulations were made regarding King Ferdinand, as this was regarded as a purely internal matter, to be disposed of as the Bulgarian people might choose. The King settled the matter by abdicating on Oct. 4 in favor of his son, who became King with the title of Boris III.

The armistice preceded by nine days the third anniversary of Bulgaria's entrance into the war.

Subsequent military operations were in the nature of fulfillment of the armistice, and had little bearing on the main issues of the war. Scattered bands of Germans and Austrians still remained in Serbia, Bulgaria, and Albania, but their resistance was negligible, and by Nov. 3 Belgrade, the Serbian capital, was recovered and the country south of the Danube had been practically cleared of the enemy.

## CRUSHING OF THE TURKISH ARMIES

Striking as had been the Bulgarian campaign, it had been equaled and perhaps eclipsed in brilliancy by the successes of General Allenby in Palestine.

The campaign that had resulted in the capture of Jerusalem had been brought to a close in April of 1918. From that time until Sept. 19 nothing of moment had occurred, except desultory combats between the Fourth Turkish Army and the troops of Hussein I., King of the Arab State of Hedjaz, who throughout the war had rendered valuable assistance to the Allies.

On the latter date Allenby struck with telling effect, and broke the Turkish line near the sea. He followed up this success by a masterly use of his cavalry and camel corps, which resulted in the encirclement of the Seventh and Eighth Turkish Armies. In two days the Turks were everywhere in flight, save a small remnant in the Jordan Valley. This held out for a short time longer, but was finally overwhelmed and the disaster was complete. Three armies had been destroyed, 80,000 prisoners and 500 guns had been captured, and all that remained was the rounding up of the refugees. The German Commander in Chief, Liman von Sanders, fled barely in time to escape capture.

From that time on the advance of the British was practically unchecked. Damascus was captured on Oct. 1, Beirut was entered on the 8th, and on the 26th British troops occupied Aleppo, the great Turkish base, and cut the Constantinople-Bagdad railway. This was the culmination of the campaign. Nothing could prevent the junction of Allenby's forces with those of General Marshall on the Tigris and Euphrates.

At that moment the latter was engaged in severe fighting on the Tigris. The battle with the Turkish forces there intrenched lasted six days, and ended on Oct. 30 in a complete victory, all the Turks being killed or captured. The Turkish forces as armies in being had been practically annihilated, and Turkey herself reduced to impotency.

Convinced of the futility of further fighting, the Turkish authorities liberated General Townshend, who had been captured by them at Kut-el-Amara, and sent him as an intermediary to the British Admiral in command in the Aegean Sea, Vice Admiral Calthorp, with the request that armistice negotiations be opened at once. The Admiral answered that conditions had already been formulated by the Allies on which they were prepared to suspend hostilities, provided the Turkish Government should send plenipotentiaries empowered to conclude an armistice. This was done promptly, and after three days of discussion the armistice was signed at the Island of Mudros on Oct. 30, to take effect on the following day.

The terms of the armistice, as in the case of Bulgaria, amounted practically to unconditional surrender. The Dardanelles and Bosporus were to be opened and access to the Black Sea accorded to the Allies, who were also to occupy the forts of the strait. Allied prisoners of war were to be repatriated immediately. Demobilization of the Turkish Army was provided for, except such troops as the Allies might choose to retain under arms as a police force. All ships were to be surrendered, and all occupied territory to be evacuated. Turkish troops in garrisons were to surrender to the nearest allied commander. Any strategic points in Turkish territory were to be occupied by the Allies at will. Germans residing in Turkey were to be sent home, and Turkey was required to end all relations with the Central Powers.

An aftermath of the armistice conference was a published assertion that a secret clause had been added which would restore Ottoman sovereignty in Armenia, Syria, and Palestine. This was emphatically denied by Lord Robert Cecil, who declared that leaving these nationalities under the shadow of Turkish oppression was absolutely inconceivable. Officially confirming this was a formal announcement issued by France and Great Britain on Nov. 7 of their firm intention to abolish Turkish misgovernment forever in the countries of the Eastern Mediterranean.

## AUSTRO-HUNGARIAN COLLAPSE

With Bulgaria and Turkey out of the war, a powerful offensive was inaugurated by Italy against the Austrian Army. In this attack fifty-one Italian divisions were assisted by three British, one Czechoslovak, and two French divisions, with a single American regiment. Opposed to them were sixty-three Austro-Hungarian divisions. The forces were nearly equal, but the Austrians were depressed by the disasters that had befallen their eastern allies, while the Italians were stimulated by the brilliant series of victories won by the Entente.

The battle began on Oct. 24 with a joint attack in the Piave and Monte Grappa regions. In both sectors the Austrain lines failed to hold. Within twenty-four hours the enemy had begun a retreat that increased in speed as their demoralization grew. By the 28th the Piave had been cleared, and British and Italian cavalry were capturing whole regiments and brigades. By Oct. 30 33,-000 prisoners had been taken. The next day this number grew to 50,000. By that time there was hardly a pretense of resistance. The Austrian retreat had become a headlong flight. Rovereto and Trent were occupied by Italian troops, Udine was entered by cavalry regiments, and the Italian colors floated over the city of Trieste. Before a halt was called by the armistice on Nov. 4 the Italians had taken 300,000 prisoners and 5,000 guns in one of the most decisive victories of the war.

## SUBMARINE DEPREDATIONS

With the war going steadily against her on land, the increasing desperation of Germany found vent in the ruthlessness of her undersea warfare. On Oct. 10 the British mail steamer Leinster, a wholly civilian vessel, with 687 passengers and a crew of 70 men, was torpedoed during a storm in the Irish Sea and went down in fifteen minutes; 480 lives were lost, including those of 135 women and children.

The Missanabie was sunk off the Irish coast Sept. 9. It was a transport, and 50 soldiers were lost. Three days later the Galway Castle, bound for South Africa, was sunk by a submarine and 189 perished.

A Japanese liner, the Hirano Maru, was torpedoed off the Irish coast Oct. 4, and only 29 out of 320 on board were saved. The U. S. S. Tampa, on convoy service, was sunk by a submarine Sept. 26, and all on board, 118, were lost.

On Sept. 30 the American steamer Ticonderoga was sunk under harrowing circumstances; 11 officers and 102 enlisted men lost their lives. In this case the most atrocious brutality was shown,

boats in the water being riddled and shots fired pointblank at men swimming about.

The American steamship Lucia, which was claimed to be "unsinkable" because of rubber-bound barrels in her hold to give her buoyancy, was torpedoed Oct. 19, 1,200 miles from the American coast. She sank the following day. Four of her crew were killed by the explosion, the rest being rescued by American destroyers. This was the last merchant ship sunk by the German submarines.

The British battleship Britannia, torpedoed on Nov. 9 near the entrance to the Strait of Gibraltar, was the last important victim of the U-boat. She sank in three and a half hours. Most of her crew were rescued.

The loss of British shipping in September was 151,593 gross tons, as compared with 209,212 gross tons in September, 1917. The losses for the quarter ended with September were 510,551 gross tons, compared with 952,938 for the corresponding period of 1917.

From the beginning of the war until Sept. 9, 1918, German submarines sank 7,157,088 deadweight tons of shipping in excess of what was constructed in that period by the world outside of the Central Powers. In the same time, however, 3,795,000 tons of enemy shipping had been seized, so that actually the allied nations on Sept. 1, 1918, had only 3,362,-088 less tons of shipping than in August, 1914. Altogether the allied and neutral nations lost during the war 21,404,913 tons. This was an average destruction of about 445,000 tons a month as the toll exacted by the submarine.

The number of American merchant ships sunk by submarines, raiders, and mines from the beginning of the war to Sept. 3, 1918, when the submarines departed from American waters, was 131, with a gross tonnage of 358,000; 447 lives were lost.

The only naval action of importance in the last phase of the war was the destruction of the naval base at Durazzo, Oct. 2. Italian and British cruisers, attended by Italian torpedo boats and American submarine chasers, made their way through the mine fields into the harbor, and after a bombardment of two hours sank all the Austrian ships and wholly destroyed the naval base. The allied squadron came out of the action unscathed, except for a slight injury to one of the British cruisers.

## THE WAR IN THE AIR

The military ascendency of the allied forces on land was closely paralleled by the supremacy which they maintained in their aerial operations. Clouds of allied planes hovered over the front of their armies, accelerating the enemy retreat, shattering their convoys, destroying their bridges, and breaking up their concentrations.

Air raids on munition plants and railway centres in the Rhine Valley were almost continuous. In three months 249 raids had been made and 247 tons of bombs dropped on strategic points at Mannheim, Treves, Metz, Frankfort, Coblenz, and Cologne. On Nov. 1 blast furnaces at Burbach, chemical factories at Karlsruhe, and railroad junctions at Baden were heavily bombed without any loss to the attackers. So heavy was the damage done that the German Government on Nov. 4 protested to Washington and proposed a cessation of air raids by both armies on places outside of the fighting zone. The appeal was fruitless, although the grim humor of it, coming from a Government that for four years had raided unfortified cities far beyond the fighting lines and repeatedly bombed hospitals, plainly marked as such, was not lost upon the world.

The Austrian Government on Sept. 9 published a manifesto declaring that all enemy aviators who might be captured while distributing propaganda would be punished with death. A stern threat of instant reprisal, if this were done, prevented the order from being carried into effect.

American aviators in the last weeks of the war did important work on the battlefront. When hostilities were suspended American airmen had destroyed 661 more German airplanes and 45 more balloons than they themselves had lost. Between Sept. 12 and Nov. 11 they had dropped 120 tons of bombs on military objectives within the enemy lines.

Political developments in the countries of the Central Powers were a reflection of the military situation. Defeat and retreat in the field resulted in demoralization and disintegration at home. By the beginning of September it was apparent to the world that the Teutonic alliance was doomed. The crumbling of the Macedonian front and the imminent collapse of Turkey deepened that conviction. Those who had drawn the sword were about to perish by the sword, and efforts were at once put forth to draw from diplomacy what had been denied by the arbitrament of war.

## AUSTRIAN PEACE OFFENSIVE

Sept. 15 the Austro-Hungarian Government addressed a communication to all belligerent and neutral powers, in which it suggested that a discussion of war aims be entered into, which, while confidential and "nonbinding," might clear away misunderstandings between the warring powers and lead to the conclusion of a treaty of peace. The note was mild and conciliatory in tone, adroitly couched, and was evidently designed to appeal to the pacifist and war-weary sentiment of the peoples to whom it was addressed. That the principle of the note, if not its exact wording, had been approved by Germany was asserted by Foreign Minister Burian, Sept. 19.

The note met with instant and, in some cases, curt rejection by the peoples and Governments of the Entente. Popular sentiment in America, as expressed through the press and by recognized leaders of public opinion, condemned it with practical unanimity. Everywhere it was regarded as a palpable trap on the part of a beaten power to escape the consequences of defeat. The refusal of the American Government was prompt to the point of abruptness. The note was handed to Secretary Lansing at 6:20 o'clock on Sept. 16, and twenty-five minutes later the President issued a reply of which the salient sentence was that " the Government has repeatedly and with entire candor stated the terms on which the United States would consider peace, and can and will entertain no proposal for a conference upon a matter concerning which it has made its position and purpose so plain."

Foreign Secretary Balfour for Great Britain and Premier Clemenceau for

France answered in a similar vein, as did Italy, three days later.

The first phase of the Austrian peace offensive was thus a total failure, and the rejection of the proposal still further increased the unrest and smoldering rebellion in the Dual Monarchy. Additional impetus was given to the Czechoslovak movement, which aimed at the creation of a republic for the Czechs of Bohemia and the Slovaks of Moravia and Silesia, embracing a territory of 48,000 square miles and a population of 12,000,000 of the Slavic race. The Czechoslovaks had already been recognized as a nation by the allied Governments. On Oct. 18 the Provisional Czechoslovak Government, with headquarters at Paris, adopted a declaration of independence, formally severing Bohemia from Austria-Hungary. On the same day Prague, the capital of Bohemia, was seized by Czechs, who raised their flag over the Government buildings. A few days of street fighting ensued, but by Oct. 28 the Czechs were in full control, the Austrian Governor had fled to Vienna, and the municipal authorities had given their adhesion to the new Government. The Republic of Czechoslovakia was formally proclaimed on Oct. 29, and Professor Thomas G. Masaryk was elected first President by delegates representing eight political parties.

Almost coincident with these events was a Conference of Oppressed Nationalites which met at Philadelphia and signed a document which united newly self-liberated peoples whose territory extended from the Baltic to the Adriatic. There was little that was definite about this new alliance. It was rather a tentative undertaking to present a united front against Germany, Austria, or any other reactionary power which might threaten the liberty which these oppressed peoples were determined to regain and maintain. Prominently represented were the Jugoslavs, Poles, and Czechoslovaks, the aspirations of all of whom could only be satisfied by the disintegration of Austria-Hungary.

That distracted Government, undeterred by the rebuff of its " nonbinding " proposition, made a new appeal to President Wilson, Oct. 7. In part the occasion for this was furnished by an address which the President had delievered in New York, Sept. 27. There he further elucidated the war aims of the United States, with the design, to use his own words, to make them sound " less like a thesis and more like a practical program." The points he made were that in the peace terms there must be no discrimination between those to whom we wish to be just and those to whom we do not wish to be just; that no special nor separate interest of any nation or group of nations not consistent with the common interest of all could be considered; that there must be no special covenants, leagues or alliances; that no special economic combinations or boycotts should be employed, except as power to do this might be vested in a league of nations as a means of discipline or control, and that all international agreements and treaties must be made known in their entirety to the world.

Shortly following this speech the Austrian note reached Washington. It reiterated the plea of having waged a defensive war, offered to conclude an immediate armistice and to enter upon negotiations for peace, the basis for which should be the fourteen points in the message of the President to Congress on Jan. 8, 1918, the four points in his address of Feb. 12, 1918, and the views expressed in the Sept. 27 address.

The President replied Oct. 18, refusing to entertain the proposal and basing his refusal upon the fact that one of the fourteen points was no longer applicable because of events that had occurred since its enunciation. The tenth of the fourteen points had demanded that the peoples of Austria-Hungary should be afforded the fullest opportunity for autonomous development. Autonomy, however, was not now sufficient, because in the interim the United States Government had recognized the Czechoslovaks as a nation, and had also indorsed the Jugoslavic aspirations for a separate national existence.

Oct. 29 Austria replied in a note which bore the marks of panic. She agreed that the Czechoslovaks and Jugoslavs were entitled to independence, declared that with this agreement nothing now stood in the way of negotiating an armistice and peace, and begged the President to enter upon these negotiations immediately without reference to any that might be pending with other Governments. This last phrase was interpreted as an abandonment of the alliance with Germany. The note was sent on the same day to the French, British, Italian, and Japanese Governments.

The appeal was transmitted to the Interallied Conference at Versailles, and Austria was notified that her request for an armistice must be made directly to General Diaz, the Italian Commander in Chief.

Emperor Charles directed that this should be done, and on Oct. 29 an Austrian officer appeared at Italian headquarters to arrange for a military capitulation. A more fully accredited commission was demanded, and this appeared on the following day. In the meantime the precise details of the armistice had been received. They were transmitted to the Austrian Government and promptly accepted. The formal document was signed on Nov. 3, to go into effect on the following day.

The terms of the armistice stripped Austria of all power to renew the war should she be so inclined. The army was to be wholly and promptly demobilized. Austrian brigades fighting with the Germans were to be withdrawn. All territories occupied by Austria since the beginning of the war were to be evacuated. Military and railway equipment in the evacuated territory was to be left intact. German troops in the Austrian Army were to be expelled. Half of the army material, artillery, and ammunition was to be surrendered to the Allies. Prisoners of war in Austrian hands were to be repatriated at once without reciprocity. A large and specified number of battleships, cruisers, destroyers, and submarines were to be surrendered, and the remaining naval vessels were to be concentrated, disarmed, and placed under allied supervision. Free movement over all parts of Austrian territory and the occupation of strategic points were to be granted to the forces of the Entente. Freedom of navigation in the Adriatic, the Danube, and all territorial

waters, together with the right to dismantle the fortifications of waterways, was also to be yielded. Stringent conditions were inserted against sabotage, concealment, or evasion in any way of the terms of armistice.

After so complete and humiliating an overthrow, the fall of the dynasty was unavoidable. The Emperor tried to weather the storm by forming a liquidation Ministry to hand over the former imperial power to the various nationalities into which the empire was dissolving. Hungary seized the opportunity to set up a separate Government, and Count Karolyi was proclaimed as head of the Hungarian Republic, which was formally established on Nov. 16. The process of disintegration went on with great rapidity. The Galician Poles took steps to join Poland, the Ruthenians inclined to unite with the Ukraine, the Jugoslavs expanded their plans to include Serbia, and the Croats seized the port of Fiume and started a rebellion against Magyar domination. The Dual Monarchy had become in fact what it had long been in spirit, a collection of nationalities with totally distinct aspirations. The once great empire of the Hapsburgs was no longer a State. It had become simply a geographical expression.

On Nov. 11 the Emperor Charles abdicated and removed with his family to the castle of Eckhartzau.

## SURRENDER OF GERMANY

Long before this sequence of events the handwriting on the wall had become legible to even the most sanguine of German statesmen. Their perception of the situation was evidenced by their diminishing peace demands and by the almost frenzied appeals to the dwindling morale of the civilian population, disheartened by the unbroken succession of defeats on the western front and the collapse of their allies on the east and south.

On Sept. 12, Vice Chancellor von Payer, in an address at Stuttgart, voiced the willingness of the Government to yield Belgium and to waive any demands for indemnities. On the same date the Kaiser made a rambling address to the workers at Essen, which clearly betokened his mental perturbation. A storm of imperial telegrams and proclamations to the army, the navy, and various civic organizations exhorted them to stand firm in their efforts to secure for Germany, if not a victorious, at least an honorable peace.

Numerous changes were made in the Constitution and in administrative officials in order to comply more fully with the requirements of President Wilson looking toward peace. A constitutional amendment was proposed requiring the consent of the Federal Council and the Reichstag for a declaration of war. Treaties also were to come in the competence of the same bodies. Cabinet Ministers could demand the right to be heard by the Reichstag. Steps were taken toward the reformation of the antiquated three-class franchise, tending toward a larger participation by the people in Governmental affairs.

Chancellor von Hertling, Vice Chancellor von Payer, and Foreign Minister von Hintze tendered their resignations Sept. 29, and were replaced by statesmen of more liberal views. Prince Maximilian of Baden was appointed Chancellor Oct. 2, on the supposition that he would be more fully persona grata with the allied nations than his conservative predecessor. Dr. W. S. Solf, a Moderate, replaced von Hintze, and Mathias Erzberger, leader of the Centrist Party, who had opposed annexations and indemnities, filled the office vacated by von Payer.

These changes were made with a haste foreign to the usual German method of procedure, but haste was urgently necessary if irretrievable disaster were to be averted. The Macedonian front had already crumbled and Turkey was known to be seeking to withdraw from the war.

Oct. 5 the new Chancellor sent a note to President Wilson through the Swiss Government accepting the program set forth by the President, especially his speech of Sept. 27, as a basis for peace negotiations and requesting him to invite the Entente nations to send plenipotentiaries to negotiate for the immediate conclusion of an armistice on land and water and in the air. Simultaneously with this request and as an elaboration of it, Prince Maximilian outlined his peace policy before the Reichstag. He emphasized the basic alteration which he claimed the German Government had undergone in the direction of popular government, offered the complete rehabilitation of Belgium, hinted that Germany would even be willing to pay an indemnity, and expressed the hope that his note to the President would secure a satisfactory peace.

The President's reply on Oct. 8 consisted of two questions and one assertion. He asked categorically whether the German Government accepted the terms set down in his addresses and whether the Chancellor was speaking for the constituted authorities who had so far conducted the war. The answers to these questions, he declared, were vital. He further stated that immediate evacuation of occupied territories by German armies was the only condition on which he would transmit the request to the allied Governments.

The questions elicited a prompt response from the German Government. It accepted unconditionally the President's terms as a basis of peace. It also agreed to the demand for evacuation and suggested the appointment of a mixed commission to regulate the procedure. It emphasized the popular basis of the Government and affirmed that the Chancellor spoke in the name of the German people.

Although this last statement was received with considerable skepticism, and the proposal of a mixed commission was viewed merely as an attempt to save the hard pressed German armies and rob the Allies of the military superiority they had established, the note might have met with a more favorable reception had it not coincided with fresh devastations in France and exceptionally brutal submarine atrocities, notably the sinking of the Leinster, to which allusion has already been made. An unmistakable hardening of tone, due largely to this, was apparent in the President's reply of Oct. 14. In this he stated that the process of evacuation was to be dictated wholly by the military advisers of the allied Governments. He condemned vigorously the inhuman practices of the Germans on land and sea and declared that there could be no cessation of arms while these continued. He also called attention to that part of the Mount Vernon speech which demanded the destruction of every arbitrary power anywhere which could separately, secretly and of its single choice disturb the peace of the world. This description, the President declared, applied to the German government authorities who had conducted the war. Unless and until convincing guarantees could be given that the Allies were dealing with a Government wholly different in character, spirit, and purpose further discussion would be unavailing.

The reply met with hearty approval in the United States and was cordially greeted by the nations of the Entente.

Germany's response was handed to President Wilson on Oct. 22. She denied in toto the charges of inhumanity on the part of her military leaders and submarine commanders, and suggested that a neutral commission be appointed to investigate the matter. Regarding evacuation and armistice, she proposed that the actual standard of power of both sides in the field should form the basis for arrangements for safeguarding and guaranteeing that standard. The statement was repeated that the peace proposal came from a Government representing an overwhelming majority of the German people.

The note was regarded by the Entente as unconvincing and unsatisfactory, and sentiment developed rapidly toward demanding nothing less from Germany than unconditional surrender. Before replying, the President communicated with the Supreme War Council of the Allies at Paris. On Oct. 23 he addressed his last letter of the series to the German Government. He agreed to take up the question of an armistice with the allied Governments, with the significant addendum, however, that the only armistice he would feel justified in submitting for their consideration was one that would make the renewal of hostilities by Germany impossible. He further stated that he had turned over all the correspondence to the Allies, with the suggestion that if their military advisers deemed an armistice desirable they should prepare·such terms as they

might think proper. He closed with the warning that if the Allies should find themselves dealing with practically the same Government that had hitherto conducted the war nothing less would be required than surrender.

The receipt of this reply caused a prolonged discussion in the German Cabinet, in which the Kaiser and Crown Prince and the military leaders joined. Oct. 26 marked the resignation of General Ludendorff. On Oct. 27 a brief note was dispatched to President Wilson; its substance was that the German Government awaited the terms of armistice to be prescribed by the allied military authorities.

During this interchange the Interallied Conference at Versailles had been busily engaged in drawing up the armistice terms which it was clearly foreseen would be ultimately requested by Germany. Nov. 4 Secretary Lansing announced that these terms had been agreed to unanimously and signed by the representatives of the Entente. The following day the Secretary announced to the German Government the willingness of the Allies to make peace on the terms laid down by President Wilson. The qualification was made, however, that the clause relating to the freedom of the seas had various interpretations and that liberty of action on that point was reserved. It was further stated that compensation must be made by Germany for all damage to the civilian population of the Allies by land, by sea, and from the air. The Secretary asserted that the President agreed with these requirements and closed with the statement that Marshal Foch had been authorized to receive duly accredited representatives of the German Government and announce to them the terms of armistice.

There was no further hesitation on the part of Germany. Delegates were appointed at once and a request was forwarded to Marshal Foch that he name a place and time for meeting the German envoys. He named Nov. 7, and on that date the delegation, headed by Mathias Erzberger, left the headquarters of the German High Command at Spa and proceeded to the French lines in automobiles bearing a white flag. They were received by French officers, who conducted them to the headquarters of Marshal Foch. These were in a railroad car drawn up in the forest of Compiègne, near the town of Rethondes. After introductions the Marshal read the terms with great clearness and deliberation. Discussions followed, the German envoys seeking to obtain some mitigation of the terms. Marshal Foch declared, however, that he was not authorized to change them except in some minor details. For three days the conference continued, the German envoys being allowed to communicate with their Government for instructions. On Nov. 11 the armistice was signed, and the most colossal war in history came virtually to an end.

The terms that had been imposed upon Austria had foreshadowed to some extent those that would be dictated to Germany. She was stunned by their severity, but the allied world felt that the conditions did not go beyond what justice and the future security of civilization demanded. The main object that had been kept in view was the prevention of any resumption of war on the part of Germany. This end the armistice achieved.

The full text of the armistice is given in this volume, and only the most important features need be referred to here. Germany was required to evacuate all occupied territories everywhere. The iniquitous treaties of Brest-Litovsk and Bucharest were annulled. Germany was to surrender 5,000 pieces of light and heavy artillery, 25,000 machine guns, 3,000 minenwerfers, 1,700 airplanes, 5,000 locomotives, 150,000 railroad cars, and 5,000 motor lorries. All these were to be in perfect condition. All submarines were to be surrendered, together with 10 battleships, 6 battle cruisers, 8 light cruisers, and 50 destroyers. The remaining naval vessels were to be disarmed and placed under allied supervision. Prisoners of war in German hands were to be yielded up without reciprocity. All territory on the left bank of the Rhine was to be occupied by the allied armies, and three bridgeheads were to be established at Mayence, Coblenz, and Cologne, each with a radius of eighteen miles. A strip of territory six miles wide on the right bank of the Rhine was to constitute a neutral zone. The period of armistice was one month, with provision for renewal if necessary.

The announcement of the signing of the armistice caused great rejoicing in all the allied nations. New York, London, Paris, and Rome were the scenes of wildest demonstrations, and to a lesser extent these were duplicated in every city and village. President Wilson announced the news to Congress in a memorable session.

On the battlefronts hostilities ceased promptly at 11 o'clock A. M. Nov. 11. All fraternizing with the enemy was strictly forbidden.

Steps were taken at once to put the terms of the armistice into effect. The Germans evacuated the occupied territory, followed at stated intervals by the allied troops in their march to the Rhine. It was arranged that of the three bridgeheads the French should hold Mayence, the British Cologne, while the American Army, under General Joseph T. Dickman, should occupy Coblenz.

The progress of the allied troops was marked by no untoward incident. The entrance of the French into the recovered provinces of Alsace-Lorraine was a triumphal procession, and the inhabitants, who had been for forty-eight years under German rule, showered the troops with flowers and acclamations. The Americans received a cordial greeting as they passed through the Duchy of Luxemburg, but their entrance upon German soil, like that of the other allied armies of occupation, was met with silence. Regulations were at once established, which, while interfering as little as possible with the ordinary mode of life of the population, safeguarded the security of the occpying forces. In general, the municipal authorities continued to function, subject to allied supervision and control.

The most spectacular feature involved in the fulfillment of the armistice terms was the surrender of the German fleet, the most amazing in history. On the morning of Nov. 21 the fleet steamed into the waters off the Firth of Forth and surrendered to Admiral Sir David Beatty, in supreme command of the allied fleets. These, including a number of American dreadnoughts, were drawn up in two lines, with guns loaded and men at battle stations, ready for instant action if any sign of treachery should be apparent. There was no lack of docility, however, and the surrender took place as stipulated. The ships were taken possession of by British crews and interned at Scapa Flow in the Orkneys, while the German mariners were placed on transports and returned to their country. Twenty of the submarines had been surrendered on the previous day to Admiral Tyrwhitt and interned at Harwich, and these were followed at intervals by other groups until all had been accounted for.

## THE GERMAN REVOLUTION

Even before the armistice was signed, the revolutionary spirit was rife in Germany. Socialist leaders in the Reichstag were loudly demanding that the Kaiser abdicate. Oct 28, Karl Liebknecht, who had been released from prison, began a Bolshevist agitation that soon assumed alarming proportions. The War Cabinet took up the question of abdication, and Dr. Delbrück was dispatched to the German Staff Headquarters at Spa to secure from the Emperor a renunciation of the throne. The men of the German Navy at Kiel mutinied on Oct. 31 and refused to take the High Seas Fleet out to battle.

A movement toward secession gained strength in the South German States. Bavaria on Nov. 8 at a great popular meeting proclaimed a republican form of government, and Kurt Eisner, a newspaper editor, assumed direction of affairs a few days later.

Mutiny continued to spread through the German Navy. Kiel, Wilhelmshaven, Cuxhaven, and other ports fell under the control of revolutionary sailors, while many vessels of the fleet were seized. In numerous other cities street fighting was followed by the hoisting of the red flag and the formation of Soldiers' and Workmen's Councils, who took control from the municipal authorities. Considering the wide extent of the uprising,

however, there was surprisingly little bloodshed.

On Nov. 9 Prince Maximilian announced that the Kaiser had decided to abdicate. Early the next day the ex-Emperor crossed the border into Holland and went to the castle of Amerongen, where he became the guest of Count Wilhelm von Bentinck. The Crown Prince also fled to Holland and was interned on the Island of Wieringen in the Zuyder Zee. Although both father and son were said to have renounced their rights to the throne, the actual documents, issued later, bore the dates of Nov. 28 and Dec. 1, respectively.

The imperial example was the signal for many other abdications of German rulers. From Nov. 8 to 14, inclusive, the Kings, Dukes, and Princes ruling Bavaria Brunswick, Württemberg, Saxony, Oldenburg, Mecklenburg, Reuss, Anhalt, Baden, and some lesser States had abdicated or fled.

On Nov. 10 Philipp Scheidemann in Berlin announced the Emperor's abdication. Prince Maximilian turned over the Government to Friedrich Ebert, a Socialist Reichstag leader, who issued a proclamation exhorting the people to remain calm and promising the speedy conclusion of a treaty of peace. Associated with him at first were Landsberg and Scheidemann, but the demands of the extremists, who promptly asserted themselves, led to the inclusion in the Cabinet of Dittmann, Haase, and Barth. Field Marshal Hindenburg put himself and his troops at the disposal of the new Government, and, despite the growing menace of Liebknecht and his followers, a fair degree of equilibrium was attained.

## THE RUSSIAN SITUATION

Chaos and destitution still reigned in distracted Russia, and the terrorism instituted by the Bolshevist régime showed no sign of abatement. The withdrawal of the Germans, in compliance with the terms of armistice, was followed in many cases by the advance of Bolshevist troops against Esthonia, Lithuania, and Poland, where local engagements seldom rising to the dignity of battles resulted.

Heavy fighting was reported from the

Volga region between Bolshevist and Czechoslovak troops, and the latter were forced to retreat from Samara. Some reinforcements were sent them by the Allies in an effort to maintain the front. It was stated Oct. 18 that the United States Government had advanced $5,000,000 to the Czechoslovak National Council and had landed $3,000,000 worth of supplies at Vladivostok for their armies.

Heavy fighting occurred on the Dvina in October between the Soviet and expeditionary forces, without decisive results. In the Archangel district the Allies scored some minor successes and drove the Bolshevists from the Ugor district in Vologda Province.

The outstanding political development was the fusion of the Siberian Government with the All-Russian Government of Ufa. The new Provisional Government that resulted had its seat at Omsk, and its authority extended over most of Siberia and parts of the provinces of Samara, Ufa, Ural, and Orenburg in Russia. Soon after its formation it sent a formal appeal to Washington for recognition on the basis of its democratic character and allied sympathies.

On Oct. 24 Foreign Minister Tchitcherin of the Soviet Government addressed a note to President Wilson asking for the conclusion of an armistice and the withdrawal of the allied troops. The note remained unanswered.

Early in November Esthonia was proclaimed an independent republic. Revel was made the capital. The new State has a territory of 47,500 square kilometers and a population of 1,500,000. Constantine Paets was chosen as first Prime Minister. Absolute neutrality was proclaimed as the policy of the State.

Finland gave amnesty to 10,000 political prisoners on Oct. 31. There was no marked political development, and the decision as to a monarchical or republican form of government remained in abeyance.

Poles in Galicia were attacked Oct. 4 by Ukrainians, who recaptured Lemberg and other cities. This was in retaliation for the announcement that Poland had annexed Galicia. Polish troops seized Cracow Nov. 5, and also occupied Warsaw. On Nov. 4 the United States recognized the Polish Government as autonomous and co-belligerent. This had previously been done by France, Great Britain, and Italy. Ignace Daszynski was chosen President of the Polish Provisional Government on Nov. 9.

## UNITED STATES

War activities in the United States were either suddenly checked or profoundly modified by the unexpectedly early ending of hostilities. The problems of war were replaced by those of peace and reconstruction, and an era was entered upon that was calculated to tax all the wisdom and statesmanship of the Government.

The question of demobilization came at once to the fore. Ships bearing troops abroad were wirelessed to return. Detachments en route to training camps were halted. Dismissal of men in the cantonments was begun promptly, and arrangements were made for shipping to bring the armies back from France.

On Nov. 11 the United States had in France a total of almost 2,000,000 officers and men. Of these, over 800,000 were combat troops. It was announced that 1,200,000 men might have to remain abroad for a considerable time, but that the transportation home of the rest would begin at once. The first transport employed for this purpose left Liverpool Nov. 23.

Surprise and some criticism were elicited by the publication of a report of the War Department, Nov. 24, showing a total of 236,117 army and marine casualties, the total death being 53,169. It had been previously estimated that the total casualties would not aggregate more than 100,000.

Nov. 16 General March, Chief of Staff, announced that within the two weeks following 200,000 men would be demobilized, and that after that the rate of discharge would be 30,000 a day.

The total cost of the war up to Sept. 5 was $20,561,000,000, of which $7,017,000,000 had been loaned to the Allies. In August the Government's expenses were $40,446 per minute.

The Fourth Liberty Loan was a great success. The approximate final figures were $6,989,047,000, or 16 per cent. more than was asked by the Government.

The figures given above are colossal. Add to them the cost of the war to the other nations of the world, and they defy the mind to grasp them. Yet they were the smallest item of the hideous toll exacted by war. The world had been sown with graves and drenched with blood. Victory was bought at a cost that staggered humanity. But liberty was saved and the future of civilization assured.

# MAJOR GEN. ROBERT LEE BULLARD

Leader of the Americans at Cantigny and Commander of the 2d
American Army Corps

*(French Pictorial Service)*

# MAJOR GEN. ENOCH H. CROWDER

A new portrait of the Provost Marshal General and chief administrator of the Selective Service act

# PERIOD XLIX.

Germany's Blackest Month—British Victories on the Somme—Recapture of Bapaume and Peronne—Piercing the Drocourt-Queant Line—Advancing Over Redeemed Ground—The Fighting on the French Front—Americans in the Soissons Sector—The Battle of St. Mihiel—Raising a New and Greater Army—President Wilson's Labor Day Appeal—Austria's Peace Conference Note—Germany's Diminishing Peace Demands—Kaiser's Speech to Krupp Workers—Russia's Reign of Terror—Progress of the Allied Expeditions—Czechs Recognized by the United States—German Claims on the Baltic Provinces—The Shearing of Rumania—Movement for Polish Independence—Montenegro's Situation—Sinkings of American Merchantmen—The Murder of Captain Fryatt—War Surgery—Keeping Our Men Fit Physically and Morally—German Peace Talk After the Retreat—Germany's War Aims in March, 1918—After the War Is Over—America's War Aims—Peace Only Through Victory—Sinking of the Lusitania—German Plotting in the United States.

# CURRENT HISTORY CHRONICLED

[PERIOD ENDED SEPT. 20, 1918.]

THE improved situation of the Allies which developed at the beginning of the fifth year of the war was so materially enhanced during the month ended Sept. 20 that the doom of the Central Powers to total defeat seemed apparent. That their fate was sealed was practically acknowledged by them when, on Sept. 16, Austria was made the medium of appeal for a " confidential and non-binding conference " as preliminary to a peace congress. This request was immediately rejected by the United States Government, while the European Allies gave unofficial indications that they would follow suit. The unanimous feeling among the Entente Governments, as expressed by authorized spokesmen, was that of an unshakable resolution to hold no peace conferences until all invaded countries had been entirely evacuated, and until the Brest-Litovsk and Bucharest treaties had been annulled; otherwise to force the fighting to unconditional surrender. That this could be accomplished was demonstrated by the continued forward sweep of the allied forces from the English Channel to the Vosges.

Every day throughout the month victory rested with the Allies; over 200,000 prisoners were captured, all territory up to the Hindenburg line was wrested from the enemy, and at numerous points the line was breached to a depth varying from five to fifteen miles, while the American Army, by wiping out the St. Mihiel salient and recovering 155 square miles of territory, held by Germany since 1914, not only removed an old menace, but turned the threat in the other direction—against the German stronghold of Metz, the key to the vital Briey iron mines. To add to the perils of the Central Powers, the offensive launched in Macedonia Sept. 14, by the Serbian-French-British-Greek Armies threatened Bulgaria's hold on Serbia and seriously menaced Bulgaria itself.

The situation in Russia became more encouraging. The allied troops made substantial progress, being received everywhere with friendly demonstrations, and the real leaders of Russia began to crystallize public action against the Bolsheviki, whose power was fast crumbling. An alliance between the Bolsheviki and Germany followed the publication by the United States Government of documentary proof that in their administration they were the bribed agents of Germany and were deliberately betraying their country for German gold.

The formal recognition of the Czechoslovaks by the United States as an independent nation, with the intimation that a similar recognition would be given the Jugoslavs and Poles by all the allied nations, foreshadowed the complete dismemberment of the Austro-Hungarian Empire and the recasting of the map of Europe as a result of the war.

The resignation of Ambassador Page was announced, and his successor was named. The month brought no other diplomatic changes of importance.

The United States held a registration of all males between 18 and 45 on Sept. 12, and about 13,000,000 were registered without any friction or confusion; it was announced that the first draft would be for youths of 19 and 20 years and for men of 32 to 36 years, inclusive; also that provision would be made for an army of 4,800,000 in 1919, and that a total of $24,000,000,000 would be the approximate outlay of the United States for army purposes in the year 1918-19. All other war activities in the United States were at high pressure, and the flood of troops to France continued without interruption, 313,000 having been landed in August and a similar number in September.

An important decision was handed down by the Federal court regarding the sinking of the Lusitania, refuting the German assertion that the vessel was armed, and declaring that the catastrophe was a monstrous crime of the German Government. This decision, an important historical document, is printed in its entirety in this issue of CURRENT HISTORY MAGAZINE.

* * *

## AMERICA'S FIRST CASUALTIES

THE United States War Department authorized the following statement on Sept. 4, 1918:

Today is the anniversary of the first casualties in the American Expeditionary Forces. The four men killed and the nine wounded were members of the Medical Department of the army, noncombatants engaged in merciful work.

On Sept. 4, 1917, a German airplane attacked the hospital group at Dannes Camiers, where the members of United States Army Bases No. 5 (Harvard unit, Boston) and No. 12 (Northwestern University, Chicago) were operating British General Hospitals Nos. 11 and 18, respectively. Five bombs fell in or close to the ward barracks, and their explosion resulted in the death or injury of the first members of the American Expeditionary Forces killed by the enemy in the performance of their duty. The names of the killed and wounded follow:

KILLED.—First Lieutenant William Fitzsimmons, Private (first class) Leslie G. Woods, Private (first class) Rudolph Rubine, Jr., Private (first class) Oscar C. Tugo.

WOUNDED.—First Lieutenant Clarence A. McGuire, First Lieutenant Thaddeus D. Smith, First Lieutenant Rae W. Whidden, Private (first class) Elmer C. Sloan, Private (first class) Allen Mason, Private Aubery S. McLeod, Private John J. Stanton, Private Hirman P. Brower, Private J. D. Ewington.

* * *

## THE KEY TO THE WAR

AT Pagny, six miles north of Pont-à-Mousson, on Friday, Sept. 13, the 1st American Army reached a terrain which the French Senator, Henry Bérenger, has called the " key to the war." If Germany had not possessed half of this terrain in 1914 she could never have made war. To be deprived of all of it now would drive her out of the war within three months, for the terrain in question provides the Kaiser's armaments with 80 per cent. of their steel.

This " key to the war " is the Bassin de Briey, the richest iron-producing region in the world. In 1916 the mines of the United Kingdom produced 13,494,658 tons of iron ore and those of the United States 39,434,797. In that year

the Bassin de Briey gave nearly 42,000,000—all to Germany.

The Bassin de Briey runs from the Belgian-Luxemburg frontier up the left bank of the Moselle at a mean distance of ten miles from the river. Its greatest length is thirty-five miles, its greatest width is twenty-one, and it has an area of 225 square miles. Once it was all French, but the treaty of Frankfort, in May, 1871, ran the frontier line in such a way that Germany got nearly half.

When the present war began, 15,000,000 tons of ore out of her total production of 22,000,000 annually came to France from her part of the Bassin de Briey. Of Germany's total annual production of 28,000,000 tons 21,000,000 came to her from her part of the Bassin de Briey. Every year since 1914 Germany has added the French share to her own. She has also mined every year 6,000,000 tons from the terrain where it laps over into Luxemburg. All this gives her a total tonnage of 49,000,000, all but 7,000,000 of which comes from the Bassin de Briey.

* * *

## AMBASSADOR DAVIS

WALTER HINES PAGE, who held the post of United States Ambassador at the Court of St. James's for six years, resigned in September on account of ill-health, and John W. Davis of West Virginia, Solicitor General of the United States, was named as his successor. Mr. Davis, at the time of his appointment, was in Switzerland at the head of the American delegation to confer with a German mission on the treatment and exchange of prisoners of war. He had been elected to Congress from the First West Virginia District, and had been appointed Solicitor General by President Wilson in April, 1913. Mr. Davis is a lawyer, 45 years of age, a graduate of Washington and Lee University, and a resident of Clarksburg, W. Va.

* * *

## COLONIES AS WAR ASSETS

GERMANY appeared late upon the field of colonial expansion; her first colony was Togoland, acquired in 1884. From that date until the beginning of the war she had acquired in colonies and dependencies an area of 1,027,820 square miles, with a native population of 12,041,603 and a white population of 25,000. The oldest retained French colony is Guiana, dating from 1626. Today her colonial possessions include 3,449,614 square miles and a population of 40,-702,528, about 1,500,000 of whom are white. Great Britain, whose colonial empire dates from the fifteenth century, has a colonial or dependent population of 400,000,000, spread over an area of 12,624,435 square miles.

Germany's colonial empire is now occupied by the Allies. In thirty years it had developed none of those features or resources which have been such a big war asset for the colonies of France and England. The material in foodstuffs alone that has been sent forth from British and French possessions for consumption by the home countries is almost incalculable.

Of the 7,500,000 soldiers and male war workers recruited by Great Britain 1,900,000 came from her oversea possessions. The latest number of the Journal Officiel tells what the French colonies have given. From 1914 till July, 1918, Algeria and Tunis had given 340,000 troops; the Sudan, Senegal, Tonkin, and Madagascar, 250,000; the French West Indies, 31,000. To this total of 621,000 fighting men should be added 238,000 laborers.

\* \* \*

## RUSSIAN AND FRENCH REVOLUTIONS

IN an attempt to draw a parallel between the Russian Revolution and the French Revolution of 1789 historians have too often sought for similarities where only contrasts existed, for a material comparison where only a psychological one is possible. Both revolutions were inevitable and both had been consciously and unconsciously prepared in a similar fashion. Russia also had her Montesquieus, her Voltaires, and her Rousseau; a peasantry which wanted land of its own; an artisan class which desired to possess factories; a bourgeoisie which craved to share the national life with the nobility; a nobility which lived off the laborers and the small capitalists, and for this reason

stood as a wall between them and royalty, forever hiding the truth from the latter.

In each country an unexpected accident precipitated revolution. Both Paris and Petrograd wanted bread. The National Guard declined to fire on the Paris mob—the Cossacks on the Petrograd mob. The monarchies were overthrown, and in each case the intellectuals and the bourgeoisie found themselves trying to establish a responsible Government, without any clear conception of what that Government should be. They appealed to the law. There was none. Knowing the monarchs were not to blame, but that it was the system which was at fault, they shielded them. Meanwhile, the masses became articulate. They mistook freedom for license. From words they passed to action as undisciplined as had been their intellectual evolution.

France had her States General; Russia her Duma. France tried to have a Constituent Assembly; so did Russia. France had her Mirabeau; Russia, her Lvoff and Kerensky. Then came the coup de main of Aug. 10, 1792, in Paris, and the coup d'état of Nov. 7, 1917, in Russia. In France the mountain gained the upper hand. In Russia, the Bolsheviki. Both came from the depths, bringing with them the illiteracy and the bestial cravings of generations of intellectual asphyxia.

So ended the first phase. Then France had her Danton and Marat; Russia, her Trotzky and Lenine. Louis XVI. was executed; so was Nicholas II. The fate of the Dauphin has been a mystery of the ages; the fate of the Czarevich seems likely to become another. Legalized terror then reigned in each country. Marat then had his Charlotte Corday. There have been several Charlotte Cordays seeking Lenine's life.

So ended the second phase. Then the Terror reigned again. It devoured itself in France. It is now feeding upon itself in Russia. In France it passed with the execution of Robespierre and the Ninth of Thermidor. Behind the back of Robespierre constructive forces had been at work which were to save France. Whether Russia is to be inflicted with a Robespierre before she can be saved is in the lap of the gods. There are forces, however, at work in Russia which were unknown in France and in her age of revolution and regeneration.

\* \* \*

### WANTON DESTRUCTION

AT Château-Thierry an American journalist, Don Martin, visited a large number of looted and wrecked private residences. As indicative of the general looting and wanton destruction which was revealed everywhere in that region, he sets forth these items of what the Germans did in one single home:

> Threw an ink bottle against a seven-foot mirror, afterward splashing ink on the walls and ceiling.
>
> Jammed a bayonet through the works of five handsome marble clocks.
>
> Tore covers and blocks of pages from costly volumes and strew more than 500 books about the floor, practically ruining a library which was very evidently the pride of a booklover.
>
> Tore a Teddy bear in two; pulled arms and legs from large dolls; smashed a doll cradle and generally wrecked a child's nursery.
>
> Smashed all the china in a cabinet and a cupboard and shattered expensive glassware.
>
> Slit oil paintings and stamped holes in pictures, which had been torn from the walls and left on the floor.
>
> Broke the keys on a costly piano.
>
> Knocked tops off vases and fancy urns.
>
> Slit tapestries and curtains to ribbons.
>
> Threw bottles against handsomely decorated walls and poured various kinds of sauces and other liquids on expensive rugs and carpets.
>
> Rifled every drawer in the house; blew open a small safe; threw trinkets and fancy articles of wearing apparel all over.
>
> Wrecked beds, dresses, and mirrors in all the sleeping rooms.

\* \* \*

### NOYON IN HISTORY

NOYON, which was recaptured by the French in September, is famed in history. Before Europe entered the Christian era Noyon, then Noviomagus Veromanduorum, was the seat of determined opposition to all-conquering Rome. In turn it was the field of stirring battle between Gaul and Roman, Roman and German barbarian, Frank and German, Frank and Frank, French-

man and Englishman, and now between Frenchmen, with English allies, and the German. The currents of history have washed high around this little city of France.

Charlemagne was crowned there in 768. Pepin the Short held his coronation there in 752. Thus the roots of the united, first-rank great power, France, reach back for their beginning to this city. Noyon was plundered and destroyed by the Normans in 859. It was ravaged by the English and Burgundians and the whole country round about completely devastated during the Hundred Years' War. It was captured and sacked by the Spaniards in 1552, and again in 1594, when Henry IV. expelled the Leaguers. It was Christianized at the close of the third century by that saint of many legends, St. Quentin. John Calvin, the great reformer, was born there in 1509.

\* \* \*

### DRINKING WATER FOR JERUSALEM

WHAT the Turks could not do at Jerusalem in 400 years of rule, the British engineers accomplished in ten weeks. The picturesque water carrier is passing. The germs that infested his leathern water bags no longer endanger the lives of the citizens, and the deadly perils which lurk in cistern water have been to a large extent removed. For its water Jerusalem used to rely mainly upon the Winter rainfall to fill its cisterns. Practically every house has its underground reservoir. But many had fallen into disrepair, and most of them required cleaning. To supplement the cistern supply the Mosque of Omar reservoir halved with Bethlehem the water which flowed from near Solomon's Pool down an aqueduct constructed by Roman engineers under Herod before the Saviour was born. This was not nearly sufficient, nor was it so constant a supply as that provided by our army engineers. They went further afield. They found a group of springheads in an absolutely clean gathering ground on the hills yielding some 14,000 gallons an hour, and this water, which was running to waste, is lifted to the top of a hill, from which it flows by gravity through a long pipe line into Jerusalem. Supplies run direct to the hospitals, and at standpipes all over the city the inhabitants take as much as they desire. The water consumption of the people has become ten times what it was last year.

* * *

### "GASLESS" SUNDAYS FOR AUTOMOBILES.

THE Fuel Administration on Aug. 27 called upon the public in States east of the Mississippi River to cease the using of all classes of automobiles, (with a few named exceptions,) motor cycles, and motor boats on Sundays until further notice, as a gasoline conservation measure. The action was taken to meet a threatened shortage of gasoline for shipment overseas, created by the increased domestic demands and extensive military operations in France. The owners and users of automobiles complied with the request with wonderful unanimity, and the strange spectacle was witnessed of city streets and country roads entirely empty of their usual Sunday traffic. This continued to be true each Sunday while the suspension lasted. Fuel Administration officials estimated that the saving of gasoline each Sunday was about 8,000,000 gallons.

* * *

### THE GREAT TASK OF THE AMERICAN RED CROSS

MAJOR JAMES H. PERKINS, head of the American Red Cross Commission overseas, made the following statement in August regarding the activities of the Red Cross in Europe:

In the last push we took care of practically all the American wounded in the French war zone. In and about Paris we have established 7,000 beds. Twice we have given sums of £250,000 to the British Red Cross, and we have contributed to the funds of the Scottish Women's Hospitals. In every direction we work with the French authorities. Through our home service, an organization that has branches in every town in America, over 300,000 families of soldiers have been helped in some way, and similar work is being done for French soldiers.

To their Red Cross we have given 10,-000,000 francs, and through our Civilian Relief work we are assisting the French authorities to establish relief centres to provide supplies for refugees and to bestow upon them the means to start life again. About 1,000 refugees a day were coming through Switzerland, many of whom were traveling twenty miles from their homes into unknown country, not knowing where they were to find shelter. The work of feeding, comforting, clothing, and helping to establish such numbers of people is stupendous. Of the courage, tenacity of purpose, and bravery of these French exiles one must speak in the highest terms of admiration. In one month 254,000 French civilians were assisted by the Civil Affairs Department, in conjunction with the American Red Cross. Children's welfare centres are part of the vast undertaking, schools for the training of district nurses are started, and in various directions succor is given to the afflicted.

The American Field Canteen Service is another branch of our industry; 1,500,000 meals were served in July to the troops. Every wounded man who goes to one of these centres is supplied with food and drink. As to nurses, there were 20,000 fully trained and registered in active service last Summer, and a campaign is being carried on to raise the number to 25,000 before Dec. 31.

* * *

### MALVY'S PARTING WORDS

M. MALVY, former Minister of the Interior, who was banished from France for five years, before his departure for Spain on Aug. 11, 1918, addressed a letter to the President of the Senate in which he said:

I have been expelled by a judgment which is at one and the same time an attack on the Constitution and the laws of the sacred right of defense. Nevertheless, desirous at this grave hour, when the fate of France is being decided, that her effort should not be weakened by any agitation, I obey the order made against me. I leave France, but I do so crying aloud that I do not and will never accept this political judgment, which turns on a question of policy.

He then states that his real crime dates from 1917, when he acted as umpire in the strikes, which he was at one time during the proceedings accused of having provoked. From this time, he says, date also the complaints against him. In the eyes of his opponents his real crime was that he had obliged the masters to meet the representatives of their employes in order to satisfy their just claims. He remains faithful "to that policy of national unity and of trust in the people, convinced that it was and remains the only policy capable of maintaining that social peace which I am happy to have been able to maintain without trouble or incident during the forty-two months of my Ministry. This social peace is a condition indispensable to victory. I love my country too much to do anything today which could hurt her. France above everything!" He is going away, the ex-Minister continues, his heart bruised by injustice, but strong in the knowledge he has been wronged. Exhorting those who may be counted his partisans, he says:

To all those who are with me in this cruel trial I address from the bottom of my heart a passionate appeal that they should continue to give, as before, the best of themselves for the national defense, which is more than ever inseparable from the defense of the republic. Let the victory of France,. which must be that of right and the independence of peoples, rest first in our cares. With it will sound the hour of retaliation, justice, and democracy. It is my consolation, as I put my foot into exile, to foresee both in the near future.

* * *

### BRITISH VOTES OF CREDIT

THE following are the details of the votes of credit of Great Britain since the war began:

| | |
|---|---|
| 1914-15 | £362,000,000 |
| 1915-16 | 1,420,000,000 |
| 1916-17 | 2,010,000,000 |
| 1917-18 | 2,450,000,000 |
| 1918-19 (to date) | 1,800,000,000 |
| | £8,042,000,000 |

This total, translated into dollars, is $40,210,000,000.

The vote of $3,500,000,000 by Parliament Aug. 2, 1918, brought the total for the current year to $9,000,000,000. The debts due Great Britain from war loans on Aug. 1, 1918, were as follows: The Dominions, $1,042,500,000; Russia, $2,-940,000,000; France, $2,010,000,000; Italy, $1,565,000,000; Belgium, Serbia, and Greece, $595,000,000.

* * *

### THE CZAR'S DEATH

THE manner of the Czar's death is a mystery. It was at first reported that he had been tried and executed on a tribunal's order. A telegram from Archangel, dated Aug. 16, stated:

No trace was found of the body of the Czar Nicholas when the Czechoslovaks captured Ekaterinburg on July 26, according to information brought to Mr. Francis

by an officer of the Czech Army, who has arrived at Archangel with dispatches from the American Consul at Ekaterinburg, after a long and perilous trip through two lines of hostile Bolsheviki. The officer said there was no definite information as to how the Czar's body had been disposed of, but the report to which most credence was given was that it had been taken to the deepest pit in the Ekaterinburg coal mine, where it was destroyed. The execution of the Czar took place on July 16. So far as the officer had been able to learn, the Commandant of the Ekaterinburg Soviet, who was reported to be a sailor, killed the Czar with a revolver. A Red Guard, who had first been commanded to kill the Czar, refused, as also did a Lettish firing party. The Commandant then drew his revolver and shot the Czar dead. The officer, however, had heard many other versions of the affair.

* * *

THE German defeats in the neighborhood of Armentières involved a German officer who is perhaps better known to the reading public of the allied nations than almost any of the German Generals. He is General Bernhardi, the author of the famous book which so frankly revealed Germany's war aims. He commands the 55th Corps of the 6th Army, which has been steadily driven back by the British across the plain of the Lys toward Armentières. The 55th Corps was badly hit in endeavoring to hold the Merville salient confronting the forest of Nieppe. It lost many positions and was badly shaken by the enfilading fire of the British batteries as it retired.

* . * *

THE famous cathedral St. Gervais at Soissons was badly battered by German guns in September. Enormous breaches were made in the splendid façade. The upper gallery was three-quarters destroyed, while the lower gallery was wrecked. The statues fell one by one from the tower. The ancient Abbey of St. Jean-des-Mignes, in which Thomas à Becket spent several years, was practically destroyed. Both towers were decapitated, while the façade was pierced in many places. The vault fell in, and the rich ornamentation of the left tower disappeared, with the exception of the statues of two saints that remained facing the enemy.

## GERMAN USE OF POISON GAS

THE report that the German Government had proposed through the Swiss Red Cross organization the abolition of the use of poison gas is nullified by the following order of the 7th German Army, issued in August, 1918. It shows that the fullest possible use is to be made of poison gas:

In order that he may have at his disposal a certain number of officers and non-commissioned officers of the active army (that is, professional soldiers who will remain in the army) who are familiar with the working of the gas service and who can be employed in the formations of this service, which it is intended to retain, the Minister of War wishes to know the names of competent officers and non-commissioned officers who have distinguished themselves in the gas service during the war and wish to remain in it after the war. Officers and non-commissioned officers of gas units now attached to the 7th Army who wish to do this are invited to send in their names to their military superiors before July 25, mentioning their unit, rank, and seniority, and also the branch of the gas service which they know and the kind of work for which they are particularly suited. Applicants mutilated in consequence of wounds should indicate the extent to which their capacity has been reduced by their injuries.

\* \* \*

## PRUSSIA AND THE SWORD

IN 1860 Bavaria was striving to bring about the cohesion of the German States and the regeneration of her neighbor Prussia by intellectual, moral suasion. Prussia was trying to do the same thing with the sword, and she and Bavaria clashed. Today King Ludwig, who in 1866 was an officer in the 2d Regiment of Uhlans, limps about with a Prussian bullet in his body—a memento of that year. It may have been a recollection of what subsequently forced Bavaria into the Prussian fold that caused the editor of the Münchener Post to write as follows on July 18:

If Prussia had known how to conquer the materialism of her ruling classes and brought about the triumph of a high ethical ideal of duty, she would have conquered Germany morally during this war. But " Prussia must not have moral conquests," decree the chiefs who have everywhere erected altars for the worship of the sword and have recently once more set forth their arrogant desires for

the present and their haughty hopes for the future. In three sittings the Prussian House of Lords made war on every fresh and new idea. It opposed the change of personal Government into a Parliamentary system, the introduction of universal suffrage, a peace by agreement, &c. Count Behr-Behrenhoff made a pathetic speech against the resolution of the Reichstag of July 19.

Yes, Prussia can renounce moral conquests! Forward! Conquer by force, by the sword, by blood, and down with ideas of moral conquest! And yet! Last session the President announced to the entire world that the ethical ideal of duty was born in Prussia, that the State of the Hohenzollerns was based on the ideas of duty and authority, and that this State, therefore, must be the centre of the German Empire. Quite the contrary was said by Frederick William IV.: " Prussia ought to resolve herself into Germany and the Germans." Instead of this Germany has humbly crystallized around Prussia.

\* \* \*

THE United States Navy has built a base hospital on the Irish coast on the grounds of an old estate.

\* \* \*

## THE AMERICAN SOLDIER'S MARCHING EQUIPMENT

THE full marching equipment of the American soldier weighs seventy pounds. Over the shoulders, attached so as to rest on the back, are shelter half, haversack, trench helmet, trench tool, and blanket roll. Strapped to the ammunition belt are canteen and first-aid package at the right and sheathed bayonet at the left.

The mess kit, containing knife, fork, spoon, cup, and a combination frying pan and plate, all of aluminium, is suspended at one end of a strap, which passes behind the neck and, crossing over the chest, hangs below the waist. On the other end of the strap are the special tools of the soldier's branch of the army—the wires and pincers of the Signal Corps or the wrench and jack of the engineer.

The shelter half is so named because it makes half of a tent in which there is just room for two men to bunk. Rations and personal belongings, such as soap, toothbrush, cigarettes, and underwear are carried in the haversack. Most extra clothing, however, is put in a dun-nage bag, which travels in a supply wagon. Blankets are rolled in a waterproof slicker and the canteen is incased in a canvas cover, which keeps the water cool.

* * *

ONE THOUSAND Victoria Crosses have been awarded since the decoration was instituted by Queen Victoria at the time of the Indian Mutiny, when 182 crosses were awarded. In the Crimean War 111 V. C.'s were won; in the South African war 78, in the Zulu war 23, and in the Afghan war 16. Nearly 200 were awarded in the present war up to September, 1916, and the thousandth on the roll was obtained by Driver Dalziel, an Australian. It is calculated that not more than half the recipients of the honor during the last four years are now alive.

* * *

THE National Industrial Conference Board asserts that the cost of living between July, 1914, and July, 1918, increased in the United States 50 to 55 per cent. The increases found for the different items that go to make up the budget of the average family were: Food, 62 per cent.; rent, 15 per cent.; clothing, 77 per cent.; fuel and light, 45 per cent.; sundries, 50 per cent.

* * *

CROPS THAT HELPED TO SAVE ENGLAND

INFORMATION collected on June 4 shows that the total arable area in England and Wales in 1918 was 12,398,-730 acres, representing an increase of 1,152,620 acres, or 10 per cent. over the arable area of 1917. This is the largest area returned for the last twenty years. The area under permanent grass is 14,-588,900 acres, a decrease of 1,246,470 acres on the year. The total area under crops and grass thus amounts to 26,987,630 acres, as compared with 27,081,480 acres in 1917. The greater part of the grass land plowed up has been placed under wheat and oats. The increase in the area under wheat is 638,260 acres, or 33 per cent., and the total under this crop in 1918 amounts to 2,556,740 acres, which is the largest since 1884. Potatoes increased

25 per cent. over 1917; the number of horses increased 3,000; cows and heifers increased 113,000; beef cattle were 27,000 less than in 1917.

* * *

NEARLY 1,000,000 men, or half the railroad employes in the United States, received increased pay as from Jan. 1, 1918. The men affected by this increase were those who did not share in the previous raising of wages, and consisted mainly of unorganized workers drawing relatively low pay. The total annual increase in wages was thereby brought up to nearly $500,000,000 since the beginning of Government control.

* * *

PEACE IDEAS OF GERMANY'S CHIEF SEAPORT

THE following resolutions were passed May 19 by the Corporation of Hamburg by unanimous vote, except of the Socialists, who voted nay:

Having regard to the empire's financial situation and to the position of the Federal States, sorely tried by war, we propose that the Senate should request the Federal Council to press at the forthcoming conclusion of peace that the following points shall be conceded, in addition to satisfactory guarantees:

(1) A sufficient war indemnity from our enemies, for which the guaranteed delivery of raw materials may eventually be substituted;

(2) The formation of great colonial possessions entirely corresponding to Germany's needs;

(3) An effective guarantee of the just German claims on foreign countries and the restoration of all rights stipulated by contracts relating to landed property, concessions, &c., appropriated during the war in enemy foreign countries;

(4) The restoration of German trade by the defeat of all possible efforts of the enemy to boycott Germany;

(5) An adequate guarantee for the free and unrestricted traffic of German ships on all seas, and particularly the granting of full equality to these ships in all enemy ports.

Having regard to the gigantic and irreparable losses, both of blood and treasure, which every further day of war involves, efforts must be made that on our side war should not be prolonged owing to demands the fulfillment of which is not an absolutely necessary condition for our existence or for our complete freedom of development.

# Germany's Blackest Month

## Her Armies Driven Back to the Hindenburg Line, Which Is Flanked by the Allies—Americans Wipe Out the St. Mihiel Salient

[PERIOD FROM AUG. 18 TO SEPT. 18, 1918.]

WITH constant losses of men, material, and terrain on the side of the enemy, the narrative of the month is a continuation of that of the preceding. The pushing back of the enemy to the Hindenburg line, however, has developed two new features. To the north and the south of the line Foch has been able to develop salients of his own which penetrate to the rear of the German line of departure of March 21. This line was also penetrated at its centre near St. Quentin on Sept. 18.

On Sept. 12 the 1st American Army began operations which ultimately annihilated the vertex of the St. Mihiel salient. Here approaches have been gained leading to the iron region of the Bassin de Briey on the north and to the fortifications of Metz on the east. There is German authority for the fact that without the steel products derived from the Bassin de Briey the enemy could not continue the war beyond three months.

A larger aspect of the St. Mihiel offensive concerns lines of communication vital to the enemy. This links it up with the operations from Flanders to Champagne. All occupied France is fed by two great trunk systems with many lateral lines running from the bases in Belgium and Northern Germany down to the front. One system runs from Lille southeast to Rheims. That covers Flanders, Artois, Picardy, and Aisne. The other runs northwest from Metz to Mézières, near the Belgian frontier. The Americans pushing back the St. Mihiel salient were on Sept. 18 a few miles from the latter, which feeds the Germans in Champagne, Argonne, and before Verdun.

There is no doubt that Ludendorff's plans for an orderly, economic retreat to the Hindenburg line, or beyond, have been seriously compromised by the constant pressure exercised by Foch and his consummate skill in enveloping positions which had been fortified for frontal attacks. The enemy has lost 80,000 prisoners and 250 guns since the last week in August, making a total of 200,000 prisoners and 2,250 guns since July 18. His divisions available for work on the Western front have been reduced from 204 to 196. As the month closes there comes the news that twenty divisions have been disbanded in order to fill gaps in others. The number of troops to a division has gradually dropped in the last two years from 20,000 to less than 13,000. Many refitted German divisions now sent back to the front have scarcely 8,000 men.

## AMERICANS AT ST. MIHIEL

On Sept. 12 the 1st American Army to be mobilized in France, operating under the American Commander in Chief, General Pershing, began an assault against the famous St. Mihiel salient, which for four years had enveloped the Plain of the Woevre, with its bridgehead on the Meuse, and, standing as guardian to the great iron fields stretching north through the Bassin de Briey to the Belgian-Luxemburg frontier, had remained as an outpost to the twenty-eight forts of Metz in the bowl of the Moselle. Its presence, together with Metz, prevented any attempt to invade German Lorraine from the lines left by Castelnau in September, 1914, when he withdrew with the 2d French Army across the border.

General Pershing's offensive had been prepared with consummate skill, with vast resources of men and material. His artillery preparation is said to have been the most scientifically concentrated on record. The 1,000 tanks which opened the way for the infantry and later for the cavalry were operated according to tactics long in experimentation but never before used in actual warfare.

In a week he had recovered an area of nearly 200 square miles, menacing the Bassin de Briey, which provides the German armaments with 80 per cent. of their steel, on the north, and the forts of Metz on the east. He had released the Verdun-Toul-Nancy railway and was less than fifteen miles from the great German trunk line which runs from Metz west to Mézières. He had captured over 20,000 prisoners, over 100 guns.

The principal attack was made north from the southern leg of the salient, where for eight months American soldiers had been attending the school of the trenches. This line runs through a marshy and gullied plain, protected on the west, south and southeast by strong French fortifications. Another attack was made from the Heights of the Meuse to the northwest, between Dommartin and Fresnes. At the same time the French wiped out the enemy's bridgehead at St. Mihiel. [See map, Page 43.]

In the first day the invaders overran the new railway which the Germans had built from Thiaucourt down to St. Mihiel as a branch to that from Metz. In the second they crossed the angle, leaving the space within, some 100 square miles, to be thrashed out by cavalry, while their front ran northwest and southeast from Fresnes through Herbeuville, Hattonchatel, St. Bénoit, Xsmmes, Jaulny, Norroy, thence east to the Moselle.

On Sept. 15 the guns of Metz began to open fire on our right wing, and the centre pressed forward for a distance of three miles on a thirty-three-mile front. Up to this date the Germans had offered no stubborn resistance. They had so far employed only six divisions; now, on Sept. 16, their line began to stiffen, and the Berlin official reports spoke of fierce artillery duels and the repulse of enemy assaults. On the 17th the Americans gained points at Ronvaux, Manheulles, Pintheville, Haumont, and north of Vandières. Traction guns at Pont-à-Mousson overlooking the Moselle Basin from the south, and others moved up on the Thiaucourt railway from Toul, began to engage the enemy's forts at Metz.

Sept. 18 was a day given over principally to gun and aircraft duels, with consolidation of our lines at Fresnes and Haumont. All along the line one and one-half miles to the northeast the Germans were concentrating guns and men.

## FLANDERS TO CHAMPAGNE

A consideration of the month's events on the rest of the front reduces itself to the simple proposition of showing

THE DIMINISHING LYS SALIENT—ARROWS INDICATE PRINCIPAL POINTS OF BRITISH ADVANCE

what Foch has done to overcome the advantages gained by Ludendorff through the five phases of the great offensive which reached its maximum expression on July 18, when the initiative passed suddenly to Foch by his surprise flank attack upon the Marne salient between Soissons and Château-Thierry.

By Aug. 18 he had shaved off a fifth of the Lys salient. On the Picardy salient he had gained the same proportional amount of territory by a broadside advance toward the Hindenburg line over a forty-mile front from Albert to Ribecourt, the centre of which had reached a point twenty-five miles from the famous line. Albert, Bray, Chaulnes, Roye, and Lassigny were on the point of being reduced. In the south the armies of the Imperial Crown Prince had been driven north over the Vesle to within ten miles of the line they had occupied north of the Chemin des Dames

## Scene of Great German Retreat From the Marne to the Aisne

THE MAP INDICATES THE SIZE TO WHICH THE "CHATEAU-THIERRY POCKET" GREW IN TWO MONTHS. THE LOWER LINE MARKS THE GERMAN POSITION OF JULY 18; THE UPPER LINE IS THAT TO WHICH THE ENEMY HAD BEEN PUSHED BY SEPT. 18, 1918. THE FRENCH AND AMERICANS HAD THUS RECOVERED PRACTICALLY ALL THE GROUND LOST DURING THE GREAT GERMAN DRIVE IN THIS SECTOR.

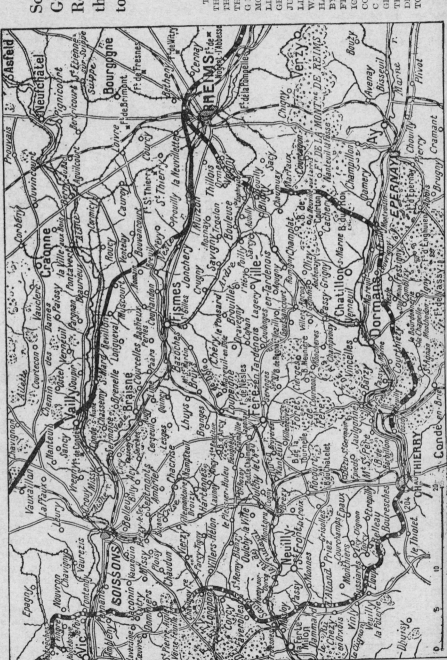

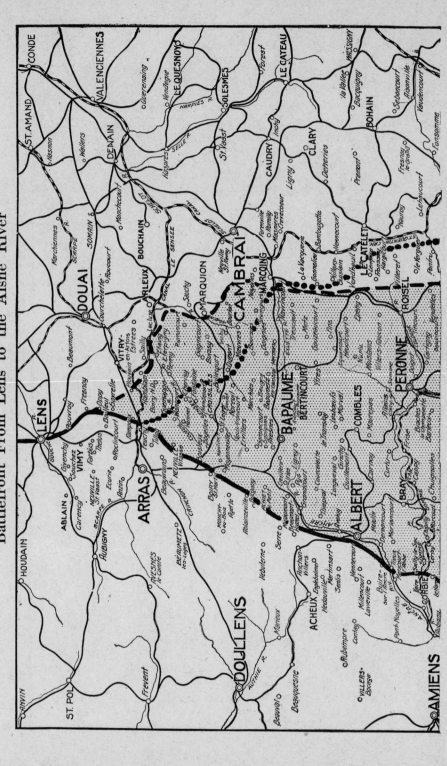

Battlefront From Lens to the Aisne River

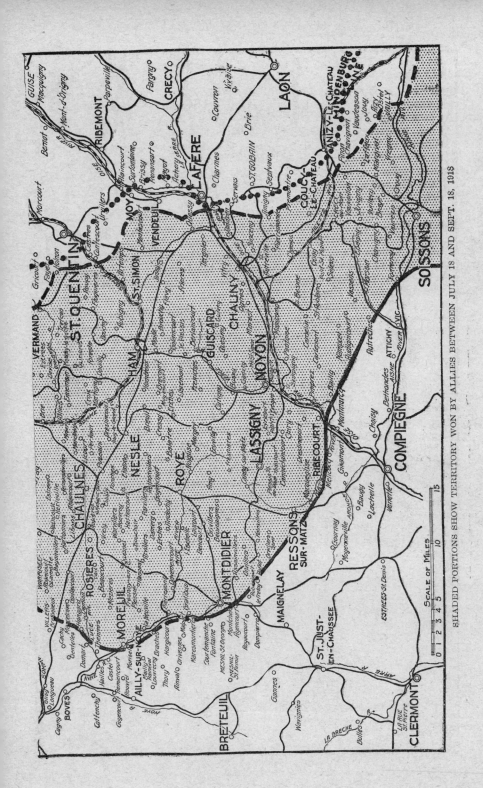

SHADED PORTIONS SHOW TERRITORY WON BY ALLIES BETWEEN JULY 18 AND SEPT. 18, 1918

on the eve of their excursion to beyond the Marne—the third phase of the offensive begun on May 27.

The story of the month reveals how Foch has progressed on these three sectors, with two notable additions. On the line east of Arras, between the Lys and the Picardy salients, he has overrun the northern flank of the Hindenburg line by forming a new salient which threatens to flank the Germans out of the Lens coal fields from the south and menaces the enemy's depots of Douai and Cambrai from the west. On the southern flank of the line he is threatening Laon from the St. Gobain Forest and the rear of the Chemin des Dames from positions respectively ten and three miles distant from their objectives. Here, as well as before Arras, he is measurably in the rear of the line from which the Germans made their offensive on March 21.

## ON THE LYS SALIENT

On the Lys salient the persistent attacks of the British have constantly taken advantage of the retreats of the enemy made necessary by the withdrawal of troops to aid other parts of the front. Here the most conspicuous successes have been the reoccupation of the strategic positions of Merville on Aug. 19, and of Mont Kemmel, with an attendant withdrawal on the part of the enemy on a twenty-mile front, and the loss of 1,500 prisoners, on Aug. 31.

From the very beginning of their assault on this line, away back on April 9, the Germans have been in a precarious situation. The salient, which by the end of that month had its centre resting on the Forest of Nippe, its northern wing on Mont Kemmel, and its southern forming the base of a triangle, (its vertex at Béthune and its sides formed by the Canal d'Aire and La Bassée Canal,) was too deep to be serviceable. It had utterly failed to attain its objectives—the ridge on the north running from Messines to the Mont des Recollets and the flanking of the Lens line south. Thus, after the initiative had passed to Foch and the ascendency of the Allies was beyond dispute, it behooved the Germans to extricate themselves from the Lys salient in

the most economical manner, qualified only by the number of troops Sir Douglas Haig thought it worth while to employ against them.

The operations which secured the reoccupation of Merville were made on a front of 10,000 yards, and reached a line running through the town from Paradis to Les Puresbecques, and, in the neighborhood of Outtersteene, 676 prisoners, together with several machine guns and trench mortars, were taken.

On Aug. 30 the Germans evacuated Bailleul, half way between Mont Kemmel and Merville. This was followed the next day by the reoccupation of Mont Kemmel by the British and the advance of their lines to the Lawe River from Vieille Chapelle to Lestrem, and to a point east of Bailleul known as Lille Mountain. The German retreat on that day is represented by the loss of three segments of the entire arc of the salient subtended by the geographic chords, Wytschaete (still in their hands)-Bailleul, Outtersteene-Merville, and Merville-Festubert. On the following day Haig was overrunning the ground between these segments. On Sept. 2 American detachments north of Wytschaete captured Voormezeele, and a few miles to the south the British gained Neuve Eglise and advanced east of Estaires. On Sept. 9 they reached a position which commanded Wytschaete from the west.

## THE BATTLE IN PICARDY

In a general way the narrative of the operations in Picardy, from Aug. 18 till Sept. 18, concerns the progress made by the Allies from Arras to Soissons to force the retirement of the Germans upon and beyond the Hindenburg line. In this narrative figure the manoeuvres of the 1st, 3d, and 4th British Armies under, respectively, Generals Horne, Byng, and Rawlinson, north of the lateral line Bray-Péronne-St. Quentin, and south of it the French armies—the 1st under Debeney, the 3d under Humbert, and the 4th and 10th, with the 32d American Division, under General Mangin. Opposed to them are the army groups of Crown Prince Rupprecht of Bavaria and the Imperial Crown Prince, in which the

Major Gen. W. R. Smith
*36th Division*
*(© Harris & Ewing)*

Major Gen. C. G. Morton
*29th Division*
*(Paul Thompson)*

Major Gen. C. S. Farnsworth
*37th Division*
*Press Illus. Service)*

Major Gen. J. N. McRae
*78th Division*
*(© Harris & Ewing)*

GENERAL DEBENEY

Commander of the French Army that captured Roye

armies of von Boehn, von Marwitz, von Hutier, and von Schwerin have been particularly concerned.

On Aug. 25, however, Byng crossed the Hindenburg line between Arras and Bapaume, and began to develop a salient in the direction of Cambrai, which soon enveloped the so-called "switch line," Drocourt-Quéant. Four days later the Americans, with Mangin, drove the Germans out of Juvigny—the initial step toward forming the line from St. Gobain south to the Aisne, which now threatens Laon, and the right-rear of the German positions south of the Chemin des Dames.

These two movements, which have progressed beyond the German line of departure of March 21, will be treated of separately after the dates mentioned in the foregoing paragraph. Prior to these dates the whole line from Arras to Soissons will be considered; after them the terrain under immediate notice will be that confined between the new salients of the Allies—before Cambrai on the north, and before Laon on the south.

By Aug. 19 the French had overrun the Lassigny massif and had taken Fresmières on the Roye highway, two miles and a half to the north. On that day the advance here was linked up with the operation in the south, across the Oise to Fontenoy, six miles northwest of Soissons. The next day came the smash from Mangin's 4th Army between the Oise and the Aisne, directed against the southern flank of Noyon, but destined to be felt, as will be seen, by the Germans north of the Vesle, fifty miles to the southeast. This attack he continued to press home until, on Aug. 29, the Americans with him drove the foe out of Juvigny, a little village, whose only importance is strategic. Meanwhile he had taken Lassigny on the 21st and Noyon on the 29th, while on his left wing Roye had fallen on the 27th and Chaulnes on the 29th. North of the Somme the British had begun a drive just north of Albert on the 21st, which gave them the town the next day. The attack north of Albert was continued persistently until it enabled the British to occupy Bapaume on the very day that the French took Noyon and the Americans drove the Ger-

mans from Juvigny. The Hindenburg line had been pierced on the 25th.

On the 30th the French in the south took possession of Mont St. Siméon, which commanded the Noyon spur and opened the way up the Oise. The next day the British captured Mont St. Quentin, which bore the same relation to Péronne. On Sept. 1 they took Péronne with 2,000 prisoners.

The foregoing operations were of great importance not only in their acquisitions, which would lead to greater things, but also in the revelations they made in regard to the enemy's growing weakness. In the north they opened up the Bapaume-Cambrai road as far as Buigny; the Roye-Pérrone-Cambrai highway to a point two miles north of Péronne. In the south they delivered the whole length of the Roye-Noyon-Soissons railway into the hands of the Allies. From Rouy-le-Petit to the Canal du Nord the Allies occupied the left bank of the Somme and its canal facing St. Quentin, fifteen miles to the east behind the Hindenburg line. An advance upon La Fère, twelve miles to the south, was also opened up the Oise. The dominating position of Thiepval northeast of Albert was overrun in a few hours on Aug. 23. In the battle of the Somme it had held out for three months.

From Sept. 1 to 6 certain strategic positions had been established—east of Péronne, Nesle, and on the right bank of the Oise; then on the latter date the whole line swept forward with an average penetration of eight miles. From the Somme eastward the line was carried twelve miles, capturing Chauny and the fortress city of Ham, once the prison house of "Napoléon le Petit." It was the following up of a German retreat going on over a front of fifty miles from the British sector before Cambrai to the Aisne south of the Chemin des Dames. What had given it its impetus was the crossing by the British of the Canal du Nord on a fifteen-mile sweep on Sept. 5.

From Sept. 8 for ten days the British concentrated to envelop St. Quentin and the French La Fère. First, the former secured Bévoir and Aubigny, while the latter crossed the St. Quentin Canal and took Dury, seven miles northwest of La Fère. Then respectively Villeveque and Vermand, Gibercourt, Rémigny, and Liez. On the 17th the British were in their old intrenchments before St. Quentin and the French in theirs before La Fère; between, however, the old line had not been reached, for the enemy still held Clastres on the St. Quentin Canal.

On Sept. 18 Rawlinson's 4th British Army and Debeney's 1st French made a surprise advance over a twenty-two-mile front which carried the outer defenses of the Hindenburg line at two points north of St. Quentin—Villeret and from Pontru to Holnon. They took 6,000 prisoners. The northern point of departure was Gouzeaucourt, ten miles southwest of Hinacourt, six miles northwest of La Fère.

## NORTH OF THE VESLE

By Aug. 1 the last of the troops of the Imperial Crown Prince had been driven back across the Vesle and that part of the Aisne between Condé-sur-Aisne and Soissons. Here they were prepared for a great frontal attack on the angle formed, with its vertex at Condé, by the Aisne and the Aisne-Marne Canal on the north and the Vesle on the south, when, on Aug. 8, Foch started his great offensive up the Somme 100 miles to the northwest. The shortening of the line from Soissons to Rheims had enabled the Crown Prince to withdraw two armies and then another. Foch had unhesitatingly taken away three armies and two American and several independent divisions. He had no thought of an expensive frontal attack. His idea was merely to exert a constant pressure which could be augmented in accordance with his advance on the northeast, between the Ailette and the Aisne—an obvious flank movement, which might break through between the Vesle and the Aisne, between the Aisne and the Chemin des Dames, or even in the rear of that great highway and that portion of the Hindenburg line which lies between Anizy and Craonne.

From Aug. 5 until Sept. 4 there were fierce patrol encounters between Americans and Germans on the north bank of the Vesle opposite Fismes. Then on the latter date the Germans beat a retreat on a twenty-mile front between Condé and Jonchery, and the next day their right wing was driven by the Americans over the Aisne west of Condé. Then from Condé up the Aisne the pressure gradually increased until the end of the month, with the enemy intrenched on the line Celles-Glennes-Les Venteaux, half way through the angle Vesle-Aisne.

We shall see how the more important events on this front were sympathetic expressions, whether in regard to the enemy or ourselves, of what was passing to the northwest of Soissons, particularly when this sector developed its front from St. Gobain to the Ailette, directly threatening Laon from the east. To that extent, therefore, it may be necessary to trespass upon ground which has no geographical connection with the angle Vesle-Aisne opening to the east.

On Aug. 20 General Mangin's 4th French Army, between the Oise and Soissons, made a movement which shook the whole line east as far as Rheims. It smashed into the German lines to a depth of two and a half miles, captured seven towns and 8,000 prisoners, and extended its front from north of Bailly to the Valpriez estate, five miles northwest of Soissons, including Champ de Merlier, Petit Maupas, Cuts, Hill 160, and Vesaponin. It gave the Allies a footing on the plateau east of Tartiers and an opening toward Camelin. An interesting circumstance of this movement was the fact that the Germans had prepared to make an attack on the same day and front, but Mangin anticipated it by half an hour. The subsequent history of this drive, forming part of the great movement against Laon, will be dwelt on under "The Move Toward Laon."

Instantly the American pressure over the rivers began to assert itself, and on Aug. 28 it was moving in force on Bazoches, fighting for the possession of Fismes and directing an artillery fire at the German bridgeheads near the Vesle-Aisne junction. The night of Sept. 5-6 was illuminated by the burning of German stores between the Vesle and the Aisne, a sign that the enemy was

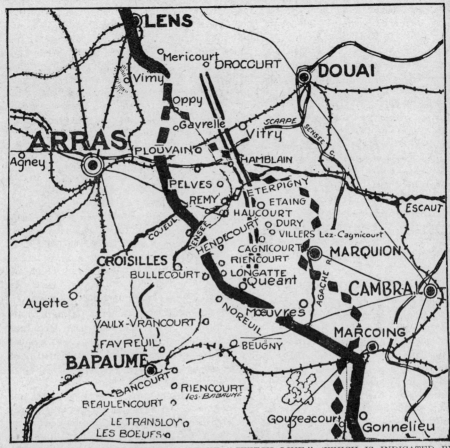

HAIG'S SMASH INTO DROCOURT-QUEANT "SWITCH LINE," (WHICH IS INDICATED BY PARALLEL LINES.) THE HEAVY BLACK LINE IS THE HINDENBURG LINE PROPER, AND THE DIAMOND DOTS INDICATE BRITISH ADVANCE TO SEPT. 18, 1918

falling back from the former. On the new front the Americans assumed the same tactics of pressure, with a flurry northeast of Glennes and Révillon, and between Vieil Arcy and Villers-en-Pravères on Sept. 11.

## MOVE TOWARD CAMBRAI

This is the story of the advance of the 1st and 3d British Armies, which, between Aug. 25 and Sept. 18, moved toward Cambrai and Douai, threatening them and the rear of the coal fields at Lens, crossing the Hindenburg line on Aug. 25, advancing down the Arras-Cambrai highway to a point further east than ever reached before, carrying the Drocourt-Quéant line, fourteen miles long, over six miles on Sept. 2, and finally developing on the enemy side of the Hindenburg

line, from just south of Lens to where the Canal du Nord crosses the line, a new salient whose perimeter came within four miles of Douai and three of Cambrai.

The steps by which this advance was made are as follows—always bearing in mind that the way to them had been paved by the capture of Albert on the south and the high ground of the Scarpe and Cojeul Rivers, respectively east and southeast of Arras, on the south: Proceeding in their advance up the Albert-Bapaume highway and the southern bank of the Scarpe, the British, on Aug. 27, captured a considerable portion of the Hindenburg line and occupied Chérisy, Vis-en-Artois, and the Bois du Sart. On the 28th, north of the Arras-Chambrai road, Canadians captured the villages of

Boiry and Pelves. A new impetus was given to the advance on the 30th, when the British reached Bullecourt, within their old lines at the battle of Cambrai of last November. The same day, however, the Germans made a desperate attempt to bar the way to the Drocourt-Quéant line; nevertheless, advances further south were made, and villages captured on the Arras-Cambrai and the Bapaume roads.

Then, as has already been said, on Sept. 2 the British crossed the Drocourt-Quéant line on a six-mile front. This formidable system of intrenched positions runs nearly in a straight line from Quéant, north to Drocourt, which lies some six miles west of Douai. Behind the line, but much nearer Douai, the Germans have yet a third series of intrenched positions. It may be added that Cambrai is protected by similarly formidable defenses, and that between that city and Bapaume runs the Hindenburg line itself.

The smashing of the Drocourt-Quéant line drove the Germans in a hasty retreat to the Canal du Nord, and on Sept. 3 Quéant, the point of juncture of the two great lines, was carried by storm in an advance on a twenty-mile front, with a penetration of six. More than 10,000 prisoners were taken by the British in this operation. Two days later, with the improved positions north and south of Péronne, the British made further progress up the Bapaume-Cambrai road.

On Sept. 12 important progress was made toward Cambrai by the capture of the villages of Havrincourt, Moeuvres, and Trescault; the British at several points also reached their old positions on the Canal du Nord.

## THE MOVE TOWARD LAON

The operations of General Mangin's 4th and 10th Armies, with the 32d American Division, which are threatening Laon and the right-rear of the armies of the Imperial Crown Prince south of the Chemin des Dames as we close this review on Sept. 18, have already been dwelt on down to Aug. 29, when the Americans driving the Germans out of Juvigny laid the foundation for the new

southern salient between the Oise and the Aisne.

The Juvigny affair was really the key to the situation subsequently produced. Here for five days succeeding Aug. 29 one American division fought four of von Schwerin's best and beat them, and gained the sobriquet of " Les Terribles." It captured 2,000 prisoners, and, on a narrow front of two miles, made a penetration of four. The taking of the village of Juvigny was a mere incident. But the occupation of the Juvigny plateau, the breaking through the railway across the front of Juvigny and Chavigny, and the gaining possession of the St. Quentin-La Fère-Soissons highway and of Terny-Sorny were events.

Incidentally Juvigny was the goal in a race between the American division and the 227th German Division. The former had marched from the front near Belfort; the latter from Metz. When the latter arrived the Americans were already pressing back the 7th German. Then were added to the enemy the 238th Division from before Rheims and the 23d Reserve Division. All were thrown back by " Les Terribles."

Meanwhile, on Sept. 1, the French troops ascended the Ailette on both banks and captured Crécy au Mont on the south and gained a footing in the wood west of Coucy le Château on the north. Between the latter and Juvigny they stormed the town of Leury and took 1,000 Germans. The next day they were threatening the woody flank to the west of the Chemin des Dames, and on Sept. 5, at Landricourt, near the edge of the Coucy Forest, having already reoccupied the famous Coucy le Château—that relic of German barbarism—they were in possession of a part of their old front as it stood before the German offensive.

On Sept. 8 the Americans could see looming up from the horizon to the northeast the twin towers of the Laon Cathedral. On that day the French of Mangin's 4th Army, taking advantage of the advance north of them made by Humbert's army, began the envelopment of that German stronghold, the St. Gobain Forest, whose outer woods begin ten miles west of Laon.

Henceforth the principal battle raged

around the approaches of the forest, where on the 9th the enemy threw in new divisions and fortified every available site with machine guns. On Sept. 15 the French captured the plateau east of Vauxaillon and the ridge northwest of Celles sur Aisne on the southern end of the sector—occupations which influenced the Germans south of the Chemin des Dames, rather than those covering the front of Laon.

On Sept. 16 General Mangin's armies made two thrusts, one against the St. Gobain Forest, the other at the Chemin des Dames. In the forest the French penetrated several groves and captured an entire enemy battalion. The thrust against the "Ladies' Road" was on a two-mile front, east of Sancy. It took Mont des Singes, northeast of Vauxaillon, and Vailly, on the north bank of the Aisne, east of Soissons.

## MACEDONIA WAKES UP

The revival of allied operations in the Balkans, begun Sept. 16, was stated by Mr. Balfour to be the prelude to an important offensive. This offensive, probably begun on account of the sending of Austrian and Bulgar armies to the western front and the waning of enemy's morale, had been expected for some time; first under Sarrail, when Rumania entered the war on Bulgaria's flank, and then, under Guillaumant, when Italy, (on the left wing of this 300-mile front,) in Southern Albania, started an offensive to gain possession of the Via Egnatia, the enemy's line from the Adriatic to Lake Ochrida, last July.

At length it has actually begun under General Franchet d'Esperey, who is believed to have a force of some 350,000 men, consisting of British, French, Ser-

bian, Montenegrin, Italian, and Russian troops, a Jugoslav division, and the new army of Greece, said to number 200,000. These are under his direct command and are acting independently of the Italian

SCENE OF ALLIED OFFENSIVE IN MACEDONIA. THE ARROW INDICATES LOCATION OF FIRST REPULSE OF BULGARIANS

and French troops on the front from Monastir to the Adriatic.

The attack was launched on a ten-mile front between the River Vardar and Lake Doiran. In two days French and Serbian troops had advanced five miles, had occupied a series of important ridges opening the way to Strumnitza, and taken 3,000 prisoners and 24 machine guns.

Through Sept. 18 the Bulgars, with their German allies, were forced back for ten miles and the front broadened to twenty. The prisoners exceeded 4,000; the guns taken, fifty. The Jugoslav division stormed the Koziak on the Bulgar's second line of defense.

# British Victories on the Somme

## Triumphant Progress Toward and Beyond the Hindenburg Line from Lens to St. Quentin

[SEE MAP, PAGES 12-13]

THE British on Aug. 8 struck their first heavy blow in the great offensive that had been begun July 18. They struck along a front of twenty-five miles in Picardy, from a point near Albert on the Somme to the River Avre, above Montdidier. This movement was rapidly extended, and by Aug. 22 embraced a front from Montdidier northward as far as Lens—more than thirty-five miles — with strong pressure on the line northward as far as Ypres, nearly twenty-five miles additional. They moved steadily forward, advancing with resistless force. The battle was still continuing on Sept. 18, at which time the British had reached at the north the defenses of Cambrai, having broken through the Hindenburg line north of Marcoing, ten to twelve miles, and were encircling the important city of St. Quentin, whose capture would force a further retirement of the Germans from that portion of France.

## CAPTURE OF ALBERT

The important town of Albert was captured Aug. 22; 1,400 prisoners and a number of cannon were taken. The fiercest battle in this region was in the sector of Miraumont, a few miles north of Albert, where the Germans resisted fiercely.

At Achiet-le-Grand the German attacks were in such strength that the British retired for a short distance from the outskirts of the town and contented themselves for the time being with pouring bullets into the enemy forces, who in their eagerness to win something, no matter how small, rushed right into the centre of the target formed by the town.

Tanks were employed to the front of the British lines almost everywhere. The battle was fought under a scorching sun, the men advancing over the dusty, shell-churned ground, open shirted or without upper garments, the sweat streaming down their half-naked bodies.

At many places heaps of German dead, mowed down by the British fire, lay baking in the sun, along with the usual débris which covers a battlefield. Efforts are always made by the burial parties to clear away the dead, but within the zone of a roaring battle it is not often possible to accomplish this task.

## GENERAL BYNG'S ATTACK

On the 22d more than 3,000 Germans were captured. Henry W. Nevinson described the initial onslaught as follows:

"Byng's attack was divided into two sections, a northern of 10,000 yards front, and a southern of 5,000 yards; and it was arranged that the southern section should come into action an hour later than the northern.

"The night was very still, but as the hours passed a wet mist formed over the earth, though the sky remained cloudless and sometimes one could see a star. So thick did the mist become that between 3 and 4 o'clock the trees were dripping with moisture almost like rain. Toward 5 o'clock the first glimmer of dawn was just perceptible.

"Suddenly, at five minutes to 5, the foggy air shook with an outburst of the British guns, and orange tongues flickered in the obscurity. For nearly three hours that torrent of smoke and fire and death continued like the incessant throbbing of a gigantic mill.

"Under this barrage the British went forward in waves, not leaping out of trenches or rushing wildly on, but walking quickly forward across No Man's Land, a second wave quickly following the first. Tanks led the first line of assault by about 100 yards."

On Aug. 23 the attack was extended along a front of thirty miles by the 3d and 4th British Armies under Generals Byng and Rawlinson. The enemy lost wide stretches of ground, numerous towns, thousands of men made prisoner, and large quantities of materials and guns. He also suffered further heavy casualties.

Crown Prince Rupprecht of Bavaria, the German commander, threw his men in before the advancing British armies in an effort to stave off the inevitable, but only to have them mown down again and again by storms of metal which poured from the British guns. One entire enemy battalion was annihilated during the fighting.

Dead Germans in great numbers were scattered everywhere over the battlefield. As an example, 400 enemy dead were observed on one small piece of ground over which the battle had swept.

With all this fierce fighting, and notwithstanding the fact that the British at many places fought over open ground against an enemy protected in " pot holes " and strong points of other kinds, the British losses everywhere were extraordinarily light.

## ENTERING BAPAUME

On Aug. 24 the British captured the dominating position of Thiepval, northeast of Albert, in the face of machine-gun and rifle fire, and reached the outskirts of Bapaume, capturing 2,000 prisoners and bringing their total in ten days to over 16,000. The Associated Press correspondent in describing the action on the 24th wrote:

" While Field Marshal Haig's men pressed forward with mighty strides on the main battlefront today, they had to fight for every yard of ground. Considerable numbers of guns and prisoners have been captured all along the line, and the British have again inflicted the heaviest possible casualties on the enemy. The ground over which the battle has been fought was invariably littered with dead Germans.

" New German divisions continue to arrive in the zone, only to be stood up before the advancing British and mowed down. While they have been able to check in a measure the Allies, they have been unable to stay their continuous forward movement.

" There are stories of less than a dozen men being left in some of the German companies which had participated in the recent fighting. Soldier prisoners captured today expressed themselves generally as having lost faith in the higher command, while non-commissioned officers attributed the defeats to the inefficiencies of the German air service and, more especially, to the presence of many untrained recruits in the older divisions. Some are said to have deserted while on the way to the front to participate in this battle."

## CHANGE IN SITUATION

The British continued their advance on Aug. 26 and 27 in face of stiffer resistance, capturing many towns, thousands of prisoners, and enormous numbers of guns. The situation as it appeared Aug. 27 is thus described by Philip Gibbs, who had returned to the front after an absence of several weeks:

" When I went away it was Rupprecht's army that was the chief threat against us, and it was an army of perhaps 250,000 fresh troops, apart from those in line waiting to be hurled against us if the German Crown Prince could do without them. We knew then that some of Rupprecht's divisions had been sent down hurriedly to his relief, but the question still remained whether the armies holding our part of the battlefront would still be strong enough to attack us or strong enough to check any attempt of ours to advance against them.

" Since then the tide has turned in an astonishing way. It is now the enemy who is on the defensive, dreading the hammer blows that fall upon him day after day, and the initiative of attack is so completely in our hands that we are able to strike him at many different places.

" Since Aug. 8 we must have taken nearly 50,000 prisoners and nearly 500 guns, and the tale is not yet told because our men are going on, taking new strides, new batches of Germans, and more batteries.

" The change has been greater in the minds of men than in the taking of territory. On our side the army seems to be buoyed up with the enormous hope of getting on with this business quickly. They are fighting for a quick victory and a quick peace so they may get back to normal life and wipe this thing clean from the map of Europe and restore the world to sane purposes. That is, I am sure, their hope, and for almost the first time in very truth they see something of its reality in sight.

"But there is a change also in the enemy's mind. Those German soldiers and their officers are changed men since March 21, when they launched their offensive. They no longer have even a dim hope of victory on this western front. All they hope for now is to defend themselves long enough to gain peace by negotiation. Many of them go even further than this and admit they do not care how peace comes so long as there is peace. They are sullen with their own officers, and some of those whom I saw today were more than sullen."

## CANADIANS' BRILLIANT WORK

Mr. Gibbs, under date of Aug. 27, described the work of the Canadians as follows:

"The arrival of the Canadians was an immense surprise to the Germans. The last heard of them was outside of Roye after their glorious advance on the left of the French, and the last thing in the world which the enemy expected was to find them right in the north beyond Arras. That was a brilliant piece of secret manoeuvre. Before the German had any inkling of their presence the Canadians were advancing upon them yesterday morning with a sweep of shellfire in front of them. Without encountering much resistance, they swung around by Guemappe and Wancourt over the high ground on each side of the Cojeul. Germans of the 214th Division, made up of men from Rhineland, Stettin, Lower Schleswig, and Hessians, were aghast at this sudden assault, and either retired or gave themselves up in the early stages of the Canadian advance. Their resistance stiffened on the crest of Monchy Hill, and there was fierce fighting all night in the trench on the top of Wancourt Spur.

"But the Canadians were determined to get this place, and with great individual gallantry and good leadership and most dogged spirit, they worked around the machine guns which were holding them off and rushed them in the darkness. By morning they held

the spur, and this body of Canadians, who had taken over 820 prisoners yesterday morning, added another 150, with many machine guns, most of which were captured in the valley below the ridge. All told, the Canadians and Scots attacking with them had taken about 1,800 prisoners.

"The highest point most desired by the Canadians was the old Wancourt tower on the tip of the crest, and this they gained in time for a new departure this morning, having to change their direction three times, owing to the lie of the ground, and face south instead of east after the beginning of the battle, which is always a difficult operation.

"A little further north other Canadian troops, who had crossed Orange Hill and Monchy, that hill which dominates many miles of country, so that the loss of it a few months ago was serious to us, advanced again this morning to two woods on equally high ground beyond for which our men strove many times in vain in May of last year. Those are the Bois du Sart and the Bois de Vert, which we used to see like green eyes staring down on our lines around Wancourt and Henin, and from which always there used to come wicked machine-gun fire when any of our troops moved in the open valley below.

"The success of our infantry is the more remarkable because in this battle very few tanks have been used, and machine-gun nests had to be taken in many cases without their help."

## HINDENBURG LINE BROKEN

On Aug. 28 the British pressed the Germans with especial ferocity. The important town of Croisilles, on the Hindenburg line, was taken, and the Germans were forced back to the so-called "switch line" of Drocourt-Quéant. Mr. Gibbs described the crossing of the Hindenburg line as follows:

"This advance gives a sense of the enormous movement behind the British lines, and there is not a man who is not stirred by the motion of it. They are feeling that they indeed are getting on with the war. It is like a vast tide of life moving very slowly but steadily.

"At Pozières and elsewhere the British have regained many of their old ammunition dumps, with valuable stores, which will come in use again. Everywhere over the old ground now recaptured there are clumps of British shells, and the earth is littered with them, lying in piles and gleaming in the rain and sun. So fast have the engineers worked that trains are now puffing up into places taken only a few days ago, and this morning I saw how all the pioneers and railway men and labor battalions, like an enormous army of ants, are working on those old battlefields to make a little order out of chaos and get on with the war, like the riflemen who are walking in front of them.

" Life is resumed in the fields and villages, which for the Summer months have been places of the great dearth. Today I saw men cooking food in parts of houses without roofs and on the lee side of shell-broken walls where only three days ago there was the menace of immediate slaughter to any living thing that passed that way."

# Recapture of Bapaume and Péronne

## By PHILIP GIBBS

[COPYRIGHTED]

AUGUST, 29, 1918. — Bapaume has been taken today, and from the hills north of the Scarpe, beyond Arras, right away down the line across the old Somme battlefields by Ginchy and Guillemont and Morval, where the British troops are pressing forward, and further still in the Australian fighting zone by Feuilleres and Belloy, above the Somme this side of Péronne, the enemy is retreating, and his men are trying to get away behind their rearguards before they are caught and killed.

In places the German machine gunners and rearguard lines are maintaining a fierce resistance in order to gain time for a more orderly retreat of the German divisions, and this defense is strongest on the northern half of the Australian front, perhaps to delay the capture of Péronne until they may have time to remove their enormous stores.

Upon our 1st and 3d Army fronts, from Bapaume and Bullecourt to the north of the Arras-Cambrai road, the German Army is stealing away in the darkness and daylight from all the country west of the Somme and from the battlefields beyond Delville Wood above. The British are trudging after them, kept up by the elation of a victorious advance, which is better than wine to them, because many of these men who are now following up the Germans in big strides are the same men who, in March last, had to fall back over the same ground under overwhelming odds. The change of fortune is balm to their spirits, and every yard of the way is a splendid revenge.

### ELATION OF THE TROOPS

Because they have the enemy on the run they are eager to go on till they can walk no further. Officers and men, like many I have met today, are high spirited, full of odd jokes and laughter, excited a little beyond the reserve and quietude of the English way, because Fritz is still hopping it, as they say, and every hour brings them news of more villages recaptured, more woods from which the Germans have fled, more ground gained on the right or left.

So I found the Australians this morning, and in another place some Welsh officers who had been moving forward day after day until they were miles away from where they started and far out in the wilderness of the Somme battlefields.

" The Old Dragon," said one of the officers of the Welsh troops, " has his tail sticking up straight as a crowbar, and Welshmen have a right to be proud of themselves, because since the 23d, when they attacked across the Ancre, they have captured place after place, with thousands of prisoners, smashed through the enemy every time he tried to stand, and scared him out of his wits."

With English troops on the right and

left, it was the Welsh who waded the Ancre up to their necks, and with the British barrage falling behind them, because they had gone too far, attacked and took the heights of Usna Hill at the bayonet point and afterward stormed the fortress position of Thiepval, which broke the enemy's main line of resistance, and then, with other troops, swept across the Pozières Ridge and Contalmaison and La Boiselle and Orvillers, through the Mametz Wood and Eseynd to Basentin le Grande.

"Mametz Wood, captured by the Welsh in 1916, has been recaptured in 1918. Hurrah!" was the wire sent to headquarters when the Welsh gained the wood on Aug. 25.

## DELVILLE WOOD RETAKEN

This morning they captured Delville Wood, the old Devil's Wood, which made a black chapter of history in 1916, and then went on to Ginchy and away toward Morval with English troops on their right through Guillemont. The British had Delville Wood for a time a day or two ago and then fell back from it day before yesterday under fierce shelling, but it is again theirs this morning, as I saw for myself when I went up to it and then took the field track toward Ginchy.

The British turned their heavies on it in the night and flung eight-inch shells among its dead trees, so that the enemy fled from its terror. Three men did not escape, but slept stolidly like dead men through all the gunfire until awakened. This morning, when the Welshmen went in, I saw coming down the road from Longueval under escort three white-faced fellows who still looked drugged by sleep but were sheepish as they passed.

I have had many strange and thrilling experiences on the battlefields of the Somme, from the time when the British fought yard by yard in 1916, so that every fold of the ground was the arena of a new battle and every clump of shelled trees, every ditch, every mound and heap of ruins was the scene of some terrible episode, until a few days after March 21, when I saw the British coming back across Pozières Ridge with the enemy in close pursuit, and German shells falling in old places which for years had been immune from fire.

But today many of those old emotions were eclipsed by the glad sense of being able to go once more up the Albert-Bapaume road, past La Boiselle, and through Contalmaison to the ridge at Longueval and Delville Wood, with the wonderful feeling that once again some foul spell had been lifted from these fields and that there was room to roam in them again—these places that are held by the heroic valor of the British, now that the enemy has been driven back to his vanishing line of retreat.

## DEAD AMID OLD GRAVES

To us who have followed this war in body and in spirit those upheaved and mangled fields are sacred ground, strewn with the graves of men who fell there. Their graves are there still, as I saw today, with the white crosses put up to them still standing above the turmoil of earth. The enemy had not touched them and the British shellfire had not destroyed them.

So far as I could see, the only difference since the enemy sprawled back here and stayed a little while and then was flung back again is that many bodies of gray clad men lie among the shell craters, and that the roads and tracks are littered with dead horses, so that the air is pestilential with foul odors and, everywhere among the old trenches and new, with their white, upturned chalk and the litter of barbed wire, are fresh German notice boards pointing the way to firing lines and observation posts and giving the directions of tracks—nach Mametz, nach Longueval nach Ginchy. They had tried to camouflage some of their tracks by screens made of rushes, and had dug deep shelters under banks and in old trenches in order to escape from the harassing British fire.

In shell craters and ditches lie their helmets, gas masks, rifles, and equipment, and here and there is the wreckage of a field gun or limber, untouched but abandoned by the enemy in their flight, and strewn over all the ground are vast numbers of unexploded shells.

## BACK IN BAPAUME

Aug. 30.—The places captured by the British today and last night are so many that the mere list of them is long, from north of the Scarpe, where the Scotsmen are on the outskirts of Plouvain, after their long and gallant fighting, to Bullecourt, which the Londoners and West Lancashire troops took yesterday, going further east today than we have ever been before and away down south beyond Bapaume and toward Péronne.

I picked some roses today in Bapaume, red rambler roses, which would make a garland for the steel helmet of one of the New Zealand boys, to whom the honor is most due for the capture of the town. Bapaume is not a fragrant place for rose lovers, and when I went into it early this morning, while a new battle was in progress outside, German shells were smashing among the houses, and there was a smell of corruption and high explosives in its ruined streets.

It is the second time we have entered Bapaume in triumph after stern fighting up a long, long trail. I shall never forget the thrill of that first entry, on March 17 of last year, when I had the luck to go in with the Australians up the long road from Albert, past Posières and Le Sar and the Butte de Warlencourt, and those frightful places where thousands of British had fallen on the way. It seemed then that Bapaume was the goal of victory, and, in spite of the dreadful sights about, one's spirit rose as one passed each shell crater and drew nearer to the town.

A repetition of experiences is never quite so fresh in sensation as the first adventure, yet, to get again into Bapaume after its loss last March, when the German Army came rolling the tide back over the Somme battlefields, was a thing worth doing. It was another landmark of history, made this time by the New Zealanders and English regiments fighting beside them.

I went up through Miraumont and the valley of the Ancre, across which the Welsh went wading to capture the heights of Thiepval on Aug. 28. It was a valley of abomination, and the dawn lightened its trees, sticking out of deep swamps, from which there rose wafts of stench, where dead things lay rotting. Sandbag emplacements, where men had little shelter from storms of fire, were white against the charred earth, and black stumps were everywhere for miles up this valley to Irles and Achiet-le-Petit and Grevillers and other places near Bapaume where the British had been fighting hard these last few days.

All this tumult of the tortured earth, all these pits dug by shells, all this wild destruction of places ruined in the first year of the war and mangled ever since were strewn with relics of German life and German death, newly littered here. Their great steel helmets punctured by bullets or torn like paper by shell splinters lay in thousands, with gas masks and rifles and cartridge belts and gray coats.

Along every mile of the way lay rows of stick bombs, never used against the British, and dumps of unexploded shells, hideous in their potentiality. A few dead horses lay on each side of the tracks, as they had gone trudging up with the British transport before being shot. Beside one horse lay a dead white dog, the pet of the transport column.

For a picture of war an artist like Orpen should have been here, but the men hereabout had other work to do. They were getting on with the business of bringing up guns across the wild wastes of cratered ground, filling up pits in the roads for the transport to pass, tearing up broken rails that new ones might be laid, riding and marching forward to support their comrades in another day of fighting.

They were mostly New Zealanders on this way, and although bad stuff was flying about—the enemy was crumping Grevillers and Achiet-le-Petit and scattering "high velocities" about in a vicious, random way — many of these lads did not trouble themselves to wear steel helmets, but kept to their slouch hats with the dandy red band.

## CAPTURE OF PERONNE

Sept. 1.—Péronne has fallen today in consequence of the Australians' brilliant attack yesterday which resulted in the capture of Mont St. Quentin.

One of the fine features of the capture of Mont St. Quentin was the rapid way in which the Australians moved their guns forward over the Somme and fired at close range on the enemy. This was largely due to the work of their engineers at the river crossings. At one of these they discovered several land mines laid by the Germans with trip wires artfully concealed, but they routed them out and prevented their explosion.

Part of the secret of the light Australian losses in this attack was the quick way in which they dived into the German trenches before clearing them, getting shelter there after they had taken 150 prisoners, so that the hail of machine-gun bullets passed harmlessly over their heads.

In the fighting from Aug. 26 until yesterday morning they took fully ten times more prisoners than their own total casualties, which must be a record in this war.

The individual gallantry of the men reached the high summit of audacity, as when an Australian Corporal in a recent action one day heard his comrades debating how they could destroy an enemy post which was giving them great trouble and said to them: "That's all right, I'll take it." He slipped one Mills bomb in his pocket, crawled through tall corn, jumped into the German trench, felled the first man he saw, and by sheer force of spirit so cowed the garrison of the German post that one officer and thirteen men surrendered to him.

## FOUR WEEKS' CHANGES

It is in the centre of our battlefront, by Bullecourt and Riencourt and Ecoust and Vraucourt, now recaptured by us today, that the enemy has been putting up the fiercest resistance, and that our men have had hard and bitter fighting.

In less than four weeks we have almost completely reversed the table of fortune, so that he has been smashed back twenty miles and more, and all the country between Amiens and Bapaume and Amiens and Péronne is cleared of his men, except of those who lie dead in tne ditches and craters, while north of the Scarpe we have gone further than ever before in this war, and further north still the Germans are forced to withdraw from positions which they gained by enormous sacrifice without our being troubled to fight them.

That is a wonderful chapter of history, and the triumph of it, the marvel of it, is that these victories have been gained very largely by those very troops who sustained the full brunt of the German offensive in March and again in April.

## CAPTURE OF QUEANT

Sept. 3.—More than 10,000 prisoners behind our lines are the best human proof of yesterday's victory when our troops broke the Drocourt-Quéant line, and today the enemy is in hard retreat from a wide belt of country north and south of the Arras-Cambrai road in a desperate hurry to escape lest his transport and troops may be encircled by our men, who are pressing their pursuit.

The capture of Quéant last night by our naval brigades, with Pronville beyond it, gives us the enemy's most important pivot where the Drocourt line joined the main Hindenburg line, which has been completely turned, so that this fortress position on which the Germans set their hopes of safety in defense is now in jeopardy.

Lowland Scots of the 17th Corps are walking along the Hindenburg line southeast of Quéant, clearing it of any men who may still be in hiding there, while the naval men of the Drakes and Hoods and Ansons and the Marines are following the line of the Hindenburg support trenches and curving downward to the Valley of the Hirondelle River and across its slopes to get astride the Bapaume-Cambrai road, which is the enemy's line of retreat for all the heavy transport now scurrying away, and burning their stores behind them.

The German command has scraped up every unit of every division which still gave some hope of fighting quality in order to counterattack us with ferocity and gain back their Hindenburg line. Ten divisions were identified against us in the region of Cagnicourt and Dury, and we took prisoners of every company of every regiment.

Behind our present front which is moving forward so quickly there is for many miles a stricken wilderness. There are no landmarks here, as even there are on Somme battlefields, where at least there are rivers and roads and natural features upon which the imagination may fasten for remembrance, but here beyond Neuville-Vitasse and Boiry and Croisilles there is nothing but a landscape of bare monotony rising and falling slightly from one slope to another without highroads cutting across it, without a river or a valley to break its lines, without even ruins more than rubbish heaps of brick which once were hamlets.

Trenches marked by hummocks of white chalk zigzag over this infernal desolation, where tangles of barbed wire, all rusted to the color of withered bracken; piles of abandoned shell gleaming wet in the rain, thousands of German stick bombs, gas masks, helmets, boots, rifles, shattered gun limbers, lorries slashed to pieces by explosives, and huts broken to matchwood are flung about between tumbledown dugouts, deserted gunpits, overturned blockhouses, dead horses, and deep shell pits.

Through this plague-stricken land, mile after mile to the far horizon, our men are marching and our guns are going up and our tents are pitched and our wounded come walking down. Even to them it has become familiar, so that they do not turn their heads to study how this obscenity of a wilderness of death is changed to different tones of evil or of grimness when the sunlight breaks through the rainclouds and washes it all with its pale gold light, revealing more sharply a detail of it all, or how it is darkened when the sun is hidden by a black mass of clouds piled up above the distant slopes.

Yet there is one feature of the landscape to which the men turned their heads when they marched up to battle. It is the only thing left standing in all this ruin behind our lines with some character and meaning beyond a mere ruin. In the centre of Croisilles, which is quite destroyed, so that hardly one brick stands whole upon another, there is a Calvary of life size. The figure of Christ has been smashed from the cross and lies with face upward on a little hillock, but the Madonna is still left, almost unscarred, I think, and the figure of St. John stands out above all this wreckage with a queer gesture of pity for the evil that has been done.

There were numbers of dismounted cavalrymen among our prisoners, wearing a yellow band around their caps, and belonging to the 7th Cavalry Division, which has been almost completely destroyed during the last twenty-four hours. These men curse the fate which brought them to the west front after an easy time in Russia, where they knew nothing of British barrages and believed the war was won.

In one camp not far from Arras there are today several thousands of prisoners, belonging to ten different divisions, and, looking at them, one might well wonder whether at last one might be justified in believing that the German Army is beginning to crack.

## SCENES BEHIND THE FRONT

Today the battle was in full progress and our guns were firing heavily, and now and then German shells came over to ruined villages on either side of this winding road, bursting with gruff coughs, and flinging up vomits of smoke and death. Through the black rainclouds the sun shone upon these frightful places, these huddles of brick and timber that gashed the skyline with their ribs and fragments, and upon the wreckage of railways and overturned engines and old gunpits and earthworks out of which we had hurled the enemy on our recent progress. That was the background of the road, and along the road itself came an incessant stream of men and mules and guns. It was like a long frieze on a living panel in some picture of war.

A stream going one way was made up of an endless chain of batteries and gun limbers going forward to follow up the enemy, and battalions were marching up in support, played up part of the way by their bands, and there were pioneers to make the way straight for the guns and ammunition and all the supplies, and ambulances, with their red crosses burning through all this black etching of guns and wagons. The other way, coming away from the battleline, were the walking wounded and prisoners and stretcher bearers. On one side was the spirit of victory moving forward, and on the other side the human price of victory and the tragedy of defeat. Crowds of German prisoners came stumbling back in small groups of twenties and fifties, odd dozens of pairs of men, and single figures hobbling slowly and painfully, with drooping bodies and their big steel helmets bent to their chests. Many were wounded, their heads all bloody and their faces like masks of blood, or with broken arms or bullet wounds in their legs; others were worse than that, so that they could not walk and seemed already dead. They were carried shoulder high on stretchers by unwounded comrades, one man to each corner of the stretchers, trudging slowly down that crowded way.

### PROCESSIONS OF WOUNDED

Our wounded and the German wounded mixed together and helped each other. Some of the Germans carried one badly wounded man as they carried their own. I saw many groups of English and Canadian and German soldiers walking together with arms about each other's neck, propping each other up, tumbling together, resting together for a time in the shelter of ditches and under ruins by the wayside. Some of them had picked up bits of timber and were using them as crutches or sticks to help them on the way, and others, after coming so far, dropped and waited for an ambulance to pick them up later in the day. Companies of wounded prisoners marched down in military formation with their own officers at their head, without escort. The officers called out words of command to them, as though on their own side of the lines; and I saw some battalion commanders among them walking gravely through with a beaten look.

There were many boys among them, but sturdy enough to make good fighting men, and their high steel helmets gave them a grim look. Many, however, wore their field caps, and by the numbers on their shoulder straps one could see many different regiments. After their first terror, they showed gladness at their escape, and many of them showed gratitude to our men by stopping them on the roadway and offering them iron crosses or pictures from their pocketbooks.

# Piercing the Drocourt-Quéant Line

[SEE MAP ON PAGE 17]

THE ASSOCIATED PRESS, on Sept. 2, thus described the battle which resulted in piercing the Drocourt-Quéant line, (the " switch line " to the Hindenburg positions:)

" The fighting was as furious as any since the war began and increased in intensity as the British battled their way forward, meeting the ever-growing resistance of the enemy, who had put in every available man and was rushing up reserves at the rear. Thousands of prisoners have been captured. The roads to the British rear are jammed with them.

" There has been fierce fighting in Dury, which was taken by the British, and Mount Dury, which the Germans held in great strength, was stormed. The British went on after killing enormous numbers of the enemy. The Germans died fighting here, as elsewhere. Cagnicourt Wood and Cagnicourt have been captured, and there has been heavy fighting in Buissy, northeast of Quéant, where large numbers of prisoners have been captured. Similar progress has been made against the northern end of the Drocourt-Quéant line for some distance.

" All during the night there was very heavy fighting around the British positions, which were almost jammed up against the great German defense system. Piles of dead Germans were one of the results. In one enemy attack a Sergeant with a machine gun killed six Germans who tried to rush him.

" It was soon after 5 o'clock in the morning that the massed British cannon broke loose with a roar that was heard for miles in a crash barrage. The whole sky seemed ablaze, as thousands of British shells poured into the German wire and lines.

" When the barrage raised the Canadians and English swarmed over the top. Just behind them were numerous tanks of all sizes. They had been over only a minute when the enemy opened with a counterbarrage, which is said to have been by far the strongest he has put down since the British offensive began.

" The instant the British appeared the Germans in many cases jumped out of their trenches and held their hands high above their heads. In some cases, however, the advancing British met a hail of machine-gun bullets, but, notwithstanding this, they pushed on. Quickly the first line was overcome.

" By 7:30 o'clock the British had completely passed the German front and support lines. It was then that the motor machine guns dashed out on to the good roads at the German rear. Tanks also managed to get through, and they are working far in advance of the infantry.

" Some of the fast motor machine guns are reported by the airplanes to have made their way along the Canal du Nord on the roads between Douai and Marquion. Along the Arras - Cambrai road the British have made good progress, and Villers-lez-Cagnicourt, which was protected by special belts of wire and a powerful trench system, was the scene of desperate fighting. At the crossroads northeast of Cagnicourt, where the Arras-Cambrai highway crosses the Villers-lez-Cagnicourt-Saudemont road, as well as all through this district, the Germans were in great strength. The crossroads are only nine and a half miles from Cambrai, and their defense is of the utmost importance to the enemy. Reports from Dury show that the fighting was of a desperate nature before the Germans, who were massed there and were about to deliver a powerful assault against the British positions, were overcome.

" As the British made progress all along the line rocket after rocket flamingly ascended through the battle smoke from German positions as the hard pressed enemy, first here and then there, called for assistance from those in the rear. The barrage had completely unnerved the Germans. The British then smashed their way through line after line, fighting in many cases hand to hand, and bayonets were used freely.

" The wood north of Quéant was found to be full of Germans with machine guns. The fighting there was of the very hardest nature until the British cleared the wood. Tanks again did heroic service.

" Where shells had failed to break through the wire, tanks rolled it out flat and charged down into the masses of Germans. Those who did not fall before the guns were crushed, together with their machine guns.

" The streets of Dury were carpeted with German dead. Here the British captured the town Mayor, and among other prisoners taken near by were several battalion commanders. Mount Dury was stormed soon afterward, but it was taken only after a terrific struggle."

# Advancing Over Redeemed Ground

THE British continued their forward movement, advancing bit by bit each day. On Sept. 13 they captured important defenses fronting Douai, Cambrai and St. Quentin, seriously menaced those three pivotal points, the capture of which would compel a withdrawal of the Germans perhaps altogether out of Picardy and Artois. Philip Gibbs in his message Sept. 13 wrote:

" It is a queer sensation to go through this country again, beyond Bapaume, down old roads which were familiar to us last year, through these fields and villages where, amid old ruin and wreckage, the British built thousands of huts and many officers' clubs and cinema sheds, and pitched camps of tents and established workshops and camouflaged gun positions.

"For a time, which now seems like a nightmare, all that sweep of country was overrun again by the enemy and was twenty miles or more behind his lines. And now once again the evil spell has been lifted from it. The gray wolves have gone and only their lairs remain and the things that belonged to their brief tenancy—things tragic and things abominable.

"Everywhere now among the old British graves are the graves of German soldiers. They stick up out of mud and swamps in these ravaged fields with wooden crosses, different in shape from the British, and surmounted with the steel helmets camouflaged by streaks of color, belonging to the men below who walked in them down these roads.

"Dead bodies, not yet buried, and dead horses lie amid the muckheaps of these battlefields, and everywhere there are old boots, old bottles, strips of field-gray uniforms, haversacks, stickbombs, German letters, the litter of the masses of men who went away in a hurry.

"It is utterly true to say that our men are going forward with gladness and exultation. They know the risks ahead. There is nothing one can tell them about the horrors of war. They know its fearful fatigues, the beastliness of things, the stench and dust of the battlefield, the wicked snap of machine-gun bullets and the howl of the high velocities. But in spite of all that they are marching forward with a light in their eyes and eager looks, and whole armies are on the move with a grim kind of joy.

"It is an astounding pageant, these hundreds of thousands of men—English, Welsh, Canadians, Scottish, and Australians—all moving in a long reaching tide with horses and guns and transport along tracks over old battlefields, going forward mile by mile very slowly because of the surge of traffic over narrow ways, but never stopping.

"Dust rises from these moving legions in brownish clouds which the wind tosses above their steel helmets, and through this dust, in which the sun is shining hotly, there is a vision of brown masses of men with the glint of steel on rifles and helmets and twinkling colors, red and blue and green, of staff badges and pennons.

"Every man marches in a white mask of dust through which his eyes shine. Dispatch riders are threading their way through long lines of transport. The endless columns of lorries, field batteries, and gun horses are grotesque, like millers all floured from head to feet. The horses are superb and in splendid form, as though from an exhibition, and it goes to the heart to see so many lying dead on the fields after the recent battles.

"There is a great music of war over all this scene. Scottish battalions go forward to the fighting line led part of the way by their pipers, and across the battlefields come the wild cry of the pibroch and the drone of many pipes. The English battalions are marching with brass bands playing old English marching tunes, and, between whiles, merry bursts of ragtime. The crunching of gun wheels over rough ground, officers shouting orders to their men, the hooting of lorry horns and motor horns, and an incessant hum of airplanes overhead all make up a symphony which has a song of triumph in its theme.

"A French artist friend of mine watched this scene and it lighted fires in his eyes—the warrior look of our men, their splendor of physique and youth, their hardness and gravity, which seemed to him illumined by a sense of victory in their spirit. A young officer of a machine-gun section came down from the line slightly wounded, with a trickle of blood down his cheek, but there was a kind of glamour on his face as of some messenger of good fate, and seeing, perhaps, some look of understanding from the French painter who was watching him, he turned and laughed and waved his hand."

# MAJOR GEN. WILLIAM S. GRAVES

Commander of the American expeditionary force in Siberia

# GENERAL KIKUZO OTANI

The Japanese military leader who has been placed in command of
the allied forces in Siberia

(© K. Adachi)

# The Fighting on the French Front

## General Mangin's Offensive Along the Oise and Aisne Toward Laon and La Fère

WHILE the British were making their onward sweep along the Somme River in August and September the French, with Americans, were continuing their pressure without cessation along the Oise and Aisne east and west of Soissons in the direction of the Hindenburg line stretching from Berry-au-Bac to Laon and La Fère. In September CURRENT HISTORY MAGAZINE gave the details up to the capture of Fismes, on the River Vesle, and the retreat of the Germans to the north side of that stream. The pressure of the armies of Generals Mangin, Humbert, Albert, Debeney, Degoutte, Berthelot, and De Mitry, with the aid of American units, was unrelenting along the front from Montdidier to Rheims. The French armies were in closest liaison with the advancing British troops to the north. Thus the whole allied front from Rheims to Lens was being steadily pushed forward to the Hindenburg line, and at several points, particularly in the north, several miles beyond it.

This movement was not as spectacular as the brilliant exploit in driving the Germans from the Château-Thierry pocket, but it was equally important; it enabled the British to achieve their triumphant progress on the north without the appalling loss of life that would have been inevitable had the Germans not been driven forward simultaneously on the south.

## GENERAL MANGIN'S OFFENSIVE

The first important capture after Fismes was Lassigny, which was preceded Aug. 20 by a new offensive launched by General Mangin's 4th Army on an eighteen-mile front from Pimprez, opposite Ribecourt, on the Oise, to Fontenoy, on the Aisne near Soissons. Walter Duranty describes this operation as follows:

" Aug. 20.—The attack was launched at 7:10 A. M. today, and by 10 o'clock the German positions had been penetrated, despite severe resistance at various points, to an average depth of four kilometers, and several thousand prisoners had been captured.

" The attack was prefaced by violent bombardment throughout Aug. 19. This increased during the night and culminated in a tremendous drumfire between dawn and the ' zero hour.'

" The prime object of the attack was the occupation of the great central plateau between the Oise and the Aisne. Six hundred feet high on the average, its top is a flat rolling country, almost unbroken by valleys, but slopes north and south, splintering into many ravines.

" The operations of the 17th and 18th had already taken the French well up the lower slopes, and the large force of tanks that supported the attack had an admirable field for work against the German machine-gun posts on the heights. The village and the ravine of Audignicourt, a little nearer Soissons, had been evacuated by the enemy, who directed such a deluge of mustard gas there as to render the ravine impassable. The assailants were quick to appreciate the situation, and, separating into two bodies, right and left, passed the obstacle, to rejoin on the tableland. This manoeuvre resulted in the capture of a large number of prisoners in a sunken road, running northward from the village where the enemy was retreating without undue haste, under the impression that the French would be checked for a considerable period.

" At Four-à-Verre and Croisette Farm, protected by the screen of the Ourscamps Forest, the resistance offered by the enemy was most determined, though in both cases it was ineffectual.

## TEN THOUSAND PRISONERS

" Aug. 21.—Today the French took the village of La Pommeraye on the northern slope of Choisy and reached the Oise along the main road from Blerancourt to Noyon, and practically re-established the line as it was before the Chemin des Dames battle, not only at a very small expense in lives, but in the face of resistance that has cost the enemy more than 10,000 prisoners, the loss of valuable material, and further depreciation of his morale.

"It is worth emphasizing that the whole operation has been less a separate battle than a second phase of the movement initiated by the Allies Aug. 8. Foch's tactics are "nibbling," plus an occasional bite. Yesterday's stroke was a bite, but that does not mean that the allied Generalissimo lacks the caution that inspired Joffre's historic saying.

"What the spirit of the French is was illustrated by the conduct of Marechal Logis Clement Darre, who was badly wounded in the eye while commanding a tank. At the same moment he learned that an officer commanding his unit had been killed. He immediately took the vacant place and despite his own suffering directed the operations of the unit for two whole days, wearing a summary first-aid bandage.

"On the evening of the second day he had reduced the great number of machine-gun nests, taken two minenwerfer, eight trench cannon, eight machine guns, and two field guns. When decorated with the Military Medal on the battlefield, he said simply: 'I am glad to have an opportunity to show what the tanks can do in battle if rightly handled.'

## FALL OF LASSIGNY

"Aug. 22.—The Germans yesterday evacuated the whole forest of Ourscamps and Carlepont Wood—in consequence of the French progress from Pontoise along the Oise to Sempigny—and Dreslincourt massif fell into French hands like a ripe plum.

"The feature of yesterday's operations was the progress on the wings of the French armies. On the left, Lassigny was entered and the dominating height of Plemont was occupied soon afterward. During the night the pressure was maintained, and today it is announced that French cavalry has crossed the Divette at various points. Mangin's right has

pushed forward to the Oise and follows the example of the left by holding the river bank from Pontoise to Brentigny.

"On the whole front the enemy was in retreat during the night and this morning, with the French in hot pursuit. There are growing evidences of demoralization in the foe's ranks. The French once more are proving that, galvanized by victory, they can perform the impossible, despite the stifling heat and difficult country.

"An exploit of Sergeant Joseph Aigisier which won the Military Medal and War Cross on the battlefield is a typical example. After capturing a machine gun and two of its servants— he had killed two others by a daring 'Indian warfare' crawl through a cornfield under fire to a vantage point— the Sergeant became separated from the squad under his orders in a ravine where gas and shell smoke were so thick that it was impossible to see his hand before his face.

"Another company was advancing on the right. He joined them, but in the smoke and confusion of the battle's ebb and flow he again lost touch with the scattered line of skirmishers, and ran full tilt into a party of fifteen Germans, by whom he was captured after a desperate struggle in which he shot one and knocked out two others with his clubbed rifle butt.

"Sent to the rear under escort, he kept his wits about him despite the rough treatment he had just experienced, and noted all he could see of the enemy's movements and positions. When the party reached a wooded corner of the road he suddenly plunged at the nearest boche, hurling him headlong into a ditch, and through a hail of bullets dashed into the wood.

"There followed a two hours' Odyssey of adventures and hairbreadth escapes in the enemy lines, but Aigisier's luck held, and he rejoined the French successfully. Then he gave information which proved of the utmost value, and without more ado picked up the rifle and equipment of a dead comrade and returned immediately to the firing line.

"Nor is this an isolated case. I could quote hundreds like it, did space permit. With such troops, the highest hopes are legitimate, and the optimism of the whole army was never so great."

## CAPTURE OF ROYE

The important German base on the Riner Avre at Roye, which was the objective of the allied attacks for weeks, fell on Aug. 27. The final assault on the preceding day was described as follows by The Associated Press:

"Aug. 26.—Fighting in water up to their waists in the marshes along the Avre and charging the crews of machine guns who served their weapons until killed, the troops of the 3d French Army today took two of the strongest defenses of Roye. They also captured 600 prisoners and took important booty, including a large number of machine guns.

"The first attack was upon the Village of Fresnoy, two and one-half miles north of Roye, where the Germans had restored the old fortifications of 1914-17, reinforced them with wire, and installed many machine-gun nests. After a short artillery preparation, the French infantry stormed the position, rushing the concrete blockhouses and killing the gunners at their pieces.

"Fresnoy was one of the centres of enemy resistance around Roye that had held out against previous assaults, and from it the Germans had launched counterattacks in an effort to check the French offensive. Prisoners say the garrison had orders to hold out at any cost. The French attacked from the north and south simultaneously and with such dash that the enemy, although aware of the impending attack, was overwhelmed. Four hundred prisoners, including sixteen officers, were captured in the town.

"The Village of St. Mard, in the low marshlands of the Avre, south of Roye, and also a strong outpost of that town, fell into the hands of General Debeney's men this afternoon after a violent struggle. The Germans had reinforced their old defenses by flooding the ground around their concrete blockhouses with water turned out from the Avre.

"The battle opened with a hard struggle for the foot bridges over the river.

The Germans tried desperately to recapture the bridges, but were driven off by the French, who fought in water to their waists. At St. Mard, as at Fresnoy, the German machine-gun fire was silenced only when the gunners were killed at their pieces."

Roye had been encircled on three sides by the tactics of the French, which overcame the numerous machine-gun nests of the German defense. Strongly protected and heavily armed positions were turned, one after the other, until the enemy was obliged to abandon the first and then the second line of defenses of 1914, upon which he fell back after being driven out of Montdidier.

General Debeney's troops took Chaulnes on Aug. 28, thus extending their front north from Roye and releasing large forces of British troops. After this success the whole French line from Chaulnes to the Aisne was rapidly advanced, General Humbert's troops having gone forward in one day in the Noyon region over six miles.

## DESTRUCTION OF NOYON

The onward sweep of the French continued. The important town of Noyon was taken Aug. 28. Ham to the north, Couchy to the south quickly followed, and the victorious French at points went beyond the Hindenburg line. The wanton destruction of Noyon by the retreating Germans was thus described by Mr. Duranty in a dispatch dated Sept. 7:

"'Mines. Danger of death. Entry forbidden,' ran an inscription in letters two feet high on barricades that shut the main street of Noyon as the correspondent's automobile jolted over a temporary structure which had replaced the causeway, destroyed by an enormous mine crater, across the unfinished canal and halted in the square on the outskirts of the town. Another car had just arrived, and by it were standing two civilians, Senator Noël, the aged Mayor of Noyon, and his deputy, M. Jouve.

"I accompanied Senator Noël down the Rue de Paris leading to the central square. Despite his age and a constitution enfeebled by captivity, he made his way nimbly enough over the single plank that bridged a chasm torn by a mine in the main sewer that ran beneath the roadway. Devastation was as complete as the enemy could have wished. Houses on both sides were shells of crumbling walls, and the road was piled high with rubbish and heaps of stone.

"'It is natural that much would be destroyed when the town was taken by assault,' said the Senator, 'but most of this is pure wantonness. The enemy has shelled the town day and night for the last eight days, and even now, when our advance has forced his guns out of France, he sent airplanes last night and the night before to wreak a last vengeance upon the city. Here was a girls' school, you would just know there had been a building; there was an almshouse for old men, it is in the same condition; everything must be rebuilt from the foundation.'

### CALVIN'S HOUSE GONE

"We came to a square where used to stand the house of Calvin. That was one of Noyon's glories. A big pile of stones, in which not even a trace of a wall was distinguishable, was all that remained.

"Here the boche destructiveness seemed to have reached its height. Mine craters were everywhere, and the houses had evidently been burned as well as shelled. We turned to the right toward the Town Hall, which had been one of the finest pieces of Renaissance architecture in France. As we entered the little square Senator Noël for the first time gave full vent to his grief.

"'Oh, my poor Town Hall!' he cried. 'My poor Town Hall! What purpose could it serve to destroy it? Ah, the bandits, the criminals!'

"The place had been smashed with true German thoroughness. The inside was completely gutted by fire and piled with charred beams and blocks of carved stone. Just enough of the façade, its beautiful stonework mutilated by shell splinters, remained to show what had been its glory, now departed.

"'It is pure wantonness,' said Deputy Jouve. 'We have an aerial photograph taken ten days ago, just after the boche was driven out, which shows this square and the Town Hall practically intact. Now look at it. Mines have destroyed

what the shells spared. I was the last man to leave town in a car with the Senator on March 25, and now I am the first to enter it. Our hearts were saddened enough then by defeat, but now in the hour of victory they are sadder still.

"After noting that the wooden structures erected by the American Red Cross near the Town Hall were mere heaps of ashes, we moved on to the cathedral, which has been preserved as by a miracle. The roof has been pierced by a dozen shells, and the interior stonework of the right-hand tower has all been smashed. The porch before the left tower was wellnigh obliterated by a huge shell, but the interior of the building suffered little. Chairs were still arranged in rows, the high altar was wholly intact, and, though the floor was covered with broken glass and rubbish, the work of restoration will not be difficult. I remarked a strange thing in one of the side chapels, where no shells or splinters seemed to have penetrated. A picture of Christ, ten feet square, was pierced with seven round holes, one exactly in the left side, and I wondered whether the revolver of some boche brute had not added sacrilege to vandalism.

"With the exception of the cathedral and a little side street from the Rue de Paris, called Rue de Saint Eloi, there is not a single building in Noyon that escaped injury, and the Mayor reckoned less than 10 per cent. capable of reconstruction."

### DESTRUCTION OF HAM

Mr. Duranty visited Ham, recaptured a few days previously, and described the appalling destruction of the city under date of Sept. 10:

"The boches fired the town, which was practically uninjured by shellfire of friend and foe, with deliberate thoroughness, despite the fact that its position on what was virtually an island, formed by the Somme River on the north and the St. Quentin Canal on the south, made it unavailable for military purposes once the bridges were destroyed. I crossed the canal by clambering across the lock gate that had escaped destruction, and passed out on the further side by a tottering series of foot-wide planks spanning the riverbed.

"Chauny Street, leading to the market place, was piled high with the wreckage of fallen walls, and at the entrance to the square a group of poilus were risking their lives in clearing the outlet of a cellar in a house whose glowing beams still crackled into flame at each gust of wind and whose side walls threatened to fall at any minute.

"I talked with a woman named Léonie Verrier, who had hidden with her father and 15-year-old sister, and had ventured to creep out on Saturday morning, (Sept. 7.)

### FIRED BY ELECTRICITY

"'Ham,' said the woman, 'was destroyed methodically by fires simultaneously started in every quarter by electric devices. Nearly a month ago we noticed the boches had begun fixing up wires in all directions, and we commented on the strangeness of such installation at a time when everything else pointed to a German retreat. It did our hearts good to see the stream of guns, the material, and the shattered, dispirited troops that had been pouring backward through Ham for the last few weeks.

"'As time passed the boches steadily continued their preparations for departure, removing wagonloads of furniture, and, indeed, everything of any value. But the wiring parties continued their work all the more busily.

"'Last Wednesday we had the key to the enigma. That morning the French guns were very near and a few shells fell close. At noon the boches issued orders to all civilians to evacuate the town. There were only about fifty inhabitants here, and perhaps twice that number of French and Belgian youths in the boche press gangs. Some fifteen of us and six boys managed to hide in the cellars. I believe all save one or two are now safely accounted for.

"'On the night from Wednesday to Thursday we heard a sudden outburst of small explosions all around. At first we thought there was grenade fighting in the street, as the noise was not loud enough for shells or airbombs. Before

dawn, father stole cautiously out. The whole town was flaming above our heads, but our house did not catch fire until we were able to leave it.

"'The boche wires had been connected with incendiary bombs which were fired simultaneously from a central electric control. Ham burned furiously all Thursday and Friday. On Saturday morning the fire was dangerously close, and we left the cellar, to meet French soldiers shortly afterward.'"

### A WILDERNESS CREATED

George H. Perris, in a cable dispatch dated Sept. 10, threw further light on the intent of the retreating Germans to make a wilderness of the country they evacuate. He wrote:

"The field of the French advance toward St. Quentin and St. Gobain is now a wilderness in which there is not the least shelter, and scarcely any fuel is to be found. I notice that authorized writers in the German press glory in this fact.

"'A decisive struggle,' says Colonel Gaedke, 'will be made more difficult for the enemy by the devastation of the regions that now form a buckler before the German armies and will contribute to their successful defense.' An official Wolff message of Sept. 1 said the Allies would 'find for Winter only ground completely bare and devastated,' and on the following day the same agency remarked: 'The abandonment o˜ this sector [north of the Oise] was prepared with our customary care, and we have been able without being interrupted to take away from this region everything that would be of any use to the adversary.'

"'The customary care' of the German Army from the highest to the lowest commands in the execution of acts of wholesale destruction and of theft is a characteristic to which since the beginning of the war I have o˜en had to testify, at first with reluctance, afterward with a deepening, and now a long-confirmed disgust. The popular term of Hun misrepresents the facts; these are not acts of savagery, but cold-blooded and highly scientific rapine. They are not accidental, but fundamental parts of the German campaign. Cities like Noyon and scores of villages sometimes, it is true, were much damaged by bombardment, but have afterward been completely razed by fire and explosive. However, every useful article had been first removed.

"One of my companions brought away from Noyon on Sunday     of the German notice boards directing the soldiery to the 'Korps Beutesammelstelle,' or loot store, which is conveniently fixed near the station. Detailed instructions lie before me for the seizure throughout the occupied country of the wool filling of mattresses and cushions, of which it is stated 10,000 tons already had been obtained on July 3, and from which millions of uniforms had been made. Instances like this could be multiplied indefinitely."

# Americans in the Soissons Sector

## Forcing the Germans to the Aisne—A Historic General Order by Pershing

THE American forces that had participated in the first offensive, launched July 18, and that had achieved the driving of the Germans from the Marne at Château-Thierry and across the Vesle, took part in no general engagement during the month ended Sept. 18, but their pressure against the German lines was constant. So strong did it become that in the end the enemy was forced to evacuate that sector and retreated northward across the Aisne.

On Aug. 27 General Pershing issued the following order:

It fills me with pride to record in general orders a tribute to the service achievements of the 1st and 3d Corps, comprising the 1st, 2d, 3d, 4th, 26th, 28th, 32d, and 42d Divisions of the American Expeditionary Forces.

You came to the battlefield at a crucial hour for the allied cause. For almost four years the most formidable army the world has yet seen had pressed its invasion of France and stood threatening its capital. At no time has that army been more powerful and menacing than when, on July 15, it struck again to destroy in one great battle the brave men opposed to it and to enforce its brutal will upon the world and civilization.

Three days later, in conjunction with our allies, you counterattacked. The allied armies gained a brilliant victory that marks the turning point of the war. You did more than to give the Allies the support to which, as a nation, our faith was pledged. You proved that our altruism, our pacific spirit, and our sense of justice have not blunted our virility or our courage.

You have shown that American initiative and energy are as fit for the tasks of war as for the pursuits of peace. You have justly won unstinted praise from our allies and the eternal gratitude of our countrymen.

We have paid for our success with the lives of many of our brave comrades. We shall cherish their memory always and claim for our history and literature their bravery, achievement, and sacrifice.

This order will be read to all organizations at the first assembly formations following its receipt.     PERSHING.

### FRENCH GENERAL'S TRIBUTE

The following order was issued by General Degoutte and spread upon the minutes of the United States Congress on Sept. 9, 1918:

GENERAL ORDER. [TRANSLATION.]

SIXTH ARMY, COMMANDING POST,
Aug. 9, 1918.

Before the great offensive of July 18, the American troops, forming part of the 6th French Army, distinguished themselves by clearing the " Brigade de Marine " Woods and the village of Vaux from the enemy and arresting his offensive on the Marne and at Fossoy.

Since then they have taken the most glorious part in the second battle of the Marne, rivaling the French troops in ardor and valor.

During twenty days of constant fighting they have freed numerous French villages and made, across a difficult country, an advance of forty kilometers, which has brought them to the Vesle.

Their glorious marches are marked by names which will shine in future in the military history of the United States: Torcy, Belleau, Plateau d'Etrepilly, Epieds, Le Charmel, l'Ourcq, Seringes-et-Nesles, Sergy, La Vesle et Fismes.

These young divisions, who saw fire for the first time, have shown themselves worthy of the old war traditions of the regular army. They have had the same burning desire to fight the boche, the same discipline which sees that the order given by their commander is always executed, whatever the difficulties to be overcome and the sacrifices to be suffered.

The magnificent results obtained are due to the energy and the skill of the commanders; to the bravery of the soldiers.

I am proud to have commanded such troops.              DEGOUTTE, *The Commanding General of the 6th Army.*

## TAKING JUVIGNY PLATEAU

The most important operation in which the Americans participated was the capture of Juvigny Plateau, north of Soissons, Aug. 29. This plateau dominated important strategic points. Edwin L. James, THE NEW YORK TIMES special correspondent, described the operations in this district in his cables, which are copyrighted for CURRENT HISTORY MAGAZINE and extracts from which are appended:

" Aug. 28.—Leaping into a new attack three hours after reaching their sector, a small unit of American troops attacked the Germans this morning in a local operation north of Soissons. The fighting is continuing. The attacking Americans were a complete surprise to the Germans, who had the French opposed to them at midnight, and seven hours later found Yankee doughboys.

" The Americans are fighting with General Mangin's 10th French Army, with which other American troops fought so successfully a short distance away to the south of Soissons in the attack starting July 18.

" The Americans who hit the Germans this morning were brought from another part of France in camions. Under cover of the dense darkness last night they were taken to the front line to relieve the French troops. The relief was completed at 4:10 o'clock, and at 7 o'clock the Americans attacked, with the French on either side. Our troops were sandwiched between two famous French shock units.

" Our men took prisoners fifteen minutes after they started. By 9 o'clock more than 150 prisoners had been count-

ed, and more were coming in. There were officers among the prisoners, who expressed the greatest surprise that the Americans had attacked them.

## INTENSE FIGHTING

" Aug. 30.—The Americans fighting with General Mangin's army north of Soissons and pushing against stubborn German resistance to better positions won in attacks of yesterday morning and last night when they made good gains eastward in the vicinity of Juvigny and the Bois de Beaumont.

" The Germans are putting up a most stubborn resistance against the pushing of the 10th French Army, and the resistance has been marked by strong counterattacks. The Americans have seen no fighting more strenuous than this. It is a second Battle of the Wilderness.

" Over the terrain which is the battlefield of our boys today war has swept four times. Of the pretty French villages of 1914 there stand now only rows of scarred stones, making these places look from a distance like huge, unkept graveyards. The fields and valleys are so scarred by war's ravage that for miles there is not one foot of the land which is not marked by a shell hole, trench, pillbox, or some other scar of the disease from which the world is suffering. There are marks of the struggle of 1914 mixed up with traces of the struggle of 1915. Then 1917 added its scars, and now the crumpled and torn landscape is receiving a new blight as the Germans are thrown back.

" What little shelter remained the Germans have recently destroyed. They have laid the land in such dismal waste as can be realized only by seeing it. They place explosives in the cellars so that the stones of destroyed houses fall deep down and leave a level waste of what has been a French town or village. Forests of former beauty now are only broken and stark poles, tossed and torn by shellfire, and the little grass that had grown up is now stained to the dirty yellow of German mustard gas in hundreds of places.

" It is a terrible wound in the side of France which is now being cleaned so that it may be mended. True it is that it may take many years to wipe out the marks of war, but the effacing years and the love of the civilized world will help brave France in her task.

"The Americans in this sector went into the battle on Wednesday morning when they took part in local operations, bringing back some two hundred prisoners. Yesterday morning at 7 o'clock as a part of General Mangin's attacking army the American fighters, after good artillery preparation, moved forward, aided by many tanks.

### FLANKED MACHINE GUNS

"Our men swept against the machine-gun positions in the wood near Juvigny. In the midst of these woods is a little plateau which the Germans had fortified strongly with machine guns. To attack it frontally meant the loss of many men, but after a while fifty German machine gunners were surprised to find Americans leaping on them from behind. Our men had filterd through the woods and attacked the Germans from the west. They brought back nearly all these Germans as prisoners. The Germans hurled many counterattacks against our men in an effort to turn our advance into a defeat. While the line swayed, we held gains all through the afternoon.

"The Germans used a new weapon against the small tanks. This weapon is for all the world like an elephant gun. It is a big rifle, something more than half an inch in diameter, and shooting an armor-piercing bullet. In these small tanks the gunner stands with his head in the turret, and the Germans used these rifles against the turrets. Tanks must move in open ground, which means that they were exposed to snipers using this big rifle, who could have good shelter and be unmolested generally, inasmuch as the tanks are used to go ahead of the infantry."

About 4 o'clock part of the American line moved forward. Juvigny was believed to have been cleared. At least, four companies of Germans had been observed to evacuate the place and an aviator who flew over the position and who was the first airman who was not fired upon while engaged in reconnoissance

operations reported that he had seen no signs of the enemy.

The enemy, however, was there and at other positions as well. The ruins of villages and the hill to the north proved to be big nests of machine guns with supporting machine guns in the positions near by.

The Americans now settled down to a heartbreaking struggle. The men dug in, advancing one line after another.

The principal nearby support position for the Germans in Juvigny was the hill to the north. On it were concealed numbers of machine guns, but the American left wing succeeded in worming a line between it and the town, and from the other side there had been sent forward to a line beyond the objective another lot of troops who came in contact with the first detachments at a point almost directly to the east of the objective. Once the enveloping movement had been consummated the little place was taken by assault.

### TERNY-SORNY

American Labor Day, Sept. 2, gave the United States troops north of Soissons an occasion to celebrate their success in reaching Terny-Sorny and the Soissons-St. Quentin highway after five days' fighting against four German divisions. Terny-Sorny, which lies across the road, was reached Sept. 1.

The foothold on the highway gave the Americans and French on either side a good position on the plateau running along north of the Aisne. To reach this position marked the accomplishment of an objective for which the Americans started Aug. 28, when they were thrown into the line in the region of Bieuxy. On their way they took about 1,000 prisoners. A correspondent wrote on Sept. 2:

"This has been one of the most stubborn, if not the most stubborn, fights in which the Americans have been engaged so far. French communiqués day after day have called attention to the stubbornness of the bloody fight when the Germans tried to hold the key position against the French and Americans north of Soissons. The American advance of the last days brought many thrilling incidents. Our artillery received congratulations for its work in following the infantry closely and firing point-blank into pestiferous German machine-gun positions. Our seventy-fives got so close yesterday that the gun crews captured fleeing Germans.

" So marked was the enthusiasm of our artillerymen that on one occasion they found they had advanced even beyond our infantry and were doing skirmish fighting against enemy machine guns. A German battery yesterday found itself without infantry between it and the Americans, with both going the same way. Our machine gunners killed the horses at two guns and we captured the guns, both six-inch pieces.

" Our final attack, which took us to Terny-Sorny, was made after a series of three barrages. After the first barrage the Germans, not thinking there could be any other system than their own plan of one barrage before an attack, rushed from their shelters to meet the Americans. They met another barrage. They went back to shelter, to come out again after that barrage. They were then met by a third barrage.

" These tactics killed so many Germans and were so demoralizing to those remaining that our infantry, advancing behind the third barrage, was easily successful, and it was this attack which won more than 500 prisoners."

The United States troops in those five days captured nearly 1,000 prisoners, and upon a two-mile front drove the Germans back to a depth of four miles, forcing them out of Juvigny, off the Juvigny tableland, and eventually pushing them across the highly important Soissons-St. Quentin road. Four different German divisions were opposed to the one American division in the course of the five-day battle.

A correspondent wrote from the battlefront under date of Sept. 6:

" Off over the valley ahead of our men lies the Chemin des Dames, that choice sector of the famed Hindenburg line toward which the Crown Prince's " strategic victory " is taking his disappointed invaders away from France, which they

found fair, but are leaving desolate to the best of their ability. For behind him the Hun ever leaves as a memento of kultur wreckage and ashes and ruin and filth, seemingly forgetful entirely that some day the war will be taken to Germany.

" America should bear in mind that, of all the troops stretched along the Vesle front from Soissons to Rheims, Americans form comparatively a small part, perhaps an eighth. This eighth part of the task has been done well by our men, but the great burden has fallen upon the French troops.

" Here and there the fields are scarred by the ruins of the once pretty Aisne villages; despoiled by the Germans, they have been ruined by allied shells. Through glasses one could just see spires jutting upward away to the northwest, marking Laon. Nearer ran the ridge on which lies the Chemin des Dames.

" With the glasses one could see camions on the distant roads. A gun barks behind, and a moment later a cloud of dust marks the landing place of the shell. One could see figures dart from the shelter of the woods when one of our shells fell there. They were Germans. Then comes a nasty, ripping whiz, and a German shell lands half a mile ahead, and one sees Americans move hurriedly away as if another might be expected in the same place. Between shellfire and shellburst one hears the steam hammer sound of the machine gun, trying to make the American advance expensive in human material.

" In the work of clearing out the German machine gunners Americans are again using the Ford cavalry, the same consisting of machine guns mounted on Ford automobiles, which scurry up the roads where the Germans have machine-gun nests. These unarmored ' tanks ' are very successful. It will be remembered that the Americans used them to good advantage in July north of Château-Thierry.

" The German withdrawal is being made in compliance with an elaborate plan. A captured order shows the instructions issued to each unit as to just how to fall back, and what to do in case of surprises. A significant part of the order is that providing for rearguard units, which are instructed to stay behind and hold the Allies, and to withdraw only when forced to do so. One would be lacking in fairness if he did not note the bravery of these men, who practically give up nine chances out of ten when they take the assignment."

## INDIVIDUAL BRAVERY

Instances of the bravery of American officers and men on the Vesle front, where the 77th (Camp Upton) Division is fighting, were narrated by Thomas M. Johnson, the special correspondent of The New York Evening Sun with the American Army, in a dispatch dated Aug. 31. Mr. Johnson told how Private Sing Kee of Bayard Street, Manhattan, stuck to his post through a German shell storm, how Captain James A. Roosevelt kept cartridges and grenades going forward through a hot fight, and how Frederick Stouke of Second Avenue, College Point, alone captured three prisoners in a shell hole and brought in one of them, who had been wounded on the way, on his back. Captain H. E. Stadie of 270 Willis Avenue, the Bronx, ran out from his dugout and carried a wounded gunner 200 yards to a place of safety.

He tells how Captain Robert P. Patterson of Glens Falls, N. Y., went out with Corporals R. A. Straub of 6 Hamilton Terrace and P. J. Carroll of 158 East 102d Street toward the outskirts of Bazoches. They ran into a German post containing about ten men, two of whom Captain Patterson killed with a rifle, while Straub and Carroll accounted for one each.

"In company with other officers," Mr. Johnson reports, "Captain Patterson did other gallant work previously, when his men were being heavily shelled in a sunken road somewhere near Chery Chartreuve. With Captain J. O. Adler of 308 West Seventy-fifth Street, [Captain Adler was a member of the staff of THE NEW YORK TIMES and CURRENT HISTORY MAGAZINE,] Lieutenant Sutherland of 57 East 127th Street, and Lieutenant Michael J. Hayes of Cleveland, Ohio, he went on an exposed crest of a ridge, where they selected suitable cover for the men. They showed them how to dig in or take advantage of the natural protection afforded by the slope, calmly walking down to direct this or that man to protect himself, disregarding their own danger.

"The result of their brave leadership was that, although the shelling continued intensely for an hour, the men under their command suffered only four casualties, about one-third of 1 per cent. of the total force."

# Germans in Our Army

Charles H. Grasty, staff correspondent of THE NEW YORK TIMES, cabled from France on Sept. 6:

"From what I have seen in this war, I would trust all the various new elements in our population as fully as Revolutionary stock. I have never seen more true-hearted Americans than these splendid fellows from the Middle West, with their German names. I heard of one whole company in another division where German was the language spoken. Not a single case of disloyalty has appeared in the whole army, as far as I know.

"In a round way, perhaps, every fourth name in the ranks is German. We have no better soldiers. They are too confident of their own Americanism to have any sensitiveness or self-consciousness. One man, whose name is very like the word ' boche,' told me laughingly that his comrades had made it into that; but he took it good-humoredly.

"While on this general subject, I should like to say that the people one meets in Europe wonder at the American solidarity. With 10 per cent. of our people of Teutonic origin, Europeans expected internal trouble. They lost sight of the absolute and complete Americanization of the elements coming to us from Europe. While there have been some few traitors, and such cases stand out conspicuously and attract general attention, the people here think that the thorough Americanism of practically the whole German-American body is one of the wonderful things of the war."

# The Battle of St. Mihiel

## How the First Independent American Offensive Wiped Out the Famous Salient in Lorraine

THE first major operation in France by the 1st American Army, acting as an independent unit under General Pershing, was the wiping out of the famous St. Mihiel salient in Lorraine, Sept. 13 and 14, 1918. In twenty-seven hours after the offensive was launched 155 square miles of territory were recaptured from the Germans, a hostile force estimated at 100,000 was forced to evacuate the section in haste, and more than 15,000 officers and men were captured, with hundreds of guns. General Pershing in his official communiqué on Sept. 14 made the following report:

> The dash and vigor of our troops, and of the valiant French divisions which fought shoulder to shoulder with them, is shown by the fact that the forces attacking on both faces of the salient effected a junction and secured the result desired within twenty-seven hours.
>
> Besides liberating more than 150 square miles of territory and taking 15,000 prisoners, we have captured a mass of material. Over 100 guns of all calibres and hundreds of machine guns and trench mortars have been taken.
>
> In spite of the fact that the enemy during his retreat burned large stores, a partial examination of the battlefield shows that great quantities of ammunition, telegraph material, railroad material, rolling stock, clothing, and equipment have been abandoned. Further evidence of the haste with which the enemy retreated is found in the uninjured bridges which he left behind.
>
> French pursuit, bombing, and reconnoissance units, and British and Italian bombing units divided with our own air service the control of the air, and contributed materially to the success of the operation.

### THE OPERATION

A correspondent of The Associated Press described the operation as follows:

"The enemy did not offer the opposition expected of him, but that was partly due to the perfection in the conception and execution of the attack by which he was stopped. Prisoners tell how division called to division in vain for aid, little knowing that the source from which it sought help was in even more desperate straits.

"Where the German troops were willing to fight—which was not everywhere—they were frequently left in such sad case by faulty liaison work that they had no option but to surrender. One such amusing case occurred when an entire regiment, with its commander and his staff, was captured. It had been left with both its flanks in the air, and suddenly found the Americans on all four sides of it.

"After surrendering, the commander requested that his roll should be called so that he might discover how heavy had been his losses. When it was called every one answered his name but one officer and one private. The commander then suggested that, as his command was so disconcertingly complete, he should march it off in whatever direction his captors desired. So it came to pass that one was met by the astonishing spectacle of an entire German regiment marching off the battlefield under its own officers, guarded by a few joyous but ridiculously inadequate troopers, who looked, with their cowboy seat in the saddle and their reckless good humor, like Highland drovers of a bygone century herding raided cattle home.

### THE PINCERS AT WORK

"The operation, to explain it in more detail, was of the pincers type always used to nip off a salient. One claw of the pincers, some twelve miles thick, rested on the Moselle at about Pont-à-Mousson. The other, about eight miles thick, rested on the heights of the Meuse at Haudiomont, a little to the east of the river. The distance to be filled up between the claws of the pincers was about thirty miles, and the ground to be nipped off by them would be about 200 square miles.

" It was thus a pretty big operation to be put through in two days on a sector that had been as stubborn to impression as almost any on the whole front. But it has been carried out not only without a hitch of any kind, but throughout in advance of the scheduled program and in weather conditions that were unfavorable throughout for all arms, and especially for the tanks and the aircraft.

" The first day's fighting saw the southern claw of the pincers advance up to the full limit assigned to it, but the western had to face more difficult ground and more strenuous opposition. It, too, however, reached its assigned position later in the day.

" Consider now how interesting was the situation. The claws of the pincers were but four miles apart. They were pursuing a large force of the enemy ahead and away from the end, and at the same time they were inclosing an unknown but certainly also a large force of the enemy in the 200 square miles that their grip embraced. When the claws met, then the arms would have a big force of the enemy on either side of them, and they then might have to fight facing both ways.

" They took a chance, for the enemy was reported to be escaping between the claws at the rate of a thousand an hour when early on Sept. 13 they closed and trapped a so far unknown number of the enemy. A chance shot at the number of the Germans inside the salient when the operation began would be from 90,000 to 100,000. Many of the roads were lined with them on the 14th, and up to the 15th over 15,000 prisoners had been counted.

## THE RESULTS GAINED

Thomas M. Johnson, in a cable dispatch to The New York Sun, dated Sept. 17, summarized the results gained as follows:

" The 1st American Army has demonstrated that it can handle itself in action. It has passed the leading stage now. By its capable working in all its parts it shows that the ' emergency ' of last Spring when the American troops had to be amalgamated with the French and British because they could not stand alone is now over, and from now on the trend will be toward a group of American armies fighting under their own flag, own Generals and own staff, though always on an equal footing with the French and British Armies under the master command of Foch as part of a single allied force.

" That the material results of the battle of St. Mihiel are important is readily comprehensible. The wedge that the Germans had pushed into the allied line, a dagger pointing at the heart of Eastern France, has disappeared, and immortal Verdun is freed forever from menace on its right flank. The dominating heights of the Meuse are in the hands of the Allies, who therefrom command the new German position. The trunk line railroad through Commercy to the towns of St. Mihiel, Thiaucourt, and Vigneulles has been reconquered, and Pont-à-Mousson, which was formerly in the front line, is now four miles behind the front, to say nothing of the fact that some seventy villages and 3,500 kilometers of French soil are liberated."

## CHARGE UP LES EPARGES

The main defense was encountered along the western side of the salient. The Germans held a series of high hills which dominated the Woevre Plateau. It was to take these natural fortifications, equipped with every defensive device, that the Americans were ordered to attack. All previous efforts to capture Les Eparges, the highest elevation, had failed in the past.

At the conclusion of artillery preparation the French and Americans swept forward in a rush that never stopped until they had reached every height in the long series which extend southward nearly to St. Mihiel. Thousands of miles of barbed wire had been stretched at intervals back of the German front lines, and every foot of the way was through underbrush, thick with machine guns.

Nearly everywhere the American artillery played havoc with the barbed wire, tearing open paths for the infantry. Only the solid, reinforced concrete forts topping the heights seemed impervious to the fire from the heavy guns.

From Les Eparges the Allies stormed

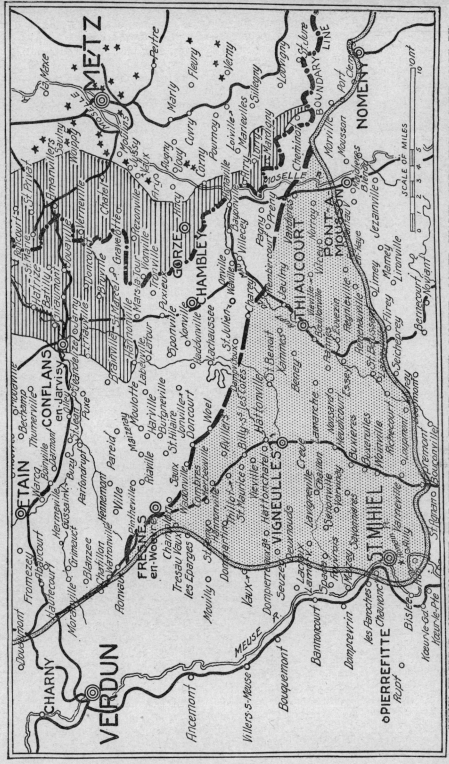

SCENE OF GREAT AMERICAN DRIVE THAT WIPED OUT THE ST. MIHIEL SALIENT. LOWER SHADED AREA SHOWS GAINS MADE BY PERSHING UP TO SEPT. 18, 1918. UPPER SHADED AREA IS BRIEY IRON BASIN, THE KEY TO VICTORY. STARS INDICATE GERMAN FORTS.

the villages of Herbeuville, Hannonville, Thillot, St. Maurice, Billy, and Hatton-châtel, and then in the depth of night entered Vigneulles, at the southern end of the line of heights. To reach these points they had to advance through thickets of machine guns.

## WELCOME TO DELIVERERS

The inhabitants of the salient were absolutely ignorant of the events of history in the last four years, knowing only what their captors had told them. Here the sad stories heard in the whole of the reclaimed districts of France were accentuated by the long years of German control, which had isolated the people from news of relatives and of world happenings.

The civilian population, consisting almost entirely of women and children because of the forcible removal of practically every male of military age, welcomed Newton D. Baker, the American Secretary of War, and Generals Pershing and Pétain when they visited St. Mihiel a few hours after it was captured.

Aged women and girls crowded about Secretary Baker and the two Generals accompanying him to express their thanks and pay homage to their deliverers. It was not merely curiosity; it was an emotional outburst following almost four years of the conqueror's suppression. The word was passed about that the small civilian was the Secretary of War of the United States, whose armies had accomplished their relief, and from half-destroyed houses and from points far removed from the centre of the village they poured forth to get a glimpse of the visitors.

A military band was brought up from the rear, the " Marsellaise " was played, and the restraint of the civilians in the presence of the visitors broke down completely. Women crowded forward ostensibly to shake the Secretary's hand, but instead they kissed his hands and wept, and then they joined in a chorus of " Vives." There were no speeches, but repeatedly Secretary Baker responded briefly to expressions of gratitude, often half-hysterically uttered by the women and children.

Every American entering the village had the same reception as that accorded to Secretary Baker and General Pershing and their party. Aged men and women seized and kissed the hands of the officers and correspondents, crying and laughing, the curiously aged children imitating their elders unknowingly. For their own compatriots, however, the greetings were deeper, and the French patrols and troops following were even more affected than those who had been delivered.

## DETAILS OF THE PROGRESS

Edwin L. James, THE NEW YORK TIMES CURRENT HISTORY MAGAZINE correspondent, in his cable of Sept. 14 gave these details:

" Our artillery preparation, which was of unprecedented intensity, started at 1 A. M. Sept. 12, and at 5 o'clock the attack on the south side of the salient began. An hour later the attack on the west side started. The big attack was successful from the start. By noon we had taken Lahayville, St. Baussant, the Bois de Mortmare and Vilcey, and at nightfall we had pushed beyond Essey, had taken the important town of Thiaucourt and had reached Villers sur Penny. By night out attack on the west, which had met some resistance, had passed St. Remy and Combres. We took 10,000 prisoners on the first day.

" On the night of the 12th we moved on into Pannes, which had been cleared by the tanks, and took Nonsard and Buxieres. We surrounded Montsec, got Woinville, and occupied St. Mihiel before 9 o'clock. On the west side we pushed in by Spada and Lavigneville and by midnight we got to Chaillon. In a brilliant advance, meanwhile, our forces, attacking near St. Remy, swept through the Forêt de Montagne, and just at midnight they occupied the western part of Vigneulles.

" Army headquarters was electrified to get the news that at 3 o'clock the forces attacking from the south had also reached Vigneulles. This meant that the St. Mihiel salient had been cut off. We did not hold all the ground south of us, paradoxical as it may sound, for in a large stretch of wood, north of St. Mihiel, we did not know what was there. By 9 A. M., Sept. 13, our forces met.

"The junction was made at Heudicourt, and we had cleaned out all the territory immediately north of the woods lying north of St. Mihiel. Meanwhile other troops had chased the Germans from Norroy and had gone into the Bois de Grandfontain and captured Jaulnay, Xammes, and St. Benoit, as well as Hattonville.

"In the afternoon we started to pry into our prize package north of St. Mihiel. This comprised the Bois de Versel, the Bois de Gaumont, and the Bois de Wawroils, and we found there several thousands of men. A Colonel and a Major sent word that they wished to surrender and were accommodated. They seemed glad to be captured and could not tire of talking about what being under our artillery fire was like. They said it was like hell.

"In those woods were tons and tons of ammunition. On the upper end a big American shell had landed on the railroad track. Just behind the break stood twenty-two cars, all loaded with big gun ammunition. There were also guns to use it. Several thousand machine guns formed part of the booty there. Among our prisoners were a considerable number of Austrians, whom the Kaiser had brought to the west front to oppose the Americans. They did not fight at all. Several hundred were taken from the 35th Austro-Hungarian Division."

## GERMAN LOOTING

When the Germans withdrew they took practically all the man power among the French civilians in thirty villages. From St. Mihiel town they took all the men between 16 and 45 years back into Germany. They had used these men during their four years' occupation of the salient. Thiaucourt, a beautiful town, was stripped of all valuables and the stores had been rifled of all supplies of every nature weeks before. At St. Mihiel the two banks of the city had been broken open and all moneys and papers taken. The city had been forced to pay a contribution of 2,000,000 francs to the Germans.

The Mayor of St. Mihiel made the following statement to THE NEW YORK TIMES CURRENT HISTORY MAGAZINE correspondent:

"The Germans exacted a heavy money toll. First there was 1,500,000 francs on their arrival—'to ransom us from sack,' said the German commander. We could never have paid even that much without the establishment of a syndicate bond system, guaranteed by forty communes in the Woevre region. Those bonds formed our money, (the unit value was 5 francs each,) and small change was supplied by paper money from Lille, Roubaix, Douai, and other occupied towns. Then the boches exacted an additional 500,000 in three installments during the last two years, nominally for the maintenance of roads, water, conduits, and the like. We met that in the same way.

"They refused to accept French money at the canteens and the market gardens established after the first year, but willingly changed it for bonds and small bills. They tried especially to get gold. They even offered a premium of 45 per cent. at their own bank, set up in the square. But the boches got precious little.

"It was in respect to 'requisitions' of furniture and mattresses that they treated us worst. All unoccupied houses were stripped first; then they took what they wanted from the rest of us."

The correspondent talked with a man of 74 whom the Germans robbed of a mattress on which he was lying sick, early this year. When he protested against the outrage, they said that the German soldiers' comfort was worth more than the lives of old Frenchmen.

"During the last two years," continued the Mayor, "they took away all metal utensils, and even bells, statues, and all water pipes they could find. As regards food, we were kept alive by the American Committee. At first we got meat (horseflesh) pretty regularly, but for the last year we have had nothing save vegetables and the daily allowance of 300 grams of very bad bread, thirty grams of fat and a little bacon. About once a month when a horse was killed or died it was distributed among us.

But we were forced to slaughter all dogs."

## PERSHING CONGRATULATED

The success of the American Army was hailed with delirious joy throughout France and produced a profound effect in all countries. President Wilson sent his "warmest congratulations on the brilliant achievement," and his "affectionate thanks." Congratulatory messages were received by General Pershing from Marshal Foch, Premier Lloyd George, Premier Clemenceau, and Field Marshal Haig; cablegrams of congratulation were received by President Wilson from the Kings of Italy and Great Britain; from President Poincaré, and the Presidents of several Central and South American States.

## BATTLEGROUND A FORTRESS

Thomas Johnson visited the salient Sept. 14 and described the battleground as follows:

" The further one goes the stronger becomes the impression of how strongly fortified was this whole place. It abounded in dugouts deep and strong and well built, while in all villages and many other places were the famous steel and concrete German pill boxes. American officers and soldiers were eating German food and drinking German beer in the captured dugouts.

" To get the full flavor of the victory the best way is to go over the battlefield from our old front line starting at Seicheprey, where the Americans had their first real fight with the enemy last April. Passing Remières Wood on the right one rides through our old trenches, then goes into No Man's Land and across to Lahayville, Sainteaussant, and Richecourt—villages that thousands of Americans have looked at longingly since Jan. 18, when the first American force took over the sector facing them. One trip over the ground is enough to show that the defenses the Americans went up against here were as strong as those on the Somme, Chemin des Dames or any other famous battle sectors of the west front.

" The greatest fortress of all was Montsec itself, and nothing that has ever been said about that solitary peak can convey an idea of how it dominated and looked down upon our old trenches around Seicheprey, Xivray, Beaumont, Rambucourt, Bouconville, and all those other towns that one is able now for the first time to name as having held the Americans ever since January. The only way to get an idea of it is to climb to the top of the Woolworth tower. It dominates New York no more than Montsec dominates its surroundings.

## STEEL DUGOUTS

" From there the boche could see every single American who walked in the road or in a trench for ten miles on a clear day. That's not the only reason why Montsec seemed a great goal. It was a symbol of the future, for they knew that when they could take it it would mean the time of the fulfillment of their promise had come. Seeing Montsec, one realizes what a veritable fortress it was, not only because of its steep wooded sides, but because of its dugouts, which were not really dugouts but subterranean chambers capable of holding thousands of men. They were made of steel, concrete, stone, mortar, brick, forty or fifty feet within the mountainside. Some built in 1915 are ornamented with the German coat of arms. They are littered with maps, papers, clothing, knicknacks, showing they were furnished in great comfort with beds, chairs, and pictures.

" The Germans had four years to do it in. These dugouts, facing north and so difficult of observation by the Allies, had fine porches, pretty tables with a splendid view across to the Meuse heights, and it was there the German officers used to drink their beer. One of them had a hammock slung under the trees and another had an open air bath tub, but great gaps showed where our shells had crashed in upon them, and one big dugout, by name 'Villa Minna,' had completely caved in. The occupants lay on their faces on the floor. In another dugout lay a dead German officer, while beside him lay a dog silently watching his dead master. He wouldn't make a responsive sign to coaxing or whistling.

# PROFESSOR THOMAS G. MASARYK

Chairman of the Czechoslovak National Committee, which has been
recognized by the Allies as the governing body of
the Czechoslovak Nation

Arras Cathedral as it appears after four years of war

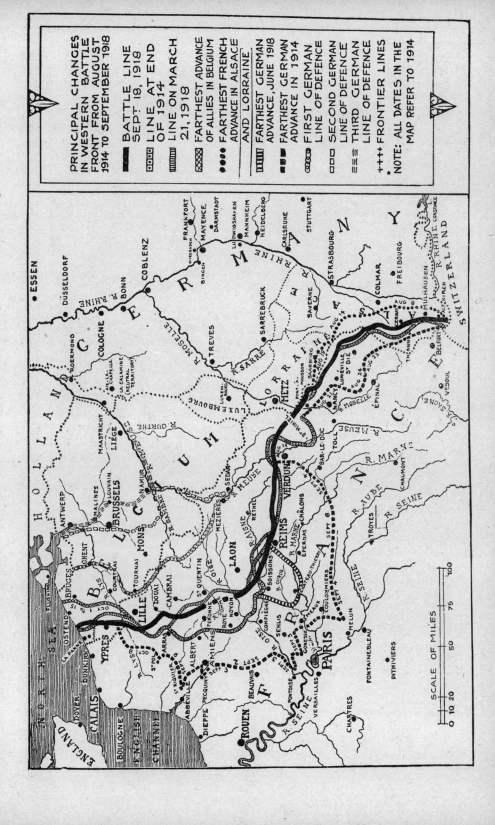

PRINCIPAL CHANGES
IN WESTERN BATTLE
FRONT FROM AUGUST
1914 TO SEPTEMBER 1918

▬▬▬ BATTLE LINE
SEPT. 18, 1918

▭▭▭ LINE AT END
OF 1914

▒▒▒ LINE ON MARCH
21, 1918

▧▧▧ FARTHEST ADVANCE
OF ALLIES IN BELGIUM

●●● FARTHEST FRENCH
ADVANCE IN ALSACE
AND LORRAINE

▦▦▦ FARTHEST GERMAN
ADVANCE, JUNE 1918

■■■ FARTHEST GERMAN
ADVANCE IN 1914

◇◇◇ FIRST GERMAN
LINE OF DEFENCE

□□□ SECOND GERMAN
LINE OF DEFENCE

═══ THIRD GERMAN
LINE OF DEFENCE

++++ FRONTIER LINES

NOTE: ALL DATES IN THE
MAP REFER TO 1914

SCALE OF MILES

0  10  20     50     75    100

" The whole top of the mountain is elaborately interlaced with paved paths railed with rustic woodwork, leading to all manner of observation posts with outlooks at every possible angle. One big, pretentious villa had been occupied by a German Brigader. The strange coincidence is that the Americans got at Château-Thierry complete information as to the exact whereabouts of everything atop Montsec. They captured maps showing the whole thing."

# Raising a New and Greater Army

## The United States Extends Draft Ages to Make All Men Between 18 and 45 Liable for Service

IN record time Congress enacted a new law extending the American draft ages to all males between 18 and 45, inclusive. President Wilson signed the bill on Aug. 31, 1918, and simultaneously issued a proclamation in which he appointed Thursday, Sept. 12, as the day of registration. The President's proclamation said in part:

Fifteen months ago the men of the country from 21 to 31 years of age registered. Three months ago, and again this month, those who had just reached the ages of 21 were added. It now remains to include all men between the ages of 18 and 45.

This is not a new policy. A century and a quarter ago it was deliberately ordained by those who were then responsible for the safety and defense of the nation that the duty of military service should rest upon all able-bodied men between the ages of 18 and 45. We now accept and fulfill the obligation which they established, an obligation expressed in our national statutes from that time until now. We solemnly purpose a decisive victory of arms, and deliberately to devote the larger part of the military man power of the nation to the accomplishment of that purpose.

The younger men have from the first been ready to go. They have furnished voluntary enlistments out of all proportion to their numbers. Our military authorities regard them as having the highest combatant qualities. Their youthful enthusiasm, their virile eagerness, their gallant spirit of daring, make them the admiration of all who see them in action. They covet not only the distinction of serving in this great war, but also the inspiring memories, which hundreds of thousands of them will cherish through the years to come, of a great day and a great service for their country and for mankind.

By the men of the older group now called on the opportunity now opened to them will be accepted with the calm resolution of those who realize to the full the deep and solemn significance of what they do. Having made a place for themselves in their respective communities, having assumed at home the graver responsibilities of life in many spheres, looking back upon honorable records in civil and industrial life, they will realize as perhaps no others could how entirely their own fortunes and the fortunes of all whom they love are put at stake in this war for right, and will know that the very records they have made render this new duty the commanding duty of their lives. They know how surely this is the nation's war, how imperatively it demands the mobilization and massing of all our resources of every kind. They will regard this call as the supreme call of their day, and will answer it accordingly.

Only a portion of those who register will be called upon to bear arms. Those who are not physically fit will be excused; those exempted by alien allegiance; those who should not be relieved of their present responsibilities; above all, those who cannot be spared from the civil and industrial tasks at home upon which the success of our armies depends as much as upon the fighting at the front. But all must be registered, in order that the selection for military service may be made intelligently and with full information.

This will be our final demonstration of loyalty, democracy, and the will to win, our solemn notice to all the world that we stand absolutely together in a common resolution and purpose. It is the call to duty to which every true man in the country will respond with pride and with the consciousness that in doing so he plays his part in vindication of a great cause at whose summons every true heart offers its supreme service.

An estimate prepared by the Provost Marshal General's office gave the number of men who would be affected by the new law as 12,788,758, as compared with 9,586,508 registered under the original service law. The Provost Marshal General's statement read in part:

At the time preparations were first being made for the registration under the law extending the ages to 18 and 45, both inclusive, the calculations of the Provost Marshal General, based on data furnished by the Census Bureau and by insurance actuaries, placed the total population of the new ages to be included at 13,000,000 in round numbers. More accurately stated, the number was 13,190,000. But, although this is the estimated number of males of those ages, the law does not require persons in active military or naval service to register, such registration being obviously impracticable for these men.

It cannot be stated with certainty just what is the number of men of these ages in the army and navy. But all of the inductions under the selective service law have been between the ages of 21 and 30; therefore, all men between the ages of 18 and 20 and 32 and 45 now in active service in the army and navy must have come in by enlistment.

The total number of enlistments in the army, navy, and Marine Corps to date is estimated at nearly 1,400,000. Of this number it is estimated that those under the age of 21 (which includes a small number under the age of 18) total about 245,000; and that the number between the ages of 32 and 45 is about 165,000, or an estimated total of 410,000 men in active military and naval service between the ages of 18 to 20 and 32 to 45. These 410,000 are, under the law, not obliged to register and must, therefore, be deducted from the 13,190,000 in making estimates as to the number who are actually due to register. This deduction will leave about 12,780,000 as the approximate number of registrants to be expected if the maximum number is attained.

To ascertain the estimated shares of those registrants to be expected in the several States the above figure of 12,-780,000 has been distributed in the same ratio shown by the registration of ages 21 to 30 on June 5, 1917. This ratio, of course, will not be exactly fulfilled in the coming registration, owing to the shifting of the industrial population, the different distribution of ages in the different States, and certain other minor considerations, but it is the nearest ratio that is attainable.

The total number of men to be obtained for general military service under the registration was estimated at 2,300,-000, of whom probably two-thirds would be between the ages of 18 and 20 years, inclusive. Youths in their nineteenth year were placed in a separate group, which was not to be drawn upon until the supply of other available men in the new classes was exhausted. The first classes to be called to the colors, it was announced, would be youths of 19 and 20 years and men of 32 to 36 inclusive.

## POLLING OUR MAN POWER

The registration of millions of youths and men in the prime of life took place quietly on Sept. 12 all over the United States. A noteworthy feature of the day was the absence of any report of disturbance or breakdown in the registration machinery anywhere in the country. In the words of Provost General Crowder, it was "a superb demonstration of the will of the American people." The following day enough of the results had been reported to show that the total registration would considerably exceed the Government's estimate. General Crowder sent this message to General Pershing:

The nation responded yesterday with an enrollment which promises to exceed all estimates, thus assuring an uninterrupted flow of man power to the army under your command.

The work of stamping the serial numbers on the cards and arranging them in classes was begun immediately by the 5,000 local boards, and the mailing of questionnaires to youths of 19 and 20 years and men of 32 to 36 years, inclusive, was started about a week later. General Crowder announced that the draft would be held as early in October as possible, and that the first 250,000 or 300,000 men of the new draft would be called to their cantonments within a few weeks thereafter. The War Department announced plans for enlarging nine or more of the cantonments to provide immediately for 77,000 more men than in the first draft, and it was stated that before Spring there would be quarters for upward of 150,000 more men than at the time of the first call.

## ARMY OF FIVE MILLIONS

The new draft made it possible to carry out the program of having eighty divisions, or approximately 4,000,000 men, in France by June 30, 1919. This great army was easily obtainable from the men eligible under the new law, as well as eighteen additional divisions to be trained and held in readiness in the United States by the same date, making a total of nearly 5,000,000 men under arms. Plans to provide supplies and equipment for that number of men were already under way before registration day. Brig. Gen. R. E. Wood, Quartermaster General, exhibited a chart of the staggering items early in September, and said to a reporter:

Here are some of the requirements of an army of 5,000,000: 17,600,000 blankets, 28,000,000 woolen breeches, 34,000,000 woolen drawers, 7,978,000 overcoats, 33,-000,000 pairs of shoes, 25,000,000 flannel shirts, 110,000,000 pairs of stockings, 7,000,000 campaign hats, 9,500,000 overseas caps. In certain items we are now ready for the army of 5,000,000; that is, either the stuff has been bought or the contracts have been let. Among items in this class are Summer undershirts, gloves, khaki coats and trousers, puttees, and barrack bags.

The General Staff notifies us thirty days ahead of a draft, and we have things fixed now so that we are not afraid of it, in whatever part of the country the demand for supplies comes. We have great storage depots in this country at Boston, New York, Baltimore, Atlanta, Chicago, St. Louis, Jeffersonville, Ind.; San Antonio, San Francisco, and El Paso. From these depots we serve the camps nearest to them. The biggest distributing depot is that in Atlanta; there are ten camps in the Atlanta district.

On the other side our stock depots are of three kinds—the one at the base section, where a forty-five-day surplus is maintained; then at the intermediate section, where the supply is for thirty days, and at the advance section, where it is for fifteen days. The key to the whole situation is the stock report.

## DRAFTS IN OTHER COUNTRIES

During the debate in Congress considerable discussion took place on the question of drafting youths of 18. To throw further light on the subject the following facts were presented and read into the record:

DRAFTING OF YOUNG MEN IN GREAT BRITAIN DURING THE EUROPEAN WAR

Under the provisions of the Military Service act of 1916, which went into effect Feb. 10, 1916, every male British subject, a resident of Great Britain, who

had reached the age of 18 and was under 41 and was unmarried or a widower without children, was deemed to have been duly enlisted in the regular army for general service with the colors or in the reserves for the period of the war.

The Statesman's Yearbook, 1918, states that all the groups of unmarried men were called out by March 18, 1916.

The Military Service act, 1916, which became law May 25, 1916, extended the liability to service to married men within the same age limits. Section 1 (1) of this act contains the following proviso:

" Provided, That steps shall be taken to prevent, so far as possible, the sending of men to serve abroad before they attain the age of 19."

Premier Lloyd George, in presenting to the House of Commons on April 9, 1918, the Government's bill raising the military age to 50, referred to this proviso, as follows:

" There was an understanding that boys under 19 years would only be used in case of emergency. We felt that the emergency had arisen, and, in so far as those who were over 18 were concerned, those who had already received six months' training, we felt it necessary that they should be sent to France."

By the terms of the recent treaty between the United States and Great Britain young men of British nationality may be drafted under the laws of the United States after they have reached the age of 20.

## DRAFTING OF YOUNG MEN IN FRANCE

### I. BEFORE THE EUROPEAN WAR

Under the military service law in force before the outbreak of the European war, namely, the Act of Aug. 7, 1913, young men were called to military service during the year following that in which they reached 19 years of age, and the class to which they belonged was designated by the calendar year in which service under this law began—that is, the year in which the twentieth birthday occurred.

### II. DURING THE EUROPEAN WAR

This draft age for beginning compulsory military service was not lowered until March 15, 1915, when an act was passed providing that—

" The class of 1916 shall be called to the colors in advance of the regular time, at such date as may be fixed by order of the Minister of War."

The class of 1916 consisted of young men who became 19 in 1915.

By the acts of Dec. 30, 1915, March 31, 1917, and March 29, 1918, (Journal Officiel, 1915, p. 9663; 1917, p. 2557; 1918, p. 2831,) the same authority was conferred upon the Minister of War to call out the classes of 1917, 1918, and 1919, respectively, in the year in which they became 19.

Circulars of the Minister of War, dated Jan. 22, 1917, and Sept. 30, 1917, (Journal Officiel, 1917, pp. 738, 7844,) show that this authority had been exercised with respect to the class of 1917 before Oct. 1, 1916, and, with respect to the class of 1918, before Oct. 1, 1917.

## DRAFTING YOUNG MEN IN GERMANY

### I. BEFORE THE EUROPEAN WAR.

Liability to military service in Germany commences with the completion of the seventeenth year. Such service is compulsory and universal, but does not actually begin until the age of 20. Every young man is enrolled in the military register during January of the year in which he completes his twentieth year. Prior to this—that is, from the seventeenth to the twentieth year, unless he has volunteered for actual service—the young man belongs to the Landsturm, a home defense force consisting of two classes, namely, the first including all men from 17 to 39 who for one reason or another have received no military training, the second class including all men over 39 up to 45, whether trained or untrained. (Constitution of the German Empire, April 16, 1871, Article 59; law relating to military service, Feb. 11, 1888, Sections 23-24; Reichsgesetzblatt, 1888, p. 18.)

### II. DURING THE EUROPEAN WAR

The Landsturm was called out for purposes of registration on Aug. 1, 1914, (Reichsgesetzblatt, 1914, p. 273.) Whether or not young men below the age of 20, except volunteers, were actually put into the military service at that time or later is not ascertainable from any official documents available in the Library of Congress. The following statement is given in Information Annual, 1916, page 259:

"According to the Lokal-Anzeiger of Berlin, June 18, all the 17-year-old boys in Germany had been ordered to report themselves to the military authorities. In Germany liability for military service begins at the age of 17 years, but in peace time actual service begins at 20."

The 1918 Statesman's Yearbook, at page 898, states that—

"By December, 1916, the whole of the 1917 class of recruits had been incorporated in the army, and by May, 1917, lads entering their seventeenth year."

The latter statement is ambiguous and does not indicate whether the 1917 class means those who completed their twentieth year or those who had completed their seventeenth year in 1917.

Nothing has been found in official sources to show that this service below the age of 20 was compulsory and not volunteer. The Berliner Tageblatt, Aug. 22, 1914, (evening edition,) page 4. contains an order of the military commander of Berlin to the effect that boys who have completed their sixteenth year may enroll for a course of military training under the instruction of retired army officers.

In a dispatch dated Paris, Aug. 20, 1918, it is stated that a number of boys of the 1919 class have been found among the latest prisoners, and that the proportion of boys taken in recent hauls indicates that practically all of the class of 1919 have been sent to the front.

## "SLACKER ROUNDUP"

A roundup of suspected slackers in the Federal districts of Southern and Eastern New York and Northern New Jersey began on the morning of Sept. 3, and proceeded vigorously for three days. Many thousands of regular and special agents of the Department of Justice, including several thousand volunteers from the American Protective League, as well as soldiers and sailors, were engaged in stopping men between 21 and 31 years of age and demanding whether they had their registration and classification cards. Those who could not produce their cards were taken to armories, police stations, and other places and held until they could prove that they had not evaded the law. The number of arrests, after three days, when the roundup was ended, was 60,187, and of these 16,505 were either ordered immediately into the service as intentional slackers or were referred back to their local boards. In the end it was stated officially that only 199 of the whole 60,000 were found to be actual draft dodgers, and that 85 of these were men not living in New York.

A vehement attack was launched in the Senate on Sept. 5 against the roundup, and after various Senators had condemned the proceedings, Senator Smoot offered a resolution calling upon the Military Affairs Committee to ascertain who was responsible and the reasons. The Chairman of the committee, Senator Chamberlain, was one of the bitterest critics of the roundup. "There is not a man in the Senate or in the country," he said, "who despises a man who undertakes to evade his military duty as much as I do, but, notwithstanding that, these men who are slackers ought to be reached by due process of law. The whole Department of Justice, the Intelligence Bureaus of the War and Navy Departments, all the American Defense Societies, the United States Marshals, and all the officers of the law have means and instrumentalities for reaching the slackers. But here we have an instance where thousands and tens of thousands of perfectly innocent men are being haled before the courts and some of them held overnight in crowded prisons, although they were perfectly innocent of trying to evade military duty."

Senators Johnson of California and Sherman of Illinois characterized the proceedings as militarism and terrorism of the Prussian type. President Wilson called on the Attorney General for a full report on all the circumstances, after which the excitement in Congress subsided.

## TOTAL CASUALTIES

While preparations were making for the drafting of a great new army, the men already in service were in the midst of constant fighting on the French front. The total casualties from the first that had been suffered by American troops up to and including those reported on Sept. 18, were as follows:

### ARMY CASUALTIES

| | |
|---|---:|
| Killed in action | 5,623 |
| Lost at sea | 291 |
| Died of wounds | 1,819 |
| Died of accident and other causes | 830 |
| Died of disease | 1,754 |
| | |
| Total | 10,317 |
| Wounded | 17,081 |
| Missing, including prisoners | 4,285 |
| | |
| Total | 31,683 |

### MARINE CASUALTIES

| | Officers. | Men. |
|---|---:|---:|
| Deaths | 37 | 919 |
| Wounded | 64 | 1,925 |
| In hands of enemy | .. | 11 |
| Missing | 1 | 151 |
| | | |
| Total | 102 | 3,006 |
| | | |
| Total | | 3,108 |

Grand total of army and marine corps casualties ...................34,791

# Who's Who in General Pershing's Army
## Names of Chief Officers and Titles of All Units in First Five Army Corps

CURRENT HISTORY MAGAZINE presents herewith a convenient and complete summary of the various military units and of the corps, division, and brigade commanders in the five American Army corps which are now facing the Central Powers on the French front. The list represents the commanding personnel of our fighting units as it stood in the first week of September, 1918. All five corps are under the personal command of General John J. Pershing.

### 1ST ARMY CORPS
Major Gen. Hunter Liggett, commanding.

*1st and 2d Divisions, Regular Army; 26th, (New England,) 32d, (Michigan and Wisconsin,) 41st, (Washington, Oregon, North and South Dakota, Colorado, New Mexico, Montana, Idaho, Wyoming, and Minnesota,) and 42d (Rainbow, troops from twenty-six States) Divisions, National Guard.*

1ST DIVISION—Major Gen. Charles P. Summerall, commanding; Lieut. Col. Campbell King, Chief of Staff; Major H. K. Loughry, Adjutant General.

1st Brigade, Infantry—Major John L. Hines; 16th and 18th Regiments; 2d Machine Gun Battalion.

2d Brigade, Infantry—Major Gen. Beaumont B. Buck; 26th and 28th Regiments; 3d Machine Gun Battalion.

1st Brigade, Field Artillery—(Commanding officer not announced;) 5th, 6th, and 7th Regiments; 1st Trench Mortar Battery.

Engineer Troops—1st Regiment.

Signal Troops—2d Battalion.

Division Units—1st Machine Gun Battalion.

2D DIVISION (U. S. M. C.)—Brig. Gen. John E. Le Jeune, commanding; Brig Gen. Preston Brown, Chief of Staff.

3d Brigade, Infantry—Brig. Gen. Hanson E. Ely; 9th and 23d Regiments; 5th Machine Gun Battalion.

4th Brigade, Infantry (Marines)—Brig.

Gen. John E. Le Jeune; 5th and 6th Regiments; 6th Machine Gun Battalion.

2d Brigade, Field Artillery—Brig. Gen. A. J. Bowley; 12th, 15th, and 17th Regiments; 2d Trench Mortar Battery.

Engineer Troops—2d Regiment.

Signal Troops—1st Battalion.

Division Units—2d Division Headquarters Troop; 4th Machine Gun Battalion.

26TH DIVISION—Major Gen. Clarence R. Edwards, commanding; Lieut. Col. Cassius M. Dowell, Chief of Staff; Major Charles A. Stevens, Adjutant General.

51st Brigade, Infantry—Brig. Gen. George H. Shelton; 101st and 102d Regiments; 102d Machine Gun Battalion.

52d Brigade, Infantry—Brig. Gen. C. H. Cole; 103d and 104th Regiments; 103d Machine Gun Battalion.

51st Brigade, Field Artillery—Brig. Gen. D. E. Aultman; 101st, 102d, and 103d Regiments; 101st Trench Mortar Battery.

Engineer Troops—101st Regiment.

Signal Troops—101st Field Battalion.

Division Units — 26th Headquarters Troop; 101st Machine Gun Battalion.

32D DIVISION—Major Gen. W. G. Haan, commanding; Lieut. Col. Allen L. Briggs, Chief of Staff; Major John H. Howard, Adjutant General.

63d Brigade, Infantry—Brig. Gen. William D. Connor; 125th and 126th Regiments; 120th Machine Gun Battalion.

64th Brigade, Infantry—Brig. Gen. E. B. Winans; 127th and 128th Regiments; 121st Machine Gun Battalion.

57th Brigade, Field Artillery—Brig. Gen. G. Le Roy Irwin; 119th, 120th, and 121st Regiments; 107th Trench Mortar Battery.

Engineer Troops—107th Regiment.

Signal Troops—107th Battalion.

Division Units—32d Headquarters Troop; 119th Machine Gun Battalion.

41ST DIVISION (Sunset)—Major Gen. Robert Alexander, commanding; Colonel Harry H. Tebbetts, Chief of Staff; Major Herbert H. White, Adjutant General.

81st Brigade, Infantry—Brig. Gen. Wilson B. Burt; 161st and 162d Regiments; 147th Machine Gun Battalion.

82d Brigade, Infantry—Brig. Gen. Edward Vollrath; 163d and 164th Regiments; 148th Machine Gun Battalion.

66th Brigade, Field Artillery—(Commanding officer not announced;) 146th, 147th, and 148th Regiments; 116th Trench Mortar Battery.

Engineer Troops—116th Regiment.

Signal Troops—116th Battalion.

Division Units—41st Division Headquarters Troop; 146th Machine Gun Battalion.

42D DIVISION (Rainbow)—Major Gen. C. T. Menoher, commanding; (Chief of Staff not announced;) Major Walter E. Powers, Adjutant General.

83d Brigade, Infantry—Brig. Gen. M.

Lenihan; 165th and 166th Regiments; 150th Machine Gun Battalion.

84th Brigade, Infantry—Brig. Gen. R. A. Brown; 167th and 168th Regiments; 151st Machine Gun Battalion.

67th Brigade, Field Artillery—Brig. Gen. G. C. Gatley; 149th, 150th, and 151st Regiments; 117th Trench Mortar Battery.

Engineer Troops—117th Regiment.

Signal Troops—117th Field Signal Battalion.

Division Units—42d Division Headquarters Troop; 149th Machine Gun Battalion.

## 2D ARMY CORPS

### Major Gen. Robert Lee Bullard, commanding.

*4th Division, Regular Army; 28th, (Pennsylvania,) 30th, (Tennessee, North and South Carolina, and District of Columbia,) and 36th (Missouri and Kansas) Divisions, National Guard; 77th (New York) and 82d (Georgia, Alabama, and Florida) Divisions, National Army.*

4TH DIVISION—Major Gen. George H. Cameron, commanding; Lieut. Col. Christian A. Bach, Chief of Staff; Major Jesse D. Elliott, Adjutant General.

7th Brigade, Infantry—Brig. Gen. B. A. Poore; 39th and 47th Regiments; 11th Machine Gun Battalion.

8th Brigade, Infantry—Brig. Gen. E. E. Booth; 58th and 59th Regiments; 12th Machine Gun Battalion.

4th Brigade, Field Artillery—Brig. Gen. E. B. Babbitt; 13th, 16th, and 77th Regiments; 4th Trench Mortar Battery.

Engineer Troops—4th Regiment.

Signal Troops—8th Battalion.

Division Units—4th Division Headquarters Troop; 10th Machine Gun Battalion.

28TH DIVISION—Major Gen. C. H. Muir, commanding; (Chief of Staff not announced;) Lieut. Col. David J. Davis, Adjutant General.

55th Brigade, Infantry—Brig. Gen. T. W. Darrah; 109th and 110th Regiments; 108th Machine Gun Battalion.

56th Brigade, Infantry—Major Gen. William Weigel; 111th and 112th Regiments; 109th Machine Gun Battalion.

53d Brigade, Field Artillery—Brig. Gen. W. G. Price; 107th, 108th, and 109th Regiments; 103d Trench Mortar Battery.

Engineer Troops—103d Regiment.

Signal Troops—103d Battalion.

Division Units—28th Division Headquarters Troop; 107th Machine Gun Batallion.

30TH DIVISION (Wild Cat)—Major Gen. Edward M. Lewis, commanding; Lieut. Col. Robert B. McBride, Chief of Staff; Lieut. Col. Francis B. Hinkle, Adjutant General.

59th Brigade, Infantry—Brig. Gen. Lawrence D. Tyson; 117th and 118th Regiments; 114th Machine Gun Battalion.

60th Brigade, Infantry—Brig. Gen. Samuel L. Faison; 119th and 120th Regiments; 115th Machine Gun Battalion.

55th Brigade, Field Artillery—(Commanding officer not announced;) 113th, 114th, and 115th Regiments; 105th Trench Mortar Battery.

Engineer Troops—105th Regiment.

Signal Troops—105th Battalion.

Division Units—30th Division Headquarters Troop; 113th Machine Gun Battalion.

35TH DIVISION—Major Gen. Peter E. Traub, commanding; Colonel Robert McCleave, Chief of Staff; Major J. M. Hobson, Adjutant General.

69th Brigade, Infantry—Brig. Gen. Nathaniel McClure; 137th and 138th Regiments; 129th Machine Gun Battalion.

70th Brigade, Infantry—Brig. Gen. Charles I. Martin; 139th and 140th Regiments; 130th Machine Gun Battalion.

60th Brigade, Field Artillery—Brig. Gen. L. G. Berry; 128th, 129th, and 130th Regiments; 110th Trench Mortar Battery.

Engineer Troops—110th Regiment.

Signal Troops—110th Battalion.

Division Units—35th Division Headquarters Troop; 128th Machine Gun Battalion.

77TH DIVISION (Upton)—Major Gen. George B. Duncan, commanding; (Chief of Staff not announced;) Major W. N. Haskell, Adjutant General.

153d Brigade, Infantry—Brig. Gen. Edward Wittenmeyer; 205th and 306th Regiments; 305th Machine Gun Battalion.

154th Brigade, Infantry—Brig. Gen. Evan M. Johnson; 307th and 308th Regiments; 306th Machine Gun Battalion.

152d Brigade, Field Artillery—Brig. Gen. Thomas H. Reeves; 304th, 305th, and 306th Regiments; 302d Trench Mortar Battery.

Engineer Troops—302d Regiment.

Signal Troops—302d Battalion.

Division Units—77th Division Headquarters Troop; 304th Machine Gun Battalion.

82D DIVISION—Major Gen. W. P. Burnham, commanding; Lieut. Col. Royden E. Beebe, Chief of Staff; Lieut. Col. John R. Thomas, Adjutant General.

163d Brigade, Infantry—Brig. Gen. Marcus D. Cronin; 325th and 326th Regiments; 320th Machine Gun Battalion.

164th Brigade, Infantry — Brig. Gen. Julian R. Lindsay; 327th and 328th Regiments 321st Machine Gun Battalion.

157th Brigade, Field Artillery—Brig. Gen. Charles D. Rhodes; 319th, 320th, and 321st Regiments; 307th Trench Mortar Battery.

Engineer Troops—307th Regiment.

Signal Troops—307th Battalion.

Division Units—319th Machine Gun Battalion.

## 3D ARMY CORPS
### Major Gen. William M. Wright, commanding.

*3d and 5th Divisions, Regular Army; 27th*

*(New York) and 33d (Illinois) Divisions, National Guard; 78th (Delaware and New York) and 80th (New Jersey, Virginia, Maryland, Delaware, and District of Columbia) Divisions, National Army.*

3D DIVISION—Major Gen. Joseph T. Dickman, commanding; Colonel Robert H. Kelton, Chief of Staff; Captain Frank L. Purdon, Adjutant General.

5th Brigade, Infantry—Brig. Gen. F. W. Sladen; 4th and 7th Regiments; 8th Machine Gun Battalion.

8th Brigade, Infantry—(Commanding officer not announced;) 30th and 38th Regiments; 9th Machine Gun Battalion.

3d Brigade, Field Artillery—Brig. Gen. W. M. Cruikshank; 10th, 76th, and 18th Regiments; 3d Trench Mortar Battery.

Engineer Troops—6th Regiment.

Signal Troops—5th Battalion.

Division Units—3d Division Headquarters Troop; 7th Machine Gun Battalion.

5TH DIVISION—Major Gen. John E. McMahon, commanding; Colonel Ralph E. Ingram, Chief of Staff; Major David P. Wood, Adjutant General.

9th Brigade, Infantry—Brig. Gen. J. C. Castner; 60th and 61st Regiments; 14th Machine Gun Battalion.

10th Brigade, Infantry—Major Gen. W. H. Gordon; 6th and 11th Regiments; 15th Machine Gun Battalion.

5th Brigade, Field Artillery—Brig. Gen. C. A. F. Flagler; 19th, 20th, and 21st Regiments; 5th Trench Mortar Battery.

Engineer Troops—7th Regiment.

Signal Troops—9th Battalion.

Division Units—5th Division Headquarters Troop; 13th Machine Gun Battalion.

27TH DIVISION (New York) — Major Gen. J. F. O'Ryan, commanding; Lieut. Col. Stanley H. Ford, Chief of Staff; Lieut. Col. Frank W. Ward, Adjutant General.

53d Brigade, Infantry—Brig. Gen. Alfred W. Bjornstad; 105th and 106th Regiments; 105th Machine Gun Battalion.

54th Brigade, Infantry—Brig. Gen. Palmer E. Pierce; 107th and 108th Regiments; 106th Machine Gun Battalion.

52d Brigade, Field Artillery—Brig. Gen. George A. Wingate; 104th, 105th, and 106th Regiments; 102d Trench Mortar Battery.

Engineer Troops—102d Regiment.

Signal Troops—102d Battalion.

Division Units—27th Division Headquarters Troop; 104th Machine Gun Battalion.

33D DIVISION—Major Gen. George Bell, Jr., commanding; Colonel William K. Naylot, Chief of Staff; (Adjutant General not announced.)

65th Brigade, Infantry—Brig. Gen. Edward L. King; 129th and 130th Regiments; 123d Machine Gun Battalion.

66th Brigade, Infantry—Brig. Gen. Paul A. Wolff; 131st and 132d Regiments; 124th Machine Gun Battalion.

58th Brigade, Field Artillery—Brig. Gen. James A. Shipton; 122d, 123d, and 124th Regiments; 108th Trench Mortar Battery.

Engineer Troops—108th Regiment.

Signal Troops—108th Battalion.

Division Units—33d Division Headquarters Troop; 112th Machine Gun Battalion.

78TH DIVISION—Major Gen. James H. McRae, commanding; Lieut. Col. Harry N. Cootes, Chief of Staff; Major William T. MacMill , Adjutant General.

155th Brigade, Infantry — Brig. Gen. Mark L. Hersey; 309th and 310th Regiments; 308th Machine Gun Battalion.

156th Brigade, Infantry—Brig. Gen. James T. Dean; 311th and 312th Regiments; 309th Machine Gun Battalion.

153d Brigade, Field Artillery—Brig. Gen. Clint C. Hearn; 307th, 308th, and 309th Regiments; 303d Trench Mortar Battery.

Engineer Troops—303d Regiment.

Signal Troops—303d Battalion.

Division Units—78th Divisi Headquarters Troop; 307th Machine Gun Battalion.

80TH DIVISION—Major Gen. Adelbert Cronkhite, commanding; Lieut. Col. William H. Waldron, Chief of Staff; Major Steven C. Clark, Adjutant General.

159th Brigade, Infantry—Brig. Gen. George H. Jamerson; 317th and 318th Regiments; 314th Machine Gun Battalion.

160th Brigade, Infantry—Brig. Gen. Lloyd M. Bratt; 319th and 320th Regiments; 315th Machine Gun Battalion.

155th Brigade, Field Artillery—Brig. Gen. Gordon G. Heiner; 313th, 314th, and 315th Regiments; 305th Trench Mortar Battery.

Engineer Troops—305th Regiment.

Signal Troops—305th Battalion.

Division Units — 80th Division Headquarters Troop; 313th Machine Gun Battalion.

## 4TH ARMY CORPS

### Major Gen. George W. Read, commanding.

*83d, (Ohio and Pennsylvania,) 89th, (Kansas, Missouri, South Dakota, Nebraska, Colorado, New Mexico, and Arizona,) 90th, (Texas and Oklahoma,) and 92d (negro troops) Divisions, National Army; 37th (Ohio) and 29th (New Jersey, Virginia, Delaware, Maryland, and District of Columbia) Divisions, National Guard.*

29TH DIVISION—Major Gen. C. G. Morton, commanding; Colonel George S. Goodale, Chief of Staff; Major James A. Ulio, Adjutant General.

57th Brigade, Infantry — Brig. Gen. Charles W. Barber; 113th and 114th Regiments; 111th Machine Gun Battalion.

58th Brigade, Infantry—Brig. Gen. H. H. Bandholtz; 115th and 116th Regiments; 112th Machine Gun Battalion.

54th Brigade, Field Artillery—(Commanding officer not announced;) 110th, 111th, and 112th Regiments; 104th Trench Mortar Battery.

Engineer Troops—104th Regiment.

Signal Troops—104th Battalion.

Division Units—29th Division Headquarters Troop; 110th Machine Gun Battalion.

37TH DIVISION—Major Gen. C. S. Farnsworth, commanding; Lieut. Col. Dana T. Merrill, Chief of Staff; Major Edward W. Wildrick, Adjutant General.

73d Brigade, Infantry—Brig. Gen. C. F. Zimmerman; 145th and 146th Regiments; 135th Machine Gun Battalion.

74th Brigade, Infantry—Brig. Gen. W. P. Jackson; 147th and 148th Regiments; 136th Machine Gun Battalion.

62d Brigade, Field Artillery—(Commanding officer not announced;) 134th, 135th, and 136th Regiments; 112th Trench Mortar Battery.

Engineer Troops—112th Regiment.

Signal Troops—112th Battalion.

Division Units—37th Division Headquarters Troop; 134th Machine Gun Battalion.

83D DIVISION—Major Gen. E. F. Glenn, commanding; Lieut. Col. C. A. Trott, Chief of Staff; Major James L. Cochran, Adjutant General.

165th Brigade, Infantry—Brig. Gen. Ora E. Hunt; 329th and 330th Regiments; 323d Machine Gun Battalion.

166th Brigade, Infantry—Brig. Gen. Malin Craig; 331st and 332d Regiments; 324th Machine Gun Battalion.

158th Brigade, Field Artillery—Brig. Gen Adrian S. Fleming; 322d, 323d, and 324th Regiments; 308th Trench Mortar Battery.

Engineer Troops—308th Regiment.

Signal Troops—308th Battalion.

Division Units—83d Division Headquarters Troop; 322d Machine Gun Battalion.

89TH DIVISION—Brig. Gen. Frank L. Winn, commanding, (acting;) Colonel C. E. Kilbourne, Chief of Staff; Major Jerome G. Pillow, Adjutant General.

177th Brigade, Infantry—Brig. Gen. Frank L. Winn; 353d and 354th Regiments; 341st Machine Gun Battalion.

178th Brigade, Infantry—Brig. Gen. Thomas G. Hanson; 355th and 356th Regiments; 342d Machine Gun Battalion.

164th Brigade, Field Artillery—Brig. Gen. Edward T. Donnelly; 340th, 341st, and 342d Regiments; 314th Trench Mortar Battery.

Engineer Troops—314th Regiment.

Signal Troops—314th Battalion.

Division Units—89th Division Headquarters Troop; 340th Machine Gun Battalion.

90TH DIVISION—Major Gen. Henry T. Allen, commanding; Colonel John J. Kingman, Chief of Staff; Major Wyatt O. Selkirk, Adjutant General.

179th Brigade, Infantry—Brig. Gen. John T. O'Neill; 357th and 358th Regiments; 344th Machine Gun Battalion.

180th Brigade, Infantry—Brig. Gen. W. H. Johnston ; 359th and 360th Regiments ; 345th Machine Gun Battalion.

165th Brigade, Field Artillery—Brig. Gen. Francis C. Marshall ; 343d, 344th, and 345th Regiments ; 315th Trench Mortar Battery.

Engineer Troops—315th Regiment.

Signal Troops—315th Battalion.

Division Units—90th Division Headquarters Troop ; 349th Machine Gun Battalion.

92D DIVISION—Major Gen. C. C. Ballou, commanding ; Lieut. Col. Allen J. Greer, Chief of Staff ; Major Sherburne Whipple, Adjutant General.

183d Brigade, Infantry—Brig. Gen. Malvern H. Barnum ; 365th and 366th Regiments ; 350th Machine Gun Battalion.

184th Brigade, Infantry—Brig. Gen. W. A. Hay ; 367th and 368th Regiments ; 351st Machine Gun Battalion.

167th Brigade, Field Artillery—(Commanding officer not announced ;) 349th, 350th, and 351st Regiments ; 317th Trench Mortar Battery.

Engineer Troops—317th Regiment.

Signal Troops—317th Battalion.

Division Units—92d Division Headquarters Troop ; 349th Machine Gun Battalion.

## 5TH ARMY CORPS

### Major Gen. Omar Bundy, commanding.

*6th Division, Regular Army ; 36th (Texas and Oklahoma) Division, National Guard ; 75th, (New England,) 79th, (Pennsylvania, Maryland, and District of Columbia,) 85th, (Michigan and Wisconsin,) and 91st (Washington, Oregon, Alaska, California, Idaho, Nevada, Montana, Wyoming, and Utah) Divisions, National Army.*

6TH DIVISION—Brig. Gen. James B. Erwin, commanding ; Colonel James M. Pickering, Chief of Staff ; Lieut. Col. Robert S. Knox, Adjutant General.

11th Brigade, Infantry—Brig. Gen. W. R. Dashiell ; 51st and 52d Regiments ; 17th Machine Gun Battalion.

12th Brigade, Infantry—Brig. Gen. J. B. Erwin ; 53d and 54th Regiments ; 18th Machine Gun Battalion.

6th Brigade, Field Artillery—Brig. Gen. E. A. Millar ; 3d, 11th, and 78th Regiments ; 6th Trench Mortar Battery.

Engineer Troops—318th Regiment.

Signal Troops—6th Battalion.

Division Units—6th Division Headquarters Troop ; 16th Machine Gun Battalion.

36TH DIVISION—Major Gen. W. R. Smith, commanding ; Colonel E. J. Williams, Chief of Staff ; Major William R. Scott, Adjutant General.

71st Brigade, Infantry — Brig. Gen. Henry Hutchings ; 141st and 142d Regiments ; 132d Machine Gun Battalion.

72d Brigade, Infantry—Brig. Gen. John A. Hulen ; 143d and 144th Regiments ; 133d Machine Gun Battalion.

61st Brigade, Field Artillery—Brig. Gen.

John A. Stevens ; 131st, 132d, and 133d Regiments ; 111th Trench Mortar Battery.

Engineer Troops—111th Regiment.

Signal Troops—111th Battalion.

Division Units—36th Division Headquarters Troop ; 131st Machine Gun Battalion.

76TH DIVISION—Major Gen. Harry F. Hodges, commanding ; (Chief of Staff not announced ;) Major George M. Peek, Adjutant General.

151st Brigade, Infantry — Brig. Gen. Frank M. Albright ; 301st and 302d Regiments ; 302d Machine Gun Battalion.

152d Brigade, Infantry—Brig. Gen. F. D. Evans ; 303d and 304th Regiments ; 303d Machine Gun Battalion.

151st Brigade, Field Artillery—Major Gen. William S. McNair ; 301st, 302d, and 303d Regiments ; 301st Trench Mortar Battery.

Engineer Troops—301st Regiment.

Signal Troops—301st Battalion.

Division Units—76th Division Headquarters Troop ; 301st Machine Gun Battalion.

79TH DIVISION—Major Gen. Joseph E. Kuhn, commanding ; Colonel Tenny Ross, Chief of Staff ; Major Charles B. Moore, Adjutant General.

157th Brigade, Infantry—Brig. Gen. William L. Nicholson ; 313th and 314th Regiments ; 311th Machine Gun Battalion.

158th Brigade, Infantry—(Commanding officer not announced ;) 315th and 316th Regiments ; 312th Machine Gun Battalion.

154th Brigade, Field Artillery—Brig. Gen. Andrew Hero, Jr. ; 310th, 311th, and 312th Regiments ; 304th Trench Mortar Battery.

Engineer Troops—304th Regiment.

Signal Troops—304th Battalion.

Division Units—79th Division Headquarters Troop ; 310th Machine Gun Battalion.

85TH DIVISION—Major Gen. C. W. Kennedy, commanding ; Colonel Edgar T. Collins, Chief of Staff ; Lieut. Col. Clarence Lininger, Adjutant General.

169th Brigade, Infantry—Brig. Gen. Thomas B. Dugan ; 337th and 338th Regiments ; 329th Machine Gun Battalion.

170th Brigade, Infantry—(Commanding officer not announced ;) 339th and 340th Regiments ; 330th Machine Gun Battalion.

160th Brigade, Field Artillery—Brig. Gen. Guy M. Preston ; 328th, 329th, and 330th Regiments ; 310th Trench Mortar Battery.

Engineer Troops—310th Regiment.

Signal Troops—310th Battalion.

Division Units—85th Division Headquarters Troop ; 328th Machine Gun Battalion.

91ST DIVISION—Brig. Gen. F. H. Foltz, commanding ; Colonel Herbert J. Brees, Chief of Staff ; Major Frederick W. Manley, Adjutant General.

181st Brigade, Infantry—Brig. Gen.

John B. McDonald; 361st and 362d Regiments; 347th Machine Gun Battalion.

182d Brigade, Infantry—Brig. Gen. Frederick S. Foltz; 363d and 364th Regiments; 348th Machine Gun Battalion.

166th Brigade, Field Artillery—Brig. Gen. Edward Burr; 346th, 347th, and 348th Regiments; 316th Trench Mortar Battery.

Engineer Troops—316th Regiment.

Signal Troops—316th Battalion.

Division Units—91st Division Headquarters Troop; 346th Machine Gun Battalion.

## UNASSIGNED TO CORPS

81ST DIVISION—Major Gen. C. J. Bailey, commanding; Colonel Charles D. Roberts, Chief of Staff; Major Arthur E. Ahrends, Adjutant General.

161st Brigade, Infantry—Brig. Gen. George W. McIver; 321st and 322d Regiments; 317th Machine Gun Battalion.

162d Brigade, Infantry—Brig. Gen. Monroe McFarland; 323d and 324th Regiments; 318th Machine Gun Battalion.

156th Brigade, Field Artillery—Brig. Gen. Andrew Moses; 316th, 317th, and 318th Regiments; 306th Trench Mortar Battery.

Engineer Troops—306th Regiment.

Signal Troops—306th Battalion.

Division Units—81st Division Headquarters Troop; 316th Machine Gun Battalion.

93D DIVISION — (Commander not announced;) Major Lee S. Tillotson, Adjutant General.

185th Brigade, Infantry—(Commanding officer not announced;) 369th and 370th Regiments; 333d Machine Gun Battalion.

186th Brigade, Infantry—Brig. Gen. George H. Harries; 371st and 372d Regiments; 334th Machine Gun Battalion.

168th Brigade, Field Artillery—(Commanding officer not announced;) 332d, 333d, and 334th Regiments; 318th Trench Mortar Battery.

Engineer Troops—318th Regiment.

Signal Troops—318th Battalion.

Division Units—332d Machine Gun Battalion.

# President Wilson's Labor Day Appeal
## A Call for Sustained War Effort

*Labor Day of 1918, Sept. 2, was observed in all industrial centres with parades of unusual size, the turnout in New York City being estimated at 60,000. The workingmen everywhere were addressed by patriotic speakers, and pledged afresh their loyalty and firm resolve to win the war. President Wilson recognized the day by issuing, on Sept. 1, the following formal appeal to organized labor and to the people generally:*

MY FELLOW-CITIZENS: Labor Day, 1918, is not like any Labor Day that we have known. Labor Day was always deeply significant with us. Now it is supremely significant. Keenly as we were aware a year ago of the enterprise of life and death upon which the nation had embarked, we did not perceive its meaning as clearly as we do now. We knew that we were all partners and must stand and strive together, but we did not realize, as we do now, that we are all enlisted men, members of a single army, of many parts and many tasks, but commanded by a single obligation, our faces set toward a single object. We now know that every tool in every essential industry is a weapon, and a weapon wielded for the same purpose that an army rifle is wielded—a weapon which if we were to lay down no rifle would be of any use.

And a weapon for what? What is the war for? Why are we enlisted? Why should we be ashamed if we were not enlisted? At first it seemed hardly more than a war of defense against the military aggression of Germany. Belgium had been violated, France invaded, and Germany was afield again, as in 1870 and 1866, to work out her ambitions in Europe, and it was necessary to meet her force with force. But it is clear now that it is much more than a war to alter the balance of power in Europe. Germany, it is now plain, was striking at what free men everywhere desire and must have—the right to determine their own fortunes, to insist upon justice, and to oblige Governments to act for them and not for the private and selfish interest of a governing class. It is a war to make the nations and peoples of the world secure against every such power as the German autocracy represents. It is a war of emancipation. Not until it is won can men anywhere live free from constant fear or breathe freely while they go about their daily tasks and know that Governments are their servants, not their masters.

This is, therefore, the war of all wars, which labor should support and support with all its concentrated power. The world cannot be safe, men's lives cannot be secure, no man's rights can be confidently and successfully asserted against the rule and mastery of arbitrary groups and special interests so long as Governments like that which after long premeditation drew Austria and Germany into this war are permitted to control the destinies and the daily fortunes of men and nations, plotting while honest men work, laying the fires of which innocent men, women, and children are to be the fuel.

You know the nature of this war. It is a war which industry must sustain. The army of laborers at home is as important, as essential, as the army of fighting men in the far fields of actual battle. And the laborer is not only needed as much as the soldier. It is his war. The soldier is his champion and representative. To fail to win would be to imperil everything that the laborer has striven for and held dear since freedom first had its dawn and its struggle for justice began. The soldiers at the front know this. It steels their muscles to think of it. They are crusaders. They are fighting for no selfish advantage for their own nation. They would despise any one who fought for the selfish advantage of any nation. They are giving their lives that homes everywhere, as well as the homes they love in America, may be kept sacred and safe, and men everywhere be free as they insist upon being free. They are fighting for the ideals of their own land —great ideals, immortal ideals, ideals which shall light the way for all men to the places where justice is done and men live with lifted heads and emancipated spirits. That is the reason they fight with solemn joy and are invincible.

Let us make this, therefore, a day of fresh comprehension not only for what we are about and of renewed and clear-eyed resolution, but a day of consecration also in which we devote ourselves without pause or limit to the great task of setting our own country and the whole world free to render justice to all, and of making it impossible for small groups of political rulers anywhere to disturb our peace or the peace of the world, or in any way to make tools and puppets of those upon whose consent and upon whose power their own authority and their own very existence depend.

We may count upon each other. The nation is of a single mind. It is taking counsel with no special class. It is serving no private or single interest. Its own mind has been cleared and fortified by these days, which burn the dross away. The light of a new conviction has penetrated to every class among us. We realize as we never realized before that we are comrades dependent upon one another, irresistible when united, powerless when divided. And so we join hands to lead the world to a new and better day.        WOODROW WILSON.

# Progress of the War

### Recording Campaigns on All Fronts and Collateral Events
### From August 17 Up to and Including September 18, 1918

## UNITED STATES

John D. Ryan on Aug. 27 was appointed Second Assistant Secretary of War, with full responsibility over the army's air service, and Benedict C. Crowell, First Assistant Secretary of War, was put in charge of the munitions program. Secretary Baker, accompanied by Mr. Ryan and other War Department officials, arrived in France Sept. 7.

The Man Power bill, providing for the drafting of men between the ages of 18 and 45, passed its final stages, and was signed by President Wilson on Aug. 31, and 12,875,000 men registered on Sept. 12.

William D. Haywood and fourteen of his chief aids in the conspiracy of the Industrial Workers of the World to overturn the American war program were sentenced to twenty years' imprisonment and fined $20,000 each. Eighty others received terms of from ten years to ten days and were fined. Sentences were imposed on Aug. 30.

Eugene V. Debs, the Socialist leader, was found guilty of violating the Espionage act and was sentenced to ten years' imprisonment.

## SUBMARINE BLOCKADE

The crew of a British oil tanker reported on Aug. 19 that a German submarine had been sunk in a running battle with the tanker off the coast of Nantucket, on Aug. 16, and on Aug. 20 another British tanker reported that she had sunk a U-boat.

Two Norwegian ships, the San José and the Nordhav, were sunk on Aug. 19; the San José was attacked off the coast of Nantucket and the Nordhav off Virginia Capes.

The British steam trawler Triumph was captured by a submarine on Aug. 20. She was turned into a raider with a German crew on board and destroyed practically the entire fleet of the Maritime Fish Corporation off the coast of Newfoundland.

Aug. 25—The Canadian steamer Eric was destroyed by shellfire off Miquelon Island; five members of the crew were wounded.

Aug. 25—The Gloucester fishing steamer J. J. Flaherty was sunk.

Aug. 26—The American fishing schooner Rush was sunk off the Canadian coast.

Aug. 28—The Newfoundland schooner Bianca was attacked but not sunk.

Aug. 29—The fishing schooner Gloaming was sunk off the coast of Nova Scotia.

Sept. 14—A steamship carrying wounded Canadian officers was attacked ninety miles off the Atlantic coast, but escaped.

Aug. 16—The American S. S. Montana was sunk in foreign waters; five of the crew were lost.

Aug. 17—The U. S. cargo S. S. Joseph Cudahy was torpedoed 700 miles off the coast of England; thirteen of the crew missing.

Aug. 21—The army chartered cargo transport Lake Edon sunk; six of the crew killed and two others missing.

Sept. 2—The U. S. steamer Onega torpedoed; twenty-six of the crew missing.

Sept. 4—American steamship Dora sunk off the French coast and on the same day the liner Persic, with 2,800 American soldiers on board, was torpedoed off the coast of England. All on board were saved, the ship was beached, and the attacking U-boat reported sunk.

Sept. 5—American troop transport Mount Vernon torpedoed off the French coast, while homeward bound, but she was able to return to port under her own steam; thirty-five of the crew killed.

Sept. 9—Canadian Pacific liner Missanabie, westward bound, torpedoed.

Sept. 12—British steamer Galway Castle sunk; 189 persons lost; among them women and children.

Aug. 17—French cruiser Dupetit Thouars sunk and thirteen of the crew missing.

Aug. 26—Seven fishing ships, three of Dutch registry, destroyed near the "free channel" in North Sea.

Six German steamers were given to Holland as reparation for ships sunk by U-boats.

Sept. 11—Portuguese steamship Leixoes torpedoed in the South Atlantic.

Aug. 21—The Spanish Government announced that German ships interned in Spanish ports would be taken to replace Spanish ships sunk by German submarines; Germany finally acceded to the decision.

Aug. 31—The Spanish ship Alexandrine attacked by a U-boat.

Aug. 31—At a meeting of the Spanish Cabinet the Foreign Minister announced the sinking of the steamship Ataz-Trendi, carrying a cargo of coal from England to Spain. One of the interned German steamers was seized in reprisal.

Losses of merchant shipping by Great Britain during July aggregated 176,479 tons.

Other allied and neutral gross tonnage sunk aggregated 136,532.

Sept. 1—Norwegian steamer Borgsdal torpedoed and sunk.

The sinking of a large German submarine, camouflaged and flying no flag, far out in the Atlantic Ocean on the morning of Sept. 3 by the American tank steamer Frank H. Buck, was officially reported Sept. 10.

## CAMPAIGN IN WESTERN EUROPE

Aug. 17—French enter German positions north of Autreches to a depth of nearly a mile on a front of more than three miles, and take Canny-sur-Matz, two miles northwest of Lassigny; Americans in Lorraine take the village of Frapelle.

Aug. 18—British in the Lys salient force Germans back along a four-mile front between Bailleul and Vieux Berquin, capturing Outtersteene, and improve their positions north of Roye; Americans gain more ground at Frapelle.

Aug. 19—French advance on a fifteen-mile front east of Ribecourt and cross the Oise to Fontenoy, capturing four villages, and capture Fresmières on the Roye highroad; British gain on a six-mile front and enter Merville; Americans and French push forward on the north bank of the Vesle.

Aug. 20—French drive ahead two and one-half miles on a fifteen-and-a-half-mile front between the Oise and the Aisne, taking seven towns and 8,000 prisoners; British push forward in the Merville sector.

Aug. 21—French take Lassigny and advance over a front of fifteen miles east and west of the Oise, driving the Germans from twenty villages; British attack on a ten-mile front from the Ancre River to the neighborhood of Moyenneville, taking seven villages, and pierce German line in Flanders near Locre half a mile on a mile front.

Aug. 22—British capture Albert in new drive in which they gain two miles on a six-mile front; French advance seven miles along the front from Lassigny to the region north of Soissons, taking several villages and crossing the Ailette River.

Aug. 23—French 3d Army crosses the Divette River in the region of Evricourt; Mangin's troops cross the Oise River and the canal at Manicamp, eight miles east of Noyon, and reach the outskirts of Morlincourt; French also make progress east of Bagneux and to the west of Crecy-au-Mont; British advance more than two miles on the six-mile front from southeast of Albert to the neighborhood of Grancourt, take nine towns, and close in on Bapaume; Americans repulse violent attacks west of Fismes.

Aug. 24.—British capture Bray and ten other towns and carry the dominating position of Thiepval Ridge; French advance at

Crecy; Americans win a half-mile front on the Soissons-Rheims front west of Fismes.

Aug. 25—British sweep on north of the Somme, taking twelve towns, and seizing and crossing the highroad between Albert and Bapaume, and carrying the new front to within 1,000 yards of the old Hindenburg line; French make progress east of Bagneux.

Aug. 26—British fight on a 30-mile front from the River Scarpe at a point east of Arras to Lihons, crossing the Hindenburg line on the northernmost sector of their attack; Canadians capture Wancourt and Monchy-le-Preux; French, in move to encircle Roye, take Fresnoy and St. Mard.

Aug. 27—British smash through the Hindenburg line for three or four miles southeast of Arras, occupying Cherisy, Vis-en-Artois, and the Bois du Sart; Scottish soldiers cross the Sensée River, seizing Fontaine-lez-Croisilles, and north of the Scarpe take Roeux and Gavrelle; English troops take Arleux-en-Gohelle and the old German line to the south; French take Roye and six other towns in an advance on a front of more than twelve miles; Americans attack Bazoches and resist assault on Fismette.

Aug. 28—French take Chaulnes and drive ahead eight miles, reaching the Somme, and recapture forty villages; British force Germans to give up Croisilles; Americans advance their lines at Chavigny and repulse German attacks at Bazoches.

Aug. 29—French take Noyon, gain a foothold on the southern slope of Mt. St. Siméon, force the crossing of the Oise at Morlincourt, take Landrimont, and capture Beaurains and Quesnoy Wood; British capture Bapaume and force a German retreat along the whole front southward to Péronne and Brie.

Aug. 30—French take Mt. St. Siméon and cross the Canal du Nord at Cantigny and Beaurains; French and American troops north of Soissons capture Chavigny and Cuffies and advance their line to the west of Crouy; British capture villages east and northeast of Bapaume, are checked at Bullecourt, but take Combles and Clery; Germans evacuate Bailleul; Americans take Juvigny.

Aug. 31—Australians storm Mt. St. Quentin and Feuillaucourt; English capture Marrieres Wood and high ground further north along the Péronne-Bapaume road; British capture Riencourt; Germans retire from the Lys salient; British take Kemmel Hill; Americans make gains eastward in the vicinity of Juvigny and the Bois de Beaumont.

Sept. 1—British take Péronne, Bouchavesnes, and Rancourt, and drive the Germans from several villages south of Bapaume; Bullecourt and Hendecourt in hands of the British; Germans lose several villages in the Lys salient; French advance on the Ailette, capturing Crecy-au-Mont and Leury; Americans forge ahead two miles beyond Juvigny; Americans fight for the first time on Belgian soil and take Voormezeele and nearby strongholds.

Sept. 2—British carry the Quéant-Drocourt "switch line" on a front of about six miles, taking several villages in a four-mile advance; Germans continue to retreat on the Lys; British occupy Neuve Eglise; Americans north of Soissons reach Terny-Sorny and the Soissons-St. Quentin highway.

Sept. 3—British push forward to Baralle, taking Quéant and thirteen other villages in an advance along a twenty-six-mile front to a maximum depth of six miles; Germans driven in hasty retreat to the Canal du Nord.

Sept. 4—Germans retreat on a front of nearly twenty miles north of the Vesle; French and American troops force a passage of the river and occupy Chassemy, Bucy-le-Long, Branelle, Vauxcere, and Blanzy; French make gains northeast of Noyon and drive the Germans before them in the territory between the Canal du Nord and the Oise; British force the passage of the Canal du Nord on a front of approximately fifteen miles northward from Moislans and advance to the east; British advance in Flanders, reaching the neighborhood of Neuve Chapelle and Laventie; Germans evacuate Lens, but British refrain from occupying it because of poison gas fumes.

Sept. 6—Germans retreat on a ninety-mile front from the posts of the Americans on the Aisne to the breaches in the Hindenburg line before Cambrai; French capture Ham and Chauny and advance east of the Canal du Nord to a depth of more than six miles at some points; British push on eastward south from the Somme, penetrating German positions nearly seven miles on a twelve-mile front, and capturing several villages; Americans south of the Aisne make progress in the region of Villers-en-Prayeres and Revillon.

Sept. 8—British make gains toward St. Quentin and Laon, capturing Villévêque and Ste. Emilie and the greater part of Havrincourt Wood; French advance along the banks of the St. Quentin Canal north of the Somme, capturing Hamel and several other villages, and advance on both sides of the Oise; Americans advance northward on the Aisne in the vicinity of Vieil Arcy, Villers-en-Prayeres, and Revillon.

Sept. 9—British gain on a four-mile front, capturing dominating positions south of Havrincourt Wood; French troops cross the Crozat Canal opposite Liez; Germans throw in new divisions to check American advance on the St. Gobain massif.

Sept. 12—First American Army attacks the St. Mihiel salient from all sides and advances on a thirty-mile front to a depth of five miles, aided by the French; St. Mihiel and several towns captured; British improve their positions between La Bassée and east of Péronne, and make important progress toward Cambrai, taking Havrincourt, Moeuvres, and Trescault.

Sept. 13—Americans wipe out St. Mihiel salient, reducing the front from forty to twenty miles, capturing 15,000 prisoners, and extending the battleline past Norroy, Jaulny, Xammes, St. Bénoit, Hattonville, Hannonville, and Herbeuville. British occupy additional territory in the region of Vermand and Jeancourt.

Sept. 14—Americans repulse counterattacks in the St. Mihiel sector and push on; French begin new attack on both sides of the Ailette River and between the Aisne and the Vesle, advancing for a distance of between one and two miles on an eleven-mile front; Mont des Singes and the villages of Allemant and Sanoy taken; British advance their lines toward Cambrai and St. Quentin and gain in the Lys region.

Sept. 15—Americans in St. Mihiel sector advance from two to three miles on a thirty-three-mile front; guns from fortress of Metz in action against them; villages of Norroy and Vilcey captured; British gain on the St. Quentin front, capturing the village of Maissemy and adjacent trench systems; French in the Chemin des Dames region capture the plateau east of Vauxaillon and the ridge northwest of Celles-sur-Aisne.

Sept. 17—Americans in Lorraine advance on extreme right of the line; Germans shell and gas the woods north of Pont-a-Mousson and near Norroy; Germans burn towns along the Moselle as American infantry advances; French guns shell Metz.

Sept. 18—British launch attack on St. Quentin defenses on a sixteen-mile line northwest of the city, occupying ten villages and crossing the Hindenburg line at Villeret and Gouzeaucourt; French attack to the right of the British and push their lines forward a mile and a quarter on the six-mile front between Holnon and Essigny le Grand; Americans build strong front line in Lorraine, and threaten Metz and the Briey coal fields.

## BALKAN CAMPAIGN

Sept. 15-16—French and Serbian troops capture first and second line Bulgarian positions along a ten-mile section of the Doiran-Vardar front.

Sept. 17—Allies progress more than five miles on a front of twelve miles, taking important ridges and the village of Gradeshnitsa; Jugoslav division, fighting with Serbs and French, reaches Koziak.

Sept. 18—Allies advance on the Macedonian front an average of ten miles—east of

Monastir—and penetrate the Bulgarian third line, opening up the region for advances into Bulgarian and Serbian territory.

## AERIAL RECORD

During August 324 German machines were destroyed or driven out of control on the western front by British airmen; 116 British fliers were reported missing. French aviators dropped 629 tons of bombs and downed 280 Teuton planes.

An allied hospital southwest of Soissons was bombed at night, Sept. 4; no casualties.

Allied aviators made many raids on German towns; Cologne was bombed Aug. 22; five persons killed, two injured.

Nine persons killed, six injured, in a raid on Karlsruhe, Aug. 23.

Sept. 2—Fifteen tons of bombs were dropped on German military works in the Rhine provinces. Three raids were made on the airdrome at Bruehl, where the hangars were demolished. The railways at Ehrang, Burbach, and Saarbrücken were bombed and fires started in the Burbach works.

Sept. 5—The railways at Metz-Sablons and Mainz and the docks and sidings at Karlsruhe bombed; extensive damage at Karlsruhe.

Sept. 7—A British squadron attacked the railways at Ehrang and the chemical works at Mannheim.

Metz and nearby cities were raided on Sept. 14, 15, and 16, over 87 tons of bombs being dropped.

Sept. 15—Allied machines dropped seventeen tons of bombs on Courcilles, Ehrang, Saarbrücken, Conlfans, and other points on the Lorraine front. Constantinople was raided several times by allied airmen; on Aug. 27 bombs and manifestoes were dropped. One person was killed and eleven wounded. Venice was bombed on Aug. 22. Some material damage was caused and several persons were wounded. Bombs were dropped on Padua Aug. 25. Some buildings were slightly damaged.

Sept. 16—Paris bombed by a large squadron; six killed, fifteen injured; one German brought down.

## NAVAL RECORD

Dutch steamer Gasconier, operated by the Belgian Relief Commission, was sunk by a mine in the North Sea Aug. 21. Six were lost.

One of a squadron of German warships cruising off the coast of the Island of Ameland, Sept. 6, ran into a mine or was torpedoed.

## RUSSIA

Japanese forces landed at Vladivostok on Aug. 12 and joined the French and British, and on Aug. 13 the Japanese Government announced that under an agreement with China troops were being sent through Manchuria to protect the border from the Bolsheviki and Teuton prisoners. On Aug. 19 word was received that China had sent troops to the Siberian border.

American forces were sent to guard the railroad between Vladivostok and Nikolsk, thus releasing Czechoslovak troops.

The Japanese General Kikuzo Otani took command of the allied forces in Siberia on Aug. 17.

Ministers of neutral countries addressed a note to Foreign Minister Tchitcherin, Aug. 26, protesting against the fresh demands which he made in connection with arrangements for the departure of allied Consuls and missions from Moscow.

The British Embassy at Petrograd was sacked by Bolsheviki Aug. 31, and Captain Cromie, the British attaché, was killed. Great Britain demanded reparation and interned the Bolshevist Envoy at London as a hostage.

Word was received on Sept. 8 that the Soviet Government would agree to the exchange of diplomats with Great Britain if the neutral powers would undertake to guarantee that the Bolshevist representatives in London were given a safe conduct home.

Eleven Englishmen, including R. H. B. Lockhart, the British Consul General at Moscow, were imprisoned by the Reds in the Fortress of St. Peter and St. Paul.

On Aug. 26 the Reds were driven back fifteen miles on the Ussuri River front and on Aug. 28 Japanese cavalry occupied Krasnoyarsk.

On Sept. 1 Japanese cavalry occupied Iman, at the junction of the Iman and Ussuri Rivers. On the Manchurian front General Semenoff's Cossacks reached the fortifications of Borgia on the Trans-Siberian Railway, and Japanese cavalry took Chingyang. On the same day the Bolshevist Council at Blagovieshtchensk, capital of the Amur Province, declared war on China because of China's sending troops to the Northern Manchurian front.

Announcement was made on Sept. 4 that Major General William S. Graves had arrived at Vladivostok to assume command of the American forces there.

Announcement was made on Sept. 5 that Czechoslovaks had captured Chita, the capital and largest city of Transbaikalia. On the same day allied troops occupied Obozerskaya and peasants captured Nizhni-Novgorod on the Volga.

Khabarovsk, at the junction of the Amur and Ussuri Rivers, was occupied by Japanese forces, Sept. 7.

On Sept. 11 announcement was made that American troops had arrived safely at Archangel.

Vologda was captured by the White Guards, Sept. 11. It was burned by the Reds before they evacuated it.

Simbirsk, on the Volga, was captured by the Reds, Sept. 14.

General Horvath attempted by a coup d'état to assume control of all the Russian military forces in the Far East, Aug. 25, but was obliged to relinquish his pretensions to a dictatorship at the demand of the Allies.

On Sept. 12 word was received that the Entente Goverments had refused to recognize the Horvath Government and had appointed a committee to administer municipal affairs.

Nikolai Lenine, the Bolshevist Premier, was shot on Aug. 30 at Moscow by Dora Kaplan, a revolutionist. Drastic measures were taken by the Soviet Government. Thousands of persons were sent to Petrograd and summary execution was decreed for all persons in Moscow found with a weapon. Mlle. Kaplan was executed on Sept. 4, and, by Sept. 8, twenty-six British officials had been arrested and threatened with death should Lenine die.

Leo Kameneff, Vice President of the Workmen's and Soldiers' Deputies, was appointed Acting Premier in Lenine's place.

The reign of terror instituted by the Bolshevist Government brought forth a joint protest from neutral diplomats, Sept. 8. They announced that their Governments would expel all Russian Bolsheviki if the Soviet Government did not stop the wholesale execution of civilians and officers and other drastic measures against its political opponents.

Up to Sept. 9, 512 counter-revolutionaries had been killed as a reprisal for the murder of Moses Uritzky, Chairman of the Petrograd Commission for the suppression of a counter-revolution. In Smolens, thirty-four landowners and the former Moscow Archimandrite, Nakari, were shot as a reprisal for the attempt on the life of Lenine. Many important personages, including Grand Dukes and ex-Ministers, were held as hostages to prevent a fresh attempt at a counter-revolt.

Admiral A. V. Razvozoff, former Commander in Chief of the Russian naval forces in the Baltic, was reported murdered in Petrograd, Sept. 12.

General Soukhomlinoff, former Minister of War in the Russian Imperial Cabinet, was court-martialed and shot on Sept. 6.

Three supplementary agreements to the Brest-Litovsk treaty were signed at Berlin, Aug. 27. They conceded to Russia routes of commerce and free ports in Esthonia and Livonia; Germany dropped her claims in the Caucasus, but obtained the promise of its oil supply; the independence of Georgia was recognized, and the indemnity demanded of Russia was partly shifted to Ukraine and Finland. Official information received by the American State Department showed that an offensive and defensive alliance with Germany was involved in the treaty, and Russia's commercial affairs were to be controlled by Germany for five years.

The first portion of the Russian war indemnity was reported to have been paid to Germany Sept. 7, amounting to $1,500,000,000.

The United States Committee on Public Information, on Sept. 14, made public a series of official communications between the German Imperial Government and the Russian Bolshevist Government and the Bolsheviki themselves, showing that Lenine and Trotzky were German agents, that the Bolshevist revolution was financed by the German Imperial Bank and arranged for by the German General Staff, and that the treaty of Brest-Litovsk was a betrayal of the Russian people by German agents.

Representatives of the former Esthonian Diet and Government, in a declaration to allied and neutral countries, repudiated the Brest-Litovsk treaty, Aug. 25.

## MISCELLANEOUS

On Sept. 14 the Austro-Hungarian Government invited all belligerent Governments to enter into non-binding discussions at a secret conference at some neutral meeting place, with a view to the calling of a peace conference. The suggestion was immediately rejected by the United States Government in a curt note forwarded to Austria Sept. 17.

An unofficial report was received on Sept. 15 that Germany had made a definite peace offer to Belgium. It was stated that Belgium had flatly rejected the offer. The story was denied by Berlin.

Word was received on Sept. 7 that a treaty of alliance had been concluded between Germany and Finland under which the entire man power of Finland was put at Germany's disposal.

Prince Frederick Charles of Hesse declared his willingness to accept the crown of Finland.

The Swedish Government entered into an agreement with Great Britain, France, and the United States under which these Governments agreed to the rationing of Sweden in return for the use of 400,000 tons of Swedish shipping, the use of some Swedish products, including rich Swedish iron ores, and certain other conditions. Announcement to this effect was made Aug. 22. A similar arrangement with Denmark was also agreed to, announced Sept. 19.

Word was received on Sept. 6 that General von Linsingen had placed the City of Berlin and the Province of Brandenburg in a state of siege, providing for a fine or imprisonment for persons inventing or circulating untrue rumors calculated to disquiet the populace.

Secretary Lansing announced on Sept. 3 that the United States Government recognized the Czechoslovaks as a belligerent nation and the Czechoslovak National Council as a de facto belligerent Government.

# Austria's Peace Conference Note

## Proposal for a "Confidential" Discussion
## Is Promptly Rejected by the United States

THE Austro-Hungarian Government on Sept. 15, 1918, addressed a communication and note to belligerent and neutral powers and the Holy See suggesting a meeting for a preliminary and "non-binding" discussion of war aims with a view to the possible calling of a peace conference.* It was transmitted to the United States Government through the Swedish Government. The official text of the introductory communication follows:

An objective and conscientious examination of the situation of all the belligerent States no longer leaves doubt that all peoples, on whatever side they may be fighting, long for a speedy end to the bloody struggle. Despite this natural and comprehensible desire for peace, it has not so far been possible to create those preliminary conditions calculated to bring the peace efforts nearer to realization and bridge the gap which at present still separates the belligerents from one another.

A more effective means must therefore be considered whereby the responsible factors of all the countries can be offered an opportunity to investigate the present possibilities of an understanding.

The first step which Austria-Hungary, in accord with her allies, undertook on Dec. 12, 1916, for the bringing about of peace did not lead to the end hoped for.

The grounds for this lay assuredly in the situation at that time. In order to maintain in their peoples the war spirit, which was steadily declining, the allied Governments had by the most severe means suppressed even any discussion of the peace idea. And so it came about that the ground for a peace understanding was not properly prepared. The natural transition from the wildest war agitation to a condition of conciliation was lacking.

It would, however, be wrong to believe that the peace step we then took was entirely without result. Its fruits consist of something which is not to be overlooked—that the peace question has not since vanished from the order of the day. The discussions which have been carried on before the tribunal of public opinion have disclosed proof

*See address by Baron Burian at Vienna Sept. 10, 1918, foreshadowing this formal proposal. It appears on Page 132 of this issue of CURRENT HISTORY MAGAZINE.

of the not slight differences which today still separate the warring powers in their conception of peace conditions.

Nevertheless, an atmosphere has been created which no longer excludes the discussion of the peace problem.

Without optimism, it at least assuredly may be deduced from the utterances of responsible statesmen that the desire to reach an understanding and not to decide the war exclusively by force of arms is also gradually beginning to penetrate into allied States, save for some exceptions in the case of blinded war agitators, which are certainly not to be estimated lightly.

The Austro-Hungarian Government is aware that after the deep-reaching convulsions which have been caused in the life of the peoples by the devastating effects of the world war will not be possible to re-establish order in the tottering world at a single stroke. The path that leads to the restoration of peaceful relations between the peoples is cut by hatred and embitterment. It is toilsome and wearisome, yet it is our duty to tread this path—the path of negotiation—and if there are still such responsible factors as desire to overcome the opponent by military means and to force the will to victory upon him, there can, nevertheless, no longer be doubt that this aim, even assuming that it is attainable, would first necessitate a further sanguinary and protracted struggle.

But even a later victorious peace will no longer be able to make good the consequences of such a policy—consequences which will be fatal to all the States and peoples of Europe. The only peace which could righteously adjust the still divergent conceptions of the opponents would be a peace desired by all the peoples. With this consciousness, and in its unswerving endeavor to work in the interests of peace, the Austro-Hungarian Government now again comes forward with a suggestion with the object of bringing about a direct discussion between the enemy powers.

The earnest will to peace of wide classes of the population of all the States who are jointly suffering through the war—the indisputable rapprochement in individual controversial questions—as well as the more conciliatory atmosphere that is general, seem to the Austro-Hungarian Government to give a certain guarantee that a fresh step in the interests of peace, which also takes account of past experiences in this domain, might at the present moment offer the possibility of success.

The Austro-Hungarian Government has

therefore resolved to point out to all the belligerents, friend and foe, a path considered practicable by it, and to propose to them jointly to examine in a free exchange of views whether those prerequisites exist which would make the speedy inauguration of peace negotiations appear promising. To this end the Austro-Hungarian Government has today invited the Governments of all the belligerent States to a confidential and unbinding discussion at a neutral meeting place, and has addressed to them a note drawn up in this sense.

This step has been brought to the knowledge of the Holy See in a special note, and an appeal thereby made to the Pope's interest in peace. Furthermore, the Governments of the neutral States have been acquainted with the step taken.

The constant close accord which exists between the four allied powers warrants the assumption that the allies of Austria-Hungary, to whom the proposal is being sent in the same manner, share the views developed in the note.

[The official telegram proceeds to say that the note has been drawn up in French, and runs as follows:]

# Text of the Note to the Powers

The peace offer which the powers of the Quadruple Alliance addressed to their opponents on Dec. 12, 1916, and the conciliatory basic ideas of which they have never given up, signifies, despite the rejection which it experienced, an important stage in the history of this war. In contrast to the first two and a half war years, the question of peace has from that moment been the centre of European, aye, of world, discussion, and dominates it in ever-increasing measure.

Almost all the belligerent States have in turn again and again expressed themselves on the question of peace, its prerequisites and conditions. The line of development of this discussion, however, has not been uniform and steady. The basic standpoint changed under the influence of the military and political position, and hitherto, at any rate, it has not led to a tangible general result that could be utilized.

It is true that, independent of all these oscillations, it can be stated that the distance between the conceptions of the two sides has, on the whole, grown somewhat less; that despite the indisputable continuance of decided and hitherto unbridged differences, a partial turning from many of the most extreme concrete war aims is visible and a certain agreement upon the relative general basic principles of a world peace manifests itself. In both camps there is undoubtedly observable in wide classes of the population a growth of the will to peace and understanding. Moreover, a comparison of the reception of the peace proposal of the powers of the Quadruple Alliance on the part of their opponents with the later utterances of responsible statesmen of the latter, as well as of the non-responsible but, in a political respect, nowise uninfluential personalities, confirms this impression.

While, for example, the reply of the Allies to President Wilson made demands which amounted to the dismemberment of Austria-Hungary, to a diminution and a deep internal transformation of the German Empire, and the destruction of Turkish European ownership, these demands, the realization of which was based on the supposition of an overwhelming victory, were later modified in many declarations from official Entente quarters, or in part were dropped.

Thus, in a declaration made in the British House of Commons a year ago, Secretary Balfour expressly recognized that Austria-Hungary must itself solve its internal problems, and that none could impose a Constitution upon Germany from the outside. Premier Lloyd George declared at the beginning of this year that it was not one of the Allies' war aims to partition Austria-Hungary, to rob the Ottoman Empire of its Turkish provinces, or to reform Germany internally. It may also be considered symptomatic that in December, 1917, Mr. Balfour categorically repudiated the assumption that British policy had ever engaged itself for the creation of an independent State out of the territories on the left bank of the Rhine.

The Central Powers leave it in no doubt that they are only waging a war of defense for the integrity and the security of their territories.

Far more outspoken than in the domain of concrete war aims has the rapprochement of conceptions proceeded regarding those guiding lines upon the basis of which peace shall be concluded and the future order of Europe and the world built up. In this direction President Wilson in his speeches of Feb. 12 and July 4 of this year has formulated principles which have not encountered contradiction on the part of his allies, and the far-reaching application of which is likely to meet with no objection on the part of the powers of the Quadruple Alliance also, presupposing that this application is general and reconcilable with the vital interests of the States concerned.

It is true, it must be remembered, that an agreement on general principles is insufficient, but that there remains the further matter of reaching an accord upon their interpretation and their application to individual concrete war and peace questions.

To an unprejudiced observer there can be no doubt that in all the belligerent States, without exception, the desire for a peace of understanding has been enormously strengthened; that the conviction is increasingly spreading that the further continuance of the bloody struggle must transform Europe into ruins and into a state of exhaustion that will mar its development for decades to come, and this without any guarantee of thereby bringing about that decision by arms which has been vainly striven after by both sides in four years filled with enormous sacrifices, sufferings, and exertions.

In what manner, however, can the way be paved for an understanding, and an understanding finally attained? Is there any serious prospect whatever of reaching this aim by continuing the discussion of the peace problem in the way hitherto followed?

We have not the courage to answer the latter question in the affirmative. The discussion from one public tribune to another, as has hitherto taken place between statesmen of the various countries, was really only a series of monologues. It lacked, above everything, directness. Speech and counter-speech did not fit into each other. The speakers spoke over one another's heads.

On the other hand, it was the publicity and the ground of these discussions which robbed them of the possibility of fruitful progress. In all public statements of this nature a form of eloquence is used which reckons with the effect at great distances and on the masses. Consciously or unconsciously, however, one thereby increases the distance of the opponents' conception, produces misunderstandings which take root and are not removed, and makes the frank exchange of ideas more difficult. Every pronouncement of leading statesmen is, directly after its delivery and before the authoritative quarters of the opposite side can reply to it, made the subject of passionate or exaggerated discussion of irresponsible elements.

But anxiety lest they should endanger the interests of their arms by unfavorably influencing feeling at home, and lest they prematurely betray their own ultimate intentions, also causes the responsible statesmen themselves to strike a higher tone and stubbornly to adhere to extreme standpoints.

If, therefore, an attempt is made to see whether the basis exists for an understanding calculated to deliver Europe from the catastrophe of the suicidal continuation of the struggle, then, in any case, another method should be chosen which renders possible a direct, verbal discussion between the representatives of the Governments, and only between them. The opposing conceptions of individual belligerent States would likewise have to form the subject of such a discussion, for mutual enlightenment, as well as the general principles that shall serve as the

basis for peace and the future relations of the States to one another, and regarding which, in the first place, an accord can be sought with a prospect of success.

As soon as an agreement were reached on the fundamental principles, an attempt would have to be made in the course of the discussions concretely to apply them to individual peace questions, and thereby bring about their solution.

We venture to hope that there will be no objection on the part of any belligerents to such an exchange of views. The war activities would experience no interruption. The discussions, too, would only go so far as was considered by the participants to offer a prospect of success. No disadvantages would arise therefrom for the States represented. Far from harming, such an exchange of views could only be useful to the cause of peace.

What did not succeed the first time can be repeated, and perhaps it has already at least contributed to the clarification of views. Mountains of old misunderstandings might be removed and many new things perceived. Streams of pent-up human kindness would be released, in the warmth of which everything essential would remain, and, on the other hand, much that is antagonistic, to which excessive importance is still attributed, would disappear.

According to our conviction, all the belligerents jointly owe to humanity to examine whether now, after so many years of a costly but undecided struggle, the entire course of which points to an understanding, it is possible to make an end to the terrible grapple.

The Royal and Imperial Government would like, therefore, to propose to the Governments of all the belligerent States to send delegates to a confidential and unbinding discussion on the basic principles for the conclusion of peace, in a place in a neutral country and at a near date that would yet have to be agreed upon—delegates who were charged to make known to one another the conception of their Governments regarding those principles and to receive analogous communications, as well as to request and give frank and candid explanations on all those points which need to be precisely defined.

The Royal and Imperial Government has the honor to request the Government of ——, through the kind mediation of your Excellency, to bring this communication to the knowledge of the Government of ——.

[The names of the intermediary Government and of that adressed in the particular note dispatched are left blank.]

# The Reply of the United States

The official communication from Austria-Hungary was handed to Secretary of State Lansing in Washington at 6:20 o'clock, Sept. 16; at 6:45 o'clock the following abbreviated reply of the United States Government was made public by the Secretary of State:

I am authorized by the President to state that the following will be the reply of this Government to the Austro-Hungarian note proposing an unofficial conference of belligerents:

"The Government of the United States feels that there is only one reply which it can make to the suggestion of the Imperial Austro-Hungarian Government. It has repeatedly and with entire candor stated the terms upon which the United States would consider peace and can and will entertain no proposal for a conference upon a matter concerning which it has made its position and purpose so plain."

The full text of the reply of the United States, in the form in which it was handed to the Swedish Minister, W. A. F. Ekengren, was made public by Secretary Lansing on Sept. 18. It was as follows:

Department of State,
Sept. 17, 1918.

Sir: I have the honor to acknowledge the receipt of your note, dated Sept. 16, communicating to me a note from the Imperial Government of Austria-Hungary, containing a proposal to the Governments of all the belligerent States to send delegates to a confidential and unbinding discussion on the basic principles for the conclusion of peace. Furthermore, it is proposed that the delegates would be charged to make known to one another the conception of their Governments regarding these principles and to receive analogous communications, as well as to request and give frank and candid explanations on all those points which need to be precisely defined.

In reply I beg to say that the substance of your communication has been submitted to the President, who now directs me to inform you that the Government of the United States feels that there is only one reply which it can make to the suggestion of the Imperial Austro-Hungarian Government. It has repeatedly and with entire candor stated the terms upon which the United States would consider peace, and can and will entertain no proposal for a conference upon a matter concerning which it has made its position and purpose so plain.

Accept, Sir, the renewed assurances of my highest consideration.

[Signed] ROBERT LANSING.

Mr. W. A. F. Ekengren, Minister of Sweden, in charge of Austro-Hungarian interests.

## Britain's Answer Indicated by Mr. Balfour.

Arthur J. Balfour, the British Foreign Secretary, in a statement made Sept. 16, regarding the Austrian note, said: "It is incredible that anything can come of this proposal." The calamities imposed by the continuation of hostilities were so overwhelming, he said, that he would never treat with disrespect any peace proposal.

"But," he went on, "I cannot honestly see, in the proposals now made to us the slightest hope that the goal we all desire—the goal of a peace which shall be more than a truce—can really be attained."

Coming after the recent speech of Friedrich von Payer, the German Imperial Vice Chancellor, [See Page 69,] Mr. Balfour continued, "This cynical proposal of the Austrian Government is not a genuine attempt to obtain peace. It is an attempt to divide the Allies." No coalition ever had been so strong as the allied coalition and the enemy would not succeed in breaking it.

Conversations such as were proposed by Austria-Hungary undoubtedly would have great value under certain circumstances. They would serve to smooth out obscurities such as questions of pride, &c., but the questions now between the belligerents were clearly defined.

"I am not taking the proposals of two years ago, or of last year, but of last week," Secretary Balfour said. "The German Vice Chancellor, speaking for the German Government, clearly and without obscure verbiage, showed where Germany stood on the question of Belgium, Alsace-Lorraine, the German colonies, and the Brest-Litovsk and Bucharest treaties."

It could not be more clearly set forth than it was by von Payer that Germany intended to pay no indemnity to Belgium. The Vice Chancellor indicated that Germany did not believe in the principle of indemnities, and yet at the same time she was squeezing millions of dollars out of Russia.

"This," the speaker went on, "was for the wrongs Russia is supposed to have done Germany. How can those wrongs be compared with the devastation and ruin which Germany is wreaking on Russia now?"

Regarding the question of colonies, Secretary Balfour said:

"The colonies are one question on which there is no misunderstanding. We stand on one side and Germany on the other."

Referring to the lack of concerted effort by the Central Powers, as emphasized by the von Payer speech and the Austrian note, the Foreign Secretary commented on the clumsiness of German diplomacy. He continued:

Take Belgium, for example. The phrase von Payer uses is a very curious one, but I suppose it is intended to mean that Germany feels that she really must restore Belgian independence. She does not say what she is going to do to restore Belgian prosperity or that indemnities are to be given to the country she wasted, brutalized, and ravaged.

But it seems that if Belgium will consent to make certain modifications in her internal arrangements she is to be allowed to get back her independence. Explicit though it be, it explicitly refuses that which we think obviously just, namely, restoration of and indemnity to Belgium, which has been so monstrously treated.

Von Payer stated that the German boundaries should remain intact, which, of course, means that Germany will keep Alsace-Lorraine. How are conversations going to set that right? There are no misunderstandings between the belligerents on that score.

Mr. Balfour recalled that von Payer said the Brest-Litovsk and Bucharest treaties should stand, and declared:

There is no misunderstanding there. It is in black and white, without circumspection or fine phrasing. No dexterity of dialogue is going to smooth differences of that kind. * * *

Until the Central Powers are of open mind and are prepared to discuss our views of what we believe to be right and just and for the uplift of civilization, mere conversations for practical results are useless.

They evidently think they can embitter whatever differences may exist between the allied countries and counteract the present allied successes on all fronts. I cannot bring myself to believe that this is an honest attempt at peace by understanding, but I am driven to the opposite opinion—that it is an attempt to weaken the forces in the field, which are proving too strong for them.

## Attitude of France and Italy

Premier Clemenceau foreshadowed the attitude of France regarding the note by the following statement, which was made in the French Senate, Sept. 18:

We will fight until the hour when the enemy comes to understand that bargaining between crime and right is no longer possible. We want a just and a strong peace, protecting the future against the abominations of the past.

In beginning, M. Clemenceau spoke of the gratitude the people of the allied nations feel toward "those marvelous soldiers of the Entente" by whom those nations would "at last be liberated from the barbarian menace." He recalled the threatening attitude of Germany toward pacific France, which had endured for half a century "the infamous wounds,

brutalities and tyrannies of an enemy who would not forgive us for having saved from the wreck the consciousness of right and our indefeasible claims to independence." He pointed out how, without the slightest pretext, Germany hurled herself on French territory, devastated the fields of France, burned and pillaged her towns and villages and enslaved her men, women, and children. He added:

The enemy thought that victory would cause all this to be pardoned, but fortune has changed. The day of glory has come. Our sons are completing the formidable task of their fathers, and with brotherly nations are securing a supreme victory. All right-mined humanity is with our troops, who are liberating the nations from the furor of evil force.

The address was enthusiastically received and the Senate voted to post it throughout the country.

### THE ITALIAN REPLY

A semi-official statement issued by Italy, Sept. 19, said:

The Austrian note has not yet reached the Government, but if the newspaper text is exact, Italy must point out that the proposal aiming at the creation of so-called negotiations is devoid of any real intent toward peace and the possibility of practical success.

Recent statements by Austro-Hungarian and German statesmen, excluding the ceding of territories, and the final iniquitous Brest and Bucharest treaties, render impossible the beginning of useful negotiations.

The Entente and the United States have made known their eager aspirations toward a just peace and also an essential basis whereon they see a just peace must be founded. On these points the Austrian proposal says nothing. It also says nothing with regard to the Italian aspirations. They are well known to Austria and also to the Allies, who have recognized them.

These aspirations are summed up in the accomplishment of Italian unity through the liberation of Italian populations still subject to Austria.

Until Austria recognizes these particular aims, as well as the general ones for which the Allies are fighting, Italy will not abandon the struggle, aiming at the creation of a humanitarian organization which will make safer a lasting peace, liberty and justice.

### NO ACTION BY POPE

Foreign Minister Burian on Sept. 14 sent the following note to the Pope through the Apostolic Nuncio, Di Bouzo, at Vienna:

After four years of unheard-of struggle and gigantic sacrifices, the battle devastating Europe has not brought a decision. Animated by a spirit of reconciliation, Austria-Hungary has decided to approach all belligerents and invite them to pave the way toward peace by a confidential and unbinding exchange of views. With full gratitude, Austria-Hungary remembers the touching appeal the Pope sent to the belligerents last year. Firmly convinced that the Pope also today, (a word missing from cabled text,) that long-suffering mankind soon will again enjoy the blessings of peace, we confidently hope he will sympathize with the note and support it with his moral influence.

It was announced from Rome Sept. 19 that the Vatican would not reply.

### GERMANY APPROVED NOTE

Baron Burian set at rest speculation as to whether Germany had approved the note by an announcement made at Vienna Sept. 19, that the Austrian proposal to the belligerents for a secret peace conference had been considered for weeks, and that the step was taken "after consultation with our allies and being certain of their approval in principle."

The German and Austrian press caustically criticised the failure of the step. The curt rejection of the proposal increased the profound unrest and revolutionary agitation both in Germany and Austria. The Kaiser, von Hindenburg, and other military leaders sought to raise the drooping spirits of their people by means of encouraging manifestoes and fervent appeals to "save the Fatherland from despoilers."

# Germany's Diminishing Peace Demands
## Friedrich von Payer, German Vice Chancellor, Mentions Belgium and Yields Indemnities

THE German Vice Chancellor, Friedrich von Payer, delivered the following significant address at Stuttgart on Sept. 12, 1918, indicating the extent to which the German Government was willing to reduce its peace demands:

In former peace negotiations the middle and lower classes, when it came to the council table, fell quietly into the background.

That time is now past, and the Governments will conclude the coming peace treaties in close harmony with the entire people.

The main thing for them in peace is not the acquisition of land, treasure, and glory; they aim, nowadays at least, at the conclusion of a lasting peace, and therefore there will be no peace of conquest. * * *

Russia collapsed because she could not maintain internal cohesion. Our victories and those of our allies now have given the subjects of that colossal empire an opportunity to liberate themselves. It is unthinkable that Germany would contribute to the restoration of the despotic Russian Empire, which, by its mere existence, always menaced the world.

We cannot hand over Poland to Russia, nor can we assist in having Finland again placed under the Russian yoke. We cannot leave to their fate the border States which lie on the German frontier and the Baltic to be subjected against their will to Russian imperialism or thrown into the perils of civil war and anarchy.

In fact, these States, having come to an understanding with us as those most nearly interested, can only be an advantage to the world, and we can never permit any one to meddle with us in this matter from the standpoint of the present European balance of power, or rather British predominance.

For the rest, the territorial possessions which existed before the war can everywhere be restored. A preliminary condition for us and our allies is that all the territory should again be restored which we possessed on Aug. 1, 1914. Germany must, therefore, in the first place, receive back her colonies, in which connection the idea of an exchange on the ground of expediency need not be excluded.

We Germans, as soon as peace is concluded, can evacuate the occupied regions. We can, when once things have been got to that stage, restore Belgium. If we and our allies are once again in possession of what belonged to us and if we first are sure that in Belgium no other State will be more favorably placed than we, then Belgium, I think I may say, can be given back without incumbrance and without reserve. * * *

It is hypocrisy to represent Belgium as the innocent victim of our policy and to clothe her, as it were, in the white garment of innocence. The Belgium Government—and that is what matters, not the Belgian people —took an active part in Great Britain's policy of encircling Germany.

There is still the question of war indemnities from one or the other party. Had Germany been allowed to pursue her work in peace, there would have been no war or injury. There can be no question, therefore, of our paying, but only whether we should receive compensation for the injuries inflicted on us. We are deeply convinced that as the innocent and attacked party we have a right to indemnification. To go on prosecuting the war, however, to that point would cost us such heavy sacrifice, irreparable by money, that we prefer, on calm reflection, and even with our favorable military situation, to abandon this idea, quite apart from the question of jeopardizing a future peace which would be inevitable if compensation were forcibly urged.

Unrealizable conditions of peace, of course, could not be laid down for our participation in the peace negotiations. We laugh at the idea that we should first penitently ask for mercy before we are admitted. We laugh at the fools who babble of revenge. I have wished only to show that peace by understanding will bring nothing humiliating for us nor a period of misery and wretchedness.

Strong and courageous in the consciousness of our invincibility, equal among the nations of the earth, we will lead a life of labor, but also with contentment and with an assured future. In common with others we will protect the world's peace from future dangers.

It would be an illusion to count on will to peace in those circles among our enemies which are responsible for the opening and the continuing of hostilities. For years they have been living on the inflaming of war passions. They cannot admit to their countrymen that their aims are unattainable and that their sacrifices have been made in vain. Others among those peoples will think differently. Moreover, they will prevail sooner or later. Until then, however, there remains nothing for us to do but to defend our lives. We place on the shoulders of our enemies the responsibility for the blood which will yet be shed, but whoever will not hear must fall. On our outer and inner front the will to destruction of our enemies will be shattered. Germany's strength, capacity, courage, and self-sacrifice, to which for four years we owe everything, must teach them that it has become hopeless for them to continue to wage this baneful war.

Despite everything, the peace treaty will have purely positive contents. The nations of the earth cry out for preservation from the further misery of wars, for leagues of nations, for international courts of arbitration, and agreements regarding equal disarmament, which cries the enemy Governments have made their own, and the fulfillment of which would not be wrecked by the German Government's opposition. We are, on the contrary, ready to collaborate to the best of our ability.

We desire a disarmament agreement on the condition of complete reciprocity applied not merely to land armies, but even to naval forces. In pursuance of the same idea and even going beyond it, we will raise in the negotiations a demand for freedom of the seas and sea routes, for the open door in all overseas possessions, and for the protection of private property at sea. And if negotiations take place regarding the protection of small nations and of national minorities in individual States, we shall willingly advocate international arrangements which will act for deliverance in countries under Great Britain's domination.

[*For earlier peace utterances of the month see Page 131.*]

# Kaiser's Speech to Krupp Workers

## An Appeal to Labor in Which the German Emperor's Tone Is Somewhat Altered

[DELIVERED SEPT. 12, 1918, AT ESSEN]

*After preliminary remarks of welcome to the men and thanks for their labor, the Kaiser proceeded:*

INDUSTRIAL mobilization, without distinction of age or sex, has constituted a demand such as never before was made on the German people, and yet it was responded to willingly and joyfully. In that connection I should like, above all, to express my warm thanks as the country's father to the women as well as the girls and the men for their self-sacrificing performance of their duty despite their harassing cares.

No one among our people should imagine I am not conversant with this. In my journeyings through the land I have spoken with many a widow, many a peasant, many a member of the Landwehr and the Landsturm, whose hearts were heavy with cares, but who glowed with the thought of duty first. I have been touched by your cares to the depths of my heart. What paternal suggestion could do to diminish the burden as far as possible has been done. Much could have been done otherwise, and it is no wonder there is dissatisfaction here and there.

But to whom, after all, do we owe this? Who spoke at the very beginning of the war of starving out the German women and children? Who was it who introduced terrible hatred into this war? It was the enemy.

Every one of you in the remotest corner of the Fatherland knows that I left no stone unturned to shorten the war as far as possible for you and your people and for the entire civilized European world. In December, 1916, I presented the enemy public with a clear and unambiguous offer of peace in the name of the German Empire and my allies. Jeers, mockery, and contempt were the answer.

He up above knows my sense of responsibility. Repeatedly during the past months the responsible leaders of the Imperial Government have unambiguously given to understand, to every one who wished to understand, that we are at all times ready to offer the hand to peace.

To make peace, two are needed. If either is unwilling, the other cannot, presuming that he does not overthrow the other. Thus we are confronted with the enemy's absolute will to destruction. And against this absolute will to destruction we must place our absolute will to preserve our existence.

Our brave army out there has shown you this will and deed. Whether in assault, or withdrawal, or trench fighting, the only thing that matters is that the enemy should lose as much as possible. That has occurred and continues to occur.

### CLAIMS NAVAL VICTORY

Our death-defying navy also has proved that. It beat the enemy at the Skagerrak, despite his great superiority. Our U-boats, like a consuming worm, gnaw at the enemy's vitals more than our enemies will admit.

Even though, in the opinion of many among you, it is lasting too long, every German man and every German woman must, as witnesses of these incomparable heroic deeds of our army and our navy, be aware we are fighting and struggling for existence and that we must make the utmost effort to defend ourselves victoriously, not only through the work but as regards the thoughts of our people.

Many among you have often asked themselves during this long war: "How did such a thing happen? Why did we have to undergo such a thing after forty years of peace?" I think it is a question well worthy of an answer and which must be answered for the future—for our children and our grandchildren. I have thought long on the matter and have come to the following answer:

In this world good clashes with evil. That is how things have been ordered from on high—the yes and the no; the no of the doubting mind against the yes of the creative mind; the no of the pessimist against the yes of the optimist; the no of the unbeliever against the yes of the champion of faith; the yes of Heaven against the no of Hell.

You will acknowledge that I am right in describing this war as the product of a great negation. And do you ask what negation it is? It is the negation of the German people's right to existence. It is the negation of all our kultur, a negation of our achievements, of all our work.

The German people was industrious, meditative, assiduous, imaginative in all domains. It worked with body and soul. But there were people who did not wish to work but to rest on their laurels. Those were our enemies. We got close to them through our profitable work and the development of our industry, science, and art; through our popular education and social legislation. Thereby our people throve, and then came envy.

## TO BLAME WAR ON ALLIES

Envy induced our enemies to fight, and war came upon us. And now when our opponents see that their hopes have been deceptive and how our mighty generals, after whom your new workshops are rightly named, have dealt them blow upon blow, hatred springs up. We only know the honest wrath which deals the enemy the blow, but when he lies prostrate and bleeding we extend to him our hand and see to his recovery.

Hatred manifests itself only among peoples who feel themselves beaten. If, therefore, such terrible hatred exists among our enemies, it owes its origin to the fact that their calculations have been wrong. Every one who knows the character of the Anglo-Saxons knows what it means to fight them—how

tenacious they are. We do not know when the struggle will end, but one thing we do know, namely, that we must fight the battle through.

And now, my friends, let me draw your attention to something more. You have read what recently happened in Moscow—the mighty conspiracy against the present Government. The parliamentary governed, democratic British Nation has endeavored to overthrow the ultra-democratic Government which the Russian people had begun to construct, because this Government, considering the interests of its fatherland, wishes to maintain its people in the peace for which it clamors.

But the Anglo-Saxon does not yet desire peace. That is how things are. It is proof of his feeling of inferiority that the Anglo-Saxon has recourse to such criminal means.

Everything now depends on our final exertions, everything is at stake, and because our enemies know it, because they have the greatest respect for the German Army, because they see they cannot overcome our army and navy, they are trying to overcome us by means of internal disintegration and to weaken us by false rumors.

These do not emanate from the German people. They are artificial productions. But whoever hearkens to such rumors, whoever passes on unsubstantiated news in the railway workshop or elsewhere, sins against the Fatherland, he is a traitor and is liable to severe punishment, no matter whether he be a Count or a workman.

I know very well every one of you will acknowledge that I am right in this matter. Believe me, it is not easy for me to bear every day the anxiety and the responsibility for a nation of 70,000,-000, and for more than four years be a spectator to all the difficulties and increasing distress of the people. * * *

## THE GERMAN WAR GOD

How can we please God and soften His heart? By doing our duty! In making our Fatherland free! Consequently it is our duty to hold out with all our strength in the fight against our enemies.

Each one of us has received his appointed task from on high. You at your hammer, you at your lathe, and I on my throne. We must all, however, build on God's assistance. Doubt is the greatest ingratitude toward the Lord, and now I ask you all simply and honestly: Have we, then, really ground for doubt?

Just look at the four years of war! What immense achievements we have behind us! Half the world stood against us and our loyal allies, and now we have peace with Russia and peace with Rumania, Serbia, and Montenegro is finished.

Only in the west do we still fight, and is it to be thought that the good God will abandon us there at the last moment? We should be ashamed of the faint-heartedness which comes when one gives credence to rumors. From the facts which you yourselves have experienced forge for yourselves a firm belief in the future of your Fatherland. We often at home and at the front, in church and in the open air, have sung: "Ein feste Burg ist unser Gott." So it is resounded in the blue vault of heaven and in the thunderclouds. The nation from which such a hymn originated must be invincible.

My request, my demand of you and through you to all the workers who have proved themselves so admirable and capable, and through you again to the entire German people, is this: For me and for my relations to my people my words of Aug. 4, 1914, hold good. I know no party. I know only Germans.

It is now no time for factions. We must all now combine into a block, and, here, the most appropriate word is to be as hard as steel, and a block of the German people welded into steel shall show its strength to the enemy.

Whoever, therefore, is determined to obey this summons, whoever has his heart in the right place, and whoever intends to keep faith, let him stand up.

Now promise me on behalf of the entire German labor, "We intend to fight and to hold out to the last, so help us, God." Whoever so intends let him answer "Yes."

[The assembly loudly chorused "Yes," and the Emperor continued:]

I thank you. With this "Yes" I go now to the Field Marshal. Now it is for every one of us to fulfill his vow of duty and to exert his body and mind to the utmost for the Fatherland. Every doubt must be banished from mind and heart.

Our watchword now is, The German swords are raised, hearts are strong, and muscles are taut. On to battle against everything that stands against us, no matter how long it lasts, so help us God. Amen. And now, farewell.

# Baiser Au Drapeau

### Par STEPHAN BORDESE

Cette fois, la blessure est grave
C'en est fini. Soldats, un brave!
Si j'ai mal défendu ma peau
Tant pis pour moi, mais le drapeau!
Prenez-le, mes enfants, courage!
Ne permettez pas qu'on l'outrage
    Hardi, je meurs!

Ce n'est pas moi qu'il faut défendre,
Mais le drapeau, venez le prendre
Qu'il ne me soit pas arraché.
De sang français je l'ai taché
En le pressant sur ma blessure,
Gardez-le d'une flétrissure
    Vite, je meurs!

Drapeau, fleur du champ de bataille
Ta tige meurt sous la mitraille,
Mais avant, laisse-moi poser
Sur ta soie un dernier baiser
D'amour, d'honneur et d'espérance,
Pour les fières couleurs de France
    Adieu, je meurs!

# Russia's Reign of Terror

## Internal War Between Social Revolutionists and Bolsheviki—Attacks on Allied Diplomats

### [PERIOD ENDED SEPT. 15, 1918]

EARLY in September, 1918, the world received information from Russia shedding considerable light on the secession of the Social Revolutionaries of the Left from the Bolshevist ranks, which had occurred in July, 1917, and which had won the Soviet Government an implacable enemy. The Bolsheviki and the Social Revolutionists had split on Lenine's policy of pitting the poor peasants against the well-to-do farmers, and also on the Government's attitude toward Germany. The defection was led by Miss Spiridonova, a Social Revolutionist, who had been one of the leading spirits of Soviet Russia, and who had rendered invaluable service to the Bolsheviki. At the All-Russian Soviet Congress on July 4, 1918, she made a speech in which she violently denounced Lenine's policies, pointing out that the majority of the workmen and peasants are not with him. She was ready, she announced, to fight, with bomb in hand, for the peasants against their oppressors. She shook her fist at the box of the German Ambassador, saying that Russia would never become a German colony.

Shortly after the break between the Social Revolutionists and the party in power a series of successful terroristic acts led to the death of prominent German and Soviet officials. Miss Spiridonova was arrested, but, contrary to first reports, she did not share the fate of a great number of her comrades, who were executed by the Bolshevist authorities.

An attempt on Premier Lenine's life was made in Moscow on Friday night, Aug. 30. The attack was made by a young woman student, Dora Kaplan, a member of the Social Revolutionary Party, who fired three shots at the Bolshevist leader. The wounds inflicted, although not fatal, were so serious that Lenine temporarily retired from his post and was replaced by Leo Kamenev, Vice President of the Petrograd Soviet. Dora Kaplan was arrested on the scene of the assault and executed on Sept. 4.

On Aug. 31 Moses Uritzki, Chairman of the Commission Extraordinary for Combating the Counter-Revolution, was assassinated in Petrograd by a young man who, when arrested, gave the name of Leonid Kannegiessers.

Two attempts were made on the life of Dr. Karl Helfferich, the German Ambassador at Moscow, who hurriedly left the Russian capital after a stay of a few days. His post was offered to Scheidemann, Ebert, and Eisler, but these Socialist leaders declined the offer, whereupon the Counselor of the German Embassy at Moscow became the Chargé d'Affaires.

### REIGN OF TERROR

To these acts the Bolsheviki opposed a reign of terror. The Commission Extraordinary for Combating the Counter-Revolution issued the following decree:

> The criminal adventures of our enemies force us to reply with measures of terror. Every person found with a weapon in his hand will be immediately executed. Every person who agitates against the Soviet Government will be arrested and taken into a concentration camp and all his private property seized.

A great number of houses were searched and many persons arrested. Numerous priests and men of prominence, such as former Ministers Verkhovski and Prince Shakhovskoy, Social Revolutionists, were reported to have been seized by the Bolsheviki as hostages. Several hundred Russian officers were said to have been shot. Up to Sept. 9, 512 persons were shot and twenty-six British officials arrested in connection with the assassination of Uritzki, while thirty-four landowners and the former Moscow Archimandrite

Makary were executed in retaliation for the attempt on Lenine's life. A report, dated Sept. 12, told of the murder in Petrograd of Rear Admiral Razvozov, former commander of the Russian Baltic Fleet. An earlier report announced the arrest of Kerensky's relatives. The arrest of Prince Kropotkin at Petrograd and the murder of General Brusiloff, former Russian Generalissimo, were also reported. According to a dispatch of Sept. 10, the Bolshevist newspapers are demanding a "mass terror" against the propertied classes and the Social Revolutionists. Neutral diplomats filed a protest to Foreign Minister Tchitcherin against the attitude of terrorism taken by the Moscow Government toward its political enemies.

## AN AMERICAN'S EXPERIENCE

"The struggle," telegraphed on Sept. 7 an American correspondent who had recently escaped from Russia, "has passed the stage of class war. Every man is at every other man's throat." The Bolshevist reign of terror is strikingly depicted in the story told by Roger Simmons, an American sent to Russia by the United States Government, of how he was arrested by the Soviet authorities and escaped death by execution. The following is a passage from this narrative:

While in prison I talked with dozens of men condemned to death, many not knowing why. I learned from men past hope of the travesty of trials before the revolutionary tribunals, and also saw men ordered shot for merely criticising Commissioners. During the year I spent studying the forests I lived among simple people and saw the injustice of the old régime, and learned to have much sympathy for the Bolshevist movement, but in prison I saw it turned to hate and vengeance without caring how innocent the victims.

In speaking of the trial to which the prisoners of the Bolsheviki were subjected, Mr. Simmons says: "They all were led before half a dozen men with raging eyes who asked a few questions, conferred, and then convicted. Few were found innocent. One had a jury of twelve, but the jury was instructed by the Judge to bring in a verdict of guilty."

On Sept. 10 the Russian Embassy at Washington made public a message received by it directly from Nicholas Tchaikovsky, Premier of the Government of Northern Russia. The text of the document follows:

Archangel, Aug. 31.—In the region of Northern Russia the yoke of the Bolsheviki is thrown off. In accord with the Allies, the Government of the region of Northern Russia, not recognizing the peace treaty of Brest, has set as its aim the expulsion of the Germans out of the boundaries of Russia and the creation anew of a great and indivisible Russia.

Owing to the initative of the League of Regeneration of Russia, composed of representatives of all political parties, except the extreme ones, the Government of the region of Northern Russia was formed by delegates of the Northern Provinces to the Constituent Assembly and by representatives of the Zemstvos and towns of the region.

The municipalities and judicial bodies are reconstituted. The Russian Army is again created and on the basis of discipline. The Allies are aiding us. Mobilization has been declared in the northern region.

Desiring to secure real liberty and a democratic régime, the Government of Northern Russia, joining hands with other regional Governments, has as final aim the formation of a single Government for the whole of Russia based on universal suffrage.

The Government of Northern Russia appeals to all Russian citizens to rally around the banner of salvation of their native country, of the liberties gained, and the rebirth of Russia.

NICHOLAS TCHAIKOVSKY,
President of the Government of Northern Russia.

The Government of Northern Russia is composed of members of the Constituent Assembly, who were elected by the Northern provinces under Kerensky. It is known as the Supreme Administration of the Region of the North, and is backed by Social Revolutionists and the Menshevik wing of the Social Democrats. A volunteer army is in process of organization. The Government is trying to meet its pecuniary difficulties by raising money by subscription and by printing notes in England.

On Sept. 8, Tchaikovsky's Government was overthrown, and the Premier, together with several other members of the Government, arrested. The perpetrators of the coup d'état were anti-German and anti-Bolshevist. The allied representatives at Archangel, however, demanded immediately that Tchaikov-sky's Government be restored to power, and the request was complied with.

## THE SAMARA ASSEMBLY

It became known late in August that 200 members of the Constituent Assembly which had been dissolved by the Bolsheviki met in the City of Samara and formed a Government ready to assume control of Russia. The Samara Assembly was reported to have elected a triumvirate with directorial powers, consisting of General Alekseyev, the well-known military leader, and Stepanov and Avksentyev. The Samara authorities came to an understanding with the Orenburg and Ural Governments on the basis of a federated Russia and a war against Germany in alliance with the Entente, but it failed to form a similar agreement with the Siberian Government.

Purely military movements directed against the Soviet Government by the peasantry have become an important feature of the situation throughout the North and East of European Russia. The peasants have made serious attempts to wrest from the Bolsheviki Nizhni-Novgorod and Petrograd itself. Anti-Bolshevist movements are reported in the Provinces of Vologda, Vladimir, Uyatka, and Oryol.

## GENERAL HORVATH'S COUP

A Vladivostok dispatch dated Aug. 25 announced that General Pleshkov, acting in the name of Lieut. Gen. Horvath, the anti-Soviet military leader in Siberia, had assumed control of all the Russian troops in the Far East in defiance of the will of the Siberian Government. General Horvath's self-appointed dictatorship lasted scarcely an hour. The allied representatives at Vladivostok made it clear to General Horvath's representative that the Allies were resolved to uphold the authority of the Siberian Government against any dictatorial rule. Thereupon, General Horvath submitted. The small body of Russian volunteers who had gone over to the would-be dictator were disarmed and removed from Vladivostok, and the incident was closed without bloodshed.

It was reported on Sept. 13 that the Entente representatives had taken over the municipal administration of Vladivostok as a step toward stabilizing self-government in Siberia.

A dispatch from Petrograd, dated Aug. 17, estimated the number of German troops occupying the Ukraine at 500,000. The peasant risings continued and the railroad strike was reported to be on the increase. Late in August the Petrograd daily, Pravda, reported that a peasant army of 40,000 was fighting German forces co-operating with Ukrainian Government troops near the Skvira railway in the Government of Kiev. The town and district of Dymera in the same Government were declared by the German army commander in a state of siege. It was in this region that about 1,200 German mutineers, with a number of machine guns, joined the peasant rebels and assisted them in fighting the German forces.

## SENTIMENT IN UKRAINE

The situation in the Ukraine is vividly depicted in letters written home by German soldiers. Here is an extract from one written by a member of the 76th Regiment of the Landwehr and dated June 16:

> I am still at Kiev, but let me tell you one thing: it is much more terrible here than in the trenches, for there the enemy is before you, while here the opposite is true. The people are so badly disposed toward us that they would devour us alive if they could, but they cannot. For here there are all too many foreigners. So long as we stay here the people will not be able to do anything, for there are too many German and Austrian troops. Police patrols are everywhere. In spite of all this, a great disaster occurred. It happened on June 6, at 10:15 in the morning. Ten ammunition depots were blown up. * * * The dead and wounded number 1,700. The men of the 2d Landwehr Regiment had trouble with the Ukrainians. I tell you, I'd like to leave Kiev today rather than tomorrow. Of course, it is always well to get money, but of what good is it if one is not sure of one's life? You never know what may come next.

A widespread sentiment in favor of reunion with Great Russia was reported to be in existence, but Germany showed no signs of changing her policy of supporting Hetman Skoropadski's dictatorial régime. A Berlin dispatch reported the speeches exchanged by the German Emperor and Skoropadski at a luncheon in Berlin. Emperor William said that Ukraine owed its existence as a State to Germany. He referred to the happy lot of the Ukrainians in the following words:

Henceforth a citizen can follow his vocation undisturbed and a peasant can cultivate the soil in safety and enjoy the fruits of his labor. There still remains much to do, but under the direction of your Highness Ukraine already has made considerable progress in internal consolidation and has thereby assured to itself a basis for future development.

The Germans succeeded in getting only one-eighth of the grain which the Ukraine was to supply under the provisions of the Brest-Litovsk treaty. Germany, on the other hand, failed to supply the Ukrainians with manufactured goods. Arrangements were reported to be under way whereby the Ukraine was to hand over to Russia 6,000,000 to 9,000,000 pounds of flour in return for textile fabrics, and also supply Russia with sugar.

## INDEMNITIES FROM PEASANTS

According to a letter from Kiev, published in a Ukrainian paper, the Austro-German forces were assisting the land-owners in raising large indemnities from the peasants. "With the object," says the cabled summary of the letter, " of enforcing payment of contributions troops come to villages during the night. Bombs and machine guns announce their arrival. The panic-stricken population are assembled before the Town Hall, surrounded, and ordered to pay so many hundreds of thousands of rubles, being threatened with the pillage and burning of the village. Profiting by experience, the peasants fetch money, but the sum being insufficient, the soldiers beat the peasants with rifles and whips." According to a dispatch of Sept. 12, revolted peasants exterminated the German garrison in the village of Brusilovka. A bloody clash occurred also between the Germans and Ukrainian village folk in the Government of Mohilev.

Similar conditions prevailed in White Russia. The systematic Germanization of Esthonia continues. According to information furnished by an official Esthonian courier and made public on Aug. 31, Esthonian music was forbidden and the national life of the people was suppressed in other ways. Shortly before this representatives of the Esthonian Diet and Government, which had been dissolved by the Germans, had repudiated in the name of the Republic of Esthonia the treaty between Berlin and the Soviet Government regarding the Baltic provinces. The Moscow Government had previously renounced all claims to the former Baltic provinces. A Geneva dispatch, dated Aug. 2, announced that General von Harbou was going to be appointed head of the military administration of a new territorial unit, " the Baltikum," consisting of Courland, Livonia, and Esthonia.

Information came through on Sept. 1 to the effect that Duke William of Urach had been selected to be King of Lithuania, and that Vilna was to be the capital of the new kingdom. Early in August it was reported that a considerable Lithuanian force, under the command of General Kaimaitis, was fighting the Soviet troops and had captured Vitebsk.

## AFFAIRS IN FINLAND

At the first session of the Russo-Finnish peace conference, held on Aug. 2, President Enckel of the Finnish delegation made a speech, in which he said:

The Finnish Senate, (Government,) once drawn into the international whirlwind, will naturally exercise its political activity in accord with the ally who aided it to triumph over the internal enemy. This fact holds no danger of a disadvantage to us, we are sure. We are convinced that the common interest of Finland as well as of Russia and Germany impels us to an amicable agreement and will lead us to it.

The recent policies of the present rulers of Finland are in keeping with this statement of alliance with Germany. A dispatch from Copenhagen, dated Sept. 7, reported that an alliance had been formed between Germany and Finland, which put Finland's entire man power at the disposal of Germany. Several dispatches conveyed the impression that Finns were fleeing their country to avoid the military and labor conscription which the Germans are forcing on the people.

On Aug. 22 a Finnish delegation left for Germany for the purpose of offering the crown of Finland to a German Prince. Prince Frederick Charles of Hesse was reported to have expressed his willingness to become the King of the Finns. He was said to be touring the country and conferring with various political leaders. He is accompanied by a strong guard. Sept. 26 was set as the date for the election of a King by the Finnish Diet.

Up to Aug. 19, 32,701 persons were arrested in Finland in connection with the suppression of the Finnish revolution. Of this number 15,555 persons were, up to Aug. 15, unconditionally sentenced and 13,732 conditionally; 1,775 persons were acquitted. A Finnish newspaper asserted that 20,000 of the Red Guards convicted for participating in the recent revolution would be sent to Germany as slaves.

## BARGAINING AWAY POLAND

The Polish Central Committee has recently made public a secret treaty regarding the status of Poland, which the Soviet Government had concluded with Germany. Dated Jan. 16, 1918, the document is signed by the German plenipotentiaries, von Tauber, Erich von Schunemann and Rausch, and on the Russian side by Krylenko, Volodarsky, Zalkind, Uritsky, Raskolnikov, Teurabend, Antonov, Dzierzinsky, and Ekrypkin. The text of the treaty follows:

1. The Polish policy is to be conducted by the German Government.

2. The Russian Government agrees not to interfere in any way whatever in the organization of Poland; in consequence it does not have the right to interpellate or protest in connection with the question of separating the metallurgic basin and coal mines of Dombrowa and annexing them to Germany, nor in the question of limiting the rights of persons of Polish origin in so far as the petroleum industry of Galicia is concerned; nor in the question of the separation and the Government of the Polish province of Khelm; nor in the question of the German customs policy; nor in the question of the German economic policy in Posen and the Austro-Hungarian policy in Galicia, as well as

in the Russian provinces which have been detached from Russia.

3. The Council of the People's Commissaries has the right of remaining in contact with the revolutionary and democratic centres existing in Poland with the purpose of spreading revolutionary ideas by sending to Poland agitators registered in the lists of the German bureaus of instructions in Petrograd and Warsaw.

4. The sending of agitators to Germany and Austria-Hungary will be stopped by the Council of People's Commissaries.

5. The Council of People's Commissaries will have to watch the groups of Polish chauvinists in order to prevent them from raising voluntary forces for a teritorial army in Russia.

6. Russia will have to consider the crossing of Ukrainia or Luthuania by Polish forces as a declaration of war by Poland to the Austrian and German empires, and Russia will lend her assistance to Germans and Austrians in crushing these armies.

7. The Council of People's Commissaries, by the interposition of its representatives at the future peace congress, will have to protest in the name of socialism and the abolition of wars against the formation of a Polish army and of a Polish Ministry of War.

8. The Council of People's Commissaries, with the assistance of its financial agents, will have to see to it that Russian citizens should not invest their own capital, nor that of the French, English, or Americans, in municipal, industrial, railroad or maritime enterprises in Poland.

9. If the German or the Austro-Hungarian Governments deem it necessary to completely modify their political relations in regard to Poland, the Government of the People's Commissaries agrees to recognize the new course of affairs and to defend it against the obstacles which may arise and against the opposition on the part of the former allies of Russia.

The treaty was signed by German and Bolshevist representatives mentioned above, and was dated Jan. 16, 1918.

## SUPPLEMENTARY TREATIES

On Aug. 27 three agreements supplementary to the Brest-Litovsk treaty were signed in Berlin by the representatives of the two contracting parties. Commenting upon the new treaties Premier Lenine declared that Germany had conceded to the Soviet Government full liberty of nationalizing Russian national economy, and, in addition, returned to Russia a number of towns and provinces.

An article in the North German Ga-

The demonstration at the Victor Emmanuel Monument in Rome, July 4, 1918, when Italians for the first time celebrated America's Independence Day

American troops on the front in Alsace celebrating the 4th of July, 1918, in a German town

(© Underwood & Underwood)

zette indicates that the supplementary treaties relate mostly to Russia's relations with the border States, which were formerly Russian provinces. The underlying principle is that of " not causing or supporting the forcible disunion of former Russian territory." The Baltic States of Esthonia and Livonia are assured independence, but at the same time Russia is given free ports on the Baltic and trading routes to that sea. Of all the Caucasian States the independence of Georgia alone is recognized, while the Baku territory, with its rich naphtha deposits, is left in Russia's hands, with the understanding that Russia pledges itself to place a portion of the naphtha at the disposal of Germany.

Russia agrees to pay to Germany an indemnity of 6,000,000,000 marks, ($1,-500,000,000,) of which sum 1,000,000,000 marks will be jointly paid by the Ukraine and Finland. Germany recognizes as legal expropriations in Russia, which affect natives and foreigners alike, but German property should not be further expropriated, nor shall the new Russian inheritance laws apply to Germans. According to a London dispatch, a portion of the Russian war indemnity amounting to 250,000,000 rubles ($125,000,000) was dispatched from Moscow to Berlin on Sept. 7.

A dispatch from Ambassador Francis at Archangel, which reached Washington on Sept. 10, threw new light on the contents of these supplementary treaties. Under them Germany guarantees Russia against attack either by or through Finland in the event of Russia's undertaking an offensive against the Allies in the north. Germany agrees also to guarantee the security of the Russian coastal and fishing fleets in Russian waters after the territory of the Soviet republic is cleared from allied troops.

Thus during the month under record the relation between Berlin and Moscow has come nearer to being one of conciliation and united action. At the same time the hostility of the Soviet authorities toward the Entente Allies reached what may be properly termed a state of war.

The allied Ambassadors left Vologda for Archangel on July 26. Fearing apparently that the Ambassadors might become a rallying point for the anti-Bolshevist elements in the north, the Soviet authorities insisted that the allied envoys should either go to Moscow or leave the country. As the Ambassadors refused to go to Moscow, they were ordered to leave. In reply to this order, delivered by Mr. Radek, Ambassador Francis is reported to have said: " If I leave the country, I leave only to return."

Foreign Minister Tchitcherin hastened to declare that the departure of the Ambassadors did not mean the severance of relations between the Allies and Russia. Lenine, however, announced before the Executive Committee that a state of war existed between the Soviet Republic and the allied countries. When called upon by the allied officials to explain this statement, Mr. Tchitcherin said that what the Bolshevist Premier really meant was " a state of defense." But in the meantime the Soviet authorities in Petrograd informed Robert W. Imbrie, the American Vice Consul at Petrograd, that a state of war existed between Russia and the United States. Thereupon the Vice Consul lowered the American flag on the consulate, turned over the interests of the United States to the Norwegian Consul and notified all Americans to leave the country.

Late in August De Witt C. Poole, American Consul General at Moscow, was still awaiting a safe conduct from the German Government. On Sept. 9 he was arrested in Moscow on the charge of having been involved in an attempt to bribe the Lettish troops, the Bolshevist Praetorian Guard.

### BRITISH EMBASSY SACKED

On Aug. 31 the British Embassy in Petrograd, situated on Palace Quay, was sacked by mobs and troops, and an English Captain who defended it was murdered. The British Government sent the following protest to the Bolshevist authorities:

An outrageous attack has been made on the British Embassy at Petrograd, its contents have been sacked and destroyed, Captain Cromie, who tried to defend it, was murdered, and his body barbarously mutilated. We demand immediate reparation and the prompt punishment of any one responsible for or concerned in this abominable outrage.

Should the Russian Soviet Government fail to give complete satisfaction, or should any further acts of violence be committed against a British subject, his Majesty's Government will hold the members of the Soviet Government individually responsible and will make every endeavor to secure that they shall be treated as outlaws by the Governments of all civilized nations and that no place of refuge shall be left to them.

You have already been informed through M. Litvinoff that his Majesty's Government was prepared to do everything possible to secure the immediate return of the official representatives of Great Britain and of the Russian Soviet Government to their respective countries. A guarantee was given by his Majesty's Government that as soon as the British officials were allowed to pass the Russo-Finnish frontier, M. Litvinoff and all the members of his staff should have permission to proceed immediately to Russia.

We have now learned that a decree was published on Aug. 29 ordering the arrest of all British and French subjects between the ages of 18 and 40, and that British officials have been arrested on trumped-up charges of conspiring against the Soviet Government.

His Majesty's Government has therefore found it necessary to place M. Litvinoff and the members of his staff under preventive arrest until such time as all British representatives are set at liberty and allowed to proceed to the Finnish frontier free from molestation.

It was previously reported that, according to an order of the Commission Extraordinary for Combating the Counter-revolution, all Allied subjects between the ages of 16 and 45 were being interned on the charge of assisting the anti-Bolshevist elements. A cable dated Sept. 11 declared that the Bolsheviki held at least a thousand British subjects as hostages and threatened to take revenge on them if attempts were made on the life of the Bolshevist leaders.

### FAMINE IMPENDING.

Food conditions in Great Russia continued to grow worse. Starvation prevailed in the cities, and potatoes and vegetables were the chief food resources of Moscow and Petrograd. In Moscow the control of the food supply exercised by the Soviet through the agency of the Provisioning Commission broke down completely, and the people took the food supply into their own hands. In the north, the food ration in some places consisted of two pounds of oats weekly per person. Epidemics of cholera and hunger typhus were reported all along the Volga and in the northern provinces.

The Soviet Government has entered into an agreement under which Germany is to get Russian goods, such as cloth and leather, which the Russians themselves badly need. A dispatch of Sept. 12 conveys the impression that Russian workmen, railroad men and even troops bitterly resented the shipment of goods to Germany and in many cases were effectively checking it. Railroad traffic was further crippled by strikes and the surging tide of civil war.

### A BOLSHEVIST DECREE

The Decree on the Nationalization of Foreign Trade in Russia, which follows, is a sample of recent Bolshevist legislation in the field of economic reform:

1. The entire foreign trade is nationalized. Commercial agreements with foreign countries and various commercial concerns abroad with regard to the purchase and sale of products of every kind are to be completed in the name of the Russian Republic by specially authorized bodies. All commercial agreements with foreign countries as regards exports and imports without the direct sanction of these bodies are forbidden.

(N. B.—Special instructions will be issued regarding postal packets and travelers' luggage entering or leaving the country.)

2. The body intrusted with the administration of the nationalized foreign trade is the People's Commissariat for Trade and Industry.

3. For the organization of import and export the People's Commissariat for Trade and Industry will establish a Council for Foreign Trade. To this council belong representatives of the following bodies, institutions, and organizations:

(a) The bodies responsible for the army, navy, agriculture, food, traffic, foreign affairs, and finance.

(b) Representatives of the central bodies for regulating and administering various branches of production.

(c) Central organizations of the co-operative societies.

(d) Central administrative bodies of the commercial and agricultural organizations.

(e) Central administrative bodies of the

trade unions and of associations of commercial employes.

(f) Central bodies of the commercial concerns established for the import and export of essential products.

(N. B.—The People's Commissariat for Trade and Industry is empowered to add to the Council for Foreign Trade representatives of organizations not included in the above list.)

4. The Council for Foreign Trade will carry out a scheme for exchanging commodities with foreign countries. Its functions are:

(a) To determine the supply and demand of products to be imported and exported.

(b) To organize the system of supply and the purchase, with the co-operation of the proper central offices, of individual branches of industry, and, in their default, with the intermediary assistance of the co-operative societies, private agents, and commercial firms.

(c) To organize purchases in foreign countries with the aid of Government Purchasing Committees and agents, co-operative societies, and commercial firms.

(d) To determine the prices of imported and exported goods.

5. The Council for Foreign Trade will be divided into departments according to the various branches of industry and the most important groups of import and export commodities, and a representative of the People's Commissariat for Trade and Industry will officiate as Chairman of each department.

6. The present decree comes into force immediately on publication.

# Progress of the Allied Expeditions

## Japanese and Americans Help to Reopen Communications With Czechoslovaks in Central Russia

[PERIOD ENDED SEPT. 20, 1918]

THE expeditionary force of American, Japanese, British, French, and Chinese troops sent to Vladivostok to help the Czechoslovak and Russian forces in restoring the military situation in Siberia and Russia began active operations early in August, 1918. British and French contingents were first to arrive, and the Japanese under General Kikuzo Otani reached Vladivostok on Aug. 12. The two American regiments from the Philippines arrived on the 15th and 16th, astonishing the residents by their cheering as they entered the harbor. General Diedrichs, the commander of the Czechoslovak forces in Siberia, greeted them warmly and presented a memorandum to all the allied representatives setting forth the urgent need of speedy action to aid the Czechoslovaks 4,000 miles away in Eastern Russia. Major Gen. William S. Graves, commander of the American contingent, sailed from the United States with a staff of forty-three officers and 1,888 men, and reached Vladivostok on Sept. 4.

Meanwhile the Japanese and British had gone to the aid of the Czechoslovaks who were fighting the Bolsheviki and German ex-prisoners in the region north of Vladivostok, along the Ussuri River, which forms the eastern boundary of Manchuria. As soon as the Americans arrived from Manila some of them were sent to occupy points along the railway in the direction of Nikolsk, thus releasing several hundred Czechoslovaks for service on the Ussuri front. On Aug. 23 it was announced that Generals D. G. Stcherbatcheff and V. A. Tcheremisoff, former Russian leaders, had accepted commands in the Czechoslovak army.

There were two main groups of Czechoslovaks separated by thousands of miles, and the first urgent task was to establish communications between these and save the western group from being isolated through the Winter. The eastern group at Vladivostok already had the active aid of the Allies. The second and larger group was distributed along the Trans-Siberian Railway all the way from Irkutsk, on the western shore of Lake Baikal, to Samara, in European Russia, a distance of more than 2,000 miles. Between the two groups, in the region around Chita, lay a well-armed force of Bolsheviki and German or Hungarian ex-prisoners, estimated at 40,000 or 50,000 men.

The first operations of the joint allied forces, therefore, were directed against two main obstacles—the enemy stronghold along the Ussuri and Amur Rivers, north of Vladivostok, and that around Chita, in Transbaikalia. The Allies took the offensive on the Ussuri on Aug. 24, and after hard fighting drove the Red Guards fifteen miles to the north. The enemy's strength here was 8,000 infantry, with at least fourteen field guns, and his loss was 300 men. On Aug. 28 Japanese cavalry occupied Krasnoyarsk. The Bolsheviki retired to the region on the Amur River, between Khabarovsk and Blagovestchensk. Japanese cavalry and an infantry battalion captured the enemy naval base at Kbabarovsk on Sept. 7, taking seventeen gunboats, four other vessels, a wireless station, and 120 guns.

## CAPTURE OF CHITA

Meanwhile the danger to the Czechoslovaks in the interior of the continent was dissipated by an unexpected success. The isolated Czechoslovak forces had been working eastward under Colonel Gaida from Lake Baikal toward Chita, while Cossack forces under General Semenoff, supported by Japanese who had come up from China, were working westward from Manchuria toward the same point. A delayed dispatch from Consul Harris at Irkutsk, dated Aug. 13, brought word that the Bolshevist army east of Lake Baikal had been destroyed, and on Sept. 4 telegraphic communication was reopened between Irkutsk and Vladivostok—also from Irkutsk to Peking, via Penza—thus re-establishing connection for 4,000 miles between the extreme ends of Siberia.

On the same day Secretary Lansing received a telegram through the American Legation at Peking announcing that Chita, the capital of Transbaikalia and the chief stronghold of the enemy in Siberia, had been captured by Czechoslovak troops, who had joined hands with the Cossack army approaching from the other direction. Another official report stated that railway communication had been re-established between the widely separated Czechoslovak groups. Pro-Entente forces were thus in control of the Siberian and Manchurian railways all the way from Vladivostok to Samara, on the Volga River, a few hundred miles from Moscow.

## ACHIEVEMENTS OF CZECHS

The following account of how the Czechoslovaks had fought their way across Siberia was telegraphed from their field headquarters in Transbaikalia on Sept. 5:

The Czechoslovaks seized Novo Nikolaievsk on May 26, but it was only on June 11 that Irkutsk was reached, after severe fighting all the way. Thirty-nine tunnels on the Trans-Siberian Railroad had been mined, but the Bolshevist forces were taken by surprise, and only one tunnel was succesfully blown up.

In the meantime Czechoslovaks had seized Listvinichskaya, near Irkutsk, on the west bank of Lake Baikal, where they found two small damaged steamers. These vessels were hastily repaired, and after two guns were mounted and several machine guns set up on the ships, they steamed to the eastward, towing barges filled with soldiers.

By a ruse the Czechoslovaks managed to land near Misovoya, though the larger vessels came out to give battle. Shots from the Czechoslovak guns shattered the gasoline tanks and set fire to the enemy steamers. The Bolshevist sailors became panic-stricken and permitted the Czechoslovaks to land and attack them from the rear.

In the battle of Misovoya the Bolshevist forces lost forty complete trains out of sixty. Of their forces, estimated to number 20,000, some 6,000 were killed and 2,000 taken prisoner. The others fled into the woods, and their defeat demoralized the troops further to the east.

On Aug. 10, at Troitskovasavsk, 1,200 Magyars, who had styled themselves "internationalists," surrendered to Colonel Linevitch's detachment. The trophies taken by the Czechoslovaks included four steamers, several barges, and a number of automobiles and horses.

A Czecho-Russian force sent overland from Irkutsk against the Bolsheviki working the Yakutsk gold mines disposed entirely of the Red Guard, took the mines under control, and occupied Yakutsk.

The main body of the Czecho-Russian troops then proceeded along the Amur railway in pursuit of the main body of Red Guards, which withdrew from Nerchinsk to Srenensk after the capture of Chita. The Cossacks freely entered the ranks of the Czechoslovaks.

The Bolshevist Government at Moscow issued a reply to the Japanese and

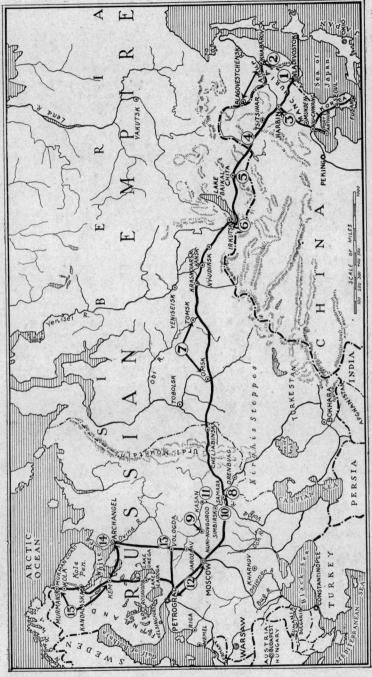

ALLIED PROGRESS IN RUSSIA: (1) BASE OF JAPANESE-AMERICAN EXPEDITION; (2) USSURI FRONT; (3) AND (4) POINTS HELD BY ALLIES; (5) CHITA, CAPTURED FROM BOLSHEVIKI; (6) AND (7) FIRMLY HELD BY CZECHOSLOVAKS; (8), (10), (11), POINTS WHERE CZECHOSLOVAKS ARE THREATENED; (9) NIZHNI-NOVGOROD, CAPTURED BY ANTI-BOLSHEVIST PEASANTS; (12) BOLSHEVIST STRONGHOLD; (13) VOLOGDA, THE POINT TOWARD WHICH BOTH EXPE-DITIONS ARE WORKING; (14) AND (15) HELD BY ALLIES' NORTHERN EXPEDITION.

American statements of Aug. 3 regarding the reasons for intervention in Russia. The version appearing in the Tageblatt of Berlin about Aug. 20 is given below:

The American and Japanese Governments have addressed a message to the Russian people in connection with the landing of their armed forces on Russian territory. Both Governments declare their armed intervention was dictated by the desire to come to the aid of the Czechoslovaks who, it is alleged, are menaced by Germans and Austrians.

The Russian Federal Republic feels compelled to make this declaration:

The statement made by the American and Japanese Governments is not based on accurate information. The Czechoslovak detachments are not menaced by either Germans or Austrians. On the soil of the Soviet Republic the battle continues between the Red Soviet Army, created by peasants and workers, on the one hand, and Czechoslovak detachments, in concert with land owners, the bourgeoisie, and counter-revolutionaries, on the other.

In this battle the workmen and peasants are defending the revolution, which is endangered by a counter-revolution aided and abetted by the Czechoslovaks.

The Soviet Government is convinced that its enemies are only attempting to blind proletarian elements of the population and they seek to deceive them by fostering in them the belief that Germans and Austrians are menacing the Czechoslovaks.

Should, however, the grounds of this attack on the Soviet Republic be really those stated in the Japanese-American message, the Soviet Government suggests that the Governments exactly formulate their wishes in the matter.

TCHITCHERIN.

### IN NORTHERN RUSSIA

The other allied expeditionary force, which had landed at Murmansk and Archangel in July and early August, continued to make progress southward from the White Sea toward Vologda, with the purpose of joining hands with the Czechoslovak forces and completing a circuit of allied control from the Pacific to the Arctic Ocean. Volunteer detachments of Russian White Guards joined in driving the Bolshevist forces southward from Archangel, and on Aug. 31 the enemy positions at Obozerskaya, seventy-five miles south of Archangel, were captured.

Thus far only American marines had taken part in this expedition, but on Sept. 11 American troops from the French front were safely landed at Archangel. These soldiers were picked men, with knowledge of the Russian or French language, and with special aptitude for enduring the rigors of a Russian Winter. They were reviewed by Ambassador Francis and the commanders of the allied forces, and were cheered as they marched through the streets of Archangel.

The Tchaikovsky Provisional Government at Archangel was overthrown by a rival faction on Sept. 8, but the allied diplomatic and military chiefs convinced the new leaders, who were friendly to the Entente, that they were acting unwisely and reinstated the Tchaikovsky Government on Sept. 12.

Progress southward continued slowly but steadily. On Sept. 14 the Bolshevist official organ, Pravda, admitted repulse. on the northern front at the hands of American, British, and French troops. The Red Guards, after an initial success, had been routed by British reinforcements and had fled in panic. A number of the Bolshevist officers, the newspaper said, had deserted to the British.

# Czechs Recognized by U. S.

## Our Country Joins Great Britain, France, and Italy in Formally Recognizing the New Nation

THE United States Government took a momentous step on Sept. 2, 1918, when it officially recognized the Czechoslovaks as a belligerent nation and the Czechoslovak National Council, which has its headquarters at Washington, as " a de facto belligerent " Government clothed with proper au- " thority to direct the military and polit- " ical affairs of the Czechoslovaks." France, Great Britain, and Italy had already recognized the Czechoslovak National Council and the Czechoslovak Army.

The official text of Secretary Lansing's announcement of recognition follows:

The Czechoslovak peoples having taken up arms against the German and Austro-Hungarian Empires, and having placed organized armies in the field, which are waging war against those empires under officers of their own nationality and in accordance with the rules and practices of civilized nations; and

The Czechoslovaks having, in prosecution of their independent purposes in the present war, confided supreme political authority to the Czechoslovak National Council,

. The Government of the United States recognizes that a state of belligerency exists between the Czechoslovaks thus organized and the German and Austro-Hungarian Empires.

It also recognizes the Czechoslovak National Council as a de facto belligerent Government, clothed with proper authority to direct the military and political affairs of the Czechoslovaks.

The Government of the United States further declares that it is prepared to enter formally into relations with the de facto Government thus recognized for the purpose of prosecuting the war against the common enemy, the Empires of Germany and Austria-Hungary.

Secretary Lansing received Professor Thomas G. Masaryk, President of the Czechoslovak National Council, at noon on Sept. 2 and formally conveyed to him the fact that the American Government had taken this important action. Pro-fessor Masaryk subsequently issued this statement:

Mr. Lansing handed me the declaration today at 12 o'clock; I read it and thanked him very heartily, as indeed I value the American recognition of our army, the National Council, and nation very highly. Mr. Lansing's explanation confirmed what I have read myself in the wording of his declaration.

The American recognition differs from the French and British in that these recognize the right to our independence directly, whereas Mr. Lansing's wording recognizes in the first place our army and the National Council. But speaking of the Czechoslovaks the declaration denotes our whole nation. The British text recognizes our National Council as the present trustee of the future Government; the United States recognizes our council directly as the de facto Government.

The United States lays stress on the belligerency and they emphasize the organization of our nation shown first in mobilizing armies and second in confiding all political affairs to the leading authority of the National Council. In accordance with the humanitarian principles of the American Constitution the military practice of our armies (this applies especially to our army in Russia) is acknowledged.

I once more would express my satisfaction and thanks to the United States Government and the President for their recognition of our national cause. I, of course, know that w also owe a good deal to American public opinion and its representatives.

## NEW NATION'S LEADERS

The headquarters of the Czechoslovak National Council formerly were in Paris. The body consists of representatives of the scattered Czechoslovak colonies, but all real authority has been in the hands of the three principal officers of the council. These are, besides Professor Masaryk, General Milan R. Stefanik, its Vice President of the council, and Dr. Edouard Benes, General Secretary. General Stefanik arrived in New York Sept. 3 from Paris. He was accompanied by his Adjutant, Captain Paul Sowneir of the French Army, Captain Ferdinand Pisecky of the Czechoslovak Army, and Lieutenant Levi of the French Army.

Professor Masaryk was a teacher in the University of Prague, as well as Deputy to the Vienna Parliament for a great many years. He left Bohemia a few months after the outbreak of the war with full authority from representatives of the Czech political parties to speak in foreign lands in the name of his people. He is 69 years old, and even before the war he was looked upon by every member of the Czechoslovak race as the " grand old man " of Bohemia. Both his official position and the reverence in which he is held by his people make his authority supreme and unquestioned.

General Stefanik was, before the war, a noted astronomer in Paris. Upon the outbreak of the war he entered the French Army as a private and soon became an officer and a daring aviator. He has been wounded several times and promoted for gallantry. He holds at present the rank of Brigadier General in the French Army. He represents the Slovak branch of the Czechoslovak Nation on the National Council.

Dr. Edouard Benes was an instructor at the University of Prague, fled from Bohemia at the first opportunity, and was placed in charge of the Paris office. He is a diplomat and an author of ability.

The Commander in Chief of the three Czechoslovak armies in Russia, France, and Italy is Professor Masaryk. The General in command of the forces in Russia is General Diedrichs. The commander of the forces on the French front is Major Gen. M. Janin. The Czechoslovaks in Italy are commanded by General Graziani.

There are 410,000 Czechoslovaks in the United States, a large proportion of them naturalized and most of those of military age have already been incorporated into the United States military forces.

The recognition of the Czechoslovaks is held to mean that America is irrevocably committed to the principle of dissolution of the Austro-Hungarian Empire as a feature of the scheme of reconstruction of Europe along the lines of nationality.

## THE BRITISH DECLARATION

The following is the text of the British declaration, issued Aug. 13 and already published in CURRENT HISTORY MAGAZINE:

Since the beginning of the war the Czechoslovak nation has resisted the common enemy by every means in its power. The Czechoslovaks have constituted a considerable army, fighting on three different battlefields, and attempting in Russia and Siberia to arrest the Germanic invasion. In consideration of its efforts to achieve independence, Great Britain regards the Czechoslovaks as an allied nation and recognizes the unity of the three Czechoslovak armies as an allied and belligerent army waging regular warfare against Austria-Hungary and Germany. Great Britain also recognizes the right of the Czechoslovak National Council as the supreme organ of Czechoslovak national interests and as the present trustee of the future Czechoslovak Government to exercise supreme authority over this allied and belligerent army.

## CZECHS AND ALSACE-LORRAINE

When President Poincaré of France presented the Czechoslovak flag to the men of that nation on the French front June 30, he referred in his speech to the fact that the Bohemian Diet had been the only organized assembly of people outside of France to issue a formal protest in 1871 against Germany's seizure of Alsace-Lorraine. The text of that protest was in part as follows:

The Czech Nation cannot but express its most ardent sympathy with noble and glorious France, which today is defending its independence and national soil, which has accomplished so much for the advancement of civilization and the principles of humanity and liberty.

The Czech Nation is convinced that such a humiliation as the tearing of a strip of territory from a nation so illustrious and heroic, so full of just national pride, would become a source of unending wars, and therefore of unending injuries to humanity and civilization.

The Czechs are a small people, but their spirit and their courage are not small. They would be ashamed by their silence to let the world believe that they approve of this injustice, or that they dare not make their protest against it because of its underlying power.

Their name must go down to history untarnished. They must and will remain faithful to the spirit of their ancestors, who were the first in Europe to proclaim the principles of freedom of conscience, and who, in the face of an enemy superior in numbers, have fought to the point of exhaustion.

## CZECHOSLOVAK ASPIRATIONS

The Czechs inhabit Bohemia, Moravia. and Austrian Silesia, which under the present Constitution are crown lands of the Austrian Empire, and lie between Austria proper on the south and the German Empire—Bavaria on the west, Saxony on the north, and Prussian Silesia on the east. The Slovaks live in the upper regions of Hungary, adjoining the Czechs to the east and southeast. The two peoples are in effect the same race; their language has only slight dialectical differences; the political division between them was erected only in 1867, when to divide the energies of the people the Slovaks were put under Hungarian rule. Czechs and Slovaks have worked together with absolute harmony for unity and independence.

" The boundaries that we hope to have set for the Czechoslovak Nation," said Dr. Masaryk to an interviewer, " will embrace Bohemia, Moravia, Silesia, and their historical boundaries. To these will be added Slovakia—that is, the northern part of Hungary, extending as far south as Presburg and to the east as far as Ungvar. This territory is about four times greater than that of Belgium. The population of the new nation will be 12,-000,000. Of these, 10,000,000 are Bohemians and Slovaks. The remainder consists of minorities.

" Our Constitution will provide for a President and two legislative chambers, a Senate and a House of Representatives, similar to yours. There will be a very elaborate system of local self-government, as a means of insuring a democracy that is not one in form alone. We shall endeavor to work out the problem of local self-government so as to render the justice of leaving the affairs of minorities in their own hands as far as possible. In reaffirming the historical boundary lines of Bohemia, Moravia, and Silesia there will of necessity be included some Germans among the population, notably in the west and north, but we

shall confer on communities of this kind the same local self-government that obtains in other parts of the country. There will be universal suffrage. We have confidence in this and a high degree of local self-government because all our people are educated."

The Czechs are one of the most highly civilized peoples in the world, and economically the most prosperous in the Austrian Empire. Their country includes most of the coal and iron deposits of the empire, the principal manufactures, and the most prosperous agricultural districts. The Slovaks have been held back by Magyar repression, but elsewhere, as in the United States, have shown that their natural capacity is as great as that of the Czechs.

The area of the Czech countries is approximately 30,000 square miles, and of the Slovak regions about 18,000. According to the census of 1910, there were about 6,500,000 Czechs and 2,000,000 Slovaks, but these figures were underestimated for political purposes, and nationalist leaders say that there are about 8,000,000 Czechs and 3,000,000 Slovaks. Among them live some 3,000,000 Germans and several hundred thousand Magyars, and the program of the independence movement provides for complete cultural autonomy for these national minorities.

## STRUGGLE FOR LIBERTY

In 1848 the Czechs came into conflict with the Pan Germans of that day, and the Hungarian revolution under Kossuth attempted to suppress the liberties of the Slovaks, with the result that all the revolutionary movements collapsed and left the Hapsburgs supreme. In 1867 defeat convinced Francis Joseph of the necessity of taking the Magyars into partnership, so the Czechoslovaks were divided between the two parts of the empire. Theoretically Bohemia was and is still an independent kingdom, and Francis Joseph even promised to be crowned King at Prague, but Bismarck's influence prevented this. Since then the Czechs have maintained a constant struggle against the Hapsburgs and the ruling races in Austria, as well as against the influence of the German Empire,

THE CZECHOSLOVAK NATION, OFFICIALLY RECOGNIZED BY THE UNITED STATES,
COMPRISES BOHEMIA, MORAVIA, SILESIA, AND SLOVAKIA, WHOSE PEOPLE DESIRE
ENTIRE INDEPENDENCE FROM AUSTRIA-HUNGARY

which regarded them as a great obstacle to its plans.

The bulk of the nation long fought for autonomy within a federalized Austrian Empire and under the Hapsburg crown, but the reign of terror with which the people's reluctance to take part in the present war was met strengthened those who demanded complete independence. Thousands of military executions, great numbers of confiscations, and arbitrary imprisonments angered the people, whose soldiers were already going over to the Russians and Serbs in great masses. Finally, in November, 1915, a committee of exiles in Paris demanded complete independence and unity of the race, and this policy at once received overwhelming support in the Czechoslovak countries.

The Czechoslovak National Committee was thereupon organized in Paris. Branches of the organization were established in the various European capitals, and another branch in the United States, where the Czechoslovak population strongly supported the national movement. France recognized the independence of the Czechoslovaks and the authority of the National Committee as a Provisional Government on July 1. The example was followed by Italy and by Great Britain. The end of the war should see the Czechoslovak people free for the first time since 1620.

## THIRD SLAVIC CONGRESS

Three important Congresses have aided the Pan Slavic movement. The declarations of the first, held at Prague on Jan. 6, and of the second, held at Agram on March 2, 1918, were recorded in the July issue of CURRENT HISTORY. The third, held in Laibach in July, has been referred to by Professor Kosch of the Czernovitz University as the third great milestone in the way to a realization of the Central European Slavdom. He gives some quotations from speeches made at that conference.

"There is no one in Bohemia," said Deputy Clofarsch, "who believes that we can negotiate with Vienna."

And another speaker, in the name of the Czechs and Poles and Jugoslavs, said: "We have joined hands. No one can part us."

Amid thunderous applause the Polish Count Skarbek shouted the Slav watchword:

"From Danzig to Trieste!"

While the Polish leader, Dr. Tertil, said to the Czechs and Southern Slavs:

"We feel we are at one with you."

The professor admits he is astounded at these signs of Slav unity and concludes:

"The motto, 'Berlin to Bagdad,' is now solemnly opposed by Slavdom's 'Danzig to Trieste' solution. It may be a motto for purposes of agitation, but it would be madness to shut one's ears to it."

The Vienna correspondent of the Weser Zeitung stated that the gathering outwardly appeared to be concerned with the foundation of a Slav National Council, just as the first meeting in Prague was apparently for the purpose of setting up a Czech national theatre, but in reality had for its aim the bringing into existence of a general Czech commonalty, which was supported by Czech, Polish, and Serbo-Croatian representatives. He added:

The official reports of the Laibach conference simply said that it had to do with the foundation of the National Council, but, as Deputy Koroschit emphatically declared, that only formed part of the whole Southern Slav organization, with headquarters at Agram; we must therefore reckon with an organization embracing all the Jugoslav lands similar in kind to the Czech National Council led by Kramersch.

The prospects for this organization are very favorable, for it is clear that the Greater Croatian movement is daily being reduced in strength by that of the pro-Entente Jugoslavs. In the south, therefore, we shall soon have similar conditions to those prevailing in the Czech regions.

The Laibach gathering was promoted according to a common plan and something like a general mobilization of Slavdom is contemplated. It is impossible to avoid the belief that the opening of hostilities will not be long delayed. Of precaution by those against whom all this is directed one hears nothing.

## The Silent Soldiers of France

*Gabriel Hanotaux, the French historian and academician, recently penned this thumbnail sketch of the French soldier for Les Annales:*

The soldier, the poilu—all honor to him! His name is legion; one sees him everywhere, but he talks very little. It is not easy to divine what is going on in his silent head; his lips often remain closed under his thick mustache. The general impression is that of cold and silent courage, just the opposite of what was expected of the French soldier. These lines from a memorandum book give the keynote:

"The country itself is not gay; an austere city, poor villages, few trees in the country; bare hills, one after the other; on the summit, cannon. Everywhere soldiers, nothing but soldiers. Everything is desolate. There is no longer a place for pity. One does not laugh, nor does one weep; one fights and kills without mercy. The life of a man does not count."

That is a picture in which there are no flowers. It is the truth. The French Army is grave. It is doing its duty, and, as the notebook says, it is fighting. The dominating idea is that of sacrifice, of willed and resolute sacrifice. As one soldier puts it: "When every shell fired is perhaps for you, the simplest way is not to think of it." Firmness in performance of duty thus becomes the dominant note. These men are the sons of a sound and healthy nation; they will bring back to their mother, France, health and strength, and—something that will do no harm—glory. This army is extending the boundaries of collective psychology; it will be a source of instruction and of wonderment for history.

H. B. K.

# German Claims on Baltic Provinces

## The Teutonic Element in Russia: Its Attempt to Rule and Its Part in the War

### By AN AMERICAN HISTORIAN

THE first germ of the present world conflict was deposited in the waters of the Baltic by Prussia and Austria when these two great powers shamelessly robbed in 1864 little Denmark of her two duchies, Schleswig and Holstein. Sadowa (1866) led straight to Sedan (1870) and, by a circuitous way over various stations, Agadir in particular, to Longwy and Verdun. John Bull had, in 1914, to atone for his fatal blunder of exactly half a century before, when he refused to join Russia in teaching Francis Joseph, Emperor of Austria, and William I., King of Prussia, a solid naval lesson about the imprescriptible rights of small nations. Very few among us are aware that the famous last interview of unsavory " scrap of paper " memory between the British Ambassador and the German Chancellor, von Bethmann Hollweg, in the first August days of 1914, was, indeed, but an unconscious expiatory continuation of that other final conference which had taken place in 1864 between Prince Gortchakoff, the then Russian Foreign Minister, and Lord Napier, when the lattter had to listen silently to the Russian statesman's stinging reproach: " Then, Milord, I doubt whether your country ever will undertake a war for a mere question of honor."

When, in 1914, William and Francis Joseph tried to repeat their game on poor little Belgium, England honorably redeemed her disastrous Baltic diplomacy of 1864.

Amid the din of guns thundering on the plains of Poland, France, and Flanders, and during the noisy housecleaning of the former empire of the Romanoffs, one further seems to neglect one of the primary fundamentals of the present war, i. e., that the decision to deliver the Baltic Sea from German control ultimately drove exasperated Russia to accept Germany's challenge.

Neither must we, finally, lose sight of the immediate and decisive rôle which the opening of the Kiel Canal—a few weeks before the beginning of the world war—played in opening the eyes of the British people as to the last goal of William's naval policy. This cut through Holstein's body was a straight challenge of John Bull's supremacy on the seven seas.

### BASIS OF GERMAN CLAIMS

The Hohenzollerns and their academic camarilla unblushingly try to bluff the whole world into the belief that the Baltic Provinces are a genuine German domain which the noble Teutonic Knights of Potsdam, Munich, and Dresden have come to free from the barbaric yoke of the Slav. What are the facts?

When, with the fall of the Roman Empire, the real recorded history of the Baltic begins, we find its coasts held by Danes, Swedes, Finns, Letto-Lithuanians, and Wends—not a trace of Germans. No doubt, about the year 1400 A. D. the control of the Baltic by the famous Hanseatic League, which, at the height of its power, claimed a membership not far short of eighty cities, was practically complete. But this mediaeval German hegemony lasted for one single decade only. In 1410, at the historic battle of Tannenberg — Hindenburg's victory at identically the same spot in 1914 may yet prove to be a boomerang for Prussia—the Poles, under the Lithuanian Kings of the House of Jagellon, crushed the power of the Teutonic Knights, attaining the height of their control over the Baltic Provinces, in 1562, by the securing of Courland.

The capture of Riga in 1621 by Gustavus Adolphus, King of Sweden, marked the beginning of a new era for that much disputed territory. The Swedish supremacy over the latter was challenged by the Hohenzollern Prince, Frederick William, known as the Great Elector, (1640-1688.) The crucial conflict was fought out in the Northern War (1700-1721) be-

MAP SHOWING LOCATION OF BALTIC PROV-
INCES—ESTHONIA, LIVONIA, COURLAND,
AND LITHUANIA

tween Peter the Great and Frederick I., King of Prussia, on the one, and Charles XII. of Sweden on the other hand. Charles was defeated; his sister and successor, Ulrike Eleonore, was compelled in 1721 to sign a peace which gave Western Pomerania to Prussia, while Russia secured Livonia, Esthonia, Ingria, Carelia, and part of Finland. The final partition of Poland gave Prussia the long-

desired link between her hitherto divided Baltic possessions, while Russia acquired, through that infamous tripartite land robbery, Courland and Samogitia.

And now comes William II., trying to sum up the age-long brigandage policy of his ancestors. He makes no secret of his ambition to swallow the whole precious morsel, making of the Baltic in the real sense of the word a " mare Germanicum." Little Denmark trembles in her boots, and even Norway is afraid of the black Prussian eagle hovering over her coasts. Fortunately for them, Foch, Haig, Pétain, and Pershing will soon have brought down that ugly bird of prey.

### SMALL GERMAN MINORITY

The aborigines of Courland as well as the Livonians and Esthonians are of pure Finnish origin. The Letts and Lithuanians, two branches of the Indo-European trunk, are racially, and, as to their whole moral makeup, closer to the Slav than to the German. The latter, it must be admitted, were shrewd enough to use the hostility existing between the Letts and the Finnish tribes, playing one against the other. They thus retained the control, not without the help of their reactionary confederates, the Tchins of Moscow and Petrograd.

Their real numerical strength? Here are the official census figures of Jan. 1, 1910:

|  | Inhabitants. |
|---|---|
| Livonia | 1,455,000 |
| Courland | 741,200 |
| Esthonia | 467,400 |

In this total figure of over 2,500,000 the German element is scarcely represented by 200,000. Professor Dr. Heinrich Vogt in his pamphlet, " Vergesst nicht die deutschen Balten! " (1916,) says: " It is true, our brethren never " numbered more than 8 to 10 per cent. " of the total Baltic population. Num- " bers, however, are dead things; life and " history speak quite another language."

There has never been among the German inhabitants of the Baltic Provinces a national conscience analogous to that ruling the minds in the Fatherland or among the " lost brethren " in Austria. The Baltic Germans never have been designated by others nor felt they themselves to be a separate people or nationality. All over the vast territory they are forming only a very thin layer of the population. There never has been a genuine class of farmers among them. Quite recently one has tried, but without permanent results, to import about 15,000 German colonists from the Russian Government of Volhynia. The one old German farm settlement in the whole Baltic Provinces, the Hirschenhof, which Catherine II. founded with Bavarian farmers, has long since ceased to be; all the descendants of the first settlers have become tradesmen or artisans.

## TOOLS OF CZARISM

The truth is that the so-called Baltic-German "Irredenta" is exclusively composed of bureaucrats, traders, and professional men, who are dominated by a handful of reactionary "Junkers." The latter, with abject servility, have licked the boots of all the Czars and Czarinas for the last two centuries. They always have been the most reliable instruments of the cruel autocratic policy of the Romanoffs. The Slavs, and the Russians in particular, are a lovable, freedom-loving race, and the same can be said of the Esthonians, Livonians, Letts, and Lithuanians. These natives of the Baltic are hospitable and hard-working people, but, like the Slavs, of a somewhat dreamy nature, loving song and music. Alas! they are too pliable and prone to foreign influence. No wonder, then, that these national fragments, sparsely settled over an enormous stretch of country, proved to be, for centuries, like wax in the skillful, cruel hands of the German dynasty of the Romanoffs—the late Nicholas II. had 64.65 German blood in his veins; all Russian Empresses during the nineteenth century, with the exception of the still living Dowager Empress Maria Fedorovna, were German Princesses—and of their German tools, the hated Baltic Barons, the Plehves, the Stürmers, and so on. These big German land owners looked down upon the Russians and Poles and Ukrainians, and still more upon the Esthonians and Livonians, as upon inferior races, which were created by the German god to serve the German superman.

It is these Teutonic Junkers who, as Generals and Admirals, Governors of the provinces, courtiers, and low-grade bureaucrats, dominated the whole Governmental machinery of Russia.

Their professors and attorneys wrote the civil and penal codes of the Russian Empire; it is they who sent, during two centuries, millions of unfortunate proletarians who dared to fight on their own native soil for a crumb of bread, for a breath of freedom, to cold Siberia. They were the direct or indirect authors of the infamous pogroms; many of them were chiefs of the still more unspeakable secret police.

As far back as 1560, when Ivan the Terrible took possession of the country, which had been occupied by the Teutonic Knights, the latter appealed to the German Princes for help. "Scraps of papers" with golden promises were solemnly forwarded, hiding the ugly fact that the empire was at that time too weak, too much rent by inner dissensions, to be in a position to send practical succor to its distant lessee among the Slav and Finnish "barbarians."

Let us skip a span of time of exactly three and a half centuries, landing in the year of grace 1905 on the estates of our Baltic Junkers. The Lettish revolution had broken out, a Lettish Republic had been proclaimed. The Germans, faithful to their reactionary policy, clung to the Government of the Czar. But the Slavic-Lettish worm began at last to turn. A great number of German castles and estates were burned; many owners were put in prison or killed outright. When their confederates, the corrupted functionaries of the Central Government of Petrograd, fled from the country in terror, the situation of the German Barons and the German "intelligenzia" became desperate indeed. The large forests, owned by the Junkers, were declared State property of the new republic, and the rest of the German estates began to be parceled out among the poor Lettish farmers.

The hour of expiation had come at last. The haughty German aristocrats who believed that they were absolute lords of the country had to flee for their lives; those who remained offered their services to the Russian Army, which was sent to suppress the revolution—and suppressed it was, according to the ethical rules of Prussian militarism.

The respite, however, was but of short duration. When the world war broke out the Russian people, whose national conscience was aroused to an unexpected pitch by the Teutonic challenge, insisted upon the uprooting of Germandom throughout the empire, and in the Baltic Provinces in particular. The Letts again joined the anti-German movement. The poor Teutons got a dose of their own medicine; they did not feel safe in their own homes; they were watched and spied upon by their Lettish servants. In that ominous hour they may have caught an echo of the curse the former Polish owners of the estates had uttered against their heartless spoliators who, on their knees, after the cruel suppression of the Polish revolt of 1863, received the bloodstained booty from the Russian Court.

The heavens threatened to fall. The agrarian banks throughout the Baltic Provinces received the order from Petrograd to buy up as many German estates ("Rittergüter") as possible and to distribute them among the 300,000 Russian peasants who were settled, in 1913, in the country along the Russian-Prussian frontier from Memel to Thorn. German schools were closed. The Lutheran-German pastors were persecuted, in many cases condemned to prison sentences. In brief, the "Deutschthum" received its deathblow. There was no spark of hope left in the breasts of the dejected sons of Germania of ever being redeemed by the Fatherland. "What do they care there about us?" was the cry of despair of the Baltische Deutsche. When, indeed, encouraged by the great victories of Hindenburg in Poland, Baltic-German delegations were sent to Germany asking whether their constituents could expect to be "delivered" some day, they were given the cold shoulder! The hottest among the jingoes emigrated to Germany.

Worse, however, was yet to come: A ukase threatened to send the proud Junkers and their henchmen to Siberia and on Feb. 2, 1915, the late ex-Czar Nicholas II. signed another decree whereby all German landowners were deprived of their property!

After the Germans had taken Libau, and German cavalry patrols had penetrated deep into the surrounding country, the miserable German "colonists" had a new ray of hope. But hardly had the German troops withdrawn than the Russian soldiers fell on the Teutons, threw the few large landowners that still remained in the country into prison and burned their estates.

I believe I have said and proved enough, yea, more than enough, to convince even the most obstinate cryptophilo-German that a great deal of the patriotic pose of the Hohenzollerns and their royal and princely confederates is nothing but humbug; that their principal aim is the annexation of land "which they have neither sown nor plowed"; that they see in the Baltic Provinces a fertile territory which is as large as entire Southern Germany, in brief, a precious supplement to their present estate.

Knowing in their heart of hearts how loathed their rule is by the "small nations," to whom they like to appear in the first critical hours of transition in the shining armor of "liberators," the Germans have made up their mind to use Poland, the Ukraine, the Baltic Provinces, and Finland as a kind of sandbag to keep off the baccilli of Bolshevism of which they are more afraid than of the bullets of the former army of the Czar. "No immigration to Germany" has become one of their favorite slogans in their great eastern "War of Liberation."

Well, there will soon be again a solid eastern front, formed by the Yanks, Japs, Czechoslovaks, British, and French; there will be a forced "emigration" of Germans on an enormous scale on both fronts, and the fleeing troops on the eastern will be begged to take with them the 2,000,000 German farmers who have been "colonized" throughout the Russian Empire from the time of Catherine II., the cousin and imperial agent of Frederick II.

NOTE—A diplomatic dispatch received in Washington on Sept. 10, 1918, stated that the plans of the Berlin authorities for dividing the Baltic Provinces of Russia into administrative districts had just been executed. Henceforth these regions are to constitute a single " military administration of the Baltic Provinces," with its seat at Riga. They are placed under the authority of the commanding officer of the town and of von Goesler, the Administration Chief, who, up to the present, has been head of the administration in Courland. The administration of the provinces includes a provincial administration for Courland, with its seat at Mittau; an administration for Livonia, with its seat at Riga, and another for Esthonia, with its seat at Reval. The head of each provincial administration is called the " Captain of the Province."

The town of Riga constitutes in itself a special administration district, placed under the authority of the Captain of the town. Lithuania constitutes the military administration of Lithuania, the seat of which is Vilna. The territory under the command of Lieut. Col. von Harbou, with whom is associated the Privy Councilor, Tisler, as head of administration, is divided into five districts.

# The Shearing of Rumania

## Further Details of the Bucharest Treaty and Subsidiary Treaties Imposed by Germany

*The following summary of the concessions exacted from Rumania by the Central Powers is based on sources vouched for by the Paris Temps, which published it July 30, 1918, and from which it is here translated for* CURRENT HISTORY MAGAZINE:

WHEN the invaders entered Rumania they found in the occupied territory more than 3,500,000 tons of cereals or oleaginous grains, the whole vineyard crop of 1916, a large number of fowls, and a stock of domestic animals amply sufficient for the food and farming needs of the country. They left only enough to preserve the life of the inhabitants, without whom there would be no laborers to cultivate the fields. The rest was divided into two parts; about one-half was confiscated, the other half requisitioned, the requisition price being fixed at two-thirds of the market price. The losses thus inflicted on the owners are estimated at more than $400,000,000.

For the year then current the Rumanian people were authorized to consume an average of 500 grams (about 17 ounces) of Indian corn per head each day. In certain regions all the provisions were requisitioned, and the peasants have had to purchase back, at increased prices, enough food to preserve life. The invaders also requisitioned 70 per cent. of the wine and fruit, and the total production of meat, wool, eggs, milk, butter, and cheese. The German military authorities have fixed the number of eggs that each hen is expected to lay and the quantity of milk that each cow must furnish under penalty of a fine to be paid by the owner or the community.

The Germans have realized great profits—1,000 per cent. and more—by reselling to the Rumanian people a portion of the products seized, and this system continues to be applied on a large scale. Thus Rumania has to give up to the Central Powers 125,000 tons of wheat at the requisition price, and has to buy an equivalent amount in Bessarabia at the market price; this operation alone entails a loss of $14,000,000. As the treaties of Bucharest stipulate that all the products of Rumanian farms and vineyards shall be sold to the Central Powers for nine years at prices fixed by the conquerors, it may be seen that the ruinous experiences of the recent past are merely a foretaste of what the future has in store.

All the requisitions levied in Rumania by the invaders have to be paid for by the Rumanian Government under the peace treaty. The Government must also become responsible for the notes issued by the invaders through a German bank at Bucharest, authorized by them to issue paper money. The Rumanian State likewise must advance the sums necessary to pay for the future purchases of the Central Powers, for the

American troops in Paris on July 4, 1918, parading along the Avenue
du Président Wilson (formerly the Avenue du Trocadéro)

French soldiers repairing a subterranean trench which was demolished by the enemy's shells

A tunnel in the Verdun region constructed by the Germans and
captured by the French

latter are not in a position to square their accounts with industrial products delivered to Rumanian consumers. The monetary situation is so disturbed by these extortions that the price paid to Rumanian farmers for their wheat represents less than $1.40 per quintal, (220 pounds.) Besides, the Rumanian State finds itself a " debtor " to the Central Powers for the board and keep of their troops of occupation and prisoners of war; this is the object of the loan, estimated at $500,000,000, which Rumania is about to negotiate at Berlin and Vienna.

After the invasion the lands were divided into three categories. In four departments of Wallachia, in the Dobrudja, regions considered to be in the army zone, the German military authorities are exploiting the resources without rendering an account to anybody, even to the sequestration administrators named by the German economic organization. It is forbidden to go and inspect any place, even since the signing of peace. Back of the army zone a part of the land has been turned over to German and Austrian organizations. The estates are exploited in behalf of the absent owners. The accounts, under control of a German bank in Bucharest, are kept in such a way that the proprietors pay for the support of numerous German and Austrian agents, and become the debtors, as far as possible, of those who occupy their property. When the land is used for cereals or livestock it is easy to make the accounts show a deficit, either through fraud or through the ridiculous prices fixed for requisitions. But the forests themselves are not immune from these methods; a case is cited of a Rumanian company in Bucharest that has been invited to hand over $76,000 to the German Kommandantur for the trouble which the Germans have taken to cut a great quantity of wood.

Finally, some lands have been claimed by the German and Austrian authorities —by reason of work done on them—for periods extending beyond the declaration of peace. When a farm is given to an individual whose services the invader wishes to recompense, it is generally at a very moderate rental, and certain proprietors have thus seen their revenues reduced by one-half. It should be added, however, that the proprietors have often succeeded in bettering or canceling disadvantageous contracts by handing an appropriate bribe to the occupying authorities.

The invaders have dismounted and carried away the motors and machinery belonging to Rumanians or to other allies. Most of this machinery has been sent to Bulgaria, where an industry is being built up with Austro-German capital. Besides, courts set up by the occupying authorities have adjudged retrospective suits which German firms brought against Rumanians. These suits, sometimes based on very old claims that were long ago liquidated, have been the more advantageous for the Germans in that the Rumanians in many cases were not aware of the claims filed against them.

In the cities the homes of officials, officers, and other residents who have fled into Moldavia have been pillaged openly. A great number of other houses have been plundered under various pretexts: requisitions, perquisitions, &c. Germans of every rank have participated in the thefts. It was noticed especially that a Prince of Schaumburg, belonging to the German Legation at Bucharest, personally directed the pillage of houses in which he had been received before the war, and whose precious objects he knew about. In the houses inhabited by enemy officers the devastations and orgies were worst of all. The only residences spared are those occupied by Turkish officers.

The cities thus despoiled have none the less been hit with forced contributions for the maintenance of German troops. Municipalities have even been obliged to provide furniture to install Germans in houses which other Germans had emptied. These various exactions are added to the general contributions which the German command has levied upon Rumania, one amounting to $50,000,000, and the other, announced during the peace negotions, reaching $80,000,000. The whole is an instructive sample of a German peace.

# Movement for Polish Independence

## Declaration at Versailles Supported by a National Polish Movement

THE declaration of the representatives of the Entente Powers at Versailles, June 3, 1918, favoring " a free and independent Poland with access to the sea," produced a profound impression throughout Poland. In the Warsaw State Council M. Swiezynski on June 26 spoke upon this declaration on behalf of the Inter-Party Club. It must be remembered that this club, which consists of fifty members, (the total of the State Council being 107 members,) represents three-quarters of the elected members of the council. M. Swiezynski spoke as follows:

At the same time, when the entire world has recognized the Polish question as an international problem and the Polish national and political aims as just, and their realization as a condition of the new order of the world, an order based on right and liberty; at the time when the solemn declaration, (the declaration of Versailles,) by responsible statesmen has given these aims positive and collective expression—at this moment nothing has taken place on Polish territory to show that the powers which have today the practical possibility of confirming their promises by deeds are guided by a real intention of restoring the Polish State.

### The Inter-Party Club at Warsaw published the following declaration:

Taking into consideration the declaration made after the meeting of the Prime Ministers of France, England, and Italy, in which it was stated that the " creation of an independent and united Polish State, with access to the sea, is one of the conditions of a just and lasting peace and of the rule of right in Europe," the undersigned parties belonging to the Inter-Party Club declare that the above statement will meet with a sincere response in the soul of the Polish Nation, the nation which during more than a century of slavery has always longed for the restoration of Poland, (here is a space left by the censor,) independent and united, (here again a blank space.)

The Inter-Party Union of Galicia, which consists of three democratic parties, (the National Democrats, the People's Party, and the National Union,) has made the following statement:

The Warsaw Cabinet, which was appointed by the Regency Council under the leadership of M. Steczkowski, but which remains in complete dependence upon the foreign authorities, has issued a statement directed against the declaration of the meeting at Versailles, the declaration which recognized that the creation of a united and independent Poland with free access to the sea was one of the conditions and guarantees of a lasting peace.

Such a step on the part of the so-called Polish Government of Warsaw, the result of following foreign interests and demands, is not only in contradiction of the promises made by M. Steczkowski when he accepted the Premiership, but also it is in contradiction of the national interests, for it is degrading to the national dignity, it ignores the natural and historic rights of the nation, and is in conflict with the deepest desires and rightful claims of the great mass of the Polish Nation. The real sentiments and real will of the Polish people found their expression in motions, passed with the greatest enthusiasm as the essence of Polish national policy on the 28th of May, by the joint meeting of the Polish Deputies to the Diet and to the Vienna Parliament. The Polish Nation has accepted the Declaration of Versailles, the declaration which is identical with the motions of May, 1917, and which is in accordance with the manifesto of President Wilson, as a step toward a just solution of the Polish problem, which insists on the international significance of this problem. (Ten lines are deleted by the censor.)

The elected members of the Warsaw State Council, three-quarters of whom belong to the Inter-Party Club, the Inter-Party Circle of the Kingdom of Poland, and the Inter-Party Union in Galicia, represent the overwhelming majority of Poles.

# Montenegro's Situation

## Why the People Wish to Give Up Their Dynasty for a Greater Jugoslav State

### By V. R. SAVITCH

[OF THE SERBIAN CONSUL GENERAL'S STAFF IN THE UNITED STATES]

THE position of Montenegro in the present world struggle is a paradox. While a most conspicuous feature of the war is the fight for independence of the smaller nations, Montenegro is fighting for a quite opposite end. Montenegro wants to lose her independence, to be relieved of an honorable position as a separate nation, and to find peace and prosperity by merging her existence with that of Serbia in the larger racial union of a free Jugoslavia. As there is reason in every paradox, so the Montenegrin paradox is based on an irrefutable logic which to be perfectly understood requires from the reader only a little patience and attention.

First of all, Montenegro is not really a distinct nation, large or small, but a part of the Serbian Nation, possessing a distinctly Serbian national consciousness. A Montenegrin is rather proud of his local name and history, but he likes you to understand that his very pride is imbedded in his larger Serbian national sentiment. He prides himself on the fact that, among all other Serbs, he has never failed in his national duty and has sacrificed more than any other part of the nation for the common Serbian ideals. Foreigners visiting the Balkans have been surprised to find all Jugoslavs with a very highly developed national consciousness, but the Montenegrins occupy the first rank in that regard. Every Montenegrin is a warrior, and there is scarcely any Montenegrin family without its own historian. The historian in this case is a bard who delights his audience (usually his own household) with the stories of the warlike achievements of his forefathers, of his clan and his nation, in which a record of his own deeds and of his living relatives is very often interwoven. This gives rise to the ever-growing ballads recited with the accompaniment of the gooslé, (the national instrument,) and the great ruler of Montenegro, Bishop Radé, said: "There is no house with men in it where the gooslé is not heard."

The Black Mountain produces few of the commodities of life. A generation ago commerce was a rather shameful occupation for a son of Montenegro. His life consisted of making history, i. e., of fighting, and, in his leisure time, in listening to that record of which he was an active and conscious part. For a Montenegrin, being void of any other worldly interest, past and present, merged in his vision, and for the acts of his daily life he always took example from his beloved heroes of the ballads, Marko Kralevitch or Milosh Oblilitch. To say to a Montenegrin that he is equal to Oblilitch is the greatest compliment he can conceive. And Milosh Oblilitch was that Serbian Knight who in the battle of Kossovo in 1389 slew the Turkish Sultan, Murad I.

In the battle of Kossovo the Serbian Empire was defeated, but the Serbian Nation was not subdued. After that battle many a Serbian squire, leaving the fertile plains to the Turk, fled to the Black Mountain, where for five long centuries he never ceased to fight for Serbian freedom. That fight was to him a religious duty, bequeathed by the martyrs of Kossovo, sung by the bards, preached by the Church, and strengthened by examples in every-day life. Therefore, among Serbs he wishes to be a Montenegrin, yet he would be offended if a foreigner should take him solely for a Montenegrin; he does not recognize any value in the existence of Montenegro apart from a larger Serbian life and ideals. Montenegro has been a stronghold of Serbian tradition and liberty for five centuries. Like a rock, it withstood all the onslaughts of the infidels. And now, when the Turkish tide has definitely receded, Montenegro desires to be relieved of her duty, as there is no reason to continue to be a sentinel on the mount, and demands to be merged into the national unity of Jugoslavia with all the Serbs, Croats, and Slovenes; such must be the outcome if Europe is to find peace.

## BEGINNING OF THE NATION

Historically, Montenegro is a continuation of the life of mediaeval Zeta, which for centuries was an integral part of the Serbian Kingdom, or, rather, that very kingdom. In reality the Serbian State life started in Zeta around the Lake of Scutari. Serbian independence was first asserted in the Black Mountain after a defeat of the Byzantine army by the first Serbian ruler, Voislav. In the tenth century his son received from Rome the title of King and made Scutari the first Serbian capital. The founder of the greatest Serbian dynasty, Stephan Nemanja, was born in Zeta, which remained always a part of the kingdom of that dynasty. The Serbian Emperor, Dushan, who ruled in Zeta as heir apparent to the throne, in the fourteenth century decentralized his empire in mighty feudal provinces. After his death Zeta, in the second half of the fourteenth century, emerged as an independent State ruled by two Princes, Balsha I. and Balsha II. Balsha II. bequeathed the throne to Ivan Cruojeovitch. He was succeeded by his son George, who vainly resisted the Turks, but who was obliged to abandon to their invasion a greater part of his dominion, and in 1496 crossed the Adriatic in search of help and refuge in Italy, where he died without an heir. The remaining part of Zeta, consisting of the unconquerable Black Mountain, continued its resistance to the Turks and received the present name of Montenegro later on in the seventeenth century.

During many centuries, until 1851, the Government of Montenegro was represented by a confederation of clans, each independently governed by a chieftain elected by a popular assembly of all male members of the clan. The unity of those clans was expressed by a Bishop, whom all the clans recognized as their spiritual head. But in order to avoid jealousy the Bishop came from different clans in turn, or indifferently from other Serbian provinces under the Turk.

## THE SERBIAN CHURCH

Although by that time Serbian State life had been completely annihilated by the Turks, yet there remained an institution representing national unity and keeping alive the memory of the Serbian Empire. This was the Serbian Church, with its patriarch at Ipek. The Montenegrin Bishops journeyed to Ipek to be consecrated by the patriarchs, thus deriving their authority from the highest Serbian spiritual authority. When the Patriarchate of Ipek was abolished the Montenegrin Bishops found their way to Russia to be consecrated by the Russian Church. These Bishops exercised no authority in civil or military matters. Their sole functions were to appoint the priests for every clan. Taxes were never collected; when the last Bishop Radé attempted to collect a tax of 20 cents from every household, in 1847, he himself and his agents were expelled from the domains of many clans.

From the beginning of the eighteenth century the line of Bishops became fixed in the family of Njegosh-Petrovitch owing to the greater authority which the first Bishops of that family acquired by their virtues and wisdom. Bishop Peter I., after his death, was proclaimed a saint, and until recently his name carried religious and spiritual authority among the Montenegrins. The jealousy of the other clans was not awakened, because the clan of Njegosh was one of the smallest. Besides Peter I., venerated as a saint, this line of Bishops gave to the Serbian Nation Radé Petrovitch-Njegosh, greatest of all Serbian poets, with whom ended the line of the Montenegrin Bishops in 1851.

Greek Orthodoxy being the religion of Montenegro, the Bishops were celibates and chose for successors the most talented youths of their family, not being bound by rules or rights of succession.

This period of the Montenegrin history, for simplicity of life, stern virtues, and heroic struggles with the enemy, may be fairly compared with the period when the Judges ruled in Israel. It was a time of which their poets said:

Oh, for other nations of the world to see Glorious this Cross still never vanquished! They with folded arms would not lazily stand Whilst for Cross you suffer untold agony; Neither should they as barbarians you brand, For, whilst they slept, you bravely perished.

The last Bishop Radé, who led a more worldly life than his predecessors, appointed as his successor his nephew, Danilo; he refused to enter the Church and assumed the title of Prince in 1851. He left no son and was succeeded in 1860 by his nephew Nicholas, the present ruler of Montenegro.

## UNDER PRINCE NICHOLAS

During this reign Montenegro has greatly changed. The simple organization of patriarchal clans was replaced by a modern State administration, and the warlike tribesmen, among whom the family feuds threatened the unity and welfare of the people, were welded into a single community. Montenegro doubled and tripled her territory, her independence was recognized by all the European States, and from a principality she has been elevated to the rank of kingdom. Owing to improved communications, Montenegro came in contact with the outer world, and all the spiritual currents of the life of modern nations found their way there.

In 1861 Prince Nicholas married a beautiful girl of a notable Montenegrin family, and she gave him a numerous progeny—three sons and seven daughters; the latter indeed brought fortune to the Petrovitch dynasty. His eldest daughter, Zorka, in 1883 was wedded to Peter Karageorgevitch, the present King of Serbia. Two others, Militza and Stana, married Grand Dukes of Russia. Ana married a German, Prince Battenburg, and Helen, the most beautiful and most popular of all, became the Queen of Italy. The youngest, Xeniya, and Vera are unmarried.

Prince Nicholas began his reign in the simple traditional way of his predecessors. During the first decade he dreamed and sang only of the union of Montenegro and Serbia. Thus, in 1866, he began negotiations with the Serbian Prince, Michael, with that end in view. In a letter to Prince Michael he thus poetically expressed himself in regard to the time when unity should be achieved: " I shall take a gun in my hand and be a sentinel at thy palace gate." But later this romantic attitude gave way to different feelings and ambitions. In the war against Turkey, in 1876-78, Montenegro doubled her territory. Prince Nicholas was then very highly esteemed by all Serbians; although he could not be compared as a poet to his granduncle, Bishop Radé, yet he was recognized as a bard of no mean merit, and one of his patriotic songs was accepted as a national hymn by all Serbians. As a leader of his mountaineers he was lauded as a prince and patriot. In view of the developing struggle in Serbia against that unpopular and autocratic rule of the Obrenovitch dynasty, he might have aspired to secure the Serbian throne for his heirs. He attained the zenith of his fortune when Emperor Alexander III. of Russia, on the occasion of a visit of Prince Nicholas in 1888, honored him in an official toast as " his sole friend."

## NATION'S CHANGED ATTITUDE

But the last generation has witnessed a great change in this respect. Prince Nicholas ruled in the old autocratic way. During fifty years of his reign he made no concessions to the new democracy which was filtering into Montenegro from Europe. He neglected national education, and the scanty resources of the country were rather monopolized by himself, his family, and some few courtiers. There was no line of demarkation between his private purse and the budget of the State, and he was many times accused of having appropriated funds sent by Russia for the relief of povertystricken Montenegrins. Emigration of Montenegrins increased from year to year, but the private wealth of King Nicholas was enormously augmented.

Soon the lustre of his aureole faded, and King Nicholas today is regarded by his people as a petty, Oriental tyrant, vainglorious and cruel, caring only for the interests of his own family. This judgment prevails among the younger Montenegrin generation, who regard him, moreover, as an insincere Serb and a shrewd politician, always exploiting national sentiment for the promotion of his family ambition. They assert that all his professions of fidelity to national ideals are imposed upon him by the national consciousness of the Montenegrins, but he always has foiled the realization of any practical scheme for unity through delays and subterfuges. They condemn his national as well as his internal policy. Some believe his character was the same from the very beginning of his career, while others incline to the belief that he became greedy and ambitious in his old age, when his judgment grew impaired under the pressure of ever-increasing vanity and the inordinate ambition of his numerous family. His sons obtained no proper education and enjoyed no popularity in Montenegro, and his unmarried daughter, Xeniya, is credited with being a domestic tyrant and his real ruler.

In 1905 King Nicholas granted a Constitution to Montenegro, and since that date he has come into direct conflict with a younger generation imbued with democratic ideals. He tried persecutions and brought the country to the verge of revolution, from which Montenegro was spared owing only to the external events which absorbed the entire attention and demanded all the energy of the Montenegrins.

In the crisis created by the annexation of Bosnia and Herzegovina in 1908, as well as in the Balkan wars of 1912 and 1913, Montenegro fought on the side of Serbia. As a result of the last wars, the Montenegrin territory was increased again, and the barrier which separated Montenegro from Serbia was at last annihilated. This proved a new source of trouble to King Nicholas. The national sentiment of the Montenegrins was aroused against any boundary being set between the two sister countries. They protested and demanded absolute union with Serbia, and in 1913 the Montenegrin Parliament urged this solution of the internal national problem. The negotiations with Serbia were conducted in 1914

with that object in view. Meanwhile the world war broke out.

## MONTENEGRO BETRAYED

There was no treaty of alliance signed between Serbia and Montenegro, but national sentiment prompted the Montenegrin Government to declare war on Austria-Hungary and Germany as soon as Serbia was attacked. Fighting at the side of Serbia, Montenegro endured the same hardships and sustained equal sacrifices with Serbia. But the end of the Montenegrin campaign was wholly different. Serbia saved intact her honor and as much as possible of her army, never suing for peace. But when the trail of the Serbian Army was still on Montenegrin soil the Montenegrin Government tried to obtain peace from the enemy. Confusion followed, and, as a consequence, although peace was not obtained, the Montenegrin Army and Government remained in the country, with the exception of King Nicholas, who hastily fled to Italy with the Prime Minister and some few of his personal entourage. The Allies, especially Great Britain, were estranged from King Nicholas by his action regarding peace, and particularly because of the demobilization of his army.

The Motenegrins who were able to escape to friendly countries are deeply indignant over what they call the betrayal of Montenegro and of their national honor. By this surrender to the enemy the Montenegrins feel that their history was sullied, and in consequence King Nicholas and his family lost the last vestige of prestige that yet adhered to them. In this situation he tried to place the responsibility for his acts on his Prime Minister, Lazar Mijuskovitch, but the latter vigorously rebuked him in an open letter published in France and Italy May 20, 1916, and, communicating with all the allied Governments, he accused King Nicholas of treason and double dealing. He concluded as follows:

I believe that all the sins of your Majesty, of your family, and your entourage, and of myself as well, cannot be attributed to the Serbian people of Montenegro, who have always fulfilled their Serbian duty in resisting their enemies and in sacrificing everything for the realization of the Serbian ideals. Therefore, I believe that there will come out from their midst men who will not allow that people should be made responsible before the world for sins not their own, and that the Montenegrins shall enter unsullied the Commonwealth of Serbia, as they have deserved it by their century-long struggle for freedom and unity of the whole Serbian Nation.

## A FORMAL PROPOSAL

After the resignation of Lazar Mijuskovitch in May, 1916, King Nicholas intrusted the Premiership to Andrey Radovitch. The latter, well aware of the feeling of the people and the disposition of the Allies, considered that King Nicholas and his dynasty could be saved only through a union of Serbia and Montenegro, and by the fusion of both dynasties, Karageorgevitch and Petrovitch. Therefore, on Aug. 6, 1916, he submitted to King Nicholas a formal proposal for his approval. In it Mr. Radovitch said:

The union of Montenegro and Serbia with the rest of the Jugoslav lands will entail the fusion of the two dynasties which have unquestionably in the past rendered great services to the Serb and Slav cause; the circumstance that the grandson of your Majesty is today Prince Regent of Serbia facilitates the execution of this project.

Your Majesty, after a reign of almost sixty years, and his Majesty the illustrious King Peter, because of his advanced age and frail state of health, both deserve to rest, so that you may watch with a glad and quiet mind, like true fathers of the country, the development of the young Jugoslav State under the guidance of the grandson of your Majesty, the son of his Majesty King Peter. The young Jugoslav sovereign would be surrounded by the Princes Petrovitch-Njegosh and Karageorgevitch. Her Majesty Queen Milena [King Nicholas's wife] would occupy the highest place of honor in the State, that of Queen Mother.

The succession to the throne could be most equitably arranged, viz., as follows: First, Prince Danilo, (heir to the Montenegrin throne,) then the descendants of the present Prince Alexander, and then, alternately, the other Princes of the two dynasties.

The King delayed from day to day any reply to this project, and a second memorandum was submitted to him on Jan. 11, 1917, expressing the positive request for an immediate decision, failing which the resignation of the Cabinet would follow. This document, which was followed by the resignation of the Cabinet, concluded in the following terms:

In the memorandum of Aug. 6 I have drawn attention to the other reasons which make it our duty to labor for the unification of the Serbian people and eventually of all the Jugoslavs; in this way Serbia, as well as Montenegro, would bring her historic mission to an end and enter, on a footing of equality with the other Serbian lands, and, in the given case, with the Jugoslav lands also, into one great State.

As I am convinced that this line of action is the only salutary one, both for the Montenegrins, who are profoundly convinced that, of all the Serbs, they stand to be the greatest gainers by the union, and for the dynasty as well as for the respect and esteem which your Majesty enjoys among the Serbs, the Slavs, and the Allies, I pray your Majesty to take into consideration that I cannot work in a different direction, and that if your Majesty does not approve of this action I shall be compelled to beg your Majesty graciously to accept my resignation.

With the most profound devotion, I am your Majesty's obedient servant,

A. RADOVITCH.

## REPLY OF NICHOLAS

Mr. Radovitch resigned, but immediately organized among the Montenegrins a movement for national unity without paying any regard longer to the views and interests of King Nicholas. This activity met with the greatest success, but King Nicholas sought to oppose the movement. On May 15, 1917, he submitted to his Cabinet a note which reads:

Sometime ago a very little group of unsatisfied men, gathered in a committee under A. Radovitch's Presidency, adopted the right to speak in the name of the Montenegrin people. This committee took the liberty not long ago to apply to the Government of Russia and of the United States. The royal Montenegrin Government is hereby compelled to disown this committee, which hasn't any right to appear as the interpreter of the Montenegrins. The Montenegrins also consider the Royal Government of Montenegro, which is still acknowledged by the Allies, as the only representative of their interests, of their national aspirations and faithful guardian of their political individuality.

But the Nicholas Cabinet, formed after the resignation of Mr. Radovitch, under the Presidency of General Matanovitch, itself refused to indorse the note of its sovereign. In a memorandum of May 15, 1917, the Ministers, in setting forth the reasons for their action, vigorously protested against King Nicholas's suggestion that Montenegro wished to continue her life as a separate nation. They said:

The status quo ante is not possible in the Balkans. The national consciousness for unity in all the classes of our people is awake and expansive. The idea of unity has become a creed—a religion of the masses. This faith has been created by the thousands of national martyrs throughout the centuries and by the blood shed in rivers on all our battlefields.

It is clear that all self-exclusion, then, is in opposition and is opposing every serious and sincere mutual understanding with Serbia, the necessity of which in several instances we have apprised your Majesty. Also we approached you with the proposal explaining the fact that it is high time negotiations should be commenced with Serbia. The same proposal we again at this moment bring before your Majesty, firmly believing that your Majesty shall accept and give your authorization for it.

Bearing in mind the above-mentioned factors, which are clear as the living truth, and which picture the future of the whole of our people, the Royal Government find that the safety of our smaller country and her national dynasty is coupled with the work which is in harmony with the ideal of the people, and therefore it is not able to accept the form of the note mentioned, not wishing to create the impression that Montenegro wants division and separation from her brothers in blood and language.

## RESIGNATION OF CABINET

As a consequence of King Nicholas refusing to give to the Matanovitch Cabinet a mandate to start negotiations for union with Serbia, the Cabinet sent in its resignation, which reads in part:

Since the very day on which were pulled down the centuries-old barriers between Montenegro and her brothers by blood and language, and especially between her and Serbia, the problem of State reconstruction was imposed upon her. The new situation demanded a new form of the State. The present separation, being obsolete and impracticable, has become impossible in the future. My Cabinet, sharing with me this point of view, prepared a program with which your Majesty expressed his complete agreement.

Your Majesty, it follows from every-thing set above that the main task of the Government was the reconstruction of our relation with Serbia in preparing a concrete proposal for reunion, which, after it should be accepted by both parties here, should be approved by competent institutions of our countries after our return into the fatherland. The preparation of this proposal could not be delayed, as our relations to our allies depend on it, who wish to create a strong Jugoslav State as a bulwark against the German onrush. The road for improvement of our relations with the Allies leads directly over this internal Serbian question, by which your royal Majesty's Government has to give a measure of its sincerity and loyalty. Many times my administration has put orally before your Majesty these weighty reasons, requesting you to give it the necessary mandate for the preparation of such a project in concert with the representatives of our sister, Serbia. In requesting it the royal Government was inspired by a broad view of our national policy, as the only way to a good end, otherwise it is fatally condemned to take a road of anti-national aims and of a policy of separation which must bring catastrophe to the country and the dynasty. Inspired by such motives, the royal Government on May 15 of this year put before your Majesty a written memorandum asking that your Majesty should please to give it the much-desired mandate. Its hope, to our regret, has been frustrated. The bad consequences following it have undermined the last vestiges of prestige enjoyed by it, since your refusal could not be interpreted otherwise than as a wavering between the two belligerent camps in regard to international politics.

Besides this, your Majesty has judged opportune to touch upon some big and delicate questions a solution of which would be contrary not only to the spirit of this Government's program, but also to the Constitution.

The telegram your Majesty has sent to his Majesty the Italian King is a negation of our Jugoslav ideal, which demands one and inseparable Jugoslavia. The Royal Government must not pass in silence this act of your Majesty.

Your Majesty, with deep regrets and soul pain I see that the execution of a national policy is impossible where the dynastic reasons prevail.

In drawing consequences from the above facts it remains to me to tender my resignation to the Presidency of your royal Government, sincerely thanking you for the confidence granted to me.

Your Majesty's devoted
BRIGADIER MILE MATANOVITCH,
*President of the Montenegrin Government.*
Neuilly, June 5, 1917.

## THE KING DISOWNED

Since that time the policy of King Nicholas has been denounced by all Montenegrins regardless of party differences, and all divisions of parties have united with the organization started by Radovitch. King Nicholas was unable to find any Montenegrin of standing to accept the portfolio of Prime Minister. At last he chose Eugene Popovitch, born in Spalato, Dalmatia, who had never become a Montengrin citizen, had never lived there, and had visited Montengro only once, in 1910, on the occasion when Prince Nicholas assumed the title of King. Likewise his colleagues and diplomatic representatives appointed to the allied countries are men who never played any part in the political or social life of the country, and who were without followers, friends, or interest in Montenegro.

The Montenegrins have resolutely reached a decision. For them the union of Serbia and Montenegro is already achieved in the present adversity, and they have resolved to defend its future with all means at their disposal, whether King Nicholas desires it or not. As to him, the best course seems to be not to push matters to extremes, and to revert to Radovitch's project, provided he does not wish to die an exile from the country over whose destiny he has presided so long.

The meaning and importance of Montenegro in the Serbian national life can be briefly put thus: Montenegro represents a last reserve which the Serbian Nation is drawing upon whenever its life is at its lowest ebb. When Byzantium and Bulgaria were in the height of their power, Serbian independence could assert itself only in the fastness of the Black Mountain. When the Serbian might was at its full power, Montenegro, owing to her scanty economic resources, could play no rôle and was relegated to a secondary position. But, again, when a new crisis broke out and Serbian life reached the nadir of its misery under the prolonged Turkish yoke, Montenegro reassumed her full importance and brilliantly discharged her function of being the guardian of Serbian liberty and tradition.

> They rose to where their sovereign eagle sails.
> They kept their faith, their freedom on the height.
> Chaste, frugal, savage, armed by day and night.
>          * * * Rough rockthorne
> Of Freedom! warriors beating back the swarm
> Of Turkish Islam for five hundred years.
> Great Tsernagora, never since thine own
> Black ridges drew the cloud and brake the storm
> Has breathed a race of mightier mountaineers.    —Alfred Lord Tennyson.

The Montenegrins argue that they have no historical and economic basis for an independent State life in the new conditions that will be after this war. They demand unity because they have nobly played their part and ended their task. But the present writer believes that their part is far from being ended, and that they will have in the Serbian Commonwealth a still, if possible, nobler task. Jugoslavia can be nothing but a democracy. But there are different democracies, with lower and higher ideals. The Montenegrins have still preserved in their social and family life stern virtues of chastity, frugality, bravery, and loyalty to higher moral ideals. Their presence in the Serbian or Jugoslav Commonwealth will be a sure guarantee that their democracy will not sink to base commercialism or anarchistical monstrosities.

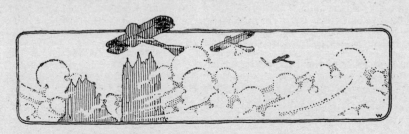

# Sinkings of American Merchantmen

## Methods and Deeds of Our Naval Crews on Armed Steamships in Fighting German Submarines

### By ALLAN WESTCOTT

[DEPARTMENT OF ENGLISH, UNITED STATES NAVAL ACADEMY]

COMMERCE warfare is essentially the weapon of the weaker naval belligerent, and from the outset of the war Germany has made this her primary means of attack upon her enemy supreme on the sea. At first she employed the traditional method of commerce raiders and cruisers in distant waters; it was only when these were driven to cover or destroyed that she resorted to the submarine.

But the possibilities of this new weapon, as she soon discovered, were greatly limited, if it were employed with due regard for the rights of neutrals and the traditional requirements of international law. Guarantees of visit and search, safety to passengers and crew, effective blockade within clearly defined and reasonable limits—all these cobwebs of legalism Germany accordingly brushed aside, at first with some stealth, but openly and defiantly in her "unrestricted warfare" proclamation of Feb. 1, 1917. This declared her adoption of the only method, in fact, by which submarine commerce warfare can be made to yield profitable results—that of sinking on sight in practically unlimited areas. She declared her purpose to shut off commerce with Europe by an immense barred zone, covering nearly the entire Mediterranean and the waters east of a line from Iceland to Cape Finisterre. "The new policy," as President Wilson said in words it is now well to recall, "swept every restriction aside. Vessels of every kind, whatever their flag, their character, their cargo, their destination, were to be ruthlessly sent to the bottom without warning."

The first reply of the United States to this challenge was to arm her ships, the vessels to retain their character as merchantmen, and to defend themselves only if attacked. But this was obviously a half measure, and as the President said in his war message, "ineffectual" against an enemy that not only sunk on sight, but threatened, with what might almost be regarded as a touch of sardonic humor, to treat the gun crews of these ships as pirates and beyond the pale of law. For this compelling motive, among a multitude of other and deeper grievances, we declared war.

The armed guards, thus placed aboard our merchant vessels in a somewhat anomalous relation to the ship's personnel, have, however, remained, and have constituted an important factor in the campaign against the submarine. When the British began to arm their ships, they were able to provide only small crews, sometimes not more than one or two trained gunners, and in the diplomatic situation then existing it was desirable to make these strictly subordinate at all times to the master of the ship, who was ordinarily a member of the Naval Reserve. The United States adopted the more difficult, but more effective, policy of putting aboard enough men to maintain lookouts and man the guns completely both night and day, and gave to the naval officer authority as to when to engage, and control of the fire when in contact with the enemy.

### OUR FIRST ARMED STEAMER

The first vessel to be supplied with an armed guard was the Manchuria of the American Line, which sailed from New York March 16, 1917. The St. Louis, St. Paul, and other transatlantic passenger steamers were also soon provided with crews from the navy, under officers of Lieutenant's or Lieutenant Commander's rank.

But with the declaration of war came

the stiffer problem of immediately extending this protection to as many as possible of the merchantmen in the European service, and supplying crews for the 200 or more ships that the Ordnance Bureau of the Navy soon succeeded in arming with good 3-inch to 6-inch guns. Navy gunners—spotters, trainers, pointers, &c.—are not made in a day, nor was it desirable to cull from the fleet in wartime a great number of its best trained men. A compromise was decided upon by which the chief petty officers in command—for the most part Chief Gunner's Mates, Chief Boatswain's Mates, and Chief Masters at Arms—and a nucleus of experienced seamen were taken from the fleet, the crews being then filled out from the training stations ashore. At these stations the recruits had such gunnery and other drill as time permitted, but it was inevitable that some of the youths who fought our guns in the war zone were afloat on their first voyage. It was such lads as these, too, who in more than one instance had to take to small boats in bitter Winter weather a hundred or more miles from land, as in the case of the Actaeon, sunk by torpedo off Cape Finisterre, Nov. 24, 1917. The armed guard boat, with twenty gunners and four of the ship's crew, without a compass and without the armed guard commander, who had fallen overboard and been picked up by another boat, sailed and drifted off the coast for eleven days until at last they came ashore at a little hamlet in Spain with three men dead from exposure and exhaustion and another who afterward died.

Yet the crews were made of the right stuff, and were quickly imbued with the fine standards of the service whose uniform they wore. It is sufficient evidence of their quality that, while many an armed ship has been torpedoed by surprise, and while many a submarine has been driven off or disconcerted in its attack by quick, accurate fire from a ship's guns, there are at present only two instances of an American ship with gun crew aboard which has been overcome in a stand-up, give-and-take fight by the gunfire of a submarine.

## TWO MEMORABLE ENCOUNTERS

Each of these instances carries with it a stirring tale. The tanker Campana, attacked on Aug. 6 of last year, surrendered only when her ammunition was exhausted after four hours and ten minutes of fighting. She was hit four times and set on fire. At the end of three hours, seeing the ship was outranged, the Captain wished to surrender, but the gun crew held on as long as they had shells. The submarine afterward took the Captain, Chief Gunner Delaney, and four of the naval crew aboard and carried them to Germany, where at last reports they are still prisoners of war.

The other ship, the tanker Moreni, was bound for Genoa with a cargo of gasoline when she was attacked in the U-boats' favorite hunting ground off Gibraltar. In command of the armed guard was Chief Petty Officer Copassaki, a Cretan by birth, an American by allegiance, and a navy fighter by virtue of inherent character and twenty-two years' service. It adds nothing to the pleasure of such an affair to engage from the topside of a cargo of high combustibles; yet this commander and crew fought till their steering gear was shot away and their ship swinging in wild and lurid circles, leaving behind a path of flames. "Come on," cried Copassaki, when they at last decided to abandon ship, "here's a chance to make a name for yourselves," and he brought up a machine gun to mount in the boat's bow. The vessel was still under headway and the boat capsized when it struck the water, spilling gun and gunners overboard and spoiling what promised to be an extraordinary encounter between a machine gun and a submarine.

"We swam around," writes Copassaki in his report, (from which the machine gun episode is omitted as insignificant,) "until we could get to the capsized boat and turn it over. The submarine called the boats alongside and the commander congratulated us, shaking hands with the Captain, and telling us it was the best fight they had ever seen put up by a merchant vessel."

For the men from training stations, and also for the sailors from the clean,

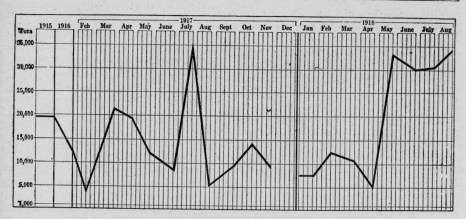

GRAPHIC CHART SHOWING AMERICAN MERCHANT TONNAGE SUNK BY U-BOATS FROM THE
BEGINNING OF 1915 TO THE END OF AUGUST, 1918

well-found, well-regulated ships of our navy, this shift into the merchant service was suffering a sea change, indeed. They went into vessels of every description, from fast liners to wind-jammers and eight-knot tramps, and they sailed to every port of friendly Europe, from Saloniki to the Murmansk coast. They came in for all kinds of experiences, from fighting U-boats to quelling mutinies and unloading cargo when strikes held them up in port. Illustrative of such experiences is that of a boatswain's mate who discovered a gang of Bolshevist stevedores in Archangel plundering a cargo of Red Cross supplies. He presented his case before the local Soviet that evening with vigor and favorable results.

They were thrown in also with the polyglot crews of our rapidly expanding merchant marine—bold fellows enough, or they would not be where they were, and many of them loyal Americans by birth or adoption, but with an element among them sullen and suspiciously neutral. In one ship the frequency of engine troubles, which kept putting the vessel behind the convoy, led to the placing of a guard in the engine room night and day, after which no more ground glass was found in the oil.

According to a clause in the agreement signed by owners of vessels when naval crews were put on board, the owners pledged themselves "to quarter and subsist the armed guard both at sea and in port in a manner satisfactory to the commander of the armed guard without expense to the Government or to the members of the armed guard." This the owners have tried to live up to, but unreliable stewards have sometimes given rise to complaints. Grumbling over grub is a sailor's license, but ordinarily not matter for official report. One grievance, however, was too serious to pass over. "The climax of the food question," so it is stated, "came when we found a wad of hair in the peach stew." To make matters worse, the Captain accused the gunners of inserting the hair.

With crews and officers of the two services thus brought together, it is surprising that more friction has not developed; but it is clearly a case where diplomacy is essential, and it is well for both navy and merchant service to realize that the two are mutually dependent and must get on together. There is a case, indeed, where a nervous Captain objected to target practice lest it shake loose the rivets of his decrepit ship. And there is another case, in which, however, both master and naval officer co-operated, where in the presence of the enemy an excited fireroom party had to be driven below at the point of the pistol. But, in general, the armed guard report usually contains a passage somewhat as follows: "Most cordial relations existed throughout the voyage. The attitude of the ship's officers and crew was all that could be wished." When a vessel is taken over by the navy, the ship's company comes under naval discipline, which in wartime is the only rational state of affairs. With the immense development of our naval auxiliary training stations, it will be possible to supply naval crews for many ships of our new merchant fleet.

## NARRATIVE OF GUN DUELS

The actual work done by the armed guard is well revealed in the reports of their engagements. These of late have become fewer, and the voyages less exciting, partly because there are fewer of the enemy and the ships commonly sail in protected convoy, but partly also because the submarine has learned to avoid surface action with an armed ship. If the vessel is unarmed and out of convoy, she is, of course, thrown upon the U-boat Captain's tender mercy, as illustrated in recent encounters off our coast. Unless she have speed to escape, which may require well above twelve knots, the enemy may bombard her as effectively as his wretchedly bad shooting permits, loot her, and sink her with bombs.

The best narratives are those of the gun duels, of which, including the Campana and Moreni affairs, there are perhaps a dozen in which American vessels have taken part. On June 14, 1917, in the period when it was still deemed expedient to arm sailing vessels and send them into the war zone, the schooner Glynn was sailing quietly through the Mediterranean, protected by two six-pounders and a naval crew of a warrant officer and six men. About twilight a submarine spotted her as an easy victim, opened on her at 4,500 yards, and came in at full speed. Shots splashed close to the Glynn and tore through her sails. The gun crew held their fire until the two craft were on parallel courses at 3,000 yards, and then threw in several rounds in rapid succession, which, in the words of the officer in command, "hit all around her." The submarine went down, and though the vessel was beating through the vicinity all that night, she was not further troubled.

The steamer Navajo on July 4, 1917, was working slowly through a morning mist in the English Channel when two shots, not in celebration of our national anniversary, broke the quiet. A submarine had seen the Navajo's superstructure, and as the mist broke away at the moment she was herself sighted about a mile distant. Then ensued a running chase in which the submarine fired forty rounds and the steamer twenty-seven. Only one of the submarine's shots took effect, striking under the port counter and causing a leak. The twenty-seventh shot from the Navajo hit and burst just forward of the enemy's conning tower, near the ammunition hoist, and caused a second explosion plainly heard on the ship. "The men who were on deck at the guns and had not jumped overboard," so reads the report, "ran aft, the submarine canted forward at an angle of almost 40 degrees, and the propeller could be plainly seen lashing the air." Then she plunged under. On the results of this action skeptical shore authorities would probably pass a doubtful verdict. "There was a submarine in the vicinity," they would say, "and she may have been injured." At all events, from then on the Navajo had a peaceful Fourth of July.

## U-BOATS THAT "HAD ENOUGH"

At nearly midnight on Oct. 30, in the Bay of Biscay, the steamer Borinquen nearly ran over a submarine lying quietly on the surface not a hundred yards off. It seems to have been a mutual surprise. The men at the forward gun were a bit nervous in the ten seconds or more that their gun bore, and did not get in a shot, but the after gun fired as it came in range. The first shot was a miss at 100 yards; the second, at 200 yards, struck the conning tower, and the third hit and exploded. After the fourth shot fired at the U-boat as she lay apparently helpless in the trough of the seas, she went down "stern first in an almost upright position." The Borinquen did not stop to gather more convincing souvenirs. And so it is still said that there is no positive proof that a merchantman's guns have ever sunk a submarine.

As a last instance may be taken the story of the Nyanza, attacked on a Sunday morning at 9:30 on Jan. 13, 1918. A periscope, silver painted, appeared

1,000 yards on the port beam, and a moment later a torpedo was sighted, which cleared the ship by a scant ten feet. The submarine fell rapidly astern, then came to the surface, started her oil engines, and gave chase, opening fire with shrapnel at 7,000 yards, or about four miles. She had guns forward and aft of the conning tower, and yawed as she came on in order to use them both. Altogether she scored five hits out of about 200 shots, fighting cautiously at long range. " She had the range good again at 11:15," says the gun commander, but at that moment the ship's stern gun was also on the target and fired several shots, which caused the submarine to " come broadside on and keel over." Then she disappeared. Whether injured or not, she had had enough.

## ARMING OF SHIPS JUSTIFIED

But the typical encounter is not such as these cited. Ordinarily the only target offered to the ship is the fanlike wake of a periscope sighted for a few seconds as the submarine aims her torpedo, and perhaps seen again as she rises astern to view results. Or the only warning may be the torpedo itself, seen a hundred yards or so from the ship. It is a maxim of the armed guards that there is no such thing as a foolish alarm. The object dimly discerned with the glass may be a bit of wreckage, a rock, a porpoise, a tide riffle, or even a friendly patrol boat. In any case it is safer— and affords good target practice—to take a shot.

It would be almost impossible to estimate the full number of actual engagements, to distinguish the real from the imaginary, or to determine the number of instances in which a submarine has

been driven off, injured or destroyed. Roughly speaking, about 100 American vessels were sunk by submarines up to Aug. 1, 1918. Of these the great majority were unarmed. Considering that by far the greater number of our steamships in submarine-infested waters have been provided with armed guards, it is evident that the ratio of losses to total number in the case of unarmed ships has been far greater than in the case of those carrying guns.

It may be admitted that the arming of merchant vessels is a means of defense of less decisive importance than offensive measures directed toward cutting off the enemy at their bases, and well-developed systems of escort and patrol. Still the guns justify their employment if they serve to keep the submarine beneath the surface, force her to use her torpedoes, and hinder her from securing good position and aim for torpedo attack. To accomplish these objects the guns must at least equal those employed in the more recent types of under-water craft. The Navy Department has, in fact, announced that it is putting guns aboard as heavy as the ship's structure and mounts will stand.

In the recent operations off our coast the enemy has confined his encounters almost entirely to unarmed vessels. This, together with favorable Summer weather, has made it possible to avoid some of the illegalities of submarine warfare, though, as shown by the loss of life in the Carolina sinking, the safety of passengers and crew is by no means duly regarded. The arming of our coastwise vessels may perhaps, therefore, be adopted against methods of Schrecklichkeit which are likely to recur at any time.

# List of American Merchant Ships Sunk by the Enemy

THE following list of 131 American merchant ships sunk by German submarines, raiders, and mines was compiled by CURRENT HISTORY MAGAZINE from news reports covering the whole period from Jan. 28, 1915, when the William P. Frye, the first American vessel, was torpedoed, to Sept. 3, 1918, when the German submarines ceased their operations in American waters. The American gross tonnage loss foots up in round numbers to 344,000, not counting twenty smaller schooners and fishing vessels whose tonnage could not be ascertained, and whose tonnage figures remain blank in the table. Estimating these at 14,000 tons, the total loss is 358,000 tons. The total number of lives lost—counting the missing as lost—is 447.

KEY TO MARKS.—(*) *Sunk by torpedo;* (†) *Sunk by mine;* (‡) *Sunk by a raider;* (§) *Missing.*

| Name. | Date. | Gross Tonnage. | Lives Lost. | Locality. |
|---|---|---|---|---|
| Wm. P. Frye,‡ sailing ship | Jan. 28, 1915 | 3,274 | 0 | South Atlantic. |
| Evelyn,† steamship | Feb. 19, 1915 | 1,963 | 1 | Borkum Island. |
| Carib,† steamship | Feb. 23, 1915 | 2,087 | 3 | North Sea. |
| Greenbrier | Mar. 4, 1915 | 3,331 | 0 | North Sea. |
| Gulflight,* oil steamer | May 1, 1915 | 3,262 | 4 | Scilly Islands. |
| Seaconnet,† or *, schooner | June 18, 1915 | 2,294 | 0 | Yarmouth. |
| Leelanaw,* freighter | July 26, 1915 | 1,924 | 0 | Orkney Islands. |
| Vincent,† sailing ship | Sep. 27, 1915 | 1,604 | 0 | Cape Orloff. |
| Lanao,* steamship | Oct. 28, 1916 | 692 | 0 | Portuguese coast. |
| Columbian,* steamship | Nov. 8, 1916 | 8,579 | 0 | Cape Ortegal. |
| Chemung,* steamship | Nov. 28, 1916 | 3,032 | 0 | Cape de Gata. |
| Housatonic,* steamship | Feb. 3, 1917 | 2,643 | 0 | Scilly Islands. |
| Lyman M. Law,* sailing ship | Feb. 12, 1917 | 1,300 | 0 | Off Sardinia. |
| Algonquin,* steamship | Mar. 12, 1917 | 1,806 | 0 | West of Bishops Rock. |
| Vigilancia,* freighter | Mar. 16, 1917 | 4,115 | 15 | Irish coast. |
| City of Memphis,* freighter | Mar. 17, 1917 | 5,252 | 0 | South of Fastnet. |
| Illinois,* tanker | Mar. 18, 1917 | 5,220 | 0 | Irish coast. |
| Phineas W. Sprague, sailing ship | Mar. 21, 1917 | 800 | 0 | ............ |
| Healdton,* tanker | Mar. 21, 1917 | 4,448 | 21 | North Sea. |
| Aztec,* freighter | Apr. 1, 1917 | 3,725 | 28 | Off Brest. |
| Marguerite, schooner | Apr. 4, 1917 | 1,553 | 0 | 35 miles S. W. Sardinia. |
| Missourian,* steamship | Apr. 5, 1917 | 6,984 | 0 | Near Porto Mauridio. |
| Seward,* freighter | Apr. 7, 1917 | 3,271 | 0 | 20 miles off Banyuls. |
| Abraham Woodward,* schooner | Apr. 22, 1917 | 744 | 0 | ............ |
| Margaret B. Rouss,* schooner | Apr. 27, 1917 | 782 | 2 | 40 miles off Monaco. |
| Vacuum,* steamship | Apr. 28, 1917 | 2,551 | 21 | North coast of Ireland. |
| Rockingham, steamship | May 1, 1917 | 4,365 | 2 | Off Gibraltar. |
| Hilonian,* freighter | May 18, 1917 | 2,921 | 4 | Off Genoa. |
| Francis M.,* sailing ship | May 18, 1917 | 1,229 | 0 | Off Gibraltar. |
| Barbara,* sailing ship | May 24, 1917 | 838 | 0 | English Channel. |
| Dirigo,* sailing ship | May 31, 1917 | 3,005 | 0 | Off Gibraltar. |
| Petrolite,* tanker | June 10, 1917 | 3,710 | 0 | Off Gibraltar. |
| Moreni,* tanker | June 12, 1917 | 4,045 | 2 | Off Gibraltar. |
| Galena,* sailing ship | June 25, 1917 | 1,048 | 0 | Ushant Island. |
| Orleans,* steamship | July 4, 1917 | 2,808 | 4 | Off French coast. |
| Massapequa,* steamship | July 7, 1917 | 3,193 | 0 | Off French coast. |
| Mary V. Bowen,* schooner | July 8, 1917 | 2,153 | 0 | Mediterranean. |
| Kansan,* steamship | July 9, 1917 | 7,913 | 4 | Off French coast. |
| Hildegaard,* schooner | July 10, 1917 | 595 | 0 | English Channel. |
| Grace,* steamship, reported | July 17, 1917 | 4,858 | 3 | Mediterranean. |
| Archbold,* tanker | July 20, 1917 | 8,264 | 5 | Mediterranean. |
| Carmela,* bark | July 27, 1917 | 1,379 | 0 | English Channel. |
| John Hays Hammond,* schooner | July 27, 1917 | 130 | 0 | ............ |
| John Twohy,* schooner | July 27, 1917 | 1,020 | 0 | Off Azores Islands. |
| Motano,* tanker | July 31, 1917 | 2,730 | 24 | English Channel. |
| Campana,* tanker | Aug. 6, 1917 | 3,580 | 0 | 143 miles w. of Ile de Re. |
| Christiane,* bark | Aug. 7, 1917 | 363 | 0 | Near Azores. |

| Name. | Date. | Gross Tonnage. | Lives Lost. | Locality. |
|---|---|---|---|---|
| Carl F. Cressy,* schooner | Aug. 23, 1917 | 898 | 0 | Coast of Spain. |
| Laura C. Anderson,* schooner | Aug. 30, 1917 | 960 | 0 | English waters. |
| Susana,* steamship, reported | Sep. 15, 1917 | 3,613 | 0 | ............ |
| Platuria,* tanker | Sep. 15, 1917 | 3,445 | 9 | Mediterranean. |
| Ann J. Trainer,* schooner | Sep. 16, 1917 | 426 | 0 | Off Brest. |
| Henry Lippit,* schooner | Sep. 23, 1917 | 895 | 0 | ............ |
| Pauline,* bark | Sep. 25, 1917 | 1,327 | 0 | ............ |
| Lewis Luckenbach,* steamship | Oct. 16, 1917 | 3,905 | 11 | English Channel. |
| Jennie E. Richter,* schooner | Oct. 16, 1917 | 647 | 0 | Off Cape Villano, Spain. |
| Antilles,* transport | Oct. 17, 1917 | 6,878 | 70 | French coast. |
| D. N. Luckenbach,* steamship | Oct. 27, 1917 | 2,929 | 5 | Off French coast. |
| Rochester,* steamship | Nov. 2, 1917 | 2,551 | 4 | Off Ireland. |
| Schuylkill,* steamship | Nov. 25, 1917 | 2,206 | 0 | Mediterranean. |
| Acteon,* steamship | Nov. 25, 1917 | 5,000 | 2 | Off Spain. |
| Harry Luckenbach,* steamship | Jan. 6, 1918 | 2,798 | 8 | ............ |
| Julia Frances,* schooner | Jan. 27, 1918 | 183 | 0 | Portuguese coast. |
| Monitor,* sailing ship, reported | Jan. 18, 1918 | .... | 0 | Canary Islands. |
| Owasco,* steamship | Jan. 25, 1918 | 4,580 | 2 | Off Spanish coast. |
| Alamance,* steamship | Feb. 5, 1918 | 4,370 | 6 | Few miles from Liverpool |
| Santa Maria,* tanker, reported | Feb. 28, 1918 | 8,300 | 0 | Off Irish coast. |
| A. E. Whyland,* schooner | Mar. 13, 1918 | 130 | 0 | ............ |
| A. A. Raven,* steamship | Mar. 14, 1918 | 3,405 | 7 | English Channel. |
| Atlantic Sun,* tanker | Mar. 18, 1918 | 2,333 | 2 | Scotch coast. |
| Chattahoochee,* steamship | Mar. 26, 1918 | 5,088 | 0 | English coast. |
| Lake Moor,* steamship | Apr. 11, 1918 | 4,500 | 46 | European waters. |
| City of Pensacola,* steamship | Apr. 29, 1918 | 705 | 0 | ............ |
| Tyler,* steamship | May 2, 1918 | 3,928 | 11 | Off French coast. |
| Wm. Rockefeller,* tanker | May 18, 1918 | 7,157 | 3 | European waters. |
| J. G. McCullough,* or †, freighter | May 18, 1918 | 1,985 | 1 | European waters. |
| Hattie W. Dunn,* schooner | May 25, 1918 | 436 | 0 | Off Delaware Capes. |
| Hauppauge,* schooner | May 25, 1918 | 1,500 | 0 | Off Delaware Capes. |
| President Lincoln,* transport | May 31, 1918 | 18,168 | 27 | En route to France. |
| Winneconne,* schooner | June 2, 1918 | 1,896 | 0 | Off Delaware Capes. |
| Isabel B. Wiley,* schooner | June 2, 1918 | 776 | 0 | Off Delaware Capes. |
| Sam C. Mengel,* schooner | June 2, 1918 | 1,100 | 0 | Off Delaware Capes. |
| Jacob M. Haskell,* schooner | June 2, 1918 | 1,778 | 0 | Off Delaware Capes. |
| Edward H. Cole,* schooner | June 2, 1918 | 1,791 | 0 | 50 miles S. E. Barnegat. |
| Texel,* steamship | June 2, 1918 | 3,220 | 0 | 60 miles off N.Y. Harbor. |
| Carolina,* steamship | June 2, 1918 | 5,093 | 13 | Off Delaware Capes. |
| Edward Baird,* schooner | June 4, 1918 | 279 | 0 | Off Cape Charles. |
| Argonaut,* steamship | June 5, 1918 | 4,826 | 0 | Scilly Islands. |
| Pinar del Rio, steamship | June 8, 1918 | 2,504 | 0 | 75 miles off Md. coast. |
| Mauban,* freighter, reported | June 11, 1918 | 1,253 | 0 | Off Italian coast. |
| Californian,* steamship | June 22, 1918 | 5,658 | 0 | ............ |
| Covington,* transport | July 1, 1918 | 16,399 | 6 | Off French coast. |
| Westover,* supply ship | July 11, 1918 | 5,000 | 10 | European waters. |
| Lansford,* schooner | July 21, 1918 | 830 | 0 | Off Cape Cod. |
| 740,* schooner | July 21, 1918 | 680 | 0 | Off Cape Cod. |
| 766,* barge | July 21, 1918 | 527 | 0 | Off Cape Cod. |
| P. R. R. 403,* barge | July 21, 1918 | 422 | 0 | Off Cape Cod. |
| Perth Amboy,* tug | July 21, 1918 | 221 | 0 | Off Cape Cod. |
| Robert and Richard,* schooner | July 22, 1918 | 140 | 0 | Off Cashe Bank. |
| Tippecanoe,* steamship | July 25, 1918 | 6,187 | 1 | ............ |
| Lake Portage,* steamship | Aug. 3, 1918 | 1,998 | 0 | Off French coast. |
| Rob Roy,* schooner | Aug. 4, 1918 | .... | 0 | Off Seal Island, Yarmouth coast. |
| Annie M. Perry,* schooner | Aug. 4, 1918 | .... | 0 | Off Seal Island. |
| Muriel,* schooner | Aug. 4, 1918 | .... | 0 | Off Seal Island. |
| O. B. Jennings,* tanker | Aug. 4, 1918 | 7,800 | 0 | Off Virginia coast. |
| Luz Blanca,* tanker | Aug. 5, 1918 | .... | 2 | 40 miles W. of Halifax. |
| Merak,* steamship | Aug. 6, 1918 | 3,224 | 0 | Cape Hatteras. |
| Stanley L. Seaman,* schooner, rep. | Aug. 10, 1918 | .... | 0 | 110 miles east of Cape Hatteras. |
| Kate Palmer,* schooner | Aug. 10, 1918 | .... | 0 | 60 miles off Nantucket. |
| Anita May,* schooner | Aug. 10, 1918 | .... | 0 | 60 miles off Nantucket. |
| Progress,* schooner | Aug. 10, 1918 | .... | 0 | 50 miles off Nantucket. |
| Star Buck,* schooner | Aug. 10, 1918 | .... | 0 | 50 miles off Nantucket. |

| Name. | Date. | Gross Tonnage. | Lives Lost. | Locality. |
|---|---|---|---|---|
| Reliance,* schooner | Aug. 10, 1918 | .... | 0 | 50 miles off Nantucket. |
| Oldtime,* schooner | Aug. 10, 1918 | .... | 0 | 50 miles off Nantucket. |
| Cruiser,* schooner | Aug. 10, 1918 | .... | 0 | 50 miles off Nantucket. |
| Earl and Nettie,* schooner | Aug. 10, 1918 | .... | 0 | 50 miles off Nantucket. |
| Lena May,* schooner | Aug. 10, 1918 | .... | 0 | 50 miles off Nantucket. |
| Frederick R. Kellogg,* tanker | Aug. 13, 1918 | 4,450 | 7 | 10 miles off Barnegat (salvaged.) |
| Dorothy Barrett,* schooner | Aug. 15, 1918 | 2,008 | 0 | 20 miles off Cape May. |
| Cubore,* steamship | Aug. 15, 1918 | 7,300 | 0 | European waters. |
| Madrugada,* schooner | Aug. 16, 1918 | 1,613 | 0 | Off Winter Quarter Shoal |
| Montanan,* steamship | Aug. 16, 1918 | 6,659 | 5§ | Foreign waters. |
| Joseph Cudahy,* tanker | Aug. 17, 1918 | 3,302 | 13§ | 700 miles off Eng. coast. |
| A. Platt Andrews,* schooner | Aug. 20, 1918 | .... | 0 | Canadian coast. |
| Lake Edon,* cargo transport | Aug. 21, 1918 | .... | 6 | European waters. |
| Sylvania,* schooner | Aug. 21, 1918 | 136 | 0 | Canadian coast. |
| Francis J. O'Hara,* schooner | Aug. 21, 1918 | .... | 0 | Canadian coast. |
| J. J. Flaherty,* schooner | Aug. 25, 1918 | 162 | 0 | Off Miquelon Island. |
| Rush, schooner | Aug. 26, 1918 | .... | 0 | Off Canadian coast. |
| Onega,* steamship, reported | Sep. 3, 1918 | .... | 26§ | Off English coast. |
| Dora,* steamship | Sep. 4, 1918 | 7,037 | 0 | 400 miles off French coast. |

# The Submarine War

## Recent Depredations and the Steady Gain in New Construction —A German Shipping Intrigue

### [PERIOD ENDED SEPT. 12, 1918]

LOSSES of allied and neutral merchant shipping during July were slightly •heavier than during June, as the following figures, in terms of gross tonnage, show:

| | British. | Allied & Neutral. | Total. |
|---|---|---|---|
| June | 161,062 | 114,567 | 278,629 |
| July | 176,479 | 136,532 | 313,011 |

Compared with the adjusted losses in May, the July shipping casualties showed a decrease in British vessels lost of 55,-300 tons and an increase in allied and neutral vessels of 3,829. Compared with the July figures of 1917 the combined British, allied, and neutral losses showed a decrease of 262,938 tons.

The British losses in July exceeded the building figures in United Kingdom yards by 34,531 gross tons, but during the same month a total of 12,220 tons was completed for British account, reducing the deficit to 22,311, as compared with the average monthly deficit in the first six months of 1918 of nearly 90,000 tons.

The production of 340,145 tons of shipping by American yards brought the total amount of new construction in the United States to over 2,000,000 tons. A statement issued by the Shipping Board showed that the deliveries for the month had set a new record in America and Great Britain. The deliveries comprised forty-four steel vessels, including one from Japan, totaling 260,645 deadweight tons, and twenty-two wood and composite vessels, totaling 78,500 deadweight tons, a grand total of 340,145 deadweight tons. The greatest previous records were 294,036 deadweight tons in June, constructed in the United States, while the greatest previous record in Great Britain was in May, when 295,911 deadweight tons were produced.

The August output brought the total for the first year of ship construction in the United States up to 333 vessels, with a total tonnage of 2,190,489. The first delivery was on Aug. 30, 1917. The first million tons was delivered in May, 1918, nine months from the first delivery.

Among the more important American vessels sunk by submarines during the month were the following:

U. S. S. Cubore, 7,300 tons, on Aug. 15.

U. S. S. West Bridge, 8,800 tons, on Aug. 16.

U. S. cargo steamship Joseph Cudahy, 3,302 tons, on Aug. 17.

S. S. Lake Edon, an army chartered cargo transport, on Aug. 21.

S. S. Onega, on Aug. 30.

Fifty-eight members of the crews of these ships were lost or listed as missing.

## TROOP TRANSPORT ATTACKED

The large troopship Persic, with 2,800 American soldiers on board, was torpedoed Sept. 6 about 200 miles off the English coast, but all on board, including the crew, were saved, and the Persic was prevented from sinking by its watertight bulkheads and was afterward beached. This attack marked a new and more desperate enemy policy in that the Persic was a unit of a large convoy, and the torpedo was fired despite the presence of warships. The sea was smooth, and the rescue of the troops was made by British and American destroyers, which immediately came alongside, so that the men, instead of getting into lifeboats, clambered down ropes to the decks of the warships. There was no sign of panic among the soldiers, most of whom were from Chicago and Cleveland, and the whole operation of rescue was carried out in swift and orderly fashion. Other destroyers instantly went in pursuit of the submarine, and its destruction was unofficially reported. Several soldiers testified to having seen the U-boat lifted out of the water by a depth bomb and then disappear.

The Persic was the fourth American transport torpedoed with troops on the way to the war zone. The other three were the Tuscania, the Moldavia, and the Oronsa. The Tuscania was sunk in February, 1918, off the north coast of Ireland with 1,912 officers and men of the Michigan and Wisconsin Guardsmen, of whom 204 were lost. There were only 250 on board the Oronsa, and all were saved with the exception of three of the crew, who were drowned when she was torpedoed off the coast of Ireland on April 30, 1918. The Moldavia was torpedoed while carrying 500 troops to France from this country, and fifty-five were lost.

The American troop transport Mount Vernon, formerly the German merchant steamship Kronprinzessin Cecilie, was torpedoed on Sept. 5, off the coast of France while on its return trip, and thirty-five men of the crew were killed by the explosion of the torpedo. The ship, however, was safely navigated back to a French port. Among those on board, unharmed, was United States Senator James Hamilton Lewis of Illinois. Secretary of War Baker, who was on his way to France in the same part of the Atlantic, later cabled to Secretary Daniels:

I have just visited and viewed the Mount Vernon. The high spirited morale of its men and the masterful seamanship of its Captain [Douglas E. Dismukes] and officers made such a stirring story of heroism that I wish all the nations might know the splendid way in which the huge transport met and foiled the attempt to destroy it at sea. The traditions of your service are enriched by the conduct of this occasion.

The attacks upon merchant ships off the Atlantic Coast of the United States and Canada continued until Sept. 3, when they suddenly ceased. The principal victims were fishing vessels. The submarine operations on the Newfoundland banks were supplemented by those of a captured trawler, the Triumph, 250 gross tons, which was manned by a crew of twenty-one from the U-boat. Nearly a score of small fishing craft were destroyed before the work of both raider and U-boat mysteriously ceased.

## DESTRUCTION OF U-BOATS

The sudden pause in the enemy's submarine raid in United States waters was partly explained on Sept. 10, when the Captain of the American tank steamer, Frank H. Buck, reported to the Navy Department that on Sept. 3 his vessel had sunk a large German submarine far out in the Atlantic in a running fight. The navy's summary of the report was as follows:

On Sept. 3, at 8:25 A. M., an enemy submarine was sighted on the starboard beam at 14,000 yards. The submarine opened fire with two 6-inch guns. We answered fire with forward gun. We saw the shot fall about 400 yards short, and immediately swung stern forward to submarine, using after gun. Our shots were very close to the submarine, and the sub-

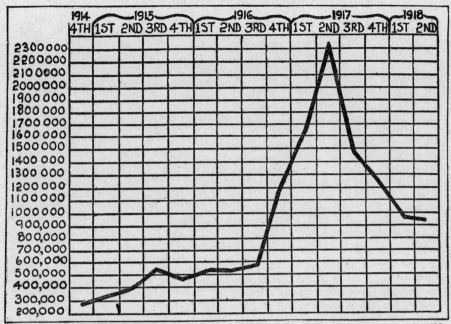

| | 1914 | | | 1915 | | | | 1916 | | | | 1917 | | | | 1918 | |
|---|---|---|---|---|---|---|---|---|---|---|---|---|---|---|---|---|---|---|
| | 4TH | 1ST | 2ND | 3RD | 4TH | 1ST | 2ND | 3RD | 4TH | 1ST | 2ND | 3RD | 4TH | 1ST | 2ND |

CHART OF SINKINGS OF ALLIED AND NEUTRAL SHIPS UP TO THE MIDDLE OF 1918.
SUBMARINE "FRIGHTFULNESS" REACHED ITS CLIMAX IN THE SECOND
QUARTER OF 1917 AND HAS STEADILY DECLINED SINCE THEN.

marine's shrapnel was bursting very near to us, some of the pieces falling upon our decks amidships. We changed our course frequently, which seemed to upset the submarine's aim and range. As soon as the submarine saw our range was equal to hers she hauled away from us. Up to that time she had been closing in on us.

Before the submarine could get out of range our twenty-eighth shot from the after gun apparently hit her stern. The twenty-ninth shot hit her just forward of the conning tower, near and under the waterline. The bow immediately shot up into the air very suddenly, then settled and went down out of sight, the stern making a half turn toward us, and then it disappeared.

Upon the shot striking the submarine we saw very closely a terrific explosion and black smoke which enveloped the submarine. I am positive that we destroyed her, as she sank almost instantly after the shot struck her.

The engagement lasted twenty-nine minutes. Some of the fragments of the submarine fell on our deck and were picked up. The submarine was about 300 feet long, of the early type of German submarine, with high bow, and had two 6-inch guns close to the conning tower, fore and aft. She fired in salvos, using about sixty shots all together. She was camouflaged, and flew no flag.

A statement by Premier Lloyd George in the House of Commons that 150 German U-boat Commanders had been disposed of was substantiated by the publication on Sept. 6 of the names of the officers referred to. Most of them were dead; some were prisoners of war, and a few interned in neutral countries where they took refuge. Among the Commanders named were:

Kapitan Lieutenant Schweiger, who, while in command of the U-20, torpedoed the Lusitania in May, 1915. The U-20 was lost on the Danish coast in 1916, but Schweiger survived and was in command of the U-80, which was lost with all hands in September, 1917.

Kapitan Lieutenant Paul Wagenführ, who sank the steamer Belgian Prince July 31, 1917, and drowned forty of the crew whom he had ordered to line up on the submarine's deck when the U-boat was about to submerge. His submarine, the U-44, was sunk with all hands about a fortnight later.

Kapitan Lieutenant Rudolph Schmeider, who torpedoed the steamer Arabic in August, 1915.

The statement added that it was significant that the authors of particularly atrocious crimes had expiated them speedily after their commission. It said that the names of such men were carefully noted by the British Admiralty, and that special endeavors were made to bring their active careers swiftly to an end.

Several commanders, it was added, had escaped retribution by finding refuge in shore appointments. Prominent among those named as having escaped retribution, but whom the British Navy has on its list, were, according to the statement:

Korvetten Kapitan Max Falentiener, who was responsible for many sinkings of vessels, among them the Norwegian steamer Magda, the Spanish steamer Pena Castillo, the Italian steamer Ancona, and the British steamer Persia.

Kapitan Lieutenant Wilhelm Werner for the sinking of hospital ships.

Korvetten Kapitan Freiherr von Forstner, who, when in command of the U-28, sank the British steamers Falaba and Aguila.

## AIRPLANES VERSUS U-BOATS

The use of airplanes to combat submarine warfare is described in a dispatch dated July 23 and sent from Brindisi, Italy, by G. Ward Price, correspondent of The London Times:

About eight times in the last five months the bald statement has appeared in the English press that "British airplanes bombed the Austrian dockyard at Cattaro," and in addition to this there have been half a dozen photographic and reconnoissance flights as well. Few people who have read these stilted official statements realize what they mean.

The air defenses of Cattaro are as formidable as the importance of the base there warrants. There is a tremendous anti-aircraft fire and, besides that, a force of fast Austrian airplanes ready to attack our fliers under conditions of great advantage to themselves. This flight, indeed, which is one of the most important defensive measures against enemy submarines which we possess, is also among the most risky enterprises undertaken anywhere by the Royal Air Force.

Our machines go over the Gulf of Cattaro generally four at a time. They carry about three-quarters of a ton of bombs, and, not content with dropping these, they take some of the best airplane photographs I have ever seen, as illustrations of their work. When you study these pictures, taken in successive raids, you realize the effect which our persistent air attacks have had upon this nest of Austrian sea-serpents. In the first photograph taken, when our machines went over to drop bombs for the first time, you

see about a dozen submarines lying close together in their dockyard on the north side of the gulf, as snug as can be. The Gulf of Cattaro is a long rambling place, divided up into several compartments. They were well inside it, and they felt so safe that they could all lie alongside and be friendly.

When the first bombs began to drop about them, they thought better of this and decided that it would be wiser to separate a little. Accordingly, in the photograph of the next couple of raids you find them divided up, some on one side, some on the other. But even so, they were not safe, and the rule was made that when the British planes came over all the submarines should at once move out into the gulf and submerge. So the next picture shows them all scuttling off like so many water-beetles, with a British bomb in full flight through the air toward them. And in the later photographs it is hard to find any submarines at all. They are all under water, hiding. And even if the submarines themselves are not hit during our raids, as there is good reason to hope they may have been, the workshops and stores are hit.

There were developments of several phases of international questions arising out of the German submarine campaign, the most important being the stand taken by the Spanish Government, (which is described elsewhere.) To compensate Holland for vessels sunk by U-boats Germany turned over to three Dutch shipping companies six ships which were interned in Java ports. The Peruvian Congress on Sept. 5 approved an arrangement reached between the Peruvian and United States Governments for the use of eight German vessels interned at Callao.

The French Government on Aug. 29 issued a decree under which safe conducts issued to neutral vessels by an enemy country would not be recognized by the Allies.

## WAGNER'S SHIP INTRIGUE

All the vessels of the American Transatlantic Company and the Foreign Transport and Mercantile Corporation were seized on Sept. 5 by the Alien Property Custodian on the ground that both of these enterprises were entirely German owned. With the seizure of these interests the Government concluded an investigation which began three years previously, when Richard G. Wagner, President of the newly formed American Transatlantic Company, first endeavored to have eleven so-called Danish steamships transferred to American registry, thereby placing them under the protection of the American flag.

At that time it was charged that the capital with which Wagner purchased the vessels was supplied by Hugo Stinnes, an influential figure in Hamburg shipping circles, and the United States Government for that reason hesitated to register them. Not long afterward, however, Wagner convinced the Government that there was no German money in the enterprise, and the vessels were admitted to American registry. For three years Wagner continued the deception, concealing the real ownership of his corporation from the French, British, and American Governments.

Recently, however, further facts were produced against him, and the renewal of the investigation by the Alien Property Custodian resulted in a complete confession by Wagner, in which he admitted that he had sworn falsely and that the money with which these companies were organized and with which the ships were purchased had been supplied by persons of German affiliations, and that practically no money belonging to American citizens had ever been invested in the companies.

This disclosure was significant in view of the fact that the seizure of four vessels of the Transatlantic Company in 1915,, the Saginaw by the French, the Hocking, the Kankakee, and the Genessee by the British, led to an effort on the part of Ambassador von Bernstorff's staff of propagandists to agitate dissension and a break between this Government and England, on the ground that the vessels were American owned. Under the direction of von Bernstorff this agitation actually assumed nationwide proportions, the general conclusion at that time being that these ships were really American owned.

The value of the ships of the American Transatlantic Company and the Foreign Transport and Mercantile Corporation was indicated, according to the Alien Property Custodian, by the fact that the Hudson Bay Company had offered to pay $7,500,000 for them, and that Wagner had refused to sell for less than $8,000,000. When the London Board of Trade objected to the payment of more than $7,500,000 Wagner refused the offer altogether, although it meant a profit of approximately $5,000,000, the original investment in the ships having been about $2,600,000. Again in February, 1917, the Compagnie Generale Transatlantique had a thirty days' option to purchase the ships for $9,300,000.

Richard G. Wagner, President of the companies, was born in Milwaukee fifty-six years ago. His father was a German, who changed his name from Wagenkneckt to Wagner.

## Spain Seizes Ninety German Ships

Spain, where pro-German influences had been particularly strong ever since the outbreak of the war, was at last roused in August, 1918, to vigorous measures as a result of the destruction of Spanish ships by German submarines. Following a meeting of the Cabinet at San Sebastian, the following official statement was issued on Aug. 21:

As a consequence of the submarine campaign more than 20 per cent. of our merchant marine has been sunk, more than 100 Spanish sailors have perished, a considerable number of sailors have been wounded, and numbers have been shipwrecked and abandoned. Ships needed exclusively for Spanish use have been torpedoed without the slightest pretext, serious difficulties resulting to navigation.

The Government has believed that it is. unable, without failing in its essential obligations and without setting aside neutrality, to defer the adoption of measures necessary to guarantee Spanish maritime traffic and to protect Spanish crews and passengers.

Consequently the Government has decided to address the Imperial German Government and declare that, owing to the reduction of tonnage to its extreme limit, it will be obliged in the case of new sinkings to substitute therefor German vessels interned in Spanish ports.

This measure does not imply the confiscation of the ships under definite title. It would be only a temporary solution until the establishment of peace, when Spanish claims also will be liquidated.

Our Ambassador at Berlin has received instructions to bring this decision to the notice of the German Government. The Spanish Government does not doubt that the German Government will appreciate the circumstances determining this resolution and will recognize that Spain, in holding to the neutrality she has practiced since the beginning of the war, has sacrificed many of her rights and legitimate conveniences when it has been possible without affecting the dignity of Spain and her national life.

The decision of the Government to assure for itself sufficient tonnage, which is indispensable to its existence, does not affect its firm resolve to maintain strict neutrality.

Germany's reply was an energetic protest against the taking over of interned ships. The Spanish Government was informed that Germany could not discriminate in favor of Spain, that the submarine campaign could not be given up, and that it was hoped Spain would remain really neutral.

After a Cabinet meeting on Aug. 31 the Spanish Government decided to take over all the German steamships, numbering about ninety, which were lying in Spanish ports.

# The Murder of Captain Fryatt
## Official Report by His First Officer

*William Hartwell, who was the First Officer of the British steamer Brussels at the time of its capture in 1916, and who is interned in Holland, wrote the following account of the arrest and execution of Captain Fryatt on the second anniversary of his death. Captain Fryatt was killed by the Germans for having tried to ram a submarine that was attacking his ship. Mr. Hartwell's report was sent to C. Busk of the Great Eastern Railway.*

SIR: This being the first opportunity since the capture of the Brussels in 1916, I will endeavor to give you details of the capture and happenings up to July 27, this being the date of Captain Fryatt's death. I beg to report that on June 22 the steamship Brussels left Rotterdam with cargo and passengers for Tilbury, stopping at the Hook of Holland. She left the Hook Quay at 11 P. M. on that day, the weather being very fine and clear. All saloon and cabin lights were extinguished before passing the North Pier Light. Directly after passing it, a very bright light was shown from the beach, about four miles north of the Hook, followed by a bright star, such as a rocket would throw. After a lapse of ten minutes this was repeated. On both occasions Captain Fryatt and myself remarked upon it, as we had never seen similar lights on any previous occasions. After passing the Maas Light Vessel, all Board of Trade Regulation Lights were darkened. Five miles west of the light vessel a very small craft, probably a submarine not submerged, commenced Morseing the letter " S " at intervals. No other lights were visible.

After running for one hour and thirty minutes, an extra sharp lookout was kept for a steamer that was going in the same direction and without lights, the port and starboard lights of the Brussels being put on for the time being. At 12:46 craft without lights were seen at a point on the starboard bow, traveling at a great speed in the opposite direction. These proved to be German destroyers of the latest type, five in all. Two came alongside on the starboard side, and one on the port side, the other two following close behind. During the time the destroyers were approaching their commanders were shouting orders to stop, asking the name of the ship, and threatening to fire on us. No firing occurred, however. As soon as Captain Fryatt was assured that the destroyers were German, he gave orders for all passengers to be ready to take to the boats if necessary, and quietly instructed me to destroy all dispatches and official papers. His instructions were carried out, and as the last bag was destroyed German seamen, armed with pistols and bombs, appeared on the starboard alleyway. I passed through the saloon to the deck and met more German seamen, who were driving all the crew they could find over the rail on to the destroyers. I was ordered over the rail, but refused to go, and then met the officer who came on board to take charge. He requested me to show him to the bridge, which I did. He greeted Captain Fryatt, and congratulated himself over the great prize.

## ANGRY GERMAN OFFICER

Satisfied that all was well, the destroyers left and made for Zeebrugge. The course was given for the Schouwenbank light vessel, and the order was given for full speed ahead, but no reply came from the engine room, as the engineers had been driven over the side with the majority of the crew. This greatly excited the German officer, who drew his revolver and threatened to shoot Captain Fryatt and myself if we failed to assist him, and to blow up the ship if the orders to the engine room were not complied with at once. It was some minutes before the German officer could be convinced that the engineers and most of the crew were on the destroyers. He then ordered his own men to the engine room, and instead of going full speed ahead, the engines were put on full speed astern. This also angered the officer, and matters became very unpleasant on the bridge. I was ordered to go to the engine room to inform the Germans of their mistake. By this time the steam was greatly falling back, owing to the stokers being away, and the order was given that all on board, except Captain Fryatt and myself, should maintain steam till the ship arrived at Zeebrugge. On reaching the Schouwenbank light vessel the German flag was hoisted, and directly after the Flushing mail boat for Tilbury passed quite close. Captain Fryatt was assured that soon after her arrival at Tilbury the capture of the Brussels would be reported. The Brussels was met and escorted by several airplanes to Zeebrugge, where the destroyers were already moored. On arrival at Zeebrugge the Brussels was moored alongside the Mole. The engineers and crew all returned. The crew were sent to their quarters and kept under armed guard. The officers and engineers were placed under a guard in the smokeroom, and Captain the same in his room. The Belgian refugees were closely searched, and landed at Zeebrugge. After a stay of about five hours the Brussels left and proceeded to Bruges under her own steam.

For some reason Captain Fryatt was kept in his cabin, and I was sent to the bridge, not to assist or officiate in any way, but simply to stand under guard and to be questioned at intervals by the Germans if they could get the right answers. During the passage from Zeebrugge to Bruges both sides of the canal were thronged in places, and both the soldiers and the marine Landsturm were greatly excited. On reaching Bruges the crew were taken off and sent to a waiting shed. Only Captain Fryatt and myself, with many German officers, remained on board. After we had been questioned at lunch Captain Fryatt and I were photographed, and we then joined the crew in the shed, being afterward taken to a building in the town. All of us, including stewardesses and twenty-five Russians, were packed in, and there was scarcely standing room.

## PACKED IN CATTLE TRUCKS

After some hours, following a request to the prison commandant, the stewardesses were allowed separate quarters in the top of the building. Otherwise they were treated in the same way as male prisoners until they were separated to go to a different camp. At 3 A. M., on June 25, orders came for all to be ready for the train to Germany, the stewardesses joining us at the station. At 5 A. M. we all left, closely packed, in cattle trucks, and on arrival at Ghent we were escorted to very dirty and unhealthful quarters underground. At 5 A. M. on the following day we left Ghent for Germany, via Cologne, where the stewardesses and Russians were separated to go to other camps. After being exhibited at Berlin, as at Hanover and other stations, the rest went to Ruhleben, where they arrived at 5 P. M., June 28. Two days later Captain Fryatt and I received orders to the effect that we were to be prepared to leave the camp at 8 P. M. for Bruges on ship's business.

We arrived at Bruges at 7 A. M., on July 2, after visiting Ostend by mistake on the part of the escort. We reported to the port commandant at 9 A. M., and were taken from him to the town prison and put in cells. From then onward we were treated as criminals. We were occasionally visited by German officials and questioned as to the submarine and other subjects, on which Captain Fryatt made a clear and open statement to the Germans, with nothing condemning to himself. From the time of being placed in the prison at Bruges to July 15 I saw Captain Fryatt and spoke to him on several occasions, after which I never spoke to him until one hour before he was shot.

I will endeaver to make you understand the so-called tribunal or trial. On July 24 Captain Fryatt and myself were questioned and cross-questioned in the prison, and, so far as I could learn, Captain Fryatt never added to or departed from his opening statement. It was then that we were first informed of the tribunal that was to follow. On July 26 we were told to be ready for the tribunal, which was to take place at Bruges Town Hall on the 27th at 11 A. M. On July 27 at 9 A. M. the door of the cell was opened, and an escort was waiting. To my surprise, four of the crew were in the waiting cell. Each man was escorted to the Town Hall, Captain Fryatt and I being the last to go, and placed under a strong guard until the trial began.

At 12 noon Captain Fryatt was called into his place before the so-called bench, and repeated his previous statement. I followed and answered questions that appeared to be ridiculous, not appearing either to defend or condemn Captain Fryatt. At the same time an officer in uniform appeared, and, approaching Captain Fryatt and myself, informed us in broken English that he was for the defense. The Naval Commandant of the port conducted the trial, and also acted as interpreter. At 4 P. M. the Naval Commandant informed us that all was over so far, and that the decision rested with the naval officers, who had retired to another room, and the verdict would be made known after we had returned to our cells. The officer for the defense then spoke again, and said he would do his utmost to save Captain Fryatt.

### CONDEMNED TO BE SHOT

After being again placed in the cells, the chief warder of the prison came to me at 5:30 P. M. and told me I was to go and stop with Captain Fryatt, as that was his last night. I then met Captain Fryatt, who was very much distressed, not so much because of the verdict, but of the unfair and cowardly manner in which everything was done. He told me himself that he was to be shot on the next morning, and after having a talk for about an hour—it was then 6:30 P. M.—the prison official took his watch from his pocket and said that in a short time the escort would be there, and Captain Fryatt would be shot at 7 P. M. The last twenty-five minutes I spent with him were appalling. At 6:55 P. M. I wished him "good-bye," and promised I would deliver his last messages, which were many, and returned to my cell.

Punctually at 7 P. M., a very short distance from the prison walls, a band commenced to play, and poor Fryatt was no more. Late the same evening an official came to my cell and described to me, in the best way he could, how Fryatt died. He was shot by sixteen rifles, the bullets of which penetrated through his heart, carrying with them the clothes he was wearing through the body and out at the back.

Sir, I was and am still proud of Captain Fryatt's manly conduct right up to the last, and I may add that there was not a German present at the trial who could face him.

# War Surgery

## What Medical Science and the United States Army Hospitals Are Doing for Wounded Soldiers

**B**RIG. GEN. R. E. NOBLE, Chief of the Overseas Service of the Medical Department of the United States Army, who has 22,000 medical officers under him, estimates that, with 4,000,000 men in France, we shall need in this country 200,000 hospital beds. This includes all necessary service, not only debarkation and general hospitals, which will take care of those returned from abroad, but embarkation and base hospitals, where those who become ill while in training or before sailing are given medical attention. There are forty-two base hospitals in operation at the camps, besides the large one established in New York City by Columbia University, a pioneer in its field, which has trained many attendants and handled some of the early cases of wounded brought from France.

But as a rule it is not considered advisable to send returning sick and wounded to base hospitals. The effect on newly drafted or enlisted men would be deleterious. The most economical plan would be to have one big general hospital with accommodations for, say, 160,000, but the objection to such a plan outweighs its advantages. The depressing psychological effect of such an enormous group of disabled men would retard individual recovery. Besides, the distribution of general hospitals throughout the country provides opportunity for the soldier to be returned close to his home, so that he may receive the cheerful stimulation of visits from his friends and relatives.

When plans already formulated have been carried out, our hospital facilities will be ample, and each general hospital will be fitted for the extended treatment of every known kind of disability.

Americans wounded in battle are first cared for at the base hospitals in France. Only those who will not be sufficiently recovered within six months to return to the front are sent back to the United States. These are estimated at 15 per cent. of the total wounded. The men to be returned are classified in France according to wounds, sickness, and disability. They are tagged with this classification, so as to expedite upon their arrival their distribution to the different general hospitals.

Two debarkation hospitals are in readiness in New York, one on Ellis Island and the other on Staten Island, and the Greenhut store, Eighteenth Street and Sixth Avenue, is being equipped, giving a total bed capacity of 5,651. Four other debarkation hospitals, three in New York City and one at Long Beach, are being put in readiness. They will practically double existing facilities.

When a patient arrives from overseas, his name, the extent of his injuries, and his condition are promptly communicated to his immediate relatives. As soon as he is able to make the journey, he is sent to a general hospital for special treatment.

### GENERAL HOSPITALS

There are twenty-seven general hospitals in this country. They are as follows:

|  | Normal Capacity. | Maximum Capacity. |
|---|---|---|
| Hot Springs, Ark | 266 | 286 |
| Fort Bayard, New Mexico | 1,283 | 1,283 |
| San Francisco | 1,197 | 1,233 |
| Takoma Park, D. C. | 1,560 | 2,010 |
| Williamsbridge, N. Y. | 977 | 1,045 |
| Fort McHenry, Md. | 966 | 1,066 |
| Colonia, N. J., (Rahway) | 539 | 539 |
| Fort Porter, (Buffalo) | 212 | 212 |
| Fort Ontario, (Oswego) | 233 | 471 |
| Fort McPherson, (Atlanta) | 1,200 | 1,900 |
| Roland Park, Md. | 102 | 102 |
| Otisville, N. Y. | 566 | 712 |
| Lakewood, N. J. | 865 | 865 |
| Cape May, N. J. | 700 | 700 |
| Biltmore, N. C. | 448 | 588 |
| Fort Oglethorpe, Ga. | 1,100 | 1,700 |
| Corpus Christi, Texas | 255 | 314 |
| New Haven, Conn. | 200 | 220 |
| Markleton, Penn. | 160 | 160 |
| Dansville, N. Y. | 250 | 250 |
| Boston | 288 | 288 |
| Waynesville, N. C. | 316 | **391** |

| | Normal Capacity. | Maximum Capacity. |
|---|---|---|
| Aza'ea, N. C. | 1,000 | 1,000 |
| Whipple Barracks, Ariz. | 155 | 207 |
| Denver | 1,000 | 1,000 |
| Richmond, Va. | 284 | 284 |
| Fort Des Moines, Iowa | 1,159 | 1,159 |
| Hoboken, N. J. | 663 | 763 |

At many of these hospitals extensive improvements are being made, and some are of entirely new construction. At the Walter Reed Hospital, at Tacoma Park, D. C., where special provisions are made for amputation work, additional hospital buildings are being erected at an estimated cost of $733,400. At Denver, Col.; Otisville, N. Y., and Azalea, in the heart of the North Carolina Mountains, there will be quarters for 2,650 tubercular patients, constructed at a cost to the Government in round numbers of $3,000,000. At Norfolk, Va., at the Norfolk Quartermaster Terminal, the Government has spent over $200,000 to build a new 120-bed hospital. Additional accommodations for 150 nurses have been provided at Fort McPherson, Ga. The Lakewood and Florence in the Pines Hotels at Lakewood, N. J., have been leased for hospital purposes at an annual rental of $58,600. The capacity of the General Hospital at Fort Oglethorpe, Ga., has been increased by the erection of two-story convalescent barracks.

During the six months ended June 1, 1918, the Government spent $25,173,477 on new buildings and improvements for army hospitals of all kinds. In August the general hospitals were ready to receive 17,447 patients, and it was estimated that the construction then under way would give an additional 7,027 beds, providing for a total of 24,474 sick and wounded men by the end of 1918. These figures should be augmented by beds for 185 patients in the Mary Imogene Bassett Hospital at Cooperstown, N. Y., which has been offered to and accepted by the Government. Here special attention will be given nervous conditions among aviators. This hospital will have at its command the resources of the Pathological Laboratory of Cooperstown.

The War Department announced on Sept. 9 that the Grand Central Palace in New York City had been leased for use as a surgical reconstruction hospital for the period of the war and three months after, at an annual rental of $395,000 and maintenance. It will be remodeled to accommodate 3,000 patients, and is expected to be ready for occupancy by Dec. 1.

Modern medicine and surgery have made the present war the least destructive to human life, in proportion to the numbers engaged, of any in the history of the world. That is what the most eminent physicians and surgeons assert. This statement, considered in conjunction with the length of allied casualty lists, at first seems incredible, but it must be borne in mind that in other wars we reckoned the number engaged in thousands, while in this one the figures run well up in millions, and aside from actual soldiers, in no other conflict have there been within the firing line so many people who were not fighting, but erecting hospitals, barracks, and officers' quarters, treating and nursing wounded, engineering the construction of railroads, storehouses, bridges, and all the means by which a modern army is provisioned, cared for, and transported.

In the civil war 7 per cent. of the soldiers perished yearly. Dr. Woods Hutchinson is authority for the statement that the annual death rate in the allied armies is 3 per cent., while an official survey made for Congress places the French mortality for 1917 as low as 1.375 per cent. Again, during the civil war from 20 to 50 per cent. of those injured in battle never recovered; but now from 70 to 80 per cent. of the wounded are returned to the front within forty days. Of the men who live six hours after being injured 90 per cent. recover, and 95 per cent. of those who reach the casualty clearing houses are saved.

Five-sixths of the deaths in the civil war resulted from what are now known as preventable diseases. The medical catastrophes of the Spanish-American war are still fresh in the recollection of this generation. The havoc which typhoid and other diseases of intestinal origin wrought among the troops who were never engaged in battle is a memory filled with shame. Those diseases were preventable then as now, but medical science had not progressed as it has in the present day. Modern methods of inoculation and sanitation have triumphed over disease and modern surgeons have accomplished results almost beyond belief.

## INOCULATION AGAINST DISEASE

Typhoid has been practically abolished by inoculation. In the civil war there were 79,462 cases of typhoid, and 29,336 deaths. In the Boer war there were 58,-000 cases, and 8,000 deaths. In the Spanish-American war, when our army numbered 107,973, there were 20,738 cases of typhoid, and 1,580 deaths. In the United States Army, from Sept. 17 of last year to Jan. 18 (one month longer than the duration of the war with Spain) there were 742,626 men in various camps and cantonments, and only 119 cases of typhoid. Inoculation is now compulsory.

Cholera is under control by disinfecting drinking water and vaccinating against it. Dysentery is being held down to a low rate by water sterilization and latrine sanitation. Preventive measures have robbed spinal meningitis—at one time one of the most baffling and cruel of plagues—of its terrors. Epidemic meningitis, which in earlier wars was dreaded under the name of "spotted fever," is now successfully treated by means of a curative serum. "Trench fever," a sickness which rarely kills, but which is the most prolific source of disability with which our armies have to contend, has not been done away with, but at least its source—the body louse—has been determined, and the question now becomes one of prevention and sanitation.

The most frightful scourges of former wars have been tetanus (lockjaw) and gaseous gangrene. Soil highly fertilized with animal excrement, like that of France, contains in large numbers the spores of tetanus and gaseous gangrene bacilli. From the earth they gain access to the clothing of men. When particles of cloth or dirt, as frequently happens, are carried into wounds by bullets or shell fragments, tetanus or gaseous gangrene, or both, frequently develop. To Dr. C. G. Bull of the Rockefeller Institute belongs the discovery of the antitoxin for the gas bacillus. Recent experiments have proved that a single serum injection may be made carrying the antitoxins for both tetanus and gaseous gangrene. As soon as possible after a wounded man is picked up he is inoculated, and both of these diseases are now practically under control.

## CARREL-DAKIN TREATMENT

The greatest addition to the modern knowledge of antisepsis came through the discoveries of Dr. Dakin in experimenting with chlorine preparations. It remained for Dr. Alexis Carrel to develop a way to use the solution compounded by Dr. Dakin. He worked with Dr. Dakin, and they experimented with 200 antiseptics before the hypochlorite solution was perfected. Dr. Carrel then invented a method of application which made it practical. His work was done in New York, at the Experimental Hospital, built for studying the diseases of the war and treatment of the wounded, and located just below the Rockefeller Institute on Sixty-fourth Street and the East River.

Dr. Carrel's invention is a unique mode of wound irrigation. It consists of a system of little rubber tubes, pierced here and there for the liquid to flow out. The wound is cleansed, the tubes are laid in and fed from a glass container which hangs above the bed. The flow is regulated by stopcocks. Of the wounded treated at Compiègne by this method, 99 per cent. were healed by first intention. Whereas formerly amputations frequently resulted in painful stumps, and the healing process consumed from six to eighteen months, now, when treated with the Dakin solution they heal quickly, and artificial legs can almost always be fitted within from four to six weeks after the treatment is first given.

The latest method of treating wounds includes the excision of all contaminated tissue, muscle, and even bone. This is on the theory that it is better and more economical to do the thing well at first than to risk a spreading of the infection and a second amputation. The use of the knife as a vital factor in cleansing wounds was the discovery of Dr. Pierre Duval of the French Army. Every bit of infected or suspected tissue is removed. When the wound may be declared " mechanically clean " it is usually closed. That is a matter of surgical technique. Under this treatment many severe wounds heal in two weeks. This means an enormous saving in man power, bandages, nursing, and surgical attention.

In connection with this treatment the transfusion of blood taken from slightly wounded but healthy men, who are willing to make the sacrifice, is freely used. It has been discovered that blood for transfusion can be kept for several weeks without deteriorating. Every casualty clearing station now endeavors to have in its icebox in readiness for emergencies about thirty pints of blood.

## CREATING NEW FACES

To another French surgeon, Dr. de Villeon, is due the discovery of a method of operating on the lungs for the successful removal of foreign matter. To expedite the examination of the wounded, the American Army Medical Department has developed a mobile X-ray outfit which may be taken to the front line trenches. A very important phase of surgery is the restoration of faces of persons supposed to be permanently disfigured. To reach the desired effect a photograph of the man, taken before his injury, is studied by a skillful French sculptor who has given three years to this work. He makes a careful model of the face in plaster, which is used by the surgeon as a guide. By transplanting bits of cartilage and bone from the man's ribs or legs, holding them in place by paraffin or the plastic material used by dentists, and then bringing over them portions of skin lifted from the forehead or cheek or neck—skin which is left with some natural attachment to aid its nutrition—a new face is actually built up, and one which is not only agreeable in appearance, but which resembles the man's former likeness. This work is being done in England, where twelve surgeons are working in collaboration with the sculptor. A reconstruction clinic has been established in New York.

In this war, as in no other in history, careful consideration has been given to the future of individuals who have been crippled in battle. For years in this country more men have annually been totally or partially disabled by industrial accidents than have been incapacitated by the war in Europe. These injured men left to fend for themselves have, in many cases, lost their grip on their self-respect, taken to drink, and, slowly deteriorating, have become either a menace to life and property or wards of the State. Comparatively little of a constructive nature has been done to aid them. There has been no scientific concerted effort in their behalf, and, paradoxically enough, it has remained for war, that great destructive power, to arouse intelligent employers from their apathy toward this enormous economic waste. The application of methods of reclamation to the injured in battle will be bound to have its reaction for good toward those disabled in industrial life.

## IN OTHER COUNTRIES

Already our associates in the war have made great strides in the right direction. The reclamation of the crippled is a matter not of sentiment, but of sound common sense. It is better business to train a man to be self-supporting than to provide for his maintenance in an institution at the public expense. The benefit to the race is, in proportion, even greater than that to the individual. Men unfit for further military service may yet be of great use to the nation in industrial fields.

Belgium, whose man-power depletion has been the most severe, was the first nation to use her men over again. It has been a profitable venture. Not only has the large Belgian re-educational centre of Port Villez been self-supporting, but it has repaid to the Belgian Government its first cost. The men receive not only 43 centimes a day, the regular pay of the Belgian soldier, but also 5 to 20 centimes an hour, according to the nature of their work, and, in addition, surplus profits are funded for the men. Forty-three trades are taught at Port Villez. A large part of the output is material, equipment, and tools made for the Belgian Army.

After the war, in all European nations,

the problem of the rehabilitation of the disabled will be an important, perhaps a determining, factor in their economic future. Germany recognizes this. It is stated that Germany uses back of the lines 85 to 90 per cent. of her disabled, and the remaining 10 to 15 per cent. are entirely self-supporting. The German policy is "to make every man self-supporting no matter how little of him there may be left." France has made provision for the vocational training of her wounded soldiers, but complete action has been retarded because of the difficulties of her position. England is teaching those blinded in battle massage, telephone operating, boot repairing, mat making, basket weaving, joinery, poultry farming, and market gardening. Scotland has a National Neurasthenic Hospital for men suffering from shell shock.

## VOCATIONAL TRAINING

Canada has taken most constructive action in this important matter. One of her hospitals best equipped for vocational training consists of the buildings and grounds—800 acres—of the old Ontario Reformatory at Guelph. Here there is a woolen mill, machine, broom, tailor, shoe and woodworking shops, and a lime kiln. A herd of eighty cows furnishes the means for the men to learn dairying. The nearby Ontario Agricultural College teaches them scientific farming. Canada's Military Orthopaedic Hospital at North Toronto has a factory where crippled men learn to make artificial limbs. The Newmarket Convalescent Hospital specializes in mental diseases and their cure through healthful occupation. Whitby Convalescent Hospital has a vocational training building. This work is also done at the Military Hospital at Manitoba and the Red Cross Hospital at Calgary. At Calgary also the Institute of Technology has a special training course in the various crafts, and the University of Saskatchewan provides free education in farm work, while the Department of Agriculture at Saskatchewan is in constant touch with farmers who will take returned men for practical training.

A magazine with the avowed purpose of interesting the public in the reconstruction of disabled soldiers and sailors is edited in the office of Surgeon General William C. Gorgas. Colonel Roosevelt and Charles M. Schwab were contributors to the August number. Both urged the necessity of viewing the matter from the sane standpoint that a man's real worth is measured by his brains and not by his possession of a full complement of legs and arms. Mr. Schwab makes the striking statement that "it is the duty of the business men of America to take these men at their intrinsic value; to employ them, not from a sense of duty, but *because a trained man who has been taught to think is a valuable asset.*"

From the moment the disabled American soldier comes out from under the influence of the anaesthetic he is constantly reminded that his future is whatever he is willing to make it. A corps of "cheer up" men, themselves cripples of various kinds, has been organized at the base hospitals in France, on hospital transports, and in the reconstruction wards in the United States. Through their efforts, example, and precept the injured man is from the first stimulated to use his brains in his own behalf. The education of his family and relatives is an important factor. They must discard maudlin pity for real helpfulness. They must make the soldier feel that his family, friends, and community expect him to prove himself a real hero by continuing to play a man's part in life, no matter how great his handicap.

## PSYCHOLOGICAL EFFECTS

The vocational training of injured and crippled men has three aspects. First, the teaching of light and easy crafts, which may be followed at the bedside or even in bed. The psychological effect of this training is its most valuable result. It is not difficult to imagine the mental condition of a man who, once able-bodied, useful, and active, is now facing life as a semi-invalid—one who will always have to be careful—or who must return to the world minus a leg or an arm. Perhaps he can no longer expect to take up the work which he performed before he gave his health in the service of his country. Unless something is done to rouse him from morbid introspection, from despair, his recovery will be great-ly retarded, or he may die. In case of a lingering convalescence, without hope or a real interest in life, he faces the danger of a deteriorating manhood, an inertia which refuses to be shaken off, a growing willingness to permit himself to be provided for by his friends or by the State. This might happen to men of the highest calibre under adverse conditions; indeed, the more sensitively tuned the nervous system, the more refined and imaginative the individual, the greater the danger.

Here the teacher of bedside vocational training steps in and prescribes an easy task, which is interesting. Many clever men have devoted the spare hours of convalescence to solving a foolish but intricate picture puzzle. The vocational training supplements the interest provided by the picture puzzle with something which is really useful. Under its guidance disheartened men take on a new lease of life. They grow eager, alert, and hopeful.

As their recovery proceeds, the men who are able to move about come under the influence of the curative workshop. Here they are taught to use the ordinary tools of the carpenter and machinist, or perhaps given some light work out of doors. A man with stiff fingers, who looks askance at spring dumbbells and other like apparatus, will cheerfully spend the morning grasping a big duster, cleaning up. An invalid with a stiff ankle is offered, for instance, fret work, where his foot drives the fret saw almost subconsc'ously while his hands guide the work and his mind is busy with his task. Without knowing it, he is exercising the necessary muscles quite as well as he would on a less absorbing pedal massage or stationary bicycle. All the shops have their special parts in the work. Whatever the men are given to do is designed not only to amuse and interest them, but to exercise the limbs and muscles looking toward the restorati n of health, always keeping in view as much as possible the third step—training for their ultimate work in the world. For, unless they are fit to go back to the tasks which they performed before they entered the serv-ice, they must be given new vocations. The endeavor is to suit a man's training to his personal inclinations as well as to the nature and extent of his disability.

Canadian figures show that 20 per cent. of the men returned unfit for military service require vocational training. Of these one-half must be equipped for an entirely new kind of work.

The report to Congress estimates that for each 1,000,000 men sent overseas 100,000 will be returned unfit, and of these 10,000 will require partial and 10,000 complete vocational training. Of 516 cases treated in four hospitals, 134 men were able to return to full military duty, 210 are fit for limited service, and 172 are eligible for discharge. In the last group twelve are helpless or institutional cases, 121 are able to return to their former occupations, and 39 must have complete vocational training.

## WONDERFUL ARTIFICIAL LIMBS

To aid the appearance and efficiency of the crippled, many new and valuable types of artificial arms and legs have been invented. An artificial leg adopted by the Government is the invention of Major David Silver, Medical Corps, U. S. A. It is said that a cripple, after he has become accustomed to it, may learn to walk with almost natural movements. No crutch or support is necessary. The foot movement is simulated by a jointed instep. The invention has been tried successfully by a soldier who had lost both legs. When it is properly clad and booted it is difficult for a casual observer to detect its artificiality.

The Red Cross Institute for Crippled and Disabled Men at 311 Fourth Avenue, New York City, maintains a training school and acts as a clearing house for men who have been taught. The institute has a room fully equipped with facilities for enabling the cripple to make his own limbs. Here plaster casts of stumps are taken and finished limbs are adjusted. Here, too, are displayed not only artificial feet and legs, but arms and hands almost perfect in their imitation of nature. But the latter are for dress only. At work an armless man uses the devices which will best aid him to fulfill his task. His working arms are fitted not with hands, but with tools, chucks and hooks, which may be interchangeably adjusted—whatever will most adequately take the place of the hand which he has lost.

Already cripples have been placed in good positions. The Kohler & Campbell Company, the Empire Art Metal Company, the Automatic Company, the Eagle Pencil Company, Untermeyer & Robbins, the Ford Company, and the Fox Film Company are among the large institutions employing reclaimed men.

Pennsylvania is the pioneer State, as such, in enabling injured soldiers to get on their feet again. The Bureau of Employment of the Pennsylvania Department of Labor and Industry maintains card files, which, compiled from a Statewide questionnaire to employers of all kinds of labor, contain a list of 42,111 jobs open to crippled soldiers and sailors. Many of them are skilled tasks which may be performed by men who have lost one or both legs or an arm.

## THOUSANDS OF NURSES

By the end of the Summer of 1918 15,000 women had enlisted in the American Army as nurses and been inducted into active service. By the end of the year 28,000 of them will have been mustered in, 20,000 will have been assigned to foreign service, and 8,000 will be on duty with the army in the making, which still remains at home. When the United States became a part of the conflict the army nursing corps numbered only 372 women. On the anniversary of that occasion it was 8,500 strong, with a call for 5,000 more by June and 20,000 more by the end of the year.

# A Miracle of the New Surgery

## By Harold Begbie

### [By arrangement with The London Chronicle]

THE operating room is full of light. It is spacious and uncrowded. The smell of drugs is not oppressive. A little group of quiet people are gathered in the centre. I notice two nurses standing perfectly still. Just beyond these women are three or four men, masked and gloved. I am introduced to Major Gillies, who bows to me and then turns to his patient.

The patient is sitting upon the operating table. He is naked to the waist, and the whole of his flesh is painted a reddish yellow with iodine. It is only by an effort that I can bring myself to look at his face. What I see I dare not describe. I hear one of the greatest surgeons in England whisper to a doctor at my side, "Did you ever see an anaesthetic more perfectly administered?" They are raptured by the perfection of the patient's repose. I can see that the patient is a man and I can see that once upon a time this man had a face; but I am thinking not of the anaesthetist, not even of the damnable wickedness of war; only how long I shall be able to stand looking at this dreadful creature who is still a man.

Major Gillies is about to operate. The patient's position is not quite suitable. He puts a yellow gloved hand on the patient's yellow shoulder and touches him. The effect upon me is like a shock. What was something like a man, seems of a sudden to be a figure stuffed with straw. The figure flops to one side, soulless, boneless.

"You understand what we are going to do?"

I shake my head.

Major Gillies points with his knife to the man's chest. There, faintly marked on the reddish-yellow flesh, as it were with thin pencil strokes, is the shape of a face. "These spots here are the eyes; this is where the nose will be, and here you see the mouth we shall give him." Good God, it searches me to the bone! That penciled face on the man's chest, like a mask; and above that penciled face on the chest, the old blasted and shattered face that a few days ago had the beauty and freshness of youth; why do surgeons speak of these things as a landscape gardener of his plans?

Some one whispers to me: "You see those little swellings on the shoulder? Those are bits of bones which have been taken from the man's ribs and placed there to form the cartilage of the nose. What is going to happen is this: the whole face on the chest, when everything is ready, will be lifted up and placed over the disfigured face; the nose will be built up with the cartilage taken from the ribs —it will be lined with the real living skin; the tissue, fed naturally by blood, will grow in its new place like a graft; and then all scars will be removed. The man's face will be as natural and real a face as any in the world."

Very well, let me see how long I can stand it. But how hot it is now, how suffocating! * * *

There is silence now. The knife gets to work. The miracle has actually begun. I glance at the nurses; they are like statues. I watch the dresser at his work. How simply, how easily he follows the surgeon's knife! I am looking below the skin, seeing behind the beautiful covering of man's wonderful but awful body. I begin to feel * * * How hot it is! My mouth is dry. Yes, it is wonderful, most wonderful, this science of surgery. A miracle; but I can't stand it. Let me get out. What a disturbance I should make dropping down in my surplice. Have I the strength to walk across the room? Yes, if I go now. Now, now; as quietly as I can. * * * Outside the theatre, I am shown photographs. He who shows them to me, a lawyer who has volunteered to serve as registrar, is enthusiastic in a depreciating manner. "Oh, yes," he keeps saying, "we are getting on, getting on; science isn't doing so badly; look at this photograph—not so bad, is it? No, not so bad; oh, yes, we are getting on—getting on."

It is easier, with my surplice off, smoking a cigarette by an open window, thus to follow the wonders of surgery. What photographs these are! Mr. Derwent Wood, the most imaginative of our English sculptors, in the early days of the war made masks for disfigured soldiers, so wonderful that across a room they looked natural. But now surgery is its own sculptor. A revolution has come. A new face is grafted on, and grows there, and becomes a real face—not a mask that hides horror. I am shown photographs so repulsive that they could not be published. A splash of lead in the centre of a boy's face turns it to a caricature so inconceivably laughable that you gasp and shudder. But these are photographs of men when they enter the Queen's Hospital at Sidcup. Look at the last photographs of them before they go back again to the trenches. They are as handsome and smiling as any youth in the world. These new faces are as real as your face, veritable faces, unscarred, lovable, beautiful. And in many cases only six months separate the one photograph from the other. "Oh, yes, we are getting on—not so bad, not so bad."

General Gouraud addressing his cavalry at the time of the pursuit of the Germans northward to the Aisne

German hand grenade throwers clad in steel armor

A British soldier of today in armor standing alongside a man in an ancient suit of mail

# Keeping Our Men Fit Physically and Morally

## By EDWARD FRANK ALLEN

[Author of " Keeping Our Fighters Fit "]

THE twin Commissions on Training Camp Activities—one for the War Department and one for the Navy Department—were appointed by Secretary Baker and Secretary Daniels early in the war. In the Summer of 1916, when our troops were encamped on the Mexican border, Secretary Baker sent Raymond B. Fosdick as a special agent of the War Department to study the problem of the soldiers' environment. Conditions in the towns near which the camps were situated were far from satisfactory. There was no provision for any sort of legitimate amusement or relaxation, nothing to compete with the lure of red-light districts and saloons. Many men who under normal conditions would avoid the evils of prostitution and alcohol fall victims in such circumstances.

When Mr. Fosdick made his report to the Secretary of War it became evident that to normalize the conditions obtaining in and around the camps where fighting men were stationed would be to supply competitive forces for combating these evils and their usual attendant result, venereal disease.

The War Department Commission on Training Camp Activities was appointed at the beginning of our war with Germany. Shortly afterward a similar commission was appointed by the Navy Department, and Mr. Fosdick was made Chairman of both. It was the first time in history that a Government had looked beyond the machinery of fighting to the personal and moral welfare of the fighters. Linked together under the supervision of the commissions are such organizations as the Y. M. C. A., the Knights of Columbus, and the Jewish Welfare Board, all of which minister to the social and religious needs of the men in camp; the American Library Association, which maintains and directs the camp libraries, and the Playground and Recreation Association of America, which provides for the soldier and sailor when away from camp. Under the direct management of the commissions are the military athletics, camp singing, the Liberty Theatres, and the Division of Law Enforcement, with which are connected sections on social hygiene for both men and women outside the camps.

## RESULTS ACHIEVED

Their work has in less than a year and a half shown remarkable results. In the army and navy the venereal disease rate has been reduced 50 per cent., and our country holds the enviable record of having the cleanest set of fighting men in the world. The co-operation of the whole country has been enlisted in the campaign to keep it so, and as a result of the activities of the commissions much social good has been accomplished. Eighty-two cities have abolished their red-light districts; a number of States are establishing reformatories for the rehabilitation of prostitutes and delinquent women and girls; many cities are providing detention houses and venereal disease hospitals where the hardened offender, the beginner, and the young girl may receive attention and provision may be made toward their rehabilitation. Laws and administrative machinery for dealing with prostitution and the liquor traffic have in a large number of States and cities been remodeled in accordance with the War Department's program. There has, in fact, been a nation-wide awakening to the importance of the matter.

" Cheerful environment " is provided by giving the men such a combination of recreation and physical exercise as will modify the abnormality of military camp life. Prominent in the recreational field are the club facilities of the Y. M. C. A., the Knights of Columbus, and the Jewish Welfare Board. Their buildings furnish a social background to camp life, a gathering place for the men off duty, where wholesome amusement and relaxation go hand in hand. Freedom from restraint characterizes these clubs. There is usually a player-piano or two and a phonograph, and when the buildings are crowded it is not unusual for all of them to be in use at once. Men are always found writing letters at the desks, for one of the aims of these organizations is to keep the home fires burning. In the chimney corner men congregate to read and smoke, and on the floor of the larger room that is a part of some of the houses there is apt to be a basket ball game in progress.

Every night in the week there is an interesting event in one or more of the buildings. One night there will be a movie show, and the next there may be a boxing exhibition or an amateur vaudeville. Religious services are held from the same platform. And, what is more to the point, no meetings are held by any of the organizations to which all the troops in camp are not invited. Indeed, the admission of such organizations to the army camps and naval training stations was on the express condition that their activities must not be limited to any particular constituency. Denominational and racial lines are disregarded, and a broad spirit of co-operation prevails.

In these buildings, especially the Y. M. C. A., is carried on the educational work of the missions. Some alien soldiers cannot understand English, and the all-inclusive draft has gathered in a small percentage of illiterates. Classes in elementary English have been formed for their instruction, and, further than this, there are courses in languages, especially French, mathematics, history, and other higher branches of learning, many of which serve practical purposes in various lines of military activity. It is estimated that at this time [Sept., 1918] over 100,000 men are enrolled in these educational classes, the majority being students of French.

## THE HOSTESS HOUSES

In a similar classification with that of the clubs are the hostess houses, which are maintained by the Young Women's Christian Association. They provide a place wherein the fighting men may meet their womenfolk who visit them in camp. They solve the problem of the woman who arrives at a cantonment tired, hungry, and bewildered, and with no definite idea of how to find the man she has come to see; for, besides a very comfortable and attractive sitting room, there are rest rooms, a cafeteria, and secretaries who can locate the desired person in the shortest possible time. So homelike is the atmosphere of these houses that their use has widened far beyond the original sphere for which they were intended. Their popularity has become a byword, and even the old line officers who at first objected to their having a place in camp are now among their most enthusiastic supporters.

Athletics occupies an important place in the program of the Commissions on Training Camp Activities. Most of the camp athletic directors appointed by the commissions have been made officers, with the rank of Captain, and their work is directed solely toward the task of making better soldiers, the recreational side being merely a valuable by-product. The big idea behind military athletics as directed by Dr. Joseph E. Raycroft, the member of the War Department Commission, and Walter Camp, the member of the Navy Department in charge of this work, is that it is absolutely essential in making a fighting man.

## BOXING AND BASEBALL

Take, for instance, the matter of boxing as practiced in the army. Experience has shown that as preliminary instruction in bayonet fighting it is invaluable, for almost every thrust of the bayonet has its counterpart in the manly art. " Bayonet fighting is boxing with a gun in your hands," the soldiers are told, and for the best preparation for hand-to-hand combat the foremost American exponents of boxing have been engaged as instructors in the camps. Boxing, moreover, trains men to be alert and to disregard punishment; it makes determined, aggressive fighters. Other sports as well have a distinct military training value, while participation in recreative activities of an athletic nature counteracts the inevitable monotony of the professional training work and develops a group spirit and solidarity in the various units. Besides, it was recently characterized by one of the leading authorities on mental and nervous diseases as one of the most important factors in preventing the occurrence of the condition known as " shell shock."

Sports today are being promoted on a scale that is unparalleled in history. In one of the Western cantonments there are not infrequently sixteen baseball games going on at the same time in one big field. A football game between teams representing two camps brought in gate receipts of $40,000. At another camp there are twenty-six football gridirons, with a seating capacity of 18,000. Games of soccer have frequently occurred in which 400 players have participated, with from eight to ten balls in use. Two thousand men run cross-country races at one time. These are but a few indications of how our men are being made fit for fighting—and after.

## LIBRARY BUILDINGS

There are thirty-six library buildings in the various army camps and naval training stations of this country that provide reading matter for the soldiers and sailors. This branch of the commissions' work is handled by the American Library Association under the direction of Dr. Herbert Putnam, Librarian of Congress, and has already attained to a high degree of usefulness. The buildings are of wood, about a hundred feet long and forty feet wide, and, having been designed by a library architect, they are well adapted to their purpose. There is a librarian in charge of each, and one or more assistants.

The majority of books circulated are fiction, but there is an unusually high percentage of demands for technical books of all kinds, owing to the fact that men have been called to unaccustomed tasks and are reading up on a vast variety of subjects. They are also reading books of information about the war and the countries at war. The following subjects were represented in the circulation of one day at Camp Meade, Md.: French history, mechanics, topography and strategy in war, self-propelled vehicles, hand grenades, field intrenchments, bridges, chemistry, physics, astronomy, geology, hydraulics, electricity, mediaeval history, civil engineering, geography, American history, surveying, materials of construction, general history, masonry and concrete.

Not only do the libraries operate in the training camps, but their service extends also to many smaller posts and to innumerable warships, patrol vessels, and transports. Books are shipped overseas in specially designed cases and distributed by Chaplains, Red Cross workers, and others. Some even find their way into the trenches. The whole service is devoid of " red tape " and is planned to meet the widest possible requirements.

## THEATRES FOR SOLDIERS

On the well-substantiated theory that contentment makes for efficiency, the plan of the Commissions on Training Camp Activities for a string of Liberty Theatres in the army camps was built. In each of thirty camps today there is a fully equipped theatre with seating capacity of from 1,200 to 3,000, constructed on the most modern lines as regards utility and safety. Plays that have been successfully tried out on Broadway are presented by capable casts, so that the soldiers may see the same shows as their friends in civil life. The admission prices are 10, 25, and 50 cents, but soldiers who are fortunate enough to have been presented with a " Smileage Book "—which are sold to the public for sending to their soldier friends—pay their way in with coupons.

The Liberty Theatres are also used for the more pretentious motion-picture shows, athletic exhibitions, lectures, amateur performances, and regimental " sings."

Singing is being developed in our army and navy as never before in the history of any nation. As a definite part of camp drill—for so it is regarded by the War and Navy Departments—it has a distinct military value. A well-known officer said that theoretically music is a gratuity, a luxury, but that practically it has proved itself to be a necessity. These sentiments are typical among military men, and consequently singing in the army and navy is making tremendous progress. Besides promoting morale and esprit de corps, it has a marked physical effect that has been proved again and again when it has been introduced on the march. General Wood recently said, " There isn't anything in the world, even letters from home, that will raise a soldier's spirits like a good, catchy marching tune." Another officer expressed it thus:

It is monotony that kills the men off. A man gets tired of drill, tired of doing the same thing in barracks, even tired of getting shot at. We need company leaders to teach the men new songs; we need instructors to show the men how to get up their own minstrel shows and dramatic entertainments. Everything that can be devised by way of wholesome amusement toward breaking up the monotony is a direct help in making better soldiers and in keeping the standards high.

The commissions have placed a song leader in every army camp and naval training station, and aboard many battleships as well. Their work has shown remarkable results, and its influence is being felt in France today.

The well-being of the soldier and sailor on leave is being provided for by the War Camp Community Service, the organization promoted by the American Playground and Recreation Association, into whose hands this phase of the work was placed by the commissions. There are at this writing over 200 cities and towns which have clubs for the use of the fighting men under the direction of the War Camp Community Service, and many thousands of volunteer workers have given the movement a nation-wide impetus.

It has proved a very satisfactory solution of the problem of social conditions arising from the proximity of camps to cities and from the shore leave of thousands of sailors. These men are assured of sleeping accommodations and food at the lowest possible cost, club facilities without cost, and in many cases the personal hospitality of private families. They are protected against extortion by merchants and others, they are given facilities for sightseeing and attending entertainments, and, best of all, they are made to feel at home in the community.

It must not be forgotten that the work of the Commissions on Training Camp Activities was conceived as an efficiency measure. Its purpose is to make better fighters and better men, and the results thus far attained have more than justified its creation.

## American Indians in the War

The total Indian population of the United States is only 335,998. Of these just about half are citizens, 50,000 still wear skins and blankets, while only 30 per cent. read and write English. There are less than 33,000 male Indians of military age. Yet there are over 6,000 Indians in the United States Army, 85 per cent. of them volunteers, and several hundred more in the navy, every one a full citizen. Fourteen tribes are represented in the service, and when young enough the chiefs themselves have enlisted. In rank our Indian soldiers scale down from Major to private, and almost

every branch has lured some Indians. One Indian helps run a flock of balloons, and there are many in the Aviation Corps. Some have become proficient in wireless telegraphy, and there are others scattered through various technical divisions of the army. Wherever Indian soldiers are found they are reported as earnest, efficient, silently observant, and equal to the best. Above all, they are anxious to fight. On the first three Liberty Loans the Indians of the United States subscribed more than $13,000,000—between $30 and $40 per capita.

# German Peace Talk After the Retreat

## Political Leaders of Germany and Austria-Hungary Change Their Tone in War-Aims Speeches

*The allied victories in France provoked a fresh peace offensive among the Central Powers; during August and September the German and Austrian authorities made various statements suggestive of peace overtures. The German Emperor and his chief lieutenants no longer spoke of "a peace with victory"; on the contrary, they declared that the nation was in danger, and that the struggle was being conducted as a war of defense. The chief utterances on this subject are here placed on record.*

### By KAISER WILHELM

[Message Sent Sept. 5, 1918, to the Municipality of Munich]

THE German people understand the difficulty of the present decisive battles against an enemy filled with hatred, jealousy, and the will to destruction, but has unanimously decided to devote all its strength to defend against its enemies' assaults its sacred soil and its kultur, which it had won in peaceful work.

### By FIELD MARSHAL VON HINDENBURG

[Manifesto Issued Sept. 6, 1918]

We are engaged in a severe battle with our enemies. If numerical superiority alone were to guarantee victory, then Germany would long since have lain crushed on the ground. The enemy knows, however, that Germany and her allies are not to be vanquished by arms alone.

[Von Hindenburg then refers to leaflets dropped on the German lines, of which he says 10,000 are gathered up daily. Some of the leaflets, according to von Hindenburg, read: "Your fight is hopeless. America will cook your goose. Your submarines are of no use. We construct more ships than you sink. Your trade is destroyed and we shall cut off your raw materials after the war; then Germany's industries must famish. You shall never see your colonies again." He continues:]

What are the facts? In the east we have forced peace, and in the west we also are strong enough to do so despite the Americans. But we must be strong and united. * * * Why does the enemy incite colored people against the German soldiers? Because he wants to annihilate us.

The enemy knows what strength resides in our State and Empire and endeavors to open wounds in the German body politic with leaflets and rumors. He endeavors to sow dissension and distrust among the Federal States. We seized on Lake Constance many thousands of leaflets which were being sent to Bavaria to stir up feeling against the North Germans. There have always been traitors to the Fatherland, witting and unwitting. They mostly dwell in neutral countries in order not to be obliged to share our battles and deprivations or be executed as traitors. * * * Be on your guard, German Army.

### By THE GERMAN CROWN PRINCE

[Authorized Interview Published Sept. 4, 1918, in the Budapest Az Est]

If Germany had wanted war, we should not have chosen this moment. No moment could have been more unfavorable for Germany. How will the end come? Through the enemy perceiving that they are not equal to the winning of their colossal stake, and that they cannot win as much as they are bound to lose.

The enemy attacks and the withdrawal on our front at several places are often wrongly interpreted in some circles. Some of our people are too accustomed to a continuous advance, and when a battle occurs wherein the enemy attacks and we have to defend ourselves, the situation is not always correctly understood. In judging the situation, both military and political, we must never forget one thing—that we are waging a war of defense. The war is one of annihilation only for the enemy, not for us.

We want to annihilate none of our enemies. We mean, however, to hold our own.

Regarding the American forces in France, I've found that the majority don't know what they are fighting for, but we feel, of course, the effect of the entry of the Americans. They have sent over very much material and are now sending very much human material. We speak openly of victory. The word victory must not be understood to mean that we want to annihilate the enemy, but only that we mean to hold our own and not let ourselves be vanquished. The moment England entered the war that was clear to me and I always emphasized it.

It was clear that England would take advantage of the opportunity. Belgium, after all, was only a pretext. England intervened because German competition was unbearable. We are fighting for our existence. I repeat, our aim therefore can only be to safeguard ourselves.

The enemy assault doubtless will continue for some time, but our enemies must themselves see that they will not be able to attain their aim. Our troops are fighting splendidly and I attribute to their courage that such colossal superiority in strength does not crush us.

The French fight brilliantly and are bleeding to death. They do not hesitate at any sacrifice. With the English, the individual man is very good and tenacious, but the leadership is deficient. Among the Americans I've found that the majority do not know what they are fighting for. I asked an American prisoner what they were fighting for and he answered, " For Alsace," and to the question, " Where is Alsace? " he replied, " It's a big lake."

## By CHANCELLOR VON HERTLING

[Address to Prussian Upper House, Sept. 5, on Reform and the Franchise]

The Government considers that its task is to bring to fulfillment the royal pledge expressed in the July message. As all the sons of the Fatherland are defending the Fatherland, there is now no question of social discrimination at the next election.

The object is one which I undertook to achieve when I accepted office and upon which I intend to stand or fall, but it is no question of Ministerial responsibility in the ordinary political sense. My honest conviction is that with this serious question the protection and the preservation of the crown and the dynasty are at stake.

Therefore, endeavor to find a road that leads to an understanding. The Government sees no possibility of approving the bill in the form in which it came from the lower house.

I fully appreciate the scruples regarding the introduction of general, equal suffrage, but at the present time these scruples must give way to greater tasks, namely, the protection of the most precious treasures of our political life—the dynasty and the crown. The Government will exercise no pressure on you.

## By BARON BURIAN

*Austro-Hungarian Foreign Minister*

[Address to German Newspaper Men at Vienna, Sept. 10, 1918]

Isn't it a crime against humanity even to think of completely pulling down a structure which has become historical— and which certainly here and there needs improvement, but is only in need of improvement—in order to found a paradise in future on its ruins? The defect in this, however, is that in accordance with the destructive methods of our enemies it can only be created with a much too great sacrifice.

Count the past hecatombs of this war. Think of those to come and ask whether striving to attain war aims at such a price is justifiable—war aims in which the principle of justice is put foremost— without investigating whether an understanding could not be reached by a fair application of that principle.

It is unthinkable that even the most confident hopes of final victory could permit the enemy in the long run to avoid considering whether the most terrific exertions and sacrifices can longer be justified in order to carry through principles which are not the enemy's monopoly or to regulate the affairs of other peoples who can manage them quite as well themselves.

I believe that careful and sincere investigation would bring many on the other side to realize that they often are fighting for imaginary things. It may be an ungrateful task to want to communicate one's own perceptions of things to the enemy.

The enemy group can, if it wishes, convince itself that in all questions of humanity and justice and of future international relations it will encounter on the part of our group no opposition and will be in line with our existing progressive aspirations. But at the same time it will meet our determination to continue steadfastly to stand up for our good right.

Our adversaries need only provide an opportunity in a calm exchange of views —some sort of direct informative discussions is thinkable which would be far from being peace negotiations—of discussing and weighing everything which today separates the belligerent parties, and no further fighting will, perhaps, be needed to bring them closer together.

But I would not delude you with baseless prospects of peace at a moment when the war fever still is shaking the world. I must, however, talk to you of peace because we all honestly want it and because we are certain there is an ever-growing number of like-minded persons in all enemy countries.

We desire to contribute to the best of our ability to a mutual understanding and help to pave a way for conciliation. But, so long as necessary, we shall hold out in a loyal and resolute joint defense.

I am certain that this war must cost this tormented earth a terrible amount of bloodshed and an immeasurable destruction of precious possessions before the end can be reached by the military overthrow of the enemy, if, indeed, this at all is possible.

We are oppressed by the same cares, but we are not downhearted. You can convince yourself here that we, just as in Germany, with head erect and without fear or arrogance, are waging a defensive war, rejecting all responsibility for the prolongation thereof, which was criminally and quite uselessly forced upon us by the enemy.

No party can be sure of the issue until the end of a war, but it is not to be expected that either party should renounce the possibility of a military victory.

## By COUNT CZERNIN
*Former Foreign Minister of Austria-Hungary*
[Statement at Vienna Sept. 10, 1918]

We must not again try to stray from peace by understanding, or otherwise the war will continue until friend and foe alike have perished. The opposition to disarmament is the greatest test of all obstacles to peace. Therefore, I regard this opposition as a serious mistake.

I must admit that the league of nations is envisaged by Entente statesmen and intends to secure Entente predominance and therefore is inacceptable to us. But I deny that no single form could be found that would impose equal rights and duties upon all States.

From the banks of the Danube this call ought to go forth to the world: " Wake up, wake up from the bad dreams of blood and force, for a new and better future must be shaped. War as a political means must be combated." The day will come when millions in all countries will repeat this call.

## By COUNT VITZHUN VON ECKSTAEDT
*Foreign Minister of Saxony*
[Address at Dresden Sept. 10, 1918]

The more we speak of peace the further away it is. The enemy's means of success have plunged him into a kind of warlike folly which makes conciliation impossible. * * * We must, therefore, hold out. We can trust the army and the high command, but popular confidence is tottering. Why? Because Germany, having no enemy in the Fatherland, becomes too oblivious of the risks incidental to war. We must deal more energetically with enemy agents in our midst. Put forth all our strength into the war and forget our differences. Then we may win.

## By Dr. W. S. SOLF
*German Colonial Secretary*
[Address Before German Society of Berlin Aug. 21, 1918]

The Chancellor declared last month in the Reichstag to all who wished to hear that we do not intend to retain Belgium in any form whatsoever. Belgium shall arise again after the war as an independent State, vassal to no one. Nothing stands in the way of the restoration of Belgium but the enemy's will to war.

How small a part regard for Belgium plays in the plans of the Entente is most clearly shown by an extract from the American press, which England's Minister of Propaganda, Lord Northcliffe, printed with enthusiastic approval in one of his papers. THE NEW YORK TIMES wrote:

> Germany's assurance that she does not intend to retain Belgium is neither of interest nor value. The Allies will drive the Germans out of Belgium and France.

Referring to this Lord Northcliffe says in The Evening News of July 16:

> We rejoice to hear such a clear, resounding voice from America. That is the way to speak. Germany must be destroyed in the sense of THE NEW YORK TIMES, we mean destroyed by bloody and absolutely irreparable defeats on the battlefield, so that nothing remains of Germany but the bones of her dead soldiers in France and Belgium. There is no other way.

Thus speak the protectors who for the sake of Belgium have drawn their swords.

I dare say that the safeguarding of our colonial future is not only the aim of our Government and certain groups of individuals, but it has become an aim of the German people. A lively consciousness now extends far into the workers' circles that the retention of our colonies is a vital question for the honor of Germany as a great power. Our colonial war aims are second to no other in national importance. The growing realization of German workers as to Germany's position is especially gratifying in view of the plans of our enemies, which have been clearly revealed during the last few days.

## REPLIES TO MR. BALFOUR

Mr. Balfour formally announced Great Britain's claim for the annexation of our colonies and did not hesitate to advance on moral grounds this claim for annexation. He not only concerns himself as to our colonial methods, but goes into high politics with all sails set. Mr. Balfour, in his speech, announced the British creed, which amounts to representing Britain's right to world domination as something self-evident, and morally annihilating Germany's claim to be a great power.

Mr. Balfour asserts that intellectual Germany is dominated by the mailed fist doctrine. Here there are Chauvinistic jingoes, people who worship the eternal yesterday, and anxiously and without understanding await the approach of a new era. Before the war these people formed a small group without political influence on the Government, which constantly combated them. During the war their number, indeed, has increased, not because the struggle for German supremacy in the world had taken deeper root, but because their ranks were swelled by numerous sober and solicitous patriots.

Among these are many who before the war held high ideals about an understanding of peoples, good-will, and fair play in international relations, but whose political creed broke down under the experiences of the war.

Where does the blame lie? Nowhere but in the spirit which animates our enemies—that spirit which is a dishonor and has turned to scorn the grand ideal of a league of nations by a simultaneous demand for a commercial war against Germany.

If I believed that the spirit which at present seems to prevail in England, which speaks clearly in Mr. Balfour's speech, and which was manifested against us in the Pemberton-Billing case—if I had to believe that this spirit would always have the upper hand in England, then I also would advocate that the war should be fought to the death.

I am, however, firmly convinced that, before the end of the war comes, an intellectual revulsion must and will supervene against this knockout spirit. Otherwise the realization of a league of nations remains a Utopian war aim.

## DEFENDS BREST PEACE

Mr. Balfour's second charge is directed against our Eastern policy. To this I reply that the Brest-Litovsk peace came about by agreement between the Russian and German Governments; that the frontier peoples of Russia, after centuries of oppression, should be permitted to live their own national life, for which object they had been striving. This agreement on the fate of the border peoples is a fact of world importance which never can be erased from history.

Not about the aim, but about the ways and means leading to conferring their own national life upon these peoples, did the Russian and German conceptions differ. Our conception was and is that the path to freedom shall not lead through anarchy to wholesale murder. Between the first bursting of the bonds and full capability for self-determination of the border peoples there lies a natural transitory period. Until the regulation forces should co-operate in the various countries, Germany felt called upon to protect these communities in their own, as well as in the general, interest, as indeed she has been called upon to do by both national majorities and minorities.

The Brest-Litovsk peace is a framework, and the picture which is to appear within is only sketched in rough lines.

England forfeited the right to act as moral champion of the Russian border States in their unparalleled time of suffering. During the war they repeatedly appealed to England for help. It was always denied them.

## ASSAILS CZECH RECOGNITION

The recognition of the Czechoslovaks— those landless robber bands—as an allied power is the logical keystone of the singular structure of Anglo - Russian friendship.

The economic distress in the territories occupied by us is undoubtedly great, but it is cynicism when England laments this, because her hunger blockade is directed against the occupied territories just as it is directed against us, against neutrals, and against the whole world. * * *

The time must come when between peoples and peoples something like an impulse of confidence shall germinate; when oppressed human nature shall revolt against false doctrines, hated and threatening to suffocate the innermost human affinities. Mr. Balfour feared such a reaction, and this is precisely why

he directed accusations not solely against the German Government, but against the German people itself. * * * Our enemies do not want peace by negotiation.

There are today groups and men who can be regarded as centres of the European conscience. In these centres there stirs something like recognition of the fact that the way into the open can only be found if the war - waging nations awaken to the knowledge of their common tasks. * * * The victorious march of the common aims is certain. Mr. Balfour can postpone that victory, but he cannot prevent it.

## By LORD ROBERT CECIL
*British Under Secretary for Foreign Affairs*
[Summary of a Reply to Dr. Solf, Issued Aug. 23, 1918]

Lord Robert said that the British Government had been collecting and soon would publish evidence of Germany's brutality and callousness in governing her colonies, after which the world would agree that the colonies could not be restored to Germany.

Lord Robert said that Dr. Solf's utterances were a very remarkable " essay in psychology," which seemed to indicate that sections of German opinion were beginning to realize that the attitude taken by the Pan Germans must be disastrous to the future of Germany. He added, however, that it was not his view that the Pan Germans were done for, as in the last resort they would always dominate Germany.

The speaker referred to Dr. Solf's statement about Belgium, saying that it appeared to represent an advance toward decency, but it was not clear. He challenged Dr. Solf to say whether he meant that Germany was prepared to give up Belgium and to restore the damage done. " Let him say this in plain language so that the whole world will understand," he added.

The Under Secretary asserted that only a few weeks ago Dr. von Kühlmann (former Minister of Foreign Affairs) was ousted because he said Germany could not have things all her own way, and declared that the German Chancellor (Count von Hertling) also had been made to explain away a phrase he uttered about the restoration of Belgium.

Referring to the Brest-Litovsk treaty, Lord Robert said that any one who had seen the way the so-called independent States were created would see that it had been done so that they would have as little independence as possible.

" When Foreign Secretary Balfour recently said that the German colonies could not be restored, he was speaking only what the conscience of mankind would have him say." Lord Robert continued: " Premier Lloyd George said months ago that the question of the colonies would be settled at the Peace Conference, but Mr. Balfour's more recent statement ruled out the possibility that they would be restored."

Turning to Dr. Solf's mention of a league of nations, the speaker said:

" Devoted as some of us are to the conception of a league of nations, we see no hope of the success of any such scheme unless preceded by victory, until it is acknowledged by Germany that her whole military system is criminal."

He said that only last April the Germans, in the flush of victory, were talking of a continent from Flanders to Egypt, and saying that the only peace possible was a German peace.

The Under Secretary asserted that as far as the Allies were concerned they had made up their minds that the only way to obtain peace was on the field of battle, and they were determined to carry on the war to victory.

# Germany's War Aims in March, 1918
## An Instructive Symposium

*A German publishing house, Montanus, at Siegen, published a book in March, 1918, containing contributions from nineteen German Deputies—representing all parties except the Minority Socialists—on German war aims. The symposium very clearly revealed the feeling of an overwhelming majority of Germans on the subject of peace terms at the time when the great offensive campaign of 1918 was launched in France. The following extracts were made by The London Times:*

HERR WILHELM BLOS, Socialist Member of the Reichstag, writes: " The fundamental condition for us all is that Germany shall remain the conqueror in the world war, or, at any rate, shall not be defeated." Herr Eduard David, the Socialist leader, contributes a violent denunciation of French Socialism, in which he declares that Jaurès was murdered because he possessed evidence of French responsibility for the war, and that the German Socialists only did their duty in defending their assaulted country. David talks a good deal about democracy, but he admits that the German Socialists " agreed to the peace in the East," although " it contains the danger of future wars." On the other hand, they advocate " the self-determination of the peoples," first, because it is " practicable," secondly, because it is " ethical," but finally, because it is " the only

guarantee that the peace will be respected in Russia." Here is the calculation:

However things may shape in Russia, the populations will remain the final Court of Appeal. Thereby we achieve for all time the dissolution of the coalition against us.

Take next the views of the so-called " Liberals " and of the Centre Party. Herr Müller, the well-known Radical Deputy for Meiningen, writes:

After the exclusion of Russia, we must not state any but general points of view; our special demands for Belgium, France, and the Colonies we must hold back for the present. We want no conquests for their own sake; we want them only as permanent security against future assaults and " encirclements," and we need elbow room for our work—not upon a paper, but upon a real foundation. For treaties are today hardly worth the paper they are written on, (sic.) From these two aims everything also will follow—the " freedom of the seas," the assurance of our greatest possible independence of foreign imports, and much else. Our new neighbor States in the East must give us settlement land for the increase of our national strength.

The well-known Centre Party leader in the Reichstag, Herr Pfeiffer, says that the war was never anything but an economic duel between Germany and England:

It was a duel, criminally provoked by England, who thought that she was still the stronger, but already compelled to fear that the existence and the continuation of this strength was being disputed. * * * One can understand the idea of revenge in the case of France and also in the case of Italy, but anybody who looks into the eyes of the English politicians, cold as ice and hard as steel, knows that for them there was no question of real sentiment or ideal patriotism, but that for them only naked business interests turned the scales.

For Herr Pfeiffer the result of the war must be a "greater Germany"— with economic and territorial guarantees, "freedom of the seas," and all the rest of it. Count Spee, Centre Party Deputy in the Prussian Diet, wants merely a German world, finally healed by German kultur. What a blessing it is, he observes, that German statesmen are not compelled to declare their war aims publicly, "like Lloyd George and Clemenceau," who have thus "to expose themselves to the coarsest abuse of their enemies."

Herr Schlee, a National Liberal member of the Reichstag, says:

I cannot see why we should bear the tremendous cost of this war, which was forced upon us. Like Herr Helfferich, I consider it obvious that our enemies, who caused this war, must also bear its cost— in so far as they can in any way be got at. The fact that they have not at present the necessary money is a matter of indifference. They can owe us the money or most of it, pay the interest on the debt, and pay off the debt little by little. * * *

I consider it inadvisable to talk at present about the amount of the war indemnity to be paid to us, and about the extent and the character of the securities which we require. There will be time enough to talk about that after the war, and then we shall also have to see to it that the countries which we take away from our enemies shall be unable to do us any harm in future. For reasons both of law and morality I consider it evident that the German people must be better off

after the war than it was before. During the whole period of its existence the German people has fertilized the whole world with its ideas, and for centuries (sic) it has lived in peace with its neighbors.

Several of the Deputies are much concerned about their duty to God. For example, Count Wilhelm Hoensbroech, a member of the Upper House of the Prussian Diet, sees Islam in revolt against its "oppressors," and Persia, India, and Egypt "in conflagration," and he is much concerned lest Germany should interfere with the judgment of "Divine Providence" upon "proud England." His last word is that all the German demands must "harmonize with national needs and bow to the authority which God has given to the Germans."

As for the avowed Pan Germans, there is an astonishing contribution by Herr Bacmeister. He wants everything. Now that Germany holds the coast of Flanders, she sees for the first time how important it is for her to keep it. She sees that in future her navy must be able to destroy British trade on the outbreak of war. Again, she sees that the fortresses of Liége and Namur, and an enemy Antwerp, are preposterous obstacles to a smooth invasion of France. And it is clear that Germany must have more agricultural land and abundant supplies of fodder and materials of every kind in order to fight the next war in comfort. Germany's war aims, in fact, are dictated by the experience of the last four years. The principles of action are so simple:

The future necessities of Germanism must by themselves alone determine the aims of the war. The interests of Germanism must be satisfied without any consideration for the interests of foreign peoples. Given military and economic necessities, Germany's might must be established even in places where the decision hitherto rested with foreign peoples. Any difficulties which may arise must be faced.

Herr Bacmeister constructs a long list of "necessities." It is obvious that Germany must hold the line of the Meuse and the Sambre. It is equally obvious that Germany must dominate the communications, and therefore must hold the Belgian railways and canals. As for coal and iron, Germany must keep what she wants. Hence she must "correct" the French and Luxemburg frontiers. In the east, it is obvious that Germany must take plenty of land for the settlement of her peasants. As the alliance with Turkey is vital, the Balkan States must be permanently subordinated to Austria-Hungary, and there must be an end of Serbia. Germany must, of course, dominate the Danube. Indemnities would be good, but a " broadening of the basis " of German economic strength by annexations in east and west, and the recovery of world trade would be better. The only way to settle the Alsace-Lorraine question is by smashing France, and the only way to settle the Italian question is by smashing Italy. All talk is useless; the power of the sword alone must decide:

> It sounds paradoxical, but it is true; a peace by agreement, without a clear military decision, means ultimately the maintenance of the old antagonisms—that is to say, of the causes of war—and so means not a true peace, but an armistice. At the moment when the English Government fears that the continuation of the war will imperil the English Empire, it will be ready for peace. Then the war will be as good as lost. The English Government will not admit this, but will proceed to conversations among the statesmen. Then these conversations will be profitable and successful. Why? Because the power of the sword will have decided.

# After the War Is Over

## A Striking Appeal for International Partnership in Business During the Transition Period

### By PREMIER LLOYD GEORGE

[ADDRESS DELIVERED BEFORE A LARGE DEPUTATION OF THE CHIEF MANUFACTURERS OF GREAT BRITAIN, WHO SOUGHT A DECLARATION OF THE GOVERNMENT'S POLICY TOWARD INDUSTRY AFTER THE WAR]

THERE are two considerations, at least, that delay declarations on the part of the Government as to their final views. First of all, there is the one that our time has been absorbed, especially during the last few months, by the demands of the great battle. The second is, that we must necessarily, in whatever policy we proclaim, keep in touch and be in complete accord, first of all, with our dominions; and, secondly, with our allies. There is a good deal of discussion about a league of nations, and I am certainly one of those who believe in it. But there are two leagues of nations which are already in existence; the first is the British Empire, and the second is the Great Alliance against the Central Powers. And whatever decision we come to must be one in which we can march hand in hand and side by side with those two great league of nations of which we are members. We have been discussing this problem in the course of the last few weeks with the dominions, and we had discussions with our allies in 1916, before America came in. The Paris resolutions were arrived at in 1916. Up to the present time America has expressed no opinion upon the Paris resolutions, and it is vitally important that the policy of America and the policy of this country should be in complete agreement on economic problems as well as on other problems. All I am permitted to say at the present moment is, that I am very hopeful, because agreement among the Allies on these great problems means that the economic fate of the world will be in the hands of the great allied powers who are federated together at present.

The less we talk of the theories of the past and the more we deal with the realities and the needs of the present the better the national progress we shall make. I will tell you why. In the war we have been a united people in defending the empire. I want us to be a united people again in the reconstruction of the empire. And more than that. There is nothing which you have said today that would lead me to believe that there are any insuperable difficulties in our continuing united. You have raised some issues of the most vital importance with regard to our industries. The essential industries of this country must be not merely maintained but strengthened. This war has taught many of us useful lessons, and I hope those lessons are not confined to one party. I have no doubt there are men in the party to which I belong who have been taught many things they did not quite appreciate before. May I respectfully hope that there are men in the other party who also have been taught a few things. These are the days when courage is needed, and there is no greater demand on courage than, when you have made up your mind that a certain course is the right one to take, to take it without any regard to anybody who taunts you that you are inconsistent with what you have done before. The country must come first and not the career or consistency of any man or of any party.

## ESSENTIAL INDUSTRIES

During the war we have undoubtedly discovered that there were industries in this country that were essential not merely from the commercial point of view, but from the point of view of national defense and security. Under no conditions, whatever it costs, should we let those industries down in the future. There, I think, we ought to have the most complete agreement, and I do not doubt for a moment that you will get it. The best method of securing those industries against unfair attack, against unfair competition, the best way in which you can secure their development and secure that they shall go on growing and increasing with a view to the strengthening of the country, is a matter which will require the very deepest consideration; and it is a consideration which no Government could possibly avoid giving to it at the earliest possible moment.

There are two or three things which I should like to say upon that particular problem. The longer the war lasts the sterner must be the economic terms we impose on the foe. And I think the sooner he realizes that the better. He is fighting in order to impose his own economic terms upon the Allies. He will never succeed in doing so. As far as that is concerned we must be in a position to determine the conditions which we regard as fair without having them imposed upon us by the will of the enemy. And if he goes on fighting, imposing greater burdens upon us, destroying our young manhood, and guilty also of outrages which shock humanity and which make it difficult to shake hands with him when the war is over, the sterner will be the terms that will be imposed upon him.

When peace comes I have no doubt that there will be a good deal of confusion, that there will be a time when all the organizing capacity of the nation and all its individual strength will be required in order to prevent something which is worse than confusion. A fact of much importance is that there will be arrears of work which it will take us years to make up, even in manufacture. A great difficulty will be raw material; where to get it and how to get it. Another difficulty will be transport, and you will find that during the first years of peace these will be difficulties that will require special consideration of a totally different character even from that which has been predicted in the very able speeches which have been delivered here today. These questions will demand the most careful consideration. You will require the most complete understanding with our allies and a complete understanding with our dominions, because it is most important that you should carry along with you the people who have contributed with you to the common sacrifices.

## VALUE OF STATE AID

No one ever dreams of continuing the present system of control after the war. The strength of this country has been very largely in the ingenuity, the self-reliance, the adaptability, and the resource which come from individual effort.

All the same, do not let us despise what the German has won from combination, and in the future, although I do not in the least deprecate the individuality which has come out of the old British methods, there is a lesson of the war which even the Germans have taught us, in the effect of the assistance of State action, of State help, of State encouragement, of State promotion, and of combined effort among those who are engaged in all the industries of the country. Let us learn our lessons wherever they come from, even from the Germans.

But no one would ever dream of continuing the present system of rigid meticulous interference which is essential in a war. War, if it is to be victorious, must be waged by a disciplined nation; and a disciplined nation must mean interference. You tear a man out of his business—he may be the only one who is conducting it—and you send him away at 1s. 7d., or whatever it is, a day, to a trench in France. That is interfering with a man's business. The war is essentially interfering with business at every turn, and you cannot avoid it. And let me say this: magnificently as the business and industrial community of this country has shown its capacity to organize itself for war—and there has been nothing comparable to it in the whole history of the world—I quite agree that when the war is over all the constant interference which may be absolutely essential now in order to direct and to concentrate the whole strength of the nation upon the war must disappear.

But there are two or three things that must remain even then until we get over the transition period. You are not going to get raw material without Government interference to a considerable extent. You have also to organize transport. You have got to see that the dominions, who are also in arrears in respect of British manufactures, shall have their fair share. We have to do more than that. We must not forget the countries who have been fighting side by side with us, and who will be entitled to the assistance of Great Britain in the re-equipment of the essential conditions of their industrial and national life. You might have perhaps from an enemy source an order which will be more remunerative to you than an order which would come from Great Britain, from the dominions, or from our allies. I think we ought to see that the people who have been fighting together should be served first. Do not let us make the mistake of dissolving partnership the moment this fighting is over. The world will not come right at once, and, if you dissolve partnership with all these great peoples—a partnership cemented with blood—there will be men quite ready to take advantage of it, even when the war is over.

Therefore, it is vital that when the war is over and when the transition period has come, when there will not be enough to go round, we must keep the partnership going and help each other to the end, so that the brotherhood shall remain.

[The address closed with the statement that what decision was finally reached would be " with the concord and good-will and cooperation which have existed between us and our allies."]

# America's War Aims

## What the United States Will Demand as a Just and Righteous Peace

### By HENRY CABOT LODGE

#### United States Senator from Massachusetts

[AN ADDRESS DELIVERED IN THE UNITED STATES SENATE, AUG. 23, 1918, BY THE REPUBLICAN LEADER OF THE SENATE]

THE Germans, repulsed and losing, will undoubtedly resort to their other weapon, which they have used more than once during this war with terrible effect. They will begin an insidious and poisonous peace propaganda. With this weapon they have succeeded in disorganizing Russia, reducing that great country to a wreck and removing it for the time being as a military factor. With the same weapon they brought about the Italian defeat on the Isonzo, which was the result of treachery and disintegrating propaganda and not of straight fighting, because the Italians, when unbetrayed, have shown since then at the Piave the finest fighting qualities and have thrown Austria back in crushing defeat.

It is the German propaganda which we shall be obliged to face in the ensuing months, and it therefore seems to me of the last importance to know exactly what we mean by peace. Generalities will not serve. It must be, it is commonly said— we have all said it—a just and righteous peace. But what is a just and righteous peace? What are the conditions that would make it so? What is the irreducible minimum? We intend to make the world safe for democracy. But what exactly do we mean by democracy? If we mean, as we undoubtedly do, the democracy of England, France, Italy, and the United States, we can all understand it; but the Bolsheviki masquerade under the name of democracy, and the Bolsheviki, by a combination of treachery, corruption, and ignorance, have reduced Russia to servitude under Germany and have engendered a form of democracy as dangerous to the world as the Government of the Hohenzollerns.

But assuming, as we do, when we say we must make the world safe for democracy that we mean our own conception of democracy, how is it to be made safe? That, again, is a vague term which must be answered, and can only be answered by definition.

We are fighting and our allies are fighting with us for security; for independence; for the right of nations, great and small, to govern themselves in their own way; for organized races and peoples to have the opportunity to govern themselves in independent States; for the sanctity and observance of treaties; for the general disarmament of nations. How are these things to be secured? The details are really far more important than the general propositions, in which we all agree. Broadly speaking, there is only one way to obtain this security of the nations, this safety of democracy, this preservation of freedom and civilization, and that is by reducing Germany to a condition where by no possibility can she precipitate another war for universal conquest, with all its attendant horrors, upon an unoffending world. Again we are faced by details. How is this to be done? I see only one way in which it can be done, and I will enumerate the results, the hard facts, the essential conditions to which we must attain.

Belgium must be restored.

Alsace and Lorraine must be returned to France—unconditionally returned— not merely because sentiment and eternal justice demand it, but because the iron and coal of Lorraine must be forever taken from Germany.

Italia Irredenta—all those areas where the Italian race is predominant, including Trieste—must go back to Italy.

Serbia and Rumania must be established in their independence.

Greece must be made secure.

Most important of all, if we are to make the world safe in the way we mean it to be safe, the great Slav populations now under the Government of Austria—the Jugoslavs and the Czechoslovaks, who have been used to aid the Germans, whom they loathe—must be established as independent States.

The Polish people must have an independent Poland.

And we must have these independent States created so that they will stand across the pathway of Germany to the east. Nothing is more vital than this for a just, a righteous, and an enduring peace.

The Russian provinces taken from Russia by the villainous peace of Brest-Litovsk must be restored to Russia. The President, as you all remember, has announced the vast importance of sustaining Russia. If Germany continues to hold a large part of Russia, the world for years to come will be under the shadow of another great war which will surely be precipitated upon us when Germany has developed her Russian possessions to the point of yielding her men, money, and supplies.

Constantinople must be finally taken away from Turkey and placed in the hands of the allied nations as a free port, so as to bar Germany's way to the east and hold the Dardanelles open for the benefit of mankind.

We must not be beguiled into concessions to Turkey in the hope of separating her from Germany. It would be a miserable outcome to have Turkey retained in Europe, a curse to her subjects and neighbors, a plague spot, and a breeder of wars. Her massacres must not under any pretense be condoned nor her iniquities rewarded. Let Turkey and Bulgaria share the fate of their master and be so treated that they will be unable again to trouble the world.

Palestine must never return to Turkish rule, and the persecuted Christians of Asia Minor—the Syrians and the Armenians—must be made safe.

These are the principal conditions which alone will give us a victory worth having, and when we talk about a complete peace and a just and righteous peace, let it be known to all the world that this is what we mean. It is idle to talk about our not annihilating the German people. Nobody, of course, has any such idea. It could not be done even if we wished to do it. We are not engaged in this war to try to arrange a government for Germany. The German people must do that themselves, and they will get precisely the government that they desire and deserve—just as they now have the government they prefer, whose purposes and ambitions and barbarism they share and sustain. Our part and our business is to put Germany in a position where she can do no more harm in the future to the rest of the world. Unless we achieve this we shall have fought in vain. Congress and the President had no right to declare war unless they meant to do precisely this thing. Nothing less would justify our action.

We are pouring out the best blood of the country, the blood of our chosen youth, upon the altar of patriotism. We are making every sort of pecuniary sacrifice. We are bearing an immense burden of taxation. We are mortgaging with our loans the future of coming generations. We have set aside for the time being the Constitution under which individual liberty has been preserved and the country has grown and prospered. We have adopted measures which lead, if unchecked, to the building up on the one hand of a great bureaucracy such as that which crushed and ruined Russia and which on the other are stimulating the development of State socialism. It is our intention to return, as our laws show, to the old restrictions, protections, and rights of the ordered freedom of the Constitution.

We are taking these vast risks, we are bearing these huge burdens, we are making these unspeakable sacrifices of life with a brave and cheerful spirit; but we have no right to do all these things unless we win the prize and reach the goal which alone can warrant and justify them. The results which we must have, and which I have ventured to outline, can never be ob-

The village of Bouresches, at the edge of Belleau Wood, northwest of Château-Thierry, after its capture by Americans, June 7, 1918. (Note the shell holes)
(© Times Photo Service)

Women and children who had remained in Château-Thierry during the fighting for the town emerging from their shelters after the Germans were driven back

(© *Underwood & Underwood*)

tained by a negotiated peace. Lord Lansdowne—and he is not alone—appears to think that this war can be ended by a peace formulated by eminent representatives of the nations in the old way. He does not seem to have gone beyond the methods of 1815 and the Congress of Vienna.

As this war is utterly different from any war that the world has ever known, so must the peace which concludes it be utterly different from any peace which the world has ever known. It cannot be a peace of bargain, of give and take, and of arrangement. No peace that satisfies Germany in any degree can ever satisfy us. It cannot be a negotiated peace. It must be a dictated peace, and we and our allies must dictate it. The victory bringing such a peace must be won inside, not outside, the German frontier. It must be won finally and thoroughly in German territory, and can be so won nowhere else.

In no other way can we secure the safety for which we are fighting. In no other way can we justify the sacrifices we are making. To this supreme end our efforts must be addressed. I do not underrate the difficulties. I do not underestimate the obstacles to be overcome. But the difficulties and the obstacles must alike be crushed, set aside, and overridden. The United States occupies, fortunately, a position in which she will be able to speak with a powerful voice. We seek no territory, no material gain for our own country. We seek only the safety of civilization and freedom and the assurance of our own absolute independence and our right to live our own lives and settle our own problems in our own way. There is no territory by which we could be bribed or influenced, no trade advantage by which we could be tempted. There is no personal profit which can turn us from the one great object. Our sole purpose is to put Germany finally and completely in a position where she can never again attempt to conquer and ruin the world as she has done in the last four years. This purpose can be accomplished. We shall do it, but we must be above all propositions of a bargained peace, all suggestions of negotiations; deaf to every voice which would divert us from the path; deaf alike to the whimper of the pacifist and to the wheedling or truculent appeal of the helpers of Germany. When Germany is beaten to her knees and the world is made safe by the arrangements which I have suggested, then, and not before, we shall have the just and righteous peace for which we fight. In this way and in no other shall we obtain it. We shall obtain it because we are going to win. Let us but be true to ourselves, and we shall not then be false to any man.

## Vagaries of Inventive Minds

The Inventions Department of the British Ministry of Munitions reports having received the following extraordinary suggestions for dealing with hostile aircraft:

The clouds are to be frozen artificially and guns mounted on them; heavy guns are to be suspended from captive balloons; the moon is to be covered with a big black balloon; airplanes are to be armed with scissors or scythes, like Boaricea's chariot, or to trail bombs behind them on a long cord; heat rays are to be projected for the purpose of setting Zeppelins on fire; electric waves to paralyze the magnetos. One of the most popular suggestions of all is to attach a searchlight to an anti-aircraft gun, get the light on the object, and shoot along the beam; but, unfortunately, the path of a shell is quite different from that of a ray of light. To prevent the polished lines of a railway showing at night, the last car of the last train, according to another correspondent, was to *camouflage* them by dribbling blacking as it went along.

Other proposals were: A balloon carrying magnets hung on strings to attract the rifles out of men's hands; a shell to contain fleas or other vermin inoculated with disease; a shell with a man inside it to steer it at the target; the squirting of cement over soldiers so as to petrify them; the sending of snakes into enemy trenches by pneumatic propulsion.

# Peace Only Through Victory

## By GILBERT M. HITCHCOCK

### *United States Senator From Nebraska and Chairman of Foreign Relations Committee*

[ADDRESS IN THE UNITED STATES SENATE, AUG. 27, 1918, FAVORING THE MAN POWER BILL]

AS a nation we are confronted with a great menace and are in the midst of a great world crisis. Not only must we from now on produce the greatest military man power of any nation on our side of the conflict, but we must help to finance our associate nations, help to feed them, and furnish to them much of the raw material and finished products that they require. This means that we must mobilize and conserve our man power at home. The men most valuable at home must be kept at home to support families or to work in essential industries.

The productiveness of the United States must be maintained at its highest point. This means not only the production of the soil and of the industries, but it means also the production of revenues derived from taxes and the production of credit derived from the sale of bonds. This can only be done by taking for military service those least needed in the field of production and business. To make the choice as broad as possible it is necessary at this time, in my opinion, to go as low as 18 years and as high as 45.

To my mind it is almost as important to success that the United States should avoid impairing its powers of production and supply as it is to furnish man power. We must furnish steel and copper and ships and food and lumber and transportation and ammunition and cotton and wool and sugar and coal and motors and hundreds of other products directly needed in the war, not only by ourselves, but by the allied nations. But, more then that, we must furnish money and credit not merely for ourselves, but to some extent for them, and this can only be done by enormous taxes and equally enormous bond sales, and these are only possible while the country is prosperous and productive. To keep it prosperous and productive we must avoid taking men in essential or useful occupations who are important or essential to those occupations.

Nothing less than a great military disaster will burn into the mind of Germany the lesson she must learn if the world is to be made safe for democracy. The German people must become convinced that their system is wrong. They must be shown that the system of military autocracy built up and developed in fifty years is a failure.

When that time comes the German people will be willing to give a guarantee of peace. They will be willing to accept the democratic theory of self-government. They will be willing to agree to the independence of small nations. They will be willing to accept justice in place of force as the international standard, but they will not be ready to do these things and repudiate military autocracy until they have tasted defeat. And, so, I am reconciled to the idea of extending the age limits of the draft, because nothing but a great military triumph can bring a real and a permanent peace. President Wilson expressed the thought in terse and striking phrase at Baltimore, when he declared the purpose of the American people. He said:

> Force, force to the utmost, force without stint or limit, the righteous and triumphant force which shall make right the law of the world and cast every selfish dominion down in the dust.

Under the present age limits we have raised over 3,000,000 men, without materially encroaching upon those in deferred classifications. Under the proposed extension provided in this bill we can increase our forces to more than 5,000,000 without calling married men who are supporting families and without taking men or boys needed in essential industries.

With such a force the road to victory and to peace may be comparatively short. The harder we hit, the shorter the fight and the lower the cost and loss.

THE LUSITANIA, THE MOST FAMOUS VICTIM OF THE U-BOAT

# Sinking of the Lusitania
## Judicial Analysis of the Deed by the United States District Court

*The Federal District Court of New York, in a decision written by Judge J. M. Mayer and filed Aug. 24, 1918, held that the steamer Lusitania of the Cunard Steamship Company, torpedoed by a German submarine May 7, 1915, was an unarmed merchant vessel which had no explosives of any kind on board. The decision absolves the steamship company from damages in the sixty-seven suits, involving $6,000,000, that had been brought against it on the ground that the vessel carried ammunition and high explosives, and had been improperly navigated while passing through the submarine zone off the Irish coast. The decision officially reviews the facts, and for the first time pronounces an American judicial verdict regarding one of the most tragic episodes of the war. The full text, constituting a document of profound historical significance, is as follows:*

UNITED STATES DISTRICT COURT, SOUTHERN DISTRICT OF NEW YORK.—IN THE MATTER OF THE PETITION OF THE CUNARD STEAMSHIP COMPANY, LTD., AS OWNER OF THE STEAMSHIP LUSITANIA, FOR LIMITATION OF ITS LIABILITY.—MAYER, DISTRICT JUDGE:

ON May 1, 1915, the British passenger-carrying merchantman Lusitania sailed from New York bound for Liverpool, with 1,257 passengers and a crew of 702, making a total of 1,959 souls on board, men, women, and children. At approximately 2:10 on the afternoon of May 7, 1915, weather clear and sea smooth, without warning, the vessel was torpedoed and went down by the head in about eighteen minutes, with an ultimate tragic loss of 1,195.

Numerous suits having been begun against the Cunard Steamship Company, Limited, the owner of the vessel, this proceeding was brought in familiar form by the steamship company, as petitione.

to obtain an adjudication as to liability and to limit petitioner's liability to its interest in the vessel and her pending freight, should the court find any liability.

The sinking of the Lusitania was inquired into before the Wreck Commissioner's Court in London, June 15, 1915, to July 1, 1915, and the testimony then adduced, together with certain depositions taken pursuant to commissions issued out of this court and the testimony of a considerable number of passengers, crew, and experts, heard before this court, constitute the record of the cause.

It is fortunate, for many reasons, that such a comprehensive judicial investigation has been had; for, in addition to a mass of facts which give opportunity for a clear understanding of the case in its various aspects, the evidence presented has disposed, without question and for all time, of any false claims brought forward to justify this inexpressibly cowardly attack upon an unarmed passenger liner.

## UNARMED: NO EXPLOSIVES

So far as equipment went, the vessel was seaworthy in the highest sense. Her carrying capacity was 2,198 passengers and a crew of about 850, or about 3,000 persons in all. She had 22 open lifeboats capable of accommodating 1,322 persons, 26 collapsible boats with a capacity for 1,283, making a total of 48 boats with a capacity for 2,605 in all, or substantially in excess of the requirements of her last voyage. Her total of life belts was 3,187, or 1,959 more than the total number of passengers, and, in addition, she carried 20 life buoys. She was classed 100 A1 at Lloyd's, being 787 feet long over all, with a tonnage of 30,395 gross and 12,-611 net. She had 4 turbine engines, 25 boilers, 4 boiler rooms, 12 transverse bulkheads, dividing her into 13 compartments, with a longitudinal bulkhead on either side of the ship for 425 feet, covering all vital parts.

The proof is absolute that she was not and never had been armed nor did she carry any explosives. She did carry some 18 fuse cases and 125 shrapnel cases, consisting merely of empty shells without any powder charge, 4,200 cases of safety cartridges, and 189 cases of infantry equipment, such as leather fittings, pouches, and the like. All these were for delivery abroad, but none of these munitions could be exploded by setting them on fire in mass or in bulk, nor by subjecting them to impact. She had been duly inspected on March 17, April 15, 16, and 17, all in 1915, and before she left New York the boat gear and boats were examined, overhauled, checked up, and defective articles properly replaced.

There is no reason to doubt that this part of her equipment was in excellent order when she left New York. The vessel was under the command of a long service and experienced Captain and officered by competent and experienced men. The difficulties of the war prevented the company from gathering together a crew fully reaching a standard as high as in normal times, (many of the younger British sailors having been called to the colors,) but, all told, the crew was good and, in many instances, highly intelligent and capable. Due precaution was taken in respect of boat drills while in port, and the testimony shows that those drills were both sufficient and efficient. Some passengers did not see any boat drills on the voyage, while others characterized the drills, in effect, as formally superficial. Any one familiar with ocean traveling knows that it is not strange that boat drills may take place unobserved by some of the passengers who, though on deck, may be otherwise occupied or who may be in another part of the ship, and such negative testimony must give way to the positive testimony that there were daily boat drills, the object of which mainly was to enable the men competently and quickly to lower the boats.

## BOAT DRILLS WERE HELD

Each man had a badge showing the number of the boat to which he was assigned, and a boat list was posted in three different places in the ship. Each day of the voyage a drill was held with the emergency boat, which was a fixed boat, either No. 13 on the starboard side or No. 14 on the port side, according to the weather, the idea, doubtless, being to accustom the men quickly to reach the station on either side of the ship. The siren was blown and a picked crew from the watch assembled at the boat, put on life belts, jumped into the boat, took their places, and jumped out again.

Throughout this case it must always be remembered that the disaster occurred in May, 1915, and the whole subject must be approached with the knowledge and mental attitude of that time. It may be that more elaborate and effective methods and precautions have been adopted since then, but there is no testimony which shows that these boat drills, as practiced on the voyage, were not fully up to the then existing standards and practices. There can be no criticism of the bulkhead door drills, for there was one each day.

In November, 1914, the Directors of the Cunard Company, in view of the falling off of the passenger traffic, decided to withdraw the Lusitania's sister ship, Mauretania, and to run the Lusitania at three-fourths boiler power, which involved a reduction of speed from an average of about twenty-four knots to an average of about twenty-one knots. The ship was operated under this reduced boiler power and reduced rate of speed for six round trips until and including the fatal voyage, although at the reduced rate she was considerably faster than any passenger ship crossing the Atlantic at that time. This reduction was in part for financial reasons and in part "a question of economy of coal and labor in time of war." No profit was expected and none was made, but the company continued to operate the ship as a public service. The reduction from twenty-four to twenty-one knots is, however, quite immaterial to the controversy, as will later appear.

Having thus outlined the personnel, equipment, and cargo of the vessel, reference will now be made to a series of events preceding her sailing on May 1, 1915.

## GERMANY'S WARNING

On Feb. 4, 1915, the Imperial German Government issued a proclamation as follows:

### PROCLAMATION

1. The waters surrounding Great Britain and Ireland, including the whole English Channel, are hereby declared to be war zone. On and after the 18th of February, 1915, every enemy merchant ship found in the said war zone will be destroyed without its being always possible to avert the dangers threatening the crews and passengers on that account.

2. Even neutral ships are exposed to danger in the war zone, as in view of the misuse of neutral flags ordered on Jan. 31 by the British Government and of the accidents of naval war, it cannot always be advoided to strike even neutral ships in attacks that are directed at enemy ships.

3 Northward navigation around the Shetland Islands, in the eastern waters of the North Sea and in a strip of not less than thirty miles width along the Netherlands coast is in no danger

VON POHL,
Chief of the Admiral Staff of the Navy.
Berlin, Feb. 4, 1915.

This was accompanied by a so-called memorial, setting forth the reasons advanced by the German Government in support of the issuance of this proclamation, an extract from which is as follows:

Just as England declared the whole North Sea between Scotland and Norway to be comprised within the seat of war, so does Germany now declare the waters surrounding Great Britain and Ireland, including the whole English Channel, to be comprised within the seat of war, and will prevent by all the military means at its disposal all navigation by the enemy in those waters. To this end it will endeaver to destroy, after Feb. 18 next, any merchant vessels of the enemy which present themselves at the seat of war above indicated, although it may not always be possible to avert the dangers which may menace persons and merchandise. Neutral powers are accordingly forewarned not to continue to intrust their crews, passengers, or merchandise to such vessels.

## THE AMERICAN PROTEST

To this proclamation and memorial the Government of the United States made due protest under date of Feb. 10, 1915. On the same day protest was made to England by this Government regarding the use of the American flag by the Lusitania on its voyage through the war zone on its trip from New York to Liverpool of Jan. 30, 1915, in response to which, on Feb. 19, Sir Edward Grey, Secretary of State for Foreign Affairs, handed a memorandum to Mr. Page, the American Ambassador to England, containing the following statement:

It is understood that the German Government had announced their intention of sinking British merchant vessels at sight by torpedoes without giving any opportunity of making any provisions for saving the lives of noncombatant crews and passengers. It was in consequence of this threat that the Lusitania raised the United States flag on her inward voyage and on her subsequent outward voyage. A request was made by the United States passengers who were embarking on board her that the United States flag should be hoisted, presumably to insure their safety.

The British Ambassador, the Hon. Cecil Spring-Rice, on March 1, 1915, in a communication to the American Secretary of State regarding an economic blockade of Germany, stated in reference to the German proclamation of Feb. 4:

Germany has declared that the English Channel, the north and west coasts of France, and the waters around the British

Isles are a war area and has officially notified that all enemy ships found in that area will be destroyed, and that neutral vessels may be exposed to danger. This is in effect a claim to torpedo at sight, without regard to the safety of the crew or passengers, any merchant vessel under any flag. As it is not in the power of the German Admiralty to maintain any surface craft in these waters, this attack can only be delivered by submarine agency.

Beginning with the 30th of January, 1915, and prior to the sinking of the Lusitania on May 7, 1915, German submarines attacked and seemed to have sunk twenty merchant and passenger ships within about 100 miles of the usual course of the Lusitania, chased two other vessels which escaped, and damaged still another.

### THE CHANGED COURSE

It will be noted that nothing is stated in the German memorandum, supra, as to sinking enemy merchant vessels without warning, but, on the contrary, the implication is that settled international law as to visit and search and an opportunity for the lives of passengers to be safeguarded will be obeyed, " although it may not always be possible to avert the dangers which may menace persons and merchandise."

As a result of this submarine activity, the Lusitania, on its voyages from New York to Liverpool, beginning with that of Jan. 30, 1915, steered a course further off from the south coast of Ireland than formerly.

In addition, after the German proclamation of Feb. 4, 1915, the Lusitania had its boats swung out and provisioned while passing through the danger zone, did not use its wireless for sending messages, and did not stop at the Mersey Bar for a pilot, but came directly up to its berth.

The petitioner and the master of the Lusitania received certain advices from the British Admiralty on Feb. 10, 1915, as follows:

Instructions with Reference to Submarines, 10th February, 1915.
Vessels navigating in submarine areas should have their boats turned out and fully provisioned. The danger is greatest in the vicinity of ports and off prominent headlands on the coast. Important landfalls in this area should be made after

dark whenever possible. So far as is consistent with particular trades and state of tides, vessels should make their ports at dawn.

On April 15 and 16, 1915, and after the last voyage from New York, preceding the one on which the Lusitania was torpedoed, the Cunard Company and the master of the Lusitania received at Liverpool the following advices from the British Admiralty:

Confidential Daily Voyage Notice 15th April, 1915, issued under Government War Risks Scheme.
German submarines appear to be operating chiefly off prominent headlands and landfalls. Ships should give prominent headlands a wide berth.
Confidential memo. issued 16th April, 1915:
War experience has shown that fast steamers can considerably reduce the chance of successful surprise submarine attacks by zigzagging—that is to say, altering the course at short and irregular intervals, say in ten minutes to half an hour. This course is almost invariably adopted by warships when cruising in an area known to be infested by submarines. The underwater speed of a submarine is very slow and it is exceedingly difficult for her to get into position to deliver an attack unless she can observe and predict the course of the ship attacked.

Sir Alfred Booth, Chairman of the Cunard Line, was a member of the War Risks Committee at Liverpool, consisting of ship owners, representatives of the Board of Trade and the Admiralty, which received these instructions and passed them on to the owners of vessels, including the Cunard Company, which distributed them to the individual masters.

On Saturday, May 1, 1915, the advertised sailing date of the Lusitania from New York to Liverpool on the voyage on which she was subsequently sunk, there appeared the following advertisement in THE NEW YORK TIMES, New York Tribune, New York Sun, New York Herald, and the New York World, this advertisement being in all instances except one placed directly over, under, or adjacent to the advertisement of the Cunard Line, regarding the sailing of the Lusitania:

Travelers intending to embark on the Atlantic voyage are reminded that a state of war exists between Germany and her allies and Great Britain and her allies. That the zone of war includes the waters adjacent to the British Isles. That in accordance with formal notice given by the Imperial German Government, vessels flying the flag of Great Britain or of any of her allies are liable to destruction in those waters, and that travelers sailing in the war zone on ships of Great Britain or her allies do so at their own risk.

IMPERIAL GERMAN EMBASSY,
April 22, 1915.    Washington, D. C.

## CUNARD LINE NOT ADVISED

This was the first insertion of this advertisement, although it was dated more than a week prior to its publication. Captain Turner, the master of the vessel, saw the advertisement or "something of the kind" before sailing, and realized that the Lusitania was included in the warning. The Liverpool office of the Cunard Company was advised of the sailing and the number of passengers by cable from the New York office, but no mention was made of the above quoted advertisement. Sir Alfred Booth was informed through the press of this advertisement on either Saturday evening, May 1, or Sunday morning, May 2.

The significance and construction to be given to this advertisement will be discussed infra, but it is perfectly plain that the master was fully justified in sailing on the appointed day from a neutral port with many neutral and noncombatant passengers, unless he and his company were willing to yield to the attempt of the German Government to terrify British shipping. No one familiar with the British character would expect that such a threat would accomplish more than to emphasize the necessity of taking every precaution to protect life and property which the exercise of judgment would invite.

And so, as scheduled, the Lusitania sailed, undisguised, with her four funnels and a figure so familiar as to be readily discernible not only by naval officers and marines, but by the ocean-going public generally.

The voyage was uneventful until May 6. On approaching the Irish coast on May 6 the Captain ordered all the boats hanging on the davits to be swung out and lowered to the promenade deckrail, and this order was carried out under the supervision of Staff Captain Anderson, who later went down with the ship. All bulkhead doors which were not necessary for the working of the ship were closed, and it was reported to Captain Turner that this had been done. Lookouts were doubled, and two extra were put forward and one on either side of the bridge; that is, there were two lookouts in the crow's-nest, two in the eyes of the ship, two officers on the bridge, and a quartermaster on either side of the bridge.

## ALL STEAM POSSIBLE ORDERED

Directions were given to the engine room to keep the highest steam they could possibly get on the boilers, and in case the bridge rang for full speed, to give as much as they possibly could. Orders were also given that ports should be kept closed.

At 7:50 P. M., on May 6, the Lusitania received the following wireless message from the Admiral at Queenstown: "Submarines active off south coast of Ireland," and at 7:56 the vessel asked for and received a repetition of his message. The ship was then going at a rate of 21 knots per hour.

At 8:30 P. M. of the same day the following message was received from the British Admiralty:

To All British Ships 0005:
Take Liverpool pilot at bar and avoid headlands. Pass harbors at full speed; steer mid-channel course. Submarines off Fastnet.

At 8:32 the Admiralty received a communication to show that this message had been received by the Lusitania, and the same message was offered to the vessel seven times between midnight of May 6 and 10 A. M. of May 7.

At about 8 A. M. on the morning of May 7, on approaching the Irish coast, the vessel encountered an intermittent fog, or Scotch mist, called "banks" in seafaring language, and the speed was reduced to 15 knots. Previously the speed, according to Captain Turner's recollection, had been reduced to 18 knots. This adjustment of speed was due to the fact that Captain Turner wished to run the last 150 miles of the voyage in the dark, so as to make Liverpool early on the morning of May 8, at the earliest time when he could cross the bar without a pilot.

Judging from the location of previous submarine attacks, the most dangerous waters in the Lusitania's course were from the entrance to St. George's Channel to Liverpool Bar. There is no dispute as to the proposition that a vessel darkened is much safer from submarine attack at night than in the daytime, and Captain Turner exercised proper and good judgment in planning accordingly as he approached dangerous waters. It is futile to conjecture as to what would or would not have happened had the speed been higher prior to the approach to the Irish coast, because, obviously, until then the Captain could not figure out his situation, not knowing how he might be impeded by fog or other unfavorable weather conditions.

On the morning of May 7, 1915, the ship passed about twenty-five or twenty-six, and, in any event, at least eighteen and a half miles south of Fastnet, which was not in sight. The course was then held up slightly to bring the ship closer to land, and a little before noon land was sighted, and what was thought to be Brow Head was made out.

### SHIP'S SPEED INCREASED

Meanwhile, between 11 A. M. and noon, the fog disappeared, the weather became clear, and the speed was increased to 18 knots. The course of the vessel was S. 87 E. Mag. At 11:25 A. M. Captain Turner received the following message:

Submarines active in southern part of Irish Channel, last heard of twenty miles south of Coningbeg. Light vessel make certain " Lusitania " gets this.

At 12:40 P. M. the following additional wireless message from the Admiralty was received:

Submarines five miles south of Cape Clear, proceeding west when sighted at 10 A. M.

After picking up Brow Head and at about 12:40 P. M., the course was altered in shore by about 30 degrees, to about N. 63 or 67 E. Mag., Captain Turner did not recall which. Land was sighted which the Captain thought was Galley Head, but he was not sure, and therefore held in shore. This last course

was continued for an hour at a speed of 18 knots until 1:40 P. M., when the Old Head of Kinsale was sighted and the course was then changed back to the original course of S. 87 E. Mag.

At 1:50 P. M. the Captain started to take a four-point bearing on the Old

THE CROSS NEAR KINSALE HEAD MARKS THE PLACE WHERE THE LUSITANIA WAS SUNK

Head of Kinsale, and while thus engaged and at about 2:10 P. M., as heretofore stated, the ship was torpedoed on the starboard side. Whether one, two, or three torpedoes were fired at the vessel cannot be determined with certainty. Two of the ship's crew were confident that a third torpedo was fired and missed the ship. While not doubting the good faith of these witnesses, the evidence is not sufficiently satisfactory to be convincing.

There was, however, an interesting and remarkable conflict of testimony as to whether the ship was struck by one or two torpedoes, and witnesses, both passengers and crew, differed on this point, conscientiously and emphatically, some witnesses for claimants and some for petitioner holding one view and others called by each side holding the opposite view. The witnesses were all highly intelligent, and there is no doubt that all testified to the best of their recollection, knowledge, or impression, and in accordance with their honest conviction. The weight of the testimony (too voluminous to analyze) is in favor of the " two torpedo " contention, not only because of some convincing direct testimony, (as, for instance, Adams, Lehman, Morton,) but also because of the unquestioned surrounding circumstances. The deliberate character of the attack upon a vessel whose identity could not be mistaken, made easy on a bright day, and the fact that the vessel had no means of defending herself, would lead to the inference that the submarine commander would make sure of her destruction. Further, the evidence is overwhelming that there was a second explosion. The witnesses differ as to the impression which the sound of this explosion made upon them—a natural difference due to the fact, known by common experience, that persons who hear the same explosion even at the same time will not only describe the sound differently, but will not agree as to the number of detonations. As there were no explosives on board, it is difficult to account for the second explosion, except on the theory that it was caused by a second torpedo. Whether the number of torpedoes was one or two is relevant, in this case, only upon the question of what effect, if any, open ports had in accelerating the sinking of the ship.

## WHERE TORPEDOES STRUCK

While there was much testimony and some variance as to the places where the torpedoes struck, judged by the sound or shock of the explosions, certain physical effects, especially as to smoke and blown-up débris, tend to locate the areas of impact with some approach of accuracy.

From all the testimony it may be reasonably concluded that one torpedo struck on the starboard side somewhere abreast of No. 2 boiler room and the other, on the same side, either abreast of No. 3 boiler room or between No. 3 and No. 4. From knowledge of the torpedoes then

used by the German submarines, it is thought that they would effect a rupture of the outer hull thirty to forty feet long and ten to fifteen feet vertically.

Cockburn, senior Second Engineer, was of opinion that the explosion had done a great deal of internal damage. Although the lights were out, Cockburn could hear the water coming into the engine room. Water at once entered No. 1 and No. 2 boiler rooms, a result necessarily attributable to the fact that one or both of the coal bunkers were also blown open. Thus, one torpedo flooded some or all of the coal bunkers on the starboard side of Nos. 1 and 2 boiler rooms, and apparently flooded both boiler rooms.

The effect of the other torpedo is not entirely clear. If it struck midway between two bulkheads, it is quite likely to have done serious bulkhead injury. The Lusitania was built so as to float with two compartments open to the sea, and with more compartments open she could not stay afloat. As the side coal bunkers are regarded as compartments, the ship could not float with two boiler rooms flooded and also an adjacent bunker, and, therefore, the damage done by one torpedo was enough to sink the ship.

To add to the difficulties, all the steam had gone as the result of the explosions, and the ship could not be controlled by her engines.

Little, senior Third Engineer, testified that in a few seconds after the explosion the steam pressure fell from 190 to 50 pounds, his explanation being that the main steam pipes or boilers had been carried away.

The loss of control of and by the engines resulted in disability to stop the engines, with the result that the ship kept her headway until she sank. That the ship commenced to list to starboard immediately is abundantly established by many witnesses.

Some of the witnesses, (Lauriat and Adams, passengers; Duncan, Bestic, and Johnson, officers,) testified that the ship stopped listing to starboard and started to recover and then listed again to starboard until she went over.

This action, which is quite likely, must have resulted from the inrush of water on the port side. There can be no other adequate explanation consistent with elementary scientific knowledge; for, if the ship temporarily righted herself, it must have been because the weight of water on the two sides was equal or nearly so. The entry of water into the port side must, of course, have been due to some rupture on that side. Such a result was entirely possible, and, indeed, probable.

The explosive force was sufficiently powerful to blow débris far above the radio wires—i. e., more than 160 feet above the water. The boiler rooms were not over sixty feet wide, and so strong a force could readily have weakened the longitudinal bulkheads on the port side in addition to such injury as flying metal may have done. It is easy to understand, therefore, how the whole pressure of the water rushing in from the starboard side against the weakened longitudinal bulkheads on the port side would cause them to give way and thus open up some apertures on the port side for the entry of water. Later, when the water continued to rush in on the starboard side, the list to starboard naturally again occurred, increased and continued to the end. As might be expected, the degree of list to starboard is variously described, but there is no doubt that it was steep and substantial.

A considerable amount of testimony was taken upon the contention of claimants that many of the ship's ports were open, thus reducing her buoyancy and substantially hastening her sinking. There is no doubt that on May 6 adequate orders were given to close all ports. The testimony is conclusive that the ports on Deck F (the majority of which were dummy ports) were closed. Very few, if any, ports on E deck were open, and, if so, they were starboard ports in a small section of the first class in the vicinity where one of the torpedoes did its damage. A very limited number of passengers testified that the portholes in their staterooms were open, and, if their impressions are correct, these portholes, concerning which they testified, were all, or nearly all, so far above the water that they could not have influenced the situation.

There was conflicting testimony as to the ports in the dining room on D deck. The weight of the testimony justifies the conclusion that some of these ports were open—how many it is impossible to determine. These ports, however, were from twenty-three to thirty feet above water, and when the gap made by the explosion and the consequent severe and sudden list are considered, it is plain that these open ports were not a contributing cause of the sinking, and had a very trifling influence, if any, in accelerating the time within which the ship sank.

From the foregoing the situation can be visualized. Two sudden and extraordinary explosions, the ship badly listed so that the port side was well up in the air, the passengers scattered about on the decks and in the staterooms, saloons and companion ways, the ship under headway and, as it turned out, only eighteen minutes afloat—such was the situation which confronted the officers, crew, and passengers in the endeavor to save the lives of those on board.

## HEROISM OF PASSENGERS

The conduct of the passengers constitutes an enduring record of calm heroism with many individual instances of sacrifice and, in general, a marked consideration for women and children. There was no panic, but, naturally, there was a considerable amount of excitement and rush and much confusion, and, as the increasing list rendered ineffective the lowering of the boats on the port side, the passengers, as is readily understandable, crowded over on the starboard side.

The problem presented to the officers of the ship was one of exceeding difficulty, occasioned largely because of the serious list and the impossibility of stopping the ship or reducing her headway.

The precaution of extra lookouts resulted in a prompt report to the Captain, via the bridge, of the sighting of the torpedo. Second Officer Heppert, who was on the bridge, immediately closed all watertight doors worked from the bridge, and the testimony satisfactorily shows that all watertight doors worked by hand were promptly closed. Immediately after Captain Turner saw the wake of the torpedo there was an explosion and then Turner went to the navigation bridge and took the obvious course, i. e., had the ship's head turned to the land. He signaled the engine room for full speed astern, hoping thereby to take the way off the ship, and then ordered the boats lowered down to the rail and directed that women and children should be first provided for in the boats. As the engine room failed to respond to the order to go full speed astern, and as the ship was continuing under way, Turner ordered that the boats should not be lowered until the vessel should lose her headway, and he told Anderson, the Staff Captain, who was in charge of the port boats, to lower the boats when he thought the way was sufficiently off to allow that operation. Anderson's fidelity to duty is sufficiently exemplified by the fact that he went down with the ship.

Jones, First Officer, and Lewis, Acting Third Officer, were in charge of the boats on the starboard side and personally superintended their handling and launching. Too much cannot be said both for their courage and skill, but, difficult as was their task, they were not confronted with some of the problems which the port side presented. There, in addition to Anderson, were Bestic, Junior Third Officer, and another officer, presumably the Second Officer. These men were apparently doing the best they could and standing valiantly to their duty. Anderson's fate has already been mentioned, and Bestic, although surviving, stuck to his post until the ship went down under him. The situation can readily be pictured even by a novice.

## BOATS WERE DAMAGED

With the ship listed to starboard, the port boats, of course, swung inboard. If enough man power were applied, the boats could be put over the rail, but then a real danger would follow. Robertson, the ship's carpenter, aptly described that danger in answer to a question as to whether it was possible to lower the open boats on the port side. He said: ·

No. To lower the port boats would just be like drawing a crate of unpacked china along a dock road. What I mean is that if you started to lower the boats you would be dragging them down the rough side of the ship on rivets which are what we call "snap-headed rivets"—they stand up about an inch from the side of the ship, so you would be dragging the whole side of the boat away if you tried to lower the boats with a 15-degree list.

That some boats were and others would have been seriously damaged is evidenced by the fact that two port boats were lowered to the water and got away, (though one afterward filled,) and not one boat reached Queenstown.

Each boat has its own history, (except possibly Boats 2 and 4,) although it is naturally difficult, in each case, to allocate all the testimony to a particular boat.

There is some testimony, given in undoubted good faith, that painted or rusted davits stuck out, but the weight of the testimony is to the contrary. There were some lamentable occurrences on the port side, which resulted in spilling passengers, some of whom thus thrown out or injured went to their death. These unfortunate accidents, however, were due either to lack of strength of the seaman who was lowering, or possibly, at worst, to an occasional instance of incompetency due to the personal equation so often illustrated, where one man of many may not be equal to the emergency. But the problem was of the most vexatious character. In addition to the crowding of passengers in some instances was this extremely hazardous feat of lowering boats swung inboard from a tilted height, heavily weighted by human beings, with the ship still under way. It cannot be said that it was negligent to attempt this, because, obviously, all the passengers could not be accommodated in the starboard boats.

On the starboard side, the problem, in some respects, was not so difficult, while, in others, troublesome conditions existed quite different from those occurring on the port side. Here the boats swung so far out as to add to the difficulty of passengers getting in them, a difficulty intensified by the fact that many more passengers went to the starboard side than to the port side and, also, that the ship maintained her way. Six boats successfully got away. In the case of the remaining boats, some were successfully lowered but later met with some unavoidable accident, and some were not successfully launched (such as Nos. 1, 5, and 17) for entirely explainable reasons which should not be charged to inefficiency on the part of the officers or crew.

## CREW NOT INEFFICENT

The collapsible boats were on the deck under the open lifeboats, and were intended to be lifted and lowered by the same davits which lowered the open boats after the open boats had gotten clear· of the ship. It was the duty of the officers to get the open boats away before giving attention to the collapsible boats, and that was a question of time. These boats are designed and arranged to float free if the ship should sink before they can be hoisted over. They were cut loose and some people were saved on these boats.

It is to be expected that those passengers who lost members of their family or friends, and who saw some of the unfortunate accidents, should feel strongly and entertain the impression that inefficiency or individual negligence was widespread among the crew. Such an impression, however, does an inadvertent injustice to the great majority of the crew, who acted with that matter-in-fact courage and fidelity to duty which are traditional with men of the sea. Such of these men, presumably fairly typical of all, as testified in this court, were impressive not only because of inherent bravery, but because of intelligence and clearheadedness, and they possessed that remarkable gift of simplicity so characteristic of truly fearless men who cannot quite understand why an ado is made of acts which seem to them merely as, of course; in the day's work.

Mr. Grab, one of the claimants and an experienced transatlantic traveler, concisely summed up the situation when he said:

They were doing the best they could— they were very brave and working as hard as they could without any fear. They didn't care about themselves. It was very admirably done. While there was great confusion, they did the best they could.

It will unduly prolong a necessarily extended opinion to sift the voluminous testimony relating to this subject of the boats and the conduct of the crew and something is sought to be made of comments of Captain Turner, construed by some to be unfavorable but afterward satisfactorily supplemented and explained, but if there were some instances of incompetency they were very few and the charge of negligence in this regard cannot be successfully maintained.

In arriving at this conclusion, I have not overlooked the argument earnestly pressed that the men were not sufficiently instructed and drilled; for I think the testimony establishes the contrary in the light of conditions in May, 1915.

I now come to what seems to be the only debatable question of fact in the case, i. e., whether Captain Turner was negligent in not literally following the Admiralty advices and, also, in not taking a course different from that which he adopted.

## RESPONSIBILITY OF· CAPTAIN

The fundamental principle in navigating a merchantman, whether in times of peace or of war, is that the commanding officer must be left free to exercise his own judgment. Safe navigation denies the proposition that the judgment and sound discretion of the Captain of a vessel must be confined in a mental straitjacket. Of course, when movements are under military control, orders must be strictly obeyed, come what may. No such situation, however, was presented either to petitioner or Captain Turner. The vessel was not engaged in military service nor under naval convoy. True, she was, as between the German and British Governments, an enemy ship as to Germany, but she was unarmed and a carrier of not merely noncombatants, but, among others, of many citizens of the United States, then a neutral country, at peace with all the world.

In such circumstances the Captain could not shield himself automatically against error behind a literal compliance with the general advices or instructions of the Admiralty, nor can it be supposed that the Admiralty, any more than the petitioner, expected him so to do. What was required of him was that he should seriously consider and, as far as practicable, follow the Admiralty advices and use his best judgment as events and exigencies occurred; and if a situation arose where he believed that a course should be pursued to meet emergencies which required departure from some of the Admiralty advices as to general rules of action, then it was his duty to take such course, if in accordance with his carefully formed deliberate judgment. After a disaster has occurred, it is not difficult for the expert to show how it might have been avoided, and there is always opportunity for academic discussion as to what ought or ought not to have been done; but the true approach is to endeavor, for the moment, to possess the mind of him upon whom rested the responsibility.

Let us now see what that responsibility was and how it was dealt with. The rules of naval warfare allowed the capture and, in some circumstances, the destruction of an enemy merchant ship, but, at the same time, it was the accepted doctrine of all civilized nations (as will be more fully considered infra) that, as Lord Mersey put it, " there is always an obligation first to secure the safety of the lives of those on board."

The responsibility, therefore, of Captain Turner, in his task of bringing the ship safely to port, was to give heed not only to general advices advanced as the outcome of experience in the then developing knowledge as to submarine warfare, but particularly to any special information which might come to him in the course of the voyage.

Realizing that if there was a due warning, in accordance with international law, and an opportunity, within a limited time, for the passengers to leave the ship, nevertheless that the operation must be quickly done, Captain Turner, on May 6, had taken the full precautions, such as swinging out the boats, properly provisioned, which have been heretofore described. The principal features of the Admiralty advices were (1) to give the headlands a wide berth; (2) to steer a midchannel course; (3) to maintain as high a speed as practicable; (4) to zigzag, and (5) to make ports, if possible, at dawn, thus running the last part of the voyage at night.

## FOLLOWED HIS INSTRUCTIONS

The reason for the advice as to keeping off headlands was that the submarines lurked near those prominent headlands and landfalls to and from which ships were likely to go. This instruction Captain Turner entirely followed in respect of Fastnet, which was the first point on the Irish coast which a vessel bound from New York to Liverpool would ordinarily approach closely, and, in normal times, the passing would be very near, or even inside of Fastnet. The Lusitania passed Fastnet so far out that Captain Turner could not see it. Whether the distance was about twenty-five miles, as petitioner contends, or about eighteen and one-half miles, as claimant calculates, the result is that either distance must be regarded as a wide berth, in comparison with the customary navigation at that point, and, besides, nothing happened there. At 8:30 P. M. on May 6 the message had been received from the British Admiralty that submarines were off Fastnet, so that Captain Turner, in this regard, not only followed the general advices, but the specific information from the Admiralty.

At 11:25 A. M. on May 7 Captain Turner received the wireless from the Admiralty plainly intended for the Lusitania, informing him that submarines (plural) were active in the southern part of the Irish Channel and when last heard of were twenty miles south of Coningbeg Light Vessel. This wireless message presented acutely to the Captain the problem as to the best course to pursue, always bearing in mind his determination and the desirability of getting to the Liverpool Bar when it could be crossed while the tide served and without a pilot. Further, as was stated by Sir Alfred Booth, " The one definite instruction we did give him with regard to that was to authorize him to come up without a pilot." The reasons for this instruction were cogent and were concisely summed up by Sir Alfred Booth during his examination as a witness as follows:

> It was one of the points that we felt it necessary to make the Captain of the Lusitania understand the importance of. The Lusitania can only cross the Liverpool Bar at certain states of the tide, and we therefore warned the Captain, or whoever might be Captain, that we did not think it would be safe for him to arrive off the bar at such a time that he would have to wait there, because that area had been infested with submarines, and we thought therefore it would be wiser for him to arrange his arrival in such a way, leaving him an absolutely free hand as to how he would do it, that he could come straight up without stopping at all. The one definite instruction we did give him with regard to that was to authorize him to come up without a pilot.

The tide would be high at Liverpool Bar at 6:53 on Saturday morning, May 8. Captain Turner planned to cross the bar as much earlier than that as he could get over without stopping, while at the same time figuring on passing during the darkness the dangerous waters from the entrance of St. George's Channel to the Liverpool Bar.

## DECISION OF THE CAPTAIN

Having thus in mind his objective, and the time approximately when he intended to reach it, the message received at 11:25 A. M. required that he should determine whether to keep off land approximately the same distance as he was when he passed Fastnet, or to work inshore and go close to Coningbeg Lightship. He determined that the latter was the better plan to avoid the submarines reported in midchannel ahead of him.

When Galley Head was sighted the course was changed so as to haul closer to the land, and this course was pursued until 1:40 P. M., at which time Captain Turner concluded that it was necessary for him to get his bearings accurately. This he decided should be done by taking a four-point bearing, during which procedure the ship was torpedoed. It is urged that he should have taken a two-point bearing or a cross bearing, which would have occupied less time, but if, under all the conditions which appealed to his judgment as a mariner, he had taken a different method of ascertaining his exact distance and the result would have been inaccurate, or while engaged in taking a two-point bearing the ship had been torpedoed, then somebody would have said he should have taken a four-point bearing. The point of the matter is that an experienced Captain took the bearing he thought proper for his purposes, and to predicate negligence upon such a course is to assert that a Captain is bound to guess the exact location of a hidden and puzzling danger.

Much emphasis has been placed upon the fact that the speed of the ship was eighteen knots at the time of the attack instead of twenty-four, or, in any event, twenty-one knots, and upon the further fact (for such it is) that the ship was not zigzagging as frequently as the Admiralty advised or in the sense of that advice.

Upon this branch of the case much testimony was taken, (some in camera, as in the Wreck Commissioners' Court,) and, for reasons of public interest, the methods of successfully evading submarines will not be discussed. If it be assumed that the Admiralty advices as of May, 1915, were sound and should have been followed, then the answer to the charge of negligence is twofold: (1) that Captain Turner, in taking a four-point bearing off the Old Head of Kinsale, was conscientiously exercising his judgment for the welfare of the ship, and (2) that it is impossible to determine whether, by zigzagging off the Old Head of Kinsale or elsewhere, the Lusitania would have escaped the German submarine or submarines.

As to the first answer I cannot better express my conclusion than in the language of Lord Mersey:

> Captain Turner was fully advised as to the means which in the view of the Admiralty were best calculated to avert the perils he was likely to encounter, and in considering the question whether he is to blame for the catastrophe in which his voyage ended I have to bear this circumstance in mind. It is certain that in some respects Captain Turner did not follow the advice given to him. It may be (though I seriously doubt it) that had he done so

his ship would have reached Liverpool in safety. But the question remains: Was his conduct the conduct of a negligent or of an incompetent man? On this question I have sought the guidance of my assessors, who have rendered me invaluable assistance, and the conclusion at which I have arrived is that blame ought not to be imputed to the Captain. The advice given to him, although meant for his most serious and careful consideration, was not intended to deprive him of the right to exercise his skilled judgment in the difficult questions that might arise from time to time in the navigation of his ship. His omission to follow the advice in all respects cannot fairly be attributed either to negligence or incompetence.

He exercised his judgment for the best. It was the judgment of a skilled and experienced man, and although others might have acted differently, and, perhaps, more successfully, he ought not, in my opinion, to be blamed.

As to the second answer, it is only necessary to outline the situation in order to realize how speculative is the assertion of fault. It is plain from the radio messages of the Admiralty, (May 6, 7:50 P. M., "Submarines active off south coast of Ireland"; May 6, 8:30 P. M., "Submarines off Fastnet"; the 11:25 message of May 7, supra; May 7, 11:40 A. M., "Submarines five miles south of Cape Clear, proceeding west when sighted at 10 A. M.,") that more than one submarine was lying in wait for the Lusitania.

## LUSITANIA WAS HELPLESS

A scientific education is not necessary to appreciate that it is much more difficult for a submarine successfully to hit a naval vessel than an unarmed merchant ship. The destination of a naval vessel is usually not known, that of the Lusitania was. A submarine commander, when attacking an armed vessel, knows that he, as the attacker, may and likely will also be attacked by his armed opponent. The Lusitania was as helpless in that regard as a peaceful citizen suddenly set upon by murderous assailants. There are other advantages of the naval vessel over the merchant ship which need not be referred to.

It must be assumed that the German submarine commanders realized the obvious disadvantages which necessarily attached to the Lusitania, and, if she had evaded one submarine, who can say what might have happened five minutes later? If there was, in fact, a third torpedo fired from the Lusitania's port side, then that incident would strongly suggest that, in the immediate vicinity of the ship, there were at least two submarines.

It must be remembered also that the Lusitania was still in the open sea, considerably distant from the places of theretofore submarine activity and comfortably well off the Old Head of Kinsale, from which point it was about 140 miles to the Scilly Islands, and that she was nearly 100 miles from the entrance to St. George's Channel, the first channel she would enter on her way to Liverpool.

No transatlantic passenger liner, and certainly none carrying American citizens, had been torpedoed up to that time. The submarines, therefore, could lay their plans with facility to destroy the vessel somewhere on the way from Fastnet to Liverpool, knowing full well the easy prey which would be afforded by an unarmed, unconvoyed, well-known merchantman, which from every standpoint of international law had the right to expect a warning before its peaceful passengers were sent to their death. That the attack was deliberate and long contemplated and intended ruthlessly to destroy human life, as well as property, can no longer be open to doubt. And when a foe employs such tactics it is idle and purely speculative to say that the action of the Captain of a merchant ship, in doing or not doing something or in taking one course and not another, was a contributing cause of disaster or that had the Captain not done what he did or had he done something else, then that the ship and her passengers would have evaded their assassins.

I find, therefore, as a fact, that the Captain and, hence, the petitioner were not negligent.

The importance of the cause, however, justifies the statement of another ground which effectually disposes of any question of liability.

It is an elementary principle of law that even if a person is negligent recovery cannot be had unless the negligence is the proximate cause of the loss or damage.

## GERMANY INTERVENED

There is another rule, settled by ample authority, viz.: that, even if negligence is shown, it cannot be the proximate cause of the loss or damage if an independent illegal act or a third party intervenes to cause the loss.

Jarnagin v. Travelers' Protective Assn., 133 F. R. 892.

Cole v. German Savings and Loan Soc., 124 F. R. 113.

See also, Insurance Co. v. Tweed, 7 Wall. 44.

Railroad Co. v. Reeves, 10 Wall. 176.

Insurance Co. v. Boon, 95 U. S. 117.

The Young America, 31 F. R. 749.

Goodlander Mill Co. v. Standard Oil Co., 63 F. R. 400.

Claimants contend strongly that the case at bar comes within Holladay v. Kennard, 12 Wall, 254, where Mr. Justice Miller, who wrote the opinion, carefully stated that that case was not to be construed as laying down a rule different from that of Railroad Company v. Reeves, supra. An elaborate analysis of the Holladay and other cases will not be profitable; suffice it to say, neither that nor any other case has changed the rule of law above stated, as to the legal import of an intervening illegal act of a third party.

The question, then, is whether the act of the German submarine commander was an illegal act.

The United States courts recognize the binding force of international law. As was said by Mr. Justice Gray in the Paquete Habana, 175 U. S. 677, 700:

International law is part of our law, and must be ascertained and administered by the courts of justice of appropriate jurisdiction, as often as questions of right depending upon it are duly presented for their determination.

At least since as early as June 5, 1793, in the letter of Mr. Jefferson, Secretary of State, to the French Minister, our Government has recognized the law of nations as an " integral part " of the laws of the land.

Moore's International Law Digest, I., P. 10.

The Scotia, 14 Wall, 170, 187.

The New York, 175 U. S., 187, 197.

Kansas v. Colorado, 185 U. S., 125, 146.

Kansas v. Colorado, 206 U. S., 46.

To ascertain international law, " resort must be had to the customs and usages of civilized nations; and, as evidence of these, to the works of commentators and jurists. * * * Such works are resorted to by judicial tribunals * * * for trustworthy evidence of what the law really is."

The Paquete Habana, 175 U. S. 677; (and authorities cited.)

## RIGHTS OF HUMANITY

Let us first see the position of our Government, and then ascertain whether that position has authoritative support. Mr. Lansing, in his official communication to the German Government dated June 9, 1915, stated:

But the sinking of passenger ships involves principles of humanity which throw into the background any special circumstances of detail that may be thought to affect the cases, principles which lift it, as the Imperial German Government will no doubt be quick to recognize and acknowledge, out of the class of ordinary subjects of diplomatic discussion or of international controversy. Whatever be the other facts regarding the Lusitania, the principal fact is that a great steamer, primarily and chiefly a conveyance for passengers, and carrying more than a thousand souls who had no part or lot in the conduct of the war, was torpedoed and sunk without so much as a challenge or a warning, and that men, women, and children were sent to their death in circumstances unparalleled in modern warfare. The fact that more than one hundred American citizens were among those who perished made it the duty of the Government of the United States to speak of these things and once more with solemn emphasis to call the attention of the Imperial German Government to the grave responsibility which the Government of the United States conceives that it has incurred in this tragic occurrence, and to the indisputable principle upon which that responsibility rests. The Government of the United States is contending for something much greater than mere rights of property or privileges of commerce. It is contending for nothing less high and sacred than the rights of humanity, which every Government honors itself in respecting and which no Government is justified in resigning on behalf of those under its care and authority. Only her actual resistance to capture or refusal to stop when ordered to do so for the purpose of visit could have afforded the commander of the submarine any justification for so much as putting the lives of those on board the ship in jeopardy. This principle the Government of the United States understands the explicit instructions issued on Aug. 3, 1914, by the Imperial German Admiralty to its commanders at sea to have recognized and embodied as do the naval codes of all other nations, and upon it every traveler and seaman had a right to depend. It is upon this principle of humanity, as well as upon the law founded upon this principle, that the United States must stand. * * *

The Government of the United States cannot admit that the proclamation of a war zone from which neutral ships have been warned to keep away may be made to operate as in any degree an abbreviation of the rights either of American shipmasters or of American citizens bound on lawful errands as passengers on merchant ships of belligerent nationality. It does not understand the Imperial German Government to question those rights. It understands it, also, to accept as established beyond question the principle that the lives of noncombatants cannot lawfully or rightfully be put in jeopardy by the capture or destruction of an unresisting merchantman, and to recognize the obligation to take sufficient precaution to ascertain whether a suspected merchantman is in fact of belligerent nationality or is in fact carrying contraband of war under a neutral flag. The Government of the United States therefore deems it reasonable to expect that the Imperial German Government will adopt the measures necessary to put these principles into practice in respect of the safeguarding of American lives and American ships, and asks for assurances that this will be done. See White Book of Department of State entitled " Diplomatic Correspondence with Belligerent Governments Relating to Neutral Rights and Duties, European War, No. 2," at p. 172. Printed and distributed Oct. 21, 1915.

## CONCEDED BY GERMANY

The German Government found itself compelled ultimately to recognize the principles insisted upon by the Government of the United States, for, after considerable correspondence, and on May 4, 1916, (after the Sussex had been sunk,) the German Government stated:

The German submarine forces have had, in fact, orders to conduct submarine warfare in accordance with the general principles of visit and search and destruction of merchant vessels as recognized by international law, the sole exception being the conduct of warfare against the enemy trade carried on enemy freight ships that are encountered in the war zone surrounding Great Britain. * * *

The German Government, guided by this idea, notifies the Government of the United States that the German naval forces have received the following orders: In accordance with the general principles of

visit and search and destruction of merchant vessels recognized by international law, such vessels, both within and without the area declared as naval war zone, shall not be sunk without warning and without saving human lives, unless these ships attempt to escape or offer resistance. See Official Communication by German Foreign Office to Ambassador Gerard, May 4, 1916. (White Book No. 3 of Department of State, pp. 302, 305.)

There is, of course, no doubt as to the right to make prize of an enemy ship on the high seas, and, under certain conditions, to destroy her, and equally no doubt of the obligation to safeguard the lives of all persons aboard, whether passengers or crew.

Phillemore on International Law, 3d Ed. Vol. 3, p. 584;

Sir Sherston Baker on " First Steps in International Law," p. 236;

G. B. Davis on " Elements of International Law," pp. 358, 359;

A. Pearce Higgins on " War and the Private Citizen," pp. 33, 78, referring to proceedings of " Institute of International Law at Turin " in 1882;

Creasy on International Law, p. 562, quoting Chief Justice Cockburn in his judgment in the General Arbitration;

L. A. Atherby-Jones on " Commerce in War," p. 529;

Professor Holland's Article, Naval War College, 1907, p. 81;

Oppenheim on International Law, 2d Ed. Vol. 2, pp. 244, 311;

Taylor on International Law, p. 572;

Westlake on International Law, 2d Ed., p. 309, Part II.;

Halleck on International Law, Vol. II., pp. 15, 16;

Vattel's " Law of Nations," Chitty's Ed., p. 362.

## FROM LAW OF NATIONS

Two quotations from this long list may be given for convenience, one stating the rule and the other the attitude which obtains among civilized Governments. Oppenheim sets forth as among violations of the rules of war:

(12) Attack on enemy merchantmen without previous request to submit to visit.

The observation in Vattel's " Law of Nations " is peculiarly applicable to the case of the Lusitania:

Let us never forget that our enemies are men. Though reduced to the disagreeable necessity of prosecuting our right by force of arms, let us not divest ourselves of that charity which connects us with all mankind. Thus shall we courageously defend our country's rights without violating those of human nature. Let our valor preserve itself from every stain of cruelty and the lustre of victory will not be tarnished by inhuman and brutal actions.

In addition to the authorities supra are the regulations and practices of various Governments. In 1512 Henry VIII. issued instructions to the Admiral of the Fleet which accord with our understanding of modern international law. (Hosack's Law of Nations, p. 168.) Such has been England's course since. (22 Geo. 2d C. 33, 2 Sec. 9, 1749; British Admiralty Manual of Prize Law 188, Secs. 303, 304.)

Substantially the same rules were followed in the Russian and Japanese regulations, and probably in the codes or rules of many other nations. Russian Prize Regulations, March 27, 1895, (cited in Moore's Digest, Volume VII., p. 518.) Japanese Prize Law of 1894, Article 22, (cited in Moore, supra, Volume VII., p. 525.) Japanese Regulations, March 7, 1904, (see Takahashi's Cases on International Law during Chino-Japanese War.)

The rules recognized and practiced by the United States, among other things, provide:

> (10) In the case of an enemy merchantman it may be sunk, but only if it is impossible to take it into port, and provided always that the persons on board are put in a place of safety. (U. S. White Book, European War, No. 3, p. 192.)

These humane principles were practiced both in the war of 1812 and during our own war of 1861-65. Even with all the bitterness (now happily ended and forgotten) and all the difficulties of having no port to which to send a prize, Captain Semmes of the Alabama strictly observed the rule as to human life, even going so far as to release ships because he could not care for the passengers. But we are not confined to American and English precedents and practices.

While acting contrary to its official statements, yet the Imperial German Government recognized the same rule as the United States, and prior to the sinking of the Lusitania had not announced any other rule. The war zone proclamation of Feb. 4, 1915, contained no warning that the accepted rule of civilized naval warfare would be discarded by the German Government.

## DID NOT DISPUTE RULE

Indeed, after the Lusitania was sunk, the German Government did not make any such claim, but in answer to the first American note in reference to the Lusitania the German Foreign Office, per von Jagow, addressed to Ambassador Gerard a note dated May 18, 1915, in which, inter alia, it is stated in connection with the sinking of the British steamer Falaba:

> In the case of the sinking of the English steamer Falaba, the commander of the German submarine had the intention of allowing passengers and crew ample opportunity to save themselves. It was not until the Captain disregarded the order to lay to and took to flight, sending up rocket signals for help, that the German commander ordered the crew and passengers by signals and megaphone to leave the ship within ten minutes. As a matter of fact, he allowed them twenty-three minutes, and did not fire the torpedo until suspicious steamers were hurrying to the aid of the Falaba. (White Book N. 2, U. S. Department of State, p. 169.)

Indeed, as late as May 4, 1916, Germany did not dispute the applicability of the rule, as is evidenced by the note written to our Government by von Jagow of the German Foreign Office, an extract of which has been quoted supra.

Further, Section 116 of the German Prize Code, (Huberich and Kind translation, p. 68,) in force at the date of the Lusitania's destruction, conformed with the American rule. It provided:

> Before proceeding to a destruction of the vessel the safety of all persons on board, and, so far as possible, their effects, is to be provided for, and all ship's papers and other evidentiary material which, according to the views of the persons at interest, is of value for the formulation of the judgment of the prize court, are to be taken over by the commander.

Thus, when the Lusitania sailed from New York, her owner and master were justified in believing that, whatever else had theretofore happened, this simple, humane and universally accepted principle would not be violated. Few, at that time, would be likely to construe the warning advertisement as calling attention to more than the perils to be expected from quick disembarkation and the possible rigors of the sea after the proper safeguarding of the lives of passengers by at least full opportunity to take to the boats.

It is, of course, easy now in the light of many later events, added to preceding acts, to look back and say that the Cunard Line and its Captain should have known that the German Government would authorize or permit so shocking a breach of international law and so foul an offense, not only against an enemy, but as well against peaceful citizens of a then friendly nation.

But the unexpected character of the act was best evidenced by the horror which it excited in the minds and hearts of the American people.

### GERMANY IS RESPONSIBLE

The fault, therefore, must be laid upon those who are responsible for the sinking of the vessel, in the legal as well as moral sense. It is, therefore, not the Cunard Line, petitioner, which must be held liable for the loss of life and property. The cause of the sinking of the Lusitania was the illegal act of the Imperial German Government, acting through its instrument, the submarine commander, and violating a cherished and humane rule observed, until this war, by even the bitterest antagonists. As Lord Mersey said, " The whole blame for the cruel destruction of life in this catastrophe must rest solely with those

who plotted and with those who committed the crime."

But, while in this lawsuit there may be no recovery, it is not to be doubted that the United States of America and her allies will well remember the rights of those affected by the sinking of the Lusitania, and, when the time shall come, will see to it that reparation shall be made for one of the most indefensible acts of modern times.

The petition is granted and the claims dismissed, without costs.

JULIUS M. MAYER,
District Judge.

Aug. 23, 1918.

### ADDENDUM

The grounds upon which the decision is put render unnecessary the discussion of some other interesting questions suggested.

As to the exception to interrogatory 20, brushing aside all technical points, I am satisfied that the withheld answer relates to matters irrelevant to the issues here. It certainly cannot be expected, in wartime, that an American court will ask for the disclosure of information deemed confidential by the British Admiralty, nor can I see any good reason for delaying a decree until some future date when the information may be forthcoming; for it seems to me that no matter what other general advices of the Admiralty may have been given prior to May 7, 1915, the result of this case must be the same.    **D. J.**

# Treasures Destroyed at Louvain

When the Germans burned the Library of Louvain the world lost forever the galleries in which Emperor Charles V., master of the greater part of Europe, meditated on ancient science. The 250,000 manuscripts reduced to ashes on Aug. 27, 1914, can never be replaced. Complete collections of the sixteenth century editions of Virgil, nineteen editions of Terence made in the sixteenth century, ten of Sallust, seventeen of Quintilian, complete sixteenth century editions of Tacitus, Seneca, Martial, Ovid, Horace, Juvenal, Livy, Lucretius, Lucian, Cicero, and Caesar were destroyed. Rare copies of Aristotle and the Greeks were lost. There vanished also first editions of the Bible that were priceless, and whole libraries of ecclesiastical history and of civil law, besides illuminated texts with initials and borders created by the patient and devoted labors of monks of Spain, Germany, and the Netherlands.

# German Plotting in the United States

## A Summary of Authenticated Facts Issued by the Committee on Public Information

EARL E. SPERRY, Professor of History in Syracuse University, has compiled for the United States Government an official summary of known and proved facts concerning "German Plots and Intrigues in the United States During the Period of Our Neutrality," which is published through the Committee on Public Information. In the introduction the following statement by the President of the United States is quoted, being a part of his address to Congress asking for a declaration of war against Germany:

> One of the things that have served to convince us that the Prussian autocracy was not and could never be our friend is that from the very outset of the present war it has filled our unsuspecting communities, and even our offices of government, with spies and set criminal intrigues everywhere afoot against our national unity of counsel, our peace within and without, our industries and our commerce. Indeed, it is now evident that its spies were here even before the war began; and it is unhappily not a matter of conjecture, but a fact proved in our courts of justice, that the intrigues which have more than once come perilously near to disturbing the peace and dislocating the industries of the country have been carried on at the instigation, with the support and even under the personal direction of official agents of the Imperial Government accredited to the Government of the United States.

The facts upon which President Wilson based this indictment are contained in a large array of documents. Among these, says Professor Sperry, are telegrams from the German Government to its diplomatic representatives in the United States; letters and telegrams exchanged by them with their hired agents here; records of financial dealings, as checks, receipts, bankbooks, deposit slips, orders to banks that money be paid and acknowledgments thereof; reports of subordinates to superiors; hotel registers and lists of telephone calls. Of particular value are the counterfoils and stubs in the checkbook of Captain von Papen, on which he habitually recorded memoranda revealing the purpose for which the checks were drawn, and the cashbook of Wolf von Igel, von Papen's secretary, with its daily record of persons to whom he made payments. In addition, much information was gleaned from the criminal prosecution of certain German agents, and consisted of confessions and sworn testimony. Professor Sperry adds:

> The commander in chief of Germany's agents here was Count Johann von Bernstorff, Imperial German Ambassador to the United States. His coadjutor and able adviser during some months was Constantin Theodor Dumba, the Austro-Hungarian Ambassador. His chief lieutenants in the execution of his plans were Captain Franz von Papen, Military Attaché of the German Embassy; Captain Karl Boy-Ed, its Naval Attaché; Dr. Heinrich F. Albert, Commercial Attaché, and Wolf von Igel, who also had diplomatic status. Assisting this central group were many of the Consuls of Germany and Austria-Hungary scattered over the United States, and beneath them were the rank and file of obscure servitors who carried out the plans conceived by the General Staff in Berlin and sent to the German Ambassador.
>
> Franz von Rintelen, although a leader in similar enterprises, was not a member of this band nor responsible to Ambassador von Bernstorff. He had a separate supply of funds and operated as a free lance.

## INTIMIDATING WORKMEN

The brochure first deals with the attempts of German agents to prevent the export of military supplies. It quotes the following circular, which originally appeared in French papers as from the German General Headquarters:

CIRCULAR OF NOVEMBER 2, 1914.

*General Headquarters to the military representative on the Russian and French fronts, as well as in Italy and Norway:*

In all branch establishments of German

banking houses in Sweden, Norway, Switzerland, China, and the United States special military accounts have been opened for special war necessities. Main headquarters authorizes you to use these credits to an unlimited extent for the purpose of destroying factories, workshops, camps, and the most important centres of military and civil supply belonging to the enemy. In addition to the incitement of labor troubles, measures must be taken for the damaging of engines and machinery plants, the destruction of vessels carrying war material to enemy countries, the burning of stocks of raw materials and finished goods, and the depriving of large industrial centres of electric power, fuel, and food. Special agents, who will be placed at your disposal, will supply you with the necessary means for effecting explosions and fires, as well as with a list of people in the country under your supervision who are willing to undertake the task of destruction.        (Signed) Dr. E. FISCHER.

Details are given of the efforts of the German and Austrian Ambassadors to prevent the export of munitions by forcing factory employes—through coercion and intimidation—to leave their positions. The instrument used for this purpose was a so-called employment bureau, conducted by one Liebau, which pretended to find work for men who had left munition factories for conscientious reasons. That coercion and intimidation were regularly used by the bureau to drive employes from munition factories has been proved by an examination of over 5,000 letters and other papers in its files. The Austrian Government reinforced these efforts by circulating in this country, through the foreign-language press, a proclamation which threatened with a penalty of ten to twenty years' imprisonment all subjects who after working in such plants returned to their native land. Captain von Papen also sent out a circular letter of similar import.

Success rewarded these energetic efforts to harass American manufacturers. Liebau's monthly report, made to the German Embassy for February, 1916, contains the following statements:

Since the bureau began its work in August, 1915, through February, 1916, 2,828 Germans and 1,638 subjects of the Austro-Hungarian Monarchy have been provided for. The total number of applicants is now 8,000. Of these 60 per cent came from factories producing munitions and war material, and 40 per cent. would have been employed in such plants if the agency had not provided for them. * * *

Engineers and persons in the better class of positions * * * were persuaded by the propaganda of the bureau to leave war material factories. * * *

The commercial employment bureaus of the country have no supply of unemployed technicians. * * * Many disturbances and suspensions which war material factories have had to suffer, and which it was not always possible to remove quickly, but which on the contrary often led to long strikes, may be attributed to the energetic propaganda of the employment bureau.

In addition, strikes were systematically fomented in all parts of the country by means of an organization regularly financed by the German Government. This conspiracy was in charge of Franz von Rintelen, who is now in a Federal penitentiary. The amount of money at Rintelen's disposal was stated by the Treasurer of the fund to have been $508,000.

## PRESSURE ON CONGRESS

The German-American National Alliance had long endeavored to weld persons of German descent in the United States into a compact body, to be used, when desirable, in the interests of Germany. After the war began, prominent German-Americans organized and supported other societies which aimed to persuade or intimidate members of Congress into adopting pro-German policies.

One of these organizations was the American Embargo Conference, established to prevent the export of munitions. That it was recognized as a valuable tool of the German Government and probably received money from Berlin is shown by the following telegram (Sept. 15, 1916) from Count Bernstorff to the German Foreign Office:

The Embargo Conference in regard to whose earlier fruitful co-operation Dr. Hale can give information is just about to enter upon a vigorous campaign to secure a majority in both houses of Congress favorable to Germany and request further support. There is no possibility of our being compromised. Request telegraphic reply.

The Embargo Conference distributed to voters over 5,000,000 telegrams demanding an embargo on munitions, and at a fixed date 250,000 of these identical messages poured into Washington. The conference paid to the telegraph companies in Chicago alone the sum of $20,-000. It also distributed pamphlets and circular letters demanding an embargo and denouncing American makers of munitions.

Although the officers of the conference asserted that it was supported by small popular subscriptions, its cashbook shows that the $57,000 received from July, 1915, to June, 1916, consisted of sums varying from $400 to $1,000, and given, as a rule, by prominent German-Americans of New York, Chicago, Cincinnati, and Detroit. One gift of $5,000 came from an international banking firm in New York City.

The Embargo Conference apparently served the German Government well, for Count von Bernstorff, in the following telegram to Berlin, requests $50,000 to be spent either on this or on a similar organization aiming to force pro-German policies on Congress:

> I request authority to pay out up to $50,000 (fifty thousand dollars) in order, as on former occasions, to influence Congress through the organization you know of, which can perhaps prevent war.
> I am beginning in the meantime to act accordingly.
> In the above circumstances a public official German declaration in favor of Ireland is highly desirable, in order to gain the support of the Irish influence here.

The actual bribery of Congressmen apparently was intended by Franz von Rintelen. According to Meloy, he supplied Lamar (who was convicted along with him) with money to be used in procuring the passage of resolutions by Congress which should embarrass the Government in the conduct of its relations with Germany. Both Congressman Buchanan and ex-Congressman Fowler received money for their assistance in attempting to bribe Congress. That such was Rintelen's intention was also stated explicitly by George Plochman, Treasurer of the Transatlantic Trust Company, where Rintelen kept his accounts.

The official summary next deals with the efforts of Foreign Secretary Zim-

mermann, through Ambassador Bernstorff at Washington and the German Ambassador at Mexico City, to provoke a war between Mexico and the United States, full details of which, with official documents, were printed in CURRENT HISTORY MAGAZINE in April, 1917.

### BOMBS IN STEAMSHIPS

Then follow the revelations regarding the placing of incendiary bombs with time fuses in the holds of outgoing steamers, setting fire to their cargoes at sea. The bomb shells were manufactured from designs by Dr. Walter T. Scheele, a German chemist of Hoboken, on the Friedrich der Grosse of the North German Lloyd Line, and were then taken to Dr. Scheele's laboratory and filled with combustibles.

When the conspirators were tried one of the witnesses called was a detective who belonged to the New York bomb squad and had worked on the case. Under the pretense that he was a German Secret Service man employed by Wolf von Igel, he had succeeded in making an appointment with Captain von Kleist, Superintendent of Scheele's factory, and thus recounted the conversation with him:

> We sat down and we spoke for about three hours. * * * I asked him the different things that he did, and said if he wanted an interview with Mr. von Igel, my boss, he would have to tell everything. So he told me that von Papen gave Dr. Scheele, the partner of von Kleist in this factory, a check for $10,000 to start this bomb factory. * * * He told me that he, Mr. von Kleist, and Dr. Scheele and a man by the name of Becker on the Friedrich der Grosse, were making the bombs, and that Captain Wolpert, Captain Bode, and Captain Steinberg had charge of putting these bombs on the ships; they put these bombs in cases and shipped them as merchandise on these steamers, and they would go away on the trip and the bombs would go off after the ship was out four or five days, causing a fire and causing the cargo to go up in flames. * * * He also told me that they have made quite a number of these bombs; that thirty of them were given to a party by the name of O'Leary, and that he took them down to New Orleans where he had charge of putting them on ships down there, this fellow O'Leary.

Between 300 and 400 bombs were manufactured, and fires were started by them on thirty-three ships sailing from New York alone. Four of the bombs were found at Marseilles on a vessel which sailed from Brooklyn in May, 1915. The evidence collected in the case led to the indictment of the following men for feloniously transporting on the steamship Kirk Oswald a bomb or bombs filled with chemicals designed to cause incendiary fires: Rintelen, Wolpert, Bode, Schmidt, Becker, Garbade, Praedel, Paradies, von Kleist, Schimmel, Scheele, Steinberg, and others. The last three named fled from justice, Scheele being supplied with $1,000 for that purpose by Wolf von Igel. He eluded the Federal authorities until April, 1918, when he was found hiding in Cuba under the protection of German Secret Service agents. All the others except Schmidt were found guilty and sentenced, on Feb. 5, 1918, to imprisonment for eighteen months and payment of a fine of $2,000 each. It was proved during the trial that Rintelen had hired Schimmel, a German lawyer, to see that bombs were placed on ships.

Schmidt, von Kleist, Becker, Garbade, Praedel, and Paradies had already been tried for conspiracy to make bombs for concealment on oceangoing vessels, with the purpose of setting the same on fire. All were found guilty, and on April 6, 1917, von Kleist and Schmidt were sentenced to two years' imprisonment and a fine of $5,000 each; the others to six months' imprisonment and a fine of $500 each. Wolpert and Bode, also indicted, obtained the privilege of a separate trial, which has not yet been held.

## BOMBS ON SHIP RUDDERS

Robert Fay, a former officer in the German Army, who came to the United States in April, 1915, endeavored to prevent the traffic in munitions by sinking the laden ships at sea. In recounting the circumstances of his arrival here to the chief of the United States Secret Service Fay said:

I had in the neighborhood $4,000. * * * This money came from a man who sent me over * * * [named] Jonnersen. The understanding was that it might be worth while to stop the shipment of artillery munitions from this country. * * *

I imagined Jonnersen to be in the [German] Secret Service.

After stating that he saw von Papen and Boy-Ed and that neither would have anything to do with him, apparently because suspicious of his identity, Fay continued:

I did not want to return [to Germany] without having carried out my intention, that is, the destruction of ships carrying munitions. I proceeded with my experiments and tried to get hold of as much explosive matter as in any way possible. * * *

Fay and two confederates were arrested in a lonely spot near Grantwood, N. J., while testing an explosive. During his examination at Police Headquarters in Weehawken immediately after the arrest he was questioned as follows:

Q. That large machine you have downstairs, what is that? A. That is a patent of mine. It is a new way of getting a time fuse. * * *
Q. Did you know where Scholz [Fay's brother-in-law] had this machine made? A. In different machine shops. * * *
Q. What material is it you wanted [from Daeche, an accomplice]? A. Trinitrate of toluol (T. N. T.) * * *
Q. How much did the machinery cost? A. Roughly speaking, $150 or $200. * * *
Q. What would be the cost of making one and filling it with explosive? A. About $250 each. * * * If they had given me money enough I should simply been able to block the shipping entirely.
Q. Do you mean you could have destroyed every ship that left the harbor by means of those bombs? A. I would have been able to stop so many that the authorities would not have dared [to send out any ships].

It was proved during Fay's trial that his bomb was a practical device, and that its forty pounds of explosive would sink any ship to which it was attached.

Fay and his accomplices, Scholz and Daeche, were convicted of conspiracy to attach explosive bombs to the rudders of vessels, with the intention of wrecking the same when at sea, and were sentenced, on May 9, 1916, to terms of eight, four, and two years respectively in the Federal penitentiary at Atlanta. Dr. Herbert Kienzle and Max Breitung, who assisted Fay in procuring explosives, were indicted on the same charge, but have not been tried. Both are interned.

Other instances are cited, with sworn

testimony, which definitely connected the German Consul General at San Francisco and other German officials in this country with the conspiracy to blow up ships and factories in the United States, as well as tunnels, munition works, and vessels in Canada.

A chapter is devoted to the conspiracy conducted in the United States in January, 1916, through the German Embassy, to destroy the Canadian Pacific Railway and to carry on sabotage (destruction of machinery) in works in the United States and Canada.

Full details are given of the evidence in the attempt of Paul Koenig, head of the Bureau of Investigation of the Hamburg-American Line, to blow up the Welland Canal. The plot was hatched and financed by the German Embassy. Details are also given of the trial and conviction of one Albert Kaltschmidt, a prosperous citizen of Detroit. There was documentary evidence that he had received many thousands of dollars from the German Embassy to be employed in plots to blow up factories, railroads, and tunnels in Canada. The cases are also cited of Werner Horn, who was financed by the German Embassy to blow up the international bridge on the Grand Trunk Railway between Canada and the United States, and the conspiracy of the German Consul General, Franz Bopp, at San Francisco, to blow up the tunnels through which the railway passes under the Selkirk Mountains in British Columbia.

## FORGERY OF PASSPORTS

The third chief purpose of Germany's diplomatic officials in the United States was to send troops and munitions to the Central Empires. When the war began, in July, 1914, large numbers of German reservists were living in America, and in order to avoid capture on their way home many of them sought under false names to obtain passports as American citizens. They thus violated the law that American passports shall be issued only to citizens of the United States, and also discredited genuine passports, thereby causing delay and distress to American citizens abroad. Their action also was a violation of America's neutrality and

endangered its national honor and safety.

In order to have at hand an adequate supply of counterfeit passports, the German Embassy maintained an office in New York City, directed by Captain von Papen, where they were forged by wholesale. German Consuls in distant cities, as Chicago and St. Paul, were informed concerning this office and sent there for passports the reservists from their several localities.

It was shown from the papers of Hans A. von Wedell, who managed the forged passport office, that he had received from the German Embassy in November and December, 1914, nearly $3,000 for these operations.

## FRAUDULENT MANIFESTS

German agents in the United States also endeavored to give military aid to their country by sending coal and other supplies to German warships which were raiding commerce in both the Atlantic and Pacific Oceans. Such action was a violation of American neutrality, and in order to evade the law the conspirators took false oaths before Federal officials concerning the ownership of vessels, the nature of their cargoes, and their destination. These acts, even more than the use of forged passports, were likely to cause friction between the United States and countries with which it was at peace.

The Hamburg-American Line, through its high officials in New York, repeatedly defrauded the United States by procuring false manifests. Among those involved were Dr. Buenz, Managing Director; George Koetter, Superintending Engineer; Adolph Hachmeister, Purchasing Agent, and Joseph Pappinghaus, who together worked up an elaborate machinery to deceive the Government. They confessed at their trial that they had sent out twelve ships, which were proved by the Government to have fraudulent papers and all of which were captured and interned before reaching their destination. Nine of these vessels were chartered, and the Hamburg-American Line paid to the owners for their losses about $1,400,000. The following copy of Captain Boy-Ed's account at a

New York bank indicates that he had large sums at his disposal for conducting Germany's naval operations from the United States and that he reimbursed the Hamburg-American Line for this and other expenditures:

1914  RECEIVED FROM
July 24, National Bank of Commerce $250,000
July 26, A. Vogel...................... 70,000
Aug. 1, National City Bank......... 100,000
Aug. 1, Speyer & Co................ 100,000
Aug. 2, National City Bank......... 200,000
Aug. 3, Speyer & Co................ 500,000
Aug. 5, Bayer Company, Inc........ 300,000
Aug. 16, Kuhn, Loeb & Co........... 35,000
Aug. 24, Interest...................... 1,941
Oct. 26, National City Bank......... 300,000
Oct. 27, Kuhn, Loeb & Co............ 150,000
Oct. 29, Kuhn, Loeb & Co...........1,250,000
Dec. 1, Interest..................... 5,253
           —————
          $3,262,197
Oct 24, Paid to Hamburg-American
  Line.......................$1,200,000
Dec. 2, Paid to Hamburg-American
  Line.......................1,961,365

## PERJURY AS A WEAPON

Gustav B. Kulenkampf of New York, who was employed by the Hamburg-American Line to draw up the false manifests, stated at the trial that he received $750,000, which was subject to the order of Captain Boy-Ed, Naval Attaché of the German Embassy, and was largely spent on the Pacific Coast. His evidence proved that, like the forgery of passports, fraud and perjury were committed under the direction of German officials protected by the diplomatic privileges which all civilized nations consider sacred. Buenz, Koetter, and Hachmeister were found guilty of conspiracy to defraud the United States, and were sentenced in December, 1915, to eighteen months in the Federal penitentiary at Atlanta. Pappinghaus was sentenced to a year and a day.

Similar means were employed by German agents on the western coast under the direction of Captain Boy-Ed to send provisions and coal to German raiders in the Pacific.

Perjury was also employed in a notable instance to justify Germany's conduct. When the passenger liner Lusitania was sunk by a submarine on May 7, 1915, with its great load of noncombatants, the German Government and its Ambassador in America asserted that she was in law and fact a ship of war, because laden with ammunition and armed with four cannon. In order to prove this statement, Ambassador von Bernstorff sent to the Department of State four affidavits swearing that the Lusitania was armed. Three of these were worthless as testimony, and the fourth had been procured by Paul Koenig of the Hamburg-American Line from Gustav Stahl, a German reservist. Federal officials knew that the Lusitania was not armed and that Stahl must have sworn falsely. He was accordingly tried for perjury, confessed his guilt, and was sentenced to eighteen months in the Federal penitentiary at Atlanta.

The report cites the violation of parole by the officers of the German cruisers Prinz Eitel and Kronprinz Wilhelm. They pledged their word of honor to our Government, which had opened the harbor for their protection, that they would not escape from the jurisdiction of the United States, and accordingly were allowed every liberty.

Several officers of the Kronprinz Wilhelm purchased a yacht after some weeks had passed, on the pretense that it was for pleasure cruises. They secretly stocked it with supplies and one night sailed away. They were given the necessary funds for their escape by the German Consul at Richmond, and Captain Boy-Ed filed a message at Sayville, asking the German authorities in Berlin for instructions for these officers. Paroled German officers at San Francisco and Guam also violated their oaths to remain within the jurisdiction of the United States.

A Military Information Bureau was established in this country to collect data concerning the production of war materials in the United States and transmit the information to Germany.

## CONSPIRACY AGAINST INDIA

Germany's effort to incite revolution in India by conspiracies conducted in the United States also furnishes a chapter in this long indictment. Federal officials collected a great amount of evidence proving the connection of the

German Consul General in San Francisco and his staff with this expedition against India. When this evidence was presented to the Grand Jury, the following persons were indicted in March, 1917, "for feloniously conspiring to set on foot a military enterprise to be carried on from within the territory of the United States against India * * * the object and purpose being to initiate mutiny and armed rebellion in India and to overthrow the Government" : Franz Bopp, Eckhart H. von Schack, William von Brincken, Hans Tauscher, F. von Papen, George Rodiek, (German Consul at Honolulu;) Ernest Sekunna, Wolf von Igel, Har Dayal, Ram Chandra, Bhagwan Singh, Chandra Kanta Chakraberty, and Haramba Lal Gupta.

The case was tried in the Federal court at San Francisco, Cal., in March, 1918. All were convicted, except one American of very minor importance and two Hindus, one of whom killed the other and in turn was killed in the courtroom by a court official.

Under German leadership and financed by German money, a group of conspirators in Chicago was planning a simultaneous invasion of India from Siam. Among the Hindus who took part in this expedition was Sukumar Chatterji. After his arrest in Bangkok he made a statement to Brig. Gen. Dudley Ridout, commanding the British troops in the Straits Settlements, in which he stated the aims and methods of the revolutionary party, its ramifications in the Orient, and narrated the events of this particular enterprise.

When the Federal authorities presented to the Grand Jury the evidence which they had collected concerning this plot, the following persons, among others, were indicted for " feloniously conspiring to set on foot a military enterprise against the territory and dominions of the King of Great Britain and Ireland and Emperor of India": G. H. Jacobsen, Kurt von Reiswitz, A. H. Wehde, G. P. Boehm, H. L. Gupta, Jodh Singh, J. N. Sanyal, C. K. Chakraberty, and one Scholz, otherwise called Sterneck. The indictment specifies these among the overt acts committed:

Said Kurt von Reiswitz, [German Consul General in Chicago,] on or about May 6, 1915, at Chicago * * * gave to William Wilms a check for $20,000, the proceeds of which were to be used to incite said subjects to rebellion.

Said Kurt von Reiswitz, on or about June 30, 1915, at Chicago, caused to be given to Albert H. Wehde the sum of $20,000, for the use of Albert H. Wehde in inciting said subjects to * * * rebellion. * * *

Said Kurt von Reiswitz, on or about May 7, 1915, at Chicago, caused to be given to * * * George Paul Boehm the sum of $1,500 to be used by [him] in defraying his expenses in traveling from Chicago to India to engage in such rebellion.

Jacobsen, Wehde, Boehm, and Gupta were found guilty on Oct. 20, 1917, of conspiracy and of violating the neutrality of the United States. The first three were sentenced on the first charge to imprisonment in the Federal penitentiary at Leavenworth, Kan., for two years, and to pay a fine of $10,000; on the second indictment to imprisonment for three years and to pay a fine of $3,000, the sentences of imprisonment to run concurrently. Gupta was sentenced to imprisonment for one year and six months and a fine of $100 on both indictments.

Telegrams from Chakraberty to Zimmermann, the German Secretary for Foreign Affairs, show that the plans concerning India continued during the year 1916.

## PAYING FOR PROPAGANDA

A chapter is also devoted to the efforts to provoke rebellion in Ireland through Irish revolutionists in this country, full details of which were printed in CURRENT HISTORY MAGAZINE, June and July, 1916. Then follows a chapter showing receipts of moneys paid to Edwin Emerson, James F. J. Archibald, and Miss Ray Beveridge for spreading German propaganda in this country in 1915 and 1916; also receipts for moneys paid Marcus Braun, the editor of a newspaper called Fair Play; George Sylvester Viereck, the owner of a paper called The Fatherland, and for other publications, the funds for which came from the German Embassy.

The aims of German propagandists in

the United States were to prove the justice of Germany's cause and the warmth of her friendship for the American people; to procure from Congress an embargo on munitions shipped to the Allies, (although Germany sent to the United States a commission with ample funds to buy such supplies for her own use, which commission organized or bought out steamship companies and chartered many vessels to transport its purchases to Germany;) to encourage pacifism by teaching the waste and wickedness of war; to provoke strife between America and the allied States, especially England and Japan. So eager were the German agents to cause friction between the United States and England that Paul Koenig attempted through perjury to manufacture evidence that supplies were being sent from New York to British warships. Ambassador von Bernstorff took a direct and active part in purchasing the services of those who would aid Germany by creating opinion in her favor.

## FINANCES OF GERMAN AGENTS

The diplomatic staff of Germany in the United States had a generous supply of money with which to carry on its operations. The essential features of its financial system are described by Frederick A. Borgemeister, confidential adviser to Dr. Albert, who was disbursing agent for the German Embassy. In a statement which he made Aug. 11-13, 1917, at Fort Oglethorpe, Georgia, before Federal officials, he said that $7,-000,000 worth of short-term German Treasury notes were sold by an American banking house early in April, 1915, and was then asked:

Q. What became of that $7,000,000? A. The $7,000,000 were partly used for the purchase of materials, raw materials, of foodstuffs, ships, and the remainder was placed at the disposal of the German Embassy at Washington.

Q. That means at the disposal of J. von Bernstorff? A. Yes, Sir.

Q. How much would that remainder be, using your best recollection? A. I should say about $4,000,000 and probably a little more.

Mr. Borgemeister was then asked in substance this question:

Q. What in the aggregate were the transactions of your office prior to the proceeds of the April loan [1915]? A. I should say about $5,000,000.

Q. That is, the whole sum total of the financial operations which were handled in your office exclusive of the April loan of $7,000,000 was $5,000,000? A. Yes. Let me think it over again—between four and five millions.

A sale of one-year notes of the German Empire realized $3,600,000, which was paid into Dr. Albert's account. At another point in his examination Mr. Borgemeister said, "We constantly received through American correspondents of the Deutsche Bank funds as we required." Besides the money realized from the sale of securities there was available, for example, $300,000 at one New York bank and $400,000 at another, and loans were also made from American banks. The total balances in the many banks where Dr. Albert had deposits varied from $1,000,000 to $5,-000,000. Toward the close of his examination Mr. Borgemeister was asked:

Q. During the time that you were retained with Dr. Albert down to the time of your resignation, covering the years 1915 and 1916, what would be the approximate amount of money which went through the H. F. Albert office, in the aggregate; please do the best you can in this estimate? A. I should say between fifteen and twenty millions.

## VON PAPEN'S FUNDS

How Captain von Papen obtained the large sums necessary for the execution of his many projects is thus explained:

Q. Please explain when von Papen wanted money who he went to to get it. A. I believe he communicated with the Ambassador. And we would be instructed to place certain funds at his disposal. * * *

Q. On what instructions would Heynen and yourself [with power to sign checks] act in transferring funds from the H. F. Albert account to the von Papen account? A. Only on instruction of Dr. Albert or on instruction of the embassy approved by Dr. Albert. * * *

Q. * * * Can you tell the disbursements by Dr. Albert's office to von Papen's office? A. There were large amounts. We would receive instructions from the Ambassador to make payments, or to hold so much money at the disposal of von Papen, and von Papen would receive this money and sign receipt by himself or von Igel, von Papen's assistant.

Mr. Borgemeister then stated that substantial amounts were paid to both Captains von Papen and Boy-Ed, and was then asked this question:

Q. What are we to understand that you mean by substantial amounts? A. I mean fairly large amounts. I would say that the entire payment during that time might have been close to a million. Of course, remember that we had funds, had not only the fund of $7,000,000; we had other funds at our disposal which had been at the office when the $7.000,000 became available to us. * * *

Q. Are we to understand that the disbursement to von Papen between the first of April and the middle of June, 1915, aggregated approximately $1,000,000? A. Yes, Sir, as far as I can estimate it.

Q. Between * * * the middle of June, 1915, and the time von Papen returned to Germany can you estimate the amount of money which was conveyed from the H. F. Albert accounts in various banks to von Papen on checks which were signed by Mr. Heynen and yourself? * * * A. It was a substantial amount in total. * * *

Q. Would that mean it was in excess of a million? A. I should say yes, it might be between one and two millions.

Captain von Papen also received funds, deposited to his credit in a Washington bank, directly from the German Embassy. Some of these deposits, a list of which follows, were made by Ambassador von Bernstorff himself:

### 1914

| | | |
|---|---|---:|
| Sept. | 9, Bernstorff | $1,116.20 |
| Sept. | 24, Bernstorff | 1,110.00 |
| Oct. | 21, Bernstorff | 1,000.00 |
| Nov. | 4, German Embassy | 583.10 |
| Nov. | 25, German Embassy | 2,000.00 |
| Dec. | 7, Bernstorff | 2,583.10 |

### 1915

| | | |
|---|---|---:|
| Jan. | 9, German Embassy | $3,000.00 |
| Jan. | 15, German Embassy | 2,000.00 |
| Feb. | 5, Bernstorff | 2,000.00 |

### 1915 (Continued)

| | | |
|---|---|---:|
| Feb. | 24, German Embassy | 1,500.00 |
| Feb. | 25, German Embassy | 3,600.00 |
| Feb. | 26, German Embassy | 1,749.30 |
| May | 26, German Embassy | 1,166.20 |
| June | 1, German Embassy | 583.10 |
| July | 20, German Embassy | 1,154.30 |
| Sept. | 7, German Embassy | 2,500.00 |
| Oct. | 14, German Embassy | 2,500.00 |

The above list is compiled from photographic copies of letters to the bank and of letters from it to Captain von Papen, advising him of the deposits, and from his checkbook. He also received from the Consul General in New York City, on March 19, 1915, $5,000, and from various unknown sources other sums.

Captain Boy-Ed received substantial amounts, said Mr. Borgemeister, from Dr. Albert, and also received funds directly from Germany.

### AN OFFICIAL LIE

All the criminal plots and conspiracies narrated in the foregoing pages were undertaken prior to the Summer of 1915. The German Government, nevertheless, in December of that year, sent to the United States for publication in the press the following authorized official lie:

*"The German Government has naturally
"never knowingly accepted the support
"of any person, group of persons, society,
"or organization seeking to promote the
"cause of Germany in the United States
"by illegal acts, by counsel of violence,
"by contravention of law, or by any
"means whatever that could offend the
"American people in the pride of their
"own authority."*

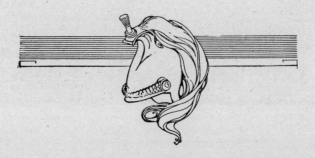

# INTERNATIONAL CARTOONS
## OF THE WAR

[Italian Cartoon]

## They Shall Not Pass

—From Il 420, Florence.

# Along the Marne

—*From La Victoire, Paris.*

"Nach Paris!"

# Proud of the Americans

—*From La Victoire, Paris.*

FRANCE: "They are chic!"
BRITAIN: "Well, they are our children!"

# An Elastic Offensive

—From The San Francisco Chronicle.

# Not to His Taste

—From *The Passing Show, London.*

WILHELM: "Vy can't I bid for von mitout de oder?"
AUCTIONEER: "Because they are inseparable!"

# Popular Pastime—Driving Nails Into Hindenburg

—*From The New York Tribune.*

# Yes, It's Uncle Sam—But Not as They Had Pictured Him

—From The New York Herald.

# Their Place at the Board

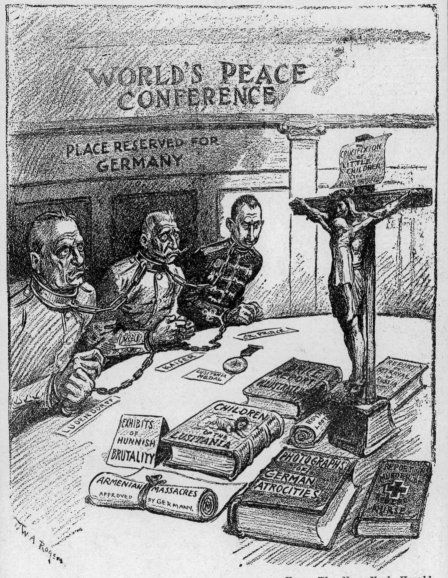

—From The New York Herald.

# After the War

—From The Passing Show, London.

"All dressed up and nowhere to go!"

# Old Home Week

HINDENBURG LINE

—From The New York World.

# A Vision: Peace on Earth!

—*From Nebelspalter, Zurich.*

# Legacy to the Unborn

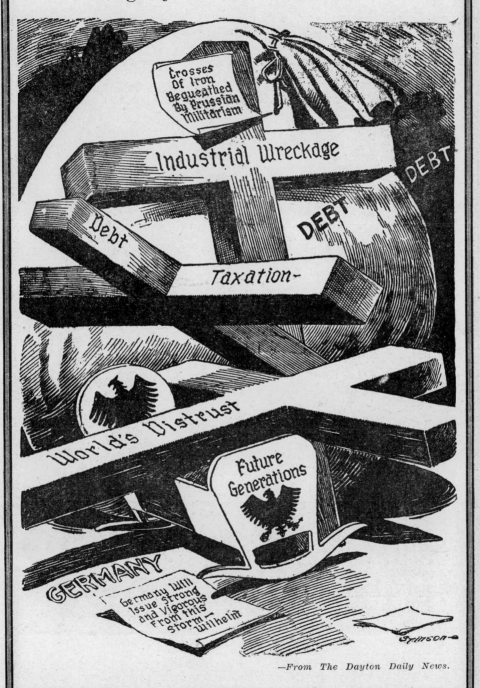

Crosses
Of Iron
Bequeathed
By Prussian
Militarism

Industrial Wreckage

DEBT

DEBT

Debt

Taxation-

World's Distrust

Future
Generations

GERMANY

Germany will
issue strong
and vigorous
from this
storm—
Wilhelm

—From The Dayton Daily News.

# "Over the Hills to the Poorhouse"

—*Central Press Association.*

## The Fool Trap

## Four Years Ago

"You will be back in your homes before the leaves have fallen."—Kaiser in August, 1914.

## "The Hit Dog Howls"

## The Sound of Wood on Bone

—From The Brooklyn Eagle.

# A Wayside Shrine

—*Central Press Association.*

## The Rhine Whine

—*Passing Show, London.*

## A Belated War Measure

—*London Opinion.*

THE KAISER: "He is the Schwein-
hund who discovered America!"

## What Doth It Profit a Man—?

—*St. Louis Post-Dispatch.*

## The Fifth Year

—*St. Louis Globe-Democrat.*

## The Other Crown Prince Also Retires

—The Dallas News.

## The Poor Nut!

—Detroit News.

## "Gott! It Will Soon Become a Truth"

—Dayton Daily News.

## Memories

—Detroit News.

# The Yankee Tomcat

—*From the Westminster Gazette.*

THE PUP: "There's a new Tomcat, father, see me go for him!"

FATHER: "What's the matter?"

THE PUP: "It was the wrong Tomcat, father!"

[Dutch Cartoon]

# The Central Quartet Out of Tune

—*From De Amsterdammer, Amsterdam.*

FIRST VIOLIN WILHELM: "What do I hear? Is it discord?"

## Enlightened

## More Power to Him

## Troublesome Pets

## When Willie Comes Marching Home

—*From The San Francisco Chronicle.*

# Peace on Earth—the Kaiser's Way

—From The Sydney Bulletin.

## Of German Extraction

—From The New York Times.

# JOHN W. DAVIS

American Ambassador to Great Britain, Succeeding Mr. Page

# DISTINGUISHED ALLIED LEADERS

Left to Right: Field Marshal Haig, President Poincaré, Marshal
Foch, and King George

**Major Gen. E. A. Helmick**
*28th United States Infantry*
(© *Press Illustrating Service*)

**Major Gen. John L. Hines**
*Headquarters Staff, American Expeditionary Force*
(© *Press Illustrating Service*)

**Major Gen. W. L. Kenly**
*Chief of Military Aeronautics*
(© *Harris & Ewing*)

**Major Gen. William T. Johnston**
*Fort Bliss, Texas*
(© *Press Illustrating Service*)

**Major Gen. Thomas H. Barry**
*Camp Grant, Rockford, Ill.*
(© *American Press Association*)

**Major Gen. Henry P. McCain**
*Adjutant General*
(© *Press Illustrating Service*)

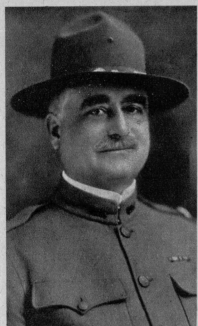

**Major Gen. William Weigel**
*In United States Army Since 1887*
(© *Press Illustrating Service*)

**Major Gen. Grote Hutcheson**
*Embarkation Chief, Newport News*
(© *Harris & Ewing*)

PRINCE MAXIMILIAN OF BADEN

Appointed German Chancellor in October, 1918, to Succeed Count
von Hertling

# MILITARY LEADERS IN THE EAST

**General Franchet d'Esperey**
*Chief of Allied Forces in the Balkans*

**General Danglis**
*Commander of the Greek Army*
*(© Photo by Paul Thompson)*

**General Semenoff**
*Anti-Bolshevist Leader in Siberia*

**General Liman von Sanders**
*Commander of Turkish Armies in*
*Palestine*
*(© American Press Association)*

Generalissimo of the Allied Armies, with Marshal's Baton in His Hand

# GENERAL MANOURY

The French Victor at the Ourcq

Americans, Britishers, and Czechoslovaks Greeting the Japanese Troops at Vladivostok

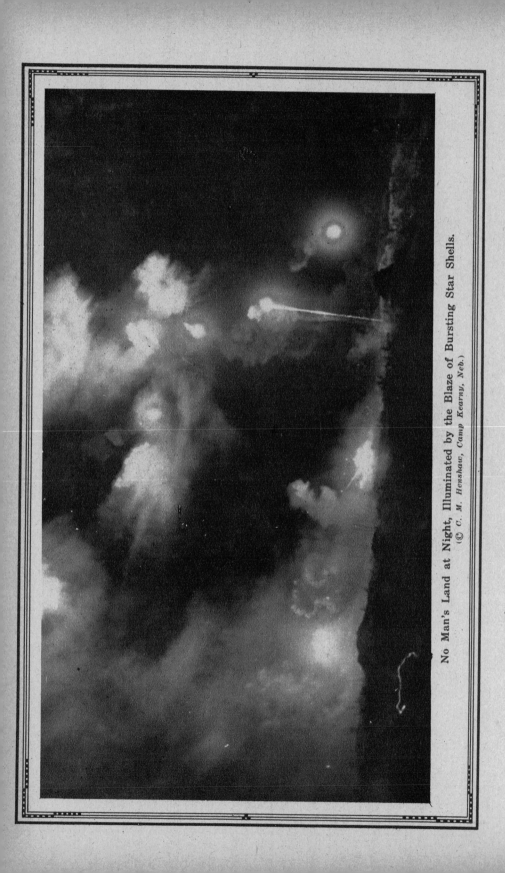

No Man's Land at Night, Illuminated by the Blaze of Bursting Star Shells.

(© *C. M. Henshaw, Camp Kearny, Neb.*)

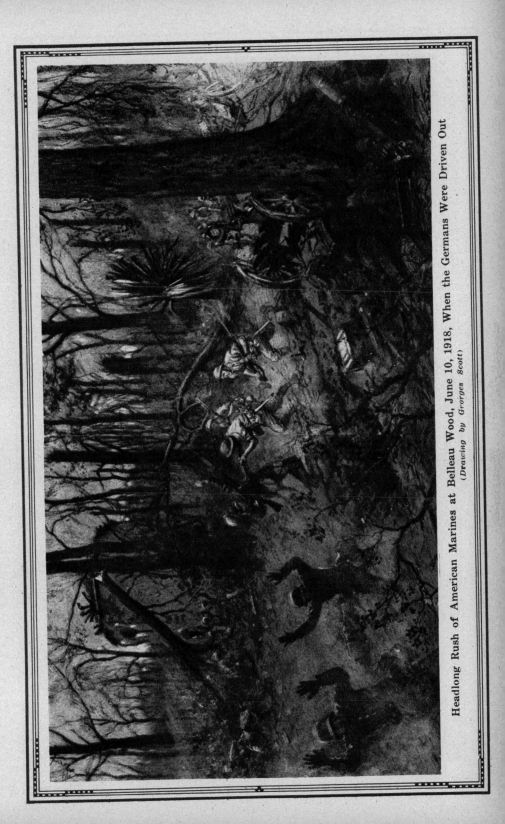

Headlong Rush of American Marines at Belleau Wood, June 10, 1918, When the Germans Were Driven Out
(*Drawing by Georges Scott*)

Hauling a Heavy American Gun Across a French River with the Aid of Tractors and a Block and Tackle

(© *International Film Service*)

French Airplane Releasing Bombs While Under Heavy Shrapnel Fire

The Ancient Town of Nazareth, Palestine, Captured by the British

(© *Underwood & Underwood*)

OVERSEA CAP

PONCHO AND BLANKET

BAYONET

KNAPSACK

STEEL HELMET

CARTRIDGE BELT

WATER BOTTLE

HAVERSACK

FIRST AID PACKAGE

GAS MASK

ENTRENCHING TOOL

SPRINGFIELD RIFLE

PUTTEES (SPIRAL)

PUTTEES (SPIRAL)

**United States Infantryman When Fully Equipped for Field Service**
(*Committee on Public Information*)

Fifth Avenue, New York City, Dressed for Fourth Liberty Loan Campaign

# PERIOD L.

Great German Retreat—New Zealand's Decree on Germany's Colonial Ambitions—Driving the Germans from Belgium—From St. Quentin to the Argonne—The Battle for Argonne Forest—The Taking of St. Mihiel Salient—Devastation of Evacuated Regions—Pushing War Activities at Home—United States the Largest Insurance Company—Prince Maximilian's Peace Drive—The Kaiser's Exhortations—President Wilson's Peace Program—Submarine Depredations—Fate of 150 U-Boats Officially Attested—Library Facilities for Our Soldiers—The Government Takes Over the Nation's Colleges—Turkey's Disaster in Palestine—Bulgaria's Surrender—The Albanian Nationality—Progress of the Allies in Russia—Lenine and Trotzky German Agents—Rasputin's Assassination—The Franco-Russian Alliance—Luxemburg and Germany—Metz in 1870: A Reminder of Its Fall—German Trench Defense Methods—Cuba's Part in the World War—Land Settlement for ex-Service Men—German Crimes in Southwest Africa—Mesopotamian Operations—A Soldier's Amazing Career—Changes in the German Government.

# CURRENT HISTORY CHRONICLED

## AN EPOCH-MAKING MONTH

OCTOBER, 1918, the fifty-first month of the war, witnessed the most momentous events since the outbreak of the world conflict. It was in this period that the strategy of the Generalissimo of the allied forces, Marshal Foch, which was first manifested in the offensive launched in the Château-Thierry pocket, July 18, saw its brilliant consummation. Within three months from that date Bulgaria unconditionally surrendered, Turkey met supreme disaster in the field and was practically out of the war, Austria-Hungary became panicstricken in the face of impending disintegration and sued for peace—which was definitely rejected, except at the price of the dissolution of the empire—while Germany's military pride was humbled into the dust by the forced retreat of her armies along the whole front from the North Sea to the Alsatian Mountains as defeat after defeat befell her on every sector. Further humiliation came when she hurriedly evacuated the entire Belgian Coast on Oct. 17 to avoid the capture of all the forces of the German right wing, and quitted the important industrial districts of Northeastern France, surrendering the important cities of Lille, Douai, Cambrai, Roubaix, La Fère, Laon, St. Quentin, and the Argonne Forest to the victorious allied arms. On Oct. 6, forced by military disasters and domestic upheaval, the German Government appealed to President Wilson for an immediate armistice and peace on the terms laid down by the President in his public utterances since Jan. 8, 1918. The Kaiser's Government was compelled to suffer a further derogation of its pride by witnessing the rejection of this plea on account of the distrust its trickery and atrocities had produced, and was confronted with the alternative of unconditional surrender or certain defeat in the field. This crisis, one of the epoch-making points in political history, with the kaleidoscopic events that followed in quick sequence, made the month's record

a fascinating and catastrophic narrative. The phases of this culmination are treated separately in the various chapters of this issue of CURRENT HISTORY MAGAZINE.

* * *

## REBUILDING LOUVAIN

ON Sept. 1 an impressive ceremony took place on the Belgian front in commemoration of the burning of Louvain and the Louvain Library. Among those present were the King and Queen of the Belgians and their son, General Roqueril, head of the French mission, and a considerable number of French and Belgian officers and men. M. Etienne Lamy, Secretary of the Académie Française, said it was the German desire to destroy everything that was not the product of their own so-called culture. There would be an international inquiry into the crime of Louvain. The Secretary of the International Reconstruction Fund said the whole of the civilized world was supporting the movement to re-establish the library. Its resurrection would be a universal work.

In a letter addressed to a meeting of men of letters at Havre for the restoration of the library, M. Emile Boutroux of the French Academy wrote:

Before the destruction of this library men belonging to one or another university, school, or society, professing some confession, right or not, seemed to be divided by such radical differences as made any kind of rapprochement impossible. In the presence of the ashes of Louvain humanity has forgotten these distinctions. It has felt outraged, violated in that which, says Pascal, is the very principle of its dignity, its thought, mirror of divine wisdom, the only instrument capable of seeking truth. Spontaneously and in unity of spirit, it has dedicated itself to the work of reparation. Intimate union, says Aristotle, is achieved by common work for a beautiful cause. The martyrdom which crowned the heroism of Belgium has been a bond of union for all men of good-will.

While we combine our efforts to repair—alas! only as much as possible—the injury done to humanity at large by the burning of Louvain, we also, if I mistake not,

pledge each other to put an end to these
feuds of opinions and beliefs, as fruitless
or baleful as they are contrary to human
dignity, and to consecrate all our forces,
first to fight as long as may be necessary
the declared enemy of liberty and all true
civilization, and, secondly, to solve those
numerous and arduous questions which
impose themselves on humanity in its
effort to realize the material, intellectual,
and moral perfection of which its nature
is capable. Louvain in ruins is no longer
a rare collection of precious things; it is
the rallying point for all minds devoted to
the higher interests of humanity.

* * *

## POOLING WAR INDUSTRIES

THE Allies have put into operation the
centralized control of all the economic forces of the nations at war with
Germany. The plan was worked out by
President Wilson's war advisers in conjunction with the allied missions, and received the approval of the President and
the Premiers of the Entente nations.
The co-ordination of effort embraces the
five interallied councils—war, shipping,
munitions, food, and finance—and the
scope of their operations is limited to
the following cases:

Where two or more Governments are
interested in supplies which must be
transported overseas, to supplement de-
ficiencies in local production.
Where several sources of supplies should
be agreed upon, together with the allotment and method of their distribution or
utilization.
Where there might, without agreement,
be competition between Governments in
procuring supplies or a wasteful duplica-
tion of productive effort.

The committees deal directly with virtually all materials and commodities for
the prosecution of the war. These include nitrates, tungsten, and tin, international pooling agreements for which
have recently been effected in Paris and
London, nonferrous metals, iron and
steel, hides and leather, rubber, wool, and
all other raw materials or manufactured
products of which there may be a
shortage, or where competitive and shipping conditions, and the local production
and distribution situation make control
desirable. Pooling agreements for these
latter will be effected as the necessity
arises.

The plan seeks to secure in the economic sphere results comparable with
those obtained in the field through the
unified military command.

* * *

## PRESENTING THE BATON TO MARSHAL FOCH

THE baton of a Marshal of France,
the nation's highest military honor,
was presented to General Ferdinand
Foch on Aug. 23, 1918. The ceremony
took place at his headquarters and was
striking in its simplicity. The Marshal
was found busied with his maps and
wearing on his sleeves seven stars, the
distinctive mark of his new dignity. A
company of infantry was drawn up in
the garden before the château. Marshal
Foch, accompanied by General Pétain and
a score of other eminent soldiers, waited
for a few minutes in front of the troops.
Then the band struck up the "Marseillaise," as motor cars bearing a distinguished party of statesmen from Paris
rolled through the gates. Among those
who alighted were President Poincaré,
Premier Clemenceau, M. Leygues, Minister of Marine, and M. Loucheur, Minister of Armaments.

The President and Marshal Foch
walked together down the line of troops.
Then the Generals grouped themselves,
and M. Poincaré, standing opposite Marshal Foch, recited the services, in recognition of which France had conferred
upon him the highest military honor in
its gift. The names of the Marne, the
Yser, the Somme, and the battles of the
present year followed each other in
quick succession, and at the close of his
eloquent peroration the President handed
to the Marshal the velvet-covered and
gold-starred baton, which symbolized the
gratitude and confidence of France.

The distinction is one that of late has
been rarely bestowed. With the exception of Joffre no one has been raised to
the rank for forty years past. It was
under the reign of Philip Augustus that
the Marshal of France was first recognized as Commander in Chief of the
army. Previous to that time he was subordinate to the constable, who held supreme military power. Under Francis I.
the number of Marshals was raised to
two, under Henry III. to four, and under
Louis XIV. to twenty. Napoleon used the
title as a stimulant to the ambition of

his soldiers, but with the downfall of the Second Empire the title fell largely into abeyance. The rarity of its bestowal increases the value of the honor conferred on the Commander in Chief of the allied forces.

\* \* \*

## ST. QUENTIN

ST. QUENTIN, in the centre of the Hindenburg line, was occupied on Oct. 1 by the Fourth British Army under Rawlinson and the First French under Debeney. It is the key to the trunk line between France, Belgium, and Northern Germany—the railway system, Lille-Rheims. It lost its tactical value for the Germans after their retreat to the Hindenburg line in the Spring of 1917, but recovered it in their offensive of last March, when von Hutier's attempt to drive his "shock" troops between the ill-fated British Fifth Army and the French Sixth almost succeeded.

During their period of occupation the Germans tried to turn the town into a miniature Paris. Both have a Champs Elysées, and in St. Quentin, in order to enhance the illusion, the Germans renamed the Faubourg St. Jean the Faubourg St. Germain, and the Faubourg d'Isle, across the Somme, the Quartier Latin. Previous to the first retreat the theatres, restaurants, and hotels did a thriving business as befitted the headquarters of the Second German Army. For three Winters it was the gayest city behind the German front. Doubtless, in the circumstances, the inhabitants learned many valuable military secrets, which may account for the fact that, when they withdrew, the enemy took with them the entire population of over 50,000.

St. Quentin has several historical edifices still standing, but more imperishable memories. Ascending the hill from the railway station by the Somme, the first of the British troops to enter the town came upon the slightly damaged structure of the Hôtel de Ville, a fine piece of Gothic. To the right at the other end of the "common" are the ruins of the church, in a crypt of which reposed the dust of the Christian martyr, Carus Quintius, whose name is preserved in both town and church.

St. Quentin saw some fighting in the war of 1870. The Boulevard du Huit Octobre commemorated the successful defense of the town on Oct. 8 against the Prussians. Later Faidherbe desperately withstood the attacks of the Bavarian, von Goeben, until the general armistice ended hostilities. The town also has several links with English history. In 1557, when the Spanish King, Philip II., was the husband of Queen Mary, their troops defeated the French Army at St. Quentin, under the famous Admiral Coligny. The battle was fought on St. Lawrence Day, and Philip raised the grim pile known as the Escorial in honor of the saint. The town was also part of the dowry of Mary Queen of Scots when she married Francis II. She drew a revenue from it until her death.

\* \* \*

## NAZARETH

NAZARETH, which was taken by the British in the advance through Palestine, is the place where Jesus spent His early youth and taught in the synagogue. Down to the time of Constantine it was a small village, occupied by Samaritan Jews, and in the year 600 it was taken by the Turks. In the year 1,000 the Greek Emperor Zimisces took the village and subsequently the Crusaders transferred thither the bishopric of Scythapolis. The town was rebuilt by Emperor Frederick II. in 1229 and was visited by Louis IX. of France.

In 1517, when the Turks conquered Palestine, the Christians were compelled to leave Nazareth. In 1620 the Franciscans, aided by Fakreddin, established themselves in the town and it enjoyed a renewal of prosperity.

The Bible relates that it was here that the Angel Gabriel appeared before the Virgin Mary to announce the conception of Christ. Upon the spot a Latin convent called the Annunciation, or the House of the Virgin, stands now, surrounded by many other buildings, dating back only to the eighteenth century. The present town has a population of about 11,000, mostly Christians. The buildings here are all flat-topped stone houses, built on a declivity, made picturesque by hedges of olive and fig trees.

### CONFERENCE REGARDING AMERICAN PRISONERS OF WAR

AN American-German War Prisoners' Conference began at Berne, Switzerland, Sept. 24, 1918, under the Presidency of Paul Dinichert, Swiss Minister Plenipotentiary. The conference was opened by President Calender of Switzerland.

The American delegates included John W. Garrett, Minister to the Netherlands; John W. Davis, the new Ambassador to London; General Kernan, representing the army; Captain Hough, representing the navy; Colonels Grant, Shartle and Ashburn, Commander Stone of the navy, Mr. Story of the Department of Justice, and Major Perkins of the American Red Cross.

The Germans included Prince Hohenlohe-Langenburg, Count Montgelas, Colonel von Fransecky, Councilor von Keller, Major Draudt, and Captain Wilke von Hindenburg of the navy.

Prince Ernst Hohenlohe-Langenburg, Chairman of the German delegation, was born in 1863. From 1900 to 1905 he was Regent in Saxe-Coburg-Gotha for Duke Karl Eduard, a minor, and later he was a member and for a short time President of the Reichstag. Count Adolph Montgelas, head of the American section of the German Foreign Office, served for a time in the embassy at Washington. He married Miss Fanny Dickinson Hazeltine, daughter of Dr. Charles S. Hazeltine of Grand Rapids, Mich, who was the American Consul at Milan under President Cleveland. Captain von Hindenburg, designated Envoy Extraordinary and Minister, is a nephew of Field Marshal von Hindenburg.

No official report of the results of the conference had been announced up to Oct. 20.

\* \* \*

### A SUPERFLUOUS MEDAL

THE Carnavalet Museum in Paris has obtained from Basle, Switzerland, a replica of the only medal remaining of a large issue which was struck off in 1914 by the Germans to commemorate their capture of Paris; the entire supply, except the single medal at the Basle Museum, was destroyed after the failure of the Kaiser's armies to reach Paris.

The medal is of an aluminium alloy. On one side is an iron cross, with " W " and a crown, and the date " 1914." On the obverse is a figure of the Eiffel Tower and the Arc de Triomphe, the two dates 1871 and 1914, and the inscription, " Entry of the German troops into Paris." This medal was obviously struck with a view to the Kaiser's being in Paris in August, 1914. His hopes not being realized and the supply of metal running short, the tell-tale stock was melted down. It is stated that tens of thousands of these medals had been made.

\* \* \*

### CAMBRAI

BAPTISTE COUTAING, who was born and lived in Cambrai in the fifteenth century, there invented a fine linen cloth or muslin which, taking its name from the place, is known as " cambric " the world over. The French, however, call it " batiste," after the inventor's name.

Cambrai, which was captured by the Third British Army under General Byng, Oct. 9, is traversed by three arms of the River Scheldt, which, on French territory, is called the Escaut. Cambrai is thirty-two miles south-southeast of Lille. It had a population of about 30,000, mostly engaged in the manufacture of cloth.

From the Roman Camaracum, it became, in the Middle Ages, the capital of a small Episcopal province, the Dukes of Burgundy, and then the German Emperors, acting as their châtelains. Here in 1508 was formed the famous League of Cambrai, comprising Maximilian, Louis XII., Pope Julius II., and Ferdinand of Aragon, against Venice. Twenty-one years later Margaret of Austria and Louise of Savoy, acting, respectively, for Charles V. and Francis I., signed the " Paix des Dames "—the women's peace—the famous Peace of Cambrai.

The town has belonged to France since 1679. In 1815 it surrendered to the Duke of Wellington. Fénelon, the diplomat and author, was born and lived here, and his name is preserved in the Place Fénelon.

Cambrai has few buildings of the very remote past; most of them date from the seventeenth or eighteenth century. But there remains the Château de Selles in the northwest corner of the town, its restorations even dating back to the eleventh century. The Belfry, in the Rue St. Martin, dates from the fifteenth century.

* * *

### LIEUTENANT OF LONDON TOWER

GENERAL SIR IAN HAMILTON, commander of the ill-starred Gallipoli expedition, which was caustically condemned by a commission, was appointed in September to the post of Lieutenant of the Tower of London, succeeding Sir Horace Smith-Dorrien, who was made Governor of Gibraltar. His selection to this lucrative post was a surprise, in view of the criticism levelled at him for the failure in the Dardanelles. The office of Lieutenant of the Tower dates from the reign of Edward II., who first created the post for Sir Giles de Oudenard, and ever since it has been filled by distinguished commanders of the British Army, the title being that of His Majesty's Lieutenant of the Tower. Above the Lieutenant is the Constable of the Tower, a still more ancient office, created by William the Conqueror in the year 1068 for Sir Geoffrey de Mandeville, and now held by the octogenarian Field Marshal Sir Evelyn Wood, V. C.

* * *

### CRIME IN ENGLAND LESSENED BY WAR

THE report of the Prison Commissioners of England and Wales shows that in the 138 prisons the following decreases occurred in the prison population:

| Daily Average— | 1914. | 1918. |
|---|---|---|
| Convict prisons | 2,704 | 1,393 |
| Local prisons | 14,352 | 7,335 |
| Borstal institutions | 928 | 720 |
| Detention | 171 | 70 |
| Reformatories | 81 | 3 |

The report states that in 1903 one person out of every 175 in the community was or had been in prison; in 1913 the number had fallen to one in every 271, and since the war started it had dropped to one in 1,127. The fall during the war was attributed chiefly to improved social conditions, the call on the manhood of the nation, and the diversion of many persons from idle and unprofitable lives, with endless opportunities for crime, to useful employment, while in many cases intense patriotism had led persons not only to abstain from evil themselves, but to do good work by their example and encouragement to others. Twenty years ago there were 20,000 youths between 16 and 21 in prison annually, and now there were only 4,000, while, owing to the efforts of the after-care societies, between 70 and 80 per cent. were saved from a life of crime.

As a result of appeals made to the patriotism of prison workers the average output of prison labor was nearly $45 per head more than before the war, and more than 17,000,000 articles, representing nearly 12,000 a day, had been distributed from the prisons for war purposes. Many former inmates of prisons had made good by acts of sacrifice and gallantry, and not a few had been promoted and decorated.

* * *

### HOLLAND'S IDLE SHIPPING

THE War Trade Board announced on Oct. 17 that negotiations would be resumed at once for a rationing agreement with Holland. Throughout the Summer Holland remained the one neutral country in Europe that had not concluded a commercial agreement with the United States. Norway, Sweden, Denmark, Spain, and Switzerland all had signed such agreements. Secretary Lansing on Sept. 20 issued a statement showing the friendly attitude of the United States in this matter. A tentative agreement with the Netherlands Government similar to those with the other European neutrals had been reached in January, 1918, by which the United States was to have furnished 100,000 tons of bread cereals, 140,000 tons of petroleum products, 26,000 tons of cotton goods, 35,000 tons of coffee, and about 100,000 tons of various other articles of which Holland stood in great need, but this arrangement was rejected by the Netherlands authorities, though at least 50,000 tons of shipping lay idle in Dutch harbors. This paralysis of Dutch tonnage was understood to be due to German threats to destroy all shipping that might be used in carrying supplies to Holland. Between America and the Dutch East Indies, where there was no submarine activity, Dutch vessels moved freely. Holland's change of policy is attributed to the altered military situation on land and sea.

\* \* \*

### CREDITS TO ALLIED NATIONS

THE following credits had been established and cash advances made in favor of foreign Governments by the United States up to Sept. 3:

|  | Credits Established. | Cash Advances. |
|---|---|---|
| Belgium | $154,250,000 | $144,030,000 |
| Cuba | 15,000,000 | 5,000,000 |
| France | 2,065,000,000 | 1,780,000,000 |
| Great Britain | 3,745,000,000 | 3,482,000,000 |
| Greece | 15,790,000 | ........ |
| Italy | 760,000,000 | 730,000,000 |
| Rumania | 6,666,666 | ........ |
| Russia | 325,000,000 | 187,729,750 |
| Serbia | 12,000,000 | 9,005,000 |
| Total | $7,098,706,666 | $6,337,764,750 |

The obligations received from foreign Governments are in the form of or are held as demand notes, carrying interest at rates not less than those borne by the respective issues of Liberty bonds of the United States, and the Treasury Department receives assurances from the Department of State as to the authority of the foreign representatives to execute the obligations on behalf of their respective Governments.

\* \* \*

### THE USE OF SHOTGUNS IN WAR

THE German authorities on Sept. 19 transmitted through the Swiss Legation a protest against the Americans' use of shotguns in guarding prisoners of war, declaring that this was a violation of The Hague Convention and announcing that every American prisoner " found to have in his possession such guns or ammunition belonging thereto forfeits his life." Secretary Lansing replied on Sept. 29 denying that the use of shotguns was forbidden by The Hague Convention, and stating that the weapon was

lawful and that its use would not be abandoned. He added this sentence:

> Moreover, if the German Government should carry out its threat in a single instance it will be the right and duty of the Government of the United States to make such reprisals as will best protect the American forces, and notice is hereby given of the intention of the Government of the United States to make such reprisals.

Shotguns are used by the American Army in general police work and in guarding prisoners, being preferred in such army work over the high-power rifle, because the latter would endanger persons not intended to be hit.

\* \* \*

THE latest church census in England shows a decrease of 135,542 communicants in two years in the Established Church; the free churches are less in membership in the same period by 74,827; the net shrinkage in ten years in Sunday schools in all churches in England is 545,161 scholars and 19,234 teachers.

\* \* \*

THE Finance Minister of Rumania introduced on Aug. 24, 1918, a bill in the Chamber of Deputies for war credits amounting to $400,000,000, of which $120,000,000 is appropriated to cover damages caused to private property in Rumania by the war. Indemnities of from 25 to 75 per cent. will be paid for damage suffered; where the damage exceeds $20,000, 25 per cent. will be allowed.

\* \* \*

THE Kaisertreuen, the party of the Kaiser in Germany, issued a statement in August, asserting that the German Socialist newspaper, Vorwärts, receives each year as a subsidy from the German Government from $60,000 to $125,000; also that the Berliner Tageblatt annually receives $500,000 from official sources. The definite statement is also made that Rudolf Mosse, publisher of several important German daily newspapers, receives a $900,000 annual subsidy from the Government.

# GREAT GERMAN RETREAT

## How Foch's Flank Strategy Turned the Enemy Out of the Gigantic Salient in Belgium and France

### [PERIOD FROM SEPT. 18 TO OCT. 18, 1918]

IN the last week of September Marshal Foch appeared suddenly to change one of his first principles of strategy and to resort to frontal attacks on a large scale—in Champagne and then in Flanders. It was a paradox, however, for only locally were they delivered against the enemy's front, and even here there was no change in the details of flanking the enemy out of defended positions; in relation to the great salient of German occupation in France, however, they were gigantic flank move-. ments at the extremities of this salient. The masterly co-ordination of decisive effects revealed Pershing's operations on the St. Mihiel salient as part of a pinching-out process on a prodigious scale.

Champagne and Flanders mark the third phase of the great movement begun on July 18. Three days earlier Ludendorff had reached the maximum of his territorial expansion in France. He had developed the Lys, the Picardy, and the Marne salients, and by so doing had stretched his active front from 195 to 250 miles.

He could expand no further. Foch held the sectors connecting the arcs of these salients, and had, almost unnoticed, secured the strategic positions on their perimeters. The Crown Prince's excursion across the Marne on July 15 was a desperate expedient. It failed. Then everywhere, but in precise tactical sequence, Foch began three days later to utilize the positions he had gained. His doubted army of manoeuvre suddenly materialized and was utilized with telling effect. Ludendorff, smashed here and there, at times simultaneously a hundred miles apart, could not hold his front. He had not the men. Foch drove in the three salients one after the other.

That was the first phase. He next developed two salients of his own at the extremes of the Hindenburg perpendicu-lar—against Cambrai on the north and Laon on the south. That was the second phase. By Oct. 15 the world was observing the third—the attacks on the extremities of the great arc whose cord was represented by 200 miles of Belgian frontier.

The German view of the first two phases of the Foch movement—in the light of the German offensive and retreat—is indicated by these words of General Ardenne in the Berliner Tageblatt:

> The three great attacking actions from March 21 to July 15 caused the enemy losses amounting to 1,225,000 men. Then, when on July 15 the attempted surprise failed, and, in spite of his losses, the enemy's numerical superiority was ready, the German command, swift as lightning and without any hesitation, knew how to find the transition to the now necessary, but momentary, defensive. That is a strategic masterpiece which merits admiration. Moltke once said that the defensive could, under certain conditions, be the stronger form of combat, especially if, in sections of ground which are particularly favorable for defense and inaccessible to hostile enemy flanking attacks, a numerically inferior force compels superior enemy forces to costly frontal attacks. The German command adopted this principle in the battles since July 15.

The expounder of this "strategic masterpiece" overlooked or ignored the psychological objective in the Foch strategy—the obsession of the enemy's mind by the idea of defeat and the conviction of useless death. With what success Foch has attained this objective the loss of the enemy's morale is abundantly demonstrating. His casualties are believed to be twice the number alleged by General Ardenne to have been suffered by the Allies up to July 15. The number of prisoners and guns lost by the enemy since July 15 is upon record; it is 300,000 soldiers and nearly 5,000 guns.

As for Foch's material objectives, the

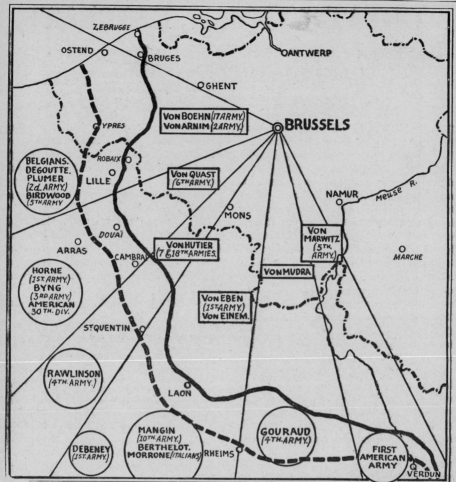

WHERE THE ALLIES FORCED THE GREAT GERMAN RETREAT. THE BROKEN LINE SHOWS
BATTLEFRONT OF SEPT. 18, AND THE HEAVY LINE THAT OF OCT. 18, 1918.

sequence of the events between Sept. 18 and Oct. 18 falls into a strategic line of development which at the end becomes chronological. Two events took place toward the end of last month's period of review which had a potent influence on the future: the penetration of the outer works of the Hindenburg line at its centre on Sept. 18 and the elimination of the St. Mihiel salient in the week succeeding Sept. 12.

The former made possible (1) the development of the attack against Cambrai, (2) the move against Laon, and (3) a further penetration at the centre of the Hindenburg line and the advance beyond St. Quentin. When these three movements had reached a certain stage

the two great flank attacks made possible (4) the advance of the Franco-American armies in the Champagne on Sept. 26, which was a strategic corollary of the affair of St. Mihiel of a fortnight before, and finally, (5) the great movement begun in Western Belgium on Sept. 28. Let us examine the details of these events according to the foregoing numerical sequence.

## I. TO CAMBRAI AND BEYOND

This sector, associated with the various battles of Arras, and particularly with the ill-fated battle for Cambrai of last November, is fed on the German side by two railways, both proceeding from Valenciennes, one to Douai and the other

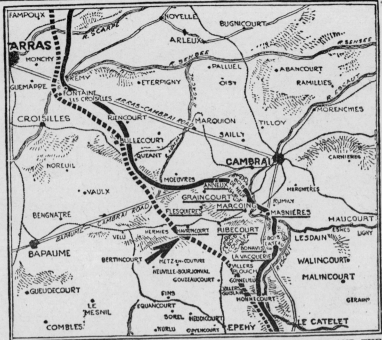

WITH HORNE AND THE FIRST BRITISH ARMY ON HIS LEFT AND THE 30TH AMERICAN DIVISION ON HIS RIGHT, BYNG AND THE THIRD ARMY TOOK CAMBRAI

to Cambrai. To the Allies the natural obstructions were the Sensée Canal from Douai south and the Scheldt or Escaut Canal, which is joined by it half way between Valenciennes and Cambrai, and the artificial obstruction, the Hunding line, constructed by the Germans between the Scarpe and the Oise.

The assault made on Sept. 18 by Rawlinson's Fourth British Army and Debeney's First French against the front of the Hindenburg line, which carried the outer defenses of that line at two points northwest of St. Quentin, (at Villeret and from Pontru to Holnon,) in the British sector, was counterattacked the following day by the Germans throughout the entire extent of the Allies' advance of twenty-two miles—from Gouzeaucourt to Hinacourt—with an intense concentration both in artillery preparation and massed infantry attacks on the British sector between Gouzeaucourt and Havrincourt Wood.

This counterattack being thrown back, the circumstance, while relieving Rawlinson and Debeney, opened the way on the former's left for a further demonstra-

tion by Byng and the Third British Army. Here Moeuvres, seven miles west of Cambrai, was completely reoccupied. On Sept. 25 the 30th American Division was injected between Byng and Rawlinson and, on Sept. 27, the Americans and Byng with the First British Army under Sir Henry Horne on their left made an advance from a fourteen-mile front in the direction of Cambrai, crossing the Canal du Nord and the ramifications of the Hindenburg line at several points, capturing several villages and 6,000 prisoners. Continuing their attack the next day, they captured several towns made famous by the battle of Cambrai of last November — Marcoing, Noyelles, Cantaing, and Fontaine - Notre Dame, and their prisoners were increased to 10,000, their captured guns to over 200.

On Sept. 29 the Americans with Rawlinson's left wing pressed forward on a thirty-mile front, from before St. Quentin to the Sensée Canal. In the south the British crossed the Scheldt Canal; in the north the Americans took Bellecourt and Nauroy and reached the suburbs of Cambrai. The advance upon Cambrai

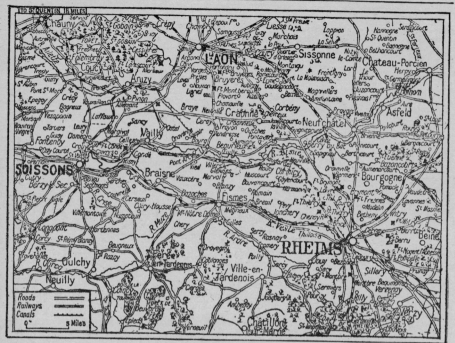

WHERE THE FRENCH ARMIES OF MANGIN AND BERTHELOT CO-OPERATED NORTH OF
RHEIMS WITH THE ITALIANS UNDER MORRONE

forced the Germans to evacuate the Lens coal fields on Oct. 3, and four days later an advance of Horne on a four-mile front placed the British in Oppy and Biache-St. Vaast, six miles to the southwest of Douai. At the same time Byng crossed the Scheldt Canal in the vicinity of Aubencheul-au-Bac, five miles northwest of Cambrai.

On Oct. 9 Cambrai was occupied by an advance over a thirty-mile front which covered both this city and St. Quentin. This was coincident with a German retreat from beyond Arras to beyond St. Quentin.

Henceforth the advance of the Allies east of Cambrai became identified with the St. Quentin front, although the advance east beyond Lens continued to be independent of it. Here the British on Oct. 11 made a thrust toward Douai, the Germans evacuating strong positions to the north of the Sensée River. In the two days following the British made other gains here and eastward from Lens.

On Oct. 17 the British carried the line of the Selle River on the whole front south of Le Cateau and established themselves on the railway beyond the town, taking 3,000 prisoners. On the 18th they took Zazeuel, east of Le Cateau.

## II. LAON

A year ago General Pétain attempted to reach Laon by a frontal attack northward over the Chemin des Dames and the Ailette. Foch approached it from the flanks—from the St. Gobain Forest on the west and the Berry-au-Bac-Asfeld line of the Aisne on the southeast. Its strategic value had been discounted by modern weapons; its tactical value remained immense. It was an important observation post, and was the junction of two trunk lines of supply, one from Hirson, the other from Mézières.

On the night of Sept. 19-20 the Germans made five successive counterattacks east of the Ailette and an equally vain attempt to cross the Vesle at Jonchery. Similar attacks were repulsed by Mangin on the following night. On the 28th the Fort de Malmaison fell, which placed him on the left-rear of the Chemin des Dames—the " Ladies' Road,"

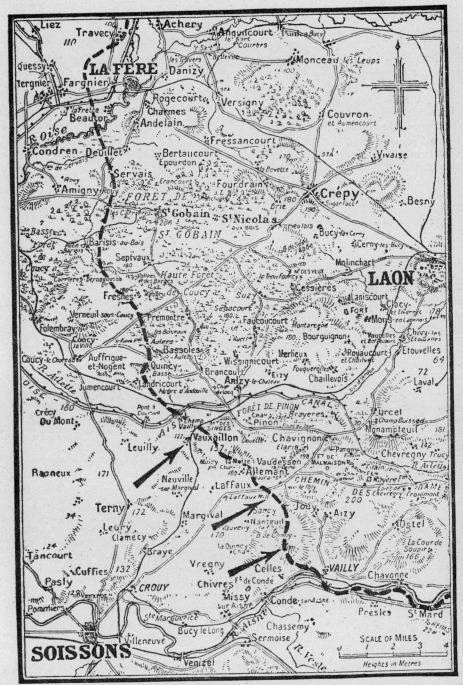

MOVEMENT ON MANGIN WITH THE TENTH FRENCH ARMY AND LINE OF DEPARTURE
OF SEPT. 18

which occupies a ridge running east from the Laon-Soissons highway to Craonne, buttressed by its three plateaus, fourteen miles away, overrun by Pétain from the south in October, 1917. From this line started the German drive to the Marne on May 27.

On Sept. 28-29 Mangin advanced behind the Chemin des Dames, covering the ground between it and the Ailette for a distance of two miles. On Oct. 2 between the Aisne and the Vesle he took several towns—Pouillon and Thil and the massif of St. Thierry. On his right General Berthelot co-operated with him by capturing Couroy, north of Rheims, Degoutte having meanwhile been sent north to aid the drive in Flanders, which had begun on Sept. 28.

The objective of Berthelot was obviously Berry-au-Bac, ten miles north of Rheims and five miles southeast of Craonne, thus in his turn broadening the front of the Champagne offensive, which had been begun by Gouraud and Pershing on Sept. 26. Berry-au-Bac, the great German supply exchange depot between Laon and Rethel, was occupied on Oct. 7. Between this date and the 12th Mangin had occupied nearly the entire length of the Chemin des Dames and the Germans were retreating from the Craonne plateaus.

The next day the great objectives sought for on the sector between La Fère and Rheims were attained by Mangin— the St. Gobain massif after a severe fight, and the strongholds of La Fère and Laon almost without firing a shot. Thus the connecting link of advance was made with Debeney and Rawlinson on the left and with Gouraud and Pershing on the right, and the vertex of the great German salient in France was entirely obliterated. After that the advance from the Oise southeast to the Aisne was rapid.

## III. BEYOND ST. QUENTIN

The front of St. Quentin had three formidable defenses. From west to east they were the Hindenburg line, with elaborate outworks, the Somme and St. Quentin Canals, and behind these waterways the southern section of the Hunding line. It was the distributing centre for

a considerable section of the German front, having a direct triple track connection with the fortress of Maubeuge, fifty miles to the northeast, near the Belgian frontier.

Rawlinson and Debeney were quick to take advantage of their penetration of the western ramifications of the Hindenburg line, made on Sept. 18. While the British made secure their reoccupation of Moeuvres and penetrated Havrincourt Wood, the French on the south went beyond Essigny-le-Grand and the Moisy Farm, five miles south of St. Quentin. On the 22d Debeney captured the woods north of Ly-Fontaine, while his patrols north of La Fère reached the Oise. From their positions east of Holnon to Hill 123, south of Holnon, and along the Ham-St. Quentin highway, via Hill 138 and Dallon height, the Germans made a determined stand behind mine fields and pitfalls as defenses against the tanks. On Sept. 24 the French gained the famous Epine de Dallon, the scene of the beginning of the defeat of the Fifth British Army on March 21. The next day the British reached Selency, only two miles west of St. Quentin. On the 30th Thorigny and Le Tronquoy, respectively three and four miles north of St. Quentin, were captured by the British, and on Oct. 1 Debeney's troops penetrated the city as far as the canal. The next day they formally took possession of the place, from which the Germans had deported the entire population of 50,000.

Henceforth operations east of St. Quentin were to be linked up with those identified with Cambrai, although not to any great extent until after the capture of that city on Oct. 9. Meanwhile, the British northeast of St. Quentin pressed on beyond Le Catelet and Beauvoir, forcing the passage of the Scheldt Canal, while to the southeast began a successful attack upon the German intrenchments of Neuville, St. Amand, and Itancourt. By the 6th the British had measurably broadened their passage over the Scheldt Canal, while the French had captured the heights southeast of Chardon-Vert.

In the great drive of the 9th, which covered the fronts of both Cambrai and

St. Quentin, the British captured scores of towns and villages and drove the Germans from their partly completed fortifications at Le Cateau, which after St. Quentin had been the headquarters of the Second German Army, and by the

PRINCIPAL FIELD OF OPERATION OF RAWLINSON WITH THE FOURTH BRITISH ARMY

10th Solesmes, ten miles east of Cambrai, had been occupied, as well as Fressies, northeast of Iwuvy. On the next day, pressing their advance north of the Sensée River, the British reached the suburbs of Douai and Cuincy. The French crept up the western bank of the Oise and reached a point only twenty-five miles west of the German stronghold of Hirson, on the frontier.

On Oct. 17, Rawlinson's right wing, in close co-operation with the French Army of Debeney, north of the Oise, made an advance of two miles across the highway east of Bohain and captured Andigny-les-Fermes.

## IV. CHAMPAGNE OFFENSIVE

The sector from Rheims east to the Côtes de Meuse, although lacking extensive lines of communication from the German side, had two great natural

defenses. On the west there was the Aisne River, which formed an arc to the north of the front from the Argonne Forest westward, with a perpendicular of twenty miles; on the east was the Argonne, with its uneven surface and great trees. But twenty miles north of the apex of the arc of the Aisne—from Rethel, now invested by the French—is the great railway junctions of Mézières, which had connections with Lille to the northwest and still has them with Metz to the southeast.

The attack began on Sept. 26, just two days before the great Belgian-British offensive in Flanders—the French under General Gouraud from the Suippe east to the Argonne Forest, and the First American Army from the forest east to the Meuse, north of Verdun.

In the first day the French advanced from three to four miles and the Americans from five to six, taking the towns of Gercourt, Guisy, Montfaucon, Cheppy, and Verennes. The French took Servon, which had been in the hands of the enemy since the retreat from the Marne, together with the Butte de Mesnil and Navarin Farm. By the end of the second day 10,000 prisoners had been captured. The Americans advancing down the Meuse and the Aire had captured Charpentry, Véry, Epinonville, and Ivoiry, bringing them within cannon range of the Kriemhilde line of enemy defenses, which extended from Grand Pré east to Damvillers, eight miles beyond the Meuse. The French had descended the Aisne arc for a distance of two miles in the direction of Vouziers, the railway junction.

On Sept. 28 the French captured Somme-Py and the Americans made two miles down the Aire and came in contact with the Kriemhilde line where it had its bridgehead at Brieulles, near the Meuse. Between Sept. 29 and 30 Gouraud, in his sector, made a rapid advance, gaining positions which commanded the railway junction of Challerange and the high ground extending northwest to Machault, bringing him within five miles of Vouziers. Meanwhile the Germans were concentrating their forces along the Kriemhilde line to oppose the American First Army. Apremont was taken and held by the Americans.

On Oct. 4 the Americans went over the Kriemhilde line, the last enemy organized line of defense south of the Belgian frontier, cutting through two Prussian Guard divisions on their way. The French in their sector evacuated Challerange, allowing the enemy to waste his artillery on it, but advanced north of Auberive and Somme-Py to the west. On the 5th the Germans made a great retirement before Gouraud's left wing over a front of twelve miles, and descended the Suippe River for a distance of three. The Americans extended their penetration of the Kriemhilde line beyond Romagne. The French instantly took advantage of the German retreat, and the next day pursued them on a broad front north and northeast of Rheims, driving the en-

PLACE OF JUNCTION OF GOURAUD'S FOURTH FRENCH ARMY AND THE FIRST AMERICAN ARMY

emy back eight miles in the direction of the Suippe, where it runs from east to west north of the Cathedral City.

On the 7th the Americans drove the Germans from the heights commanding the Aire Valley—Hills 242, 244, and 269. On the same day the taking of Berry-au-

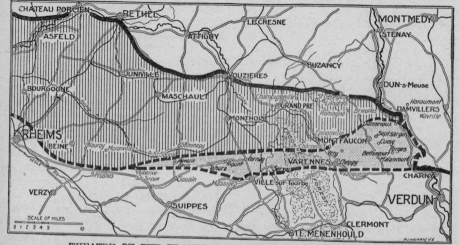

THEATRE OF THE FRANCO-AMERICAN DRIVE BEGUN SEPT. 26

Bac by Berthelot on Gouraud's left linked up the two armies in a common advance which took Rheims out of range of the enemy's cannon for the first time since its investment in the Autumn of 1914. For three days the Americans, who had dug in on the heights of the Argonne, defended themselves against severe attacks of the enemy. By the 11th the French had taken over the entire line of the Suippe, while the Americans had begun to develop a new advance east of the Meuse. The line of contact through the northern tip of the Argonne Forest ran west and east.

On Oct. 12 it was officially announced that in sixteen days the Fourth French Army had taken thirty-six towns and villages, 21,567 prisoners, and 600 guns. The next day it took Vouziers and reached the great curve of the Aisne at its most northern point between Château-Porcien and Rethel.

On Oct. 15 the First American Army went beyond St. Juvin, stormed the defenses of St. Georges, and took Hill 299. It gained complete supremacy of the air from the northern course of the Aisne to the Meuse. It further expanded its positions on the right bank of the latter.

On Oct. 16 the Americans occupied the important strategic point of Grand Pré, on the northern bank of the Aire, at the vertex of the Argonne Forest. The next day they took the defenses of Romagne, which gave them complete control over the Côte de Chatillon and consolidated their positions beyond the Kriemhilde line. Meanwhile, the French west of Grand Pré had captured Notre Dame de Liesse and had advanced toward Rethel as far as the village of Acy-Romance. Violent counterattacks were made against the divisions of General Guillaumat on the road from St. Germainmont to Gerzicourt.

On the 18th the French crossed the Aisne near Vouziers. The Americans by a surprise attack captured Bantheville, north of Romagne, and Talma Farm, northwest of Grand Pré.

## V. FLANDERS

As the month closes the front from

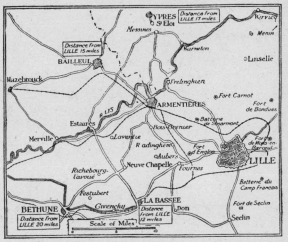

SCENE OF BIRDWOOD'S OPERATIONS WITH REHABILITATED FIFTH ARMY. ON HIS LEFT IS PLUMER WITH THE SECOND, ON HIS RIGHT HORNE WITH THE FIRST.

Lens to the sea is the great theatre of interest. Here the German retreat is being conducted on a vast scale, with the evacuation of towns left practically intact. The retreat followed an attack under the personal direction of King Albert. In the first week the enemy lost 12,000 prisoners and 130 guns. This number was doubled by Oct. 15.

On Sept. 28, while the British fleet bombarded the coastal defenses and points of communication from Nieuport to Zeebrugge on the North Sea, the Belgian Army, under King Albert, and the Second British Army, under General Plumer, went over the German lines on a ten-mile front between Dixmude and Passchendaele Ridge, north of Ypres. They captured the whole of the Houthulst Forest and extended their front to the line of Woumen, Pierkenshoek, Schaep, Baillie, and Broodseynde—a penetration of five miles—and captured 4,000 prisoners and an immense amount of supplies. On the following day, the Belgians took Dixmude, Zarren, Stadenberg, Passchendaele, Moorslede, and part of Westroosebeke, and reached a point

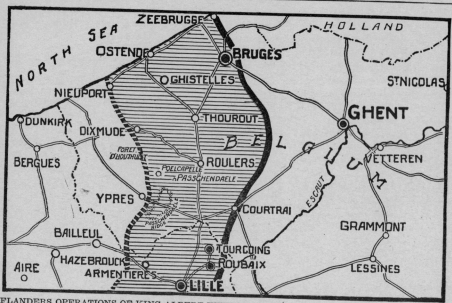

FLANDERS OPERATIONS OF KING ALBERT WITH DEGOUTTE'S FRENCH ARMY AND PLUMER'S
SECOND BRITISH ARMY

two miles west of Roulers. More than 1,500 prisoners were added.

On Sept. 30, Roulers was taken by the Belgians, while the British, advancing over their old battlefield of last year, overran Passchendaele Ridge and came within two miles of the railway junction of Menin. The next day the Allies crossed the Roulers-Menin road, while the British expanded the salient to the southeast, reaching the Lys River on a four-mile front between Warneton and Wervicq.

The French Army under General Degoutte joined this sector on Oct. 2, and a great enveloping movement, with Lille as its objective, was begun, which quickly obliterated the remnants of the Lys salient developed by the Germans on April 9, as the second phase of their great offensive. On the 2d also the Belgians went beyond Roulers to the northeast, taking Hooglede and Handzeeme, and the British captured Rolleghencapelle, between Roulers and Courtrai. Further south they made an advance astride of La Bassé Canal, threatening Lens from the northwest, and reoccupied Armentières, taken by the enemy on April 9.

For ten days there was a consolidation of positions by the Allies; then, on Oct. 14, they made a furious attack from Comines to the sea in the general direction of Ghent and Courtrai.

The results were in the following days overwhelmingly apparent. There were gradually developing signs that the Germans were preparing to evacuate the Belgian coast, falling back behind the Lys, possibly behind the Scheldt. The Belgians advanced north of the line of Handzeeme-Courtemarck for a distance of eight miles. In the centre the French, under Degoutte, took the Hooglede Plateau, while their cavalry crossed the Roulers-Thourout road and advanced toward Lichtervelde. Together with the British, under Plumer, they captured Winckelhoek and Lendelede and reached the Courtrai-Ingemunster railway.

On Oct. 16 the great retreat of the Germans from Western Belgium began under the ever-accelerating pressure of the Allies. The Belgians advanced astride the Thourout-Bruges and the Thourout-Ostend roads. The French cavalry rushing toward Thielt came to within seven miles of the Ghent-Bruges Canal. The British reached Quesnoy and captured several towns along the Lys, crossing that river east of Comines.

Further south the rehabilitated British Fifth Army, under General Birdwood, began the envelopment of the important and historical French city of Lille, which he occupied, when the Germans evacuated it, on the 17th.

On the second day of the German retreat from Western Belgium, Ostend and Zeebrugge, the German submarine bases on the coast, were evacuated, as were all the towns westward of the line—Bruges, Lophem, Thielt, Meulebeke, Courtrai, Tourcoing, Roubaix, Lille—an irregular front of over fifty miles, which since Oct. 14 had rendered over 15,000 prisoners.

## EXIT BULGARIA

[See map on Page 275]

The offensive begun by the army of the Allies under the French General, Franchet d'Esperey, on Sept. 14, on the Macedonian front, was brought to a sudden close on Sept. 30 by the unconditional surrender of Bulgaria, which had opened negotiations with the allied Commander in Chief on the 28th by asking for an armistice for forty-eight hours. Henceforth the chief concern of the British Army was to see that Bulgaria kept the terms of her surrender, while that of the French, Italian, and Serbian, with their Czechoslovak and Jugoslav auxiliaries, was to clear Serbia, Montenegro, and Albania of their Teuton enemies.

By Sept. 18 the Allies had extended their line of departure beyond Monastir on the west and beyond Lake Doiran on the east, over a front of 100-odd miles On the north, with a penetration of forty miles, they were forcing their way up the Vardar toward Uskub, Serbia, and were threatening the Bulgarian town of Strumnitza from the left bank beyond the mountain barrier. Their prisoners were averaging 5,000 a day.

The French official report on the closing operations against Bulgaria reads as follows:

By Sept. 22 the Serbians had succeeded in cutting the communications of the First Bulgarian Army, operating along the Vardar, and those of the Bulgarian Second Army and the Germans north of Monastir. Displaying extraordinary endurance, courage, and a spirit of sacrifice, all the allied forces joined in the attack on Sept. 18 against the enemy positions at Doiran, capturing this region from important Bulgarian forces.

Beginning Sept. 21, the Italian, Greek, and French troops in the region of Monastir moved forward in their turn. On the 22d a general pursuit began. It was conducted with ardor and splendid energy.

On the 23d the Serbians and French crossed the Vardar in the direction of Krivolak. On the 24th French cavalry entered Prilep. On the 25th Ishtib and the formidable barriers to Veles were captured. The British opened up the road to Strumnitza, which they entered on Sept. 26. The same day the Serbians reached Kochana and Veles and the Italians, French, and Greeks were marching on Kichevo.

On the evening of Sept. 26 the Bulgarians asked that hostilities be suspended, announcing that they were sending plenipotentiaries.

In the course of these glorious operations, which the hurried sending of German reinforcements could not check, the allied armies took a great number of prisoners and an immense quantity of war material.

Allied aviators took a most active part and gave very great help in the fighting. They constantly sent back information to the command, and without cessation they attacked enemy troops and convoys with machine guns, causing disorder among the enemy forces and preventing them from escaping from the advancing infantry.

There were reports that Austrian and German troops were hurrying to the support of the Bulgars and that their Governments would never permit Bulgaria to withdraw from the war; nevertheless, the surrender prevailed, and the first of the new month saw the Teuton forces fighting rearguard actions in Serbia and Albania. In the latter Berat was reoccupied by Italian troops on Oct. 3, and the French diverted west from the Vardar into Montenegro. The Serbians, with a Czechoslovak division, ascended the Vardar to the Morava River, and on Oct. 13 they occupied Nish, the war capital of Serbia, thereby cutting the Orient Railway, the only rail link between Berlin and Constantinople.

In Albania, Durazzo, whose naval forces had been demolished by the allied ships, including American submarines, on Oct. 1, was occupied by Italian troops on the 13th. The next day they entered Elbasan and invested Tirana, twenty miles to the northwest.

The subsequent developments of the

campaign to free Serbia and Montenegro from enemy occupation are filled with political meaning. On Oct. 17 a French column of cavalry reached Ipek, just over the Serbo-Montenegrin frontier, sixty-five miles east of Oettinje. On the same day the Serbs, proceeding beyond Nish, diverted a column up the Serbian Morava and reached Krushevatz, ten miles southwest of Stolac, where a railway and highway coming east from Serajevo, the capital of Bosnia, join the Orient Railway. Serbia claims both Bosnia and Herzegovina on account of their preponderant Serb population, but to the west of Bosnia is Croatia and to the north Slavonia, two Jugoslav States which were incorporated in the Jugoslav nation proclaimed at Corfu, July 20, 1917, and subsequently expounded to the Entente at the Rome Congress of April 8-10, 1918. The Serbian invasion of these States would at once establish material communication between them and the Allies, from which hitherto they have been isolated.

## CONQUEST OF HOLY LAND

[See map on Page 271.]

On Sept. 19, British and French forces in Palestine under General Allenby attacked the Turkish position on a sixteen-mile front from Rafat to the sea. The results which followed are in a military sense the most interesting in the war. They are otherwise remarkable.

Ever since he closed his campaign last April he had apparently been held up on a sixty-mile front extending from the edge of the Plain of Sharon on the sea southeast to the River Jordan. Beyond his front were the Seventh and Eighth Turkish Armies, and on his right the Fourth, which all Summer had been in hostile contest with the troops of Hussien I., King of the Arab State of Hedjaz. It is estimated that the Turkish armies had the strength of between 100,000 and 150,000 bayonets; previous accounts had placed the figure as high as 300,000, but during the Summer there had been many desertions.

There were three successive stages to Allenby's operations: The breaking of the Turkish line near the sea; the pour-ing of his cavalry and camel corps through the breach, with the encirclement of the Seventh and Eighth Armies, and his pursuit of the refugees. At this writing he is still developing the third stage, which, by the middle of October, had carried his cavalry to Tripoli, forty-five miles north of Beirut, the capital of Syria, on the coast, and to Homs, eighty-five miles north of Damascus. He had destroyed three armies and, with the aid of the Arabs, had captured 80,000 prisoners and 500 guns. The enemy Commander in Chief, the German Field Marshal, Liman von Sanders, narrowly escaped capture.

This rapid campaign, which opened the way to Aleppo, within 100 miles of which his cavalry was manoeuvring when it occupied Homs on Oct. 8, was simultaneous with an attack of Arabs against the Fourth Army, east of the Jordan. It immediately drove the Seventh and Eighth north upon Mount Ephraim and gained possession of the Tul Keram-Messudieh railway, between which and the sea the cavalry poured through.

This cavalry proceeded north along the western mounds of the Mount Ephraim range and then turned east toward the Jordan, thus placing itself in the rear of the two Turkish armies by occupying the valley between El Afule and Nazareth. The circle was completed on the 22d. Meanwhile, the army of the King of Hedjaz had attempted, but with less success, a similar manoeuvre against the Fourth Army. However, he had prevented the retreat of this army, cutting its communications north by destroying the Damascus-Medina railway at Derat, east of the Sea of Galilee.

By the 26th, while specially appointed detachments were picking off groups of prisoners south of the Haifa-El Afule-Bésan-Derat line, the patrol cavalry occupied the town on the Sea of Galilee known to the post Biblical geography as the Lake of Tiberias. East of the Jordan, Amman, on the Damascus railway, was also occupied. Finally, on Oct. 1, a strong British force and a detachment of the Arab Army took possession of the famous city of Damascus and at once began to organize work for the cavalry further north.

A certain concentration of enemy forces remained at Aleppo, although they had been heavily drawn upon to obstruct the advance through Mesopotamia of General Marshall and the Anglo-Indian Army. The main body of Marshall's forces was reported to be still south of Mosul on the Tigris. A 700-mile caravan trail runs to Mosul across the desert from Aleppo. Further north the Bagdad railway is in operation as far east as Ras-el-Ain, about half way to Mosul.

## New Zealand's Decree on Germany's Colonial Ambitions

SIR JOSEPH WARD, Finance Minister of New Zealand, with the concurrence of Premier Hughes of Australia and W. F. Massey, the Premier of New Zealand, announced to the British Empire League at London July 16 that they had a positive mandate from their people, through resolutions passed at public meetings and unanimous declarations of the citizens, to inform the people of Great Britain that the New Zealand public would never tolerate the handing back to Germany of Samoa, New Guinea, and the Marshall Islands, the former German colonies in the Pacific Ocean. He proceeded as follows:

On one occasion Bismarck put this question to the British Government: " What parts of the Australian continent are claimed by Britain? " Do the people of the Motherland know that an attempt was made to Germanize South Australia? Have they ever heard of the " Dutch Heritage " and the " World Empire " scheme of the early eighties with its inner and outer circles, the former of which was to embrace the African coast and the latter the Australian colonies and the Falkland Islands? I recall this to show how limitless and all-pervading have been German aims and ambitions, and how that must be so again if we lapse into indifference. As long as Germany has a foothold in the Pacific she will ever stand a menace to our security and our peaceful development. German penetration in the Pacific was brought about in the early eighties during the international scramble for new territory. We out there had seen the danger for years, but it required an infinitude of patience and the acceptance of many snubs and rebuffs before the

Motherland could be induced to annex Fiji and other territories.

After recalling the action of Queensland with regard to taking formal possession of New Guinea in 1883, which was not approved by the Secretary of State for the Colonies at that time, Lord Derby, and after giving illustrations of the difficulties and complications which ensued, Sir Joseph referred to the Intercolonial Conference, which met in December, 1882, and passed the following resolution:

" The further acquisition of dominion in the Pacific south of the equator by any foreign power would be highly detrimental to the safety and well-being of the British possessions in Australasia, and injurious to the interests of the empire."

Despite that, Germany, in August, 1884, annexed part of New Guinea, and what was the attitude of the British Government then? Lord Granville was " able to assure Count Münster that her Majesty's Government had no desire to oppose the extension of German colonization in the islands of the South Seas which are unoccupied by any civilized power. * * * The extension of some form of British authority in New Guinea will only embrace that part of the island which specially interests the Australasian colonies, without prejudice to any territorial question, beyond those limits." That might be described as effusiveness to Germany and partial surrender to the colonial point of view when it was too late.

Such was the story of the advent of Germany into the Pacific. A similar story might be told of Samoa. What he had said already was enough to justify this contention that the present attitude of New Zealand and Australia regarding the possible return of the former German colonies was no flash-in-the-pan of a hastily formed and ill-considered opinion, but was the latest and most logical outcome of a mature, well-defined, and well-reasoned policy of very long standing.

# Driving the Germans From Belgium

## Battles That Won Cambrai and Lille in France and Forced the Enemy Out of Flanders

### By PHILIP GIBBS

*The British offensive that began on Aug. 8, 1918, under Field Marshal Haig in Northeastern France and Flanders, the first phases of which were recorded in the September issue of* CURRENT HISTORY, *was continued with increasing success during the month ended Oct. 18. Those eventful weeks witnessed the capture of St. Quentin, Cambrai, Douai, and the important industrial cities of Lille, Roubaix, and Courtrai, while in Belgium, with the aid of the Belgian Army, the enemy was driven from Ostend, Zeebrugge, and Bruges, and was forced to retire with all speed from the whole English Channel region. The victorious allied armies, consisting of British, Belgian, French, and American units, by the middle of October were advancing at a speed that promised to drive the Germans entirely from Belgium and Northern France within a month and send them back to their last line of defense on the Meuse at the German frontier. The events of this great campaign were narrated day by day in the copyrighted cable dispatches of Philip Gibbs for* THE NEW YORK TIMES *and its affiliated publication,* CURRENT HISTORY MAGAZINE. *The most striking portions of Mr. Gibbs's brilliant eyewitness descriptions are here presented in a continuous narrative, beginning with his pen picture of how Bourlon Wood fell to the Canadians on Sept. 27:*

THE storm clouds had not passed just as the dawn broke, and those fields had a wild, bad look as they were dimly revealed by the rising curtain of day. Lights glimmered from the windows of huts built in these wastes and tents glowed red as the soldiers behind the lines rose and lit their lamps.

Camp fires began to burn outside the old dugouts where sandbags were whitening in the dawn. Already the airmen were outside their hangars, scenting the wind and looking to their machines for the first flight over the battlelines. The kite balloons were in battle array all across the sky, according to the swing of the line, and presently the sun rose and the clouds were dispersed by a fleet wind. Above their snowy peaks there was a lake of blue and those balloons of the British watching the drama of battle below them glistening and white.

I was not in time to see the first barrage fire, which began just at dawn without any preliminary bombardment, but it was terrific when I arrived in sight of Bourlon Wood and Moeuvres in the valley below. On the right all the guns were slogging away with rapid fire, with the heavies—monstrous 9.2—far behind where I stood, and the field batteries well forward. The noise of their shells came rushing through the sky like great birds, beating their wings.

For miles stretching down below Ridges from Inchy and Moeuvres southward to Savincourt, I could see gun flashes and bursts of greenish smoke as lyddite shells were fired. There was a tremendous barrage of fire all about Bourlon Wood, to the left and right of it, and in the sweep across Flesquières.

### PANORAMA OF BATTLE

The business of the battlefield was in full activity. Supporting troops were on the move marching in Indian file along duckboards leading to the front line or standing in groups under the shelter of sunken roads waiting for orders to get ahead. Gun limbers were crawling up many of the tracks with new stores of ammunition. Horse ambulances with canvas hoods, on which the Red Cross was painted like a flag, were being driven amazingly near to the battlelines, and bodies of the Royal

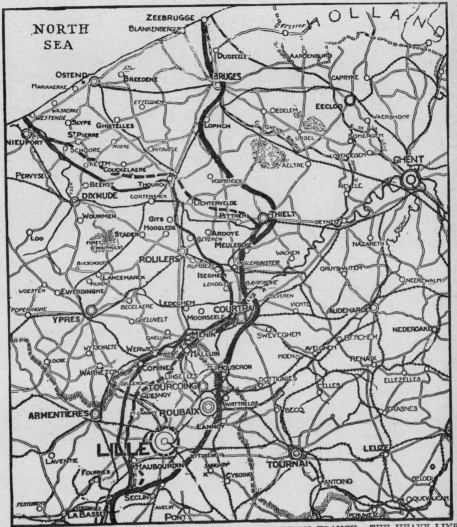

SCENE OF GERMAN RETREAT IN BELGIUM AND NORTHERN FRANCE.  THE HEAVY LINE
INDICATES BATTLEFRONT ON OCT. 18, 1918

Army Medical Corps were laying out new field hospitals and putting up tents in full view of Bourlon Wood, except for a fringe of bushes here and there. It was a wonderful panorama of battle.

*On Sept. 29 the Belgians captured Dixmude, the first break in the German right flank, and the British continued their progress toward Cambrai. The chief struggle that day was on the Scheldt Canal, north of St. Quentin; here the Hindenburg line was again breached.* Mr. Gibbs wrote:

This attack began in a dense fog.

It produced a weird effect such as I had never seen in this war. Bodies of men were moving in close array following up the first assault columns, but they could only be seen as through a glass, darkly, and no man was visible twenty paces ahead. Gun transports and batteries moved up the tracks toward the canal crossing, at Bellenglise, and as the mist shifted for a moment one saw them as ghost figures of men and beasts, and then a minute later they disappeared and one seemed in utter loneliness except for the sound of wheels going over the rough ground and the tramp of horses' hoofs and the march of men.

Everywhere hidden in this fog were the guns. They were in sunken roads and infolds of fields and out in the open country and under cover of woods, but one could see nothing of them, not even a flash of them, but hear only their vast tumult of fire and rush of shells overhead, then something very horrible. In this darkness and noise it was as though an infernal nightmare were let loose around me. It was impossible to know one's whereabouts or gauge one's risk of hostile fire.

Immense shell craters in one patch of ground near one's position at the moment showed that the German guns had marked down this place, and that their shells had furrowed there a little while before being blind. One listened, and there was a sense of reassurance, because only rarely did one hear the whine of hostile shells or the snarl of German shrapnel. All shells but a few were going one way, and it was the British way, forward from the British guns.

## STORMING THE CANAL

North of the 9th Corps, on the right of the attack, Australians and Americans stormed the canal, where a thousand yards were above the ground on their front and a thousand yards below, north and south of Bellicourt. Their left boundary was just below Vendeuville, where other English troops formed the flank and tried to bridge the canal.

The line in front of the American and Australian front was terrific in its original strength, for besides the wide canal there was a great belt of wire and many trenches. However, this morning the wire had been well cut by the British guns, and tanks were with the British to force a passage beyond and keep down machine-gun fire if they could get across.

They went across by the marvelous valor of the men, who established their bridges in spite of a heavy German barrage. This by good luck fell mostly behind them, and few of the British wounded were hurt in their desperate eagerness to keep close to their own barrage fire, the Americans being less experienced in this than the Australians, who were mostly veterans.

Notwithstanding the annihilating British bombardment, there was a fierce machine-gun fire from the enemy, and the British had hard going at first, but they broke down all resistance and, having passed to the other side of the canal, went ahead with the tanks around Bony and Bellicourt, where they had their worst fighting, and toward the next organized line of German resistance known as the Massinères-Beaurevoir line.

In these last three days, the most successful in all these years of war, we have struck the enemy a smashing and decisive blow from the sea to Verdun, and the Hindenburg line is now a farce—a farce and a tragedy which will shock the people of Germany to their hearts, because it breaks their last hopes of safety.

## THE LABOR OF BATTLE

I should like to write about the courage and splendor of all our men who have the spirit of victory in their hearts and are taking all risks and daring everything with the eager desire to press on and on.

It is mighty labor, for fighting is hard work all the time, and not joyous excitement, as some folks think. It is a surge and struggle forward of hundreds of thousands of men down narrow ways choked with traffic, over fields under fire, through ruined villages into which shells are falling, or where they may fall at any second.

It is a labor of moving guns over rough ground with mules and horses that have been going for many days, so that some of them drop dead, and there is a trail of dead horses of which some have been killed by shrapnel and some by shells and some by bombs.

It is a labor of armies of men making roads through ground just captured and pushing out railway lines into deeper desolation. It is a labor of engineers and pioneers making the way of the army straight, and lastly, it is a labor of gunners and infantry hungry for sleep, firing their guns until they are red hot, then moving to fire on new targets, and, if they are infantry, marching, marching, marching in support of those ahead, passing through them to new attacks, resisting counterattacks when they have won a battle, having no chance for rest until they in turn are leap-frogged by comrades coming up behind.

Gunner officers are hoarse with shouting orders and haggard from lack of sleep. Infantry officers snatch sleep if they can in any ditch or behind any broken wall, while shells are bursting close and their men are digging a little cover before the next advance.

It is a superhuman effort of physical strength and will power, but throughout our armies, as I have seen them during the last three days, there is a grim sense of meeting an enemy on the run and smashing him so beyond recovery that ever after this he will have to back and back before us until he is cleared out of Belgium and France.

## AMERICANS IN BATTLE

*In his cable letter on Sept. 30, describing the fierce fighting around Cambrai, Mr. Gibbs wrote of the American troops as follows:*

One of the German surprises yesterday was to meet American troops in the attack against them on this front. It was no surprise to those who had seen them moving up day by day nearer the fighting zone, so that as the British passed them they said to each other:

" These men are out for business, and, by Jove, how well they look."

These two divisions with men of New York State and North and South Carolina and Tennessee were quartered in shell-broken village, full of history, made by English troops these four years of war, so that every ruined cottage in them is scrawled over with English and Scottish names.

The Americans had come newly to these places and had the look of new men—so fresh, so keen, so unscarred by the tragedy of war, which leaves its imprint on men's faces and gives them a certain look in the eyes not to be mistaken.

They looked very young, many of these American boys, but hard and fit, and I watched them putting up their camps and their pup tents and going up with their guns and transport to the edge of the battlefield. They drew nearer and went further into the stricken land among the shell craters and all the wreckage of human life, and then on the first day of this new battle yesterday I saw some of them coming down with their prisoners, escorting them proudly and smiling back to the Tommies, who said: " Well done, Yanks; that's a good beginning. Keep it up."

They came marching through the white fog which veiled everything yesterday morning, and I saw their staff officers driving up the roads this side of the Scheldt Canal and the American guns and transport threading their way through the British streams of traffic.

They were keen to attack, full of confidence and enthusiasm because they believed that they would do well and help in the day of the big victory, and they led the assault on one sector of the canal by Bellicourt, where the Australians were to pass through then to the extension of the attack.

Later in the day they stormed through the German lines, secured the canal crossings, and struck on toward Gouy and Mauroy, and the only fault to find with them was the laughing criticism from veterans in the British ranks that they set the pace too hard and were too eager to get forward. That is a fault on the right side, the gift of the freshmen in this hard old university of war, where men learn to be cautious of possible snags and make very sure of the ground behind them before they tread on again.

Their courage yesterday was magnificent, and they went straight into deadly risks without shirking the hazard. They had done and learned enough in one day to call themselves veterans, for a battle like this crowds much into a few hours.

## HEROIC BRITISHERS

One of the finest episodes beyond all doubt was the crossing of the canal by the Midland men of the 46th Division of Leicesters and Staffords and others whom I first met several years ago near Armentières. They had to get across the Scheldt Canal by Bellenglise, where it is eighteen yards wide and very deep.

German guns were trained upon it,

its banks bristled with machine guns, and its bridges were mined, but the Midland men went down to that gully of death, went down in a thick white fog through which there was a frightful tumult of guns as I heard them in the darkness and through which howled German shells searching for their bodies and a long tattoo of machine guns and the swish of thousands of bullets.

With life belts around their tunics and small rafts and ladders and sections of wooden bridges they went down to the edge of the canal, not knowing what comrades fell, not pausing. Some men went down the chalky banks, plunged into the almost ice-cold water and swam across under fire, and some used their rafts and built bridges.

The Midland men of the Forty-sixth streamed across and the tanks went with them to their side of the canal. In an hour or two, or less, the strongest system of defense on the western front had been broken and carried and the Hindenburg line had been made a byword forever, and the barrier upon which all German hopes had been built was behind our lines, with our men away beyond it.

The Forty-sixth Division, fanning out as it went over the whole corps front, took over 4,000 prisoners and a large number of guns, and as the men crept into the hostile ground and fought those who preferred to fight they saw the result of the forty-eight hours of bombardment which had gone before their advance, and it was an appalling sight, because of the number of dead who lay everywhere.

## THE FIGHT FOR CAMBRAI

*Oct. 1 was a critical day in the battle for Cambrai. The Canadians had a fierce struggle over the Scheldt Canal, which swings in a close loop around that city. Mr. Gibbs wrote:*

Yesterday, under intense German fire from many guns and savage machine gunning, the Canadians had drawn back again from Blécourt and Abancourt, north of Cambrai, and it was decided by the Canadian command to cease all efforts in this direction until more guns were in position to provide a heavier barrage, behind which the troops could

make a stronger advance on the whole corps front. This was done, and this morning at 5 o'clock, after a complete reorganization of the artillery and infantry dispositions—not an easy task in the darkness and slashing rain—a new battle was begun.

The barrage fire was intense and murderous, and the enemy replied by a line of fire that also was very fierce five minutes after the Canadian guns opened their hurricane bombardment, with a creeping barrage for the men to follow.

The Canadians advanced with the greatest courage, and, in spite of this shelling and intense machine gunning at close range, were not balked of their main purpose. The 3d Canadian Division on the right did all its men had been asked to achieve, but on the left the troops were held up for a time by a terrible artillery concentration. The 4th Canadian Division had severe fighting around Cuvillers and Bantigny, but are securing their positions in that neighborhood, and the 1st Canadians apparently entered Abancourt, but had to fall back temporarily owing to a girdle of high explosives which barred their way.

## IN CAMBRAI'S SUBURBS

*In August and September the British captured on the western front 123,618 prisoners and 2,783 guns. In a fair day's fighting on the St. Quentin-Cambrai front, beginning with Sept. 27, they engaged and defeated thirty-six German divisions, approximately 432,000 men. Describing the battle of Oct. 2, Mr. Gibbs wrote:*

The battle this morning on this southern side of Cambrai was being fought by infantry without much artillery support, as it was close fighting in the suburbs of the city, where a long street, called the Faubourg de Paris, strikes out of Cambrai into the open fields, and where every house in it is a machine-gun fort.

To the right the ridge from which our men fought this morning up to Rumilly was also quiet, though all through the night until after the new advance of ours at dawn it was on fire, with bursts of shells.

I saw the ruins of the village of Rumilly, close to a belt of slaughtered trees, and from its neighborhood there came the slashing sound of intense machine-gun fire. Across field tracks our men were marching to support their comrades in that open country, and behind them some guns of ours, big fellows who split the sky with their noise when they fire, were moving slowly forward and taking up new positions, so that for a little time they were silent.

Three of our kite balloons were amazingly far forward over Boulon Wood, staring down into the German lines and taking the risk of German shrapnel, which was bursting about them. Their observers had to take to their parachutes twice yesterday when a German fighting scout circled round them and was only driven off in the nick of time by one of our air patrols.

Away north there was also unusual quietude after the fierce bombardment lasting for two days, and here there is close fighting in the northern suburbs of Cambrai. It is here that the Canadians have been fighting in their greatest struggle against massed reserves of the enemy, who tried to bear them down by weight of numbers, by superiority of machine-gun fire, and by fierce counterattacks forced hard by men brought fresh into this infernal struggle.

### FIERCE OPPOSITION

Against the Canadians and English divisions on their left the Germans now have nine divisions reinforcing the First Guards Reserve and 18th Reserve Divisions, with thirteen marksmen detachments and artillery of thirteen divisions, and machine gun strength, giving them four light and four heavy machine guns to each camp front—a strong sweep of fire in close-range fighting.

All day yesterday there was a ceaseless and severe struggle on both sides, and after the Canadian attack in the early morning, when they gained ground at Ramillies, Cuvillers, and Blécourt and entered Morenchies and Arancourt, the Germans counterattacked again and again with almost fanatical courage.

They advanced in close formation down the valleys of Bantigy and Rail-

lencourt and were seen by Canadian observers, who called to the Canadian guns. Our artillery had human targets at short range and fired for hours with open sights.

Their shells raked the German ranks, tore gaps in them and laid out men in heaps. Others came up to take their places and struggle on to break the Canadian lines, and again the guns took them for their targets and killed large numbers of them. There was a massacre of men in those valleys and the British guns were served until they were too hot to fire, but still, under cover of sunken roads and embankment cuttings, the German infantry made their way, regardless of all losses, and forced a passage into some of the ruined villages which the Canadians had captured that morning by most resolute spirit, though many of their comrades fell, and succeeded in making some of the Canadian battalions fall fack to the outskirts of those places.

All the Canadians say the number of German dead strewn about this ground is horrible to see, but they have taken this toll of the enemy not without paying a severe price themselves for the ground they still hold, and after all their days of fighting since their first glorious advance south of Amiens on Aug. 8 their present actions are a marvelous achievement.

### CROSSING SCHELDT CANAL

*Meanwhile, the Belgian troops, in close liaison with French and British, continued their advance in Flanders, and by Oct 2 were before Roulers, an important railroad centre, and held Houthulst Wood and Zarren, menacing the entire German right flank. On Oct. 3 the passage of the Scheldt Canal was forced by English and Irish troops at Gouy and Le Catelet and both villages were taken. The same day the Germans evacuated Lens and Armentières and were in retreat on a twenty-mile front between those two strongholds, which were occupied by the British. Mr. Gibbs wrote on Oct. 4:*

Men who captured the further bank of the Scheldt Canal can take anything, and because the Germans could not hold this line they can hold no line. I went along a great length of it today and was astounded that our men could get across with such little loss. It has steep banks 90 to 100 feet high on each side of the canal cutting high and dry by Bellenglise, but with 5 or 6 feet or more of water twenty yards wide between that village and Bellicourt. Some miles away when it goes into the tunnel it is perfectly prepared for defense with communication trenches leading from the lower ground beyond to high banks, where were machine-gun and field-gun emplacements having a perfect field of fire should any men be rash enough to advance over the ridge to the western bank. Our men were rash enough, and over the canal are bridges of planks by which they passed and in water rafts on which they floated.

The canal passes under a hill through a tunnel five miles long. There were only dead Germans in the tunnel now, and dead in such a way that the sight of them revived that gruesome story of the German Kadaver Anstalt, or corpse factory, which some time ago deceived the credulous.

It was at Bellicourt, by the entrance of the tunnel, that the Americans made their attack last Sunday and continued fighting with the Australians as their comrades for some days later. Those young American soldiers came into their first big battle full of courage and impetuous desire. Leading the advance, they broke the strongest defenses of the Hindenburg line up by Bellicourt, stormed their way across the canal to the machine guns on the other bank, and went forward that day like huntsmen in a chase that must never be forgotten. In one of the greatest battles of the war, when we crossed the Scheldt Canal and broke the last barrier of the enemy's defensive positions, it was these Americans who stormed one of the most formidable sectors of the line and overpowered the enemy.

## CAPTURE OF CAMBRAI

Oct. 9.—At 4 o'clock this morning, in darkness except for the light of the stars, Canadian and English troops, pressing close from the north and south, joined hands in the chief square of Cambrai.

This morning the enemy is in retreat behind their rearguards, and the whole city of Cambrai is in our hands, but since its capture successive explosions have been going on which have practically reduced the town to ruins.

For a long distance south of Cambrai the German Army is hard in flight, blowing up bridges and burning villages, and our troops are away eastward trying to keep in touch with the enemy rearguards.

This morning I went into Cambrai. As on that day now nearly two years ago, when I went first into Bapaume on a morning of history, this entry into our newly captured town was the end of a long phase of war which had reached a victorious climax, and the journey I made up the long, straight road past Fontaine Notre Dame was full of interest and gave me a sense of drama beyond ordinary scenes of war, because to get to Cambrai our army has fought a long and hard fight since those days in November last when our men first came in sight of the city and then had to fall back again, and since last March, when, under the weight of the German onslaught, they had to retreat almost as far back as Amiens, and Cambrai seemed then a world away.

## CITY OF EMPTY HOMES

But in two months to this very day they have not only fought their way back to their old front lines, but are now far into country which was never ours before, and Cambrai itself is their prize, while the enemy, broken forever in his strength, is in hard retreat beyond.

Truly, today is a glorious day for British arms, and the honor of it goes to the private soldiers and young officers of the English, Irish and Scottish, Welsh, Canadian, Australian, New Zealand, and American forces who, with untiring courage, have fought every yard of this way, have stormed the strongest lines ever made in war, and beaten down every deadly obstacle with which the enemy has tried to bar their way.

Everywhere were German signs revealing the enemy's life in this town, and one notice painted on many walls showed that the German soldiers have their moving pictures like our men in the rest billets. But in one doorway there was posted up a notice in French, and its words dug into one's mind the human tragedy which had happened here a few weeks ago, the tragedy of the city's abandonment by the people who had their homes here and their business and their interest in life, and suddenly, at the command of the enemy, in whose grip they were, had to leave everything and go away deeper into bondage.

It was a proclamation by the German commandant of Cambrai, Gross by name, stating that in the interest of security the inhabitants of Cambrai would be evacuated to a region further removed from the war zone. They were ordered to leave on Sept. 7 and 8, and each day trains carrying 15,000 people would leave the station. Every inhabitant must have his identity and work card, and would be allowed only such baggage as could be carried on a long march. So these people could take only a few small belongings with them, and they had to leave behind all their furniture and property of any bulk to become the booty of German looters.

What touched one most was the wreckage of the smaller houses and little shops and restaurants. I looked into houses where women's sewing machines still stood on tables, as they had done their work with their babes around. Perambulators stood on thresholds, and children's dolls lay on floors as they had been dropped because of the terror that had followed the notice on the walls signed by Commandant Gross. China and glass were in cupboards and on kitchen tables unbroken, amidst a litter of clothes turned over by German soldiers searching for things to take away.

## MILES OF DEVASTATION

Oct. 10.—I drove forty miles this morning, the whole depth of the British advance since Aug. 8, and every mile of it was haunted by memories of bloody fighting and every landmark of broken brickwork or dead trees or twisted iron was a place where the British troops had done heroic and deadly things.

It was when going through Arbencheul and Villers-Outreaux beyond the Great Canal, which the British crossed one famous Sunday, and through the Beaurevoir line with its belts of rusty wire, which they stormed in their last big battle, that I saw fresh tracks of the strife and relics that always tell one when only a day or two have passed since the war was here.

Along that road and in the ditches on either side lay dead horses and overturned gun limbers and smashed guns. I have never seen the road so strewn with dead beasts, not even the Menin Road in Flanders. Every yard along the way shell holes had punctured the banks on either side and artillery teams, driving at a gallop toward Villers-Outreaux, had been slashed by fire. It was a way of the German retreat and a way of horror.

Villers-Outreaux was the place the Welshmen attacked in pitch darkness two nights ago, when they closed in upon the German garrison and fought their machine gunners and then stormed the village from end to end, taking many prisoners. The British side of it was damaged in the usual way by shelling and the walls were smashed to rubbish heaps, but the centre of the village, which is a large place, was hardly touched, and the buildings around its old market place were unscarred by the battle.

At Selvigny, where there are more than 500 civilians, I chatted with many of the women and children and with elderly men, who had not been taken away like all the male civilians between 16 and 60, whom the Germans had driven before them on their retreat.

These people told me many tragic things, a tragedy of small nagging things which every day in hostile hands had fretted their spirit and their pride. The Germans had robbed them of everything. In their houses they had stolen their linen and their window curtains. They had killed their fowls and then laid hands on some of the supplies, such as lard and any kind of fat.

"Were you really hungry?" I asked a woman who was packing some things into a perambulator before leaving for a safer place, and she said in French, which is better than English for this phrase, " There was too much for death, but not enough for life."

## WANTON DESTRUCTION

The curé of Selvigny, with whom I had a long talk, told me how he had saved his church from destruction. " I know they meant to destroy it," he said, " because I saw German soldiers put bombs at each corner of the tower and carry up cases of explosives into the loft. Then I saw them fix wires across the little cemetery, and I knew that unless the English came quickly my dear little church would be blown up. But tonight before they came I crept out and searched for the wires and, by good luck, found them without being seen. I cut them, and then came back feeling very joyful and yet a little afraid lest my track should be discovered."

At Selvigny, Walincourt and other villages all around the people make embroidery and tulle, and for this work have delicate and expensive machines. French inhabitants from the district of the Somme were ordered to break the machines, which their poor owners would not do, even though they died for their refusal, and this destruction was carried out before their eyes as part of the general scheme to destroy French industries. A curé took away some of the delicate parts of the machinery and hid them, but this was discovered, and he was fined 100 marks and the machinery was broken up and scattered outside his doors.

There seem to have been elaborate preparations to destroy the whole area around Caudry les Bains, Esnes, and all the towns and hamlets north and south and east of Cambrai. The British were too quick for them, and that country as far east as Le Cateau is undestroyed in their hands, and many poor people have been liberated from the enemy, including 4,000 at Bohain. So by the rapid pursuit the retreat was for a time thrown into some confusion, and the British airmen, flying low over their roads of retreat, came back sometimes with descriptions of wild stampedes.

The British tanks were after them yesterday. I saw these monsters crawl through undestroyed hamlets on the edge of the enemy's rearguard line, watched with amazed eyes by Frenchwomen who had heard much about their power and fearful habits from German soldiers, but now saw them for the first time passing their cottage doors, leaving deep tracks behind them as they waddled down the narrow ways. Truly they look terrifying things, full of deadly menace.

## SWEEPING BEYOND CAMBRAI

Oct. 11.—The great battle raging southeast of Cambrai is on a front of nearly thirty miles today, it having been extended to the north. The British are gaining everywhere. There is virtually no enemy infantry opposition.

The only resistance worth mentioning is coming from the enemy machine gunners. The bulk of the enemy artillery seems to have fled so far east of the battleground as to be out of range.

It was American troops from Tennessee and North and South Carolina who captured Vaux-Andigny and St. Souplet and the country just north and south of those towns. The Americans quickly left Vaux-Andigny behind, but on reaching the headwaters of the River Selle they encountered a heavy enemy machine-gun fire from the east bank. Hot fighting is in progress here, and the enemy is gradually being thinned out by the American fire.

Nearly 10,000 French civilians have been liberated from the Germans by the advancing British and Americans. Four thousand civilians were found in Bohain alone. They were in a pitiful condition, having been without food for three days when rescued. Tears of joy coursed down the emaciated cheeks of the liberated men and women.

The 2,500 civilians rescued from the Germans at Caudry rushed from the town as the British stormed toward it, waving their arms and cheering. The Germans had robbed them of all their belongings.

## TALES OF CAPTIVES

Oct. 13.—Amid all this fighting and beyond it there is another drama of a most strange and pitiful kind. It is the tragedy of those French civilians whom our men are now meeting as they capture village after village, where these old people and young women and children are waiting in their cellars for deliverance, hearing the approach of the battle, the louder noise of our guns, the crash of shells above the deadly rattle of machine-gun fire down their streets, and at last the cheers or tramp of our men.

On the roadside and in the villages just taken I meet these people and talk with them, and the look of them and the things they say, such tragic and passionate things, such simple and frightful things, reveal the world of agony in those human hearts, divided from us for four years by the German lines and now coming through to us as the barrier is broken.

Yesterday I met many of them on a far journey through those places which our men have just captured. On one road, crowded with our guns and transports, and amid the noise of a loud bombardment through the early morning mist, I met a group of women and girls with their children standing as though waiting for some hand of fate to help them. It was cold, and they had shawls on their heads, but shivered.

"Where are you from?" I asked, and they said, "We have just come out of Le Cateau."

The enemy was still in the outskirts of Le Cateau, and there was a little hell up there. A girl pulled her shawl from her face, and said:

"We have been in our cellars for four days without food. The bombardment began and some women were killed. The Germans wanted us to get away, but we said: 'We will wait for the English though we die.'"

The girl thrust an arm through her shawl and the emotion of all that she had seen and suffered made her white face flame.

"Oh, the dirty brutes!" she said, and then laughed with queer mirth and said:

"They are getting punished now. It was very funny a week ago. 'The English will never get to Le Cateau.' they said, and I said, 'Wait a bit.' 'They won't get Cambrai,' they said, 'because we are killing them in heaps,' but I said, 'Soon it will be your turn to die.'

Then, a few days ago, they became scared and had a big fright. The high officers went away in a hurry and I waved my hands as they passed and said, 'It is time to go, my fine devils, eh?' Then the Commandateurs rushed off with their papers, and I laughed to see them, and then the Sergeant Major went, and the Sergeants and signalmen, and I knew the English were after them, aud in our cellars when the shelling began we waited and listened and said: 'The devils have gone, and we shall be free again.'"

The girl and the women around her broke into passionate words, their breath steaming in the wet mist, and every word was a flame of hatred for the enemy in whose hands they had been for four years. And then they wept a little at the remembrance of that misery.

## BOHAIN A WRECK

The approach to Bohain was sinister. There was a loud noise of gunfire close behind a thick curtain of mist. Many dead horses lay along the road, with broken guns and gun limbers. There were new shell pits on each side of the road and the Germans had blown up deep craters on the highway.

It had been an immense German junction for detraining troops and stores, and I passed over six broad gauge lines and vast sidings. They had had ordnance stores here and ammunition dumps, but had cleared away most of their material and had blown up what they could not save, so that there was a wild litter of twisted iron and wreckage of sheds and trains.

Three men came and spoke to me, one a handsome middle-aged man with a spade beard and a distinguished way of speech, the second a little old gnome-like man of 70 or so, with a laborer's rugged face, and the third a tall man with a short black beard and high cheekbones and a queer light in his eyes. It was the man with the spade beard who spoke first and faster. He took my hand and said:

"You are an English soldier. Come and see what the Germans have done in Bohain. Go round these streets and speak to our women. Go to our Town Hall, which cost great sums of money, and see how before they left they blew it up and burned it to the ground. Go to our factories, which were filled with machinery, by which our people earned their bread before the war, and you will see that they have left nothing, not one bar of iron, not one little wheel—nothing! nothing! Tell your soldiers and your people that the Germans are devils, bandits, brigands, pigs, and brutes, and tell them how they made your prisoners suffer, how they starved them, so that they dropped dead as they walked."

## SUFFERINGS OF PRISONERS

He pointed to a little field through a gap in the red brick houses and said: "There are graves of English soldiers who starved to death in Bohain." He pointed to a doorway close to us and said: "Outside that house I saw one of your men drop down dead from hunger." The two other men said the same kind of things.

A few days ago there were heartrending scenes when 5,000 males, between the ages of 14 and 60, were sent away further into the German lines. They were assembled in the chief square, where they carried little parcels and handbags, and from their wives and mothers and children there rose loud wailing, and all the men wept as they embraced those who were dear to them, and there was agony of human hearts.

## BATTLES IN FLANDERS

*On Oct. 14 Belgian and French troops in close co-operation carried by assault enemy positions on a front of twelve miles between Handzaeme Canal and the Roulers-Menin road. Many villages were taken and the City of Roulers fell to the French. The same day the British advance approached Courtrai. Philip Gibbs wrote on Oct. 15:*

The battle in Flanders, which began yesterday morning and is continuing today in the direction of Thourout and Courtrai, is being fought by combined Belgian, French, and British armies under the supreme command of King Albert.

The British Second Army, under General Sir Herbert Plumer, is on the right of this group of armies, with the Belgians on the left between Roulers and Menin, and the French in the centre around Roulers itself, which they had the honor of taking.

This international action has gained important success along the whole line of attack, and it is interesting in that the number of prisoners captured were almost exactly the same for the troops of each nation, amounting to about 4,000 yesterday, which brings them up to some 12,000 in all. The British troops also captured some 50 guns.

In describing the scenes yesterday when the British and Belgian troops marched along the same tracks and encamped side by side in the same fields of those four old Flemish battlefields and came back together along the tracks for walking wounded, I was unable to include the French soldiers in this forbidding picture of war, because they were still an official secret. But the color of their sky-blue uniforms, the long trail of their blue carts over the heights of Passchendaele, and their columns of guns, going forward to the battleline, were interwoven with the masses of Belgian infantry moving forward to their objectives and with the khaki of the English, Scottish, and Irish battalions.

After four years of war in many fields of battle they are sterner and graver looking in mass than the English soldiers, who still contrive to find a joke or two along the line of march, and they were leaner looking, more sharply cut in profile than the Belgians in their yellow helmets. But seeing them, one marveled that after all these years of sacrifice France could still put in the field such wonderful battalions, in which each man seemed picked because of his hardihood and fitness.

## EVACUATION OF LILLE

Oct. 17.—The enemy has abandoned Lille and Turcoing, those great industrial towns of Northern France, which he has held so long as his trump cards in his devil's gamble of this war, and we are following him up. We have taken Lambartzede on the coast and captured Ostend. From one end of the line to the other the German armies are in retreat from great portions of France and Belgium, and it is the landslide of all their ambitions and their military power.

Today I have seen scenes of history which many people had been dreaming through all these years, until at last they were sick with deferred hope. I have seen Belgian and French soldiers riding through liberated towns, cheered by the people who had been prisoners of war in their own houses for all these dreary years, under a hostile rule which was sometimes cruel and always hard, so that their joy now is wonderful to see, and makes something break in one's heart at the sight of it, because one understands by these women's faces, by the light in the children's eyes, and by the tears of old bearded men what this rescue means to them and what they suffered.

This regaining of Lille is the most wonderful occurrence since the combined offensive of the Allies on the western front in August last, and is the prize of many victories won by the heroism of young officers and men and by the fine strategy of Marshal Foch, whose brain has been behind all these movements of the men.

One feels that the horror of this war is lifting, and that the iron ramparts of the enemy, so strong against us year after year in spite of desperate efforts of millions of gallant men who dashed themselves against those barriers, have yielded at last and that many gates are open for our men to pass through on their way to victory.

*Mr. Gibbs's account may be supplemented with this dispatch of Oct. 18 from a correspondent of the Petit Journal of Paris:*

I have just witnessed the most touching spectacle of my life. The whole city, in a delirium of joy, was ready to throw itself upon us, the first to enter Lille. Tonight at 9 o'clock, near Armentières, an officer shouted to us: " Lille is taken! " We speeded our auto on the road of victory. Two miles from Lille two young girls ran out in front of our auto, crying amid sobs of joy: " They have gone! They have gone! Vivent les Anglais! Vive la France! "

We went a little further, and then a huge shell hole obliged us to abandon our machine and proceed on foot. Two more girls, who had run out of the city to meet their deliverers the sooner, cried, while tears streamed down their cheeks, " They won't come! "

A hack appeared, and we got in, but a crowd, every member of which was weeping, seized us. One man climbed on our shoulders. Another shouted to us: " My name is Guiselin. I am City Counselor. The Germans offered me a million to betray my country. The cowards, the cowards! " and then he burst into sobbing.

Carried by the crowd, we arrived at the City Hall. Deputy Mayor Baudon stood at the door. When we entered every one rushed to embrace us. An old man, with white hair, stood with a violin at the top of the grand staircase and played the " Marseillaise." Outside the crowd seethed like a sea. We were the first messengers from the motherland.

" Speak, speak to us! " they cried. We opened the windows and told of our victory. A shout went up that filled the city. We told of the Bulgarian capitulation. Again the cheers rang out. We told of the Turkish promise to quit the war, and again the crowd cheered. Then we told them that President Wilson had refused to grant an armistice and demanded Emperor William's head. The crowd, in a frenzy, tossed everything it could lay hands on into the air.

At the prefecture the Acting Prefect, M. Regnier, embraced us, and there was a fresh outburst of cheering from the crowd. It was for Mayor Delsalle and for his son, a French officer of the Legion of Honor and wearing the War Cross. This officer, an aviator, heard at 11 o'clock that the city had been freed. He leaped into his machine, flew quickly to Lille, and landed in the Place du Théâtre. Alighting, he rushed home to his father. His was the first French uniform the liberated citizens had seen, and the sight of it increased their delirium of joy.

There remain 120,000 inhabitants in Lille. The Germans had carried off all the male population more than 14 years of age. The city is not greatly damaged, and the public buildings are intact.

# From St. Quentin to the Argonne

## How Mangin and Rawlinson Crushed the Keystone of the Hindenburg Line in the Champagne

WHILE the British were driving out the enemy in the north, and the Americans were breaking through on the other wing of the great salient that stretched from the channel to Switzerland, the French were smashing away at the centre between Arras and Rheims. This Champagne offensive was carried on by French and American forces on the right under Generals Mangin, Gouraud, Debeney, and Berthelot, and by British and American forces on the left under Rawlinson. Victories were gained by both groups despite great natural obstacles of terrain and weather. The most vital result was the capture of the Chemin des Dames, with the delivery of the Rheims region; at the same time Cambrai, St. Quentin, Laon, and La Fère, all strongholds of the Hindenburg line, were captured. The events on this part of the front were narrated each day by George H. Perris and Walter Duranty in their copyrighted dispatches for THE NEW YORK TIMES and its affiliated publication, CURRENT HISTORY MAGAZINE.

Describing the relentless pressure against the Chemin des Dames on Sept. 22, Mr. Duranty cabled:

"When the history of the war comes to be written, full justice will be done to the work of General Mangin's army during the month of September, which the more striking operations elsewhere now tend somewhat to obscure. In fact, so gradual has been the progress and so lacking in sensational incident that were it not for the historic name of the Chemin des Dames to mark the goal of the effort, Mangin's soldiers might fancy that their advance, foot by foot, accompanied by some of the most desperate fighting of the whole war, was scarcely noticed by the rest of the world.

"Skillful manoeuvre has been the secret of this success. The German position as a whole is being patiently turned from the southwest just as an individual post of defense or a fortified village is outflanked and carried in detail.

"It is a parallel of the operation against the equally difficult massif of Thiescourt, where Humbert's men pushed steadily round toward Lassigny, while simultaneously 'nibbling' their way forward by 'infiltration' through the heart of the massif. But against Mangin the resistance is stiffened greatly by the fact that the enemy is close to the Hindenburg defenses.

"Counterstroke after counterstroke follows every French advance. On the night of Sept. 10 the Prussian Guards attacked six times in a vain attempt to win back the important position of Laffaux. On the night of the 19th another crack division broke five times against the stubborn defense of a French unit that had just won the farm of Moisy.

"It is a pitiless struggle, with little quarter on either side, in the ravines and caverns that are features of the country. In this confined space grenades are as mortal as shells, and flamethrowers turn the underground darkness into a hell of agony and fire.

"Yet the advance is as constant as it is imperceptible to the outside world. Now the French Army is almost within reach of Malmaison, the true key to the Chemin des Dames position. And, what is hardly less important, it is doing its share in a far greater operation. That consists in 'nailing' the enemy to battle along the Hindenburg line from Arras to Rheims."

### MALMAISON PLATEAU

On Sept. 29 the Malmaison front, which had been invested by a concentric movement of General Mangin's army, was abandoned by General von Carlowitz, who retreated behind the Ailette.

This made inevitable the evacuation of the Chemin des Dames. Two days previously, General Gouraud, battling east of Rheims, captured Somme-Py with more than 10,000 prisoners. Mr. Perris wrote on Sept. 27:

" Today the army disinterred itself. Like a wakened giant, it shook its stiff limbs and laughed aloud. I saw several thousand German prisoners starting on their backward journey, and even they seemed to reflect the prevalent mood. To judge by the number of smiling faces, never was there a body of soldiers more glad to be rescued from their country's service. Every considerable victory is an occasion for a general shift. The wounded and prisoners go down; the mass of the armies moves up. Old battery positions must be hastily changed for new. Old camps, old parks and dumps, old quarters of all sorts, grown odiously familiar, are light-heartedly abandoned.

" The roads are full of this movement. The barren woods, stripped and scarred with an age of deadlock warfare, are suddenly alive with color. The endless miles of chalk-walled lanes above which it was death two days ago to show one's head already look like the remains of a distant, incredible past. Some, at least, of their tenants are taking a sun bath on the open hillsides, and, indifferent to occasional arrivals, as they call German shellbursts, watch like children some passing drama of the air—a sausage balloon falling from the sky like a smoke serpent, its white silk parachute, or the breaking globes of shrapnel vapor around the enemy raider. And always the guns are going forward, and the narrow-gauge railways are bringing up fresh piles of shell boxes.

" There is little joy in war, and I must not overstrain the impression of one of its lighter intervals. That would be to forget the architects of this victory, the men who as I write are taking the wounds and pains by which alone it could be bought. For them there is no lifting of the strain. The best one can say is that sunshine and success will for them also make a difference.

" And I can testify, especially as regards their great chief, that their boundless devotion is not forgotten. We must never forget it, is the sense of General Gouraud's most frequent and emphatic words. They are worthy of one another, these men and their large-minded, gentle, clear-willed chief."

## HAND-TO-HAND FIGHTING

Regarding the withdrawal of the enemy from Malmaison, Mr. Duranty wrote Sept. 29:

" The battle continues furious on the flanks of the great salient that is the front in France. In the centre the enemy slowly withdraws from key positions like Malmaison Fort and Pinon Forest, every foot of whose ground both he and the Allies bought before with blood. While the Belgians and British are thrusting the left claw of the giant pincers forward across the Hindenburg and Wotan lines, the Franco-Americans on the right are directing even a deadlier menace against the communications of the German centre.

" The élan of Gouraud's troops has overcome counterattacks of more than a score of boche divisions hurled against them yesterday with disregard for losses which even the Germans have seldom equaled. Again and again there was desperate hand-to-hand fighting on the trench-scarred slopes of Mount Cuvelet, whose height of 500 feet commands the lower ridges east and west. Grenades soon gave out in the heat of the contest, and the combat became a mêlée wherein knives, clubbed rifles, and bayonets played the principal part.

" So confused was the struggle that machine guns did not dare to fire lest friend might share foe's destruction. At 10 o'clock this morning the attack was resumed along Gouraud's whole front, after a night spent in organizing liaisons, regrouping scattered units, and bringing up guns, food, and supplies. By 2 o'clock the heights dominating the Aisne Valley to the northeast were securely in French possession.

" Most important feature of all, the enemy seemed unable to counterattack—in the supreme hour of battle the poverty of reserves is telling fatally. His artillery fire has also weakened. The effect of success will be equally great on the American operations east of the Argonne, for French guns command the Valley of Grand Pré, whose cleft in the trackless forests hitherto offered the enemy an easy line of communications between the right and left flanks of attack.

"Beyond it, the vital junction of Challerange is similarly dominated. Once more the historic forest of the Argonne, which Dumouriez called the French Thermopylae, is the scene of French victory over the Prussians."

## FROM SOMME TO ARGONNE

On Sept. 30 the French continued their gains, advancing to within five miles of the important German base of Vouziers, and Mr. Perris wrote:

"The region of the Somme which was taken yesterday morning was fiercely defended. Two miles east of the town there is a tunnel of the Challerange railway which was blown up in 1914, but had been repaired, and was used as a store and shelter for the reserves. The enemy evidently expected to have to evacuate this big hole, for they had mined it in nine places.

"A system of trenches four miles deep had to be reduced in this neighborhood, the tanks giving valuable assistance to the infantry. Further east, the plateau of Gratreuil, with its three crests, was obstinately defended after the capture on Friday afternoon by a clever turning movement of the villages of Gratreuil and Fontaine-en-Dormois.

"Still further east, on both sides of the valley of the upper Aisne, very strong opposition has been encountered, especially in the woods which are the outlying fragments of the Argonne Forest. I went up to trenches beyond Vienne-le-Château for the first time and realized the peculiar conditions here obtaining ever since Sarrail and de Langle de Cary, in the first Autumn of the war, inflicted defeat upon the Crown Prince. The Aisne is here only a small stream, but there is much marshy ground on either side.

"A valley opens out beyond Vienne, but it is still covered by machine-gun fire from the Argonne and from the hills on the west. Mont Cuvelot and the woods between Bouconville and Binarville were receiving a tremendous bombardment from many French batteries, thanks to which the infantry made an important advance yesterday.

"We have taken Binarville and the Allies are here only six miles from the gap of Grand Pré, between the army groups of the Crown Prince on the west and von Gallwitz on the east.

"The Northern Argonne has been throughout these years one of the most redoubtable of the boche fortresses, and its clearance without the cost of a frontal attack is one of the happiest results of the parallel Franco-American movement."

St. Quentin, the keystone of the German line of defense, was captured Oct. 1. Under that date Mr. Perris wrote:

"French troops entered St. Quentin this afternoon. Repeated explosions of great violence in the town were heard between 6 and 8 o'clock this morning. The new attack, which began at 5 o'clock last evening, brought the right of General Rawlinson's army into Levergies and enabled General Debeney to cross the Cambrai road east of Gricourt. West of St. Quentin the German trenches were very strongly held, and no ground could be won. Further south the front was slightly advanced beyond the roads from Giffecourt to Urvillers, and thence to Vendeuil on the Oise.

"The army of General Mangin is steadily clearing the south bank of the Ailette as far east as the canal reservoir, whence its front runs southeast by Ostel to the Aisne. Here a body of Italian troops has captured the village of Soupir. The recovery of the Aisne heights is thus proceeding by regular stages, but it is to be noted that this time the enemy's retreat is taking a northeasterly, not a northerly, direction, and that to protect this movement the hill block between Rheims and the Aisne is being vigorously defended.

"The marching wing of the Belgians, British, and French in the north, and the French and Americans in the south enjoy a somewhat freer development than the British and French in the centre and open more varied prospects.

"It would not be discreet to enter

upon any full discussion of these possibilities, but a glance at the map will show that General Gouraud before Monthois and Challerange, and General Pershing at Vilosnes, on the Meuse, are only about thirty miles from Sedan and Longwy, respectively, and that the shortest line from Roulers in Belgium to Vilosnes passes far behind St. Quentin and the Ailette.

"The capture of Binarville and Conde, in the Aisne Valley on his right, and of Marvaux on his centre, has greatly strengthened Gouraud's front, and the German forces northwest of Rheims may soon find themselves in a salient difficult to hold."

## NEARING THE ARGONNE

On Oct. 3 the French made sweeping gains from St. Quentin eastward to the Argonne region, further relieving Rheims, and capturing Challerange, with 2,800 prisoners. Mr. Duranty thus described the operations:

"The best troops of the German Army had been accumulated for the defense— Guards, Jaegers, and other units that had distinguished themselves throughout the war. The French emphasize the good quality of the prisoners, both from a military viewpoint and physically, and as regards equipment. Their orders were uncompromising to the highest degree. Thus the 200th Jaeger Division, whose defense is still being maintained in Fourmilier Wood and on the Hill of Notre Dame des Champs, north of Sainte Marie, had these instructions: 'You must make a determination to hold out to the very end enter the heart and life's blood of every soldier. No inch of ground must be abandoned without immediate counterattack. It must be a point of honor for officers to force their men everywhere to resist until death.'

"This division is the flower of the army. They wear a special green uniform with insignia of edelweiss and antlers on their caps, and the letter C in memory of the Carpathians, where their record was magnificent.

"Such was the general quality of the defenders, and the abundance of reserves available permitted them immediately to replace any unit that did not seem to come up to the standard. Thus the 15th Bavarians, who weakened, were withdrawn after one day in the line. It is worth noting that this division appears to have been less than eager to fight— an ominous symptom of the state of mind of the Bavarians, whereof other instances have occurred recently.

"Despite all the Germans could do, Gouraud's men have penetrated far into the second battle zone on the centre and right of the front, where a threat toward the vital point of Vouziers is most dangerous. Challerange fell yesterday, and the French are now attacking the village of Mouron on the northern side of the Grand Pré defile, which is thus closed to the enemy. To pass the Argonne their railroad communication must now traverse the valley of Quatre Champs, some ten miles to the north. Further west, Orfeuil was occupied this morning, which facilitates operations against the hills north of Ste. Marie.

"And the victory is being won at a cost so light that it would be deemed incredible if I could state the figures. Never do Gouraud or his subordinates forget that manoeuvre is the key to success, and always a flanking wood or other vital point of the defense positions is smashed by artillery before the infantry is sent forward."

## FALL OF RHEIMS SALIENT

Under date of Oct. 8 Mr. Perris wrote: "The dogged pressure and manoeuvring skill of General Berthelot on the west and of General Gouraud on the east have had a sudden and dramatic result. The four-year-old German salient before Rheims has burst. Von Mudra has abandoned the whole pocket, thirty miles wide and eight miles deep, and has fled to the line of the small Rivers Suippe and Arnes, pursued closely by French cavalry and infantry. Those fearsome citadels, Brimont and Nogent l'Abbesse, and the Moronvillers Hills have fallen without the need to fire a shot. Thousands of prisoners and many guns have been taken. French soldiers are in a state of high enthusiasm, and one has the sense of the corresponding collapse into despair, if not actual panic, on the other side. This was the strongest part of the Crown Prince's line—a bad day, indeed, for the Hohenzollerns. It is a pure triumph of good generalship and indomitable pluck.

"On Thursday General Gouraud's army had carried by assault the second main defensive system of von Einem's neighboring front, running from Mont Blanc north of Somme-Py, by the Medeah Farm, past the villages of Orfeuil, Liry, and Monthois, and including Challerange. On the left of this the battle was splendidly sustained by the American division which first distinguished itself in Belleau Wood, near Château-Thierry. On Friday the attack was extended to the west. Here the German engineers had expended all their ingenuity in fortifying the height of Nôtre Dame des Champs, beyond Ste. Marie-a-Py building successive tiers of pillboxes by which the whole valley was enfiladed. The position, however, was turned by the northwest, and when it had been cleared out a rapid advance was made to the northwest, St. Souplet being captured, and five miles further north St. Etienne, in the Arnes Valley. Autry Station was taken, lost, and finally recovered.

"During the evening the push on the left was strengthened by the occupation of Vaudevincourt and Dontrien, villages lying on the Suippe at the foot of the Moronvillers plateau. At the same time General Berthelot's army on the other side of the Rheims salient had reached Bermericourt and had begun to throw bridges over the Aisne-Marne Canal eastward. After the collection of 2,500 prisoners and twenty heavy cannon in its march from the Vesle it was not disposed to overestimate its adversary. Von Mudra felt the pincers closing upon him. * * *

"General Gouraud's outposts had discovered the beginning of the retreat on the east side of the mountains. It was at once followed over the foothills, and at dawn yesterday Berthelot's army pushed across the canal in force at several points.

"Nine German armies, those of Below, Marwitz, Hutier, Boehn, Carlowitch, Eberhard, Mudra, Einem, and Gallwitz, are now in peril. It would be rash to expect a sudden débâcle, but the development of events has been so rapid and upon such an immense scale that even that is possible."

## FALL OF CAMBRAI

On Oct. 9 Cambrai was taken after being almost totally destroyed by the retreating Germans. Hardly stopping there, the armies of Mangin, Gouraud, and Debeney swept on. Mr. Duranty on Oct. 13 wrote:

"Today's news locates Gouraud's troops on the south bank of the Aisne from Vouziers, where they have established a bridgehead on the further bank, to Asfeld, west of which cavalry and automitrailleuses have thrust forward to the Laon-Rheims railroad. Further west the Fifth Army, in conjunction with Mangin's forces, has occupied more than half of the Laon massif. On Mangin's left Debeney yesterday, after a furious struggle, succeeded in crossing the Oise River and the Sambre-Oise Canal.

"In a word, the Germans are retreating from an untenable salient, but the menace of the French and British advance on its left flank is still deadly. The Germans cannot regard themselves as safe from that danger until they have reached the Valenciennes-Avesnes-Hirson-Mézières-Sedan line, almost coincident with the Franco-Belgian frontier. Even there they have no defenses to be compared in strength with the Hindenburg system or the Champagne lines that the Allies have so triumphantly broken, and during their retreat American pressure on their extreme left toward Sedan may involve them in wholesale disaster."

## LAON AND LA FERE

The taking of Laon and La Fère on Oct. 14, together with the previous captures of Cambrai and St. Quentin, completed the demolishment of the key positions of the famous Hindenburg line. Mr. Perris wrote on Oct. 14:

"I have just come down the lines from Laon. The town is very little damaged, the interesting old cathedral and other public buildings being intact. But all the houses and shops left by their occupants at the beginning of the war have been completely emptied of their contents, and the Acting Mayor gives a grievous account of the German exactions in the form of fines and taxation.

"The worst complaint of the thousands of inhabitants who have borne the enemy yoke for nearly four years, is of the system of compulsory labor to which every able-bodied adult and youth had been subjected. Even when elderly men accompany them as the war lords were going shooting in the neighborhood they made the girls beaters.

"General Mangin had a great reception when he entered the town, children wearing tricolor ribbons and waving extemporized flags, and old folk laughing and crying in their joy at being delivered. The German retreat may be measured by the fact that General Mangin's artillery moved up twelve miles in the thirty-six hours."

Mr. Perris's summary of the situation was as follows on Oct. 16:

"Marshal Foch continues his general pressure, which is accentuated now on one part of the front, now on the other. He has proved markedly superior to Ludendorff. His methods give the enemy no breathing time to strengthen his threatened points. The consequence of this succession of German defeats, added to the knowledge that Germany cannot hope for victory, has produced discouragement, if not demoralization, which is certainly a leading factor in the situation, and may be more serious than one can prove.

"By the end of last week there remained behind the German front as a general reserve no more than thirty divisions, half of which had only just been withdrawn from the fighting line for reconstruction, and only a dozen were rested. These jaded troops had to face a host constantly recruited by the American arrivals and perfectly confident of the result.

"Army orders taken on the battlefield show that strikes, bad feeling, and the army's demand for men have resulted in a decline of manufactures, and that both guns and munitions are lacking. The field artillery has been reduced by several hundred batteries, and the heavy batteries have been reduced from four to three divisions.

"In three months of the allied offensive we have captured on the western front more than 4,600 cannon, and, including the wear and tear, the loss must be 5,000 pieces, which is a third of the German artillery on the western front, and a quarter of the whole. It may be doubted whether the enemy has half as many airplanes as the Allies, and in many other directions he is badly handicapped. When to these elements of numbers and material, leadership and morale, it is added that Germany has no longer an ally to count upon, is no longer sure of victory, and that her spirit and unity are broken, it will be seen that her position is desperate."

# The Battle for Argonne Forest

## How the American First Army Drove the Germans From a Vital Stronghold by Desperate Fighting

### By EDWIN L. JAMES

*The First American Army launched an attack Sept. 26, 1918, between the Meuse and Aisne Rivers, directly east of Rheims, on a front of twenty miles. The chief objective was to clear the Argonne Forest and reach the high plain beyond, which would clear the way for an advance toward Sedan and the German frontier. The task involved the penetration of the Kriemhilde line, one of the chief defensive works of the German front. An advance in this sector menaced the only transportation lines by which the Germans could withdraw, except through Belgium. The supreme importance of protecting these lines was apparent to the German command, and here were concentrated the Prussian Guards and the flower of the army, with instructions to resist to the death. The American Army confronted the task with indomitable determination and skillful strategy. For three weeks they maintained a furious assault, and on Oct. 17 they stood before the shattered German front, with the Argonne Forest and the main strategetic points beyond it safely in their hands. Edwin L. James described this advance in daily cable letters to THE NEW YORK TIMES, which were copyrighted for its affiliated publication, CURRENT HISTORY MAGAZINE, and are herewith given:*

SEPT. 26, 1918.—The brunt of the attack in the centre fell to the corps commanded by Major Gen. Hunter Liggett. Troops from Kansas, Pennsylvania, and Missouri stormed, despite the stubborn resistance of the Prussian Guard, the towns of Varennes, Montblainville, Vauquois, and Cheppy. The tanks did stout work at Varennes. Our airplanes had full supremacy. Tonight the troops are pressing forward beyond the old German defense line. Malancourt, Bethincourt, Montfaucon, and Dannevoux have been taken, with 5,000 prisoners the first day.

This second effort of America's First Army came just two weeks after the beginning of the successful stroke at the St. Mihiel salient. There is little doubt that General Foch and General Pershing surprised the German command. It is known that the enemy expected the attack on the St. Mihiel sector and had rushed new troops there.

At 11:30 o'clock last night our artillery began heavy work east of the Meuse, and this was followed by strong raids. Meanwhile, at 2:30 this morning, the artillery work for our real attack began, and was followed just three hours later by the start of the infantry.

Our young soldiers left the trenches, scarred by four years of war, and started north over the war-rocked No Man's Land on an enterprise which had proved so costly to other allied efforts. A few hundred yards took them into the first line of the Hindenburg series of defenses. This was taken at 7 o'clock. By 9 o'clock the second line had been taken, and by noon our troops had passed the whole Hindenburg line ahead of schedule.

### FIGHTING PRUSSIAN GUARD

Sept. 27.—The villages of Charpentry, Véry, Epinonville, and Ivoiry were taken by the First American Army today, showing a handsome gain for the day's fighting against heavy and fresh German forces.

Late counterattacks in force were made against our troops, but netted the Germans no gains worth having. The heaviest of these counterattacks fell on troops commanded by General Cameron. These units hail from Ohio, New Jersey, Maryland, Virginia, Oregon, Washington, Colorado, Wyoming, and Montana. Many of them, although in battle for the first time, successfully withstood savage counterattacks by Prussian Guard troops late in the afternoon. We have taken more than 100 guns. The prisoners so far counted total 8,000.

The American advance today precipitated engagements of great intensity. Our fighters met the sternest kind of resistance from some of the best soldiers of the German Army. Two-thirds of the advancing line is composed of American soldiers from the Meuse westward to the left of the Argonne Forest, with the French Army fighting northward along the rest of the line, the whole movement covering more than half the front from north of Rheims to north of Verdun.

This morning the Germans threw in at least four divisions against the Americans, and they have brought up within twenty-four hours several times that number to oppose our further advance. Despite all this we made satisfactory progress, hitting strategic points along the Dannevoux-Montfaucon line and pushing in strong forces.

During the first twenty-four hours of the attack the American First Army, moving like clockwork on a schedule, drove back the German line for almost a uniform depth from the Meuse to the Aisne, for some distances as great as fifteen kilometers, but averaging about ten. According to its schedule, the French Fourth Army pushed its front over the Hindenburg line to an extreme depth of six kilometers.

The American attack was made with a great concentration of guns and airplanes. Our ample supply of guns enabled us to gas far-back locations, where the Germans were reported concentrating. The hardest problem for the tanks was the masonry work of the Hindenburg line, which often rose sharply several feet above the level of the ground. Then, too, the Germans had built stone walls, reinforced with bars of steel, across roads and streets forming part of their line. One road had four of these walls in half a kilometer. We blasted them away after the doughboys had climbed over them.

Then there were the traps which the Germans had built. They had hollowed huge holes in the roads and covered them neatly with a few inches of surfacing. Tanks running over them simply sank out of sight. We had rather good luck avoiding these, and when a tank fell into one, two big trucks were hitched to it and pulled it out.

## NETWORK OF TRENCHES

It is difficult for one who has not seen the sight to imagine the quantity of barbed wire used and the extent of the burrowing the two armies have done opposite each other in four years. It seemed that there was wire enough to circle the globe several times, and that if all the trenches in the Aire Valley alone were put end to end they would reach New York. There are big trenches, little trenches, communicating trenches, simple ditches, and trenches fitted with palatial dugouts and electric lights. One German command had running water and framed pictures on the walls.

One of the most interesting places taken is Vauquois, where the Germans had added to the existing caves until they had tunnels which reached away back under the hill north of the town. I am told that the aggregate length of all these tunnels is forty kilometers. Here were kept men and supplies. A captured document showed that the Germans were ordered to hold this place at all costs.

Against the best efforts of crack German troops we made important gains. Perhaps 200,000 fresh troops have arrived back of the German line. Today we pierced several points of this line running through Montfaucon and Donnevoux, the Germans falling back after stubborn resistance.

In the Forest of Argonne the Americans today met many machine-gun nests in all possible places of protection. Our boys did great work against the line, and their spirit is shown by the fact that 230 of these gunners were marched back as prisoners, all carrying their weapons, which the American guards forced them to pile in front of their division headquarters. Those who did not bring guns brought American wounded.

By the side of General Pershing, in command of the First American Army,

Secretary of War Baker watched the development of the battle yesterday. He expressed the greatest enthusiasm over the achievements of Young America at war.

## THE KRIEMHILDE STELLUNG

Sept. 29.—After a three days' struggle through mile after mile of seemingly insuperable barriers, constituting the Germans' formidable defense of masonry, steel, wire and pitfalls, the First American Army today is fighting on in the rain to the fourth and last line of those defenses known as Kriemhilde Stellung. I have spent the day exploring a part of what beyond doubt is the greatest piece of military defense work the world ever saw. There is nothing to compare to it, because there never was anything like it. For instance, in Argonne Forest the Americans had to cut their way through a zone of barbed wire two and a half miles, through wire nailed to trees through the forest and reaching sometimes ten feet high. This wire ran in every direction and often was hidden in the underbrush. Other underbrush held hidden entrapments and ordinary trench wire. In this two-and-a-half-mile zone there were innumerable trenches, forming three distinct systems, and between them and over them everywhere there was barbed wire. The communication trenches ran beneath this wire.

Turn your attention to the all-night fighting in the Argonne Forest and realize what our men are going through. It is raining and there is inky darkness. The boche is shelling heavily and pouring gas into all the valleys. Our men must travel on the hills. Those hills are being raked by thousands of German 77s.

The Americans in the advance hit the barbed wire. Rifles are slung across shoulders and pliers are pulled out. Busily our men cut wire after wire. The noise they make brings the nasty rat-a-tat of a Hun machine gun from a tree on the other sile of the wire. Then another and another, and twenty machine guns are going.

Their aim is poor, and their flashes give our rifles a chance. Our doughboys pile through that wire fence and through the underbrush and stack up against another fence ten feet further on. The range has been telephoned back to the boche batteries and shells begin to fall all around.

They cut that barbed wire and then stumble on to concealed wire entanglements covered with brush. They climb these. All the time, from the dark, German snipers and machine gun men, always with time enough to fall back, are taking their toll. Now our line comes upon a broad trench with more wire. In the dark our boys leap across it; some fall into it. Others get over at the first attempt and pull out their pliers to cut more wires.

All this time it is raining and cold, very cold. The inky blackness there in the forest is broken by streams of fire from machine guns and the intermittent flash of some German sniper, seeming to taunt the youthful Americans struggling against such devilish odds.

## TASK FOR STOUT HEARTS

It takes stout hearts, it takes real men to stand this. But it was over two and a half miles of this sort of terrain that one American division tore its way through the Argonne Forest. This was the worst part. Further on the wire was less frequent, and our men in the Argonne, having crashed through the Bois d'Apremont, are now reaching a zone where the roads are good, and the advance is easier.

Since the French tried vainly to take it in 1915 the Germans had used the Argonne Forest as a rest area—a sort of recreation ground for their war-worn troops, and had built such defenses as they thought would defy all attempts frontally. For three years the Argonne has been a kind of pleasure resort for boche fighters. It is worth years of any one's life to see what they had built there on the pretty wooded slopes and through tangles of verdant beauty.

There were underground palaces with electric illumination and with hotel ranges to cook for the officers. On a slope just a mile back of the front line there is an enormous cave fronting north. Its front was built of brownstone, on which had been chased pillars and other carvings. Above its big portals was the word "Offizierhaus," and above that an enormous iron cross. In this club there were a large dining hall and perhaps ten rooms. The inside was lined with concrete and wooden floors had been laid. At the dining table were mahogany chairs, filched from some nearby French château. Over the General's place hung an electric call bell, and electric lights were strung down the middle of the table. It represented the luxury of war. This was just one of hundreds and hundreds of these dug-in and scientifically made dwelling places.

The whole world has heard of the trenches of the Hindenburg line. I had often heard them spoken of as being made of concrete. I would call them masonry. Out in front would be small trenches for the outpost, connecting backward with the first main trench. This was no trench of mud-covered walls and duck boards, yielding into slimy mud under the step. These trenches are lined with cement, with cement floors, along each side of which ran a little drainage ditch.

Each watching soldier had a steel and concrete post with steps leading to it. Nothing could be more complete. Connecting this trench to others in the rear ran communicating trenches of cement, covered with iron roofing and camouflaged and leading back to the officers' underground residences and the men's quarters. Further back were other underground houses for supplies and ammunition, and so on.

### AMERICAN AIRMEN

Two weeks ago, when the First American Army struck the blow at the St. Mihiel salient, five-sevenths of the airmen who were working with the army were other than American. But in the present effort of the First American Army between the Meuse and the Aisne we are using only American airmen. Fighters, observers, pilots, bombers—all are American. It is the first operation of American troops in which this has been true.

Of course the greater part of the airplanes which those aviators are using are not American made, but more of our planes are arriving every week from the United States.

Not only are the airmen of the First American Army taking care of our front between the Meuse and the Aisne, but they are also caring for the front from the Meuse to the Moselle at the same time. They are doing the job excellently. We have air supremacy in all parts of the battlefront, and for the first six hours of the fight not one enemy plane got over the American line. In three days, despite the prevailing bad weather, the American aviators downed sixty German airplanes and twelve observation balloons.

Day bombing is very dangerous work, because it takes the airplanes far back of the lines in full visibility, and these planes are less quick than the enemy's present machines. This fact led yesterday to what perhaps was one of the biggest single air combats of the war. To a series of points north of Verdun were sent thirty-four bombing fours. They were attacked by thirty-six Fokkers in battle formation. Under skillful leadership our planes kept a solid formation, and in returning accounted for seven Fokkers. Five of our aircraft did not get back.

### WHAT NEW YORKERS DID

*The fighting on Sept. 29 and 30 and on Oct. 1 and 2 was furious. The Germans resisted to the death, and the battleline swayed to and fro in the Argonne Forest, yet each day ended with some slight gains for the Americans. On Oct. 2 General Pershing reported that within the week the Americans had taken 120 guns of all calibres, 750 trench mortars, 300 machine guns, 100 tank guns and thousands of artillery shells and hundreds of thousands of rounds of small arms ammunition. Mr. James wrote:*

Oct. 1.—After three days' stubborn resistance against the unfaltering pressure of the American First Army the Germans tonight are withdrawing their advanced elements on the left of our Aisne-Meuse sector, pulling their troops northward in the vicinity of the Argonne Forest toward the Kriemhilde positions.

The troops which have done such

valiant fighting in the Argonne Forest, overcoming the four-year-old German defenses, believed by the boche to be impregnable, are New York troops. They come from Manhattan, Brooklyn, the Bronx, Long Island, and Westchester mostly. These youngsters were trained at Camp Upton and have fought with the spirit of seasoned veterans under most difficult weather conditions.

When they started against the Hindenburg line they had to cut their way through two and a half miles of barbed wire defenses against German machine gun, rifle, and artillery fire as well as gas.

The Germans have some excellent fighters in this sector—men with iron nerve. Yesterday morning a company of about a hundred men found an unguarded path through the woods and actually went through the American line and attacked our advance troops from behind. About the same time advancing troops came up behind the Germans, trapping them. As a result of the fight we brought back sixty of the hundred as prisoners, most of the others being killed. The physical condition of the German soldiers is excellent. As a class their bodily stamina is such as can stand more suffering than our American soldiers.

## KRIEMHILDE LINE BROKEN

Oct. 4.—The Americans are astride the Germans' Kriemhilde line, the last organized defense system between them and the border of Belgium. After a day of terrific fighting, following an attack at 5:30 o'clock this morning, the First American Army drove back the Germans to a line two kilometers north of Binarville and Fleville and north of Gesne to Brieulles. Two Prussian Guard divisions were cut to pieces, one being taken out of the battle entirely.

All day the Germans made the strongest sort of defense, with absolute disregard for their losses. In the Argonne Forest they hurriedly felled trees, wired them, and placed machine guns before our advancing troops. Against the concerted efforts of the German troops, Wisconsin, Illinois, Western Pennsylvania, Virginia, and West Virginia forces and

regular troops, under Major Gen. Bullard, drove the enemy back into the Bois de Forest.

We are on the Kriemhilde line for some distance. The defense system on which the Germans have been working feverishly since our attack of Sept. 26 is now deeply bitten into. Breaking this line means that the fighting north of it will be with the opposing forces on equal terms, and the Germans no longer will have the advantage of organized positions, fortified with steel and masonry lines and intricate wire defenses.

## DESPERATE FIGHTING

*On Oct. 4 General Pershing reported the resumption of the attack on the Meuse and important advances by the forces under Major Gen. R. L. Bullard, consisting of troops from Illinois, Wisconsin, Western Pennsylvania, Virginia, West Virginia, and regulars. Mr. James thus described the German counterattacks:*

Oct. 5.—The German high command, by means of new troops, artillery, and additional aerial forces, threw terrific resistance against the First American Army on the Argonne-Meuse front today. Desperate efforts to drive our men back down on the Aire Valley failed with heavy losses to the Germans.

The enemy have a deep salient in the Argonne Forest, which is protecting their heavy concentration in the woods and hills in the vicinity, and show their intention to pay almost any price to hold their Argonne stronghold.

Our troops found themselves today up against strong machine-gun nests well organized in the trench positions on the left, which form part of the Kriemhilde line, on which our right rests. Repeated German counterattacks nowhere won anything.

Today's artillery activity on the part of the Germans was the heaviest since our attack started. Ours was also heavy. On top of the hill on which the ruins of Montfaucon perch I watched the artillery and machine-gun duel this afternoon. The air was filled with German shells, and more than an equal number of ours returning. The German attack on our line three miles ahead could be seen clearly. One could hear the rat-tat-tat of dozens of machine guns going at the same time.

The air activity was most intense all day, both Americans and Germans venturing far over one another's lines and precipitating scores of combats. The German aviators were very daring. Our day bombers did extensive work.

Today's fighting showed that the Germans had concentrated their artillery and airplanes on the front of the First American Army. Starting at an early hour this morning, the German heavies shelled our roads and villages, paying special attention to the roads out of Montfaucon, Nantillois, Cierges, the Bois de Septarges, and Bois de Forges. This artillery fire was well directed by heavy swarms of airplanes, which came over our lines in large aggregations, sometimes as many as thirty machines in a group.

Since Sept. 28, by a stubborn, expensive effort, the Germans in the Meuse-Aisne area had held the Americans pretty much on the line reached in the first two days' attack, which started on the 26th. By throwing in heavy divisions supported by a concentration of artillery back of the Kriemhilde line they had interposed a human wall against our advance north of Montfaucon and against the Aire Valley, as well as in the Argonne Forest. In addition to this, a number of violent counterattacks were made against the First Army.

All this effort was to protect a vital position, the pivot point of the eastern wing of the great salient forming the Germans' western front. Against this heaviest sort of fighting the Americans hold their own, and, having gotten up their artillery and built roads for supplies, this morning they slammed ahead again to put the boche across the last organized defense line before our troops this side of the French border. Our progress all day was slow, but with the methodical sureness of a well-oiled machine.

## ENEMY'S SHOCK TROOPS

Oct. 6.—The fighting since early this morning is characterized as perhaps the bitterest the Americans have yet seen. It is grueling, soul-trying fighting, with the heroics and sensationalism taken out. The best troops Germany has have been hurled without success against our lines. These shock troops are working independently of the heavy concentration of other troops that are blocking our advance with the heaviest concentration of machine guns war has seen.

An official report says that on one stretch of the front the Germans have a machine gun for every five yards of the line. The German concentration of artillery also is ponderous, the guns being grouped in masses in a zone two and a half miles deep. The short front between the Argonne and the Meuse is the one most vital to the whole line. An advance by the Americans to any great depth would imperil the whole east wing of the German salient stretching from the sea to the Moselle River.

The nature of the infantry fighting in this sector is marked by advances by our troops until the line becomes dented by being held up by German machine guns in sheltered places. As our advance troops move ahead these spiteful weapons open up, and then ensues a bloody contest for the reduction of the nests. This occurs and reoccurs from hour to hour.

Our front from the Argonne to the Meuse is ablaze and the sky is lighted up by the constant glow from hundreds and hundreds of guns on both sides, speaking without cessation in one of the bitterest battles of the world war.

## FIGHT FOR HILL 240

We have had bitter fighting for possession of Hill 240 in the Aire Valley, and tonight we hold it securely despite strong attempts by the Germans to regain the height. Hill 269, northeast of Hill 240, was reached during the afternoon.

German forces fought with might and main to save Hill 240 from falling into the hands of the Americans on Friday, the 4th. Even when the Americans commanded the east, west, and south slopes of the height the enemy attempted to send up reinforcements from the north.

This hill is an important observation point, commanding positions for miles over the plateau west of the Meuse. It is shaped like an inverted cup. On the north slope were the German artillery emplacements, the hill being honey-combed with dugouts. This area resembles an Indian village of Arizona. Each dugout entrance was found to be protected by earthworks strengthened with great wooden and steel props.

On the summit of the hill and among the clutters of shell-shattered stone farmhouses were nests of machine guns. On the southern slope the Germans had erected a steel tower, in which they had installed powerful telescopes. This tower was used when the instruments could not be used on the ground during heavy artillery firing.

Throughout the 4th the Americans fought for possession of the hill. The last German machine gunners did not surrender until toward evening. As the Americans advanced toward the height they divided their forces so that they flanked it on both sides.

After clearing Boyon Wood, the Americans pressed on, despite torrents of machine gun bullets that were turned against them by the concealed enemy. Several times the Americans thought the last German had been accounted for, when the machine gun fire was reopened. Then the Armerican artillery was called upon, and the summit and sides of the hill were subjected to an intense bombardment. American riflemen and machine gunners, from positions to the west, south, and east, aided materially in the fight until the last German fled over the top of the hill.

In the course of the battle German ammunition wagons attempted to reach the enemy forces, but they were caught by the rifle fire, many horses and drivers being killed and the rest being compelled to retreat. German machine gunners tried to protect the wagons, but they were smothered by the American fire.

Americans who were in the fight assert that on one occasion the Germans on top of the hill raised the white flag, but when the Americans started forward the enemy's guns reopened fire. The Americans fell back, and a redoubled rifle and artillery fire was opened on the position of the enemy. Soon after-ward Hill 240 fell to the American attackers.

## OTHER HEIGHTS CAPTURED

Oct. 7.—After a day of bitter fighting they have driven the Germans from the heights west of the Aire Valley and are commanding the Argonne Forest from our line to the end of the jungle at Grand Pré. These heights include Hills 242, 244, and 269, on the crests of which our troops have dug in. This is the best advance we have made against the Argonne stronghold since the drive of the First American Army started on the morning of Sept. 26.

Our attack this morning was started by the troops on the line from Fleville, five kilometers southward, the troops moving due west. A short time after this attack started, at 6:30, the troops holding the line through the forest attacked northward. We used little artillery preparation, but put down heavy barrages ahead of our men.

This fire, while doing considerable damage to the Germans' communications, did not succeed in cutting the wire, because the thick woods deflected the shells to a great extent. The heavy wire entanglements had to be cut by the advancing infantry. Tanks, of course, could not be used to attack the forest.

Our attack was aided by a heavy mist, which enabled us to get upon the German positions before being seen. This precipitated a large amount of hand-to-hand fighting. The mist later developed into a cold rain, which still continues.

It is impossible to exaggerate the difficulties of the task of taking the Argonne Forest, so long regarded as impregnable. The Germans have thousands of steel and concrete positions bristling with machine guns, innumerable trenches running in all directions through the jungles, and many funnel-shaped traps commanded by nests of machine guns. They are fighting with desperation against the Americans, who are determined to wrest their highly prized stronghold from them.

Today's victory gives us an immediate advantage in the possession of the commanding heights west of the Aire Valley and aids observation, which is most difficult in the tangle of woods and jungle. Most of the hills are tortured bare of all trees and vegetation, but in the ravines and valleys thick woods give excellent shelter to friend and enemy.

### APPROACHING GRAND PRE

Oct. 9.—The battle today has given us all of the Argonne Forest except the imperilled salient, which is still in German hands.

We have taken the important heights just south of the village of Marcq, and from thence the line runs tonight westward to where our forces join the French at Lancon. Today the French advancing toward Grand Pré have taken Lancon and Grand Ham and have reached Senue.

Attacking against divisions freshly thrown in, the Americans pushed through the Kriemhilde line today between Cunel and Romagne, after bitter fighting, in which artillery played an important part. East of the Meuse we held the positions won yesterday, despite violent attacks by the Germans this morning, and we have advanced our line to Sivry and into Chaune Wood. Two thousand prisoners were taken today. In the Argonne we advanced upward from the north end of Apremont Wood and westward from a line before Cornay.

The machine-gun fighting was very heavy. Our troops went forward this morning in a heavy fog, which proved a big help. The reports show we are chewing bit by bit the German position in the northern end of the Argonne Forest. The fighting is as bloody and difficult as any the war has seen. It should put an end to the present talk about German morale. Their machine gunners fight generally until they are killed and effect a formidable barrier to any advance. The nature of the terrain gives excellent positions for machine gun defense.

Despite the protection of the ravines, hills, and woods being to their advantage, the German losses have in the two days in the Argonne been terrific. The losses in dead are particularly high, and the situation makes it difficult for the Germans to get out their wounded.

Surrounded in a fastness of the Argonne Forest three days, a target all the while for German artillery and machine guns, without food for the last thirty-six hours, a battalion of American soldiers has been rescued in an attack led by Lieut. Col. Gene Houghton of Racine.

The story of these men is one of the classics of the war. On Friday night, (Sept. 27,) participating in an attack on German positions deep in the forest, they had to advance in single file. Pushing on against stern opposition they gained their objectives to find at dawn Saturday Germans not only in front of them but behind and on both sides.

Their position was three kilometers northeast of Binarville, on the western edge of the Argonne Forest. The Germans had found an opening on their left and, using a trench, filtered in fully a thousand men behind our battalion out there. In trenches on both sides the enemy installed many machine guns and went about corraling what they regarded as their sure prey.

On Saturday morning other Americans discovered the plight of their comrades, who were from seven companies and numbered 463 men. The French on our left attacked at the same time in an effort to release the Americans. The attack failed, but as it developed probably saved the Americans because it divided the German attack on them from the south.

On Sunday three more attempts were made to reach them, and all failed. On that day fourteen airplane missions were undertaken in their behalf, dropping two tons of food and considerable ammunition for the sequestrated men. Pigeons were also dropped by parachute, so that messages could be sent back. Our aviators could not see anything of the missing men.

Knowing Monday morning that the food of the soldiers was about gone, the Americans set about a fresh attempt to rescue them. Our attack on the forest from the east helped in a determined effort made from the south and late that night the troops broke through and reached the exhausted but still determined band. More than three-fourths of them were safe.

When the men had been for a long time without food and almost wholly without ammunition, and when many were weak from exhaustion, but not one despairing, an American who had been taken prisoner by the Germans suddenly appeared at the little camp surrounded in the valley.

The man had been sent blindfolded from the German headquarters with a typewritten note to Major Whittlesey, reading:

"Americans, you are surrounded on all sides. Surrender in the name of humanity. You will be well treated."

Major Whittlesey did not hesitate a fraction of a second.

"Go to hell!" he shouted. Then he read the note to those around him, and his men, despite their weariness and hunger, and in imminent danger every moment, cheered so loudly that the Germans heard them from their observation posts. Major Whittlesey is a nephew of Charles W. Whittlesey, a lawyer, of New York City.

## ARGONNE FOREST CLEARED

In the capture of nearly all of the Argonne Forest, the American troops have effected one of the notable achievements of the world war. It is by far the biggest thing our troops have yet done. In a word, they have taken what was regarded so long as an impregnable position and one for the possession of which hundreds of thousands of men have died in the last four years and two months.

The Argonne Forest is about fifty kilometers long, extending from Grand Pré on the north to Thiaucourt on the south. Before our attack on Sept. 26 the line crossed the forest about twenty kilometers south of Grand Pré through Chatade Wood. The Americans had been told that the Argonne Forest could not be taken frontally, and so, when our drive started, the plan was to advance up the Aire Valley on the east and up the Aisne Valley on the west of the forest, pinching it out.

The story of how they did it is one of the most stirring of the war. Across the forest, which hides a series of hills and ravines and dense jungles, ran the famed Hindenburg line, four kilometers deep, with trenches by the hundreds and with lines of wire at short intervals for a

depth of two and a half miles. The rocks and trees and holes formed shelters for thousands of machine guns. The road had been mined or blown up. Artillery could not be used with effect. The Germans were protected by uncounted pillboxes, dugouts, and ready-made positions, running always to the southern side of the crests of the hills, and on these hills the most of our advance was made. The Germans had every crosstrail and road under the exact range of guns further back. It was a veritable hell through which the boys from New York were ordered to go, and they went.

It was a case of cutting a path through the wire and filtering through single file. This gave the Germans a chance which they took advantage of a number of times to get around behind the Americans and engage in bitter hand-to-hand fighting. On and on our boys worked their way through Gruerie Wood and into Apremont Wood. This progress was made during the first two days. For eight days our progress was piecemeal until Sunday, ten days after we had started, our real success began as the boche gave way before our never-ceasing pressure. It is the biggest victory that General Pershing has yet won.

## IMPORTANCE OF RESULTS

*The Americans pressed forward on Oct. 11 and 12, gaining important new ground beyond the Argonne Forest. On the 13th, 14th, and 15th they drove their wedge deeper into the Kriemhilde line, taking important positions beyond. Mr. James wrote:*

Oct. 15.—There are graveyards everywhere, German graveyards from which one might imagine the countless thousands whom Prussian militarism has sent to their graves are watching silently the loss of what they died to gain.

A tribute should be paid to the hardihood of the American boys fighting this battle, one of the bitterest of the war. Most of them never lived, much less spent days and nights outdoors, in such climate, for which there is no counterpart in America. Rain and rain, nothing but rain, day after day, penetrating cold all the time, and no shelter except holes in the ground and pup tents.

But in the rain and cold with fires taboo the American spirit is holding fast and the doughboys are figuring that they can stand it, because the boche has to. To break up the Kriemhilde Stellung is the job given the Americans to do and they are going to do it.

How great is the importance attached by the Germans to holding back the Americans is shown in a recent order of General von der Marwitz, Commander in Chief of the Fifth Army, which has reached American intelligence officers. The order reads:

> It is on the unconquerable resistance of the Verdun front that depends the fate of a great part of the western front, perhaps even of our nation. The Fatherland must rest assured that every commander and every man realizes the greatness of his mission and that he will do his duty to the very end. If they do this, the enemy's attack will, as heretofore, break against our firm will to hold.

Oct. 16.—Grand Pré was captured to-day by the American troops. East of this not inconsiderable town we drove our wedge deeper across the Aire River into the edge of the Bois des Loges, reaching a line two miles north of Chevieres. Meanwhile the French on the left pushed their line forward west of Grand Pré.

Grand Pré is an important defense point before the Kriemhilde line, and was held by the Germans against repeated attacks by the Americans for three days. It is a junction point for railways that feed the enemy. The Germans continue a determined effort to hold back the Americans, and are succeeding in making the advance painful and slow.

When we attacked on Sept. 26 between the Aisne and the Meuse, the Germans had four divisions in line on this battle-front. Since then they have had thirteen whole divisions and the equipment of two more divisions, making a total of fifteen extra divisions, of which eight were fresh and two were rushed from the Champagne front, despite important progress being made there by the French Fourth Army. The reinforcement has been four divisions to each division in the line when our drive began.

# The Taking of St. Mihiel Salient
## Immensity of the Operation

*A correspondent of The Chicago Tribune summarized the preparations of the First American Army for the capture of the St. Mihiel salient and the results obtained as follows:*

IN order to take 152 square miles of territory and seventy-two villages, captured in the crushing of the St. Mihiel salient, the American Army first had to evolve preparations on colossal lines, because the actual action brought into the plan hundreds of elements, all of which had to co-ordinate smoothly. The figures given are estimates made by officers directly in touch with the operations.

First, we issued 100,000 detail maps covering in minutest detail the character of the terrain of the St. Mihiel salient, including natural defenses, and telling how each was manned and by what enemy units. These maps were corrected in some instances as late as the day before the battle opened, and were sup-plemented by 40,000 photographs. These were for the guidance of the artillery and infantry, and were scattered among the officers of the whole army a few hours before the zero hour.

Five thousand miles of wire was laid in the St. Mihiel salient and on its borders before the attack, and immediately after the Americans advanced 6,000 telephone instruments were connected with these wires throughout the battle zone.

When the battle opened on the morning of Sept. 12, 1918, trucks started northward at a speed of seven miles an hour, unreeling wires across No Man's Land until they reached points where the reels had to be carried by Signal Corps men afoot.

Such work made it possible for American officers whose troops had flanked the foe's trenches to telephone back, informing the artillery of the exact location of the enemy trenches and in a few minutes bringing a deluge of metal on the boche.

Telephone squads carried these lines up to the fighting front on Thursday morning and soon in the triangular battle ground there was a telephone system in operation that would have been adequate to handle the telephone business of a city of 100,000, and it was going at top efficiency. The branch lines were connected with the main axis, which was established through the middle of the salient. Ten thousand men were busily engaged in operating the system. Many of the phone exchanges were on wheels. Several thousand carrier pigeons supplemented the Signal Corps.

We captured a tremendous quantity of German signal supplies, 500 miles of German wire, many switchboards, one radio truck, and numerous batteries.

In the midst of the battle other Signal Corps men took more than 10,000 feet of movie film depicting war scenes and many thousands of photographs.

Extensive hospital facilities were arranged, including thirty-five hospital trains, 16,000 beds in the advanced areas, and 55,000 others further back. Happily, less than 10 per cent. of the hospital facilities were needed, and therefore our surgeons and nurses were enabled to give the finest care to our wounded and sick, and every attention to the German wounded.

In the course of the operation our guns fired approximately 1,500,000 shells. Forty-eight hundred trucks carried men and supplies into the lines. They were assisted by miles of American railroads of standard and narrow gauge, and the cars were pulled by engines marked " U. S. A."

In addition to restoring this big territory to France with an unprecedentedly small force the Americans liberated two railroads and a canal from the menace of the boche artillery. We took 15,188 prisoners and the following spoils: One hundred and eleven guns, including twenty-five of large calibre and seventy-eight Austrian 77s; forty-two trench mortars, two hundred machine guns, thirteen trucks, including an ambulance; thirty box cars, four locomotives, five caissons, forty wagons, and thirty-six narrow-gauge cars.

The quantity of captured munitions is still unestimated, but one spot alone yielded 4,000 shells for 77s and 350,000 rounds of rifle cartridges. Twelve thousand hand grenades were found in one place. Four ammunition dumps were taken. Large quantities of food, clothing, trinkets and many documents bring up a total which makes our first venture as an individual unit assume characteristic American proportions.

## Devastation of Evacuated Regions

The Germans continued to ruin and devastate all towns evacuated up to the middle of October, when President Wilson's mention of such acts as obstacles to peace, coupled with the French Chamber's formal notification that Germany would have to pay for the restoration of all cities thus wanontly burned, was followed by a sudden change of policy. The German newspapers on the evening of Oct. 17 published an official notification that the German Army command had " brought military measures into accord with the steps taken for the conclusion of peace," and that the German armies had received orders to cease all devastation " unless absolutely forced to follow this course by the military situation for defensive reasons." Accordingly, when Lille, Roubaix, Tournai, and other cities in France and Belgium were evacuated they were spared.

But before this change occurred Cambrai, Douai, Laon, Lens, and other cities were looted and burned. Noyon was wantonly destroyed with explosives fired by electric devices after its evacuation. The same thing was repeated on a scale a hundredfold greater in the Aisne region.

The pillage of Laon was progressive. It began with the arrival of the first troops, who looted every house and building that was not inhabited at the time. Later on, the pillage extended to houses that were inhabited. It reached its height on the departure of the general staff of the German Army commanded by General von Heeringen. With the staff disappeared all the furniture of the City Hall. The furniture of private houses was " requisitioned " sometimes, and sometimes simply taken. Five million eight hundred thousand francs in cash (about $1,160,000) was the sum exacted from the town, part of it under the guise of a war contribution and part as fines for different so-called infractions of the commandant's rules.

Of the 10,000 houses which constituted the garden city of Lens, formerly a workingman's paradise, not one remains standing. Every house has been deliberately razed and the gardens which surrounded most of them have been ruined for a long time to come. The mines in every case have been flooded. The pumping alone will require nearly two years. At the great Courrieres mines, where one or two pits are already in course of restoration, every scrap of the surface organization, which was reputed the best in France, has been destroyed systematically to the last limits.

Measures were taken two or three years ago to begin the work of restoration immediately after the Germans were driven out. Even in view of this foresight, however, it is not believed that coal production can be resumed in the Lens mine field before eighteen months or two years, and even then only a very small proportion of the former output will be obtainable. Experts report that at least five years will be required before the pits can be brought back to their normal output.

The mines in the Lens and Douai districts before the war produced 12,000,000 tons of coal a year. All these mines were kept working during the whole period the Germans occupied the localities concerned, and an enormous quantity of coal was extracted by them. Step by step as the Allies advanced, however, the mines were systematically ruined. In order to prevent use being made of the mines which the Allies wrenched from the enemy the Germans made each mine an enormous tank into which all the surface water overhead was carefully directed. The work of rehabilitating the French mines has been taken in hand by a specially created Government department.

## The Part the Pigeons Played

ONE of the most important factors of the defense in the Eastern Champagne on July 15, 1918, was the smooth working of the Information Service under the German bombardment. Each pillbox fort in the covering zone was supplied with a crate of carrier pigeons, and the birds carried back news of every movement of the enemy and every phase of the fight to the command posts. One officer commander, with experience of intelligence work, interrogated German prisoners who were brought into his pillbox as they arrived, and sent back the information derived from the bewildered Germans by pigeon post almost as quickly as it could have been telegraphed.

In another case the garrison of a pillbox sent back by pigeon a request that artillery should immediately open on the ground around their stronghold, taking no thought for their own safety, as the Germans were about to surround them.

# Pushing War Activities at Home

## New Draft Involving Nearly 13,000,000 Men Doubles the Size of the United States Army

[PERIOD OF SEPT. 18 TO OCT. 18, 1918]

PURSUANT to the United States Government's plan to have approximately 5,000,000 men under arms before the Summer of 1919, the third draft registration, embracing all male citizens between the ages of 18 and 45, inclusive, took place throughout the country on Sept. 12, 1918, as recorded in detail in the preceding issue of CURRENT HISTORY. Provost Marshal General Crowder had estimated that about 12,-780,000 should be the number of new registrants if all the men between 18 and 21 years and 32 and 45 years, inclusive, responded to the call under the Selective Service act. The actual total, as announced a month later, was 12,966,594, or more than 186,000 in excess of the estimate. With the men previously registered under the first and second drafts this made a grand total of 23,456,021 registered since the country entered the war.

Youths who had not yet completed their nineteenth year were placed in a separate group to be called last into service, and questionnaires were promptly dispatched to youths of 19 and 20, and to men of 32 to 36, inclusive, preparatory to sending them to cantonments for training as soon as possible after the draft.

On Sept. 30 the drawing to decide the order in which the registrants should be called into service took place at Washington in the same room of the Senate Office Building where the first draft had been held. President Wilson, blindfolded with a cloth taken from the covering of one of the chairs used at the signing of the Declaration of Independence, drew the first number amid cheers from the onlookers. The capsule that he drew bore the number 322, which meant that each man who happened to have this number opposite his name in the local registration lists throughout

the country would be the first to be called to the colors there in his class.

The drawing of the rest of the 17,000 key numbers went on continuously for the next twenty hours, when Provost Marshal General Crowder took the last

PRESIDENT WILSON, BLINDFOLDED, ABOUT TO DRAW THE FIRST CAPSULE FROM THE JAR THAT DETERMINED THE FORTUNES OF 13,000,000 MEN.

capsule from the big bowl. Thus ended the drafting of a grand total of more than 23,000,000 potential soldiers, including the 9,000,000 or more in the first draft, July 20, 1917, and the 1,000,000 youths in the second draft who had reached the age of 21 by June 5, 1918.

The third draft differed from its predecessors in that it allowed enlarged opportunities for exemption. Men under the earlier drafts had to offer their own claims for exemption. At the time of the third draft, in view of the increasing labor shortage, the Government invited employers to file claims in behalf of employes engaged in essential industries, with the assurance that such claims would be seriously considered, even though the registrant himself might decline to claim exemption. It was announced that each of the 156 district draft boards would have the assistance of a Board of Industrial Advisers in deciding questions of exemption; the latter board was to consist of three members, one appointed by the Department of Labor, one by the Department of Agriculture, the third by the District Board itself. In large districts, such as New York and Chicago, the number of advisers would be increased.

The "master list" of 17,000 draft numbers, after being carefully rechecked by the military authorities at Washington, was printed in a 68-page pamphlet and mailed on Oct. 5 to the more than 4,500 local exemption boards in the United States. With the lists went instructions as to the method to be used in classifying registrants, so that no difficulty should be encountered in fixing the order in which men of Class 1—aged 19 to 36 years, inclusive—were to be called to the training camps. Many men had already presented themselves for examination, waiving exemption, and preparations were well under way to have the camps partly filled by the end of October.

### SPANISH INFLUENZA

During September and October, however, an epidemic of the disease known as Spanish influenza gained increasing headway throughout the country, especially in the training camps, where its frequent complication with pneumonia caused many fatalities. On Oct. 11, for instance, the influenza cases reported to the Surgeon General numbered 12,024, pneumonia cases 2,824, and deaths 892. The figures each day for several weeks were similarly large. At the date named the total number of influenza cases at camps since the beginning of the epidemic had reached 223,000; pneumonia cases, 27,907, and deaths, 8,335. By Oct. 17 the deaths in army and navy camps had exceeded 11,000.

In view of these facts General Crowder canceled the calls for the entrainment between Oct. 7 and 11 of 142,000 men who had been inducted into service under previous drafts, while the calling of the men of the new draft to the cantonments was temporarily suspended. Meanwhile, the epidemic swept the whole country, causing the closing of schools, churches, theatres, and seriously handicapping business in all the larger cities. Illinois had 300,000 cases on Oct. 16, Pennsylvania 300,000, Virginia 200,000, and other States reported similar figures. The War Department announced, however, that there would be no pause in the transportation of troops overseas.

### COST OF ENLARGED ARMY

A bill officially designated as "the first Appropriation bill for the fiscal year ending June 1, 1919," was introduced in the House of Representatives on Oct. 16. It carried a total of cash and authorizations of $6,645,755,666, of which $6,152,062,704 was for the army, $107,217,778 for the navy, and $86,-475,183 for civil service, including $70,-000,000 to pay dependents of soldiers. The total of the estimates was $8,886,-131,651. This amount was sought in addition to $17,500,000,000 provided by the annual Army bill and the Fortifications bill. It will bring the total of appropriations and authorizations for the year up to $36,000,000,000.

The following statement was made by General March, Chief of Staff, concerning the forces for whose support, equipment, and transportation these great sums are designed:

We propose to have 4,850,000 men, involving eighty divisions in France and eighteen divisions at home. The estimated status of the army on Sept. 17 shows that there are in the United States 1,422,768 men; there are in France, or on the high seas, en route to France, 1,708,-437 men; there are in Siberia, our island possessions, and elsewhere, including the Panama garrison and Alaska garrison, 69,958 men. This gives us for the entire American Army, as well as it can be estimated today, 3,201,162 men. That does not include marines, but the number of marines turned over to the army in France or embarked for there is 19,821.

In drawing up the military program, we have determined, first, the maximum number of troops we propose to use abroad, and then the number of troops necessary to hold in the United States to feed into those divisions. We have determined that number abroad at eighty divisions.

The scheme that has been worked out for the whole fiscal year of the number of divisions per month that will have to be obtained in order to keep the machine going corresponds quite closely to the number of troops that we are sending abroad each month. For instance, in July we shipped six divisions abroad. As those six divisions went, carrying 300,000 men, we got from General Crowder 300,000 more men to take their places. In August the same thing happened.

General March announced on Oct. 11 that 1,900,000 American troops had been transported to Europe, and on Oct. 19 he told a Senate committee that the number sent abroad had passed the 2,000,000 mark.

## INTERESTING DETAILS

General Crowder stated on Oct. 16 that of the 2,750,000 men who would have to be called to maintain the program of ninety-eight divisions, 50 per cent. would come from the 19 to 36 class, leaving 1,350,000 to be supplied by the 37 to 45 and 18 to 19 classes. The immensity of the military program is indicated in detached items, such as General Crowder's announcement that motor cycles with side cars were to be constructed to carry 233,000 fighting men; that the army aviation program contemplated training 30,000 aviators, of whom 8,390 were already in France and 6,210 in this country. It was stated that there would be a total of 450 flying squadrons, that 329 balloons had been produced to date, that thirty-nine balloon companies were already organized, and that there were enough balloons ready to equip 162 companies.

An indication of the scope of the supply problem is seen in the fact that at one French port 147 warehouses have been built, each 500 feet in length. At this place the working force includes 13,000 engineer troops, 7,000 stevedores, 8,000 civilian laborers, 1,000 German prisoners and 1,000 infantry, in all 30,-000 men carrying on American activities at this one port. The five main French ports have a capacity for unloading 30,-000 tons of army goods every day, or an average of about thirty pounds per man for every American soldier in France.

Food Administrator Hoover stated, Sept. 21, that in the year ending July 1, 1919, it would be necessary to ship abroad for the American Army and the allied and neutral nations 17,550,000 tons of meats, fats, breadstuffs, sugar and feed grains. This total, he said, represented 5,730,000 tons more than were shipped in the year ended July 1, 1918, and would require continued self-denial on the part of the American people.

## FOURTH LIBERTY LOAN

The Fourth Liberty Loan campaign—for the floating of $6,000,000,000 in war bonds bearing 4¼ per cent. interest—began Sept. 28 and ended Oct. 19. The loan was the largest in history; the subscriptions fell somewhat below the estimated rate of progress during the earlier weeks of the campaign, but a whirlwind effort at the end brought the total to a figure well above the desired $6,000,-000,000.

The campaign was marked by interesting incidents in every city. Some of those in New York may be recorded as typical. President Wilson visited New York on "Liberty Day," Oct. 12, and marched at the head of a great parade. Fifth Avenue was decorated with flags to an extent unprecedented and was temporarily rechristened the "Avenue of the Allies," under which name it gave the title to a memorable poem by Alfred Noyes.

Later President Wilson autographed the subscriptions made at a New York theatre, where $750,000 was raised. Miss Geraldine Farrar, an opera star, sang $2,000,000 out of the pockets of those present at a dinner. Mr. Schwab at another dinner raised $52,000,000. A young girl climbed a ladder of fifty rungs in Wall Street, each rung counting for a ubscription for a $50 bond. A large sum was realized at a young folks' gathering, where the star part was played by a small dog, who snarled violently at every mention of the Kaiser. Douglas Fairbanks flew from Washington to New York in a Curtiss biplane, with a 16-cent stamp on a tag in his buttonhole to indicate that he was third class mail matter, and sold $2,000,000 in bonds at the journey's end. The five New York Borough

Presidents assembled on Oct. 18 at the Altar of Liberty in Madison Square to await the coming of homing pigeons, the order of whose finish was to decide the way in which the officials should subscribe $260,000 to the loan.

## United States the Greatest Insurance Company

The War Risk Insurance Bureau is now carrying a total of soldiers' insurance greater than the combined risks of the twenty largest insurance companies in the world. By Sept. 1, 1918, the insurance on the lives of soldiers and sailors issued by the Government amounted to twenty billions of dollars. This was more than one-half the total of all other insurance on lives in the United States.

The limit of insurance that the men are permitted to take is $10,000. At the outset, the Government estimated that not more than half the men entitled to it would take out insurance. It was thought also that the policies would not average more than $2,000 each. Both of these forecasts were incorrect; 80 per cent. have taken out policies, and the average policy is for $8,200.

The enlisted man with family is required to allot one-half his pay, or $15 per month, to his family. The Government adds $15 per month to this for the wife and $7.50 for each child up to a total of $50 per month. At the time of the summary on which these statements are based 780,000 checks were being sent out monthly. In June disbursements amounted to $21,000,000.

The policy's value is based on the American Experience Tables of Mortality at 3½ per cent. interest, without expense loading, the Government paying the expenses. The $10,000 policy entitles the beneficiary to $57.50 per month for twenty years; a total of $13,800.

It is planned to arrange for commutation of these monthly payments and the discharge, in whole or in part, by a lump payment whose present value will equal that of the twenty years of monthly payments.

The law creating the War Risk Bureau was passed in October, 1917. The rate established makes the insurance of the soldier or sailor at 30 years of age about $8 per annum per $1,000. The rate, under the same conditions, that was fixed on by the insurance companies when they were negotiating with the Government was $37.50. In the Government view this was far too high, and was based on an excessive estimate of deaths that would occur in the service. Hence the decision of the Government to undertake the work itself.

One advantage expected to result from national insurance is a reduction in pensions to be paid after the war. The high-water mark in civil war pensions was reached forty years after the end of the war. It is proposed under the present plan to make the insurance indemnities take the place of pensions, with the advantage over the latter of giving the beneficiary the bulk of his money at the start, when he presumably needs it most. This is not to say that a pension plan in some form may not be later established. On that point the Government has not pronounced a decision.

# Prince Maximilian's Peace Drive

## Text of the New German Chancellor's Correspondence With President Wilson

PRESIDENT WILSON'S Metropolitan Opera House speech in New York on Sept. 27, 1918, which will be found in full on Pages 251-254 of this magazine, became the basis of a new attempt on the part of the Central Powers to secure a negotiated peace. Continued German reverses on the western front and the collapse of Bulgaria in the Balkans had greatly increased the desire of the Kaiser to conclude some kind of peace before meeting irretrievable disaster in France and Belgium. Information reaching Washington through diplomatic channels indicated that Field Marshal von Hindenburg himself, confronted with lack of ammunition as well as of man power, was the chief force behind the demand for a new Chancellor and a new peace drive, despite the failure of the one attempted a month before through Austria-Hungary.

Prince Maximilian of Baden succeeded Count von Hertling as Imperial Chancellor on Sept. 30, and proceeded at once, in conjunction with Austria-Hungary and Turkey, to launch the new movement for peace negotiations. He was ready to make greater concessions than Germany had ever offered before. On the night of Oct. 4-5 he sent to President Wilson, through the Swiss Government, the following note:

The German Government requests the President of the United States to take in hand the restoration of peace, acquaint all the belligerent States with this request, and invite them to send plenipotentiaries for the purpose of opening negotiations.

It accepts the program set forth by the President of the United States in his message to Congress on Jan. 8, and in his later pronouncements, especially his speech of Sept. 27, as a basis for peace negotiations.

With a view to avoiding further bloodshed, the German Government requests the immediate conclusion of an armistice on land and water and in the air.

## TEXT OF REICHSTAG SPEECH

The foregoing note was followed on Oct. 5 with an important speech before the German Reichstag, in which the new Chancellor outlined his peace policy. The text of this address, as cabled by The Associated Press, is as follows:

In accordance with the Imperial decree of Sept. 30, the German Empire has undergone a basic alteration of its political leadership. As successor to Count George F. von Hertling, whose services in behalf of the Fatherland deserve the highest acknowledgment, I have been summoned by the Emperor to lead the new Government. In accordance with the Governmental method now introduced, I submit to the Reichstag, publicly and without delay, the principles upon which I propose to conduct the grave responsibilities of the office.

These principles were firmly established by the agreement of the Federated Governments and the leaders of the majority parties in this honorable House before I decided to assume the duties of Chancellor. They contain, therefore, not only my own confession of political faith, but that of an overwhelming portion of the German peoples' representatives—that is, of the German Nation—which has constituted the Reichstag on the basis of a general, equal, and secret franchise, and according to their will. Only the fact that I know the conviction and will of the majority of the people are back of me has given me strength to take upon myself conduct of the empire's affairs in this hard and earnest time in which we are living.

One man's shoulders would be too weak to carry alone the tremendous responsibility which falls upon the Government at present. Only if the people take active part, in the broadest sense of the word, in deciding their destinies; in other words, if responsibility also extends to the majority of their freely elected political leaders, can the leading statesman confidently assume his part of the responsibility in the service of folk and Fatherland.

My resolve to do this has been especially lightened for me by the fact that prominent leaders of the laboring class have found a way in the new Government to the highest offices of the empire. I see therein a sure guarantee that the new Government will be supported by the firm confidence of the broad masses of the people, without whose true support the whole undertaking would be condemned to failure in advance. Hence, what I say today is not only in my own name and those of my official helpers, but in the name of the German people.

## PROGRAM OF NEW GOVERNMENT

The program of the majority parties, upon which I take my stand, contains, first, an acceptance of the answer of the former Imperial Government to Pope Benedict's note of Aug. 1, 1916, and an unconditional acceptance of the Reichstag resolution of July 19, the same year. It further declares willingness to join a general league of nations based on the foundation of equal rights for all, both strong and weak.

It considers the solution of the Belgian question to lie in the complete rehabilitation (wiederherstellung) of Belgium, particularly of its independence and territorial integrity. An effort shall also be made to reach an understanding on the question of indemnity.

The program will not permit the peace treaties hitherto concluded to be a hindrance to the conclusion of a general peace.

Its particular aim is that popular representative bodies shall be formed immediately on a broad basis in the Baltic provinces, in Lithuania, and Poland. We will promote the realization of necessary preliminary conditions therefor without delay by the introduction of civilian rule. All these lands shall regulate their Constitutions and their relations with neighboring peoples without external interference.

In the matter of international policies I have taken a clear stand through the manner in which the formation of the Government was brought about. Upon my motion, leaders of the majority parties were summoned for direct advice. It was my conviction, gentlemen, that unity of imperial leadership should be assured, but not through mere schismatic party allegiance by the different members of the Government. I considered almost still more important the unity of ideas. I proceeded from this viewpoint, and have, in making my selections, laid greatest weight on the fact that the members of the new Imperial Government stand on a basis of a just peace of justice, regardless of the war situation, and that they have openly declared this to be their standpoint at the time when we stood at the height of our military successes.

I am convinced that the manner in which imperial leadership is now constituted, with the co-operation of the Reichstag, is not something ephemeral, and that when peace comes a Government cannot again be formed which does not find support in the Reichstag and does not draw its leaders therefrom.

The war has conducted us beyond the old multifarious and disrupted party life, which made it so difficult to put into execution a uniform and decisive political wish. The formation of a majority means the formation of a political will, and an indisputable result of the war has been that in Germany, for the first time, great parties have joined together in a firm, harmonious program and have thus come into position to determine for themselves the fate of the people.

## ALTERATION OF CONSTITUTION

This thought will never die. This development will never be retracted, and I trust, so long as Germany's fate is ringed about by dangers, those sections of the people outside the majority parties and whose representatives do not belong to the Government will put aside all that separates us and will give the Fatherland what is the Fatherland's.

This development necessitates an alteration of our Constitution's provisions along the lines of the imperial decree of Sept. 30, which shall make it possible that these members of the Reichstag who entered the Government will retain their seats in the Reichstag. A bill to this end has been submitted to the Federal States and will immediately be made the subject of their consideration and decision.

Gentlemen, let us remember the words spoken by the Emperor on Aug. 4, 1914, which I permitted myself to paraphrase last December at Karlsruhe: "There are, in fact, parties, but they are all German parties."

Political developments in Prussia, the principal German Federal State, must proceed in the spirit of these words of the Emperor, and the message of the King of Prussia promising the democratic franchise must be fulfilled quickly and completely. I do not doubt, also, that those Federal States which still lag behind in the development of their constitutional conditions will resolutely follow Prussia's example.

For the present, as the example of all belligerent States demonstrates, the extraordinary powers which a condition of siege compels cannot be dispensed with, but close relations between the military and civilian authorities must be established which will make it possible that in all not purely military questions, and hence especially as to censorship and right of assemblage, the attitude of the civilian executive authorities shall make itself heard and that final decision shall be placed under the Chancellor's responsibility.

To this end, the order of the Emperor will be sent to the military commanders. With Sept. 30, the day of the decree, began a new epoch in Germany's internal history. The internal policy whose basic principles are therein laid down is of deciding importance on the question of peace or war.

The striking force which the Government has in its strivings for peace depends on whether it has behind it the united, firm, and unshakable will of the people. Only when our enemies feel that the German people stand united back of their chosen leaders—then only can words become deeds.

## PROTECTION OF LABOR

At the peace negotiations the German Government will use its efforts to the end that the treaties shall contain provisions concerning the protection of labor and insurance of laborers, which provisions shall oblige the treaty-making States to institute in their respective lands within a prescribed time a minimum of similar, or at least equally, efficient institutions for the security of life and health, as for the care of laborers in case of illness, accident, or invalidism.

Of direct importance are the conclusions which the Government in the brief span of its existence has been able to draw from the situation in which it finds itself and to apply practical'y to the situation. More than four years of bloodiest struggle against a world of numerically superior enemies are behind us, years full of the hardest battles and most painful sacrifices. Nevertheless, we are of strong heart and full of confident faith in our strength, resolved to bear still heavier sacrifices for our honor and freedom and for the happiness of our posterity, if it cannot be otherwise.

We remember with deep and warm gratitude our brave troops, who, under splendid leadership, have accomplished almost superhuman deeds throughout the whole war and whose past deeds are a sure guarantee that the fate of us all will also in future be in good and dependable hands in their keeping. For months a continuous, terrible, and murderous battle has been raging in the west. Thanks to the incomparable heroism of our army, which will live as an immortal, glorious page in the history of the German people for all times, the front is unbroken.

This proud consciousness permits us to look to the future with confidence. But, just because we are inspired by this feeling and the conviction that it is also our duty to make certain that the bloody struggle be not protracted for a single day beyond the moment when the close of the war seems possible to us which does not affect our honor, I have, therefore, not waited until today to take a step to further the idea of peace.

Supported by the consent of all duly authorized persons in the empire, and by consent of all our allies acting in concert with us, I sent on the night of Oct. 4-5, through the mediation of Switzerland, a note to the President of the United States, in which I requested him to take up the bringing about of peace and to communicate to this end with all the belligerent States.

## NEW GOVERNMENT'S VIEWS

The note will reach Washington today or tomorrow. It is directed to the President of the United States because he, in his message to Congress Jan. 8, 1918, and in his later proclamations, particularly in his New York speech of Sept. 27, proposed a program for a general peace which we can accept as a basis for negotiations.

I have taken this step not only for the salvation of Germany and its allies, but of all humanity, which has been suffering for years through the war.

I have taken it also because I believe the thoughts regarding the future well-being of the nation which were proclaimed by Mr. Wilson are in accord with the general ideas cherished by the new German Government and with it the overwhelming majority of our people.

So far as I am personally concerned, in earlier speeches to other assemblages, my hearers will testify that the conception which I hold of a future peace has undergone no change since I was intrusted with the leadership of the empire's affairs.

I see, hence, no distinction whatever between the national and international mandates of duty in respect of peace. For me the deciding factor is solely that all participants shall with equal honesty acknowledge these mandates as binding and respect them, as is the case with me and with the other members of our new Government. And so, with an inner peace, which my clear conscience as a man and as a servant of the people gives me, and which rests at the same time upon firm faith in this great and true people, this people capable of every devotion, and upon their glorious armed power, I await the outcome of the first action which I have taken as the leading statesman of the empire.

Whatever this outcome may be, I know it will find Germany firmly resolved and united either for an upright peace which rejects every selfish violation of the rights of others or for a closing of the struggle for life and death to which our people would be forced without our own fault if the answer to our note of the powers opposed to us should be dictated by a will to destroy us.

I do not despair over the thought that this second alternative may come. I know the greatness of the mighty powers yet possessed by our people, and I know that the incontrovertible conviction that they were only fighting for our life as a nation would double these powers.

I hope, however, for the sake of all mankind that the President of the United States will receive our offer as we mean it. Then the door would be opened to a speedy, honorable peace of justice and reconciliation for us, as well as for our opponents.

On the same day Prince Maximilian sent a telegram to Baron Burian, Austro-Hungarian Foreign Minister, saying: "The glorious deeds of our armies, and the determination of our peoples to defend themselves in loyal co-operation with their Governments, will, with God's help, lead us to an honorable peace." Baron Burian replied that all his thoughts and efforts were "in loyal co-operation with the Imperial German Government, directed toward bringing the blessing of an honorable peace as soon as possible to our admirable armies and peoples."

## AUSTRIA'S EXPLANATION

An elucidation of the peace efforts of the Central Powers, intended for the people of Austria-Hungary, appeared in the Vienna newspapers of Oct. 6, with the explanation that the article emanated from "well-informed circles." Its evidently official origin and its rapid sketch of past peace efforts entitle it to a place in the record of the subject. It reads as follows:

It is first to be emphasized that this step by Austria-Hungary, Turkey, and Germany is not to be regarded as a decision taken suddenly under the stress of military events. It constitutes rather, in the history of our peace policy, the last link in the chain of logical and continual evolution, regard being paid at the same time to the latest internal political developments in Germany.

As is known, the point of departure of our peace policy was Baron Burian's note of December, 1916. The step then taken was of a very vague character. The conditions were not described, but only indicated in broad outlines.

In the course of the development the conditions have become crystallized. During February, March, and April expressions regarding a general and just peace without annexations or compensations came into currency.

Subsequently the idea of establishing an international court of arbitration and a reduction of armament was discussed, and, further, the principle of freedom of the seas was proclaimed, and, finally, the principle was set forth that economic wars and economic oppression after the war must be prevented. Out of these guiding principles has arisen the present program.

All these points, it will be recalled, were accepted by Count Czernin, (former Austrian Foreign Minister,) in speeches and interviews, as a suitable basis for peace negotiations, and finally received the approval also of the German Reichstag, so that uniformity in the conception of the allies (Teutonic) thereby found expression.

Then followed the peace note of Pope Benedict, whose proposals and fundamental ideas were accepted by us as forming an acceptable basis. Only President Wilson, in his note of Jan. 8, 1918, in his fourteen points made proposals and proclaimed principles which substantially accorded with the program of the Central Powers.

Count Czernin and Count von Hertling described President Wilson's proposals, apart from a reserve regarding certain points, as a suitable basis for peace. The Austro-Hungarian delegations and the German Reichstag have described their attitude toward these proposals in a similar manner. It should be noted also that it was always President Wilson who occupied himself with a concrete peace program, while the Entente adhered to its intentions of conquest. Then came Baron Burian's last proposal for a preliminary discussion by the belligerent powers.

## NEW HOPE OF PEACE

The proposal was rejected by President Wilson, not, however, with the intention of cutting off peace discussion, because in his speech of Sept. 27 he again reverted to it and in an objective manner set forth the necessity of a just peace—a peace that would not be one-sided, but just to both sides, and thus fulfill the principle of high justice to all.

At this moment of the proclamation of this principle of equal justice for all parties it became clear that it was possible in this manner to come near to attaining peace, because the principle of the elimination of any one-sided preference provides for the solution of a group of difficult questions.

In the consideration of the further circumstance that owing to the internal political change in Germany certain difficulties were cleared out of the way, it became clear that a uniform decision of the Central Powers regarding peace could be affected. On this day of the new German Government's entering office we are in a position to undertake a step which reaches as far back as the beginning of 1917.

This step was not born of the events of the moment but continually had won its way through in the course of a natural development.

In the circumstances we expect our step will lead to rapprochement and discussion. At the same time in expressing this hope we do not know how the Entente and President Wilson will view this step. It is, however, politically justified on the ground alone that President Wilson represents sole power and is not politically bound to the Entente.

In a formal manner it is also pointed out that our step is not to be interpreted as a request for mediation. This is out of the question, as only a neutral could act as mediator. We approach President Wilson because the points formulated by him represent a basis on which we could negotiate.

Our step will assuredly be regarded generally as one of great historic moment. In the note it is expressed with full clearness that the much-calumniated Central Powers are pursuing no imperialistic policy, and, moreover, their conditions are in full accord with their program of defense.

Should our proposal not be accepted, then our opponents will have to undertake full responsibility. The note is presented separately because the allies (Teutonic) are represented in America by protecting States—we by Sweden, Germany by Switzerland.

The note at this moment has already been handed to the American Ministers at Stockholm and Berne.

In Berlin excited crowds on the evening of Oct. 6 tore from the hands of newsdealers special editions of the newspapers containing the speech of Prince Maximilian amid shouts of " Peace has come! " " Peace at last! " A note of doubt and warning against overconfidence, however, pervaded a large section of the German press, apart from the Pan German irreconcilables. President Wilson's New York speech of Sept. 27, hitherto ignored by the German press, appeared in full in Berlin newspapers of Oct. 5, and everything was done by the Government to centre attention and responsibility upon the President in the matter.

## PRESIDENT'S FIRST REPLY

Replying to the note of Prince Maximilian, President Wilson sent the following through the Swiss Chargé d'Affaires to the German Chancellor:

*DEPARTMENT OF STATE,*

Washington, D. C., Oct. 8, 1918.
Sir: I have the honor to acknowledge,

on behalf of the President, your note of Oct. 6, inclosing a communication from the German Government to the President, and I am instructed by the President to request you to make the following communication to the Imperial German Chancellor:

" Before making reply to the request of the Imperial German Government, and in order that that reply shall be as candid and straightforward as the momentous interests involved require, the President of the United States deems it necessary to assure himself of the exact meaning of the note of the Imperial Chancellor. Does the Imperial Chancellor mean that the Imperial German Government accepts the terms laid down by the President in his address to the Congress of the United States on the 8th of January last and in subsequent addresses, and that its object in entering into discussions would be only to agree upon the practical details of their application?

" The President feels bound to say with regard to the suggestion of an armistice that he would not feel at liberty to propose a cessation of arms to the Governments with which the Government of the United States is associated against the Central Powers so long as the armies of those powers are upon their soil. The good faith of any discussion would manifestly depend upon the consent of the Central Powers immediately to withdraw their forces everywhere from invaded territory.

" The President also feels that he is justified in asking whether the Imperial Chancellor is speaking merely for the constituted authorities of the empire who have so far conducted the war. He deems the answer to these questions vital from every point of view."

Accept, Sir, the renewed assurances of my high consideration.

ROBERT LANSING.

To Mr. Frederick Oederlin, Chargé d'Affaires of Switzerland, ad interim in charge of German interests in the United States.

This reply, being of an unexpected nature, caused a vast variety of comments on both sides of the Atlantic. Mingled sentiments of approval and of disappointment that the President had refrained from abruptly rejecting the German overtures were expressed at Washington and elsewhere, but the prevailing view was one of willingness to await results. In England the press comment was overwhelmingly favorable. In France the note was regarded as a clever diplomatic move, placing the task of a difficult reply upon the German Government.

## GERMANY'S FIRST REPLY

The response of the German Government to President Wilson's queries bore the signature of Dr. W. S. Solf, the Colonial Secretary, who had been appointed Imperial Foreign Secretary on Oct. 6. His message, wirelessed from Nauen, picked up in France and cabled to Washington, appeared in the newspapers of the United States on the 13th, though the official text, coming through diplomatic channels, did not reach Washington until the next day. It employed the phrase " German Government " instead of " Imperial German Government " throughout its text, which follows:

BERLIN, Oct. 12, 1918.

*In reply to the questions of the President of the United States of America, the German Government hereby declares:*

The German Government has accepted the terms laid down by President Wilson in his address of Jan. 8 and in his subsequent addresses on the foundation of a permanent peace of justice. Consequently its object in entering into discussion would be only to agree upon practical details of the application of these terms. The German Government believes that the Governments of the powers associated with the Government of the United States also take the position taken by President Wilson in his address.

The German Government, in accordance with the Austro-Hungarian Government, for the purpose of bringing about an armistice, declares itself ready to comply with the proposition of the President in regard to evacuation. The German Government suggests that the President may occasion the meeting of a mixed commission for making the necessary arrangements concerning the evacuation.

The present German Government, which has undertaken the responsibility for this step toward peace, has been formed by conferences and in agreement with the great majority of the Reichstag. The Chancellor, supported in all his actions by the will of this majority, speaks in the name of the German Government and of the German people.

(Signed) SOLF,
State Secretary of Foreign Office.

Comment in Berlin and Vienna was reported to be unanimous in expressing the view that the German Chancellor's note was an unselfish peace offer, in which Germany, undefeated, was willing to sacrifice her military advantage over the Allies for the good of humanity. The German people generally leaped to the conclusion that the offer would be accepted. The excitement was said to be extraordinary. An Amsterdam dispatch to a London paper declared: " People in " Berlin are kissing one another in the " streets, though they are perfect stran- "gers, and shouting peace congratulations " to each other. The only words heard " anywhere in Germany are ' Peace at " last.' "

## PRESIDENT'S SECOND REPLY

The interval between the first and second notes of the President was marked by fresh devastations in France and by new submarine atrocities, notably the sinking of the British mail steamer Leinster, with the loss of hundreds of lives of noncombatants, including more than a hundred women and children. These events helped to shape his second reply, which was addressed to the Swiss Chargé d'Affaires at Washington, and which read as follows:

DEPARTMENT OF STATE,

WASHINGTON, Oct. 14, 1918.

*Sir: In reply to the communication of the German Government, dated the 12th inst., which you handed me today, I have the honor to request you to transmit the following answers:*

The unqualified acceptance by the present German Government and by a large majority of the German Reichstag of the terms laid down by the President of the United States of America in his address to the Congress of the United States on the 8th of January, 1918, and in his subsequent addresses justifies the President in making a frank and direct statement of his decision with regard to the communications of the German Government of the 8th and 12th of October, 1918.

It must be clearly understood that the process of evacuation and the conditions of an armistice are matters which must be left to the judgment and advice of the military advisers of the Government of the United States and the allied Governments, and the President feels it his duty to say that no arrangement can be accepted by the Government of the United States which does not provide absolutely satisfactory safeguards and guarantees of the maintenance of the present military supremacy of the armies of the United States and of the Allies in the field. He feels confident that he can safely assume that this will also be the judgment and decision of the allied Governments.

The President feels that it is also his

duty to add that neither the Government of the United States nor, he is quite sure, the Governments with which the Government of the United States is associated as a belligerent will consent to consider an armistice so long as the armed forces of Germany continue the illegal and inhuman practices which they persist in.

At the very time that the German Government approaches the Government of the United States with proposals of peace its submarines are engaged in sinking passenger ships at sea, and not the ships alone, but the very boats in which their passengers and crews seek to make their way to safety; and in their present enforced withdrawal from Flanders and France the German armies are pursuing a course of wanton destruction which has always been regarded as in direct violation of the rules and practices of civilized warfare. Cities and villages, if not destroyed, are being stripp ? of all. they contain, not only, but often of their very inhabitants. The nations associated against Germany cannot be expected to agree to a cessation of arms while acts of inhumanity, spoliation, and desolation are being continued which they justly look upon with horror and with burning hearts.

It is necessary also, in order that there may be no possibility of misunderstanding, that the President should very solemnly call the attention of the Government of Germany to the language and plain intent of one of the terms of peace which the German Government has now accepted. It is contained in the address of the President delivered at Mount Vernon on the Fourth of July last. It is as follows:

"The destruction of every arbitrary "power anywhere that can separately, "secretly, and of its single choice disturb "the peace of the world; or, if it cannot "be presently destroyed, at least its "reduction to virtual impotency."

The power which has hitherto controlled the German Nation is of the sort here described. It is within the choice of the German Nation to alter it. The President's words, just quoted, naturally constitute a condition precedent to peace, if peace is to come by the action of the German people themselves. The President feels bound to say that the whole process of peace will, in his judgment, depend upon the definiteness and the satisfactory character of the guarantees which can be given in this fundamental matter. It is indispensable that the Governments associated against Germany should know beyond a peradventure with whom they are dealing.

The President will make a separate reply to the Royal and Imperial Government of Austria-Hungary.

*Accept, Sir, the renewed assurances of my high consideration.*
(Signed) ROBERT LANSING.
Mr. Frederick Oederlin, Chargé d'Affaires of Switzerland, ad interim in charge of German interests in the United States.

## APPROVED BY THE ALLIES

This answer was regarded with universal approval by the allied nations. Senators and Representatives at Washington, irrespective of party, expressed themselves as in thorough accord with the note. Senator Lodge of Massachusetts, ranking Republican of the Foreign Relations Committee, who had voiced serious doubts as to the wisdom of the first reply, expressed relief at the explicit and uncompromising attitude of the second. "The President's last clause," he said, "in which he in substance declines to carry on any discussions with the German Government, is eminently satisfactory, and will, I am sure, bring a great sense of relief to the American people, who, I am certain, desire an unconditional surrender won by the armies in the field." Senator Hitchcock, Democrat, who is Chairman of the Foreign Relations Committee, expressed similar views, and Senator Reed of Missouri said of the note:

It is in accord with the universal voice of America and with the demands of humanity throughout the world. It is an unequivocal demand that the Hohenzollerns shall get out. That means, of course, the destruction of the military autocracy of Germany, and with it, necessarily, would go the House of Hapsburg.

England hailed the reply as exactly suited to the situation. Winston Spencer Churchill, Minister of Munitions, declared in a speech at Manchester that President Wilson's "stern and formidable answer to Germany" would be wholeheartedly indorsed by all the allied countries. The London press comment was unanimously favorable. The same was true of the Paris press, which dwelt especially upon the diplomatic effects of the incident in the German Empire itself. The Paris Temps said:

It will not consolidate the authority of the Prussian Staff nor the personal prestige of the Kaiser, nor the popularity of the dynasty or imperial régime. The directors of Germany sought public debate.

They have it. The first result is that they appear in the eyes of their people, gasping for peace, as the principal obstacles to peace.

The President's second reply had the effect of a cold douche upon Germany. The German newspapers were divided in their comment, some voicing anger and defiance, others seeing hope of peace despite the wording of the note. A tendency toward some kind of acceptance of its terms, notably by the semi-official organs, was evident. The North German Gazette's comment was typical; it said that the answer to the American note would naturally require a thorough discussion, but that the German Government would be led by a spirit of conciliation even now, being animated by the wish to end the bloodshed and to make its decision in consideration of the wishes of the German people.

## AUSTRIA-HUNGARY'S NOTE

The text of Austria-Hungary's note proposing an armistice and peace negotiations on similar grounds to those proffered by Germany was made public Oct. 19, 1918, along with President Wilson's rejection of the proposal. The Austrian note, which was transmitted through the Swedish Legation, was as follows:

*Legation of Sweden, Washington, D. C.,*
*Oct. 7, 1918:*
[Translation.]

Excellency: By order of my Government I have the honor confidentially to transmit herewith to you the following communication of the Imperial and Royal Government of Austria-Hungary to the President of the United States of America:

" The Austro-Hungarian Monarchy, which has waged war always and solely as a defensive war, and repeatedly given documentary evidence of its readiness to stop the shedding of blood and to arrive at a just and honorable peace, hereby addresses itself to his Lordship, the President of the United States of America, and offers to conclude with him and his allies an armistice on every front on land, at sea, and in the air, and to enter immediately upon negotiations for a peace for which the fourteen points in the message of President Wilson to Congress on Jan. 8, 1918, and the four points contained in President Wilson's address of Feb. 12, 1918, should serve as a foundation, and in which the viewpoints declared by President Wilson in his address of Sept. 27, 1918, will also be taken into account."

Be pleased to accept, &c.,
W. A. F. EKENGREN.
*His Excellency, Mr. Robert Lansing, Secretary of State of the United States, Washington.*

## PRESIDENT WILSON'S REPLY

The text of the reply handed to the Swedish Minister was as follows:

Sir: I have the honor to acknowledge the receipt of your note of the 7th inst., in which you transmit a communication of the Imperial and Royal Government of Austria-Hungary to the President. I am now instructed by the President to request you to be good enough through your Government to convey to the Imperial and Royal Government the following reply:

" The President deems it his duty to say to the Austro-Hungarian Government that he cannot entertain the present suggestions of that Government because of certain events of utmost importance, which, occurring since the delivery of his address of the 8th of January last, have necessarily altered the attitude and responsibility of the Government of the United States.

" Among the fourteen terms of peace which the President formulated at that time occurred the following:

" ' (X) The peoples of Austria-Hungary, whose place among the nations we wish t see safeguarded and assured, should l accorded the freest opportunity of autono mous development.'

" Since that sentence was written and uttered to the Congress of the United States, the Government of the United States has recognized that a state of belligerency exists between the Czechoslovaks and the German and Austro-Hungarian Empires, and that the Czechoslovak National Council is a de facto belligerent Government, clothed with proper authority to direct the military and political affairs of the Czechoslovaks. It has also recognized in the fullest manner the justice of the nationalistic aspirations of the Jugoslavs for freedom.

" The President is therefore no longer at liberty to accept the mere ' autonomy ' of these peoples as a basis of peace, but is obliged to insist that they and not he shall be the judges of what action on the part of the Austro-Hungarian Government will satisfy their aspirations and their conception of their rights and destiny as members of the family of nations."

Accept, Sir, the renewed assurances of my highest consideration.
ROBERT LANSING.

A third note from Germany was on its way to Washington when these pages went to press.

# The Kaiser's Exhortations

While the German Cabinet was undergoing reorganization and the German armies were suffering daily reverses Kaiser Wilhelm was attempting to stir the nation to new efforts for victory. Addressing the soldiers at Rufach, Alsace, late in September—before Bulgaria's surrender—he said:

Neither the French nor the Americans will break through our front in Alsace-Lorraine. We shall defend with the last drop of our blood these provinces which belong to us and which the Almighty has intrusted to us to administer as His stewards, and we shall keep them for the benefit of their inhabitants and the glory of God. Our faithful allies are with us in this. The last drop of blood of every Austrian and Hungarian soldier, the last drop of blood of every Bulgarian and Turkish soldier, will be shed before our enemies wrest from us land which belongs to Germany. Our enemies can not and will not succeed. We are under Divine protection.

On Sept. 30, 1918, the Kaiser sent the following telegram to the Westphalian Patriotic Society:

Germany is decided to utilize all force to fight this enforced defensive war until a victorious end is secured and the Fatherland protected for all time against foreign oppression. A glance at the magnificent successes of our heroic sons and their able leaders ought to protect the German people, even in the changeable fortunes of war, against unworthy discouragement and unjustified doubt.

In a message to the Fatherland Party, Oct. 1, he said:

I have the confident hope that the whole German people in these most serious times will resolutely gather around me and give their blood and wealth until the last breath for the defense of the Fatherland against the shameful enemy plans. Such a unanimous resolve to exist will and must, with God's help, succeed in breaking the enemy's will to war, and secure for the Fatherland the peace it is worthy of among the peoples of the world.

Responding to a demand for the establishment of a dictatorship in Germany, Herr von Berg, chief of Emperor William's civilian cabinet, sent the following reply to the citizens of Hanover on Oct. 3:

His Majesty confidently expects in the present times that the entire German people will unanimously and trustfully support the Kaiser and the empire, and with its competent labors pursue only one aim, staking its blood and treasure to free the Fatherland from threatening dangers.

The following proclamation to the German Army and Navy was issued by the German Emperor on Oct. 6:

For months past the enemy, with enormous exertions and almost without pause in the fighting, has stormed against your lines. In weeks of the struggle, often without repose, you have had to persevere and resist a numerically far superior enemy. Therein lies the greatness of the task which has been set for you and which you are fulfilling. Troops of all the German States are doing their part and are heroically defending the Fatherland on foreign soil. Hard is the task.

My navy is holding its own against the united enemy naval forces and is unwaveringly supporting the army in its difficult struggle.

The eyes of those at home rest with pride and admiration on the deeds of the army and navy. I express to you the thanks of myself and the Fatherland.

The collapse of the Macedonian front has occurred in the midst of the hardest struggle. In accord with our allies, I have resolved once more to offer peace to the enemy, but I will only extend my hand for an honorable peace. We owe that to the heroes who have laid down their lives for the Fatherland, and we make that our duty to our children.

Whether arms will be lowered still is a question. Until then we must not slacken. We must, as hitherto, exert all our strength tirelessly to hold our ground against the onslaught of our enemies.

The hour is grave, but, trusting in your strength and in God's gracious help, we feel ourselves to be strong enough to defend our beloved Fatherland.

WILHELM.

Emperor William was quoted by the Cologne Gazette on Oct. 10 as having said to the German Industrial Association, in answer to its vow of confidence:

The hour is grave! We are fighting for the future of the Fatherland and for the protection of the soil of the homeland. To that end we need the united action of the intellectual, moral, and economic powers of Germany. On the co-operation of those powers our invincibility rests. The will for defense must bind all separate views and separate wishes into one great unity of conception. God grant us something of the spirit of the war of liberation.

# President Wilson's Peace Program

## Text of Address Delivered in Metropolitan Opera House, New York, Sept. 27, 1918

MY FELLOW-CITIZENS: I am not here to promote the loan. That will be done—ably and enthusiastically done—by the hundreds of thousands of loyal and tireless men and women who have undertaken to present it to you and to our fellow-citizens throughout the country; and I have not the least doubt of their complete success, for I know their spirit and the spirit of the country. My confidence is confirmed, too, by the thoughtful and experienced co-operation of the bankers here and everywhere, who are lending their invaluable aid and guidance. I have come, rather, to seek an opportunity to present to you some thoughts which I trust will serve to give you, in perhaps fuller measure than before, a vivid sense of the great issues involved, in order that you may appreciate and accept with added enthusiasm the grave significance of the duty of supporting the Government by your men and your means to the utmost point of sacrifice and self-denial. No man or woman who has really taken in what this war means can hesitate to give to the very limit of what they have; and it is my mission here tonight to try to make it clear once more what the war really means. You will need no other stimulation or reminder of your duty.

At every turn of the war we gain a fresh consciousness of what we mean to accomplish by it. When our hope and expectation are most excited we think more definitely than before of the issues that hang upon it and of the purposes which must be realized by means of it. For it has positive and well-defined purposes which we did not determine and which we cannot alter. No statesman or assembly created them; no statesman or assembly can alter them. They have arisen out of the very nature and circumstances of the war. The most that statesmen or assemblies can do is to carry them out or be false to them. They were perhaps not clear at the outset; but they are clear now. The war has lasted more than four years and the whole world has been drawn into it. The common will of mankind has been substituted for the particular purposes of individual States. Individual statesmen may have started the conflict, but neither they nor their opponents can stop it as they please. It has become a peoples' war, and peoples of all sorts and races, of every degree of power and variety of fortune, are involved in its sweeping processes of change and settlement. We came into it when its character had become fully defined and it was plain that no nation could stand apart or be indifferent to its outcome. Its challenge drove to the heart of everything we cared for and lived for. The voice of the war had become clear and gripped our hearts. Our brothers from many lands, as well as our own murdered dead under the sea, were calling to us, and we responded, fiercely and of course.

## ISSUES OF THE WAR

The air was clear about us. We saw things in their full, convincing proportions as they were; and we have seen them with steady eyes and unchanging comprehension ever since. We accepted the issues of the war as facts, not as any group of men either here or elsewhere had defined them, and we can accept no outcome which does not squarely meet and settle them. Those issues are these:

*Shall the military power of any nation or group of nations be suffered to determine the fortunes of peoples over whom they have no right to rule except the right of force?*

*Shall strong nations be free to wrong weak nations and make them subject to their purpose and interest?*

*Shall peoples be ruled and dominated, even in their own internal affairs, by arbitrary and irresponsible force or by their own will and choice?*

*Shall there be a common standard of right and privilege for all peoples and nations or shall the strong do as they will and the weak suffer without redress?*

*Shall the assertion of right be haphazard and by casual alliance or shall there be a common concert to oblige the observance of common rights?*

No man, no group of men, chose these to be the issues of the struggle. They *are* the issues of it; and they must be settled—by no arrangement or compromise or adjustment of interests, but definitely and once for all and with a full and unequivocal acceptance of the principle that the interest of the weakest is as sacred as the interest of the strongest.

This is what we mean when we speak of a permanent peace, if we speak sincerely, intelligently, and with a real knowledge and comprehension of the matter we deal with.

We are all agreed that there can be no peace obtained by any kind of bargain or compromise with the Governments of the Central Empires, because we have dealt with them already and have seen them deal with other Governments that were parties to this struggle, at Brest-Litovsk and Bucharest. They have convinced us that they are without honor and do not intend justice. They observe no covenants, accept no principle but force and their own interest. We cannot "come to terms" with them. They have made it impossible. The German people must by this time be fully aware that we cannot accept the word of those who forced this war upon us. We do not think the same thoughts or speak the same language of agreement.

## JUSTICE IMPERATIVE

It is of capital importance that we should also be explicitly agreed that no peace shall be obtained by any kind of compromise or abatement of the principles we have avowed as the principles for which we are fighting. There should exist no doubt about that. I am, therefore, going to take the liberty of speaking with the utmost frankness about the practical implications that are involved in it. If it be in deed and in truth the common object of the Governments associated against Germany and of the nations whom they govern, as I believe it to be, to achieve by the coming settlements a secure and lasting peace, it will be necessary that all who sit down at the peace table shall come ready and willing to pay the price, the only price, that will procure it; and ready and willing, also, to create in some virile fashion the only instrumentality by which it can be made certain that the agreements of the peace will be honored and fulfilled.

That price is impartial justice in every item of the settlement, no matter whose interest is crossed; and not only impartial justice, but also the satisfaction of the several peoples whose fortunes are dealt with. That indispensable instrumentality is a League of Nations formed under covenants that will be efficacious. Without such an instrumentality, by which the peace of the world can be guaranteed, peace will rest in part upon the word of outlaws, and only upon that word. For Germany will have to redeem her character, not by what happens at the peace table, but by what follows.

And, as I see it, the constitution of that League of Nations and the clear definition of its objects must be a part, is in a sense the most essential part, of the peace settlement itself. It cannot be formed now. If formed now, it would be merely a new alliance confined to the nations associated against a common enemy. It is not likely that it could be formed after the settlement. It is necessary to guarantee the peace; and the peace cannot be guaranteed as an afterthought. The reason, to speak in plain terms again, why it must be guaranteed is that there will be parties to the peace whose promises have proved untrustworthy, and means must be found in connection with the peace settlement itself to remove that source of insecurity. It would be folly to leave the guarantee to the subsequent voluntary action of the Governments we have seen destroy Russia and deceive Rumania.

## A PRACTICAL PROGRAM

But these general terms do not disclose the whole matter. Some details are needed to make them sound less like a thesis and more like a practical program. These, then, are some of the particulars, and I state them with the greater confidence because I can state them authoritatively as representing this Government's interpretation of its own duty with regard to peace:

*First, the impartial justice meted out must involve no discrimination between those to whom we wish to be just and those to whom we do not wish to be just. It must be a justice that plays no favorites and knows no standard but the equal rights of the several peoples concerned;*

*Second, no special or separate interest of any single nation or any group of nations can be made the basis of any part of the settlement which is not consistent with the common interest of all;*

*Third, there can be no leagues or alliances or special covenants and understandings within the general and common family of the League of Nations;*

*Fourth, and more specifically, there can be no special, selfish economic combinations within the league and no employment of any form of economic boycott or exclusion except as the power of economic penalty by exclusion from the markets of the world may be vested in the League of Nations itself as a means of discipline and control;*

*Fifth, all international agreements and treaties of every kind must be made known in their entirety to the rest of the world.*

Special alliances and economic rivalries and hostilities have been the prolific source in the modern world of the plans and passions that produce war. It would be an insincere as well as an insecure peace that did not exclude them in definite and binding terms.

The confidence with which I venture to speak for our people in these matters does not spring from our traditions merely and the well-known principles of international action which we have always professed and followed. In the same sentence in which I say that the United States will enter into no special arrangements or understandings with particular nations let me say also that the United States is prepared to assume its full share of responsibility for the maintenance of the common covenants and understandings upon which peace must henceforth rest. We still read Washington's immortal warning against "entangling alliances" with full comprehension and an answering purpose. But only special and limited alliances entangle; and we recognize and accept the duty of a new day in which we are permitted to hope for a general alliance which will avoid entanglements and clear the air of the world for common understandings and the maintenance of common rights.

I have made this analysis of the international situation which the war has created, not, of course, because I doubted whether the leaders of the great nations and peoples with whom we are associated were of the same mind and entertained a like purpose, but because the air every now and again gets darkened by mists and groundless doubtings and mischievous perversions of counsel and it is necessary once and again to sweep all the irresponsible talk about peace intrigues and weakening morale and doubtful purpose on the part of those in authority utterly, and if need be unceremoniously, aside and say thir s in the plainest words that can be found, even when it is only to say o again what has been said before, qu e as plainly if in less unvarnished terms.

As I have said, neither I nor any other man in Governmental authority created or gave form to the issues of this war. I have simply responded to them with such vision as I could command. But I have responded gladly and with a resolution that has grown warmer and more confident as the issues have grown clearer and clearer. It is now plain that they are issues which no man can pervert unless it be willfully. I am bound to fight for them, and happy to fight for them, as time and circumstance have revealed them to me as to all the world. Our enthusiasm for them grows more and more irresistible as they stand out in more and more vivid and unmistakable outline.

And the forces that fight for them draw into closer and closer array, organize their millions into more and more unconquerable might, as they become more and more distinct to the thought and purpose of the peoples engaged. It is the peculiarity of this great war that while statesmen have seemed to cast about for definitions of their purpose and have sometimes seemed to shift their ground and their point of view, the thought of the mass of men, whom statesmen are supposed to instruct and lead, has grown more and more unclouded, more and more certain of what it is that they are fighting for. National purposes have fallen more and more into the background and the common purpose of enlightened mankind has taken their place. The counsels of plain men have become on all hands more simple and straightforward and more unified than the counsels of sophisticated men of affairs, who still retain the impression that they are playing a game of power and playing for high stakes. That is why I have said that this is a peoples' war, not a statesmen's. Statesmen must follow the clarified common thought or be broken.

## ISSUES MUST BE CLEAR

I take that to be the significance of the fact that assemblies and associations of many kinds made up of plain workaday people have demanded, almost every time they came together, and are still demanding, that the leaders of their Governments declare to them plainly what it is, exactly what it is, that they are seeking in this war, and what they think the items of the final settlement should be. They are not yet satisfied with what they have been told. They still seem to fear that they are getting what they ask for only in statesmen's terms—only in the terms of territorial arrangements and divisions of power, and not in terms of broad-visioned justice and mercy and peace and the satisfaction of those deep-seated longings of oppressed and distracted men and women and enslaved peoples that seem to them the only things worth fighting a war for that engulfs the world. Perhaps statesmen have not always recognized this changed aspect of the whole world of policy and action. Perhaps they have not always spoken in direct reply to the questions asked because they did not know how searching those questions were and what sort of answers they demanded.

But I, for one, am glad to attempt the answer again and again, in the hope that I may make it clearer and clearer that my one thought is to satisfy those who struggle in the ranks and are, perhaps above all others, entitled to a reply whose meaning no one can have any excuse for misunderstanding, if he understands the language in which it is spoken or can get some one to translate it correctly into his own. And I believe that the leaders of the Governments with which we are associated will speak, as they have occasion, as plainly as I have tried to speak. I hope that they will feel free to say whether they think that I am in any degree mistaken in my interpretation of the issues involved or in my purpose with regard to the means by which a satisfactory settlement of those issues may be obtained. Unity of purpose and of counsel are as imperatively necessary in this war as was unity of command in the battlefield; and with perfect unity of purpose and counsel will come assurance of complete victory. It can be had in no other way. "Peace drives" can be effectively neutralized and silenced only by showing that every victory of the nations associated against Germany brings the nations nearer the sort of peace which will bring security and reassurance to all peoples and make the recurrence of another such struggle of pitiless force and bloodshed forever impossible, and that nothing else can. Germany is constantly intimating the "terms" she will accept; and always finds that the world does not want terms. It wishes the final triumph of justice and fair dealing.

# Submarine Depredations

## Total Sinkings in Four Years 21,404,913 Tons—
## Decreased Totals for Current Month

### [PERIOD ENDED OCT. 15, 1918]

DURING the period from August, 1914, to September, 1918, German submarines sank 7,157,088 deadweight tons of shipping in excess of the tonnage turned out in that period by the allied and neutral nations. That total does not represent the depletion of the fleets at the command of the allied and neutral nations, however, as 3,795,000 deadweight tons of enemy ships were seized in the meantime. Actually, the allied and neutral nations on Sept. 1, 1918, had only 3,362,088 less tons of shipping in operation than in August, 1914.

These details of the shipping situation were issued by the United States Shipping Board along with figures to show that, with American and allied yards under full headway, Europe's danger of being starved by the German submarine was apparently at an end. The United States has taken the lead of all nations in shipbuilding, and it is expected that within a few months more the submarine losses will have been overcome.

In all, the allied and neutral nations have lost 21,404,913 deadweight tons of shipping since the beginning of the war, showing that Germany has maintained an average destruction of about 445,000 deadweight tons monthly. During the latter months, however, the sinkings have fallen considerably below the average, and allied construction passed destruction for the first time in May last.

The losses of the allied and neutral shipping in August, 1918, amounted to 327,676 gross tonnage, of which 176,401 was British and 151,275 allied and neutral, as compared with the adjusted figures for July of 323,772, and 182,524 and 141,248, respectively. British losses from all causes during August were 10,887 tons higher than in June, which was the lowest month since the introduction of unrestricted submarine warfare.

An official statement of the United States Shipping Board, issued Sept. 21, 1918, sets forth the following facts:

### STATUS OF WORLD TONNAGE, SEPT. 1, 1918
#### (Germany and Austria excluded)

| | Deadweight Tons. |
|---|---|
| Total losses (allied and neutral) August, 1914-Sept. 1, 1918 | 21,404,913 |
| Total construction (allied and neutral) August, 1914-Sept. 1, 1918 | 14,247,825 |
| Total enemy tonnage captured (to end of 1917) | 3,795,000 |
| Excess of losses over gains | 3,362,088 |
| Estimated normal increase in world's tonnage if war had not occurred (based on rate of increase, 1905-1914) | 14,700,000 |
| Net deficit due to war | 18,062,088 |

In August, deliveries to the Shipping Board and other seagoing construction in the United States for private parties passed allied and neutral destruction for that month. The figures:

| | Gross (Actual) Tons. |
|---|---|
| Deliveries to the Shipping Board | 244,121 |
| Other construction over 1,000 gross | 16,918 |
| Total | 261,039 |
| Losses (allied and neutral) | 259,400 |
| America alone surpassed losses for month by | 1,630 |

NOTE.—World's merchant tonnage, as of June 30, 1914, totaled 49,089,552 gross tons, or, roughly, 73,634,328 deadweight tons. (Lloyd's Register.)

The rapid progress American shipbuilding has made in the first year of the present Shipping Board is shown by the following table of launchings:

| Date. | Composite Wood Ships. | | Steel Ships. | | Contract Ships. | | Requisitional Steel Ships. | | Total | |
|---|---|---|---|---|---|---|---|---|---|---|
| | Number. | Deadweight Tons. | Number. | Deadweight Tons. | Number. | Deadweight Tons. | Number. | Deadweight Tons. | Number. | Deadweight Tons. |
| August, 1917 | .. | .... | .. | .... | .. | .... | 16 | 127,055 | 16 | 127,055 |
| September, 1917 | .. | .... | .. | .... | .. | .... | 12 | 61,930 | 12 | 61,930 |
| October, 1917 | .. | .... | .. | .... | .. | .... | 19 | 131,126 | 19 | 131,126 |
| November, 1917 | .. | .... | .. | .... | 1 | 8,800 | 19 | 135,805 | 20 | 144,605 |
| December, 1917 | 2 | 7,500 | .. | .... | 2 | 17,600 | 21 | 134,730 | 25 | 159,830 |
| January, 1918 | .. | .... | .. | .... | 1 | 8,800 | 15 | 103,700 | 16 | 112,500 |
| February, 1918 | 4 | 14,500 | 1 | 4,000 | 3 | 21,150 | 23 | 132,200 | 31 | 171,850 |
| March, 1918 | 10 | 36,000 | 1 | 4,000 | 6 | 51,650 | 27 | 167,266 | 44 | 258,916 |
| April, 1918 | 16 | 55,500 | 1 | 4,000 | 7 | 45,850 | 22 | 119,880 | 46 | 225,230 |
| May, 1918 | 30 | 108,200 | 2 | 7,500 | 14 | 85,025 | 28 | 164,530 | 74 | 365,255 |
| June, 1918 | 22 | 78,700 | 1 | 3,500 | 13 | 74,300 | 13 | 77,050 | 49 | 233,550 |
| July, 1918 | 53 | 187,700 | 3 | 11,000 | 35 | 218,725 | 33 | 216,986 | 124 | 634,411 |
| August, 1918 | 33 | 111,350 | 4 | 14,500 | 48 | 176,400 | 13 | 88,730 | 98 | 390,980 |
| Total | 170 | 599,450 | 13 | 48,500 | 130 | 708,300 | 261 | 1,660,988 | 574 | 3,017,238 |

A world's record was established in September, when seventy-four vessels built in this country were completed and turned over to the United States Shipping Board. The addition to America's merchant marine tonnage amounted to 369,330, whereas the previous high-water mark in deliveries of completed vessels was reached in August, when 339,313 deadweight tons of new shipping were turned over by the builders.

September deliveries from American shipyards greatly exceeded deliveries from British yards in the same month. The British deliveries, as cabled to Chairman Hurley of the Shipping Board by Consul General Skinner in London, amounted to 231,635 tons. Thus the American and British tonnage totals 600,965.

### LOSSES OF NEUTRALS

Figures compiled in Holland and reaching Washington Sept. 23 show the losses that the Dutch Nation has suffered from submarine depredations from the beginning of the war to the end of 1917. In this period 217 Dutch ships were sunk with a loss of 693 lives. The number of Dutch merchant ships sunk in 1917 alone is sixty-one, of a gross capacity of 91,017 registered tons; that of fishing vessels, fifty. One hundred and four lives were lost on merchant ships and 142 on fishing craft, leaving 133 widows, 389 children, 25 mothers, 10 fathers, 8 mothers-in-law, 8 fathers-in-law, and 1

grandfather unprovided for. Besides, 20 sailors were wounded, and 1,345 lost all their belongings. The vessels were fired at without warning, and in most cases the crews were left to take their chances in the open boats, irrespective of the weather conditions or of the distance from land. Crews taken captive to Germany were kept imprisoned for weeks, with insufficient food and bedding. Any goods plundered remain unpaid for.

Norway lost eight vessels in September, with an aggregate tonnage of 11,943. Six sailors were drowned.

The Italian Navy reports increasing success in combating German and Austrian submarines in the Mediterranean. In 1917 Italy's losses in tonnage on one occasion reached as high a figure as seventeen ships a month, but now these losses have been reduced to two ships a month.

Negotiations between Madrid and Berlin resulted in an agreement by Germany to allow Spain to replace Spanish ships sunk by submarines with German ships interned for the duration of the war, but exacted pay for the use of these vessels. Further, the offer applies only to ships sunk outside of the German prohibited zone, within which Germany reserves the right to sink vessels without compensation.

### THE MONTH'S TRAGEDIES

While the German Government was making strenuous efforts for peace its submarines continued to work with their most ruthless methods. The month brought an increased number of sinkings of troopships, but the act that most deeply exasperated the Allies was the torpedoing of the British mail steamer Leinster, Oct. 10, in the Irish Sea. This wholly civilian vessel, carrying 687 passengers and a crew of 70 men, was struck down without warning in a very rough sea, sinking in fifteen minutes, and 480 persons perished, including 135 women and children. This act was regarded as in the same class with the sinking of the Lusitania, and its effect was reflected in President Wilson's stern note of Oct. 14.

Other important losses included that of the British transport Missanabie, sunk by a torpedo off the Irish coast Sept. 9. The ship sank in seven minutes, with a loss of fifty lives. On Sept. 12 the British steamer Galway Castle, on her way to South Africa, was torpedoed and sunk with a loss of 189 lives. On the night of Oct. 4 the Hirano Maru, a Japanese liner, was sunk by a submarine off the Irish coast and only 29 out of the 320 persons on board were saved.

The Mallory Line freighter San Saba was sunk by a floating mine off Barnegat Oct. 4. Only four of her crew of thirty-seven are known to have been saved.

The American steamer Buena Ventura, on her way from Bordeaux to a Spanish port, was torpedoed and sunk Sept. 16, with a loss of twenty-five lives.

The United States steamer Tampa, while on convoy service, was lost with all on board, 118, through a submarine attack off the English coast on Sept. 26.

## HELPLESS MEN SHELLED

Typical brutality marked the torpedoing Sept. 30 of the Ticonderoga, formerly the German steamship Camilla Rickmers, causing the death of 11 naval officers and 102 enlisted men. The Ticonderoga, east bound, was handicapped by bad coal, and engine trouble developed and she fell behind the other vessels. She was discovered by a U-boat at daybreak in longitude 37 west, about 1,700 miles from the American coast. The first the men

on board knew that they had fallen prey to an undersea boat was when a torpedo struck their vessel. It did not hit a vital spot, however, and the Captain crowded on steam in hopes of getting away. The gun crews went to their stations. Said one survivor who told the story:

Our guns did not fire more than five or six shots, so quickly did the shells from the submarine strike down both guns and their crews. The forward gun was shot away nearly at once, as the submarine was not more than a mile away and kept coming nearer, and the after gun and its crew were as quickly done for. The men went to the boats, but it was no use, as the flying shrapnel was spraying the decks and men fell by scores either killed or badly wounded.

All of the eight boats were riddled with the flying fragments of shell with the exception of one, and this, the only one fit to put over, was filled with men. Some of these were killed as they attempted to lower themselves over the ship's side. One raft also was got away and all the time the Hun commander did not slacken his shellfire.

Finally, in desperation, one man overboard swam to the side of the submarine, which was less than a quarter of a mile away firing almost point blank at us, and hailed an officer, asking him in God's name to stop. The Lieutenant who answered pointed a revolver at him, saying that if he did not swim back he would shoot him.

When our boat had only seventeen in it we were ordered alongside and made to tie up, while the shelling of the dead and dying on the sinking ship kept up. Questions were put to the leader of our boat which he refused to answer, and suddenly the submarine submerged, and only the parting of the rope with which we were tied fast to the U-boat prevented our going down with it.

Several collisions exacted a heavy toll in lives. Seven men were lost when the United States freighter Westgate, of 5,800 tons, was sunk Oct. 7 in a collision with the steamer American, 500 miles off the Atlantic Coast. The United States destroyer Shaw collided with a British vessel in British waters Oct. 9, and fifteen of her men were killed, although she succeeded in reaching port under her own steam.

Much graver was the loss, Oct. 11, of the American transport Otranto, through a collision in the British Channel with the P. and O. liner Kashmir. The latter crashed into the transport, bow on, during a furious storm, and the Otranto sank in a few minutes. Splendid heroism was shown by the soldiers and crew, and discipline never faltered. The British destroyer Mounsey did gallant work in rescue, but of the 700 American soldiers on board 365 were lost.

Vice Admiral Sims, speaking in London Oct. 10, said that the average number of enemy submarines operating against merchant ships and transports across the Atlantic was about eight or nine, but that sometimes it ran up to twelve or thirteen. That was all the submarines the enemy could keep out at a time, he declared.

Around the British Isles, Vice Admiral Sims said, there were about 3,000 anti-submarine craft in operation day and night. Of American craft there were 160, or 3 per cent. of the total, and it was about the same in the Mediterranean. There were about 5,000 anti-submarine craft in the open sea, cutting ou, mines, escorting troopships and merchant vessels, and making it possible for the Allies to win the war.

# Fate of 150 U-Boats Officially Attested

## British Admiralty Statement

*The British Admiralty on Sept. 6, 1918, made public the following statement:*

ALTHOUGH it is not intended to adopt the practice of giving proof of official utterances of his Majesty's Ministers, it has been thought desirable to give the names of the commanding officers of 150 German submarines which have been disposed of, in order to substantiate to the world the statement made by the Prime Minister in the House of Commons on Aug. 7, and denied in the German papers, that "at least 150 of these ocean pests had been destroyed." The statement includes no officers commanding the Austrian submarines, of which a number have been destroyed, and does not exhaust the list of German submarines put out of action.

The fate of the officers is given, and it will be seen that the majority (116) are dead; twenty-seven are prisoners of war, six are interned in neutral countries where they took refuge, and one succeeded in returning to Germany.

[*The chief official ranks in the following list are Kapitanleutnant—Captain Lieutenant; Oberleutnant—First Lieutenant.*]

Albrecht, Kurt, (Kapitänlt.,) dead.
Albrecht, Werner, (Oberlt. z.S.,) dead.
Amberger, Gustav, (Kapitänlt.,) prisoner.
Amberger, Wilhelm, (Oberlt. z.S.,) dead.
Arnold, Alfred, (Oberlt. z.S.,) prisoner.
Bachmann, Günther, (Oberlt. z.S.,) dead.
Barten, Wilhelm, (Oberlt. z.S.,) dead.

Bauck, W., (Kapitänlt.,) dead.
Bauer, Cäsar, (Kapitänlt.,) dead.
Bender, Waldemar, (Kapitänlt.) This officer was not lost when his submarine sank, and he succeeded in returning to Germany.
Berckheim, Egewolf Freiherr von, (Kapitänlt.) dead.
Berger, Gerhardt, (Kapitänlt.,) dead.
Bernis, Kurt, (Kapitänlt.,) dead.
Branscheid, Albert, (Oberlt. z.S.,) dead.
Braud, Charles, (Oberlt. z.S.—Res.,) dead.
Breyer, Herbert, (Oberlt. z.S.,) prisoner.
Buch, Gustav, (Kapitänlt.,) dead.
Degetau, Hans, (Oberlt. z.S.,) dead.
Dieckmann, Victor, (Kapitänlt.,) dead.
Ditfurth, Benno von, (Oberlt. z.S.,) dead.
Edeling, Karl, (Kapitänlt.,) dead.
Ehrenthaut, Otto, (Oberlt. z. S ) dead.
Eitester, Max, (Kapitänlt.,) dead.
Feddersen, Adolf, (Lt. z.S.—Res.,) dead.
Fircks, Wilhelm Freiherr von, (Kapitänlt.,) dead.
Fischer, Karl-Hanno, (Lt. z.S.,) dead.
Fröhner, Eberhardt, (Lt. z.S.,) dead.
Fürbringee, Gerhardt, (Kapitänlt.,) prisoner.
Furbringer, Werner, (Kapitänlt.,) prisoner.
Gaister, Hans, (Oberlt. z.S.,) dead.
Gebeschus, Rudolf, (Kapitänlt.,) dead.
Gercke, Hermann, (Korv. Kapitän.,) dead.
Gerlach, Helmut, (Kapitänlt.,) dead.
Gerth, Georg, (Kapitänlt.,) prisoner.
Glimpf, Herman, (Oberlt. z.S.,) dead.
Graeff, Ernst, (Kapitänlt.,) prisoner.
Gregor, Fritz, (Oberlt. z.S.,) dead.
Gross, Karl, (Oberlt. z.S.,) dead.
Günther, Paul, (Oberlt. z.S.,) dead.
Güntzel, Ludwig, (Kapitänlt.,) dead.
Gunzel, Erich, (Kapitänlt.,) dead.
Haag, Georg, (Lt. z.S.,) dead.
Hansen, Klaus, (Kapitänlt.,) dead.
Hartmann, Richard, (Kapitänlt.,) dead.
Hecht, Erich, (Oberlt. z.S.,) dead.

Heinke, Curt, (Oberlt. z.S.,) dead.
Heller, Bruno, (Oberlt. z.S.,) dead.
Hennig, Heinrich von, (Kapitänlt.,) prisoner.
Heydebreck, Karsten von, (Oberlt. z.S.,) dead.
Hirzel, Alfred, (Oberlt. z.S.,) dead.
Hoppe, Bruno, (Kapitänlt.,) dead.
Hufnagel, Hans, (Kapitänlt.,) dead.
Keyserlingk, Harald von, (Oberlt. z.S.,) dead.
Kiel, Wilhelm, (Oberlt. z.S.,) dead.
Kiesewetter, Wilhelm, (Kapitänlt.—Res.,) interned.
Klatt, Alfred, (Oberlt. z.S.,) dead.
Kolbe, Walther, (Oberlt. z.S.,) dead.
Konig, Georg, (Kapitänlt.,) dead.
Korsch, Hans Paul, (Oberlt. z.S.,) dead.
Kratzsch, Paul, (Kapitänlt.,) dead.
Frech, Günther, (Kapitänlt.,) prisoner.
Kreysern, Günther, (Oberlt. z.S.,) dead.
Kroll, Karl, (Korv. Kapitän,) dead.
Küstner, Heinrich, (Oberlt. z.S.,) dead.
Lafrenz, Claus P., (Kapitänlt.,) prisoner.
Launburg, Otto, (Oberlt. z.S.,) prisoner.
Lemmer, Johannes, (Kapitänlt.,) dead.
Lepsius, Reinhold, (Oberlt. z.S.,) dead.
Lilienstern, Rühle von, (Oberlt. z.S.,) dead.
Lorenz, Heimut, (Oberlt. z.S.,) interned.
Lorenz, Herman, (Kapitänlt.,) dead.
Löwe, Werner, (Oberlt. z.S.,) dead.
Lühe, Vicco von der, (Oberlt. z.S.,) prisoner.
Menzel, Bernhard, (Oberlt. z.S.,) dead.
Metz, Arthur, (Oberlt. z.S.,) dead.
Metzger, Heinrich, (Kapitänlt.,) interned.
Mey, Karl, (Oberlt. z.S.,) dead.
Mildenstein, Christian, (Oberlt. z.S.,) dead.
Moecke, Fritz, (Oberlt. z.S.,) dead.
Mohrbutter, Ulrich, (Oberlt. z.S.,) prisoner.
Moraht, Robert, (Kapitänlt.,) prisoner.
Mühlau, Helmut, (Kapitänlt.,) prisoner.
Muhle, Gerhardt, (Kapitänlt.,) dead.
Müller, Hans Albrecht, (Oberlt. z.S.,) dead.
Neumann, Friedrich, (Oberlt. z.S.,) prisoner.
Niemer, Hans, (Oberlt. z.S.,) interned.
Niemeyer, Georg, (Oberlt. z.S.,) dead.
Nitzsche, Alfred, (Oberlt. z.S.,) dead.
Noodt, Erich, (Oberlt. z.S.,) prisoner.
Petz, Willy, (Kapitänlt.,) dead.
Platsch, Erich, (Oberlt. z.S.,) dead.
Pohle, Richard, (Kapitänlt.,) dead.
Prinz, Athalwin, (Kapitänlt.,) dead.
Pustkuchen, Herbert, (Oberlt. z.S.,) dead.
Reichenbach, Gottfried, (Oberlt. z.S.,) dead.
Reimarus, Georg, (Oberlt. z.S.,) dead.
Remy, Johannes, (Kapitänlt.,) dead.
Röhr, Walther, (Kapitänlt.,) dead.
Rosenow, Ernst, (Kapitänlt.,) dead.
Rücker, Claus, (Kapitänlt.,) dead.
Rumpel, Walther, (Kapitänlt.,) dead.
Saltzwedel, Rudolf, (Oberlt. z.S.,) dead.
Sebelin, Erwin, (Kapitänlt.,) dead.
Sueffer, Rudolf, (Kapitänlt.,) dead.
Schmettow, Graf M. von, (Kapitänlt.,) dead.
Schmidt, Georg, (Kapitänlt.,) dead.

Schmidt, Siegfried, (Oberlt. z.S.,) dead.
Schmidt, Walther G., (Oberlt. z.S.,) interned.
Schmitz, Max, (Oberlt. z.S.,) dead.
Schmitz, Walther, (Oberlt. z.S.,) prisoner.
Schneider, Rudolf, (Kapitänlt.,) dead. This was the officer who torpedoed the steamship Arabic on Aug. 19, 1915.

THE PARTS SHADED WITH HORIZONTAL LINES INDICATE BRITISH MINE BARRIERS, WHICH PROTECT THE NORTH SEA FROM GERMAN DEPREDATIONS

Schultz, Theodor, (Oberlt. z.S.,) dead.
Schurmann, Paul, (Oberlt. z.S.,) dead.
Schwartz, Ferdinand, (Oberlt. z.S.,) dead.
Schweinitz und Krain, Graf von, (Kapitänlt.,) dead.
Schwieger, (Kapitänlt.,) dead. This was the officer who, whilst in U-20, torpedoed the Lusitania on May 7, 1915. U-20 was lost on the Danish coast in November, 1916, but Kapitänlt. Schwieger survived to bring disaster to another submarine, U-38, which was lost with all hands in September, 1917.
Sittenfeld, Erich, (Kapitänlt.,) dead.
Smiths, Wilhelm, (Oberlt. z.S.,) prisoner.
Soergel, Hans, (Oberlt. z.S.,) dead.
Sprenger, (Kapitänlt.,) prisoner.
Steckelberg, Oscar, (Oberlt. z.S.,) interned.
Stein zu Lausnitz, Freiherr von, (Oberlt. z.S.,) dead.
Steindorff, Ernst, (Oberlt. z.S.,) dead.
Stenzler, Heinrich, (Oberlt. z.S.,) dead.
Stosberg, Arthur, (Oberlt. z.S.,) dead.
Stoss, Alfred, (Kapitänlt.,) prisoner.
Stöter, Karl, (Oberlt. z.S.,) dead.
Stuhr, Fritz, (Kapitänlt.,) dead.
Suchodoletz, Ferdinand v., (Kapitänlt.,) dead.
Tebbenjohanns, Kurt, (Kapitänlt.,) prisoner.

Träger, Friedrich, (Oberlt. z.S.,) dead.
Utke, Kurt, (Oberlt. z.S.,) prisoner.
Valentiner, Hans, (Oberlt. z.S.,) dead.
Voigt, Ernst, (Oberlt. z.S.,) dead.
Wachendorff, Siegfried, (Oberlt. z.S.,) dead.
Wacker, Karl, (Oberlt. z.S.,) dead.
Wagenfuhr, Paul, (Kapitänlt.,) dead. This was the officer who sank the steamship Belgian Prince on July 31, 1917, and so barbarously drowned forty of the crew whom he had ordered to line up on the submarine's deck. The submarine (U-44) was sunk with all hands about a fortnight after this outrage.

Walther, Franz, (Oberlt. z.S.,) dead.
Weddigen, Otto, (Kapitänlt.,) dead.
Wegener, Bernhard, (Kapitänlt.,) dead.
Weisbach, Erwin, (Kapitänlt.,) dead.
Weisbach, Raimund, (Kapitänlt.,) prisoner.
Wendlandt, Hans H., (Oberlt. z.S.,) prisoner.
Wenninger, Ralph, (Kapitänlt.,) prisoner.
Wigankow, Günther, (Oberlt. z.S.,) dead.
Wilcke, Erich, (Kapitänlt.,) dead.
Wilhelms, Ernst, (Kapitänlt.,) dead.
Willich, Kurt, (Kapitänlt.,) dead.
Wutsdorff, Hans Oskar, (Oberlt. z.S.,) prisoner.
Zerboni di Sposetti, Werner von, (Oberlt. z.S.,) dead.

## SENATOR THOMPSON'S FIGURES

*Further light on the subject of German submarines was given on Sept. 18 by Senator William H. Thompson of Kansas in a speech in which he told the Senate:*

The submarine is no longer a serious menace to transportation across the seas. It is, of course, an annoyance and a great hindrance, and as long as there is a single submarine in the waters of the sea every effort must be made by the allied powers to destroy it, for it is an outlaw and must not exist. The truth is that Germany never had more than 320 submarines all told, including all construction before and since the war.

We have positive knowledge of the destruc-

tion of more than one-half of these submarines, and we also know that it is practically impossible for Germany to keep in operation more than 10 per cent. of those remaining. It is therefore reduced to a negligible quantity so far as its ultimate effect upon the result of the war is concerned.

I saw a reliable statement in France to the effect that there is one ship of some character leaving the eastern shores of America for the war zone every six minutes, and it is only a few vessels which are ever torpedoed, estimated at about 1 per cent. This is less than the loss by storm and accident in the earlier days of transportation and is not much greater than such loss now. We must bear in mind that we read only of the ships which have been torpedoed and see but little account of the hundreds of ships which pass over the ocean safely and undisturbed. Three hundred thousand soldiers are conveyed across the Atlantic every thirty days, and an average of about 500,000 tons of freight carried to the French coast. There are warehouses in only one of the many ports of France with a capacity of over 2,000,000 tons.

It is to the navy that this credit for the destruction of this outlaw seagoing craft is due. The navy is and has been the backbone of this war, the same as it has been of almost every great war in history. Without the allied navy the submarine would have perhaps accomplished its nefarious purpose in starving the European allies and in preventing them from securing the necessary munitions of war to defend themselves. It has utterly failed in this respect. The Allies are amply supplied with food, and there are provisions enough on hand now, if every ship should be sunk, to last the Allies and armies for months. The destroyer is the ship which has brought Germany to her knees in submarine warfare and will keep her there. We have not enough destroyers, and it is for this reason we are obliged in this great transportation problem to run risks which would not be taken under ordinary conditions. If every ship was escorted by a sufficient number of destroyers I doubt if there would be a single ship of any consequence sunk, except by the merest accident.

# Library Facilities for Our Soldiers

## By FLORENCE A. HUXLEY

[MANAGING EDITOR, THE LIBRARY JOURNAL]

HUNDREDS of thousands of American soldiers in France who two years ago could not have told what the letters "A. L. A." stood for now speak enthusiastically of the work of the American Library Association in promoting their interest in books and helping them to win the war. Before America entered the war the libraries of the country had been busy gathering literature on the countries involved and data on the issues at stake, and in general had tried to help the American people to an intelligent understanding of its great import. The library buildings were being used as meeting places for the Red Cross chapters and for the numerous other organizations devoted to relief work of various kinds. But when America came forward to take her rightful place with the other allies, the librarians felt that there was a broader service for them to render. In May, 1917, Walter L. Brown, librarian of the Buffalo Public Library and President of the American Library Association, appointed a committee "to assemble the various suggestions that had been made and to bring them before the association with some sense of proportion, possibly with recommendations as to which might be most practical and most helpful to the Government." This preliminary committee comprised: Herbert Putnam, Librarian of Congress, Chairman; Arthur E. Bostwick, Librarian of the St. Louis Public Library; R. R. Bowker, editor of The Library Journal; Gratia Countryman, Librarian, Minneapolis Public Library; M. S. Dudgeon, Secretary, Wisconsin Library Commission; Alice S. Tyler, Director, Western Reserve Library School, and J. I. Wyer, Jr., State Librarian of New York.

At the annual conference of the A. L. A. in Louisville in June, 1917, this committee made its report. It recommended that a War Service Committee of seven be appointed by the President of the association, with power to appoint subcommittees or auxiliary committees as needed, and that arrangements be made for the possible erection, equipment, and maintenance, under the auspices of the association, of district library buildings in each of the sixteen main cantonments then under construction. The report was adopted as read, and a special committee was appointed, consisting ultimately of the following personnel: J. I. Wyer, Jr., Chairman; Gratia Countryman, E. H. Anderson, Director of the New York Public Library; Frank P. Hill, Librarian of the Brooklyn Public Library; Electra C. Doren of the Dayton Public Library; William H. Brett of the Cleveland Public Library, and Charles Belden of the Massachusetts State Library, (now Librarian of the Boston Public Library.)

## BOOKS FOR CANTONMENTS

The position of this committee was still more firmly established by authority conferred by the Federal Government in a letter from the War Department Commission on Training Camp Activities, more familiarly known as the Fosdick Commission. This letter, dated June 28, 1917, asked that the American Library Association assume responsibility for providing adequate library facilities in the thirty-two cantonments and National Guard camps expected to be opened by Sept. 1. Here, in less than a week, was a doubling of the work which the association had tentatively suggested. The opportunity was eagerly seized, however, and at a meeting of the A. L. A. Executive Board in August the War Service Committee was given full authority to solicit funds with which to proceed with the work of supplying books to all soldiers and sailors in this country and abroad, and to enter upon active work at once.

In October, 1917, Dr. Herbert Putnam

was made General Director, and the work was consolidated at the Library of Congress, where permanent headquarters have since been maintained. Prior to his appointment, working through sub-committees and with almost no money, the War Service Committee during the Summer months had yet been able, with the generous help of Edward L. Tilton, a Mew York architect, to perfect plans for library buildings and their equipment; arrange with publishers for liberal discounts on books purchased; prepare and print a suggested list of titles for camp libraries; organize a book campaign which resulted in the collection and shipment of many thousands of books to camps, often far in advance of the arrival of any librarian or A. L. A. representative; establish collecting and sorting stations in New York, Chicago, and a dozen other populous centres; inaugurate a personnel roster, send a few volunteer librarians to camps, where they were housed in Y. M. C. A. buildings pending the erection of separate library buildings, and, finally, organize its first campaign for funds.

## FORTY-THREE CAMP LIBRARIES

This campaign was launched in September under the Chairmanship of Dr. Frank P. Hill. The original time set for its culmination was the week of Sept. 24, but in many places it was continued to a later date. When this War Finance Committee finally closed its account on Jan. 19, 1918, the sum of $1,570,386.44 had been received in cash, and additional subscriptions had been reported, but not received, which would bring the grand total up to $1,727,554.25. This sum included a grant of $320,000 from the Carnegie Corporation of New York, for the erection of thirty-two library buildings at an estimated average cost of $10,000 each.

By January most of these thirty-two buildings had been erected and put into use, together with another at Camp Perry, identical in plan, the gift of an anonymous friend. Today there are forty-three large camp libraries in operation on this side of the water—forty-one of them in separate buildings. Every Y. M. C. A. and K. of C. hut, every Y.

W. C. A. hostess house, every Jewish Welfare Board building, every Salvation Army house, may have its branch of the nearest camp library, with anywhere from 500 to 2,000 books. There are at the time of writing—though the figures will be far exceeded before publication—1,547 such stations in operation, under the careful supervision of the camp librarian, exactly as the branches and stations of any city library are administered.

In addition, 315 small military camps and posts (52 of them aviation camps, including schools and repair depots) have been equipped with book collections, under the general charge of traveling library supervisors; 138 naval and 26 marine stations, and 242 vessels have been supplied with libraries; and 143 hospitals and Red Cross houses have been provided with books. This hospital service is a very important and rapidly growing phase of the work, and is being developed at a pace that keeps the association a little breathless. Special hospital librarians are being appointed in every camp, as well as in the base and deportation hospitals. Books are taken to the men in every ward by the librarian in charge, who stops to chat at each bedside, trying to find just the right book for every individual case.

In the administration of all the camp libraries and stations more than 250 trained librarians have already been engaged. Many of them have been volunteers; others have been given leaves of absence and their salaries continued by their home libraries. Where such an arrangement is impossible, the association has paid them $1,200 and their living expenses, or rather less than the pay a Second Lieutenant receives. As much as possible has the fund of the association been conserved for books and necessary administrative expenses.

## WHAT THE SOLDIERS READ

The average camp library building is about 40 by 100 or 120 feet, and contains from 15,000 to 30,000 volumes. The arrangement of book shelves varies slightly in the different camps, but in general they are placed so as to form attractive alcoves, where comfortable

Windsor chairs invite the men to stop and read. In the evenings and the hours when the men have leisure, every chair will be full and men will be seen standing all about the long room, book in hand, absorbed in story or study.

When the library was still in process of formation it was assumed that fiction would be the main demand, and that the men would read chiefly for recreation. In general this has not been found to be the case. Given the choice between a first-rate novel and a book on his branch of military service or on the business in which he was interested before entering the army, in about seven cases out of ten the soldier leaves the novel on the shelf. As a result of this unanticipated demand for serious books the association has already been obliged to purchase over 600,000 technical books on a wide range of subjects. Fiction has been supplied in generous quantities by the public, both in the early book campaign and in the later nation-wide appeal which was made in March, when over 3,000,000 books were supplied—over 500,000 contributed in New York City alone.

The appreciation of the men has been unexpected and overwhelming. There were many skeptics in the early days who said that the average soldier would not have either time or inclination to read. They had failed to take into account the fact that our men are not average soldiers. The young man of today has learned that he must read to succeed in his business, whatever his line may be.

## CHIEF LINES OF INTEREST

Typical questions asked and answered in a day run about as follows:

Who is the Sultan of Turkey?
How many months in the year is the Baltic navigable?
Is Alan Seeger American or English?
How much space in a line of march is required for a motor cycle?
Is there such a place as hell—and is there a Princess of hell?
What day of the week was July 4, 1915?

The librarian in charge of service on the Mexican border, on a single visit to Eagle Pass, received requests for books on the following subjects—not at all an unusual list: The metric system; algebra; chemistry of gunpowder; Spanish dictionaries, readers, and grammars; army paper work; machine guns; Italian books; Speakers, (readings and recitations;) lettering; geometries; Haweis—"Music and Morals"; gas engines; Bernhardi—"Great Britain, Germany's Vassal"; geography of the Philippine Islands.

Many of the books read show that the men are making after-the-war preparations. Very few plan to make the army or navy their permanent profession, and they use their leisure time, and their hours of convalescence in the hospitals, to fit themselves for better jobs in peace times. Books on business practice, advertising, cost accounting, farming, electricity, are always in demand.

For the men in isolated camps or outposts boxes of fifty volumes are prepared and forwarded, with a message that if the box does not contain material on subjects of particular interest to that group of men, a letter of request is all that is necessary to bring the desired volume to the reader. "The book you need when you want it," is the slogan of the A. L. A. War Service, and if the association does not have in its own stores the exact volume requested, it undertakes to get it either by purchase or by borrowing from some nearby public library.

## BOOKS FOR NAVAL MEN

The work overseas has grown apace. With the service in this country established early in 1918, Dr. M. L. Raney, Librarian of Johns Hopkins University, was sent to Europe to survey the field there and discover the best means of carrying the A. L. A. service to our rapidly growing army on foreign soil. Arrived in England, his first duty was to call on Admiral Sims. He found him rather cold to the idea of library service for the army and navy. The battleships all had libraries, said Admiral Sims, and the chief naval base had a fine club house with an excellent library. However, he gave Dr. Raney a pass to all naval stations under his command. Armed with this, Dr. Raney crossed to Paris, where at the Naval Headquarters the library idea was hailed with delight. They passed him on to an Admiral on active convoy duty along the coast of France, and every man he met on board the ships was equally enthusiastic. He found men preparing to take Annapolis examinations, but lacking textbooks. Cables were called into service and in a surprisingly short time the necessary books had been forwarded from America and were in the hands of the men. That settled the service to the navy. Admiral Sims became an ardent propagandist for the A. L. A., and asked for libraries everywhere, in naval bases, aviation fields, mine-sweeping bases—even, said Dr. Raney in his report of this work, " on his pet battleships that, in February, would never, never need us."

Following the success of his mission with the navy Dr. Raney proceeded to the general headquarters of the army. Armed with approving letters from Major J. H. Perkins, Commissioner for Europe for the Red Cross, and from E. C. Perkins, chief of the Y. M. C. A. of the A. E. F., Dr. Raney laid the whole plan of the A. L. A. before General Pershing in a single document. Two days later (on Feb. 22, 1918—significant date) he received the official indorsement of the plan, including the allotment of fifty ship tons per month free cargo space for the transportation of reading matter, and the duty of receiving the books was added to the tasks of the chief Quartermaster of the A. E. F. The latter at once caused a proper warehouse to be erected for their handling at one of the great debarkation ports, without cost to the association. Since that time 1,030,458 books have been shipped overseas.

## THE WORK IN FRANCE

Dr. Raney returned to this country early in the Spring and, while retaining direction of the work, was succeeded in the active service overseas by Burton E. Stevenson, the novelist and librarian, who organized the first and one of the most successful camp libraries at Camp Sherman, Chillicothe, Ohio. At headquarters in Paris Mr. Stevenson, with Mrs. Stevenson as assistant, began preparing collections of books to forward to the various units, large and small, of the American Army. On July 4 a cablegram announced to the members of the association then assembled in annual conference at Saratoga that the day had been celebrated by placing collections of books on every one of the American hospital trains in France.

In August permanent headquarters were set up at 10 Rue de l'Elysée, in a magnificent building that until fifteen years ago was the residence of the Papal Nuncio to France. " Here," Mr. Stevenson writes, " I am planning to set up a real American public library which will act as a reservoir and central distributing point for the whole of France. What I am trying to do is to institute, in the principal camps, a system somewhat similar to that which we started in the camps in America, by which the boys may look toward our Paris headquarters for advice and assistance. * * * The work is of the most inspiring kind and the demand for books on the part of our men is almost unbelievably great."

This means that in France, and later also in England, as in this country, every permanent camp and school will have its own separate building, with branches in all the huts of the various welfare organizations, and traveling libraries for the men in the smaller units, right up to the front-line trenches. Permission has recently been received from the Army Post Office to forward volumes requested by individual readers under a franking privilege from the reservoir collections set up at Paris and Gievres. This means that any officer or enlisted man can get any book he wants, and return it when he is finished, without cost. A room in the Hotel Mediterranée, which is army department headquarters in Paris, has been set aside for the special purpose of handling these franked books.

## LIBRARIES ABSOLUTELY FREE

Against the advice of some, the association has been insisting on the idea of absolutely free service to the soldier and sailor, and their faith has been justified. Above every case of books in every station overseas is a card on which is printed this message from the Commander in Chief:

> These books come to us overseas from home. To read them is a privilege. To restore them promptly unabused a duty.
> (Signed)    JOHN J. PERSHING.

Another poster in all branch libraries reads as follows:

> These books are loaned on the honor system. If you fail, it fails. America is far away, tonnage scarce, and books precious. Play square with the other fellow; he has played square with you.

Besides the fifty tons cargo space allotted for books each month, every transport that goes over carries a collection of several hundred volumes for the use of the men on shipboard. These books are shipped in specially constructed boxes, which have a centre shelf and can be set up and used as bookcases as soon as opened. Each box holds about seventy volumes, of which about ten are usually of a technical nature, the rest being a selected lot of fiction and biography. These boxes are in charge of the Y. M. C. A. secretaries who sail on each transport, and who see that the books are repacked and forwarded after the ship reaches port.

Magazines also are being sent across. Special arrangements have been made with publishers so that remainders of each month's issue are sent over in bulk. Over 5,000,000 of the so-called Burleson magazines have already been distributed in this country through the agency of the American Library Association, going to camp reading rooms, barracks, outposts, hospitals, troop trains, and wherever reading matter is desired.

When there have been shortages of books there have always been the magazines to fall back on, and in many cases they have furnished the only information on the many new subjects of the day—topics still too new to have gotten into book form.

## GROWTH OF LIBRARY SERVICE

For the year 1919 greatly increased service has been planned. In the United War Work Campaign of November, 1918, now at hand, the American Library Association hopes to secure at least $3,500,-000. The budget which has been prepared and adopted for the expenditure of this sum has some interesting items. They include the construction of twelve large and ten smaller library buildings in overseas camps, together with the rental of five other buildings, besides the Paris and London headquarters; the addition of ten large and ten smaller buildings to those in use in this country, as well as extensive alterations in the ones already in use; the expenditure of more than $1,500,000 in the purchase of additional books and magazines for which there is a crying need, and $1,000,-000 in the maintenance and equipment of the service. Items which are little considered, such as the provision of shipping cases for the 2,500,000 volumes which it is planned to send overseas during the next twelve months, will cost at least $75,000. A much larger sum than the one specified could be used advantageously for the purchase of books. The variety of demands grows daily as the possibilities of the book in the winning of the war are realized more and more by officers and men alike in the service.

# The Government Takes Over the Nation's Colleges

THREE HUNDRED AND FIFTY-NINE colleges and universities taken over by the Government! That was the revolutionary war measure adopted on Oct. 1, 1918, by the Federal authorities of the United States with regard to our higher institutions for academic training. The step was not mandatory but voluntary on the part of the schools included in the scheme; but scarcely a college from the Atlantic to the Pacific refused to respond to the appeal of the War Department. Loyalty demanded acceptance of the program, and 150,000 young men entered college to become soldiers, not scholars.

On campuses—now known by the sterner name of military reservations— they marched forth in military alignment to enroll for the newer tasks of learning how to fight. At the same moment—12 o'clock by Eastern time— the student soldiers throughout the land took the oath of allegiance to the American flag, which was raised in every college simultaneously from ocean to ocean; they listened to messages from President Wilson, General Pershing, and other high officials; then passed, still in civilian clothes, for their first parade in review before the officers of the new army posts. Collectively they had become a regular military unit, the Student Army Training Corps, each man under orders and entitled to a soldier's pay.

In every college these new recruits were addressed by eminent civilians or soldiers, and listened to this message from President Wilson, their Commander in Chief:

The step you have taken is a most magnificent one. By it you have ceased to be merely individuals, each seeking to perfect himself to win his own place in the world, and have become comrades in the common cause of making the world a better place to live in. You have joined yourselves to the entire manhood of the country and pledged, as did your forefathers, " your lives, your fortunes, and your sacred honor " to the freedom of humanity.

The enterprise upon which you have embarked is a hazardous and difficult one. This is not a war of words; this is not a scholastic struggle. It is a war of ideals, yet fought with all the devices of science and with the power of machine. To succeed you must not only be inspired by the ideals for which this country stands, but you must also be masters of the technique with which the battle is fought. You must not only be thrilled with zeal for the common welfare, but you must also be master of the weapons of today.

There can be no doubt of the issue. The spirit that is revealed and the manner in which America has responded to the call are indomitable. I have no doubt that you, too, will use your utmost strength to maintain that spirit and to carry it forward to the final victory that will certainly be ours.

## WAR DEPARTMENT'S OFFER

The plan for this revolutionary step was laid before the colleges in a circular letter and statement sent out on Aug. 28 by Colonel Robert I. Rees of the General Staff at Washington. The statement outlined the method by which every college student was to be voluntarily inducted into the Student Army Training Corps, becoming " a soldier in the United States Army, uniformed, subject to military discipline, and with the pay of a private." The War Department undertook to furnish officers, uniforms, rifles, and equipment, and to assign the students to military duty, after a few months, either at an officers' training camp or in some technical school, or in a regular army cantonment with troops as a private, according to the degree of aptitude shown on the college campus.

At the same time a circular letter to the Presidents of colleges arranged for a contract under which the Government became responsible for the expense of the housing, subsistence, and instruction of the students. The preliminary arrangement contained this provision, among others:

The per diem rate of $1 for subsistence and housing is to govern temporarily, pending examination of the conditions in the individual institution and a careful working out of the costs involved. The amount so fixed is calculated from the experience of this committee during the last five months in contracting with over 100 collegiate institutions for the housing and subsistence of over 100,000 soldiers in the National Army Training Detachment. This experience indicates that the average cost of housing is 15 to 20 cents per day; subsistence, (army ration or equivalent,) 70 to 80 cents per day. The tuition charge is based on the regular per diem tuition charge of the institution in the year 1917-18.

A permanent contract was arranged later under these governing principles:

The basis of payment will be reimbursement for actual and necessary costs to the institutions for the services rendered to the Government in the maintenance and instruction of the soldiers with the stated limitation as to cost of instruction. Contract price will be arrived at by agreement after careful study of the conditions in each case, in conference with authorities of the institution.

The War Department will have authority to specify and control the courses of instruction to be given by the institution.

The entity and power for usefulness of the institutions will be safeguarded so that when the contract ends the institutions shall be in condition to resume their functions of general education.

The teaching force will be preserved so far as practicable, and this matter so treated that its members shall feel that in changing to the special intensive work desired by the Government they are rendering a vital and greatly needed service.

The Government will ask from the institutions a specific service; that is, the housing, subsistence, and instruction along specified lines of a certain number of student soldiers. There will be no interference with the freedom of the institution in conducting other courses in the usual way.

The contract will be for a fixed term, probably nine months, subject to renewal for a further period on reasonable notice, on terms to be agreed upon and subject to cancellation on similar terms.

## STUDENTS TO BE OFFICERS

Why this intensive military training in our colleges for the period of the war? The answer is, to develop officers for handling the growing army. We have at present approximately 1,900,000 men in France. About 900,000 are on the fighting line. The United States Government plans to select 3,000,000 men by the new draft law, including those between the ages of 18 and 45. It hopes to have an army of 5,000,000 men, trained, equipped, and in the field by the opening of the Spring campaign. Such a number will make it possible to put 4,000,000 men on the front, with 1,000,000 behind the lines.

In round numbers, it requires 200,000 officers to handle an army of 5,000,000 men. Sixty thousand officers are now greatly needed, especially Second Lieutenants. These officers are to be developed in our colleges during this academic year, so far as acceptable leaders can be found.

Experience has taught that, as a class, college men make the best officers. Eighty per cent. of the officers of the army today are college graduates, many of them having been trained at West Point. While there are a goodly number of our ablest officers who came up from the ranks, or stepped out of business or professional life into official military position, after a brief period of training, without having ever studied in college, still, college men are and always will be the army's major source of officer supply. The reasons are apparent: The college man possesses a more or less trained mind. The knowledge of mathematics required of an army officer he has already in some measure. The writing of a military order clearly and accurately is not difficult for him by reason of his knowledge in language. Moreover, his mind, because it is trained, is more to be relied on in a sudden call for quick decision.

The Government started its program of encouraging intensive military drill in American colleges in the Spring of 1918. The plan at that time was to divide the country into three districts, east, central and west, with headquarters for army tactics at Plattsburg Post, N. Y.; Fort Sheridan, Ill., and Presidio, San Francisco, Cal. Provision was made for the colored college men at Howard University, Washington, D. C. The colleges and universities of these several districts were invited to send students to the post designated for them on the basis of ten for every one hundred students of the college body, together with one member of the Faculty for every one hundred students. Nearly all the colleges accepted the invitation.

## RESULTS AT PLATTSBURG

The work of the several camps may be illustrated by a brief statement of what has been accomplished at Plattsburg during the Summer period. Preceding the larger gathering of students at this post, 2,800 students came to Plattsburg on June 3 from military colleges, in accordance with the law requiring them to spend one month every Summer in intensive military training at some assigned camp. These young men were known as the R. O. T. C., viz., Reserve Officers' Training Corps. They did so well that the commanding officer of the post asked that 25 per cent. of them remain for the task of assisting in the larger school that was to follow. Six hundred and four of the number remained, and so far as age permitted received the commission of Second Lieutenant on Sept. 16, 1918.

On July 18 students began to pour in from 187 Eastern and Southern colleges that had accepted the Government's invitation to give two months' intensive military training to 10 per cent. of the male student body. By Aug. 10 3,250 men had reported for their work. They were called S. A. T. C., viz., Student Army Training Corps. These men were organized into twenty-four companies. They labored assiduously, both in study and drill, and with marked enthusiasm and efficiency. On Sept. 3 the commanding officer said to a distinguished audience, " In six weeks we have developed here an excellent organization bcause we have a group of men who have trained minds." Not only have these students trained minds, but they are morally clean and physically fit. On entering the camp every young man was carefully examined by a competent physician, and in not one case was there found a trace of venereal disease. Think of it! Such men are the flower of American manhood, on whom we can confidently rely for the leadership necessary for victory.

## RAPID ADVANCEMENT

Practically all the men in the camp, 20 years of age or over, received commissions at the close of the training period and went directly into the army as officers. Those under 20 returned to college, after Sept. 16, to take up the intensive program of military study and drilling of their fellow-students. Thirteen hours a week are given to such work. All students of the draft age will be inducted into the training corps, except the physically defective. The students below 18 years will be enrolled, but not inducted into the military unit. There is high authority for the statement that the students who may be returned at 20 years of age will be allowed to remain in college about two months, those 19 six months, and those 18 nine months before going into the army as officers. Virtually none of the men who return to college this Fall will be in school next year, should the war continue.

Thus our colleges have become little West Points for the remainder of the war. All college work is incidental to the military program. The great purpose of our educational institutions is to win the war, and to this end they have made large sacrifices. Long before the United States entered the war the students of most of our colleges and universities had begun preparations for the coming crisis. Gathered in groups, discussing current problems and listening to lectures on international relations, they naturally foresaw the storm. The universities of California, Chicago, Northwestern, Harvard, Yale, Princeton, Columbia, Johns Hopkins, and scores of others were making ready for the fray. And when war was declared against Germany the graduates and students of our American colleges were in the van as volunteers.

On Sept. 3 and 4 eighty-seven college Presidents counseled at the Plattsburg Post as to how the college curriculum could be adjusted to the military requirement. What a revolution in academic life! Imagine if you can some dear old professor, 70 years of age, who has taught algebra, geometry, and calculus all his pedagogical days, after a certain fashion, never changing, trying to adjust his instruction to the present-day military program! Surely there will be a shaking up of the dry bones in many of our colleges. To quote a broad-brained college President, " It will turn us upside down for a while, but will prove to be a blessing in the long run."

# Turkey's Disaster in Palestine

## Rout and Capture of Two Ottoman Armies by British Force End the Turk's Power as a Belligerent

THE campaign against the Turks in Palestine, begun Sept. 18, 1918, was a brilliant success for the Allies, and developed into so serious a disaster for the Turks that by Oct. 12 it was semi-officially reported that the Turkish Government had opened negotiations for a separate peace, its entire forces being in a state bordering upon collapse. As a result of the disasters in Palestine and Mesopotamia Enver Pasha, who for years had been the commanding and controlling figure in Turkey, was overthrown on Oct. 8, Talaat Bey, Grand Vizier and Minister of the Interior, having surrendered his portfolio four days previously. Ahmed Tewfik Pasha, formerly Ottoman Ambassador in London, was appointed Grand Vizier in succession to Talaat Pasha. An Athens dispatch filed Sept. 26, but not received in America until Oct. 8, stated that there had arrived at Mitylene, on behalf of Rahmi, Governor of Smyrna, three parlementaires to enter into peace negotiations. One of the emissaries was a Greek, one an Englishman, and one a Turk.

No further details were obtainable at the time, but the hypothesis was that the Vilayet of Smyrna had revolted from the Government of Constantinople. This province covers the western end of Asia Minor and has an area of 25,801 square miles and a population of 2,500,000.

Various dispatches of an unofficial character came to Europen capitals announcing that revolution had broken out at sundry points in the Turkish Empire, and all the indications pointed to the conclusion that Turkey could no longer remain as a belligerent, and that its unconditional surrender was only a question of days.

### ALLENBY'S ADVANCE

General Allenby's new offensive, which began on Sept. 18, 1918, was an unbroken succession of victories. The British forces, in close liaison with the Arabs, under King Hussein, advanced rapidly on a line from the Mediterranean at Haifa, extending across Palestine to the Arabian desert. Damascus, the capital of Syria, was taken on Oct. 1, and was occupied by the British forces and a portion of the Arab Army. The British pushed forward rapidly. By Oct. 8 they had occupied the towns of Zaleh and Rayek, respectively thirty-three and thirty miles northwest of Damascus. On the same day a French naval division entered the important port of Beirut, 160 miles northwest of Damascus, and the Allies thus had an unbroken front from that port to the desert, and were rapidly advancing northward toward Aleppo, the main base of the Turkish Armies in Asia Minor. The capture of Aleppo was inevitable, as the Turkish forces were in rapid retreat and in a state of demoralization.

The British forces along the Euphrates and Tigris also began a forward movement toward Mosul, with a prospect of coming soon into contact with General Allenby's army, thus establishing an unbroken and victorious front from the Mediterranean across Mesopotamia into Persia. It was reported on Oct. 8 that Persia was being evacuated by the Turks.

General Allenby's forces captured between Sept. 18 and Oct. 5 more than 71,000 prisoners and 350 guns, besides 8,000 prisoners taken by the Arabs. Included in these figures were the Turkish commanders of the 16th, 19th, 24th, 53d, and composite divisions, the commander of the Maan garrison, Ali Verbi Pasha, and German and Austrian troops numbering more than 206 officers and 3,000 privates.

The landing of French naval forces at Beirut was enthusiastically received by the populace. The territory in Syria through which the British and French troops advanced was conceded to France by a treaty.

It was reported from Paris on Sept. 26 that Palestine would be administered under an agreement reached between the British, French, and Russian Governments in 1916. When the Bolshevist authorities took control in Russia they published a number of secret diplomatic documents found in the archives in Petrograd. Among them was a convention negotiated by Russia, France, and Great Britain under which Alexandretta, in Asiatic Turkey, was to be a free port and Palestine was to be a protectorate under the three Governments. Both France and Great Britain have since officially announced that Palestine should be an autonomous State, and pledges have been given that the Zionistic Jews shall be safeguarded in the erection there of a Jewish (Zionistic) State.

## THE FIRST BLOW

General Allenby began his offensive on Sept. 18, and it proved a complete surprise to the Turks. An official version of the initial attack says:

Preparations for this battle entailed a good deal of marching. The troops were always moved by night and remained hidden in the orange and olive groves in the daytime. The British mastery of the air prevented enemy observers from seeing any change in the dispositions and the movements of large columns. Troops of all arms were thus concealed skillfully in a country where the marching of men raises huge columns of dust, and the Turk, too, possessed positions that commanded a wide range. But he remained mystified, which is the finest tribute that could be given to the work of the British staff.

The infantry opened a way for the cavalry to pass through, and then there was a wonderful spectacle of long columns of British yeomanry and Australian light horse and picturesque Indian cavalry moving over a wide expanse of country throughout the coastal sector of the plain of Sharon to get to the enemy's rear.

The initial successes were achieved on the historic plain of Esdraelon or Jezreel, where the Israelites fought battles, as recounted in the Book of Revelation and parts of the Old Testament. The region is famous as the battlefield of Armageddon and, according to Revelation, is to be the scene of the decisive battle at the end of the world.

Nazareth, captured in this advance, is at the northern edge of the plain, west of the hills of Galilee and southeast of Acre, Tul Kerani, and Nablus, which were taken the first day. All through the region are the remains of two old civilizations, the ruins of the tribes mentioned in the Bible and the later civilization of the Roman colonies.

Beisan, another ancient town occupied in the initial advance, lies in the Valley of the Jordan, not far from the river, about fifty-five miles northeast of Jerusalem and directly east of the plain of Esdraelon, although to reach it from that region a traveler would pass through the depression between the Hills of Galilee and the Hills of Ephraim. This town was a centre of the Romans during their control of the land, and the remains of an acropolis, a Roman bridge, a theatre, fragments of houses and columns, and many excavated tombs may be seen there yet. Only a few hundred persons live near the town now.

## HISTORIC DAMASCUS

The capture of Damascus, capital of Syria, by the troops of General Allenby, opened the way to Aleppo, on the Constantinople-Bagdad Railroad, 180 miles to the north. Damascus is the most beautiful and, after Bagdad, the most historically romantic city in Asiatic Turkey. It is situated in a fertile plain at an altitude of 2,350 feet, at the base of the Anti-Libanus; its water supply still survives as one of the marvels of Jewish engineering work, with many improvements wrought by the Arabs; its population is 150,000.

Prior to the war, it was the headquarters for the Fifth Turkish Army Corps, and later were drilled in the fields about the city the Seventh, Eighth, and Fourth Armies, which have just been annihilated by Allenby.

More than any other city under Turkish rule, Damascus has preserved its ancient buildings and architecture. The five-mile city wall, which the Crusaders besieged in vain in 1148, is still there with its seven gates, and through the

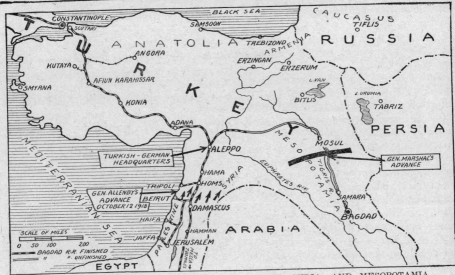

**SCENE OF BRITISH SUCCESSES IN PALESTINE, SYRIA, AND MESOPOTAMIA**

city still runs the "street called Straight" where St. Paul had his abode. It is said that the description of Paradise in the Koran was taken from the appearance of Damascus.

Once conquered by King David, it soon achieved independence and attacked the Kingdom of Israel itself. Then conquered by Assyria, it later successively became a colony of Greece and of Rome. In the seventh century came the Arabs, who made it a great show city, a seat of learning, and of metal arts, the most famous of which was the making of sword blades. From the sixteenth century it has alternately surrendered to Egyptian and Turkish conquerors. In 1841 it was finally restored to Turkey together with Syria.

### IN THE JORDAN VALLEY

On Sept. 20 the enemy resistance had collapsed everywhere save on the Turkish left in the Jordan Valley. General Allenby in his official report describes the operations on that day as follows:

Our left wing, having swung around to the east, had reached the line of Bidieh, Baka, and Messudich Junction, and was astride the rail and roads converging at Nabulus.

Our right wing, advancing through difficult country against considerable resistance, had reached the line of Khan-Jibeit, one and one-fourth miles northeast of El-Mugheir and Es-Sawieh, and

was facing north astride the Jerusalem-Nabulus road.

On the north our cavalry, traversing the Field of Armageddon, had occupied Nazareth, Afule, and Beisan, and were collecting the disorganized masses of enemy troops and transport as they arrived from the south. All avenues of escape open to the enemy, except the fords across the Jordan between Beisan and Jisr-ed-Dameer were thus closed.

East of the Jordan Arab forces of the King of the Hedjaz had effected numerous demolitions on the railways radiating from Derat, several important bridges, including one in the Yurmak Valley, having been destroyed. Very severe losses have been inflicted on the masses of Turkish troops retreating over the difficult roads by our air services.

A German airplane, later ascertained to have been carrying mails, landed in the midst of our troops at Afule. The pilot, who believed the place still to be in Turkish hands, destroyed the machine and its contents before he could be secured.

### COMPLETENESS OF VICTORY

W. T. Massey, the official correspondent with the British troops, in a dispatch dated Sept. 23, thus described the completeness of the victory in the early advances:

"More than 260 guns have been located in our lines, and possibly more will be found. Artillery ammunition in vast quantities has been found everywhere. Some of the depots are acres in extent. As the Turks only manufacture small arms ammunition, if they try to raise new armies to take the place of these destroyed, they must call on Germany for every gun, transport, and instrument of war required.

"Today saw one of the most remarkable sights which a soldier ever gazed upon. From Balata, where the road from Nabulus falls through craggy hills and narrow passes to Wadi Farah, there is a stretch more than six miles long covered with débris of the retreating army. In no section of Napoleon's retreat from Moscow could there have been a more terrible picture of hopeless, irretrievable defeat.

"In this area alone were eighty-seven guns of various calibres, fully 1,000 horse and oxen drawn vehicles, nearly 100 motor lorries, cars filled with kitchens, watercarts, and a mass of other impedimenta. The road was black with the carcasses of thousands of animals and bodies of dead Turks and Germans.

## AMAZING AIRPLANE WORK

"This was the work of the Irish, Welsh, and Indian infantry. The artillery pressure behind the indomitable British and Australian airmen in front of the infantry had forced the enemy over the hills into the road, and just as the guns began to shell the retiring transport airmen swooped down to 200 feet and bombed the head of the column. Once that was accomplished, time only was required to finish the job, and this was done with surprising thoroughness. One flight after another took up the work, until the whole column was one vast broken mass.

"The enemy troops, seeing escape with the vehicles was impossible, fled to the hills. Some who had endeavored to find an outlet up the Beisan road fell into the hands of cavalry waiting for them. Others, accepting the inevitable, sought refuge in our lines.

"For effectiveness of systematic bombing it is difficult to find a parallel to this destroyed column. The operations working up to this débâcle were magnificently conducted."

The capture of the important town of Amman, lying on the Hedjaz Railway

about forty-five miles northwest of Jerusalem, is thus described by Mr. Massey in a dispatch dated Sept. 26:

"I have just returned from witnessing the mounted men's triumphant capture of Amman, and can speak of the splendid handling of the troops in a country where nature had raised enormous barriers against an attacking army.

"The Anzac mounted division east of the Jordan was assisted by some infantry, including a battalion of British West Indians, whose gallant bayonet charge on the Jordan's banks won the admiration of the colonial veterans. They knew the country, having made two dashing raids and inflicted damage on the Hedjaz Railway. They drove the Turks and Germans out of Amman, though the presence there of Germans indicated what deep importance the enemy set upon this section of the line.

"At the moment when Allenby's plans overwhelmed the two Turkish armies in Palestine, the Anzacs began a movement to harass the Turkish Fourth Army over the Jordan. They had to get across several miles of flat country, under enemy observation, and enter the Gilead mountain chain—almost impenetrable except for one pass to Es Salt. Until the pass was won, only pack transport was possible. The cavalry moved up goat tracks and were in Es Salt on the third day after the operations began east of the Jordan.

"The enemy, fearing an advance against the town months ago, made a strategic road west of Es Salt and had wired one valley, and all the approaches thereto had been covered by many machine guns. The New Zealanders declined a frontal attack. They got over the crags of the hill, threatened the enemy flank, and compelled a retirement on the town. There was not much fighting at Es Salt. Between 600 and 700 prisoners were taken.

"On Sept. 24 the cavalry got to Suwcileh, half way on the Amman road, and at dawn yesterday began operations against Amman. An Australian light horse brigade moved from the right in the Ain Sir direction, continually driving over the rough plateau the Turkish cavalry.

"Infantry accounted for a number of detachments of prisoners, mounted on little wiry horses, very unlike the British mounts, causing surprised interest as they passed through the lines. On the right the brigade made good progress, and at noon had got into excellent position southwest of Amman."

Major Gen. Sir Frederick B. Maurice, in commenting on General Allenby's strategy, wrote as follows on Sept. 24:

The more one studies General Allenby's operations the more admirable they appear, and the manner in which the movements of the infantry and cavalry were

synchronized though separated by wide stretches of difficult hilly country is as perfect an example of co-operation of two arms in a decisive battle as is to be found in the pages of history.

Little less remarkable is the speed with which the mass of horsemen, with sufficient supplies and munitions to make them independent for several days, was got across the maze of our own and of the Turkish trenches in the plain north of Jaffa. This argues most careful and thorough staff work and preparation.

Field Marshal Liman von Sanders, who commanded three Turkish armies of about 100,000 men in Palestine, fled on Sept. 20 when the first disaster overtook his troops, and was reported to be in Constantinople on Oct. 5.

# Bulgaria's Surrender

## King Ferdinand, His Armies Shattered, Is Forced to Capitulate and Abdicate

THE vigorous offensive begun in the Balkans by the allied armies on Sept. 16, 1918, led swiftly to the most important developments in that portion of Europe since the early days of the war. Within the next two weeks the Bulgarian forces had been split into two helpless segments, the Bulgarian Government had been compelled to surrender and make a separate peace with the Allies, King Ferdinand had abdicated in favor of his son Boris, and Germany, confronted by the first break in the ranks of the Central Powers, saw Turkey isolated and helpless and the Pan German dream of empire in the Orient shattered.

From the base at Saloniki the British and Greek troops struck at the enemy on the right, in the region of Lake Doiran, while the Serbians and French shattered the enemy's centre, driving forward on a twenty-five-mile stretch across the Czerna River; meanwhile a large Italian army was dealing heavy blows at the left, where the enemy's line extended west into Albania. By Sept. 23 the British held Doiran, the Serbians had captured the formidable Drenska Massif, a great natural defense of Prilep,

with that city itself, and the First Bulgarian Army in that region, finding itself cut off from the Second Army in the Doiran region, fled in disorder. On Sept. 24 the Second Army also was in full retreat, the Serbians had crossed the Vardar, and the pursuit continued along the whole front from Monastir to Beleu.

Veles, the principal railway centre of Old Serbia, was captured by the Serbians on the 25th, and the British and Greek troops invaded Bulgaria near the fortress of Strumnitza, capturing it the next day. This opened a way for the Allies toward the gates of Sofia itself. By Sept. 29 the Bulgars were burning their stores in the important base of Uskub, which the Serbians and French, advancing from Veles, entered on the 30th. The Bulgarian First Army was caught between the two allied advances, and its destruction was becoming inevitable. King Ferdinand's desperate appeal for German aid brought no results; Germany had troubles of her own on the west front. Bulgaria had come to the end, and nothing remained but to surrender. Malinoff, the Premier, had long been in favor of making peace with the Entente, and pacifist crowds besieged the Government building in Sofia demanding surrender and voicing bitter anger against King Ferdinand for the plight into which he had brought the nation.

## PROPOSAL FOR ARMISTICE

King Ferdinand assembled his Grand Council on Sept. 23, with the result that a formal demand was made on Berlin and Vienna for immediate assistance. It met with evasive replies. Meanwhile revolution and anarchy threatened the King at home, and the anti-German feeling in Sofia had reached the point where a massacre of all the Germans in the city was feared. Ferdinand gave way to the wishes of his Cabinet and people, and, despite the fact that at Nauheim a month before he had personally promised Kaiser Wilhelm to remain faithful to the alliance, he gave his consent to a movement for unconditional surrender to the Entente.

An official Bulgarian statement dated Sept. 24, but not published until four days later, was as follows:

In view of the conjunction of circumstances which have recently arisen, and after the position had been jointly discussed with all competent authorities, the Bulgarian Government, desiring to put an end to the bloodshed, authorized the Commander in Chief of the army to propose to the Generalissimo of the armies of the Entente at Saloniki a cessation of hostilities and the entering into of negotiations for obtaining an armistice and peace. The members of the Bulgarian delegation left yesterday evening in order to get into touch with the plenipotentiaries of the Entente belligerents.

The leaders of the Ministerial bloc of the Bulgarian Parliament, according to advices from Sofia, published the following official note in connection with the Government's proposal for an armistice:

In accordance with orders of the leaders of the Ministerial bloc, the Government at 5 o'clock Wednesday afternoon [Sept. 25] made an official offer of an armistice to the adversary. The leaders of the bloc are in accord that the army and the people must maintain military and public discipline, which is so necessary for a happy issue in these times, which are decisive for the recently begun work of peace.

News of these developments came suddenly to the outside world on Sept. 28, in the announcement that the Bulgarian Government was sending delegates to negotiate peace with General Franchet d'Esperey, Commander in Chief of the allied armies in Macedonia. A high Bulgarian officer had presented himself at Saloniki in behalf of General Terodow, commanding the Bulgarian Army, and had asked a suspension of arms for forty-eight hours to permit the arrival of authorized delegates from the Bulgarian Government, who were on their way with the assent of King Ferdinand to arrange terms of peace. In view of the possibility that all this might be merely a military ruse, General d'Esperey sent the following reply:

My response, which I send through a Bulgarian officer bearing the letter in question, cannot be, by reason of the military situation, other than the following:

I can accord neither an armistice nor a suspension of hostilities tending to interrupt the operations in course. On the other hand, I will receive with all due courtesy the delegates, duly qualified, of the Royal Bulgarian Government, to which your Excellency alludes in the letter. These delegates to present themselves in the British lines, accompanied by a parlementaire.

(Signed) FRANCHET D'ESPEREY.

## TERMS OF SURRENDER

The Bulgarian delegates arrived at Saloniki on Sept. 28. They were General Lonkhoff, commander of the Bulgarian Second Army; M. Liapcheff, Finance Minister, and M. Radeff, a former member of the Bulgarian Cabinet. On the evening of the 29th an armistice was signed, General d'Esperey signing for the Entente Allies and the three Bulgarian delegates for their Government. The terms of the surrender were submitted to the Entente Governments and received their approval, and hostilities ceased officially at noon, Sept. 30. The Bulgarian delegates to Saloniki were accompanied by the American Chargé d'Affaires at Sofia, Dominic I. Murphy; though he went merely as an observer, the Washington Government ordered his return to Sofia, indicating the American Government's desire to have no part in these pourparlers.

The armistice was a purely military convention and contained no provisions

MAP OF BALKAN FRONT SHOWING BATTLELINE AT TIME OF BULGARIA'S SURRENDER

of a political character. Its terms, as summarized for the press, were as follows:

> Bulgaria agrees to evacuate all the territory she now occupies in Greece and Serbia, to demobilize her army immediately, and surrender all means of transport to the Allies.
>
> Bulgaria also will surrender her boats and control of navigation on the Danube and concede to the Allies free passage through Bulgaria for the development of military operations.
>
> All Bulgarian arms and ammunition are to be stored under the control of the Allies, to whom is conceded the right to occupy all important strategic points.
>
> The military occupation of Bulgaria will be intrusted to British, French, and Italian forces, and the evacuated portions of Greece and Serbia, respectively, to Greek and Serbian troops.
>
> The armistice means a complete military surrender, and Bulgaria ceases to be a belligerent.
>
> All questions of territorial rearrangement in the Balkans were purposely omitted from the convention.
>
> The Allies made no stipulation concerning King Ferdinand, his position being considered an internal matter—one for the Bulgarians themselves to deal with.
>
> The armistice will remain in operation until a final general peace is concluded.

Thus, nine days before the third anniversary of Bulgaria's decision to cast her lot with Germany, she had made a full surrender to the Allies. On Oct. 8, 1915, the Sofia Government had issued a manifesto announcing Bulgaria's decision against the Entente. This action had been merely the result of a secret treaty signed by Germany and Bulgaria in the preceding July.

Bulgarian troops began evacuating Serbia on Oct. 1. When hostilities had ended the Serbians held a line from Uskub eastward through the mountains to the Bulgarian border near Charevo. They continued to advance into their own oppressed country day by day, meeting no opposition from Bulgarian troops, but fighting German and Austrian forces at some points. An official statement issued from German Headquarters on Oct. 6 announced the withdrawal of all the German troops who had been fighting in the ranks of the Bulgarian Army. At the same time Germany rushed all available forces to Sofia and other strategic points in Bulgaria and Serbia with the object of holding territory in these countries as long as possible. A dispatch from Rumania declared that 250,000 troops had been withdrawn from that country to go to Sofia, and signs of an anti-German uprising in Rumania at once began to appear.

## NAVAL BLOW AT DURAZZO

A further reverse for the Central Powers in the Balkan Peninsula came on Oct. 2, when the Austrian naval base at Durazzo was destroyed by allied warships. Italian and British cruisers, protected by Italian torpedo boats and American submarine chasers, succeeded in making their way through mine fields into Durazzo Harbor. An intense bombardment lasting two hours and aided by airplanes destroyed the naval base on the shore and sunk the Austrian ships found at anchor. Italian sailors, in the teeth of a hot enemy fire, torpedoed an Austrian destroyer and a steamer, while twelve American submarine chasers sunk two enemy submarines. The only damage suffered by the allied squadron during the operations was a slight injury to a British cruiser from a torpedo fired by a submarine.

In the interior of Albania on Oct. 7 Italian troops captured Elbasan after crushing stubborn Austro-Hungarian resistance, and Italians were already operating in the coastal region close to Durazzo.

The Serbians, with the other allied troops, swept rapidly northward from Uskub after the Bulgarian collapse, intent upon driving the remaining Germans and Austrians out of Serbia and beyond the Danube. On Oct. 13 they captured Nish after a day's vigorous fighting. This made a definite cut in the famous Orient Railroad from Berlin to Constantinople, and the German authorities announced that henceforth trains on this line would run only to the Serbian border, but that passengers might be able to go further by means of local trains. The Serbian peasants, unearthing weapons which escaped confiscation by the troops of occupation, were aiding the Allies to drive out the retreating invaders.

The spirit of the Serbs in this campaign to recover their native land was described by Ward Price in a dispatch of Sept. 30 as follows:

The Serbs began their drive with an assault on those precipitous heights on the Czerna bank, the crest of which the Bulgarians had intrenched. So steep was the climb toward the enemy positions that the Bulgars could only oppose the advancing Serbs by leaning over their parapets to drop bombs. Twice before the Serbs had attacked these formidable mountains in vain. "We felt that the third time would change our luck," said a young Serbian officer whom I knew well, "and if it did not, what could we do better than go for-

ward to die as close as possible to the homes we long to win back again from our enemies?"

It was this resolve to do or die that carried the Serbs right ahead over obstacles that every cold-blooded observer would have said were humanly impassable. Undoubtedly the rapidity of the Serbian push enabled them to live to great extent on the captured enemy supplies and materials. I am told of a Bulgar battery trying to get away, all of whose drivers were shot down by Serbian rifle fire from heights beside the road. The Serbs then came down and found the battery practically complete with transport and 20,000 rounds of ammunition. They lost no time, but carried two of the captured guns forward to a position from where they could shell a Bulgarian howitzer battery, which they captured in its turn.

## FERDINAND'S ABDICATION

King Ferdinand of Coburg abdicated the throne of Bulgaria on Oct. 4 in favor of his son, Crown Prince Boris, and left Sofia the same night for Vienna. On his way through Budapest he told the Bulgarian Consul there that he intended in the future to devote himself to his favorite pursuits, chiefly to botany. He denied playing a double game, and said he had always wished to remain faithful to his allies. " But unexpected circumstances which transformed the situation," he declared, " compelled my abdication and forced me to quit Bulgaria in the interests of the people. They were unwilling to continue the war, and there was opposition between them and me. Serious troubles broke out in Sofia. I was unwilling to be an obstacle to the general desire for peace, so I left." Before leaving Sofia he issued the following manifesto:

By reason of a succession of events which have occurred in my kingdom and which demand a sacrifice from each citizen, even to the surrendering of one's self for the well-being of all, I desire to give as the first example the sacrifice of myself.

Despite the sacred ties which for thirty-two years have bound me so firmly to this country, for whose prosperity and greatness I have given all my powers, I have decided to renounce the royal Bulgarian crown in favor of my eldest son, his Highness the Prince Royal Boris of Tirnovo.

I call upon all faithful subjects and true patriots to unite as one man about the throne of King Boris, to lift the country from its difficult situation and to elevate new Bulgaria to the height to which it is predestined.

Before signing his declaration of abdication, he received the party leaders, all of whom expressed approval of his decision. The abdication was announced by Premier Malinoff at a crowded session of the Bulgarian Parliament, and the news was received by the Deputies with the greatest interest. Premier Malinoff, explaining to the Deputies the situation leading up to the surrender, said:

We know of the profound misery which has overwhelmed the country and we deplore it. We know the wrong was due largely to not receiving succor from our allies, but this is past, and our duty now is to repair as far as possible the results of the national catastrophe.

Ferdinand's popularity with his people has been waning rapidly since it became apparent to Bulgarians that he had erred grievously in plunging the country into war on the side of the Teutonic powers. Advices from Sofia had indicated that before the armistice with the Entente was signed King Ferdinand was trembling for his throne and feared that a revolution might upset the whole dynasty.

King Ferdinand took the Bulgarian throne in 1887, but his election as monarch was not confirmed by the great powers until 1896. He married Marie Louise de Bourbon, eldest daughter of Duke Robert of Parma, in 1893. Her death occurred in 1899, and in 1908 Ferdinand married Princess Eleanore of the house of Reuss, who died in 1917.

Prince Boris in a manifesto to the Bulgarians announcing his accession to the throne said he would adopt the name of Boris III. He reminded his people that he was born in Bulgaria, (Jan. 18, 1894,) and belonged to the Orthodox faith. He promised to respect the Constitution and invited the people to rally round the throne.

The accession of Prince Boris was received enthusiastically by the populace, according to a dispatch from Sofia. The bells of all the churches were rung. Addressing a large crowd from the palace, Boris said: "I thank you for your manifestation of patriotic sentiments. I have faith in the good star of Bulgaria, and I believe that the Bulgar people, by their good qualities and cooperation, are directed to a brilliant future."

The Bulgarian Cabinet offered its resignation to the new King, who expressed his confidence in it and asked the Ministers to retain their portfolios. The first decree signed by King Boris was one demobilizing the Bulgarian Army.

All Germans, Austro-Hungarians, and Turks were ordered to leave Bulgaria within a month. By Oct. 10 the German-Turkish exodus from Bulgaria had been greatly accelerated. Officers, soldiers, and civilians were arriving in Vienna on freight cars, and long convoys of artillery and foodstuffs received the right of way. Passenger trains were reaching Vienna twelve to twenty hours late. Steamer service on the Southern Danube had been discontinued.

# The Albanian Nationality

## By CONSTANTINE A. CHEKREZI

[FORMERLY SECRETARY TO THE INTERNATIONAL COMMISSION OF CONTROL FOR ALBANIA]

ONE of the vexatious Balkan questions which the coming peace conference—or probably the Entente Allies alone—will soon be called upon to settle in a definitive manner is that of Albania. The Albanian nationality is not very well known today, but in the course of history it has played an important rôle in the Balkan Peninsula, besides being the oldest nationality in Southeastern Europe.

History and legend afford no record of the arrival of the Albanian race in the Balkan Peninsula. None the less, it is now pretty well established that the Albanians are the direct descendants of the earliest Aryan immigrants, who were represented in historical times by the kindred Illyrians, Macedonians, and Epirots. The Albanian language, as spoken today, is the only surviving representative of the Thraco-Illyrian group of languages, which formed the primitive speech of the Balkan Peninsula. Its groundwork and grammar are distinctly Indo-European, but the language is entirely different from the neighboring tongues.

In ancient times the Albanians constituted the kindred kingdoms of Illyria, Epirus or Molossia, and Macedonia. Foremost among the Kings of those remote times stands the famous Pyrrhus of Epirus, and Teuta, the celebrated Queen of Illyria. Owing to her peculiar geographical situation, Albania has been successively invaded by various races, such as the Gauls, the Romans, the Goths, the Slavs, and finally the Turks, but the natives have either driven out or absorbed the invaders.

During the first half of the fifteenth century the kingdom of Albania stood as the main bulwark of Christianity in the Balkan Peninsula, under the celebrated national hero, George Castriota, or Scanderbeg, (Prince Alexander,) as the Turks surnamed him for his military valor. After his death Albania suc- cumbed to the repeated attacks of the Turks, in 1478, last among the Balkan nationalities. She remained under the Turkish domination for about 450 years, but the Albanians managed to live practically independent under the nominal sovereignty of the Sultan.

In 1910-12 the overzealous Young Turks tried to destroy that internal independence of Albania, but in the end they were forced to recognize it officially, thanks to the desperately determined resistance of the Albanians.

## ALBANIAN STATE CREATED

In the Fall of 1912 the Balkan Alliance, formed of Bulgaria, Serbia, Greece, and Montenegro, declared war against Turkey. The Albanians declared their independence in November of the same year; but, as a result of their unexpected triumphs over Turkey, the Balkan allies sought to partition even the territories of Albania among themselves. These plans were frustrated, however, by the intervention of Austria and Italy, who had interests of their own to protect in Albania. An acute international crisis ensued, and, but for the timely mediation of Great Britain, the European war would have broken out two years earlier than it did.

The question of Albania was then referred to the Ambassadorial Conference at London, which recognized the independence of Albania on Dec. 20, 1912. The conference undertook also the task of the delimitation of the frontiers of the new State, which it placed under the collective protection of the six great powers. But in order to satisfy the irreconcilable views and aspirations of the Balkan States, as well as those of the great powers, the territory of Albania was cut down to an absurd minimum, while the largest part of it was handed over to Serbia, Montenegro, and Greece. From the very day of the creation of the new State there have been a great many misgivings as to its ability of ever standing on its own feet, owing to the merciless treatment it had received at the hands of the conference.

In definitive fulfillment of their task, the powers assigned to Albania, on the proposal of Italy, the German Prince of Wied, who was to be the hereditary ruler of the young kingdom. But the acute rivalry of Austria and Italy, each striving to get the upper hand, with the customary intrigues and machinations of the Balkan States, the indifference of the other European powers, the total lack of any administrative organization, the empty coffers of the new-born State, the impairment of its physical faculties by the Conference of London, and, finally, the outbreak of the European war, rendered the position of the Prince untenable, and he was forced to retire to his estate in Prussia on Sept. 3, 1914, after a disheartening reign of only six months.

## ALBANIA IN THE WAR

On leaving Albania the Prince of Wied handed over his authority to the International Commission of Control, a body consisting of one delegate from each of the six great powers, with an Albanian representative. This commission had been empowered by the London Conference to assist the Albanian Government in running public affairs and to control every action that exceeded the limits set by the Provisional Constitution. But the International Commission fared as badly as had the Prince, being without funds and without efficient means for the execution of its decrees. Moreover, it could not be rationally expected that the delegates of Austria and Germany would co-operate for the sake of Albania with the delegates of Great Britain and France while the two groups of Governments were at war.

As a consequence the International Commission soon dispersed, and the country was left without any government at a critical moment when international morals had relaxed—after the violation of Belgian neutrality by Germany —and when each State was watching its neighbor to discover any slackening in its power of resistance.

## ESSAD PASHA

One month after the flight of the Prince, Essad Pasha, his former Minister of War, whom Prince William had condemned to perpetual exile for plotting against his sovereign authority, hastily returned to Durazzo, the late provisional

MAP OF ALBANIA, SHOWING ITS RELATION TO OTHER BALKAN COUNTRIES.

capital. Essad Pasha came back to Albania with a medley of hirelings recruited from among the Albanians assigned to Serbia. This was done with the authorization of the Serbian Government, which even provided the funds for their equipment. Essad Pasha now set up a multi-colored Government, the so-called " Government of Central Albania or of Durazzo," made up of ignorant peasants and of some vagabond old Turks. His constant effort was to set up by any means available a Government under his Presidency, so as to figure later before the world as an unjustly dispossessed ruler or sovereign in the same class as King Peter of Serbia and King Nicholas of Montenegro.

The Government of Essad Pasha had

hardly been formed when the rebels who had attacked Durazzo and besieged Prince William within its walls turned their arms against the alien Government of the Pasha. They attacked Durazzo, in the same old way, but the Pasha found shelter under the protecting fire of the Italian Navy, which rushed to his aid, and which alone was able to check the advance of the rebels and to save Essad Pasha and his capital. Thenceforth the dominion over which the "Government of Central Albania" was ruling was confined to the small peninsula of Durazzo. The rebels remained encamped at the gates of the besieged city, and the Italian squadron was constantly moored in the Bay of Durazzo ready for action against them. This curious situation lasted up to the day when the Serbian and Montenegrin troops came to the relief of Essad Pasha. Meanwhile Essad Pasha persisted in speaking and acting on behalf of Albania, which stood in arms against him and his alien Ministry.

## INVASION OF ALBANIA

In the meantime the troops of King Constantine of Greece had reoccupied the southern provinces of Albania, the Government of Athens having declared that the occupation was intended to be only provisional. On Dec. 25, 1914, Italian marines and soldiers landed at Valona, the chief seaport of Albania, and occupied the city, which is situated at the bottom of one of the best natural bays in Europe. The Government of Rome declared that the occupation of Valona by Italian troops was necessary in order to safeguard the interests of the Albanian State, which had been jeopardized by the Greek occupation of the territory adjoining Valona.

At the beginning of the following year, 1915, the Serbians and Montenegrins felt tempted by the action of the other neighbors of Albania. They, therefore, started the invasion of Northern and Central Albania, in spite of the angry protests of Italy and the remonstrances of the Entente Allies, who advised the Governments of Belgrade and Cettinje not to scatter their forces, as they were all sorely needed in the war

against Austria-Hungary. But the Serbians and Montenegrins, taking no heed, overcame the Albanians in a series of bloody and desperate battles, and occupied Northern and Central Albania.

Essad Pasha was relieved for the moment, but in the Spring of 1916 the Teuton-Bulgarian armies entered on their decisive campaign against the Serbians and Montenegrins, and the latter were forced to withdraw their forces from Albania. Into this country, however, their decimated armies fell back, shortly afterward, in their retreat toward the Adriatic. The Austrians occupied Northern and Central Albania, and Essad Pasha, who in the meantime had declared war against the Central Powers, was forced to transfer his Government and his insignificant army to Saloniki, where he posed as a victim of the war, a dispossessed ruler. It is only lately that the Allies have begun to realize that his influence and authority in Albania do not extend beyond his immediate followers in Saloniki. Had the Allies realized this when it was yet time, the Albanians, who were struggling against Essad Pasha, would have been on their side against the Central Powers, and the Serbian retreat through the mountains of Albania would not have proved so disastrous.

During the late Summer of 1916 the Italian expeditionary forces in Albania began their southward march, and gradually drove the troops of King Constantine from Southern Albania. The process of the occupation of these southern provinces by the Italians was brought to an end in the month of December, 1916. During that same month a French detachment of the army of Saloniki expelled the Greek royalist troops from the district of Koritza, (or Korcha,) which has been raised into an independent Albanian Republic.

## UNDER ALLIED OCCUPATION

On Italy's entering the war the Government of Rome stated that one of the war aims of the Italian people was the re-establishment of the independence and integrity of the Albanian State. In pursuance of this policy the Italian Government declared the independence and unity of Albania. On June 3, 1917, General Ferrero, commander of the Italian expeditionary forces in Albania, issued an official proclamation to the Albanians by which he declared, in the name of his Government, the independence and unity *of the whole* of Albania "under the shield and protection of the Italian Kingdom."

The question of how far this protection goes has been raised and discussed many a time, but no definite answer has yet been given. This particular point, however, assumes great importance in view of the announced evacuation of Albania by the Austrians. On Oct. 3, 1918, the Vienna Government issued the following statement: "We have withdrawn our divisions from Albania. This was rendered necessary by events on the Bulgarian front." This means, of course, that very soon the whole of Albania will be under either wholly Italian or mixed allied occupation, and the phrase "under the shield and protection of the Italian Kingdom" calls for interpretation.

## PRESENT CONDITIONS

To understand exactly the position of this oldest people in the Balkans one must have a general idea of the conditions prevailing therein. As reliable statistics are wanting with regard to all countries under the Turkish domination, the population of the Albanian principality cannot be stated with exactness. Whitaker's Almanack places it at 2,000,000, but I think it would be reasonable to reduce this figure to 1,500,000. On the other hand, it is estimated that the whole Albanian race numbers 3,500,000, dispersed in Serbia, Montenegro, Greece, Macedonia, and Italy. The Conference of London allotted to Serbia alone almost 1,000,000 Albanians. The area of the Albanian State as delimited by the London Conference is about 11,000 square miles, or about the same area as that of the State of Maryland.

Wild stories have long been current in regard to the conditions of the population. The phrases "semi-barbarous," "wild," "uncivilized," &c., have been used indiscriminately in fanciful narratives regarding Albania. While one cannot deny that Albania is backward in civilization owing to her incessant struggles against Turkish domination for 440 years, the average Albanian is not any worse than the average Balkanian, be he Greek or Bulgarian or Rumanian or Serbian.

Considering the fact that the Turkish Government has never allowed the establishment of Albanian schools, the wonder is that the Albanians have been able to maintain their standard of intellectual development, which is far above the level reserved for them by the Turks.

Brigandage, despite the prevailing myth on the subject, is practically unknown in Albania. The native is too proud and chivalrous—and these are his two main national characteristics—to lower himself to the condition of highwayman. Miss Helen Stanhope of Chelsea, Mass., was not harmed or interfered with in any way during her travels in Albania, but she was immediately captured and held for ransom by a band of Bulgarian highwaymen as soon as she stepped out of Albanian territory.

As to the reputed fanaticism of the Albanians and their constant religious strife, it may be said that religious toleration exists in Albania to a degree found nowhere else in the Balkans. Divided as the Albanians are into Moslems, Roman Catholics, and Greek Catholics, they have always managed to get along far better than Catholics and Protestants in Western Europe. In Albania there are today families in which one brother is a Moslem and another a Christian, yet they live in perfect harmony within the walls of the same home.

In general the people of Albania are characterized by an innate and irresistible love for liberty, by intelligence and practical spirit, and by great eagerness for progress and civilization. The country is very rich in natural resources, such as forests, mines, fisheries, but abnormal conditions thus far have rendered impossible their development and exploitation.

# The Republic of Koritsa

The war has developed a curious historical episode in Albania in the form of the little Republic of Koritsa, or Korce, to use the official Albanian spelling. This impromptu republic originated in the late Autumn of 1916 in the brilliant brain of a French cavalry Colonel. The bulk of Albania was at that time occupied by the Austrians. In the south the Italians held Avlona, on the Adriatic, but between them and the allied Saloniki forces was a solid wedge of Austrians and King Constantine's unfriendly Greeks.

In the Autumn General Sarrail pushed forward in a northwesterly direction and occupied Koritsa and the region near Lake Malik. This was the first time that French troops from Saloniki had found themselves in Albanian territory, and the Colonel in command was faced with the problem of setting up a civil administration. Northeast lay Serbia and southeast lay Greece, but Koritsa was neither. According to the Treaty of Bucharest, the only legal instrument recognized by the Allies, it was part of Albania. The Colonel solved the difficulty by proclaiming Koritsa, and the caza, or administrative district of which it is the capital, to be an autonomous Albanian republic, under the protection of the Allies.

General Sarrail, confronted with a fait accompli, accepted the situation, and Koritsa has remained a republic. A council of twelve elders, mixed Musulman and Christian, was set up as the governing body, Essad Pasha uttered a blessing in Albanian, a flag was devised, a Post Office system instituted, and stamps issued.

All did not go without a hitch. The two-headed eagle, which flaunted so bravely on the flag and the first stamp issue, roused antagonism, and was said to be not the genuine Albanian bird beloved of Skanderbeg and all good Shkipetari, but a monstrous Austrian imperial creature.

Yet, on the whole, Koritsa greatly enjoyed its autonomy, even if it realized that the days were coming when it would be merged in some larger whole. Meantime, owing to various advances of the Allies, it gained several extensions of territory.

Allied arms made steady progress in Albania during the Autumn. Italian troops pushing northward entered Elbasan on Oct. 7, 1918, after crushing stubborn Austro-Hungarian resistance. At the same time Italian forces in the coastal region were approaching Durazzo, while the Austrian naval base at Durazzo was destroyed by Italian, British, and American warships on Oct. 2. The clearing of hostile forces out of Albania proceeded rapidly in the weeks that followed.

# Progress of the Allies In Russia

## New Provisional Government Established at Ufa Aspires to Restore the Russian Front

### [PERIOD ENDED OCT. 15, 1918]

ALLIED military operations on Russian territory made steady progress during September and October. On the North Russian front the fighting in the second half of September resulted in an advance of fifty miles southward along the River Dvina. The operations were conducted by British troops associated with American, Serbian, and Russian detachments, and the advance was pushed along both banks of the river simultaneously. The Soviet forces retired to Kotlas, in the Government of Vologda, 235 miles from Archangel, the enemy ships sowing mines as they fled. Some hundred prisoners were captured, a number of Soviet vessels sunk, and several guns captured, together with a good deal of munitions. On Oct. 3 the Americans held a village situated on the River Vaga, which is a tributary to the Dvina, midway between Shenkursk and the Bolshevist base, Baelsk. The American detachment played an important part in restoring Archangel to normal life.

Americans were also fighting in Eastern Siberia. They co-operated with the Japanese in the capture of Blagoviestchensk, the capital of the Amur Province, which took place on Sept. 18. Fifteen thousand Austro-German prisoners were reported to have been disarmed there by the Japanese. The Japanese also occupied Alexeievsk and took 2,000 Teuton prisoners. The enemy retreated up the Zeya River. The Japanese cavalry, partly with the aid of General Semenoff's troops, had previously occupied Chita, (Sept. 6,) and Merchinsk, (Sept. 10,) in Transbaikalia. On Sept. 22 Japanese cavalry, marching eastward from Chita and northwest from Blagoviestchensk, effected a junction at Rufulov. The next day it occupied Zeya-Pristan, on the River Zeya, 240 miles north of Blagoviestchensk. The allied forces entered on Sept. 27 the town of Banbuki, where they seized nine steamers, many railway cars, and a large supply of war materials. According to a Tokio dispatch of Oct. 4, the Soviet troops abandoned the gold mining districts in Transbaikalia.

According to a Peking dispatch of Sept. 23, the Germans and Austro-Hungarians in Russia were ordered by the German Emperor on Sept. 10 to join the Soviet forces and to oppose Japan and her allies.

### CZECHS ON THE VOLGA

On Sept. 11 the Czechoslovak forces in Siberia were reported to be concentrating at Irkutsk and preparing to move westward with a view to relieving their comrades in European Russia, and shortly afterward began the movement of Czech units to the Volga front, which was hard pressed by the enemy owing to lack of munitions. In the middle of September the Soviet forces occupied Volsk, Simbirsk, and Kazan. According to a Petrograd dispatch of Sept. 30 the latter city was recaptured by the Czechoslovaks. The Bolsheviki laid the fall of Kazan to the behavior of the Lettish troops intrusted with the defense of the city. It was stated that all the officers of the 3d Lettish Regiment were sentenced to death " for failure to keep the regiment in its proper position and for having tolerated meetings while the battle was in progress."

In Northeastern Russia the number of armed Czechs and Russians was estimated at 60,000, and they were believed to be outnumbered by the Bolshevist forces. Their situation was perilous.

On Oct. 11 General F. B. Maurice thus summarized the military situation in Russia:

In Russia the position is that, thanks to the intervention of the allied forces which landed at Vladivostok, our position

MAP OF RUSSIA SHOWING CHIEF CENTRES OF WAR ACTIVITY

as far as Lake Baikal is practically assured. Between Lake Baikal and the Urals the Czechoslovaks are supreme, and they control the Trans-Siberian Railway for some 400 miles west of the Urals as far as Kazan and Samara. Intermittent warfare is being waged between the Czechoslovak and Bolshevist forces, in which the former have, on the whole, held their own, but are in need of assistance. Between the lower Volga and the Caucasus the Cossacks, who are anti-German and anti-Bolshevist, are in control. But the whole of the rest of Russia west of the Volga, with the exception of Archangel and the Murman coast, is in the hands either of the Germans or of the Bolsheviki.

## THE UFA GOVERNMENT

Late in September the Russian Embassy at Washington received a report to the effect that a number of the members of the Constituent Assembly, which was elected in the Fall of 1917, had held a national convention in the City of Ufa and set up a central government for the whole of Russia. On Oct. 7 the newly established Ufa Government informed the Russian Ambassadors throughout the world, as well as the allied Governments,

that it had taken over the power as a successor to the Provisional Government which was overthrown by the Bolsheviki. Regarding the composition of the convention and the personnel of the directorate created by it, we find the following information in the manifesto issued by the new Government:

The National Convention was composed of :

1. The present members of the Constituent Assembly and representatives of the committee of the same assembly.

2. Representatives of the Temporary Government of Siberia, the Regional Government of the Urals, the Temporary Government of Esthonia.

3. Representatives of the Cossacks of Orenburg, Ural, Siberia, Irkutsk, Semiretchensk, Enisseni, and Astrakhan.

4. Representatives of the Government of the Bashkirs, the Kirguio, the Turkestan, and the Turko-Tartars of interior Russia and Siberia.

5. Representatives of the Convention of Municipalities and Zemstvos of Siberia, the Ural, and the Volga.

6. Representatives of the following parties and organizations: Socialist Revolutionists, Social Democrats, (Mencheviks,) Socialist Labor Party, Constitu-

tional Democrats (Narodnaia Svoboda) of the Social Democratic organization "Iedinstvo," and of the Association of the "Rebirth of Russia."

In a unanimous effort to save the Fatherland, to re-establish its unity and its independence, the Convention has decreed to transmit the supreme power over the whole territory of Russia to the Provisional Government, composed of five persons:

Nicholas D. Avksentieff, Nicholas I. Astroff, Lieut. Gen. Vassili G. Boldyreff, Peter V. Vologodski, Nicholas V. Tchaikovsky.

The program of the new Provisional Government is formulatetd in some detail in its constitutive act. This document follows:

### GENERAL PRINCIPLES

1. Until the moment of the convocation of the Constituent Assembly, the Russian Provisional Government is the sole possessor of supreme power over the whole territory of Russia.

2. On the order of the Russian Provisional Government all functions of supreme power temporarily exercised by Regional Governments are transmitted to the Provisional Government.

3. Definition of the limits of the power of the Regional Governments, which are to be founded on the principles of broad regional autonomy and in accord with the program stated below, is confided to the judgment of the Russian Provisional Government.

### OBLIGATIONS OF THE GOVERNMENT TOWARD THE CONSTITUENT ASSEMBLY

The Russian Provisional Government accepts the following obligations:

1. The Provisional Government will aid the Convention of Members of the Constituent Assembly, which is acting as a State institution, in its work, aiming to secure the attendance of members of the Constituent Assembly and to prepare for the opening of the session of the assembly as elected in November, 1917, at the earliest possible date.

2. All acts of the Government will be based on the sovereign and unquestionable right of the Constituent Assembly. The Government will take vigilant care that the subordinate administrative institutions shall not infringe the rights of the Constituent Assembly or retard in any way the beginning of the Assembly's activities.

3. The Government will, without delay, report concerning all its acts to the Constituent Assembly, from the very beginning of its activities; it owes entire submission to the Constituent Assembly as the only possessor of sovereign power in Russia.

### IMMEDIATE AIMS OF THE PROVISIONAL GOVERNMENT

In endeavoring to reconstitute the unity and independence of Russia, the Provisional Government sets forth as its immediate aim:

1. A struggle for the liberation of Russia from the power of the Bolshevist Soviets.

2. The reintegration in Russia of adjoining regions which were detached or separated.

3. Annihilation of the treaty of Brest-Litovsk and of all other international treaties concluded after revolution of March, 1917, either in the name of Russia or in the name of its provinces, by any authority except the Provisional Government.

4. Restoration of treaties with the allied nations.

5. Continuation of war against the German coalition.

In its interior policy the Provisional Government pursues the following aims:

### MILITARY AFFAIRS

1. The creation of a single and powerful Russian Army beyond the influence of political parties and subordinate, through its military chiefs, to the Russian Provisional Government.

2. Exclusion of intervention by military authorities in the domain of civil authorities except in the fighting zone of the armies or regions declared by the Government, in cases of extreme necessity, in conditions of siege.

3. Establishment of strict military discipline based on law and humanity.

4. Interdiction of political organizations into the army and its entire isolation from politics.

### CIVIL AFFAIRS

1. Liberated Russia must be constituted in accordance with liberal principles of regional autonomy, taking into consideration the geographical, economic, and ethnographical differences. The national organization and federation of the State will be determined by the Constituent Assembly, possessor of the supreme power.

2. The Government secures to national minorities which do not occupy definite territories the free development of their national culture.

3. The Government secures to the liberated parts of Russia the re-establishment of democratic municipalities and Zemstvos, fixing immediately the nearest possible date for the new elections.

4. The Government secures the realization of civil liberties.

5. The Government will take necessary measures actually guaranteeing public security and order.

## ECONOMIC REGULATIONS

1. To cope with the economic disorganization.

2. Development of productive forces of the country with the aid of private capital, Russian as well as foreign, and of personal initiative.

3. Legal regulation of commerce and industry.

4. Increase the productiveness of labor and reduce the nonessential expenditure of national revenues.

5. Development of labor legislation, protection of labor and regulation of the conditions of employment and discharge of workmen.

6. The Government recognizes full liberty of unions.

7. Relative to questions of supplies, the Government stands for abolition of State monopoly of wheat and abolition of fixed prices, continuing at the same time to regulate distribution of products existing in sufficient quantities, and will organize State warehouses with the aid of private commerce and co-operative societies.

8. In the sphere of finance the Government will combat the depreciation of paper money in working out the reconstitution of the fiscal system, increasing the direct income tax and the indirect taxes.

9. The Constituent Assembly alone has the right to solve definitely the agrarian question, and the Government cannot admit any modification which would impede the work of the Constituent Assembly. It, therefore, temporarily leaves the exploitation of the soil to its present holders and resumes activities aiming to regulate and increase to the utmost the exploitation of the soil, in conformity with the peculiarities of the regional customs.

## ORDER OF SUBSTITUTION OF MEMBERS OF THE GOVERNMENT

The Provisional Government, possessor of supreme power, exercises this power in accordance with the above principles. Until the convocation of the Constituent Assembly the members of this body cannot be recalled and are not responsible to anybody for their activities.

The following persons are chosen to serve as substitutes for members of the Provisional Government who may be obliged to quit their functions:

Andrew A. Argunoff, Vladimir A. Vinagradoff, General Michael V. Alexeieff, Vassili V. Sapojnikoff, and Vladimir M. Zenzinoff.

In case of the absence of one of the members of the Provisional Government their substitution will take place in the following manner:

N. B. Avksentieff would be replaced by A. A. Argunoff.

N. I. Astroff would be replaced by V. A. Vinagradoff.

Lieut. Gen. V. G. Boldyreff would be replaced by General Michael V. Alexeieff.

P. V. Vologodski would be replaced by V. V. Sapojnikoff.

N. V. Tchaikovsky would be replaced V. M. Zenzinoff.

So as fully to realize the activities of the Government, those members of the Provisional Government who are at present absent are replaced in order designated in the preceding article.

Members of the Provisional Government will take a solemn oath when assuming their functions.

The new Provisional Government is supported by former Premier Kerensky, who on Oct. 10 asked the British Government to accord formal recognition to it. The Entente Governments, however, decided to wait for further evidences of its ability to act for the Russian Nation.

The Ufa Government commenced the formation of a new national army. The first step in this direction was the mobilization of the classes of 1918 and 1919 by the Autonomous Siberian Government of Omsk. The 200,000 young recruits are being trained by 30,000 officers. The Academy of the General Staff is at Tomsk, Western Siberia.

## REIGN OF TERROR

The feeling of insecurity in Soviet circles has resulted in a state of affairs repeatedly described by eyewitnesses as a Reign of Terror. The month of July, which witnessed the execution of Nicholas II. by the Ural Soviet, may be considered the beginning of that reign. The fifth Soviet Congress, which took place shortly before the murder of the Czar, passed a resolution to the effect that " all counter - revolutionary plots must be suppressed without mercy," and that " the revolutionary proletariat and the poorest peasantry must answer these criminal plots with mass terror against the middle classes." It was also in July that Pravda, the official organ of the Communist Party, (the Bolsheviki,) wrote editorially, " Watch out, you of the middle classes; you are just as mortal as the Czar whom you have so passionately supported," while the Northern Commune, a Petrograd daily, declared that the time had come when " the application of terror is a necessity and when revolutionary force can maintain itself only by the merciless suppression of its enemies."

A correspondent of The London Daily Chronicle, who was arrested and imprisoned, together with other Englishmen, in the Peter and Paul Fortress after the assassination of Commissary Uritsky, wrote to his paper that prison conditions were much worse than under the old régime. The prisoners he saw in the fortress were mainly former officers. "Most of them," he said, "had not been examined and some had been confined without any accusation being made against them for over a month."

A member of a group of seventy-six Englishmen from Moscow, who reached London on Oct. 3, was quoted as saying that "in recent months executions have run into 100 a week, for no reason except that the victims, sent to their death without trial, were formerly officers or wealthy people." The same person is credited with the story of an officer's wife allowed to bring food to her husband for four days after he had been shot, and of another woman who was told by Commissary Jacob Peters that her husband had been shot by mistake. It was reported early in October that Alexander J. Gutchkov, War Minister in the first Provisional Government, was murdered by robbers and ex-Premier Alexander Trepov had been assassinated.

The State Department at Washington authorized the following statement: "All persons coming out of Russia report the existence of appalling conditions. Slaughter of representative people and former officers is taking place. These are shot without trial, and the only charge offered is that of being 'dangerous to the Soviet.' One detail is that officers are shot at night in the cellars, guns being muffled by silencers."

## TERRORIST DECREE RESCINDED

The situation was discussed at a meeting of the Central Executive Committee of the Soviets, and, according to a Moscow daily, the authorities rescinded the reign of terror at the instance of Premier Lenine and decided to return to orderly methods of government. The decree failed to change the situation. A proposal to free the political prisoners was

defeated in the Soviet, and M. Zinoviev, a Bolshevist leader, was quoted as saying that it was the duty of every revolutionist to be a terrorist.

According to a dispatch to the Leipziger Abendzeitung of Sept. 21, a soldier in Kursk fired twice at Trotzky, but the bullets missed their mark. A later dispatch reported a renewal of the attempts to assassinate Soviet officials.

Dewitt C. Poole, acting American Consul General in Moscow, arrived in Stockholm on Sept. 26. An order for his arrest, signed by the Extraordinary Commission, arrived two hours after he passed the Finnish frontier. Information received by the State Department at Washington was to the effect that, late in September, several hundred English and French citizens, officials among them, were imprisoned in the Fortress of Peter and Paul and also in the Moscow Kremlin. Among the allied officials arrested by the Bolsheviki were the Ministers formerly credited to the Rumanian Government, including American Ambassador Charles J. Vopicka.

The British and the Russian authorities came to an agreement regarding the exchange of their representatives and subjects. On Sept. 25, Litvinov, the London representative of the Soviet Government, left for Russia, together with a group of his compatriots. He was to stay aboard a ship until the British in Russia were safe.

## AMERICA'S PROTEST

On Sept. 21 the American Government, through Secretary of State Lansing, sent an appeal to all the associated and neutral Governments urging them to express their condemnation of the reign of terror in Russia. The text of the document follows:

This Government is in receipt of information from reliable sources revealing that the peaceable Russian citizens of Moscow, Petrograd, and other cities are suffering from an openly avowed campaign of mass terrorism and are subject to wholesale executions. Thousands of persons have been shot without even a form of trial; ill-administered prisons are filled beyond capacity, and every night scores of Russian citizens are recklessly put to death; and irresponsible bands are venting their brutal passions in the daily massacres of untold innocents.

In view of the earnest desire of the people of the United States to befriend the Russian people and lend them all that is possible of assistance in their struggle to reconstruct their nation upon principles of democracy and self-government, and acting therefore solely in the interest of the Russian people themselves, this Government feels that it cannot be silent or refrain from expressing its horror at this state of terrorism. Furthermore, it believes that in order to check the further increase of the indiscriminate slaughter of Russian citizens all civilized nations should register their abhorrence of such barbarism.

You will inquire, therefore, whether the Government to which you are accredited will be disposed to take some immediate action, which is entirely divorced from the atmosphere of belligerency and the conduct of war, to impress upon the perpetrators of these crimes the aversion with which civilization regards their present wanton acts.

Most of the countries of the world indorsed this note, and the diplomatic representatives of Norway and Holland in Soviet Russia protested jointly against Bolshevist terrorism.

## THREE GERMAN TREATIES

On Sept. 7 the German papers published the text of the three treaties which were signed between Russia and Germany on Aug. 27 and ratified by the Central Executive Committee of the Soviets on Sept. 2. They are known as the German-Russian Supplementary Treaty, the German-Russian Financial Agreement, and the German-Russian Private Law Agreement, and are very elaborate. Extracts from the main clauses of the first two treaties follow:

In Clause 1 of the German-Russian Supplementary Treaty to the Brest peace treaty it is stated: " In so far as this has not yet been done, German-Russian commissions will immediately be formed to fix the demarcation lines for all fronts where German and Russian troops face one another. These demarcation lines shall be so drawn that there are neutral zones between the respective fronts, which zones must not be trodden by any members of the respective armies, with the exception of parlementaires. In so far as there is not yet regular traffic between the respective fronts, such traffic will be established by the demarcation commissions."

Clause 2, which deals with the separation movements in Russia, says inter

alia: " In so far as is not otherwise prescribed in the peace treaty or in this supplementary treaty, Germany will in no wise interfere in the relations between Russia and parts of its territory, and will thus in particular neither cause nor support the formation of independent States in those territories."

Clause 3, dealing with North Russian territory, says: " Germany undertakes that no attacks of any sort shall be made on Russian territory from the Finnish side, while Russia will employ all means at its disposal, in defense of its neutrality, to expel Entente forces from the North Russian regions."

Clause 4, dealing with Esthonia, Livonia, Courland, and Lithuania, says: " Russia, taking account of the position at present existing in Esthonia and Livonia, renounces sovereignty over these regions, as well as all interference in their internal affairs. Their future fate shall be decided in agreement with their inhabitants." The clause then sets forth arrangements to facilitate Russian commerce via Esthonia, Livonia, Courland, and Lithuania, providing that Russia shall receive free harbor zones at Reval, Riga, and Windau, where the storage and packing of goods imported from or consigned to Russia can take place without hindrance, and exports and imports from Russian customs districts can be regulated by Russian officials.

According to Clause 5, Germany will evacuate Russian Black Sea territory, with the exception of the Caucasus which she occupied, when the peace treaty which is to be concluded between Russia and the Ukraine has been ratified.

In Clause 6 Russia agrees that Germany shall recognize Georgia as an independent State. Russia will promote the extraction of raw oil and raw oil products in the Baku district in so far as lies in her power, and will give Germany a quarter of the supplies obtained, or at least a certain number of tons monthly, yet to be agreed upon. In so far as the yield may be sufficient for the delivery of this fixed quantity, it will be supplemented by supplies obtained elsewhere.

In Clause 7 Germany recognizes the Russian ownership of the warships confiscated by the Germans after the ratification of the peace treaty, as well as Russia's claim to compensation for the Russian supplies seized by German troops after the conclusion of peace, except for those seized in the Ukraine and Finland.

## ENORMOUS INDEMNITY

Clause 1 of the Russo-German Finance Agreement stipulates that Russia will pay Germany six milliard marks ($1,500,-000,000) for the indemnification of Germans who suffered loss through Russian measures, regard being paid to corresponding Russian counterclaims and the value of the stores seized in Russia by the German forces since the conclusion of peace. Of these six milliards an amount of one and a half milliard marks will be paid by a remittance of 245,564 kilograms of fine gold and 545,440,000 rubles in bank notes. This remittance will be made in five installments, namely, 42,860 kilograms of fine gold and 90,900,000 rubles in bank notes to be paid on Sept. 19, 1918, and four amounts of 50,676 kilograms of fine gold and 113,635,000 rubles in bank notes to be paid respectively on Sept. 30, Oct. 31, Nov. 30, and Dec. 31, 1918. One milliard marks will be settled by the delivery of Russian goods in amounts of fifty million marks each by Nov. 15 and Dec. 31, 1918, amounts of 150,000,000 marks each by March 31, June 30, Sept. 30, and Dec. 31, 1919, and 300,000,000 by March 31, 1920. Two and a half milliards will be settled by Dec. 31, 1918, by means of bonds to be taken up in Germany by the Russian Government, such loan bearing interest at 6 per cent. from Jan. 1, 1919, and to be redeemed by amortization of one-half of 1 per cent., together with the saved interest. The question of the remaining one milliard marks is reserved for special agreement in so far as its payment is not taken over, with Germany's assent, by the Ukraine and Finland in their negotiations with Russia regarding property. Clause 2 of the Financial Agreement deals with the handing over of respective bank deposits and credits. Clause 3 deals with the adjustment of certain differences in the respective oconomic systems of the two countries.

The news came on Oct. 11 that the Finnish Diet, at a public meeting, had chosen Prince Frederick Charles of Hesse as King of Finland. The Agrarian and Socialist members had abstained from voting, as a protest against the election.

## THE BATTLE FOR BREAD

By the middle of October the downfall of the Bolshevist régime was being hastened more by hunger than by political enemies. On the eve of the first anniversary of the proletariat dictatorship it faced the most terrible famine in modern history. An American who had just come out of Russia told The Associated Press correspondent at Stockholm of widespread military preparations among the peasants against the Lenine-Trotzky Government, due wholly to impulses of self-preservation. In many places the wheat and oats crops were in the hands of armed peasant organizations, which were guarding them against the Bolsheviki. In three districts of the Vyatka Government alone the peasants had organized and armed 15,000 men, chiefly returned soldiers, to resist Soviet attempts to take their grain. The peasants were paying the soldiers 500 rubles each monthly. The correspondent continues:

The food crusaders sent from Moscow and Petrograd meet with such resistance that many who escape death join the anti-Bolshevist forces and assist in tightening the noose of starvation about Petrograd and Moscow, the two Soviet strongholds, which are undergoing a hunger siege far more death-dealing than the spasmodic revolutionary outbreaks directed against them by the Social Revolutionists and the Social Democrats.

Infant mortality in Petrograd has increased to 50 per cent. School statistics show from 57 to 87 per cent. of the enrolled children are absent on account of illness. The situation is growing worse daily, and the juvenile population of Petrograd will practically be wiped out this Winter unless food is provided from foreign countries. According to Captain William B. Webster of the American Red Cross, who has just come from Petrograd, starvation is claiming thousands, especially aged and infirm persons without resources, who are unable to get food at the Government restaurants or return to their native villages.

Arrival at Archangel of a relief ship which left an American port in August with 4,600 tons of food, drugs, and other supplies for allied soldiers and destitute civilians in Northern Russia was announced Oct. 12 by the American Red Cross. The cargo was valued at $1,500,-000, the amount originally appropriated for relief at that point.

## AN AUSTRIAN REPORT

To counteract the effect of Bolshevist propaganda among the Austro-Hungarian soldiers the Austrian Bureau of Propaganda published a pamphlet compiled by an official commission which visited Russia. Curiously enough, the pamphlet begins by admitting that the Central Powers had used Lenine as their accredited agent to weaken Russia, dissolve its political institutions, and wipe out its army. This cynical confession is followed by a graphic description of the results in the political, military, industrial, and economic field. Terrors, alarms, panic, distress, hunger, misery, murder, and anarchy are the results, so much so that the question now arises whether the Central Powers have any interest in further sustaining Soviet rule. The pamphlet minutely describes the disorder and anarchy in the Bolshevist administration.

The commercial and industrial population and a large part of the peasants, says the pamphlet, long for the overthrow of Soviet rule, and it was significant that when Krylenko ordered the return to the colors of some troops who had been dismissed not one man obeyed his order. Those who grasped power under the Soviet standard did so for selfish motives, to tyrannize over others, and, adds the pamphlet,

The hands of even the most prominent leaders are not clean of bribery, and bribery is rampant among the smaller fry, who simply reek with corruption. In the army discipline is a thing of the past. Soldiers throw off their uniforms and go home or return to their regiments at will. Nobody dares stop them. If at home they find nothing to eat they simply return to their regiments to have food, but not to fight, unless it is to shoot down civilians. Thus, in the fortress of Dünaburg (Dvinsk) there were at one time no fewer than 200,000 of these soldiers who were there only for the rations they got or exacted from the population and peasants. They held political meetings as a pastime, made noisy demonstrations, fired their rifles at night to terrify the people, changing their commanders every day and sometimes bastinadoing them.

## RUIN OF INDUSTRY

The disorder and anarchy of Soviet rule described by the Austrian document almost presaged the crime at the British Embassy. It says:

The police no longer exist in Russia. Any one professing himself a Bolshevik can commit any crime with impunity. Street murders, mobbing, rioting, and lynching are common occurrences. They are almost a pastime of the Bolsheviki. In Petrograd the tram service and the lighting are suspended, the schools are closed for weeks, miscreants and idlers abound in the streets and attack sledges, carriages, or any passing vehicle. They often undress the people merely to rob them of their clothes, and let them go

away naked. Rifle shots are heard constantly in the streets, drink shops are looted, and when the crowds get a chance they summarily lynch these malefactors. No regular administration of justice exists. The Judges are selected at random, and the scenes in the Soviet courts of justice have no parallel in any civilized land. The courts are invaded by the crowd, and the public, when it does not like a Judge, simply hustles him out and decides the case itself. Savage scenes sometimes follow. An old Admiral, accused by some blackguards, was thus sentenced to death with some others, but as he was too weak to walk he was put on the shoulders of another man likewise condemned to death, and before they had gone far they were both shot down.

Some time ago at Sevastopol Bolshevist sailors killed the engine drivers in a station, amid indescribable scenes of savagery, simply because they had refused to start the trains at the arbitrary commands of the sailors. The Bolsheviki represent no idealist system, no civil movement, but simply terrorism and the dissolution of all civilized society. They are not the expression of the majority of the Russian people, as is proved from the fact that they attained power only by violence. They refused to permit the meeting of the Constituent Assembly because, despite all their efforts, they obtained only one-third of the votes. They have ruined all industry, commerce, and social life in Russia. The great textile factories at Morosoff, near Moscow, where by far the largest amount of cloth was produced in Russia, were ruined after only five days of Socialist and Bolshevist management.

Similar scenes and results followed in the great steel works of Petrograd, in the Neva works, and at the Putiloff works, and Petrograd sent half a million of idle workers to Moscow. All industry is at a standstill. The setting up of a boiler and engine alone costs now from 150,000 to 200,000 francs, ($30,000 to $40,-000,) and the repairs of a single locomotive cost 1,400,000 francs, ($280,000.) The chemical industry no longer exists. The production of sugar, which amounted to 100,000,000 sacks, descended to 40,000,000, and finally to 10,000,000. The postal and telegraphic services are in a complete state of anarchy, and a letter may take from four to six weeks to get from Moscow to Petrograd, if it gets there at all. The railway material is going to ruin. The former rolling stock is dilapidated and is not replaced by new. The Austro-Hungarian Commission had difficulty in finding a locomotive to take their train from Petrograd to Dvinsk, and they finally got one which could go only at the rate of ten miles an hour.

# Lenine and Trotzky German Agents

## Secret Documents Unearthed in Petrograd Prove That Bolshevist Leaders Are Paid Traitors

### [First Installment]

THE United States Government, through its Committee on Public Information, sent a special representative to Russia in the Winter of 1917-18 to learn the underlying truth concerning the chaotic conditions there. This representative, Edgar Sisson, came into possession of some seventy documents which in their entirety constitute complete proof of what the world had long suspected, namely, that Lenine and Trotzky and other members of the Bolshevist Government of Russia were paid German agents who were systematically betraying the Russian people—even the workingmen whom they pretended to represent—and were working from first to last for the Imperial German Government under the direction of German officers in Petrograd.

Mr. Sisson sent these incriminating documents to George Creel, head of the Committee on Public Information, embodying them in a report, with explanatory notes appended to the translations. Many of the documents are originals annotated by Bolshevist officials. The others are photographs of originals. The two main series are corroborated by a third set of typewritten circulars, (see appendix later,) of which only two originals are possessed, but all of which fit perfectly into the whole pattern of German intrigue.

These documents show that the Bolshevist revolution was arranged for by the German Great General Staff and financed by the German Imperial Bank and other German financial institutions. They show that the treaty of Brest-Litovsk was a betrayal of the Russian people by the German agents, Lenine and Trotzky; that a German-picked commander was chosen to "defend" Petrograd against the Germans; that German officers have been secretly received by the Bolshevist Government as military advisers, as spies upon the embassies of Russia's allies, as officers in the Russian Army, and as directors of the Bolshevist military, foreign, and domestic policy. They show, in short, that the present Bolshevist Government is not a Russian Government at all, but a German Government, acting solely in the interests of Germany and betraying the Russian people, as it betrays Russia's natural allies, for the benefit of the Imperial German Government alone.

The first document is a photograph of a report made to the Bolshevist leaders by two of their assistants, informing them that, in accordance with their instructions, there had been removed from the archives of the Russian Ministry of Justice the order of the German Imperial Bank "allowing money to Comrades Lenine, Trotzky, 'and others' for the propaganda of peace in Russia"; and that, at the same time, "all the books" of a bank in Stockholm had been "audited" to conceal the payment of money to Lenine, Trotzky, and their associates by order of the German Imperial Bank.

This report is indorsed by Lenine, with

his initials, for deposit in "the secret department" of the Bolshevist files. And the authenticity of the report is supported by Document No. 2, which is the original of a report sent by a German General Staff representative to the Bolshevist leaders, warning them that he has just arrested an agent who had in his possession the original order of the German Imperial Bank referred to in Document No. 1, and pointing out that evidently "at the proper time steps were not taken to destroy the above-mentioned documents."

## TEXT OF REPORT

CURRENT HISTORY MAGAZINE herewith presents—in two installments—the complete text of Mr. Sisson's report, with photographic reproductions of a few of the documents in the original Russian:

Three groups of documents are subjected to internal analysis in the material that follows. One group consists of originals, one group consists of photographs of documents believed still to be in the file rooms of the Russian Bolsheviki, and the third (the appendix later) of typewritten circulars that have not been traced to their originals except in the case of two of the number. The chief importance of the third group is that its appearance inspired the efforts that led to the uncovering of the other groups. And they fit into the fabric of the whole.

The first set of these appendix circulars came into my hands on Feb. 2, in Petrograd. An additional set appeared the following day at an office where I frequently called. A third appeared in another quarter a day afterward. One set was in Russian and two in English. On Feb. 5 I held all three sets. A possible explanation for their appearance at this time and their intent is given in the appendix.

By themselves they were plausible but not substantiated. Having first performed the obvious duty of analyzing them for surface values and transmitting them and the analyses to Washington, I turned, therefore, to the task of further investigations. It is not yet possible to name those who helped, but in two weeks' time the judgment of facts became apparent.

The material is presented in its report form, with the addition of some later data. For instance, I was not able to learn until several weeks after I left Russia that the German order (which I possessed) naming the Russian who was to "defend" Petrograd had been obeyed.

The text of the documents discloses both the methods and the effects of the German conspiracy not alone against Russia, but the world. With each document is the indications of whether it is an original or photograph. With each document is an interpretative note.

### DOCUMENT NO. 1

*VERY SECRET*

PEOPLE'S COMMISSARY
FOR FOREIGN AFFAIRS.

*Petrograd, Nov. 16, 1917.*

TO THE CHAIRMAN OF THE COUNCIL OF PEOPLE'S COMMISSARS:

In accordance with the resolution passed by the conference of People's Commissars, Comrades Lenine, Trotzky, Podvoisky, Dykenko, and Volodarsky, the following has been executed by us:

1. In the archives of the Ministry of Justice from the dossier re "treason" of Comrades Lenine, Zinovieff, Koslovsky, Kollantai and others, has been removed the order of the German Imperial Bank, No. 7433, of the second of March, 1917, for allowing money to Comrades Lenine, Zinovieff, Kameneff, Trotzky, Sumenson, Koslovsky and others for the propaganda of peace in Russia.

2. There have been audited all the books of the Nia Bank at Stockholm containing the accounts of Comrades Lenine, Trotzky, Zinovieff and others, which were opened by the order of the German Imperial Bank, No. 2754. These books have been delivered to Comrade Muller, who was sent from Berlin.

Authorized by the Commissar for Foreign Affairs.

F. ZALKIND,
E. POLIVANOFF.

NOTE.—*The Russian Council of People's Commissars was dominated by the President, Vladimir Ulianov (Lenine); the then Foreign Minister, Leon Trotzky, now War Minister, and the Ambassador to Germany, A. Joffe. The marginal indorsement in writing is " To the secret department, B. U." This is the fashion in which Lenine is accustomed to initial himself. The English equivalent would be V. U. for Vladimir Ulianov. So, even if there existed no further record of German Imperial Bank order No. 7433, here would be the proof of its contents, and here is the link connecting Lenine directly with his action and his guilt. The content matter of the circular exists, however, and herewith follows:*

Order of the 2d of March, 1917, of the Imperial Bank for the representatives of all German banks in Sweden:

Notice is hereby given that requisition for money for the purpose of peace propaganda in Russia will be received through Finland. These requisitions will emanate from the following: Lenine, Zinovieff, Kameneff, Trotzky, Sumenson, Kozlovsky

Kollontai, Sivers, and Merkalin, accounts for whom have been opened in accordance with our order No. 2754 in the agencies of private German businesses in Sweden, Norway, and Switzerland. All these requests should bear one of the two following signatures: Dirschau or Wolkenberg. With either of these signatures the requests of the above-mentioned persons should be complied with without delay.

No. 7433, Imperial Bank.

*I have not a copy of this circular nor a photograph of it, but Document No. 2, next in order, proves its authenticity at once curiously and absolutely. Particular interest attaches to this circular because of Bolshevist public denial of its existence. It was one of several German circulars published in Paris in the Petit Parisien last Winter. The Petrograd Bolshevist papers proclaimed it a falsehood. Zalkind, whose signature appears not only here but on the protocol, was an Assistant Foreign Minister. He was sent in February on a mission outside of Russia. He was in Christiania in April when I was there.*

*Have photograph of the letter.*

### DOCUMENT NO. 2

*NO. 1645 SECRET*

[G. G. S., Nachrichten Bureau, Section R, No. 292]

FEBRUARY 12.

TO THE CHAIRMAN OF THE COUNCIL OF PEOPLE'S COMMISSARS:

The Secret Service Department has the honor to inform you that there were found on the arrested Captain Konshin two German documents with notations and stamps of the Petersburg secret police (Okrana) which show themselves to be the original orders of the Imperial Bank, No. 7433, March 2, 1917, concerning the opening of accounts for Messrs. Lenine, Sumenson, Koslovsky, Trotzky, and other active workers on the peace propaganda, by order No. 2754 of the Imperial Bank.

These discoveries show that at the proper time steps were not taken to destroy the above-mentioned documents.

For the head of the Department:

R. BAUER,

ADJT. BUKHOLM.

N 1645. Секретно.

G. G.-S.
NACHRICHTEN-BUREAU.

Section R.
№ 92

12 Февраля 1918 г.

Г. Председателю Совѣта Народныхъ Комиссаровъ.

Развѣдочное Отдѣленіе имѣетъ честь сообщить, что найденные у арестованнаго кап. Коншина два германскихъ документа съ помѣтками и штемпелями Петербургскаго Охраннаго Отдѣленія, представляютъ собою подлинные приказы Имперскаго Банка за № 7433 отъ 2 Марта 1817 года объ открытіи счетовъ г.г. Ленину, Суменсонъ, Козловскому, Троцкому и другимъ дѣятелямъ на пропаганду мира, по ордеру Имперскаго Банка за № 2754.

Это открытіе доказываетъ, что не были своевременно приняты мѣры для уничтоженія означенныхъ документовъ.

Начальникъ Отдѣленія R. Bauer

Адъютантъ

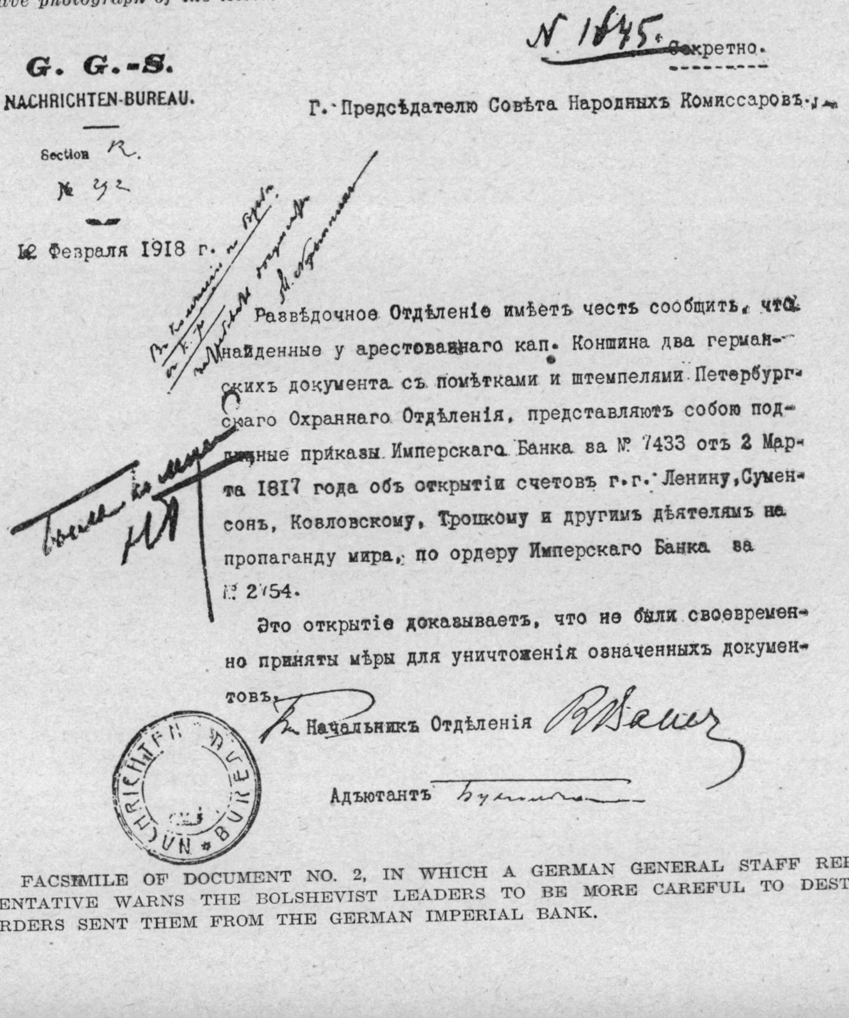

FACSIMILE OF DOCUMENT NO. 2, IN WHICH A GERMAN GENERAL STAFF REPRESENTATIVE WARNS THE BOLSHEVIST LEADERS TO BE MORE CAREFUL TO DESTROY ORDERS SENT THEM FROM THE GERMAN IMPERIAL BANK.

ПРОТОКОЛЪ

Сей протоколъ составленъ нами _ Ноября 1917 года
въ двухъ экземплярахъ въ томъ, что нами съ согласія
Совѣта Народныхъ Комиссаровъ изъ дѣлъ Контръ-Развѣ-
дочнаго Отдѣленія Петроградскаго Округа и бывш. Де-
партамента Полиціи, по порученію Представителей Германскаго Генеральнаго Штаба въ Петроградѣ изъяты:

1. Циркуляръ Германскаго Генеральнаго Штаба за
№ 421 отъ 9 Іюня 1914 г. о немедленной мобилизаціи
всѣхъ промышленныхъ предпріятій въ Германіи и

2. Циркуляръ Генеральнаго Штаба Флота Открытаго
Моря за № 93 отъ 28 Ноября 1914 г. о посылкѣ во враж-
дебныя страны спеціальныхъ агентовъ для истребленія
боевыхъ запасовъ и матеріаловъ.

Означенные циркуляры переданы подъ росписку въ
Развѣдочное Отдѣленіе Германскаго Штаба въ Петроградѣ

полномоченные Совѣта Народныхъ Комиссаровъ

Означенные въ же ояшемъ протоколѣ циркуляры № № 421 и 93, а также
одинъ экземпляръ этого протокола получены 3 Ноября 1917 г. Развѣдочнымъ
Отдѣломъ Г.Г.Ш. въ Петербургѣ.

Адъютантъ

FACSIMILE OF THE ORIGINAL OF THE PROTOCOL (DOCUMENT NO. 3) IN WHICH
BOLSHEVISTS AGREE TO HAND OVER TO THE GERMAN GENERAL STAFF TWO IN-
CRIMINATING GERMAN CIRCULARS.

NOTE.—*Observe the thoughtfulness with which Bauer, a careful man, set down exactly what was in the document, thereby permitting the contents to rise again from the ashes to which perhaps he committed the damaging paper. He admits that the documents found were truthful originals. The world will thank him and Germany will not.*

*I have the original letter. It bears marginal indorsements " Referred to the Commission for Fighting Counter-revolution. Demanded documents. M. Skripnik," and an illegible comment by N. Gorbunov, Lenine's other Government Secretary. The letter is directed to Lenine. Did Skripnik get the documents? I do not know.*

*The letter is remarkable otherwise, for the arrested Captain Konshin mentioned is a German officer, Lieutenant Otto, who appears elsewhere as an agent in the German double-crossing intrigue in the Ukraine. What was behind the mystery of his arrest? What was his fate?*

### DOCUMENT NO. 3
[V. K. D. No. 323—2 inclosures]
### PROTOCOL

This protocol, written by us on the 2d of November, 1917, in duplicate, with the consent of the Council of People's Commissars is taken from the department of secret service of the Petrograd district and the former department of police, (Okrana,) on instructions of the representatives of the German General Staff in Petrograd:

1. Circular of the German General Staff, No. 421, dated June 9, 1914, concerning the immediate mobilization of all industrial enterprises in Germany, and

2. Circular No. 93, dated November 28, 1914, of the General Staff of the high sea fleet, concerning the sending into enemy countries of special agents for the destruction of war supplies and materials.

The above noted circulars were given over under signed receipt into the secret service department of the German staff in Petrograd.

Authorized by the Council of People's Commissars.

F. ZALKIND,
E. POLIVANOFF,
(Illegible, but may be Mekhanoshin.)
A. JOFFE.

The Circulars No. 421 and No. 93 mentioned in this protocol and also one copy of this protocol were received on the 3d of November, 1917, by the secret service department of the German General Staff in Petrograd.

HENRICH, *Adjutant.*

**GR. GENERALSTAB.**
**CENTRAL ABTHEILUNG.**

Section M.

№—- --
*Berlin.*

# CIRCULAR

vom 9 Juni 1914

an Bezirkscommendanten.

Nach 24 Stunden vom Empfang des vorliegenden Circulars alle Besitzer der Industrieunternehmungen telegraphisch zu benachrichtigen die Packete mit mobilisations—gewerblichen graphischen Darstellungen und Plänen zu eröffnen, die im Circular der Kommission von Graf Waldersee und Caprivi vom 27 Juni 1887 angewiesen sind.

№ 421 Der Mobilisationsabtheilung.

CIRCULAR OF JUNE 9, 1914, ORDERING ALL INDUSTRIAL CONCERNS IN GERMANY TO OPEN THE SEALED ENVELOPES CONTAINING THEIR " INDUSTRIAL MOBILIZATION PLANS AND REGISTRATION FORMS," SO THAT THEY MIGHT BE PREPARED FOR THE WAR FOR WHICH THE EXCUSE HAD NOT YET BEEN FOUND.

NOTE—*The circulars inclosed are in German, and are as follows:*

[1. Gr. General Staff, Central Abtheilung, Section M. No. (blank), Berlin.]

CIRCULAR OF JUNE 9, 1914

TO BEZIRKSCOMMENDANTEN:

Within twenty-four hours of the receipt of this circular you are to inform all industrial concerns by wire that the documents with industrial mobilization plans and with registration forms be opened, such as are referred to in the circular of the Commission of Count von Waldersee and Caprivi, of June 27, 1887. No. 421, Mobilization Section.

[2. General Staff of the high sea fleet, No. 93]

CIRCULAR OF NOVEMBER 28, 1914

TO MARINE AGENTUREN AND FLOTTENVEREINEN:

You are ordered to mobilize immediately all destruction agents and observers in those commercial and military ports in Canada and America where munitions are being loaded on ships going to Russia, France, and England, where there are storehouses of such munitions, and where fighting units are stationed. It is necessary to hire through third parties who stand in no relation to the official representatives of Germany agents for arranging explosions on ships bound for enemy countries, and for arranging delays, embroilments, and difficulties during the loading, dispatching, and unloading of ships. For this purpose we are especially recommending to your attention loaders' gangs, among whom there are many anarchists and escaped criminals, and that you get in touch with German and neutral shipping offices as a means of observing agents of enemy countries who are receiving and shipping the munitions.

**G. S. der HOCHSEEFLOTTE.**

№ 93.

## CIRCULAR

vom 28 November 1914.

den Marineagenturen und den Flottenvereinen.

Es wird Ihnen vorgeschrieben sofort alle Agenten-Beobachter und Agenten—Vertilger in diesen Handels und Militär-Häfen zu mobilisieren, wo Schiffe zur Lieferung der Kriegsammunition nach England, Frankreich, Kanada, Vereinigte Staaten der Nord-Amerika und Russland aufgeladen sein können, wo Niederlagen für solche Ammunition sich vorfinden und auch wo Marine-Kriegseinheiten stehen.

Es ist durchaus nothwendig durch dritte in keiner Verbindung zu officielen Vertreten Deutschlands stehende Personen Agenten zu erwerten, um Explosionen auf in feindliche Länder sich begebenden Schiffen zu veranstalten, um Verspätigungen, Verwierungen sowie Missverständnisse bei Beladung, Absendung und Ausladung der Schiffe zu bewirken.

Zu diesen Zweck empfehlen wir Ihrer Aufmerksamkeit ganz besonders Ladungs-Vereinigungen (Artelen), unter welchen viele Anarchisten und entlaufene Verbrecher sich finden, ferner deutsche und neutrale Transport-Comptoirs und auch Agenten feindlicher Länder bei Emfang und Absendung des Kriegsmaterials.

Die dazu nöthigen Geldsummen werden laut Ihrer Aufforderung zur Verfügung gestellt, um das unentbehrliche Personal zur Erreichung des angegebenen Zweekes zu miethen und zu bestechen.

Nachrichten-Bureau des Gen. Stabes der Hochseeflotte.

König.

ORDER FROM THE GERMAN GENERAL STAFF OF THE HIGH SEA FLEET, DATED NOV. 28, 1914, CALLING FOR THE MOBILIZATION OF "ALL DESTRUCTIVE AGENTS AND OBSERVERS" IN THE UNITED STATES AND CANADA FOR THE PURPOSE OF PREVENTING THE SAILING OF SHIPS FROM AMERICAN PORTS TO RUSSIA, FRANCE, AND ENGLAND.

Money required for the hiring and bribing of persons necessary for the designated purpose will be placed at your disposal at your request.

Nachrichten Bureau of the General Staff of the High Sea Fleet.

KOENIG.

NOTE.—*Both the circulars bear the penciled notation that the German Secret Service Bureau at Petrograd has received them, signed Agasfer, the cipher signature of Major Luberts, head of the bureau, as will be shown in Document No. 5. The German intent here was to remove from the records of the old Russian Government the evidence, first, that Germany was beginning in June, 1914, its active preparations for the war that surprised the world in August, 1914, and, second, to remove the evidence of its responsibility for incendiarism and explosions in the United States, a country with which Germany was then at peace. The result was to give new evidence of the truth of the charges.*

*Have original of the protocol and have the printed circulars.*

---

DOCUMENT NO. 4

[G. G. S., Nachrichten Bureau, Section R, No. 35]

Jan. 17, 1918.

To the Commissar of Foreign Affairs: The section has received exact information that the leaders of the Socialist Party now ruling in Russia, through Messrs. Fuerstenberg and Radek, are in correspondence with Messrs. Scheidemann and Parvus regarding the destruction of the traces of the business relations of the party with the Imperial Government. We also know that the demand was caused by the demand of leading groups of German Socialists, who saw in the said communications a danger to the cause of world Socialism. By order of the staff I have the honor to request the submitting of this question to special discussion in the presence of the representative of our staff and Mr. von Schoenemann.

For the head of the department.

M. WAAL.

NOTE.—*The world penalty, therefore, was apparent to some Germans. Of the personalities named in the letter, Scheidemann, the leader of the German Government supporting wing of the Socialist Party, is the most notable. Once before he has been named in relation to the " business relations " of the Russian Bolsheviki with the Imperial Government, writing a letter from Berlin Aug. 25, 1917, to a " Mr. Olberg," in which he stated that 150,000 kroner had been placed at Olberg's disposal at Fuerstenberg's office through the Nia Bank. (See appendix later.) Now Fuerstenberg by this time, January, in Petrograd at Smolny, is trying to help Schei-*

*demann in covering up old trails. Radek is a clever Polish-Austrian Jew who came from Switzerland with Lenine. He and Trotzky between them staged the public play-acting at Brest-Litovsk. Von Schoenemann was the accredited German representative to the Bolshevist foreign office. He is named later in Document No. 5. Parvus is a handler of German propaganda money, with headquarters at Copenhagen, and is credited with being the directing force behind Joffe.*

*Have photograph of this letter.*

---

DOCUMENT NO. 5

[Gr. (Great) General Staff Central Abtheilung, (Division,) Section M, October, 1917, Berlin]

SECRET DEPARTMENT 31

To the Council of People's Commissars: In accordance with the agreement which took place in Kronstadt in July of the present year between officials of our General Staff and leaders of the Russian revolutionary army and democracy, Messrs. Lenine, Trotzky, Raskolnikov, and Dybenko, the Russian division of our General Staff operating in Finland is ordering to Petrograd officers for the disposal of the information department of the staff. At the head of the Petrograd division will be the following officers, who use the Russian language perfectly and who are acquainted with Russian conditions:

Major Luberts, cipher signature Agasfer.

Major von Bölke, cipher signature Schott.

Major Bayermeister, cipher signature Ber.

Lieutenant Hartwig, cipher signature Heinrich.

The espionage department, in accordance with the agreement with Messrs. Lenine, Trotzky, and Zenovieff, will have the surveillance of the foreign embassies and military missions and on the counter-revolutionary movement, and also will perform the espionage and counter-espionage work on the internal fronts, for which purpose agents will be assigned to the espionage cities.

Coincidentally, it is announced that at the disposal of the Government of People's Commissars are assigned consultants to the Ministry of Foreign Affairs, Mr. von Schoenemann, and to the Ministry of Finance, Mr. von Toll.—Chief of the Russian Division, German General Staff, O. Rausch; Adjutant, U. Wolff.

(*And below on the same letter:*)

To the Commissariat on Foreign Affairs: The officers indicated in this paper have been before the Military Revolutionary Committee and have agreed on conditions with Muravieff, Boie, and Danishevski with regard to their mutual activities. They have all come under the direction of the committee. The consultants will appear as called for.—Chairman Military Revolutionary Committee, Council of Workers' and Soldiers' Deputies, A. Joffe; Secretary, P. Krushavitch.

NOTE.—*Here is the working compact. If Rausch was then in Berlin he presumably came immediately afterward to Petrograd. It is more probable that the letter was written in Finland than Berlin. In some other letterheads on which Berlin is printed the word is run through with a pen. Stationery was hard to get in Petrograd. Major Luberts became the head of the information or intelligence bureau, (Nachrichten bureau.) Kronstadt was the midsummer headquarters of Lenine. Raskolnikoff will be referred to in connection with the project to sell the Russian fleet to Germany. Dybenko was the commissar of the fleet, the Naval Minister, a driving man and keen-witted. Zinovieff is the President of the Petrograd Soviet, during the Winter the most powerful of the local bodies of the Russian Soviets. He is Jewish and well educated. Joffe, in the letter of Bolshevist acceptance of the German compact, again stands forth for what he is, the spokesman, after Lenine, in all matters of supreme importance to Germany.*

*Have photograph of the joint letter.*

---

### DOCUMENT NO. 6
[Gr. General Staff, Central Division, No. 813, Nov. 19—]

To the Council of People's Commissars: This is to advise you that the following persons have been put at the disposal of the Russian Government as military advisers: Major Erich, Major Bode, Major Sass, Major Zimmerman, Major Anders, Lieutenant Haase, Lieutenant Klein, Lieutenant Breitz.

These officers will choose a cadre of the most suitable officers from the list of our prisoners, who will likewise be at the disposal of the Russian Government, as was agreed at the conference in Stockholm when Lenine, Zinovieff, and others were traveling through to Russia.—Head of the Russian Section, German General Staff, O. Rausch; Adjutant, U. Wolff.

NOTE.—*Major Anders took the Russian name Rubakov, and Major Erich the Russian name Egorov. Lenine and Zinovieff passed through Germany and Stockholm together.*

*Have photograph of letter.*

---

### DOCUMENT NO. 7
[G. G. S., Nachrichten Bureau, Section R, Jan. 12, 1918]

#### CONFIDENTIAL

To the Commissar of Foreign Affairs: By the order of the local department of the German General Staff, the intelligence section has informed us of the names and the characteristics of the main candidates for the re-election of the General

Executive Committee. The General Staff orders us to i sist on the election of the following people: Trotzky, Lenine, Zinovieff, Kamenoff, Joffe, Sverdlov, Lunacharski, Kollontai, Forbrizius, Martov, Steklov, Golman, Frunze, Lander, Milk, Preobrajenski, Sollers, Studer, Goldberg, Avanesov, Volodarski, Raskolnikov, Stuchka, Peters, and Neubut. Please inform the President of the Council of the General Staff's wish.—Head of Department, Agasfer; Adjutant, Heinrich.

NOTE.—*The indorsements are: "Copy handed to chairman council workmen and soldiers' deputies, N. 956." "Delivered to Comrade Zinovieff and to secret department"; signature illegible. Jan. 12 Russian calendar fell in the early part of the week of the All-Russian Soviet Convention in Petrograd, the week after the forcible dissolution of the constituent assembly. The election came at the end of the week and was a perfunctory re-election of practically the whole former executive committee of commissars. Lacking the exact list, I nevertheless can state that the present executive committee was drafted from this group. The name there surprising to me is that of Martov, the leader of the Mensheviks, though it is my recollection that this party of opposition was allowed representation.*

*Martov is an able writer, was associated with Trotzky in his Paris journalistic venture, but was supposed to have split with him in Russia. The evidence that he is still agreeable to Germany is pertinent. Mme. Kollontai, the only woman on this list, was the commissar of public welfare. She was sent abroad for foreign propaganda in February, but did not get beyond Scandinavia and later returned to Russia. Kameneff, who went out of Russia with Kollontai, also sought to return, but was arrested by the Finnish White Guards (not the Germans) on the Aland Islands, and his release was the subject of negotiations. He is Trotzky's brother-in-law. Sverdlov was temporary chairman of the all-Russian soviet. Lunacharski is commissar of education.*

*Steklov is editor of the official paper Isvestia. Volodarsky, who has lived in the United States, was in close confidence with Lenine. He was killed in Moscow the last week in June. Agasfer, who delivered the order in behalf of Rausch, is Major Luberts.*

*Have photograph of letter.*

---

### DOCUMENT NO. 8
[Reichsbank No. 2, Jan. 8, 1918]

#### VERY SECRET

TO THE COMMISSAR OF FOREIGN AFFAIRS:

Information has today been received by me from Stockholm that 50,000,000 rubles of gold has been transferred to be put at the disposal of the representatives of the People's Commissars. This credit has been supplied to the Russian Government in order to cover the cost of the keep of the Red Guards and agitators in the country. The Imperial Government considers it appropriate to remind the Soviet of the people's commissars of the necessity of increasing their propaganda in the country, as the antagonistic attitude of the south of Russia and Siberia to the existing Government is troubling the German Government. It is of great importance to send experienced men everywhere in order to set up a uniform Government. —*Representative of the Imperial Bank, von Schanz.*

NOTE.—*Members of the Red Guard were paid from 12 to 16 rubles a day, whereas soldiers were paid hardly that number of kopeks. This letter shows where the money came from. The Bolshevist Government also required factory owners to pay regular wages to their workers while the latter served in the Red Guard. The notation on letter indicates that it was referred to Menshinski, the Financial Minister, whose expert councilor was the German, von Toll. Menshinski personally conducted the wrecking of the Russian banks, a manoeuvre that deprived all opponents of Bolshevism of their financial means of warfare. It was a classic job of destruction, done in the name of reconstruction. Have photograph of this letter.*

## DOCUMENT NO. 9
[Reichsbank No. 8, Jan. 12, 1918, Berlin]
*VERY SECRET*

TO THE COMMISSAR OF FOREIGN AFFAIRS:

I am instructed to convey the agreement of the Imperial Bank to the issue of a credit of 5,000,000 rubles for the dispatch of the assistant naval commissar, Kudriashoff, to the Far East.

On arrival at Vladivostok he should visit the retired officer of the Russian Fleet, Mr. Panoff, and instruct Buttenhoff and Staufacher, who are known to Panoff, to come to see him. Both the mentioned agents will bring with them Messrs. Edward Shindler, William Keberlein, and Paul Diese, (or Deze.) With these persons it is necessary to think out a plan for carrying out the Japanese and American war materials from Vladivostok to the west. If this is not possible then they must instruct Diese (or Deze) and his agents to destroy the stores. Shindler must acquaint Kudriashoff with the Chinese agents at Nikolsk. These persons should receive the agreed amounts and should be dispatched to China to carry on an agitation against Japan.—*President of the Imperial Bank, von Schanz.*

NOTE.—*If this plan was developed to a climax it was hot by Kudriashoff. He was killed on his passage through Siberia two or three weeks later and it was reported that a great sum of money was taken from his body by his murderers, who were said to be two Cossacks. Most of the German agents*

*named in this letter were still active in Siberia in the Spring, as shown by Document No. 29.*
*Have photograph of this letter.*

## DOCUMENT NO. 10
[Reichsbank No. 5, Jan. 11, 1918]

TO THE CHAIRMAN OF THE COUNCIL OF PEOPLE'S COMMISSARS:

My Dear Mr. Chairman: The industrial and commercial organizations in Germany interested in trade relations with Russia have addressed themselves to me in a letter, including several guiding indications. Permit me to bring them to your attention.

1. The conflict of the Russian revolution with the Russian capitalists absolutely does not interest German manufacturing circles, in so far as the question does not concern industry as such. You can destroy the Russian capitalists as far as you please, but it would by no means be possible to permit the destruction of Russian enterprises. Such a situation would produce a constant ferment in the country, supported by famine of materials and, in consequence of that, of products also. The English, American, and French capitalists take advantage of this disorder and understand how to establish here corps of their commercial agents. It is necessary to remember that German industry in the first years after the general peace will not be in a position to satisfy the purchasing demand of the Russian market, having broad similar parallel tasks in the Near East, in Persia, in China, and in Africa.

2. It is essential, therefore, to conduct a canvass and gather statistical information with regard to the condition of industry, and, in view of the absence of money in Russia, to address in business conversations whichever is desired of the groups of German Commercial Banks.

3. Trade with Germany may be in the first period almost exclusively exchange for wheat and for any remaining products to receive household necessities. Everything which exceeds the limits of such trade should be paid for in advance to the amount of 75 per cent. of the market value, with the payment of the remaining quarter in a six months' period. In place of such an arrangement, probably, it would seem to be possible to permit, privately, the taking of German dividend shares on the Russian financial market, or solidly guaranteed industrial and railroad loans.

In view of the indicated interest of German manufacturers and merchants in trade relations in Russia, I cordially beg you, Mr. Chairman, to inform me of the views of the Government regarding the questions touched upon, and to receive the assurances of my sincere respect.—*Repre-*

*sentative of the Imperial Bank and Stock Exchange in Berlin, G. von Schanz.*

NOTE.—*The engaging attitude of the German manufacturers toward Russian capitalists is the feature of this letter, apart from the cordial and evidently understanding expressions of the representative of the German Imperial Bank to that supposed enemy of the capitalists of all nations, Lenine. The letter was sent to the secret department by Secretary Skripnik. Perhaps some day von Schanz will disclose Lenine's answer.*

*Have photograph of letter.*

---

### DOCUMENT NO. 11

[Reichsbank, No. 12378, Berlin, Dec. 28, 1917]

#### RESOLUTION

of conference of representatives of the German commercial banks convened on proposal of the German delegation at Petrograd by the management of the Imperial Bank, to discuss the resolutions of the Rhine - Westphalian Industrial Syndicate and Handelstag.

1. All loans are canceled, the bonds of which are in the hands of German, Austrian, Bulgarian, and Turkish holders, but payment must be realized by the Russian treasury in the course of a 12 months' term after the conclusion of separate peace.

2. The purchase is permitted of all Russian securities and dividend-bearing paper by the representatives of the German banks at the rate of the day on the open market.

3. After the conclusion of separate peace, on the expiration of 90 days, there are re-established all the shares of private railway companies, metallurgical industries, oil companies, and chemical pharmaceutical works. The rating of such papers will be made by the German and Austrian Stock Exchanges.

4. There are banished and for five years from date of signing peace are not to be allowed English, French, and American capital in the following industries: Coal, metallurgical, machine building, oil, chemical, and pharmaceutical.

5. In the question of development in Russia of coal, oil, and metallurgical branches of industry there is to be established a supreme advisory organ consisting of 10 Russian specialists, 10 from the German industrial organizations, and the German and Austrian banks.

6. The Russian Government must not interfere in the region of questions connected with the transfer to the benefit of Germany of two mining districts in Poland—Dombrosky and Olkishky—and to Austria of the oil region in Galicia. The transfer of the latter will be only in the form of limitations of the right of making claims, land allotments, and application of capital for the production and refining of oil.

7. Germany and Austria enjoy the unlimited privilege of sending into Russia mechanics and qualified workmen.

8. Other foreign mechanics and workmen during five years after the conclusion of peace between Russia and Germany are not to be allowed to enter at all.

9. The statistical department of producing and manufacturing industries with the corresponding Government organ must be controlled by German specialists.

10. Private banks in Russia arise only with the consent and according to the plan of the Union of German and Austrian Banks, whereby the rating of the stocks of the banks on all Exchanges of the New and Old World will be handled by the group of the Deutsche Bank.

11. At the ports of Petrograd, Archangel, Odessa, Vladivostok, and Batum will be established, under the leadership of specialists from Germany, special statistical economic committees.

As regards the tariff, railway and shipping rate policies to regulate the Russo-German-Austrian trade relations, this part of the economical treaty will be discussed by the special Tariff Council of the Handelstag.—*Chairman von Grenner; Secretary Berenbluet.*

NOTE.—*The penned indorsement on the photographed copy of the resolution is " Chairman of the Central Executive Committee-Commissar Menshinsky requests that this resolution should be taken under advisement, and to prepare the ground in the Soviet of the Workmen's and Soldiers' Deputies, in case the Council of People's Commissars will not accede to these requests. Secretary R. Raskin." Menshinsky is Minister of Finance. All of these terms, wholly punitive to American, English, and French capital, could lurk in the secret section in the present German-Russian treaty. I do not know the fate of the resolution on this, its early winter appearance.*

*Have besides the notated photograph a printed copy of this circular.*

---

### DOCUMENT NO. 12

[Gr. General Staff, Nachrichten Bureau, Section R, No. 780, Feb. 25, 1918]

#### *SECRET*

TO THE CHAIRMAN OF THE COUNCIL PEOPLE'S COMMISSARS:

After conferring with the People's Commissar Trotzky, I have the honor to ask you to urgently inform the agents of the Secret Service at Stafka, Commissars / Feierabend and Kalmanovich, that they should work as formerly in complete independence and without the knowledge of the official staff at Stafka and the General Staff in Petersburg, and particularly General Bonch-Bruevich and the Secret

Service of the northern front, communicating only with the People's Commissar Lieutenant Krylenko.—*For the head of the department, R. Bauer; Adjutant, Bukholm.*

NOTE.—*Across the top is written " Inform Mosholov, N. G., (Gorbunof's initials.) In the margin is written " Passed on to the Commissar of War, M. Skripnik." The significance of this letter is that it is to Lenine; that the two chief secretaries of himself and the council passed it on for action; and that Trotzky and Lenine on Feb. 27 were continuing to hamper the Russian commander at a moment when the German Army was threatening Petrograd. Mosholov was one of the Commissars on the staff of Krylenko, the Commissar representing the Council of Commissars in the command of the Russian military forces. His achievements as a disorganizer were notable. This letter indicates that he had the confidence of Germany. Have original letter.*

## DOCUMENT NO. 13

[Gr. General Staff, Nachrichten Bureau, Section R, No. 753, Feb. 25]

### VERY SECRET

TO THE CHAIRMAN OF THE COUNCIL OF PEOPLE'S COMMISSARS:

According to reports of our Secret Service in the detachment operating against the German troops and against the Austrian Ukrainian corps, there has been discovered propaganda for a national rising and a struggle with the Germans and their allies, the Ukrainians. I ask you to inform me what has been done by the Government to stop this harmful agitation.—*For the head of the department, R. Bauer; adjutant, Heinrich.*

NOTE.—*Across the top is written " Urgent to the Commissars of War and Special Staff. M. Skripnik." The last sentence is underscored, and in the margin appears a question marked, initialed " L. T." The first is Lenine's order through his secretary and the second may possibly be taken as Trotzky's opposition to any action. The loss of the Ukraine by counter-German intrigue was a sore point in prestige with him. But the essential obedience to Germany was not lessened. Have original letter.*

## DOCUMENT NO. 14

[G. G. S., Nachrichten Bureau, Section R, No. 278-611, Feb. 7]

TO THE COMMISSAR OF FOREIGN AFFAIRS:

According to information of the Secret Service Department it has been ascertained that the promise given personally by you, Mr. Commissar, in Brest-Litovsk, that socialistic agitational literature would not be circulated among the German troops is not being fulfilled. Tell me what steps will be taken in this mat-

ter.—*For the head of the department, R. Bauer; adjutant, Heinrich.*

NOTE.—*Brusque words to the Foreign Minister of the Soviet Government of Workmen, Soldiers, and Sailors of the Russian Republic, delivered not by an equal in official rank, but by the deputy of a German Major at the head of an information department of the German Government. Did Trotzky resent or deny the imputation? Instead he wrote with his own hand in the margin,"I ask to discuss it.—L. T." Thus he admits that he did give the promise at Brest-Litovsk. The question raised concerns only the measure of obedience to be required.*

*Have original letter.*

## DOCUMENT NO. 15

[The counterespionage with the Stavka. No. 311, special section, Jan. 29, 1918]

### A WARNING

TO THE CHAIRMAN OF THE COUNCIL OF PEOPLE'S COMMISSARS:

The counterespionage at the Stavka advises that at the front is being spread by unknown agitators the following counter, revolutionary literature:

1. The text of circulars of various German Government institutions with proofs of the connection of the German Government with the Bolshevist workers before the passing of the Government into their hands. These leaflets have reached also the German commanders. The supreme commander has received a demand from Gen. Hoffman to stop this dangerous agitation by all means possible.

2. A stenographic report of the conversation of Gen. Hoffman with Comrade Trotzky, whereby it was supposedly proposed to the latter to make peace on conditions of considerable concessions on the part of the Central Empires, but on the obligation of the Russian Government to stop the socialization of the life of the State. Comrade Trotzky supposedly offered the termination of the war without peace and the demobilization of our army. When Gen. Hoffman announced that the Germans would continue the advance, Trotzky supposedly replied, " Then under the pressure of force we shall be forced to make peace and fulfill all demands."

This document has created indignation among the troops. Against the Council of People's Commissars are heard cruel accusations.—*Commissar S. Kalmanovich.*

NOTE.—*This letter is a warning of the slow rising but coming storm that will sweep these boldest pirates of history from the country they have temporarily stolen. To get a real understanding of the meaning of the second and important section of the letter, it must be pointed out that until Feb. 1 the Russian calendar was 13 days behind the Western European calendar. The real date of this letter, therefore, is Feb. 10. This is the date Trotzky's " No peace no war " pronounce-*

*ment was made at Brest-Litovsk. The news of it did not reach even Petrograd until the next day. Yet on that day printed circulars were being distributed at the front stating that Trotzky had agreed to do the very thing he did do, and giving an augury of events that did take place a week later when Germany did begin its advance and when the Bolsheviki did fulfill all demands. The fact is that simple truth was being told. Nor is the means by which it was secured at all obscure. A few daring and skillful Russians had found a means to get information from Brest-Litovsk.*

*The circulars referred to in the first paragraph are of course those already familiar to Washington from February dispatches.*

*The following naive comment adds to the attractiveness of the letters: " The committee for combating the counter-revolution states that these circulars were sent from the Don, and the stenographic report was seized in transmission from Kiev. Its origin is undoubtedly Austrian or from the Rada.—M. Skripnik."*

*Have photograph of letter.*

### DOCUMENT NO. 16
[Counterespionage, Stavka, Jan. 21, 1918, No. 215]

TO THE COMMISSARIAT OF FOREIGN AFFAIRS:

We hereby advise you of the arrival in Mogilev of the following German officers, who are being ordered to England, France, and America:

Zanwald, von Weine, Pabst, Mayer, Gruenwaldt, and Baron Schilling. They have been granted passports, sent here by Commissar Trotzky.

Von Weine, with a Danish passport in the name of Hansen, a merchant of Copenhagen, is to proceed to England.

Baron Schilling is ordered to the United States of America with a Norwegian passport in the name of Dr. Joseph Brun.

Gruenwaldt has instructions to proceed to France with a Russian passport in the name of Ivan Kalnin.

The remaining persons are to make a journey through Finland and Sweden, supplied with papers from the German staff, in order to follow up the counter-revolutionary work of countries allied to us.—*Chief of Counterespionage Feierabend.*

NOTE.—*A young German who said he was a deserting officer and that his name was Mayer sought the aid of the embassy, the military mission, and myself in getting to America. He was a good-looking young Prussian, had lived in New York, spoke English with very little accent, and claimed to have been converted to the President's views on peace requisites. He said he had walked across the lines as a deserter because he could stand no more of German war and that he wanted to go to the United States to talk and write against Germany. I was not re-*

*ceptive. He said he was a Lieutenant. There is no record at our military control office in Christiania of a passport to Dr. Joseph Brun.*

*Have a photograph of letter.*

### DOCUMENT NO. 17
[Commissar for combating the counter-revolution and pogroms, No. 2, Jan. 5, 1918, Petrograd]

TO THE PEOPLE'S COMMISSARIAT FOR FOREIGN AFFAIRS:

The Plenipotentiary Commissar for combating the counter-revolution and Comrad Antonoff request the Commissariat for Foreign Affairs to issue passports for going to Denmark to the following comrades, who are going to the allied countries to conduct peace propaganda:

To England are going: Comrades Adolf Pavlovich Ribba, Ilia Julieavich Uritski, Vladislav Antonovich Dashkevich.

To France: Rimma Lvovna Orlovna, Vladimir Konstantinovich Schneur.

To America: Isai Borisovich Kahn, Mark Vlasievich Gritsker, Sofia Arturovna Mack.

All the named comrades will visit at Copenhagen the premises of the staff, where they will receive neutral passports for the trip to the named countries. At the disposal of the dispatched will be placed the necessary means for combating in the press with the imperialists of England, France, and the United States. Their confidential addresses will be transmitted to you later on the arrival of the named comrades at the places of their destination. Authorized Commissaries: A. Shilinski, F. Zubert.

NOTE.—*Trotzky indorsed this note " To be urgently executed. L. T."*

*The plan of peace propaganda campaign in the allied countries is plainly outlined. These Bolshevist-German agents will preach international Bolshevism and will charge the countries at war with Germany with the very imperialistic offenses of which Germany is guilty. This also was the method used in Russia by the Bolshevist-German press in attacking the United States, England, and France. In the formula of this propaganda imperialism relates not only to territory but to business enterprise. The agents listed above likely sought entrance under different names. They and the centres from which they work should be recognized, however, by their words and their works. The commissars who sign are members of commission for combating the counter-revolution.*

*Have photograph of letter.*

### DOCUMENT NO. 18
[Gr. General Staff, Central Department, Section M, No. 951, Dec. 20, 1917]
*SECRET DEPT. AFFAIR 31-a*

TO THE COMMISSARIAT OF FOREIGN AFFAIRS:

According to the negotiations between

Russian and German peace delegations at Brest-Litovsk, the Russian section of the German General Staff have the honor to request the hastening of the departure of agitators to the camps of Russian prisoners of war in Germany for the recruiting of volunteers, who will be sent to the English and French troops for the purpose of observation and peace propaganda.

Simultaneously the staff requests the following sailors to be sent to Germany: Shishko, Kirshu, Matviev, and Dratchuk. They will receive special instructions when traveling through Brest-Litovsk.— *Chief of the Russian Section German General Staff, O. Rausch; Adjutant, U. Wolff.*

NOTE.—*This request was referred to the commissariats on military and naval affairs. A marginal question asked by E. P. (probably Polivanoff): Is "Dratchuk at Black Sea?" He was at Sevastopol and may not have been sent. The others went, visited the camps for war prisoners in Germany, and then returned to Russia. Shishko in February was Commissar of the Naval College in Petrograd.*
*Have photograph of letter.*

### DOCUMENT NO. 19
[Counterespionage at the Stavka, Jan. 16, 1918.]

TO THE COUNCIL OF PEOPLE'S COMMISSARS:

I hereby bring to the notice of the Council of People's Commissars that through our front, on the personal permission of the Supreme Commander, have passed 100 German officers and 250 noncommissioned officers, who proceeded to our internal fronts; part of the German officers have gone to the front in the Don region, part to the front against Dutoff, and part to Eastern Siberia and the Trans-Baikal for the surveillance, and, if it shall be possible, to oppose the Japanese occupationary detachment and the counterrevolutionary Trans-Baikal Cossack officers.—*Counterespionage Official, P. Arkipoff.*

NOTE.—*An odd comment gives interest to this letter. It is "An accusation or a silly accusal for personal benefit," signed illegibly. Apparently the letter passed through the hands of some honest man not in the confidence of the gang.*
*Have photograph of letter.*

### DOCUMENT NO. 20
[The Counterespionage with the Stavka, Jan. 8, 1918]

TO THE COUNCIL OF PEOPLE'S COMMISSARS:

The Supreme Commander Krylenko has received an offer from the Supreme Commander of the German Army to send to the disposal of the German Staff 10 reliable officers of the revolutionary army. The said persons must arrive at Warsaw, where they will receive their further structions. The aim of the trip is to visit the camps of our prisoners of war on the propaganda of peace ideas. The staff points out the desirability of sending Dzevaltovsky, Siemashko, Saharoff, and Volodarsky.—*For the Chief of the Counterespionage, S. Kalmanovich.*

NOTE.—*Dzevaltovsky was an officer of the Life Guards Grenadier Regiment and an agitator who aroused the soldiers at the time of the ill-fated June advance. Volodarsky has been referred to previously. He was assassinated a few weeks ago at Moscow. Kalmanovich was a Commissar on the staff of Krylenko, the talking man who was assigned to disorganize the army. In actual army rank Krylenko was a Sub-Lieutenant.*
*Have photograph of letter.*

### DOCUMENT NO. 21
[Gr. General Staff, Central Division No. 759, Nov. 1, 1917]

TO THE COUNCIL OF PEOPLE'S COMMISSARS:

In accordance with an inquiry from the German General Headquarters I have the honor to request you to inform me at the earliest possible moment the exact quantity of ammunition at the following places: Petrograd, Archangel, Kazan, Tiflis.

You must also state the quantity and storage place of the supplies which have been received from America, England, and France, and also the units which are keeping guard over the military stores.— *Head of Department, O. Rausch; Adjt., U. Wolff.*

NOTE.—*This is a request made upon a country which America, England, and France still regarded at that date as an ally.*
*Have photograph of letter.*

### DOCUMENT NO. 22
[General Staff of the High Sea Fleet, No. 79, Jan. 10, 1918]

*VERY SECRET*

The Petrograd representative of the supreme sea command has received by wireless from Kiel orders to propose to the Council of People's Commissars to place at the disposal of our agents at Vladivostok—Buttenhof, Staufacher, and Franz Walden—several steamships. On these ships must be loaded the goods indicated by our named agents and also persons indicated by them and be sent as directed to ports of the United States, Japan, and British colonies in Eastern Asia. In case of absence of free tonnage in Pacific ports it is necessary to charter ships sailing under a foreign flag. The object of sending the ships is to carry to enemy countries agents, agitators and agents-destructors. All the expenses and risk the Petrograd agency of the supreme naval command takes for account of the naval operations fund.— *Capt. Lieut. Rudolph Miller.*

NOTE.—*The indorsement of Lenine's secretary, Skripnik, is "reported." The active Vladivostok agents have been referred to previously. The threat of the arrival of German agents through Pacific ports is apparent.*

*Have photograph of letter.*

### DOCUMENT NO. 23

[General Staff of the High Sea Fleet, No. 850, Jan. 14, 1918]

*VERY SECRET*

TO THE COUNCIL OF PEOPLE'S COMMISSARS:

According to instructions of the German high sea command, transmitted today to me by Radio A, I apply to the Russian Government with a proposal to take measures to deliver to the Pacific by railway three of our submarines, disassembled. On the conclusion of peace negotiations and the conclusion of peace between Russia and Germany this transporting must be begun immediately, whereby on the conclusion of the war the transported vessels will remain at the disposal of the Russian Government.— *Capt. Lieut. Rud. Miller.*

NOTE.—*The letter is indorsed "Reported. Secretary Skripnik." The transporting, according to the categorical demand, was to begin immediately after peace was signed. These are the only two communications of Captain Miller that appear.*

*Have photograph of letter.*

### DOCUMENT NO. 24

[Commissar for Combating the Counter-Revolution and Pogroms, No. 445-63, Jan. 21, 1918]

TO THE COMMISSAR OF WAR SKLIANSKY:

Our agency on the Fuhrstaskaya informs us that two unknown people have been noticed to visit the American Embassy three times.

Major Luberts begs to point out to Commissar Podvoisky the necessity of keeping a watch over the movements of these two persons. I await your instructions.—*Commissar A. Kozmin.*

NOTE.—*Major Luberts believed in identifying visitors to the American Embassy. Podvoisky was the Minister of War.*

*Have photograph of letter.*

### DOCUMENT NO. 25

[G. G. S., Nachrichten Bureau, Section R, No. 168, Dec. 17, 1917]

*VERY SECRET.*

TO THE COMMISSAR ON FOREIGN AFFAIRS:

At the request of the commission on combating the counter-revolution of Dec. 17, the intelligence section has the honor to forward a list of men watching the missions of the countries allied to Russia:

The British Embassy is watched by German scouts Luze, Telman, Possel, Franz, and Gezel; Russian agents Ovisannikov, Gluschenko, and Baliasin.

The French Embassy is watched by German scouts Silvester, Butz, Folhagen; Russian agents Balashev, Turin, Gavrilov, Sadavnokov, and Shilo.

The U. S. A. Embassy is watched by German scouts Strom, Buchholtz, Fasnacht, Todner; Russian agents Spitzberg, Sckolnitzky, Tarasov, and Vavilov.

The Rumanian mission is watched by German scouts Suttner, Baider, Wolf; Russian agents Kuhl, Kikitin, Zolotov, and Arkipov.

The Italian Embassy is watched by German scouts Kuhlder, von Geze, Goin, and Burmeister; Russian agents Salov, Alekseievsky, and Kuzmin.

These agents must fulfill all instructions of the commission for combating with counter-revolution, sabotage, looting, &c.—*Head of department, Agasfer.*

NOTE.—*The German, Major Luberts, (Agasfer, see Document 5,) therefore, was the keeper of ambassadorial hostages of the allied countries in Russia throughout the Winter. The names listed above were unidentifiable in the establishments of at least the British and the American Embassies. All may have been outside watchers. The method of outside surveillance is shown in Document No. 27.*

*Have photograph of letter.*

### DOCUMENT NO. 26

[G. G. S., Nachrichten Bureau, Section R, Feb. 23, 1918]

PERSONAL TO THE COMMISSAR OF FOREIGN AFFAIRS:

According to my personal conversation with the Chairman of the Council of People's Commissars, it has been decided to delay the departure of the Italian Embassy from Petersburg, and, as far as possible, to search the embassy baggage. Of this decision I count it my duty to inform you.—*For the head of the department, R. Bauer; Adjutant, Heinrich.*

NOTE.—*Across the top of letter is written by Trotzky "Instruct," and signed with his initials, L. T. It is here set forth laconically that a German officer of the General Staff and Lenine in conference ordered the search of the baggage of the Ambassador of a country friendly to Russia and at war with Germany, and that Trotzky gave the instructions for carrying out the order. A clerk's note at the bottom is additionally specific, "To be given to Blagonravoff." The last named was the Commissar of Martial Law in Petrograd. The Italian Embassy train was delayed for more than twenty-four hours when it sought to depart, some days later. Petroff, Assistant Foreign Minister, told me on March 2, with a great show of indignation, that " the Italians had given a diplomatic passport to the embassy cook." So, he said, it was right to search the train. If they had better luck than they did when they held up and searched the Italian Ambassador in his automobile almost in front of the Hotel Europe I did not hear of it. Document 27 tells of the robbery.*

*Have original letter, No. 26.*

## DOCUMENT NO. 27

[Commissar on completing the counter-revolution and pogroms, No. 71, Petrograd, Feb. 14]

### SPECIALLY SECRET—PERSONAL

TO THE PEOPLE'S COMMISSAR ON FOREIGN AFFAIRS:

Our agents investigated the Italian Embassy. I. E. Maeror, Imenitski, and Uroy followed up the Ambassador and conducted a search of him in the street, with a confiscation. Documents regarding relations with German diplomats and the special papers of the Ambassador to the allied Ambassadors, mentioned by you, were not found. In order to mask the attack several articles listed in the protocol furnished by Comrade Imenitski were taken from the Ambassador.

The watch on the British and American Ambassadors and the Serbian Minister has been intensified. The supplementary observation point on the British Embassy has been established in the Marble Palace—Lieut. Bekker and a member of the Central Executive Committee of the Council of Workmen's and Soldiers' Deputies, Frunze.

On the French Embassy, on the French Quay, house No. 8, Comrade Peters, member of the Central Executive Committee of the council, etc.

On the North American Embassy observation has been established at Fuhrstatskaya Street, house No. 23, apartments Nos. 1 and 4, in the latter Comrades Goldberg and Spitzberg carrying on the observation very successfully. Telephones have been installed in the above-mentioned places. General management of the surveillance has been intrusted to Alfred von Geigendorf.—*Commissar Mitopovich; for Secretary R. Bateski.*

NOTE.—*The marginal comment by Trotzky's secretary, Markin, is " Follow up." Most of the names in this letter, including the signatures at end, are unfamiliar. Peters, placed in charge of French observation, is a Lettish sailor, active and able, a former resident of England. The robbery of the Italian Ambassador took place late in the evening on a lighted frequented central street and was a day's sensation. The observation point on*

*the American Embassy was a yellow apartment house almost opposite the entrance. After I got this information I tested the watch and always saw a head or hand retreating from a window. But I doubt if the watchers profited much by studying the visitors to the Embassy.*

*Have photograph of letter.*

## DOCUMENT NO. 28

[Gr. (Great) General Staff, Central Abtheilung, Section M, No. 369, Feb. 24]

### CONFIDENTIAL

TO THE COMMISSAR OF FOREIGN AFFAIRS:

According to instructions of the Imperial Government, I have the honor to ask you to provide in the shortest possible time a list showing what commercial boats, auxiliary cruisers, and transports may be sent into the waters of the Pacific Ocean, where the German Government intends to form, for the purpose of opposing the American-Japanese trade, a powerful commercial fleet flying the Russian flag.

At the same time I call to your attention the data that in your Baltic Fleet your sailors are selling from the warships the launches, small fittings, copper, and bronze parts of machines, &c. Would it not be the proper time to raise the question of selling to Germany these war vessels which are being stripped and disarmed?

Please communicate the decision of the Government.—*Head of the Russian Section of the German General Staff, O. Rausch; Adjutant, U. Wolff.*

NOTE.—*Opposite first paragraph is notation " Ask Lomof. Markin." Latter was one of Trotzky's secretaries. Opposite paragraph second Markin makes notation " Refer to Raskolnikoff." Latter is a commissar on naval general staff, who conducted conferences with German officers in Kronstadt in March, April, and July, 1917, and an active aid to Dybenko in stirring up the Russian fleet to revolt. Do not know who Lomof is. The importance of the first paragraph as indicating the use against America to which Germany intends to put Russia is self-evident. The ludicrous picture painted in the second paragraph at once intensifies the shame of the ending of the fine new Russian Navy and 'discloses the German hope of securing and refitting the vessels.*

*Have original letter.*

## DOCUMENT NO. 29

[G. G. S. Nachrichten Bureau, Section R, No. 883, Mar. 9, 1918]

### VERY SECRET

TO THE COMMISSION FOR FIGHTING THE COUNTER-REVOLUTION:

It is herewith communicated that for watching, and if necessary attacking, the Japanese, American, and Russian officers who may command the expeditionary rorces in Eastern Siberia, our agents, Staufacher, Krieger, Geze, Walden, Buttenhoff, Dattan, and Skribanovich, take charge, and to whom it is necessary that either Commissar Kobozeff or any of those named by the commission must apply.—*Head, R. Bauer.*

NOTE.—*Comments to " Telegraph Kobozeff " and " Telegraph Streaberg " of illegible signature appear on letter, and below it is the order " the list," initialed " D. Z.," corresponding with the signing habit of Dzerzhinski, Chairman of the commission for fighting the counter-revolution. Below this order appears the list of addresses, as follows:*

*Reported according to List No. 3.*

1. *Staufacher, Vladivostok, Panoff's house.*
2. *R. Krieger, Nikolsk, Ussurisky.*
3. *Deze or Geze, Irkutsk, drug store Zhinzheroff.*

4. *F. Walden, Vladivostok, his own house.*
5. *Buttenhoff, Khabarovsk, firm Kunst & Albers.*
6. *A. Dattan, Tomsk, Nechayefskaya Street.*
7. *Kuzberg, Harbin, office of the Chinese-Eastern Railway.*
8. *G. Skribanovich, Blagoveschensk, house of Kunst & Albers.*
9. *Panoff, Vladivostok, his own house.*

*This letter was sent me after I left Petrograd and reached me April 5. It is important not only for content, indicating as it does the names and addresses of agents destructors who are called upon for increasing activity against the United States and Japan to make the Pacific Ocean a new area of terror, but showing that the German General Staff was continuing after the Brest-Litovsk " Peace " to work actively with the Russian Bolshevist Government.*

*Have original letter.*

[Conclusion in Next Issue]

# Rasputin's Assassination

## By AN EYEWITNESS

*Dr. Stanislaus de Lazovert, a former Colonel in the Russian Army under the Czar, gave out in New York Sept. 24, 1918, the following as the true version of the killing of Gregory Rasputin, the Black Monk, on Dec. 31, 1916:*

THE shot that ended the career of the blackest devil in Russian history was fired by my close and beloved friend, Vladimir Purishkevitch, Reactionary Deputy of the Duma.

Five of us had been arranging for this event for many months. On the night of the killing, after all details had been arranged, I drove to the Imperial Palace in an automobile and persuaded this black devil to accompany me to the home of Prince Yusupoff, in Petrograd. Later that night M. Purishkevitch followed him into the gardens adjoining Yusupoff's house and shot him to death with an automatic revolver. We then carried his riddled body in a sheet to the River Neva, broke the ice and cast him in.

The story of Rasputin and his clique is well known. They sent the army to the trenches without food or arms, they left them there to be slaughtered, they betrayed Rumania and deceived the Allies, they almost succeeded in delivering Russia bodily to the Germans. Rasuptin, as a secret member of the Austrian Green Hand, had absolute power in Court. The Czar was a nonentity, a kind of Hamlet,

his only desire being to abdicate and escape the whole vile business. Rasputin continued his life of vice, carousing and passion. The Grand Duchess reported these things to the Czarina and was banished from Court for her pains.

This was the condition of affairs when we decided to kill this monster. Only five men participated in it. They were the Grand Duc Dumitre Pavlovitch, Prince Yusupoff, Vladimir Purishkevitch, Captain Suhotine and myself.

Prince Yusupoff's palace is a magnificent place on the Nevska. The great hall has six equal sides and in each hall is a heavy oaken door. One leads out into the gardens, the one opposite leads down a broad flight of marble stairs to the huge dining room, one to the library, &c. At midnight the associates of the Prince concealed themselves while I entered the car and drove to the home of the monk. He admitted me in person.

Rasputin was in a gay mood. We drove rapidly to the home of the Prince and descended to the library, lighted only by a blazing log in the huge chimneyplace. A small table was spread with cakes and rare wines—three kinds of the wine were poisoned and so were the cakes. The monk threw himself into a chair, his humor expanding with the warmth of the room. He told of his successes, his plots, of the imminent success of the German arms and that the Kaiser would soon be seen in Petrograd.

At a proper moment he was offered the wine and the cakes. He drank the wine and devoured the cakes. Hours slipped by, but there was no sign that the poison had taken effect. The monk was even merrier than before. We were seized with an insane dread that this man was inviolable, that he was superhuman, that he couldn't be killed. It was a frightful sensation. He glared at us with his black, black eyes as theough he read our minds and would fool us.

And then after a time he rose and walked to the door. We were afraid that our work had been in vain. Suddenly, as he turned at the door, some one shot at him quickly. With a frightful scream Rasputin whirled and fell, face down, on the floor. The others came bounding over to him and stood over his prostrate, writhing body. It was suggested that two more shots be fired to make certain of his death, but one of those present said, " No, no; it is his last agony now."

We left the room to let him die alone, and to plan for his removal and obliteration.

Suddenly we heard a strange and unearthly sound behind the huge door that led into the library. The door was slowly pushed open, and there was Rasputin on his hands and knees, the bloody froth gushing from his mouth, his terrible eyes bulging from their sockets. With an amazing strength he sprang toward the door that led into the gardens, wrenched it open and passed out.

As he seemed to be disappearing in the darkness, F. Purishkevitch, who had been standing by, reached over and picked up an American-made automatic revolver and fired two shots swiftly into his retreating figure. We heard him fall with a groan, and later when we approached the body he was very still and cold and —dead.

We bundled him up in a sheet and carried him to the river's edge. Ice had formed, but we broke it and threw him in. The next day search was made for Rasputin, but no trace was found. Urged on by the Czarina, the police made frantic efforts, and finally a rubber was found which was identified as his. The river was dragged and the body recovered.

I escaped from the country. Purishkevitch also escaped. But Prince Yusupoff was arrested and confined to the boundaries of his estate. He was later released because of the popular approval of our act. Russia had been freed from the vilest tyrant in her history; and that is all.

## Great Britain's Part in the War

W. F. Massey, Prime Minister of New Zealand, told a London press representative in the Autumn of 1918 that one of the most abiding impressions he would carry back to his distant dominion was that Great Britain had never before reached such heights of greatness as she had reached in this war. He added:

" The historian of the future, looking back in half a century from now, will realize that the men of the first seven British divisions who assisted in rolling back the tide of war from the very gates of Paris, and who many of them made the supreme sacrifice in doing it, gave their lives and shed their blood in the greatest cause ever contended for by humanity. He will realize what civilization owes to Britain—the nation which, without a moment's hesitation, flung the pick of her manhood into the breach, and stemmed the torrent which was sweeping to destruction the civilization which it had taken centuries of effort to build up."

# The Franco-Russian Alliance

## Official Records Cited to Prove That It Was Purely for Defense

THE French Government, on Sept. 19, 1918, issued a Yellow Book regarding the Franco-Russian Alliance of 1892. Its object was to establish by official records that the alliance was purely defensive; that it was not specially directed against Germany, but was intended to maintain the status quo, and was not entered into to enable France to reconquer Alsace-Lorraine, as has been asserted by German statesmen. The book contains 107 documents. The principal one is the text of the convention between the two nations, which emphasizes the strictly defensive character of the alliance. It follows:

France and Russia, being animated by an equal desire to preserve peace, and having no other aim but to provide for the necessities of a defensive war provoked by an attack of the forces of the Triple Alliance against either the one or the other, have agreed to the following resolutions:

1. If France is attacked by Germany, or by Italy supported by Germany, Russia will employ all the forces at her command in attacking Germany. If Russia is attacked by Germany, or by Austria supported by Germany, France will employ all the forces at her command in fighting Germany.

2. In case the forces of the Triple Alliance or of one of the powers which belong to it should mobilize, France and Russia, upon the first intimation of the event, and without any preliminary meeting being necessary, will immediately and simultaneously mobilize the whole of their forces and will place them near their frontiers.

3. The available forces which can be used against Germany on France's part amount to 1,300,000 men and on Russia's part to 700,000.

4. Ways and means of corresponding in time of war will be studied and provided for in advance.

5. France and Russia shall not conclude a separate peace.

6. The present convention shall continue in force as long as the Triple Alliance.

7. All the clauses enumerated above shall be kept strictly secret. It is the determination of France and Russia to unite solely for all speed and haste so that Germany must fight in the east and west at the same time.

8. The headquarters staffs of the armies of the two countries will hold counsel together from time to time in order to prepare and facilitate the execution of the measure stated above. They will communicate to each other in times of peace all the information relating to the armies of the Triple Alliance.

## GENERAL MIRIBEL'S REPORT

One of the most interesting documents is a report by the French General, de Miribel, with the approval of M. de Freycinet, then French War Minister, which Foreign Minister Ribot forwarded Feb. 4, 1892, to Count de Montebello, French Ambassador to Petrograd, to be handed to the Czar. This report reveals what was the original French view of the basis on which should be constructed the military convention with Russia, which was afterward, on Dec. 30, 1892, approved by the Czar and a few days later by the French Government. General de Miribel's report was as follows:

France and Russia being both animated by the same desire to preserve peace, the present note has been drawn up exclusively from the point of view of a defensive war, provoked by an attack of the forces of the Triple Alliance against either one or other of these two powers or against both at once.

The note assumes that the two powers have decided to practice toward each other the principle of entire reciprocity; that is to say, if either one of them be attacked the other will go to her help with every active means available.

Rapidity being more than ever essential to conditions of success, active measures must be taken by both countries immediately the danger is known. Consequently the note assumes that mobilization will be simultaneous in France and Russia and that it will follow in a few hours the mobilizing of the forces of the Triple Alliance.

## ESTIMATE OF FORCES

As it does not appear that the other European powers will have taken an effective part in hostilities, calculations as to the military forces given below refer only to the five countries—Germany, Austria-Hungary, Italy, France, and Russia.

Section 1. Germany will place on foot as field troops in the first line sixty-two infantry divisions grouped in army corps consisting of three or two divisions, which will be supported immediately by eleven divisions of Landwehr to a total of seventy-three divisions of infantry, nine divisions of independent cavalry, and 3,564 guns, or 1,550,000 men, who would be concentrated at the frontier toward the fourteenth day. The remainder of the German forces will remain at first in German territory.

Italy will place in the first line in addition to her Alpine troops nine army corps on a peace footing and four divisions of militia, making a total of twenty-two infantry divisions, twenty-two battalions of Alpine troops, two divisions of independent cavalry, and 1,092 guns, or 360,000 men, who would be concentrated near the Alps from the fifteenth day. The remainder of the Italian forces will at first be retained in Italian territory.

Austria will place in the first line fourteen army corps on a peace footing of three divisions brought up to war strength, making a total of forty-two divisions of infantry, eight divisions of independent cavalry, and 1,776 guns, or 900,000 men, who would be concentrated on the Russian frontier from the sixteenth day as concerns the first ten corps and from the twentieth to the twenty-fifth day for the last four. The remainder of the Austrian forces would be held within the frontiers at first, either to keep surveillance on Bosnia and Herzegovina or to guard military centres and home defense.

The forces of the Triple Alliance in the first line therefore would be 137 infantry divisions with their divisional cavalry, nineteen divisions of independent cavalry, and 6,432 field guns, or a total of 2,810,000 men.

France will place in the first line very nearly the same forces as Germany, and after having provided for the defense of Algiers, Tunis, and for home and coastal defense, will dispose of seventy-five divisions of infantry, seven divisions of independent cavalry, and 3,370 guns, or 1,550,000 men, who would be concentrated at the frontiers from the fourteenth day.

Russia will place on a field footing forty-eight infantry divisions reinforced by twenty-one reserve divisions. After providing for the safety of her various frontiers, chiefly with her reserve divisions, Russia will have available twenty-two army corps of three divisions each, making a total of sixty-six infantry divisions of four battalions per regiment, twenty divisions of cavalry with an average of twenty-four squadrons per division, one-half of which may be considered as having to be used as army corps cavalry, 80,000 Cossacks of second

and third qualities, and 3,290 guns, 1,600,-000 men, part of whom, owing to the big number of troops already in Poland, would be concentrated somewhat rapidly, but the concentration of the remainder of which would be at a rather later date, especially as concerns Cossacks of the third class.

## FORCES ALMOST EQUAL

Paragraph 2 of the French Yellow Book, dealing with the Franco-Russian alliance, reads:

The total Franco-Russian forces would therefore have to be a total value of 141 divisions of infantry with their divisional cavalry, sixteen divisions of independent cavalry, and 7,160 guns, or a total of 3,150,000 men.

It may therefore be said that the forces of the two sides would be nearly equal, for if the numbers are in favor of France and Russia, rapidity of concentrations is in favor of the Triple Alliance.

### Section 2 reads:

The French General Staff is penetrated by the principle that in such a struggle the essential object is to prosecute the destruction of the principal enemy. The defeating of the others must inevitably follow. In a word, once Germany were conquered, the Franco-Russian armies would be able to impose their will on Austria and Italy.

Following this order of ideas, France would devote her entire strength to the struggle against Germany. Her plan will be to maintain in front of the twenty-two Italian divisions, as well as for the protection of her African posessions and fortresses, only the forces strictly necessary for the purpose; and in her plan of concentration she has allocated more than five-sixths of her first-line troops, or sixty-five divisions, to face the German armies.

With these sixty-five divisions France will attack Germany all along the line in such fashion that she will be unable to divert any of her western forces toward the east to threaten Russia.

If Russia adopts a similar policy, she will leave to face the Austrian armies only the force which is indispensable, and throw her whole remaining force against Germany.

## RUSSIA'S POSITION

The position of Russia as against Austria, however, cannot be exactly compared with that of France against Italy. While between the last two countries there exists a natural frontier which is difficult to cross, Russia, on the other hand, is scarcely separated from Austria. She has, moreover, to fight in support of the Slavs and to discourage the Poles. Allowing for those differences, however, the whole of Russia's surplus forces should be directed against Germany.

Eleven Russian corps of three divisions, thanks to their exceptional solidity and the superiority of their effectives over those of the Austrian army corps, (regiments of four battalions in place of three), appear to be entirely sufficient to stop and conquer the fourteen army corps that Austria can place in line.

When their provision to meet Austria has been made, Russia would still have available eleven army corps, or thirty-three divisions. These forces, added to the sixty-five divisions of the French Army, would be sufficiently powerful, especially if they arrived in time, to make an end of the German Army.

Merely to unite these eleven army corps against Germany will not be sufficient, however. It is further necessary that these corps shall be concentrated with very great rapidity, which will be the only means of disconcerting an adversary who calculates, thanks to the rapidity of his railway transport machinery, to throw himself first on France and conquer her, and then to turn against Russia. This is the plan which must be upset.

Every step must therefore be taken for the purpose of bringing into action as quickly as possible elements of the Russian Army designed to combat Germany. The corps which are to compose this army must consequently be selected, and their points of assembly determined in such a way that their advance will be easy and that the German concentrations can be reached in a short period of time.

Whatever efforts Russia may make, she cannot avoid, in view of the present conditions of her means of communication, being behind time as compared with Germany. But from this sole fact, that Russia will be getting ready to march forward, Germany will be compelled to immobilize a portion of her forces on her eastern frontier, and will have to relinquish all hope of being able to transport her troops backward and forward, east and west.

## QUICK ACTION A NECESSITY

### Section 3 of the Yellow Book reads:

To sum up, the one thing necessary for both France and Russia in order to unite all favorable factors of the campaign to be undertaken in common is that from the moment that the signal for hostilities is given by the Triple Alliance the two powers must rapidly throw against Germany the whole of their forces which are not required to contain the secondary enemy. The importance of this secondary enemy will alone decide the relative importance of the forces that will have to be used to contain him.

France estimates that she can contain Italy with one-sixth of her forces, and in this way she would be able to come to the help of Russia in case of need with sixty-five of her seventy-five divisions.

It is no exaggeration to assume that Russia will be able to master Austria with one-half of her forces, and that she will be able to go to the aid of France with the other half, or thirty-three of her sixty-six divisions.

The Yellow Book shows that the Franco-Russian naval agreement, which came much later, really originated with Russia. A letter from the French Ambassador at Petrograd, to Poincaré, then Premier and Foreign Minister, dated Feb. 6, 1912, states that " the Russian Minister of Marine told me this evening that he had been authorized to inform me officially that the Emperor would be very satisfied for direct relations to be established between the General Staffs of the French and Russian Navies, similar to those which have existed since 1892 between the General Staffs of the armies of the two countries."

# Luxemburg and Germany

THE betrothal of Princess Antonia of Luxemburg to Crown Prince Rupert of Bavaria, announced Aug. 26, 1918, confirmed the fact that the ruling house of Nassau had thrown off all reserve and openly gone over to the Germans. The bride is nineteen and the betrothed fifty, a widower. It is asserted that the union was arranged for political reasons by the German Chancellor, Count von Hertling, so that at the peace conferences Germany might defend the dynastic rights of the House of Nassau and bring the country into the German Federation.

The editor of the Telegraaf, a leading Dutch newspaper issued at The Hague, made the following statement regarding the betrothal:

Luxemburg was overrun in August,

1914, by Germany, which twice committed perjury, violated two treaties, that of 1867, whereby the eternal neutrality of the Grand Duchy was expressly proclaimed by Prussia, and the treaty of 1902, whereby Germany bound herself never to employ the Luxemburg railways for the transport of troops and war material.

Since then the unfortunate little country has learned the horrors of occupation. Germany established garrisons there, requisitioned the railways and the post and telegraphs; expelled the Ministers of foreign powers from the country, depriving Luxemburg by so doing of even the appearance of independence; abolished the immunity of the people's representatives; still keeps the export of goods so strictly under supervision that it is really at a standstill; interferes in disputes between Luxemburg employers and workers; stretches the network of espionage over the whole country; arbitrarily imprisons and condemns to death or deportation civilians known for their freedom of thought and action; compels Luxemburgers living in Germany to serve in the German Army; exposes the country to the constant danger of incalculable catastrophe from the Allies' air attacks; in a word, treats Luxemburg as conquered territory and the Luxemburgers as a conquered people.

This violation of treaties, followed by terrorization, raised to the highest pitch the hatred of Germany which has always been one of the main characteristics of the Luxemburgers' national feeling. More ardently than ever do the Luxemburgers sing the popular version of their national song, which declares that, above all, " Prussians will we not become."

The Grand Ducal family alone has no share in their feelings. Its sympathies are openly for the intruder. During the twenty-eight years of its Government the dynasty of the 'Nassauers has forgotten nothing and learned nothing. It always remembers its foreign origin, turns its back on the essential character of Luxemburg, and, as it is German, has surrounded itself with Germans. Those holding offices of dignity at Court are exclusively chosen from the Prussian, Bavarian, and Austrian nobility. These foreigners, paid by the sovereign, neglect no opportunity to treat her subjects with contempt, to ridicule their language, manners, and customs, and to thwart their aspirations. The Luxemburg people have always been angry at this foreign camarilla's insulting arrogance and anti-patriotic zeal. The press opposed it, various Deputies interpellated, and the late Minister of State, Herr Paul Eyschen, made a discreet representation to Court. In vain. The family of Nassau continued to seek its advisers outside the country, and in 1914 the Grand Duchess Maria Adelaide's *entourage* was quite as German as the Grand Duke Adolf's suite when he ascended the throne in 1890.

When the first German gangs streamed over the country these wonderful representatives of a so-called neutral Court were soon sauntering in the streets of the capital, showing the way to the intruders' advance guard, fraternizing in Merl camp with German officers. Some days later the younger among them disappeared, for, like every German of position, the reserve officers followed the voice of " the German Fatherland," which called them to arms. The Grand Duchess did not dismiss them. They retained their titles and salaries, and the unusual spectacle was observed of Luxemburg courtiers fighting in the ranks of the army which, like a coward, had murdered Luxemburg's independence.

# Metz in 1870: A Reminder of Its Fall

## How Bazaine Surrendered

*The flattening of the St. Mihiel salient, followed by the advance of the first American Army in the direction of Metz and the bombardment of that city's defenses, revives the story of the intrigue by the Germans in the Franco-Prussian War of 1870, when " discussions" such as were proposed by Austria in her note of Sept. 14, 1918, were opened with Marshal Bazaine, the French Commander. The London Telegraph recalls the circumstances as follows:*

IT is a circumstance worthy of being noted that this activity of the advance fortress of Germany is reported on the very day when it became known that Austria-Hungary had sent out an invitation to a " confidential and non-binding discussion " between the belligerents. There was something of the kind before the fall of Metz. The parallel is not only interesting, but contains its own warning to the Allies. The story of the enemy's intrigue of 1870 is still somewhat obscure, but it is established that the Germans managed to open up some sort of " confidential and nonbinding discussion " with Bazaine, the French Commander. What its precise character was is still uncertain, but the pourparlers, marked by much secrecy, served the enemy's purpose. When the hour came to strike, a curt demand was made for the surrender of the fortress and its great army. Bazaine decided that there was no alternative but compliance, and on Oct. 28 the capitulation was consummated.

The moral lies on the surface. The Marshal was, of course, tried by court-martial on his subsequent release by the Germans. He was sentenced to degradation and death, with a recommendation to mercy, which was not without effect. He eventually escaped to Italy, and died in Madrid on Sept. 23, 1888. In the light of fuller knowledge of German methods, it may be permissible to wonder whether the whole truth of the matter has yet been revealed!

And now that the limelight of the world again beats down on Metz, a summary of the main incidents of the siege may be of interest:

Metz, Aug. 11, 1870.—The Emperor went this morning to visit the troops who have taken a position around Metz.

Metz, Aug. 12.—French official communiqué reported that the army was concentrated at Metz, and rapidly revictualing and receiving reinforcements.

Paris, Aug. 14.—Metz is now in a perfect state of defense, and fully provisioned for a siege. No persons are allowed to take up residence there without being provided with at least forty days' provisions.

Aug. 18.—Great battle reported west of Metz. According to German reports the King cut off the French communication with Paris. The French were driven out of strong positions and thrown back toward Metz.

The Prussians were some 220,000 strong, and the French from 100,000 to 120,000, but the French, whose accounts were exceedingly meagre, claimed to have driven the Prussians into the quarries of Janmont. The battle lasted for nine hours, and, according to the Germans, " the losses of our troops are unfortunately commensurate with the greatness of their heroic achievements against the strong French posts which they stormed."

In three battles during this week the French were reckoned to have lost 50,000 combatants in killed, seriously wounded, and prisoners, the last item figuring for not less than 20,000 or 25,000.

Aug. 23.—Bazaine and his soldiers were surrounded from the Moselle on the north of Metz to the Moselle on the south, and completely cut off from Paris. For two days the French Government had received no communication from the Army of the Rhine.

Aug. 25.—A message from Paris (dated Aug. 23) said Metz was completely isolated.

Aug. 27.—Our special correspondent with the army of General Steinmetz gives an account of an engagement on Aug. 14 with the enemy at Vallières, four miles from Metz. After an action of four hours, in which the First Army Corps was dreadfully handled, the Seventh Army Corps was called up. The French retired and abandoned positions. The Prussian losses were very heavy.

Daily Telegraph, Sept. 15.—First bombardment of Metz. Our correspondent with the German Army at Ars said, on Sept. 8, their losses were trifling—one man killed and three wounded. Prices of edibles at Ars were " something fearful." Eggs, 6d each; fowls, 7f each; salad, 2f; small melon, 3f; cup of coffee, 5 sous, wtihout milk or sugar; hay, 3 sous per pound; kilo of oats, 5f; fillet of beef, about 1 pound, 3f; sugar " you cannot buy."

Sept. 18—The cordon is being tightly tied around Metz, our correspondent stated. " The truth of the various statements respecting the condition of the troops in Metz can be pretty accurately tested by the fact that a healthy horse slaughtered yesterday was sold in that unfortunate town at 2 francs per pound. A horse that had died from sickness or disease was sold at 10 sous cheaper per pound."

Sept. 21—Deserters declare the soldiers and people of Metz are in terrible straits from hunger, drought, and sickness. The water supply has been cut off.

On Sept. 26 and 27 there was severe fighting before Metz. Hunger had commenced its fearful inroad. French troops fought for food and forage.

Royal Headquarters at Versailles on Oct. 8 reported that on the previous night the whole garrison at Metz, including the guard, made a sortie to the north of both banks of the Moselle. The attack was repulsed, the French losing 2,500 men and the Prussians 600.

Oct. 28 was announced the capitulation of Metz on the previous day, after a blockade of seventy days from the date of the decisive battle of Gravelotte, on Aug. 18. The surrender of General Bazaine's army included three Marshals of France, 50 Generals, 500 staff officers, and 173,000 men, 16,000 of the latter being sick.

# German Trench-Defense Methods

## Nature of the Famous Hindenburg Line, Which the Allies Smashed by Hard Fighting

*Toward the end of 1917 the Germans transformed their whole system of trench defenses, especially in comparatively level country. Early in 1918 M. d'Entraygues of the Paris Temps made a detailed study of the new methods. His article, here translated for* CURRENT HISTORY MAGAZINE, *is of especial interest as throwing light on the task of the allied armies in breaking through the Hindenburg line.*

FOR a long time, but especially after November, 1916, uniform and precise instructions fixed the general outline of the German defense system from the sea to the Vosges. The system consisted of three successive barriers, which I have indicated in Fig. 1 by the letters A, B, C. Intervals of nearly two miles separated these barriers from each other, and each was made up of three lines of continuous trenches protected by wire entanglements and dotted with deep dugouts or shelters, especially fortified points, called blockhouses, redoubts, centres of resistance, points of support, reinforced these barriers wherever the nature of the terrain permitted or demanded it.

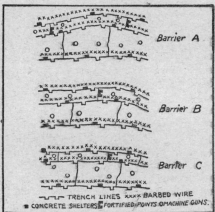

FIGURE 1

Barrier A was the first position to be defended—with the greatest stubbornness —against enemy attacks, if need be with reinforcements from Barrier B. If this first position was taken, the fight continued over Barrier B and then over Barrier C. Before the front was really pierced the enemy had to occupy A, B, and C successively.

This plan of organization has for some time been materially modified. In August, 1917, the German General Staff published new instructions which substitute "defense by depth" for "linear or extended defense." Each of the barriers consists no longer of three parallel lines of continuous trenches 100 or 200 yards apart, but of a great number of successive trenches, continuous or discontinuous, parallel or divergent, succeeding each other over a zone that may have a depth of several miles, the whole guarded as before with fortified works arranged so as to sweep the intervals between them with gunfire and to continue their resistance in all directions even if they are surrounded and isolated.

Fig. 2 gives a sketch of one of the old defense barriers after its transformation under the new system. It is no longer an affair of three parallel trenches, but of eight successive trenches or portions of trenches, protected by wire entangle-

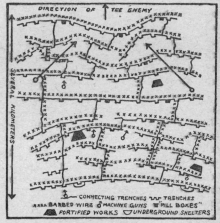

FIGURE 2

ments. And instead of eight there may be ten, twelve, or even more, if the nature of the ground requires it.

Under the new system it is no longer a matter of the first, second, or third line. The first barrier is called the covering zone (Vorfeldzone) or zone of ordinary fighting. Its foremost lines are simply tunnels or narrow shelters in which the lookouts keep watch; then, as one goes back further from the enemy, the trenches become deeper, more substantial, and fuller of men and war material. The object of this first zone is to give a permanent view of the enemy, and also, in case of attack, to furnish a resistance that will seriously weaken the force of the assailant.

The second zone is called the great combat zone, (Grosskampfzone.) As in the preceding zone, one finds here a system of trenches and fortified works supporting each other to a great distance toward the rear, with points of support, " pillboxes," and groups of dugouts. The machine guns are arranged here in chessboard style, some crossing their fire, so as to sweep the space between two fortified works, others flanking these works and permitting the decimation of the assailant with lines of fire formed by communication trenches perpendicular to the general direction of the line of defense. It is in this second zone that the brunt of the attack is to be received and repulsed, however violent it may be.

The third and last barrier is called the rear zone of combat, (Rückwärtigekampfzone,) and it is here that the enemy must finally be stopped if he has carried the two other zones.

A comparison between the official instructions regarding this new system and those governing the old methods reveals the nature of the tactics now employed by the Germans. In 1916 the General Staff provided for " a first position solidly built, with an ample depth of continuous lines * * * and with other analogous positions behind this." Now it prescribes that the defense shall be conducted " not in a line, but in a defensive zone spread out to a depth, if need be, of several kilometers." In 1916 the General Staff said: " The fighting in or

for the first line has become the fight for the first position." It says today: " The fighting should be done, not around the *lines*, but in *zones of combat*." It adds these details:

The zones ought to be far enough apart so that the enemy artillery cannot bombard two of them at the same time. The men and materials should be so arranged that the density of the fire and the strength of the resistance shall increase steadily from the first to the last line of the zone. The concrete works will be reserved for the first zone, the deep dugouts for the rear zone. The connecting trenches will be organized so as to form flanking lines. Supplementary shelters and emplacements for artillery will be built for use in case those aimed at in the course of the battle should become untenable. The zones of combat will be constructed by the combatant troops under direction of the division and group officers; the one in the rear will be organized by sappers under the direction of special officers of the General Staff. The trenches will be constructed on the rear slope of a hill whenever the forward slope can be overlooked by the observation post, and whenever the machine guns can act effectively upon the terrain attacked. (See Fig. 3.)

FIGURE 3

The thought dominating the German General Staff in these new methods is this: The primary object is no longer to defend the first line of trenches considered as the principal position, but to attract the enemy into the great combat zone after having weakened him as much as possible in the covering zone. The arrangement of the forces, line behind line, to a great depth places the enemy up against greater and more numerous difficulties the further he penetrates, so that when he finally reaches the real zone of decisive combat he has endured such losses that the defense, which is awaiting him with all its forces, has every facility for driving him back to his own lines. If he should succeed in penetrating to the rear zone he is supposed to be unable to hold it, being too badly shattered by long and painful fighting.

# Cuba's Part in the World War

## By GEN. MARIO G. MENOCAL
### President of the Cuban Republic

[STATEMENT AUTHORIZED BY PRESIDENT MENOCAL IN HAVANA, SEPT. 15, 1918]

THE same day President Wilson sent to the Congress of the United States his famous message relative to the declaration of war against Germany—that is to say, on the 6th of April, 1917, and almost at the same time that the Congress passed, with exceptional solemnity, that memorable declaration—Cuba spontaneously and resolutely took the same attitude. Inspired by the unanimous sentiment of the people of Cuba, as revealed by unmistakable signs, I had the honor to send to the Cuban Congress my message of April 7, in which I surveyed the unheeded protests against repeated violations of international law by the German Empire, and especially against the submarine campaign, made by the United States, and added an appeal to Congress for a declaration of war against the Imperial German Government.

The Cuban House of Representatives and Senate, unanimously and in the midst of utmost enthusiasm, adopted, in conformity with the recommendations of the Presidential message, a joint resolution declaring war.

The spontaneity and decision of these acts impart to them a very high and patriotic significance. No recommendation of the Government of the United States moved the will of the Government of Cuba or excited the generous passions of her people. None was necessary. The horror universally inspired by the haughty and violent attitude in which an imperialistic power, vain of its might, attempted to impose upon the world an intolerable domination was joined in the Cuban people with the energetic will, the noble ambition to cooperate with all their strength and with all their resources in the sacred defense of the liberty and sovereignty of all peoples against the malignant and menacing military power.

## NO DISSENTING VOICES

There was no discrepancy of opinion among any portion of the people or any opposition to these unanimous determinations. Party discord and animosity ran very high in consequence of the seditious movement brought about in February by the leaders of the Liberty Party, and which I had put down with all necessary energy. It might well have been feared that this political situation would be an obstacle to the declaration of war, to the policy of action to be adopted therewith. It did not turn out thus, for public opinion unanimously decided for war and it was unanimously proclaimed in both houses of Congress by the representatives of the people, and all needed powers and authority to wage war were granted me.

This declaration was soon vigorously put into practice, within the limits of the possibilities of the country, sparsely populated but of great spirit and proverbial wealth derived from its immense production of sugar and tobacco.

A relatively considerable number of large German steamships were held by the war in Cuban ports. I ordered their immediate seizure, as the Governments of all the belligerent nations have done in similar cases, and turned them over to the United States to use them freely in the prosecution of the war. The Red Cross had been established in Cuba years before, but in a very modest way and with very limited resources. Without loss of time steps were taken to reorganize it, and it was very soon reconstituted under the active Presidency and direction of my wife, Sra. Mariana Seva de Menocal, who succeeded in gathering around her a considerable number of ladies and gentlemen of distinguished social position for that purpose, and measures were taken immediately to raise funds, which now amount to a large sum, and which have been applied, and are being applied, strictly in the aid of similar institutions of the nations at war and their gallant soldiers. Conformably with this noble inspiration, a law recently approved by me—to which I gave my support, both before and after its enactment—provides a fund for aiding the Allies, out of which the public treasury has remitted a quarter of a million dollars to different countries.

## CUBAN BOND ISSUE

Upon my express recommendation the Congress authorized an issue of $30,000,-000 in bonds for raising necessary funds and new taxes to meet interest and amortization charges of the bonds—taxes which have produced more revenue than all calculations, leaving a large surplus. It having been declared by the Government of the United States, in accord with the allied Governments, that sugar was a commodity of prime necessity, the production and consumption of which should be regulated, the Government of Cuba lent its co-operation in the control of production and price and to a plan for the exportation and shipment of the entire crop, which amounted this year to 3,500,000 tons, the greatest in our industrial history. Food distribution was also subjected to severe regulations in agreement with the food authorities of the United States.

In several messages I recommended to Congress in connection with the declaration of war the implanting of obligatory military service in order that the country might dispose of all the military forces necessary for its defense and for repairing to the theatre of war which might be assigned in case the participation of its armed forces should be considered necessary. The obligatory military service bill has been passed. It is now a law and will soon be put in force, and the country equipped with a military organization consistent with its means and its aims.

To the same end of frank co-operation the Government of Cuba authorized the sending of American troops to different points in Cuba for military instructions and preparations. For the same purpose a goodly number of officers and enlisted men of the Cuban Army were sent to the United States to complete and perfect their training for war.

## SENDING OF TROOPS ABROAD

The law establishing obligatory military service empowers the President to take steps for sending a contingent of our present regular army to the European battlefields, reinforced by such volunteers who wish to go and who have already, indeed, begun to enlist in considerable number. The President is also authorized to send military missions to the United States, England, France, and Italy.

Effective measures were adopted by executive decree against espionage and enemy propaganda, and a large number of German and Austrian subjects were on specific charges or reasonable suspicion interned in a camp provided ad hoc. And in the contingency that these decrees might prove deficient for the purpose sought, the passage of a law of ample scope has recently been obtained, giving the Government a strong repressive hand.

With the assistance of American experts the censorship of mail and telegraphic correspondence has been established and is operating with full rigor and efficiency.

The Fourth of July, anniversary of the independence of the United States, and the 14th and 21st of July, celebrated in France and in Belgium as pariotic fêtes, have been declared legal holidays.

Great public and official manifestations have been held in honor of Italy.

## WAR AGAINST AUSTRIA

On Dec. 6, 1917, I sent a message to Congress requesting a declaration of war between the Republic of Cuba and the Imperial and Royal Government of Austria-Hungary, predicated upon the same ground as my message of April 7 and upon the important consideration that the Austro-Hungarian Government, intimately allied with that of Germany, had not ceased to second both on land and on sea the unjustifiable conduct of the latter, thus meriting equally with the latter the just reprobation of nations allied for the maintenance of international law and the rights of civilization and humanity; a course in which I was influenced also by the similar action of the Government of the United States. The Congress responded to my request by adopting the joint resolution of Dec. 16 by which the existence of a state of war between the Republic of Cuba and the Imperial and Royal Government of Austria-Hungary was declared, and the same powers vested in me as conferred by the joint resolution of April 7, 1917.

Cuba is showing her decided purpose to co-operate, to the extent of her power and by all means within her reach, in the triumph of the cause of liberty, democracy, and international justice, and to support without reserve the noble and disinterested action of the United States in this glorious effort. Near neighbors as we are of the great North American nation, we Cubans are able to observe with our own eyes the civic enthusiasm, the heroic decision, and the unparalleled effort of the United States in men, in war material, and in resources of all kinds which exceed anything that has ever before been seen in the world. This very proximity to the United States, and the constant intercourse between the two peoples growing out of the strong bonds of gratitude which join Cuba with the great nation which helped her decisively twenty years ago to gain her independence after long and devastating wars, and which on two occasions—that is, after two interventions—left her in full possession of her independence, her sovereignty, and her laws, without interfering with her administration or government, gives Cubans a peculiar insight into the high and disinterested motives with which the United States is already taking a predominant part in the war, which events have reserved for that country in order to uphold and save the principles of liberty and justice, and consequently the existence and sovereignty of small States, the freedom of the seas, the rights of neutrals, the faithful observance of international treaties, free self-determination of all peoples and the free co-operation of all nations in the maintenance of peace and international law,

through a decisive victory over the Central Powers of Europe, and over the military despotism which they seek to impose upon the civilized world.

## EXAMPLE OF UNITED STATES

The people of Cuba have before their eyes the splendid picture afforded by the Americans from one extreme to the other of their immense territory, overflowing with faith, enthusiasm, and decision for the great causes whose defense they have assumed without a thought for any material interest, without any aim of conquest of territory, nor of advantages or compensations, which in no event could offset their incomparable sacrifices. Neutrality afforded them gigantic profits for their trade and capital, most solicitously sought by Europe, without incurring extraordinary expenditures or loss of life or exceptional effort; and they did not hesitate to abandon that neutral position, impelled by the noble purpose of defending the freedom of the seas, the inviolability of right, and the respect due the sovereignty of states, incurring enormous expenditures, contracting internal debts of stupendous figures never equaled, in order to lend financial assistance to the allied nations through heavy advances, imposing upon their people severe restrictions in consumption, with the consequent privations, in order to send to Europe vast quantities of supplies and munitions; limiting the freedom of domestic traffic with unrivaled abnegation in order to supply all kinds of war material to Europe; and, finally, accomplishing the greatest maritime and military effort on record in transporting in a few months, despite the enemy submarines, a million and a half soldiers splendidly equipped for war and ready to enter immediately into action 3,000 miles away from home and decide with their most valiant co-operation the destinies of the world.

With this great and noble example before them, the people of Cuba feel themselves more and more intimately convinced that all the democracies of America have their place of honor at the side of the great American Nation which, with her allies in Europe, defend at the cost of the hardest sacrifices the ideals of modern civilization, the right of all peoples, strong or weak, great or small, to a life of freedom and the full exercise of their sovereignty.

NOTE.—Since General Menocal wrote this article the Cuban Government has announced its intention of sending 25,000 trained officers and men to France for immediate service. The Congress at Havana has voted $2,500,-000 to be distributed among Red Cross organizations of the allied countries. Cuba's budget this year, most of it devoted to war purposes, is $64,000,000. A hospital unit of 100 doctors and nurses has been equipped and sent to the front. Brig. Gen. J. Marti,

Cuban Secretary of War, said at the beginning of October:

"We have established training camps in Cuba, both military and naval, and through the courtesy of the United States we have placed officers at Key West and Pensacola for instruction. France has detailed two Cuban aviators, who have achieved brilliant records in France with the Lafayette Escadrille, to act as instructors in our aviation school. We have purchased additional equipment and materials necessary to make this arm of our service effective, and we expect soon to receive the supplies we need from the United States. The Cuban Government will withhold nothing it possesses that can be used to advantage by our allies in the fight against Prussian militarism."

# Land Settlement for Ex-Service Men
## Measures Adopted by Great Britain, Canada, and Australia for Giving Farms to Soldiers
### By S. ZIMAND

THE President of the British Board of Agriculture and Fisheries appointed a department committee in July, 1915, to consider what steps could be taken to promote the settlement and employment on the land of discharged sailors and soldiers. The final report, in two parts, together with the minutes of evidence taken before the department committee, was published in 1916. Part I., bd. 8192, deals with the settlement of ex-service men on small holdings, and Part II., bd. 8277, with employment.

There were representatives on the committee dealing with land settlement, of the House of Commons, the Development Commission, the small holding Commissioners, and the landed interests. The committee heard a large number of witnesses and inspected a number of small holdings in various parts of the country, including one large farm, agricultural colleges, and some land on the coast ripe for reclamation.

As a result of this investigation, the Small Holding act came into force on Aug. 23, 1916, (Public General Acts VI. and VII., George V., 1916, Chapter 38.) This act empowers the Board of Agri-

culture and Fisheries, with the consent of the Treasury, to acquire, by agreement, lands suitable for the purpose of providing experimental small holding colonies during the continuance of the present war and a period of twelve months thereafter, and provides that in the selection of persons to be settled on the land so acquired the board shall give preference to persons who have served in the naval or military forces of the Crown in the present war.

The total area of the land for the time being acquired by the board for this purpose must not at any time exceed 4,500 acres in England, (excluding Monmouthshire,) or 2,000 acres in Wales and Monmouthshire, or 6,500 acres in all. The board, with the consent of and subject to the regulations made by the Treasury, may promote the formation or extension of societies on a co-operative or copartnership basis, having for their object, or one of their objects, the establishment of profitable working holdings provided under this act, whether in relation to the purchase of acquisites, sale of produce, credit banking, or insurance, or guaranteeing advances made by the society, upon such terms and conditions as to the rate of interest and repayment and other securities as the board thinks fit.

This act applies, with small modifications, to Scotland, but does not extend to Ireland.

## FARM COLONIES

On the passing of the act, a Land Settlement Committee was appointed to assist the President of the Board of Agriculture to carry on the establishment of the pioneer colonies provided in the act on the lines of the report of the Departmental Committee on Land Settlement and to work in co-operation with the War Pension Statutory Committee.

The farm colonies branch was formed to carry on the work. In 1917 the Board of Agriculture and Fisheries acquired three estates in England and one in Wales, and worked out the following scheme for the land settlement plan: The settlers work on a colony either as individual small holders or as members of a community.

A man is required to work as an ordinary laborer for the first year, which is regarded as a period of probation. At the end of that time he will either be offered a holding or allowed to share in the profits. There are two kinds of colonies—the small holding system and the private sharing system.

Under the small holding system the colony begins as one large farm under the management of a director. Applicants are employed as workers upon it, at a rate of wages, for a period of probation of not less than one year, and at the end of that period any approved applicant will be allotted, at low cost, an area of land. Even when all the small holdings have been taken up, a certain portion of the estate will be retained as a central farm under the management of the director. A co-operative depot will be established for each colony through which settlers will be able to purchase what they need and also dispose of their produce.

The Government does not propose to make direct advances of capital to ex-service men desirous of taking up holdings, but industrious men may start to work on the central farm, and at the same time cultivate some acreage on their own account. In the selection of settlers for the colonies preference will be given to those whose wives or other relatives have acquired some knowledge of farm work.

## PROFIT-SHARING SYSTEM

Under the profit-sharing system the colony will be managed by a director as one farm, settlers being employed by him at the current rate of wages, but receiving in addition a share of any profits arising out of the farming operations. Each settler will be provided, if desired, with about half an acre of land adjoining or near his cottage.

The profits, after the current rate of interest (5½ per cent.) on capital and working expenses, &c., has been paid and after allocating a percentage to a reserve fund, will be divided between capital, management, and labor. In other words, each settler will receive a dividend on the amount of his wages for the year.

In connection with land settlement and employment of ex-service men on the land, the Corn Production act was passed at the end of 1917. The main purpose of this act is to guarantee a minimum price to the grower for a fixed period, until that branch of national activity has been firmly established, to insure to the laborer a statutory wage which will prevent sweating and also brighten his outlook; lastly, to allow the ordinary laws of supply and demand to operate in the interests of the consumer, and to secure to the grower the minimum price by paying him the difference between the average selling price and the open market in the figure guaranteed by Parliament.

(a) The minimum wage per week for agricultural labor should be 25 shillings. (b) The minimum price for wheat and oats should be guaranteed from 1917 to 1922.

In accordance with the Corn Production act, an Agricultural Wage Board was established. This board consists of thirty-nine members, of whom seven are appointed as impartial members and the remainder as representatives of employers and workers, respectively.

## LAND FOR CANADIANS

In Canada the Dominion Government controls Crown lands in the Provinces of Manitoba, Saskatchewan, and Alberta, and a portion of British Columbia. The Government proposes to reserve—in the above-named provinces—large areas of land for ex-soldiers under special conditions. These conditions, summarized, are as follows:

That administration of the reserve land shall be exercised by the Lands Settlement Board, consisting of three members possessing an intimate and practical knowledge of Western Canada and its farming conditions. It is intended to grant to suitable and approved ex-service men 160 acres of Crown lands each, free of charge. The classes entitled to participate include honorably discharged ex-service men from the forces of Canada or the United Kingdom, and the widows of sailors and soldiers from those parts of the empire whose husbands died while in active service. The Settlement Board will be empowered to grant a loan of $2,000 to each approved applicant, to be spent in erecting a house and purchasing implements and stock and generally in preparing the land for settlement. This loan will be a first mortgage on the homestead. It will be advanced at a low rate of interest and will have to be repaid within fifteen years.

The first repayment may be deferred for two or three years after the settler has entered upon the land, at the discretion of the Settlement Board. Applicants for land or loans must have previous farming experience before they can be eligible. However, ex-service men who do not already possess such experience can be placed for training upon the demonstration farms of the Dominion or Provincial Government, or placed with the selected and approved farms in the existing organizations of the Government. In either case he would be employed at the current rate of wages.

Regulations for the granting of the loans were approved in May, 1918, by the Governor in Council. The Provincial Governments have also passed legislation providing schemes for settling ex-service men on the land.

## IN AUSTRALIA

At the successive conferences between the Commonwealth and State authorities of Australia the first steps have been taken toward the establishment of a comprehensive scheme to enable ex-service men to take advantage of the offers of land made by the States, and the Commonwealth and State Governments have decided to give—with certain reservations—the same facilities for British soldiers as for Australian soldiers who desire to settle on the land. The Commonwealth will find the funds (estimated at £22,000,000 in all) and the States the necessary lands, while a joint board, consisting of a Minister for each State and a Commonwealth Minister, will supervise operations.

The necessary machinery for the repatriation of soldiers was provided in a bill passed by the Federal Parliament of Australia in September, 1917. The bill provides for the creation of a central commission of seven private persons, to be appointed by the Government and presided over by the Minister. The duties of the commission will be administrative. Its regulations and decisions will be executed in each State by a State board composed in each case of seven private citizens. The State boards will be advised and assisted in their work by special local committees in all parts of the country. All members alike of the commission, State boards, and the local committees will serve in an honorary capacity. The commission and all subordinate posts will include returned soldiers and will prescribe by regulations the nature and extent of the activities embraced in the work of repatriation. The State boards will deal with applications submitted by returned soldiers, who will register their names before discharge. The object in view is to secure a complete network of labor agencies.

The Federal repatriation policy includes, as its main points, the establishment of curative workshops attached to the hospitals; arrangements with private employers to enable such men to get the advanced training referred to, and the provision of facilities for young men who went to war in the middle of their apprenticeships to complete their tuition, the Government accepting the responsibility of supplementing their wages to enable them to do so. For the encouragement of small holding industries, such as hog raising, the Government guarantees the market and organizes the handling and selling of the products. The establishments for slaughtering and treatment will be finally handed over as a co-operative concern to the settlers. Provision will be made for those desiring it in the form of assistance in the establishment of residences in urban areas.

## New Zealand's Provision for Soldier Settlers

Arrangements have been made by the New Zealand Government, and are already in operation, by which those returned soldiers who desire to take up farming in the dominion may have the opportunity of doing so. Suitable blocks of Crown lands have been set aside, so that subdivision and road-making may be proceeded with in readiness for the returning soldiers. Blocks of privately owned lands have been purchased, some of which have been surveyed for closer settlement purposes, and are already occupied by soldier settlers. Many of them have, however, been kept for the main body of the New Zealand Expeditionary Force when the war comes to an end.

Speaking of the financial arrangements which have been made with a view to enabling soldier settlers to farm their lands, W. F. Massey, the Prime Minister, said in September, 1918:

> Over 700 soldier settlers have already been provided with land, and, so far as it is possible to judge, most of them are doing well and on the road to success. The new settlers get the land at cost price, and financial assistance is given to those requiring it, up to £500 being lent in most cases, but in special cases £750 may be advanced on the recommendation of the Land Board. Five per cent. interest is charged, and the conditions are made as easy as possible. If an intending settler wants land for sheep farming or dairy farming or the growing of cereals or fruit growing or poultry farming, the Land Board will endeavor to suit him, and it is generally successful.

If, however, a soldier prefers to settle in one of the cities or towns, and desires to become the owner of his own house, Mr. Massey explained, he can take advantage of the Workers' Homes act and have a cottage built or bought for him on terms. Previous experiments in military settlements in New Zealand, he admitted, had not been successful, principally for the reason that the settlers were allowed to sell their interest in their sections. In the present scheme sale was not permitted for a number of years, except in the case of death or some serious family or financial trouble. In order that partially incapacitated men might have an opportunity of supplementing their pensions arrangements have been made by the New Zealand Government for them to attend technical schools to obtain a knowledge of occupations which do not require a term of apprenticeship. In such cases the Government allows the learner £1 per week in addition to his pension during the period of his tuition.

In other cases, where the partially incapacitated soldier is unskilled or is unable by the nature of his injuries to follow his usual occupation, the Government has made arrangements for him to learn a new trade. After consultation with the trade union authorities the amount which the beginner is able to earn is fixed, and the difference between this rate and the minimum wage payable in that particular industry is contributed by the State.

NOTE.—Regarding the repatriation of Australian soldiers, it was officially stated in September that the Commonwealth Repatriation Scheme had already involved the expenditure of nearly £3,000,000. Since 1915 nearly 60,000 members of the Australian Imperial Forces had returned to Australia, and situations for upward of 50,000 of these had been provided by the Repatriation Department. Settlers on the land are allowed £500 on loan as working capital; advances are also made for the acquisition of businesses.

# German Crimes in Southwest Africa

## Official Records Revealing Cruelties Inflicted on Natives Under German Colonial Rule

WHEN the German forces in Southwest Africa had capitulated in July, 1915, the task of restoring order in the former German protectorate was intrusted to a British administrator, E. H. L. Gorges, Secretary for the Interior after the establishment of the South African Union. The terms of the capitulation had provided that the civil population and the reservists then under arms should be allowed to resume their normal vocations, and immediately there arose a strong demand for native labor. The occupying authorities, however, found labor conditions in a deplorable state. The German masters regarded their native servants as slaves, without rights, and amenable only to the lash, while the natives regarded their oppressors as inveterate enemies from whom there was no escape. In the course of the uphill task of creating better relations between the whites and the blacks the British administrators have found it necessary to institute what amounts to a complete social revolution, repealing all the obnoxious provisions in the German native code and substituting milder ones whose success had been proved through years of use in the Transvaal.

Mr. Gorges, meanwhile, prepared a memorable report on the German treatment of the natives of Southwest Africa, based on German official archives found at Government House, Windhuk, and accompanied by records of certain trials under the German régime, and by the writings of Leutwein, the German Governor from 1894 to 1905; Paul Rohrbach, Professor Karl Dove, and other German authorities. This report was published in London on Sept. 12, 1918, as a Government Blue Book, and is now accessible to the world.

The main report deals, in a first section, with the attitude of the German administration and of the German settlers toward the natives since the first days in which they came into contact, and shows the methods by which Germany established her authority over the territory. This section was compiled by Major T. L. O'Reilly, Attorney of the Supreme Court of South Africa, Transvaal Provincial Division, and Military Magistrate of Omaruru, in the Southwest African Protectorate. He had been in the country in an official capacity for nearly three years, and was well acquainted with the country and its inhabitants. The second section of the report is devoted to an analysis of the position of the natives under the criminal law, and was prepared by A. J. Waters, Crown Prosecutor for the Protectorate, who had been stationed at Windhuk since October, 1915. The Administrator observes:

> Enough is, I think, contained in this report to leave no doubts as to the terrible courses pursued both by the German Colonial Administration, acting either under the orders or with the acquiescence of the Berlin Government, and by individual Germans settled or stationed in the country; or as to the deplorable plight the natives fell into under the brutalities and robberies to which they were systematically subjected.

### GERMAN GOVERNOR'S PROTEST

How systematic were these atrocities is disclosed by the Government files at Windhuk, which show that, from 1910 onward, the German authorities were in a constant state of nervous apprehension. They were always expecting another native rising. Unwarned by the lesson of the earlier insurrections, officials and settlers heedlessly pursued their "terrible courses." Of the state of affairs as late as 1912 the following confidential circular addressed by Governor Seitz to his Magistrates in May of that year is eloquent enough:

The Imperial Governor of G. S. W. A.
            Windhuk, May 31, 1912.

*To all Magistrates.*
*Secret and Personal.*

Within recent weeks I have received information from various quarters to the effect that a desperate feeling is becoming prevalent of late among the natives in certain areas of the country.

The reason which is unanimously given for this fact is that brutal excesses of Europeans against the natives are alarmingly on the increase—it is much to be regretted in this connection that even police officials have become guilty of such offenses in a few cases—and that such offenses do not find the punishment before the courts of law which they ought to receive according to the sense of justice of the natives.

In consequence thereof the natives are supposed to despair of the impartiality of our jurisdiction and to be driven into a blind hatred of everything that is white, and as a final result would resort to self-help, that is, another native rising.

It is quite evident that such feelings of hatred among the natives, if amelioration of their lot is not energetically provided for, must lead within a short space of time to a renewed and desperate native rising, and consequently to the economic ruin of the country.

It is therefore in the interests of the whole European population that persons who rage in mad brutality against the natives, and who consider their white skin a charter of indemnity from punishment for the most brutal crimes, be rendered innocuous by all possible means. Because a people who make a claim to be regarded as a dominant race must first of all keep clean their own ranks.

If the crimes committed by Europeans against natives do not find punishment at all, or no sufficient punishment, it will become impossible in future to act with that severity in the cases of crimes committed by natives against Europeans which is imperative in the general interest.

I have no influence on the jurisdiction as far as Europeans are concerned, but I shall, as far as that is possible, take care by administrative measures that the doubtlessly existing critical conditions are counteracted.

Above all things I intend to order, as such cases arise, that Europeans who persist in ill-treating their native servants in a brutal manner shall no longer be supplied with native labor.

However, an effectual alteration will only be possible if the white population itself, who, as far as I feel, condemns such brutalities of rough elements to the utmost, does not leave such individuals, who are a danger to the common weal, in any doubt about its attitude on the question, and actively cooperates to prevent such crimes or to bring them to justice in cases where they have occurred.

And as I am convinced that it will be possible for the District Councils to influence their co-citizens in this respect, I request that you will inform the District Councils in the strictest confidence of the contents of this communication at their next meeting.

I trust that with the assistance of the European population it will be possible to create conditions which will reinstate in the natives a confidence that they will find protection from the Europeans against the brutal excesses of a few individuals.

You are requested to confirm the receipt of this communication.

            (Signed)          SEITZ.

## EXTERMINATING THE HEREROS

The report tells the story of how the German authorities exterminated the native Hereros. When Germany annexed the country in 1890 they were believed to possess well over 150,000 head of cattle. After the rinderpest scourge of 1897 they still owned something like 90,000 head. By 1902, less than ten years after the arrival of the first German settlers, the Hereros had only 45,898 head of cattle, while the 1,051 German traders and farmers then in the country owned 44,487. The policy of robbing and killing the natives had by that time received the sanction of Berlin. By the end of 1905 the surviving Hereros had been reduced to pauperism and possessed nothing at all. In 1907 the Imperial German Government by ordinance prohibited the natives of Southwest Africa from possessing live stock.

The wholesale theft of the natives' cattle, their only wealth, with the direct connivance and approval of the Berlin Government, was one of the primary causes of the Herero rebellion of 1904. The revolt was suppressed with characteristic German ruthlessness. But the Germans were not content with a mere suppression of the rising; they had decided upon the practical extinction of the whole tribe. For this purpose Leutwein, who was apparently regarded as too lenient, was superseded by von Trotha, noted for his merciless severity. He had played a notorious part in the Chinese Boxer rebellion, and had just suppressed the Arab rising in German East Africa by the wholesale massacre of men, women, and children. As a preliminary von Trotha invited the Herero chiefs to come in and make peace, "as the war was now over," and promptly shot them in cold blood. Then he issued his no-

SOUTHWEST AFRICA, A FORMER GERMAN PROTECTORATE, WHOSE FUTURE MUST BE DECIDED BY THE ALLIES.

torious "extermination order," in terms of which no Herero—man, woman, child, or babe—was to receive mercy or quarter. "Kill every one of them," he said, "and take no prisoners."

These orders, says Mr. Gorges, were only too faithfully carried out. The evidence of natives of other tribes, who were eyewitnesses of the atrocities which took place, is presented in the report, and their narratives bear on the face of them the stamp of truth. There is, for example, the story of the native who for two years acted as groom to von Trotha, and who declares that during the whole of that time he knows of no instance in which prisoners were spared.

When leaving Okahandja General von Trotha issued orders to his troops that no quarter was to be given to the enemy. No

prisoners were to be taken, but all, regardless of age or sex, were to be killed. General von Trotha said, "We must exterminate them, so that we won't be bothered with rebellions in the future." As a result of this order the soldiers shot all natives we came across. It did not matter who they were. Some were peaceful people who had not gone into rebellion; others, such as old men and old women, had never left their homes; yet these were all shot.

## HEARTLESS CRUELTY

In this way, it is noted, thousands of harmless and peaceful Berg-Damaras—who had nothing to do with the rebellion—met the same fate as the Hereros. Other quotations from the evidence of native eyewitnesses are appended:

(a) A German soldier found a little Herero baby boy about nine months old lying in the bush, and brought it into the camp. The soldiers formed a ring, and started throwing the child from one to another and catching it as if it were a ball. The child was terrified and hurt, and was crying very much. After a time they got tired of this, and one of the soldiers fixed his bayonet on his rifle and said he would catch the baby. The child was tossed into the air toward him, and as it fell he caught it and transfixed the body with the bayonet. The child died in a few minutes, and the incident was greeted with roars of laughter by the Germans, who seemed to think it was a great joke.

(b) I went with the German troops right through the Herero rebellion. The Afrikaner Hottentots of my werft were with me. We refused to kill Herero women and children, but the Germans spared none. They killed thousands and thousands. I saw this bloody work for days and days and every day. Often, and especially at Waterberg, the young Herero women and girls were violated by the German soldiers before being killed.

(c) I went with the German troops to Hamakari and beyond. They killed thousands and thousands of women and children along the roadsides. They bayoneted them and hit them to death with the butt ends of their guns. They were lying exhausted and harmless along the roads, and as the soldiers passed they simply slaughtered them in cold blood. Mothers holding babies at their breasts, little boys and little girls; old people too old to fight and old grandmothers, none received mercy.

From the testimony of another witness it appears that some of the choicest forms of frightfulness with which the war has made the world familiar were not new to the Germans:

On one occasion I saw about twenty-five prisoners placed in a small inclosure of thorn bushes. They were confined in a very small space, and the soldiers cut dry branches and piled dry logs all round them—men, women, and children and little girls were there. When dry branches had been thickly piled up all round them the soldiers threw branches also on the top of them. The prisoners were all alive and unwounded, but half starved. Having piled up the branches, lamp oil was sprinkled on the heap, and it was set on fire. The prisoners were burned to a cinder. The Germans said, " We should burn all these dogs and baboons in this fashion." The officers saw this, and made no attempt to prevent it. From that time to the end of the rising the killing and hanging of Hereros was practically a daily occurrence. There was no more fighting. The Hereros were merely fugitives in the bush. All the water-holes on the desert border were poisoned by the Germans before they returned. The result was that fugitives who came to drink the water either died of poisoning or, if they did not taste the water, they died of thirst.

This gruesome story by eyewitnesses (comments the Administrator) could be continued until the report would probably·require several thick volumes. Evidence of violation of women and girls is overwhelming, but so full of filthy and atrocious details as to render publication undesirable.

## POLICY OF EXTERMINATION

One more quotation may be added, from the testimony of a European who acted as transport driver to the Germans. He states:

The hanging of natives was a common occurrence. A German officer had the right to order a native to be hanged. No trial or court was necessary. Many were hanged merely on suspicion. One day alone I saw seven Hereros hanged in a row, and on other days twos and threes. The Germans did not worry about rope. They used ordinary fencing wire, and the unfortunate native was hoisted up by the neck and allowed to die of slow strangulation. This was all done in public, and the bodies were always allowed to hang for a day or so as an example to the other natives. Natives who were placed in jail at that time never came out alive. Many died of sheer starvation and brutal treatment. * * * The Hereros were far more humane in the field than the Germans. They were once a fine race. Now we have only a miserable remnant left.

This last statement is amply proved by official German statistics. Out of between 80,000 and 90,000 souls, only about 15,000 starving and fugitive Hereros were alive at the end of 1905, when von Trotha relinquished his task. In 1911, after all rebellions had been suppressed and tranquillity restored, the Government had a census taken. The figures, reproduced below, speak for themselves:

|  | Estimate, 1904. | Official Census, 1911. | Decrease. |
|---|---|---|---|
| Hereros | 80,000 | 15,130 | 64,870 |
| Hottentots | 20,000 | 9,781 | 10,219 |
| Berg-Damaras | 30,000 | 12,831 | 17,169 |
|  | 130,000 | 37,742 | 92,258 |

In other words, 80 per cent. of the Herero people had disappeared, and more than half of the Hottentot and Berg-Damara races had shared the same fate. Dr. Paul Rohrbach's dictum, " It is applicable to a nation in the same way as to the individual that the right of existence is primarily justified in the degree that such existence is useful for progress and general development " comes forcibly to mind. These natives of Southwest Africa had been weighed in the German balance and had been found wanting.

From the figures above quoted it will be apparent that the treatment of the Hottentots and other native races of the territory was the same as that meted out to the Hereros. The story here told of German intercourse with these tribes is a consistent record of treachery, robbery, and cruelty, followed by revolt, its merciless suppression, and the virtual enslavement of the surviving remnants.

When the Hereros and Hottentots finally surrendered and " peace " was made they were sent to forced labor on the harbor works at Luderitzbucht and Swakopmund and also on railway construction. Of 3,500 Hottentots and Kaffirs sent to Shark Island, all but 193 died there. How these unhappy people fared is told by some of the victims themselves. Two extracts must suffice:

About 600 men, women, and children prisoners were in an inclosure on the beach, fenced in with barbed wire. The women were made to do hard labor just like the men. They were put in spans of eight to each cart, and were made to pull, like draft animals. Many were half starved and weak, and died of sheer exhaustion. Those who did not work well were brutally flogged with sjamboks. I even saw women knocked down with pick handles. The German soldiers did this. I personally saw six women (Herero girls) murdered by German soldiers. I was there for six months, and the Hereros died daily in large numbers as a result of exhaustion, ill-treatment, and exposure.

When von Trotha left we were advised of a circular which the new Governor, von Lindequist, had issued, in which he promised to spare the lives of our people if we came in from the bush and mountains where we lived like hunted game. I went to Okambahe, near my old home, and surrendered. We then had no cattle, and there were only a few thousands of us left, and we were walking skeletons, with no flesh, only skin and bones. I was sent down with others to an island at Luderitzbucht. There on that island were thousands of Herero and Hottentot prisoners. Men, women, and children were all huddled together. We had no proper clothing, no blankets, and the night air of the sea was bitterly cold. The wet sea fogs drenched us and made our teeth chatter. The people died there like flies that had been poisoned. The little children and the old people died first, and then the women and the weaker men. No day passed without many deaths. We begged and prayed and appealed for leave to go back to our own country, which is warmer, but the Germans refused.

German native policy after the suppression of the rebellions was, in short, directed to the complete subjugation of the native races. Mr. Georges supplies statements by natives made on oath which give some idea of the reign of terror which existed up to 1914, and adds: " Instances of cruelty, injustice, and barbarism might be multiplied almost indefinitely. Instances of gross and bestial conduct, which for sheer depravity and immorality are well-nigh unbelievable, are also contained in the file of affidavits, but they are hardly fit for publication."

As an instance of the methods in which justice was meted out to the natives of the territory, the case of Lieutenant Venuleth, an officer of the German forces, may be noted. This officer in June, 1915, caught two natives, (one of whom was a woman,) charged with stock theft, and he proceeded to hold a court-martial on them, in which he acted as President of the court, and supplied practically the only evidence taken, with the result that the natives were condemned and shot. Lieutenant Venuleth was subsequently arrested by the British authorities and tried for murder, and a record of the trial has already been published in the Parliamentary paper, (Cd. 8,371.) As the court which tried him observed:

The whole procedure was hopelessly bad. The accused, Venuleth, was at once President and complainant. According to his own account, the only evidence was his own remarks and the statement of Schulze, a member of the court. No charge was made against the natives accused. They were not present; no evidence was heard; they were convicted and sentenced in their absence. They were found guilty and shot. Now it is difficult to mention any principle of justice and law which has not been violated, if this court really meant to try those natives.

Attention may be directed also to the case of Ludwig Cramer, which is described in full in the report. Cramer was accused of assaulting certain native women, and was eventually sentenced to four months' imprisonment and a fine of $675. The amazing inadequacy of this punishment can only be realized by reading the full account of the nature of assaults committed. It is sufficient to say that two of the victims were flogged by Cramer to such an extent that one died after fourteen days' hospital treatment and the other, after being released from hospital as incurable, died six months later.

The report is illustrated with photographs of men executed by the primitive method of hanging, of the bodies of women flogged nearly to death, and of the chains and fetters with which the natives were tortured by their captors—ghastly but eloquent testimony to the meaning of German rule.

# Mesopotamian Operations

## Report of the Commander in Chief Covering the Period From September, 1917, to March, 1918

LIEUT. GEN. SIR W. R. MAR-SHALL, Commander in Chief of the Mesopotamian Expeditionary Force, submitted to the British War Office a report for the six months ended March 31, 1918, which was officially published in September. In this period the chief engagement was at Khan Baghdadi, on the Euphrates, where the Turks were crushed and pursued beyond Ana. On the Diala front the British in this period captured the Sakaltutan Pass and drove the Turks back through Kifri. The most important portions of General Marshall's report are as follows:

I assumed the command of this force on Nov. 18 last on the death of the late lamented Lieut. Gen. Sir Stanley Maude, and now have the honor to submit a report on the operations in Mesopotamia from Oct. 1, 1917, till March 31 of this year. The last dispatch of General Maude covered the period April 1 to Sept. 30, 1917, [printed in CURRENT HISTORY MAGAZINE for April, 1918,] and concluded with the operations which resulted in the capture and occupation of Ramadi, on the Euphrates. At the commencement of the period covered by the present dispatch this force was opposed on the northeast by Turks, who were holding the hills known as Jebel Hamrin, while up the Tigris they were intrenched in front of Daur, and the left wing was secure at Ramadi. At the beginning of October it was decided to clear the Turks from the left bank of the Diala and occupy the Jebel Hamrin, astride of that river, in order that the control of the canals might be in our hands. All our objectives were gained, and a position astride the Diala gorge, protecting the headworks of the canals, was seized and consolidated.

To insure a perfect system of communication in the new forward area considerable work was necessitated. The main canals, i. e., Khalis, Mansuriya, Khorassan, Mahrut, Haruniya, and Ruz, as well as their numerous distributaries, were rapidly bridged—often at more than one place—and this mobile bridging equipment was subsequently replaced by more permanent structures capable of carrying heavy loads. Seventy-five bridges of various sizes were built in this area alone, and the Jebel Hamrin, which prior to our occupation was a roadless tangle of hills, was gradually pierced by a very complete and convenient number of roads suitable for wheeled traffic. These roads have involved heavy work, not only in digging but in rock-cutting through the hills and in metaling over the sandy flats. While the operations referred to above were in progress the 18th Turkish Army Corps on the Tigris undertook a counterdemonstration against our troops on that line, and in the middle of October advanced as far as El Huweslat, eight miles north of Samarra, where they proceeded to intrench themselves. General Maude decided to attack before they had time to consolidate their position to any great extent.

## ARMY'S HIGH MORALE

General Marshall then refers to the death of General Maude from cholera on Nov. 19, 1917; he pays a touching tribute to his predecessor and refers in detail to the high morale which existed in the army, due to General Maude's wonderful powers of organization. He proceeds:

The Turkish Army, on the contrary, was low in morale, and desertions from it were numerous and frequent; on the Tigris and Euphrates they had retreated out of rapid striking distance, and only on our right flank was there a good opportunity of hitting them. Toward the end of November, therefore, I determined to attack that part of the 13th Turkish Army Corps which was holding the Diala River above Mansuriya, the passes over the Jebel Hamrin and Kara Tepe. The Turkish forces were well placed for defense, and the task set to our troops included the forcing of the passages of the Diala and Nahrin Rivers, as well as the Sakaltutan and Abu Zenabil Passes through the Jebel Hamrin. The operations were intrusted to Lieut. Gen. Sir. R. Egerton, while an independent force of cavalry under Major Gen. L. C. Jones was ordered to demonstrate up the Adhaim River and prevent strong reinforcements being brought down against our attacking force from the line Tuz Kermatli-Kirkuk. On Dec. 5 a combined column pushed forward against Kara Tepe, (which was carried.) The features of the day's fighting were the determination and dash of the infantry, their close support by the artillery, and the valuable co-operation of the Flying Corps with both. During these operations our troops received valuable assistance from the Russian detach-

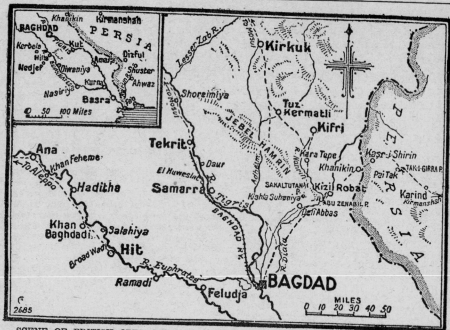

SCENE OF BRITISH OPERATIONS IN MESOPOTAMIA UNDER GENERAL MARSHALL

ment under Lieut. Col. Bicharakhov. Our casualties were very small, in spite of the difficulties of terrain, and the operation reflected great credit on the commanders and staffs concerned, as well as on the regimental officers and men. On Dec. 9 Khanakin was occupied and the communications in that area improved.

## ON THE EUPHRATES

On the Euphrates Ramadi had been captured in September, and the months from October to December were occupied by the troops in that area in consolidating their forward positions and in establishing a sense of security among the surrounding tribes. Several bridges were thrown across the River Euphrates, and the development of the forward area was taken in hand so as to relieve the strain on transport, which had to bring supplies by road from Bagdad until the railway was completed on Dec. 21.

During December and January it was evident that the Turks were being reinforced, the bulk of their troops being near Hit, and as their strength grew their patrols were pushed down stream as far as Uqbah and Nafata. I accordingly issued orders to Major Gen. Sir H. T. Brooking, commanding the troops on the Euphrates front, to capture Hit and its garrison as soon as his arrangements were completed and the state of the ground permitted. [After describing the operations, which were quite successful, the dispatch says:] The total prisoners taken were the commander and staff of the 50th Turkish Division, the commandant of

Ana, two regimental commanders, 213 officers, and 5,022 other ranks, inclusive of Germans. Twelve guns, forty-seven machine guns, and great quantities of rifles, ammunition, and stores were also captured. The amount of ammunition found at Ana, being too large to be brought away, was blown up, and on March 30 the troops were gradually withdrawn down the Euphrates to previously arranged positions.

## FAMINE CAUSED BY TURKS

With the advent of the new year, the weather, which had been unexpectedly good in December, became consistently wet. Continuous operations on any large scale were rendered out of the question, and the greatest strain was thrown on the lines of communication and supply formations. Toward the end of the month the state of famine to which the Turks had reduced Northern Persia made it incumbent on me to endeavor to open the main trade route via Kirmanshah in order to get supplies to the poor inhabitants of the towns and villages, and to provide them with an outlet for their home manufactures. With this object in view I increased the garrison of Kasr-i-Shirin, and pushed small posts toward Kirmanshah. A large amount of tribal labor was also employed in improving the road, which was in a lamentable state of disrepair. The continuance of wet weather up to the present date, coupled with snow on the high ground east of the Tak-i-Girra pass, has rendered the maintenance of troops along the road a matter of extreme difficulty. In addition to the operations on the Diala, Tigris, and Euphrates, and the activities toward Kirmanshah, to which I have referred, numerous minor operations have been carried out on all fronts.

## RELIGIOUS CITIES

In the time of my predecessor the Civil Commissioner, Sir Percy Cox, had strongly urged that the whole of the Euphrates line from Feludja to Nasiriya should be brought under military and civil control, but at that time circumstances did not permit of any extension of our military responsibilities. By the middle of December, 1917, however, the military position had completely changed owing to the magnificent success gained by General Allenby in Palestine. I therefore considered that the time was ripe to establish a firm control of the line of the Euphrates, and by that means encourage and assist in the development of the rich agricultural lands in that area. To that end I issued orders for troops to be dispatched from Nasiriya and Bagdad to garrison various villages, thus establishing through communication by river between Basra and Feludja and controlling the development of local resources throughout the lower Euphrates Valley.

The extension of military control over this area was also desirable in order that the Sheiks of important towns like Kerbela, Nedjef, Hilla, and Diwaniya might be brought more closely into the sphere of British influence and that pro-Turk sympathizers might be expelled. Care was taken not to establish troops in either of the religious cities of Kerbela and Nedjef, and they were quartered at a distance. The inhabitants of Nedjef are, for the most part, well-disposed holy people, but there is in addition a proportion of irreconcilables in the town. On Jan. 12 some of these fired on the troops exercising near the town, causing a few casualties. Not wishing to injure a town which is full of sacred memories for Mohammedans, I decided to punish two of the leading Sheiks who were known to be responsible for the offense, and to levy a heavy fine. The Sheiks, however, fled before they could be arrested, and they became outlaws. The fine was paid.

After this incident matters seemed to be going on satisfactorily when, on March 21, to my great regret, the political officer in Nedjef, Captain W. W. Marshall, was murdered. No reason was given for the act, as the deceased officer was universally liked. I immediately ordered a blockade of the town until all those implicated in the murder were given up, and surrounded it by a cordon of military posts joined by barbed wire. While I am prepared to go to extreme measures if necessary in order to exact reparation for so foul a deed, I feel confident that by blockade methods I shall cause all the delinquents to be surrendered. When these have been removed the further punishment of the town will be a matter for subsequent consideration.

Meantime, the development of the Hilla area has proceeded apace. Many hundred tons of seed grain have been planted, and to assist in bringing the harvest into Bagdad a branch line down to Hilla is being made, which is expected to be open for traffic by the middle of May. I have every confidence that this scheme will prove beneficial and enable this force to be dependent largely on local produce.

## LINES OF COMMUNICATION

The maintenance of the line of communication defenses along both the Tigris and Euphrates has been carried out with marked efficiency. On the Tigris the only trouble caused has been due to losses by theft from trains and boats, especially between Kurna and Amara. This district is inhabited by marsh tribes, who in their native swamps are afforded complete immunity against attack by land, as they retreat rapidly into their boats, leaving nothing of value behind. The tribes between Basra and Nasiriya have been absolutely quiet, and have made no hostile movement. I have nothing but praise for the patrols, railway guards and escorts, whose work has brought out qualities of self-reliance and devotion to duty. The defenses at Fao have been consolidated and improved, and the examination service of ships entering the Shatt-el-Arab has been effective. During the six months under review 581 vessels other than British and 8,466 native craft have been examined.

One of the principal features of the lines of communication has been the rapid development of the port of Basra by the completion of the dockyard and of the first set of wharves, earlier planned, as well as the continuance of the arrangements for improving the working of ocean shipping. A large island at Magill has been raised by dredging to take ocean ships on one side and to load river steamers on the other. The auxiliary annex of Nahr Umr has also given very great assistance with little outlay of material. All this work reflects great credit on the construction branch of the Port Administration and Conservancy. The period covered by this dispatch contains the worst months of low water, when every day was a constant anxiety with regard to river navigation, and the river was kept open only by the most unremitting care of the buoying establishment. The river-borne tonnage has steadily improved, and the organization of the Inland Water Transport has shown a very high state of efficiency. Considerable progress has also been shown in the development of the railways in all sections of the lines of communication, and in the improvements of the river ports of Amara and Kut-el-Amara.

The report compliments the various

auxiliary services, such as nursing, medical, sanitary, Red Cross, ordnance, remount, and proceeds as follows:

The Irrigation Department, as such, has been recently constituted, though irrigation work was carried out previously, chiefly on the Euphrates. The work done can only be described as extraordinary, and I look forward to a great development in this direction next year. The excellent results already achieved are due to the untiring zeal and energy of all ranks in a country where, until recently, there was no military control. The period has been one of constant construction work and of steadily increasing demands on the Railway Department. Floods have caused several interruptions, but the service of trains has been maintained with great success in face of difficulties inherent to lines rapidly constructed in a new country, where all material has had to be brought from overseas. The Department of Local Resources has, in addition to its former duties, taken over the control of grass farms,

the feeding of the civil population, and the arrangements for the collection and transportation of the coming harvest. Tanneries, and a poultry farm primarily to supply hospitals, are being formed. The blockade system has been carefully regulated, and ample evidence is available of severe shortage of supplies among the Turkish troops, resulting in increased desertions and loss of morale. The department has been conducted with considerable ability. Agriculture has made great progress, and my especial thanks are due to C. C. Garbett, First Revenue Officer, for the initiative displayed and the valuable work done by him in this connection. The latest estimate for the coming harvest is most gratifying. I hope, by the institution of a properly constituted Department of Agriculture and by its co-ordination with the Irrigation Department, that a very large increase will be shown next year in the agricultural development of this country.

**The dispatch ends with recommendations for distinguished service awards.**

# A Soldier's Amazing Career

The Paris Journal describes the remarkable career of a private French soldier named Bertrand. The narrative is vouched for to that newspaper by Bertrand's Lieutenant:

Bertrand wears the French Legion of Honor, Military Medal, Military Cross with seven palms and five stars, British Military Cross, Belgian Military Cross, French Colonial and Morocco Medal, the Life-Saving Medal, and also a ribbon for wounds, as he has lost one arm and one leg, and has been otherwise mutilated, besides receiving some thirty bayonet wounds. He is 26. He enlisted at 18, and fought in Morocco, where he saved two officers and won the Military Medal. At the outbreak of the war he went through the Charleroi and Marne battles. At the latter he captured two German field kitchens, having killed the cooks and brought the kitchens with food ready to eat into the French lines. On the Yser and the Somme, fighting with the British troops, he made ten German prisoners with his own hands, and won the British Military Cross. He was five times taken prisoner and five times escaped. After that he volunteered for the Near East, and at Monastir with one or two comrades he kept four machine guns firing and held an enemy battalion

at bay, with the result that 200 prisoners were made. After that at Monastir he saved his Captain and a nurse. In this affair he lost an arm, and was otherwise mutilated. He was sent back to France, and forty-eight hours after sailing his boat was torpedoed, and the explosion blew off his leg. He amputated the remainder of the limb himself with his own knife. He fell into the sea, and managed with his one arm to hang on to a floating spar. Then he caught sight of the ship's skipper, who had had both arms blown off. He managed to pick him up, and both men remained on the raft for three days and three nights. For this Bertrand was awarded the Life-Saving Medal, the only medal left to him to win.

This astounding career has been accompanied by the extraordinary tragedies of his family. His father enlisted at 53 at the beginning of the war, and was killed on Sept. 2, 1914. His four brothers have all died for their country; the last surviving one had lost both arms and both legs and was blinded, and mercifully died a few months ago. Bertrand's old mother has just died also, overcome by the succession of tragedies, and Bertrand remains alone of the family with his sister aged 9, of whom he is the sole support.

# INTERNATIONAL CARTOONS OF THE WAR

[Canadian Cartoon]

## "What Stands in the Way of Peace?"

[LANSDOWNE IN HIS PACIFIST LETTER]

From The Halifax Herald.

Only a Bloodstained Beast

# The Kings

—From *Nebelspalter, Zurich.*

"This is a time in which Monarchs must stand together."
[From the letter of the Emperor Karl to King Ferdinand]

# The Thinker

—From The Baltimore Sun.

" If only I hadn't——"

## [Italian Cartoon]
## The Crown Prince Moves in Haste

*Il 420, Florence.*

## [English Cartoon]
## Escorting Him Home

*—Passing Show, London.*

## [Spanish Cartoon]
# The Miracle of the Neutral Ship

Esquella of Barcelona issued a special number devoted to "Ex-Votos," or modernized versions of the mediaeval pictures with which pious persons celebrated unusual occurrences. The above picture bears the legend: "Ex-voto of an honest sailor, devoted to the Holy Lady of Bonanova, patroness of mariners, for the miracle of having arrived in port without being torpedoed, a miracle the more remarkable when it is remembered that the vessel was completely neutral."

## The Lord of the World

—*Ulk, Berlin.*

[In accordance with Germany's plan to create enmity between Japan and America, this cartoon shows England, the United States, France, and China all kneeling to the Mikado.]

## Her New Partner

" After the Sioux Indians the United States has sent the Apaches to France."— *German news item.*

—*Kladderadatsch, Berlin.*

FRANCE: "Mon Dieu! the real Apache."

## Wilson's Trip to the Front

—*Ulk, Berlin.*

[The German cartoonist represents the President as saying: " Though the whole world goes to ruin, I am not going to let *my* war be spoiled."]

## Berlin's Boast

—*Der Brummer, Berlin.*

It does not matter how they screech,
  or how Poincaré crows
For victory they'll never reach—it
  never backward goes.

# The Dance of Death

—*From De Amsterdammer, Amsterdam.*

GERMANIA: "Enough! Enough! Have done!"
DEATH: "You chose me for a partner, you will continue to dance!"

# The Chancellor and Belgium

—*From De Amsterdammer, Amsterdam.*

VON HERTLING: "We hold Belgium as a PAWN."

# Paying the Debt

—From The Dayton News.

## "Peace—Kamerad!"

## We Hit From the Shoulder

## Grasping a Salient Feature!

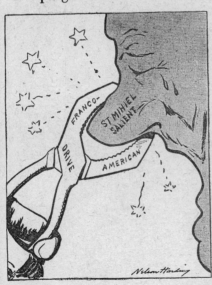

## Don't Try to Talk With Your Mouth Full!

—*Brooklyn Eagle.*

# The Rejected Gift

—*From La Baionnette, Paris.*

"It was a solid peace, too, for it came from the Krupp works."

[Italian Cartoon]

# The Kaiser's Change of Mind

—From *Il 420, Florence.*

IN 1915: "The armies of the Entente are as mosquitos to Germany."
IN 1918: "Who would have thought those mosquitos could bite so hard!"

# Changing His Step

—*From The Cleveland Plain Dealer.*

**The goose step and the Rhine trot.**

# A Bird in the Hand

—From *The Knickerbocker Press, Albany.*

# A Fool There Was

*—From The St. Louis Globe-Democrat.*

DEFEAT (unmasking): "Kiss me, my fool, kiss me!"

## Implacable Pursuit

—Central Press Association.

## "Wilson Said 'No,' Your Majesty"

—New York World.

## Line Out of Order ]

—Central Press Association.

## Goose-Stepping for Peace

—New York Tribune.

## Restrictions "Under There"

—*San Francisco Chronicle.*

## Pity the Blind

—*San Francisco Chronicle.*

## Feeding the Lion

—*Newark Evening News.*

## "Treatin' 'em Rough"

—*Newark Evening News.*

## The Rats Are Beginning to Leave

—*New York Tribune.*

## The Awakening

—*New York Times.*

## Kultur in Russia

—*New York Herald.*

## All in One Day

—*New York World.*

## The Fortune Teller

—Satterfield Syndicate.

## Why We Are Fighting

—St. Louis Republic.

## Coming Home to Roost

—Dallas News.

## Peace for Christmas? Not in That Stocking!

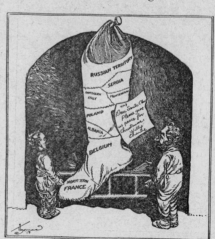

—Detroit News.

# Changes in the German Government

## Amendments Made on Account of President Wilson's Peace Program

CHANGES were made in the German Cabinet and also in constitutional and franchise provisions affecting the Government, all tending to conform more or less with President Wilson's requirements respecting peace. Chancellor von Hertling, Vice Chancellor von Payer, and Foreign Minister Von Hintze tendered their resignations Sept. 29, 1918, and these were accepted by the Emperor.

Count von Hertling, a conservative by instinct and training, had tried to steer a middle course and thus had deprived himself of the support of all parties. His support of the electoral reform measure, even in its emasculated form, angered the Pan Germans. The Moderates charged that he had "no program and no will," while the Socialists distrusted his sincerity and declared that he was absolutely frigid toward democratization and parliamentarization. Dr. von Payer, who followed his chief into retirement, was regarded as sharing the same defects, though in a lesser degree. Von Hintze, though his appointment had met with the enthusiastic approval of the Junker element, had proved to be a colorless figure during his term of office.

On Oct. 2 Prince Maximilian of Baden was appointed Chancellor. He is the heir presumptive to the grand ducal throne of Baden, and was born July 10, 1867. His expressed views on the war have been moderate, and his elevation was largely due to the belief that he would be an acceptable spokesman for Germany in dealing with the allied nations. A speech that he made to the Upper Chamber in Baden, of which he was President, on Dec. 15, 1917, in which he declared that "the sword alone will never be able to tear down the opposition to us" lent color to this belief. Soon after his appointment, however, the publication of a private letter in which he cast ridicule upon the sincerity of his previous professions greatly weakened his position, and at once rendered his tenure of office uncertain.

Dr. W. S. Solf, who succeeded von Hintze as Imperial Foreign Secretary, retained at the same time the Colonial portfolio. He has been a Moderate in politics and his speeches on the war have been marked by self-restraint.

Von Payer's functions were taken over by Mathias Erzberger, a leader of the Centrist Party, who opposed indemnities and annexations. Minor offices in the Cabinet were filled by the appointment of Dr. Eduard David, a Socialist leader in the Reichstag, as Under Secretary for Foreign Affairs, and of Herr Bauer, also a Socialist, as Secretary of State for the Imperial Labor Office. Philipp Scheidemann, Majority Socialist leader, was made a Secretary of State without portfolio.

Shortly after the appointments, and in apparent harmony with the purpose that dictated them, it was announced on Oct. 16 that Germany's Federal Council had accepted the proposed amendment to the Constitution, Paragraph 2 of Article II., making it read:

The consent of the Federal Council and the Reichstag is required for a declaration of war in the empire's name, except in a case where imperial territory has already been invaded or its coasts attacked.

Paragraph 3 of Article II. was amended to read:

Treaties of peace and treaties with foreign States which deal with affairs coming under the competence of the imperial law-giving bodies require the consent of the Federal Council and the Reichstag.

Cabinet Ministers were no longer to be required to be members of the Federal Council, but were at all times to have the right to be heard by the Council. They were also to have the right to demand to be heard by the Reichstag.

It was explained by the semi-official Wolff Bureau that these changes were in accord with the Emperor's decree of Sept. 30, in which he declared his will to be " that the German people shall henceforth more effectively co-operate in deciding the Fatherland's destinies."

The Election Commission of the Prussian House of Lords, in its reconsideration of the franchise measures, eliminated the clause granting an extra vote to men over 40 years of age. The period of residence required in an election district was reduced from one year to six months and other changes were made. The proportional franchise was accepted for a number of election districts containing large cities.

A decree by the Emperor, dated Oct. 4, was as follows:

> On your proposal I decree that the social and political affairs of the empire, which heretofore have pertained to the Imperial Economic Ministry, shall henceforth be dealt with by a special central authority, under the name of the Imperial Labor Minister, under direct control of the Imperial Chancellor. You will have to provide for the allocation of work for the officials requisite in virtue of this decree.

Another step toward the reform of Prussia's antiquated three-class franchise was taken by the adoption, Oct. 12, of the following resolution by the Conservative faction in the Prussian Diet:

> In the hour of the Fatherland's greatest distress and in realization that we must be equipped to fight hard battles for the integrity of the Fatherland's soil the Conservative Party of the Diet considers it a patriotic duty to lay aside all internal conflict and be ready to make heavy sacrifices to attain the ends in view. The members of the party believe that a far-reaching radicalization of the Prussian Constitution will not advance the welfare of the Prussian people, but are, nevertheless, prepared to abandon their opposition to the equal franchise in Prussia, in accordance with the latest decision of their friends in the House of Lords, in order to assure a harmonious front against the outside world.

The empire created by the German Constitution of April 14, 1871, consisted of four kingdoms, six grand duchies, five duchies, seven principalities, three free cities, and one territory, all under the Presidency of the King of Prussia, with the title of German Emperor. All the officials of the empire are appointed by him.

It is not a union of equal States, for Prussia drew up the instrument, and some States declined to join except on their own terms. Thus Prussia has the hereditary right to the Presidency and her representation in the Federal Council is seventeen out of a possible sixty-one, and the number of her representatives in the Reichstag is 236 out of 397. Prussia also has the casting of a vote in case of a tie in the Federal Council, and the Chirmanship of all standing committees save one. Other States which have special privileges are Bavaria, Württemberg, Baden, and Saxony. The Constitution contains a guarantee that no State so privileged shall be deprived of its rights without its consent.

Just as the King of Prussia is the German Emperor, so the Prime Minister of Prussia is Chancellor of the Empire. The Chancellor, whose title is Reichskanzler, countersigns the laws passed by the Federal Council, which represents the individual States of the empire, and by the Reichstag, which represents the empire as a political entirety, after which they are promulgated by the Emperor, with whom they originated.

The Chancellor also presides at the Federal Council, and supervises a body of Secretaries, who independently attend to the business of the empire—foreign affairs, finance, justice, &c.,—but they do not, strictly speaking, form a Ministry or Cabinet, for they are responsible only to the Chancellor, who is responsible to the Emperor.

Whatever changes may be made in the method of appointing members to the Federal Council or electing the members of the Reichstag, whatever changes may be made in the Constitutions of the various States of the empire, so long as the articles in the Constitution of April 16, 1871, which pertain to the power of the German Emperor, remain as they are, the empire will continue, from father to son, under the absolute government, rule and reign of the Hohenzollerns.

The amendments made to the Constitution on Oct. 16 left this supreme power inviolate, while they made the Reichstag, in certain cases, a party to the responsibility of the Federal Council.

# Progress of the War

## Recording Campaigns on All Fronts and Collateral Events
## From September 18 Up to and Including October 18, 1918

### UNITED STATES

The Fourth Liberty Loan campaign opened Sept. 28; closed Oct. 19, with more than $6,000,000,000 subscribed.

Germany sent an ultimatum to the United States Government Sept. 29, demanding that America cease arming troops with shotguns, and threatening to execute prisoners in reprisal. The American Government replied, justifying the use of shotguns and announcing that if the threat of reprisals were carried out, America would retaliate.

### SUBMARINE BLOCKADE

The American steamship Tampa was sunk off the English coast on Sept. 26; 118 men lost.

The American steamer Ticonderoga was torpedoed Sept. 30, about 1,000 miles from the American coast, while on its way to France. Eleven naval officers and 102 men were lost, and two officers were made prisoners by the submarine.

The American transport Amphion, homeward bound, had a two hours' running fight with a submarine 800 miles off the Atlantic Coast on the morning of Oct. 12. Eight American men were wounded, but the ship reached port safely.

Norway lost eight vessels in September.

Word was received on Sept. 20 of the sinking of the French liner Amiral Charner, bound for Malta. Six lives were lost.

The Spanish steamer Francoli was torpedoed Oct. 4.

Three hundred lives were lost when the Japanese liner Hirano Maru was sunk off the Irish coast Oct. 5.

The Italian cargo carrier Alberto Treves was torpedoed 300 miles off the Atlantic Coast Oct. 8.

The Irish mail boat Leinster was torpedoed in the Irish Channel Oct. 10, with a loss of 408 lives.

Figures given out by the United States Shipping Board Sept. 21 showed that during the period from August, 1914, to September, 1918, German submarines sank 7,157,-088 tons of shipping in excess of the tonnage turned out in that period by the allied and neutral nations; 3,795,000 tons of enemy ships were seized, the net loss to the allied and neutral nations on Sept. 1, 1918, being 3,362,088 tons. In all, the allied and neutral nations had lost 21,404,193 tons of shipping since the beginning of the war, and the total construction was 14,-247,025 tons.

**Sinkings in August amounted to 327,676** gross tons, of which 176,401 was British and 151,275 allied and neutral.

The British Admiralty announced on Oct. 2 that in the second quarter of 1917 the world's merchant shipping suffered a loss of 2,236,934 tons, but in the months of June, July, and August, the total was 932,556 tons—a reduction of 58 per cent.

### CAMPAIGN IN WESTERN EUROPE

Sept. 19—British advance into the Hindenburg line outposts northwest of St. Quentin and captured Lempire and Gauche Wood; French enter Contescourt and occupy Castres and Benay.

Sept. 20—American guns shell Metz forts; British recapture the fortified village of Moeuvres, seven miles west of Cambrai, advance their lines more than a mile, and advance on a front of more than two and a half miles northeast of La Bassée; French capture Essigny-le-Grand and gain northeast of Vailly.

Sept. 21—British break into the Hindenburg line east of Epehy and near Hargicourt.

Sept. 23—Germans give up Vendeuil, on the Oise; British capture strong positions northwest of St. Quentin.

Sept. 24—British and French attack on adjacent fronts, gaining about seven miles northwest, west, and southwest of St. Quentin.

Sept. 25—British capture Selency.

Sept. 26—First American Army launches an attack between the Meuse and the Aisne Rivers, on a twenty-mile front, smashing through the Hindenburg line for an average gain of seven miles and taking twelve towns.

Sept. 27—Americans continue their drive west of Verdun; French advance east of Rheims, gaining five miles in two days' fight and taking more than a dozen villages and important strategic points; British attack in Cambrai sector on a fourteen-mile front, crossing the Canal du Nord and piercing the Hindenburg line at several points.

Sept. 28—Americans reach the Kriemhilde line at Brieulles and advance; French take Fort Malmaison, southeast of Laon, and gain in Champagne; Belgians and British attack on a ten-mile front in Flanders, from Dixmude to a point north of Ypres, advancing more than three and a half miles; British close in on Cambrai, taking many towns.

Sept. 29—British strike on a thirty-mile front from St. Quentin to the Sensée River, aided by the Americans, who capture

Bellicourt and Nauroy; English division crosses the Scheldt and captures the garrison of Bellenglise; Americans fight on to the Kriemhilde line, capturing Brieulles-sur-Meuse and Romagne; French advance two miles on the Chemin des Dames; Belgians take Dixmude and advance.

Sept. 30—British force their way into the outskirts of Cambrai and St. Quentin; British take Messines Ridge and Gheluwe; Americans advance slightly in the Argonne; French advance on a front of seven and a half miles between the Aisne and the Vesle Rivers.

Oct. 1—French troops enter St. Quentin and extend their lines east of the city; Germans driven from Aisne hills northwest of Rheims; British take northern and western suburbs of Cambrai; Americans push ahead in the Aisne-Meuse sector and repulse German counterattacks in the region of Cierges and at Apremont; Germans prepare to evacuate Belgium.

Oct. 2—Germans begin evacuation of Lille and begin a retreat on a wide front on both sides of La Bassée Canal as Allies continue enveloping movement north and south of Lille, Roubaix, and Turcoing; Belgians take Hooglede and Handzaeme; British take Le Bezet in move to encircle Armentières; last known German line of defense between Cambrai and St. Quentin broken by British capture of the front extending from Beaurevoir to Fonsomme; Cambrai mined by the Germans, but British patrols enter the city; all of St. Quentin won by the French and positions south of the city carried; French advance north of the Vesle.

Oct. 3—British break German line on an eight-mile front from Sequehart to the Scheldt Canal north of Bony, capturing several towns, and penetrate German positions about five miles; Germans evacuate Armentières and Lens, and retreat on twenty-mile front; French make sweeping gains from St. Quentin eastward to the Argonne region, clearing the country north and west of Rheims.

Oct. 4—Americans break the Kriemhilde line and drive Germans back to a line two kilometers north of Binarville and Fleville; Americans join French in the Champagne and take part in operations north of Somme-Py; fighting in the streets of Cambrai; Germans continue to retreat on the Lens-Armentières front.

Oct. 5—Germans evacuate Lille; British cross the Scheldt Canal on the eight-mile front between Crèvecoeur and Le Catelet; Germans retreat on wide front north of Rheims and in Champagne.

Oct. 7—British advance on a four-mile front north of the Scarpe and capture Oppy and Biache-St. Vaast; French take Berry-au-Bac; Americans gain in the Argonne region, taking Châtel-Chehery and commanding positions on the Aire.

Oct. 8—British, American, and French forces shatter twenty miles of Hindenburg defense system from Cambrai southward, advancing to an average depth of three miles.

Oct. 9—British take Cambrai, and advance nine miles on a twenty-mile front, defeating thirty German divisions; Americans break through the Kriemhilde line between Cunel and Romagne; French take Vaux les Mauron and Bazancourt.

Oct. 10—British push their lines to the banks of the Selle on the ten-mile reach between Solesmes and St. Souplet, capturing Le Cateau; French north of the Aisne gain the plateau of Croix-Sans-Tête and cross the Aisne Canal near Villers-en-Prayères; Americans press forward in the Argonne Forest.

Oct. 11—British press in to the northeast of Cambrai, capturing Iwuy and Fressies; Germans abandon their line along the Sensée River; British close in on Douai; French force an evacuation of thirty-seven miles in a six-mile thrust on the Suippe front; Germans evacuate the Chemin des Dames; Americans clear the Argonne Forest.

Oct. 12—French enter Vouziers and hold southern slopes of the Returne Valley; British capture more villages southeast of Cambrai.

Oct. 13—Germans evacuate Laon without a fight; French take La Fère and occupy the massif of St. Gobain; British take suburbs of Douai.

Oct. 14—French capture Roulers in allied drive on twelve-mile front between the Handzaeme Canal and the Roulers-Menin Road; British and French menace Courtrai; Americans advance west of the Meuse; French capture and pass beyond Sissonne.

Oct. 16—Germans begin evacuation of the Belgian coast region; British forces drive closer to Lille; Americans capture Grand Pré.

Oct. 17—British enter Lille and Douai; Germans evacuate Ostend and British naval forces enter harbor; Belgian patrols enter Bruges; British and American attack on a nine-mile front northeast of Bohain and advance two miles.

Oct. 18—Allies occupy Zeebrugge, Blankenberghe, and Thielt; British occupy Roubaix and Turcoing, capture villages to the southeast of Douai, and advance east of Le Cateau; Americans advance north of Romagne and take Bantheville; Germans withdraw from Loges and Bantheville Forests and Bois Hadois.

## BALKAN CAMPAIGN

Sept. 17-18—British and Greek troops begin drive in the region of Lake Doiran; Serbs, French, and Greeks capture forty-five villages, take a foothold on the hills of Kuchkov, and cross the Perez River.

Sept. 21—Serbs east of Monastir advance nine miles, liberating ten villages.

Sept. 23—Allied armies drive Germans and Bulgars back on a front of more than ninety miles; Italians on the left wing cut First Bulgarian Army at Prilep off from communication with Second Army in the Doiran section; Serb, French, and Greek forces in the centre cross the Drenska mountain range and cut the German-built railroad from Prilep to Gradsko.

Sept. 24—Allies advance on a front of twenty miles in Macedonia; French and Serbs capture Prilep; British occupy Doiran and advance northward; passing Kara Oghular; Serbs establish themselves on the eastern bank of the Vardar between Demirkapu Pass and Krivolak.

Sept. 25—Bulgars retreat toward Veles, pursued by Serbs, who cross the Vardar River northwest of Gradsko, Krivolak-Ishtib road cut.

Sept. 26—Serbs capture Veles and Ishtib; British and Greek forces invade Bulgaria from the Doiran region.

Sept. 27—British capture Strumnitza City; Serbs enter Kochana; Bulgaria asks for armistice.

Sept. 30—French enter Uskub; Serbs Charevo; hostilities with Bulgaria officially ended as armistice is signed.

Oct. 2—Bulgarian troops evacuate Serbia; Austrians resist vigorously in the region of the Albanian border.

Oct. 3—Austrian troops withdrawn from Albania; Italians occupy Berat without a fight and advance beyond; German troops in Macedonia move northward and fortify the Rumanian bank of the Danube River.

Oct. 4—Greek troops enter Seres and occupy the Demir-Hassar Pass; Teutons plan new front in Northern Serbia and Bulgaria.

Oct. 8—Greeks occupy Drama.

Oct. 9—Italians in Albania occupy Elbasan.

Oct. 11—Teutons reinforced in Serbia; Serbs advance toward Nish.

Oct. 13—Allies take Nish.

Oct. 15—Italians take Durazzo.

Oct. 17—Serbs capture Alexinatz and Krushevatz; Teuton forces in Western Serbia retire into Montenegro, after evacuating Diakova.

## CAMPAIGN IN ASIA MINOR

Sept. 19—British and French forces in Palestine, under command of General Allenby, attack Turkish positions on a front of sixteen miles, breaking through the Turkish lines between Rafat and the sea and advancing twelve miles.

Sept. 22—Turkish army between the Jordan and the Mediterranean virtually wiped out by the British, who advance sixty miles from their original positions and occupy Nazareth, El Afule, and Beisan; Hejaz Arabs east of the Jordan destroy railroads and bridges.

Sept. 23—British cavalry, pushing up the Mediterranean coast, occupy Haifa and Acre; Turks east of the Jordan cut off on the Damacus-Medina railroad to the north, and retire southward on Amman.

Sept. 26—British reach the Sea of Galilee and occupy Tiberias, Semakh, and Es-Samra, also Amman, on the east of the Jordan on the Hejaz Railway.

Sept. 27—British cavalry drives Turks northward through Mezeris and joins hands with Arab forces of the King of the Hejaz.

Oct. 1—Damascus taken by the British, aided by the Arabs.

Oct. 6—British occupy Zahieh and Rayak.

Oct. 16—British seize Tripoli and Homs.

## AERIAL RECORD

Mannheim, Karlsruhe, Boulay, Frescaty, and Morhange were bombed Sept. 19. One German machine was brought down and one allied machine was reported missing.

American aviators performed noteworthy feats in the Argonne region. On the night of Oct. 9 an expedition of over 350 planes bombed many towns. One man was lost.

British airmen destroyed 383 German airplanes on the western front in September.

## NAVAL RECORD

American, British, and Italian warships destroyed the Austrian naval base at Durazzo and the warships anchored there, Oct. 2.

Beirut was entered by a French naval division, Oct. 7.

## RUSSIA

The American Government sent a communication to all neutral and allied Governments urging them to condemn the slaughter and barbarism involved in the Bolshevist reign of terror, Sept. 21. Appeals to this effect were also issued by the Ukrainian Council and the Russian Duma and Russian Imperial Council. A decree rescinding the reign of terror was issued by the Bolshevist Government, Sept. 26.

The allied and Czechoslovak forces made some progress in their fighting against the Bolsheviki in Siberia and in European Russia. On Sept. 18 the Japanese captured Blagoviestschenck, the capital of Amur, and Alexievsk. The Austro-German forces at Kopka laid down their arms, and another formation retreated to the upper reaches of the Zaya River. On Sept. 21 Entente naval units and allied troops operating along the River Dvina sank two enemy ships and captured three guns. Many towns along the Dvina River were occupied by American and allied forces. Kadish, in the Province of Archangel, was occupied, and Karelia was reported cleared of the enemy, who were driven back over the Finnish border, Oct. 18.

Martial law was declared in Vladivostok Sept. 25, by Colonel Butenko, Provisional Commander of the Armed Forces of the Maritime Province.

A new Government, with the controlling power vested in the Constituent Assembly, was organized at Ufa Sept. 24, at a conference which was attended by many members of the Pan Russian Constituent Assembly and presided over by the Socialist Revolutionary leader Avskentieff, former Minister of Agriculture and of the Interior. The conference was organized and supported by President Malinoff of the National Czech Council. It took over the reins of power in succession to the Provisional Government of 1917.

Russia abrogated the treaty of peace with Turkey Oct. 5.

## PEACE MOVES

Germany announced her readiness to participate in the exchange of ideas on peace proposed by Austria Sept. 20. Bulgaria replied to the Austrian note, accepting President Wilson's views on the settlement of Balkan conflicts in accordance with the rights of nationalities.

On Sept. 28 Bulgaria asked the Allies for an armistice of forty-eight hours, with a view to making peace. Great Britain replied immediately, calling for unequivocal submission. Bulgaria surrendered unconditionally to the Allies. The armistice was signed at Saloniki Sept. 29, and hostilities ceased officially at noon Sept. 30. Bulgaria agreed to evacuate all occupied territory in Greece and Serbia, to demobilize her army immediately, and to surrender all means of transport to the Allies. The evacuation of Serbia was begun at once.

Austria-Hungary appealed to President Wilson, Oct. 5, to conclude an armistice immediately and to start negotiations for peace.

On Oct. 6 the German Chancellor, Prince Maximilian of Baden, sent a note to President Wilson proposing a peace parley on the President's principles, and asking for an armistice.

President Wilson replied, Oct. 8, asking if his terms were fully accepted, and if the Chancellor spoke for the people. He also called for the evacuation of invaded territory before an armistice could be asked.

On the same day Turkish emissaries were sent to the Allies from the Province of Smyrna to secure peace.

Germany replied to President Wilson's note, partially accepting his terms, Oct. 12, but asking for a mixed commission on the evacuation of invaded territory.

President Wilson answered this second note, Oct. 13, declaring that there would be no armistice so long as the armed forces of Germany continued their barbarous methods of warfare, that there would be no agreement with an autocratic German Government, and that the evacuation of invaded territory would be under direction of the allied military chiefs alone.

President Wilson replied to Austria's request for peace on Oct. 19 by a refusal, stating that the independence of the Czechoslovak and Jugoslav nations had been recognized by the United States Government, and with these nations would rest the decision as to any terms proposed by Austria.

## MISCELLANEOUS

German forces of occupation began to retire from Rumania Sept. 27.

German troops evacuated Finland at the request of the Finnish Government Oct. 11.

Talaat Bey, Turkish Minister of the Interior, resigned, Oct. 4.

The allied Governments decided formally to recognize the belligerent status of the Arab forces fighting with the Allies against the Turks in Palestine and Syria, Oct. 4.

The British Government recognized the Polish National Army as autonomous, allied, and co-belligerent, Oct. 16.

King Ferdinand of Bulgaria abdicated in favor of Crown Prince Boris, Oct. 4.

Emperor Charles of Austria-Hungary issued a manifesto announcing his decision to unite Croatia, Slavonia, Bosnia, and Herzegovina in one State, Oct. 11. On the same day Dr. Alexander Wekerle, the Hungarian Premier, resigned.

A general strike broke out in Prague, and on Oct. 17 word was received that at a meeting of the Hungarian Parliament a proclamation was read declaring Hungary to be an independent State. It was also reported that Baron von Hussarek, the Austrian Premier, announced that Austria was to be transformed into Federal States.

On Oct. 18 Emperor Charles proclaimed steps for the organization of Austria on a federalized basis, Baron Burian resigned as Austrian Premier, the Provisional Government of the new Czechoslovak Nation proclaimed its independence of Austria-Hungary, and the Czechs seized Prague.

Count von Hertling, the Imperial German Chancellor, resigned, Sept. 27, and the German Cabinet was reorganized with Prince Maxmilian of Baden at its head.

The Prussian upper house rejected a motion to introduce suffrage based on vocations and passed a direct suffrage measure, with the addition of an extra vote for persons over 50 years of age, Oct. 2.

The German Federal Council accepted the measure calling for further parliamentarization of Germany, Oct. 13.

On Oct. 16 the Prussian Diet withdrew opposition to equal franchise and the Federal Council accepted the proposed amendment to the Constitution restricting the right of the Emperor to declare war and make treaties.

# WOODROW WILSON

President of the United States, Who Helped to Shape the Larger
Issues at the Peace Conference

(© *Underwood & Underwood*)

# RAYMOND POINCARE

President of France, Who Held His Nation Steadfast for Victory
Through the War's Darkest Days

*(Photo Brown Bros.)*

# KING GEORGE V.

Head of the British Empire, Who Won Increased Loyalty of All His Dominions During the War

# KING VICTOR EMMANUEL

Italy's King, Who Broke the Triple Alliance and Joined the Entente
Against Germany

KING ALBERT OF BELGIUM

Ruler of the Little Nation That Received the First Blow of the War-
Mad German Invaders

# ROBERT LANSING

American Secretary of State and Head of the United States Delegation to the Peace Conference

(© *Harris & Ewing*)

# DAVID LLOYD GEORGE

British Prime Minister and the Most Conspicuous English Organizer
of Victory

*(Central News Photo Service)*

# GEORGES CLEMENCEAU

Premier of France, Whose Inspiring Courage Carried the Nation
Through the Last Crisis

# VITTORIO ORLANDO

The Italian Premier, Who Helped to Organize the Victory Over
Austria-Hungary

# ADMIRAL SIR DAVID BEATTY

Commander in Chief of the British Grand Fleet and Victor in the
Battle of Jutland
*(Photo Central News Service)*

# VICE ADMIRAL WILLIAM S. SIMS

Commander of the United States Fleet in the Atlantic During the War

# MARSHAL FERDINAND FOCH

Commander in Chief of all the Allied Armies and the Universally
Recognized Organizer of Victory

Victor in the First Battle of the Marne, Which Saved France from
Conquest

# FIELD MARSHAL SIR DOUGLAS HAIG

Commander in Chief of the British Armies in France, Whose Military
Genius Is Everywhere Acclaimed

# GENERAL ARMANDO DIAZ

Commander in Chief of the Italian Armies and Victor in the Second
Battle of the Piave
*(International Film Service)*

# GENERAL JOHN J. PERSHING

Commander of the American Armies, Who Personifies America's
Amazing Military Achievements

*(Feldman Studios)*

# PERIOD LI.

End of the War: Story of Germany's Surrender—Announcing the Armistice in America—President's Address Announcing an Armistice—Text of Armistice Signed by Germany—The March to the Rhine—Surrender of German High Seas Fleet—Germany in Revolution—The Collapse of Austria-Hungary—Turkey's Surrender to the Allies—Story of the Capture of Damascus—Overseas Transportation of U. S. Troops—German Methods in Alsace-Lorraine—The Franco-German Armistice in 1871—The War in Its Last Phases—The Aviators' Share in the Victory—Final Acts of Oppression—How Peace Came to the Battlefronts—The Redemption of Belgium—French Armies' Final Victories—The Battle That Won Sedan—The Blasted Valley of the Somme—Breaking the Hindenburg Line—Growth of Commissioned Personnel of the U. S. Navy—End of the U-Boat Warfare—The North Sea Submarine Barrage—The Czechoslovak Republic—Poland's Move for Independence—The Mid-European Union—Terrorism Versus Order in Russia—The Czech Exodus: A Siberian Epic—Final War Activities in United States—American, British, and German Losses—Austria's Ultimatum to Serbia: Serbia's Reply.

# END OF THE WAR

## Germany's Capitulation and the Historic Words and Acts That Preceded the Signing of the Armistice

THE war came to an end on Monday, Nov. 11, 1918, at 11 o'clock A. M., French time; 6 o'clock, Washington time. The armistice, which was imposed upon Germany by the Allies and the United States, was signed by the German plenipotentaries at 5 o'clock A.M., Paris time; midnight, Washington time.

The conclusion of the armistice followed within three weeks after the dispatch of a note from the German Government to President Wilson, in which it was affirmed that a fundamental change had been made in the German Government in " complete accord with the principle of the representation of the people based on equal, universal, secret, direct franchise," with the further announcement that orders had been issued to submarine commanders precluding the torpedoing of passenger ships, and asking that steps be taken to arrange an armistice which would contain no " demand which would be irreconcilable with the honor of the German people and with the opening of the way to a peace of justice." This note was dispatched on Oct. 21, 1918.

On Oct. 23 President Wilson replied by agreeing to take up with the Allies the question of an armistice, but said the only armistice which he would submit for consideration would be one that would leave the Allies in a position to enforce any arrangement entered into and make a renewal of hostilities by Germany impossible, with the significant addition that if the Government of the United States " must deal with the military masters and the monarchical autocrats of Germany now, or if it is likely to have to deal with them later in regard to the international obligations of the German Empire, it must demand, not peace negotiations, but surrender."

On Oct. 25 the German War Cabinet considered the reply of the President, and the note was discussed in sectional meetings of the Reichstag members. It was at this juncture that the first mutterings of serious discontent with the Government reached the outside world. On Oct. 25 a dispatch was allowed to go from Berlin stating that an enormous crowd had assembled before the Reichstag building calling for the abdication of the Kaiser and the formation of a republic. That the then existing Government did not contemplate the surrender of Alsace-Lorraine was indicated by a statement made by the Foreign Secretary, Dr. Solf, to the Reichstag that " the Cabinet would continue the reforms already undertaken in the government of Alsace-Lorraine, but would not anticipate the solution of that problem." The Foreign Secretary contended that "Polish annexation demands were not in accordance with the peace program of President Wilson."

A vote of confidence was given the Chancellor by the Reichstag on this day, the vote standing 193 to 52.

On Oct. 27 another note was sent President Wilson by the German Foreign Secretary declaring that far-reaching changes had occurred in Germany's constitutional structure and that peace negotiations were being carried forward by the people's Government, "in whose hands rests, both actually and constitutionally, the power to make the deciding conclusions," and closing with the statement that "the German Government now awaits the proposals for an armistice."

On Oct. 28 matters were advanced by receipt of a note from the Austrian Government declaring that all the conditions laid down by the President for the entry into negotiations for an armistice were accepted. This note was followed on the 29th by another from the Austrian Government urging that the negotiations for an armistice be hurried, thus indicating that Austria's complete surrender had been decided upon.

Meanwhile in Berlin the Crown Council was practically in continuous session under the Presidency of Emperor William and profound agitation was observed among Reichstag members and extreme nervousness in German military circles.

## FORMULATING ARMISTICE TERMS

On Oct. 31 it was announced from Paris that the heads of the allied Governments and Colonel E. M. House, special representative of the United States Government, were holding informal meetings in Paris.

The following Ministers and military and naval chiefs of the Allies had arrived in Paris on the 30th: Premier Lloyd George, Foreign Minister Balfour, War Secretary Milner, Field Marshal Haig, Sir Eric Geddes, Admiral Wemyss, and General Wilson of Great Britain, Admiral Benson and Vice Admiral Sims of the United States, Premier Orlando, Vice Admiral di Revel, and Foreign Minister Sonnino of Italy.

Colonel House took a residence in Paris on the left bank of the Seine, not far from the French Ministry of War. He was in daily consultation with the Ministers and military heads of the allied Governments.

On Oct. 31 the representatives of the allied Governments held a formal meeting at Versailles to consider the armistice terms for Austria, which would foreshadow the terms to be submitted to Germany.

At Versailles the business was over in a couple of hours, and a long line of automobiles with the representatives of the powers returned to Paris. The reason for the trip to Versailles was that it was the headquarters of the Supreme War Council, which theoretically takes no decision except at Versailles.

The very atmosphere of Versailles was surcharged with the importance of the events. The presence of numerous uniformed officials of the allied nations, with Councilors, Prime Ministers, and

personages of high estate, lent to the scene a dignity which reflected the nature of the colossal questions to be decided, directing the destiny of the new order of world politics.

## SCENES AT VERSAILLES

Automobiles glided over the asphalt and cobblestone streets of France's ancient seat of government bearing world figures. Some carried the highest army staffs in dazzling uniforms; others bore naval chiefs in their black uniforms, variegated with gold stripes in profusion and patterned according to their country's orders, while now and then limousines with distinguished civilians rushed by, claiming the right of way seemingly because of the high positions of the occupants in the world's affairs.

Trianon Palace was isolated. The deliberations of the Premiers, Ministers, and naval and military chiefs were conducted amid the quietude of a woodland dell, retained in all its beauty by the French Government since the days of Louis XIV., and used afterward by successive sovereign, including Napoleon.

Trianon Palace, nestling in clusters of giant trees, surrounded by a picturesque park and resplendent with flower gardens and serpentine walks, stands within the very shadow of the Louis XIV. Palace, in the north wing of which, in the " Galérie des Glaces," Wilhelm I., grandfather of the German Emperor and then King of Prussia, was proclaimed first German Emperor in 1871.

To make more secure the isolation of the palace for the conferences, all traffic in its direction was stopped. Guards of French soldiers, British, Americans, and Italians stood on duty at various posts. During the sessions the guard about the palace was considerably reinforced, so as to prevent the slightest possibility of any unauthorized person approaching the grounds.

## PRELIMINARY CONFERENCE

An informal conference took place at the home of Colonel E. M. House, President Wilson's personal representative, in the forenoon prior to the assembling at Versailles. Among those present were

M. Clemenceau and M. Pichon, respectively the French Premier and Foreign Minister; Signor Orlando and Baron Sonnino, the Italian Premier and Foreign Minister, and David Lloyd George, the British Prime Minister. This gathering was preparatory to the formal meeting.

In addition to the French, Italian and British representatives, Dr. M. R. Vesnitch, the Serbian Minister to France, and Eleutherios Venizelos, the Greek Premier, attended.

The Americans present, in addition to Colonel House, were Arthur H. Frazier, Secretary of the American Embassy; Joseph C. Grew and Gordon Auchincloss, who acted as secretaries for Colonel House; General Tasker H. Bliss, the representative of the United States in the War Council, with General Lockridge and Colonel Wallace as secretaries, and Admiral Benson, with Commander Carter and Lieutenant Commander Russell as his secretaries.

The last to arrive at the conference was Marshal Foch. He was alone, without aid or orderly.

## COUNCIL IN SESSION

The Supreme War Council resumed its sessions at Versailles on Nov. 1 to consider the armistice terms which would be submitted to Austria and Germany.

General Tasker H. Bliss, representative of the United States, was the first delegate to reach the Trianon Palace Hotel, arriving at 1:50 P. M. He was followed soon by Premier Clemenceau, Marshal Foch, Field Marshal Sir Douglas Haig, Colonel House, and David Lloyd George, the British Prime Minister.

The deliberations in connection with the armistice proposition were participated in by Belgian and Japanese representatives, the day's meeting having to do with Germany. When Austrian affairs were discussed the day before, Serbian and Greek representatives were in attendance, because of their particular interest in Austrian matters.

The session was held in the large chamber on the main floor of the Trianon Palace, with windows overlooking the garden. The hall has little ornamentation beyond a marble clock and candelabra upon a mantel topped with massive mirrors. Immediately in front of this extends a wide mahogany table the entire length of the room, with the members facing one another on two sides.

The entire aspect was one of business, the meeting being devoid of formalities. Each member had before him a large blotting pad with all desk requisites. Colonel House sat on the left side next to Premier Orlando of Italy, with Premier Clemenceau directly opposite.

A stenographer at a desk in a corner took notes of the official proceedings. The uniforms of the Generals and Admirals participating gave a touch of color to the scene, but the prevailing tone was one of a civilian gathering, as the larger part of the membership was made up of Premiers and other high civilian officials.

The deliberations proceeded with complete privacy. Guards along the Boulevard of the Queen kept the crowds from approaching the iron gate leading to the palace.

## CLOSING IN ON GERMANY

The conference continued its sessions daily, and during this period the political unrest in Germany continued to develop fresh intensity, with extreme agitation in all the larger cities and more pronounced and insistent demands by popular assemblies for the abdication of the Kaiser. During all this time the allied armies on the western front from the North Sea to Switzerland continued to deliver hammer blows on the shattered German lines and the latter were steadily retreating from Belgium and France with enormous losses.

On Nov. 3 the armistice with Austria was signed in the field, imposing drastic terms, which are given in full elsewhere, and on the same day the German Kaiser issued a decree addressed to the German Imperial Chancellor in which he accepted the transfer of " fundamental rights of the Kaiser's person to the people," and acknowledged the adoption of the changes in the German Government which had been demanded by the Allies. The reports, however, indicated that he was firmly resisting the pressure coming from all sides that he abdicate.

On Nov. 4 the drastic terms of the Austrian armistice were made public and at the same time it was officially announced that the allied Governments and the United States had come to a complete agreement on the terms Germany must accept.

On Nov. 5 a note was handed to the Swiss Minister, who represented Germany at Washington, by Secretary of State Lansing, in which he stated that Marshal Foch had been authorized to receive German delegates and to communicate to them the terms of an armistice. [The text of this note appears on page 388.]

The German Government took instant action. On Nov. 6 it was announced from Berlin that a German delegation to conclude an armistice and take up peace negotiations had left for the western front.

## PRELIMINARY TO THE ARMISTICE

On Nov. 7 the following documents relating to the armistice negotiations were made public at Paris:

"There was received the 7th of November at 12:30 A. M. the following from the German high command, by order of the German Government, to Marshal Foch:

The German Government, having been informed through the President of the United States that Marshal Foch had received powers to receive accredited representatives of the German Government and communicate to them conditions of an armistice, the following plenipotentiaries have been named by it:
Mathias Erzberger, General H. K. A. von Winterfeld, Count Alfred von Oberndorff, General von Grünnel, and Naval Captain von Salow.
The plenipotentiaries request that they be informed by wireless of the place where they can meet Marshal Foch. They will proceed by automobile, with subordinates of the staff, to the place thus appointed.

"A German wireless dispatch received Nov. 7 at 1 P. M. said:

German General Headquarters to the Allies' General Headquarters; the German Commander in Chief to Marshal Foch: The German plenipotentiaries for an armi-

stice leave Spa today. They will leave here at noon and reach at 5 o'clock this afternoon the French outposts by the Chimay-Fourmies-La Capelle-Guise road. They will be ten persons in all, headed by Secretary of State Erzberger.

"Orders were given to cease fire on this front at 3 o'clock P. M. until further orders.

"On Nov. 7 at 1:25 A. M. Marshal Foch sent the following to the German command:

If the German plenipotentiaries desire to meet Marshal Foch and ask him for an armistice, they will present themselves to the French outposts by the Chimay-Four-

WHERE THE GERMAN ENVOYS PASSED THROUGH THE BATTLELINES—ON THE LA CAPELLE ROAD.

mies-La Capelle-Guise road. Orders have been given to receive them and conduct them to the spot fixed for the meeting.

"The following wireless dispatch in German was received at 1:50 P. M.:

German General Headquarters to the Allied General Headquarters: The Supreme German Command to Marshal Foch: From the German outposts to the French outposts our delegation will be accompanied by a road-mending company to enable automobiles to pass the La Capelle road, which has been destroyed.

"The following wireless in German was received at 6 P. M.:

The German Supreme Command to Marshal Foch: By reason of delay the German delegation will not be able to cross the outpost line until between 8 and 10 o'clock tonight at Haudroy, two kilometres northeast of La Capelle.

## ARRIVAL OF ENVOYS

The German plenipotentiaries sent to receive the armistice terms from Marshal Foch arrived at allied General Headquarters Nov. 8 at 6 A. M. The terms were delivered to them, with a formal demand that they be accepted or refused within seventy-two hours.

A message from the German envoys to the Imperial Chancellor and the German high command, sent by the French wireless, was picked up at London Nov. 8. It asked that a courier be sent back as soon as possible with instructions. The message read:

> From the German Plenipotentiaries for an Armistice to the Imperial Chancellor and the German High Command:
>
> Friday morning at Allied General Headquarters the plenipotentiaries received the conditions of an armistice, as well as a formal demand that they be accepted or refused within seventy-two hours, expiring on Monday morning at 11 o'clock, French time.
>
> The German proposal for an immediate conclusion and provisional suspension of hostilities was rejected by Marshal Foch.
>
> Please acknowledge receipt and send back courier as soon as possible with your latest instructions. Sending of fresh delegates is not necessary for the moment.
>
> A German courier bearing the text of the conditions of the armistice has been sent to Spa, no other means of communication being practicable.

The French Wireless Service gave out a dispatch sent by General Winterfeld of the armistice delegation, to the German high command, announcing that a courier, Captain Helldorff, would cross the lines between 6 o'clock and 8 o'clock P. M. Nov. 8, and that the French command had taken measures for his safety.

The delegates crossed the allied line near La Capelle late on the night of Nov. 7. The white flag bearers reached the left wing of General Debeney's army at 10 P. M. They arrived at the place indicated by the allied supreme commander within the French lines about 2 o'clock A. M. Nov. 8 and passed the remainder of the night there. They were taken to a house at Rethondes, six miles east of Compiègne and thirty miles from Marshal Foch's headquarters, where preparations had been made to receive them.

## MEETING MARSHAL FOCH

The automobiles conveying the delegates carried white flags and were preceded by a trumpeter. Some French soldiers under an officer approached them on the road just outside the lines.

The delegates established their identity and showed their credentials. The members of the German party were then blindfolded and the delegates proceeded to the place where they spent the night.

Generals Winterfeld and von Grünnel wore uniforms of the rank of General. Von Salow was in the uniform of an Admiral of the fleet. Mathias Erzberger and Count von Oberndorff were in plain civilian dress.

They stayed over night at the house to which they were conducted, and were then taken to a place in the Department of the Aisne, which was the meeting place fixed by Marshal Foch. This trip required about four hours.

The delegates were received by Marshal Foch at Rethondes at 9 o'clock on the morning of Nov. 8 in a railroad car, in which the Commander in Chief of the allied force had his headquarters.

When the Germans' credentials had been opened and verified, Mathias Erzberger, leader of the enemy delegation, speaking in French, announced that the German Government had been advised by President Wilson that Marshal Foch was qualified to communicate to them the Allies' conditions and had appointed them plenipotentiaries to take cognizance of the terms and eventually sign an armistice.

## HEARING THE TERMS

Marshal Foch then read the terms in a loud voice, dwelling upon each word. The Germans were prepared by semi-official communications for the stipulations as a whole, but hearing set forth in detail the concrete demands seemed to bring to them for the first time full realization of the extent of the German defeat.

They made a few observations, merely pointing out material difficulties standing in the way of carrying out some quite secondary clauses. Then Erzberger asked for a suspension of hostilities in the interests of humanity. This request Marshal Foch flatly refused.

The delegates, having obtained permission to send a courier to Spa and communicate with that place by wireless, withdrew. Marshal Foch immediately wrote an account of the proceedings and sent it by an aid to Premier Clemenceau, who received it at noon.

With the Commander in Chief at the time of the interview were Major Gen. Maxime Weygand, his assistant; Vice Admiral Sir Rosslyn Wemyss, First Lord of the British Admiralty, and the American Vice Admiral, William S. Sims. Admiral Sims took no part in the negotiations and soon afterward returned to London.

## CROSSING THE LINES

When the French command received the German headquarters' wireless dispatch announcing the start of the armistice delegation, the delegates were directed to present themselves between 8 and 10 o'clock P. M. Nov. 7 at a certain point on La Capelle road. The crossroad was clearly marked by the beams of several searchlights. At the same time the order was given in the French lines that hostilities should be suspended over a distance of several miles in the region of the meeting place.

The three automobiles bearing the German delegates arrived at 9:15 P. M. at the crossroad, preceded by a group of German pioneers charged with making the shell-damaged road passable. The German delegates were received by officers whom Marshal Foch had sent to guide them. These officers got in the automobiles, and, with the window curtains drawn, proceeded to the Château Francfort in Compiègne Forest, belonging to the Marquis de l'Aigle.

Owing to the lateness of the hour, the delegates were conducted to the apartments assigned them, where they took refreshments. The next morning they again entered the automobiles and were taken to the station at Rethondes, where they found Marshal Foch in his special train.

The abdication of the Kaiser and the revolution in Germany occurred the day following the receipt of the armistice terms, Nov. 9, but no decision was announced respecting the acceptance of the armistice.

The German courier bearing the text of the armistice conditions arrived at German headquarters at 10 o'clock A. M.

Nov. 10. The courier, Captain Helldorf, was long delayed while the German batteries persisted in bombarding the route he had to follow.

The German delegates had suggested on Nov. 9 that the courier's mission might be attempted by airplane. The French high command saw no objection to this and offered to furnish a machine on condition that the German high command pledge itself that the airplane would not be fired at. A rapid message was sent to German headquarters, which was replied to without delay as follows:

"We grant free passage to the French airplane bringing our courier. We are issuing orders that it shall not be attacked by any of our machines. For the purpose of recognition it should carry two white flags very clearly marked."

The orders from the German headquarters staff, however, were inoperative as regarded the land batteries, for on La Capelle road the enemy's fire, despite reiterated requests to desist, went on without intermission.

A French airplane, piloted by an officer of the French Air Service, was soon available, and the pilot was ordered to hold himself ready to start on his journey. About that time a message came from General Headquarters, announcing that orders for the cessation of fire had been given to the batteries directed against La Capelle road, and that Captain Helldorf was at liberty to start by automobile. Almost immediately the German fire ceased, and the courier set out on the road for Spa at 3:20 o'clock in the after oon.

German headquarters was notified of his departure, and informed that he might be expected to arrive in the evening. But the road was long and hard, and many delays occurred.

Nineteen hours after the German courier reached the German headquarters—at 5 o'clock A. M. Paris time, Nov. 11—the armistice was signed and the official announcement was made at Washington at 2:40 A. M., Nov. 11, by the Secretary of State. President Wilson was notified immediately by telephone.

# Announcing the Armistice in America

PRESIDENT WILSON, in spite of his broken sleep, was up early in the morning of Nov. 11, and by his direction arrangements had soon been made for the joint session of the Senate and the House. Each legislative body met separately at noon in accordance with custom, and in a few minutes each had adopted the concurrent resolution essential to holding the joint meeting requested by the President. The time fixed was 1 o'clock P. M., Nov. 11, and at that hour the stage was all set in the hall of the House of Representatives for the historical event that was soon to pass.

The galleries were crowded with men and women. By far the greater proportion of the spectators were wives, daughters, and other female relatives or friends of Senators, Representatives, and high Government officials.

In the President's pew, the front row of the gallery to the left of the presiding officer's rostrum, sat Mrs. Wilson and the President's daughter, Mrs. William G. McAdoo, wife of the Secretary of the Treasury. Occupying chairs on the floor were members of the Cabinet, General March, the army's Chief of Staff, men engaged prominently in Government war activities, and many former Senators and Representatives. One member of the present House, La Guardia of New York, was there in the uniform of an army aviator.

## SUPREME COURT JUSTICES

The very centre of the stage, as it were, was occupied by the nine Justices of the Federal Supreme Court. They sat in chairs placed in the area directly in front of the rostrum. If, in all the enthusiasm that punctuated the President's address, any one may be credited with having led the applause, the palm should go to the distinguished Chief Justice of the United States, Edward Douglass White. On a par with his enthusiasm was that of a former member of the highest judicial tribunal, Charles E. Hughes, the man who had lost the Presidency to Woodrow Wilson, whose triumph he now applauded.

Owing to the fact that many Senators and Representatives had not returned to Washington from their homes, where they had been participating in the political campaigns, hardly half the membership of Congress was present and there were scores of vacant benches on the floor.

The Representatives present seemed hardly a handful when they appeared at the opening of the House session. The Senators, led by Vice President Marshall, arrived in the hall of the House shortly before 1 o'clock, and after being duly announced took seats in the forward rows of benches. As it was a joint session, the Vice President sat beside Speaker Clark on the rostrum. Then the Speaker and the Vice President, each in turn, announced the appointment of a committee of Senators and Representatives to escort the President to the chamber, and everything was ready for the historic moment.

As usual, President Wilson reached the Capitol well before the time set for his appearance at the joint session. Outside the main entrance to the House wing a great crowd had gathered.

Before going to the Capitol the President had written in lead pencil on a half sheet of note paper a proclamation to the people announcing the conclusion of hostilities and had then given orders that the employes of all Government departments should have a holiday. The word had gone forth that he was to address the Congress and hundreds of Government workers made their way to Capitol Hill to get a peep at as much of the great show as it was their privilege to see.

## PRESIDENT CHEERED IN STREETS

As the President, attended by his Secret Service guards, alighted from his motor car at the entrance to the House wing, a cheer went up from the people gathered there and he lifted his top hat and smiled in a way to show his happiness. It was two minutes past 1 o'clock when he appeared in the House Chamber escorted by a committee of Senators and Representatives.

" The President of the United States! " shouted Joseph Sinnott, Sergeant at Arms of the House, as the President stepped through a doorway to the left and rear of the rostrum.

In an instant the whole company was on its feet. There was handclapping, but this dignified, deferential mode of greeting did not satisfy those who were full of the enthusiasm that came from the knowledge that America and her European associates had won the great war. The cheering was mild at first, but it grew in volume, and the presiding officers made no attempt to enforce the rule that spectators in the galleries must not indulge in demonstrations.

During the minute—it seemed longer— that the cheering lasted, the President smiled the same happy smile that he had given those who had greeted him outside of the building. His face showed no effect of his broken rest. He seemed the personification of physical vigor and did not look his sixty-one years. He wore a trim-fitting black tailcoat of the sort known to fashion as a morning garment, and to the man on the street as a cutaway, light gray trousers, with a light cravat. He shook hands with Speaker Clark and Vice President Marshall, and as the applause ended took from his pocket some narrow typewritten sheets and began to read to an audience that held its breath in sheer intensive interest.

At the very outset of his address the President read the conditions that Germany was obliged to accept to obtain an ending of the war that her ambition had brought about. He read the written words without any effort at dramatic effect. At first his voice was low and a bit husky. But it soon cleared, and he could be heard in the furthermost corners of floor and galleries.

The President's announcement that the German authorities had accepted and signed the terms of armistice brought a faint round of handclapping. But a moment later, when he made known that the second condition imposed upon Germany was the immediate evacuation of invaded countries, his auditors could not restrain their delight. He read the

names of the countries to be evacuated— Belgium, France, Alsace-Lorraine, Luxemburg.

It was the mention of Alsace-Lorraine that brought the spectators cheering to their feet. And how they cheered!—not very long—but heartily.

The President's audience listened intently, but with hardly any display of feeling, to the concluding portion of his address, in which he indicated that the Allies must be helpful to the conquered people of Germany.

When he told that the representatives of the victorious Governments in the Supreme War Council at Versailles had unanimously agreed to assure the peoples of the Central Empires " that everything that is possible in the circumstances will be done to supply them with food and relieve the distressing want that is in so many places threatening their very lives," some faint applause came.

The suggestions of a charitable and helpful attitude toward Germany, however, brought no demonstration from those who listened to the President.

It was 1:30 o'clock when the President completed the reading of his address. He had taken twenty-seven minutes to read it. As he turned to leave the House, after bowing to his auditors and again shaking hands with Speaker Clark and Vice President Marshall, another demonstration began that lasted until the President was well out of hearing. Then the Senate went back to its own chamber and the House adjourned, while the President, returning to the White House in his motor car, passed great throngs of joymakers, who cheered him without stint.

On Nov. 11 President Wilson issued the following proclamation prior to his address to Congress:

" My Fellow-Countrymen: The armistice was signed this morning. Everything for which America fought has been accomplished. It will now be our fortunate duty to assist by example, by sober, friendly counsel, and by material aid in the establishment of just democracy throughout the world.

" WOODROW WILSON."

# The President's Address Announcing An Armistice

*President Wilson, after reading in person the full terms of the armistice to the joint session of Congress, delivered the following address:*

THE war thus comes to an end; for, having accepted these terms of armistice, it will be impossible for the German command to renew it.

It is not now possible to assess the consequences of this great consummation. We know only that this tragical war, whose consuming flames swept from one nation to another until all the world was on fire, is at an end and that it was the privilege of our own people to enter it at its most critical juncture in such fashion and in such force as to contribute, in a way of which we are all deeply proud, to the great result. We know, too, that the object of the war is attained; the object upon which all free men had set their hearts; and attained with a sweeping completeness which even now we do not realize. Armed imperialism such as the men conceived who were but yesterday the masters of Germany is at an end, its illicit ambitions engulfed in black disaster. Who will now seek to revive it?

The arbitrary power of the military caste of Germany, which once could secretly and of its own single choice disturb the peace of the world, is discredited and destroyed. And more than that—much more than that—has been accomplished. The great nations which associated themselves to destroy it have now definitely united in the common purpose to set up such a peace as will satisfy the longing of the whole world for disinterested justice, embodied in settlements which are based upon something much better and more lasting than the selfish competitive interests of powerful States. There is no longer conjecture as to the objects the victors have in mind. They have a mind in the matter, not only, but a heart also. Their avowed and concerted purpose is to satisfy and protect the weak as well as to accord their just rights to the strong.

## FEEDING THE HUNGRY

The humane temper and intention of the victorious Governments have already been manifested in a very practical way. Their representatives in the Supreme War Council at Versailles have by unanimous resolution assured the peoples of the Central Empires that everything that is possible in the circumstances will be done to supply them with food and relieve the distressing want that is in so many places threatening their very lives; and steps are to be taken immediately to organize these efforts at relief in the same systematic manner that they were organized in the case of Belgium. By the use of the idle tonnage of the Central Empires it ought presently to be possible to lift the fear of utter misery from their oppressed populations and set their minds and energies free for the great and hazardous tasks of political reconstruction which now face them on every hand. Hunger does not breed reform; it breeds madness and all the ugly distempers that make an ordered life impossible.

For with the fall of the ancient Governments, which rested like an incubus on the peoples of the Central Empires, has come political change not merely, but revolution; and revolution which seems as yet to assume no final and ordered form, but to run from one fluid change to another, until thoughtful men are forced to ask themselves, With what Governments and of what sort are we about to deal in the making of the covenants of peace?

With what authority will they meet us, and with what assurance that their authority will abide and sustain securely the international arrangements into which we are about to enter? There is here matter for no small anxiety and misgiving. When peace is made, upon whose promises and engagements besides our own is it to rest?

## ORDER THE FIRST REQUISITE

Let us be perfectly frank with ourselves and admit that these questions cannot be satisfactorily answered now or at once. But the moral is not that there is little hope of an early answer that will suffice. It is only that we must be patient and helpful and mindful above all of the great hope and confidence that lie at the heart of what is taking place. Excesses accomplish nothing. Unhappy Russia has furnished abundant recent proof of that. Disorder immediately defeats itself. If excesses should occur, if disorder should for a time raise its head, a sober second thought will follow and a day of constructive action, if we help and do not hinder.

The present and all that it holds belong to the nations and the peoples who preserve their self-control and the orderly processes of their Governments; the future to those who prove themselves the true friends of mankind. To conquer with arms is to make only a temporary conquest; to conquer the world by earning its esteem is to make permanent conquest. I am confident that the nations that have learned the discipline of freedom and that have settled with self-possession to its ordered practice are now about to make conquest of the world by the sheer power of example and of friendly helpfulness.

The peoples who have but just come out from under the yoke of arbitrary government and who are now coming at last into their freedom will never find the treasures of liberty they are in search of if they look for them by the light of the torch. They will find that every pathway that is stained with the blood of their own brothers leads to the wilderness, not to the seat of their hope. They are now face to face with their initial test. We must hold the light steady until they find themselves. And in the meantime, if it be possible, we must establish a peace that will justly define their place among the nations, remove all fear of their neighbors and of their former masters, and enable them to live in security and contentment when they have set their own affairs in order. I, for one, do not doubt their purpose or their capacity. There are some happy signs that they know and will choose the way of self-control and peaceful accommodation. If they do, we shall put our aid at ·their disposal in every way that we can. If they do not, we must await with patience and sympathy the awakening and recovery that will assuredly come at last.

# Text of Armistice Terms Signed by Germany

The corrected text of the armistice between Germany and the Allies and United States, as it finally stood when the envoys signed it, is in full as follows:

### I.—MILITARY CLAUSES ON WESTERN FRONT

One—Cessation of operations by land and in the air six hours after the signature of the armistice.

Two—Immediate evacuation of invaded countries: Belgium, France, Alsace-Lorraine, Luxemburg, so ordered as to be completed within fourteen days from the signature of the armistice. German troops which have not left the above-mentioned territories within the period fixed will become prisoners of war. Occupation by the allied and United States forces jointly will keep pace with evacuation in these areas. All movements of evacuation and occupation will be regulated in accordance with a note annexed to the stated terms.

Three—Reparation beginning at once to be completed within fifteen days of all the inhabitants of the countries above enumerated, (including hostages, persons under trial or convicted.)

Four—Surrender in good condition by the German armies of the following war material: Five thousand guns, (2,500 heavy, and 2,500 field,) 25,000 machine guns, 3,000 minenwerfer, 1,700 airplanes, (fighters, bombers—firstly, all of the D 7's and all the night bombing machines.) The above to be delivered in situ to the allied and United States troops in accordance with the detailed conditions laid down in the note (annexure No. 1) drawn up at the moment of the signing of the armistice.

Five—Evacuation by the German armies of the countries on the left bank of the Rhine. The countries on the left bank of the Rhine shall be administered by the local troops of occupation. The occupation of these territories will be carried out by allied and United States garrisons holding the principal crossings of the Rhine, (Mayence, Coblenz, Cologne,) together with the bridgeheads at these points of a thirty-kilometer radius on the right bank and by garrisons similarly holding the strategic points of the regions. A neutral zone shall be reserved on the right bank of the Rhine between the stream and a line drawn parallel to the bridgeheads and to the stream and at a distance of ten kilometers, from the frontier of Holland up to the frontier of Switzerland. The evacuation by the enemy of the Rhinelands (left and right bank) shall be so ordered as to be completed within a further period of sixteen days, in all, thirty-one days after the signing of the armistice. All the movements of evacuation or occupation are regulated by the note (annexure No. 1) drawn up at the moment of the signing of the armistice.

Six—In all territories evacuated by the enemy there shall be no evacuation of inhabitants; no damage or harm shall be done to the persons or property of the inhabitants. No person shall be prosecuted for offenses of participation in war measures prior to the signing of the armistice. No destruction of any kind shall be committed. Military establishments of all kinds shall be delivered intact, as well as military stores of food, munitions, and equipment, not removed during the time fixed for evacuation. Stores of food of all kinds for the civil population, cattle, &c., shall be left in situ. Industrial establishments shall not be impaired in any way and their personnel shall not be removed.

Seven—Roads and means of communication of every kind, railroads, waterways, main roads, bridges, telegraphs, telephones, shall be in no manner impaired. All civil and military personnel at present employed on them shall remain. Five thousand locomotives and 150,000 wagons in good working order, with all necessary spare parts and fittings, shall be delivered to the associated powers within the period fixed in annexure No. 2, and total of which shall not exceed thirty-one days. There shall likewise be delivered 5,000 motor lorries (camion automobiles) in good order, within the period of thirty-six days. The railways of Alsace-Lorraine shall be handed over within the period of thirty-one days, together with pre-war personnel and material. Further, the material necessary for the working of railways in the countries on the left bank of the Rhine shall be left in situ. All stores of coal and material for the upkeep of permanent ways, signals, and repair shops shall be left in situ. These stores shall be maintained by Germany in so far as concerns the working of the railroads in the countries on the left bank of the Rhine. All barges taken from the Allies shall be restored to them. The note, annexure No. 2, regulates the details of these measures.

Eight—The German command shall be re-

sponsible for revealing within the period of forty-eight hours after the signing of the armistice all mines or delayed action fuses on territory evacuated by the German troops and shall assist in their discovery and destruction. It also shall reveal all destructive measures that may have been taken, (such as poisoning or polluting of springs and wells, &c.) All under penalty of reprisals.

Nine—The right of requisition shall be exercised by the allied and United States armies in all occupied territories, subject to regulation of accounts with those whom it may concern. The upkeep of the troops of occupation in the Rhineland (excluding Alsace-Lorraine) shall be charged to the German Government.

Ten—The immediate repatriation without reciprocity, according to detailed conditions which shall be fixed, of all allied and United States prisoners of war, including persons under trial or convicted. The allied powers and the United States shall be able to dispose of them as they wish. This condition annuls the previous conventions on the subject of the exchange of prisoners of war, including the one of July, 1918, in course of ratification. However, the repatriation of German prisoners of war interned in Holland and in Switzerland shall continue as before. The repatriation of German prisoners of war shall be regulated at the conclusion of the preliminaries of peace.

Eleven—Sick and wounded who cannot be removed from evacuated territory will be cared for by German personnel, who will be left on the spot with the medical material required.

## II.—DISPOSITION RELATIVE TO THE EASTERN FRONTIERS OF GERMANY

Twelve—All German troops at present in the territories which before belonged to Austria-Hungary, Rumania, Turkey, shall withdraw immediately within the frontiers of Germany as they existed on August First, Nineteen Fourteen. All German troops at present in the territories which before the war belonged to Russia shall likewise withdraw within the frontiers of Germany, defined as above, as soon as the Allies, taking into account the internal situation of these territories, shall decide that the time for this has come.

Thirteen—Evacuation by German troops to begin at once, and all German instructors, prisoners, and civilians as well as military agents now on the territory of Russia (as defined before 1914) to be recalled.

Fourteen—German troops to cease at once all requisitions and seizures and any other undertaking with a view to obtaining supplies intended for Germany in Rumania and Russia, (as defined on Aug. 1, 1914.)

Fifteen—Renunciation of the treaties of Bucharest and Brest-Litovsk and of the supplementary treaties.

Sixteen—The Allies shall have free access to the territories evacuated by the Germans on

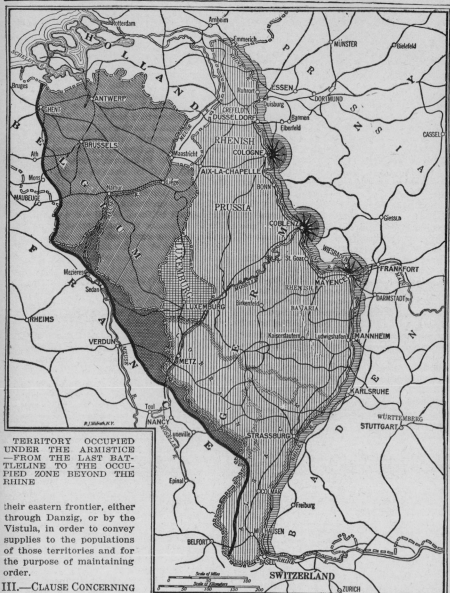

TERRITORY OCCUPIED
UNDER THE ARMISTICE
—FROM THE LAST BAT-
TLELINE TO THE OCCU-
PIED ZONE BEYOND THE
RHINE

their eastern frontier, either
through Danzig, or by the
Vistula, in order to convey
supplies to the populations
of those territories and for
the purpose of maintaining
order.

### III.—Clause Concerning East Africa

Seventeen—Evacuation by all German forces
operating in East Africa within a period
to be fixed by the Allies.

### IV.—General Clauses

Eighteen—Repatriation, without reciprocity,
within a maximum period of one month in
accordance with detailed conditions hereafter to be fixed of all interned civilians,
including hostages, (persons?) under trial or
convicted, belonging to the allied or associated powers other than those enumerated
in Article Three.

Nineteen—The following financial conditions
are required: Reparation for damage done.
While such armistice lasts no public securities shall be removed by the enemy which
can serve as a pledge to the Allies for the
recovery or reparation for war losses. Immediate restitution of the cash deposit in
the national bank of Belgium, and in general immediate return of all documents,
specie, stocks, shares, paper money, together with plant for the issue thereof, touching public or private interests in the invaded
countries. Restitution of the Russian and
Rumanian gold yielded to Germany or taken
by that power. This gold to be delivered

in trust to the Allies until the signature of peace.

## V.—NAVAL CONDITIONS

Twenty—Immediate cessation of all hostilities at sea and definite information to be given as to the location and movements of all German ships. Notification to be given to neutrals that freedom of navigation in all territorial waters is given to the naval and mercantile marines of the allied and associated powers, all questions of neutrality being waived.

Twenty-one—All naval and mercantile marine prisoners of the allied and associated powers in German hands to be returned without reciprocity.

Twenty-two—Surrender to the Allies and United States of all submarines (including submarine cruisers and all mine-laying submarines) now existing, with their complete armament and equipment, in ports which shall be specified by the Allies and United States. Those which cannot take the sea shall be disarmed of the personnel and material and shall remain under the supervision of the Allies and the United States. The submarines which are ready for the sea shall be prepared to leave the German ports as soon as orders shall be received by wireless for their voyage to the port designated for their delivery, and the remainder at the earliest possible moment. The conditions of this article shall be carried into effect within the period of fourteen days after the signing of the armistice.

Twenty-three — German surface warships which shall be designated by the Allies and the United States shall be immediately disarmed and thereafter interned in neutral ports or in default of them in allied ports to be designated by the Allies and the United States. They will there remain under the supervision of the Allies and of the United States, only caretakers being left on board. The following warships are designated by the Allies: Six battle cruisers, ten battleships, eight light cruisers, (including two mine layers,) fifty destroyers of the most modern types. All other surface warships (including river craft) are to be concentrated in German naval bases to be designated by the Allies and the United States and are to be completely disarmed and classed under the supervision of the Allies and the United States. The military armament of all ships of the auxiliary fleet shall be put on shore. All vessels designated to be interned shall be ready to leave the German ports seven days after the signing of the armistice. Directions for the voyage will be given by wireless.

Twenty-four—The Allies and the United States of America shall have the right to sweep up all mine fields and obstructions laid by Germany outside German territorial waters, and the positions of these are to be indicated.

Twenty-five—Freedom of access to and from the Baltic to be given to the naval and mercantile marines of the allied and associated powers. To secure this the Allies and the United States of America shall be empowered to occupy all German forts, fortifications, batteries, and defense works of all kinds in all the entrances from the Cattegat into the Baltic, and to sweep up all mines and obstructions within and without German territorial waters, without any question of neutrality being raised, and the positions of all such mines and obstructions are to be indicated.

Twenty-six—The existing blockade conditions set up by the allied and associated powers are to remain unchanged, and all German merchant ships found at sea are to remain liable to capture. The Allies and the United States should give consideration to the provisioning of Germany during the armistice to the extent recognized as necessary.

Twenty-seven—All naval aircraft are to be concentrated and immobilized in German bases to be specified by the Allies and the United States of America.

Twenty-eight—In evacuating the Belgian coast and ports Germany shall abandon in situ and in fact all port and river navigation material, all merchant ships, tugs, lighters, all naval aeronautic apparatus, material and supplies, and all arms, apparatus, and supplies of every kind.

Twenty-nine—All Black Sea ports are to be evacuated by Germany; all Russian war vessels of all descriptions seized by Germany in the Black Sea are to be handed over to the Allies and the United States of America; all neutral merchant vessels seized are to be released; all warlike and other materials of all kinds seized in those ports are to be returned and German materials as specified in Clause Twenty-eight are to be abandoned.

Thirty—All merchant vessels in German hands belonging to the allied and associated powers are to be restored in ports to be specified by the Allies and the United States of America without reciprocity.

Thirty-one—No destruction of ships or of materials to be permitted before evacuation, surrender, or restoration.

Thirty-two—The German Government will notify the neutral Governments of the world, and particularly the Governments of Norway, Sweden, Denmark, and Holland, that all restrictions placed on the trading of their vessels with the allied and associated countries, whether by the German Government or by private German interests, and whether in return for specific concessions, such as the export of shipbuilding materials, or not, are immediately canceled.

Thirty-three — No transfers of German merchant shipping of any description to any neutral flag are to take place after signature of the armistice.

## VI.—DURATION OF ARMISTICE

Thirty-four—The duration of the armistice

is to be thirty days, with option to extend. During this period if its clauses are not carried into execution the armistice may be denounced by one of the contracting parties, which must give warning forty-eight hours in advance. It is understood that the execution of Articles 3 and 18 shall not warrant the denunciation of the armistice on the ground of insufficient execution within a period fixed, except in the case of bad faith in carrying them into execution. In order to assure the eexcution of this convention under the best conditions, the principle of a permanent international armistice commission is admitted. This commission will act under the authority of the allied military and naval Commanders in Chief.

### VII.—THE LIMIT FOR REPLY

Thirty-five—This armistice to be accepted or refused by Germany within seventy-two hours of notification.

---

*This armistice has been signed the Eleventh of November, Nineteen Eighteen, at 5 o'clock [A. M.] French time.*

> F. FOCH.
> R. E. WEMYSS.
> ERZBERGER.
> A. OBERNDORFF.
> WINTERFELDT.
> VON SALOW.

# Notes That Led Up to the Armistice

## Conclusion of Diplomatic Correspondence Between the German Government and President Wilson

THE first two notes from Germany and the first two replies of President Wilson in the interchange begun by Prince Maximilian on Oct. 6, 1918, relative to an armistice and peace, were printed in the preceding issue of CURRENT HISTORY MAGAZINE. This diplomatic correspondence with Berlin and Vienna was continued by President Wilson up to a point where he handed over the further formulation of terms of surrender to the Interallied War Council at Versailles. The concluding notes in the series, beginning with Germany's third, written in reply to the President's note of Oct. 14, are given below.

### GERMANY'S THIRD NOTE

This German reply was dated Oct. 20; it became public unofficially by wireless on Oct. 21, and the official German text was handed to President Wilson by the Swiss Chargé d'Affaires at Washington on the 22d, along with an English translation sent by the German Government. This official translation read as follows:

In accepting the proposal for an evacuation of the occupied territories the German Government has started from the assumption that the procedure of this evacuation and of the conditions of an armistice should be left to the judgment of the military advisers and that the actual standard of power on both sides in the field has to form the basis for ar-

rangements safeguarding and guaranteeing this standard. The German Government suggests to the President to bring about an opportunity for fixing the details. It trusts that the President of the United States will approve of no demand which would be irreconcilable with the honor of the German people and with opening a way to a peace of justice.

The German Government protests against the reproach of illegal and inhumane actions made against the German land and sea forces and thereby against the German people. For the covering of a retreat, destructions will always be necessary, and they are in so far permitted by international law. The German troops are under the strictest instruction to spare private property and to exercise care for the population to the best of their ability. Where transgressions occur in spite of these instructions the guilty are being punished.

The German Government further denies that the German Navy in sinking ships has ever purposely destroyed lifeboats with their passengers. The German Government proposes with regard to all those charges that the facts be cleared up by neutral commissions. In order to avoid anything that might hamper the work of peace, the German Government has caused orders to be dispatched to all submarine commanders, precluding the torpedoing of passenger ships, without, however, for technical reasons, being able to guarantee that these orders will reach every single submarine at sea before its return.

As a fundamental condition for peace the President prescribes the destruction of every arbitrary power that can separately, secretly, and of its own single choice disturb the peace of the world. To this the German Government replies: Hitherto the representation of the people in the German Empire has not been endowed with an influence on the formation of the Government. The Constitution did not provide for a concurrence of representation of the people in decisions of peace and war. These conditions have just now undergone a fundamental change. A new Government has been formed in complete accordance with the wishes of the representation of the people, based on equal, universal, secret, direct franchise. The leaders of the great parties of the Reichstag are members of this Government. In the future no Government can take or continue in office without possessing the confidence of a majority of the Reichstag. The responsibility of the Chancellor of the empire to the representation of the people is being legally developed and safeguarded. The first act of the new Government has been to lay before the Reichstag a bill to alter the Constitution of the empire so that the consent of the representation of the people is required for decisions on war and peace. The permanence of the new system is, however, guaranteed not only by constitutional safeguards, but also by the unshakable determination of the German people, whose vast majority stands behind these reforms and demands their energetic continuance.

The question of the President—with whom he and the Governments associated against Germany are dealing—is therefore answered in a clear, unequivocal manner by the statement that the offer of peace and an armistice has come from a Government which, free from any arbitrary and irresponsible influence, is supported by the approval of an overwhelming majority of the German people.

(Signed) SOLF,
*State Secretary of Foreign Affairs.*
*Berlin, Oct. 20, 1918.*

Germany's reply was universally regarded in Entente countries as unsatisfactory, especially in its lack of guarantees of genuine reforms in the Kaiser's Government. In some quarters there was a sentiment in the United States against the continuance of these long-distance parleys, and Senator Poindexter of Washington offered a resolution on Oct. 21 to make it unlawful for " any official of this Government to answer in any way " any note from Germany regarding peace or an armistice until Germany had surrendered unconditionally. This sentiment did not crystallize into definite action, but President Wilson got into close communication with the Supreme War Council at Paris before replying to the note.

## MAXIMILIAN TO THE REICHSTAG

Meanwhile the new German Chancellor appeared before the Reichstag on Oct. 22 and delivered a speech in which he said:

The President's first answer to the peace move of the German Government has in all countries brought the question of a peace of justice or a peace of violence to the highest point. President Wilson's last note did not make clear to the German people how this public agitation will end. His next answer will, perhaps, bring definite certainty. Until then we must in all our thoughts and in our actions prepare for both eventualities—first, that the enemy Governments are anxious for war, in which case there is no choice for us but to put ourselves in a posture of defense with all the strength of our people driven to the last extremity.

Should this necessity arise, I have no doubt that the German Government, in the name of the German people, will issue a call for national defense in the same way that it spoke for the German people when it took action for peace. He who honestly took a stand on the basis of peace will also undertake the duty of not submitting to a peace of violence without a fight. The Government which would act otherwise would be left to the mercy of the fighting and working people. It would be swept away by public opinion.

There is also another possibility. The German people must not be blindly brought to the conference table. The German people today has the right to ask, if peace is realized on the basis of President Wilson's conditions, what they mean for our future. Our answers to the President's question must be framed on the German people's understanding of that question. What it now wants is clearness.

The decision will be of stupendous import. It will not be our strength that will decide, but it will be what is thought to be right in free discussion with our opponents that will give the decision. This is a great effort for a proud people accustomed to victory. The legal questions involved will not stop at our national boundaries, which we will never of our own accord open for violence.

The principles upon which we have agreed as a rule of conduct also involve internal questions. From many quarters it has been represented to me that an acceptance of President Wilson's conditions would mean submission—anti-German submission—to an anti-German court of justice which would decide legal questions entirely from the viewpoint of its own interests. If that is the case, why then is it the extreme apostles of force in the Entente fear the council chamber as the guilty fear the court of justice?

The essence of President Wilson's program for a League of Nations cannot be achieved when all peoples have not the right of national self-determination. This realization of community law means the abandonment of part of the unqualified independence which hitherto has been the indication of sovereignty, both by us and others. Should we at home maintain as fundamental the national egoism which until a short time ago was the dominating force of the people's life, there would be no restitution and no renovation for us. There would be a feeling of bitterness which would cripple us for generations.

But if we comprehend that the significance of this frightful war is, above all, victory for the idea of justice, and if we do not resist this idea, but submit with all good faith, then we shall find in it a cure for our present wounds and a reservoir of future strength.

Field Marshal von Hindenburg issued a general order stating that he approved the peace move, and was supporting the Government in it. The Crown Prince issued a briefer order to his army group referring to the exchange of diplomatic notes, and warning his officers not to modify their battle lines without express orders. Another order emanating from the German high command said:

Diplomatic negotiations with a view to terminating the war have begun. Their conclusion will be all the more favorable in proportion as we succeed in keeping the army well in hand, in holding the ground conquered, and in doing harm to the enemy. These principles should guide the direction of the combat in the days that are to follow.

All these documents were captured from the 5th Bavarian Division.

## PRESIDENT'S THIRD ANSWER

Secretary Lansing sent President Wilson's reply to Germany's third note the day after the official copy had been received. It was inscribed " From the Secretary of State to the Chargé d'Affaires of Switzerland, ad interim in charge of German interests in the United States." Following is the text:

DEPARTMENT OF STATE,
WASHINGTON, D. C., Oct. 23, 1918.

*Sir: I have the honor to acknowledge the receipt of your note of the 22d transmitting a communication under date of the 20th from the German Government and to advise you that the President has instructed me to reply thereto as follows:*

Having received the solemn and explicit assurance of the German Government that it unreservedly accepts the terms of peace laid down in his address to the Congress of the United States on the 8th of January, 1918, and the principles of settlement enunciated in his subsequent addresses, particularly the address of the 27th of September, and that it desires to discuss the details of their application, and that this wish and purpose emanate, not from those who have hitherto dictated German policy and conducted the present war on Germany's behalf, but from Ministers who speak for the majority of the Reichstag and for an overwhelming majority of the German people; and having received also the explicit promise of the present German Government that the humane rules of civilized warfare will be observed both on land and sea by the German armed forces, the President of the United States feels that he cannot decline to take up with the Governments with which the Government of the United States is associated the question of an armistice.

He deems it his duty to say again, however, that the only armistice he would feel justified in submitting for consideration would be one which should leave the United States and the powers associated with her in a position to enforce any arrangements that may be entered into and to make a renewal of hostilities on the part of Germany impossible.

The President has, therefore, transmitted his correspondence with the present German authorities to the Governments with which the Government of the United States is associated as a belligerent, with the suggestion that, if those Governments are disposed to effect peace upon the terms and principles indicated, their military advisers and the military advisers of the United States be asked to submit to the Governments associated against Germany the necessary terms of such an armistice as will fully protect the interests of the peoples involved and insure to the associated Governments the unrestricted power to safeguard and enforce the details of the peace to which the German Government has agreed, provided they deem such an armistice possible from the military point of view. Should such terms of armistice be suggested, their acceptance by Germany will afford the best concrete evidence of her unequivocal acceptance of the terms and principles of peace from which the whole action proceeds.

The President would deem himself lacking in candor did he not point out in the frankest possible terms the reason why extraordinary safeguards must be demanded. Significant and important as the constitutional changes seem to be which are spoken of by the German Foreign Secretary in his note of the 20th of October, it does not appear that the principle of a Government responsible to the German people has yet been fully worked out or that any guarantees either exist or are in contemplation that the alterations of principle and of practice now partially agreed upon will be permanent. Moreover, it does not appear that the heart of the present difficulty has been reached. It may be that future wars have been brought under the control of the German people, but the present war has not been; and it is with the present war that we are dealing. It is evident that the German people have no means of commanding the acquiescence of the military authorities of the empire in the popular will; that the power of the King of Prussia to control the policy of the empire is unimpaired; that the determining initiative still remains with those who have hitherto been the masters of Germany. Feeling that the whole peace of the world depends now on plain speaking and straightforward action, the President deems it his duty to say, without any attempt to soften what may seem harsh words, that the nations of the world do not and can not trust the word of those who have hitherto been the masters of German policy, and to point out once more that in concluding peace and attempting to undo the infinite injuries and injustices of this war the Government of the United States cannot deal with any but veritable representatives of the German people who have been assured of a genuine constitutional standing as the real rulers of Germany.

If it must deal with the military masters and the monarchical autocrats of Germany now, or if it is likely to have to deal with them later in regard to the international obligations of the German Empire, it must demand, not peace negotiations, but surrender. Nothing can be gained by leaving this essential thing unsaid.

*Accept, Sir, the renewed assurances of my high consideration.*

(Signed) ROBERT LANSING.

Mr. Frederick Oederlin, Chargé d'Affaires of Switzerland, ad interim in charge of German interests in the United States.

The President's action in calling for surrender and in turning over the matter to the military commanders in France met with unmixed approval in Paris and London. In Washington a like sentiment prevailed, though some Congressmen and Senators held that there should have been no discussion whatever with the enemy. Ex-President Taft declared that the note was so near to being a demand for unconditional surrender that " even a German can see it, and, we hope, will stop sending notes." Ex-President Roosevelt the next day sent a telegram to Republican leaders in various parts of the country assailing Mr. Wilson's " fourteen points " as a " thoroughly mischievous " basis for peace negotiations. " Let us dictate peace by the hammering guns," he wrote, " and not chat about peace to the accompaniment of the clicking of typewriters."

## FOURTH GERMAN NOTE

The German War Cabinet discussed President Wilson's note in a long session on Oct. 24, and on Friday, Oct. 25, there was a meeting of the Crown Council, in which the Crown Prince as well as the Kaiser took part, with all the Secretaries of State, including the Chancellor and the War Cabinet Ministers. The resignation of General Ludendorff followed the next day, and on Oct. 27 the results of the Crown Council meeting were embodied in a brief reply to President Wilson, which reached him on the 28th through the same channels as its predecessors. The official German text was translated by the Swiss Embassy as follows:

The German Government has taken cognizance of the reply of the President of the United States. The President knows the far-reaching changes which have taken place and are being carried out in the German constitutional structure. The peace negotiations are being conducted by a Government of the people, in whose hands rests, both actually and constitutionally, the authority to make decisions. The military powers are also subject to this authority. The German Government now awaits the proposals for an armistice, which is the first step toward a peace of justice, as described by the President in his pronouncements.

(Signed)          SOLF,
State Secretary of Foreign Affairs, Berlin, Oct. 27, 1918.

Diplomatic and press comment in the Entente countries was almost unanimous in regarding this note as an acceptance of the idea of surrender. The President had laid down the principle that the armistice must be on terms which would preclude Germany from renewing hostilities, and to that principle the German reply gave tacit consent. Nothing remained but for the Entente War Office and Admiralties to formulate the program of military and naval measures with which the Central Powers must comply before an armistice could be granted.

Though neither President Wilson nor Secretary Lansing had answered the latest communications from Berlin, the German Government sent a fifth note, which reached Washington on Oct. 30, through the Swiss Legation. It was officially described as a memorandum, and its contents were not given to the public at the time.

From this point onward the German Government's communications were carried on directly with Marshal Foch until the signing of the armistice.

Secretary Lansing issued this statement at 9 o'clock in the evening of Nov. 4:

According to an official report received this evening, the terms of the armistice to be offered to Germany have just been agreed to unanimously and signed by the representatives of the Allies and the United States in Paris. The report further states that diplomatic unity has been completely achieved under conditions of utmost harmony.

## PRESIDENT'S FINAL NOTE

The diplomatic correspondence begun by Prince Maximilian on Oct. 5 was closed on Nov. 5 by the following note, which Secretary Lansing handed to the Swiss Minister for transmission to Germany:

DEPARTMENT OF STATE,
Nov. 5, 1918.
*From the Secretary of State to the Minister of Switzerland, in charge of German interests in the United States.*

*Sir:* I have the honor to request you to transmit the following communication to the German Government:

In my note of Oct. 23, 1918, I advised you that the President had transmitted his correspondence with the German authorities to the Governments with which the Government of the United States is associated as a belligerent with the suggestion that, if those Governments were disposed to accept peace upon the terms and principles indi-

cated, their military advisers and the military advisers of the United States be asked to submit to the Governments associated against Germany the necessary terms of such an armistice as would fully protect the interests of the peoples involved and insure to the associated Government the unrestricted power to safeguard and enforce the details of the peace to which the German Government has agreed, provided they deem such an armistice possible from the military point of view.

The President is now in receipt of a memorandum of observations by the allied Governments on this correspondence, which is as follows:

"22—The allied Governments have given careful consideration to the correspondence which has passed between the President of the United States and the German Government. Subject to the qualifications which follow, they declare their willingness to make peace with the Government of Germany on the terms of peace laid down in the President's address to Congress of January, 1918, and the principles of settlement enunciated in his subsequent addresses.

"They must point out, however, that Clause 2, relating to what is usually described as the freedom of the seas, is open to various interpretations, some of which they could not accept. They must, therefore, reserve to themselves complete freedom on this subject when they enter the peace conference.

"Further, in the conditions of peace laid down in his address to Congress of Jan. 8, 1918, the President declared that invaded territories must be restored as well as evacuated and freed. The allied Governments feel that no doubt ought to be allowed to exist as to what this provision implies. By it they understand that compensation will be made by Germany for all damage done to the civilian population of the Allies and their property by the aggression of Germany by land, by sea, and from the air."*

I am instructed by the President to say that he is in agreement with the interpretation set forth in the last paragraph of the memorandum above quoted. I am further instructed by the President to request you to notify the German Government that Marshal Foch has been authorized by the Government of the United States and the allied Governments to receive properly accredited representatives of the German Government and communicate to them terms of an armistice.

*The number "22" attached to this memorandum is the index number of the statement, each of those adopted by the allied conference being numbered.

*Accept, Sir, the renewed assurances of my highest consideration.*

(Signed) ROBERT LANSING.

MR. HANS SULZER,

Minister of Switzerland,

In charge of German interests in the United States.

The next day the German Government sent peace plenipotentiaries to receive the terms of armistice from Marshal Foch, and on Nov. 11 the terms were signed. The terms imposed and the story of Germany's surrender appear elsewhere in these pages.

# The March to the Rhine

## As the Germans Withdrew, the Allied Armies Advanced Toward Germany Amid Popular Rejoicings

THE withdrawal of the German armies from the occupied portions of France and Belgium, in accordance with the terms of the armistice, began on Tuesday, Nov. 12, the allied armies and the Americans moving forward into the evacuated regions. The departure of the invaders, with their surrender of munitions and the liberation of prisoners in the occupied territory, was accomplished without a hitch and in apparent good faith.

A period of fifteen days after the signing of the armistice had been granted the Germans to evacuate Belgium, Luxemburg, and Alsace-Lorraine. On Nov. 21, after ten of the fifteen days allotted the allied armies had passed beyond Brussels, had penetrated into Luxemburg, and had reached Saarbrücken and the line of the Rhine to the Swiss border. In these ten days the Belgians had advanced fifty miles, the Americans and British thirty, and the French forty, and the entire front was being advanced from eight to ten miles a day. Antwerp was formally occupied Nov. 17, Mülhouse Nov. 17, Antwerp Nov. 18, Brussels, by the King of the Belgians on Nov. 22, and Strassbourg on Nov. 23. Everywhere the advancing troops were welcomed by the inhabitants. The demonstrations by the people in Alsace and Lorraine were marked by undisguised joy; even in Luxemburg, which was believed to have strong German leanings, the American troops were cordially received. The occupation of Antwerp, Brussels, and Metz produced scenes of unexampled enthusiasm, which were participated in wholeheartedly by all the population.

### ADVANCE OF AMERICANS

The actual advance of the American Army began at 5:30 o'clock Sunday morning, Nov. 17. Units forming the American Army of occupation were chosen with regard to their military accomplishments since they came to France. The advance was made in columns and not in the order of battle so long followed. But it was not forgotten that, technically, at least, there was still a state of war. Nothing was left to chance, and every precaution was taken to guard against surprises.

Care was taken to have the force well echeloned. The advance guard, well in advance of the main force, was followed by engineers, who were instructed not only to repair roads, reconstruct bridges, and clear the way generally, but to inspect keenly every object and position that might be a trap. The Germans sent word that the way was open and the mines removed, except in cases which they designated. Water also was inspected carefully and none permitted to be used until pronounced pure.

The arrangements in force were such that, although advancing much as it might along the country roads of the United States, the entire formation could be altered almost in minutes to battle formation. Divisions moving on the front had others in support, and the flanks were carefully covered. In addition, a long line of observation balloons was maintained behind the lines, moving slowly forward, observing the movements of the retreating Germans. The aviators, however, had little to do. They moved up somewhat later, ready for immediate action.

The advancing Americans were flanked by the armies of France, and on Sunday evening the advanced elements of the Americans crossed the Belgian border. The French Fifth Army, on the left, and the French Tenth Army, on the right, advanced abreast the Americans, while far along the line to the left and right the allied troops continued to march toward the line agreed on in the armistice. It was arranged that the armies should march two days and rest two.

## BRIEY BASIN OCCUPIED

The first important town reached by the advancing Americans was Montmédy. The entrance into this city, in the Briey coal basin, was witnessed by Edwin L. James, correspondent of THE NEW YORK TIMES and CURRENT HISTORY MAGAZINE, who wrote on Nov. 17:

" When the doughboys reached this once pretty little city French flags were flying from every window, and 800 or 900 townsfolk, dressed in their sorry best, with tears streaming down their faces, welcomed their deliverers. Those French flags had been hidden in little nooks and corners unknown to the Germans for four years, hidden and guarded, against this glorious day, which the brave French folk never doubted was coming to them. The Stars and Stripes floated from the City Hall. There was no set ceremony—there had been no time for that, for the enemy had left but twelve hours before we entered.

" The celebration was the better because spontaneous. Every soul in the town just stood by and cheered for the Americans. When it was learned they would stop there for the night every home was thrown open to them, and apologies were made for the plight the Germans had left the houses in. Two hours after the Americans got there—it was the 2d Division—the 5th Marines had their good band out in the square playing ' Hail! Hail! The Gang's All Here! '

" All the shops in town were open,

their windows filled, for the most part, with empty boxes, for the Germans had left little, but it showed the spunky nature of the French people. When the Germans left Montmédy they looted and pillaged everything lootable and pillageable. They took all food, all cattle, even supplies sent to the civilians by the American relief. They tore the furnishings of houses to pieces in those last hours.

" All day thousands after thousands of released prisoners passed our advancing soldiers, coming into our lines. There were Americans, British, French, Italians, men of all the armies which had been fighting against the Germans. Some said they had been released and told to move in this direction. Others said the Germans just went away and left them unguarded.

## MARCH TOWARD GERMANY

" It was in the cold, gray dawn this morning that the army started on the march to Germany. Moving northeast from the line where the First and Second Armies stopped fighting at 11 o'clock on Nov. 11, the victorious troops got under way for one of the most notable marches ever made under the Stars and Stripes. Our army went forward as to battle. It went forward prepared for whatever might come. No brass bands were playing at the head of the troops, no flags waving. The Americans went up the roads as if the enemy might be around the next turn, for, although the armistice has stopped fighting and no one really expects it to start again, we are still at war with Germany, and if the army of occupation has to start war again it can do it.

" No conquering General rode at the head of our troops. Patrols of eight men under Sergeants went first. Then came marching squads of infantry, and back of them light artillery, followed by supply trains. In the vanguard went all the equipment of an army going to war. The whole movement was made on a war footing. We moved forward from a line running roughly from Mouzon, Stenay, Damvillers, Fresnes, and Thiaucourt, on a front of fifty-six miles.

" Thrills came to the Americans, all

veterans of this war, as they marched over the land which the Germans had fought so hard to hold, over the heights from which 77s and machine guns had pumped murderous fire into their ranks. The men felt exultation that their easy march was the reward of victories of the soul-trying days of the last month and the month before."

## AMERICAN THIRD ARMY

The American army of occupation was designated as the Third Army, under command of Major Gen. John T. Dickman. The divisions leading were the 2d and 32d of the corps commanded by General Hines, and some divisions of the 3d and 4th Corps, General Muir commanding.

Supporting the 3d Corps went the 42d Division, commanded by General MacArthur, and in support of the 1st and 3d Divisions the 4th Corps, commanded by General Hirschey. The divisions on the line were carefully selected. The 2d was commanded by Major Gen. John A. Lejeune, commander of the marines, who won honors beginning at Belleau Wood and added to them at Château-Thierry, St. Mihiel, and Champagne. On the right was the 32d Division, renowned for its work north of the Marne, later at Soissons, and also in the recent operations. It was made up of men from Michigan and Wisconsin and commanded by General Haan.

The 1st Division was one of regulars, commanded by General Frank Parker. The 3d Division, also made up of regulars, was commanded by General Preston Brown. Both these regular divisions were made up of picked men.

Along the road from Verdun to Spincourt, a distance of about twenty-five miles, released prisoners of various nationalities traveled toward Verdun in great streams, passing the Americans going in the opposite direction. Many of the former prisoners were attired in cast-off German uniforms and had their effects in wheelbarrows, carts, hand trucks, and baby carriages. For the most part the prisoners were well clothed, but hungry.

The American troops entered Briey,

the heart of the Lorraine iron fields, at 11 o'clock, Nov. 18. There were arches across the main street and the town was bedecked with flags. Fifteen hundred civilians greeted the troops. After a welcome by the Briey officials, the 38th Infantry Band of the 3d Division gave a concert. Then the Americans lunched from rolling kitchens, a large number of released Russians also being fed. Outwardly Briey showed few indications of the war, the buildings being intact, but there were German signs everywhere pointing in the direction of ammunition dumps and the various headquarters. On a decorated arch, under which the Americans passed, was a home-made American flag four feet in length flanked by the French colors. The flag, which had been made by three French girls, had eleven stars and seven red and white stripes.

Before the war the population of Briey numbered about 2,500. Civilians employed in the mines by the Germans received pay of four to six francs a day. The Germans abandoned a large number of trucks and portable dynamos in Briey, owing to their haste to withdraw their troops.

Smoke streaming from the chimneys of many mines greeted the advancing Americans, for a number of mines were in actual operation, and there were fires under the boilers in other mines so as to keep the pumps going. Several mines had been flooded by seepage, having been idle for two or three years. The Germans had removed the machinery for other purposes. Most of the mines had been operated until Nov. 10, when the Germans began to release the Russians and others who had been employed in this work.

## RECEPTION AT VIRTON

Mr. James, cabling on Nov. 18, described as follows the reception at Virton, a Belgian border town, as typical of the attitude of the people:

" This pretty little Belgian city of Virton belongs to the Americans tonight, it and everything in it, the willing gift of 4,000 inhabitants, to whom the doughboy from America today brought deliverance after fifty months under the yoke of the boches, who left it so little ahead of the Americans' entry that some of them were overtaken.

"When I reached here at 11 o'clock this morning the 9th Regiment of the 2d Division had arrived. Standing in the town in marching formation, the troops were the centre of cheering and weeping Belgians, dressed in their best clothes, who at once notified the American Major that their homes were open to him. They told us that the boche had just left. Later I learned that a Lieutenant, leading the advance patrol, had reached Virton before the last German infantry had left, and that a German Major, about to leave, had got out of his automobile and shaken hands with the American Lieutenant and said: 'Well, I must be going.' The Major got into his car and sped away.

"A few moments after my arrival at Virton I saw a German Major and three Lieutenants walking nonchalantly up the street. The Americans who saw them gasped and grasped their rifles, until their commander told them that German surgeons had been left behind by agreement with the American commander.

"It is fair to state that Virton is in excellent condition. It is untouched by the ravages of war. No shell holes, no bomb craters, no burned houses were seen. The little city looked beautiful in the clear sunshine. It has as many residents as before the war. But they tell bad tales of the boche. They say that he kept the city in good shape because he had headquarters there and didn't expect to leave so soon.

"I could not help comparing Virton with pillaged Montmédy, which I saw yesterday, where everything worth looting had been stolen. In Virton the shops were well stocked with German and Dutch goods, and I actually went into a hotel, ordered lunch, and had an excellent meal. They had bread left by the Germans in exchange for white flour they had taken. They had meat killed this morning, sugar sent by the American Relief Committee, and tea which the landlady assured me had been hidden for four years.

"The Germans took practically all food from Virton, but left everything else. In Montmédy they had destroyed everything of value, even burning a warehouse full of cabbages which they couldn't take away. There was another interesting difference in the German policy in the two places. In Montmédy all payments were made by the Germans in French money, in Virton in German money. My conclusion is that the Germans believed that for years to come Virton would be a German city. In the last hours they did not loot it out of policy."

## THROUGH LUXEMBURG

The advance of the Americans through Luxemburg on Nov. 20, 21, and 22 was in the nature of a parade. Everywhere the troops were warmly welcomed. Mr. James cabled on Nov. 20:

"The American troops shoved their lines across the German frontier today. The frontier was crossed opposite Briey and Audun-le-Roman, and at points between these two places. On the left American marines occupied the town of Arlon, Belgium, where the day was proclaimed a holiday. Thousands of civilians greeted the Americans, who entered Arlon early in the morning. To the south the Americans went into Fontoy and Vitry in Lorraine and several villages to the northeast of Vitry.

"Swinging northward from Metz the American 1st Division crossed into Luxemburg just before noon, [Nov. 20,] entering Esch, a mining town of 20,000 inhabitants. The civilians expected the Americans Thursday, but when the vanguard appeared the news spread quickly. The whistles at the mines were blown, bells were rung, children were excused from schools, stores were closed, and the afternoon was proclaimed a holiday.

"In the store windows and public buildings along the principal streets there were pictures of President Wilson, drawn by an artist of Esch, who had worked night and day to complete by hand as many drawings as possible. Pictures of President Poincaré, Marshal Foch, and King Albert also were prominently displayed.

## CROSSING THE BOUNDARY

" To the 1st Division fell the honor of crossing the Lorraine line, the advance guard entering Aumetz soon after 9 o'clock. For three days the civilians of Aumetz had been looking for the Americans, expecting them every minute. There had been no school all week, and the children had been drilled in singing and flag-waving to receive the advancing army.

" Two hundred pupils, attired in fancy dress, that of the girls being of the colors of France, and the boys carrying the red and yellow colors of Lorraine, a home-made American flag and tricolored bunting of France, met the troops at the archway over the road entering the town from Audun-le-Roman. By the time the marching troops reached Esch the civilians were ready to receive them. The children tossed flowers at the soldiers as they passed through the streets.

" The Esch Band, which had been called to assemble in a hurry, led the march of the civilians to the City Hall, where the Mayor and officials received the military officers. After midday even the mines closed in order to give the workers, many of whom are women and girls, an opportunity for assembling in the square, where formal ceremonies were held. The advance guard later advanced beyond Esch, but division headquarters was established there for the night.

" At Fontoy the streets were decorated and civilians were out in force to receive the Americans. Fontoy is a railroad centre. Here the Americans found twenty-one locomotives in good condition and a yard full of passenger cars, flatcars, and freight cars. The roundhouse also is in such condition that it can be used by the Americans.

" It may be said in passing that the Luxemburg towns were left in good shape. There were no signs of looting or wrecking. The shops were well stocked, and food seemed plentiful, though dear. Luxemburg appears to stand not to be a loser by the American occupation. It doesn't seem to have suffered from the German occupation, either. A cynic might be excused for saying that Luxemburg was playing both ends against the middle.

## JOY IN ARLON

" For real, downright joy I never saw anything to equal the sights at Arlon today. Arlon is a little Belgian city of some 20,000 inhabitants, and is beautiful beyond compare. Today they had hundreds and hundreds of fête trees, just like our Christmas trees, all along the streets, and they bore tinsel and Japanese lanterns. Overhead were bowers of fir tree branches, and along the streets were pretty girls and handsome women and cheering men and brass bands and the gendarmes. Don't forget the gendarmes. Their uniforms, not worn for four years, had been dug up and burnished so that each ' copper ' looked no less than a Major General.

" When the 6th Marines came marching up the main street pandemonium broke loose. While over in Luxemburg one had wondered if they meant it, there was no room for doubt in Arlon. There were a thousand home-made American flags, and everywhere banners and big signs reading, ' Hail, generous Americans! ' They had not been able to get cloth enough to make all the flags they wanted, and so hundreds had been painted on big sheets of paper. What if the paint did run—the flags were still recognizable.

" Just a final touch was given to the picture when a wizened old woman ran up the street waving an edition of a newspaper, with the ink still wet, and across the front page in big type, ' The Day of Glory Has Arrived.' The marines quickly bought all her papers and read what noble fellows they were.

## CLEANING AFTER THE FOE

" The German withdrawal is losing some of its first neatness. More and more trucks are being left behind, and a considerable number of stragglers are trying to enter our lines. Reports say that the German officers, who seem to be trying to observe all the provisions of the armistice, are having increasing trouble with their men, most of whom think only of getting home and away from the army, of which they are sick.

This does not apply to the Prussians, but generally to all the other elements of the enemy's forces.

" About two-thirds of our front is moving through Luxemburg, with the rest passing across Lorraine. The French are on our right and left.

" Residents of French and Belgian towns are busy cleaning up after the Germans. In every village one sees fires burning the clothes and other personal equipment which the invaders left behind them. The rooms they occupied in private houses are being aired and fumigated, while the towns are busy cleaning the public buildings they used, in many of which is found indescribable filth. Beasts could not have left more disgusting evidences of their presence than the German officers left in the Hôtel de Ville at Arlon."

## GREETED BY GRAND DUCHESS

When the Americans passed through Luxemburg they were reviewed by General Pershing from the balcony of the palace of the youthful Grand Duchess, who stood beside him with members of the Cabinet and gave evidences of gratification at the withdrawal of the Germans.

Prior to the entry of the troops General Pershing in a proclamation assured the public that the American Army would remain only as long as was necessary, and while it was in Luxemburg would conduct itself in conformity with the civil law. The proclamation was distributed among the troops as well as among the population.

General Pershing entered the city ahead of his troops. The American Commander in Chief and his staff drove into the capital in automobiles. The General was greeted by thousands of cheering Luxemburgers and with the blowing of sirens and the ringing of church and school bells.

The 18th Infantry of the 1st Division were the first American troops to enter the city. The Americans were greeted by thousands of civilians, who lined all the streets through which the troops marched, school children tossed flowers in their pathway, and to each soldier was presented a bouquet of chrysanthemums.

Forty civic societies participated in the parade of welcome. Every building flew the flag of Luxemburg with here and there American flags. The chief political party of Luxemburg issued a proclamation which referred to the troops as " our deliverers, the glorious troops of the Entente and America." The declaration protested against the invasion of Luxemburg in 1914 by the Germans, asserted that their country had been humiliated, affirmed that the people at all times were pro-ally, expressed gratification over delivery from German oppression, and urged that they be allowed " to remain what we are."

## FRENCH ENTRY INTO METZ

General Pétain, Commander in Chief of the French Armies, who was made a Marshal of France by the French Cabinet on Nov. 19, entered Metz at the head of the Tenth Army the same day. The official French report of the entry tersely said:

The entire population went out to meet our troops, loudly acclaiming them. The old city of Lorraine, captive for forty-seven years and finally reunited to France, has manifested in a never-to-be-forgotten way its love for the mother country. In Alsace our soldiers received yesterday the same moving welcome in the loyal town of Colmar.

Mr. James, in describing the occupation, wrote as follows:

" I went to Metz to see the historic entry of the conquering French fighting men. The thing was too big to grasp, too much for the 70,000 population to realize. They seemed dazed. Down the faces of aged men and women who were French before Germany stole Lorraine tears of joy ran in streams. But the great mass of the population seemed dazed. They cheered and cheered, these younger folks, but I thought the tears of the old folks best told the story of Metz. It was incongruous to hear voices in German praising the appearance of French poilus, but they meant it, none the less, with few exceptions.

" The streets and squares were packed when early this afternoon the blast of trumpets told that the conquering heroes were coming. Overhead swept fifty airplanes, dropping miniature French flags, and from a distance came the strains of the 'Marche Lorraine.' And then French cavalry, and then French Generals and more officers, and then the poilus.

" As they swept into the square before the great cathedral—those handsomest soldiers God ever made—the real French and mongrel French broke into a great demonstration of joy. Then there came some trusty 75s and more infantry and more bands; and so on for two hours Mangin's soldiers swept through the city and the barracks the Germans had built and had just left, and Metz was French again."

Another correspondent thus described the entry into Metz:

When Marshal Pétain appeared on the Esplanade, mounted on a fine white charger and followed by the entire General Staff, with American and British officers attached, a shout went up that drowned the whirr of the dozen or more airplanes flying overhead, and the crowd surged forward, breaking the line of guards in places, to get a glimpse of the victorious commander.

Still mounted, Marshal Pétain, surrounded by a brilliant group of Generals and superior officers, took up his position in front of the statue of Marshal Ney to review the troops, comprising the 38th Division of Infantry, with its artillery, under General Pougin; a detachment of the 1st Corps of Cavalry, under General Feraud; other mounted troops under General de Boissieu, two escorting squadrons from the 1st Moroccan Division, and a detachment of tanks.

The staff of the Tenth Army, which General Mangin was prevented from heading because of the accident he had met with, was lined up directly in front of the Marshal, while General Fayolle, commanding the central group of armies, stood near the Commander in Chief just in front of the Ney statute, which the various superior officers saluted in passing. Enthusiastic cheers of " Long live France!" greeted every flag as it appeared.

The day was one of notable enthusiasm throughout, which thus failed to diminish. Bands, with torches, appeared as soon as the light began to fade, and jubilant processions continued gayly to circulate through the town until a late hour. Meanwhile, from the French lines all around the fortress there was a display of fireworks, which brightly lighted the sky, signal fuses and star shells serving as skyrockets.

People unaccustomed to any other

tongue than the German for years began many days ago brushing up their knowledge of French in preparation for this occasion, and although the majority of the population undoubtedly has a perfect acquaintance with no other tongue than the German, little of that language is now heard in the streets.

Other things German had disappeared over night, including the statues of the German rulers, which had been hauled down by the citizens. William I. had toppled over from the horse of his equestrian monument, while Frederick III., who for many long years had pointed a menacing finger at France from the pedestal upon which he stood, had come down with a rope around his neck.

## KING ALBERT IN GHENT

The King of the Belgians formally entered Ghent on Nov. 13. On that day Philip Gibbs wrote:

" Today in Ghent there are vast cheering crowds, and King Albert is making his triumphal entry into his city, and the sun is shining with a golden light upon all the old roofs of Ghent and upon the crowded balconies from which banners hang.

" The King and Queen came riding in with the young Prince, escorted by Belgian, French, and British Generals, and as they came white flowers were thrown from all the balconies, and their petals fell about like confetti. They took up a position outside the old club in the Place d'Armes, and cheers swept round them in storms. Then there was a march past of Belgian troops, men who had fought on the Yser in the old bad days of mud and blood and those who, in the last days, had stormed their way through with guns and cavalry. They had flowers in their rifles and on their helmets and looked like veterans as they marched under their heavy packs.

" The Queen of the Belgians wore a light habit with a little linen cap and was a simple figure. There next to her was the tall King, whose face has been bronzed and hardened by four years in the field with his men. It is a great day for Belgium, and the air is full of music and the gladness of a brave people whose courage has won through to victory.

" Ghent was the last Belgian town to be rescued before the armistice. The

Germans had clung to it as the pivot of their retreat, holding the canal in front of it by machine-gun fire, and it was not until 2 o'clock on Monday morning (Nov. 11) that they went away. Twelve Belgian soldiers were the first to enter, at 7 o'clock, led by a young Belgian Lieutenant, whom I met last night, and a few minutes afterward all the streets were filled with the citizens of Ghent shouting, cheering, embracing these soldiers and each other.

" The enemy had gone after four years of oppression, and as dawn came it rose upon a day of liberty. Bells rang out from all the churches and from the old belfries of Ghent there were joyful carillons. The Belgian troops marched in, and their artillery passed through, and the people covered them with flags, and the music of their bands was overwhelmed by shouts of ' Vive la Belgique.' "

## OCCUPATION OF ANTWERP

Mr. Gibbs also witnessed the entry of the King and Queen into Antwerp on Nov. 19. He cabled under that date:

" To the pealing of bells in the great cathedral and the cheers of massed crowds, the King of the Belgians made a state entry into the City of Antwerp today by the bridge across the Scheldt, known as the Tête de Flandres, and with the Queen drove around the streets to the Hôtel de Ville in an open carriage.

" Antwerp is a noble old city, with broad streets and squares and big public buildings, and these were all draped with long banners, and across the highways were streamers and flags. In a village outside, through which the King passed, the people had placed Christmas trees adorned with little flags and Chinese lanterns, as if for the coming of Father Christmas with the spirit of peace.

" Physically the people of Antwerp have not suffered in this war, but their joy at liberation, the enthusiasm with which they greeted King Albert, the stories they told me, are proof enough that they suffered in a mental way severely enough to make them feel that a horror had been lifted from them by the retreat of the Germans. The first man I met had been in prison three

months for jostling a German officer while he was disputing with a friend over a point of grammar, and then he was suspended by the arms to a wall for fourteen days because he received a packet of chocolate and would not sell it to the Prison Governor who coveted it, saying: ' I do not make commerce with Germans.' Thousands of people went to prison for trivial offenses like this or for their refusal to pay fines.

## ENTRY OF RULERS

" During the formal entry of the King and Queen into Antwerp their cars were laden with flowers, which had been given to them. On the steps of the Hôtel de Ville the sun glinted on the gold work on that masterpiece of the Flemish guilds; and now from scores of windows more flowers fell, so that they drove through a flurry of red and white petals.

" Before they went to the saluting base there was a procession which made emotion pass down the lines of the people like a wave. It was a crowd of men walking very slowly by the help of crutches and sticks, with a banner above them. Some of them were in the uniform of the Belgian Army of 1914, and others wore armlets of the Belgian colors. They were the men who had been in the siege of Antwerp in October of the first year of the war, and with their bodies had barred the way for a little while to the invading hordes.

" The march past of the Belgian troops who had fought in the later battles at Dixmude and at Pervyse, on the mud banks of the Yser and at Merckem, a month or two ago, was a stirring thing to see. The people had been waiting for them to come into this city again after four long years. Just four years ago I used to see men like this, covered with mud and blood, laid out in rows on stretchers. I saw many of them die. These men, who marched through Antwerp today, had lived to see the liberation of their country, and they were the lucky ones.

" There was a Te Deum in the cathedral, but I could get no further than the transport, because of the crowds there straining to get a glimpse of the King.

Before the high altar I could see the "Descent from the Cross," with its rich color like a great bouquet or painted window through which the light shines, and above the people long silken banners were draped from the tall pillars. The air was heavy with incense; and music and the murmur of voices came down the aisles, meeting the murmurous whispering of those about me; and through the open door out there in the square, where other crowds were around the statue of Peter Paul Rubens.

"All over Antwerp bells were ringing, their notes mingling in a strange clashing melody, and from the belfry of the cathedral the chimes of the gay carillons came tinkling down. They were playing 'The Marseillaise.'"

## BRUSSELS EVACUATED

A demonstration occurred at Brussels on Nov. 10 in sympathy with the revolutionary outbreaks in Germany. Several thousand German soldiers were making manifestations, and at length got beyond control of their officers and hoisted the red flag from the balcony of the Governor's house. Rioting ensued, and a number of soldiers and civilians were killed.

The last detachment of German troops left Brussels on Nov. 17.

The ceremony proclaiming the liberation of Brussels was performed that day in the Grand Place at 10 o'clock. The square was packed with people and former prisoners, while the windows and balconies were crowded with onlookers. Newsboys were shouting the names of newspapers which had been suppressed by the Germans and which reappeared that day.

Burgomaster Le Monier, heralded by a fanfare of trumpets, appeared at the Leon Staircase, accompanied by an Alderman, and announced the liberation of the capital. His speech was continually interrupted by cheers from the crowd, which swore that the murders and robberies committed by the Germans would never be forgotten.

The Belgian flag was then hoisted over the Hôtel de Ville, while the great mass of people in the square waved the national colors. The "Brabançonne" was sung and this was followed by the anthems of the Allies.

The excitement of the people reached its zenith when a procession was formed. It was headed by an old banner of the revolution of 1830, a symbol of Belgian liberty. The procession, ever growing larger, marched to the Place des Martyrs, where there is a monument to the heroes of the 1830 revolution. Here Burgomaster Le Monier made a patriotic speech.

After fifty months of captivity in Germany, Burgomaster Max came into his own again. The Municipal Council met to receive him at the Hôtel de Ville. The Dutch Minister, many prominent citizens, and officers of the allied armies were present. Burgomaster Max was loudly cheered when he entered the hall and took his seat at the Aldermen's table. Acting Burgomaster Le Monier welcomed him with a flattering address and formally relinquished the Burgomaster's seat to Max, who made a short address.

## KING ALBERT IN BRUSSELS

King Albert formally entered Brussels, accompanied by the Queen and their children, on Nov. 22. He entered his capital in brilliant Autumn sunshine, amid the joyous demonstrations of the populace. On the preceding evening the Belgians had again formally reoccupied the city of Louvain, which had been practically destroyed by the Germans. President Wilson sent the following congratulatory telegram to King Albert of Belgium, at Brussels:

"At the moment that you re-enter Brussels at the head of your victorious army, may I not express the great joy that it gives to me and to the American people to hail your return to your capital, marking your final triumph in this war, which has cost your nation so much suffering, but from which it will arise in new strength to a higher destiny?"

# Surrender of German High Seas Fleet

## Seventy-one Warships and Two Squadrons of U-Boats Delivered to Britain and Interned in the Orkneys

THE first surrender of German naval vessels under the armistice was the delivery of twenty submarines to Admiral Tyrwhitt of the British Navy off Harwich at sunrise on Nov. 20, 1918. The following day nineteen more were delivered. The most spectacular event, however, was the surrender of the German High Seas Fleet to Admiral Beatty and the allied armada off the Firth of Forth on the morning of Nov. 21, the greatest naval capitulation in history. The vessels surrendered were nine battleships, five battle cruisers, seven light cruisers, and fifty destroyers. One destroyer, while on its way across the North Sea, had struck a mine and sunk.

The rendezvous appointed for the act of surrender was thirty to forty miles east of May Island, opposite the Firth of Forth. The forfeited ships were sighted by the allied columns at 9:20 o'clock docilely following their British pilot, the light cruiser Cardiff, which, with destroyers and other small craft, had ranged ahead of the allied fleet. The enemy studiously complied with Admiral Beatty's orders. Every vessel steaming out to meet the German vessels flew battle ensigns and was ready for instant action, with its men at battle stations and guns in position for the prompt annihilation of the enemy's forces if their mission proved to be other than peaceful. Five American battleships, the New York, Texas, Arkansas, Wyoming, and Florida, were prepared to fire every gun in forty seconds after the signal was given.

The main allied fleet extending over a line fourteen miles long in the Firth of Forth began to weigh anchor at 1 o'clock A. M., Nov. 21. The Scotch mist which for days had obscured the harbor was swept away by a stiff breeze and the moon shone brilliantly out of a clear sky. The ships quickly took their stations in the long double line they held throughout the day. British battle cruisers led the way, followed by dreadnoughts. Admiral Beatty's flagship, the Queen Elizabeth, led the squadron in the northern column. The American warships fell into line behind Admiral Beatty's craft, balancing a British squadron similar in power to the opposite file.

The rendezvous was approximately fifty miles distant, and the ships gauged their speed to arrive at the appointed place at 8 o'clock. At 5 o'clock a signal summoned the men into battle stations and, except for the officers on the bridges, the ships' companies were hidden behind the bulwarks of steel. When dawn broke the sea was again covered with mist, which reduced the visibility to less than 8,000 yards.

## ENEMY FLEET SIGHTED

Eyes straining through the murky haze finally were rewarded. Off the starboard bow the Cardiff, trailing an observation kite balloon, came steaming in. Close behind her came the first of the German ships, the great battle cruiser Seydlitz, which was flying the flag of Commodore Togert. After her came four others of the same type, the Derflinger, Von der Tann, Hindenburg, and Moltke. They moved along three cable lengths apart.

Immediately following them were nine dreadnoughts, the Friedrich der Grosse, flagship of Rear Admiral von Reuter; the Koenig Albert, Kaiser, Kronprinz Wilhelm, Kaiserin, Bayern, Markgraf, Prinzregent Luitpold, and the Grosser Kurfürst.

Three miles astern of the battleships came seven light cruisers, the Karlsruhe, bearing the ensign of Commodore Harder; the Frankfort, Emden, Burnberg, Brummer, Köln, and Bremen.

Then came another gap of three miles and German destroyers came steaming in five columns abreast, with ten destroyers to a column.

Six miles separated the allied columns, and squarely between them the Cardiff brought her charges, all steaming at the stipulated speed of ten knots. As ordered, their guns were in regular fore-and-aft positions, and, as far as powerful glasses could determine, there was no sign to provoke suspicion. Until all the major ships had been swallowed up in the enveloping allied columns the latter never for a moment relaxed their alert watch. Over the Germans circled a British dirigible, which acted as eyes for the allied ships.

## INTERNED IN ORKNEYS

When the leading German ship had reached the western end of the flanking columns, the allied ships put about in squadrons. Quickly re-forming their lines, they proceeded to escort the enemy into the Firth of Forth. By noon the last wisp of fog had dispersed and a splendid view of the vast array of war craft could be obtained. Holding steadily to its course, the great fleet reached May Island at 2 o'clock. The captive Germans were piloted to anchorages assigned to them and British ships from the southern column closed in as guards. The northern column steamed on to the regular anchorages higher up the Firth.

Inspection parties from the Grand Fleet boarded the Germans to make sure that all conditions of the armistice were observed. The enemy vessels were later interned in Scapa Flow in the Orkney Islands. Part of the crews remained for maintenance work and the remainder were returned to Germany.

Admiral Beatty's signal, after the German fleet had been moored at the appointed place, was: "The German flag is to be hauled down at 3:57, and is not to be hoisted again without permission." A surrender on such a gigantic scale had no precedent in naval history.

The tonnage of the vessels surrendered approximated 410,000, divided as follows:

| BATTLE CRUISERS— | Tons. |
|---|---|
| Seydlitz | 25,000 |
| Derflinger | 28,000 |
| Hindenburg | 27,000 |
| Moltke | 23,000 |
| Von der Tann | 18,000 |

| DREADNOUGHTS— | Tons. |
|---|---|
| Friedrich der Grosse | 24,113 |
| König Albert | 24,113 |
| Kaiser | 25,000 |
| Kronprinz Wilhelm | 25,000 |
| Kaiserin | 24,113 |
| Bayern | 28,000 |
| Markgraf | 25,293 |
| Prinzregent Luitpold | 24,113 |
| Grosser Kurfürst | 25,293 |

| LIGHT CRUISERS— | |
|---|---|
| Karlsruhe | (?) 4,000 |
| Frankfort | 5,400 |
| Emden | 5,400 |
| Broomberg (?) | 4,000 |
| Breslau (?) | 4,000 |
| Köln | (?) 4,500 |
| Bremen | 4,000 |

| DESTROYERS— | |
|---|---|
| Fifty—Averaging 600 tons | 30,000 |

## THE U-BOAT SURRENDER

The first twenty German submarines were surrendered to Rear Admiral Reginald W. Tyrwhitt thirty miles off Harwich at sunrise on Nov. 20. The Admiral received the formal surrender on board his flagship, the Curacao.

The submarines went some twenty miles further in the North Sea in charge of their own crews. They were then boarded by British crews and interpreters and proceeded to Parkeston Quay, near by. The British naval force that received them consisted of five light cruisers and twenty destroyers. High above the squadron hung a big observation balloon.

The squadron, headed by the flagship, then steamed toward the Dutch coast, followed by the Coventry, Dragon, Danale, and Centaur. Other ships followed in line, with their navigation lights showing. The picture was a fine one as the great vessels, with the moon still shining, plowed their way to take part in the surrender of the German U-boats.

Soon after the British squadron started the "paravanes" were dropped overboard. These devices are shaped like tops and divert any mines which may be encountered, for the vessels were now entering a mine field. Almost every one on board donned a life belt and just as the sun shone above the horizon the first German submarine appeared in sight. Soon after 7 o'clock twenty submarines were seen in line accompanied by two German destroyers, the Tibania and the Sierra Ventana, which were to take the submarine crews back to Germany after the transfer.

All the submarines were on the surface, with their hatches open and their crews standing on deck. The vessels were flying no flags whatever and their guns were trained fore and aft, in accordance with the terms of surrender.

A bugle sounded on the Curacao and all the gun crews took up their stations ready for any possible treachery. The leading destroyer, in response to a signal from the Admiral, turned and led the way toward England and the submarines were ordered to follow. They immediately did so. The surrender had been accomplished.

## STEAMING TO HARWICH

Each cruiser turned, and, keeping a careful lookout, steamed toward Harwich. On the deck of one of the largest of the submarines, which carried two 5.9 guns, twenty-three officers and men were counted. The craft was estimated to be nearly 300 feet in length. Its number had been painted out. Near the Ship Wash Lightship three large British seaplanes, followed by an airship, were observed. One of the submarines was seen to send up a couple of carrier pigeons and at once a signal was flashed from the Admiral that it had no right to do this. When the ships had cleared the minefield and entered the war channel the " paravanes " were hauled aboard. On reaching a point some twenty miles off Harwich the ships dropped anchor and Captain Addison came out on the warship Maidstone.

When the enemy boats were sighted there were only two or three members of each crew on deck, but as the details of the surrender worked out during the morning and early afternoon more Germans appeared from below decks. They appeared a sullen, but well fed, lot when

the first British officers stepped aboard and curtly saluted. British sailors followed the officers, and the Germans went to the forward deck as the British and German officers went below to examine the first submarine to be taken over. The German commander briefly answered questions regarding the machinery, but said nothing else. Evidence of strain and deep chagrin was unmistakably written on the faces of the German officers. The machinery was generally in good shape, but the vessels were extremely dirty and devoid of all unessentials. Everything indicating the names of the craft had been removed, although the Germans, conforming to instructions, readily told the names of their boats.

British crews were then put on board the submarines to take them into the harbor. With the exception of the engine staffs, all the German sailors remained on deck. The submarines were then taken through the gates of the harbor and the German crews transferred to the vessels which were to take them back to Germany. As the boats went through the gates the white ensign was run up on each of them, with the German flag underneath.

Each German submarine commander at the transfer was required to sign a declaration to the effect that his vessel was in running order, that its periscope was intact, that its torpedoes were unloaded, and that its torpedo heads were safe.

Orders had been issued forbidding any demonstration, and these instructions were obeyed to the letter. There was complete silence as the submarines surrendered and as the crews were transferred. So ended a historic event and the first portion of the German submarine fleet was in the hands of the British Navy.

Nineteen additional submarines surrendered on Nov. 21.

# Germany in Revolution

## Abdication of the Kaiser and Organizing of Republican States Follow Military Collapse

OCT. 27, 1918, dawned a fateful day for Germany. For many it signified a parting of the ways. The previous week had closed with the resignation of Ludendorff, and astonishing freedom of speech by the Socialist Deputies Ebert, Ledebour, and Kühle in the Reichstag. Demand for peace and popular government had risen to an open summons to the Kaiser to abdicate. Deputy Kühle even went so far as to voice the threat that "abdication would not save the Kaiser from trial as the man who caused the war." But with the Kaiser still "watching events calmly," and Hindenburg remaining as chief of the General Staff, much uncertainty was manifest in the current of events, shot through, as it was, by "the wild propaganda of the Conservatives in favor of the old régime." Mainly outstanding, the resignation of Ludendorff signified the downfall of militarism in Germany.

The day following, Oct. 28, two men occupied the centre of the political stage, Dr. Karl Liebknecht and von Hindenburg. On Dr. Liebknecht's release from prison, around him had gathered the extreme Radicals of Bolshevist tendencies. Moderate Socialists, for whom Vorwärts was the spokesman, viewed with alarm the swiftly rising tide of the extremists under Liebknecht's leadership. By them it was hoped Ludendorff's military head would act as a popular tranquilizer. "If von Hindenburg went, the Kaiser would be the next to fall, slithering the whole political power into the hands of the extreme Socialists and the four million disgruntled soldiers returning from the front."

As straws in the current, reports of mutinous German troops in garrison came through to the outer world. Also, there was said to have been a panic in the Rhine Provinces at the prospect of the enemy being permitted to occupy Coblenz and Cologne.

On the Wednesday following Ludendorff's retirement, Lieut. Gen. Groener was appointed to occupy the position of First Quartermaster General of the German Army. General Groener's proved capability as a transport organizer was held to point to his competence for the task of withdrawing the German armies from France and Belgium. In 1916 he had been bitterly attacked in the Reichstag for his ruthless suppression of munition strikers, and later for oppression in collecting food and raw materials in the Ukraine.

### DISCUSSING ABDICATION

A telegram from Berlin quoted the Kaiser as saying, with reference to his possible abdication: "In any case, if the moment comes when the interest of Germany demands it, I should abdicate and would do so without hesitation; but the moment does not seem to have come yet."

From Nov. 1 to Nov. 4 a political storm raged with increasing fury around the question of the Kaiser's abdication. On Thursday the Berlin Vossiche Zeitung stated that the abdication question was discussed at the latest meeting of the War Cabinet, and Vice Chancellor Delbrück had left for the front on an important mission for Chancellor Maximilian, presumably to present the Emperor with an abdication document.

What seemed to be a singularly inauspicious claim to the Imperial Crown of Germany was promptly put forward by the Bavarian Premier on behalf of the Bavarian royal family, should Emperor William abdicate. The claim, whatever it might have been worth in those shadowy hours for German royalty, was based mainly on the fact that two members of the Wittelsbach family of Bavaria had worn the imperial purple of the Holy Roman Empire of the Germans.

Presently the wildest reports sped one after the other out of Germany. Immediate peace was demanded by Socialist organizations in flaming manifestoes. The Kaiser had slipped away in the dead of night from Berlin and taken refuge at Army Great Headquarters. This was after the War Cabinet had debated his abdication. Complete submission to the Allies was said to be advised by Count Reventlow, the violent exponent of Pan-Germanism and bitter reviler of all things English. The Kaiser was said to be surrounded by pessimists of the species of Scheidemann, Secretary of State without portfolio. A majority of the War Cabinet was declared to be in favor of the Kaiser's remaining on the throne. No sign of the Kaiser's abdication. All seemingly chaos and confusion.

## KAISER'S REFORM DECREE

On Nov. 3 Prince Maximilian officially released a decree of the Kaiser, giving his full support to reforms, dated Oct. 28. It read as follows:

Your Grand Ducal Highness:

I return herewith for immediate publication the bill to amend the Imperial Constitution and the law of March 17, 1870, relative to the representation of the Imperial Chancellor, which has been laid before me for signature.

On the occasion of this step, which is so momentous for the future history of the German people, I have a desire to give expression to my feelings. Prepared for by a series of Government acts, a new order comes into force which transfers the fundamental rights of the Kaiser's person to the people.

Thus comes to a close a period which will stand in honor before the eyes of future generations. Despite all struggles between invested authority and aspiring forces, it has rendered possible to our people that tremendous development which imperishably revealed itself in the wonderful achievements of this war.

In the terrible storms of the four years of war, however, old forms have been broken up, not to leave their ruins behind but to make a place for new, vital forms.

After the achievements of these times, the German people can claim that no right which may guarantee a free and happy future shall be withheld from them.

The proposals of the allied Governments which are now adopted and extended owe their origin to this conviction. I, however, with my exalted allies, indorse these decisions of Parliament in firm determination, so far as I am concerned, to co-operate in their full development, convinced that I am thereby promoting the weal of the German people.

The Kaiser's office is one of service to the people. May, then, the new order release all the good powers which our people need in order to support the trials which are hanging over the empire and with a firm step win a bright future from the gloom of the present.        WILHELM, I. R.

Berlin, Oct. 28, 1918.
(Countersigned.)
    Max, Prince of Baden.

The Associated Press correspondent at Amsterdam on Nov. 4 summarized popular sentiment in Germany as follows:

The Kaiser question is the topic of general discussion in Germany. The German War Cabinet has gone into the problem very fully during the last few days, and, inter alia, it decided to allow press and public discussion of the question.

People who come from Germany tell me that among the masses a highly inflamed feeling is shown toward the Crown Prince. "I don't think he could walk in safety down Unter Den Linden," is what one traveller says. The Kaiser has few of the people on his side, but the hottest hate of the people is reserved for his son.

The most democratic members of the Government, I learn, insist on both of them going, and there is a section of the Ministry which has openly told Prince Max that it would be well to do away with the crown altogether, now that the people's representatives have put their hands to the plow of reform.

## SECESSION OF STATES

Meanwhile, it was reported that some of the South German States, particularly Bavaria, had threatened to secede and proclaim independent republics. A panic had swept over financial centres, causing a widespread hoarding of currency. The German Moderate press again showed concern over the Bolshevist danger, attributed to the propaganda of the Russian Embassy. The formation of a Workers' and Soldiers' Committee was noted for the first time in Berlin.

On Nov. 5 the Chancellor, Prince Max, issued a manifesto to the people, beseeching them to believe that the Government was working for an early peace and comprehensive democratic reforms, reminding them that equal suffrage in Prussia was already "assured."

At the same moment such papers as the Deutsche Tageszeitung, the Cologne Volkszeitung, and the Tageblatt asserted that Germany was not beaten in the field, that "the German armies could resist Foch's armies," and that there were "weak spots in the Allies' political liaison" which enabled Germany to reject impossible armistice terms.

With the appearance of red flags on the streets of Stuttgart and shouts of "Down with the war—Long live the Social Revolution," the Kaiser was declared to have decided to keep his throne as a democratic monarch after the pattern of the Kings of England and Italy. In response to an ultimatum of abdication from the Socialist Party the Kaiser replied that "he could not at the moment of peace undertake the terrible responsibility of handing over Germany to the Entente and delivering up the country to anarchy."

On Nov. 8 it was telegraphed from Munich that at a great popular meeting, which included soldiers, fiery speeches were delivered demanding the abdication of the Kaiser, renunciation of the right to succession by the German Crown Prince, and the formation of a republican form of government in Bavaria. The crowd, a mile long, marched to the palace, where the Ministers endeavored to appease them.

### REVOLT IN THE NAVY

On the same day news came through via Amsterdam of widespread revolts in Germany. Practically the whole German fleet had fallen into the hands of revolutionary sailors, who, in conjunction with Workmen's and Soldiers' Councils ashore, had gained control of Kiel, Wilhelmshaven, Heligoland, Borkum, and Cuxhaven. Initial fighting began on the battleship Kaiser on Friday, the 7th. After resistance on the part of the officers, two of whom were killed, the Imperial flag was hauled down and the red flag of the revolution hoisted in its place. Other ships immediately followed suit, together with all the submarine crews. On the following day the Governor of Kiel capitulated to the revolutionaries on these terms:

1. Recognition of the Soldiers' Council.
2. Better treatment of the men on ships and ashore.
3. Abolition of the salute.
4. Equality for officers and men as regards victuals.
5. Abolition of the officers' casinos.

6. Release of all persons in prison for refusal to obey orders.
7. No punishment for men who had not returned to their ships.

During the excitement Prince Henry of Prussia, the Kaiser's brother, made a spectacular escape from Kiel in an auto flying the red flag. He was shot at by marines. After some further adventures he managed to reach the Danish border and pass over into safety. There he was joined by Count zu Reventlow. Almost simultaneously a strike of workers was declared in Hamburg, which quickly developed into a revolt. Artillery firing between royal and revolutionary combatants took place in the streets. Several casualties were reported.

### THE KAISER'S ABDICATION

On Nov. 9 a wireless message from Berlin announced that the German Imperial Chancellor, Prince Max of Baden, had issued the following decree:

> The Kaiser and King has decided to renounce the throne. The Imperial Chancellor will remain in office until the questions connected with the abdication of the Kaiser, the renouncing by the Crown Prince of the throne of the German Empire and of Prussia, and the setting up of a regency have been settled. For the regency he intends to appoint Deputy Ebert as Imperial Chancellor, and he proposes that a bill shall be brought in for the establishment of a law providing for the immediate promulgation of general suffrage and for a constitutional German National Assembly, which will settle finally the future form of government of the German Nation and of those peoples which might be desirous of coming within the empire.

This was the only document or official utterance of any kind given to the world in proof of the assertion that the Kaiser had abdicated. Even after his retirement to Holland there was widespread disbelief in the genuineness of his permanent renunciation of the throne. A general upheaval throughout Germany, however, immediately followed Prince Max's issuance of the Kaiser's decree. A Socialist republic was proclaimed in Bavaria, with Herr Kurt Eisner at its head. Throughout the Rhine industrial regions the movement spread like wildfire, the hoisting of the red flag over public buildings in numerous cities being accompanied by a stoppage of work. Thus,

Hamburg, Bremen, and Altona went over to the revolution. While contested in some places, on the whole it was accomplished with an astonishing lack of disorder.

## REVOLUTION IN BERLIN

In Berlin but a few hours on Sunday, the 10th, sufficed for a complete triumph. It began at 9 o'clock in the morning. At that hour a general strike was started, and shortly afterward thousands of soldiers, carrying red flags and accompanied by armed motor cars, began to pour into the centre of the city from the outskirts. With them came workers from outlying factories. A little later trains began to arrive, bringing 3,000 sailors from Kiel. They were received in the streets with the utmost enthusiasm.

Presently these arrivals broke up into detachments and occupied the bridges, public buildings, street corners, &c., fraternizing with the populace. Almost as by magic red flags appeared everywhere, and officers in the streets and barracks stripped off their cockades and epaulettes—in very few cases was compulsion necessary—and threw them away. Hundreds of Iron Crosses could be picked up in the streets.

Scheidemann, in announcing the abdication of the Kaiser from the front of the Reichstag building, was accorded a tremendous reception. The hoisting of the red flag over the Kaiser's palace was greeted with thunderous cheers. From the Wolff Bureau a message of democratic triumph was transmitted to the whole world. " The revolution has gained a glorious and almost bloodless victory."

## NEW CHANCELLOR'S ADDRESS

Friedrich Ebert, the new Chancellor, immediately issued the following address:

Citizens: The ex-Chancellor, Prince Max of Baden, in agreement with all the Secretaries of State, has handed over to me the task of liquidating his affairs as Chancellor. I am on the point of forming a new Government in accord with the various parties, and will keep public opinion freely informed of the course of events.

The new Government will be a Government of the people. It must make every effort to secure in the quickest possible time peace for the German people and consolidate the liberty which they have won.

The new Government has taken charge of the administration, to preserve the German people from civil war and famine and to accomplish their legitimate claim to autonomy. The Government can solve this problem only if all the officials in town and country will help.

I know it will be difficult for some to work with the new men who have taken charge of the empire, but I appeal to their love of the people. Lack of organization would in this heavy time mean anarchy in Germany and the surrender of the country to tremendous misery. Therefore, help your native country with fearless, indefatigable work for the future, every one at his post.

I demand every one's support in the hard task awaiting us. You know how seriously the war has menaced the provisioning of the people, which is the first condition of the people's existence. The political transformation should not trouble the people. The food supply is the first duty of all, whether in town or country, and they should not embarrass, but rather aid, the production of food supplies and their transport to the towns.

Food shortage signifies pillage and robbery, with great misery. The poorest will suffer the most, and the industrial worker will be affected hardest. All who illicitly lay hands on food supplies or other supplies of prime necessity or the means of transport necessary for their distribution will be guilty in the highest degree toward the community.

I ask you immediately to leave the streets and remain orderly and calm.

At the same time Field Marshal von Hindenburg placed himself and the German Army at the disposal of the new People's Government, having asked the Cologne Workmen's and Soldiers' Council to send delegates to German Main Headquarters.

## SWING OF PENDULUM

News of these events had scarcely been flashed over the cables when a struggle between the Moderate Socialists and the Extremists or " Reds " developed. First, control of the new Government rested in the hands of the Moderate triumvirate—Ebert, Landsberg, and Scheidemann. But the Extremists quickly proceeded to make their power felt. Concession to Extremists resulted in places in the Government being offered to Haase, Liebknecht, and Barth. Erzberger of the Centrist Party and Gothein of the Progressive People's Party were also offered seats.

That the Revolutionary Government was resisted in spots was evidenced by reports from Antwerp and elsewhere of fighting between royalist and revolutionary troops, and the Third German Squadron persisted in keeping the Imperial flag at the masthead. Also, Field Marshal von Mackensen, in command of the army of occupation in Rumania, announced his refusal to recognize the Revolutionary Government as constitutional.

On Nov. 9 and 10 fighting broke out in Berlin around the Royal Castle and spread to other parts of the city. Its origin was a demand for a Constitutional Assembly by the Extremists. What threatened a triumph for the "Reds" was, however, quickly dissipated. "Kultur" reasserted itself. The party of Dr. Karl Liebknecht was relegated to political obscurity, and the Councils of Workers' and Soldiers' Delegates were said to be well under control. The demand for a Constituent Assembly was held to be unnecessary at the moment. Presently a new government sprang into being entitled the Government of Plenipotentiaries.

Meanwhile, German crowns continued to fall like overripe fruit in late Autumn, as the following list shows:

King of Bavaria.................Nov. 8
Duke of Brunswick..............Nov. 9
King of Württemberg............Nov. 10
King of Saxony.................Nov. 11
Grand Duke of Oldenburg........Nov. 11
Grand Duke of Mecklenburg......Nov. 11
Prince of Reuss................Nov. 12
Grand Duke of Saxe-Weimar......Nov. 13
Prince of Lippe-Detmold........Nov. 13
Prince of Waldeck-Pyrmont......Nov. 14
Duke of Anhalt.................Nov. 14
Grand Duke of Baden............Nov. 14

## FLIGHT OF THE KAISER

Nov. 9 was the date when the German Emperor signed his letter of abdication at German Grand Headquarters at Spa in the presence of the Crown Prince and Field Marshal von Hindenburg. Up till the last hour the Kaiser had refused to yield to the inevitable, and had gone so far as to try to prevent the German armistice delegation from reaching the French lines. In this attitude he was supported by a group of his personal staff officers. Hindenburg, however, was insistent that delay would have the most terrible results. An urgent message from Philipp Scheidemann presented to the Kaiser a hopeless situation. The Kaiser signed the abdication. "It may be for the good of Germany," were reported to have been his words as he appended his signature. He was "deeply moved" and "his hand shook" as he read the fateful document. Thereupon the Crown Prince signed away his imperial birthright.

Early on the following Sunday morning the Kaiser, accompanied by his personal staff, arrived in automobiles at Eysden, near Maastricht, on the Dutch frontier. A royal train of sleeping and dining cars rolled into the station of the quiet little village an hour and a half later. While waiting for official permission to enter Holland as a refugee, the Kaiser was the object of much curiosity among the country folk gathered to the spot. The former ruler was seen by them in a General's uniform, impatiently striding up and down, chafing over formalities to which he had never before been subjected. When these were finally settled, there was again a long wait on the royal train before arrangements were made for him to take up his residence at Count Goddard Bentinck's château of Amerongen. Three weeks previously forty large cases had arrived at Count Bentinck's castle containing various treasures, including crown jewels, and on Nov. 18 more than 200 sacks, each containing a hundredweight of German gold, were delivered there. It is noteworthy that Amerongen had housed a former monarch in exile, Charles II. of England.

The Crown Prince, after being several times reported shot by his own soldiers, finally reached the Holland border and was temporarily interned at Maastricht. On Nov. 21 he left for Mosterland, an isolated fishing hamlet on the little island of Wieringen, near the Dutch naval station at Helder. In this lonely spot he was to be interned.

# The Situation in Germany Summarized

*A correspondent of The New York Times succeeded in sending the first direct cables from Berlin on Nov. 16 and 17, 1918, which were copyrighted for* CURRENT HISTORY MAGAZINE. *From these the following details were procured:*

Nov. 16.—A week ago Berliners went to bed to a painful degree in an absolute monarchy, and when they awoke the next morning they found themselves in a most radical republic. It was like a dream, people said; but after celebrating and wondering, as the case might be, for twelve hours, the people have sobered up quickly under the pressure of the awful realities of the general situation, and almost everybody today is resolutely putting his shoulder to the wheel, or at least trying to readjust his shattered conception of the world to the hard facts. The long war and its fearful sacrifices have schooled this people, and, of course, after the fearful and absolutely unexpected military catastrophes, nothing whatever could really stun them any more.

Today the revolution is an accepted fact, and everybody, to outward appearances, goes quietly about his business. True, many, even among the uninitiated, saw it coming, and nearly the whole people, excepting the very small reactionary percentage, had for weeks been asking: " Why doesn't he go?  Why doesn't he quit? "

And this for his once so terrible Majesty, William the Second! When finally he went, it was too late to prevent a complete change of everything.  The revolution was already progressing, Max von Baden's so-called People's Government being far too weak to stop the silently swelling tide of liberty.

Though many would have liked to see emerge from the catastrophe a Government more on the lines of the Western democracies, for the present nearly all intelligent people are thankfully recognizing that none but the strong organization of the Social Democratic Party could possibly have saved the situation from the utter chaos to which the ex-Kaiser's criminally selfish attitude seemed to doom the German people.

So far the Socialist Government certainly has made good.  Everything is orderly and quiet.  The masses of the people, after the first few days, returned to work.  There were no flowers, no music, no alcohol about this revolution, nor were there bonfires, or much gunpowder spent, as proved by the scant traces at the Royal Palace and the cafés in Unter den Linden.

It is only just to state that the present Government is extremely fair in its attitude toward the employes of the former régime, leaving as many as possible in their old positions.  Perhaps too many, the extremists claim, since there is the danger of laying a viper on one's own bosom; for there cannot be any doubt that many of the old officials, especially of the higher ranks, would rejoice in the failure of the present Government, no matter at what cost to their own country.

Despite all these tremendous difficulties, things are going astonishingly smoothly, considering the appalling difficulties.  What seemed the most immediate danger to the Ebert Government, namely, the rupture of the two large groups of Socialists which support it, has happily been avoided by their making common cause.

Around Cologne, Berlin, and other great cities cordons of soldiers are being formed to divert the threatening flood of returning soldiers into harmless channels, if possible. Much has been done for reform in municipal government in Berlin, Hamburg, and all other cities. Everywhere the old form of election for city parliaments has been replaced by a secret, universal ballot.  In Berlin the people's new Police President, Eichhorn, has abolished the much-hated political branch, and also abolished the hated name of " Schutzmann " (" protector,") which has been replaced by " Watchman."

The watchmen no longer carry sabres, but go unarmed until they can be furnished with rubber clubs.  Meanwhile, they are aided by members of the Council of Soldiers, who are carried through the streets on autos formerly in the military service. They carry rifles and machine guns and are the terror of housebreakers and plunderers, with whom they make very short work.

Considering the circumstances, however, there have been astonishingly few cases of robbery and similar crimes. Among the autos now employed in patrolling the city are some that formerly belonged to the ex-Kaiser, and their horns, sounding the combination of notes familiar to all Berliners, created no little astonishment and mirth when they were heard on their new duty as they raced for the first time along the crowded Roten Linden, (Red Lindens,) as that famous street—the Unter den Linden that was—is named now.

For weeks, even before the revolution, there had been a steady run on German banks all over the country, not only causing an extremely painful dearth of currency, but the banks in many cities, among them Berlin, being compelled to print so-called Notgeld, ("money of necessity," or substitute for paper money,) which will be canceled after the present stringency.

Since the revolution certain little groups of Independent Socialists have done much to increase alarm by making irresponsible statements in their organs regarding certain aggressive measures against individual wealth, insisting, for instance, that iron, coal, and potash mines and other industrial concerns be taken over by the Government before the National Convention takes place. Freiheit, one of these new organs of the Independent Socialists, said that by doing so now the National Convention would face accomplished facts that would be extremely difficult to change.

To reassure the public the Government on Nov. 17 made public the following statement, signed by Ebert and Haase:

First, we do not intend to confiscate any bank or savings bank deposits nor any sums in cash or banknotes or other valuable papers deposited in the bank safes.

Secondly, we do not intend to cancel any subscriptions to the Ninth War Loan, or any other war loan, or in any other way to impair the legitimacy of those loans. The Government, however, is determined to enforce the strictest measures that large fortunes and great incomes shall contribute appropriately toward the public expense.

Thirdly, salaries, pensions, and other claims on the State, held by officials, employes, officers, wounded and other soldiers and their relatives, will remain absolutely valid.

The members and employes of the former Royal Theatre and Opera House formed a council for the administration of the two houses until Dr. Suedekum, now Minister of Finance, is ready to take them over.

The Council of Waiters is another creation of the demands of the new times. In the first session this council decided on the abolition of the tips system. In future regular salaries will be demanded by the waiters. It was also decided to induce restaurant and hotel keepers gradually to discharge the waitresses who took the men's positions during the war, in order that there should be room for the men returning from the war.

The Centrist and all parties other than the Socialists sent out appeals to their members, urging them not to stand passively aside, but to take part in the reconstruction of the country. On Nov. 19 a large number of well-known men and women of all classes in all parts of the country published a similar document, urging organization of the democratic party, which is to take the place of the old party forms that crumbled to dust on Nov. 9. Extracts from this document read:

What is desired now is that all those circles of men and women who do not wish to be pushed aside should unite and recognize the new order of things and emphasize their right to co-operate for the common welfare. This union must constitute itself as the great democratic party of the united nation. No program shall be announced today, but our fundamental principle must be faith in the republican form of State, which we are to defend against any reaction. The decision of the new Constitution must be left to the National Convention.

Our second principle shall be that liberty is inseparable from law and order and the political equality of all citizens, and that Bolshevist or reactionary terrors will not be tolerated. Today only sweeping efforts will be effective, and wealth must make great sacrifices if ur happy or reactionary results are to be avoided from the outset.

Socializing ideals must take the place of monopolistic systems. Large State domains and great estates of landlords must be parceled out to the peasants. War profiteers must be properly assessed, while the rights of laborers, officials, and employes must be adequately readjusted, as also those of war prisoners and their dependents. Every able individual of whatever class must have his chance. To ward off any attempts of a dictator and arbitrary force, steps must immediately be taken for the election of a National Convention.

The document is signed by many men of high repute, among them Franz von Liszt, Hugo Preuss, who has just been appointed State Secretary of the Interior; Bernhard Dernburg, Frau Theodor Barth, Herr Dove, Vice President of the Reichstag; Herr Fischbeck, State Secretary; Theodor Wolff, the editor; Hellmuth von Gerlach, an editor, who has just been appointed Under Secretary; Rudolph Mosse, and von Richthofen. There are also bank Directors, well-known merchants, officers, and high officials among the signers.

# The Collapse of Austria-Hungary

## Utter Defeat in Second Battle of the Piave Leads to Surrender and Break-up of the Empire

[See maps on Pages 430 and 432]

AUSTRIA-HUNGARY was the third and last of Germany's allies to surrender and make a separate peace with the Entente. The débâcle that led swiftly to this ending was one of the most overwhelming in history. In the second battle of the Piave the Italians in a single week swept the Austrian forces out of Northern Italy, entered Trent in the Alps and Trieste on the Adriatic, captured 300,000 Austrians, and forced Austria-Hungary's unconditional surrender on Nov. 3, 1918, a date immediately added to the list of Italian holidays. Following this overwhelming military defeat and surrender Emperor Charles abdicated and the Dual Empire began disintegrating into separate States representing the various nationalities formerly held together under Hapsburg rule.

The story of this amazing climax begins with the sudden blow struck by General Diaz on Oct. 24 and 25 against the Austrian lines in the Monte Grappa region, between the Brenta and Piave Rivers, while a British unit attacked along the lower Piave and a French unit took Monte Seisemol on the Asiago Plateau. Nearly 3,000 prisoners were taken the first day. By Oct. 30 the Italians had captured Monte Grappa, with 33,000 prisoners, and were driving the Austrians back along the whole front from the Alps to the sea. The 332d American Infantry Regiment by that time was taking an active part in the fighting in the Brenta region.

With the fall of Monte Grappa the enemy army in the mountains was definitely cut off from the one in the plains, and both began to flee in increasing confusion. By Nov. 1 the one in the south was in utter rout, and the Italians, already across the Livenza River, had taken 80,000 prisoners and 1,600 guns. Vienna was imploring an armistice. Meanwhile the pursuing Italians were inflicting terrific losses on the invaders, and the whole stretch of country, in the mountains and on the plains for a distance of seventy miles, was littered with the bodies of Austrian dead.

There were tumbled heaps everywhere of the fantastic débris of abandoned war material, colossal stores, mounds of foodstuffs, and equipment of every kind, some of which had been hidden away in caves and underground labyrinths of the Grappa and Asiago Plateau. The total value of those war hoards alone amounted to many millions of dollars.

The fleeing enemy had to pass through Feltre, which was dominated by Italian guns, and here his losses were very heavy. To prevent the Austrians from burning their enormous food depots in that city the inhabitants, especially the women, assailed the foe ferociously with weapons of all kinds, which they had managed to conceal since the days of invasion, and succeeded in saving the stores. On Nov. 3, the day of the signing of the armistice, the Italian War Office announced that both Trent and Trieste had been captured, and that Italian cavalry had entered Udine. Church bells were run all over Italy, and parades and illuminations followed in Rome and elsewhere. American officers met in the street were greeted with "Viva America! Viva Wilson!" by the jubilant throngs.

## OFFICIAL SUMMARY

An official summary of the battle issued by the Italian War Office on Nov. 4 read as follows:

The war against Austria-Hungary, which, under the high guidance of the King, the supreme leader of the Italian Army, inferior in numbers and material, began May 24, 1915, and which, with unbending faith and tenacious valor, has been conducted uninterruptedly and bitterly for forty-one months, has been won.

The gigantic battle engaged in on Oct. 24, in which fifty-one Italian divisions and three British, two French, one Czechoslovak, and one American regiment participated against sixty-three Austro-Hungarian divisions, is ended.

The daring and very rapid advance of the 29th Army Corps on Trent, closing up the enemy's armies in Trentino, who were overcome to the west by troops from the Seventh Army and to the east by the First, Sixth, and Fourth Armies, brought about the total collapse of the enemy's front.

From the Brenta to the Torre, with irresistible dash, the Twelfth, Eighth, and Tenth Armies and cavalry divisions are driving the fleeing enemy constantly further away. On the plains the Duke of Aosta is advancing rapidly at the head of his unconquered Third Army, with the purpose of reclaiming those positions which the enemy holds.

The Austro-Hungarian Army is destroyed. It suffered very heavy losses in the fierce resistance of the first days of the struggle, and in pursuit it has lost an immense quantity of material of all kinds, nearly all its stores and depots, and has left in our hands about 300,000 prisoners,

with their commands complete, and not less than 5,000 guns.

This defeat has left what once was one of the most powerful armies in the world in disorder and without hope of returning along the valleys through which it descended with haughty assurance.

An Associated Press dispatch from the Italian headquarters in the direction of Trieste declared that this defeat of the Austrians had been ten times as costly to the enemy as the defeat suffered a year earlier at Caporetto had been to the Italians. A correspondent with the Italian Army in the mountains at Trent wrote on Nov. 6 that, while the redeemed city was rejoicing, the fleeing Austrian troops were suffering horrors comparable to those of Napoleon's retreat from Moscow. He continued:

Great masses of men wait for long hours to move a few feet or a few hundred yards, to halt anew on a road littered with the carcasses of horses, pieces of shells, pistols, rifles, broken down auto trucks, and machine guns. Many Austrians are dying from sheer fatigue and starvation and not wounds. The Italians are doing all they can to hurry up food supplies. This is difficult, and in the meantime dead horses are eaten, the flesh being cooked by the roadside by fires kindled by the soldiers.

Large bodies of Austrians are helpless. The correspondents passed between Overto and Trent, a distance of sixteen miles, an unending column of men marching none knew whither. They asked orders from an officer who was with the correspondents. When asked if they knew about the armistice, they said: "We want food. Food is the only thing we are interested in. We are indifferent to war and peace and death—everything but food."

It is estimated that nine Austrian divisions were taken with their staffs. Thirty-nine divisions were partially disorganized and fifteen, although in bad condition, are retreating from the advancing Italians. These troops, while equipped for their retreat, are without orders, and go traveling here and there like droves of sheep.

President Wilson sent the following message to the King of Italy on Nov. 4:

May I not say how deeply and sincerely the people of the United States rejoice that the soil of Italy is delivered from her enemies? In their name I send your Majesty and the great Italian people the most enthusiastic congratulations.

WOODROW WILSON.

Secretary Lansing, through Ambassador Sharp at Paris, also sent the following message to Baron Sonnino, Italian Minister for Foreign Affairs, then in Versailles, attending the sessions of the Supreme War Council:

At the moment of the complete victory of the Italian arms I take this means of conveying to you my most sincere congratulations. The Government of the United States admires the valor of the Italian armies and unites with the Italian Nation in this hour of rejoicing and of triumph.

The Italian Government on the same day named a parliamentary mission to carry to the United States certain precious manuscripts as gifts to show the appreciation of Italy for the help given by the Americans. The manuscripts were original codices written by Christopher Columbus, Amerigo Vespucci, and Giovanni da Verrazano.

# Armistice and Preliminary Notes

Austria-Hungary's first note of the series leading up to the armistice had been handed to President Wilson on Oct. 7, and the text of it, along with the President's reply of the 18th, was printed on Page 249 of the preceding issue of CURRENT HISTORY MAGAZINE. On Oct. 29 the Vienna Government answered President Wilson, asking that immediate negotiations for peace and an armistice be entered into without awaiting the results of exchanges with Germany. This note was sent through the Swedish Government at Stockholm and read as follows:

LEGATION OF SWEDEN,
Washington, D. C., Oct. 29, 1918.

Excellency: By order of my Government, I have the honor to beg you to transmit to the President the following communication from the Imperial and Royal Government of Austria-Hungary:

" In reply to the note of the President, Mr. Wilson, to the Austro-Hungarian Government, dated Oct. 18 of this year, and about the decision of the President to take up, with Austria-Hungary separately, the question of armistice and peace, the Austro-Hungarian Government has the honor to declare that it adheres both to the previous declarations of the President and his opinion of the rights of the peoples of Austria-Hungary, notably those of the Czechoslovaks and the Jugoslavs, contained in his last note. Austria-Hungary having thereby accepted all the conditions which the President had put upon entering into negotiations on the subject of armistice and peace, nothing, in the opinion of the Austro-Hungarian Government, longer stands in the way of beginning those negotiations. The Austro-Hungarian Government therefore declares itself ready to enter, without waiting for the outcome of other negotiations, into negotiations for a peace between Austria-Hungary and the Entente States, and for an immediate armistice on all the fronts of Austria-Hungary, and begs the President, Mr. Wilson, to take the necessary measures to that effect."

Be pleased to accept, Excellency, the assurances of my high consideration.

W. A. F. EKENGREN.

His Excellency, Robert Lansing, Secretary of State of the United States, Washington, D. C.

The Austro-Hungarian Government communicated this note also to the French, British, Japanese, and Italian Governments, begging the approval and support of these nations. The note was generally interpreted as indicating both the approaching dissolution of the Dual Empire and the abandonment of the alliance with Germany. Referring to the phrase " without awaiting the result of other negotiations," the Paris Temps said: " In these words the son of the Minister who concluded the Austro-German alliance gives official notification that the alliance has been torn up." The Journal des Débats said: " If Secretary Lansing answers the appeal made to him, it will be easy for him to say, 'There is no occasion to pursue the subject, as neither Austria-Hungary nor a common Minister of Foreign Affairs exists.'"

## SUPPLEMENTARY NOTE

The same day, Oct. 29, Count Andrassy had sent a supplementary note addressed directly to Mr. Lansing, Secretary of State, and asking for his personal intervention with President Wilson for an armistice on all fronts. The text, as telegraphed from Vienna via Basle, Switzerland, read as follows:

Immediately after having taken direction of the Ministry of Foreign Affairs and after the dispatch of the official answer to your note of Oct. 18, 1918, by which you were able to see that we accept all the points and principles laid down by President Wilson in his various declarations and are in complete accord with the efforts of President Wilson to prevent future wars and to create a League of Nations, we have taken preparatory measures, in order that Austrians and Hungarians may be able, according to their own desire and without being in any way hindered, to make a decision as to their future organization and to rule it.

Since the accession to power of Emperor-King Charles his immovable purpose has been to bring an end to the war. More than ever this is the desire of the sovereign of all the Austro-Hungarian peoples, who acknowledge that their future destiny can only be accomplished in a pacific world, by being freed from all disturbances, privations, and sorrows of war.

This is why I address you directly, Mr. Secretary of State, praying that you will have the goodness to intervene with the President of the United States in order that in the interest of humanity, as in the interest of all those who live in Austria-Hungary, an immediate armistice may be concluded on all fronts, and for an overture that immediate negotiations for peace will follow.

### SEMI-OFFICIAL STATEMENT

The following semi-official statement regarding the Austro-Hungarian Government's reply to President Wilson was issued at Vienna on Oct. 29:

Austria was obliged to conform to the methods of President Wilson, who had successively replied to the three members of the Triple Alliance, and act apart from her allies. The monarchy, which has formally adopted President's Wilson's line of action, shares his opinion, as was shown by the Emperor's manifesto to the peoples, which, in proclaiming the federalization of the monarchy, exceeded President Wilson's program.

However, the complete reorganization of Austria can only be carried out after an armistice. If Austria-Hungary has declared herself ready to enter into negotiations for an armistice and for peace, without awaiting the result of negotiations with other States, that does not necessarily signify an offer of a separate peace. It means that she is ready to act separately in the interests of the re-establishment of peace.

Austria-Hungary's offer to negotiate a separate peace caused anger and dismay in the German Reichstag, especially among members of the National Party, who held that such action was unnecessary, as the situation was assuming a form in which co-operation with Germany would be possible. In other German quarters a certain sense of relief was expressed, on the ground that Count Andrassy's action would leave Germany free to act in her own interest. A movement looking toward the joining of Austrian Germans with Germany was at the same time in evidence.

# How Austria-Hungary Signed the Armistice

Meanwhile revolution was agitating the whole of the Dual Empire, and its dissolution had begun. Emperor Charles and Empress Zita arrived in Vienna from their palace near Budapest on Sunday morning, Oct. 27, and the Emperor at once received Count Julius Andrassy, his new Foreign Minister, and Professor Lammasch, the Austrian Premier. The Premier was instructed to form a " liquidation Ministry " of impartial officers whose duty should be to bring about a speedy peace and transfer the reins of power from the imperial to the various National Governments during the transition period. At the same time orders were given for a military capitulation to General Diaz, the victorious Italian commander.

Toward the evening of Oct. 29 an Austrian officer was seen coming from the enemy trenches close to Serravalle, above Ala, in the Adige Valley. He bore a white flag, and several Italian officers advanced to meet him. He proved to be a Captain, who said he had come to discuss the steps necessary for an armistice. As he had no authoritative papers he was sent back with a message that a more fully accredited mission should be sent before the subject could be discussed. The next day a white flag was again hoisted, and at the head of a group that approached the Italian trenches appeared General von Weber, an Austrian corps commander. The party consisted of eight persons and included another General and naval and military officers.

There were also civilians, either diplomatic or Government representatives, and secretaries and typists.

They were treated with courtesy, and when General von Weber had formally stated his mission and shown that he was the bearer of proper credentials he and his party were driven in motor cars on Oct. 31 to the Villa Giusti, close to General Diaz's headquarters. At 9 o'clock in the morning General Badoglio, the Chief of Staff, drove with an escort of cavalry to the villa, and on his arrival all the troops present saluted and bugles were sounded.

Entering the villa, General Badoglio found all the Austrian mission standing in a line in the drawing room awaiting him. General von Weber was in full uniform, wearing the stars and ribbons of his orders. General Badoglio saluted him and upon seating himself asked the Austrian General his errand. General von Weber replied that he had come to ask the conditions upon which an armistice would be granted. General Badoglio answered that within an hour he would let him know the general lines of such an armistice contained in a written message. He then left the room, and the written message in question was at once sent to the villa.

Meanwhile telegrams were exchanged with Versailles, and during the afternoon the precise details under which an armistice would be granted were received from Signor Orlando, the Italian Prime Minister, and again in written form handed to General von Weber. During the evening one of the Austrian envoys left by motor car for Serravalle with a draft of the conditions to communicate to the Austrian Government.

## TEXT OF ARMISTICE

As a result of these pourparlers the following armistice was signed by General Diaz on Nov. 3, to go into effect at 3 o'clock Nov. 4:

*One*—The immediate cessation of hostilities by land, by sea, and by air.

*Two*—Total demobilization of the Austro-Hungarian Army and immediate withdrawal of all Austro-Hungarian forces operating on the front from the North Sea to Switzerland. Within Austro-Hungarian territory, limited as in Clause Three, below, there shall only be maintained as an organized military force a (?) reduced to pre-war effectiveness.

Half the divisional, corps, and army artillery and equipment shall be collected at points to be indicated by the Allies and United States of America for delivery to them, beginning with all such material as exists in the territories to be evacuated by the Austro-Hungarian forces.

*Three*—Evacuation of all territories invaded by Austro-Hungary since the beginning of the war.

Withdrawal within such periods as shall be determined by the Commander in Chief of the allied forces on each front of the Austro-Hungarian armies behind a line fixed as follows: From Pic Umbrail to the north of the Stelvio it will follow the crest of the Rhetian Alps up to the sources of the Adige and the Eisach, passing thence by Mounts Reschen and Brenner and the heights of Oetz and Zoaller. The line thence turns south, crossing Mount Toblach and meeting the present frontier Carnic Alps. It follows this frontier up to Mount Tarvis, and after Mount Tarvis the watershed of the Julian Alps by the Col of Predil, Mount Mangart, the Tricorno, (Terglou,) and the watershed of the Cols di Podberdo, Podlaniscam, and Idria. From this point the line turns southeast toward the Schneeberg, excludes the whole basin of the Save and its tributaries. From the Schneeberg it goes down toward the coast in such a way as to include Castua, Mattuglia, and Volosca in the evacuated territories.

It will also follow the administrative limits of the present province of Dalmatia, including in the north Lisarica and Trivania, and to the south territory limited by a line from the (Semigrand) Cape Planca to the summits of the watersheds eastward, so as to include in the evacuated area all the valleys and water courses flowing toward Sebenico, such as the Cicola, Kerka, Butisnica, and their tributaries. It will also include all the islands in the north and west of Dalmatia from Premuda, Selve, Ulbo, Scherda, Maon, Paga, and Puntadura, in the north, up to Meleda, in the south, embracing Santandrea, Busi, Lisa, Lesina, Tercola, Curzola, Cazza, and Lagosta, as well as the neighboring rocks and islets and passages, only excepting the islands of Great and Small Zirona, Bua, Solta, and Brazza.

All territory thus evacuated shall be occupied by the forces of the Allies and the United States of America.

All military and railway equipment of all kinds, including coal belonging to or within those territories to be left in situ and surrendered to the Allies, according to special orders given by the Commander in Chief of the forces of the associated powers on the different fronts. No new destruction, pillage, or requisition to be done by enemy troops in the territories to be evacuated by them and occupied by the forces of the associated powers.

*Four*—The Allies shall have the right of free movement over all road and rail and water ways in Austro-Hungarian territory and of the use of the necessary Austrian and Hungarian means of transportation. The armies of the associated powers shall occupy such strategic points in Austria-Hungary at times as they may deem necessary to enable them to conduct military operations or to maintain order.

They shall have the right of requisition on payment for the troops of the associated powers wherever they may be.

*Five*—Complete evacuation of all German troops within fifteen days, not only from the Italian and Balkan fronts, but from all Austro-Hungarian territory.

Internment of all German troops which have not left Austria-Hungary within the date.

*Six*—The administration of the evacuated territories of Austria-Hungary will be intrusted to the local authorities, under the control of the allied and associated armies of occupation.

*Seven*—The immediate repatriation without reciprocity of all allied prisoners of war and internal subjects of civil populations evacuated from their homes, on conditions to be laid down by the Commander in Chief of the forces of the associated powers on the various fronts. Sick and wounded who cannot be removed from evacuated territory will be cared for by Austro-Hungarian personnel, who will be left on the spot with the medical material required.

## NAVAL CONDITIONS

*One*—Immediate cessation of all hostilities at sea and definite information to be given as to the location and movements of all Austro-Hungarian ships.

Notification to be made to neutrals that freedom of navigation in all territorial waters is given to the naval and mercantile marine of the allied and associated powers, all questions of neutrality being waived.

*Two*—Surrender to the Allies and the United States of fifteen Austro-Hungarian submarines completed between the years 1910 and 1918, and of all German submarines which are in or may hereafter enter Austro-Hungarian territorial waters. All other Austro-Hungarian submarines to be paid off and completely disarmed and to remain under the supervision of the Allies and the United States.

*Three*—Surrender to the Allies and the United States with their complete armament and equipment of three battleships, three light cruisers, nine destroyers, twelve torpedo boats, one mine layer, six Danube monitors, to be designated by the Allies and the United States of America. All other surface warships, including river craft, are to be concentrated in Austro-Hungarian naval bases to be designated by the Allies and the United States of America and are to be paid off and completely disarmed and placed under the supervision of the Allies and the United States of America.

*Four*—Freedom of navigation to all warships and merchant ships of the allied and associated powers to be given in the Adriatic and up the River Danube and its tributaries in the territorial waters and territory of Austria-Hungary.

The Allies and associated powers shall have the right to sweep up all mine fields and obstructions, and the positions of these are to be indicated.

In order to insure the freedom of navigation on the Danube, the Allies and the United States of America shall be empowered to occupy or to dismantle all fortifications or defense works.

*Five*—The existing blockade conditions set up by the allied and associated powers are to remain unchanged and all Austro-Hungarian merchant ships found at sea are to remain liable to capture, save exceptions which may be made by a commission nominated by the Allies and the United States of America.

*Six*—All naval aircraft are to be concentrated and impactionized in Austro-Hungarian bases to be designated by the Allies and the United States of America.

*Seven*—Evacuation of all Italian coasts and of all ports occupied by Austria-Hungary outside their national territory and the abandonment of all floating craft, naval materials, equipment and materials for inland navigation of all kinds.

*Eight*—Occupation by the Allies and the United States of America of the land and sea fortifications and the islands which form the defenses and of the dockyards and arsenal at Pola.

*Nine*—All merchant vessels held by Austria-Hungary belonging to the Allies and associated powers to be returned.

*Ten*—No destruction of ships or materials to be permitted before evacuation, surrender, or restoration.

*Eleven*—All naval and mercantile marine prisoners of the allied and associated powers in Austro-Hungarian hands to be returned without reciprocity.

# Break-up of the Empire—The Emperor's Abdication

The irretrievable disaster of the Austro-Hungarian armies in Italy led swiftly to the dissolution of the Dual Empire. By the end of October the Hus-sarek Ministry at Vienna had resigned and the empire was already breaking up into independent States. Emperor Charles acquiesced in the inevitable by appointing Professor Lammasch as head of a liquidation Ministry to hand over the former imperial powers to the various national Governments.

Serious rioting took place in Budapest on Oct. 28 when the followers of Count Michael Karolyi sent a deputation to ask Archduke Joseph to appoint Karolyi Premier. This was the beginning of a swift and comparatively bloodless revolution that aimed to make Hungary a republic. On Oct. 30 a considerable body of revolted troops, armed with machine guns and munitions, made public demonstrations and acclaimed the new order. The troops were acting in agreement with the Hungarian National Assembly. Count Stephen Tisza, the former reactionary Hungarian Premier, was assassinated on Nov. 1 by three soldiers who entered his home in Budapest.

Announcement of the success of the revolution in Budapest was made in a message sent by Count Michael Karolyi to the Berliner Tageblatt. This read:

Revolution in Budapest and National Council took over Government. Military and police acknowledge National Council completely. Inhabitants rejoicing.
(Signed)   KAROLYI,
President National Council.

Count Karolyi announced to the Hungarian National Council on Nov. 2 that Emperor Charles had freed the Hungarian Government of its oath of fidelity and left it free to decide its future form of government. A republic was formally proclaimed on Nov. 16, with Karolyi as Governor.

Meanwhile Vienna had become the centre of a revolution which aimed to create "the German State of Austria" under a distinct Government. The movement began on Oct. 30 with a demonstration of students and workmen in front of the Parliament building, when President Dinghofer of the National Council announced from the steps of the Diet that the National Government would take over the whole administration the next day. "But without the Hapsburgs!" shouted the crowd. An officer in uniform then called on the officers to remove their imperial cockades, which was done "with enthusiasm," and the imperial standard, flying before the Parlia-

ment building, was hauled down upon the order of President Gross of the Austrian lower house. There were strong elements in favor of union with Germany under a republican form of government.

Similar movements of independence were in progress among other nationalities. The Galician Poles moved to join Poland, and the Galician Ruthenians desired to unite with the Ukraine. The Jugoslavs were planning to join Serbia, and the Croats, having seized Fiume, had started to revolt from the Magyars. The Czechs of Bohemia had already organized their republic, as related elsewhere in these pages.

The proclamation announcing the abdication of Charles V. as Emperor of Austria-Hungary was issued on Nov. 11 and read as follows:

Since my accession I have incessantly tried to rescue my peoples from this tremendous war. I have not delayed the re-establishment of constitutional rights or the opening of a way for the people to substantial national development. Filled with an unalterable love for my peoples I will not, with my person, be a hindrance to their free development. I acknowledge the decision taken by German Austria to form a separate State. The people has by its deputies taken charge of the Government. I relinquish every participation in the administration of the State. Likewise I have released the members of the Austrian Government from their offices. May the German Austrian people realize harmony from the new adjustment. The happiness of my peoples was my aim from the beginning. My warmest wishes are that an internal peace will be able to heal the wounds of this war.   (Signed)   CHARLES.
(Countersigned)   LAMMASCH.

After signing his abdication the ex-Emperor and his family went in an automobile to his castle at Eckhartsau, fifteen miles away, where he remained for some time in retirement.

The most disturbing element everywhere was the lawlessness of the radical "Green Guards," who gained many dangerous recruits from the hundreds of thousands of hungry soldiers from the battlefronts. By the last week in November some portions of the former empire were reported in a state bordering on chaos.

# Turkey's Surrender to the Allies

## Text of the Terms Under Which Turkey Laid Down Her Arms on Oct. 31, 1918

TURKEY was the second of the Central Powers to surrender to the Allies. General Allenby's capture of Damascus and his rout of two Turkish armies at the end of September and beginning of October opened the way to Aleppo and to final Turkish defeat. His British cavalry and armored cars entered Aleppo on Saturday morning, Oct. 26, and cut off the Turkish traffic on the Constantinople-Bagdad railway at that point. This railroad, the artery that fed the Turkish forces opposing General Marshall on the Tigris and Euphrates, had already been cut off from Berlin by the surrender of Bulgaria. On Oct. 29 General Marshall's forces on the Tigris, after a stubborn fight, defeated the Turks at Kaleh Sherghat and cut off their communications with Mosul. The main objectives of both the Mesopotamian and Palestine expeditions had been attained. The remaining Turkish forces were checkmated and helpless.

Turkey laid down her arms on Oct. 31, 1918, after signing an armistice which, like that of Bulgaria a month before, was tantamount to unconditional surrender.

The armistice was signed at Mudros, on the Island of Lemnos, in the Aegean Sea, and one of the leading actors in the preliminary events was General Townshend, the British commander who had surrendered to the Turks at Kul-el-Amara two years and a half before. When the Turkish authorities saw that their cause was lost they liberated General Townshend and sent him to inform the British Admiral in command in the Aegean Sea that they wished to open immediate negotiations for an armistice. The British replied that if the Turkish Government sent fully accredited plenipotentiaries, Vice Admiral Calthorp, the British commander, was empowered to inform them of the conditions upon which the Allies would agree to stop hostilities and could sign an armistice on these conditions in their behalf. The Turkish plenipotentiaries arrived at Mudros, and after three days of parley, concerning which General Allenby as well as the Entente Governments were kept fully informed, the armistice was signed on the evening of Oct. 30, to take effect at noon the next day.

Meanwhile the hard fighting on the Tigris, which had begun on Oct. 24, had ended on the 30th with the capture of the entire Turkish force on that river. The prisoners were estimated at 7,000, with much material. Ismail Hakki had surrendered with one entire division and the best part of two others.

### TERMS OF ARMISTICE

The terms imposed upon Turkey by the allied powers were as follows:

*First*—The opening of the Dardanelles and the Bosporus and access to the Black Sea. Allied occupation of the Dardanelles and Bosporus forts.

*Second*—The positions of all minefields, torpedo tubes, and other obstructions in Turkish waters are to be indicated and assistance given to sweep or remove them, as may be required.

*Third*—All available information concerning mines in the Black Sea is to be communicated.

*Fourth*—All allied prisoners of war and Armenian interned persons and prisoners are to be collected in Constantinople and handed over unconditionally to the Allies.

*Fifth*—Immediate demobilization of the Turkish Army, except such troops as are required for surveillance on the frontiers and for the maintenance of internal order; the number of effectives and their disposition to be determined later by the Allies, after consultation with the Turkish Government.

*Sixth*—The surrender of all war vessels in Turkish waters or waters occupied by Turkey. These ships will be interned in such Turkish port or ports as may be directed, except such small vessels as are required for police and similar purposes in Turkish territorial waters.

*Seventh*—The Allies to have the right to occupy any strategic points in the event of any situation arising which threatens the security of the Allies.

*Eighth*—Free use by allied ships of all ports and anchorages now in Turkish occupation and denial of their use by the enemy. Similar conditions are to apply to Turkish mercantile shipping in Turkish waters for the purposes of trade and the demobilization of the army.

*Ninth*—Allied occupation of the Taurus Tunnel system.

*Tenth*—Immediate withdrawal of Turkish troops from Northern Persia to behind the pre-war frontier already has been ordered and will be carried out.

*Eleventh*—A part of Transcaucasia already has been ordered to be evacuated by Turkish troops. The remainder to be evacuated if required by the Allies after they have studied the situation.

*Twelfth*—Wireless, telegraph, and cable stations to be controlled by the Allies. Turkish Government messages to be excepted.

*Thirteenth*—Prohibition against the destruction of any naval, military, or commercial material.

*Fourteenth*—Facilities are to be given for the purchase of coal, oil fuel, and naval material from Turkish ' sources, after the requirements of the country have been met. None of the above materials is to be exported.

*Fifteenth*—The surrender of all Turkish officers in Tripolitania and Cyrenica to the nearest Italian garrison. Turkey agrees to stop supplies to and communication with these officers if they do not obey the order to surrender.

*Sixteenth*—The surrender of all garrisons in Hedjaz, Assir, Yemen, Syria, and Mesopotamia to the nearest allied commander ,and withdrawal of Turkish troops from Cilicia, except those necessary to maintain order, as will be determined under Clause 5.

*Seventeenth*—The use of all ships and repair facilities at all Turkish ports and arsenals.

*Eighteenth*—The surrender of all ports occupied in Tripolitania and Cyrenica, including Misurata, to the nearest allied garrison.

*Nineteenth*—All Germans and Austrians, naval, military, or civilian, to 'be evacuated within one month from Turkish dominions, and those in remote districts as soon after that time as may be possible.

*Twentieth*—Compliance with such orders as may be conveyed for the disposal of equipments, arms, and ammunition, including the transport of that portion of the Turkish Army which is demobilized under Clause 5.

*Twenty-first*—An allied representative to be attached to the Turkish Ministry of Supplies, in order to safeguard allied interests; this representative to be furnished with all aid necessary for this purpose.

*Twenty-second*—Turkish prisoners are to be kept at the disposal of the allied powers. The release of Turkish civilian prisoners and prisoners over military age to be considered.

*Twenty-third*—An obligation on the part of Turkey to cease all relations with the Central Powers.

*Twenty-fourth*—In case of disorder in the six Armenian vilayets, the Allies reserve to themselves the right to occupy any part of them.

*Twenty-fifth*—Hostilities between the Allies and Turkey shall cease from noon, local time, Thursday, the 31st of October, 1918.

An additional clause, made public two days later, dealt with the Russian region of the Caucasus, as follows:

Allied control officers are to be placed on all railways, including such portions of the Transcaucasian railways as are now under Turkish control; these must be placed at the free and complete disposal of the allied authorities, due consideration being given to the needs of the population. This clause is to include the allied occupation of Batum. Turkey will raise no objection to the occupation of Baku by the Allies.

## EVENTS IN TRANSCAUCASIA

This supplementary clause relates to the chaotic situation in Transcaucasia. Ever since the Bolshevist revolution in Russia the region between the Black and Caspian Seas had been a storm centre. To save themselves from the anarchy that spread over the rest of Russia the peoples of this region had organized the Federal Republic of the Caucasus in the Autumn of 1917. The Government consisted of Tartars, Georgians, and Armenians, representing 5,500,000 inhabitants and an area of 250,000 square kilometers. To these were added nearly 200,000 Armenian refugees from Turkey. The new organization succeeded for a time in preserving order; but when the Bolshevist Government at Petrograd undertook to hand over the districts of Batum, Kars, and Erivan to Turkey, a crisis arose, and serious differences developed between the Tartars and Armenians, weakening the Governmental control.

Not content with Batum and the other regions designated in the treaty, Turkey sent a force from Tiflis about July 20,

1918, to seize the oil wells of Baku, on the Caspian Sea. Baku was defended by small contingents of Armenians and Russian Bolshevists, who in this case were on the side of the Allies; and these

CAUCASUS REGION, CONTROL OF WHICH WAS ASSUMED BY THE ENTENTE ALLIES

were joined on Aug. 15 by a small British force, which had come all the way from India, by way of Persia. A month later, however, the British had to withdraw. A British report laid the blame for this withdrawal upon the instability of the Armenian contingent at Baku, and this charge, later declared unjust, gave rise to two interesting official letters, which are reproduced at the end of this article.

A German-Bolshevist treaty, signed Aug. 27, left Baku definitely to the Russians, but the Turks, who were already quarreling with the Bulgarians over other items of the spoils, proceeded shortly afterward to take possession of the city and its rich oil trade. Here they remained until the Turkish collapse. A Moscow dispatch of Oct. 30 announced that they had evacuated Baku without fighting. The supplementary clause in the armistice of Oct. 31 closed this chapter by placing both Baku and Batum in the hands of the Allies.

### EFFECTS OF SURRENDER

George Nicoll Barnes, a member of the British War Cabinet, stated on Nov. 1 that the armistice with Turkey could have been signed earlier, but that the Allies were committed to a free Arab State under the King of the Hedjaz, with Aleppo as the capital, and that there had been no hurry to get Turkey

out of the war until after Aleppo and other places necessary to this project had been captured. He added that the British had for some time been assembling ships at the mouth of the Dardanelles, and that these had already started through the strait. A large fleet of mine sweepers was at work clearing the Dardanelles of the maze of mines and other obstructions that barred the way through the Bosporus to the Black Sea. Mr. Barnes added:

There is now nothing to prevent the fleet from going into the Black Sea and up the Danube to Germany's back door, and if the Germans are going to defend their territory they must divide their remaining forces between the western front and the back door, at which we shall soon be knocking.

### PALESTINE PERMANENTLY FREE

Lord Robert Cecil, Assistant Foreign Secretary, on the same day emphatically denied a published assertion that a secret agreement had been signed with Turkey which would restore Ottoman sovereignty in Armenia, Syria, and Palestine. He said:

There is no secret undertaking, engagement, or bargain of any sort or kind, as far as the British Government is concerned. Nothing concerning territorial arrangement has been settled at all. I cannot conceive of any solution that would leave these nationalities under the shadow of Turkish oppression.

He was particularly emphatic in his allusions to the Armenians, and pointed out that two clauses of the armistice terms especially provided for their protection, and the Allies had reserved the right to occupy their vilayets in case of disorder. "The armistice terms," he went on, "amount to unconditional surrender, and especially important is our right to occupy the Taurus tunnel system." Lord Robert added that nothing in the armistice would hamper the Allies in making such disposition of European Turkey as they wished at the peace conference.

Turkey entered the war in November, 1914. For her unprovoked bombardment of Sebastopol Russia declared war on her on Nov. 3; France and Great Britain two days later. Turkey issued a formal declaration of war against the Entente

THE TURKISH EMPIRE, WHOSE FATE IS TO BE DETERMINED AT THE PEACE CONFERENCE

Allies on Nov. 23, 1914. Meanwhile, however, military operations had begun against Turkey on Nov. 5, and Great Britain had annexed the Island of Cyprus.

Turkey entered the war a few weeks after the German warships Breslau and Goeben had sought shelter in the Dardanelles, which was at once blockaded by the allied fleet. In April, 1915, allied troops were landed on the Gallipoli Peninsula, but the campaign failed and the allied troops were withdrawn in December of the same year. The British began a campaign up the Tigris in November, 1914. They advanced to within nineteen miles of Bagdad a year later, but were defeated and forced to retreat to Kut-el-Amara, where they were later forced to surrender. Early in 1917 the British renewed the offensive in Mesopotamia and continued it successfully until they were within a few miles of Mosul at the time of the armistice.

Turkey sent armies against the British in Egypt and against the Russians in the Caucasus. The Egyptian campaign failed in February, 1915. That in the Caucasus was driven back by the Russians through Armenia. In Palestine the allied drive under General Allenby resulted in the clearing of the whole country and the capture of the impor-

tant base of Aleppo. The Russian campaign in the Caucasus was rendered fruitless by the rise of the Bolsheviki to power.

For several weeks after the United States declared war on Germany Turkey took no action, but on April 21, 1917, she severed diplomatic relations. There was, however, no declaration of war by either country.

## ARMENIA'S SERVICE TO THE ALLIED CAUSE

The following correspondence, embracing a plea by Lord Bryce for justice to the Armenian people and a reply by the British Secretary for Foreign Affairs recognizing the services rendered by the Armenians to the allied cause, contains also an official declaration that the Allies' policy toward them remains unaltered:

Hindleap, Forest Row, Sussex,
Sept. 30, 1918.

My Dear Balfour: Boghos Nubar Pasha, (the son of old Nubar,) who is the head of the Armenian National Council in Paris, has sent me a copy of the communication which that council has addressed to you, expressing a wish that I would support its request that his Majesty's Government should, if possible, do something to remove the painful impression which has been created by the terms of the statement regarding the conduct of the Armenians at Baku. Those terms have greatly distressed the Armenians in England also.

I need not repeat the arguments contained in the letter of the Armenian National Delegation, but may observe that through the whole course of the war the Armenian people as a whole have both done and suffered what well entitles them to our sympathy and consideration. Some 700,000 or more have been massacred because the Turks and Germans assumed them to be in sympathy with the Allies. They have enlisted in large numbers both in France and in America, and many were anxious to serve in the force which we at one time thought of landing at Alexandretta, near which there was a large Armenian population, now nearly exterminated.

In the French armies they have distinguished themselves by their exceptional valor. During the earlier years of the war they were the best fighters in the Russian Army of the Caucasus, and chiefly contributed to the capture of Erzerum. When the Bolsheviki abandoned the Caucasian provinces they held out heroically alone, having been deserted by the Russian troops, defending themselves and their districts till overwhelming enemy forces compelled them to make terms at Erivan, where they were entirely without support. I believe that there and at Baku they had little or no artillery.

It would be a grave discouragement to the Armenians both in France and in European Russia, who are doing their best for the allied cause, if it were supposed that we are placing a stigma on the Armenian Nation as a whole. Very sincerely yours, BRYCE.

### LORD R. CECIL'S REPLY

Foreign Office, Oct. 3, 1918.

MY DEAR LORD BRYCE: Mr. Balfour has been much concerned at the view taken by Boghos Nubar Pasha, in his letter to him to which you refer, regarding the communiqué reporting the events at Baku, and asks me to reply in his name.

The Baku Armenians were not only an isolated remnant, but no doubt their task was made impossible from the outset by the disorganization which prevailed and had thrown open to the Turks the Transcaucasian Railway leading to the gates of the city. Whatever may have happened at Baku, the responsibility cannot be laid at the door of the Armenian people.

The National Delegation, commissioned by his Holiness the Katholikos in 1913 to obtain from the civilized world that justice to Armenia which has been delayed with such terrible consequences, have given many proofs, under the distinguished Presidency of his Excellency Boghos Nubar Pasha, of their devotion to the cause of the Allies, as being the cause of all peoples striving to free the world from oppression.

The Council at Erivan threw itself into the breach which the Russian breakdown left open in Asia, and after organizing resistance to the Turks in the Caucasus from February to June this year, was at length compelled by main force to suspend hostilities. Great Britain and her allies understand the cruel necessity which has forced the Armenians to take this step, and look forward to the time, perhaps not far distant, when allied victories may reverse their undeserved misfortunes.

Meanwhile, the services of the Armenians to the common cause, to which you refer in your letter, have assuredly not been forgotten; and I venture to mention four points which the Armenians may, I think, regard as the charter of their right to liberation at the hand of the Allies:

(1) In the Autumn of 1914 the Turks sent emissaries to the National Congress of the Ottoman Armenians then siting at Erzerum and made them offers of autonomy if they would actively assist Turkey in the war. The Armenians replied that they would do their duty individually as Ottoman subjects, but that as a nation they could not work for the cause of Turkey and her allies.

(2) On account, in part, of this courageous refusal, the Ottoman Armenians were systematically murdered by the Turkish Government in 1915. Two-thirds of the population were exterminated by the most cold-blooded and fiendish methods—more than 700,000 people, men, women, and children alike.

(3) From the beginning of the war that half of the Armenian Nation which was under the sovereignty of Russia organized volunteer forces, and, under their heroic leader Andranik, bore the brunt of some of the heaviest fighting in the Caucasian campaigns.

(4) After the breakdown of the Russian Army at the end of last year these Armenian forces took over the Caucasian front, and for five months delayed the advance of the Turks, thus rendering an important service to the British Army in Mesopotamia. These operations, in the region of Alexandropol and Erivan, were, of course, unconnected with those at Baku.

I may add that Armenian soldiers are still fighting in the ranks of the allied forces in Syria. They are to be found serving alike in the British, French, and American Armies, and they have borne their part in General Allenby's great victory in Palestine.

Need I say, after this, that the policy of the Allies toward Armenia remains unaltered? If your letter and Nubar Pasha's make it necessary for the British Government to do so, I am quite ready to reaffirm our determination that wrongs such as Armenia has suffered shall be brought to an end and their recurrence made impossible. Yours sincerely, ROBERT CECIL.

### ABOLISHING TURKISH RULE

France and Great Britain issued a formal announcement on Nov. 7, 1918, that it was their intention to abolish Turkish oppression forever in the countries of the Eastern Mediterranean and to establish

Governments deriving their authority from the free choice of the native populations. The statement, made public through the British and French legations at Washington, was as follows:

The aim of France and Great Britain in carrying on in the Near East the war let loose by Germany's ambitions is the complete and final liberation of the peoples so long oppressed by the Turks and the establishment of Governments and administrations deriving their authority from the initiative and the free choice of the native populations.

In view of following out this intention, France and Great Britain are agreed to encourage and hold the establishment of native Governments and administrations in Syria and Mesopotamia actually liberated by the Allies, and in the territories they are now striving to liberate, and to recognize them as soon as effectively established.

Far from seeking to force upon the populations of these countries any particular institution, France and Great Britain have no other concern than to insure by their support and their active assistance the normal working of the Governments and institutions which the populations shall have freely adopted, so as to secure just impartiality for all, and also to facilitate the economic development of the country in arousing and encouraging local initiative by the diffusion of instruction, and to put an end to discords which have too long been taken advantage of by Turkish rule.

Such is the rôle that the two allied Governments claim for themselves in the liberated territories.

Dispatches at the same time announced the transfer of British and French troops to occupy the Dardanelles and Bosporus.

# Story of the Capture of Damascus
## By W. T. MASSEY

*Mr. Massey, as British official war correspondent with Allenby's army in Palestine and Syria, witnessed the brilliant operations that put Turkey out of the war. In the November number of* CURRENT HISTORY MAGAZINE *some extracts were given from his narrative of the early stages of the British offensive. Reviewing the later operations, toward the end of September, 1918, Mr. Massey wrote:*

OUR progress was rapid, and the extent of our advance, on a very wide front, is so great that it may be the impression at home that we were weakly opposed. That would be wholly wrong. A document which has been captured shows that the ration strength of the Eighth Army was 39,783 men, of the Seventh Army 28,575, of the Jordan Group 5,223, and of the Fourth Army 21,899. On the lines of communication were 4,958 men, and of animals there were 39,234.

These figures may be exaggerated. But it is clear that General Allenby was opposed by an army of over 100,000, who, at any rate in places, fought strongly, and at times got to grips both with bomb and bayonet. The prisoners exceed 70,000. The dead I believe are not more than 10,000. Many got away home by other roads.

It will take some time to collect all the facts to show the completeness of General Allenby's victory, but sufficient data are available demonstrating how absolute has been the annihilation of the Turkish forces.

We have learned much from captured documents illustrating the strength of the enemy opposed to us. In the equipment of the Turkish Army large support was given by the Germans. In the Yilderim army group there were 509 guns, including thirty in the repair shops. Of the balance we have captured over 350 of various calibres. There has not been time to search the hundreds of square miles of mountainous country, but doubtless others are hidden in the hills with many hundreds of machine guns and an enormous amount of gun ammunition.

With the Turks were 15,635 Germans, including several battalions of infantry, machine-gun companies, artillery, and the remainder technical troops running the railways, transport, signal service,

&c. There was thus a large stiffening of Germans, with many technicians, and they were generally found wherever the enemy put up a strong resistance. The prisoners include a large number of Germans and Austrians.

The sheiks of the Ruwalla tribe, one of the most powerful in Arabia, brought 3,000 horsemen and the Haurani peasantry others, so that when near Deraa there was a force of 11,000 camelry, horsemen, and Arab irregulars with the column, which on Sept. 16 got to the Hedjas Railway, south of Deraa, and blew up the line.

Next day the north town was destroyed, with six kilometers of railway and an important bridge. On the night of the 18th they cut the line between Deraa and Nablus, in the Yarmuk Valley, burning the station of Mezerib and the rolling stock, with six German lorries. The following day they moved south of Deraa, having made a complete circle round the town, and blew up the bridge. An armored car saw two airplanes and riddled them with bullets.

## FREQUENT BOMBING RAIDS

As the line was repaired it was again destroyed, so that the enemy's railway communication between Damascus and the main Turkish Army was broken for five days. The Amman garrison was cut off for eight days. Wherever the Arabs camped enemy planes bombed them, flying low and using machine guns. At one period near Deraa the enemy planes made frequent bombing raids, but were ineffectual to prevent the complete disorganization of the railway service. When General Allenby's attack began the Arabs fought their way up the railway line. One section, under Shereef Nasser, marched seventy miles in twenty-four hours, fighting part of the way, and reached the outskirts of Damascus on Sept. 30.

The work of the Air Service has been most praiseworthy. The difficulty of the cavalry keeping contact with the vast front has been overcome by the untiring energies of the airmen. One pilot for four days had an average of eight hours each flying day, and on occasions had to fly low, subjected to heavy machine-gun fire. His machine returned from one expedition with seventy-four bullet holes, but was unhit in any vital part. Our planes south of Amman secured the surrender of 2,000 Turks. The pilot, seeing a long-drawn-out column, dropped a message to say that if they did not surrender they would be bombed. He returned to the aerodrome and six machines shortly afterward were sent out with bombs, and while circling the ground the signal was laid out recalling them; the Turks had hoisted the white flag.

## CAVALRY'S ACHIEVEMENTS

*Mr. Massey paid this tribute to the work of the cavalry around Damascus in his dispatch of Sept. 30:*

The operations of the last few days afford an illustration that the rôle of cavalry in present-day warfare over a front so wide as this makes it almost impossible to keep touch with the daily movements. General Allenby's mounted troops are being supremely successful, never missing an opportunity of hitting hard and swiftly, following up one big movement immediately by another equally vigorous, until the three cavalry divisions have today converged on Damascus. Troops from the Northern and Southern Hemispheres are now looking on the most ancient of living cities. Masses of British Yeomanry and Australian and Indian Horse, a force larger probably than was ever before assembled under one command, have outmanoeuvred the Turkish forces, dealing the death blow to the Seventh and Eighth Armies before attacking the Fourth Army over the Jordan. Only those who have seen the superb cavalry of General Allenby's army could appreciate the possibilities, and not many of those in Palestine dreamed it was possible that Damascus was within reach of the wide stretch of the cavalry arm.

In ten days the mounted troops have covered fully 150 miles, in a country that yielded no food for man or beast, and are now practically surrounding the white city, set in a most beautiful green frame. The glorious gardens, rendered more refreshing to eyes used to the glare of the

Eastern sun by comparison with the desolate, stony hills overlooking the verdant scene from all sides, are momentarily put to military uses by the enemy. In the mud-walled garden inclosures are nests of machine guns which at present we have not attempted to disturb. There are obvious signs that the Turk's days of possession of the city are numbered. Since the morning the enemy has been burning vast stores, and there have been numerous explosions of ammunition and petrol. Military establishments are ablaze, and the enormous wireless installation for communication with Constantinople and Berlin has been blown up. From the position of the fires it is believed that the two railway stations have been destroyed.

## FIRES IN DAMASCUS

So far the city seems to have escaped, though with the high wind the huge fires are dangerous, the city being built mainly of wood. Every soldier looking on the city hopes it will be preserved, but it would be in keeping with the blighting influence of the Turk on everything he touches if by his action Damascus, which has changed hands many times in the 4,000 years of its life, should be destroyed for the first time by the Turks. Happily, that fate appears to be unlikely.

As a preliminary to jumping off for this jeweled goal, a portion of the cavalry moved to Deraa with orders to advance up the eastern road. A larger column took Tiberias and secured the bridge over the Jordan south of Lake Hule. The blowing up of the central arch of the ancient structure did not prevent the crossing, owing to the swimming of the river by an entire Australian regiment. Yesterday the cavalry halted at Kuneitra while supplies were brought over the steep, winding road from the Jordan Valley, many miles of which are absolutely the worst surface in the world for highways. It is a mass of unrolled lava boulders strewn in the roadway. Progress was extremely difficult for wheels, but the cavalry's spirit surmounted all obstacles.

As the sun was setting last night the move forward from Kuneitra began with the weird and impressive spectacle of thousands of horsemen passing in the darkness. There was no sound save the horses' hoofbeats and the rumble of wheels. The Australian Mounted Division led, the Yeomanry and Indian cavalry following. Hardly any part of the country was visible in the gloom, except where the irregular crest of Mount Hermon blotted out the stars. Less than a dozen miles on the journey a brisk action delayed the advance for three hours. They were precious hours, for we knew that what remained of the Fourth Army was trekking north to Deraa, partially disorganized and with scanty transport, and we were anxious to bag the whole lot.

On the steep, rough hills overlooking the road, with a wadi in front, several hundred Turks and Germans waited with machine guns, with a couple of field guns well placed to cover the road. They had the advantage of the light of the waning moon. We got them in flank with a few casualties, and took prisoners. Those escaping up the hill were captured early in the morning. The German machine gunners were greatly surprised by the rapidity of our advance. At 8 o'clock our troops on the western road reached the southwestern edge of the hills holding Damascus in their hollow. There was one small but effective charge on the plateau, and strong opposition athwart the road at Kaukeb, ten miles from Damascus, the enemy striving hard to delay our advance until the destruction of the stores in the city's environs was complete.

## IN SIGHT OF THE GOAL

At noon there was a spirited mounted attack at Kaukeb by the Australian Light Horse, who overrode the enemy in a brilliant charge, and enabled the brigade's cavalry to ride forward along the road west of the city and pursue the enemy attempting to get away on the Rayak road. This advance, within visual range of the Damascus minarets, has already yielded many prisoners. The regiment of Light Horse and one of French cavalry are just sending in 3,500 between them, while the Australian brigade brought machine guns into action on two hills dominating the road and killed all the transport animals and many men who blocked the road. Another force went across country to intercept parties of Turks retiring on Damascus in front of Deraa and heavily shelled the enemy before they reached the villages on the southern outskirts of the city.

*Damascus itself was captured on Oct. 1, and that day Mr. Massey wrote:*

General Allenby's triumphant march northward into Syria early this morning drove the Turks completely out of possession of Damascus, and there is now not a Turkish soldier in the city nor a Turkish official doing duty. The appearance of the Australian Mounted Division northwestward of the city at noon yesterday set the seal on the doom of the Turkish Government in the place on which Arabs centre their eyes. Today the city was enveloped by British, Australian, and Indian troops, and the King of the Hedjaz's Arab army has marched in. The few Turks who got away are scattered and demoralized. Fully 12,000 Germans and Turks are prisoners. In and about the city a number of guns have been captured. The roads are a shambles where the enemy resisted. Transport has been smashed and most of the material left behind has been destroyed by the Germans, though some valuable transport, including a complete park of cavalry limbers, was untouched. The prisoners captured since Sept. 19 are probably more than 60,000.

## AN AMAZING WELCOME

I was under the impression that Damascus would display the usual Arab calmness of demeanor and accept our appearance as Kismet, while appreciating the prospect of a change from bad to good government, and would receive us with their customary immobile features, giving no outward and visible sign of their inward feelings.

I rode into the town with an armored-car officer when the road was deemed unsafe owing to snipers in those luscious gardens surrounding this fascinating and truly Oriental city. I was amazed at the heartiness of the welcome accorded the British uniform. The people were far from taking our victory as an ordi-

nary incident of life. They threw off their stolid exterior, and received us with ecstatic joy. They closed their shops and made a holiday, put on festival dress, and acclaimed the day as the greatest in the 4,000 years of the history of Damascus. Only a few British officers have as yet entered the city, but each has been received with the same whole-hearted fervor. Here, at least, they have seen what the British name stands for. At Jerusalem the British Army was welcomed by all sects and creeds with deep feelings of thankfulness, but their condition, rendered pitiable through starvation, prevented their welcome from being so demonstrative, though equally sincere, as today's. When a soldier appeared in the streets of Damascus he was surrounded by the excited and delighted throng. Crowds gathered to hear the news. When I told some English-speaking people, of whom there are many, of the latest victory on the western front and of the Bulgarian armistice their enthusiasm was remarkable.

But they were more keenly interested in General Allenby's army's tremendous stride through Palestine and Syria. The enormous captures of prisoners and war material, of which they had no conception, more than anything else, meant to them the finish of the Turk. They said: " You are settling our long accounts with them." The thoroughness with which it has been done gave them the impression that our army was composed of supermen. With eyes unused to complete and orderly equipment, they admired the soldierly turnout of the men who have fought and ridden a hard 150 miles, and acclaimed them their deliverers. They looked upon this army as the saviors of the downtrodden peoples of this part of the East. This amazing tribute to Britain and British freedom lasted all day; at nightfall the population gave a firework exhibition of captured Verey lights. Even the street of St. Paul called " Straight " was illuminated from end to end.

The opportunities for rejoicing were increased by the arrival of the Arab Army, which operated on our right flank. Our cavalry during the march from Deraa arrived at Damascus at 6 this morning, the northwestern outskirts being occupied by the Australian Mounted Division last night. Soon after daybreak the Arab Army entered the city, and the streets became alive with picturesquely clothed Arabs on light steeds, almost overburdened with elaborately appointed saddlery. Arab horsemen and camelry dashed about the streets, proclaiming the victory and making much noise and continually firing their rifles. This lasted till midnight, and the inhabitants, tired out and happy, allowed the city to become normally calm.

### REJOICING IN BEIRUT

*Beirut was taken by a French naval force on Oct. 7, and shortly afterward was entered by a division of Allenby's forces. The relief of the inhabitants at redemption from Turkish control was equal to that of the people of Damascus. Mr. Massey thus described it:*

Of all the scenes of war I have witnessed, nothing impressed me more than the extraordinary demonstrations of welcome accorded the infantry advance up the coast to Beirut. When our Expeditionary Force first landed in France I saw the French people's expression of thankfulness and relief at our troops' assistance. Their outward and visible signs of joy were eclipsed by Syria, where all classes and creeds united to acclaim the British and Indian infantry as deliverers of the land from the oppressive rule of centuries. Ancient Acre and Tyre threw off their customary calm, but not till Saida—Sidon of old— was reached did the population show their real feelings. When the Yeomanry approached, the people rushed to tear down palm leaves to build triumphal arches, decorate houses, and hang out carpets.

The infantry in Saida the next day could not pass through the streets, choked with the population, till the people had passed to the balconies and roofs of the houses, where they stayed all day, cheering deliriously, untired, and devoutly thankful. Other towns were equally enthusiastic. When the corps commander entered Beirut the people threw flowers and sprayed perfumes in front of his car. Whenever a British uniform is seen the crowds surround it, shout in English, "Hooray," and clap hands. British prestige has never stood higher. The exemplary behavior of our splendid troops is commented upon everywhere. The population regard them as the vanguard of a glorious and chivalrous army bringing a new and enlightened rule of freedom, justice, and liberty.

The infantry's march from Haifa was a splendid achievement. The division of Scottish, English, and Indian troops which was the first in Bagdad was the first infantry in Beirut. The Hertford and Lancashire Yeomanry entered the town yesterday, while a British armored car had been in the previous day. French warships were in the port.

The infantry in seven days marched 100 miles from Haifa, making roads half the way, and joining the metaled highway north of Tyre. Only those who have been with the infantry can appreciate the magnitude of the march. Mere tracks were converted into roads. One colossal obstacle, in which a series of steps was cut in rock, was made into a road for wheels in three days.

## Democracy

### By WILLIAM MILL BUTLER

Great mother of a new-born race,
All earth shall be thy dwelling place;
Democracy, thy holy name
Shall set the continents aflame,
Shall thrill the islands of the sea,
And keep thy children ever free.

[PUBLICATION AUTHORIZED BY THE SECRETARY OF THE NAVY, HON. JOSEPHUS DANIELS]

# Overseas Transportation of United States Troops

### By Commander CHARLES C. GILL, U. S. N.

[*Approved by Rear Admiral Albert Gleaves, Commander of the Cruiser and Transport Force, United States Atlantic Fleet*]

PREVIOUS to 1916 the idea of a United States overseas expeditionary force numbered by millions would have been generally regarded as a remote if not impossible contingency. Consequently no extensive peace-time preparations had been made for such an undertaking. The task of providing a transport fleet was, therefore, a pioneer work. Ships had to be obtained, officers and crews enrolled and trained. It was necessary to provide docks, storehouses, lighters and tugs, coaling equipment, repair facilities, and all the varied machinery for operating and maintaining a large transportation service. An efficient administrative organization had to be developed.

Such, in brief, was the problem confronting Rear Admiral Albert Gleaves, then Commander of the Destroyer Force of the Atlantic Fleet, when, on May 29, 1917, he received orders designating him Commander of United States Convoy Operations in the Atlantic in addition to his other duties.

The work of the navy in connection with the transportation of troops to France constitutes a distinct phase of the present war. The attending political and military circumstances incident to the collapse of Russia, the critical situation on the western front, and the threat of the German submarine combined to make this phase of special significance. Throughout the year following the entry of the United States into the war the military and naval developments were such that the safe transportation across the Atlantic of troops and supplies became a problem of more and more pressing importance.

The United States Army in France was a decisive factor in obtaining speedy victory. The transportation of this army overseas under naval protection was, therefore, a major operation of first importance. A large share of this urgent mission devolved on the United States Navy, and its successful accomplishment in the face of great difficulties is another page to the record of the service in keeping with its past history and traditions.

Much confusion of thought has existed as to just how the vast work of transporting a United States Army numbering 2,079,880 souls to Europe has been accomplished. It is unfortunate that misinformation should be disseminated respecting an operation in which the different organizations concerned performed their respective functions in utmost harmony and co-operation.* All have done their allotted parts splendidly and efficiently. All share in the satisfaction resulting from the successful accomplishment of a difficult and urgent undertaking.

At the time the United States entered the war the enormous toll of shipping gathered by the U-boat in the East Atlantic and the boast of von Hindenburg that the submarine blockade of England would starve her out and win the war, indicate the seriousness of the naval situation in those waters at that

---

*As an instance of more or less prevalent misinformation: Recently in the press reference was made by high authority to " Seven great British liners which have carried 60 per cent. of the American soldiers abroad since March." The actual figures are:

Total United States soldiers carried since the end of March, 1918, 1,505,624.

The seven largest ships of a foreign ally carried in all 10.37 per cent. of the above total. In the same period a single ship of the United States naval transport service carried 5 per cent. of the total.

time. Inasmuch as the principal field of British naval activities was the North Sea and English Channel, the task of breaking the U-boat blockade in the Atlantic naturally became the immediate mission of the United States Navy. The prompt dispatching of destroyers, yachts, and all other available craft of a type useful against the submarine to the East Atlantic, and the splendid work these vessels and others later sent to augment their strength have done in cleaning up these waters of U-boat devastation is a matter of record, the importance of which in winning the war is conceded from all quarters. This was the first step in preparation for sending the United States Army overseas.

The next step was the development of the transport service and the convoy and escort system. In this work the Cruiser and Transport Force co-operated with the destroyers and other anti-submarine craft abroad. In addition, Great Britain, France, and Italy supplied troop ships. As would be expected from Great Britain's enormous merchant marine, she was able to supply the greatest carrying capacity. She had the ships ready for this use, and 48¼ per cent. of the American Army was transported in British steamers; 2½ per cent. were carried in French ships, and 3 per cent. in Italian. The remaining 46¼ per cent. were carried in United States ships, and all but 2½ per cent. of these sailed in United States naval transports.

All the troops carried in United States ships were escorted by United States men-of-war; that is, cruisers, destroyers, converted yachts, and other anti-submarine craft. Also for the most part the troops carried in British, French, and Italian ships were given safe conduct through the danger zones by United States destroyers. Roughly, 82¾ per cent. of the maximum strength of the naval escorts provided incident to the transportation of United States troops across the Atlantic was supplied by the United States Navy, 14⅛ per cent. by the British Navy, and 3⅛ per cent. by the French Navy.

The declaration of war with Germany found the United States without a transport fleet and without a merchant marine capable of supplying ships for transporting a large military expedition. It is a remarkable and noteworthy example of American ingenuity and zeal that, starting with almost nothing at the beginning of the war, a United States naval transport service has been built up which has carried almost a million soldiers to Europe. In spite of the determined efforts of submarines to prevent it this has been accomplished without the loss of a single soldier by the hand of the enemy.

The splendid co-operation of the army has made this possible. The army organized and developed an efficient system for loading and unloading the ships at the terminal ports. The navy transported the troops and safeguarded them en route.

On homeward-bound voyages, however, we have not been so fortunate. In a measure this has been due to need of concentrating maximum naval escort protection on troop-laden convoys. Frequently this necessitated lighter escort for the ships returning, and it was on these homeward-bound vessels that the submarines scored their successes. The United States Naval Transports Antilles, President Lincoln, and Covington were torpedoed and sunk. The Finland and Mount Vernon were torpedoed, but were able to reach port for repairs. The United States armored cruiser San Diego struck a mine laid by a German submarine and was sunk.

The service was not without hazard, as is shown by the fact that more than half of the war casualties in the United States Navy were suffered in the Cruiser and Transport Force. Nor were enemy guns and torpedoes the only menace—danger from fire and internal damage was enhanced by the machinations of enemy secret agents, and the likelihood of collision was increased by the necessity of manoeuvring without lights in convoy formation vessels manned for the most part by inexperienced crews.

In connection with the operation of the ships special mention should be made of the volunteer and reserve personnel, particularly the officers and men from the United States merchant marine service who enrolled in the navy for the

# Table Showing Total of United States Troops Transported and the Ships That Carried Them

Prepared by Ensign WALTER LOGAN, U. S. N., Statistical Officer, Cruiser and Transport Force, United States Atlantic Fleet.

| | Carried by United States Naval Transports | No. of United States Naval Transports Sailed | Carried by British Ships | Number of British Ships Sailed | Carried by British-Leased Italian Ships | No. of British-Leased Italian Ships Sailed | Carried by Other United States Ships | Number of Other United States Ships Sailed | Carried by Other Ships (French, Italian, &c.) | Number of Other Ships Sailed (French, Italian, &c.) | Total United States Troops Transported | Total Ships Sailed | Percentage Carried by United States Naval Transports | Percentage Carried by British Ships | Percentage Carried by British-Leased Italian Ships | Percentage Carried by Other U. S. Ships | Percentage Carried by Other Ships | Under United States Naval Escort | Under British Naval Escort | Under French Naval Escort | Percentage Under U. S. Naval Escort | Percentage Under British Naval Escort | Percentage Under French Naval Escort |
|---|---|---|---|---|---|---|---|---|---|---|---|---|---|---|---|---|---|---|---|---|---|---|---|
| **1917.** | | | | | | | | | | | | | | | | | | | | | | | |
| May | 1,035 | 3 | 508 | 2 | 0 | 0 | 0 | 0 | 0 | 0 | 1,543 | 5 | 67 | 33 | 0 | 0 | 0 | 258 | 1,285 | 0 | 17 | 83 | 0 |
| June | 8,855 | 9 | 1,080 | 1 | 0 | 0 | 5,156 | 8 | 0 | 0 | 15,091 | 18 | 59 | 6½ | 0 | 34½ | 0 | 15,032 | 59 | 0 | 99 | 1 | 0 |
| July | 5,281 | 8 | 7,299 | 6 | 0 | 0 | 0 | 0 | 296 | 1 | 12,876 | 15 | 41 | 57 | 0 | 0 | 2 | 10,063 | 2,566 | 247 | 78½ | 20 | 1½ |
| Aug. | 4,310 | 6 | 11,890 | 7 | 0 | 0 | 1,109 | 2 | 2,094 | 2 | 19,403 | 17 | 22 | 61 | 0 | 6 | 11 | 12,259 | 4,129 | 3,015 | 63 | 21 | 16 |
| Sep. | 13,917 | 15 | 19,671 | 12 | 0 | 0 | 0 | 0 | 0 | 0 | 33,588 | 27 | 41 | 59 | 0 | 0 | 0 | 17,432 | 12,898 | 3,258 | 51½ | 39 | 9½ |
| Oct. | 25,098 | 14 | 13,013 | 9 | 0 | 0 | 0 | 0 | 1,916 | 1 | 40,027 | 24 | 62½ | 32½ | 0 | 0 | 5 | 36,893 | 3,134 | 0 | 92½ | 7½ | 0 |
| Nov. | 9,988 | 9 | 10,669 | 7 | 0 | 0 | 1,235 | 2 | 1,830 | 1 | 23,722 | 19 | 41½ | 46 | 0 | 4½ | 8¼ | 13,246 | 10,476 | 0 | 56½ | 43½ | 0 |
| Dec. | 37,445 | 16 | 11,370 | 9 | 0 | 0 | 0 | 0 | 0 | 0 | 48,815 | 25 | 77 | 23 | 0 | 0 | 0 | 42,783 | 6,032 | 0 | 87½ | 12½ | 0 |
| **1918.** | | | | | | | | | | | | | | | | | | | | | | | |
| Jan. | 25,662 | 16 | 20,514 | 9 | 0 | 0 | 0 | 0 | 1,879 | 1 | 48,055 | 26 | 53 | 42½ | 0 | 0 | 4½ | 35,827 | 12,228 | 0 | 75 | 25 | 0 |
| Feb. | 39,977 | 17 | 9,259 | 4 | 0 | 0 | 0 | 0 | 3 | 1 | 49,239 | 22 | 81½ | 18½ | 0 | 0 | 0 | 48,795 | 444 | 0 | 99 | 1 | 0 |
| Mar. | 56,278 | 26 | 27,626 | 14 | 0 | 0 | 1 | 1 | 1,895 | 4 | 85,710 | 45 | 65 | 33 | 0 | 0 | 2 | 73,095 | 12,615 | 0 | 85 | 15 | 0 |
| Apr. | 67,553 | 27 | 47,362 | 20 | 2,626 | 2 | 737 | 11 | 1,794 | 3 | 120,072 | 63 | 56 | 39½ | 2 | 1 | 1½ | 91,308 | 28,764 | 0 | 75½ | 24½ | 0 |
| May | 96,273 | 33 | 133,795 | 75 | 12,127 | 6 | 3,288 | 22 | 2,231 | 5 | 247,714 | 141 | 39 | 53½ | 5 | 1½ | 1 | 220,463 | 26,652 | 599 | 88½ | 11 | ½ |
| June | 115,256 | 36 | 140,172 | 70 | 14,465 | 7 | 6,003 | 11 | 4,538 | 4 | 280,434 | 128 | 41¼ | 50 | 5 | 2¼ | 1½ | 244,631 | 30,912 | 4,891 | 87½ | 11 | 1½ |
| July | 108,445 | 33 | 175,526 | 89 | 11,502 | 7 | 4,020 | 13 | 11,866 | 5 | 311,359 | 147 | 35 | 56½ | 3½ | 1 | 4 | 258,332 | 46,329 | 6,698 | 83 | 15 | 2 |
| Aug. | 116,401 | 36 | 137,745 | 74 | 9,376 | 6 | 8,495 | 15 | 14,358 | 9 | 286,375 | 140 | 41 | 48 | 3 | 3 | 5 | 237,920 | 22,572 | 25,883 | 83 | 8 | 9 |
| Sep. | 107,025 | 35 | 134,576 | 69 | 7,052 | 4 | 5,511 | 18 | 5,506 | 3 | 259,670 | 129 | 41 | 52 | 3 | 2 | 2 | 224,298 | 20,681 | 14,691 | 86 | 8 | 6 |
| Oct. | 72,092 | 43 | 94,214 | 57 | 11,098 | 7 | 4,709 | 17 | 1,950 | 3 | 184,063 | 127 | 39 | 51 | 6 | 3 | 1 | 130,274 | 51,454 | 2,335 | 70½ | 28½ | 1 |
| To Nov. 11. | 1,191 | 9 | 10,698 | 12 | 0 | 0 | 235 | 3 | 0 | 0 | 12,124 | 24 | 10 | 88 | 0 | 2 | 0 | 7,451 | 4,673 | 0 | 61¾ | 38¼ | 0 |
| Total | 912,082 | 391 | 1,006,987 | 546 | 68,246 | 39 | 40,499 | 123 | 52,066 | 43 | 2,079,880 | 1,142 | 43¾ | 48¼ | 3 | 2½ | 2½ | 1,720,360 | 297,903 | 61,617 | 82¾ | 14⅛ | 3⅛ |

period of the war. These have rendered splendid service, and the interests of the United States for the future require that the cordial relations of co-operation established between the merchant marine and the navy be maintained. In the larger transports it was the policy of the department to have the Captains, executive officers, chief engineers, gunnery officers, senior medical officers, and senior supply officers detailed from the regular navy and the remainder of the officer complement filled from the various classes of reserve and volunteer officers. This worked very well, and too much credit cannot be given the latter for the loyal service rendered and the aptitude shown in adapting themselves to naval war conditions.

In special cases it was possible, after a certain amount of experience had been gained, to relieve heads of departments, originally assignments of regular naval officers, by reserve officers. For example, in the case of the Harrisburg, Louisville, Plattsburg, Manchuria, Mongolia, and Finland, after a few trips the reserve Captains took over command of the ships. Credit is also due the navy yards, provisions and clothing depots, medical supply depots, and the ship repair plants which supplemented the navy yards in performing the work incident to making ready and keeping in service this large United States Naval Cruiser and Transport Force, commanded by Rear Admiral Gleaves, and numbering, at the time of the armistice, twenty-four cruisers and forty-two transports, manned, exclusive of troops carried, by about 3,000 officers and 42,000 men.

•  [SEMI-OFFICIAL]

# German Methods in Alsace-Lorraine
## Personal Narratives of Citizens Who Witnessed Atrocities in the First Days of the War

*Though Alsace and Lorraine were a part of Germany, they were treated with the same cruelty as Belgium and Northern France, and the fatal phrase, " Man hat geschossen," (" Somebody shot at us,") caused as many victims as elsewhere. Two narratives of citizens who were present at the massacres and incendiarism in Bourzwiller, Alsace, and Dalheim, Lorraine, are herewith translated for CURRENT HISTORY MAGAZINE from Nouvelles de France, a Paris semi-official publication. They are typical of what happened also in Sengern, Lauterbach, Dornach, and other towns. The narrative of a citizen of Bourzwiller, whose name was withheld to protect him from German reprisals, is as follows:*

THE French arrived in Bourzwiller on Aug. 8, 1914. On the 9th, about 9 o'clock in the evening, the Germans, owing to their great numerical superiority, again succeeded in making themselves masters of the village. On Aug. 10, between 2 and 3 o'clock in the morning, two half sections of the 110th and 111th Infantry Regiments forced their way into the courtyard of a house, the one shortly after the other. The great obscurity and the state of enervation into which the soldiers had fallen caused them to confound friends and enemies, and the first noise provoked rifle shots, a thing inevitable in the circumstances. Four soldiers wounded by their comrades cried out in their pain. This attracted the attention of a Captain who was coming to find out from his men the cause of the shots. One soldier asserted that they had been fired upon from the windows of the house.

Meanwhile the owner of the house had approached and had heard the accusation. He told the Captain that it was baseless, because he and his whole family had been refugees in the cellar since 11:30, and before that he had locked every room in the house. As the soldier persisted in his charge, the proprietor treated him as a liar and begged the officer to investigate for himself as to the truth of what had been stated. Eight men were selected to visit the house from garret to cellar under the farmer's guidance.

## TURN RIFLES ON COTTAGE

At this juncture one of the soldiers who had remained in the courtyard declared he had seen some one shoot from a little house that stood beside the main residence. The Captain gave credence to these assertions, and without further preliminaries ordered his men to fire through the two windows of the cottage. The rifles set fire to the straw which had been laid in the rooms to receive the wounded.

The proprietor ran up and begged the Captain to desist; no one could have shot from there, he said, because there was nobody in the cottage. The officer was compelled to admit the truth of this statement, for no one left the burning house. The farmer was permitted to extinguish the flames with the aid of some soldiers, but the fire had attained considerable proportions and he ran great risks. His niece, who had rushed out to get the fire pumps, was brutally repulsed by the soldiers, who cried, "Raus mit dem frechen Frauenzimmer!" ("Get back, you hussy!") The farmer went himself in search of the pumps and succeeded in putting the fire out.

Another villager who had come to help him suddenly saw, to his stupefaction, his wife forced up against a wall in the midst of a group of soldiers. He ran and demanded that she be set free. By way of reply he was immediately arrested—without cause—along with six other inhabitants. One of the latter, of whom the Germans had demanded six loaves of bread and who could furnish only three, was thrown into the gutter and threatened with bayonets. A Captain passing the spot had him bound and taken to Illfurt, where he and the others were liberated.

When the four wounded soldiers were being carried into the house the proprietor and his family were forced to leave it. They were taken into the fields and there placed under guard by German soldiers, along with many other inhabitants. Eight Frenchmen who had been hiding in Bourzwiller were also taken there. Troops passing them hurled the grossest insults at the prisoners, threatening them with cruel punishments and unanimously demanding their immediate execution. "Kill them, the dogs!" ("Schlagt sie tot, die Hunde!") cried cynical voices on all sides. Two hundred yards away German batteries were firing in the direction of Mülhouse, and the shells, which were flying over their heads, caused inexpressible fear in these peaceful Alsatians. Finally, after six hours of this punishment, deliverance came. The Germans marched away to Mülhouse and abandoned the village and its inhabitants.

## AN AGONIZING NIGHT

About 8 o'clock in the evening of Aug. 14 a rumor ran like a train of powder through the village, filling the inhabitants with a joy which none tried to conceal: the arrival of the French was expected. But consternation followed when a German officer appeared in the street at the head of a patrol and ordered everybody indoors. Two soldiers went into one house, where wine was given them and their canteens were filled with brandy. Thus abundantly provided with drink, they returned to mount guard in the forest of Bourzwiller—in the direction of Kingersheim. Night came, bringing an agonizing silence. Thick clouds, precursors of a storm, covered the sky.

About 3 o'clock in the morning of Aug. 15 came the first clap of thunder; at the same moment a cannon shot rang out. One inhabitant rose with all his family and went down into the cellar. Through the cellar window he saw the Trantzer tile works in flames, and seven men, deployed in a skirmish line, who were firing on Bourzwiller. Behind the hill on the road to Kingersheim about sixty men were answering the fire of these sharpshooters. At the same time a military truck was arriving from Kingersheim with soldiers in helmets and dark blue uniforms, belonging to a Württemberg regiment. Near the church in Bourzwiller a patrol of the 136th German Infantry opened fire on the truck and killed a dragoon, an Alsatian native of Ribeauvillé, who was passing on horseback.

Near the church is the house of Benjamin Schott. Awakened by the firing, the proprietor rose and, seeing the storm, went out, lantern in hand, with his farm hands to place under cover his wagons laden with sheaves of wheat. When he heard the bullets whistling he retraced his steps on the run to seek safety for his family and himself in the cellar. The soldiers of the 136th Regiment asserted that he had killed the dragoon; they set fire to his house and made prisoners of him and all his family, consisting of his wife, who was with child, and his five children, the oldest 14 years of age.

These also were arrested: Nick Ignace, with his son and daughter; the widow Schmitt and her children, including a boy of 16, and Jean-Baptiste Biehler, an old man of 95 years. Schott was maltreated, thrown down, then taken with the others to a field a hundred yards from the house. Meanwhile the soldiers were setting fire to his house; in their anger they even hurled the children's savings banks through the windows.

## CITIZENS EXECUTED

About 5 in the morning the Germans shot the following named persons before the eyes of their wives and children: Benjamin Schott, Nick Ignace and his 17-year-old son, Schmitt, the 16-year-old son of widow Schmitt; Jean-Baptiste Biehler, who was 95 years old and wore two pairs of spectacles. Seventeen volunteers had been found to execute these five Alsatians. Almost at the same time a man named Fritsch, who had come out to see what was happening, was killed on the Kuneyl doorstep at the muzzle of a rifle.

The relatives of those who had just been shot were held under guard in the fields by sentinels. From time to time the soldiers went into the woods and

fired in the direction of the village. Those who remained behind did not hesitate to accuse the Alsatians, "that drove of hogs," ("diese Schweinebande!") of firing upon them.

Between the Kingersheim road and the Bernheim and Kuneyl factories the Germans arrested seventy persons and took them to Mülhouse. At their head walked —— and his son, who had nothing on but his shirt. His wife, half naked, had to endure the coarse gibes of the soldiers for two hours.

Fifty-six houses were systematically burned. Bourzwiller that morning was nothing but a vast bed of glowing coals. The soldiers went from one house to another and carried out their work of destruction with straw and petroleum, which the inhabitants were compelled to place at their service.

When a villager asked a soldier why they were in such a rage against this innocent community he received the significant reply: "Everybody, innocent or guilty, ought to be stood up against a wall." He and his family were arrested and compelled to look at the bodies of their dead neighbors, then led away to the place where almost all the inhabitants had been herded together—"this drove of hogs," as one officer remarked.

From the forest came rifle shots. Then came the order to take "this band of brigands" to Kingersheim, keeping the civilians on the two sides of the road and the soldiers between them, so that in case of stray bullets the civilians should be the first to be hit. On the way most of them were abandoned and fled in crowds, seeking refuge in the homes of relatives, friends, or acquaintances. This was the end of the Bourzwiller tragedy.

## TOLD BY ANOTHER WITNESS

An Alsatian soldier gave the following information regarding the incidents at Bourzwiller:

On Aug. 14 the 1st Battalion of the 136th Regiment of Infantry was at Rixheim. About 2 o'clock in the morning of Aug. 14 we were awakened and sent in the direction of Bourzwiller. A truck that had followed the same route had been fired upon and lost two drivers.

The battalion stopped before the village and captured the café near the tile works about 4 o'clock in the morning.

The soldiers talked of nothing but the Bourzwiller affair. They said that civilians had opened fire on the troops in the night and that they were to be punished at once. The conversation was suddenly interrupted by shots. The battalion ran to their stacked arms and marched on the village, two companies on the right of the road and two on the left. One witness asserts that at the moment when the first battalion entered the village it received a volley from the right. The bullets passed on into the woods without hitting any one. Two groups of the third section, which were marching in the direction of the church, were fired upon from the roof of the tile works. The men took shelter in the ditch by the roadside and opened fire on the factory. Volunteers were sent to set it on fire, and the groups of sharpshooters retired toward the village with the main body of troops, who had entered the forest in order to reach the village under cover. The battalion resumed its advance and began to visit the houses and set fire to them by order of the officers. Straw was piled under the beds and set on fire; at the same time the barns were burned.

## CRUEL TREATMENT

The population was assembled and taken into a wood in front of the village; there were men, women, children, very old men, who were not even allowed time to dress. The women, with uplifted hands, implored the soldiers for pity, but the only reply was to threaten them with bayonets. Men were also dragged away on the charge of having arms in their houses; it seems that a revolver was found in one man's pocket.

Captain Kuehne (3d Company of the 136th) ordered the witness, who had no desire to take part in these scenes of barbarity, to set fire to a house. The man refused, saying that an Alsatian could not do such an act, adding that it had by no means been proved that the citizens had fired on the troops. Kuehne did not insist, and did not molest the soldier. He even remarked to Commandant Trotz von Solz that they were taking a grave responsibility if they executed civilians and burned the village. But the commander insisted on the complete carrying out of his orders.

Five men had been condemned to death on the pretext that they had been found with firearms; these he ordered brought, stood them up in two rows, and had them shot by the men of the 1st Company. The unfortunate Alsatians, calm and resigned, looked death courageously in the face; their hands had not been bound or their eyes bandaged. All fell dead at the first volley except one young man of 17 years, who remained standing, and whom two or three soldiers had to finish off. The Major of the 1st Battalion, Captain Derichs of the 1st Company, and Kuehne of the 3d were present at the execution.

The women and children were compelled to pass in front of the bodies, which lay in a pool of blood, in order that the sad spectacle might be engraved deep in their memories.

# Narrative of a Citizen of Dalheim

*A resident of Dalheim, whose name is withheld, wrote the following in German:*

Immediately after the proclamation of a state of siege, Dalheim, a little village in Lorraine, was garrisoned with an infantry company, (the 8th of the 131st Regiment,) which was then replaced by the 3d Battalion of the 23d Bavarian Infantry. On Aug. 18 the village at length drew a long breath. A little after noon the Bavarians departed, and a few hours later the population welcomed the French Hussars with open arms. Dalheim has had few such happy hours. The Hussars passed the night there, and on the 19th they attacked Morhange.

Unfortunately the brave little band could not hold its own against the Bavarian masses that attacked it on the morning of the 20th. Our 20th Corps had to retire to the hills of Marthil, while the inhibitants of Dalheim, who were not aware of the situation, remained plunged in their dream of liberation. The wounded made their way to Dalheim, which soon became the centre of small infantry engagements, (evening of Aug. 20.) The resistance was brief and ineffectual; then the Bavarian troops, which in the morning had taken and pillaged Marthil, entered Dalheim and did the same there. Everything was booty for them. They respected nothing. Women and young girls were violated. Nothing escaped the Vandals. There was a reign of terror.

## KILLING THE INHABITANTS

At nightfall on Aug. 21 some rifle shots rang out. Immediately the troops, excited by heavy drinking, rushed out of the village, while artillery was placed in position on the Grandes Portions and the Chemin de Bellange, 600 yards east of the village. About three batteries hurled volleys of incendiary shells on the village, which took fire on all sides. And while the people were running madly about, the infantry, excited by alcohol, took the flaming village by assault.

A tailor, Theophile Fristot, was killed by a bullet in the back as he stood in the corridor of his home. Robert Calba, a boy of 15, son of Androphile Calba, was shot at the muzzle of a rifle as he stood before his father's house, and was finished off with bayonet thrusts. An officer killed the old innkeeper, Julien Gézard, with a revolver shot in the back of the neck and ran him through with his sabre. The curate, Prosper Calba, was slashed with a knife and with a sabre; the former Mayor of Dalheim, Louis Sommer, who was ill, perished in the flames. And unfortunately many of our beloved defenders, who had been wounded, suffered the same fate, as the people, despite their devoted efforts, had not succeeded in removing them all from the burning buildings. And those who had been snatched from this danger were dispatched by the victorious Germans. Fourteen were dragged into the vineyards and shot without respite or trial.

Meanwhile the infamous horde was assembling the women and children with kicks and blows of rifle stocks. To the sound of drums the men were led away to Morhange, where they had to remain until noon of the 22d lying in the water on the parade ground without power to budge. Whoever lifted his head received a blow on the skull with a rifle butt. Jules Fristot died on the way there. François Michel died a little later from meningitis caused by blows. François Paulin is completely paralyzed in the legs as a result of the cruel treatment he received. The same treatment followed the men on their journey to Faulquemont and their railway trip to Deux-Ponts, where they were interned.

While this was going on, the women, girls, and children were chased like wild animals through the vineyards, and the soldiers carried their shameless conduct to the extent of tearing the clothes from the bodies of their victims and leaving them entirely naked. These barbarous acts continued until the next morning. Others amused themselves by burning with torches the houses that had escaped the shells.

## GERMAN EXCUSES

In order to give some appearance of judicial sanction to these proceedings the Germans published various interpretations.

*First Explanation:* " After a rather violent combat the Bavarian troops succeeded, in the forenoon of Aug. 20, 1914, in carrying the hills of Marthil-Bellange; the French retired, passing through Dalheim, and the German troops pursued them energetically beyond the village. As the second reserve column was passing through that locality the curate was asked whether the village had been evacuated by the French. Receiving an affirmative reply, our troops penetrated in compact masses into the village. At the moment when they arrived near the church a volley from the belfry shot down the officers and men at the head of the troops. The belfry was taken by assault and fourteen Frenchmen were captured. Immediate search of the houses resulted in the discovery of a quantity of firearms that showed recent usage. The curate, the schoolmaster—a gun still warm was found in the latter's bed—and the French soldiers caught in the belfry were shot. The inhabitants involved in the high treason are imprisoned at Deux-Ponts. The military court will determine their fate."

*Second Explanation* (as set forth in the indictment): "While the 10th Bavarian Regiment was resting, a man named Paul Becker attacked a territorial from behind, attempting to shoot him with a revolver, while several shots were fired from the windows at our troops."

*Third Explanation* (published in the Saarbrück Gazette): "The troops of the —— battalion of the —— regiment of Bavarian infantry were camped at the entrance to the village. Some territorials who were going to the village in quest of water were greeted with bullets, quite as much from inhabitants as from French soldiers who had hidden in the church. Investigation has shown that the inhabitants did some of the shooting. A shotgun still warm was found in the bed of the schoolmaster. The curate, the schoolmaster, and fourteen Frenchmen were executed. The village was given over to the soldiers. The men were taken to Deux-Ponts and imprisoned."

The court-martial at Deux-Ponts in October, 1914, pronounced the inhabitants of Dalheim innocent, establishing the falsity of the accusations; nevertheless, the inhabitants of Dalheim were not liberated until February, 1916. Their imprisonment of nineteen months was aggravated by harsh treatment and innumerable vermin. (Victims: François Bertaigne, a farrier, who died in October, 1914, and several others whose names we do not know.) At Dalheim only two or three houses remain in the lower village and four in the lane called La Cour; all are more or less damaged. In February, 1916, no indemnity had yet been paid to the inhabitants; they had received no grant of funds and no aid.

Another informant, a soldier of the 132d Infantry Regiment, testified:

Bavarian troops, including the 22d Infantry Regiment, had occupied the country around Dalheim at the beginning of August. On the 18th the Bavarian army retired to the Metz-Strassburg line. On the 19th the French advanced, and on the morning of the 20th came into contact with the enemy. The battle of Morhange was fought, in the course of which the French, being inferior in numbers, had to retire before the Germans, who were concentrated between Morhange and Saarbrück.

In the course of the afternoon this retreating movement passed Dalheim, and when the German reserves stopped back of the village they were fired upon, undoubtedly by Frenchmen hidden in the ravines of the vineyards and in the orchards north of the village. They had intended to enter the village by the "lane of the torrent." This path crosses the road, on the east of which the Germans had stopped, and ends at the kitchen-garden of the house that bears the number 60.

## POLICY OF FRIGHTFULNESS

Hearing the fusillade, the Germans threw themselves upon the inhabitants living near this path and inflicted seven or eight bayonet stabs upon a man named Jules César, aged 39, who lived at No. 59, while the tailor, Theophile Fristot, was dragged from his house and shot without any form of trial. Almost at the same time the German artillery opened fire from the high ground two-thirds of a mile to the northwest of the village, burning several houses. The curate, Prosper Calba, who had declared that the French had left the village, was dragged out of the town and shot by order of the commander. The fowl and cattle along the roads were killed by the soldiers with rifle shots, and this fusillade put their comrades into a rage; the latter believed that the inhabitants had fired from the windows.

A young surveyor offered his services to the Germans to make a house-to-house search. This offer was ignored and several houses were burned. Straw and wood were heaped in the church, and it also was given over to the flames. Later the charred body of the Mayor's father was found in the cellar of the Mayor's home. It was almost impossible to save anything; many cattle and horses perished in the flames. At the Guerber home fourteen head of cattle, all the pigs, all the fowl, the furniture, and the reserves of hay, wheat, and rye were burned. The draft horses were taken away by the soldiers and the colts left running at large in the fields.

At Quatre-Chemins, in an isolated house, Christophe Baquel, a veteran of the Crimea, and his wife were grievously wounded by projectiles and died a few days later. A young boy, Robert Calba, who, trying to hide himself, was fleeing through the unharvested fields, was killed by a bullet. In their terror the inhabitants took refuge in cellars, awaiting their fate with anguish. About thirty houses were destroyed by fire; likewise the church, whose belfry still stands in spite of the flames. On the morning of the 21st the inhabitants were herded together like animals, forced to hold up their hands, and, with a few exceptions, taken away to Morhange. Then about ten other houses in the quarter known as Lorraine were destroyed by the Teutons. The remaining women and children begged the soldiers to take them to other villages, because the sight of the burning and devastation was unbearable.

On Saturday, Aug. 22, an aged man was walking toward a well near the road to fill a pail with water. At the same instant a military automobile came along and stopped long enough to enable an officer to shoot down the unfortunate man with a revolver.

The sixty-five men who had been arrested on the 21st were taken to the drill ground at Morhange. Some of them had left home in wooden shoes, some in slippers and shirt sleeves, and, owing to terror, had eaten nothing for several days. On the drill ground they were ordered to lie down with their faces toward the sun and were told that before night they would all be shot. However, on higher orders, they were taken with a convoy of French war prisoners to Puttelange, where they were placed in railway cars. On the journey, at Bertrange, Jules Fristol collapsed of inanition and died. His body was thrown over the side of the railway embarkment. In the villages of Lorraine the people offered food to the suffering prisoners, but the Bavarians repulsed them

brutally. In the villages of Germany, on the other hand, the reception of the prisoners by the population was hostile. Stones flew, insults were uttered, pitchforks and canes were brandished to frighten them.

The scenes at Deux-Ponts beggar description. After their many torments the inhabitants of Dalheim were imprisoned in that city. For six weeks their only food was bread and water. Their bed was rotten straw. On Sept. 11 young Paul Becker was condemned to death by court-martial on the pretext that he had fired at a reservist. The sentence was suspended, however, on account of false testimony.

In October the treatment of the prisoners improved. Some old men, the ill and the weak, were set at liberty. Those who were fit for military service were incorporated on Dec. 6, 1914, in the 9th Regiment of Grenadiers, at Stargard, Pomerania, the others were sent home in March, 1916, with the exception of Celestin Becker, the father of the young man mentioned above. He is working in the neighborhood of Kreuzwald.

Most of the crops of 1914 were destroyed by the fire or could not be harvested; the crops of 1915 and 1916 were requisitioned by the military authorities without indemnifying the inhabitants. In 1915 the wronged families received a monthly allowance of 20 to 40 marks as advance payments on the indemnity to be paid by the State. In 1916 a commission composed of the Sub-Prefect of Château-Salins, the Prefect of Lorraine, and several other eminent persons came to Dalheim to see what repairs could be made on houses damaged by the bombardment and fire. Attention was paid only to houses that were still standing; no thought can be given to the reconstruction of buildings in ruins until the conclusion of peace.

The foregoing facts were gathered by the narrator from his mother in Dalheim, from civilian prisoners who had been liberated, and from his brother and his uncle. Besides, in the course of the war he has met several German soldiers who were present at the tragedy of Dalheim.

# MAJOR GEN. PETER C. HARRIS

Adjutant General of U. S. Army, Succeeding Major Gen. H. P. McCain

(© *Harris & Ewing*)

Major Gen. Guy Carleton
*in Service in France*

Major Gen. John A. Lejeune
*Commanding Marine Corps in France*
*(Harris & Ewing)*

Major Gen. William H. Hay
*Formerly Commanding 134th In-*
*fantry Brigade*
*(© Harris & Ewing)*

Ass't Surgeon Gen. M. W. Ireland
*Serving in France*
*(© Harris & Ewing)*

FRIEDRICH EBERT

First German Chancellor After the Abdication of Kaiser Wilhelm II.
(© *Central News Service*.)

# SOME OF THE KAISER'S LEADERS

**Dr. W. S. Solf**
*Imperial Foreign Secretary*

**Dr. Eduard David**
*Under Secretary of Foreign Affairs*

**Philipp Scheidemann**
*Leader of Moderate Socialists*

**Lieut. Gen. Groener**
*Ludendorff's Successor*

**Mathias Erzberger**
*Head of German Envoys*

**General H. K. A. von Winterfeld**
*German Envoy*

**Major Gen. Weygand**
*Marshal Foch's Adjutant*

**Admiral Wemyss**
*British Admiralty Chief*

**Lieut. Capt. von Schräder**
*Who Sank the Justicia*

**Lieut. Capt. Schwieger**
*Who Sank the Lusitania. Lost with*
*U-88, Sept. 1917*

**Lieut. Capt. Steinbauer**
*Who Sank the Kingstonian.*

**Lieut. Capt. M. Valentiner**
*Who Sank the Persia and Was Later*
*Killed*

COUNT MICHAEL KAROLYI

Newly Chosen President of Hungarian National Council

**General Jekow**
*Commander in Chief of the Bulgarian Armies*

**Major Gen. Townshend**
*Former British Commander at Kut-el-Amara*

**Boris III.**
*Who Succeeded Ferdinand as Czar of Bulgaria*

**Mohammed VI.**
*New Sultan of Turkey*

WAR INDUSTRIES BOARD—Seated from Left to Right, Are: Rear Admiral F. F. Fletcher; Robert S. Brookings, Chairman Price-Fixing Committee; Bernard N. Baruch, Chairman, and Hugh Frayne, Labor Representative. Standing, from Left to Right: H. P. Ingels, Secretary; Judge E. B. Parker, Priorities Commissioner; George N. Peek, Commissioner of Finished Products; J. Leonard Replogle, Steel Administrator; Alexander Legge, Vice Chairman; Major Gen. George W. Goethals, Army, and Albert C. Ritchie, General Counsel.

Ruins of the Church of Notre Dame des Brebières, Albert, Formerly One of the Most Stately Structures in France

One of the Mammoth Guns That Shelled Paris from the St. Gobain Forest, 75 Miles Distant. This Picture, Taken from a German Paper, Was Drawn by One of the Gun Crew. The Gun Was 90 Feet Long, and Threw a Projectile of 200 Pounds, Which Rose 20 Miles in the Air and Reached Paris in Three Minutes.

The Street of Sadi Carnot, Béthune, France, showing the Mere Skeletons of Once Beautiful Buildings

*(© British Official Photo, from Underwood & Underwood)*

The Shattered Church at Ribecourt, on the Oise, After the French Had Recaptured the Town

*(© French Official Photo, from Underwood & Underwood)*

A Square in the Ruined Town of Merville, France, the Scene of Some
of the Fiercest Fighting of the War

The Railway Line at Albert, France, Half an Hour After the Germans
Had Been Driven from the Town

A Procession of Tanks of the New French Type, Small But Swift,
Rushing to the Front Line in Pursuit of the Retreating Germans

Cemetery at St. Mihiel, France, Where German Soldiers Who Died
During German Occupation of the Town Were Buried

The Gun That Fired the First American Shot in the World War, from the Lorraine Sector, on Oct. 23, 1917

French Memorial Society Honoring Graves of American Soldiers Who Fell at Belleau Wood and Château-Thierry

## GERMAN WAR MAKERS

This is a composite of photographic portraits grouped by an artist. The portraits are those of the Kaiser's most trusted leaders at the beginning of the war. The Kaiser himself is in the foreground. The standing figures from left to right are: General von Bülow, General von Mackensen, General von Moltke (deceased), Crown Prince Friedrich Wilhelm, General von François, General Ludendorff (resigned), General von Falkenhayn, General von Einem, General von Beseler, ex-Chancellor von Bethmann Hollweg, General von Heeringen. Seated from left to right are: Crown Prince Rupprecht of Bavaria, Duke Albrecht of Württemberg, General von Kluck (deceased), General von Emich (deceased), General von Haeseler, General von Hindenburg, Admiral von Tirpitz (resigned).

# The Franco-German Armistice in 1871

## Summary of the Peace Terms Exacted From France by Germany Forty-seven Years Ago

### By J. W. DUFFIELD

WHEN France sought an armistice from Prussia on Jan. 23, 1871, the nation lay in utter defeat. So complete a débâcle in so short a time had not been known in modern warfare. In six months there had been seventeen great battles and 150 minor engagements. Almost all of these, with the exception of the French initial success at Saarbrück—which had been little more than an outpost skirmish—had resulted victoriously for the invaders. The French had fought bravely, but had been deficient in preparation, equipment, and leadership. Four hundred thousand French soldiers had been made prisoners of war. Incompetence had caused the surrender at Sedan. Incompetence and treachery combined had brought about the capitulation of Metz. Seven thousand cannon and 600,000 small arms had fallen into the hands of the Prussians. The Emperor, Napoleon III., was a prisoner at Wilhelmshöhe. The Empress Eugénie had fled to Chiselhurst. The Prince Imperial had also found asylum on English soil at Hastings. The monarchy had vanished, leaving to its republican successor the task of obtaining what terms it could from the conquerors.

The Third Republic was proclaimed on Sept. 4, the day of the Empress's flight from Paris. Its chief spirit and most potent voice was M. Thiers, eminent as a statesman and historian. Other prominent leaders were Favre, Simon, Gambetta, Trochu, Arago, Ferry, and Rochefort, men of radical or moderate republican antecedents. Most of them had opposed the declaration of war, Thiers especially having been so vehement in his opposition that his house had been mobbed by the war-mad populace. But now that France was threatened with defeat, they were a unit for its defense. Favre, who, by the irony of fate, was afterward to carry the plea for an armistice to Bismarck, declared on the first day of the new republic that "not one foot of soil, not one stone of a fortress shall be surrendered to Germany." In this he had the unanimous support of his colleagues, and energetic measures were at once taken to put Paris into condition for defense.

### SIEGE OF PARIS

But on Sept. 19, exactly two months after the date when war had been declared, the army of Crown Prince Frederick William laid siege to Paris. By himself he would probably not have succeeded, for the city was fairly well provisioned, strongly garrisoned, and the people were determined to resist to the last. But successes in other parts of France released German armies which came to swell the ranks of the besiegers, and the lines tightened around Paris like the folds of a giant anaconda. Nor could the frequent and desperate sorties of the besieged cause the coils to relax.

Other efforts were put forth to save the doomed city and nation. Gambetta, the greatest orator and most flaming spirit of France, escaped from Paris in a balloon and proceeded to Bordeaux, where he put forth herculean efforts to raise new armies. Thiers, in late September and early October, visited London, Vienna, Florence, and St. Petersburg, trying to secure the aid of neutral powers. None cared, however, to intervene. From Oct. 30 to Nov. 6 Thiers under a flag of truce had several interviews with Bismarck. These were more or less of an informal character and ran the gamut from threat to persuasion. To tentative suggestions of a truce Bismarck was deaf. The man of "blood and iron" remained true to his sobriquet. It was either fight or surrender.

In the meantime, conditions in Paris had become desperate. The inhabitants were on the verge of starvation. Rats, cats, dogs, horses, even the animals in the Zoo had been eaten. No help or supplies could reach them from without. Ammunition was failing, and the soldiers, faint with hunger and exposure, had scarcely enough strength left to carry their weapons. One last despairing sortie was made and failed. The end had come.

## NEGOTIATING WITH BISMARCK

On Jan. 23, 1871, invested with authority by the Government of National Defense to act as its representative, Jules Favre visited Bismarck at Versailles to secure if possible an armistice. The Chancellor had been notified of his purpose and was awaiting him.

In the duel of wits that ensued, the combatants were unequally matched. Favre had little or nothing to bargain with; besides, having been shut up in Paris, he knew little of actual conditions in other parts of France. Bismarck's knowledge was circumstantial and exact. Favre was in the position of a card player whose opponent holds all the trumps.

In strict keeping with the traditions of the old diplomacy, the conference began with each statesman trying to hoodwink his opponent. Favre declared that Paris had provisions enough to last six months. Bismarck countered with the statement that he had already begun negotiations with the imperial family. Neither believed the other.

Favre warned Bismarck that the garrison of Paris were going to make a sortie in overwhelming force, and that Bismarck, if he were obdurate, would have to bear the responsibility for the bloodshed that would ensue. Bismarck smilingly accepted the responsibility.

After this preliminary fencing, a serious discussion ensued, a discussion involving so many important points that repeated conferences were necessary for six days before they were finally adjusted.

A difference in point of view was developed at the outset. Favre sought simply an armistice, a cessation of actual fighting for a space, during which, or after which, the question of final peace terms could be brought up if desired. Bismarck wanted to have peace conditions woven in with the terms of the armistice. Favre, moreover, had only Paris in view, as regarded the armistice; the fighting could go on in other parts of France. Bismarck would hear of no terms that did not include the whole nation.

Another point concerning which Bismarck and Emperor William were genuinely perplexed was the authority of the French Government as then constituted to make any peace that would endure. It was true that the monarchy had vanished; but there was no guarantee that it might not be restored. The Third Republic, which had come into being on Sept. 4 and had had its headquarters at Bordeaux during the latter part of the year, was self-proclaimed. It had no mandate from the nation. It might at any time be challenged and overthrown. It carried in itself no certainty of stability.

The objection was justifiable, though there is no doubt that it was emphasized by the unwillingness of the Hohenzollern dynasty to deal with a republic. It was overcome, however, by the agreement of Bismarck that it would not be allowed to stand in the way of an armistice, provided that a National Assembly should be elected that might be regarded as expressing the will of the nation and be qualified to settle the terms of a treaty of peace, if peace should be ultimately decided upon.

As to whether the armistice should include Paris alone or all of France, a compromise was effected. Belfort, in the east of France, was one of the places where the French forces were holding out with a fair prospect of success. Bismarck demanded that the fortress be surrendered. Favre insisted that this should be excluded from the zone of the armistice. He also insisted that if the German General, Werder, were allowed to continue the siege, the French General, Bourbaki, who was preparing to go to the relief of the fortress, should be permitted to continue his operations. After considerable debate this zone of warfare was excepted from the operation of the proposed armistice, in the following terms:

The military operations in the territory of the Department of Doubs, Jura, and Côte d'Or, as well as the siege of Belfort, shall continue independently of the armistice until an agreement shall be arrived at regarding the line of demarkation, the tracing of which through the three departments has been reserved for an ulterior understanding.

## SIGNING THE ARMISTICE

The conditions ultimately arrived at as regarded the French capital were that the soldiers in Paris were to be made prisoners of war but were not to be removed from the city. All were to be disarmed, with the exception of a remnant who were to act as a police force. The artillery of the forts protecting Paris was to be dismounted and the forts themselves were to be garrisoned by Germans. All material of war in them was to be surrendered.

As soon as these conditions should be fulfilled, the Germans were to permit food to enter the city. It was agreed that the German troops as a body should not enter Paris while the armistice was in force. The date of the expiration of the armistice was set at Feb. 19, at noon. This, it was calculated, would afford sufficient time for the election of a National Assembly, which should decide whether the war should go on or negotiations for peace be inaugurated.

At 8 P. M. on Jan. 28, 1871, the armistice which had been signed earlier that same day became effective; the Germans were ordered to stop firing, and Favre, on the order of the Council of National Defense, telegraphed to Gambetta at Bordeaux: "We have signed an armistice. See that it is executed everywhere."

Steps were immediately taken for a national election. There was but one issue—that of peace or war. An overwhelming majority was returned in favor of peace. When the Assembly convened at Bordeaux on Feb. 17, Thiers was appointed Chief of Executive Power and authorized to open negotiations looking toward peace. He chose a Ministry

and repaired at once to Versailles. The armistice had almost expired, but an extension to March 12 was granted, Bismarck exacting, however, as a compensation for this concession, that the German troops should make a triumphal entry into Paris. In the interim, the mooted question of Belfort had been settled by the course of events.

Bourbaki, moving to the relief of the city, had been attacked and badly defeated. In the battles of Jan. 15-17 he lost 10,000 men, and in the retreat that followed on the 27th his remaining army of 85,000 men was forced over the Swiss boundary, disarmed and interned. Bourbaki attempted to commit suicide. Belfort itself, a few days later, deprived of hope of succor, surrendered to the Germans.

It had been expected by the French plenipotentiaries that the German demands in the peace preliminaries would be severe. But they were staggered when they learned that France would be required to cede the greater part of Alsace and Lorraine and pay an indemnity of six milliards of francs. The French delegates protested vehemently and indignantly. The provinces, they said, were among the fairest of France, and to take them would be striking at the nation's heart. The 6,000,000,000 francs were an indemnity unheard of and not to be considered. It was pointed out that 2,000,000,000 were sufficient to pay the expenses that Germany had incurred. For several days the protests and arguments continued, but Bismarck was inexorable in the main, although he finally conceded that Belfort should remain French and that the six milliards should be reduced to five, equivalent to about $1,000,000,000. The sum was to be paid in installments covering a period of four years. Until the amount was fully paid the Germans were to occupy stipulated French zones and fortresses.

## PEACE TREATY TERMS

The chief provisions of the preliminary peace treaty of Versailles finally arrived at were as follows:

I.—France was to cede to Germany all of Alsace except Belfort, and to cede one-fifth part of Lorraine, including Metz and Thionville.

II.—Five milliards of francs were to be paid as an indemnity. Of this amount, 1,000,000 was to be paid in 1871, and the balance in installments extending over three years. Interest was to be paid at the rate of 5 per cent. on all unpaid installments, dating from the signing of the treaty.

III.—German troops were to begin the evacuation of France as soon as the treaty was ratified. The region of Paris was to be evacuated at once. As security for payment, certain zones of French territory, together with border fortresses, were to remain in German occupation, these zones to be evacuated one after the other as the installments were paid.

IV.—There were to be no requisitions in the occupied territory, but the German armies there stationed were to be maintained at French expense.

V.—The inhabitants of the annexed territories could choose where they wished to live, and no hindrances would be placed in the way of their migration.

VI.—Prisoners of war were to be set at liberty immediately.

VII.—Negotiations for a final treaty were to be opened after the ratification of the preliminary treaty.

VIII.—The administration of occupied territories was to be carried on in general by French local authorities, subject, however, to German military control.

IX.—The treaty was to confer no rights whatever on Germans in French territory not occupied.

X.—The treaty must be ratified by the National Assembly of France.

## GERMAN ARMY IN PARIS

On Feb. 26 this preliminary treaty was signed. It was conveyed at once by Thiers to the French National Assembly, sitting at Bordeaux. Although the harshness of the terms was deplored and denounced, the prostrate condition of France left no alternative, and the treaty was ratified on March 2 by a vote of 546 to 107.

On March 1 the German Army entered Paris, German arms were stacked in the Place de la Concorde and the Elysées Palace was ablaze with light as the German high command held festival. After remaining one day, they marched out again, and on March 12 Versailles was evacuated and the National Assembly transferred its sittings to that city.

Peace with the invader had become a *fait accompli* and only awaited formal consummation at the final peace conference, which was to be held at Frankfort in May. The interval was a stormy one, for in that period the Commune filled Paris with bloodshed and outrage. That wild time of excesses—which were finally suppressed by the National Assembly—had no bearing on the peace negotiations, except that it again gave rise to some questioning on the part of Germany as to the stability of the Government with which it was dealing. This matter, however, was satisfactorily adjusted, and by the final treaty of peace, signed in Frankfort on May 10, 1871, the Franco-Prussian war came formally to an end. The final treaty differed in no essential respect from the treaty of Versailles.

The payment of the indemnity was made in advance of the scheduled dates. By the end of 1873 the last franc had been paid and the last soldier of the German army of occupation had left French soil.

## ALSACE AND LORRAINE

The demand for Alsace-Lorraine was the one unforgivable thing that rankled in the bosom of France. Thiers voiced the general sentiment of the world, outside of Germany, when he said: " It is " one of those monuments of a human " weakness which does not know how to " stop in success, and which, perpetu- " ating in peace the passions of war, de- " posits fresh germs of hostility, even in " the treaties destined to bring it to an " end."

When the National Assembly at Bordeaux ratified the Treaty of Versailles the representatives of the alienated provinces drew up and presented to the Assembly a formal protest, known to history as the Declaration of Bordeaux. Its concluding paragraphs are as follows:

In brief, Alsace and Lorraine protest highly against all cession; France cannot consent to it, Europe cannot sanction it. In support of this we call upon our fellow-citizens of France, and upon the Governments and nations of the whole world, to witness that in advance we hold null and void all acts and treaties, votes or plébiscites, which shall consent to abandoning to the stranger all or part of our provinces of Alsace and Lorraine.

We proclaim by these presents forever inviolable the right of citizens of Alsace and Lorraine to remain members of the French Nation, and we swear, both for ourselves and for those we represent, likewise for our children and their descendants, to claim it eternally by all ways and means and against all usupers.*

Bismarck himself declared cynically to France's first envoy to Germany after the war that he knew perfectly well that

*The Declaration of Bordeaux was printed in full in CURRENT HISTORY MAGAZINE August, 1917.

he had no right to take Alsace and Lorraine, which were bound to be a source of trouble to Germany. " If this were a " permanent peace," he went on, " we " would not have done it; but there is " going to be another war, and then Ger- " many will need those provinces for " strategic purposes."

" The whirligig of time brings its revenges," and there is a dramatic element in the fact that in the very building at Versailles where Thiers and Favre besought an armistice for France, the Interallied War Council in November, 1918, framed the terms of an armistice to be imposed upon the autocracy that had sought to humble and dominate the world.

# The War in Its Last Phases

## Germany, Deserted by Her Allies, Keeps Her Shattered Armies Fighting in Retreat to the End

### [Period from Oct. 18 to Nov. 11, 1918.]

THE concluding phases of the great war on the western front were naturally influenced by the surrender of Turkey and Austria-Hungary, which followed that of Bulgaria, already recorded; also by the political events which were taking place in the countries of the enemy, and by the exchange of diplomatic notes between them and the Entente leaders, both political and military.

Ludendorff's and then General von Lossberg's retreat tactics, pitted against the consummate strategy of Foch and the hammer-like blows of Pershing, form a sequel to the events set forth last month. There was a continuation of the two great flank movements—that begun in Champagne on Sept. 26 and that in Flanders two days later, the former prosecuted against formidable opposition and the latter practically a march of occupation with merely rear-guard and machine-gun interference.

As a background for the rapidly moving scenes there should be constantly

kept in mind this geographical picture: South of the movement from west to east in Flanders there were on Oct. 18 two enemy salients, one between the Scheldt and the Oise, the other between Le Cateau and Rethel, on the Aisne. They had little influence on the movements in Flanders, but a tremendous influence on the movements of Gouraud and the First American Army in Champagne and Argonne and the Meuse region, retarding their advance and enabling the Germans to oppose that advance with great desperation, if not with vigor and skill.

### I. CLEARING UP BELGIUM

The work since Oct. 18 of following up the Germans in Belgium, where Crown Prince Rupprecht was reported to have again superseded von Boehn, devolved principally upon the Belgians under King Albert, the French army under Degoutte, and the British Second, Fifth, First, and Third Armies under respectively Plumer, Birdwood, Horne, and Byng. With the

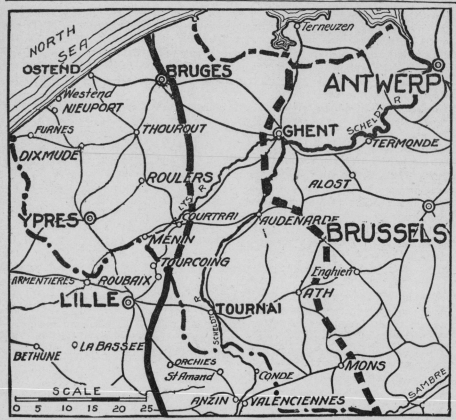

LAST BRITISH AND BELGIAN ADVANCE IN THE NORTH: THE TWO BATTLELINES
INDICATE THE PROGRESS MADE FROM OCT. 18 TO NOV. 11 WHEN THE FIGHTING CEASED
UNDER THE ARMISTICE TERMS.

close of the last review the line had extended from Zeebrugge on the coast,
southeast of Bruges, on Courtrai, east of
Roubaix, Lille, Douai, and Cambrai. The
objective of these armies, whether in
Belgium or France, was to reach as soon
as possible the line of the Scheldt River,
where it was known the enemy was constructing formidable fortifications.

In relation to the line as far as Metz,
it was a flank attack just as that conducted by Gouraud and Pershing in
Champagne and the Argonne at the other
end But here there nas not the formidable resistance with which the Americans met 150 miles to the southeast.
Here there was an organized retreat on
the part of the enemy conducted with
great rapidity; there he yielded only after the most stubborn resistance.

By Oct. 20 the Belgian infantry had occupied Ostend and Bruges and had over-

come severe machine-gun resistance,
which had been maintained between
Whnghen and Thielt. The Second British Army, in the terrain south of the
Lys, had crossed the Courtrai-Mouscron
railway, and had gone four miles beyond
the road toward Brussels. The coast of
the Dutch frontier had been cleared.

In the five following days the Belgians
and French made an attack on the Lys
Canal toward Ghent, crossing the canal
and taking 11,000 prisoners. The First
British Army between Valenciennes and
Tournai took Bruay, Bleharies, and Es-
tain, and then pushed on through
Raismes Forest into the Condé loop of
the Scheldt. Further south the Third
Army gained an eight-mile stretch on
the Valenciennes-Avesnes railway.

From the 20th to the 30th of October
there were marches and consolidations
of lines and positions and a skirting of

the Dutch frontier to the east, then on the 31st another big slice of important territory was torn from the enemy on a fifteen-mile front between the Deynze on the Lys and Avelghem on the Scheldt. In this operation the American 30th Division was still bracketed with Byng's Third Army. Numerous towns and villages were thus released—Pergwyk, Tiergheim, Anseghem, and Winterken.

On Oct. 31 the Second British Army, in co-operation with the French and Belgians, drove the enemy toward Audenarde on the line of the Scheldt—Audenarde, the town fourteen miles south-southwest of Ghent, where, in 1708, Prince Eugene of Savoy and Marlborough defeated the French under Vendome.

On Nov. 3 the Belgian Army made nearly ten miles along the Dutch frontier, and its front passed east of Ertvelde and Everghem, reaching the Terneuzen Canal, practically liberating the entire region as far as this waterway. The British also succeeded in moving detachments to the right bank of the Scheldt in the region of Pofter. These movements brought the Allies to within five miles of Ghent.

## II. CROSSING BELGIUM

The advance of the allied front from beyond Cambrai and St. Quentin had for central figure Rawlinson with the Fourth British Army; on his left were the 30th and later the 27th Division of the 2d Corps of the American Army; on his right was the First French Army under Debeney. Their objectives were the railway junction at Valenciennes, the fortress of Maubeuge, and the fortified camp at Hirson, all south of the Franco-Belgian frontier. Before the armistice went into effect they were beyond the frontier at several points, so that their front presented an almost right angle with the line of the Belgian, French, and British armies on their left.

In the early hours of Oct. 20 the British attacked the enemy's positions on the line of the Selle River north of Le Cateau and succeeded in crossing the river and, further north, in reaching, in spite of the increasing resistance of the enemy, the line Haveluy-Wandignies-Hagage-Brillon-Beuvry. Two days later they pressed forward on a twenty-five-mile front, extending from Pont-à-Chin (northwest of Tournai) to Thiant, (southwest of Valenciennes.) They won ground beyond the Scheldt, and their patrols reached the suburbs of Valenciennes. The next day the Fourth Army swung south of the town. The American 30th and 27th Divisions notably contributed to this manoeuvre of the Fourth Army, particularly on the 25th, when it reached Le Quesnoy-Valenciennes railway on a front of six or seven miles and took over 3,000 German prisoners. On this date the line of the Scheldt formed a continuous front as far south as the Sambre, but the railway was still free for the Germans from Le Quesnoy as far as Hirson, thirty miles to the southeast.

Then on Nov. 1 the British began to put the pincers on Valenciennes, in which the Canadians captured between 2,000 and 3,000 prisoners, in spite of spirited counterattacks on the high ground west of the Preseau-Valenciennes road.

The next day the Canadian troops, under General Currie, entered the city and even went beyond to St. Saulve on the road to Mons, the scene of the British defeat in the last week in August, 1914. Valenciennes had been occupied by the Germans since the 27th of August, 1914.

On Nov. 4 the British armies were engaged on a thirty-mile front between the Scheldt and the Oise-Sambre Canal. It was an advance for the First, Third, and Fourth Armies with the two American divisions. They captured 10,000 prisoners and 200 guns, and many places, including Landrecies (south of the Mormal Forest) and Catillon, and carried their front more than three miles east of the Oise-Sambre Canal.

Simultaneous with this movement the First French Army, under Debeney, forced a passage of the canal to an average depth of two miles, taking 3,000 prisoners and 15 guns and releasing several villages.

From the front thus established daily advances were made until the fighting ended, first forcing the enemy to retreat

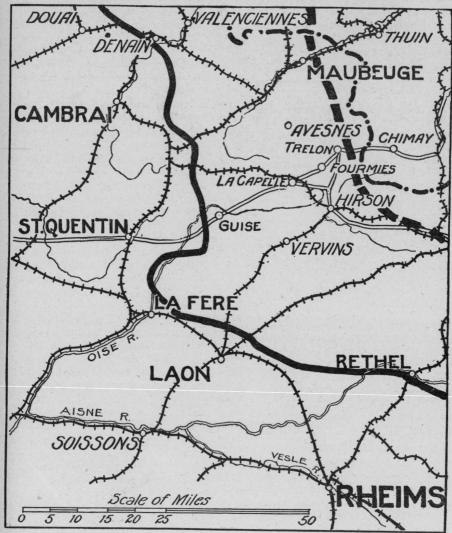

SCENE OF LAST FIGHTING IN CENTRAL SECTOR, FROM VALENCIENNES TO RETHEL.
THE TWO BATTLELINES SHOW PROGRESS MADE BETWEEN OCT. 18 AND NOV. 11, WHEN
THE FIGHTING CEASED.

on a seventy-five-mile line from the
Scheldt to the Aisne and then as far up
the Aisne to Gouraud's advanced position at Rethel, thus trespassing upon the
sectors whose events are now to be recorded.

### III. THE OISE-AISNE FRONT

From the Oise-Aisne front as it was
on Oct. 18 the greatest distance to be
traversed to the frontier lay before the
Tenth French Army under Mangin, with
Debeney on his left and Berthelot, with

whom the Italians under Marrone were
bracketed, and Gouraud on his right.
His objective was to reach the frontier
between Hirson and Mézières. Before
hostilities ceased he had captured Hirson
and had penetrated over the border.

Mangin, having captured Laon and
broken the German hold on La Fère,
pressed rapidly forward between the
Oise and the Aisne and soon caught up
with Gouraud's advance from the south
across the latter river. On the right of
Mangin his flank was cleared by the

Czechoslovak forces recapturing the village of Terron, north of Vouziers, on Oct. 24. On the same day the French crossed the Oise Canal opposite Longchamps, southeast of Le Cateau, and came within two miles of the strong German positions at Guise. This was a movement which greatly relieved General Debeney's First Army, which had been held up by stout German resistance between Mont d'Origny and the Serre Valley. Debeney's late advance carried suddenly ahead of Mangin when he reached the heights overlooking the valley of the Péron and the line east of Ribemont.

On Oct. 25 a formidable advance was made by the French which pierced the Hunding line. Mangin, holding the centre, took Mortiers, on the south bank of the Serre. On his left was General Guillaumat, who advanced on a four-mile sector between Sissonne and the Aisne, while still further on his left Debeney made a raid with tanks between the Oise and the Serre. The climax of the advance was Guillaumat's attack over the Hunding positions between St. Quentin-Le Petit and Herpy, west of Château-Porcien, on the Aisne.

Henceforth Debeney was to act in concert with Mangin rather than with Rawlinson. By the end of October he had driven beyond the Oise, forced the Péron River, and taken Bois-les-Pargny. He and Mangin kept the flank well harassed when the Germans began their great retreat from the Scheldt to the Aisne, reaching on Nov. 7 the railway between La Capelle and Hirson on the general line Effry and Origny-en-Thierache, and further east along the Thon, an affluent of the Oise, as far as Leuze.

On Nov. 8 the French reached the outskirts of Mézières, took the Thon bridgeheads, and were almost within striking distance of Hirson and Maubeuge. They held the southern bank of the Meuse from near Mézières to near Bazeilles. The next day Maubeuge fell to Rawlinson's army; French cavalry passed through Hirson on their way over the Belgian frontier, and Mézières was closely invested.

## IV.—AISNE-MEUSE FRONT

In continuing their fight toward the frontier the Franco-American advance lay over the Aisne-Meuse watershed. Theoretically these two rivers, with the Germans fortified on the right banks, presented formidable obstacles if the object were frontal attacks. But the fact that both descended from within the allied lines gave both the Fourth French Army under Gouraud and the First American Army a singular advantage. What the Americans had done in the preceding month on the Aire in clearing the Argonne Forest and the French had measurably performed in regard to the Aisne the Americans were to accomplish, even more effectually, in regard to the Meuse. Advancing astride of the river until encountering formidable resistance on the right bank, they would then form a bridgehead several miles down stream and thus enfilade the enemy between, always avoiding a costly frontal attack across stream. When the end came the Franco-American line was within five miles of the frontier, having gone beyond Sedan, invested Montmédy, and occupied a front southeast to Pagny, eight miles above Metz on the Moselle, via Stenay, Baalon, Damvillers, and St. Hilaire, facing the most famous battlegrounds of 1870 in Lorraine and the great iron fields of the Bassin de Briey, without which Germany could not have prosecuted the late war for three months.

When last month's review closed on Oct. 18 the situation presented by the fronts of Gouraud's Fourth Army and the First American Army was as follows: On the left the Germans still retained a salient from Rethel northwest to Le Cateau which Debeney and Mangin were to smash in; Gouraud had been held in his descent of the Aisne at Vouziers, twenty-five miles south of Mézières. From Vouziers his line fell south of the river until Rethel was reached with a maximum distance of five miles south of Attigny. On his right the Americans, over a fifty-mile front almost due east over the Meuse, were in the centre three miles south of Buzancy and on the Meuse right wing ten miles south of Stenay. The next day the Germans re-

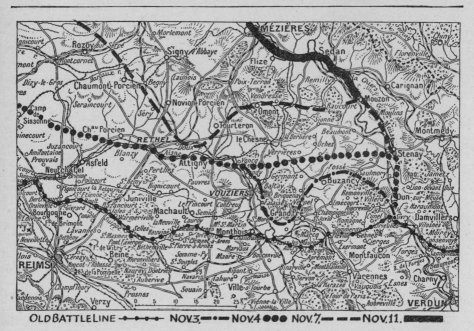

OLD BATTLE LINE •→•→•  NOV. 3.■—•—■  NOV. 4 ●●●  NOV. 7.—  — ■ NOV. 11.■━━━

SCENE OF THE BATTLE OF THE MEUSE, IN WHICH THE AMERICAN FIRST ARMY TOOK SEDAN, WITH THE SUPPORT OF GENERAL GOURAUD'S FORCES ON THE LEFT.

treated before the American centre to the Freya Stellung, a couple of miles behind the Kriemhilde line, already pierced by the Americans. This Freya line crossed the Meuse south of Dun, climbed Hill 26, and ran north of the Andon Valley, Bantheville, and thence west to the Bois Bourgogne. It was the last protection for the great trunk railway which ran parallel to it on the average of ten miles to the north—from Mézières to Metz, via Sedan, and Montmédy. This railway with its lateral lines had supplied the entire enemy front from Rheims east to the Moselle.

Here the great closing battle of the war was fought. Down to Oct. 26 the Americans fought fiercely to reach the last German line of defense. Having reached it, it then became their business to render the great railway inoperative. This they also did. Meanwhile, the French on their left did little until Nov. 1, being hampered, in their turn, by the operations which were obliterating the German salient, Le Cateau-Rethel.

On Oct. 19-20 the First American Army forged ahead on the northern edge of Bantheville Forest and in the region of Bourrot, capturing a few hundred

Germans, but meeting at every point an ever-stiffening resistance. The next day they occupied Brieulles and the Bois de Foret and lost and won Bantheville several times. Then on the 23d they broke through the Freya defenses on a two-mile front, which they broadened until the 26th, when they brought up their huge sixteen-inch naval guns, and the bombardment of the railway began. This bombardment was aided by numerous air squadrons, which dropped bombs upon the enemy's troop centres. The fire was principally concentrated on the line between Sedan and Montmédy. Ancreville Ridge was captured on Oct. 30, and the way was open to Sedan and the frontier.

Then on Nov. 1 Gouraud's front was again in movement, and swept across the Aisne, where it had been held between Vouziers and Rethel on a twelve-and-a-half-mile line, but meeting with violent resistance on the Alleux Plateau and the Croix-aux-Bois defile. The next day the Freya defenses for almost their entire length fell into the hands of the Americans. The enemy's line had here been weakened by the withdrawal of five Austrian divisions. By the 4th observers reported that the railway line had been completely shattered at Montmédy and Conflans. This was a crowning success, for in attempting to keep this railway intact the enemy had sacrificed over 100,000 men.

Then, down to the time the last shot was fired, the American advance observed two distinct directions: one was an expansion of the centre, which cut through the Sedan line and occupied that city on Nov. 6; the other concerned the descent of the Meuse from the positions north of Verdun with a consolidation of the line southeast across the Woevre to the Moselle. Here the heights of the Woevre were captured and the forts of Metz brought within easy range of the great American naval guns, which, however, were not employed.

When hostilities ceased the whole situation forecast two great events which were never to take place: the reduction of the Metz forts and the advance of the Second American and French armies into Lorraine over the battlefield made famous by Castelnau in the early days of the war.

## ITALY'S GREAT VICTORY

In the story which recorded the last efforts of Germany to bring to a successful conclusion her highly organized retreat in France and Belgium, what was taking place in Italy hardly received its proportional attention—there had been so many stories to the effect that, on account of the internal political situation in each country, both the Italian and the Austro-Hungarian military authorities were content to let the war be settled on the western front. The deciding factor, however, that the Italian Army was waiting on the orders of Foch, was quite forgotten. Ever since April Foch had been in supreme command and the Italian Army had been the right wing of the great army of the Allies which extended from the North Sea to the Adriatic—just as the Austrian Army in Italy had been the left wing of the enemy covering the same battlefront under the supreme command of Ludendorff.

In anticipation of the drive beyond the Marne which was to seal Germany's fate on July 18, Ludendorff ordered an attack of the Austrian Army from the Asiago, Grappa, and Piave positions which had been secured by the defeat of the Italians at Caporetto in the previous October. The attack was made on June 15-16, and on June 25-26 was so powerfully counterattacked by the Italians directed by General Diaz as to be rendered abortive. The Italians secured certain strong positions in the mountains and cleared the entire Piave right bank of the enemy, who, however, still clung to some river islands below Il Montello.

Between the last week in August and the middle of October Diaz gained several more strategic positions, principally in the mountains, and then on Oct. 19 Foch ordered him to attack. It was a most propitious moment for victory. In Belgium and France the German retreat had assumed proportions which precluded a stand west of the Meuse. In Austria-Hungary the defeat in June as well as political turmoil amid the subject peoples had had a depressing effect upon the heterogeneous armies of Emperor Charles. Bulgaria had surrendered to the Allies and Turkey was trying to do so.

By Oct. 24 the great Italian offensive was well under way. Between that date and Nov. 4, when the terms of the armistice went into effect at 3 P. M., Diaz captured 300,000 prisoners and 5,000 guns, and the utter annihilation of the entire military forces of Emperor Charles was in sight.

In this gigantic battle, begun on the first anniversary of Caporetto, fifty-one Italian divisions, three British, two French, and one Czechoslovak division and one American regiment participated against sixty-three Austro-Hungarian divisions. The battle divides itself into two great tactical movements:

First, the daring and rapid advance of the Italian 29th Army Corps closed up the enemy's forces in the Trentino; there these forces west and east of the Adige were separately attacked and defeated by the Seventh, First, and Fourth Italian Armies. Second, this manoeuvre enabled the assault from the Brenta down the Piave to the sea to be pressed forward without fear of a flanking movement on the part of the enemy. The forward movement was made by the

# Italy's Final Victory

SCENE OF THE SECOND BATTLE OF THE PIAVE: THE SOLID BLACK LINE SHOWS THE BAT-TLEFRONTS OF OCT. 24 AND THE BROKEN LINE MARKS THE PO-SITION OF THE ITALIAN FORCES AT THE TIME OF THE AUSTRIAN DEBACLE ON NOV. 3, WHEN THE ARMISTICE ITAL-IAN ARMISTICE WAS SIGNED.

Twelfth and Eighth Armies, by the Tenth, under Lord Cavan, containing, in addition to the Italians, the allied major detachments, and by the Third Army, under the Duke of Aosta, on the lower Piave.

## THE BATTLE IN DETAIL

Early on the morning of Oct. 24 the Italians deluged the enemy's positions in the Asiago and Monte Grappa regions with artillery fire; there the British and French minor detachments entered the enemy's advanced positions and captured prisoners and munitions. Meanwhile, the Italians themselves crossed the Ornic River in the Grappa region and captured Monte Solarole and parts of Monte Prassolan and Monte Pertica. On the Piave the British of the Tenth Army captured the island Grave di Papadopoli and other river garrisons of the enemy, occupying their positions.

Within twenty-four hours after the offensive had begun the Italians had captured 3,000 prisoners; the enemy's line in the Grappa region was giving way and he was retreating from his positions on the left bank of the Piave. By the 26th the Tenth Army was crossing the Piave in force, and next day a bridgehead had been firmly established at Valdobbiadene by the Twelfth Army. By the 28th the three Piave armies were well across the river, while British and Italian cavalry were pressing the enemy's rear guards and capturing thousands of prisoners. By the 30th 33,000 prisoners had been taken. On that date the Third Army on the extreme right entered the battle, with the 332d American Regiment on its left.

From now on until the end there was a rapid, enthusiastic advance along the entire front, with the Eighth and Tenth Armies in the lead. The former by the first of November had rushed beyond Vittorio; the latter had crossed the Conegliano-Oderzo highway. The Austro-Hungarian retreat had become a flight, in which the enemy when overtaken freely surrendered and made no attempt to remove his vast supplies of munitions. By the first of November also the Twelfth, Eighth, Tenth, and Third Armies

had reached the Livenza, and established bridgeheads there, with the cavalry covering the ground between that river and the Tagliamento. To the northeast the advance beyond the railway terminal at the City of Belluno had completely destroyed communication between the Austrians in the Trentino and those in Veneto. The number of prisoners had increased to 50,000.

Up to the eve of the armistice 100,000 Austrians had been taken, together with 2,200 guns. In the Trentino the cities of Rovereto and Trent had been occupied; on the plains Udine, the former headquarters of Cadorna, had been overrun by the Italian cavalry; on the Adriatic the great Austrian seaport of Trieste was in possession of the land and sea forces of King Victor Emmanuel III., and there the tricolor was flung to the air from the tower of San Giusto. When the armistice went into effect the next day the Austro-Hungarian military forces had been defeated in the field in a manner which was never to be suffered by the Germans in Belgium and France. The armistice providing a capitulation saved the armies of Emperor Charles from death or a voluntary surrender where they stood. After a duel of forty-five weeks with her ancient enemy Italy came forth the supreme victor.

## THE END IN TURKEY

After the annihilation of the Seventh, Eighth, and Fourth Turkish Armies by General Allenby on the terrain between the Plains of Sharon and the River Jordan by rapid movements which began on Sept. 19 the succeeding events in Palestine and Syria down to the time of the Turkish surrender on Oct. 31 were little more than patrol operations for the occupation of the principal towns evacuated by the Turks. The same may be said of the movements of General Marshall's army, operating 450 miles across the desert to the east in the valleys of the Tigris and the Euphrates.

The rapidity with which Allenby's cavalry and camel corps moved is illustrated by the fact that on Oct. 1, less than a fortnight after the campaign had begun, detachments, together with a part of the Arab army of the King of Hedjaz, en-

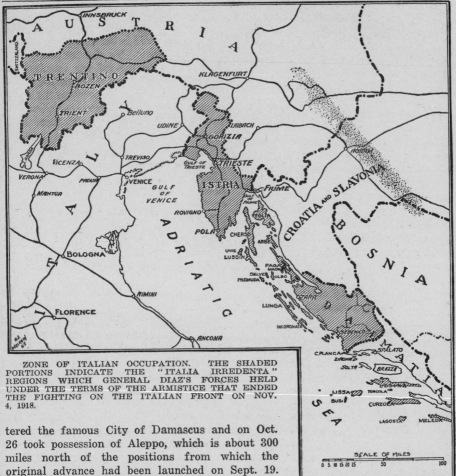

ZONE OF ITALIAN OCCUPATION. THE SHADED PORTIONS INDICATE THE "ITALIA IRREDENTA" REGIONS WHICH GENERAL DIAZ'S FORCES HELD UNDER THE TERMS OF THE ARMISTICE THAT ENDED THE FIGHTING ON THE ITALIAN FRONT ON NOV. 4, 1918.

tered the famous City of Damascus and on Oct. 26 took possession of Aleppo, which is about 300 miles north of the positions from which the original advance had been launched on Sept. 19.

This crowning achievement, just five days before Turkey surrendered, had been made by forced marches, but over a country which, according to authoritative reports, revealed little evidence of the enemy's depredations. Aleppo is about 185 miles north of Damascus and seventy miles east of the Mediterranean. Just above it is the junction of the railway line from Constantinople, via the Scutari ferry across the Bosporus, and the Damascus railway running down through Syria and Palestine to Medina, in the kingdom of Hedjaz. The former line, part of which is called the Bagdad Railway, may or may not be entirely linked up with Mosul, on the Tigris, south of which the forces of Marshall were operating on the other side of the Syrian desert.

Although Allenby, with his army made up of some Italian and French detach-

ments, aside from his original Anglo-Egyptian forces and the Arab army on his right, had opened his decisive campaign on Sept. 19, it was not until a fortnight before the Turkish surrender that Marshall, with the Anglo-Indian army, started to decrease the seventy-five miles of terrain which separated him from Mosul. His delay is explained by the fact that not only did he have to keep his right wing in Northern Persia well protected, but had also been obliged to send a force to relieve the Armenians in the Caspian region.

As he began his advance north he encountered some opposition from the Turks, who had fortified themselves south of Kerkuk, on his right, and across the Tigris near Fatah, on his centre. On Oct. 23, however, the Turkish forces were in full retreat from these positions, and, on his extreme right wing, had evacuated Tabriz, in Persia. His column in the Caspian region was still waiting on eventualities in the vicinity of Baku, which, after occupation, it had been obliged to evacuate, together with the Armenians.

On the very last day of the war Marshall was still heavily engaged with the Turkish forces north of Kaleh Sherghat, where he captured over 1,000 Turks, and his armored cars were on the point of executing an enveloping movement similar to that performed by Allenby's cavalry, when, with the Arab army, it had practically surrounded three Turkish armies seven weeks before.

## CLEARING UP THE BALKANS

The practically unconditional surrender of Bulgaria on Sept. 30 still left the allied armies under General Franchet d'Esperey occupied with the Austrians and Germans in Serbia and Montenegro, and the Italian Army in Albania with the Austrians there, until the Austro-Hungarian Government accepted the armistice, which went into effect on Nov. 4.

As last month's review closed a French column had reached Ipek in Montenegro; the Serbs were at Krushevatz, on their way to Serajevo, in Bosnia; other allied columns had penetrated up the Orient Railway beyond Nish in the direction of Belgrade, and had reached the Rumanian frontier near Radujevac and Vidin, and were preparing to cross the Danube. Meanwhile, the main British and French armies and Italian cavalry

were seeing that the terms of the Bulgarian surrender were being carried out in that territory. Two-thirds of the Serbian land had been recovered.

By Oct. 21 a Serbian column had reached Trstenik in the direction of the Bosnian frontier, while further east another had reached Zajecar, twenty-eight miles south of the Danube at Negotin and forty-five miles northeast of Nish. On the Danube at Vidin the French had cut the Austro-German river communication to Turkey via Bulgaria and had captured the enemy's supply and naval flotilla.

On Oct. 23 French troops entered Negotin, while further west the Serbians smashed the German line of Rajhani-Stalatz. Meanwhile, the Italian advance in Albania was encountering little opposition, for, as the Austrians withdrew, the native bands invariably hoisted the Italian tricolor. On Oct. 30 the Serbian cavalry on its way to Belgrade reached Semendria, twenty-four miles southeast of the old capital, and on Nov. 3 Belgrade itself was occupied. The country south of the Danube by that date had been practically cleared of the Austrians and Germans, while on the west the Second Serbian Army had reached the Bosnian frontier and a Serbian flying column had occupied Serajevo.

Even after the Austro-Hungarian capitulation of Nov. 4 the pursuit of the Germans still continued into Hungarian territory north of the Save and Danube, where, it was reported, the Hungarians welcomed the Serbians.

# The Aviators' Share in the Victory

## German Protest Against Raids

ALLIED supremacy in the air, which had long been pronounced, became overwhelming in the last weeks of the war. The initiative there, as well as on land, passed definitely into the hands of the Entente. The retreat of the Germans from the occupied parts of France and Belgium was greatly accelerated by the effective work of the allied aviators.

Bridges were destroyed, convoys shattered, enemy concentrations broken up, to a degree beyond precedent. Nor was the activity confined to the western front. There were important operations in six separate theatres of war, from the coast of Belgium to the fringes of the Syrian desert. Heavy destruction was wrought on the Palestinian front, in the Balkan battle zone, on the Piave, and in the Monte Grappa region.

British reprisal raids on munition plants and railroad centres in the Rhine Valley continued without abatement. In three months British aviators raided towns in that region 249 times and dropped 247 tons of bombs on strategic points. Great damage was inflicted. Mannheim, Treves, Metz, Sablons, Frankfort, Düsseldorf, Coblenz, and Cologne suffered heavily. Attacks were made Oct. 29 on the Morhange and Frescati airdromes, on factories at Mannheim and Saarbrücken, and on railway junctions at Longuyon, Tecouviez, and Thionville. In the air fighting that accompanied the raid thirty-two enemy machines were destroyed and ten driven down out of control. On Nov. 1 British air forces dropped bombs on railroad junctions at Baden, on chemical factories at Karlsruhe, and on blast furnaces at Burbach. The raiders returned without the loss of a plane.

So great was the agitation aroused by air raids upon the German cities that on Nov. 4 the German Government sent the following protest to Washington:

> The German aerial forces have been under orders since the beginning of October of this year only to make bomb attacks which are directed solely against important hostile military objects within the immediate area of operations of war. These orders were issued on the assumption that the enemy aerial forces were to receive similar instructions.
>
> In assuming this the German people find themselves disappointed. A short time ago the enemy made bomb attacks on the German towns of Wetvlar, Kaiserslautern, Mannheim, Ludwigshafen, Freiburg, Forbach, and Wiesbaden, claiming numerous victims among the civilian population. Nor has occupied territory been spared.
>
> It is evident that Germany can refrain from aerial attacks on enemy territory behind the area of operations only if, on their side, the enemy from now on will reciprocate and also refrain from making aerial attacks outside the area of military operations.
>
> In the expectation that the intention, shared by the other side, to further humanity and preserve important objects of culture, will meet with the understanding of the opponents, the German Government proposes to the Governments of the other belligerent countries that corresponding

instructions be issued without delay to their aerial forces, informing it of the measures taken.

In view of the repeated raids of German air forces in the last four years not only on defenseless towns in France, England, and Belgium, but also on hospitals plainly marked and far beyond the fighting zones, the German protest brought forth no immediate response, though the last air raid on London had been made on May 29, 1918.

Evidence accumulated that the dropping of propaganda material by allied aviators over enemy lines was seriously disturbing the Central Powers. An Austrian army order, published in the Allgemeine Tiroler Anzeiger of Sept 9, ran as follows:

> Enemy airplanes landing in our lines must be absolutely prevented from getting away again. Information of landing of enemy airplanes must immediately be notified by telegram. In order that the troops, gendarmes, and civil population should work in close co-operation, the local military commander should notify the fact at the same time to the military authorities at Innsbruck and Linz, to the Provisional Governor of Salzbourg, and to the Provincial Gendarmerie Commanders.
>
> Further distribution of manifestoes and proclamations by enemy aviators constitutes a crime against the State. Any aviator who distributes such manifestoes or is even found carrying them, thereby places himself outside the limits of international law and will be considered guilty of a crime punishable with death.

From among the hundreds of dramatic incidents in the air fighting on the western front this one may be cited: Two British aviators, flying low in one machine, brought about the surrender of sixty-five Germans, and without leaving their airplane shepherded the party across No Man's Land to the British lines. The pilot and his observer had been attacked from a trench and sunken road. The pilot dived and replied to the enemy fire with his machine guns, killing one and wounding three. The Germans in a panic ceased firing and hoisted a white handkerchief. As there were no British infantrymen in that neighborhood, the pilot descended to within fifty feet of the ground and ordered the Germans out of the trenches, circling around them to insure that none escaped. All were safely brought in and handed over to the nearest British troops. The aviators then resumed their patrol.

Our fighting in the air started last April with one squadron up near Toul. This grew to four squadrons by the end of May. But America's real entrance as an air power dates from the latter part of June, when our airmen entered the Marne fighting. Roughly speaking, our air service took part in three large operations—first, the Marne fighting; second, the St. Mihiel battle, and third, the struggle north of Verdun. By the middle of October, 1918, our aviators had brought down between 500 and 600 German planes.

Testimony given before the House Appropriations Committee in Washington by Colonel H. H. Arnold of the Air Service showed that 11,000 American aviators had already been trained, of the 30,000 provided for in the aviation program. On Nov. 1 there were 8,390 American fliers in France and 6,210 in this country. At that time about 2,500 fighting airplanes of all kinds had been shipped to France, more than 8,000 training planes had been built, and the production of Liberty motors had reached 1,000 a week.

When hostilities were suspended on Nov. 11 our American aviators had destroyed 661 more German airplanes and 35 more German balloons than the Americans had lost. The number of enemy airplanes destroyed by the Americans was 926 and the number of balloons 73. Two hundred and sixty-five American airplanes and 38 balloons were destroyed by the enemy.

On the day of the signing of the armistice there were actually engaged on the front 740 American airplanes, 744 pilots, 457 observers, and 23 aerial gunners. Of the machines, 329 were of the pursuit type, 296 were for observation, and 115 were bombers. Between Sept. 12 and Nov. 11 the air forces operating with the First Army dropped 108,984 kilograms (about 120 tons) of high explosives on the enemy lines, supply depots, and railheads.

# Final Acts of Oppression
## Devastation and Suffering Marked the Pathway of the Retreating German Armies

REVELATIONS of hardships and cruelty suffered by the inhabitants of occupied territories followed in the wake of the retreating German armies. The last atrocities of the invaders had taken such forms as the enforcement of peasant labor, deportations to Germany, wholesale requisitions, pillage, and the needless destruction of cities and villages. Dr. Woods Hutchinson described the situation in recaptured regions of Belgium and France on Sept. 22, 1918, as follows:

"When crossing the beautiful Pays Reconquis last May, lovely still even in its utter desolation, my farm-bred eye was caught by one redeeming feature in the scene of destruction, a soft green background for the picture of horror and despair. This was the waving green seas and sheets of wheat which shimmered over all the fields, over every foot of tillable soil, and rippled right up to the edge of the roadway and to the foot of the shapeless heaps of ruins which had once been human homes.

"It was so far the best crop of wheat that I had seen anywhere in France that it provoked inquiries. Then I found that it had been grown under instructions from Berlin, from the Wilhelmstrasse itself, after this fashion: Sixty per cent. of all the plowable soil was taken over and cultivated by the German Army itself, with its own artillery horses and tractors. Twenty per cent. of the land was cultivated by the peasants and the army together, while the remaining 20 per cent. was cultivated by the peasants themselves, under the direction and watchful eye of the German officials. All that the army grew it took for itself, and half of the crop which it had cultivated jointly with the peasants, so that all that the peasant had left was 30 per cent. of his former crop, and the bulk of this was purchased for the use of the army and paid for in promissory notes, redeemable and payable after the close of the war! Which was extremely nourishing for the peasant and his family.

" The net result was that the German Army which occupied Northern France and Belgium grew, with the assistance of the peasants, all the grain that was required for themselves and their horses, and even sent some back for the civilian population at home.

" And I was informed that the same methods and the same results were enforced on the Russian and on the Rumanian fronts also.

" The reason for the joint cultivation of one-fifth of the land was apparently to get the German under-officers acquainted with the members of the peasant population and their various working capacities. When this had been ascertained, every old man or old woman, every mother of a family, every boy or girl over the age of 12, was assigned a certain number of hours' work each day, either upon the land, or cutting wood, or washing the soldiers' clothing, or cooking, or making roads, or digging trenches, or, if house-ridden, sewing sandbags. A book was issued to each one, in which was written down the number of hours per day required or the amount of piece work to be turned out. This had to be inspected and signed each week, and in some cases each day, by the local officer, and at the end of the week turned in to the military police officer in charge of the district. If the bearer of the book could not then show that he or she had performed the full task of work required he was flogged, imprisoned, or otherwise severely punished, and threatened with deportation into Germany to work in the munition factories or the mines."

## DEPORTATION OF CITIZENS

Deportations of French and Belgian inhabitants continued to the end of the German occupation. With reference to the labor of prisoners of war within the German lines a British White Paper of Oct. 29 stated: " Some prisoners were forced to work often within the fire of their own guns. On one occasion 1,300 to 1,500 prisoners were billeted in an old church. ' The place was fearfully crowded and we had only straw to lie on, which got filthy and verminous; but the crowd was such that many of us were unable to sit or lie down.' "

The following official document for the forcible conscription of the women in Lille, Easter week, 1916, was discovered after the Germans evacuated the city:

All inhabitants of households, with the exception of children under 14 years and their mothers, and with the exception as well of aged people, must prepare at once for their deportation in an hour and a half. An officer will make the final decision as to which persons shall be conducted to the camp of assembly. For this purpose all inhabitants of households must assemble before their habitations; in case of bad weather it is permitted to remain in the lobby of the house; the door must be kept open.

All pleas will be useless. No inhabitant of the house, even those who are not to be transported, will be permitted to leave the house before 8 in the morning, German time.

Each person will be entitled to ten kilograms of luggage. If there is excess of weight the entire luggage of such person will be refused without any consideration. It is absolutely necessary to provide one's self in one's own interest with utensils for eating and drinking, and also with a woolen blanket, good boots, and linen. Every person must carry his or her identity card.

Any one who endeavors to avoid transportation will be ruthlessly punished.

ETAPPEN,
Kommandantur.

## WHOLESALE REQUISITIONS

The following estimate of the total of enforced contributions exacted from the Belgians during the period of German occupation was made by Belgian officials on Oct. 20:

Local contributions and fines levied by Germany on Belgium in 1914, £8,000,000.

War contributions from November, 1914, to October, 1916, £38,400,000.

War contributions, seven months, to May, 1918, £23,000,000.

War contributions from May, 1917, to May, 1918, £28,000,000.

War contributions from June to October of the current year, £15,000,000.

Raw materials and machinery taken by the Germans were reckoned by them in January, 1915, at £80,000,000. The damage to December, 1914, estimated by the North German Gazette, amounted to £200,000,000. This makes a grand total of £384,200,000, [$1,921,000,000.]

These items do not include material destruction and requisitions since January, 1915, which alone must be reckoned at several hundred million pounds.

During the Winter of 1916 Belgian workingmen to the number of 1,750,000 were deported to Germany. The future production of these men was thus totally lost to their country.

## PILLAGE AT BRUGES

Of pillage Perry Robinson, in his cable dispatches, wrote on Oct. 21:

" In Bruges on Friday night all civilians were told to stay within doors until 11 o'clock next day. The order was obeyed, and it gave the German soldiery the finest opportunity they had had for looting. A ring or knock would be heard at the door of a shop or house. On the door being opened two or three German soldiers were within with pistols ready. At one private house the owner opened the door and was met with a demand for shirts. He said he had no shirt but the one he wore and those at the laundry.

" ' What time is it? ' asked one of the soldiers. The man took out his watch and immediately they demanded the watch and then ordered him to take them into his house and give them any other watches and jewelry he had. They carried off three timepieces and some rings.

" At various shops I heard similar stories of men coming and ringing at the door, and then, while flourishing a revolver, filling their pockets with whatever caught their fancy. Of course, there has been in these towns the same continuous thieving as at Lille and elsewhere—the same abuse of ' requisitions ' and the same terrorism.

" In Ostend all empty houses were stripped clean of everything, as were also the great hotels. These last furnished rich hauls of ' requisitioned ' goods. The kitchen battery of a big hotel has about ten coppers on an average, which, of course, are all gone, also all mattresses and woolen goods—all taken under formal requisition. Then every day soldiers came in and took one thing after another. The guardian of one hotel told me how they came with sacks and carried off things that were portable, and finally removed all the furniture, either to be sent to Germany or sold or used to furnish dugouts."

## EXPERIENCES AT LIEGE

In a dispatch to THE NEW YORK TIMES Nov. 4 the following appeared:

" Liége is full of soldiers, mostly those returning from the front. Besides a large house already emptied of its occupants to accommodate Prince Rupprecht, more and more houses are being evacuated in the city. There are many signs that a large number of troops are expected.

" German officers are as insolent and arrogant as ever, and either turn the people out of their houses altogether or allow them to live in garret or cellar, or, if alone, an officer often chooses the largest and finest rooms for himself, without any consideration of the occupants. All the hospitals except one have been taken by the military, and the sick are turned out, in spite of the large numbers of patients at present.

" Houses which have been occupied by officers during the war are entirely spoiled and plundered of their valuables. Oriental carpets are taken with the excuse that the wool is requisitioned, and of course anything of bronze or brass is valuable; vases, works of art, pictures, old furniture, and clocks, as in the seventies, are looted.

" All these are taken and sold in Germany or Holland. The hunt for brass, copper, and bronze has been untiring in the last few months. Walls are broken and cellars ransacked to find hiding places.

" An order was issued a few weeks ago that even all water faucets in houses would be removed. However, this order was countermanded a week ago, when the ardent search for metal was also abandoned. People are asking whether this is an indication of peace. Fines are no longer imposed for hoarding or hiding."

## SELLING STOLEN FURNITURE

The Norwegian Journal Morgenbladt of Christiania received a significant letter from a correspondent, who described as follows the traffic that had developed in the sale of furniture stolen from Belgium:

The importation of furniture [into Norway] is one of the activities promoted by the war—all the more unexpected because it overthrows the ancient foundations of the philosophy of law and the rights of people. " It is permitted to exact war contributions from the conquered, that is the State, but it is not permitted to appropriate private property; that would be robbery," says Kant, one of the thinkers oftenest cited by the exporters of the furniture in question.

Indeed, as Kant would say, this furniture is stolen from French and Belgian homes. The traffic is so flourishing because the cost price defies competition and the supply exceeds the amount which the furniture makers could furnish, at any rate in Norway.

The Speditions und Lagerhaus Akt Ges., Aix-la-Chapelle, and a great many other old and new firms, as announced in the Koelnische Zeitung, furnish information and estimates in regard to the transportation of furniture from the Belgian cities to Germany and Austria-Hungary.

We do not, however, find the furniture cheap, for it has passed through many hands, the express company, the speculators, and the retailers. But, in the first place there is not much expense except the estimates made by the above mentioned firm and others. And these estimates include only the expense for transportation by railroad, upholsterers, movers, and damage; and not even these expenses when the furniture has been removed by an official order. " The dining room suite was charming," wrote the wife of a German officer to her husband; " now you must try to get us a salon in the Empire style."

" Furniture from belligerent countries." But it is not hidden in the sombre shop of a receiver of stolen goods. It is posted in the rue de l'Université (Universitetsgaten) on the sign of the shop and in all the houses and in the advertising columns of the papers. It is purchased by our " nouveaux riches." The most beautiful pieces were already sold, said the man whom I found in the shop.

" The furniture comes from numerous Belgian and French homes," he said; " it comes directly from France; I am selling it for a Norwegian who is traveling."

## GHASTLY DEVASTATION

A graphic description of the devastation and ruin left in the wake of the German armies was cabled by Walter Duranty on Oct. 19 to THE NEW YORK TIMES:

" Words cannot express the utter desolation of the Passchendaele battlefield. Already Ypres is a deplorable ruin, whose central square, which was once a thing of beauty, flanked by the marvelous Cloth Hall and the thousand-year-old houses, now resembles the outskirts of a new American town.

" Grass and weeds are the tragedy of Ypres; one cannot even tell where the houses stood or the roads once ran. But the appalling shell-torn waste that is the battlefield of Flanders surpasses the wildest visions of Doré in ghastliness and gloom. For nearly four miles the road of rotting planks that is the sole passage across the ridges winds amid acres of shell holes merging one into another.

" No single tree or bush or hedge or building remains to tell that human beings once cultivated this desert. Here lie a rusting tank and three broken caissons. Further on is a hole that was a dugout where men lived and died. Everywhere are shattered concrete, barbed wire in crazy festoons, convex roofs of corrugated iron that gave some shelter against the elements, planks by millions for roadways, and faded crosses that mark innumerable graves.

" This frightful realization of Macbeth's ' blasted heath ' is the resting place of tens of thousands of brave men to whom death must have been a relief from more than mortal hardship. Now only rats—huge, gaunt, and hungry since the humans have departed—inhabit the accursed spot, and run sluggishly across the road before the automobiles and then bump slowly over the shell holes."

## DESTRUCTION OF CITIES

That this picture is not singular to one front is proved by other correspondents. Of Douai one wrote: " Not one of several hundred houses is in a livable condition. * * * The south and east sides of the Grand Place were blown to the ground. A number of houses in the southern part of the town were burned apparently out of sheer caprice. The handsome City Hall was stripped of its candelabra and the archives there were thrown about in confusion." Again of Audenarde this was written: "Today the city is deserted, the doors of the dwellings are left wide open; through the shattered windows one can easily judge from the disorder of the bedding that the inhabitants must have fled in a hurry, surprised as they were by this criminal bombardment. Not a soul is encountered, and a shower of shells continues the destruction, wrecking houses and monuments. The beautiful Town Hall seems irremediably damaged. While I am writing, the bombardment is going on." An Associated Press correspondent with the French Army in Champagne wrote on Oct. 23:

"The region along the Retourne abounds with indications of willful devastation of villages that were never within range of artillery, but were found razed to the ground. In others, where houses were still erect, they were mined for slow destruction, while the purely military installations, such as barracks built by the Germans for their own troops, were left intact. Orders for the burning of Juniville, a large village in the valley of the Retourne, arrived on the day of evacuation. The Germans had built comfortable quarters, with casinos, officers' clubs, moving-picture theatres, hotels, and rest houses for the soldiers in the village. The people pleaded with the officers to spare their homes, but the torch was put to every house. The village was one vast brazier when the French entered it. Mont St. Remy shared the same fate.

"Châtelet, Alincourt, Bignicourt, and Ville-sur-Retourne were partially saved because the French troops pressed the Germans there so closely that the sappers left behind to do the work were surprised. Some of these men fled before they could set off the mines which had been prepared. Others were captured."

An instance of mining a church was reported on Nov. 4 by the officer commanding the American troops on the British front south of Le Cateau. "By means of wires," he wrote, "the charge was connected with the monstrance on the high altar in such a way that if the sacred vessel were moved an explosion would have brought the church down on the heads of the worshippers."

# How Peace Came to the Battlefronts

## The Wave of Rejoicing That Swept Over the Allied Armies and Nations

*When the signing of the armistice between the Entente Powers and Germany ended the war on Nov. 11, 1918, the reaction from the tension of the conflict found expression in great demonstrations of joy throughout the allied world. The victorious nations gave themselves up to holiday. Strangely enough, the relief and delight found more unrestrained expression among the civil populations than among the men who had carried on the grim work of fighting. New York, London, Paris, Rome, went wild with uncurbed enthusiasm, and their example was followed on a smaller scale in every city and village of the Allies. Edwin L. James cabled from the American front in France the day the armistice was signed:*

NOVEMBER 11, 1918.—They stopped fighting at 11 o'clock this morning. In a twinkling of an eye four years' killing and massacre stopped, as if God had swept His omnipotent finger across the scene of world carnage and cried, "Enough!"

In fact, it seemed as if some good spirit had helped set the stage for the ending of the great tragedy. They told me at the front today that never before had the telephones and wireless worked so well. All our divisions, all our regiments, all our companies, got the word to quit at 11, and quit they did.

History will record that the Americans fought to the last minute. Aye, more, they fought to the last second. I picked the sector northeast of historic Verdun on the scarred hills where were buried German hopes, to spend what may be the world's greatest day. On this front we attacked this morning at 9:30 o'clock, after heavy artillery preparation.

Reaching the front this morning, expecting to find quiet reigning in view of the imminence of the cessation of hostilities, I found the attack in full swing, with every gun we had going at full speed, and roaring in a glorious chorus, singing the swan song of Prussianism. It was a glorious chorus drowning the discord of German shell-fire. We were attacking.

Picture, if you will, that scene at 10:30 this morning. Back in the rear every one knew that the war was to stop at 11 o'clock, but in the front line no one knew except the officers. The doughboys knew nothing except their orders were to attack. They had heard rumors, but at 10:30 they were chasing the Germans back from their last hold on the hills east of the Meuse. At 10:40, at 10:50, at 10:55 they were fighting on. What could be more dramatic than when at 11 the platoon leaders in the front line sharply called the order, "Cease firing!" and explained that hostilities had been called off?

## THE LAST SALVO

If one listened then, one heard just at 11 the great salvo from all our guns, and then silence. They tell me the men stood as if numbed with shock, and then smiles spread over their faces and they broke into laughs as they listened and learned the Germans, too, had called off the war.

Then through the fog across the ravine they saw the boches spring from their positions and shout and sing with joy. They saw white flags in the cold wind and they saw the boches waving their hands in invitation to come over. But strict orders had been issued to our men against fraternizing, and the Germans, getting no encouragement, kept on their side of No Man's Land.

When all this happened I was standing with a grizzled American General at Beaumont, just back of the line of one of our crack divisions.

"It's so big," said he, "that I cannot grasp it at all," and then he pulled from his pocket a paper, and handing it to me, said, "Here's the order that stopped the war."

What he handed me was a copy of the order written, I understand, by Marshal Foch, the self-same order being issued to all the allied troops this morning.

It was just after 11 o'clock when a General invited me to go from within the last front line. We started walking eastward from Beaumont. Over terrain torn so that there was not one inch that had not its shell hole, we climbed the heights of the Bois de Wavrille. Toiling through rack and ruin, stumps and wire and fallen trees, we came after an hour to the eastern edge of the Bois de Wavrille from which the Germans had been driven this morning.

## IN VIEW OF THE ENEMY

Across a ravine lay the Bois Herbebois, with St. André Farm a mass of stones on the slopes nearest us. Half way up the hill toward the Bois Herbebois ran a road, and that road was the front line. Along it were doughboys ready if the boche changed his mind about stopping hostilities.

Right up the hill was the German line at the end of the woods. We could see Germans walking about. With a French Captain and an American Major I started across, but the General called us back. Going up to the hill near St. André Farm, we got a good look at the boche lines, where the Germans appeared as unconcerned as if on a picnic. Out fifty yards ahead of our front line was a dugout from which curled smoke. In it were three boches cooking supper. A platoon of our men wanted to go get them, but a Lieutenant ruled against it, so the Germans went on cooking supper.

Over these hills, the scene of bloody

warfare since the war started and the scene of perhaps the world's most bitter battle when the Crown Prince tried to take Verdun, an almost unearthly calm rested. Where the roar of a million and one shells had so often torn the air one could have heard a sparrow twit had the ruthless war left a sparrow there. Torn and twisted and tortured was that land. Of all the woods no tree was left whole. There were only blackened and stark sticks. Of pretty villages there were only moss-covered and shattered stones, of roads not one trace was left. Over all were sombre shadow and silence that would have seemed ominous had one not known that it was harmless. The war had stopped.

### THE FIRST CAMPFIRES

While we were there at the front Germans could be seen getting back, as if seeking sleeping quarters for more comfort. As we left the scene cold dusk was settling in a wet blanket over the landscape. As we reached the edge of the woods the General called my attention to hundreds of campfires lining the hills as far as the eye could see. It was the first time fire had burned on the front line since the days when the Kaiser ran amuck and started more than he and his misled people could finish. Germany stopped at the eleventh hour.

As we came back along the roads the landscape seemed to be filled with cheering Americans. The news had spread everywhere and our men were behaving just as a victorious football team and its fans after the last game of the season. No Fourth of July in the United States ever saw such fireworks as tore their red, green, and blue streaks across the foggy sky.

And what we saw at Verdun would stir the pulse of a dead man. Poor, torn, suffering Verdun! It had been suddenly changed to a place of glory. Gathering darkness hid its wounds, and what one saw was the French Tricolor and the Stars and Stripes flying from the house-tops and parapets, searchlights showing their glory in all its splendor. At the top of the grizzled fortress walls a band, half French and half Yankee, was playing all the tunes it knew, while through the streets marched rejoicing Yankees and their allies, whom they love. What could be more fitting for allied victory than that immortal Verdun should celebrate it?

### FRATERNIZING FORBIDDEN

*To ward off danger from fraternizing the following orders were issued by the American military authorities to their brigade commanders:*

1. You are informed that hostilities will cease along the whole front at 11 o'clock A. M., Nov. 11, 1918, Paris time.

2. No allied troops will pass the line reached by them at that hour in date until further orders.

3. Division commanders will immediately sketch the location of their front line. This sketch will be returned to headquarters by the courier bearing these orders.

4. All communication with the enemy, both before and after the termination of hostilities, is absolutely forbidden. In case of violation of this order severest disciplinary measures will be immediately taken. Any officer offending will be sent to headquarters under guard.

5. Every emphasis will be laid on the fact that the arrangement is an armistice only, and not a peace.

6. There must not be the slightest relaxation of vigilance. Troops must be prepared at any moment for further operations.

7. Special steps will be taken by all commanders to insure strictest discipline and that all troops be held in readiness fully prepared for any eventuality.

8. Division and brigade commanders will personally communicate these orders to all organizations.

### FIRES OF HELL PUT OUT

*The rejoicings at Mons and Ghent on the two days following the signing of the armistice were described by Mr. Gibbs as follows:*

Nov. 12.—Last night, for the first time since August in the first year of the war, there was no light of gunfire in the sky, no sudden stabs of flame through the darkness, no long, spreading glow above the black trees where for four years of night human beings were being smashed to death.

The fires of hell had been put out. It was silent all along the front. With the beautiful silence of nights of peace, we did not stand listening to the dull rumbling of artillery at work, which had been the undertone of all closer sounds for 1,500 nights, nor for sudden heart beats at explosions shaking the earth and air, nor say in whisper to ourselves, " Curse those guns! " At 11 o'clock the order had gone to all batteries to cease fire. No more men will be killed, no more be mangled, no more be blinded. The last boyhood of the world was reprieved on the way back from Mons.

I listened to this silence which followed the going down of the sun and heard the rustling of russet leaves and the little sounds of night in peace, and it seemed as though God gave a benediction to the wounded soul of the world. Other sounds rose from towns and fields in the yellowing twilight, and in the deepening shadow world of the day of armistice. They were sounds of human joy.

Men were singing somewhere on the roads, and their voices rang out gladly. Bands were playing, as all day on the way to Mons I heard their music ahead of the marching columns. Bugles were blowing.

## BRITISH TROOPS GAY

In villages from which the enemy had gone out that morning round about Mons crowds of figures surged in the narrow streets, and English laughter rose above the silvery chatter of women and children. British soldiers were still on the march with their guns, and their transport, and their old field cookers, and all along their lines I heard these men talking to each other gayly as though something had loosened their tongues and made them garrulous.

Motor cars streaked through Belgian streets, dodging traffic, and now and then, when night fell, rockets were fired from them, and there came gusts of laughter from young officers, shooting off their pistols into the darkness to celebrate the end of hostilities by this symbol of the rising stars, which did not soar so high as their spirits. From dark towns like Tournai and Lille these rockets rose and burned a little while with a white light.

Our aviators flew like bats in the dusk, skimming tree tops and gables, doing Puck-like gambols above the tawny sunset, looping and spiraling and falling in steep dives which looked like death for them until they flattened out and rose again. And they, too, these boys who had been reprieved from the menace which was close to them on every flight, fired flares and rockets, which dropped down to the crowds of French and Flemish people waving to them from below.

Late into the night there were sounds of singing and laughter from open windows in towns which had been all shuttered, with people hiding in their cellars a week ago or less, and British officers sat down to French pianos and romped about the keys and crashed out chords, and led a chorus of men who wanted to sing any old song.

## ON THE ROAD TO MONS

It was worth going to Mons yesterday. I stopped at brigade headquarters on the way, and an officer there said:

" Hostilities will cease at 11 o'clock this morning, and thank God for that! "

Everywhere the news had gone ahead of me. Soldiers assembled in the fields for morning parade were flinging their steel helmets up and cheering. As they marched through villages they shouted out to civilians, " Guerre fini, guerre fini, boche napoo! " And the women and children came running to them with Autumn flowers, mostly red and white chrysanthemums, and they put them in their tunics and in the straps of their steel helmets.

Thousands of flags appeared suddenly in villages where no French or Belgian flag could be shown without fines and imprisonment until that very morning, when liberty had come again and every Tommy in the ranks had a bit of color at the end of his rifle or stuck through his belt, and every gun team had a banner floating above their limber or their guns, and their horses had flowers in their harness.

For miles there was a pageant on the roads, and as there moved one way endless tides of British infantry, and cavalry, and artillery, and transport, with all that flutter of flags above them, with the great banners of Belgium and France like flames above them, another tide moved the opposite way, and that had its flags and its banners.

It was the pitiful, heroic tide of life, made up of thousands of civilians, people who that morning had come back through the German lines. They were men from 15 to 60 who had been taken away from Cambrai and Courtrai, Lille, and Roubaix, and Tourcoing, Tournai and Valenciennes and hundreds of towns and villages in the wake of the enemy's retreat, because to the very end the German command conscripted this manhood to forced labor.

## SCENES AT GHENT

Nov. 13.—I passed last night in Ghent and saw the joy of this city of Belgium after its liberation. It was the last Belgian town to be rescued before the armistice. The Germans had clung to it as the pivot of their retreat, holding the canal in front of it by machine-gun fire, and it was not until 2 o'clock on Monday morning that they went away.

Twelve Belgian soldiers were the first to enter, at 7 o'clock, led by a young Belgian Lieutenant, whom I met last night, and a few minutes afterward all the streets were filled with the citizens of Ghent shouting, cheering, embracing these soldiers and each other.

The enemy had gone after four years of oppression, and as dawn came it rose upon a day of liberty. Bells rang out from all the churches as they are now ringing while I write, and from the old belfries of Ghent there were joyful carillons.

The Belgian troops marched in, and their artillery passed through, and the people covered them with flags, and the music of their bands was overwhelmed by shouts of " Vive la Belgique."

It was beyond the British sphere of action, and yesterday when I went into Ghent with two other men the sight of our uniforms aroused new enthusiasm, and crowds surrounded us with outstretched hands and words of thanks to England. It was astonishing how many people spoke English in those crowds of men and women who pressed close to tell of things they had suffered, and again,

as always in these captured cities, of the awful misery of British prisoners.

Darkness came into this Old World town, with its tall Flemish houses of red brick and stepped gables, unchanged in many parts since Charles II. was in exile here, and with its Hotel de Ville and Palais de Justice richly sculptured by Flemish craftsmen who were great artists, and with its churches and cathedrals and belfries, whose bells have rung above the city through many centuries of joy and woe—darkness came, but not in the hearts of the people nor in their windows. For the first time in five Winters of war they lighted their lamps with open shutters, and from many windows there streamed out bright beams which lured one like a moth to candlelight because of its sign of peace. There were bright stars and a crescent moon in the sky, silvering the Flemish gables and frontages between black shadows and making patterns of lace in the Place d'Armes below the trees with their Autumn foliage.

In these lights and in these shadows the people of Ghent danced and sang until midnight chimed. They danced in baker's dozens, with linked arms, men and girls together, singing in deep voices and high voices, all mingling, so that when I went to my bedroom and looked out of the casement window it rose in a chorus from all over the city, like music by Debussy.

## KING ALBERT'S ENTRY

Today in Ghent there are vast cheering crowds, and King Albert is making his triumphal entry into his city, and the sun is shining with a golden light upon all the old roofs of Ghent and upon the crowded balconies from which banners hang.

The King and Queen came riding in with the young Prince, escorted by Belgian, French, and British Generals, and as they came white flowers were thrown from all the balconies, and their petals fell about like confetti. They took up a position outside the old club in the Place d'Armes, and cheers swept around them in storms. Then there was a march past of Belgian troops, men who had fought on the Yser in the old bad days of mud and blood, and those who, in the last days, had stormed their way through with guns and cavalry. They had flowers in their rifles and on their helmets, and looked like veterans as they marched under their heavy packs.

The Queen of the Belgians wore a light habit with a little linen cap, and was a simple figure. There next to her was the tall King, whose face has been bronzed and hardened by four years in the field with his men. It is a great day for Belgium, and the air is full of music and the gladness of a brave people whose courage has won through to victory.

## CELEBRATION IN NEW YORK

The United States held a premature jubilation on Nov. 7, based on a false cablegram, but there was enough emotion left, when the real and authentic news of the signing of the armistice arrived before daylight Nov. 11, to start a celebration in New York City that lasted without interruption for fully twenty-four hours, and while it was going on stopped all kinds of business in the city except theatrical performances and the dispensing at retail of food.

And what was true of New York was true of the nation. Throughout the country there were joyous celebrations of the signing of the armistice, marked by parades and the ringing of bells. Every city, village, and hamlet thus expressed its emotion at the victorious ending of the war.

Yet it was not altogether the same kind of celebration that had occurred when the premature news was celebrated. That event had let off much surplus steam, and nothing else could quite get up the enthusiasm which was then manifested. When the premature peace report dropped suddenly, as if out of the skies, on a city which had not expected the news at that particular moment, New York was like a city which found itself saved after entertaining gloomy forebodings. On every countenance in the street, in the early hours of that day before the peace report was known to be false, there was a heartfelt,

unconscious smile of rapture, an outward token of the coming to every man and woman of glad tidings of great joy. The devil was dead, and everybody felt a particular personal interest in his demise.

This first spontaneous expression of relief on Nov. 11 had already been discounted; there was more of a prearranged air about the celebration. But if it was deliberate, it was none the less heartfelt, none the less of universal appeal. The whole city joined in celebrating the final and complete disappearance of German autocracy, a disappearance whose surprising fullness was not known when the false peace report came. And so, while there was not the impressive revelation of a people's soul which was evoked by the false news, there was none the less a celebration which the City of New York will hold in its memory for many years.

Whistles, sirens, and bells kept up a constant din the entire day; all business was suspended; the streets were packed and jammed; spontaneous processions formed in every block; effigies of the Kaiser hanging and in coffins were conspicuous; dense snowstorms of bits of paper filled the air and streets, and at night the city was in a state of joyous celebration that almost approached delirium.

## AT PARIS

It was to the accompaniment of great guns firing a salute to Victory along the banks of the Seine that Premier Clemenceau, speaking from the tribune of the Chamber of Deputies, told France the extent of the great triumph of the Allies. At that moment those other guns in the bitter action of four long years, from the North Sea to the Swiss frontier, had been silent for five hour.

Paris had known definitely from 11 o'clock that the armistice had been signed and that the fighting had ceased, but the great moment of the great day had been reserved for the time when Clemenceau should make the declaration in Parliament and read the conditions of the armistice.

He had hardly begun when the crowd in the Chamber heard the muffled booming of guns outside, and knew that all France was rejoicing. There were no formal preliminaries. No attempt at ceremony was needed or undertaken to add anything to one of the most impressive sessions in the history of all Parliaments. The Premier mounted the tribune almost immediately after entering the Chamber. He waited for the end of the tumult of applause, and then, without a word of introduction, began reading those conditions which were being announced simultaneously in all allied capitals.

In the terms themselves was the best possible oratory—victory as read by this wonderful old man of nearly 80. This Clemenceau, this "Tiger of France," who has known so well how to save his people. It was the Clemenceau who as a member of this same Chamber nearly fifty years ago voted against surrender to the triumphant Germany.

Often he was stopped by applause which even blotted out the sound of the guns—when, for example, he read that Alsace-Lorraine was coming back, that the submarines were to be given up, that the victorious troops were to go to the Rhine.

Only once, and then for only an instant, did this master of sarcasm allow any sarcasm to creep into his voice. It was when he had occasion to refer to the Imperial Government of Germany. Laughter swept across the Chamber, shared in even by that sparse group of the Extreme Right, known as Royalists. There was for the moment, at least, no Right, Left, or Centre. France as represented in that Chamber was united in her hour of triumph.

As he came down the tribune the venerable Premier had to stop on his way to the Ministers' bench and shake hands with his enemies, the Socialists, who crowded about him.

Applause and cheering were not enough for this session of the Chamber. The Deputies as they rose to adjourn spontaneously began singing the "Marseillaise." The hymn was taken up by the galleries and by the crowds in the corridors. It spread to the vast throng standing in the twilight outside on the river banks and bridges, and soon all Paris was singing its song of victory.

All day and everywhere the rejoicing went on, and it continued all night. From the Bastile to the Madeleine, down the Rue Royale to the great corral of captured German guns in the moonlit Place de la Concorde, up the Champs Elysées across the many bridges, singing, weeping, laughing.

## IN LONDON

King George, accompanied by the Queen and Princess Mary, drove in an open carriage to the Mansion House in London on Nov. 11 to congratulate the Lord Mayor and the citizens of London. He was everywhere greeted with extraordinary enthusiasm. The City gave itself up to wholehearted merriment and infectious joyousness. At night all London was brilliantly illuminated and the populace surged to the streets. Spread over three miles from St. Paul's to Oxford Circus and down Whitehall to Victoria the streets were full from curb to curb with laughing, jostling, happy people, and traffic difficulties were solved in the simplest fashion by turning back nearly all buses.

A marvelous night scene was witnessed off the Scottish Coast when the grand fleet celebrated the armistice. On a thirty-mile line, warships of every description were simultaneously illuminated. Myriads of sirens blew off with awesome sounds. Hundreds of searchlights played fantastically. Fireworks and star shells were shot up.

A Te Deum for victory was sung and solemn thanksgiving was offered on Nov. 12 in St. Paul's Cathedral, London. The royal family, the Government officials, all the diplomatic corps, the clergy, and over 10,000 people were in attendance.

The signing of the armistice was elaborately celebrated at Rome, and the Vatican issued a note of thanksgiving.

Throughout the entire world, in cities, towns, villages, and at countrysides, the celebrations were spontaneous and unrestrained, being signalized by the blowing of whistles, ringing of bells and impromptu processions and demonstrations of joy.

# The Redemption of Belgium

## Final Advance of the Allied Armies That Freed the Coast and Liberated Valenciennes and Ghent

### By PHILIP GIBBS

*The forced evacuation of Belgium by the German armies continued with scarcely a pause from the middle of October to the declaration of the armistice on Nov. 11. The advance of the Allies and the joy of the liberated towns as their deliverers entered were describd with his distinctive charm by Mr. Gibbs in his cable dispatches to The New York Times, which copyrighted them for its affiliated publication, CURRENT HISTORY MAGAZINE. The most memorable of these pen pictures are here presented:*

BRITISH FRONT IN BELGIUM, Oct. 18, 1918.—To go into Lille this morning was as good as anything that can come to a man who had seen four years of war, and I am glad that I have lived to see the liberation of that city. I saw the joy of thousands of people who, during all those four years, have suffered tragic things, unforgettable outrages to their liberty and spirit, and have dwelt under a dark spell of fear and have waited month after month, year after year, with a faith that sometimes weakened but never died, for the rescue that has now come to them.

It seems a miracle to them, now that it has come suddenly, and they fill their streets like people in a dream, hugging their gladness, yet almost afraid that it is unreal and that they may wake again to find the swarms of field-gray men about them and guns in their gardens and the German law hard upon them.

All the bridges had been blown up as the last act of the enemy at 1:30 o'clock yesterday morning, before his flight, and most of the British troops were still on the west and south side of the canal and had not entered the city, but they had built footbridges here and there, and I crossed on one and walked into the heart of the people, who were ready to give a warm welcome to any Englishman in khaki.

They opened their arms in great embraces of gratitude and love for those who have helped to rescue them from their bondage, and I saw the joy of vast crowds, and the light in thousands of eyes was like sunlight about one, and in a few hours one made hundreds of friends who thrust gifts into one's hands and poured out their emotion in words of utter simplicity and truth, and thanked one poor individual as though he were all the army and had done this thing alone.

It was overwhelming and uplifting. Before one had gone far up the first avenue of Lille one was surrounded by a great crowd. A lady broke through the ring, and, clasping both hands, said: " I embrace you for the gladness you have brought us." She kissed one on both cheeks, and it was the signal for general embraces.

Pretty girls came forward and offered their cheeks, and small boys pushed through to kiss the men bending down to them, and old men put their hands on one's shoulders and touched one's face with their grizzled mustaches, and mothers held up their children to be kissed.

This did not last for a few minutes. It lasted all the time I was in Lille. For hours tens of thousands of people were in the streets, and my hands were clasped by many hundreds of them, by all close enough to take my hand.

Children walked hand in hand with me for a little way as if they had known me for years, and talked all the time of their gladness because the Germans had gone. Then other children took their places and other groups gathered, and one was closed in by new crowds who seized one's hands and cried: "Welcome! Welcome! Long live England!"

## PRAYED FOR THE ALLIES

I passed today through Armentières, a town of shapeless ruin, and thought of all the death that has been there while Lille remained an unattainable place. Thousands of British have fallen around here in four years of terrible fighting, and in April last, after the German offensive, when they drove through Armentières itself, Lille seemed further away than before, and that to many of the British men was all the way from life to death.

Now, this morning I passed the last rubbish heap of ruin, the last dead tree stump, the last shell craters and barbed wire, the last dead horses on the road; and came very quickly to that great city beyond the canal, that was so close to the British lines and yet so far, where there are fine churches, colleges, shops, factories, private houses, and an enormous population of rich people and poor, all under the evil spell of German rule, all passionate against its tyrannies, torn with emotions and agonies that were hidden from the Allies until today.

Women lay awake, as they told me today, and cried out: "When will the English come?" Children wept themselves to sleep, as their mothers told me this morning, because another day had passed and the English had not come. "We had so long to wait for you, very long," said many of these people today.

## CONSCRIPTED 8,000 GIRLS

After the first terror of the German occupation and the first nagging of law which regulated all their lives, forbade them to be out in the streets after 8 o'clock in the evening, and shut them up in their houses like naughty children at 2 in the afternoon when the German commandant was annoyed with some complaint, one of their worst days came when, just before Easter, 1916, 8,000 young women of Lille were forcibly seized and sent away to work in the fields, hundreds of miles from their homes.

It was a reign of terror for every girl in Lille and for their parents. Different quarters in the town were chosen for this conscription of girls, and machine guns were posted at each end of the street, and families were ordered to gather in doorways when the German officers came around and made arbitrary choice, saying to one girl, "You," and to another, "You," and then ordered their men to take them.

Mr. Moore, a clergyman, told me that some girls whom he knew were dragged out of their beds and carried screaming away. They were girls in all conditions of life, and a young one whom I met today told me that she was chosen but escaped by threatening to kill herself rather than go, for it was to be a life of misery and horror to any girl of decent instincts.

One of them who was taken and spent six months in this forced labor told me that she had no change of linen all that time and slept on a truss of straw in an old barn, at first with men who were put into the same barn with them and then only with women.

They never had enough to eat in the early days, though the food was better later, and many of these girls fell ill from hunger, and their brothers, who were also taken, suffered. More unspeakable things happened, and there is no forgiveness in the hearts of those who suffered them.

That was the first exodus from Lille, and the second happened twelve days later, when 12,000 men and boys were sent away further into the German lines so that their labor should not be given to the Allies.

"I went when my poor boy was taken," said a lady this morning. "He was only 14, and such a child in his heart. They were laden with packs and kept in the citadel for two nights before leaving, with little food, and when they were assembled their sisters and mothers walked with them as far as allowed, weeping and crying, and the boys and men tried in vain to hide their own tears, and it was a breaking of hearts."

## JOY WITH A SOB IN IT

Oct. 20.—Under pressure of the allied armies the enemy's retreat continues, with severe rearguard fighting on the British front east of Roubaix, Douai, and Le Cateau, but every hour is giving back to Belgium and France precious soil and cities, and is liberating thousands of their people from German bondage.

These are wonderful days when the agony of war is passing from stricken souls, so that out of misery they are lifted to joy, which in itself is a kind of pain, because it is so sudden. Strong men cheer with tears streaming down their cheeks, as I saw many times yesterday in Bruges. The laughter of women breaks suddenly into sobs.

We who are witnesses of these days, having been spared the long ordeal of war and seen so much of its death and tragedy, are not untouched by this emotion. Our eyes are not dull when we go into the light of these people's gladness. There are moments when it is not easy to hide behind the mask which men try to wear when these things touch them. They are good days to live in.

Down a long, straight avenue of trees in Autumn foliage, richly colored like gold and crimson banners for this day of triumph, we went into Bruges, the most beautiful old town in Belgium—this fairy-tale city with its great belfry towering high above the little Old World houses with stepped gables and with the spires of its three tall churches in the blue sky reflected in canals which go between streets crossed by hundreds of small stone bridges.

It was as though we had stepped out of the horror of this four years of war into Flanders of the sixteenth century on a pageant day when the city was celebrating some festival of joy after the raising of a siege. From every house, with its Old World gables, floated Belgian and English flags. Balconies carved 500 years ago were draped with Union Jacks and Belgian colors. All the people of Bruges were in the streets in massed crowds outside the Hôtel de Ville, with its lacework front of stone, and before the Gruuthuus and around the gates of Bruges, with their fat old towers, like giants' castles in Grimm's fairy tales.

Every child in these crowds, and many women, carried banners, so that all the city was filled with color. Belgian soldiers marching through had garlands on their helmets and flags and flowers on their guns. The crowd swayed and surged in the streets and squares, and gusts of cheers rose up to one, and then, because we were the first English to come into Bruges, amazing things happened to us.

The words " English " and " England " were cried by thousands of people and followed us everywhere through these quaint old streets, and were called down to us from high windows, where women and children waved colored 'kerchiefs, and rose up from all that vast crowd in Grande Place by the Hôtel de Ville.

When we walked, the people of Bruges came around us, and we were embraced by all who could get close to us. Old men and young women clasped our hands, and as they spoke of their gratitude to England tears streamed from their eyes and their voices broke. They could not say all they wanted to say. Old women kissed us and hugged us, and said, " The English are our saviors," though Belgian soldiers were the first in Bruges, and praised God because their misery had passed.

As in Lille, so in Bruges, Englishwomen came out of the crowd and said: " I am English. Welcome. Thank God! Thank God! " And then they wept because their hearts had overbrimmed.

As at Lille and Roubaix and Turcoing, so in Bruges, everybody spoke a little English, even the children, because they had been learning it for four years until this day should come. They gathered around, all speaking together, all telling of the things they had suffered, all passionate against the enemy, who had been hard with them, who had robbed them, imprisoned them, outraged their liberties and their homes.

## FIFTY MILES OF BATTLE

Oct. 21.—The British troops are engaged in heavy fighting on the whole length of the front from northeast of Courtrai to southeast of Le Cateau for more than fifty miles, and in spite of the enemy's desperate resistance in order to hold the line of the Scheldt, southward from Ghent, covering Tournai and Valenciennes, they are getting close to that canal everywhere, and are beyond it between Denain and Le Cateau.

This morning's advance by the Second and Third Armies threatens the crossings of the canal, and the two historic cities of Tournai and Valenciennes will soon be within their reach.

There was terrific fighting yesterday by English, Scottish, and Welsh divisions for heights above the River Selle, and the tank corps rendered great service to the infantry by getting across to the east flank and destroying many German machine-gun nests in spite of the flooded ground.

The engineers have been wonderfully gallant in their work of throwing across pontoon bridges under heavy fire, especially under the hail of machine-gun bullets from high ground on the enemy's side, and by their courage the field gunners were able to get across close behind the infantry and open fire on hostile positions at close range.

On the Third Army front by the town of Solesmes, south of Valenciennes on the German line of resistance, there has been extremely severe fighting, and the enemy has massed artillery behind the Scheldt, with which he barraged the line of advance fiercely, using large numbers of gas shells in order to soak the woods and villages with poison vapor.

## SUFFERINGS OF COURTRAI

I went into Courtrai itself this morning. It has now been freed from the enemy, but it was not wholly a joyous entry like that into Lille or Bruges or other towns where civilian crowds have greeted any Englishman with cheers or embraces.

The people here, 25,000 to 30,000 of them, have suffered too much to have any complete reaction, yet some of them called out " Good morning," and all their men doffed their hats to us, but with gravity and a kind of dullness like people who had long been stunned by misery.

I could not wonder at that. I was chilled by the sinister spirit of this old city, so beautiful in time of peace, with its tall belfry of St. Martin's Church high above its gabled houses and the Flemish Town Hall and broad market place, where six centuries ago English merchants came to buy their cloth from Flemish burghers, and where after the battle of spurs many knights with broken armor and tattered plumes were brought in as prisoners of Flemish craftsmen who had fought against them for their liberties.

Through many centuries of history Courtrai has been a famous town in Flanders with a rich trade in cloth and wool, and from the windows of houses still standing silken banners were hung to welcome Kings like the fourth Edward of England or on the last days of the Guilds.

I remembered these things today when I went into the city across the canal with broken bridges where two days ago there was bloody fighting and where today new pits were dug by German shells, and when I went into the grand place and saw people standing in their doorway or hurrying to their vaults to escape from shellfire I thought of these contrasts of history.

## UNFORTUNATE CIVILIANS

Oct. 23. — Near Valenciennes the enemy is filtering out of the big Forest of Raismes, and the British have been able to bite off half of it, called the Forest of Vicugne, and advance around the rest of it without much resistance or risk. * * *

I am afraid that there must be many poor peasants trapped along this line of battle, woodcutters crouching in the undergrowth through which machine bullets are slashing, and wives of French charcoal burners hiding with their babies in the cellars of little farmsteads.

This has happened on the line of the advance beyond big towns, and it is a tragedy which stirs the hearts of the British troops, who go stepping day after night far from the main lines of communications into this great unknown country which they call " the blue." They give some of their bully beef to these women and children, though they are ravenously hungry after cold nights and exhausting days, and they break off hunks of bread and thrust them into the hands of boys and girls, whose pinched faces tell their tale, though they do not beg.

Lamentable things are happening in some of these places, as at St. Amand, near Valenciennes, which was captured by British cavalry. In this village the enemy had collected nearly 1,500 people who were suffering from what is called Spanish influenza. He turned one building into a hospital for them and crowded it.

Then when he left the village to escape the cavalry which had closed around it, he shelled it with mustard gas. Most of his shells fell around the hospital, though his gunners ought to have known and had pity, and these poor stricken souls, who went hiding in their cellars, so ill already that many could not stand, and though dying, (and some are now dead,) were aware of the poisonous vapor stealing into their lungs and burning them.

That has just happened, and the British are now getting these people away in ambulances as fast as they can be brought up, and this morning I saw many hospital nurses on the way to look after these gas victims.

The problem of the civilian populations liberated by the advancing British armies is serious and adding to the burden of the fighting organization. One corps east of Douai has 42,000 people on its hands, all destitute, utterly without means of getting food, in grave peril of starvation unless the army sends supplies without delay.

## DOUAI A DEAD CITY

In Douai itself there is tragedy, but of another kind without the human touch, for Douai is dead. In this home of old scholars and of many centuries of splendid history and good craftsmanship there is no life except that of a stray cat or two, like one I saw affrighted by my footsteps today in the lonely halls of the Hôtel de Ville, where upstairs and downstairs there was an utter loneliness and great silence amidst the litter of its archives flung about by German hands in search of loot.

Where are the people of Douai? No single face looked out from the windows of its old houses today. Its cathedral was a house of silence. In the dwellings cupboards were open and bare and all furniture overturned and crockery and glassware smashed by deliberate industry.

It was a noble old city, and its gables and old carvings and sixteenth century frontages would tempt an artist's hand, and everywhere a man with a knowledge of history finds the spirit of old France calling to him with the voices of its saints and scholars and Princes and burghers and fair women famous in the pages of France, but it is a city of ghosts and no human being is there, and I and two other men today were alone in it, and its solitude scared us so that we were glad to leave.

## KING ALBERT IN BRUGES

Oct. 27.—On Friday morning, [Oct. 25,] after one or two private visits, the King and Queen of the Belgians made their state entry into Bruges. The Queen rode on the left of the King, and on his right was the young Prince Leopold in the uniform of his regiment of carabineers.

Every soul in the city was in the streets or at the windows and balconies, and there were flaming fires of enthusiasm above the people, who had waited four years for the day when the entry of the brave soldier who stayed with his army in the narrow strip of ground which was all his kingdom would symbolize to them the return of their liberties.

For a time while King Albert reviewed his troops the people of Bruges held back in a hollow square, but afterward when he went up the steps of the Governor's house they broke bounds, and tens of thousands of them surged around him, cheering that tall figure which looked down upon them, with its hand at a salute, with a most joyous and wonderful emotion.

From hundreds of old houses in Bruges long banners floated with the rich colors of the Belgian flag, and on this splendid day of Autumn the trees along the canals and the walls of the houses above the stone bridges were gold and scarlet in the glory of their dying foliage, so that Bruges was like a painting in an old illuminated book, and one went with wonder into the heart of it.

A belfry rang out a joyous carillon, and from other tall towers of churches, built high like dream castles above the gabled roofs, there was the booming of deep-toned bells, very soothing below the singing notes of the belfry chimes. The voices of many centuries seemed to mingle with the shouts of the living drawn into the past history of Bruges, when there were other wars and other servitudes, and the music of the bells was the call of the old sadness of life mingled with that dancing carillon like the laughter of children who forget.

## BRUGES'S YEARS OF SORROW

Poor Bruges will not soon forget these last four years, for they have scarred the spirit of her people. Physically they have not suffered much. They put aside that part of their suffering, the dearness and scarcity of food, the lack of coal, the shabbiness of clothes that had been worn for four years—a suit of clothes costs $135—first with a shrug of the shoulders and the words, " All that was nothing." But what hurt them, what was hard to bear, was their utter helplessness under iron tyranny.

Some of them speak fairly of the German private soldier; with astonishing generosity, indeed. " They were well behaved, orderly, and, apart from the inevitable brutes among them, gave no trouble," said one of the most notable gentlemen of Bruges, and he added: " It is right and fair that we should tell that to the world." But having said that, he and other men I met denounced the German officials and the German officers of the regular army type with passionate indignation.

" They were utterly lacking in any spirituality," said a friend of mine, Mr. Jean de Brouwer. " Many of them were inspired by a kind of satanic pride and philosophy, and they have a bestiality of character which is not accidental, but deliberate and educated."

He told me stories of gross behavior which would be unbelievable if I did not have good evidence. The worst of these men were submarine commanders who infested Bruges. They were swaggering bullies, like the professional duelists in old days, taking great risks for the sake of applause and adulation from their fellows.

Later their risks became too great and their doom so almost certain that they were cowed and lost something of their braggadocio, so many of them went out and never returned. They were like men under sentence of death. They never told their losses. No German submarine was ever reported lost in their newspapers, but the people in Bruges who knew them by sight and by name in the streets and shops ticked them off.

### SECRET POLICE

Worse than the German officers of the most brutal type were the German secret police, who went about among the people as spies in plain clothes, and took venomous delight in tracking out small offenders against German law, so that they might be punished by heavy, fines or imprisonment. Hundreds of men in Bruges were fined, sometimes enormous sums, or taken to prisons in Germany for trivial reasons.

Jean de Brouwer was fined 1,500 marks for writing to the authorities in French instead of Flemish, and this was one incident in the deliberate effort made by the German authorities to sow seeds of dissension between the Flemish and French speaking populations of Belgium.

The nuns of a Flemish convent were fined 1,000 marks because one of their ladies, when asked the time by a German officer inspecting their house, pulled out a watch and gave the Belgian instead of the German time. The Superior of the convent, who happens to be an English lady, wrote the German commandant of Bruges, protesting against this fine, pointing out that all the clocks in her house were set to the German time, and that the act complained of was due to the forgetfulness of one young nun. The answer she received was insulting.

" Your letter is full of lies," was the reply, " and, being English, that is what might be expected."

The taking of wool from every home and every mattress and linen from beds and cupboards, and brass from door handles and lamps and ornaments, was galling to the people of Bruges, but in order to replace their woolen mattresses by straw they had to pay 1 mark 25 for every kilo of straw, or a hundred times more than the pre-war price, and, having taken their goods and their factories, the Germans resold the manufactured goods according to the same scale of prices.

## GERMAN DISCIPLINE BROKEN

Oct. 30.—Germany is both beaten and ruined, recent prisoners say. However, German machine gunners, who are the élite of their army, are fighting bravely and doggedly in order to gain time for retreating troops. Our pursuit has been too rapid for the enemy's plans of orderly withdrawal, and he is still holding on to his present line because he has not had enough time to do his packing up and is afraid of losing masses of material. But behind these military arrangements, which are still being carried out with method and discipline, there are bigger things, which make them only the last demonstration of German militarism in the fields of war.

In spite of Hindenburg's order that German soldiers have no concern with politics, the imminent surrender of their army leaders, the despair and passion that are breaking loose among their people, and the knowledge of defeat have broken the spirit of the German armies as a fighting machine, and they are not unconcerned with the doom that is upon them. Civilians in the newly liberated towns of Lille and Roubaix and others tell me that the breaking up of German discipline and well-being was plainly visible about a year ago and during the last six months could not be hidden.

The fighting machine and fighting spirit of these men were wearing out and withering. Their horses became so thin and starved that even in the streets of Lille they used to drop down dead. Rations of the men were reduced, and they became pinched and pallid. The arrogance of the officers, brutal beyond words in the early days to citizens of Lille, became chastened, and among the men there was a growing revolt against the officer class and "capitalists," whom they denounced as the authors of the war. They were struck in the face and slapped with whips by their officers for any trivial offense, and they cherished these things and said: "We will cut their throats when we are free of this."

## NEARING VALENCIENNES

Nov. 1.—Valenciennes was apparently closed in by Canadian troops this morning after heavy fighting, and the enemy probably will abandon it within a few hours. All the thousands of civilians who still are living there and are waiting with desperate anxiety for our entry will then be rescued from days of terror.

When I went up among the Canadians today the sound of the shellfire was terrific, and Canadian officers tell me their troops attacked today under support of a more powerful concentration of guns than they had three days ago under German counterattacks.

There were a number of farms, farmsteads, and cottages, like Targette and Chemin Vert, to the left of the village of Aulnoy, just below the Valenciennes railway, in which the enemy had organized defenses. Over these places our barrage fire rolled like a tide, wiping them off the map of France, and at the same time our guns fired a number of smoke shells, which made a dense white fog, obliterating all view of our advancing troops and putting the Germans in a haze so thick they could not see three paces about them.

## THE FOE HELPLESS

Their machine gunners could not find their human targets, and were helpless. The German infantry of the 6th Division were helpless. They were as baffled as if blankets had been flung about their heads. One German officer taken prisoner this morning with many others said his position was so hopeless in this fog that he told his company there was nothing to do but surrender, and led them forward as the Canadians advanced, to hand them over at a small place called Le Vessie. At the southern edge of Valenciennes there was a German field gun in action, firing at close range through this mist, but the Canadians closed around it and captured it.

The enemy's guns had put down a fierce line of fire before the attack started, or soon afterward, but their batteries were quickly silenced by the power of our artillery, and after that the Canadians were only faced by machine-gun fire from positions in ruined buildings and in embanked ditches where the Germans held out to the last. The Canadian casualties were not heavy, I am told by their own officers, and they were perfectly successful in reaching their objectives along the railway, which is the southern boundary of Valenciennes.

The Germans have already lost many men on this southern side of the city, and the Canadians were surprised at the number of German dead lying about the Rhonelle River after the fighting of recent days. For the survivors it is a hopeless business, for they know now that they are not only beaten in the field but in the world.

"We have been betrayed," said one of the German officers today, "and that is why we have lost the war."

He had a list of betrayals, beginning with Italy and going on to Rumania, and then to Bulgaria, and now, worst of all from his point of view, Austria. They acknowledge that with Austria out of the war they will find it impossible to fight on alone, except in a losing fight to save their pride; so humiliation and despair have entered their souls, where once arrogance had a dwelling place and a sense of victory over all the world.

## AMONG THE FLEMISH VILLAGES

Further across the French frontier toward the town of Audenarde in Belgium there is another battle in progress which began yesterday and is continuing today with Belgian, French, American, and British troops attacking side by side. It is a battle among Flemish villages and farmsteads where the peasants are still living, helplessly entangled in nets of horror with German machine gunners firing from their windows and allied troops tramping into their courtyards with naked bayonets, and the killing of men in their bedrooms and cellars.

Into the villages from which the enemy has been lately driven poison gas comes from a shellfire which is not very loud but makes a little hiss as each shell bursts and liberates its fumes.

We stopped all use of gas because of these civilians, but the Germans are using it every day, and in the Flemish villages many babies are dead and dying and our ambulances are carrying away women and girls gasping for breath and blinded by this foul weapon of war.

Our men give these village people gas masks taken from German prisoners now safe behind the lines and teach them how to use them, but it is of no avail because it needs long training and discipline to keep on gas masks any length of time.

They were fighting hard yesterday in a wood called Spitalbosch, which the enemy strongly defended behind barricades dug in great roots of trees. It was like the fighting the American troops had in the Argonne, and very difficult and perilous, but these men have gone forward with fine courage and have routed the enemy out from many of his lairs in this woodland, and by their good service have helped the progress of the French on their left, at this moment striking from Audenarde; and the country north of it breaks through the German line south of Ghent and will lead surely enough to the liberation of that Belgian city, which is yearning for the luck of Bruges.

## VALENCIENNES CAPTURED

Nov. 3.—After fierce fighting by English and Canadian troops the old City of Valenciennes, across the Scheldt Canal, was entered yesterday morning. At 7:50 A. M. the General commanding the Canadian troops which encircled the town sent this historic message: "I have the honor to report that Valenciennes is completely in our hands."

It was a fine achievement which the English troops share with the Canadians. Against these Yorkshire territorials and regulars of country regiments came the enemy's desperate counterattacks on Nov. 1 after our advance in the morning through the villages of Aulnoy and Preseau, strongly held by large numbers of German troops with orders to defend these positions to the death.

From the north all advance was made impossible by the opening of the Scheldt sluice gates, which flooded that side of the city, and the enemy's only way to escape was by the southeast, so that here he had concentrated all his available men. They fought with great courage and obstinacy, but it was unavailing against the Canadians and English, supported by an immense concentration of artillery.

Many German dead lie across the little Rhonelle River, and 4,000 prisoners were taken by the combined forces. The enemy's counterattacks were made with the help of tanks, but they broke down utterly, so that the British captured tanks and many more prisoners.

I went into Valenciennes yesterday morning soon after its capture, when there was still heavy fighting on its southeastern side, so that all the British guns were in action with enormous noise as I passed them in the outskirts of the city, and flights of shells were passing over its houses, where many civilians experienced mingled joy and fear, knowing that they were free again, but afraid of this fury of the guns around them.

## OUTLYING VILLAGES DESERTED

The way to Valenciennes from Douai was full of haunting pictures of the war, because Canadian and English troops fought through many of the villages along these roads, and those places have not escaped unscathed.

Their people have fled from those nearest to Valenciennes because of the German shells which smashed through their roofs and walls and made wreckage in many houses. Some of them have been sliced in half, so that one looks into rooms where cottage pianos and women's sewing machines and babies' cradles still stand against the furthest walls amid broken beams and plaster.

Only a few soldiers move among these abandoned villages, and yesterday, which was a foul day, with the wet mist steaming through their shell-pierced walls, which shook like sounding boards to the roar of gunfire, they smelled of tragedy. Through Orgy and

Audry to La Sentinelle—suburbs of Valenciennes on this side of the Scheldt—there was hardly a living soul about, except odd figures like shadows in the weg fog, lurking under the walls—British soldiers, as one could tell by the shape of their steel hats.

All along the railway from Douai the bridges had been blown up by the enemy and lay in monstrous wreckage across the line. Beyond, in this thick veil of mist, black slag mountains, like Egyptian pyramids, loomed vaguely. Factory chimneys were faintly penciled above them, as though this were a war in Lancashire. Dead horses, horribly mangled, lay at the roadside. The war had passed this way not long ago. It was still very close to Valenciennes, and that city was between two fires. Most of the fire came from our side. The guns were crowded in this fog, through which their flashes stabbed with sudden gusts of flame.

The monsters raised up their snouts and bellowed from the muddy fields near by, shaking the earth and sky. Field batteries, stark in the open, were hard at work, and as I passed within a few yards of them their sharp strokes hit my eardrums like the crack of hammers.

Then we came to the Scheldt Canal and saw Valenciennes spread out before us on the other side—a long, narrow city, built along the line of the Scheldt, so that one sees it from end to end, with its churches and factories and towers high above its crowded roofs.

## VIEW OF FROISSART'S CITY

Valenciennes, the old city of lacemakers, famous through a thousand years because of the history of its people and the noble men and women born within its walls and the many sieges and captures and conflicts when it became the prize of robber princes and warring empires! I thought of Sir John Froissart, that very gallant knight and mediaeval war correspondent, who was born here 500 years ago and came riding here across the bridge when there was a pageant of chivalry within its walls, and troubadours sang to the ladies of Valenciennes, with their own lace about their long white necks.

The ghost of Sir John Froissart walked

with me as I crossed and looked for the first time on this fair city and saw flames rising from its old houses on the southeast side and heard the flight of many shells whining across its roofs and the booming of many guns echoed back in deep resonance like the low notes of organ pipes, enormously long drawn. That gentle chronicler would have been sad at heart to see the peril of his city, and yet not without exultation, because of its liberation from the enemy who had held it for four years under an iron scourge.

There was still the noise of machine-gun fire somewhere on the right—long bursts of staccato shots—and I had heard from a Canadian Colonel that the enemy was still holding out in a machine-gun post in the suburb of Marly. We kept our ears alert for any " piling " of a close bullet. A German ready for death might take many sure shots from any window or cellar here before paying the price.

But where were the people of Valenciennes? The solitude was beginning to be oppressive. This was not like the entry into Lille. There were no manifestations of joy in this liberated city. The fury of that gunfire overhead had kept the people hidden in their houses.

Presently here and there I saw some faces peering out, and then a door opened, and a man and woman and their thin children appeared. The woman thrust out a skinny hand, grasped mine and began to weep. Then she talked passionately, with a strange mingling of rage and grief. " O my God! " she said. " Those devils have gone at last! What have they not made us suffer! " Her husband spoke to me over his wife's shoulder. " Sir," he said, " they have stolen everything, broken everything, and have ground us down for four years. They are bandits and brigands! " The woman held my wrists tight in her skinny hands and said: " We are grateful to the English soldiers. It is they who have saved us."

## STORMING LE QUESNOY

Nov. 5.—It was an astounding victory yesterday south of Valenciennes, about Le Quesnoy and Landrecies, and after his heavy defeat the enemy is retreating

in disorder from some sectors of his front. The 4th British Corps, commanded by General Harper, was in the centre of this attack, with the 37th and New Zealand divisions on this side of Ghissignies and Le Quesnoy.

The last-named place is a mediaeval town, defended by high ramparts and inner and outer bastions, strengthened by Vauban, the famous Engineer of Military Works under Louis XIV., and it was garrisoned by over 1,000 Germans, with orders to defend it at all costs. They were brave men, and determined to obey this command. The New Zealanders, however, were equally determined to take Le Quesnoy, and they set out to assault it frontally as soon as the attack had been launched with a powerful bombardment.

Those New Zealand boys, among whom I have been this morning, have been fighting with hardly a break since they went away from Hebuterne, near Albert, three months ago, but their spirit remains high, and yesterday they achieved one of their most heroic feats. They stormed the outer ramparts of Le Quesnoy in old-fashioned style with scaling ladders, and made breaches through the walls, as in the old days of Henry's men-at-arms, but with more peril because of machine-gun fire which swept them from the inner defenses. They gained part of the outer ramparts, but could get no further, and the German garrison remained strong inside their keep.

New tactics were adopted by the New Zealand General, who ordered one body of his men to go round Le Quesnoy on the north, and another to work round it on the south, leaving pickets all around the town. This was done, and the town was completely surrounded by the New Zealanders, who joined hands on the east side.

## A DRAMATIC SURRENDER

Some of their battalions then fought forward against determined resistance from the Germans in the villages of Herbignies and Jolimetz, where they broke their way into the enemy's artillery positions and captured many guns. Astonishing things happened there, but meanwhile the German garrison of Le Quesnoy was called upon to surrender. Messages were first dropped inside the town from British airplanes flying low above the place.

"You are completely surrounded," was the first message dropped in this way. "Enemy troops are far to the east of you. If you will surrender you will be treated as honorable prisoners of war."

The German garrison of Le Quesnoy read these words, but no order to surrender was given. Later in the morning two deputations were sent to them, each one consisting of a New Zealander officer and two German officer prisoners. Going through a breach in the outer ramparts they shouted out the summons to surrender, with the promise of honorable treatment. A few men accepted this offer and came out to give themselves up, but most of the thousand remained within their bastions and still gave no sign of capitulating.

So it was all day until evening, when, after astonishing successes further forward, the New Zealanders determined to close in upon Le Quesnoy and force its surrender at the point of the bayonet. From the outer ramparts they stormed the inner walls, which were very high and perpendicular, so that they were not easy to scale. They forced their way in despite all machine-gun fire, and after fighting in the streets of the town they received the capitulation of the remaining members of the garrison, amounting still to nearly a thousand men.

### VAST WAR MACHINE

Nov. 6.—The blow inflicted upon the enemy by the British victory of Monday south of Valenciennes, at Landrecies and Le Quesnoy was so heavy and vital that German battalions, which had escaped capture and were in reserve lines, have been forced to retreat from the Forest of Mormal and on a wide front east of it.

Haig's troops are following them closely, and behind them once again that vast machine, which is the complement of the modern army, with its engineering services, its material needed for roads, rails, and bridges, its food for men and guns, is on the move, so that the fighting men shall not be out of touch with their supplies.

No mortal can imagine what this means in terms of traffic and in human energy unless he has seen the mechanism of war. It means the surging forward of motor truck columns and transport wagons far back for scores of miles from the new front line, for when one link of the chain is extended all that chain has to be dragged ahead, and it is a chain made by hundreds of thousands of men, with all the material of their labor.

It means that the big guns have to get on the move, crawling up narrow roads on monstrous caterpillar tractors. It means that the tanks have to find new hiding places. It means that the roads are narrow channels down which battalions on the march are crowded to one side, mud-splashed and jammed by endless columns of field batteries, by motor buses and motor trucks, swaying perilously along high-cambered tracks on the edge of greasy ditches; by staffs and the transport of corps and divisional headquarters, shifting their lodgings from one village to another; by pontoon bridges on heavy wagons; by airdrome equipment, packed up for removal; by field kitchens, ammunition columns and the army of road menders who follow up the fighting men.

### AMAZING AIR BATTLE

The aviators who are hurrying the enemy's retreat have beaten all their records lately in air combats, and their most famous day, when they destroyed something like seventy hostile airplanes, has already been surpassed.

One exploit is now the talk of the army, and it seems to be as wonderful as anything that has been done by these knights-errant of the air. It happened over the Forest of Mormal, in British hands since yesterday, and there, over those dense woods with a queer kind of Eiffel Tower in the centre of them, flew a Major of one of the British flying squadrons, searching for the whereabouts of the British troops and for any German fighting plane which he might challenge to a duel.

He saw a two-seater, flying at 1,000

feet to escape the "Archies" and any other trouble, and the Major climbed up to it in a wide spiral and then from below fired at it. The German pilot and observer fell, their machine breaking in the air, and one man dropping in a parachute. Immediately a Fokker biplane came into view, and the Major heard the whistling of bullets through his plane, and then felt a hammer stroke on his left thigh. He had been hit, and for the moment was stunned.

His airplane began to spin out of control, but the Major became conscious of his danger, and, instinctively touching his levers, again got his grip on the engine. Then he saw that he was surrounded by fifteen Fokkers, crowding about him for the death shot. His defense was by attack, and by a marvelous manoeuvre he got his shots in first, and three enemies fell, but machine guns were chattering about him and bullets singing past his wires.

Another hammer blow struck him, this time shattering his left thighbone. He fainted clean away and his machine dived helplessly, but once again the spirit of the man awakened to the instinct of self-preservation and anger against those who were out to kill him. He handled his machine again, mastered it, and looked out for the Germans.

## ONE AGAINST MANY

From twelve to fifteen enemy scouts were in his sky, taking up the hunt for him. He flew at one, and saw his burst of fire set it alight, so that it began falling in flame. At the same time bullets were about him like wasps. One of them smashed his left elbow, and his arm dropped and hung loose and useless.

With one hand he managed now to steer and shoot against a new swarm of enemies that came like midges. He dived steeply to escape them, but eight more scouts chased him down. He could not avoid them, so he fought them. He fought by manoeuvring for position with every stunt known to airmen with a little morning wildness in their hearts, but this was cold, deadly skill. It was watched by ground observers, who held their breath at the sight of that one British airplane, banking, nose diving, looping, with the flock of Germans about it.

For ten or twelve minutes he juggled with his airplane to get his target among the vultures. He hit two and put them out of action, and then they had had enough, and he landed successfully. But when his machine came to a rest he did not jump out. He sat all crumpled up, with his head drooping, and it was on a stretcher that he went away. He is now in a hospital, gravely wounded, and every man out here who knows how he fought between fifty and sixty hostile aircraft and destroyed four and drove down six hopes with all his heart that this air knight will recover from his wounds.

## SCENES IN TOURNAI

Nov. 10.—The spirit of victory is in the air. The British troops are following up the retreating enemy with bands playing and are going up the roads with flags on their rifles and on their gun limbers through villages from which the German rearguard had gone only an hour or two before, and where the French and Flemish cheer them as they pass with cries of " Vivent les Anglais! "

It is glorious Autumn weather, with a sparkle of gold in the sunlight and the glint of gold on the russet leaves and shining pools along the roads. It is Sunday, and in many churches in France and Belgium and in cathedrals which escaped destruction by a narrow chance, only scathed a little by battles around the town, " Te Deums " are being sung, and people who a week ago crept to church close in the shadow of the walls, afraid of the noise of gunfire around them, and who a day or two ago saw the gray wolves of the German Army still prowling in the streets, though with a hangdog look, are now singing their praises to God because of their deliverance, almost doubting, even yet, that after four years under the hostile yoke they are free—free to speak their minds, free to display the flag of their nation, free of fines and punishment and requisitions and spying, and German police and German arrogance, free in their souls and hearts after four years of servitude under hostile rule.

So it was in Tournai today. For three weeks the people there had lived in cellars, listening to the fury of gunfire along the Scheldt Canal and closing in about them. * * * A month ago more than 10,000 went away from Tournai, but that was behind German bayonets after a rollcall of all able-bodied men, who were forced to go while their women wept for them. A week ago the roar of the bombardment increased and never ceased day or night, and the people became haggard in their cellars, because of this awful noise above them. But they were comforted by the knowledge that this British gunfire was not directed on Tournai, and they said:

"The Germans have lied again. We shall not be killed by our friends."

Then, two nights ago, above the noise of the guns there were louder noises—stupendous explosions shaking every stone of their cellars and their vaulted roofs as by an earthquake, and the people of Tournai guessed that the Germans were blowing up the bridges over the Scheldt Canal, and that it was the signal of their retreat.

## BRITISH AT MONS

Nov. 11.—The British troops knew early this morning that the armistice had been signed. I stopped on my way to Mons. Outside brigade headquarters an officer said: "Hostilities will cease at 11 o'clock." Then he added, as all men add in their hearts: "Thank God for that!"

All the way to Mons there were columns of troops on the march, and their bands played ahead of them, and almost every man had a flag on his rifle, the red, blue, and white of France, the red, yellow, and black of Belgium. They wore flowers in their caps and in their tunics, red and white chrysanthemums given them by crowds of people who cheered them on their way—people who in many of these villages have been only one day liberated from the German yoke.

The men marched, singing, with a smiling light in their eyes. They had done their job, and it was finished with the greatest victory in the world.

The war ended for the British at Mons, as it had begun there. When I went into this town this morning it seemed to me a most miraculous coincidence, and a joyful one. Last night there was a fight outside the town before the British forced their way in at 10 o'clock. The Germans left many of their guns in the gardens before they ran.

This morning Mons was full of English cavalry and Canadian troops, about whom there were crowds of townspeople, cheering them and embracing them. One old man told me of all they had suffered in Mons, but he wept only when he told me of the suffering of the British prisoners.

"What a shame for Germany," he said, "what a shame, when these things are known about your poor men starving to death! Our women tried to give them food, but were beaten for it, and fifteen days ago, down there by the canal, one of your English was killed because a woman gave him a bit of bread."

Little children came up to me and described the fighting the night before, and many people narrated the first fighting in Mons in August of 1914, when the "Old Contemptibles" were there, and fought their battle through the town and then on their way of retreat outside.

All that is now a memory. The war belongs to the past. There will be no flash of gunfire in the sky tonight. The fires of hell have been put out, and I have written my last message as war correspondent, thank God!

---

*Mr. Gibbs's eloquent descriptions of scenes in Mons and Ghent appear elsewhere in these pages under the title "How Peace Came on the Battlefronts."*

# French Armies' Final Victories

## Pen Pictures of Bruges When Entered by the Allies, and of Battles for Other Cities

### By WALTER DURANTY

*By the middle of October the French forces under Gouraud, Debeney, and Guillaumat had established a close liaison with the American First Army, which, after clearing out the Argonne Forest, was developing an advance east of the Meuse. The French attack was directed toward Vouziers and Mézières, while the Americans sought to cut the Longuyon-Sedan-Mézières railway. The fighting was stubborn and the terrain difficult, but the French stormed their way through the enemy lines with great captures of men and guns and rapidly advanced toward their objectives. Walter Duranty, after depicting conditions in Bruges and other recaptured Belgian towns, accompanied the French armies and cabled vivid descriptions of the fighting to* THE NEW YORK TIMES. *These have been copyrighted for its affiliated publication,* CURRENT HISTORY MAGAZINE, *and are given herewith.*

BRUGES, Oct. 20, 1918.—" President Wilson saved Bruges," said Town Clerk Victor, to whom I talked today. The same opinion is universal among the 50,000 people remaining in the city. " The President's reply caused a marked change in the German attitude," continued M. Victor. " Thus the commandateur had notified some two-score leading citizens ten days ago that they would be removed as hostages. We were conducted to the station for departure, when suddenly a counterorder for our release came from General Headquarters. The enemy carefully refrained from injuring buildings or works of art and confined his destruction to the arsenal and his own depots. A high Prussian officer admitted that there had been a decision to spare invaded territories henceforward as far as possible. For the Germans, fear of punishment is the beginning of clemency."

Not only Bruges's famous buildings are intact, but priceless pictures and art treasures were so well hidden before the enemy's arrival that everything has been saved. The fact is the Germans never for a moment thought that Bruges would pass from their possession, and consequently did not trouble to consider the question of removing its monuments until it was too late. In the Palace of Justice they did not touch the carved mantelpiece, a masterpiece of mediaeval art, merely saying that the space on the wall opposite it was reserved for the Kaiser's picture directly peace established their hold on the city.

Although the last boches departed during the night of Friday to Saturday, [Oct. 18-19,] the evacuation began fully three weeks ago, and for the last fortnight there had been a steady flow of documents, stores, &c., by train and barge to Antwerp. The enemy made no secret of his preparations, and on Monday, Tuesday, and Wednesday a series of explosions and fires in the arsenal and port warned the inhabitants that deliverance was near.

### ENTERING BRUGES

The first Belgian soldiers entered the city yesterday morning, but mine craters at crossroads and the destruction of the canal bridges prevented the passage of vehicles until today. It was a thrilling progress along the beflagged streets between dense rows of people who cheered to the echo every car, camion, motor cycle, or foot soldier along the route to the central square, where the chimes—the sole brasswork not unhidden that had not yet been stolen by the boches—and the famous great bell of the belfry tower were ringing for the second time during the war. The first time was that day of gloom for the inhabitants when with full pomp and music the boches announced the signature of peace with Russia, the "beginning of the allied end," as all called it.

An interesting feature was the display in the windows of shops and houses of linen and copper utensils walled up in cellars during four years to escape the German requisitions. Each copper pot, sheet, and tablecloth was proudly decked with a rosette of the Belgian colors. Portraits of the King and Queen were everywhere.

As regards food, Bruges is to be reckoned fortunate. For the poor the American Committee functioned admirably; for the rich there was wholesale smuggling from Holland, wherein the Germans readily participated. One could buy sugar at $1 per pound, coffee at $8, and tea at $10. Milk at 20 cents per pint and butter at $5 per pound were reserved for the invaders, but could nevertheless be bought sub rosa.

## GERMANS TOOK BRIBES

For the inhabitants it was a point of honor to enjoy the same comforts as the invaders, no matter at what cost or risk of fines and imprisonment. They took pleasure in buying with the complicity of German officials—generally offered at a price which now is deemed excessive. Just the same the commandateur never ceased perquisitions and pillage. From the leading printer in the town eight tons of lead type were taken with the words: " It will make missiles to fire upon your damned Belgians as Solf's payment."

As early as 1916 the price of clothes was beyond reach to any save millionaires. One girl I saw had manufactured a coat from a blanket, another from a curtain. Shoes were soled with old bicycle tires, and bicycles ran on the front wheel on felt and the rear on springs. The Germans mercilessly pillaged unoccupied houses and, as at Ostend, forced the inhabitants in many cases to yield to them choice dwellings with their contents under pain of fine.

From the outset the authority of the Burgomaster was set aside by the invaders, but until recently a local Magistrate was allowed to try civil cases.

Three months ago the Germans suppressed the court.

I visited the Port of Bruges, which formed the principal centre of the submarine campaign against the North Sea and British coast. As many as forty submarines often assembled within the huge basins of the port—to say nothing of torpedo boats, three of which still remain with their smokestacks projecting from the water, sunk to avoid capture.

M. Brandel was arrested by the Germans at the outset and imprisoned several weeks because he refused to put his services at their disposal. The Germans told him the port henceforth would be the State property of Germany, which would develop it and make Bruges a second Hamburg, through which should pass the trade of Belgium and Northern France.

With this end in view the boches had begun a vast scheme of construction of new docks to double the port area. Scores of houses had been pulled down to provide the necessary space. Five floating docks were built, and the number of cranes, dock buildings, and repair yards increased tenfold.

## GERMAN CRUELTY

Oct. 21.—German rule in Bruges was marked by a combination of cruelty and corruption without parallel since the days of Spanish tyranny in Flanders. Supreme powers over the city were vested in the port commander, Admiral von Schröder, who proved a worthy successor to the infamous Duke of Alva. By Schröder's orders hundreds of persons have been shot after the travesty of a trial on the scantiest evidence.

" For a case of espionage presumption is sufficient evidence and proof unnecessary," was one of his sayings, and another: " It is better to shoot a score of innocent people than to let one spy escape." On that system the Germans did " justice " in Flanders.

The most notorious case was the murder of Captain Fryatt. I talked today with a man named Schaloigne, whose cousin shared a cell with Fryatt during the trial. After a brief hearing the Captain was removed from the court while his judges deliberated. "I fear there is little hope," said Fryatt. "They call it a trial, but it looked like a put-up job to me. Everything was cut and dried for condemnation."

Hardly were the words out of his mouth when they came and led him away, and five minutes later the Belgian heard the fatal volley in the courtyard. Fryatt's body lies in a nameless grave in a corner of the cemetery, but it is said that the sexton has a record of the exact spot.

It is worthy of note that before his departure a few days ago the German Military Judge Zepfel, who presided at Fryatt's trial, declared: "The British will want my head in payment of Fryatt's life, but it is Schröder alone who is responsible. I simply obeyed his orders which insisted absolutely on the death penalty."

### TORTURE OF FOUR BELGIANS

An even more horrible case was that of a Belgian named De La Place and his three companions, condemned to be shot after half an hour's trial. At dawn the following morning they were led out to the courtyard of the Lancers' Barracks, where the execution took place, and were fastened to posts opposite which a firing squad was ready. Just as the last knot was being tied an officer entered the courtyard, crying: "Admiral's orders. Your appeal has been heard." And all four were taken back to prison.

Incredible as it may seem, this hideous farce was repeated a week later, with a similar respite at the last moment. Then, after another fortnight's imprisonment, during which the Belgians continued protesting their innocence of all charges against them, they faced a firing squad for the third time, and the death sentence was carried out. One of them named Gloovére had become a raving maniac since the second application of torture, but the Germans knew no mercy. Soldiers bore him out and fastened him to the execution post with the others.

### VISIT TO ZEEBRUGGE

Oct. 23.—I visited Zeebrugge today, the scene of one of the most audacious exploits in the war's history. Along the coast from Blankenburg the sandhills separating the road from the beach were honeycombed with battery positions succeeding one another absolutely without interval. There must have been hundreds of guns varying from six to twelve-inch and tons of big shells still left by the Germans. Everywhere one could see long muzzles turned seaward.

As Zeebrugge drew near, the gun emplacements in many cases were obliterated by gaping craters fifty feet across, made by aerial torpedoes or projectiles from the largest English naval cannon. The port of Zeebrugge made a striking picture in the bright midday sunshine. Just at the right of the little group of hotels and villas that formed the town begins the long mole—its entrance commanded by a battery of six-inch guns still intact—but after running out a hundred yards into the sea it curves northward for half a mile parallel with the shore, thus making a sheltered harbor in front of the mouth of the Bruges Canal, which enters the sea between two long piers some six hundred yards north of the town.

The tide was low and the wrecks of sunken ships stood high out of the water. Close against the mole and nearly at the end was the Brussels, and beyond it unknown vessels. Nearer the coast was a dredger, sunk by the Germans. Then exactly off the end of the canal was the wreck of the Thetis, the old British warship which was sunk in the famous attack. Between the still smoldering timbers of the burned pier I could distinguish other British ships, the Iphigenia and the Intrepid—long, battered masses of twisted, rusty iron.

### BLOWING UP MINES

Suddenly there came the rat-a-tat of machine guns from a flotilla of motor launches grouped off the end of the mole and a moment later an enormous column of mud and water rose a hundred feet in the air, followed by an ear-splitting explosion as the bullets fired one of the many mines that had formed a barrage at the northern end of the harbor.

I walked as far as possible along the mole. After twenty-five yards the solid concrete wall, twenty feet high and thirty feet across, gave way to the timbers of wooden pier work, under which the tide swept right up the harbor. There was a forty-yard gap in the mole, torn by the explosion of a British submarine crammed to the hatches with trinitro-toluol and driven headlong against the breakwater on the night of the attack. The inhabitants of Bruges, twelve miles away, were startled by that terrific blast, which dwarfed the roar of the bombard-ment—the heaviest in their experience.

The Germans soon bridged the gap with a pier solid enough to bear a rail-road, but the rush of water through it was steadily silting on the harbor, and rendered it almost useless in rough weather. Just where the further end of the pier rejoins the stone work the timbers had been dynamited by the Ger-mans, and a five-yard hole, over which drooped broken rails, barred further progress. * * *

For more than a month the canal was blocked entirely, German efforts to budge the concrete-filled Iphigenia be-ing vain. Finally they managed by dredging to render passage at her stern practicable for small submarines and torpedo boats at high water, but the channel remained closed to large vessels.

## ORGIES OF THE U-BOAT MEN

Oct. 24.—The U-boat men were the spoiled darlings of the German forces in Belgium. Bruges, as the central base of the whole submarine campaign against British ships, was flooded with posters entitled "England's Peril," showing a fantastic number of dots around the British Isles, each of which represented a vessel torpedoed.

While on shore the U-boat men were allowed practically unlimited license. Their pay, already very high—the low-est grade of officer received 800 marks monthly—was almost doubled by supple-mentary allowances for the period of active service. Promotion—for those who survived—was exceedingly rapid, and decorations were rained upon them. Huge awards of prize money were given for allied warships sunk, and on a slid-ing scale according to tonnage for mer-chant ships. Thus the destruction of a hospital ship or transport of 10,000 tons would be worth 1,000 marks to a new-joined midshipman, and upward or downward from 5,000 for a Lieutenant Commander to 250 for an ordinary sea-man.

The finest houses in Bruges were at their disposal as quarters, and the cream of famous Belgian wine cellars was " requisitioned " by the invaders. The favorite amusement of the U-boat oficers ashore was an orgy of cham-pagne, terminated by the demolition of every piece of crockery and furniture in the house. Several fine old mansions were set on fire as a result of such bouts, but instead of being punished the officers had a fresh dwelling imme-diately offered them.

I visited one such house belonging to a millionaire grain merchant named Ca-tulle, near the port, which had been the headquarters and officers' club for U-boat men at Bruges. The basement had been transformed into a palatiai rathskeller, whose walls bore well-exe-cuted cartoon frescoes, with rhyming mottoes, and were decked with colored brass lamps and flags taken from allied vessels. Here Prince Adalbert, the Kaiser's son, spent a plentiful leisure while at Bruges last year. Nominally the commander of a corvette, he distin-guished himself chiefly by the length and extent of his drinking bouts. With boon companions of the aristocracy he would start drinking at 7 in the evening, and the orgy would end toward dawn, only when the entire company was lying besotted under the tables.

## PILFERING FOOD

Oct. 25.—On all sides one hears of the misery of their " home folks " as related by Germans back from leave. The wholesale corruption—leading sometimes, as in the case of the Ghent supply staff, to a gigantic scandal—was due primarily to the appalling need of the German civil population. The same cause was responsible for the vast system of smug-gling from Holland. Although in the country districts of Germany there was enough hidden food, the urban popula-tions have been in many cases literally starving.

During the first six months of the war food was sent home freely from

Belgium, but when the military authorities realized, after the battle of the Yser, that they faced a long war, the whole of the immense food production of Belgium was reserved for the army. Nevertheless, officers and men going on leave persisted in carrying supplies. In vain punishments were rained broadcast and leave curtailed. It was impossible to suppress leave entirely, and the severity of the orders against the removal of food only spread the corruption wider. At the present moment the famous German discipline has in this respect broken down completely. Nothing—neither honor, duty, nor patriotism—can prevent the troops at the front from endeavoring to save the millions at home from starvation.

Now the Germans have lost the Belgian treasure house, and in a few weeks not only civilians, but the army itself, will be feeling the pinch of starvation. It is this which makes the German situation so desperate.

### DESPERATE FIGHTING

Oct. 26.—Although the armistice question for the moment overshadows the military operations, the gigantic battle on the western front continues with the utmost desperation.

The climax of the French attack is General Guillaumat's drive east of Laon against the Hunding positions, the long-prepared line protecting the German centre. It is characteristic position warfare that the poilus are waging against a quadruple trench system reinforced by concrete shelters, five lines of barbed wire, each twenty feet deep, and ground sown with anti-tank mines. Nevertheless, Guillaumat's troops have broken through on the ten-kilometer front between St. Quentin-Le Petit and Herpy. [Herpy is on the Aisne, two miles west of Château-Porcien.] In the centre of the attack the village of Banogne still holds out, but the latest information is that the French progress is steady.

With every available gun the Germans are opposing the advance by a deluge of gas and high explosive shells. They are still fighting bravely, but the vastly increased proportion of officers captured —from 5 to 7 per cent., instead of 1½

to 2, as heretofore—proves that it is difficult to maintain German discipline.

Far more startling evidence of Germany's decadence is the fact that in this hour of her crying need for soldiers some men of the 1920 class have to be kept at home—some who had reached the front were actually withdrawn—to keep down internal disturbances.

There has been hardly less bitter fighting on the front of the armies of Debeney and Mangin, who are steadily reducing the Marle-Mortiers salient. Despite savage counterattacks, Debeney's advance continues, and 800 fresh prisoners were reported this morning.

### GERMANS OUTMANOEUVRED

Oct. 27.—The great battle begun on the 24th by the armies of Debeney, Mangin, and Guillaumat against the German centre continues to rage with unabated fury. It is impossible to overestimate the importance of the fact that, while the air is filled with talk of an armistice and peace, the Germans are fighting with the utmost desperation.

Their motive is obvious: First, to prevent the rolling up of their flanks and the colossal disaster that would result from the rupture of their centre; second, to impress on the Allies that the German Army is still a force to be reckoned with and to create a current of opinion favorable to peace negotiations. It is at once a supreme sham of resistance and the final attempt to bluff the Allies and their own population into the belief that the German military situation is not yet hopeless.

Thus counterattacks in which engineers, staff orderlies, labor battalions, and every available man have been engaged have been hurled during the last thirty-six hours against Guillaumat's forces, which on the 25th had pierced to a depth of two kilometers beyond the Hunding line on the twelve-kilometer front between the River Serre and Château-Porcien. The French refused to abandon a foot of ground, but their progress was for the moment checked, and this morning's news announced a terrific bombardment of the French advanced lines before dawn, followed by more unsuccessful counterattacks. On Guillaumat's left the struggle was hardly less bitter, but Mangin forced the passage of the Serre this morning east of Crécy. On his right he is meeting counterattacks of the same violence as those directed against Guillaumat.

At the moment of cabling I learn that the Germans are retreating on the whole twelve-mile front of the First Army, (Debeney's,) whose advance guards occupied Jouquequise Farm and Bertaignemont Wood, five kilometers nearer Guise than the furthest point reached last night. The German withdrawal extends to Mangin's left, which has crossed the Serre near Assis and occupied enemy trenches without much opposition. Once more Foch has outmanoeuvred the enemy, who must abandon the Hunding Stellung, the last and most formidable bastion of the centre line.

## WEST OF THE ARGONNE

Nov. 1.—General Gouraud attacked today west of the Argonne simultaneously with a great American drive further east. Although the front of the attack is only about 7½ miles wide, from the region of Semuy to Falaise—both in the hands of the enemy—the importance of the operations is very great in relation to the American push.

Gouraud is aiming northeastward, and his successful progress in connection with the American advance on the other side of the Argonne will pinch out the forest massif north of the Grand Pré defile, whose deep ravines and fastnesses, strengthened by elaborate fortifications, have proved such a formidable obstacle to the Americans during the past weeks. In fact, American progress northward toward the all-important junction of Mézières would be impossible unless this position on their flank were reduced.

It is a daring manoeuvre that Gouraud is undertaking, as the southern part of his line for the five miles between Terron and Falaise is across the Aisne to a depth of only about a mile—a somewhat inadequate starting point for an attack—with a deep river in the rear.

During the night many footbridges were prepared and placed in position without much interference from the enemy. At 5:15 A. M. began an artillery preparation of the utmost violence, lasting thirty minutes. At 5:45 the infantry attacked in fine weather through a haze, whose cover was augmented by smoke shells. Owing to the river and broken character of the ground tanks could not be used, but the latest reports indicate very satisfactory progress.

Thus in the loop of the Aisne opposite Semuy Village, Rilly was occupied by 7:10 A. M. and the loop was cleared of the enemy—a gain of two kilometers in less than an hour and a half. Still more valuable was the capture of Voncq, further south. Hidden in mist and smoke clouds, the French charged over the railway embankment, which had been the German front line, and flung their bridges first across the canal, then the river, 100 yards beyond.

By 9 o'clock assault companies had reformed on the further bank and, regardless of machine-gun fire and a heavy artillery reaction, had begun an attack on the village. With irresistible élan they rushed the slopes of the high spur on which Voncq is situated, and by 9:55 the last defender had surrendered. This position dominated the whole valley of the Aisne to Vouziers. Further south, beyond Vandy, the advance was equally successful.

## CROSSING THE CANAL

Nov. 4.—The entry into Ghent and the great Franco-British drive toward Maubeuge and the Belgian frontier are today's pendant to the Franco-American victory in the east, similarly pointed in the direction of Mézières and the frontier of Germany.

Today I visited General Debeney's army, whose left wing is playing a part on the flank of the British attack comparable to General Gouraud's achievement in clearing the Argonne while the Americans drove forward.

It was a difficult task assigned to the French on the twelve-kilometer front north of Guise, protected by the brimful Sambre-Oise Canal. During the night the bridging preparations were completed, and at 6:30, after a brief bombardment, the engineers began their work under cover of a mist and of smoke shells. The German resistance, both with artillery and machine guns, was very strong from the outset, but by 8 large forces had effected a crossing, and their subsequent manoeuvres cleared the way for their comrades at the points where the German defense was maintained.

Before 10 o'clock the crossing was accomplished on the whole front of the attack, and the no less difficult task of advancing against a strongly posted enemy, with a waterway in the rear, was in full swing. The poilus pushed irresistibly up the slopes east of the canal, and the latest advices indicate that they have advanced to an average depth of two kilometers despite counterattacks on the left from the western horn of Nouvion Forest, which affords the usual favorable cover for the defenders.

In this supreme battle the French are fighting with a spirit and élan which, after their extraordinary and continuous efforts since March, may well be regarded as one of the greatest miracles of the war. Their dogged courage which saved the Allies in the critical three months has been fired by success into the same invincible fury of victory that animated the soldiers of Napoleon.

## THE END IN SIGHT

Nov. 6.—The Nauen wireless message announcing the departure of the armistice envoys from Berlin occasions no great surprise at French headquarters. At the same time it is pointed out that the extreme haste shown by the enemy to demand conditions, of whose severity they already have a good idea from the terms accorded their allies and the prognostications in the Swiss press, proves that the German war chiefs realize what is known here, that the military situation is no less dangerous than internal conditions. * * * Only weak rearguards oppose the allied advance. Large captures of material are everywhere reported. It is growing hourly more certain that nothing but surrender will avert disaster. For the first time I can affirm with confidence that the end is in sight.

Nov. 11.—Even in its death agony German militarism clung fast to its princi-

ple of hideous savagery. All this morning the German batteries have been pouring a deluge of high explosives and poison gas on Mézières, where 20,000 civilians—men, women, and children—are penned like trapped rats without possibility of escape.

Words cannot depict the plight of the victims of this crowning German atrocity. Westward the broad stream of the Meuse cuts them off from an army of their countrymen whose soldiers, maddened to frenzy, are giving their lives without a thought in the effort to reinforce under the pitiless hell-storm their scanty detachments on the eastern bank.

French forces which yesterday crossed the Meuse a few kilometers east of Mézières were met by a counterattack of Prussian Guards, pressed home with a determination that in other circumstances would have commanded the respect even of enemies.

At 6 last night the torment of Mézières began. Incendiary shells fired a hospital, and by the glare of a hundred fires the wounded were evacuated to the shelter of the cellars in which the whole population was crouching. That was not enough to appease the bitter bloodlust of the Germans in defeat. Cellars may give protection from fire or melinite, but they are worse than death traps against the heavy fumes of poisonous gas.

So the murderous order was given today, and faithfully the German gunners carried it out. In a town that has been protected by miles of invaded territory from war's horrors there were no gas masks for the civilians and no chemicals that might permit them to save lives with improvised head coverings. Here and there, perhaps, a mother fixes a mask, found as by miracle on the body of a dead enemy, across her son's face, that he, at least, may escape the death she knows will take her. Others may pass the shell barrier and reach, stunned and torn, the comparative shelter of the neighboring woods, but they will be fortunate exceptions. The great majority must submit to martyrdom—final testimony that civilization is a thing apart from the unclean barbarism of the boche.

# The Battle That Won Sedan

## How the American Army Cut the German Supply Line and Took the Historic City

### By EDWIN L. JAMES

*A prodigious task was assigned to the American First Army when, having cleared the Argonne Forest, it was ordered to cut the Longuyon-Sedan-Mézières railway, the most important enemy line of communication. The success of the movement would bottle up all the German armies, with only one avenue of withdrawal, through the Liége gateway. The German High Command realized the peril and threw in their crack divisions to avert it. Some of the fiercest fighting of the war ensued, but the American élan was irresistible. The cutting of the line and the capture of Sedan were graphically described by Edwin L. James, who accompanied our First Army up to the time the armistice was concluded. His dispatches to* THE NEW YORK TIMES *were copyrighted for its affiliated publication,* CURRENT HISTORY MAGAZINE, *and are given herewith:*

OCTOBER, 22, 1918.—While the attention of the world has been centred on the glorious victories of the French, British, and Belgian armies in the north, where the Germans have been driven back so many miles, the world must not forget the large degree in which that advance has been facilitated by the fact that to the Champagne and Meuse front has been drawn one-fourth of the German military strength to meet the French Fourth Army and the American First Army, whose rush threatens the whole enemy army.

The success of the American operation north of Verdun is not to be measured in kilometers gained, but in its effect on the whole situation. Since General Pershing's men launched their first attack, in the mist of the morning of Sept. 26, they have fought and put out some twenty German divisions, among which are some of the best in the German Army, such as three of the five guard divisions and the 28th, known as the Kaiser's Own. In front of us now there are some eighteen more divisions, and others are being brought up day by day to confront us.

On the front of the First American Army the last four weeks have seen some of the fiercest fighting of the whole war, where the best soldiers the Kaiser has are fighting youthful Americans under orders to hold at all costs the line which protects the Luxemburg gateway, the most important artery of the German Army. Captured German officers explain: "We have just got to hold north of Verdun." A captured order of a German General says the fate of the Fatherland may hang on the fight north of Verdun. If the Mézières-Luxemburg railroad system is reached or put under easy gunfire, all communication for the German front from in front of Laon to the Meuse falls.

### TAKING ARGONNE FOREST

In the battle we have advanced generally from fifteen to eighteen kilometers, breaking through the Hindenburg line and taking the Argonne Forest. The taking of the Argonne positions will go down in history as one of the big accomplishments of the war. It is not easy to tell the story of our fight. One reads in communiqués of stubborn resistance, or bitter and heavy counterattacks, and of continued artillery fire. But those terms have become so trite and worn from overuse that they fail to convey to the imagination real meanings.

The enemy's main resistance has been confined to the holding of the line. He has made counterattacks from time to time, but generally apparently for the purpose of frustrating our attack plans, and not to regain lost terrain. In fact, captured orders tell the Germans to make counterattacks only when success seems assured, but, on the other hand, to yield no foot of territory which can possibly be held. And so the German command has placed a large concentration of artillery against us and innumerable machine guns. Therefore the fighting resolves itself into the grueling job of reducing machine-gun nests, and the progress of the battle has become the unsensational affair to which the machine gun has reduced so much modern warfare.

One must bear in mind that the machine gun is the prime weapon for defense. This means that a certain number of men on defense, with machine guns well placed, as the Germans know how to place them, can hold back a much larger number of men who are equally good fighters. To attack these machine-gun nests, or rows of them, frontally is too expensive to be generally done. They must be reduced by manoeuvring, flanking, and surrounding. When one realizes that on some parts of our front these venomous little weapons are placed one to a yard, one realizes what a severe task our soldiers have.

### GERMAN FORCES USED UP

That the defense of their line is expensive to the Germans is proved by the replacement of twenty divisions in less than four weeks because they had been so cut up that not enough was left to function, or else so worn out that they could not stand the pressure by Pershing's men. Nearly every day brings identification of new German divisions brought from other parts of the line. We have met troops brought from Flanders, from Cambrai, St. Quentin, and, in fact, from all parts of the German front. The German lines are held in undiminished numbers in front of the American First Army, the German command taking chances elsewhere in order to try to make sure that the Americans do not break through north of Verdun.

A glance at the order of battle map shows that the concentration of divisions in front of us is so heavy that there is scarcely room to write their numbers. Only one other part of the whole front is so heavily held, and that is the Cambrai-St. Quentin sector.

In a word, the task being performed by the American First Army is part of the general battle scheme. It is the hardest, bitterest, and least sensational task of the whole battle, but some army has to do it, and Pershing gladly accepted the commission, knowing that it would be no such picnic as the reduction of the St. Mihiel salient.

I believe that fully one-sixth of the rifle strength of the whole German Army has been thrown against the American First Army in the last week. There were four divisions in front of us just before the attack. These have been reinforced by fully thirty more, which unquestionably Ludendorff could have used to advantage elsewhere had it not been for the American attack.

From this statement of facts it is hoped that those who may have doubted, because our advance is not to be measured by the same kilometer scale as is the advance in the north, will realize that we have achieved and are achieving good success. The battle is a strain upon our strength; it is likewise a strain upon the German strength. We have more strength to expend than the Germans have. Both sides are throwing thousands after thousands into the mill that grinds north of Verdun, but America's strength will have thousands to throw in when the Germans have no more thousands to throw in should the fortunes of war keep the mill grinding.

If one of the purposes of allied effort is to destroy the German military machine, then the American First Army is doing a big job.

### CAPTURE OF ST. JUVIN

Oct. 23.—It may now be told that the American unit which captured St. Juvin, east of Grand Pré, was Company H, 2d Battalion of the 306th Regiment of the 77th Division. Company H was led by Captain Julius O. Adler of New York City.

Captain Adler and twenty-six men of his company were left after the day's fighting, in which St. Juvin and Hill 182, north of the village, were captured. Company H took 352 prisoners, including a German Major.

On the morning of Oct. 12, Major Gen. Alexander, commanding the 77th Division, ordered the 2d Battalion of the 306th Infantry to take St. Juvin, where the boche, with his main position of resistance on Hill 182, held the sore spot in our line. Company H was in reserve, and at once received the commission.

Crossing the Aire River about daylight, the Americans started over the valley plain, when the Germans caught sight of them and opened up with 77s and machine guns from Hill 182. Leading his men, Captain Adler started straight for the village, having been told that only a scattering of Germans were there. As they neared the houses, more machine guns opened on them.

Captain Adler says he had forty-six men when he got into the village. Using hand grenades largely, these forty-six, scattered in squads, moved through the village swiftly, killing a number of Germans and taking sixty prisoners. Then they started off for the hill crest lying a few hundred yards north.

The few Americans there were scattered and opened fire in all quarters. The Germans, believing the Americans to be present in force, and seeing others approaching in the distance, began to surrender when Adler's men approached, while others fled. With four machine guns, Company H, or what was left of it, got in effective work; and when the Germans were cleared off the hill our men began to count their prisoners. One hundred and ninety-two more had been taken on the hill.

The less than half a hundred Americans held the position unmolested, except for artillery fire during the afternoon. On the night of Oct. 12 other American units went up on either side and consolidated the positions.

## SHOOTS TWO GERMAN MAJORS

Next morning the Germans made a counterattack in force. The small number of Americans holding the trench on the crest of the hill were forced to fall back into the village.

Captain Adler sent three runners by separate routes for reinforcements, and set about holding the Germans until aid arrived. From a German officer taken on the day before he had borrowed a heavy Leuger pistol. He was carrying his own ammunition and automatic as well. With eir of his men he engaged in a close-range fight with the Germans who had filtered into the northern end of the village.

Rounding a corner, Captain Adler ran into two German Majors leading a counterattack. His automatic was empty. Drawing his Leuger pistol, he shot one of the Majors dead and wounded the other. Seeing their leaders gone, the German driving force weakened, and the little company was doing well on its own account when ample reinforcements arrived and again occupied the trench on the crest of Hill 182.

Captain Adler came through unhurt. He is now Acting Major, commanding the 1st Battalion of the 306th Regiment. The 77th Division is composed of New York men.

## A SURPRISE ATTACK

Oct. 24.—The First American Army hit the German line two smashing blows today, one on either side of the Meuse. On the west of the stream we reached the Freya Stellung at Grand Carré Farm, north of Banthéville. East of the river our advance was larger, taking our line to Boisetraye Hill, commanding the village of that name, which lies just west of the important point Damvillers.

This attack, made in a northeastern direction, was started early in the morning under the cover of mist and succeeded from the beginning, the enemy being taken by surprise. Quickly recovering, he directed an intense artillery and machine-gun fire at Pershing's men.

The total advance was one kilometer deep on a front of three kilometers. We hold Boisehouppy, Boisbelleu, half of Boiswavrille, and Boisetraye. After the first surprise the enemy contended bitterly every foot of ground.

Our advance on Grand Carré Farm took us astride the Germans' new line of defense, the Freya Stellung. This fight was marked by intense artillery fire. About 11 o'clock the Germans started a concentrated fire on our new positions, and within fifteen minutes were dropping from eighty to a hundred shells a minute. Our own artillery reached drumfire, and held that concentration for several hours.

Despite this hell of shellfire our troops made their way over the crest running southeast of Grand Carré Farm and filtered into ravines beyond, thereby crossing the Freya Stellung.

## FIGHT FOR HILL 360

Oct. 25.—Bitter fighting has been in progress all day for possession of Hill 360, lying east of the Meuse and southwest of Damvillers, and tonight our troops hold the hill. This promontory, sticking up above other hills northeast of Verdun, gives observation over the whole area in which the Americans are operating east of the Meuse River.

The hill was of the greatest value to the Germans. When the Americans attacked it yesterday they found the enemy in deep trenches, leading into dugouts that seemed impregnable and were defended by 7s and 155s. The whole wooded hill was one great nest of machine guns. We first attacked the hill yesterday afternoon, and got half way up the thousand-foot slope, and held on until this morning at 4 o'clock, when a fresh regiment of Germans drove the Americans back down the hill.

Between 6 o'clock this morning and 3 this afternoon the Americans attacked five times, each time being driven back. At 4 o'clock another attack was made, and when I left the front at dusk word had just come in that we had two companies on the crest of the promontory, which had been cleared of the enemy.

Meanwhile a hot engagement was in progress at Belleu Wood, north of Hill 360, where a German counterattack drove back our advanced elements. After three American attacks we have reached the further edge of these woods, which have been won and lost six times in the last three days.

In the region of Grand Pré we attacked locally this morning, meeting tense and firm resistance. We made a slight advance north of Grand Pré and Bois Loges, taking some prisoners. We met and repulsed four counterattacks in this vicinity in the morning. We have strongly organized heights north of Brieulles, and control the town, which the Germans continue to shell heavily.

## SCENE IN VERDUN

Oct. 26.—Big German guns are worrying the weary stones of this torn city of Verdun, rent and tortured by four years and more of war. Here a shell screams into a moss-covered stone pile marking what once was some one's handsome home, and because the ruin is already complete it does no more harm. Another bumps its way through the rusty skeleton of what was once a pretty railroad station and for the thousandth time wracks the battered wreck. Another sticks its nose against the noble rampart of the ancient wall and tumbles into the moat as if recognizing the uselessness of spending its message of hate against the stones the Germans have tried so hard to reach in times gone by.

What could be more weird than to stand in this silent city, the historic corpse of the world's greatest slaughter, the graveyard, too, of the Germans' fondest hopes, and hear the oppressive quiet, broken by the ugly whining of the enemy's 210s coming from over the hills to the northeast?

Over these hills, whose scarred rims are torn so that the skyline looks much like a misused saw, the Americans are tearing their way into the vitals of the German Army. It is the toughest job that they ever undertook. It is one of the toughest that ever soldiers tried. The terrain is just one hill after another, one ledge rising beyond the next, with tattered woods giving the enemy the best of shelter for his machine guns.

## WORK OF SIGNAL CORPS

The Germans know every inch of ground over which we are fighting, and are enabled to make their artillery fire very accurate. In addition, it is heavy, and the enemy is expending an enormous amount of ammunition against our men fighting northeast of Verdun.

I give this instance to depict the violence of the shellfire. Behind the attacking troops run telephone lines, and the wireless has been set up. Yesterday during one attack lasting two and a half hours the telephone line was cut twenty-three times by shells, and nineteen Signal Corps men were killed in repairing it. One wireless apparatus was downed seven times in two hours.

Alarmed by the pressure of our troops, the Germans yesterday put in 800 Prussian shock troops, who gained only a temporary success, being driven back within an hour. On this front the Germans late yesterday put in a fresh division against the American divisions.

The fighting is no less severe west of the Meuse, where the Germans are contesting bitterly every foot of ground we gain and hurling frequent attacks against us. For the last twenty-four hours there has been almost constant fighting for possession of Belle Joyeuse Farm, which we have captured twice and as many times have lost.

We have had Grand Pré free from Germans three times. Twice they have come back, but now they are out and we hold a handsome margin north of the ruins of this once pretty Aire Valley town.

## BIG AMERICAN GUNS

Oct. 28.—American guns of large calibre* have begun firing on the Longuyon-Sedan-Mézières railroad, the most important German line of communication, with the object of interrupting traffic and ultimately breaking the line.

Thus the offensive of the American First Army begun Sept. 26 begins to achieve its objective. Our advance of some eighteen kilometers now makes possible the shelling of the German communication line to defend which the German command has made such enormous

*These were American 16-inch naval guns, manned by officers and bluejackets of the American Navy. Secretary Daniels authorized the statement about this time that these naval gunners on the west front were under the command of Rear Admiral Charles P. Plunkett. The first party of officers and men for the expedition had reached France on June 9. The first shipment of material left the United States on June 20. The entire organization was completed and ready to move to the battlefront in France in August. This battery went into action for the first time on Sept. 16. It continued in active operation to the end of the war.

efforts in past weeks. Of course, the nearer we get to the line the greater is the number of guns which can be used against it. It is not permitted to give details about the big guns, but it may be said that they are among the largest that have been used in the war.

Brisk local fighting continued today on both sides of the Meuse. East of the river there were heavy contacts in the Bois de la Grand Montagne and in the vicinity of Bois Bellu. We took Belleu Wood for the fifth time yesterday afternoon, only to be later driven out again. We have now retaken it again, despite terrific German artillery fire.

Just west of the Meuse our patrols pushing forward found that the Germans had deserted Clery le Grand. North of Grand Pré the Germans also withdrew from Belle Joyeuse Farm, which has changed hands eleven times in the last ten days.

## CUTTING THE SEDAN ROAD

Oct. 29.—Long-range, big-calibre American guns are again shelling the important German communication system running through Longuyon, Montmedy, Sedan, and Mézières. It is this system through Luxemburg that forms one of the two gateways between Germany and the German Army, the other clearing through Liége. The main line of the Longuyon-Sedan system runs through Montmedy, and this line up to Sed— is now the target of our giant rifles.

Any one familiar with the destructive power of big guns knows what will happen when the mammoth shells from these guns fall on a roadbed. It may fairly be said that the work of destruction of the most important artery of the German Army is now under way. To protect this road the Germans have thrown the best of their army against the Americans moving northward on the Meuse front. This has cost the enemy nearly 100,000 men so far.

The distance of our front line from the railroad is now some thirteen miles. This means that an advance of a few more miles will bring the road within accurate range of 155s, of which we have hundreds available for making sure the cutting of the German communication system. However, it should be stated that there is not the slightest doubt that every foot of this advance will be most bitterly contested by the anxious boche. Order after order has been captured calling on the German soldiers to hold the Americans at all costs and to throw them back wherever advances have been made.

## TRANSPORTING BIG NAVAL GUNS

When the word of what big German guns were doing came to America, a certain officer conceived the idea of doing some big-league shooting on account of the United States. Rifles of the desired size and range were in America. This officer persisted in his idea until he got the guns assigned to him. They were too big to go into the hold of any available ship, and so he lashed them to the decks of ships and got them to the French ports. There he was told that their weight was too great for the French roadbeds. He insisted that he would see that payment was made for any damage, and so he unloaded the rifles.

Then he was told that they would not go through the tunnels. He fixed them so they would go through the tunnels. Against many obstacles, this officer got his guns into the battle area, where they were held until the proper time came for their use. A few days ago it was decided that the time was ripe, and the guns were hauled into position, and have now been turned loose on the big-league job.

In considering the work of these guns and the potentiality of their success one must bear in mind that the railroad line at which they are shooting is the Germans' chief shuttle line, which is used to shift troops quickly from one part of the front to another. This means that if at any time up to the present the Americans had made a drive in the region below Nancy the Germans would have used this road to shift troops there. Running through Longuyon, the railroad system, in addition to running into Germany through Luxemburg, branches as the voie de rocade through the Metz area and down into lower Lorraine and Alsace.

## INFERNAL MACHINES

Boche duplicity continues to be illustrated by the high-class infernal machines he leaves behind. The ingenuity of these seems to depend upon the time Heinie has to work them out. In some regions every dugout has its little contrivance of death, but of all the assortment, the one he left at Château-Chéhéry ranks first. It was here that ammunition dumps and dugouts began to explode two days after the Germans left that place some two weeks ago. Ten days after the enemy was gone, two dugouts blew up from time bombs. Our engineers have found many types of infernal machines, such as those fixed to eight-day clocks and thermometers.

For ingenuity, one found yesterday was remarkable. Eight feet from the entrance of a handsome dugout that would make a good shelter for weary doughboys was found a cane, hanging carelessly over the balustrade of a stairway. It looked harmless, but a certain engineer Lieutenant had learned to be wary. Walking around the cane, he examined it. It appeared to be all right. Turning on his flashlight, he went over it minutely, and half way between the ferrule and the handle he saw a small black string tied. This string led to the balustrade, and down to where a person would naturally stand at the foot of the stairs when grasping the cane. Beneath this spot a four-foot-square hole was filled with an explosive corresponding to TNT.

## BREAKING THROUGH

Nov. 2.—The American First Army has broken through the German line north of Verdun and is pursuing the retreating Third and Fifth German Armies. On our left the French Fourth Army is pursuing the enemy.

Crashing through the Freya Stellung on a wide front, the Americans today captured Champigneulle, dashed on to Thénorgues, and then by storm took the important German railroad centre at Buzancy and captured Fosse, Barricourt, Villers-devant-Dun, and Doolcon. Our line has pushed on beyond those places and at many points we have lost contact with the retreating enemy.

Late today our doughboys have outrun their communications and, bad weather making aerial observation impossible, we can get no exact information at this hour of where our front line is.

The Germans put up a stiff fight at only two places today—Buzancy and Clery-le-Petit, which is over near the Meuse River. On our left, where the enemy put up such a bitter fight yesterday, he had gotten out during the night except for weak rearguards, and when he started forward along the east edge of the Forest of Boult this morning it was like child's play compared with what our men have been through for the last five weeks.

Soon these rearguards were rounded up, and there was no resistance worth speaking of from 9 o'clock up to noon. Early in the afternoon we lost contact, and commanders sent a hurry call for as many big trucks as could be spared.

### PURSUED BY TRUCKS

These trucks, which were rushed up over crowded roads, arrived about 3 o'clock. At once they were loaded with doughboys and started north after the retreating Germans. Last reports say they have not overtaken the Germans. Their joy ride, of course, was limited by the difficulties of getting up supplies and ammunition over roads made wretched by rain today.

Surely few stories of the war are more picturesque than that of the half hundred big American trucks, with our doughboys with ready rifles perched on the hoods and machine guns mounted above the drivers' heads, filled with fighting men on tiptoe for a fight, roaring northward on a grand hunt for the Germans.

What has happened is that the German armies have been worn down in the bitter battle of the last five weeks in which the Americans inflicted losses of more than 100,000, including 30,000 unwounded prisoners. After three weeks of grueling warfare we hit strongly yesterday morning, meeting the strongest resistance the enemy could put up. It was evident that when we began another intense artillery preparation this morning the Germans gave up the job

of holding the line and got out of our way. Then the Americans reaped the fruits of the bitter but unsensational battle of the last month and more.

### BUZANCY CAPTURED

It was our plan this morning to try to bring up our right, and especially our left, to the approximate line of Bayonville. Our centre corps turned to aid the left corps, only to find the left sweeping ahead. The commands were hurriedly changed and the centre turned about north. Our left swept on through Champigneulle, through the Bois des Loges, which had been taken and lost seven times, and with the centre corps surrounded the village of Thénorgues, where we counted several hundred prisoners and seventy-two machine guns.

Meanwhile, the centre, starting out just as a heavy, cold rain came on, captured Hill 313, finding resistance so slight that it surprised the men. Over the open fields they moved forward to Fosse, eleven kilometers ahead of yesterday's starting point.

Our troops then were on three sides of Buzancy. At noon we stormed the place after brisk artillery preparation, and in forty minutes we had taken this not inconsiderable town, capturing orders issued yesterday commanding the garrison to hold it at all costs.

Further to the east our troops which started from north of Remonville ran into bitter machine-gun resistance in the Bois Barricourt. Withdrawing a bit, we gave the enemy a dose of 75s and then cleared the woods. Through this barrier we swept on to Barricourt village, about on a line with Buzancy.

### RAPID GERMAN RETREAT

Nov. 3.—For the third day the American First Army has continued its sensational advanace north of Verdun against the demoralized Third and Fifth German Armies. In some sectors Pershing's men have been pursuing the enemy since dawn without catching up. The German retreat is approaching a rout. The French Fourth Army, on our left, is pushing ahead with fine speed.

From left to right we join with the French near Noirval. Our troops near

Brieulles-sur-Bar have taken Authe. In the centre we have swept on behind Champy Bois to Bois Belval. We have also taken Aucourt Farm and Beauclair. On the right we have pushed beyond Halles and Montigny. East of the Meuse great activity is reported behind the German lines.

The capture of the heights east of Beauclair, on the west bank of the Meuse, places our line seven miles from the Germans' main railroad line, the Mézières-Sedan-Longuyon system, in the vicinity of Lamouilly, which means that the line will be under range of our 75s as soon as they can be got up. We have hundreds of these accurate little guns available for cutting this line.

Nov. 4.—German resistance to the onward sweep of the Ameri·a·. First Army has developed, and late today it became apparent that the German command had effected a stand against our troops. In the afternoon bitter fighting developed along the Meuse south of Stenay, where the German Fifth Army sent up heavy reinforcements in order to prevent our crossing the river at all costs.

## CROSSING THE MEUSE

Nov. 5.—Accepting the challenge of the Germans, who threw in heavy reserves yesterday in an attempt to hold the line on the Meuse from Sivry to the north, the American First Army turned eastward today, cleared the west bank of the river from Sivry up to beyond Pouilly, and, using pontoons thrown across in the dark hours of early morning, effected passage across the Meuse at three points below Stenay. Tonight Pershing's men have crossed in force, throwing the Germans back from their defense line on the Canal de l'Est, east of the Meuse. General Liggett's men late today were fighting on the outskirts of Stenay, less than one kilometer distant from the main part of the town. * * *

There is a story of staying qualities and bravery of both doughboys and engineers in the crossing of the Meuse. Yesterday we forced the river and got small detachments across, which the Germans drove back. Twice yesterday we got a bridge over, only to have it destroyed. Under cover of intense darkness last night we got a large number of pontoons along the west bank, and, starting soon after midnight, our engineers threw three bridges across near Brieulles, many of them working in cold water up to their armpits.

Hearing a noise, the Germans started machine gun and artillery fire going. We rushed patrols across, which met the German patrols and beat them back. The German counterattack after the crossing also was stopped. By this time enemy shells had wrecked one of the bridges, so the engineers put across a fourth to give the requisite three. By the time it was daylight our men were marching across in force. I am not permitted to tell how many thousand we had got over at noon.

To the north, near Clery-le-Petit, we effected another crossing, and still one more was made. Despite continuous shelling all day, we used the crossings with little interruption of serious consequence. Our troops which crossed met heavy fighting all afternoon as they pushed the Germans back over the canal, where hundreds of the enemy were drowned.

## SIX VICTORIOUS DAYS

Nov. 6.—The success of the American First Army is developing fast into one of the greatest victories of the war. For six successive days we have driven ahead since dawn, and when the sun went down this evening our troops were within sight of Sedan, which lies six miles across low flung hills from where the triumphant doughboys rest north of Chémery. They are on their way to write a new story of Sedan which will call blessed the name of a city the French have hated to remember since the dark days of 1871.

Running across the battlefield from left to right we have pushed beyond Chémary, have reached Raucourt, passed Pourron, and are on the outskirts of Mouzon. We poured troops across the Meuse and to the east of the river smashed into German positions with striking success. We hold Lion-devant-Dun, Fontaines, the edge of the Bois St. Germain, and are nearing Stenay.

We have the boche beaten and the rearguard efforts he puts up melt quickly after we hit them. Six kilometers was the measure of our advance today just west of the Meuse. With the French Fourth Army smashing across the Aisne at many points today, coming up on our left, Pétain is pushing up toward Mézières and Charleville. General Foch's message to General Pershing gives big importance to our victory.

Reports have just come in that Stenay has been evacuated by the Germans. Word has been sent to American commanders that 850 civilians remain in the town. Reports also say that the civilian population of Montmedy has been evacuated and the population of Sedan has been told to get ready to move. The Germans have sent to the Americans a list of villages with civilians, presumably to avert bombardment. Laneuville, where 210 civilians were left by the enemy, was shelled. Because of this boche warfare the Americans were forced today to take these people back to safety.

Late today Americans at Laneuville received a message brought from Stenay asking that our men reach the people there soon with something to eat, and also get them from under the German shellfire. The Germans are able to see from the hills that we have not occupied this town, but they keep shelling it.

## CAPTURE OF SEDAN

Nov. 7.—When the German emissaries were dispatched to the front today to receive the armistice terms the German Army was all but bottled up, having only one avenue of escape—that through Liége. This bottling up was largely done by the First American Army, which is driving the last remaining Germans out of Sedan. Thus the men fighting under the Stars and Stripes have achieved what is perhaps one of the most brilliant victories of the war, and certainly the most important offensive victory.

Among the troops which reached Sedan was the 42d (Rainbow) Division, including the old 69th New York. Other divisions participating in our rush north are the 77th, (New York,) 78th, (New Jersey and New York,) 80th, (Pennsyl-

vania,) 32d, (Michigan and Wisconsin,) 90th, (Texas and Oklahoma,) the 1st, 2d, 3d, and 5th regulars, 89th, (Kansas and Nebraska,) 26th, (New England,) and the 29th, (New Jersey.)

In the First Army's remarkable six days' advance of forty kilometers it not only liberated a hundred French villages and several thousand civilians, but also captured the City of Sedan, liberating 5,000 French folk. It also cut the main German railroad system of communication from the western front through Luxemburg. Moreover, the Americans have driven the German Fifth and Third Armies, which were holding the pivot of the whole front, in full retreat.

## SET WHIRLWIND PACE

Our victorious troops set such a fast pace as to break all communication with the rear, and the weather made airplane observation impossible. That is why our commanders did not know until this morning that the doughboys had reached historic Sedan yesterday afternoon at 4 o'clock and had drawn their line along the river which cuts off a small portion of the city. Early this morning the work of putting across bridges started.

It is a sweet reward for the Americans to achieve this brilliant success after five weeks of bloody and disheartening fighting. The troops know that they broke the best German resistance that the Kaiser could put against them, and now they are reconciled, for they have changed the memory of Sedan from a sorrowful recollection to one of joy; they have changed Sedan from a name for defeat to a name for victory. Nov. 6 will go down in history along with July 18 as a great day. On July 18 the Americans and French started the offensive of the Marne and on Nov. 6 the Americans cut one of the two German communication and withdrawal lines and made the German military situation impossible.

The German retreat has been accomplished under great difficulties. American guns are hammering them as they run, and in their haste they are leaving behind uncounted millions in war material. The German Army has been swept clean of horses, and oxen have been hitched to the German guns. One report says that French cows, hitched to German 77s, are toiling far ahead, away from the pursuing Americans. Food, lumber, clothing, coal, ammunition, rifles, cannon — everything that is used in war has been left behind by the Germans in their flight, which became precipitate.

Deserters tell us of a hundred Germans from one division leaving and fleeing home, convinced that it was useless to fight the Americans any longer. An idea of the elaborate plans the Germans made to keep us back is given by the fact that at Sedan were found incomplete dams for flooding the Meuse below the city. In this they were only slightly successful, and the flood is no longer a menace to France. The Americans dynamited the dams this morning.

## SUMMARY OF THE BATTLE

Nov. 8.—Now that after one of the hardest fought and bloodiest battles of the whole war the American First Army has reached Sedan, it is perhaps fitting briefly to review the final phase of the struggle which has led to one of the most important victories the Allies have achieved.

The first phase, starting Sept. 26, took Pershing's men seven miles ahead through the Hindenburg and Völker Stellungs, but failed to break the German hold in the Argonne Forest. The second phase began on Oct. 4, and, after a grueling fight, took the First Army through the Kriemhilde Stellung, breaking the four-year hold of the Huns on the Argonne, and gave us Grand Pré. This phase lasted until Oct. 31.

One week ago yesterday the third phase began. On Nov. 1 General Liggett's army started against the Freya Stellung, forty kilometers south of Sedan, and in six days crashed through to historic Sedan, sweeping the west bank of the Meuse clear, liberating hundreds of villages and thousands of French civilians, and capturing a vast and valuable amount of war material.

Of course, the most important effect of our victory was cutting the German railroad system from Mézières through Sedan and Longuyon, which was not only an important voie de rocade, but the more important of the Germans' two lines of communication between their battlefront and the Fatherland.

In our sweep, which freed more than 700 square kilometers, we took some 10,000 prisoners and 200 guns.

When we peeped ahead in the wet dawn of Nov. 1 we had occupied the heights north and east of Grand Pré, the Bois de Bantheville, and Hill 288, as well as the hills south and on the river. We had a difficult barrier in the remaining sector of the Kriemhilde Stellung in front of the villages of St. Georges and Landres et St. Georges. By a series of fortunate local operations we had prepared an excellent jumping-off line.

## CAUGHT ENEMY UNPREPARED

The enemy expected our attack, but had planned for a date two days later than we had, which, by the way, was the same thing he did in the St. Mihiel battle. It was at 5:30 o'clock in the morning that our attack started on the whole front of more than twenty-five kilometers, preceded for two hours by intense artillery preparation, in which we fired some 200,000 gas shells. The centre of our army was held by a division which has made itself famous wherever it has appeared in battle. It was this division which made the furthest advance of the day, and alone took 3,000 prisoners. While our centre shot ahead, our left was held up at the Bois des Loges. On the right we encountered heavy resistance along the Meuse, despite which we occupied Cléry-le-Grand.

On the morning of Nov. 2 we resumed the attack at dawn. The remarkable thing about the second day was that gains were made greater than on the first day, a thing never before occurring on the western front. In the centre we not only smashed ahead for eleven kilometers, capturing the important German railhead at Buzancy, but on the right we broke the resistance, reaching Fosse, and on the left, where we had been held up, we broke the enemy's resistance so thoroughly in the morning attack and put the boche to such hurried flight that the infantrymen were loaded on to trucks and sent ahead as far as Briquenay in an effort to catch up with the enemy.

Soon after the attack was resumed on the morning of Nov. 3, it became apparent that the enemy's organization had been knocked to pieces. In three days we had defeated seventeen German divisions and broke them up so that their liaison was broken and no organized resistance could be made. Our advance on Nov. 3 enabled us to bring the German railroad through Longuyon and Montmedy under fire of our field guns.

## BROKE STENAY-ORMONT LINE

In liaison with the French Fourth Army on the left, we broke the German hold on the Bois Boult. We made good gains along the Meuse, and by night the advance had reached eighteen kilometers from the starting line of Nov. 1. Before noon on Nov. 4 we had reached the heights south of Beaumont, where we encountered the German line running from Stenay west of Ormont. We broke through this successfully, but attempts to cross the Meuse between Dun and Stenay failed under heavy German machine-gun and artillery fire from the heights east of the stream.

The roads back of the enemy on the line east of the Meuse were filled with advancing troops, which told of their determination to hold the Meuse line. Reinforcements also appeared against us west of the Meuse. This day we advanced six kilometers.

The night of Nov. 4-5 saw four pontoon bridges thrown across the Meuse under cover of heavy darkness, and shortly after midnight our troops began to pour across and continued up to noon. One bridge, which was destroyed, was replaced and the bridgeheads were maintained. While the troops on the right were gathering a firm foothold across the river, in the centre we took the town of Beaumont, finding 500 civilians there, and cleared the heights north of that place.

When we started again at dawn of Nov. 6 the German high command had given orders for a withdrawal behind the river after it had become apparent that it could not halt the Americans on this side. While our advance was not spectacular east of the Meuse, west of the river by noon we had reached the outskirts of Mouzon and passed on to seven kilometers from Sedan. Just after noon our centre started forward again, and at 4 o'clock reached the southern outskirts of the city, where the French met a decisive defeat in 1871.

On Nov. 7 we bettered our positions east of the Meuse and brought up needed supplies and ammunition west of the river, while our engineers built bridges across the river at Sedan under heavy fire from the German guns on the heights north of the city.

On the night of Nov. 7 we received word that 5,000 French civilians in Sedan were awaiting liberation. The French on our left were rapidly moving up toward Mézières and Charleville.

This brief sketch tells only a fragmentary story of the forty-kilometer advance of the American First Army, which has given to American arms credit for one of the most telling and brilliant victories of the world struggle. In no other battle in which Americans ever fought were any such numbers engaged on either side. The number engaged since the battle started far exceeds 1,000,000 men.

## NEARING THE END

Nov. 10.—The fact that this might be the last day of the war had no recognizable effect on military operations along the American front. The truth of the matter is that the United States fighting men were busy today on the greatest front they ever worked on, for we were fighting over a 115-kilometer line from Sedan east to the Moselle River near Pont-a-Mousson.

The terrific effort of the American First Army in the Meuse sector, while using up some forty-three German divisions, of course taxes us heavily. But now the Second Army has its outfit and it works well, as was shown by the success of its first operation today.

The advance of the Second Army was made from a front approximately the same as that reached following the reduction of the St. Mihiel salient by the First Army in the middle of September.

General Bullard's Second Army took over this front when the First Army was shipped north of Verdun for our great drive starting on Sept. 26.

The First Army continued to distinguish itself today by capturing the important town of Stenay, lying on the eastern bank of the Meuse, which the Germans had endeavored to hold by hundreds of machine-gun nests and by terrific artillery and machine-gun barrages from the hills beyond Stenay. Stenay was a town of some 3,000 inhabitants before the war. We found 850 civilians there who came out from their cellars and warmly welcomed their Yankee deliverers.

Operations of both the First and the Second Army continue and they will keep the boche busy on their fifty-kilometer front until called off. Every one in the American Army is looking forward to tomorrow at 11 o'clock. The army is ready for any turn the war may take.

## LAST DAY OF FIGHTING

*To Mr. James's story may be appended this Associated Press account of what the American troops did on the last day:*

Nov. 11—The line reached by the American forces at 11 o'clock today, when hostilities ceased, was being staked out this afternoon. The Germans hurled a few shells into Verdun just before 11 o'clock. Thousands of American heavy guns fired the parting shot to the Germans at exactly 11 o'clock. On the entire American front, from the Moselle to the region of Sedan, there had been artillery activity in the morning, all the batteries preparing for the final salvos.

At many batteries the artillerists joined hands, forming a long line as the lanyard of the final shot. There was a silence of a few seconds as the shells sped through the heavy mist. Then the gunners cheered. American flags were raised by the soldiers over their dugouts and guns and at the various headquarters.

News that the armistice had been signed spread rapidly along the American front from the Moselle River to the region of Sedan. Reaching the various headquarters early in the day, the news passed by wire and wireless to division and regiment, and finally from mouth to mouth to the boys in the forward lines. It was among the boys who had been under shell fire for days that there was the most genuine rejoicing.

Both sides kept up an intermittent artillery fire on Sunday as a reminder to each other that the order to cease hostilities had not been received. With nightfall the duel became weaker, each side awaiting the final word as to the set hour for desisting all firing of guns.

## THE FINAL ADVANCE

Northeast of Verdun the American infantry began to advance at 9 o'clock this morning, after artillery preparation of Ornes. The German artillery responded feebly, but the machine-gun resistance was stubborn. Nevertheless, the Americans made progress. The Americans had received orders to hold the positions reached by 11 o'clock, and at those points they began to dig in, marking the advanced positions of the American line when hostilities ceased.

Along the American front awaiting the eleventh hour was like awaiting the arrival of a new year. The gunners continued to fire, counting the shells as the time approached. The infantry were advancing, glancing at their watches. The men holding at other places organized their positions to make themselves more secure.

Then the individual groups unfurled the Stars and Stripes, shook hands and cheered. Soon afterward they were preparing for luncheon. All the boys were hungry, as they had breakfasted early in anticipation of what they considered the greatest day in American history.

Germans who came into the American line later today said their orders had been to retire with as little delay as possible. They added that they had expected to be back in their homes in Germany a week from Sunday.

# The Blasted Valley of the Somme

## By SIR GILBERT PARKER

*Sir Gilbert Parker visited the battlefields of the Somme early in October, 1918, when the Australians were still driving forward beyond the broken Hindenburg line. While his impressions were still fresh he wrote them for The London Telegraph, and the most vivid portions of his article are here reproduced.*

AT Amiens, the deserted city, was the first exhibition of the Hun desecration that I saw—nearly every shop closed, and the Hotel de la Paix only just open after a long period of quiescence, and everywhere round it were abandoned shops and deserted homes, and near by, with its shattered walls and exposed and ruined rooms, Hotel Perigord, from which hang beds and carpets and curtains as they have hung for many a day. What would have happened if the Huns had captured Amiens can best be imagined by recalling Péronne, where every house and shop was shattered and the cathedral was a mass of ruins, though three sacred figures were untouched in the destruction, as though signs should be left of this holy war against heathen horror. At least the beautiful cathedral of Amiens was standing, with only a few windows broken, with one hole through the roof and one buttress injured, and its lovely rose windows left untouched save for a few missing pieces of glass, though streets near to the cathedral were badly hammered. Also the Palais de Justice near by had escaped, but the Bureau de Change at the cathedral gates had been destroyed.

Amiens, thank Heaven, was not taken. The Australians at first prevented that, and were presently bulwarked and strengthened by the British. If Amiens had fallen a very severe blow would have been dealt to the cause of the Allies, but the same good Providence was with us as in 1914, when, being four to one in men and eight to one in arms and ammunition, the Germans did not get to Paris, as they did not get to Calais, or take Verdun, or hold Ypres, and, strangest of all, did not get to Venice. Was there a man in Europe that did not believe Venice was lost? I think not.

Who prevented it? If this is a struggle between good and evil, between right and might, then God's hand was with the Allies, and, as if in proof of it, of the reality of this Armageddon, the real Armageddon is taken, and Palestine is retaken from the Mohammedan. All these things I thought of as we went down the road with Captain Loudon, an intelligence officer of the Australian forces, from Amiens to the vicinity of Péronne, where we were to sleep, and from where we were to go to the Hindenburg line.

### AN AIRPLANE ATTACK

That night at dinner we had the first real taste of war at the front. We were sitting at dinner, when an officer said: "There's a Hun airplane. We can tell it by the difference in the vibrations. The British airplane has one continuous grind, while the German has pulsations and stops. Listen." A little later there were two sounds of bombs, and a few minutes after that the door opened, and an orderly said that a bomb had exploded in the camp, and that several men were killed and wounded. The next morning I went with the Colonel to visit the portion of the camp in which we were, and there I saw the bloody ground where men had been wiped out in an instant. It was fair battle, but it was ugly, and no man in those forces was unmoved.

After my visit to the camp we walked to Péronne, seeing American troops in driblets pass and repass, and watching the Australians drilling and on the march. One thing struck my fancy. It was the brass bands playing little columns of Australian troops, with towels on their arms and over their shoulders, on their way to baths which the Germans had left behind. I said to the officer with me, "I'm glad to see those bands; but why have you so much music?" He said, "We have seventeen bands hereabout, and can't you understand what an effect it has on the troops? First, there is the attitude of mind. A pleased mind bends more readily to discipline; and look at those men marching. Can't you see that they instinctively keep step better, and that makes for discipline. Our men are all right, but they are independent in feeling and habit, and we have to treat them like intelligent human beings."

## MOUNT ST. QUENTIN

The journey to Péronne was more than interesting; it was dramatic, for over beyond it was Mount St. Quentin, where we saw spread out all round the high plateau the great valley which could have been commanded and held successfully against a great army. Yet it was taken by a few thousand Australians, who faced this Gibraltar with proud and fearless hearts and took it. I believe that Mount St. Quentin could have been held by 500 men against 10,000, yet it was taken by Australians far fewer in number than the defending forces. They are great soldiers are the Australians, like the Canadians and New Zealanders, and they have no fear. They are worthy competitors and comrades of the British Army.

On those heights of Mount St. Quentin, where we stood exactly a month from the time it was taken, one saw the relics of the battlefield in German knapsacks, helmets, all kinds of war material, and dead bodies only partially buried; and one understood that the race which could take this apparently impregnable plateau could drive the Germans out of France and march to Berlin. And it is being done—and done fast and sure. What a change in a month! There are over 254,000 officers and men captured, and 3,669 guns, and over 23,000 machine guns, and Bulgaria is done, and Turkey will come next. And this was the army that treacherously sacked Belgium, that helped the Turks to slaughter ruthlessly the Armenians, that assisted Austria to devastate Serbia, and that has disgraced the history of mankind. The Austral-

ians have great and natural pride in their defense of Amiens, in the taking of Villers-Bretonneux, and in the battle of Mount St. Quentin. Three very remarkable events, which have had a great effect on the war and have assisted well the splendid British Army to drive the German back.

These things were much in my mind as we took the road from Australian Headquarters and Péronne to the Hindenburg line, which we were to see in the hands of British and Australian troops. It was a sad, yet glad, progress we made from Péronne to Tincourt, Marquaix, Roisel, Templeux, Hargicourt, and Villeret—sad because of the war devastation that we met, glad because the Hindenburg line was taken a week ago—and I saw it two days after it was taken—and the canal, with its underground tunnel of three miles, which had been thought impregnable. As we passed along the road the guns on either side—the 9.7 and smaller guns—were pounding away, deafening our ears, and the battle was still going on, for the Germans had recovered themselves somewhat after their heavy defeat.

## THE SHELLED ROAD

From the heights above Villeret we could see the British airplanes and several observation balloons, and in the far distance a German observation balloon, and it struck me that the German balloon could see us and the trains of artillery wagons in the narrow road, and I ventured to say that they would probably try to reach us, but was told that they had not yet recovered their poise and got their guns to work. Yet I was right, for presently we saw a shell burst directly in the road in front of us, about 250 feet away, then another and another. It was a trying moment, for the Germans were getting the range, and if they succeeded in hitting the horses and wagons in front of us, there would be great difficulty ahead of us in getting clear. But Captain C. E. Bean, an astute and admirable guide, insisted on taking another road which was not being shelled, and so we backed out of the snarl of wagons and military vans, and took another road to ruined Bellicourt, for which we were making.  As we did so, two vans filled with dead Australians were halted in the cross roads, and were fresh evidence of the fighting which had taken place at the end of last week and the beginning of this.  Let this be said for the soldiers that rode the horses or accompanied the vans, that when the shells fell so near them they showed no signs whatever of panic or anxiety, but went on their way apparently oblivious of their danger.  That they were oblivious, of course, is not true.  They must have realized their danger, but they showed no signs of it.

Oh, it was splendid, the steady, untroubled spirit of these men, and one could understand that the Hindenburg line had to pass into their hands and the hands of the Americans, who have shown such excellent bravery in all the fighting in which they have shared, and when their supply department—food, &c.—is in order, will be one of the greatest armies in the world, as it is now one of the most courageous and intelligent.  We saw a few thousands of them marching back from the Hindenburg line and the canal which they had taken, and I think I never saw a finer looking lot of men—very intelligent, lithe, and capable looking.  Those who doubted that the American and Australian, New Zealander and Canadian, would lack in discipline have been proved wrong.  They have the gift of adapting themselves to the duty of the hour, and that duty they have performed magnificently in all the fighting in which they have shared, and have subtlety and intelligence and skill to help them on their hard way.

## RELICS OF BATTLE

At last we reached the spot where we had to leave our motors, and then began a walk over the worst country I have ever seen.  Every yard had its shell hole, and as we went we saw on either hand dead bodies of Huns, with stark, discolored faces, and one lay with his head crushed to a pancake by the wheels of a tank or artillery wagon, while in a copse to the right of us were the remnants of Americans blown to pieces and many putrefying Huns.  A little later we looked down on the valley where the endless barbed wire of the Hindenburg line

was stretched, and away to the left was the town of Bellicourt, the road from which the Huns were shelling continuously.  One could hear the long swirl through the air, and then the burst of the shell and see the cloud of dirt that rose from the impact.  But their aim was bad, and I don't think they succeeded in felling many men.

But on the hillside, as we went down into the valley, we saw American soldier gravediggers putting away in the too thickly populated improvised cemetery the very many dead soldiers who had so gallantly done honor to the Stars and Stripes.  And yesterday, as it were, these were civilians like ourselves, with war as far from their thoughts as bounty is far from a miser.  And what good spirits did all soldiers whom we saw and met show!  Their day of danger was not over, but their day of victory was in their hands.  Officers in dugouts, men in carts and by the roadside, everywhere were cheerful, without being jubilant—hopeful and radiant and self-possessed.

## IN THE CANAL TUNNEL

Down into the valley we went after seeing afar the points of battle interest, like Bony and Cabaret Farm, and we made our way heavily to the canal, meeting officers who issued from their dugouts taken from the Huns to give us " the glad hand."  Down the steep sides of the canal we made our way to the entrance of the long underground ditch, and saw the spot where the Hun had made a storehouse for food and a sheltered but unhealthy home for so many of his soldiers.  It was perfectly foul, but then every officer's dugout in the German Army is foul, so we are told by British and Australian officers, and we have to clear up after their physical as after their moral presence.  The canal was dark and unsightly when I visited it, and its rough bunks, occasional tables and unsightly furnishment gave little sign of home or comfort.  It is what Captain Bean has called " a great unwholesome underground barrack."  Its people are all now our prisoners, after their comrades had lain in dugouts, and not being mopped up, had turned their machine guns on the Americans—good warfare, for which they had paid a full price, for most of them were killed by Australian infantry, who took a sweet revenge on their butchery. Even this canal did not give them security from British and Australian guns, and dead bodies of Huns were found in chambers where shells had laid them low. The endless procession of barges in the tunnel and the solidity of the construction, together with the network of barbed wire in the valley outside, made the place seem one of impregnable strength. Yet it was taken by the Americans and Australians, in spite of all forecast and expectation, and is a fit comparison with Dixmude, Loos, Ypres, Neuve Chapelle, Lens, Vimy, and a score of other places where Hun deviltry has been over-matched and our feet planted firmly and for the last time on soil from which we had been driven.

# Breaking the Hindenburg Line
## By SIR ARTHUR CONAN DOYLE

*Conan Doyle, the noted British romancer and historian, writing for The London Times, has created a pen picture of the battle near Bellicourt which is full of interest for American readers.*

Mine eyes have seen the glory of the coming of the Lord;
He is trampling out the vintage where the grapes of wrath are stored.

THE grand, sonorous, mystical lines of Julia Ward Howe rang in my head as I found myself by most unlooked-for chance an actual eye-witness of one of the historical episodes of the greatest of wars. Yes, with my own eyes I saw the rent in the Hindenburg line while the men who made it were still pushing forward from the further side of it. Even now I can hardly realize that it was so. A kindly invitation from the Australian Government explains my presence on their front, and the energy and good-will of a helpful soldier on the spot, a Captain of Australian artillery, brought about the rest. Let me try to transcribe what I saw.

It was about 11 o'clock when we reached the edge of the battlefield upon Sunday, Sept. 29. The program of the day was already clear in our heads. American divisions were to rush the front line. The Australian divisions were to pass through them and carry the battlefront forward. Already as we arrived the glad news came back that the Americans had done their part and that the Australians had just been unleashed. Also that the Germans were standing to it like men.

As our car threaded the crowded street between the ruins of Templeux, we met the wounded coming back, covered cars with nothing visible save protruding boots, and a constant stream of pedestrians, some limping, some with bandaged arms and faces, some supported by Red Cross men, a few in pain, most of them smiling grimly behind their cigarettes. Amid them came the first clump of prisoners, fifty or more, pitiable enough, and yet I could not pity them, weary, shuffling, hangdog creatures, with no touch of nobility in their features or their bearing.

The village was full of Americans and Australians, extraordinarily like each other in type. One could well have lingered, for it was all of great interest, but there were even greater interests ahead, so we turned up a hill, left our car, which had reached its limit, and proceeded on foot. The road took us through a farm, where a British anti-aircraft battery stood ready for action. There we found open plain, and went forward, amid old trenches and rusty wire, in the direction of the battle.

### EASTWARD HO!

We had now passed the heavy-gun positions, and were among the field guns, so that the noise was deafening. A British howitzer battery was hard at work, and we stopped to chat with the

Major. His crews had been at it for six hours, but were in great good humor, and chuckled mightily when the blast of one of their guns nearly drove in our eardrums, we having got rather too far forward. The effect was that of a ringing box on the exposed ear—with which valediction we left our grinning British gunners and pushed on to the east, under a screaming canopy of our own shells. The wild, empty waste of moor was broken by a single shallow quarry or gravel pit, in which we could see some movement. In it we found an advanced dressing station, with about a hundred American and Australian gunners and orderlies. There were dugouts in the sides of this flat excavation, and it had been an American battalion headquarters up to a few hours before. We were now about a thousand yards from the Hindenburg line, and I learned with emotion that this spot was the Egg redoubt, one of those advanced outposts of General Gough's army, which suffered so tragic and glorious a fate in that great military epic of March 21—one of the grandest in the whole war. The fact that we were now standing in the Egg redoubt showed me, as nothing else could have done, how completely the ground had been recovered and how the day of retribution was at hand.

We were standing near the eastward lip of the excavation, and looking over it, when it was first brought to our attention that it took two to make a battle. Up to now we had seen only one. Now two shells burst in quick succession forty yards in front of us, and a spray of earth went into the air. "Whizz-bangs," remarked our soldier-guide casually. Personally, I felt less keenly interested in their name than in the fact that they were there at all.

## VIEW FROM A TANK

We thought we had done pretty well to get within 1,000 yards of the famous line, but now came a crowning bit of good fortune, for an Australian gunner Captain, a mere lad, but a soldier from his hawk's eyes to his active feet, volunteered to rush us forward to some coign of vantage known to himself. So it was Eastward Ho! once more, still over a dull, barren plain sloping upward, with little sign of life. Here and there was the quick fluff of a bursting shell, but at a comforting distance. Suddenly ahead of us a definite object broke the skyline. It was a tank, upon which the crew were working with spanners and levers, for its comrades were now far ahead, and it would fain follow. This, it seems, was the grand stand which our young gunner had selected. On to the top of it we clambered—and there, at our very feet and less than 500 yards away, was the rift which had been torn a few hours before in the Hindenburg line. On the dun slope beyond it, under our very eyes, was even now being fought a part of that great fight where at last the children of light are beating down into the earth the forces of darkness. It was there. We could see it. And yet how little there was to see!

## GERMAN GUNS WAKE UP

The ground sloped down, as dark and heathy as Hindhead. In front of us lay a village. It was Bellicourt. The Hindenburg position ran through it. It lay quiet enough, and with the glass, or even with the eye, one could see rusty red fields of wire in front of it. But the wire had availed nothing, nor had the trench that lurked behind it, for beyond it, beside the village of Nouroy, there was a long white line, clouds of pale vapor spouting up against a dark, rain-sodden sky. "The boche smoke barrage," said our guide. "They are going to counterattack." Only this, the long, white, swirling cloud upon the dark plain, told of the strife in front of us. With my glasses I saw what looked like tanks, but whether wrecked or in hiding I could not say. There was the battle—the greatest of battles—but nowhere could I see a moving figure. It is true that all the noises of the pit seemed to rise from that lonely landscape, but noise was always with us, go where we would.

The Australians were ahead where that line of smoke marked their progress. In the sloping fields, which at that point emerged out of the moor, the victorious Americans, who had done their part, were crouching. It was an assured victory upon which we gazed, achieved so rapidly that we were ourselves standing far forward in ground which had been won that day. The wounded had been brought in, and I saw no corpses, though some friends who had reached the line to our left found eighteen American lads lying dead by the roadside. On that side the fight was very severe, and the Germans, who had been hidden in their huge dugouts, were doing their usual trick of emerging and cutting off the attack. So much we gathered afterward, but for the moment it was the panorama before us which was engrossing all our thoughts.

Suddenly the German guns woke up. I can but pray that it was not our group which drew their fire upon the half-mended tank. Shell after shell fell in its direction, all of them short, but creeping forward with each salvo. It was time for us to go. If any man says that without a call of duty he likes being under shell-fire, he is not a man whose word I would trust.

We made our way back, with no indecent haste, but certainly without loitering, across the plain, the shells always getting rather nearer, until we came to the excavation. Here we had a welcome rest, for our good gunner took us into his cubbyhole of a dugout, which would at least stop shrapnel, and we shared his tea and dried beef, a true Australian soldier's meal.

The German fire was now rather heavy. From where we sat we could see heavy shells bursting far to our rear, and there was a general atmosphere of explosion all round us, which might have seemed alarming had it not been for the general chatty afternoon-tea appearance of all those veteran soldiers with whom it was our privilege to find ourselves. As we started on our homeward track we came, first, upon the British battery which seemed to be limbering up with some idea of advancing. Further still we met our friends of the air guns, and stopped again to exchange a few impressions. They had nothing to fire at, and seemed bored to tears, for the red, white, and blue machines were in full command of the sky.

Soon we found our motor waiting in the lee of a ruined house, and began to thread our way back through the wonderfully picturesque streams of men—American, Australian, British, and German—who were strung along the road.

And then occurred a very horrible incident. One knew, of course, that one could not wander about a battlefield and not find one's self sooner or later involved in some tragedy, but we were now out of range of any but heavy guns, and their shots were spasmodic. We had halted the car for an instant to gather up two German helmets which Commander Latham had seen on the roadside, when there was a very heavy burst close ahead round a curve in the village street. A geyser of red brick dust flew up into the air. An instant later our car rounded the corner. None of us will forget what we saw. There was a tangle of mutilated horses, their necks rising and sinking. Beside them a man with his hand blown off was staggering away, the blood gushing from his upturned sleeve. Beside the horses lay a shattered man drenched crimson from head to foot, with two great glazed eyes looking upward through a mask of blood. Two comrades were at hand to help, and we could only go upon our way with the ghastly picture stamped forever upon our memory. The image of that dead driver might well haunt one in one's dreams.

Once through Templeux, and on the main road for Péronne, things became less exciting, and we drew up to see a column of 900 prisoners pass us. Each side of the causeway was lined by Australians, with their keen, clear-cut, falcon faces, and between lurched these heavy-jawed, beetle-browed, uncouth louts, new caught and staring round with bewildered eyes at their débonnaire captors. I saw none of that relief at getting out of it which I have read of; nor did I see any signs of fear, but the prevailing impression was an ox-like stolidity and dullness. It was a herd of beasts, not a procession of men. It was indeed farcical to think that these uniformed bumpkins represented the great military nation, while the gallant figures who lined the road belonged to the race which they had despised as being unwarlike. Time and Fate between them have a pretty sense of humor.

# Growth of Commissioned Personnel of the United States Navy

## By CAROL HOWE FOSTER

*Instructor in the Department of English, United States Naval Academy*

THE commissioned personnel of the United States Navy in April, 1917, included 3,800 officers, staff and line, reserve and regular. In October, 1918, it numbered approximately twenty-five thousand, and was increasing at the rate of some two thousand each month. This accomplishment and the methods followed constitute a noteworthy chapter in naval history.

The inherent democracy of the American Navy is shown by a few statistics of the Naval Reserve Force as it stood on Oct. 1, 1918. In the Naval Coast Defense Reserve there were 3,690 officers—including 692 warrant officers—and 75 per cent. of them were formerly enlisted men. Likewise in the Pay Corps Reserve 75 per cent. of the officers had been enlisted men, and in the Aviation Reserve no less than 90 per cent. of the officers had risen from the ranks. The total number of officers commissioned from the enlisted force was 8,977 in the Reserve and about three thousand in the regular navy.* Enlistment has been made the best and quickest avenue to a commission in the navy.

The navy's resourcefulness is illustrated in the enrolling of provision reserve Ensigns for ultimate submarine duty. In addition to possessing recognized engineering degrees and considerable engineering experience, applicants must be recommended by one of the following institutions: American Institute of Electrical Engineers, American Society of Mechanical Engineers, American Institute of Mining Engineers, National Research Council, or the Naval Consulting Board. By means of these civilian organizations, reservoirs of specially trained personnel have been drawn upon

and the professionally unfit have been eliminated.

In the early days of the war a few college men and Annapolis graduates were, after examination, commissioned in the Pay Corps, Corps of Civil Engineers, and Marine Corps, and then as commissioned officers fitted for their duties in the navy. There were similar openings in the Pay Corps for enlisted men in the navy and in the Marine Corps for enlisted men among the marines. A few of them after passing the required examinations were commissioned and then as officers prepared for their duties. But these were exceptional cases. The standard requirement for a staff officer was that he be a man of thorough training and special skill, already established in his profession.

Between April, 1917, and September, 1918, the various staff corps were increased as follows in their commissioned personnel: Medical from 511 to 2,667; Dental from 44 to 105; Pay from 262 to 1,679; Chaplains from 40 to 160; Naval Constructors from 83 to 268; Civil Engineers from 41 to 180. These numbers include permanent, temporary, and reserve staff officers, but do not include commissioned professors,* as none of these has been appointed since 1913. Temporary commissions are only for the period of the war.

---

*Exact figures are not available for the regular navy.

*The staff corps have an established order of precedence, and each corps wears a distinctive color between the gold stripes on sleeve and shoulder strap. First come the doctors, with dark maroon velvet as their color. Second are the dentists, marked by orange. Third are the pay officers, whose color is white. Fourth rank the Chaplains, distinguished by the cross on the collar and by stripes of black lustrous cloth between the gold stripes. Fifth is the order and dark green the color of the Professors of Mathematics; their corps is a vanishing one, inasmuch as no new appointments can be

## NAVAL RESERVE FORCE

Most line officers have been obtained by way of the various branches of the Naval Reserve Force. In the present Reserve there are five classes. Those in Class 1 must be former members of the regular navy. Those in Class 2 must be qualified for duty in combatant vessels. In Class 3, which is the largest of all, they must qualify for duty in the Naval Overseas Transport Service or the merchant marine. In Class 4, which is next to the largest, they are enrolled for the coast patrol or for special work in the naval districts, such as technical or administrative or inspection duty. Class 4 also contains a great many who are in training for transfer to Class 2 or some other class. Members of Class 5 must be qualified for ground or flying duty in aviation†

Officers for the reserve have been systematically selected in all the naval districts from the enlisted men of the coast guard, regular navy, and reserve force. Men who have some education and demonstrate unusual ability in actual competitive service are quickly picked out for unusual training and advancement. Each district sends out a weekly or monthly quota of those who seem likely to measure up to the requirements for officers of combatant or merchant ships. Officer material schools in all the districts except the ones on the Gulf are constantly passing men of promise through intensive courses in navigation, seamanship, steam and gas and electrical engineering, gunnery, torpedo work, signaling, navy regulations, &c. Students in these schools hold their enlisted ratings, Chief Quartermaster, for example, until their final examination after the normal four months' course. They are then commissioned Ensign, U. S. N. R. F., Class 4, or are transferred to general detail with appropriate ratings in case they do not prove to be competent for commission. After three months at sea as reserve Ensigns in Class 4 they may, if favorably recommended by their commanding officers, be eligible for transfer to Class 2 and subsequent examination for commission as temporary Ensigns in the regular navy.

## NAVAL AUXILIARY RESERVE

For the Naval Auxiliary Reserve a special officer material school has been established at Pelham Park, New York. Here men are trained for deck duties on merchant ships. After they have had one month of military experience and two months' service on coastwise shipping they are given a two months' course of navigation, seamanship, regulations, and signaling.

Those who desire to become engineer officers are taken for the first month to Stevens Institute, where the preliminary training in boilers, engines, and auxiliaries is given; then two months of practical work on coastwise shipping and in different repair plants near New York Harbor. The fourth month's training in organization, routine, care and upkeep, navy regulations, duties of engineer officers and assistants, is again at Stevens Institute.

Commissions in the Naval Auxiliary Reserve have also been given to seagoing officers possessing licenses in the merchant marine. They and the graduates of the deck and engineering schools just described make up the commissioned personnel of Class 3 of the

---

made. Sixth come the naval constructors, with dark violet. Seventh, and last, are the civil engineers, with light blue. Staff officers in the reserve force are distinguished by the same colors as the regulars. Formerly their colors were broken, but by an order of Aug. 27, 1918, all distinctions of uniform between reserves and regulars were abolished. In respect to uniforms it might be added that line officers both in the reserve and in the regular navy have a star on the shoulder strap and on the sleeve just above the stripes, and also an anchor on the collar.

†Both reserve and regular officers in aviation are distinguished by their olive drab uniforms with the naval shoulder straps. Other naval officers are allowed the olive drab only by special privilege, as when traveling or on inspection duty in a munition plant. Officers qualified as pilots wear a spread wing on the left breast. Naval aviators who are actually on flying duty have 50 per cent. extra pay. All reserve officers when on active duty in wartime receive the pay and allowances of regulars of the same rank and length of service, and in addition, if confirmed in grade, receive their retainer pay as reserve officers.

reserve force. In October they numbered 6,571, or about twice as many as any other class. Next year they will have to take charge of the tweny-two hundred additional ships projected by the Shipping Board and will number close to thirty thousand. In this class promotion is extremely rapid up to the grade of Lieutenant Commander. The present prospect is that some of our large steamers will have to be commanded in 1919 by men of less than one year's total sea service.

Naval aviation required fliers, inspectors, and engineers, and by October, 1918, had developed over 1,600 commissioned reserve officers. Commissions were offered to good officer material where it could best be found. Of 1,709 commissioned and warrant officers 90 per cent. had come from the enlisted force. Their training in electricity, aeronautical motors, navigation, seamanship, meteorology, photography, wireless, &c., was made possible only by the co-operation of various educational and industrial institutions like Massachusetts Institute of Technology, University of Washington, Columbia University, Packard Motor Car Company, and the seven flight training schools.

## PROMOTING ENLISTED MEN

For producing regular line officers every ship in commission—especially the large ones—has been a floating Plattsburg. All enlisted men are under close observation, and the intelligent are selected and trained as officer material. As fast as a man masters the duties of one rating he is advanced to the next. The commander of the United States naval forces operating in European waters has suggested three months as a reasonable time to serve before each promotion, but it is often shorter. Men thus advanced, through the non-commissioned grades, who have talent for leadership and can pass the necessary examinations, are commissioned at sea as temporary Ensigns in the regular navy.

If a man is excellent officer material and of good general education, but in need of special training in navigation and other technical subjects such as are taught in the officer material schools, he will probably—if he survives a hard competition—be sent to Annapolis for four months of intense work in company and competition with a few selected from the districts by competitive examination. After final examination he is commissioned Ensign, U. S. N. (T.) Temporary officers are appointed to fill vacancies created by temporary increase in the authorized enlisted strength of the active list of the navy. Temporary appointments continue in force only until otherwise directed by the President or until six months after the war.

Beginning in the Summer of 1917, reserve officers' classes at Annapolis have been graduated and commissioned as follows: 134 on Sept. 15, 1917; 285 on Feb. 1; 388 on June 8; 700 on Sept. 15, 1918; some 450 will be graduated about Feb. 1, 1919. The ships at sea and the Ensigns' School together have developed about 3,000 temporary regular line officers.

## NAVAL ACADEMY'S WORK

The most important single source of regular line officers has been the Naval Academy. Classes are now twice as large as those before the war; the present "plebes" are nearly a thousand strong. And the course of study has been compressed to three years. But the navy is still in urgent need of adequately trained deck officers. Accordingly additional quarters for 1,100 midshipmen are being completed, at a cost of three millions. Bancroft Hall will soon accommodate 2,200. Even then the Naval Academy will be unable to supply the demand for its graduates.

For other reasons besides numbers the Naval Academy has been the most important of our agencies for obtaining commissioned naval officers. No other place can give them the same grounding in the duties of both deck and engine room. No other place prepares men at so plastic and formative a period for the exercise of command. The cohesive power of our navy has been due in no small measure to the fact that positions of command, particularly in fighting ships, have been the prerogative of graduates from Annapolis. Naval commanders have been able to work together so successfully largely because they were sure of just what they could depend on from each other. They knew each other's mental and moral backgrounds. So the backbone of our navy will undoubtedly continue to be composed of regular graduates of the Naval Academy. In the resting place of John Paul Jones and of the trophy flags our navy has captured, they have taken to heart the great ideals of obedience, loyalty, pluck, and honor. Through their unique discipline and their lifelong devotion to naval duties, they are in a peculiar sense the torch-bearers of glorious traditions.

The magnitude of this achievement is matched by its quality. It has been marked throughout by the absence of graft. Appointments have been made on the basis of competitive and comparative merit. Record, personality, and examinations both physical and mental, these and all other available factors have been considered. If "pull" did in a very few cases manifest a disposition to show itself, it had such a pronounced and denounced odor that it quickly defeated its own ends. The way of the grafter and wire-puller has lain under a barrage of public opinion within and without the service. Staff officers have had to prove that they possessed competence and standing in their profession. Line officers have had to demonstrate superior force of character and superior ability in the performance of their duties. Merit has been the only principle followed.

The growth of the commissioned personnel of the navy might be summarized thus:

COMMISSIONED STAFF OFFICERS

|  | April 6, 1917. | Aug. 15, 1918. |
|---|---|---|
| Permanent | 869 | 1,634 |
| Temporary | None | 810 |
| Reserve | 128 | *2,630 |

COMMISSIONED LINE OFFICERS

|  | April 6, 1917. | Aug. 15, 1918. |
|---|---|---|
| Reserve | 552 | *13,198 |
| Temporary | None | 2,275 |
| Permanent (engin'r'g only) | None | 33 |
| Permanent (Naval Academy graduates, both deck and engineering) | 2,270 | 2,615 |
| Total staff and line | 3,819 | 23,195 |
|  |  | †1,000 |
|  |  | ‡24,195 |

* August, 1918.
† Increase estimated for Aug. 1, 1915.
‡ Total on Aug. 15, 1918.

# End of the U-Boat Warfare

## Last Sinkings Before the Recall of the Submarines, Which Ended Three Years of Terrorism

THE German Government's note of Oct. 21, 1918, requesting President Wilson to arrange an armistice, announced that orders had been issued to U-boat commanders to cease attacks on passenger ships. No sinkings were reported after that date.

The British battleship Britannia was torpedoed near the west entrance to the Strait of Gibraltar on Nov. 9, and sank three and a half hours later. Thirty-nine officers and 673 men were saved. The Britannia, which had a displacement of 16,350 tons, was 453.7 feet in length, had a speed of approximately 19 knots, and carried a peace-time complement of 777 men. Her main armament consisted of four twelve-inch guns.

The American steamship Lucia, which had her lower holds fitted with rubber-bound barrels and was believed to be unsinkable, was torpedoed and sunk on the 19th of October, 1,200 miles from the American coast. Four of the crew were killed by the explosion; the remainder were rescued. The vessel was a single-screw steamship of 6,744 gross tonnage. The Irish steamer Dundalk, 863 tons, was torpedoed in the Irish Sea Oct. 19; of the crew of 34 only 13 were rescued. No other torpedoeings of importance were reported subsequent to that date.

It was reported on Oct. 21 that all German destroyers and torpedo boats, as well as submarines, which had their bases at Ostend and Zeebrugge had escaped to German ports. At the same time Kiel Harbor was reported to be so crowded with returned submarines that some had to lie outside.

The losses of British shipping due to enemy action and marine risk during September totaled 151,593 gross tons, compared with 176,434 in August and 209,212 in September, 1917. The losses for the quarter ended with September were 510,551 gross tons, compared with 952,938 for the corresponding quarter of 1917.

The Norwegian bark Stifonder, 1,746 tons, was torpedoed Oct. 13 by a German submarine 1,000 miles off the American coast. T. Fritji, mate, and nine survivors of the crew were adrift fifteen days in a longboat until they were picked up off Barnegat, N. J. The other members of the crew were lost. When the commander of the U-boat came close alongside the bark on the morning of Oct. 13 he ordered the crew to abandon ship at once. Before placing bombs on board to sink her the German sailors took away a quantity of stores, oil, and gasoline.

## SUCCESS OF CONVOYS

In reviewing the submarine record for June, July, and August, 1918, the last active period of the U-boat campaign, The Associated Press gave the following details of the operation of the American naval convoy service, under London date of Oct. 10, 1918:

" In the tremendous arrivals this Summer period is satisfactory. Not one of the incoming troopships was lost, and every soldier was landed. Such losses as have occurred have been on outgoing ships, mainly freighters going back with little or no cargo.

" As the American naval convoy service has borne the brunt of this protection, the results achieved for the first Summer are a notable tribute to the American fleet. In the Mediterranean there are five of the allied navies cooperating in the protective service—the French, British, American, Italian, and Japanese. Here on the Atlantic Coast, however, the French and American fleets furnish the convoys and protective service, and along 300 miles of the front the

American service has a foremost part, particularly in the huge movement of troops and supplies from America.

" The monthly tonnage losses for the Summer were close around 260,000 tons, or about 50,000 tons less than the monthly losses at the opening of the year, and 100,000 tons less than the losses in March. In January the losses stood at about 300,000 tons. They mounted steadily through February and March, until the March total was around 350,000. Then a sudden drop began, and in April the losses were down to 260,000. Again they mounted slightly in May to 280,000. Then there was another fall to 240,000. In July they stood at 260,000, and this has been the level to the close of the Summer.

" The percentage of losses on the Atlantic route since the convoy system began May 25 last is less than that on any other route. In the Mediterranean the percentage of losses is about 1½, and on one exposed route it runs up to 18. But on the Atlantic route, where the American convoy is chiefly concerned, the percentage of losses is around 1 per cent.

" As to the loss of submarines, the one fact known definitely is that they are being destroyed faster than they are being built. But there are not the same exact figures as to the fluctuations of losses, as these are carefully concealed by the enemy, and the loss of an underwater craft is much less apparent than that of one on the surface. But a pretty accurate check is kept on those which disappear and the new ones taking their place.

" Among the new ones are the U-139, U-141, and U-142, built at the Germania Krupp yards at Kiel. They have a length of about 315 feet, with sixteen knots speed on the surface and nine knots under water. They each mount four guns and two machine guns, and have four 500-centimeter torpedo tubes, two forward and two aft.

" But the appearance of new boats in no way keeps pace with the loss of the old ones, which are crippled or sunk, or mysteriously disappear, leaving hardly a trace as the depth bombs do their deadly underwater work."

## VAST CARGOES CARRIED

The British Wireless Service on Nov. 6 stated that since the convoy system had been successfully adopted some 26,-000,000 tons of food and 35,000,000 tons of munitions had been brought in convoy to England and the food ships lost had been reduced from nearly 10 per cent. to 1 per cent.

In the course of the Summer 307 ships of a tonnage of 1,466,000 had carried the Argentine wheat crop to Great Britain, France, and Italy, and only one ship was lost. This may be compared with the worst period for sinkings, the week ended April 29, 1917, when 119 ships were lost.

Convoys between July 26, 1917, and Oct. 19, 1918, were 1,027 in number, containing 14,968 ships, of which only 118 were lost. The gross tonnage was 77,-057,231. The tonnage lost was 654,288. One convoy of United States troops and British ships brought 30,000 men.

The grand total of merchant ships convoyed was 85,772 and the losses were only 433.

The volume of traffic to and from the United Kingdom in less than three-quarters of this year increased by one-third, while the risk of loss was reduced one-half.

It was stated in November that the claims of neutral nations for vessels sunk by submarines would exceed $1,000,-000,000, represented by the loss of 1,500 ships, with a capacity of 2,000,000 tons; the loss of life exceeded 2,500. By ceding seven interned ships to Spain to replace as many of the eighty-seven Spanish vessels sunk, Germany admitted her liability. The mercantile marine losses of Germany's foes exceeded those of the neutrals, and there were not enough German ships to replace this tonnage. But many of these ships are now interned in neutral harbors. Spain has ninety of them.

The first steamship that entered New York Harbor with lights ablaze since the beginning of the U-boat campaign, 1915, arrived Nov. 2, 1918. The commander had received a wireless dispatch at sea the day before, informing him that the way was clear and that he could steer a direct course for port, which shortened the voyage by twenty hours. Transports and other vessels were burning their lights at sea Nov. 2 for the first time in three years.

# The North Sea Submarine Barrage

## How Our Navy Helped to Defeat the U-Boat, With the Greatest Mine Area on Record

[AUTHORIZED BY SECRETARY DANIELS, OCT. 30, 1918]

ONE of the most important accomplishments of the Bureau of Ordnance in this war has been the establishment, in co-operation with the British Navy, of the North Sea mine barrage, designed to bar, so far as possible, the egress of German submarines from their home bases into the Atlantic. For this project a new and improved type of mine was invented, many thousands manufactured and transported overseas, large bases were established abroad for assembling and issuance of mine planters, a fleet of mine layers was sent and has been maintained in foreign waters, a score of merchant vessels were fitted out and have been engaged in transportation of the material from this country, and a mine-loading plant, with a capacity of more than a thousand mines a day, was erected, and has been in operation for many months.

Rear Admiral Joseph Strauss, former Chief of the Bureau of Ordnance, is in command of the mine force abroad; Captain R. R. Belknap directs the mine planters; Captain O. G. Murfin is in charge of the forces and bases ashore, where several thousand men are engaged, and Commander S. P. Fullinwider is in charge of the Mine Section of the Bureau of Ordnance, which keeps the forces overseas supplied.

From the time this country entered the war officers of the Bureau of Ordnance contended that a most effective way of combating the submarine would be to blockade the enemy's coast by means of mines or anti-submarine devices, and urged the placing of an anti-submarine barrier around the North Sea to prevent submarines from getting into the Atlantic. They made a thorough study of the various types of barrage, including nets, nets in combination with mines and bombs, and mines alone. They concluded that mines offered the only practicable solution of the problem; but no mine then existing appeared to be satisfactory for the purpose, so efforts were concentrated on the evolution of a new type with which such a barrier could be established. The immense number required for the project and the operation of mining in such great depths of water presented new and difficult problems.

The mining section of the bureau, under the direction of Commander Fullinwider, produced a new type of mine, the success of which has surpassed all expectations. The first step was to devise a new firing device, and the officers saw possibilities in an electrical anti-submarine device which Ralph Browne, an American inventor, had submitted to the department in May, 1917, which, while not of practical value in the form submitted, embodied an element which could be utilized to advantage in a naval mine. The inventor, in collaboration with officers of the bureau, constructed a model apparatus which on test, July 9, 1917, gave gratifying results, and the bureau immediately proceeded with the design of a mine in which the apparatus could be used. The firing apparatus having been completed, other parts were designed as rapidly as possible, each part being put into manufacture as it was designed and tested. To insure the practicability of planting mines by either British or American planters, outside dimensions of the American mine and planter were made to conform to the standard British gear. Lieut. Commander H. Isherwood, R. N. V. R., worked with the bureau to accomplish this end, and assisted in designing the complicated mine anchor.

Tentative plans for a North Sea barrage were submitted to Admiral Benson, Chief of Naval Operations, on June 12, 1917; the development of a mine peculiarly adapted for use against submarines was announced July 18, and plans for a British-American joint offensive operation were submitted on July 30, 1917. After being approved by Secretary Daniels, they were submitted to the British Admiralty by Admiral Henry T. Mayo, on his visit to Europe during August and September, 1917; were accepted, in modified form, by the British authorities, and the details of the joint operation worked out. Upon Admiral Mayo's return, the Bureau of Ordnance was directed by Secretary Daniels to proceed with the procurement of the necessary mines.

At first some officials looked upon the plan as impracticable, mainly on account of the immense amount of material required and the inadequate number of mine layers available. But these difficulties were overcome and the British and American authorities agreed upon the plan which has been put into effect.

Many thousands of mines had to be produced, and as rapidly as the several parts were designed, contracts were placed for their manufacture. Coincident with this work numerous experiments and tests were made of each part. The routine method would have required the design and test of the mine and all its attachments as a whole before undertaking manufacture, but a year's time would have been lost if this routine had been followed. To obtain the new mine in large quantities, and to preserve due secrecy regarding its characteristics, a radical departure from usual manufacturing methods was adopted. The expedient was adopted of subdividing the mine into its many elements and having these elements manufactured in different commercial plants, all the parts to be finally brought together and assembled into finished mines at a mine depot. The work was divided among about 140 principal contractors and more than 400 subcontractors. The major portion of the work was done in automobile plants, which possessed the organization and equipment for quantity production.

Having the various parts made at so many points was a somewhat hazardous course to adopt, as the manufacturers would have to tool up and get into quantity production before a single mine could be assembled and tested, and such a policy could be justified only as an urgent war measure, where time was a vital consideration. For this reason Rear Admiral Earle, Chief of the Bureau of Ordnance, accepted the risk and pushed the work to the utmost. The results fully justified the means adopted, as a full year's time was saved, and the mines when finally assembled and tested under service conditions functioned as designed. The cost of the new mine is much less than that of similar products before the war, notwithstanding the higher cost of labor and material, and this is due to the quantity production methods followed out and the keen competition between contractors.

While the mine itself was being placed in production, a number of ships were converted into mine planters, a mine-charging plant with a capacity of a thousand mines a day was erected to load the mines, an important railroad shipping pier was taken over for the handling of mine material, and other necessary arrangements made. Abroad mine depots were fitted out for the assembly of mines and their issuance to the mine planters.

A fleet of more than twenty merchant vessels was taken over by the navy and fitted out for the sole purpose of transporting mine material overseas. Captain R. R. Belknap accomplished the work of procuring, fitting out, and organizing the vessels for mine planting. The task of fitting of mine bases on shore abroad was intrusted to Captain O. G. Murfin, who proceeded overseas in November, 1917. The arrangements for the receipt of the various parts, transportation, and final assembly were made rapid and automatic, and on a scale never before attained in such work. From American ports material started across early in February. Since that time there has been a constant succession of such shipments, and only one vessel carrying mine material has been sunk by submarine.

Rear Admiral Strauss was selected as commander of the mine force, and sailed in April, 1918, followed by the mine planters under Captain Belknap in May, vessels of the force reaching the bases on May 26 last. Since that time many miles of mines have been planted and the American mine layers, working in conjunction and close co-operation with the British, have made a vast area impracticable for enemy submarines.

## The Nationality of the Finns and Esthonians

THE independence of Finland adds yet another to a group of European nations which are of non-Aryan race, and some of which, like the Magyars and the Turks, and, to some extent, the Bulgars, represent recent incursions of Asiatic nomads, who have fastened themselves on European soil. The Finns and Esthonians, who are connected with all these peoples, since all are members of the Mongolian Ural-Altai group, represent, however, a far earlier incursion, if they are not even older than the Aryan races (Slavic and Scandinavian) who now almost surround them. The Finns were known under that name (Phinnoi) to Ptolemy, while it seems certain that the Esthonians are the Aestii of Tacitus. The Finns, however, call themselves Suomi, "men of the marshes," from Suo,

a marsh. With the Esthonians, they are closely akin to a group of non-Slavonic, Mongoloid peoples, like the Mordvins, the Cheremiss, the Ostiaks, the Voguls, who spread over Northern and Northeastern Russia, forming a strong element of yellow race, which has largely blended with the Russians.

In 1911, the population of Finland numbered 3,250,000, of whom 2,570,000 were Finns, 340,000 Swedes, 7,000 Russians, and less than 2,000 Germans. The Finns are, almost without exception, Lutherans, as are the Swedish upper classes in Finland. But there is practically no race difference between the Finns, on the north of the Gulf of Finland, and the Esthonians, Curlanders and Livonians, on the south of the same gulf.

# The Czechoslovak Republic

## Text of the Declaration of Independence Adopted by the Provisional Government

THE first of the new States to be organized from the ruins of the Austro-Hungarian Empire was the Czechoslovak Republic, consisting of the Czechs of Bohemia and the Slovaks of Moravia and Silesia, a total of 12,000,000 people of Slavic race, whose aspirations for liberty since the beginning of the war had found their chief spokesman in Professor Thomas G. Masaryk, President of the Czechoslovak National Council. This body, recognized by all the leading Entente Governments as the new nation's Provisional Government, had its headquarters in Paris, though Professor Masaryk remained in Washington, where he was in close touch with President Wilson, especially after our Government's recognition of the Czechoslovak Nation and Army, on Sept. 2, 1918. Formal action severing Bohemia from Austria-Hungary was taken by the Provisional Government in Paris on Oct. 18, when it adopted the following Declaration of Independence:

At this grave moment, when the Hohenzollerns are offering peace in order to stop the victorious advance of the allied armies and to prevent the dismemberment of Austria-Hungary and Turkey, and when the Hapsburgs are promising the federalization of the empire and autonomy to the dissatisfied nationalities committed to their rule, we, the Czechoslovak National Council, recognized by the allied and American Governments as the Provisional Government of the Czechoslovak State and Nation, in complete accord with the declaration of the Czech Deputies made in Prague on Jan. 6, 1918, and realizing that federalization and, still more, autonomy, means nothing under a Hapsburg dynasty, do hereby make and declare this our Declaration of Independence.

We do this because of our belief that no people should be forced to live under a sovereignty they do not recognize, and because of our knowledge and firm conviction that our nation cannot freely develop in a Hapsburg mock federation, which is only a new form of the denationalizing oppression under which we have suffered for the last 300 years. We consider freedom to be the first prerequisite for federalization, and believe that the free nations of Central and Eastern Europe may easily federate should they find it necessary.

We make this declaration on the basis of our historic and natural right. We have been an independent State since the seventh century, and in 1526, as an independent State, consisting of Bohemia, Moravia, and Silesia, we joined with Austria and Hungary in a defensive union against the Turkish danger. We have never voluntarily surrendered our rights as an independent State in this confederation. The Hapsburgs broke their compact with our nation by illegally transgressing our rights and violating the Constitution of our State, which they had pledged themselves to uphold, and we therefore refuse longer to remain a part of Austria-Hungary in any form.

We claim the right of Bohemia to be reunited with her Slovak brethren of Slovakia, once a part of our national State, later torn from our national body, and fifty years ago incorporated in the Hungarian State of the Magyars, who, by their unspeakable violence and ruthless oppression of their subject races have lost all moral and human right to rule anybody but themselves.

The world knows the history of our struggle against the Hapsburg oppression, intensified and systematized by the Austro-Hungarian dualistic compromise of 1867. This dualism is only a shameless organization of brute force and exploitation of the majority by the minority; it is a political conspiracy of the Germans and Magyars against our own as well as the other Slav and the Latin nations of the monarchy. The world knows the justice of our claims, which the Hapsburgs themselves dared not deny. Francis Joseph in the most solemn manner repeatedly recognized the sovereign rights of our nation. The Germans and Magyars opposed this recognition, and Austria-Hungary, bowing before the Pan Germans, became a colony of Germany, and, as her vanguard to the East, provoked the last Balkan conflict, as well as the present world war, which was begun by the Hapsburgs alone without the consent of the representatives of the people.

We can not and will not continue to live under the direct or indirect rule of the violators of Belgium, France, and Serbia, the would-be murderers of Russia and Rumania, the murderers of tens of thou-

MID-EUROPEAN GROUP OF NEWLY LIBERATED PEOPLES

sands of civilians and soldiers of our blood, and the accomplices in numberless unspeakable crimes committed in this war against humanity by the two degenerate and irresponsible dynasties. We will not remain a part of a State which has no justification for existence and which, refusing to accept the fundamental principles of modern world organization, remains only an artificial and immoral political structure, hindering every movement toward democratic and social progress. The Hapsburg dynasty, weighed down by a huge inheritance of error and crime, is a perpetual menace to the peace of the world, and we deem it our duty toward humanity and civilization to aid in bringing about its downfall and destruction.

We reject the sacrilegious assertion that the power of the Hapsburg and Hohenzollern dynasties is of divine origin; we refuse to recognize the divine right of Kings. Our nation elected the Hapsburgs

to the throne of Bohemia of its own free will, and by the same right deposes them. We hereby declare the Hapsburg dynasty unworthy of leading our nation, and deny all of their claims to rule in the Czechoslovak Land, which we here and now declare shall henceforth be a free and independent people and nation.

We accept and shall adhere to the ideals of modern democracy, as they have been the ideals of our nation for centuries. We accept the American principles as laid down by President Wilson; the principles of liberated mankind—of the actual equality of nations—and of Governments deriving all their just power from the consent of the governed. We, the nation of Comenius, cannot but accept these principles expressed in the American Declaration of Independence, the principles of Lincoln, and of the declaration of the rights of man and of the citizen. For these principles our nation shed its blood in the memorable Hussite wars 500 years ago; for these same principles, beside her allies, our nation is shedding its blood today in Russia, Italy, and France.

We shall outline only the main principles of the Constitution of the Czechoslovak Nation; the final decision as to the Constitution itself falls to the legally chosen representatives of the liberated and united people.

The Czechoslovak State shall be a republic. In constant endeavor for progress it will guarantee complete freedom of conscience, religion and science, literature and art, speech, the press, and the right of assembly and petition. The Church shall be separated from the State. Our democracy shall rest on universal suffrage; women shall be placed on an equal footing with men, politically, socially, and culturally. The rights of the minority shall be safeguarded by proportional representation; national minorities shall enjoy equal rights. The Government shall be parliamentary in form and shall recognize the principles of initiative and referendum. The standing army will be replaced by militia.

The Czechoslovak Nation will carry out far-reaching social and economic reforms; the large estates will be redeemed for home colonization; patents of nobility will be abolished. Our nation will assume its part of the Austro-Hungarian pre-war public debt; the debts for this war we leave to those who incurred them.

In its foreign policy the Czechoslovak Nation will accept its full share of responsibility in the reorganization of Eastern Europe. It accepts fully the democratic and social principle of nationality and subscribes to the doctrine that all covenants and treaties shall be entered into openly and frankly without secret diplomacy.

Our Constitution shall provide an efficient, rational, and just Government, which will exclude all special privileges and prohibit class legislation.

Democracy has defeated theocratic autocracy. Militarism is overcome, democracy is victorious; on the basis of democracy mankind will be recognized. The forces of darkness have served the victory of light, the longed-for age of humanity is dawning.

We believe in democracy, we believe in liberty, and liberty evermore.

*Given in Paris on the eighteenth of October,* 1918.

Professor THOMAS G. MASARYK, Prime Minister and Minister of Finance.

General Dr. MILAN R. STEFANIK, Minister of National Defense.

Dr. EDWARD BENES, Minister of Foreign Affairs and of Interior.

On the same day the Czechs seized control of Prague, the capital of Bohemia, and the Czech flag was raised over Hradschin Castle. A general strike was proclaimed throughout the country. The Austrian authorities made little attempt at resistance, and after a few days of confusion, with street fighting in Prague and Brunn, the Czechoslovak National Council gained full control. When the Czech soldiers under General Gouraud in France were told on Oct. 21 of their nation's declaration of independence a wild burst of enthusiasm ensued, and after only fifteen minutes of artillery preparation the men rushed into an attack on the German lines, and after an hour's desperate fighting captured the village of Terron, one of the most difficult positions on the Aisne.

The Czech National Committee took over the functions of the Local Government in Prague on Oct. 28. The Austrian Governor fled to Vienna, and the imperial military representatives in the Bohemian capital handed over their authority to Dr. Kramarz as local head of the National Council. The Austrian imperial symbols were removed from public buildings, imperial proclamations were torn down, and the city officials took the oath of allegiance to the Czechoslovak Republic. The next day, the 29th, the republic was formally proclaimed, and the authority of Emperor Charles became only a name in Prague.

Prague was beflagged for the occasion, and her enthusiasm was boundless. Great demonstrations expressed the joy of the people, who acclaimed the Entente and America. In other parts of the country the same high enthusiasm was shown. Everywhere there were monster meetings and patriotic speeches proclaiming the linking up of the new State with the cause championed by the Entente and America.

The news of Austria's peace offer came, indeed, as a sign that the last moments of Austrian supremacy in Bohemia had been reached. When Prague heard the news the people assembled in great throngs in the streets, embraced one another in their joy, and sang the Czech national songs. The soldiers tore the Austrian cockades from their caps and threw them away. In some cases the officers had to be forced to do so, but the vast majority of them shared the joy of the soldiers and the people, and decked their swords with ribbons of the Czechoslovak colors. The army was no longer a force to be used at the bidding of Austria-Hungary. A large number of officials took the oath of office before the Council.

A tremendous crowd gathered around the Huss Monument, and Premier Lammasch's name was loudly acclaimed. From there the crowd surged onward to the General Post Office, where a young man, amid tremendous cheering, climbed up to where the Austrian eagle was fixed and threw it down. The crowd quickly trampled it to pieces.

The National Council appointed new railway, telegraph, and postal officials and took possession of the railways as far as Bodenbach, near the frontier of Saxony. The cars were marked with the inscription, " Free Czechish-Socialist Republic." German soldiers stationed within the boundaries of the new State were disarmed without any special acts of violence. All trains carrying food to Austria or Germany were stopped and the exportation of coal was forbidden.

## MASARYK MADE PRESIDENT

Two delegations of Czech leaders—one from Prague and one from the Provisional Government in Paris—met in Geneva, Switzerland, at the end of October to formulate a Constitution for the new republic. The conference ended Nov. 2, when it had completed the draft of a Constitution patterned after that of the United States. At this conference Professor Thomas G. Masaryk was elected first President of the Czechoslovak Republic by delegates representing eight political parties. A telegram urged him to leave Washington at once for Prague. It was announced that a National Parliament would be assembled in Prague at an early date. The National Council lost no time in organizing an army, regrouping the existing forces, ordering a general revision of the lists of soldiers, and calling up new classes. All men liable to military service up to the age of 26 throughout Czechoslovakia were called to the colors in the first week of November.

From the beginning of the war the Czechs and Slovaks showed insubordination toward their German officers, who forced them to fight against their Russian kinsmen. As the conflict proceeded, more than 100,000 of them surrendered to Russia, and a large proportion of these fought on the Russian side against their former oppressors.

Probably the most dramatic episode in this connection was that which occurred when the 28th Czech Regiment of Prague surrendered to the Russians, on April 3, 1915, with all its equipment, and to the strains of Czech national music. Of the 2,000 men who surrendered, many requested permission to fight against the Austrians.

As a punishment against the regiment, a new unit of the same title was formed entirely of 20-year-old soldiers, and sent to the Isonzo front. There it was exposed to the withering fire of the Italian artillery near Gorizia. Only eighteen soldiers survived. The rest of the thousands lay dead on the battlefield. The Austrian Emperor proclaimed by an order of the day that the disgrace of the 28th Regiment of Prague had been wiped out by the sacrifices of that regiment on the Izonzo.

When Germany took over the direction of the military affairs of Austria-Hungary, the Czechoslovak regiments were dissolved, and the soldiers scattered among the Magyar and German regiments. If one hears of Bohemian regiments having fought with élan against the Italians, one must remember that they were either German or Magyar regiments, with a scattering of Bohemian soldiers. As a nation the Czechoslovaks had come over on the side of the Allies, heroically bearing the sanguinary consequences of their decision. Ninety-five per cent. of the Bohemians of military age resident in Britain volunteered in the British Army.

The Russian débâcle brought all the oppressed nations of Eastern Europe together against Austria-Hungary, and the Czechs and Slovaks led the way in active fighting. On Dec. 10, 1917, Premier Clemenceau of France authorized the organization of a Czechoslovak army, and recognized it as a belligerent unit. The epoch-making event in the general movement, however, was the Congress of Oppressed Nations at Rome, April 10, 1918, where all the conflicting claims of peoples from Poland to Jugoslavia were harmonized with those of Italy, resulting in the Pact of Rome. Premier Orlando made this statement in the Chamber of Deputies on Oct. 3:

> As early as April 21, 1918, the Italian Government concluded an agreement with the Czechoslovak National Council for the creation of a legion to fight on our front, a step which implied the recognition of a de facto Government. Since then our relations with this heroic people have been uniformly friendly, and the fraternal bonds between us have been strengthened and hallowed by the blood which its generous sons have shed in the Alps for the defense of Italy as well as of their own land. I believe I am a faithful interpreter of the soul of the whole Italian Nation when I say that the union between these two peoples will continue sincere and indissoluble and will be prolonged through fruitful economic and intellectual relations after the war.

Great Britain's formal recognition of the Czechoslovak Nation was published on Aug. 13, that of the United States on Sept. 2, and that of Japan on Sept. 9. An expeditionary force to support the Czechoslovaks in Russia was sent to Vladivostok, and the new nation became a definite military element in the war before it had become a political entity.

# Story of the Czechoslovaks
## Thirteen Hundred Years of Struggle Against German Oppression
### By DR. EDWARD BENES

[FORMER PROFESSOR OF SOCIOLOGY IN THE UNIVERSITY OF PRAGUE; MINISTER OF FOREIGN AFFAIRS IN THE NEW CZECHOSLOVAK REPUBLIC]

[*Written in the Summer of 1918*]

FROM the sixth century we Czechs in Bohemia were a free people; we were a nation; we were complete and independent. In the beginning of the seventh century began our oppression. The German barbarian set himself to destroy us. From that day, for 1,300 years, my people fought the German. They have never lost heart. They have never accepted the tyrant. Always they have opposed to the German their passion for liberty and their national consciousness. In the sixteenth century this bitter struggle came to a climax. We were defeated, wiped out, annihilated. Nothing was left of us but a few peasants. Our aristocracy was executed; our middle classes driven into exile; our working classes slaughtered. Nothing was left but those few peasants—nothing. It was the destruction of a nation. And on the north of those peasants there were Germans; on the south, Germans; on the west, Germans; and on the east, enemies just as deadly to those peasants, the brutal Magyars.

But our peasants had something in their hearts no German could destroy. There was no aristocracy to inspire them, no middle class to lead them; they were like sheep without a shepherd. Ah, but listen! In the hearts of those peasants was the undying flame of freedom. Yes; and in their souls the undying fire of national consciousness. They tilled the earth, they patiently earned their hard living, and in their homes the mother told her babe of the days that were past and of the days that would surely come again; and these people, these poor peasants, with all the might of the German crushing them to the earth, never bowed to the tyrant, never accepted the Catholic Church, never despaired. The mother sang to her baby the song of yesterday and tomorrow.

It is true to say this: At the end of the eighteenth century the Czechs of Bohemia had ceased to exist as a nation; and yet, at the beginning of the nineteenth century, that nation began to rise from the dead.

From 1840 began the passionate modern life of this arisen nation. The

Revolution in France burst the door of its sepulchre. Not a peasant in Bohemia who did not say to himself, Now I live. Those people saw what they must do. They were suffocating in tyranny. They must be free or perish. And on all sides of them was the Austrian, crushing them with the five weapons of despotism—the dynasty, the aristocracy, the bureaucracy, the church, the army. What could those peasants do? I will tell you. They said to themselves, We have no physical force wherewith to achieve freedom; very well, then, we will fashion an intellectual force—with our minds we will destroy Austria, with our brains we will achieve the ideals of the revolution. It was like the sun rising over the hills. They set up national schools; they cultivated the national literature; they taught their children that to have brains was a part of patriotism. They were only peasants, but they created a nation. Out of those little schools, out of those humble homes, came a new Czech aristocracy—doctors, professors, engineers, merchants, bankers—all of them the sons of peasants. I myself am the son of a peasant. I have four brothers—all of them are intellectuals.

We said to ourselves, We will make ourselves a nation; we will be free, we will be independent, we will be powerful. And from that moment began a boycott of the German which has lasted for nearly a hundred years. We buy no German goods. We have no dealing with the German. We have our own national banks. The German banker says to our people, Bring me your savings and I will give you 5 per cent. The Czech says, I lend my money to my national bank for 3 per cent. For years we have been economically and industrially free. We are a self-supporting nation, advanced in our industry, advancing in our culture, nowhere in all Bohemia an illiterate. And when war came, our soldiers, forced to fight on the side of Austria, deserted in hundreds of thousands. They went over not to their enemies, but to their friends—the friends of freedom. And now, in Siberia, in France, in Italy, they are fighting for democracy.

This fight has been ten million against eighty million. Tomorrow the odds will be even! We Czechs are allying ourselves with the Poles—with the Jugoslavs. There are millions of us. Our Provisional Government, sitting in Paris, receives every day letters from Czechs all over the world—in Australia, China, South Africa, North America, South America, everywhere. And all these letters say one thing—" Here is money; tell me what I can do to help." We have asked not one penny from the Allies—not a penny; and we have three armies fighting in different parts of the world for our freedom. The Slavs in Russia are listening to us. In Siberia our soldiers are the vanguard of a free and glorious Russia. One day you will see Austria crash to the ground, and on that day the heirs of the Czech peasants will receive their reward. Why? Because they have been faithful; because they have loved liberty; because their conception of life is right; because their mentality is a better mentality than the German's.

Always we have had one enemy—the German! And he has hated us because we have loved freedom.

# Poland's Move for Independence

## America's Official Recognition

IN the middle of July, 1918, Senator Hitchcock, Chairman of the Foreign Relations Committee, drafted a resolution recognizing Poland as an independent nation. The measure was not, however, laid before Congress. Early in September the movement took on new impetus, as a result of the efforts of Roman Dmowsky, President of the Polish National Committee in Paris, who had come to this country to present the claims of his people to the Washington authorities. On Nov. 4 Secretary Lansing addressed the following letter to Mr. Dmowsky:

> I beg to acknowledge the receipt of your letters of Oct. 18 and Oct. 25 requesting the Government of the United States to associate itself with the Governments of France and Great Britain by recognizing the Polish Army, under the supreme political authority of the Polish National Committee, as autonomous, allied, and co-belligerent.
>
> In reply I beg to inform you that the Government of the United States has not been unmindful of the zeal and tenacity with which the Polish National Committee has prosecuted the task of marshaling its fellow-countrymen in a supreme military effort to free Poland from its present oppressors.
>
> This Government's position with respect to the Polish cause and the Polish people could hardly be more clearly defined than was outlined by the President in his address before the Congress on Jan. 8, 1918.
>
> Therefore, feeling as it does, a deep sympathy for the Polish people, and viewing with gratification the progress of the Polish cause, this Government experiences a feeling of genuine satisfaction in being able to comply with your request by recognizing the Polish Army, under the supreme political authority of the Polish National Committee, as autonomous and co-belligerent.

In taking this step the United States was following the example of France, Great Britain, and Italy. The British Government recognized the Polish National Army as " autonomous, allied, and co-belligerent." In announcing this fact to Count Sobansky, delegate of the Polish National Committee in England, Mr. Balfour stated that the British Government had " repeatedly announced their " desire to see the creation of a united " and independent Polish State," and that Great Britain " looks forward to a time " when the present provisional arrange- " ments will come to an end, and Poland, " free and united, will shape its own Con- " stitution according to the wishes of the " people."

The Polish National Army, thus accorded allied recognition, consists of detachments fighting hand in hand with the powers associated against Germany on the soil of France, Italy, and Russia. A Polish force in France, consisting of volunteers recruited in various lands, and particularly in the United States, was created by the decree of June 4, 1917. A year later it was made an independent military organization fighting under its own flag and commanded by Polish officers exclusively. The solemn ceremony of presenting flags to the first division of the Polish Army in France, which took place on June 22, 1918, was attended by the French Minister of Foreign Affairs and by the President of the Republic of France, who addressed the assembled soldiers of Poland. The Polish Army, thus newly constituted, fought gallantly in July on the battlefields of Champagne. A Polish detachment was also present on the Italian front. Early in September a movement was reported to be on foot for the formation of a Polish Army in Siberia for the purpose of fighting westward toward its own country. A small force of Poles is co-operating with the allied expedition in the north of European Russia.

The supreme commander of all the Polish forces is General Josef Haller, formerly a Colonel in the Austrian Army. After the conclusion of the Brest-Litovsk treaty General Haller, together with his Polish regiment known as the Iron Brigade, escaped from Bukovina, joined the 2d Polish Army Corps in Russia, commanded by General Michaelis, and fought the Germans for days. Overpowered by the enemy, he retreated across the Dnieper and effected a junction with the Czechoslovaks in Southern Russia. Later he made his way to Paris by way of the Murman coast.

A number of the revolted men, namely, eighty-eight officers and twenty-six privates, who had made their way into Russia under General Haller's leadership, were captured by the Austrians and court-martialed. Facing the probability of a death sentence, the prisoners addressed an appeal to the Polish Parliamentary Club in Vienna, in which they explained that the Brest-Litovsk treaty had caused them to withdraw their allegiance from Austria, because it " aimed " to separate from our motherland ter- " ritory won through ages of martyrdom " and held by ties of blood." The reference was to the Kholm district in Poland, ceded by Austria to the Ukraine. The document continues:

Our decision was the result of deep premeditation. No one depended upon a pardon, nor did any one intend to plead for forbearance or forgiveness in the event of defeat. As Polish nationalists, our move was a deliberate demonstration in protest against an outrage. We elected to become formal partners in the general Polish manifestation. As men experienced in warfare and its usages, we selected a portion of the national battle line which belonged to us.

And now we receive, indirectly, the news that awakens fear in us that concern over our fate is present to weaken the resistance and the decided stand taken by the official Polish representation, in the face of the Governments that dismembered our country. It is said that we are threatened with the danger that the Polish Parliamentary Club, in consideration of a modification of our sentence, might be compelled to lessen the strength of the opposition and to agree to make concessions in the sphere of the general Polish political policies.

We value greatly our compatriots' love, and we were touched deeply by the generosity with which the country thought of us, but we desire to protest most energetically against relief and concessions secured for us, to the detriment of the country, by making concessions as to the ancient rights of our nation. It was our ambition to make of ourselves a power in the hands of the highest Polish authority and, in the full consciousness and realization of the rôle we assumed, we cast unfalteringly into the lot our greatest asset, the fame of a Polish soldier, established upon his blood and that most beautiful legend of a Polish army reborn.

You are not to injure us with gifts requiring too great concessions. Do not permit our personal lot to weaken the united Polish front, for the verdict and death penalty can affect us only physically. The sufferings undergone by our grandfathers and fathers we will continue as a national obligation, without complaint and resentment, and with this sincere conviction that we are serving a free, united, and independent Poland.

The verdict to be given by our motherland will mete out justice to us, and we await the verdict with confidence.

It was reported on Oct. 20 that the Polish rebels under court-martial unanimously declined the amnesty offered to them by Emperor Karl. The prisoners argued that they were soldiers of the Polish Nation and that the Austrian Government had no right to grant them pardon, just as it had no right to inflict punishment upon them.

Late in September a Polish peasant paper described the conditions prevailing in Poland in these words:

Here the German military power rules, and our Governments are powerless against it. Everywhere Germans are in command. Returning German colonists get all they need for rebuilding their homes, but the Polish peasants get no timber to rebuild with. They do not allow our peasants to touch the woods. And what is our Government doing? Now, when the foreign yoke is so heavy, our governing class does not offer its hand to the people, and understanding is impossible.

Press dispatches from neutral countries conveyed the impression generally that the Poles were subjected to as many forms of persecution as under the old Russian régime, and that some inhabitants were fleeing from their country to avoid German rule. Late in the Summer of 1918 serious disagreements arose between Germany and Austria regarding the solution of the Polish question.

At a conference at the German headquarters in August the Poles submitted a number of demands. These included, among others, maintenance of the present frontiers, access to the Baltic, recognition of Danzig as a free port, the annexation of certain Lithuanian territory, and the abolition of the divided Austro-German administration of Poland. Very little attention was given to these demands and no agreement was reached. This attempt was followed by an appeal of the Polish regency demanding the establishment of an independent Poland embracing all the territories inhabited by Poles. On Oct. 13 the Prussian Poles issued a manifesto declaring: " Nothing " but the union into one State of all " peoples living in Polish lands, a State " which shall possess full rights, can " guarantee a lasting league of Nations."

Late in October the German authorities were reported to have planned stringent measures for the suppression of Polish separation in Prussia.

On Oct. 24 the Polish National Committee addressed a message to the Italian people, which declared that legitimate representatives of all classes of the Polish population had met at Warsaw and proclaimed the union of all the Polish territories subject to Austria, Germany, and Russia. According to a later dispatch a new national Polish Government was to be formed, consisting mostly of workers' representatives. Early in November hostilities broke out between Polish and Ukrainian troops. The latter captured Lemberg and Przemysl, while the Poles seized Cracow and assumed control of affairs in Galicia.

A message from Cracow on Nov. 9 announced the formation of a Polish Republic under the Presidency of Deputy Daszynski. At the same time Professor Lammasch, the Austrian Premier, received formal notification that Poland had assumed sovereignty over Galicia. In many places there were conflicts with German troops.

# The Mid-European Union

## Declaration Signed in Independence Hall, Philadelphia, Aims at Union of Liberated Nations

EIGHTEEN representatives of nations of Central Europe formerly subject to alien domination met in Philadelphia and signed a document on Oct. 26, 1918, creating an informal union of these newly liberated nations, whose territory stretches from the Baltic to the Adriatic. The alliance was christened the Mid-European Union, and was stated to be a tentative understanding in which the new States undertook to present a united front against future aggression by Germany or any other reactionary power. The declaration of independence was signed in the same hall and at the same table as the American Declaration of Independence. Professor Thomas G. Masaryk, now President of the new Czechoslovak Republic, presided. The conference was in session two days, and at the end a new bell, modeled on the historic Liberty Bell, pealed forth as the signatures of the delegates were attached to the document. Among the signers were these:

Czechoslavs, Professor Thomas G. Masaryk; Poles, T. M. Helinski; Jugoslavs, Dr. Hinko Hinkovitch; Uhro-Ruthenes, Gregory Zatkovitch; Ukrainians, Miroslav Sichinsky; Rumanians, Captain Vasile Stoica; Italia Irredenta, Giovanni Amaglia; Greeks, Christo Vasilkaki; Lithuanians, Thomas Narusoutchius; Albania, Christo Dako, and Zionists, Ittamar Ben Avi.

Following is the text of the declaration:

In convention assembled at Independence Hall, Philadelphia, Penn., United States of America, on Oct. 26, 1918, we, representing together more than 50,000,000 people constituting a chain of nations 'ying between the Baltic, the Adriatic, and the Black Seas, comprising Czechoslovaks, Poles, Jugoslaves, Ukrainians, Uhro-Russians, Lithuanians, Rumanians, Italian Irredentists, Unredeemed Greeks, Albanians, and Zionists, wholly or partly subject to alien dominion, deeply appreciating the aid and assistance given our peoples by the Government and people of America and of the Entente Allies, on behalf of ourselves and our brethren at home, do hereby solemnly declares that we place our all—peoples and resources—at the disposal of our allies for use against our common enemy; and in order that the whole world may know what we deem are the essential and fundamental doctrines which shall be embodied in the Constitutions hereafter adopted by the peoples of our respective independent nations, as well as the purposes which shall govern our common and united action, we accept and subscribe to the following as basic principles for all free peoples:

1. That all Governments derive their just power from the consent of the governed.

2. That it is the inalienable right of every people to organize their own Government on such principles and in such form as they believe will best promote their welfare, safety, and happiness.

3. That the free and natural development of the ideals of any State shall be allowed to pursue their normal and unhindered course, unless such course harms or threatens the common interest of all.

4. That there should be no secret diplomacy, and all proposed treaties and agreements between nations should be made public prior to their adoption and ratification.

5. That we believe our peoples, having kindred ideals and purposes, should co-

ordinate their efforts to insure the liberty of their individual nations for the furtherance of their common welfare, provided such a union contributes to the peace and welfare of the world.

6. That there should be formed a league of the nations of the world in a common and binding agreement for genuine and practical co-operation to secure justice, and therefore peace, among nations.

In the course of our history we have been subject to and victims of aggressive and selfish nations and autocratic dynasties and held in subjection by force of arms. We have suffered destruction of our cities, violation of our homes and lands, and we have maintained our ideals only by stealth, in spite of the tyranny of our oppressors.

We have been deprived of proper representation and fair trial. We have been denied the right of free speech and the right freely to assemble and petition for the redress of our grievances. We have been denied free and friendly intercourse with our sister States, and our men have been impressed in war against their brothers and friends of kindred races.

The signers of this declaration and representatives of other independent peoples who may subscribe their names hereto do hereby pledge, on behalf of their respective nations, that they will unitedly strive to the end that these wrongs shall be righted, that the sufferings of the world war shall not have been in vain, and that the principles here set forth shall be incorporated in the organic laws of whatever Governments our respective peoples may hereafter establish.

A few days afterward the representatives of the Poles, through Ignace Paderewski, announced their withdrawal from the league because the Ukrainian Government had failed to relinquish portions of Galicia and was maintaining troops in regions rightly belonging to Poland.

# What Canada Has Done in the War

Canadians celebrated on Oct. 15, 1918, the fourth anniversary of the arrival in England of the first contingent of troops from the Dominion. The record of the Canadian Expeditionary Force in those four years was summarized by The London Times as follows:

| | |
|---|---|
| Regular Canadian troops at outbreak of war | 3,000 |
| Number of first contingent | 33,000 |
| Canadian soldiers sent overseas up to Sept. 1, 1918 | 400,000 |
| Troops in training | 60,000 |
| Canadian soldiers killed in action | 50,000 |
| Casualties, over | 175,000 |
| Wounded returned to the front | 40,000 |
| Returned to Canada | 50,000 |
| Number who have received decorations | 10,000 |
| Awarded the Victoria Cross | 40 |

The 1st Division went into training on Salisbury Plain about the middle of October, 1914, and sailed for France on Feb. 9, 1915. The Canadians arrived in Flanders in time for the second battle of Ypres in April, 1915, which culminated in a German defeat and the winning of much glory for Canada. Since then Canadians have fought at Festubert, (May, 1915;) Givenchy, (June, 1915;) Loos, (September, 1915;) St. Eloi, (April, 1916;) Sanctuary Wood and Hooge, (June, 1916;) the Somme-Courcelette, (September, 1916,) and Regina Trench, (October-November, 1916;) Vimy Ridge, (April, 1917;) Hill 70 and Lens, (July-August, 1917;) Passchendaele, (October-November, 1917;) Villers-Bretonneux, (March, 1918;) Amiens, Monchy, Cambrai, (1918.)

Apart from her fighting men, Canada has furnished various special corps which have proved of inestimable value to the British armies—the Canadian Forestry Corps, the Canadian Corps Salvage companies, and the Canadian Railway troops. The splendid health in which the Canadian corps has been maintained is due to the unceasing vigilance and tireless efforts of the Canadian Army Medical Corps. It is estimated that 75 per cent. of the medical profession in Canada is engaged in some professional capacity in connection with the armed forces of Canada, either at home or overseas.

# Terrorism Versus Order in Russia

## Heavy Fighting Encountered by Allied Expeditions
## The All-Russian and Siberian Governments Unite

[PERIOD ENDED OCT. 15, 1918]

AMERICAN-JAPANESE troops continued their advance along the Trans-Siberian Railroad in September and October, while other allied detachments were operating elsewhere from Vladivostok. The Japanese reached Irkutsk on Oct. 12, 1918. The Soviet forces which remained in the region of Blagoviestchensk were dispersed late in October. On one occasion the Bolshevist troops also suffered a defeat in the Ural region at the hands of Czechoslovak and Siberian forces, but events on the Eastern Czechoslovak front took a turn favorable, upon the whole, to the Soviet Army. The Czechs were forced to evacuate Samara and to retreat along the Samara-Cheliabinsk railway. According to a statement issued on Oct. 14 by the Department of Foreign Affairs in Samara, fierce battles were being fought in the Volga region.

> The Soviet troops [said the document] consist mostly of German war prisoners, and especially Hungarian and Chinese regiments and Letts, who are attacking furiously. The Czechoslovak regiments are greatly exhausted by the uninterrupted fighting. Without the immediate help of the Allies it will be impossible to hold this front.

The allied expedition in Siberia responded to this and similar appeals by rushing small reinforcements westward in an effort to maintain the Volga front. On Oct. 15 the first transport with supplies from America arrived in Vladivostok. A dispatch of Oct. 18 reported that the United States had advanced $5,000,000 to the Czechoslovak National Council and shipped $3,000,000 worth of supplies for the Czechoslovak armies.

In Northern Russia the allied troops were mainly engaged in repulsing heavy attacks by the Soviet forces on both banks of the Dvina. In the middle of October the Allies were forced to abandon some positions on the Dvina front. Later they made a slight advance. According to an official statement of Oct. 18 the allied forces operating on the Murmansk front from Kem had cleared Central and Southern Karelia, driving the enemy across the Finnish border. On the Archangel front the troops occupied Kadish, on the Emtsa River, and advanced six miles south along the Archangel-Vologda railway. Assisted by local Zyrian tribes, the Allies drove out the Bolsheviki from the Ugor district, in the Province of Vologda. A report from Archangel was to the effect that the peasants of the Dvina region were looking forward with terror to the return of the Bolsheviki. The population was facing starvation, and the American Red Cross had sent into the interior of the country (on Oct. 22) a shipload of food and other supplies.

### THE ALL-RUSSIAN GOVERNMENT

The outstanding event in the internal life of Russia in these weeks was the fusion between the All-Russian Government of Ufa and the Siberian Government, which was effected early in November. This new All-Russian Government is provisional in character and is responsible to the Constituent Assembly elected in the Fall of 1917. The plan announced is to convene the Constituent Assembly in January, 1919, so that it may either confirm the present Government in its authority or create a new governing body. The All-Russian Provisional Government is headed by Peter V. Vologodsky, Prime Minister, and Nikolai Avksentyev, President. Its seat is Omsk, Siberia, and its authority extends over practically the whole of Siberia and parts of the provinces of Samara, Orenburg, Ufa, Ural, and Archangel.

The Omsk Government was reported to be making an effort to raise a large

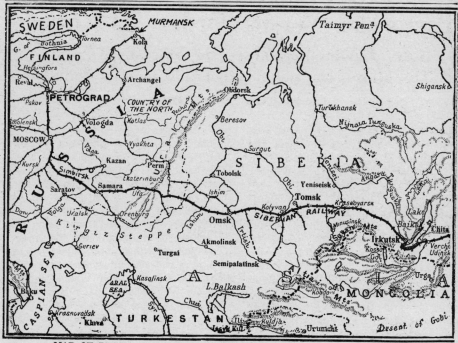

MAP OF RUSSIA AND SIBERIA SHOWING CHIEF POINTS OF ACTIVITY

army. General Ivanov-Rizov declared on Oct. 17: "A strong army under the "All-Russian Government is completing "its training at Omsk, but there is ur- "gent need of arms, equipment, and "money from the Allies." According to the General, the program of his Government included the following points: Iron discipline and no politics in the army; the suppression of Bolshevism; responsibility of the command to the Central Government. The number of recruits who responded to the appeal of the Omsk Government was estimated at 380,000. The mobilization of the classes of 1918 and 1919 was completed and General Boldyrev was appointed Commander in Chief of all the Russian forces. Mobilization of the last two years was also declared in the Region of the North, formerly under Tchaikovsky's autonomous Government, and non-commissioned officers of the reserves of the years 1888 to 1897 were called to the colors. The Government also established a Treasury at Omsk and proceeded to levy taxes. It was announced officially on Nov. 1 that the Omsk Government would soon resume the sale of vodka as a Government monopoly.

The All-Russian Provisional Government is seeking allied recognition. Early in November it addressed the following appeal to President Wilson:

It is evident that the exit of Russia from the number of belligerents and the process of dismemberment which it is suffering has a deep influence on the fate of all the other countries. Furthermore, the problems of the future of Russia should be considered by Governments and nations of the universe as a problem of their own future. Russia will not perish. She is greatly suffering, but not dead. Her national forces are regaining with remarkable quickness, and her effort to recover her unity and greatness will not cease until she attains this sublime aim.

Moreover, the reconstruction of a powerful and prosperous Russia presents itself as a condition necessary to the maintenance of order and international equilibrium. It is therefore that the new Provisional Government, into whose hands has been intrusted the supreme power by the people of Russia, the regional Governments, the convention, and committee of the members of the Constituent Assembly, the Zemstvos, and Municipalities, addresses itself to the Allied Powers. It expects to receive their aid, and considers itself in the right to demand such help insistently.

It is to the head of the great American Democracy, recognized apostle of peace and fraternity of the nations, that it makes its appeal. All aid already extended to Russia by the Allies would be in vain if the new help should arrive too late, or in insufficient quantity. Every hour of delay threatens with innumerable calamities Russia, the Allies, and other nations.

A press dispatch of Nov. 1 describes Siberia as a place of refuge for hosts of Russians, who were fleeing from the Soviet territories in quest of food and peace. These refugees were suffering dire want. They drifted into crowded cities, where they found no employment, and were taken advantage of by profiteers. The pathetic story, published late in October, of a party of Serbian civilians who arrived in Harbin in a state of destitution baffling description, after having traveled for eight months across the whole of Russia, illustrates the conditions prevailing among the wanderers moving in an endless stream from the Urals eastward. The entire country is suffering from a scarcity of manufactured goods, especially agricultural implements and industrial machinery.

## PROTEST AGAINST TERRORISM

The neutral diplomats at Moscow made a futile protest on Sept. 3 to Commissary Zinoviev against outrages of the Bolshevist terror. Later the neutral States, through E. Odier, the Swiss Minister, addressed a written protest to the Commissary of Foreign Affairs, in which they said in part:

Imbued only with the desire to vent their hatred on a whole class of citizens, and without being provided with any authority, armed men break in day and night into private dwellings, steal and plunder and arrest and throw into jail hundreds of unfortunates who have nothing to do with the political struggle, and whose only guilt consists in belonging to the bourgeois class, the uprooting of which the communist leaders urge in their newspapers and speeches. The anxious relatives of these people are refused all information as to where they are, and are not permitted either to visit them or bring them necessary food.

Such deeds of terrorization and force on the part of men professing a desire to realize human happiness are incomprehensible. They call forth the indignation of the whole civilized world, which now has knowledge of the events in Petrograd. The diplomatic corps has found it necessary to announce its shocked feelings to the people's Commissary, M. Zinoviev. It protests with the utmost energy against the arbitrary deeds that are occurring every day.

In reply the Soviet Government addressed a note " to the gentlemen representing the capitalist neutral nations," pointing out that, although it could ignore the protest as " an act of gross interference with the inner affairs of Russia," it was taking this opportunity to explain its tactics, for the reason that it considered itself " the spokesman not only of the Russian working class, but of exploited humanity all over the earth." The note further declared that the masses had been plunged into the world war by " a small clique of bankers, Generals, and bureaucrats," and that " in the entire capitalist world the white terror (of the bourgeoisie) rules over the working class." The document continues:

When the representatives of the neutral nations threaten us with the indignation of the entire civilized world, and protest against the Red Terror in the name of humanity, we respectfully call their attention to the fact that they were not sent to Russia to defend the principles of humanity, but to preserve the interests of the capitalist State. We would advise them further not to threaten us with the indignant horror of the civilized world, but to tremble before the fury of the masses who are arising against a civilization that has thrust humanity into the unspeakable misery of endless slaughter. * * * The Russian working class will crush without mercy the counter-revolutionary clique that is trying to lay the noose around the neck of the Russian working class with the help of foreign capital and the Russian bourgeoisie.

## THE MURDER MANIA

According to British and French refugees, the Soviet authorities were systematically killing off factory owners and engineers. The Britishers who were released from Moscow, together with Consul Lockhart, were quoted in a Stockholm dispatch as saying:

The murder mania is so strong among the Bolshevist officials that they even shoot their own officials. Firing squads take delight in forcing condemned men to jump from automobiles and in shooting them before the eyes of other victims.

Many executions take place on the Khodynka parade grounds. These are in charge of Lettish troops. The victims are shot with revolvers, and the bodies fall into open trenches. Wet concrete immediately is thrown over them so that it is impossible for relatives to identify and claim the bodies.

The terror abated in Moscow and Petrograd only to flare up with double strength in the provinces. The commissions for combating counter-revolution, which are responsible for the terroristic measures, were reported to have become so powerful as to defy the central and local Soviets and execute victims without reference to other Government agencies.

During the time which elapsed from the death of Uritzki, who was assassinated late in August, up to Oct. 1, sixty-eight hostages, including five priests, were shot by the Soviet authorities. According to a Petrograd dispatch Vladimir N. Kokovtzev and Prince Shoikhovskoy, former Ministers of State, were sentenced to death by the People's Court and executed.

Norman Armour, Secretary of the United States Embassy in Russia, who returned to the United States on Nov. 5, was quoted as saying: " Words are in-" adequate to describe what I saw in " Russia during the reign of terror, mis-" ery, want, and wholesale murder. The " people are starving and can get no " hearing, much less redress, from the " blood-crazed Bolsheviki." On Oct. 31 Lord Robert Cecil discussed in the House of Commons the position of British subjects in Russia. He pointed out that in bloodshed the Soviets have outdone the old Russian régime. " There has been " no pretense of justice," he said. "People " of all nationalities have been arrested " and imprisoned without any reason " being given." He added that the British Government meant " to exact justice " on the people guilty of these outrages " when they are able to get them into " their power."

The following is an extract from a telegram which, according to the Moscow Izvestia, was sent to all the Soviets by Petrovsky, Commissar for Home Affairs, in September:

All Right Social Revolutionists known to the local Soviets should be arrested immediately, numerous hostages taken from the bourgeois officer classes, and at the slightest attempt to resist or the slightest movement among the White Guards the shooting of masses of the hostages should be begun without fail.

The initiative rests especially with the local Executive Committees. Through the militia and extraordinary commissions all branches of the Government must take measures to seek out and arrest persons hiding under false names and shoot without fail anybody connected with the White Guards.

All the above measures should be put immediately into execution. Indecisive action on the part of local Soviets must be immediately reported to the People's Commissar of Home Affairs. Not the slightest hesitation will be tolerated in the using of mass terror.

These measures, the instructions declared, were necessitated by anti-Bolshevist terroristic acts, conspirators, and the wholesale shooting of Soviet partisans in Finland, in the Ukraine and in the Don region.

The German and Austro-Hungarian Consuls, who protested against the Bolshevist methods of treating political adversaries, received, according to advices from Archangel, the following reply: " Germany, which violated the neutrality " of Belgium and holds populations of " invaded countries under a brutal yoke, " is not qualified to intervene in this " question."

## GERMAN EVACUATION

In accordance with a Russo-German agreement, reached on Sept. 15, the Germans were to begin evacuating the country east of the Berezina, each of the five sections to be vacated as soon as an installment of the Russian indemnity was paid to Germany. The conditions in the territories evacuated, or to be evacuated, were depicted in the following official Russian dispatch, dated Oct. 30:

From all regions now in German occupation it is reported that the German military authorities are carrying off everything that it is possible to take to Germany. They are devastating the country. In White Russia there are no horses and no cattle because the Germans have taken them all. In the regions where evacuation is pending the fields remain unsown, because the Germans have left no seed. Children are dying of starvation. Milk cannot be obtained. Household furniture, telegraphic and telephonic instruments and appliances from many towns have been sent to Germany. The railway lines have been stripped, only wrecked and useless cars being left behind.

The Lithuanian districts evacuated by the Germans were immediately occupied by Bolshevist troops and subjected to the Soviet rule. According to a dispatch of Oct. 24, two Lithuanian delegates arrived in Copenhagen to appeal to the Allies for help against the Bolsheviki.

It was stated on Nov. 4, on the authority of the Frankfort Gazette, that Russia had stopped payments to Berlin, after having paid two installments of the war indemnity. Two days later it became known that Germany demanded the withdrawal of all Russian diplomatic representatives in Germany. The discovery that the Russian Embassy in Berlin was a centre of revolutionary propaganda was believed to be the cause of the severance of diplomatic relations between the two countries.

Commissary Tchitcherin addressed the following note to President Wilson on Oct. 24:

> As a condition of the armistice during which peace negotiations shall be begun, you in your note to Germany demanded the evacuation of occupied territories. We are ready, Mr. President, to conclude an armistice on this condition and request you to inform us when you intend to withdraw your troops from Murmansk, Archangel, and Siberia.

Ten days later it was reported from Petrograd that the Soviet Government was transmitting, through neutral diplomats, a note asking the Allies to appoint the time and place for peace negotiations, so as to put an end to the hostilities between the Entente and the Bolshevist Government.

## THE ESTHONIAN REPUBLIC

The following day Esthonia was proclaimed an independent republic. The Esthonian Republic has a territory of 47,500 square kilometers and a population of 1,500,000, of whom 96 per cent. are Esthonians; the proclamation of independence gives the following list of districts included in the territory of the new State:

Harjumaa, (Revel,) Laanemaa, (Hap-

sal,) Jurvamaa, (Weissenstein); Viruma, (Wesenberg,) with the town of Narva and its surroundings; Tartumaa, (Dorpat,) Vorumaa, (Verro,) Viljandimaa, (Fellin,) and Parnumaa, (Pernau,) comprising the islands of the Baltic Sea; Saaremaa, (the island of Oesel,) Hilu, (Nagoe,) Muhu, and others that the Esthonians have inhabited for centuries. The definite establishment of the frontiers of the Republic will be decided by a referendum * * * after the end of the war.

The Government is headed by Constantine Paets, Mayor of Revel, as Prime Minister, and a Cabinet of eight Ministers. The capital is Revel. The proclamation declared that the Esthonian Republic wished to preserve absolute neutrality, and that the Esthonian soldiers in the Russian Army would be recalled and demobilized.

In the middle of October the Lithuanians addressed to Prince Maximilian, German Chancellor, a note demanding the immediate evacuation of Lithuanian territory. The " Taryba " decided to set up a national Government and to create an army and a police force for the maintenance of order and the defense of the frontiers. Plans were also announced for the convocation of a constituent assembly.

## AFFAIRS IN FINLAND

A Stockholm dispatch of Oct. 15 described the conditions under which Prince Frederick Charles of Hesse was elected King of Finland. Nearly all the Social Democratic deputies were locked up in jail or otherwise prevented from voting. " The whole game," says Hjalmar Branting in discussing the victory of the Finnish monarchists, " is a grotesque farce played by a troupe of country actors before backwoods people who have no notion of the great currents of opinion now stirring the world. * * * Finland's fate will be settled first when the Finnish people themselves can again speak among the free nations." On Oct. 21 the King-elect was reported to have refused the Finnish throne.

On Oct. 31 the Finnish Government amnestied about 10,000 political prisoners. At the same time the allied successes were seen to be causing a marked change of sentiment in favor of the Entente.

# The Czech Exodus: A Siberian Epic

## How 50,000 Determined Men Fought Their Way
## From Moscow to Vladivostok

### By CAPTAIN VLADIMIR S. HURBAN
[OF THE CZECHOSLOVAK ARMY]

*When Captain Hurban came to Washington to report to Professor Mascryk, Commander in Chief of the Czechoslovak Army and President of the National Council, he gave the American people this lucid narrative of one of the most romantic episodes of the war:*

THE history of the origin of our army, of its operations on the Russian front, and its march around the world to the French front reads like an almost incredible romance. Our army in Russia was organized from Czech and Slovak prisoners of war under well-nigh insurmountable difficulties. We were co-operating with the Russian Army, and since the Summer of 1917 had been practically the only army on the Russian front capable of military action in the proper sense of the word. In July, 1917, during the first revolutionary offensive under Kerensky, it was only our army that really attacked and advanced.

When the Bolshevist Soviet Government signed the peace treaty at the beginning of March, 1918, our army of about 50,000 men was in Ukrainia, near Kiev. The former Ukrainian Government, to escape the Bolsheviki, threw themselves into the arms of the Germans and called for German help. When the German and Austrian armies began their advance into Ukrainia, the position of our army was almost desperate. We were in a State which had concluded peace, into which, however, the Germans were advancing and occupying large territories without resistance. The Red Guards of the Soviets did not represent any real military power.

The Germans advanced against us in overwhelming numbers and there was danger that we would be surrounded. Our rear was not covered and the Germans were liable to attack us there. We had no lines of communication behind us, no stores of materials, and no reserves; everywhere there was disorganization and anarchy, and the Bolshevist Red Guards seized the locomotives and were fleeing east in panic.

Under these circumstances Emperor Charles sent us a special envoy with the promise that if we would disarm we should be amnestied and our lands should receive autonomy. We answered that we would not negotiate with the Austrian Emperor.

### RETREAT FROM KIEV

As we could not hold a front we began a retreat to the east. Already then in agreement with the Allies (our army had been proclaimed a part of the Czechoslovak Army on the western front, and thus allied with the French Army) it was decided to transport our army over Siberia and America to France. We began the difficult retreat from Kiev. The Germans in an overwhelming force were trying to prevent our escape. About 100 miles behind us they seized the important railroad junction at Bachmac, which we were obliged to pass in our trains on our retreat to the east.

When we arrived at Bachmac the Germans were already waiting for us. There began a battle lasting four days, in which they were badly defeated, and which enabled us to get our trains through. The commander of the German detachment offered us a forty-eight hours' truce, which we accepted, for our duty was to leave Ukrainia; the truce was canceled by the German chief commander, Linsingen, but too late; our trains had already got away. We lost altogether about 600 men in dead, wounded, and missing, while we buried 2,000 Germans in one day.

In this manner we escaped from

Ukrainia. Our relations with the Bolsheviki were still good. We refrained from meddling with Russian internal affairs, and we tried to come to an agreement with the Bolshevist Government with respect to our departure, or passage through Russia. But already signs were visible that the Bolsheviki—either under German influence or because we then represented the only real power in Russia—would try to put obstacles in our way. It would have sufficed to order one of our regiments (our army was then, in March, near Moscow) to take Moscow, and in half a day there would have been no Bolshevist Government; for then we were well armed, having taken from the front everything we could carry to prevent it from falling into the hands of the Germans. Each of our regiments had 200 to 300 machine guns and nobody in Russia, to say nothing of Moscow, could have at all contemplated an attempt at opposition. Moscow, moreover, would have received us with open arms. But we were determined to leave as the army of a friendly, brother nation, an army which, in spite of all bad experiences, wished Russia the strengthening of real democracy. Although we could not sympathize with the Bolshevist Government, we as guests refrained from all action against it, and remained absolutely loyal to it.

### GAVE UP THEIR ARMS

To prove indisputably our loyalty, we turned over to the Bolsheviki everything, all our arms, with the exception of a few rifles, which we kept for our, so to say, personal safety, (ten rifles to each 100 men.) The equipment we turned over to the Bolsheviki, including arms, horses, automobiles, airplanes, &c., was worth more than 1,000,000,000 rubles, and it was legally in our possession, for we took it away from the Germans, to whom it had been abandoned by the fleeing Bolsheviki. This transfer of the equipment was, of course, preceded by an agreement made between us and the Moscow Government, by which we were guaranteed unmolested passage through Siberia, to which the Government pledged to give its unconditional support.

Already there were signs that the Ger-mans were beginning to be uneasy about our movement. Today we have documentary evidence that in March the Germans considered our progress as a naïve adventure, which would soon end in failure. When they saw, however, that the "impossibility," as they called it, was becoming a reality, they began to do their best to frustrate our efforts, and organized an army against us. As I have said, the Bolsheviki, though not exceptionally friendly to us, refrained so far from all direct action against us. Their only desire in that respect, to which they devoted much money, was to persuade our volunteers to join their Red Guard. We did practically nothing to oppose it, but we knew our men. Our people are too well educated politically and in every other way to be carried away by the methods of Lenine and Trotzky.

More dangerous was the work of German agents who, under the mask of internationalism, found their way into the Soviets. In every Soviet there was a German who exercised a great influence over all its members.

Soon there came the news that the German and Magyar prisoners of war were organizing in Siberia and were being armed by the Bolsheviki under the pretext that they were going to fight against "world imperialism." We have proved now that the Germans were planning to provoke our conflict with the Bolsheviki and to destroy us piecemeal with the aid of the armed prisoners of war.

### EIGHTY TRAINLOADS

Under such circumstances we began our pilgrimage east. I was in the first train (there were then eighty trains of us) which was to prepare the way. We were determined to leave Russia without a conflict. Notwithstanding the fact that we kept our word, that we surrendered all arms with the exception of the few necessary, our progress was hindered, and unending negotiations had to be repeated in every seat of a local Soviet. We were threatened by machine guns, by cannon, but we patiently stood it all, although the Bolshevist Red Guard could have been disbanded by a few of our volunteers. After fifty seven days of such tiresome travel our first train arrived at Vladivostok, where we were enthusiastically received by the allied units stationed there.

When the Germans saw that we, notwithstanding all their intrigue, were nearing Vladivostok, they exercised a direct pressure on Lenine and Trotzky; for the things that were later committed by the Soviets cannot any further be explained away on the ground of ignorance. The trains were stopped at different stations, so that they were finally separated by a distance of over fifty miles from one another. Provoking incidents of all kinds were the order of the day. The arming of the German and Magyar prisoners was begun on a large scale. One of the orders of Tchitcherin, the Bolshevist Foreign Minister, reads: "Dispatch all German and Magyar prisoners out of Siberia; stop the Czechoslovaks." Three members of our National Council, who were sent to Moscow for an explanation of the stopping of our trains, were arrested. At the same time our trains were attacked in different stations by the Soviet troops, formed mostly of German and Magyar prisoners.

## IRKUTSK OUTRAGE REVENGED

I will recall the Irkutsk incident. Our train—about 400 men, armed with ten rifles and twenty hand grenades—was surrounded by a few thousand Red Guards armed with machine guns and cannon. Their commander gave our men ten minutes to surrender their arms, or be shot. According to their habit, ours began negotiations. Suddenly there was heard the German command, "Schiessen!" and the Red Guards began firing at the train. Our men jumped off the train, and in five minutes all the machine guns were in their possession, the Russian Bolsheviki disarmed, and all the Germans and Magyars done away with.

The Siberian Government, which resides in Irkutsk and which, as it appeared later, ordered this attack, can thank only the intervention of the American and French Consuls that it was not destroyed by our rightly embittered volunteers.

To what extremes our loyalty was carried is shown by the fact that although perfidiously attacked, and although we disarmed the Red Guards in Irkutsk, we still began new negotiations, with the result that we surrendered all our arms, on the condition that all German and Magyar prisoners would be disarmed and disbanded, and that we would be allowed to proceed unmolested. The Siberian Government guaranteed us unmolested passage, and, taught by bitter experiences that it was dangerous to attack even unarmed Czechoslovaks, let us proceed to Vladivostok. True, this concerned only the trains in the vicinity of Irkutsk; the trains west of Irkutsk were—under the orders of Moscow—attacked in the same manner, but always with the same result; everywhere the Bolsheviki were disarmed.

The arrest of the members of our National Council took place immediately before these treacherous attacks. Then thousands of armed Germans and Magyars in the vicinity of Omsk, Krasnoyarsk, and Chita forced our men between Volga and Irkutsk to take the Siberian administration into their hands, (toward the end of June.) But even at this stage we were trying to enter into negotiations with Moscow. But Moscow, i. e., Lenine and Trotzky, proclaimed us murderers and began mobilization against us. Under these circumstances our troops were forced to take possession of the bridges over the Volga.

## WELCOMED BY POPULATION

I must mention the fact that our defense, which, as said, was necessitated by treacherous attacks and everywhere resulted in the disarmament of the Bolsheviki, was joyfully greeted by the majority of the Russian population. Anti-Bolsheviki took advantage of the situation and overthrew the Soviets. We did not interfere with their internal affairs even after the open conflict. We only disarmed those who attacked us, to make repetition of attacks impossible.

The Germans were trying to spread rumors that our volunteers committed brutalities during these battles. That is not true. The facts are these: Russian Bolsheviki taken by our troops were disarmed and sent home, but the Magyars and German prisoners, taken with arms in hand, were killed. Our purpose was made known to them beforehand. The Austrians hanged all our wounded whom they captured on the Italian front, and they attacked one of our trains of wounded in Siberia. Four years of a struggle for life have taught us to be on guard. We did no harm to German or Magyar prisoners who did not oppose us, although they were our enemies; we could have killed thousands and thousands of them, but we allowed them to leave Siberia in peace, if they desired to go home. When, however, they treacherously attacked us, they were of necessity made harmless. We made an official announcement that every German and Magyar caught by us with arms in hand would be given no quarter. On the contrary, we could cite many instances of unprecedented brutalities committed on our wounded by the German, and especially Magyar, prisoners.

In Siberia there are today some hundred thousand German and Magyar prisoners, a great number of whom are armed. It is these men who offer considerable resistance to our army; the Russian Bolsheviki surrender after the first shot.

The Bolsheviki gave a sufficient proof of the fact that they are incapable to rule. The number of their fighting supporters is very indefinite. They consist chiefly of hungry masses, loath to work, who are getting 30 to 40 rubles a day in the Red Guard. They have no workers among them. A great number of the Bolshevist officials steal just like the officials of the Czar's régime. Industry, commerce, transportation—everything—is at a standstill, and there is nothing to eat. That spells failure of the Bolshevist Government; the Bolsheviki are now doing everything to maintain their power. They obey the Germans and Austrians to keep themselves in power. The Germans, however, do not want a consolidation of Russia.

Russia needs effective, firm, friendly help, for today she is herself completely helpless. Russia needs order, which today the Russians are incapable of up-

building. The Russians are exhausted, they now have lost faith in themselves, and they need rest to recover. The majority of them are excited people, who, therefore, cannot organize.

The Allies, knowing the psychology of Russia today, and knowing the real strength of Russia, will extend their help in the proper manner. I think that our army can be of great assistance in this task; all our boys have learned Russian in the four years of war, and know how to treat the people. They know the Russian people and Russian situation, and they desire only the good of Russia. It was the Czechoslovaks who were always accused of exaggerated Russophilism by the Germans and Magyars, and it is the irony of fate that we had to suffer so much in Russia. We hope and desire that our sacrifices be not offered in vain.

## OTHER DRAMATIC DETAILS

*Captain Hurban's narrative was confirmed and amplified on Sept. 12 by an Associated Press dispatch from Vladivostok containing these graphic passages:*

General Gaida's Czechoslovaks, fighting their way through 2,000 miles of hostile territory, furnish a tale no less thrilling than that related of Cortez's drive from Vera Cruz to the ancient Aztec capital in the sixteenth century. * * * When the order came from Petrograd countermanding the permission given for the free movement of the Czechoslovaks toward Vladivostok, it found them strung out in a thin line from the Volga to Vladivostok. * * * Assisted by Cossacks and Czechs from Chiliabinsk, Colonel Kadlets, then commander of the Czech forces west of Irkutsk, fought his way west to Omsk, taking towns en route. He improved the time during the armistice to clean up the line westward to the Urals.

Meantime, with resumption of hostilities to the eastward, the Czechoslovak forces between Krasnoyarsk and Irkutsk found themselves hard pressed and near to the end of their resources. Kadlets doubled back eastward, and by a series of flanking movements, falling upon the Bolsheviki in the night, stampeded them time after time. In this way he pushed through to the relief of his countrymen at Krasnoyarsk and Irkutsk.

From Irkutsk to the southernmost point of Lake Baikal there are forty-one tunnels. It was the Czechs' aim to clear out the Bolsheviki without giving them time to blow up these tunnels, and to that end they started a small contingent overland to surprise the Bolsheviki beyond the series of tunnels. These men marched four days under greatest difficulties. They became so pressed for food supplies that they had to eat their horses. But they accomplished their object. They attacked the Bolsheviki in the middle of the night, captured their machine guns, and started them northward in disorder. The Bolsheviki succeeded in blowing up one tunnel, the last one in the series.

The Czechs and their Russian allies now had a clear track to the southern extremity of the lake, to a village named Slujianka, where the blocked tunnel presented a serious obstacle to further progress. They dragged a few light guns over the ridge and marched sev-

eral contingents of troops around the obstruction, only to find the Bolsheviki massed in force some twenty miles beyond. The Czechs and Russians suffered heavy losses in the fighting here and were forced back to within a few miles of the tunnel.

Meantime the Czechs had cleared the tunnel sufficiently to pass troops through on foot. General Gaida, who had succeeded Colonel Kadlets in command, caused decoy messages to fall into the enemy's hands, begging for help and declaring that the tunnel was hopelessly blocked and he in desperate straits, surrounded and at the end of his resources. The Bolsheviki thereupon moved southward in high spirits, throwing aside all caution. Bands played and their progress was in the nature of a triumphal march.

A few miles from the tunnel they ran into an ambush which completely demoralized them. Machine guns raked them from the hillsides and field guns shelled them front and rear. A tattered remnant of the Bolshevist army fled northward with the few trains they were able to save.

## Titanic Labors of the British Navy

Figures made public Oct. 25, 1918, on the growth of the British Navy during the war show that the fleet, including auxiliaries, had increased from 2,500,000 tons displacement to 6,500,000 tons, and the personnel from 146,000 to 406,000. Since the outbreak of the war 21,500,000 soldiers had been transported by sea, of whom 4,391 had been lost. For the requirements of the British naval and military forces more than 85,000,000 tons of stores were transshipped, while more than 24,000,000 tons were taken overseas for Great Britain's allies. Transportation was also provided for 2,000,000 animals. The organization of convoys, due to German submarine warfare, had been an important part of the work of the British Navy since March, 1917, since which time there had been 75,929 sailings, with the losses numbering only a few hundred vessels.

# Lenine and Trotzky German Agents

## Secret Documents Unearthed in Petrograd
## Show Bolshevist Leaders as Tools of Berlin

### [SECOND INSTALLMENT]

CURRENT HISTORY MAGAZINE herewith presents the second and concluding installment of the secret documents through which the United States Government has revealed the relation of master and servant existing between the Imperial German Government and the so-called Bolshevist Government at Petrograd. The Committee on Public Information sent Edgar Sisson to Petrograd to investigate, and Mr. Sisson unearthed these documents and sent them to Washington in the form of the report here reproduced. The following introduction and the explanatory notes throughout are his:

Germany made its Russian peace with its own puppet Government, the misnamed Council of People's Commissars, the President of which is Vladimir Ulianov, (Lenine,) the Foreign Minister of which was Leon Trotzky, and the Ambassador of which to Germany is A. Joffe. Germany made this peace harder upon the Russian people as punishment to the ambition of its tools in seeking to become too powerful and in hoping for a little while not only that Russia would be delivered over to them, but that they could double-cross their masters by turning a simulated German revolution into a real one.

But their craftiness was a toy in the hands of rough German force. Germany was actually double-crossing them by negotiating with the Ukrainian Rada at the moment they dreamed they were tricking Germany.

Germany, however, did not discard the Bolshevist leaders, recognizing their further use in the German world campaign for internal disorganization in the nations with which it wars, but confined them to the limited inland province which Great Russia proper has now become.

Lenine, according to statements made public as soon as Trotzky's spectacular device of "No peace—no war" failed, always was for peace on any German terms. He dominated the situation thereafter and conceded everything that Germany asked. Nor did Trotzky cease to continue to obey the German orders delivered to him both by General Hoffman at Brest-Litovsk and at Petrograd directly by the Russian division of the German General Staff, which was seated in Petrograd itself from November, and which was still there in full operation when I left, Monday, March 4, the day that Petrograd received notification that peace had been signed at Brest-Litovsk by the Russian and German delegations.

Trotzky, therefore, rests rightly under the accusation of having staged his theatrical scene as a climax to the Russian disorganization desired by Germany. The actual order he gave was for the immediate demobilization of the Russian Army, leaving the German Army unopposed.

The actual effect of the work of the Bolshevist leaders, moreover, was to enable Germany to combine its former army of the Russian front with its western army for the launching of its March offensive in France. Such has been the fruition of Russia's German-directed Bolshevism.

The following documents tell the story of the betrayal of Russia to a shameful and ruinous peace:

---

### DOCUMENT No. 30

[Gr. (Great) General Staff, Central Abtheilung, section M/R, No. 408, Feb. 26, 1918]

*SECRET*

TO THE CHAIRMAN OF THE COUNCIL OF THE PEOPLE'S COMMISSARS:

The Department of the Staff has the honor to request data of the attitude of the detachments being sent to Pskoff and to guard against all possible results if in these detachments any will carry on patriotic propaganda and agitations against the German Army.—*Head of the Russian Division German General Staff, O. Rausch; Adjutant, U. Wolff.*

NOTE.—*The Chairman of the Council of People's Commissars is Lenine. At the top of his letter is written comment "Urgent. Chairman of the Council of People's Commissars asks Voladarsky to communicate this to the agitation department. (Signed) Secretary Skripnik." Skripnik is the First Secretary of the Government, personally reporting to Lenine. A second notation in margin is "Central Executive Committee No. 823 to report. (Signed) N. G." The initials correspond with those of N. Gorbunov, Chief Secretary of the Council of People's Commissars. The detachments being sent to Pskoff at this time were composed of Red Guards and of the recruits of the new Red*

**G. G. -S.**
NACHRICHTEN-BUREAU.

Личнo.

Section *R*

№ *715*

23 Февраля 1918 г.

Господину Народному Комиссару по Иностранными Дѣламъ.

Согласно личныхъ переговоровъ моихъ съ г.Предсѣдателемъ Совѣта Народныхъ Комиссаровъ, было рѣшено задержать отъѣздъ Итальянскаго Посольства изъ Петербурга и, по возможности, произвести обыскъ посольскаго багажа. Объ этомъ рѣшеніи считаю долгомъ извѣстить Васъ.

Начальникъ Отдѣленія

Адъютантъ

DOCUMENT NO. 26: A LETTER REVEALING HOW A GERMAN OFFICER AND LENINE, IN CONFERENCE, ORDERED SEARCH OF THE ITALIAN AMBASSADOR'S BAGGAGE. ITALY WAS STILL AN ALLY OF RUSSIA. THE TRANSLATION OF THIS LETTER APPEARED IN THE PRECEDING INSTALLMENT IN THIS MAGAZINE

*Army. Pskoff was taken by the Germans without a fight.*
*Have original letter.*

DOCUMENT No. 31
[G. G. S., Nachrichten Bureau, Section R, Feb. 27, 1918]
*VERY SECRET*

TO THE PRESIDENT OF THE COUNCIL OF PEO-
PLE'S COMMISSARS:

Not having received an exact answer to my question of the 25th of February, I now have the honor to request you to inform me in the shortest possible time the numbers and kind of forces sent to Pskoff and Narva.

At the same time at the orders of the representative of our General Staff I once more remind you of the desirability of naming Gen. Parski to the post of commander in chief of the Russian armed forces, in place of Gen. Bonch-Bruevich, whose actions do not meet the approval of the German high command. Since the attacks on the lives and property of the German landowners in Estland and Lifland, which, according to our information, were carried out with the knowledge of Gen. Bonch-Bruevich, and his nationalistic

actions in Orla, his continuance in the position of General is particularly no longer desirable.—*Head of the Department, Agasfer.*

NOTE.—*Across the letter is written " Send to Trotzky and Podvoisky. (Signed) N. G." (Gorbunov's initials.) Observe the mandatory nature of the whole letter and particularly of the first paragraph. Agasfer, as has been shown, is the cipher signature of Major Luberts, head of the Petrograd Intelligence Department of the German General Staff, the chief branch of the Russian division of the German General Staff, the head of which is Major Rausch, referred to in this letter as the representative of " our General Staff." Apparently both Luberts and Rausch wrote a warning against sending any patriots to the defending forces and seemingly the Bolshevist effort at obedience as indicated in document No. 3 was not fast enough to suit the German martinets. Podvoisky was Minister of War.*

General Parski was appointed to the command of the Petrograd district, and as late as June 14 still held the post. He formerly was in command of the City of Riga, which was surrendered to the Germans without adequate defense in the early Autumn of 1917.
*Have original letter.*

Секретно.

**GR. GENERALSTAB.**

**CENTRAL NACHRICHT.**

Господину Предсѣдателю Совѣта Народныхъ Коммисса

ровъ

Section M./R

26 Февраля 1918 г.

№ 403

Berlin

Отдѣленіе Штаба имѣетъ честь просить свѣдѣній о

настроеніи направляемыхъ къ Пскову отрядовъ и пре-

достерегаетъ отъ возможныхъ печальныхъ послѣдствій,

если въ этихъ отрядахъ будетъ вестись патріотиче-

ская пропаганда и агитація противъ Германской Ар-

міи.

Начальникъ Русскаго Отдѣла

Германскаго Генеральнаго Штаба

Адьютантъ

FACSIMILE OF DOCUMENT NO. 30, IN WHICH A GERMAN OFFICER DEMANDS—AND LENINE GRANTS—DATA REGARDING RUSSIAN FORCES AT PSKOFF. THAT PLACE WAS AFTERWARD TAKEN BY THE GERMANS WITHOUT A FIGHT

### DOCUMENT NO. 32

[Gr. General Staff, Nachrichten Bureau, Section R, No. 272-600, Feb. 6, 1918]

*VERY SECRET*

To the Commissar of Foreign Affairs:

I ask you to immediately give the Turkish subject, Carp C. Missirof, a Russian passport in place of the one taken from him, which was given him in 1912 on the basis of the inclosed national passport.

Agent C. Missirof is to be sent to the staff of the Russian high command, where, according to the previous discussion between General Hoffman and Commissars Trotzky and Joffe, he will keep watch on the activity of the head of the staff, General Bonch Bruevich, in the capacity of assistant to the Commissars Kalmanovich and Feierabend.—*For the head of the department, R. Bauer; adjutant, Bukholm.*

Note.—*Here we have the behind-the-scene disclosure of the real relations between Trotzky and General Hoffman at Brest-Litovsk, stripping the mask from the public pose. Trotzky got his orders in this case and he*

carried them out. Across the top of this letter, too, he has written his own conviction, " Ask Joffe. L. T.," while Joffe, whose rôle seems to be that of the mouthpiece of Germany, has written in the margin, " According to agreement this must be done. A. Joffe." Thereby he becomes a witness for the agreement itself—that pledge between himself, Trotzky, and the Military Chief of the German Government at the Brest-Litovsk conference to betray the commander of the Russian Army when he should attempt to defend Russia against Germany. A second marginal note states that the passport was given Feb. 7, under the Russian name, P. L. Ilin.

Have original letter and the surrendered passport. Kalmanovich and Feierabend were commissars of counterespionage.

### THE UKRAINIAN DOUBLE-CROSS

How the Bolsheviki themselves were double-crossed in the Ukraine, how the Germans toyed with their puppets to disorganize Russia, with disclosures of plans for assassination of loyal Russian leaders, are shown in the following documents:

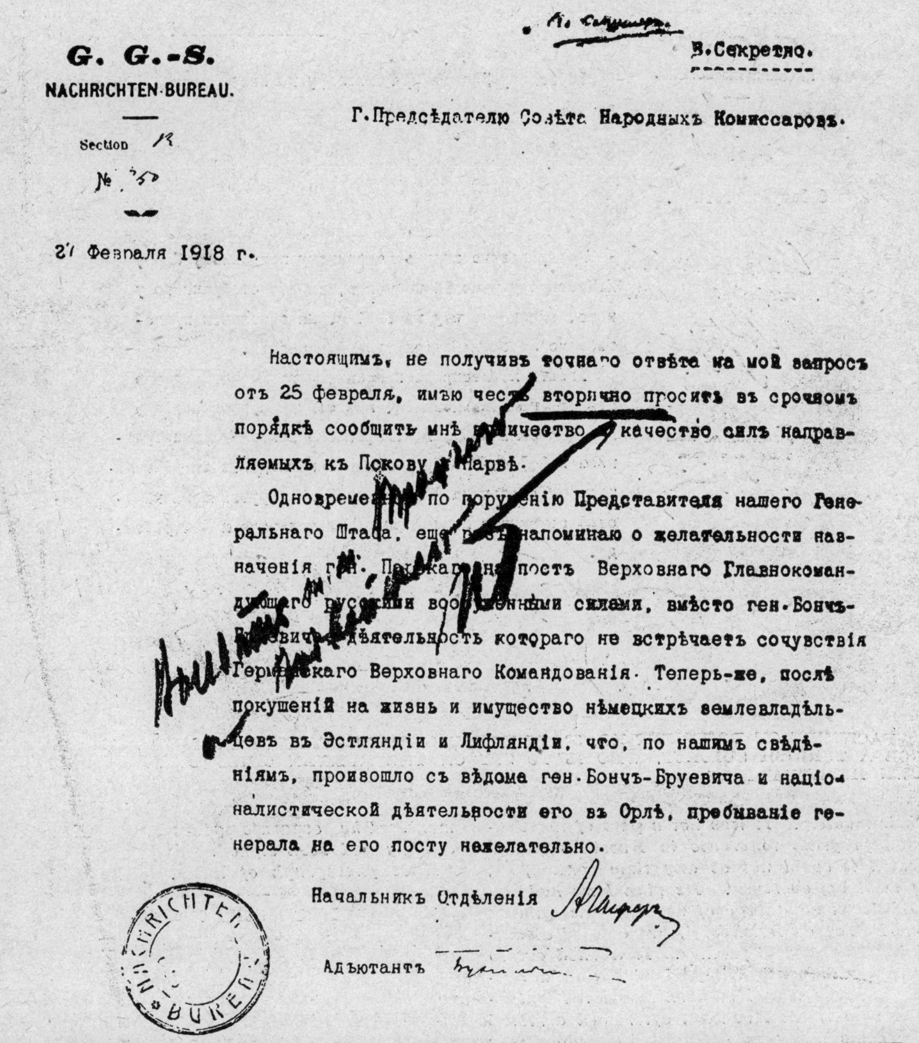

**G. G.-S.**

**NACHRICHTEN-BUREAU.**

Section *18*

№ *50*

В.Секретно.

Г.Предсѣдателю Совѣта Народныхъ Комиссаровъ.

2*7* Февраля 1918 г.

Настоящимъ, не получивъ точнаго отвѣта на мой запросъ отъ 25 февраля, имѣю честь вторично просить въ срочномъ порядкѣ сообщить мнѣ количество и качество силъ направляемыхъ къ Пскову и Нарвѣ.

Одновременно по порученію Представителя нашего Генеральнаго Штаба, еще разъ напоминаю о желательности назначенія ген. Парскаго на постъ Верховнаго Главнокомандующаго русскими вооруженными силами, вмѣсто ген. Бончъ-Бруевича, дѣятельность котораго не встрѣчаетъ сочувствія Германскаго Верховнаго Командованія. Теперь-же, послѣ покушеній на жизнь и имущество нѣмецкихъ землевладѣльцевъ въ Эстляндіи и Лифляндіи, что, по нашимъ свѣдѣніямъ, произошло съ вѣдома ген. Бончъ-Бруевича и націоналистической дѣятельности его въ Орлѣ, пребываніе генерала на его посту нежелательно.

Начальникъ Отдѣленія

Адъютантъ

FACSIMILE OF DOCUMENT NO. 31, IN WHICH A GERMAN OFFICER ORDERS THE BOLSHEVIST GOVERNMENT TO FURNISH MILITARY DATA AND PLACE A MAN OF BERLIN'S CHOICE AT THE HEAD OF THE RUSSIAN ARMY

DOCUMENT NO. 33

[Counterespionage at the Stavka, No. 63, Jan. 10, 1918]

To THE COMMISSION FOR COMBATING THE COUNTER-REVOLUTION:

The commissar on combating the counter-revolution, in a cipher telegram, No. 235, demanded the sending of special agents to Kiev and Novocherkask.

There have been sent Comrades Vlasenko, Gavrilchuk, and Korablev, who have more than once very successfully performed information service. The commissar in his cipher telegram indicates that the German and Austrian agents assigned from Petrograd, Lieutenants Otto Kremer, Blum and Vasilko, are playing a double rôle, reporting on what is happening at Petrograd, and they carry on an intensive agitation in favor of a separate peace of the Ukraine with the Central Powers, and for the restoring of order. Their work is having success.

To Siberia have been ordered Comrades Trefiley and Shepshelevich, in connection with your report of the purchase and export of gold by Austrian prisoners in Siberia. — *Director of Counterespionage Feierabend.*

NOTE.—*So stands disclosed the manner in which Germany set about to double-cross the Bolshevist servants who in success had become at times uppish in bargaining with*

**G. G.-S.**

NACHRICHTEN-BUREAU.

Section *R*

№ 272/600

5 Февраля 1918 г.

Весьма секретно.

Господину Народному Комиссару по Иностраннымъ Дѣламъ.

Прошу срочно выдать турецкому подданному Карпу Х.Миссирову русскій паспортъ, вмѣсто отобраннаго у него, выданнаго ему въ 1912 г. на основаніи прилагаемаго къ сему національнаго паспорта.

Агентъ К.Миссировъ направится въ Штабъ Русскаго Верховнаго Командованія, гдѣ согласно происшедшимъ переговорамъ между ген.Гофманомъ и Комиссарами Троцкимъ и Іоффе,-онъ будетъ нести наблюденіе за дѣятельностью Начальника Штаба ген. Бончъ-Бруевича въ качествѣ помощника Комиссаровъ Кальмановича и Фейерабенда.

Начальникъ Отдѣленія

Адъютантъ

FACSIMILE OF DOCUMENT NO. 32, IN WHICH GERMAN OFFICERS DEMAND A PASSPORT FOR A TURKISH SUBJECT, WHO IS TO SPY ON THE RUSSIAN CHIEF OF STAFF IN HIS OWN HEADQUARTERS

*their masters. It was not a part of the German program to create in Russia a power which it could not at any time control, or, if need be, overturn. Its plan here had the additional advantage of not only disciplining the Petrograd Bolsheviki, but also of disunifying Russia still further. It worked out to a separate peace with Ukraine and a separate peace with Northern Russia. Lieutenant Otto is the Kronshin afterward arrested for some unknown betrayal. See document No. 2.*

*Have photograph of letter.*

### DOCUMENT NO. 34

[Counter espionage at Stavka, No. 511, Jan. 30, 1918]

TO THE COMMISSION FOR COMBATING THE COUNTER-REVOLUTION:

You are informed that the German and Austrian officers located at Kiev now have private meetings with members of the deposed Rada. They insistently inform us of the inevitable signing and ratification of peace treaties, both between the Ukraine and the Central Powers and between Rumania and Austria and Germany.—*Chief of the Counter Espionage, Feierabend; Commissar Kalmanovich.*

NOTE.—*Corroborative of the preceding docu-*

*ment. The separate peace with Ukraine already had been signed.*

*Have photograph of letter.*

### DOCUMENT NO. 35

[G. G. S., Nachrichten Bureau, No. 181, December, 1917]

*VERY URGENT*

TO THE COMMISSAR OF FOREIGN AFFAIRS:

In accordance with your request, the intelligence section on Nov. 29 sent to Rostov Major von Boehlke, who arranged there a survey over the forces of the Don Troop Government. The Major also organized a detachment of prisoners of war, who took part in the battle. In this case the prisoners of war, in accordance with the directions given by the July conference at Kronstadt, participated in by Messrs. Lenine, Zinovieff, Kameneff, Raskolnikoff, Dybenko, Shisko, Antonoff, Krylenko, Volodarsky, and Podvoisky, were dressed in Russian Army and Navy uniforms. Major von Boehlke took part in commanding, but the conflicting orders of the official commander, Arnautoff, and the talentless activity of the scout Tulgk paralyzed the plans of our officer.

The agents sent by order from Petrograd to kill Generals Kaledine, Bogaevsky, and Alexeieff were cowardly and nonenterprising people. Agents passed through to Karauloff. The communications of General Kaledine with the Americans and English are beyond doubt, but they limit themselves entirely to financial assistance. Major von Boehlke returned to Petrograd and will make a report today at the office of the Chairman of the Council at 10 P. M.—*For the head of department, R. Bauer.*

NOTE.—*This is a cold-blooded disclosure of a German-Bolshevist plan for the assassination of Kaledine and Alexeieff, as well as proof of a condition often denied by Smolny during the Winter—that German prisoners were being armed as Russian soldiers in the struggle against the Russian Nationalists on the Don. The letter also contains the most complete list of the participants in the July conspiracy conference at Kronstadt. The marginal comment opposite the assassination paragraph is, " Who sent them!" in an unidentified handwriting. Major von Boehlke is a German officer referred to in Document No. 5. His cipher signature is Schott. Have photograph of letter.*

---

### DOCUMENT NO. 36
[G. G. S., Nachrichten Bureau, No. 136, Nov. 28, 1917]
#### VERY SECRET

To THE COUNCIL OF PEOPLE'S COMMISSARS:

In accordance with your request, the Intelligence Section of the General Staff informs the Council of People's Commissars that the Ukrainian Commission at the Austrian high command, in which participate the empowered representatives of the German Staff, has worked out a plan of the activities of the revolutionary zone to the Council of Workmen's and Soldiers' Deputies—Chudovsky, Boyardsky, Gubarsky, and Piatokov—who are under the full direction of the Austro-Hungarian high command.

The Commander in Chief of the Russian Army has been made acquainted by Schott with plans of the Austro-German high command and will co-operate with him.—*Head of Department, Agasfer.*

NOTE.—*At this early time there was harmony all around on the Ukraine program, Germans, Austrians, and the Commissars in complete brotherhood. Schott is Major von Boehlke and Agasfer is Major Luberts. Have photograph of letter.*

---

### TROTZKY AND RUMANIA

The machinations of Trotzky, inspired by the German General Hoffman, for the disruption of Rumania are disclosed in the following:

### DOCUMENT NO. 37
[Counterespionage at the Stavka]

To THE COMMISSION ON COMBATING THE COUNTER-REVOLUTION:

Commander in Chief Krylenko has requested the counterespionage at the staff to inform you that it is necessary to order the following persons to the Rumanian front immediately: From Petrograd, Commissar Kuhl, Socialist Rakovsky, Sailor Guieshin, and from the front the chief of the Red Guard Durasov. These persons should be supplied with literature and with financial resources for agitation. To them is committed the task of taking all measures for the deposing of the Rumanian King and the removal of counter-revolutionary Rumanian officers. —*Director of Counterespionage, Feierabend; Secretary, N. Drachev.*

NOTE.—*This marks the beginning of large-scale work to disorganize the Rumanian Army. That in its early Winter phases it advances disappointingly to Germany is evidenced by vengeful steps taken later by General Hoffman and Trotzky from Brest-Litovsk, when in the middle of January Trotzky, at the request of General Hoffman, ordered the arrest in Petrograd of the Rumanian Minister Diamandi. The contents of this letter, written by Joffe, were telegraphed to Washington in February and photographic copy of letter forwarded.\**

*At about the same time the Rumanian public gold reserves in custody within the Kremlin walls at Moscow were seized by the Russian Government. Diamandi was released from arrest at the demand of the united diplomatic delegations at Petrograd, but his humiliations continued, and on Jan. 28 he was ordered from Petrograd, being given less than ten hours to prepare for the departure of a party that contained many women and children. Ambassador Francis sought in vain of Zalkind, who was acting as Foreign Minister in the absence of Trotzky, again at Brest, for an extension of the time of departures.*

*The Rumanian party was thrown pell-mell on a train at midnight. It was delayed in Finland on one excuse and another, not immediately apparent, but in three weeks the Minister, leaving behind a large part of his people, was allowed to proceed to Torneo. By good luck he reached there the day after the Red Guard lost Torneo to the White Guard. That day saved his life, for on the person of Svetlitzsky, a Russian Commissar who joined him in mid-Finland and accompaned him to Torneo, was found an order to Timofeyeff, the Commissar at Torneo, to shoot him. Svetlitzsky was shot instead.*

*When I passed through Torneo the control officer talked frankly about the details, expressing the opinion that the shooting might have been a mistake, as it was not shown that Svetlitzsky was aware of the contents of*

---

*\*Letter from Joffe at Brest-Litovsk carrying General Hoffman's order through Trotzky to incite agitation against the Rumanian Army and to arrest Diamandi, the Rumanian Minister.*

the letter. Svetlitzsky, however, was an important person in Petrograd, close to Trotzky.

Our American party brought Guranesco, the First Secretary of the Rumanian delegation, out of Finland through the lines with us. He had been in Red Finland seven weeks. Behind us at Bjorneburg we left several families of Rumanians who had departed from Petrograd with the Minister. We would have liked to have brought them through the lines of the two armies, but our venture was too desperate to permit unauthorized additions to the party.

The marginal notation on this letter is " Execute," initialed " ch," the sign manual of Tchitcherin, the returned exile from England, at that time Assistant Minister of Foreign Affairs, now Minister of Foreign Affairs.

Have photograph of letter.

DOCUMENT 37A*

CONFIDENTIAL

[No. 771, Affair of Peace Deleg., To Report 4 I, Urgent (Initials)]

BREST-LITOVSK,

Dec. 31, 1917. No. 365-N. K.

TO THE COUNCIL OF PEOPLE'S COMMISSARS:

Comrade L. Trotzky has charged me to bring to the knowledge of the Council of National Commissaries the motives for his telegraphic proposal to arrest the Rumanian diplomatic representatives in Petersburg.

General Hoffman, referring to the conference which had taken place in Brest-Litovsk between the members of the German and Austro-Hungarian delegations on Dec. 29, presented to the Russian delegation in the name of the German and Austrian chief command (a deciphered radiotelegram was exhibited in this connection) a confidential demand concerning the immediate incitement of the Rumanian Army to recognize the necessity of an armistice and adopting the terms of a democratic peace pointed out by the Russian delegates. The implacability of the staff and the whole commanding force of the Rumanian Army, with regard to which the chief command of the German Army has received the most exact agency information, spoils the excellent impression produced in Germany and on all the fronts by the Russian peace proposition, which has made it possible to again stimulate the popular feeling against England, France and America and can bring about an undesirable and dangerous aggravation of the peace question up to the German

Army going over to the attack on our front and an open annexation of the territories occupied in Russia.

The General expressed his opinion that against peace might be the Cossacks, some Ukrainian regiments, and the Caucasian Army, in which case they will also doubtless be joined by the Rumanian armies, which, according to the information in possession of the German staff, enter into the calculations of Kaledine and Alexeieff. It is greatly in the interests of the German and Austrian delegations that complete harmony should prevail on the entire Russian front as regards the conclusion of an armistice and adopting the terms of a separate peace between Russia and Germany, seeing that in this event the German and Austrian chief command will propose to Rumania their terms of peace, and will be in a position to take up their operative actions on the western front on a very large scale; at the same time Gen. Hoffman, in the course of a conversation with Comr. Trotzky, twice hinted at the necessity of immediately beginning these war operations.

When Comr. Trotzky declared that at the disposal of the Council's power there are no means of influencing the Rumanian staff, Gen. Hoffman pointed out the necessity of sending trustworthy agents to the Rumanian Army and the possibility of arresting the Rumanian mission in St. Petersburg and of repressive measures against the Rumanian King and the Rumanian commanding forces.

After this interview Comr. L. Trotzky by cable proposed to arrest the Rumanian mission in Petersburg with all its members. This report is being sent by special courier—Comrade I. G. Brossoff, who has to personally transmit to Commissary Podvoisky some information of a secret character regarding the sending to the Rumanian Army of those persons whose names Comr. Brossoff will give.

All these persons will be paid out of the cash of the " German Naphtha-Industrial Bank," which has bought near Boreslav the business of the joint-stock company of Fanto & Co. The chief direction of those agents has been intrusted, according to Gen. Hoffman's indication, to a certain Wolf Vonigel, who is keeping a watch over the military agents of the countries allied with us. As regards the English and American diplomatic representatives, General Hoffman has expressed the agreement of the German staff to the measures adopted by Comr. Trotzky and Comr. Lazimiroff with regard to watching over their activity.—Member of the delegation, A. Joffe.

MARGINAL NOTATIONS

Comr. Shitkevitch: Take copies an send to the Commiss. for Foreign Afairs,

---

*The contents of this letter, written by Joffe, were telegraphed to Washington in February, and photographic copy of letter forwarded by Ambassador Francis to State Department.

personally to Comr. Zalkind. [*Passages printed above in italics marked*:] To Sanders.

Reported Jan. 4, regarding the arrest of Diamandi and others.—M. SHITKE-VITCH.

JANUARY 5, 1918.

TO THE CHANCERY:

Send an urgent telegram to Trotzky about the arrest of the Rumanian Minister.—*Savelieff.*

NOTE (as cabled Feb. 9.)—*The date is Jan. 12, western time, the eve of the Russian New Year. The Rumanian Minister was arrested that night in Petrograd, and only released on the united demand of all embassies and legations in Petrograd. Since then he has been sent out of Russia. The letter shows that Trotzky took General Hoffman's personal demand as an order for action. Most important of all, however, it strips the mask from the Lenine and Trotzky public protestations that they have sought to prevent the peace negotiations with Germany from turning to the military advantage of Germany against the United States, England, and France. The aim here disclosed is, instead, to aid Germany in stimulating feeling against England, France, and the United States, in enabling Germany to prepare for an offensive on the western front. A German bank is named as paymaster for Bolshevist agitators among the Rumanian soldiers. Is Wolf Vonigel, the Field Director, the Wolf von Igel of American notoriety? The similarity of name is striking. Finally, General Hoffman and the German staff are satisfied with Trotzky's watch over the American and English diplomats. Yoffe, who signs the letter, is a member of the Russian Peace Commission. Since this letter was written Zalkind has gone to Switzerland on a special mission.*

*July 6, 1918.—E. S.*

*He did not reach there, being unable to pass through England, and in April was in Christiania.*

---

## ESPIONAGE AND ASSASSINATION

Former disclosures of espionage operations and of assassination orders for the ruthless extermination of Russian patriots follow:

### DOCUMENT NO. 38

[Commission for combating the counter-revolution and pogroms, Dec. 14, 1917, Petrograd]

MAJ. VON BOEHLKE, ESTEEMED COMRADE:

I bring to your notice that our Finnish comrades, Hakhia, Pukko, and Enrot, have advised the commissar for combating the counter-revolution of the following facts:

1. Between the English officers and the Finnish bourgeoisie organizations there are connections which cause us serious apprehension.

2. In Finland have been installed two wireless stations, which are used by unknown persons who communicate in cipher.

3. Between General Kaledin and the American mission there is an undoubted communication, of which we have received exact information from your source, and therefore a most careful supervision of the American Embassy is necessary.

These reports must be established exactly. Our agents are helpless. Please excuse that I write on the official letterheads, but I hasten to do this, sitting here at the commission at an extraordinary meeting. Ready to service.—*F. Zalkind.*

NOTE.—*The written comment at the top of the letter is " Commissar for foreign affairs. I request exact instructions. Schott." It is von Boehlke's question, signed with his cipher name. (See Document 5.) The letter may imply that von Boehlke had, in the opinion of his good friend Zalkind, a means of internal observation at the American Embassy.*

*Have photograph of letter.*

### DOCUMENT NO. 39

[Counterespionage at the Stavka, No. 268, Jan. 25, 1918]

*VERY SECRET*

TO THE COMMISSION ON COMBATING THE COUNTER-REVOLUTION:

The 23d of January at the Stavka there took place a conference at which there participated Major von Boehlke, assigned from Petrograd. It was decided, upon the insistence of the German consultants, to send to the internal fronts the following persons, furnishing them all powers for dealing with individual counter-revolutionaries.

To the Don: Zhikhorev, Rudnev, Krogultz, and Ernest Delgau.

To the Caucasus Front: Vassili Dumbadze, Prince Machabelli, Sevastianov, and Ter-Baburin.

To the 1st Polish Corps of General Dovbor-Menitsky are assigned Dembitsky, Stetkus, Zhimiltis, and Gisman.

Be so good as to take all measures for the quick assignment and the adequate furnishing of the assigned persons with money, reserve passports, and other documents—*Senior Officer, Peter Mironov.*

NOTE.—*This is an assassination order against individuals. It was not successful against the Polish General. Dembadze and Prince Machabelli were German spies implicated in the Sukhomlinoff affair and sentenced to prison, but afterward liberated by the Bolsheviki. Lieut. Col. Dembitsky was a Bolshevist Polish officer. Baburin was an assistant chief of staff under Krylenko. The letter is indorsed " Comrade Lunarcharsky, leave with report for Comrade Zenovieff," signature illegible.*

*Have photograph of letter.*

DOCUMENT NO. 40

[Counterespionage at the Stavka, No. 51/572, Jan. 19, 1918]

To the Commission for Combating the Counter-Revolution:

There have been received two notes addressed to the Supreme Commander from the staffs of the Austrian and German High Commands. These notes inform the Stavka that the organizer of the volunteer army in the Don region, General Alexeieff, is in written communication with the officer personnel of the Polish legions at the front, with the view of getting the help of Polish officers in the counter-revolution. This information has been received by the Austrian agents from the Polish Bolshevist Comrade Zhuk, who played a large part at Rostov during the November and December battles. On the other side, the representative of the German Government, Count Lerchenfeldt, reports of the rapidly growing movement in Poland in favor of the bourgeoisie estate owners' imperialistic plan to defend with arms the greatest possible independence of Poland, with the broadening of its frontiers at the expense of Lithuania, White Russia, and Galicia.

This movement is actively supported by the popular democratic party in Warsaw, as well as Petrograd, by military organizations guided by the counter-revolutionary estate owners and the bourgeois Polish clergy.

The situation which has arisen was discussed on the 16th of January at the Stavka in the presence of Major von Boehlke, sent the Petrograd branch of the German Intelligence Bureau, and it was there decided:

1. To take the most decisive measures, up to shooting en masse, against the Polish troops which have submitted to the counter-revolutionary and imperialistic propaganda.

2. To arrest General Dovbor-Menitsky.

3. To arrange a surveillance of the commanding personnel.

4. Send agitators to the Polish legions to consult regarding the Polish revolutionary organizations known to the committee.

5. On learning of the counter-revolutionary activity of Polish officers to immediately arrest them and send them to the Stavka to the disposal of the Counterespionage.

6. To arrest the emissaries of General Alexeieff, Staff Captain Shuravsky, and Captain Rushifsky.

7. To request the Commission for Combating the Counter-Revolution with agreement with the German Intelligence Bureau at Petrograd to arrange a surveillance and observation of the following institutions and persons:

(a) The high Polish Committee.

(b) The Society of Friends of the Polish Soldier.

(c) Inter-Party Union.

(d) The Union of Polish Invalids.

(e) Members of the Polish Kolo of the former State Duma and Council.

(f) The Chairman, Lednitsky, and the members of the former committee for the liquidation of affairs of the Polish kingdom.

(g) Boleslav Jalovesky.

(h) Vladislav Grabsky.

(i) Stanislav Shuritsky.

(j) Roman Catholic Polish clergy.

(k) The Polish Treasury, through which, according to agency reports, the Governments of countries allied with Russia intend, with the assistance of the New York National City Bank, to supply with monetary resources the counter-revolutionary camp.

It is necessary to verify the private reports of several Lithuanian revolutionaries that among the church benevolent funds, which are at the disposal of the Polish clergy, are the funds of private persons who hid their money from requisition for the benefit of the State.

In case of establishment of any connection with the counter-revolution the guilty Polish institutions are to be liquidated, their leaders and also persons connected with the counter-revolutionary activity are to be arrested and sent to the disposal of the Stavka.—*For Chief of the Counterespionage, Commissar Kalmanovitch.*

Note.—*Again Germany, through Count Perchenfeldt, was intriguing on both sides. Chiefly, however, the significance of the letter is in the thoroughness of the outlined German plan to crush the threat of armed opposition from the Polish legions of the Russian Army. The troops were fired upon, as indicated. The preceding document really follows this in natural sequence. The next two further elucidate the situation for the benefit of the Poles of the outside world. Have photograph of letter.*

DOCUMENT NO. 41

[Counterespionage at the Stavka, No. 461, Jan. 28, 1918]

To the Commission for Combating the Counter-Revolution:

The special commission on the conflict with the Polish counter-revolutionary troops has begun its activity. All the conduct of its affairs has been located at the counterespionage at the Stavka, where is being collected all information on the counter-revolution on the external and internal fronts. At the commission have arrived members of the Commission for Combating the Counter-Revolution, E. Miekonoshin, I. Zenzinov, Zhilinski, and from Sevastopol Comrade Tiurin. To a conference were called agents announcing their wish to be sent for conflict with the bourgeoisie Polish officers—Dembitsky, Boleslav, Yakhimovich, Strievsky, Yasenovsky, and Adamovich. All those agents are under obligation to carry the affair to the point of open insubordination of the soldiers against the officers, and the arrest of the latter.

For emergency the commander in chief ordered to assign Nakhim Sher and Ilya Razymov for the destruction of the counter-revolutionary ringleaders among the Polish troops, and the commission recognized the possibility of declaring all Polish troops outside the law when that measure should present itself as imperative.

From Petrograd, observers announced that the Polish organizations are displaying great reserve and caution in mutual relations. There has been established, however, an unquestionable contact between the high military council located in Petrograd and the Polish officers and soldiers of the bourgeoisie estate-owning class with the counter-revolutionary Polish troops. On this matter, in the Commissariat on Military Affairs, there took place on Jan. 22 a conference of Comrades Podvoisky, Kovdrov, Boretzhov, Dybenko, and Kovalsky. The Commissar on Naval Affairs announced that the sailors Trushin, Markin, Peinkaitis, and Schulz demand the dismissal of the Polish troops, and threaten, in case it is refused, assaults on the Polish legionaries in Petrograd. The Commander in Chief suggests that it might be possible to direct the rage of the sailors mentioned, and of their group, to the front against the counter-revolutionary Polish troops.

At the present time our agitation among the Polish troops is being carried on in very active fashion and there is great hope for the disorganization of the Polish legionaries.—*Chief of Counter-espionage, Feierabend.*
NOTE.—*Have photograph of letter.*

---

## DOCUMENT NO. 42
[Counterespionage at the Stavka, Jan. 28, 1918]
TO THE COMMISSION FOR COMBATING THE COUNTER-REVOLUTION:

At the request of the Commander in Chief, in answer to your inquiry, I inform you, supplementary to the dispatch, that the funds sent with Major Bayermeister have been received here. Among the troops acting on the front against the counter-revolutionaries have been prepared several battalions for conflict with the Poles and Rumanians. We will pay 12 rubles a day, with an increased food ration. From the hired sections sent against the legionaries have been formed two companies, one from the best shots for the shooting of officers of regiments,

the other of Lithuanians and Letts for the theft of food reserves in Vitebsk, Minsk, and Mogilev Governments, in the places where the Polish troops are situated. Various local peasants have also agreed to attack the regiments and exterminate them.—*Commissar G. Mosholov.*
NOTE.—*These two documents show that the policy against these patriotic soldiers was one of merciless extermination, financed by German money, handed out by a German officer. Bayermeister is named in Document No. 5.*
*Have photograph of letter.*

The following documents show the complete surrender of the Bolshevist leaders to their German masters:

## DOCUMENT NO. 43
[Gr. (Great) General Staff, Central Abtheilung, Section M-R, No. 411, Feb. 26, 1918]
*VERY SECRET*

TO THE COUNCIL OF PEOPLE'S COMMISSARS:

According to instructions from the High Command of the German Army, I have the honor to remind you that the withdrawing and disarming of the Russian Red Guard from Finland must be commenced immediately. It is known to the staff that the chief opponent of this step is the head of the Finnish Red Guard, Yarvo Haapalainen, who has a great influence on the Russian tovarische, (comrades.) I request you to send for this struggle with Haapalainen our agent, Walter Nevalainen, (Nevalaiselle,) bearer of Finnish passport 3681, and supply him with a passport and pass.—*Head of the department, O. Rausch; Adjutant, U. Wolff.*
NOTE.—*Written at the top of the letter and signed N. G., the initials of Lenine's secretary, N. Gormunov, is the order "Send to the Commissar of Foreign Affairs and execute." In the margin is written "Passport 211—No. 392," but unfortunately the name under which the new passport was given is not mentioned. This order explains the withdrawal of the Russian Red Guard from Finland in early March and the abandonment of the Finnish Red Guard to its fate. The latter, however, took care of the disarming both of Russian soldiers and sailors as they left Finland, for the Finns needed guns and ammunition. The Russians sometimes fought, but were surrounded and disarmed. In Helsingfors while I was there in March the Red Guard and the sailors were fighting each other nightly with rifles and machine guns. One of two Finnish Red Guard leaders almost surely is Nevalainen, but under the circumstances I do not care to speculate.*
*The order to hold all foreign embassies in Red Finland was given coincidently with the appearance of one of them upon the scene. The excuse offered was that foreigners were carrying information to the White Guard. Simultaneously influence was exerted in the*

White Guard to increase difficulties in passage between the lines. It is reasonable to
place the obstacles to passage created on
both sides of the Finnish lines to German effort, for German aid was being given the
White Guard openly at the moment it was
intriguing in the inner councils of the Red
Guard. The American party cornered in Finland escaped only by persistence and good
fortune. The British Embassy party was
passed through the day before the closing
order came. The French and Italian Embassies were obliged, after a month of vain
effort, to return to Russia. Have original
letter and the surrendered passport.

## DOCUMENT NO. 44

[G. G. S., Nachrichten Bureau, Section R,
No. 283]

To THE COMMISSAR OF FOREIGN AFFAIRS:

We are told that secret service agents
attached to Stavka are following Major
Erich, who has been ordered to Kiev. I
ask you to take urgent measures to remove the surveillance of the above-named
officer.—*Head of the Department, Agasfer; Adjt. Bulkholm.*

NOTE.—*Tchitcherin, Assistant Foreign Minister, initials a marginal comment " Talk it
over." This note marks the period of ac-
cute irritation over the Ukraine between
Bolsheviki and Germans. Agasfer is Major
Luberts.*
*Have original letter.*

## DOCUMENT NO. 45

[G. G. S., Nachrichten Bureau, Section R,
No. 228, Feb. 4, 1918]

To THE COMMISSAR OF FOREIGN AFFAIRS:

By instructions of the representative of
our staff I have the honor to ask you
immediately to recall from the Ukrainia
front the agitators Bryansky, Wulf, Drab-
kin, and Pittsker. Their activity has been
recognized as dangerous by the German
General Staff.—*Head of the Department,
Agasfer; Adjt. Henrich.*

NOTE.—*An exchange of courtesies of the
same period as Document No. 44 Tchitcherin has notated it " Discuss."*
*Have original letter.*

## DOCUMENT NO. 46

[G. G. S., Nachrichten Bureau, Section R,
Feb. 3, 1918]

To THE COMMISSAR OF FOREIGN AFFAIRS:

According to instructions of the representative of our General Staff, I have the
honor once more to insist that you recall
from Estland, Litva, and Courland all
agitators of the Central Executive Committee of the Soviet of Workmen's and Soldiers' Deputies.—*Head of the Department, Agasfer; Adjutant Bukholm.*

NOTE.—*Another instance of the time when
Germany was using an iron hand of dis-*

cipline, clearing of agitators the provinces it
already had announced its intention of seizing for its own. The letter was referred by
Markin, one of Trotzky's Secretaries, to
Volodarsky, who seems to have been in
charge of the proletarian agitation in these
provinces.
*Have original letter.*

## DOCUMENT NO. 47

[G. G. S., Nachrichten Bureau, Section R,
No. 17, Feb. 17, 1918]

To THE COUNCIL OF PEOPLE'S COMMISSARS:

The Intelligence Department has received detailed information that the agitators of the Petrograd Soviet of Workmen's
and Soldiers' Deputies have completely
changed the character of the Estland
Socialists' activity, which finally led to
the local German landlords being declared
outlawed. By order of the General Staff
I ask you to take immediate steps for the
restoring of the rights of the above-men-
tionel German landlords and the recalling
of the agitators.—*For the Head of the
Department; R. Bauer.*

NOTE.—*This order for the release of the
German landlords was at once obeyed, and
the act of surrender, evidently at the direct
order of Lenine, to whom this letter is addressed, marked the end of the incipient rebellion of the Bolshevist leaders against their
German masters.*
*Have photograph of letter.*

## DOCUMENT NO. 48
### VARIED ACTIVITIES

[Counterespionage at the Stavka, Jan. 22,
1918]

To THE COUNCIL OF PEOPLE'S COMMISSARS:

By our agents it has been established
that connections between the Poles, the
Don, and French officers, and also probably the diplomatic representatives of the
allied powers, are maintained by means of
Russian officers traveling under the guise
of sack speculators. In view of this we
request you to take measures for the
strict surveillance of the latter.—*Commissar Kalmanovitch.*

NOTE—*The indorsement on this is by
Trotzky, " Copy to inform Podvoisky and
Dzerzhinsky." The former was Minister of
War, the latter Chairman of the Commis-
sion for combating the counter-revolution.
Sack speculators were food peddlers who
went into the provinces and brought food
to the cities for profitable sale. Soldiers
practically had a monopoly of the trade.*
*Have photograph of letter.*

## DOCUMENT NO. 49

[Gr. General Staff, Section R, No. 151,
Dec. 4, 1917]

To THE COMMISSARIAT OF MILITARY AFFAIRS:

Herewith the Intelligence Bureau has

the honor to transmit a list of the persons of Russian origin who are in the service of the German Intelligence Department:

Sakharoff, officer First Infantry Reserve Regiment; Praporschik Ter-Arytiuniantz, Praporschik Zanko, Yarchuk, Golovin, Zhuk, Ilinsky, Cherniavsky, Captain Postinkov, Scheueemann, Sailors Trushin and Gavrilov. All the persons mentioned are on the permanent staff of the Intelligence Department of the German General Staff.—*Head of Department, Agasfer.*

NOTE—*Have photograph of letter.*

---

### DOCUMENT NO. 50

[Gr. General Staff, Central Division, Section M., Jan. 14, 1918]

*VERY CONFIDENTIAL*

TO THE CHAIRMAN OF THE PEOPLE'S COUNCIL OF COMMISSARS:

The Russian section of the German General Staff has received an urgent report from our agents at Novocherkask and Rostov that the friction which has arisen between General Alexeieff and General Kaledine, after which the volunteer corps of General Alexeieff began the movement to the north, is a tactical step to have a base in the rear. In this way the army of General Alexeieff will have a reliable rear base protected by Cossack troops for supplying the army and a base in case of an overwhelming movement on the part of the enemy. The communications of General Alexeieff with the Polish troops have been proved by new reports of the Polish Bolshevist Commissars, Shuk and Dembitsky.—*Chief of the Division of General Staff, O. Rausch; senior aid, R. Krieger.*

NOTE.—*Important as showing that the Germans had a real fear of the military possibilities in the Alexeieff-Kaledine movement. The suicide of General Kaledine at a moment of depression, following betrayals that undoubtedly were carefully plotted, was tragically a part of the great national tragedy. Have photographs of letter.*

---

### DOCUMENT NO. 51

[Counterespionage at the Stavka, No. 263/79, Jan. 23, 1918]

TO THE COMMISSARIAT OF FOREIGN AFFAIRS:

To your inquiry regarding those agents who might be able to give an exact report of the sentiment of the troops and population in the provinces, I transmit to you a short list of the Russo-Germans agents-informers. In Voronezh, S. Sirtzof; in Rostov, Globov and Melikov; in Tiflis, Enskidze and Gavrilov; in Kazan, Pfaltz; in Samara, Oaipov and Voenig; in Omsk, Blagoveschensky and Sipko; in Tomsk, Dattan, Tarasov, and Rodionov;

in Irkutsk, Zhinizherova and Geze; in Vladivostok, Buttenhof, Pannoff, and Ellanger.—*Chief of Counterespionage, Feierabend; Commissar, Kanmanovich.*

NOTE.—*Apart from the list of agents this letter has interest from the comment " To the company of Bonch-Bruevich." The signature is illegible. Have photograph of letter.*

---

### DOCUMENT NO. 52

[Counterespionage at the Stavka, No. 395, Jan. 21, 1918]

TO THE COMMISSION FOR COMBATING THE COUNTER-REVOLUTION:

The agents of the counterespionage at the Stavka have established that the anarchists Stepan Kriloff, Fedor Kutzi, and Albert Bremsen, at Helsingfors, and also Nahim, Arshavsky, Ruphim, Levin, and Mikhail Shatiloff had during the recent days a conference with the Chief of Staff of the Petrograd army district, Shpilko. After Comrade Shpilko transmitted to the anarchists the offer of Comrade Antonoff and Comrade Bersin to recruit agents for the destruction of several counter-revolutionists, the latter expressed their willingness and immediately began the recruiting. To Kiev are assigned the following, who have been hired at Helsingfors: S. Smirnoff and Rigamann. To Odessa, Brack and Schulkovich.—*For the Chief of the Counterespionage; Commissar, C. Moshlov.*

NOTE.—*This is an assassination compact between Bolsheviki and anarchists. Antonoff, one of the chief Bolshevist military leaders, is credited with the taking of Petrograd, and was in charge of the operations against Alexeieff and Kaledine. The list of anarchists includes several notorious characters. Have photograph of letter.*

---

### DOCUMENT NO. 53

[Counterespionage at the Stavka, No. 471, Jan. 27, 1918]

TO THE COMMISSION FOR COMBATING THE COUNTER-REVOLUTION:

By us here there has been received a report from Finland, from Grishin and Bakhi, of the counter-revolutionary activity of the lawyer, Jonas Kastren. This Kastren, in the years 1914-15, recruited on German funds Finnish volunteer regiments and sent them to Germany. For facilitating the work of recruiting he represented himself as a Socialist-Maximalist, and promised support to the Workers' Red Guard. In his office many of our comrades found a cordial reception and material support. Kastren furnished to Russia German money for the propaganda of Bolshevism in Russia. He had already established in 1916 a division of the German General Staff in Helsingfors. Now he, together with Svinhuvud, Ernroth, and Nandelschtedt, is on the side of the White Guards and is aiding them with money, supplies, and arms. We are informed that Kastren works both with German and English money. It is necessary immediately to cut short the work of Jonas Kastren and his group. The Commander in Chief advises to call to Petrograd the Finnish comrades, Rakhi and Pukko, or order Grishin to Helsingfors.—COMMISSAR A. SIVKO.

NOTE.—*Kastren was still alive when I spent a week in Helsingfors in March, but he added to his chances of longevity by fleeing in early February to the White Guards headquarters at Vasa. The order for his removal came too late. Again we see Germany playing with both sides in Finland at the same time.*

*Have photograph of letter.*

## " COUNTERESPIONAGE "   CIRCULARS
### APPENDIX I

This appendix is of circulars of which (except in two noted cases) I have neither originals nor authenticated copies. A number of sets of them were put out in Russian text in Petrograd and in other parts of Russia in the Winter (1918) by the opponents of the Bolsheviki.

The circulars were declared to be copies of documents taken from the Counterespionage Bureau of the Kerensky Government, supplemented by some earlier material from the same bureau when it was under the Imperial Government. The opportunity for securing them could easily have been afforded to the agents and employes of the bureau, for most of them walked out when the Bolsheviki grasped the Government and could have taken freely of the contents of their departments.

Some of the documents were included in the publication made in Paris, hitherto referred to.

The simple test that I have applied to the circulars is that of internal analysis. To that they respond without contradicton. I have not relied on them as proof, but they fit to other fabrics of proof, and in the light of it are more valuable for themselves than they were when they stood alone.

Finally, I am now able to prove that two of the documents among these circulars—the circular of industrial mobilization of June 9, 1914, and the agents' destruction circular of Nov. 28, 1914—are authentic. I have them in the orignal German printed version of their official distribution, and I have the doubly attested Russian and German record that they, in preceding time, reposed in the files of the Secret Service of the Russian Government, from which they were taken by German order and turned over to German representatives of the German Government in Petrograd with the intent of eliminating them as international evidence against Germany. (See Document 3 of my *Report.*)

This group of circulars came into my hands the first week in February, 1918, and a few days ater two duplicate sets reached me. I prepared a digest of the set and Ambassador Francis cabled the message in code to the State Department Feb. 9.

It was nearly four weeks later before I secured the originals and all the photographs listed in my *Report.* Two of these originals were of circulars I had seen in copy form four weeks earlier. That summarizes the case of the circulars of the appendix considered as evidence.   EDGAR SISSON.

*Analysis of German conspiracy matter, with notes as prepared by me and cabled State Department in Ambassador Francis's code Feb. 9, 1918, and with some added notes, as indicated.*

### DOCUMENT NO. 54

Circular 18, February, 1914.—From the Ministry to all groups of German banks and by agreement with the Austro-Hungarian Government, the "Oesterreichische-Kreditanstalt."

The managements of all German banks which are transacting business abroad and, by agreement with the Austro-Hungarian Government, the "Oesterreichische-Kreditanstalt " Bank are hereby advised that the Imperial Government has deemed it to be of extreme necessity to ask the management of all institutions of credit to establish with all possible dispatch agencies in Luleo, Haparanda, and Vardo, on the frontier of Finland, and in Bergen and Amsterdam. The establishment of such agencies for a more effective observation of the financial interests of shareholders of Russian, French, and English concerns may become a necessity under certain circumstances, which would alter the situation of the industrial and financial market.

Moreover, the managements of banking institutions are urged emphatically to make provisions for very close and absolutely secret relations beng established with Finnish and American banks. In this direction the Ministry begs to recommend the Swedish " Nia-Banken " in Stockholm, the banking office of Furstenberg, the commercial company " Waldemar Hansen " in Copenhagen, as a concern which is maintaining (virulent) relations with Russia.

(Signature)   " N 3737,
*" Appertaining to Division, for Foreign Operations."*

NOTE.—*This is the outline of the basic financial structure begun in February, 1914, five months before war was launched, and still in operation. Notice the reappearance in subsequent Lenine messages of towns Luleo and Vardo. Likewise the reference to American banks. Olaf Ashberg, one of the heads of the Nia-Banken, came to Petrograd a month ago (January, 1918) and on way boasted that Nia-Banken was the Bolshevist bank. He was overheard by one of our own group.*

He secured from Smolny permit for export several hundred thousand gallons of oil, opened at Hotel d'Europe headquarters where both Mirbach and Kaiserling of German commissions have been entertained, negotiated with State Bank Feb. 1 contract for buying cash rubles and establishing foreign credit for Russian Government. Furstenberg is now at Smolny using the name Ganetzky, is one of the inner group, and is likely soon to be placed in charge of State Bank. Ashberg now in Stockholm, but returning.

The material in this and all notes is independent of documents and accurate.

## DOCUMENT NO. 55

Circular June 9, 1914.—From the General Staff to all military attachés in the countries adjacent to Russia, France, Italy, and Norway. In all branches of German banks in Sweden, Norway, Switzerland, and the United States special war credits have been opened for subsidiary war requirements. The General Staff is authorizing you to avail yourself in unlimited amounts of these credits for the destruction of the enemy's factories, plants, and the most important military and civil structures. Simultaneously with the instigation of strikes it is necessary to make provisions for the damaging of motors, of mechanisms, with the destruction of vessels, setting incendiary fires to stocks of raw materials and finished products, deprivation of large towns of their electric energy, stocks of fuel and provisions. Special agents, detailed to be at your disposal, will deliver to you explosive and incendiary devices and a list of such persons in the country under your observation who will assume the duty of agents of destruction.

(Signed) DR. FISCHER, *General Army Councilor.*

NOTE.—*Dated six weeks before the rest of the world knew it was to be warred upon, and even then making exact plans for a campaign of incited strikes and incendiary fires in the industrial plants and the yet uncreated munition plants in the United States.*

## DOCUMENT NO. 56

Circular June 9, 1914.—General Staff to all intendencies. Within twenty-four hours after receipt of this circular you are to inform all industrial concerns that the documents with industrial-mobilization plans and with registration forms be opened, such as are referred to in the circular of the Commission of Count Waldersee and Count Caprivi, of June 27, 1887.    N. 421, DE MOBILLIZATION.

NOTE.—*Issued on the same day as No. 55. German industry mobilized for war three weeks before the assassination of the Austro-Hungarian heir apparent, Ferdinand, and his wife.*

NOTE.—*This is the content of circular of*

which I have original German printed circular in form it was sent to German officials. See my report, Document No. 3.—EDGAR SISSON, July 6, 1913.

## DOCUMENTS 57-68

[These documents, here omitted for lack of space, are of the same general nature as the three immediately preceding.]

## APPENDIX II

*Illustrating the "offense tactics" of the Bolshevist leaders against Great Britain and the United States. A conversation by telegraph between Tchitcherin at Petrograd (who is speaking) and Trotzky at Brest-Litovsk in first week in February, a few days before Trotzky made his "No-peace-no-war" gesture, with its practical aspect of demobilizing the army and opening Russia's unarmed breast to Germany.*

With reference to the Allies the situation is evidently favorable. Separate peace will not cause a rupture. England has reconciled herself to this in advance: The recognition of us is a matter of the near future. England and America are playing up to us separately. A few days ago there appeared a so-called head of a commercial mission, Lockhart, with a letter from Litvinoff stating that the bearer is an honest man, who, indeed, fully sympathizes with us. Indeed, he is a subtle, alert Englishman; expresses very liberal views; runs down his Government. He is a type of the diplomat of the new school. At present he is not an official representative, but de facto he is an envoy, having been sent by the War Cabinet. After our recognition he will obtain an official position with us. He promises all kinds of favors from England.

He explained that, if we should not spoil the situation, our recognition is a question of the near future, but something would have to be ceded on our part. He said that no Government could tolerate intervention in its internal affairs. If we are going to raise the British people, if our agents in England will attempt to cause strikes, England will not tolerate this. It proved later that this had reference to Petroff's mission. Concerning the latter specially Lockhart said that his appointment would be difficult for England to swallow, and should he be arrested in England or not be allowed to land, we would probably reply by reprisals, and thus the whole business would be spoiled. He begged that we postpone this matter for ten or twelve days.

Simultaneously Ransome tried to persuade Petroff not to go to England. His journey in case of a conflict would put the question of a revolution in England on edge, which would be exceedingly risky. We discussed this question and decided that our strength was in attack and that whatever would happen it would be the worse for Lloyd George & Co., and the revolution would be the gainer. We sent Petroff's passport to be viséd. Lockhart came running to us. I arranged for an interview with Petroff. Lockhart stated that the question had been referred for decision to London. We said that Russia represented a part of the world's revolutionary movement and that in this was its strength. We and our comrades in England would proclaim that this is not a concrete organization of strikes. We explained the aim of Petroff's mission—i. e., the clearing up of misunderstandings between two nations. He will appeal to all organs of the British Nation. This has also been sent by radio.

Lockhart stated that he was very well impressed and promised to telegraph advising that the visé should be granted. We await further developments. He stated that according to English information the German troops on the eastern front were so badly infected by our propaganda that no second course of barrack régime could cure them. He said that our method of fighting militarism was the most effective. We listened to this and laughed up our sleeves.

NOTE.—*There in the last sentence we have it. The Bolshevist plot in Russia could be placarded a cynical farce if it were not a world tragedy. [This appendix is from an intercepted dispatch which came into the possession of Mr. Sisson.]*

# Report of a Special Committee on the Genuineness of the Foregoing Documents

When the foregoing documents were published in the newspapers their authenticity was questioned by The New York Evening Post and several of its correspondents. George Creel, Chairman of the Committee on Public Information, therefore requested Professor Joseph Schaefer, Vice Chairman of the National Board for Historical Service at Washington, to appoint a competent committee of experts to determine the truth or falsity of these charges. The committee thus appointed consisted of Dr. J. Franklin Jameson, editor of the American Historical Review and Director of the Department of Historical Research of the Carnegie Institution at Washington, and Dr. Samuel N. Harper, Professor of Russian Language and Institutions in the University of Chicago. Under date of Oct. 26, 1918, the committee made its report to Mr. Creel, and the report was appended to the pamphlet edition of the documents issued by the Government under the title, " The German-Bolshevist Conspiracy." Its essential portions are as follows:

You have also laid before us the original documents in sixteen cases, and in the other cases the photographs, on which all the translations from No. 1 to No. 53 were based, and also the mimeographed texts in Russian from which were made the translations from No. 54 to No. 68. Mr. Sisson has detailed to us, with all apparent candor, the history of his reception of the documents, and has permitted us to question him at great length as to these transactions and as to various points

relative to the papers. Several officials of the Government in Washington have obliged us by contributing other pertinent and valuable information.

In presenting the results of our investigations, we find it desirable to distinguish the documents into three groups: first, and much the largest, (I.) those presented to us in Russian originals or photographs—four-fifths of the whole set; (II.) the two documents presented to us in circulars printed in German; (III.) those documents for which no originals or photographs are presented, but the translations of which rest solely on mimeographed texts in Russian, purporting to represent originals in or from Russian archives.

In other words, our first group (I.) consists of the documents bearing the numbers 1 to 53, inclusive. Our second group (II.) consists of the two documents which appear translated in the newspaper publication as annexes to Document No. 3. They also appear, with facsimiles, after No. 3 in the proposed pamphlet; and they are identical with Nos. 56 and 58 in the appendix. Our third group (III.) embraces all the documents of Appendix I. (Nos. 54 to 68, inclusive) except Nos. 56 and 58. We comment upon these groups separately.

I. The originals and photographs composing what we have called the first group are all in the Russian language. They are typewritten (save one which is printed) on letterheads of the Petrograd bureau of the German General Staff, of the Counterespionage at the Stavka, (army headquarters,) or of other offices in Russia, German or Russian. They are dated according to the Russian calendar, (" Old Style,") up to February, 1918, when the Bolshevist Government made the change to " New Style." We have subjected them with great care to all the applicable tests to which historical students are accustomed to subject documents of the kind, and to as many others as we could devise and use, consistently with the need of making a reasonably early report. Besides studying whatever internal evidences could be derived from the papers themselves, we have, so far as we could, compared their versions of what went on with the actual facts. Upon the basis of these investigations we have no hesitation in declaring that we see no reason to doubt the genuineness or authenticity of these firty-three documents.

II. The two documents of our second group seem to us to call for a special, a less confident, and a less simple verdict. Printed in German, they purport to be official German orders of the year 1914—the one addressed on June 9 of that year, seven weeks before the outbreak of the war, by the General Staff of the German Army to district commandants, enjoining them to cause German industrial establishments to open their instructions respecting industrial mobilization; the other, dated Nov. 28, 1914, addressed by the General Staff of the High Seas Fleet to maritime agencies and naval societies, and calling on them to mobilize destructive agents in foreign harbors, with a view to thwarting shipments of munitions to " England, France, Canada, the United States, and Russia." The problem of their genuineness must be considered in connection with Documents Nos. 56 and 58 in the appendix, which are nearly identical with them, differing in sense only as Russian translations might easily differ from German originals.

The errors of typography, of spelling and even of grammar in these German circulars make it impossible to accept them as original prints of the General Staffs named. Certain peculiarities of expression tend in the same direction. In the naval circular the explanation, in parentheses, of the German word " Vereinigungen " by the Russicism Artelen (Russsian word with German plural ending) make it impossible to think of the document as one printed by the German Naval Staff for use indifferently in all the various countries in which there were German maritime agencies and naval societies. Furthermore, the reference to the United States is puzzling. On the other hand, Document No. 3, a protocol which presents exceptional evidences of genuineness, records the transfer from Russian archives into the hands of German military officials in Petrograd of two documents which it not only designates by date and number, but describes; and date, number, and description correspond to those of the two papers in question. There is other evidence in Washington of the existence of two such circulars, said to be of the dates named, in Petrograd archives in 1915. Attention should also be called to the manuscript annotations on the circulars, plainly visible in the facsimiles. On both appears, in blue pencil, a note which, properly translated, reads: " One copy

given to the Nachrichten Bureau.—Archive." That is to say, one printed copy has been handed over, in accordance with the formal record made in Document No. 3, to the Military Intelligence Bureau of the German General Staff, (a bureau which then, or soon after, was housed under the same roof with the Bolshevist Government, in the Smolny Institute,) while this present printed copy is to be put in the Russian archives. The circular dated June 9 bears also the annotation in red ink, " To the protocol [of] Nov. 2, 1917," confirming the connection asserted.

We do not think these two printed circulars to be simply forgeries. We do not think them to be, in their present shape, documents on whose entire text historians or publicists can safely rely as genuine. If we were to hazard a conjecture, it would be that they are derived, perhaps at one or two removes, from actual documents, which may have been copied in manuscript and at a later time reproduced in print. In any case they have no relation to the Bolshevist officials, except indirectly through their connection with Document No. 3, which, with or without them, shows the Petrograd office of the German General Staff desirous of withdrawing certain papers from the Russian archives, and the Bolshevist Government complying with its desires.

III. For the documents of our third group, apart from Nos. 56 and 58, we have only the Russian mimeographed texts. The originals of nearly all of them would have been written in German. We have seen neither originals nor photographs, nor has Mr. Sisson, who rightly relegates these documents to an appendix, and expresses less confidence in their evidential value than in that of his main series, Nos. 1 to 53. With such insufficient means of testing their genuineness as can be afforded by Russian translations, we can make no confident declaration. Thrown back on internal evidence alone, we can only say that we see in these texts nothing that positively excludes the notion of their being genuine, little in any of them that makes it doubtful, though guarantees of their having been accurately copied, and accurately translated into Russian, are obviously lacking.

We should say the same (except that its original is not German) of the telegraphic conversation between Tchitcherin and Trotzky, which Mr. Sisson prints as Appendix II. The letter of Joffe, on the other hand, dated Dec. 31, 1917, which he prints just after his No. 37,* stands on as strong a basis as Documents Nos. 1 to 53, for Mr. Sisson had at one time a photograph of it, derived in the same manner as his other photographs.

As to the Reichsbank order of March 2,

---

*Printed as Document No. 37A. It should be noted also that the " telegraphic conversation " referred to is taken from an intercepted dispatch which came directly into Mr. Sisson's hands. This, perhaps, was not made clear to the committee.

1917, printed by him as an annex to Document No. 1, the text there presented does not purport to represent more than its general substance. The reader is not asked to rely on its accuracy and completeness, and we should not wish to do so.

It remains to consider the specific criticisms, as to genuineness of the documents, advanced by The New York Evening Post and its correspondents. Most of them fall away when it is known that the main series of documents, Nos. 1 to 53, are written in Russian and dated in accordance with the calendar currently used in Petrograd, and when it is considered that, as is well known, the Bolshevist coup d'état was expected in that city for some time before it took place.

Thus, The Evening Post (of Sept. 16, 17, 18, 21, 1918) repeatedly scouts Document No. 5, dated in the newspaper publication " October, 1917," and Document No. 21, dated Nov. 1, 1917—letters addressed by the Petrograd bureau of the German General Staff to the Bolshevist Government—on the ground that on those dates, in the Berlin calendar, there was no Bolshevist Government, the Bolshevist coup having been delivered on Nov. 7 of that calendar. But these documents are not of Berlin, though they are typewritten on letterheads bearing that name in print, in the one case crossed out with the pen, in the other case not. Document No. 5 seems to have been written in Finland. We have been able to make out, in the photograph, the day-date in its heading. It is 25 October, i. e., Nov. 7 of New Style; and the Bolshevist acknowledgment at the bottom bears the date, not given in the newspaper publication, " 27.X.1917," i. e., Nov. 9 of New Style. In other words, more cannot be said than that the German General Staff, not unaware of preparations of which all the world was aware in Petrograd, was prompt in action. It is a slight but significant touch that Colonel Rausch, writing from Finland on the day when the expected outbreak occurred, styles the new organization " Government (Pravitelstvo) of People's Commissaries " instead of " Council (Soviet) of People's Commissaries," the designation actually adopted.

The Post's criticism (Sept. 16) of Document No. 2 on the ground of its mention of the " Petersburg Secret Police," (Okhrana,) assumed by the writer to have been destroyed on March 10 or 11, seems to us to have no conclusive weight. The old Okhrana was abolished by the revolution, but the revolutionary Government itself had of course its secert service, to which a German might continue to apply the old name.

A correspondent of The Post, Mr. E. J. Omeltchenko, in its issue of Oct. 4, rightly finds it singular that Dr. von Schanz, in Documents Nos. 8 and 9, should be represented as signing himself on Jan. 8, " Representative of the Imperial Bank," and on Jan. 12, " President of the Imperial Bank." It should be explained that the Russian word used is the same in both cases, *Predstavitel* but that the translator of No. 9 wrongly translated it " President," while the translator of No. 8 translated it rightly, " Representative."

Mr. Omeltchenko also, with reference to Document No. 8; prints figures of the gold reserves of the Reichsbank and of the Bank of Sweden, November, 1917, to January, 1918, in the belief that, if the Reichsbank had at the beginning of January given the Bolshevist officials a credit in Sweden of 50,000,000 rubles gold, these figures would show the fact. We are informed on high financial authority that the Reichsbank would be able to effect such a transaction by means much less easily traced. Mr. Omeltchenko questions the need of the transaction, but the insecurity and unsettled conditions prevailing within the boundaries of the old Russian Empire might easily account for the desire of the Bolsheviki to establish a large gold credit abroad without the necessity of actually exporting gold.

Professor Edward S. Corwin, in the same issue of The Evening Post, rightly criticises the date June 9, 1914, for Document No. 55. Its proper date appears to be Nov. 2, 1914. The mimeographed Russian text bears that date. A translator, probably by confusion with No. 56, gave it the June date.

Respectfully submitted,

J. FRANKLIN JAMESON.
SAMUEL N. HARPER.

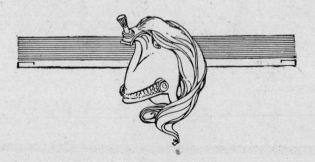

# INTERNATIONAL CARTOONS OF THE WAR

[American Cartoon]

## Nobody Home!

—From The Knickerbocker Press, Albany. (Sept., 1918.)

# A Bogus Note

—*From The New York Times.*

WILSON: "That signature is worthless—have the lady sign it."

# Preparing for the Chief Guest

—From *The Cincinnati Commercial Tribune.*

Some Essential Details Before the Table Is Really Set

# The Day of Judgment

—From The New York Herald.

# The End of an Era

—*From Paradise of the Pacific, Honolulu*

# Are They As Sorry As They Look?

—From The Passing Show, London.

# A Capture---American Style

—*From La Baionnette, Paris.*

# An Obstacle to Peace

—*From La Victoire, Paris.*

" Before I can raise my hands, alas! I must drop the swag."

## "Oh, Yes! The Kaiser Will Sit at the Peace Table!"

## The Tune Is All Right, but the Organist Will Not Do

—Atlanta Constitution.

—St. Joseph News-Press.

## Going—Going—Gone!

—From Cassell's Saturday Journal, London.

## " No Indemnities "

## Robbing the Cook

## " Hoch der Kaiser ! "

## On the Tail of the Lonesome Whine

*—From The San Francisco Chronicle.*

## After the Allied Tidal Wave

"The mill will never grind with the water that has passed."

## Where the River Jordan Flows

## It's the Only Way Out, Wilhelm!

## Peaceful (?) Evacuation of Belgium

—Central Press Association

## Too Late to Mend

## The Beast That Talks Like a Man

*I DEMAND AN HONORABLE PEACE—NO HUMILIATION ETC*

## Pleased to Meet Us!

## On His Last Legs

—From the Brooklyn Eagle

## [German Cartoons]

*—Simplicissimus, Munich (Sept., 1918)*

[This German lampoon, entitled "Wilson Goes to War," represents the President as saying: "We will fight to the last man."]

*—Simplicissimus, Munich (Oct., 1918)*

FRANCE AND ENGLAND: "Lord, may we make peace?"

WILSON: "Pay first!"

*—Lustige Blaetter, Berlin (Sept., 1918)*

"In the West day and night the path to Germany's future is being made by Ludendorff's hammer."

*—Der Ulk, Berlin (Sept., 1918)*

John Bull is represented as saying: "I hereby grant you the rights of free **and** independent nations."

[English Cartoon]

# The End of the Joy Ride

—*Passing Show, London.*

[Italian Cartoon]

# The German Sword

—*L'Asino, Rome.*

[English Cartoon]

# S. O. S.

—*London Opinion.*

[French Cartoon]

# Victory Singing

—*La Baionnette, Paris.*

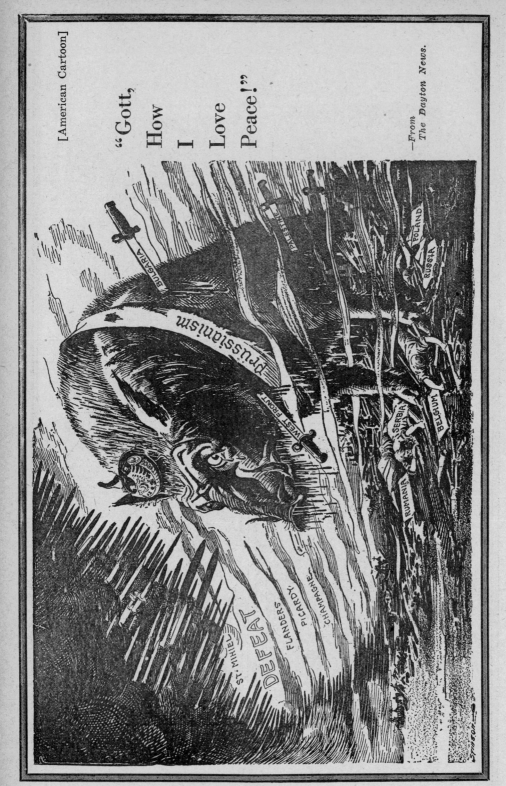

[American Cartoon]

"Gott,
How
I
Love
Peace!"

—From *The Dayton News.*

542

[Australian Cartoon]

## Reckoning-Time

—From The Sydney Bulletin.

## Shall We Celebrate ?

—*Esquella, Barcelona.*

## Insuring Peace

—*Il 420, Florence.*

KAISER: "Why are you pulling all my teeth?"

FOCH: "So that you shan't get the idea of a dinner in Paris again."

## After the Defeat

—*L'Asino, Rome.*

AUSTRIA TO GERMANY: "Don't worry; they'll decorate you, too."

## American Preparedness

—*Raemackers in London Telegraph.*

WILSON: "*You* want to sheathe the sword. I have only just begun to draw it."

## Camouflage

## "The Somme, You See, Was Papa's Verdun"

—*Montreal Daily Star.*

—*Pêle-Mêle, Paris.*

## "I Couldn't Put It Over, Gott"

## Well, Look Who's Here!

—*New York World.*

—*Dallas News.*

# Wilhelm: "See! Der Coat Makes Him a Man"

—Dayton News.

# A Dinner—Not in Paris

—New York Tribune.

Foch: "Will you carve it yourself, or shall I serve it for you?"

# The Dawn of an Idea

—Passing Show, London.

"If I didn't know petter, Fritz, I vouldt say dot der All Highest vos a verdammt liar!"

# Peace Negotiations—German Style

—New York Times.

Thief: "Hurry up! What do I get for it?"

# Final War Activities in United States

## Our Army Had Reached a Total of 3,764,677 Men, of Whom 2,200,000 Were Transported Overseas

ACTIVITIES bearing on the war continued with undiminished vigor in the United States until the signing of the armistice on Nov. 11. Following that date there was a marked slowing up in operations. Officials were cautious, because it was realized that, while hostilities had ceased, the war had not formally come to an end. Moreover, the derangement of business conditions by too sudden a cancellation of contracts had to be avoided. All further developments of war activities were governed by these considerations.

### ARMY OPERATIONS

A letter from Secretary of War Baker to President Wilson on Oct. 22 gave details regarding the number of troops transported to France. The Secretary wrote in part:

> In my letter of July 1, 1918, I informed you that between May 8, 1917, and June 30, 1918, over a million men had either been landed in France or were en route thereto. Since July 1, 1918, embarkations by months have been as follows:
>
> July ............................. 306,185
> August ........................... 290,818
> September ........................ 261,415
> October 1 to 21................... 131,398
>
> Total ........................ 989,816
> Embarked to July 1, 1918........1,019,115
>
> Grand total..................2,008,931
>
> In our overseas operations I feel that we have good reason to be proud and thankful of the results obtained. Our losses have been exceedingly small, considering the size of the force transported, and this is due to the efficient protection given American convoys by the naval forces. We also have been greatly assisted in the dispatch of troops abroad by the allocation of certain vessels from our allies, principally those of Great Britain.

The War Department announced on Nov. 11 that the American Army had reached a total strength of 3,764,677 men; of that number 2,200,000 had been sent to France, Italy, or Russia. The remainder were under arms in camps in this country.

### COST OF EACH SOLDIER

The cost of maintaining each individual of this vast force at home and abroad is thus given in a statement issued by the War Department:

> Under direction of Brig. Gen. R. E. Wood, Acting Quartermaster General of the Army, statistics have been gathered from the clothing and equipage, subsistence, conservation, reclamation, and hardware and metals divisions of the Quartermaster Corps to indicate just what it costs a year to maintain a soldier overseas and in the United States. These statistics show that the cost is $423.47 a year to equip and maintain a soldier overseas and $327.78 to equip and maintain one in the United States.
>
> Subsistence, figured at 69 cents per day, amounts to $251.85 per man overseas; figured at 52 cents per day in the United States, it amounts to $189.80 per man.
>
> The cost of the initial equipment for the soldier the first year in the United States is $115.30. The cost of the initial equipment of the soldier overseas for the first year is $42.41. This cost of $42.41 is for articles which are issued for overseas use only, and which are in addition to the regular equipment.

An idea of the immensity of supplies required by one branch of our forces overseas, for which continued financing was necessary, was shown by the following table of materials shipped from this country up to Aug. 31, 1918, by the Corps of Engineers:

| | |
|---|---|
| Rails and accessories, standard-gauge track, tons.............. | 213,000 |
| Rails and accessories, narrow-gauge track, tons.............. | 64,000 |
| Structural steel, tons............ | 45,000 |
| Corrugated iron, tons............ | 7,000 |
| Barbed wire, tons................ | 16,000 |
| Lumber, including ties, stringers, and piles, (balance purchased in Europe,) tons............... | 16,000 |
| Building materials: | |
| Wall board, tons.............. | 2,000 |
| Expanded metal, tons.......... | 5,000 |
| Nails, tons..................... | 10,000 |
| Camouflage materials: | |
| Wire netting, square yards.... | 2,000,000 |

| | |
|---|---|
| Paint, tons..................... | 1,200 |
| Burlap, square yards......... | 3,000,000 |
| Fish netting, square yards.... | 1,300,000 |
| Steel warehouse sheds (covering 2,000,000 square feet)......... | 100 |

Pontoon equipment.—Pontoon equipment for three divisions has been shipped overseas and the equipment for thirty-six additional divisions is now being freighted.

It was officially announced on Oct. 18 that the Balloon Corps of the army was to be increased by 25,000 men and 1,200 officers. Before that date it numbered approximately 11,000 men.

The largest order ever given by the Government for army vehicles was announced on Oct. 22. Contracts were placed for motor trucks, ambulances, tractors, trailers, motor cycles and bicycles, calling for an expenditure of approximately $130,000,000.

A tabulation of American Army casualties at the time the armistice was signed showed a total of slightly over 70,000, but the figures for the heaviest losses of the war were still to come. The War Department's report on Nov. 24 showed a total of 236,117 army and marine casualties; the total deaths, as announced on the same date, were 53,169.

## STEPS TOWARD MOBILIZATION

Almost simultaneously with the signing of the armistice Secretary Baker sent out a cancellation of all army draft calls, under which more than 300,000 men had been ordered to entrain for camps before Nov. 30. Delinquents under the draft still remained liable to punishment. It was stated also that classification was to continue, except for registrants between the ages of 36 and 45.

The War Department announced on Nov. 15 that the development battalions would be the first to be demobilized. These embraced about 50,000 men, who for physical or other reasons were found unsuited for active military service when they were called up in the draft.

On Nov. 16, General March, Chief of Staff, announced that 200,000 soldiers in camp in the United States were to be mustered out within the next two weeks. The arrangement provided that the rate of discharge was to be 30,000 a day thereafter.

## CANCELLATION OF CONTRACTS

In a letter from Secretary Baker to Senator Martin on Nov. 21 the Secretary said:

The armistice was signed on the 11th of November. Up to and including today the War Department has canceled contracts in process of execution effecting a total saving of $438,900,818.

On contracts which have been let, but upon which no work had as yet been done, cancellations aggregate a saving of $700,-000,000.

An order was made on the 11th of November cutting out all overtime and Sunday work. The amount saved by this order aggregates about $2,900,000 a day.

The foregoing amounts are exclusive of cancellations in aircraft production or in engineers.

In the Bureau of Aircraft Production orders have been telegraphed out stopping all production on a large number of items, including planes of various types, engines, parts, and special instruments, which aggregate, in the estimated saving, $225,000,000.

In addition to the foregoing, plans have been made to begin the demobilization of the forces under arms in this country and to begin returning at once to the United States such portions of the armed forces abroad as are not needed for the purpose of occupying enemy territory.

## THE WIRELESS TELEPHONE

John D. Ryan, Director of Aircraft Production, on Nov. 15 made public what had hitherto been an army secret—the perfection of a system of wireless telephony by which messages could be received by aviators while in flight and miles away from the sender. It had been in use in France among American fliers since February, 1918, and had proved of incalculable value in air fighting.

The transmitting set consisted of a power plant, a set box, a transmitter or microphone, and an antenna system. The power plant consisted of a generator driven on the windmill principle by the passage of the airplane through the air. It was placed somewhere in the open, usually on the running gear or on one of the wings, and its tiny propeller blade whirled vigorously as the airplane traveled along.

The so-called set box received the power from the generator, converted it and placed it on the aerials in the form of sustained or undamped waves. The voice entering the transmitter varied the electric current on the wires, which were connected as in the ordinary telephone.

The receiving set consisted of a receiving set box, a head receiver, a source of power and an antenna system. The latter was the same as the antenna system in the transmitting set. The source of power was a small storage battery. The head receiver was built into the aviator's helmet in such a manner as to exclude sounds from the motor reaching the pilot's ear and interfering with his hearing. With this apparatus it is possible for any number of aviators to hear plainly the voice of a commander giving orders five or six miles away on the ground below.

## REMOVAL OF "STATIC"

A great step forward in wireless telegraphy was announced Nov. 19 by the Marconi Wireless Telegraph Company of America. Roy A. Weagant, chief engineer of the company, it was stated, had perfected an invention which removes the "static," which had hitherto been the chief obstacle to the transmission of radio messages. An official statement by the Marconi Company read:

Ever since the genius of Marconi made wireless telegraphy a fact, the only limitation of this method of communication was the deadly phenomena of "static conditions." It was "static"—the presence of a large amount of uncontrolled electricity in the air—that at the beginning of the war often entirely prostrated the wireless service even between the most powerful stations erected in Europe and America. Static conditions were responsible for abnormal delays and for the mutilation of words in wireless messages.

It remained for an American radio expert, Roy A. Weagant, chief engineer of the Marconi Wireless Telegraph Company of America, to discover the solution of the static problem. Weagant practically had devoted his life to a study of this perplexing phenomenon, and the result of fifteen years of experimental work was about to be published to the world when the United States entered the war. Although patent applications had been made and the claims allowed by the United States Patent Office, the Weagant system was immediately placed at the disposal of the American Government, and every precaution was taken to keep the invention secret until the discovery could be safely announced. With the spirit of research that has made the navy such a magnificent arm of our military service, officials of the Navy Department assigned naval experts to co-operate with the inventor in installing experimental stations in various parts of the country. These stations are now receiving messages from all the high power wireless stations of the world.

## FOURTH LIBERTY LOAN

The Fourth Liberty Loan, the campaign for which began Sept. 28 and ended Oct. 19, was oversubscribed by nearly a billion dollars.

The approximate final figures for the loan were $6,989,047,000, which was $989,047,000, or 16.48 per cent., more than was called for. This oversubscription the Government accepted, making the total amount put into Government war loans by the people, including War Savings Stamps, $17,852,000,000. Items included in this total were: First Loan, $2,000,000,000; Second Loan, $3,808,000,000; Third Loan, $4,176,000,000, and War Savings, $879,000,000.

In the Fourth Loan every district oversubscribed. The place of honor was held by Boston, which went beyond its quota 26.44 per cent. Richmond was a close second with 25.95 per cent.

The Fourth Loan was by far the largest floated by any country during the war, and therefore the greatest in history. The nearest to it was one by Great Britain, which was between four and five billions.

Following were the approximate final figures on subscriptions to the Fourth Liberty Loan issued by the Treasury Department:

| District. | Quota. | Subscribed. | P. C. |
|---|---|---|---|
| Boston ... | $500,000,000 | $632,221,850 | 126.44 |
| Rich. ..... | 280,000,000 | 352,688,200 | 125.95 |
| Phila. .... | 500,000,000 | 598,763,650 | 119.75 |
| Cleve. .... | 600,000,000 | 702,059,800 | 117.00 |
| Dallas ... | 126,000,000 | 145,914,450 | 115.82 |
| M'n'plis .. | 210,000,000 | 241,628,300 | 115.06 |
| San Fran. | 402,000,000 | 459,000,000 | 114.17 |
| St. Louis.. | 260,000,000 | 296,388,550 | 113.99 |
| N. Y. .... | 1,800,000,000 | 2,044,778,600 | 113.59 |
| Atlanta .. | 192,000,000 | 217,885,200 | 113.48 |
| K. City .. | 260,000,000 | 294,640,450 | 113.32 |
| Chicago .. | 870,000,000 | 969,209,000 | 111.40 |

| | | |
|---|---|---|
| Total ..$6,000,000,000 | $6,954,875,200 | |
| U. S. Treas. | 33,829,850 | |
| | | |
| Total ... | $6,989,047,000 | 116.48 |

## ABOLITION OF CENSORSHIP

A tangible evidence of the ending of hostilities was the removal of censorship restrictions on all forms of communication except wireless, which still remained under the control of the navy authorities.

Censorship of telephone, telegraph, and cable lines and of the mails had been exercised during the war by a special board consisting of the Secretaries of War and the Navy, the chiefs of the Military Intelligence Bureau and the Bureau of Naval Intelligence, and George Creel, Chairman of the Committee on Public Information. To the navy was left supervision of cable terminals in this country, naval censors passing upon all outgoing messages. Matter coming in passed first over the desks of British or French censors. The abolition of the censorship restrictions occurred on Nov. 15.

## COST OF THE WAR

Some illumination was thrown on the matter of war expenses by an official statement issued at Washington on Sept. 5, which showed that the Government's expenses in August were $40,446 per minute, reaching the enormous total of $1,805,513,000 for the month and exceeding by more than $200,000,000 the highest previous monthly record of expense since the war began.

The total war cost to Sept. 5 was calculated at $20,561,000,000, of which $7,017,000,000 had been loaned to the Allies. Only a little more than one-fourth of the expense had been raised from taxation, and slightly less than three-fourths from Liberty Loans and War Stamps.

## THE FOOD SITUATION

Herbert D. Hoover was appointed by President Wilson, Nov. 9, as special representative of the United States in Europe for the determination of measures of relief for European populations, in co-operation with the various Governments concerned. Mr. Hoover still retained the title of United States Food Administrator and the work in this country was to be conducted by an exec-

utive board, with which Mr. Hoover would keep in close touch.

Mr. Hoover outlined the world's need of food in an address delivered at a conference in Washington of State Food Administrators. He said in part:

We have now to consider a new world situation in food. We have to frankly survey Europe, a Europe of which a large part is either in ruins or in social conflagration; a Europe with degenerated soils and depleted herds; a Europe with the whole of its population on rations or varying degrees of starvation, and large numbers who have been under the German heel actually starving.

The group of gamblers in human life who have done this thing are now in cowardly flight, leaving anarchy and famine to millions of helpless people.

The war has been brought to an end in no small measure by starvation itself, and it cannot be our business to maintain starvation after peace.

We must consider carefully how this situation reacts upon our people. We must consider our national duty in the matter, and we must make such changes in our policies as are fitting to the new situation. The matter of prime importance to us is how much of each commodity the exporting countries can furnish between now and next harvest and how much is necessary to the importing countries in which we have a vital interest, in order to maintain health and public order in the world.

A computation on this basis showed this situation until the next harvest: A shortage of about 3,000,000,000 pounds in pork and dairy products and vegetable oils, and of dairy feeds of about 3,000,000 tons. Of beef, there were sufficient supplies to load all refrigerating ships' capacity, and there would be enough of other foodstuffs, provided the utmost economy were practiced by the American public. North America was expected to furnish 60 per cent. of the world's supply of foodstuffs, and the United States and the West Indies would export 20,000,000 tons, as against a pre-war normal of 6,000,000 tons.

## SEIZURE OF OCEAN CABLES

On Nov. 19 the President issued a proclamation taking over the control of the ocean cable lines under the act of July 16, 1918. The proclamation ended with these paragraphs:

It is hereby directed that the supervision, possession, control, and operation of such marine cable systems hereby by me undertaken shall be exercised by and through the Postmaster General, Albert S. Burleson. Said Postmaster General may perform the duties hereby and hereunder imposed upon him, so long and to such extent and in such manner as he shall determine, through the owners, managers, Boards of Directors, receivers, officers, and employes of said marine cable systems.

From and after 12 o'clock midnight on the 2d day of November, 1918, all marine cable systems included in this order and proclamation shall conclusively be deemed within the possession and control and under the supervision of said Postmaster General without further act or notice.

## THE AIRCRAFT INQUIRY

On Oct. 3 ex-Justice Hughes rendered his report on the various activities connected with the manufacture of airplanes. He recommended the trial by court-martial of Colonel Edward A. Deeds and, in the criminal courts, of Lieut. Col. J. G. Vincent, Lieut. Col. W. G. Mixter, and Second Lieut. S. B. Vrooman, Jr.

It was set forth that the actual loss from condemned types of planes and engines would amount to perhaps $20,500,000, while disbursements in the United States up to June 30 last amounted to $106,741,490 and since June 30 to $139,186,661.

Training planes to the number of 7,324 had been produced, 1,706 of them since June 30; 2,457 service planes, 1,928 since June 30; 14,735 engines for training planes, 4,494 since June 30; 9,937 engines for service planes, 7,545 since June 30. Still later figures for De Haviland 4's increased the number delivered to 2,556 and for Liberty motors to 10,568.

The Liberty motor was declared to be a "great success for observation and bombing planes, and for this purpose had found high favor among the Allies."

Of the production program as a whole, it was said that "we have not as yet sent from this country to the battlefront a single pursuit or combat plane, as distinguished from the heavy observation or bombing planes, and, after giving due weight to all explanations, the fact remains that such pursuit planes could

have been produced in large quantities many months ago had there been prompt decision and consistent purpose."

All civilian officials of the Aircraft Board and all naval officers attached to it were freed from blame for the situation. Major Gen. George O. Squier was called "incompetent," but no worse.

## THE INFLUENZA EPIDEMIC

The scourge of Spanish influenza that had swept the country finally abated, though not until it had claimed a heavy toll of victims. Complete statistics were not at hand, but a Census Bulletin stated that in forty-six cities the total fatalities due to the disease were 82,306. This was considerably more than double the number of American soldiers who were killed in battle or died of wounds.

## THANKSGIVING PROCLAMATION

The rejoicing felt by the nation at the victorious termination of hostilities was mirrored in the Thanksgiving proclamation issued by the President Nov. 17. The proclamation, which set Nov. 28 as the date, in part follows:

It has long been our custom to turn in the Autumn of the year in praise and thanksgiving to Almighty God for His many blessings and mercies to us as a nation. This year we have special and moving cause to be grateful and to rejoice. God has in His good pleasure given us peace. It has not come as a mere cessation of arms, a relief from the strain and tragedy of war. It has come as a great triumph of Right. Complete victory has brought us, not peace alone, but the confident promise of a new day as well, in which justice shall replace force and jealous intrigue among the nations. Our gallant armies have participated in a triumph which is not marred or stained by any purpose of selfish aggression. In a righteous cause they have won immortal glory and have nobly served their nation in serving mankind. God has indeed been gracious. We have cause for such rejoicing as revives and strengthens in us all the best traditions of our national history. A new day shines about us, in which our hearts take new courage and look forward with new hope to new and greater duties.

While we render thanks for these things, let us not forget to seek the

Divine guidance in the performance of those duties, and Divine mercy and forgiveness for all errors of act or purpose, and pray that in all that we do we shall strengthen the ties of friendship and mutual respect upon which we must assist to build the new structure of peace and good-will among the nations.

## OUR OPERATIONS IN FRANCE

On the morning of Nov. 11 the United States had in France 78,391 officers and 1,881,376 men, a total of almost 2,000,000, and there were 750,000 combat troops in the Argonne sector, not including units cn other parts of the front.

Since war was declared, 967 standard gauge American locomotives and 13,174 standard gauge freight cars had been shipped over and operated, along with the operation of 350 locomotives and 973 cars of foreign origin. Engineers constructed 843 miles of standard gauge railroad, 500 miles being built between June 1 and Nov. 11, 1918.

Where railroads were unnecessary the engineers constructed miles of roadway for the operation of 53,000 motor vehicles of all descriptions.

In the construction and improvement of dockage and warehouses, the work was proportionate, the warehouses alone having an aggregate floor area of almost 23,000,000 square feet. Dredging operations were expanded and dock facilities greatly increased.

Figures gathered by The Associated Press showed also that the American Army was in no danger of food shortage, as it had on hand in France Nov. 11 390,-000,000 rations of beans, 183,000,000 rations of flour and substitutes, 267,000,-000 of milk, 161,000,000 of butter and substitutes, 143,000,000 of sugar, 89,000,-000 of meat, 57,000,000 of coffee, and 113,000,000 of rice, hominy and other foods, with flavorings, fruits, candy and potatoes in proportion. For smokers there were 761,000,000 rations of cigarettes and tobacco in other forms.

## DEMOBILIZING THE FORCES

The demobolization of the American forces in Europe began Nov. 21. A transport loaded with sick, wounded, and discharged troops left Liverpool Nov. 23. At the same time it was announced that eight divisions of National Guard and National Army troops, eight regiments of coast artillery and two brigades of field artillery would be returned immediately to the United States. The troops first to be returned were the following:

National Guard—Thirty-first, (Georgia, Alabama, and Florida;) 34th, (Nebraska, Iowa, South Dakota, and Minnesota;) 38th, (Indiana, Kentucky, and West Virginia,) and 39th, (Arkansas, Mississippi, and Louisiana.)

National Army—Seventy-sixth, (New England;) 84th, (Kentucky, Indiana, and Southern Illinois;) 86th, Northern Illinois, including Chicago,) and 87th, (Arkansas, Louisiana, Mississippi, and Southern Alabama.)

The coast artillery regiments to be returned as soon as possible were announced as the 46th, 47th, 48th, 49th, 50th, 73d, 74th, and 75th. The two field artillery brigades to be brought home are the 65th and 163d. Eighty-two aero squadrons, seventeen construction companies, and several special units will be brought home from England as soon as transportation facilities are available, General March said.

It was announced that an army of 1,200,000 would remain in Europe for some time.

It was also announced Nov. 23 that the total number of Germans taken prisoner by the Americans was 44,000; the number of American prisoners taken by the Germans was slightly in excess of 2,100.

# The American, British, and German Losses in the War

GENERAL PERSHING informed the War Department on Nov. 23 that the total casualties in the American Expeditionary . Forces had aggregated 236,117. This was three times the number estimated at the time the armistice was signed. It was explained that the discrepancy between the actual figures and the estimates based on reports up to Nov. 15, 1918, was due to the difficulty in sending by cable the full lists of casualties; moreover, it was explained that the losses by the Americans in the last four weeks of the war were much heavier than during any preceding period.

The total casualties as reported on Nov. 23 by General Pershing were as follows:

Killed or died of wounds............ 36,154
Died of disease ..................... 14,811
Deaths unclassified ................. 2,204
Wounded ...........................179,625
Prisoners ........................... 1,163
Missing ............................ 1,160
———————
Total ..............................236,117

## BRITISH AND GERMAN LOSSES

The detailed figures of the British War Office, issued late in November, 1918, giving the casualties in all the areas in which the British Armies fought, show that of the total casualties 21.6 per cent. were killed, 66.6 per cent. wounded, and 11.8 per cent. listed among the missing, including prisoners. The German proportions are practically identical for the missing and prisoners, being 11.9 per cent. The German percentage for killed, however, which is 24.9, is higher, and the percentage for wounded, which is 63.2, is lower than those reported by the British. These differences were explained by the fact that the figures for wounded as given by the Germans include only the number of men wounded, exclusive of second and third wounds suffered by the same men, whereas these additional wounds are included in the British fig-

ures as accepted casualties, thereby swelling the number of wounded.

The percentages of killed, wounded, and missing or prisoners, based on British and German official reports, are shown in the following tables:

## BRITISH CASUALTIES

### OFFICERS

| | Killed. | Wounded. | Missing. | Total. |
|---|---|---|---|---|
| France .... | 32,769 | 83,142 | 10,846 | 126,757 |
| Dardanelles | 1,785 | 3,010 | 258 | 5,053 |
| Mesopotamia | 1,340 | 2,429 | 566 | 4,335 |
| Egypt ..... | 1,098 | 2,311 | 183 | 3,592 |
| Saloniki ... | 285 | 818 | 114 | 1,217 |
| East Africa | 380 | 478 | 38 | 896 |
| Italy ...... | 86 | 334 | 38 | 458 |
| Other thea. | 133 | 142 | 51 | 326 |
| | | | | |
| Total .... | 37,876 | 92,664 | 12,094 | 142,634 |

### MEN

| | Killed. | Wounded. | Missing. | Total. |
|---|---|---|---|---|
| France .... | 526,843 | 1,750,203 | 315,849 | 2,592,895 |
| Dardanelles | 31,737 | 75,508 | 7,431 | 114,676 |
| Mesopotamia | 29,769 | 48,686 | 14,789 | 93,244 |
| Egypt ..... | 14,794 | 35,762 | 3,705 | 54,261 |
| Saloniki ... | 7,330 | 16,058 | 2,713 | 26,101 |
| East Africa | 8,724 | 7,276 | 929 | 16,929 |
| Italy ...... | 941 | 4,612 | 727 | 6,280 |
| Other thea. | 690 | 1,373 | 908 | 2,971 |
| | | | | |
| Total .... | 620,828 | 1,939,478 | 347,051 | 2,907,357 |

### TOTAL OFFICERS AND MEN

| | Killed. | Wounded. | Missing. | Total. |
|---|---|---|---|---|
| France .... | 559,612 | 1,833,345 | 326,695 | 2,719,652 |
| Dardanelles | 33,522 | 78,518 | 7,689 | 119,729 |
| Mesopotamia | 31,109 | 51,115 | 15,355 | 97,579 |
| Egypt ..... | 15,892 | 38,073 | 3,888 | 57,853 |
| Saloniki ... | 7,615 | 16,876 | 2,827 | 27,318 |
| East Africa | 9,104 | 7,754 | 967 | 17,825 |
| Italy ...... | 1,027 | 4,946 | 765 | 6,738 |
| Other thea. | 823 | 1,515 | 959 | 3,297 |
| | | | | |
| Total .... | 658,704 | 2,032,142 | 359,145 | 3,049,991 |

## GERMAN CASUALTIES

[As reported by a German socialist newspaper, Vorwärts, on Nov. 15, 1918]

| | Killed. | Wounded. | Missing. | Total. |
|---|---|---|---|---|
| All fronts.. | 1,580,000 | 4,000,000 | 650,000 | 6,330,000 |

No official figures were available Nov. 22, 1918, upon which to compute the approximate losses of the other belligerent nations in the war.

# Austria's Ultimatum to Serbia

## Full Text of the Document That Started the World War, and Serbia's Reply to It

A T 6 o'clock in the evening of July 23, 1914, the Austro-Hungarian Minister at Belgrade presented to the Serbian Government a note containing the demands of the Dual Monarchy with regard to the suppression of the Pan-Serbian movement and the punishment of Serbians alleged to have been concerned in the murder of the Archduke Franz Ferdinand, who had been shot on June 28 by an Austro-Hungarian subject. The document which sought to make Serbia a vassal of Austria-Hungary and which, with Germany's backing, started the greatest war in the history of the world, is here presented in full:

On March 31, 1909, the Royal Serbian Minister in Vienna, on the instructions of the Serbian Government, made the following statements to the Imperial and Royal Government:

" Serbia recognizes that the fait accompli regarding Bosnia has not affected her rights, and consequently she will conform to the decisions that the powers will take in conformity with Article XXV. of the Treaty of Berlin. At the same time that Serbia submits to the advice of the powers she undertakes to renounce the attitude of protest and opposition which she has adopted since October last. She undertakes, on the other hand, to modify the direction of her policy with regard to Austria-Hungary and to live in future on good neighborly terms with the latter."

The history of recent years, and in particular the painful events of June 28 last, have shown the existence in Serbia of a subversive movement with the object of detaching a part of Austria-Hungary from the monarchy. The movement, which had its birth under the eyes of the Serbian Government, has had consequences on both sides of the Serbian frontier in the shape of acts of terrorism and a series of outrages and murders.

Far from carrying out the formal undertakings contained in the declaration of March 31, 1909, the Royal Serbian Government has done nothing to repress these movements. It has permitted the criminal machinations of various societies and associations, and has tolerated unrestrained language on the part of the press, apologies for the perpetrators of outrages, and the participation of officers and functionaries in subversive agitation. It has permitted an unwholesome propaganda in public instruction. In short, it has permitted all the manifestations which have incited the Serbian population to hatred of the monarchy and contempt of its institutions.

This culpable tolerance of the Royal Serbian Government had not ceased at the moment when the events of June 28 last proved its fatal consequences to the whole world.

It results from the depositions and confessions of the criminal perpetrators of the outrage of June 28 that the Serajevo assassinations were hatched in Belgrade, that the arms and explosives with which the murderers were provided had been given to them by Serbian officers and functionaries belonging to the Narodna Obrana, and, finally, that the passage into Bosnia of the criminals and their arms was organized and effected by the chiefs of the Serbian frontier service.

The above-mentioned results of the magisterial investigation do not permit the Austro-Hungarian Government to pursue any longer the attitude of expectant forbearance which it has maintained for years in face of the machinations hatched in Belgrade and thence propagated in the territories of the monarchy. These results, on the contrary, impose on it the duty of putting an end to intrigues which form a perpetual menace to the tranquillity of the monarchy.

To achieve this end, the Imperial and Royal Government sees itself compelled to demand from the Serbian Government a formal assurance that it condemns this dangerous propaganda against the monarchy and the territories belonging to it, and that the Royal Serbian Government shall no longer permit these machinations and this criminal and preverse propaganda.

In order to give a formal character to this undertaking the Royal Serbian Government shall publish on the front page of its official journal for July 26 the following declaration:

" The Royal Government of Serbia condemns the propaganda directed against Austria-Hungary, i. e., the ensemble of tendencies of which the final aim is to detach from the Austro-Hungarian Monarchy territories belonging to it, and it sincerely deplores the fatal consequences of these criminal proceedings.

" The Royal Government regrets that Serbian officers and functionaries participated in the above-mentioned propaganda and thus compromised the good, neighborly relations to which the Royal Government was solemnly pledged by its declaration of March 31, 1909. The Royal Government, which disapproves and repudiates all idea of interfering or attempt to ' iterfere with the destinies of the inhabitants of any part whatsoever of Austria-Hungary, considers it its duty formally to warn officers and functionaries, and the whole population of the kingdom, that henceforth it will proceed with the utmost rigor against persons who may be guilty of such machinations, which it will use all its efforts to anticipate and suppress."

This declaration shall simultaneously be communicated to the royal army as an order of the day by his Majesty the King, and shall be published in the official bulletin of the army.

The Royal Serbian Government further undertakes:

1. To suppress any publications which incite to hatred and contempt of the Austro-Hungarian Monarchy and the general tendency of which is directed against its territorial integrity.

2. To dissolve immediately the society styled Narodna Obrana, to confiscate all its means of propaganda, and to proceed in the same manner against other societies and their branches in Serbia which are addicted to propaganda against the Austro-Hungarian Monarchy. The Royal Government shall take the necessary measures to prevent the societies dissolved from continuing their activity under another name and form.

3. To eliminate without delay from public instruction in Serbia, not only as regards the teaching body, but also as regards the methods of instruction, everything that serves or might serve to foment the propaganda against Austria-Hungary.

4. To remove from the military service and from the Administration in general all officers and functionaries guilty of propaganda against the Austro-Hungarian Monarchy, whose names and deeds the Austro-Hungarian Government reserves to itself the right of communicating to the Royal Government.

5. To accept the collaboration in Serbia of representatives of the Austro-Hungarian Government in the suppression of the subversive movement directed against the territorial integrity of the monarchy.

6. To take judicial proceedings against accessories to the plot of June 28 who are on Serbian territory. Delegates of the Austro-Hungarian Government will take part in the investigation relating thereto.

7. To proceed without delay to the arrest of Major Voija Tankositch and of the individual named Milan Ciganovitch, a Serbian State employe, who have been compromised by the results of the magisterial inquiry at Serajevo.

8. To prevent by effective measures the co-operation of the Serbian authorities in the illicit traffic in arms and explosives across the frontier, to dismiss and punish severely officials of the frontier service at Achabatz and Loznica guilty of having assisted the perpetrators of the Serajevo crime by facilitating the passage of the frontier for them.

9. To furnish the Austro-Hungarian Government with explanations regarding the unjustifiable utterances of high Serbian officials, both in Serbia and abroad, who, notwithstanding their official position, did not hesitate after the crime of June 28 to express themselves in interviews in terms of hostility to the Austro-Hungarian Government; and finally:

10. To notify the Austro-Hungarian Government without delay of the execution of the measures comprised under the preceding heads.

The Austro-Hungarian Government expects the reply of the Serbian Government at the latest by 6 o'clock on Saturday evening, the 25th of July.

## Austria-Hungary's Circular Note

Following the dispatch of the foregoing ultimatum to Serbia the Austro-Hungarian Government on July 24, 1914, sent a circular note to its embassies in Germany, France, England, Italy, Russia, and Turkey, explaining its action in the following terms:

The Imperial and Royal Government has felt itself compelled to forward on Thursday, the 23d inst., to the Royal Serbian Government, through its Imperial and Royal Minister in Belgrade, the following note:

(Here follows the Austro-Hungarian note to Serbia.)

I have the honor to request your Excellency to bring the contents of this note before the Government to which you are accredited, and to accompany this with the following explanations: On the 31st March, 1909, the Royal Serbian Government addressed a statement to Austria-Hungary, the text of which is repeated above. Almost on the following day Serbia's policy took a direction tending to rouse ideas subversive to the Austro-Hungarian Monarchy in the minds of the Serbian subjects, and thereby to prepare for the detachment of those districts of Austria-Hungary which adjoin the Serbian frontier.

A large number of agents are employed in furthering by all possible means the agitation against Austria-Hungary to corrupt the youth of those territories of Austria-Hungary bordering on Serbia. The spirit of conspiracy which animates Serbian political circles and which has left its bloody traces in the history of Serbia has grown since the last Balkan crisis. Members of bands who up to that time had found occupation in Macedonia have since placed themselves at the disposal of the terrorist propaganda against Austria-Hungary. The Serbian Government has never considered itself obliged to take steps of any kind against the intrigues to which Austria-Hungary has been exposed for years.

The patience which the Imperial and Royal Government has observed toward the provocative attitude of Serbia is to be attributed to the fact that she knew herself to be free from all territorial interests and to the hope which she did not abandon that the Serbian Government would eventually prize at its worth the friendship of Austria-Hungary. The Imperial and Royal Government thought that a benevolent attitude toward the political interests of Serbia would eventually call for a similar attitude from that kingdom.

Austria-Hungary expected an evolution of this nature in the political ideas of Serbia, more especially at the time following the events of the year 1912, when the Imperial and Royal Government, by its disinterested attitude, from any suggestion of ill-will, made possible the important extension of Serbia.

The sympathy which Austria-Hungary demonstrated in its neighbor nevertheless made no change in the conduct of that kingdom, which continued to permit on its territory a propaganda, the lamentable consequences of which were made evident to the whole world on June 28 this year, when the heir apparent of the Dual Monarchy and his illustrious consort fell the victims to a plot hatched in Belgrade.

In view of this state of affairs the Imperial and Royal Government found itself compelled to take a fresh and energetic step in Belgrade, of such a nature as to induce the Serbian Government to put an end to a movement which threatened the security and integrity of Austria-Hungary. The Imperial and Royal Government is convinced that in taking this step it is acting in complete harmony with the feelings of all civilized nations, which cannot agree that royal assassinations can be made a weapon to be used unpunished in political struggles, and that the peace of Europe may be incessantly disturbed by intrigues which emanate from Belgrade.

In support of these statements, the Imperial and Royal Government holds at the disposal of the Government to which you are accredited a dossier dealing with the Serbian propaganda, and showing the connection of this propaganda with the assassination of June 28.

# Serbia's Reply to the Ultimatum

Serbia's answer to the Austro-Hungarian note was sent on July 25, 1914. It conceded all the demands except two, which infringed upon its rights as a sovereign State, and these two it offered to submit to arbitration. The text of Serbia's reply follows:

The Royal Serbian Government has received the communication of the Imperial and Royal Austro-Hungarian Government of the 10th of this month and it is persuaded that its reply will remove all misunderstanding tending to threaten or to prejudice the friendly and neighborly relations between the Austro-Hungarian Monarchy and the Kingdom of Serbia.

The Royal Government is aware that the protests made both at the tribune of the National Skupshtina and in the declarations and the acts of responsible representatives of the State—protests which were cut short by the declaration of the Serbian Government made on March 18—have not been renewed toward the great neighboring monarchy on any occasion, and that since this time, both on the part of the Royal Governments which have followed on one another, and on the part of their organs,

no attempt has been made with the purpose of changing the political and judicial state of things in this respect.

The Imperial and Royal Government has made no representations save concerning a scholastic book regarding which the Imperial and Royal Government has received an entirely satisfactory explanation. Serbia has repeatedly given proofs of her pacific and moderate policy during the Balkan crises, and it is thanks to Serbia and the sacrifice she made exclusively in the interest of the peace of Europe that this peace has been preserved. The Royal Government cannot be held responsible for manifestations of a private nature, such as newspaper articles and the peaceful work of societies—manifestations which occur in almost all countries as a matter of course, and which, as a general rule, escape official control—all the less in that the Royal Government, when solving a whole series of questions which came up between Serbia and Austria-Hungary, has displayed a great readiness to treat, (prevenance,) and in this way succeeded in settling the greater number to the advantage of the progress of the two neighboring countries.

It is for this reason that the Royal Government has been painfully surprised by the statements, according to which persons of the Kingdom of Serbia are said to have taken part in the preparation of the outrage committed at Serajevo. It expected that it would be invited to collaborate in the investigation of everything bearing on this crime, and it was ready to prove by its actions its entire correctness to take steps against all persons with regard to whom communications had been made to it, thus acquiescing in the desire of the Imperial and Royal Government.

The Royal Government is disposed to hand over to the courts any Serbian subject, without regard to his situation and rank, for whose complicity in the crime of Serajevo it shall have been furnished with proofs, and especially it engages itself to have published on the front page of the Official Journal of July 13-26 the following announcement:

"The Royal Serbian Government condemns all propaganda directed against Austria-Hungary, that is to say, all tendencies as a whole of which the ultimate object is to detach from the Austro-Hungarian Monarchy territories which form part of it, and it sincerely deplores the fatal consequence of these criminal actions. The Royal Government regrets that Serbian officers and officials should, according to the communication of the Imperial and Royal Government, have participated in the above-mentioned propaganda, thereby compromising the good neighborly relations to which the Royal Government solemnly pledged itself by its declaration of the 31st of March, 1909. The Government, which disapproves and repudiates any idea or attempt to interfere in the destinies of the inhabitants of any part of Austria-Hungary whatsoever, considers it its duty to utter a formal warning to the officers, the officials, and the whole population of the kingdom that henceforth it will proceed with the utmost rigor against persons who render themselves guilty of such actions, which it will use all its efforts to prevent and repress."

This announcement shall be brought to the cognizance of the royal army by an order of the day issued in the name of his Majesty the King by H. R. H. the Crown Prince Alexander, and shall be published in the next official bulletin of the army.

1. The Royal Government engages itself, furthermore, to lay before the next regular meeting of the Skupshtina an amendment to the press law, punishing in the severest manner incitements to hate and contempt of the Austro-Hungarian Monarchy, and also all publications of which the general tendency is directed against the territorial integrity of the monarchy. It undertakes at the forthcoming revision of the Constitution to introduce in Article XXII. of the Constitution an amendment whereby the above publications may be confiscated, which is at present categorically forbidden by the terms of Article XXII. of the Constitution.

2. The Government does not possess any proof, nor does the note of the Imperial and Royal Government furnish such, that the society Narodna Obrana and other similar societies have up to the present committed any criminal acts of this kind through the instrumentality of one of their members. Nevertheless, the Royal Government will accept the demand of the Imperial and Royal Government and will dissolve the Narodna Obrana Society and any other society which shall agitate against Austria-Hungary.

3. The Royal Serbian Government engages itself to eliminate without delay for public instruction in Serbia everything which aids or might aid in fomenting the propaganda against Austro-Hungary when the Imperial and Royal Government furnishes facts and proofs of this propaganda.

4. The Royal Government also agrees to remove from the military service (all persons) whom the judicial inquiry proves to have been guilty of acts directed against the integrity of the territory of the Austro-Hungarian Monarchy, and it expects the Imperial and Royal Government to communicate at an ulterior date the names and the deeds of these officers and officials, for the purposes of the proceedings which will have to be taken.

5. The Royal Government must confess that it is not quite clear as to the sense and object of the demands of the Imperial and Royal Government that Serbia should undertake to accept on her territory the collaboration of delegates of the Imperial and Royal Government, but it declares that it will admit whatever collaboration which may be in accord with the principles of international law and criminal procedure, as well as with good neighborly relations.

6. The Royal Government, as goes without saying, considers it to be its duty to open an inquiry against all those who are, or shall eventually prove to have been, involved in the plot of June 28, and who are in Serbian territory. As to the participation at this investigation of agents of the Austro-Hungarian authorities delegated for this purpose by the Imperial and Royal Government, the Royal Government cannot accept this demand, for it would be a violation of the Constitution and of the law of criminal procedure. Nevertheless, in concrete cases it might be found possible to communicate the results of the investigation in question to the Austro-Hungarian representatives.

7. On the very evening that the note was handed in the Royal Government arrested Major Voija Tankositch. As for Milan Ciganovitch, who is a subject of the Austro-Hungarian Monarchy, and who, until June 15 was employed as a beginner in the administration of the railways, it has not yet been possible to (arrest) him. In view of the ultimate inquiry the Imperial and Royal Government is requested to have the goodness to communicate in the usual form as

soon as possible the presumptions of guilt as well as the eventual proofs of guilt against these persons which have been collected up to the present in the investigations at Serajevo.

8. The Serbian Government will strengthen and extend the measures taken to prevent the illicit traffic of arms and explosives across the frontier. It goes without saying that it will immediately order an investigation, and will severely punish the frontier officials along the line Schabatz-Losnitza who have been lacking in their duties and who allowed the authors of the crime of Serajevo to pass.

9. The Royal Government will willingly give explanations regarding the remarks made in interviews by its officials, both in Serbia and abroad, after the attempt, and which, according to the statement of the Imperial and Royal Government, were hostile toward the monarchy, as soon as the Imperial and Royal Government has (forwarded) it the passages in question of these remarks and as soon as it has shown that the remarks made were in reality made by the officials regarding whom the Royal Government itself will see about collecting proofs.

10. The Royal Government will inform the Imperial and Royal Government of the execution of the measures comprised in the preceding points, in as far as that has not already been done by the present note, as soon as each measure has been ordered and executed.

In the event of the Imperial and Royal Government not being satisfied with this reply, the Royal Serbian Government, considering that it is to the common interest not to precipitate the solution of this question, is ready, as always, to accept a pacific understanding, either by referring this question to the decision of The Hague International Tribunal or to the great powers which took part in the drawing up of the declaration made by the Serbian Government on March 18-31, 1909.

## Denunciation and Declaration of War

The Austro-Hungarian Foreign Office denounced Serbia's reply on July 27 in the following terms, and issued a formal declaration of war the next day:

The object of the Serbian note is to create the false impression that the Serbian Government is prepared in great measure to comply with our demands.

As a matter of fact, however, Serbia's note is filled with the spirit of dishonesty, which clearly lets it be seen that the Serbian Government is not seriously determined to put an end to the culpable tolerance it hitherto has extended to intrigues against the Austro-Hungarian Monarchy.

The Serbian note contains such far-reaching reservations and limitations not only regarding the general principles of our action, but also in regard to the individual claims we have put forward that the concessions actually made by Serbia become insignificant.

In particular our demand for the participation of the Austro-Hungarian authorities in investigations to detect accomplices in the conspiracy on Serbian territory has been rejected, while our request that measures be taken against that section of the Serbian press hostile to Austria-Hungary has been declined, and our wish that the Serbian Government take the necessary measures to prevent the dissolved Austrophobe associations continuing their activity under another name and under another form has not even been considered.

Since the claims in the Austro-Hungarian note of July 23, regard being had to the attitude hitherto adopted by Serbia, represent the minimum of what is necessary for the establishment of permanent peace with the Southeastern monarchy, the Serbian answer must be regarded as unsatisfactory.

That the Serbian Government itself is conscious that its note is not acceptable to us is proved by the circumstance that it proposes at the end of the note to submit the dispute to arbitration—an invitation which is thrown into its proper light by the fact that, three hours before handing in the note, a few minutes before the expiration of the time limit, the mobilization of the Serbian Army took place.

The text of the Austro-Hungarian declaration of war against Serbia, issued July 28, runs as follows:

The Royal Government of Serbia not having replied in a satisfactory manner to the note remitted to it by the Austro-Hungarian Minister in Belgrade on July 23, 1914, the Imperial and Royal Government finds itself compelled to proceed to safeguard its rights and interests and to have recourse for this purpose to force of arms.

Austria-Hungary considers itself, therefore, from this moment in a state of war with Serbia.

COUNT BERCHTOLD,
Minister of Foreign Affairs of Austria-Hungary.

After vainly pleading with the Kaiser to intervene for peace, the Czar of Russia mobilized a portion of his army to go to the aid of Serbia; Germany invaded Belgium, Great Britain declared war on Germany, and the great conflict that was to shake the world for more than four years had begun.

# Progress of the War

## Recording Campaigns on All Fronts and Collateral Events From October 19 Up to and Including November 15, 1918

### UNITED STATES

The Fourth Liberty Loan campaign closed Oct. 19. Subscriptions amounted to $6,989,047,000.

As a result of the signing of the armistice with Germany, the War Industries Board issued orders on Nov. 12 removing many restrictions on public improvements and cutting by 50 per cent. the curtailment which had been placed on forty-two classes of industries.

Secretary Daniels lifted the ban on shipping news Nov. 12.

### SUBMARINE BLOCKADE

The American steamship Lucia, which had her lower holds fitted with rubber-bound barrels, and which was believed to be unsinkable, was torpedoed and sunk Oct. 19. All except four members of the crew were rescued.

On Oct. 20 Spain received an official communication from the German Government saying that the Admiralty had ordered submarines to return immediately to their bases. On the same day word was received that the steamer Maria, which had been requisitioned by the Spanish Government, had been sunk.

Losses of British shipping due to enemy action and marine risk amounted to 151,-593 gross tons, the lowest monthly total in more than two years. Losses for the quarter ended in September were 510,551 gross tons.

Andrew Bonar Law announced in the House of Commons Oct. 29 that there had been a cessation of U-boat attacks on passenger steamships.

The British battleship Britannia was torpedoed off Gibraltar Nov. 9.

### CAMPAIGN IN WESTERN EUROPE

Oct. 19—Allied armies reach the Dutch frontier; British extend their gains east of Douai, capturing several villages, and approach Tournai; Americans and British advance southeast of Cambrai; Germans begin evacuation of Brussels; French reach the Hunding line in Champagne and capture St. Germainmont; Americans pierce the Kriemhilde line at several points between the Argonne and the Meuse and force Germans to retire to the Freya line.

Oct. 21.—Allies push forward on a ninety-mile front from the Dutch border to the Oise east of St. Quentin; Germans in Northern Belgium forced back upon Ghent and the Scheldt.

Oct. 23—Americans on the Verdun front occupy Brieulles, the Bois de Forêt, and Banthéville; British gain three miles in advance on a seventeen-mile front from Le Cateau to the Scheldt River.

Oct. 24—British drive Germans back on the whole front between the Sambre Canal and the Scheldt and take several strongholds on both sides of Valenciennes; Americans advance on both sides of the Meuse.

Oct. 25—British reach the Le Quesnoy-Valenciennes railway on a front of six miles; French attack on the Serre and the Aisne on a front of forty miles, and advance their lines at all points; Americans clear Belleau Wood of Germans and hold Hill 360 in fierce fighting.

Oct. 27—French advance on a fifteen-mile front between the Oise and Serre, gaining five miles at some points.

Oct. 29—Americans shell Conflans region; French attack on a seven-and-one-half-mile line east of Laon.

Nov. 1—First American Army attacks on a front of over fifteen miles north of Verdun, advancing nearly four miles at some points and freeing a dozen towns, aided by the French.

Nov. 2—British capture Valenciennes; Americans break through Freya line on a wide front, taking Champigneulle, Buzancy, Fosse, Barricourt, Villers-devant-Dun, and Doolcon.

Nov. 3—Americans continue advance north of Verdun, taking several towns, and joining with the French near Noirval; Franco-Belgian troops reach a line within five miles of Ghent.

Nov. 5—Germans retreat on a 75-mile front from the Scheldt to the Aisne; Americans cross the Meuse at three points below Stenay.

Nov. 6—Germans order retreat across the Meuse on the front of the American Army; Mouzon in flames; Vervins, Rethel, and other towns won; Sedan fired.

Nov. 7—Americans take Sedan; French troops east of the Oise and north of the Aisne push forward ten miles; 100 villages redeemed.

Nov. 8—French reach the outskirts of Mézières, advance beyond the La Capelle-Avesnes road, and take Thon bridgeheads; Americans drive Germans out of last dominating position east of the Meuse.

Nov. 9—French cavalry crosses the Belgian border; Hirson captured; British take

Maubeuge and Tournai; Americans clinch control on both sides of the Meuse.

Nov. 10—Americans attack on seventy-one-mile front; Stenáy stronghold taken.

Nov. 11—British take Mons; fighting ceases under armistice.

## ITALIAN CAMPAIGN

Oct. 24—Allied forces begin offensive between the Brenta and Piave Rivers.

Oct. 25—Italians advance across the Ornic River in the Monte Grappa sector and capture Monte Solarole; British capture islands in the Piave; French take Monte Sisemol, on the Asiago Plateau.

Oct. 27—Italians and British force passage of the Piave and capture several towns in new drive toward the Isonzo.

Oct. 30—Italians reach Vittorio, and drive the Austrians back along the Piave from the mountains to the sea.

Oct. 31—Italians reach Ponte nelle Alpi, thus dividing the Austrian armies, and cut off fifteen Austrian divisions between the Brenta and the Piave by the capture of the mountain pass of Vadal; Austria asks for armistice.

Nov. 1—Armistice terms handed to Austria; Italians cross the Livenza River.

Nov. 2—Italians advance northward in the Trentino as far as the Sugana Valley.

Nov. 3—Italians take Trent and Trieste; their cavalry enters Udine; fighting ceases under armistice.

## BALKAN CAMPAIGN

Oct. 19—Last remaining territory in Macedonia invaded by the Bulgarians is reoccupied by Greeks.

Oct. 21—French troops reach the Danube near Vidin, shell an enemy monitor, and drive it ashore.

Oct. 26—Serbs occupy Kralievo; Italian cavalry reaches the Bulgar frontier.

Oct. 28—Italians in Albania cross the Mati River and march on Alessio; Allies in Serbia occupy Kragujevatz and Jogodina.

Oct. 30—Austrians flee from Montenegro; Cettinje and other cities seized by insurgents; Scutari occupied by Albanian freebooters and Montenegrin volunteers.

Nov. 1—German troops withdraw to the north bank of the Danube at Belgrade.

Nov. 3—Serbian Army reoccupies Belgrade; Second Army reaches Bosnian frontier.

Nov. 4—Serbs enter Bosnia.

Nov. 10—Serbs advance north of the Danube and the Save Rivers and enter Serajevo.

## CAMPAIGN IN AISA MINOR

Oct. 25—British forces on the Tigris reach Kerkuk and the mouth of the lesser Zab.

Oct. 26—Aleppo captured by the British; Constantinople-Bagdad railroad cut at that point.

Oct. 27—British cut the road from Sherghet to Mosul and occupy Kerkuk.

Oct. 28—British occupy Kaleh Sherghat.

## AERIAL RECORD

Within six months, American aviators on the western front brought down between 500 and 600 German planes. They brought down an average of eight German fliers to each American airman lost.

British airmen bombed Karlsruhe, Bonn, Baden, Treves, and Heidelberg, Oct. 30.

Germany sent a note to the United States, Nov. 4, protesting against allied raids on German towns, and announcing that she had been limiting her bombing operations since Oct. 1.

## NAVAL OPERATIONS

The Cuban steamship Chaparra was sunk by a mine off Barnegat, Oct. 27.

The Austro-Hungarian superdreadnought Viribus Unitis, flagship of the fleet, was torpedoed and sunk by an Italian naval tank, Nov. 1.

The American steamer Saetia was sunk by a mine twenty-five miles off the Maryland coast, Nov. 9.

## RUSSIA

Foreign Minister Tchitcherin sent a note to President Wilson, Oct. 24, announcing the readiness of the Bolsheviki to conclude an armistice upon the evacuation of occupied territory and asking when American troops would be withdrawn from Russia.

On Nov. 5 it was announced that the Bolshevist Government had handed neutral Ministers a note for transmission to the Entente nations asking for the opening of peace negotiations.

Germany demanded the withdrawal of all Russian representatives in Germany, Nov. 6.

## ARMISTICE MOVES

Oct. 19—President Wilson replied to the Austro-Hungarian note of Oct. 7. He refused the proposals for peace negotiations and said that the Czechoslovaks, Jugoslavs, and other oppressed peoples must have independence.

Oct. 21—Germany replied to President Wilson's answer to her first peace note. She suggested arrangements for an armistice, announced that her submarines would be restricted, and told of Government reforms.

Oct. 23—President Wilson replied to the German note, expressing doubt as to the popularization of the German Government, and calling for surrender. He announced that the question of an armistice had been submitted to the allied Governments.

Oct. 26—Turkey made an offer of peace to the Allies that amounted virtually to surrender.

Oct. 27—Germany replied to President Wilson's note, declaring that the peace negotiations were being conducted by a People's Government, and that Germany was awaiting proposals for an armistice.

Oct. 28—Austria-Hungary sent another note to President Wilson asking that immediate negotiations be entered into without awaiting the results of exchanges with Germany. The Vienna Government conceded all rights asked for the Czechoslovaks and Jugoslavs, and requested that the President begin overtures with the allied Governments with a view to ending immediately the hostilities on all Austro-Hungarian fronts.

Oct. 29—Austria-Hungary sent a note to Secretary Lansing asking him to intervene with President Wilson for an immediate armistice.

Oct. 30—Germany sent another note to the United States telling of steps taken toward the democratization of Germany. The State Department declined to make the text public. General Diaz rebuffed the appeal of the Austrian commander for an armistice.

Oct. 31—Turkey surrendered to the Allies. An armistice was signed at Mudros, on the Island of Lemnos, to take effect at noon. An Austrian deputation was permitted to cross the fighting line in Italy for pourparlers concerning an armistice.

Nov. 1—Armistice terms given to Austrian Army.

Nov. 3—Austria-Hungary signs armistice.

Nov. 5—Secretary Lansing notifies the German Government that the Allies are willing to arrange an armistice on President Wilson's principles, and that the terms can be obtained of Marshal Foch.

Nov. 6—German armistice delegation reaches allied lines; Italian troops begin to occupy Austrian territory.

Nov. 7—Firing ceases on one section of the front to permit passage of German armistice delegation.

Nov. 8—German plenipotentiaries arrive at allied headquarters.

Nov. 11—Armistice between Germany and the allied Governments and the United States signed at 5 A. M., Paris time; hostilities cease at 11 A. M., Paris time; President Wilson addresses Congress, announcing the terms of the armistice; Dr. Solf, German Foreign Secretary, addresses message to Secretary Lansing requesting that the President intervene to mitigate conditions in Germany.

Nov. 12—Revised text of armistice announced; Germany appeals to the United States to arrange immediately for peace negotiations because of the pressing danger of famine; German troops begin evacuation of France and Belgium; allied troops move forward; Americans advance toward Metz and Strassburg.

Nov. 13—Germany again appeals to the United States for food; President Wilson says America is willing to help and promises to consult Allies; allied high command refuses to modify conditions of armistice.

Nov. 14—German women appeal to Mrs. Wilson and Jane Addams for milder armistice terms and for food.

## BELGIUM

Baron von Falkenhausen on Oct. 22 pardoned all Belgian and neutral residents condemned by military tribunals or military commanders under his jurisdiction, and ordered the release of all Belgian and neutral citizens interned in Belgium or Germany. He also appointed a committee to investigate charges of devastation and destruction during the German retreat in Belgium.

## AUSTRIA-HUNGARY

The Hungarian Cabinet, headed by Dr. Wekerle, and the Austro-Hungarian Foreign Minister, Baron Burian, resigned Oct. 25. Count Albert Apponyi was appointed Hungarian Premier. Count Andrassy was appointed Austrian Foreign Minister. He resigned Nov. 2, and on that day a new Hungarian Ministry was formed, headed by Count Karolyi.

Military insurrections occurred in Vienna and Budapest Oct. 30. The people and troops proclaimed a republic and a Soldiers and Officers' Council was set up at Vienna. The National Assembly adopted a Constitution in which there was no place left for the crown. The Austro-Hungarian Navy was handed over to the South Slav National Council and the Danube flotilla to the Hungarian Government.

The Rumanian Deputies in the Austrian Parliament constituted a separate Rumanian National Assembly Oct. 19.

A resolution for the complete disunion of Hungary from Austria was introduced by Count Karolyi Oct. 20. A pacific revolution was accomplished at Budapest beginning Oct. 23. A Hungarian National Council and Hungarian Assembly were formed. Riots occurred later, and troops fired on the adherents of Karolyi, who asked Archduke Joseph to appoint him Premier. On Oct. 29 word was received of the formation of an independent and anti-dynastic State, under the leadership of Count Karolyi, in agreement with the Czechs and South Slavs. On Oct. 30 the Hungarian Diet adopted a motion declaring that the constitutional relations between Hungary and Dalmatia, Slovenia, and Fiume had ceased to exist and that the relations between Croatia and Austria had been severed. On Nov. 3 Count Karolyi proclaimed a republic in Hungary.

The Central Executive Committee elected by the National Council of Slovenes, Croatians, and Serbians assumed political control of these nationalities Oct. 22. Croatian soldiers at Fiume revolted Oct. 24 and seized the city, but the mutiny was suppressed by Austro-Hungarian regiments. On Oct. 27 and 28 riots occurred in Croatia. On Oct. 30 the Croatian Parliament at Agram voted for the total separation of Croatia, Slavonia, and Dalmatia from Hungary. The formation of the Jugoslav Republic was announced Nov. 3.

The Czech National Council took over control of Prague Oct. 28. Count Andrassy, the Austro-Hungarian Foreign Minister, entered into diplomatic relations with members of the Czechoslovak Government in Paris. The republic of the Czechoslovaks was proclaimed Oct. 29.

German Austrian Deputies in the Austrian Parliament issued a declaration announcing the creation of the German Austrian State Oct. 22. On Oct. 30 the German Austrian National Council sent a note to President Wilson notifying him of the formation of the State. On Nov. 12 it was proclaimed a part of the new German Republic.

The Kingdom of Greater Serbia was proclaimed at Serajevo Oct. 31, and the assassins of Archduke Franz Ferdinand were released by soldiers. Bosnia and Herzegovina incorporated themselves with the Kingdom of Serbia.

The German-Bohemian Deputies proclaimed the independence of the State of German Bohemia Oct. 31, and entered into negotiations with the Berlin Government with a view to joining German Austria to Germany.

Emperor Charles abdicated Nov. 13.

## GERMANY

Dr. Karl Liebknecht was released from prison Oct. 24.

Oct. 25—Prussian upper house passes en bloc the three electoral bills.

Oct. 27—General Ludendorff, First Quartermaster General of the German Army, resigns after Reichstag adopts bill placing the military command under control of the civil Government. General Groener succeeds Ludendorff; meeting of Crown Council and dignitaries of the entire empire.

Oct. 29.—Federal Council approves bill amending the Constitution in the form as adopted by the Reichstag; Bavarian Premier notifies Berlin that the Bavarian royal family claims the imperial throne in the event of Emperor William's abdication.

Nov. 3—Kaiser decrees his full support of reforms.

Nov. 7—German fleet revolts; Kiel seized by Soldiers' Council; Schleswig seized by revolutionists; Prince Henry of Prussia in flight.

Nov. 8—Prince Maximiliam of Baden resigns as Chancellor; resignation not accepted. Bavarian Diet passes decree deposing the Wittelsbach dynasty; Bavarian Republic established. Revolutionists are in control of Hamburg, Bremen, Bremerhaven, Cuxhaven, Schwerin, and other cities, and take navy out of Kiel.

Nov. 9—Kaiser and Crown Prince adbicate; Prince Maximilian named Regent of the empire; Friedrich Ebert, Social Democrat, appointed Chancellor; Cologne, Hanover, Oldenburg, and other cities join revolt; Duke of Brunswick and his successor abdicate.

Nov. 10—King of Württemberg abdicates; former German Emperor and Crown Prince flee to Holland; crews of four dreadnoughts in Kiel Harbor and guardships in the Baltic join the Reds; Berlin and many other cities seized by revolutionists; republic promised in Schleswig-Holstein.

Nov. 11—German fleet leaders reject armistice terms; Field Marshal von Hindenburg places himself and the German Army at the disposition of the new People's Government; frontier garrisons revolt; majority Socialists reject Bolshevist program; King Friedrich August of Saxony and the Grand Duke of Oldenburg dethroned; Grand Duke of Mecklenburg-Schwerin abdicates.

Nov. 12—Reds seize Heligoland and northern fleet; Soldiers' Council formed to present its demands to von Hindenburg.

Nov. 13—Grand Duke William of Saxe-Weimar and Prince Leopold of Lippe-Detmold abdicate; republics proclaimed in Württemberg and Hesse; Grand Ducal lands seized in Hesse; eastern army with Reds; censorship lifted.

Nov. 12—Reds tighten grip on fleet and army; report that republic has been proclaimed; Soldiers' Council formed to present its demands to von Hindenburg.

Nov. 13—Former German Crown Prince interned in Holland; all-Socialist Cabinet installed at head of new Government; property of Prussian Crown confiscated.

## POLAND

On Oct. 4 Ukrainians, aided by Teuton troops, attacked the Poles in Galicia and recaptured Lemberg and other cities. This action was taken because Poland had announced the annexation of Galicia. Cracow was seized by the Poles Nov. 5. Polish troops occupied Warsaw and helped to demobilize Germans.

The United States Government recognized the Polish Army as autonomous and cobelligerent Nov. 4.

## MISCELLANEOUS

King Boris of Bulgaria abdicated Nov. 2. A peasant Government was established under the leadership of M. Stambuliwsky, who formed a republican army.

Formal meetings of the Supreme War Council at Versailles began Oct. 31.

The Finnish Government granted armistice to 10,000 revolutionaries Nov. 1.

The new Rumanian Government declared war on Germany Nov. 12.

A general insurrection broke out in Montenegro Nov. 8.

Members of the Second Chamber of Alsace-Lorraine constituted themselves into a National Council Nov. 13.